Anonymous

**History of St. Joseph County, Michigan**

with illustrations descriptive of its scenery, palatial residences, public buildings

Anonymous

**History of St. Joseph County, Michigan**
with *illustrations descriptive of its scenery, palatial residences, public buildings*

ISBN/EAN: 9783337734350

Printed in Europe, USA, Canada, Australia, Japan

Cover: Foto ©Andreas Hilbeck / pixelio.de

More available books at **www.hansebooks.com**

## 1827.

# HISTORY

OF

# ST. JOSEPH COUNTY,

### MICHIGAN,

## With Illustrations

### DESCRIPTIVE OF ITS SCENERY,

## *Palatial Residences,*

### Public Buildings, Fine Blocks, and Important Manufactories,

FROM ORIGINAL SKETCHES BY ARTISTS OF THE HIGHEST ABILITY.

PHILADELPHIA:

L. H. EVERTS & CO.,

716 FILBERT STREET.

## 1877.

# PREFACE.

To the citizens of St. Joseph county, who have so generously contributed, in various ways, and so courteously aided us, in our efforts to gather reliable data from which to compile this work,—we tender our heartiest acknowledgments. We are under special obligations to Hon. Isaac D. Toll, Hon. W. H. Cross, Captain John C. Joss, L. A. Clapp, Esq., W. B. Langley, Esq., John Hull, Esq., Hon. William Conner, and Henry Gilbert, Esq., of Kalamazoo.

Had we the space we would, with pleasure, make acknowledgment by name to each of the many persons who have rendered us material aid in our historical researches, also to the many published sources of the information compiled and presented to the public in this volume; but it would cover pages and add bulk to an already voluminous work.

We have garnered from every available source (in many cases a mere sentence only), confining ourselves as far as possible to original material, depending largely upon the memories of old settlers, and those whose lives and associations have made them familiar with the subjects portrayed. We have also, so far as practicable, classified all matter, although the labor of compilation has been materially increased thereby. Yet we feel assured that our work as a book of reference receives an added value that will more than compensate us for the increased labor and expense. We have also endeavored to make the history of each town and village after its organization up to present date complete in itself, without too much recapitulation; to avoid this entirely were impossible, though we trust that it occurs to no considerable extent.

Some incidents and anecdotes have been related more with the design to illustrate the past than to amuse the reader, for we have aimed only to show and trace the method of the change, in a concise, unpretentious way : how and by whom the wilderness has been changed to the garden, the log-cabin to the brownstone front, the track through the forest and the lone postal rider to the iron rail, fast mail, and electric wire with its lightning messenger,—the lands of the red men to the homes of the white. Honor and credit are certainly due to some. We have named many, but not all,—only a few of the leading spirits, whom to associate with was to be one of. Too much honor cannot be rendered them.

Instructions to our historians were, " Write truthfully and impartially of every one and on every subject." Their instructions have been as faithfully executed as was possible, and while some may have been omitted who should have had a place in these pages, yet especial pains has been taken to make it otherwise.

We expect criticism. All we ask is that it be done in charity, after weighing all contingencies, obstacles and hindrances that may have been involved; for if our patrons will take into account all the difficulties we have had to overcome,—the impossibility of harmonizing inharmonious memories, of reconciling perverse figures and stubborn facts, of remembering all the fathers and grandfathers where there are so many to remember, and, finally, the uncertainty of all human calculations and the shortcomings of even the most perfect,—we shall be content with their verdict.

THE PUBLISHERS.

Philadelphia, May 17, 1877.

# TABLE OF CONTENTS.

## HISTORICAL AND DESCRIPTIVE.

# ILLUSTRATIONS.

# INTRODUCTORY.

The Historian, in rescuing from oblivion the life of a Nation, should "extenuate nothing, nor aught set down in malice." Myths, however beautiful, are at their best but fanciful; traditions, however pleasing, are uncertain—and legends, though the very essence of poesy, are unauthentic. The Novelist will take the most fragile thread of a vivid imagination, and from it weave a fabric of surpassing beauty. But the Historian should place his feet upon the solid basis of FACT, and turning a deaf ear to the allurements of fancy, sift, with careful and painstaking scrutiny, the evidence brought before him, and upon which he is to give the record of what *has been*. Standing, as he does, down the stream of Time, far removed from its source, he must retrace, with patience and care, its meanderings, guided by the relics of the past which lie upon its shores, growing fainter and still more faint and uncertain as he nears its fountain, oft-times concealed in the *debris* of ages, and in mists and darkness impenetrable. Written records grew less and less explicit, and finally fail altogether, as he approaches the gloom of a fast-receding past. Memory, wonderful as are its powers, is yet frequently at fault; and only by a comparison of its many aggregations can he be satisfied that he is pursuing stable-footed truth in his researches amid the early paths of his subject.

In the Republic, founded upon popular sovereignty, the people are supreme. They are the source of power. From them springs the government of the Nation in its varied phases—National, State and Municipal. The several States of the American Union, conceding to the General Government its central power, retain their individual sovereignty, within the limits prescribed by the Federal Constitution, and, in the spirit and significance of the national legend, (*E Pluribus Unum*), are "many like the billows, and *one* like the sea." This principle of independent sovereignty runs through the whole system of the government, from the election of the Federal Executive to that of the most obscure constable or pathmaster. And it is by reason of this sovereignty that the beginning and progress of a county become no unimportant subjects to trace upon the permanent pages of history.

The ties of "home" have, ere now, thrown around sterile coasts, frozen plains and mountain cliffs the halo of the love of a patriotic people. Is it surprising, then, that the undulating, flowery prairies and open vistas of park-like lawns, which, for extent and natural beauty, far excel the baronial manors of European aristocracy, and watered with clear running streams and quiet lakes—which beautiful landscape is embraced within the limits of St. Joseph county—should charm the eyes of the forest settlers as they emerged from the dark, dense forests of New York, Pennsylvania and Ohio, and beget in their hearts a love for the surroundings of nature, that clings to them in their old age, and falls but little short of reverence when they speak of the old county, which witnessed their first struggles for life and competency. These associations have made it a sacred and almost hallowed spot.

These old pioneers are fast sinking to rest after the toils and privations of the border, whither they came, buoyed up with hope and nerved with vigor, to build for themselves and their loved ones, homes amid this beautiful scenery, while yet the whoop of the Indian and the howl of the wolf resounded on every side, and war's alarms came not infrequently, with imperious demands for blood and treasure. Here and there a white-haired veteran, bowed with the weight of years and the unremitting toil of pioneer life, remains, an interesting relic of fast-fading times. Before all of these old, hardy pioneers, whose impress was the germ of the present, and whose endowment was lofty examples of courage and unabated energy, and who have durably stamped their characteristics upon worthy successors—before these have passed away, we seek to place upon the historic page the record of whom they were, and what they did to make their county the just pride of the great Peninsular State of the American Union. Records will, be traced as far as they may yield the information sought; the memories of the pioneers will be laid under tribute; the manuscripts of the provident will give their contributions, and all sources will be called into requisition to furnish material, reliable and certain, to bring forth a truthful history of this grand county.

Individual success is a proof of triumphant energy, and pledges a like career to corresponding effort; therefore biographies of earnest, successful representative lives, intimately connected with the development of the county, will illustrate what energy, determination and indomitable will have hitherto accomplished, and can yet accomplish.

To foster local ties, to furnish examples of heroism, to exhibit the results of well-applied industry, and to mark the progress of the community, literature, art and typography, (an attractive trio), are freely employed to embellish and render invaluable a practical and interesting work.

Less than fifty years ago the first white settler built his cabin of rough, unhewn logs west of the principal meridian of the United States in the State of Michigan. Until then the solitudes of the whole territory of Southwestern Michigan, acquired in 1821 by the treaty of Chicago, had been unbroken by any sound of humanity save as that mysterious people, the mound-builders, (whose monuments alone remain to tell us they once lived), had pursued their peaceful avocations within its borders—or their Indian successors had traversed its forests and plains, or in their light canoes sped over the unruffled bosoms of its lakes in pursuit of game, or on the more bloody trail of war. Adventurous traders, *coureurs des bois*, and messengers with despatches to beleaguered posts beyond the western lakes, had indeed followed the wild tribes, for commercial purposes, or passed across its boundaries, but no mark was left to show that an actual settlement had been made, with any idea of permanency, previous to 1827, in all of its wide extent.

A half-century has wrought a wondrous change. Despite privation, danger and misfortune, farms multiplied and towns grew; highways were cut through the forests; streams were bridged; morasses drained, and the stage-coach made its weekly trip between the eastern and western lakes. Then came the railways, connecting the populous and wealthy East with the Western border, affording easy and rapid transit, and progress sprang forward, equipped for an untiring march. The productions of the soil were, as by magic, exchanged for the commerce of the seas and the manufactories of the seaboard. Education and Religion walked hand-in-hand, and together

7

wrought their beneficent mission, laying broad and deep the foundations of happiness and progress, and doing much, also, to erect the harmonious and symmetrical edifice thereon, which prosperous trade, busy manufacture and toilsome agriculture have made a demonstrable certainty.

In prosecuting our enterprise we shall essay, first, somewhat of the history of the State in its early settlement, with a brief sketch of the title to the fee of the millions of acres of prolific soil within its splendid domain, and which the National Government confers upon the settler who makes his home thereon. Then will follow an account of the county, from its earliest settlement, up to and including this present centennial year ; showing its surprising development in agriculture, trade, manufactures, political influence, population and wealth—not forgetting to do honor to the brave men, of all political faiths, who rallied to the common defence of the country when armed treason raised its bloody hand against the national life, and who bore the banner of the Peninsular State through the carnage of many hard-fought fields, onward to ultimate triumph. Brief histories of the several townships

and villages composing the county, will follow, wherein will appear the names of the early settlers, public officials, professional men, tradesmen ; with accounts of schools, churches and societies ; together with comparative statements of the business of those early days and of the present—interspersed with incidents, humorous and sad, which invariably attach to border life, but which, however graphically they may be told, cannot give to us of the present day, who have come into our pleasant places through the toils and privations of the pioneers, any realizing sense of the rugged, thorny paths those heroes and heroines patiently and hopefully trod for many long and weary years.

It cannot, then, be unimportant or uninteresting to trace the progress of St. Joseph's gratifying development, from her crude beginnings to her present proud position among her sister counties ; and therefore we seek to gather the scattered and loosening threads of the past into a compact web of the present, ere they become hopelessly broken and lost, and with a trust that the harmony of our work may speak with no uncertain sound to the future.

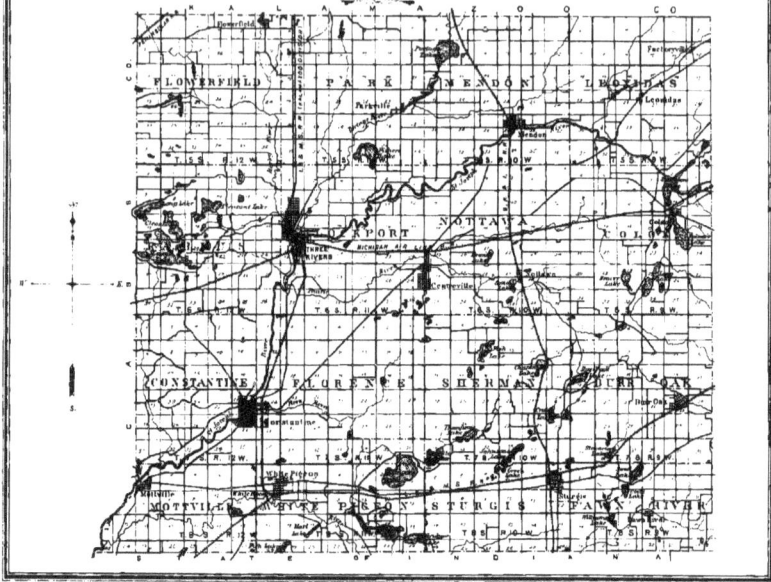

OUTLINE MAP OF
ST. JOSEPH CO.
MICHIGAN.

# HISTORY

—OF—

# ST. JOSEPH COUNTY, MICHIGAN.

## CHAPTER I.

CIVILIZATION—ITS PROGRESS—FIRST INTRODUCTION INTO MICHIGAN—FIRST PERMANENT SETTLEMENT—ORDINANCE OF 1787—ORGANIZATION OF TERRITORY—COUNTIES AND TOWNSHIPS—ADOPTION OF CONSTITUTION—DEVELOPMENT OF STATE.

In the early ages, amid the hordes of the East, civilization was born, and began its march of progress. Westward, over Assyria, India, Egypt, Greece and Rome, as those nations successively rose and fell, its waves rolled, and lapped the shores of Spain, France and Britain. Checked for a time at this *ultima thule* of the Greek and barbarian, by the repressive spirit of the middle ages, at length it overleaped the barriers interposed to its progress, and bore upon its topmost crest, over the Atlantic, a Columbus, a Cabot and a Cartier as its *avant couriers* to the New World, whose shores were bathed by the waters of two oceans. Rolling inland, over mountain, lake and river, across the ancient domain of the mound-builders, then the realm of the Iroquois and Algonquin, the first ripple of the incoming-tide broke upon the shores of Michigan in the year of grace 1641, at which time* Father Chas. Raymbault and his companion, Isaac Jogues, (Jesuit missionaries, and envoys of the king of France,) unfurled the Bourbon lilies at the Sault St. Marie, and proclaimed to an assemblage of two thousand of the red men of the Northwest, the news of salvation.

These missionaries were followed by Rene Menard in 1660, and Claude Allouer in 1665, in the Lake Superior region; and by Pere Marquette and Claude Dablon in 1668, who founded the mission at Sault St. Marie, which was the first settlement by Europeans in Michigan.

In 1671 Pere Marquette founded the mission of St. Ignace, on the north shore of the straits of Mackinac; and in 1673, after his discovery of the Mississippi—the great event of his life—he discovered and named the river St. Josephs, and explored it for some distance from its mouth.

In 1679 La Salle traversed the great lakes in the "Griffin," the first vessel ever launched thereon, and while awaiting her return, built a trading post at the mouth of the St. Josephs; and, carefully sounded the stream and buoyed its channel; and, finally, went to Illinois with Hennepin and Tonti, making the portage to the Kankakee, near the present site of South Bend, Indiana. The real settlement of Michigan, however, may be said to have commenced at Detroit in 1701, when De la Motte Cadillac, with the inseparable Jesuit and one hundred Frenchmen, took possession of that point in the name of the king of France, and which was the first permanent colony settled in Michigan. Thus this Commonwealth, which began to be colonized even before Georgia, is the oldest of all the inland States of the Union, excepting Illinois, which had a colony at Kaskaskia previous to 1700.

The French authority over Michigan, which lasted till 1760, and the English domination which succeeded, and ended nominally in 1783, but really not until 1796, brought but little progress to the country. In 1787 the northwest territory was organized under the ordinance of 1787, Michigan coming under its government and laws at the departure of the British garrison in 1796, from Detroit. The first American settler in Michigan located

_____
* This date was five years before Elliot preached to the Indians within six miles of Boston Harbor.

at Frenchtown, on the river Raisin, in 1793. In January, 1796, the northwest territory assumed the second grade of territorial government as provided by the ordinance of 1787, and the territory of Michigan, as afterwards established, constituted a single county, Wayne, in that territory, and sent one representative to the General Assembly of the northwest territory, held at Chillicothe; and the election at which this representative was chosen was the first election held in Michigan under the American government.

In 1802 the Lower Peninsula was annexed to Indiana territory by the act of Congress creating the State of Ohio. January 11, 1805, Michigan was erected into a separate territory, and General William Hull appointed governor. From that time to the glorious victory of Commodore Perry on Lake Erie, in 1813, the country was subject to the terrors and atrocities of Indian warfare, the western tribes being confederated under Tecumseh, with the British, against the United States.

After the recapture of Detroit in 1813, General Cass began a most successful administration as governor of the territory, which lasted until 1831, during which, as a historian of Michigan says, he did "more for the prosperity of Michigan than any other man, living or dead."

From 1805 to 1824, the legislative powers were vested in the governor and judges who formed the territorial government; but in the latter year Congress provided for a legislative council, to which those powers were given. The members were appointed by the President from eighteen nominees elected by the people, nine of whom constituted the council for four years. The first legislative council was held in Detroit on June 7, 1824. Emigration now began to flow into the country, and population being scattered, Congress authorized the governor, in 1825, to divide the territory into counties and townships, and to provide for the election of township officers. In 1826, the counties of Mackinaw, Saginaw, Lapeer, Shiawassee, St. Clair, Macomb, Oakland, Washtenaw, Wayne, Lenawee and Monroe were organized, and the territory west of the principal meridian to Lake Michigan—which had not been surveyed—was attached to Monroe and Oakland counties for judicial purposes. On April 23, 1827, the lands ceded by the treaty of Chicago in 1821, were formed into a township, and named St. Josephs, and attached to Lenawee county for similar purposes. The same year, Congress gave the people the right to elect the representatives to the legislative council, and the representation was apportioned among the districts and counties according to population.

In 1833 the people of Michigan memorialized Congress for an enabling act to form a State constitution, preparatory to the admission of the State into the Union; but that body refused their prayer. Thereupon Governor Stevens convened the legislative council, which ordered a census of the territory to be taken, and called a convention to frame a constitution, that "the State might demand as a right what had previously been asked as a favor." In 1834 the census was taken, showing a population of 87,273; an excess of 27,273 over the requisite number provided for in the organic law of the northwest territory. In May, 1835, the convention framed a constitution, and sent it to Congress for acceptance; but owing to the southern boundary trouble, which had been vexing the people of Ohio and Michigan for thirty years, and the political agitation of the times, the State was not finally admitted until January, 1837; the boundaries being adjusted as at present,

9

and so accepted by the people finally. From this time Michigan dates her marvelous progress in manufactures, agriculture, commerce and education, which has placed her in the very fore front of the grand galaxy of American Commonwealths. Amid her unrivaled natural beauties, and inexhaustible resources, her commercial and educational development, this proud State may well and justly say to all comers within her borders, in the language of her appropriate motto, *Si quæris peninsulam amænam, circumspice*, "If you seek a beautiful peninsula, look around you!"

## CHAPTER II.

Notwithstanding the claims made by England and France to American soil, based upon the right of discovery under the law of nations, and which claims were maintained for two hundred years at a most frightful expenditure of blood and treasure, and although the thirteen colonies, after a bloody and expensive war of seven years, succeeded to the rights of those nations in the soil of the Northwest, yet there was an adverse and prior claim to be extinguished before a free and unincumbered title in fee simple could be given to lands northwest of the Ohio river. The aboriginal inhabitants—the Indians—were the real lords proprietary of the soil of North America, and most energetic and tenacious were they in defending their title thereto, and so successful were they in that defence, that the American people, notwithstanding their rights acquired so bloodily and expensively, were under the imperative necessity of perfecting their fee in their conquests by purchase from these same proprietors, from first to last. All of the terrible Indian wars which have deluged the territory of the United States with the blood of white men, to say nothing of the extermination of whole nations of the red race, which these same wars have occasioned, have been caused and waged on account of the trespass of the pale-faces upon the Indians' land, as alleged by the latter.

In 1753 the French, by the treaty of peace following the fall of Quebec, ceded their rights in Canada and the Northwest to the English crown, and it in turn, by the treaty of peace at Versailles, after the revolution in 1783, ceded its rights in the Northwest to the United States. Several of the colonies had obtained, previous to the Revolution, certain vested rights in the territory northwest of the Ohio by charters from the British crown, and hence these lands were known by the name of "Crown Lands." These vested rights were ceded by the several States of New York, Virginia, Massachusetts, Connecticut and South Carolina, to whom they belonged, to the general government of the Union, from the year 1781 to 1787, and yet it was claimed by the Indians—and the claim made valid—that the United States had acquired by these several cessions the right of pre-emption only to the soil whenever the Indians chose to alienate their title thereto. After the great confederate council of the Eastern and Western Indians, at the Huron village, on the Detroit river, in December, 1786, the Congress of the United States accepted the construction placed by them upon the treaty with England in 1783—that they (the Indians) were no party thereto, nor included in the provisions thereof—and the government at once began measures looking to the quieting and extinguishment of the Indian title to the lands in the Northwest. A treaty was made with the Wyandot, Ottawa, Delaware and Chippewa tribes, at Fort McIntosh, in 1785, by which lands at Detroit and Mackinaw were ceded to the United States. This treaty was subsequently confirmed in 1787 by another one at Fort Harmer, and in 1795 by Wayne's treaty at Greenville. This last treaty also ceded other tracts of land at Miami Rapids, and the islands of Mackinaw and Bois Blanc.

In 1807 Governor Hull, of Michigan, made a very important treaty with the Ottawa, Chippewa, Pottawatomie and Wyandot tribes, whereby the Indians ceded to the United States all the lands lying east of the present west lines of the counties of Saginaw, Shiawassee, Washtenaw and Lenawee. In 1817 Governor Cass made a treaty with certain of the tribes, whereby the greater part of Ohio and a portion of Indiana and Michigan were ceded; and in 1819 the governor effected another treaty at Saginaw with the Chippewas, by which the United States quieted the Indian title to six millions of acres in Michigan. In 1821, by the treaty of Chicago with the Ottawas, Chippewas and Pottawatomies, all of the country west of the principle meridian, south of the Grand river to the Indiana State line, and

west to Lake Michigan, with the exception of a few reservations, was ceded and confirmed to the general government. Subsequent treaties in 1823, 1825, 1826 and 1827, at Niles, Prairie du Chien, Green Bay and St. Joseph, extinguished the Indian title throughout the then territory of Michigan, with the exception of such reservations as were made for special bands or tribes—most of the Indians in the southern portion of the territory removing west of the Mississippi.

Under the French domination in Michigan, grants of land could be made by the French governors of Canada and Louisiana, which were to be confirmed by the King of France, to make them legally pass the title. The French commandants of the posts were also allowed to grant permissions of occupancy to settlers, and these latter sometimes occupied lands without permission from any one, thus gaining a color of possessory title, under which they subsequently claimed the full right of ownership. On the accession of the English power, the British king restricted the extinguishment of the Indian title; prohibiting the English governors from issuing grants of lands, except within certain prescribed limits, and the English subjects from making purchases of the Indians, or settlements, without those prescribed bounds. Grants, purchases and settlements, however, were made, the king's proclamation to the contrary notwithstanding; and these prohibited possessions formed an important part of the ancient land claims afterwards adjudicated by the land board of Michigan.

In the "American State Papers," Vol. 1, "Public Lands," it is stated by the report of a commission on land claims in Michigan, that there were but eight legal titles passed to lands during the French and English occupancy of the country. However, there was a land-office established at Detroit, in 1804, and the evidence in support of the various land claims arising in Michigan, was gathered and submitted to Congress, which body, by subsequent acts of relief, vested the right to their lands in all actual settlers who could show a reasonable color of title thereto.

The first legal grant of land in Michigan was made in 1707, by "Antoine de la Motte Cadillac, Esq., Lord of Bonaquet Mont Desert, and Commandant for the King, at Detroit, Pont Chartrain," to "Francois Fafard Delorme;" and it was charged with a great many conditions of the old feudal tenure of Europe; the rents and quit rents were to be paid in peltries until a currency should be established, when the peltries were to be exchanged for and succeeded by the cash of the country.

The system now in vogue in conducting the surveys of the public lands, by which the territory is surveyed into townships of six miles square, and the townships subdivided into thirty-six sections, one mile square each, is the suggestion and plan of General Harrison, and was adopted by the general government.

In Michigan the principal meridian of the surveys was located on the west line of Lenawee county, where the same intersects the Ohio state line; and was run due north through the State to the Sault St. Marie. A base line was established, commencing on lake St. Clair, on the line between Macomb and Wayne counties, and running due west to lake Michigan, on the division lines of the counties intervening. Three auxiliary lines for the correction of the surveys were run; the first beginning at the meridian, on the centre line of Gratiot county, and running due west to lake Michigan; the second beginning at lake Huron, on the line between Iosco and Bay counties, and running due west to the lake; and the third beginning at Thunder bay, just south of the centre line of Alpena county, and running due west to the same general termination. There are in the survey eighteen ranges of townships west, and sixteen east of the principal meridian, in the widest part of the State. The townships number eight south, and thirty-seven north of the base line on the meridian in the lower peninsula, and run as high as fifty-eight in the upper peninsula, on Keweenaw Point.

The first survey of public lands in the State was made in 1816, in the eastern part thereof, on Detroit river and vicinity, and a portion only of that surveyed brought into market in 1818, all within the Detroit land district.

In 1823 the Detroit land district was divided, and a land-office established at Monroe, at which all entries west of the principal meridian, up to 1831, had to be made. The lands were first offered at public sale, and after all competition seemed to be over, the applications and bids would be opened and examined, pending which action the office was closed, thereby causing much delay and expense to *bona-fide* settlers, and also affording a fine opportunity for the "land sharks"—speculators—to reap a rich harvest from the real settlers who came to buy their own locations.

The public sales were finally abolished, which act, together with the adoption of the cash system, rendered the swindling tricks of the speculators less easy of performance, and as a consequence, their occupation was soon gone.

After the applications and bids at the public sales were disposed of, the land was subject to private entry at one dollar and twenty-five cents per acre, cash in hand. Previous to 1820 the price of the public lands was fixed at two dollars per acre, and the terms at one-quarter down, the balance in three equal annual payments. This system proved a delusion and a snare to the people as well as the government, for many would buy larger tracts than they could pay for, not considering sufficiently the drawbacks they were liable to, and did experience, in the settlement of a new country. The result was, that the government could not, and would not, take the improvements of the settlers, but extended their time of payment and gave them liberal discounts and concessions; and finally abolished the credit system altogether, and at the same time reduced the price of the public lands to one dollar and twenty-five cents per acre, and made it subject to private entry at that price.

In 1831 a land-office was established at White Pigeon, for lands subject to entry west of the principal meridian, but in 1834 it was removed to Bronson, now Kalamazoo.

A military board of survey, or commission, was sent out by Congress to report on the quality and quantity of lands in Michigan, for the purpose of locating on such lands the bounty land-warrants of the Revolutionary soldiers and officers, covering, in Michigan, two millions of acres. General Brown stated in the report of this commission, that there were not enough of good lands in the State to locate that amount of warrants, and therefore the Act of Congress, passed May 6, 1812, ordering the survey to be made, was repealed, and a survey of a similar quantity of lands directed to be made in lieu thereof, in Arkansas and Illinois. This report gave a bad reputation to Michigan lands, and it was not until after 1830 that the effect was removed by the representations of actual settlers, when emigration, which had mostly "passed by on the other side" to Illinois and Iowa, received a remarkable impetus, literally surging by waves into the territory. But the cloud had its "silver lining," nevertheless, for though the inaccurate and unjust report of the military board kept away the emigrants for a time, it also left them free of the bane of new countries—the land speculator, whose "tricks of trade" were so happily suppressed by the government in after years.

### CHAPTER III.

The valley of St. Joseph river, throughout its entire length nearly, contains abundant and unmistakable evidences of its once being the habitation of that unknown and mysterious people, which modern science, for want of a better appellation, has named mound-builders. That such a people once occupied the territory from the upper lakes to the Gulf, has been determined beyond question, and Foster, in his "*Pre-historic Races of the United States*," says, "with regard to their manners and customs, the past is not altogether speechless. Enough of their monuments survive, to enable us to form an intelligible opinion as to their architecture, system of defence, proficiency in art, habits and pursuits, and religious observances."

But farther than this, all is mystery. Who they were, whence they came, and whither they went, is as much a matter of speculation to-day, after all the researches of Lubbock, Baldwin, Foster, Schoolcraft, and scores of other investigators, as it was when it was first determined that the monuments scattered throughout the Ohio and Mississippi valleys were not the work of the present Indian races. The present Indians have no tradition of them, nor had they when they first came in contact with Europeans, six hundred and more years ago. But the works remain, for the present investigators to examine and theorize over, perhaps to give a clue for the future revealment of the now sealed history.

The evidences found in St. Joseph county of this ancient people, consist of garden plats or beds, mounds and fortifications. That they are ancient, is testified by the growth of trees, similar to those of the surrounding forest, upon the mounds and fortifications and beds, since the same were constructed, as large, apparently, as many of the older ones in the forest. In the township of Lockport there are garden beds still visible, bearing the same general characteristics as those described by Schoolcraft higher up the val-

ley, as follows: "Many of the lines of the plats are rectangular and parallel. They consist of low ridges, as if corn had been planted in drills. They average four feet in width and twenty-five of them have been counted in a space of one hundred feet. The depth of the walk between them is about six inches."

In Colon there are several mounds, some of which have been excavated by E. H. Crane, a professor of taxidermy and embalming and archæologist, who resides at Colon, of whom we have obtained much of the information here given of the remains in St. Joseph county. Mr. Crane opened two mounds on the farm of Phineas Farrand, in which he found all the characteristics of the works of the mound-builders, but no bones; the soil of which they were composed being porous and not capable of preserving the latter. He found flints—small ones—and in one, a fire-place. In a mound he opened on H. K. Farrand's farm, he found some remnants of bones, a very beautifully wrought celt, and some flints; and in one opened on George Teller's farm he found flints and celts. Mr. Crane has found in the mounds he has already opened in the county, nearly every form of implement known to the mound-builders, some of them very unique and handsomely wrought, and others in the rough, or first stage of work, as well as the partially-prepared blocks of stone, for working.

Within three hours' ride of Colon village, there are no less than six fortifications of these ancient people. One of them is distinctly visible yet, and is in a square form, fronting on the St. Joseph river, with an avenue leading to the rear to Bear creek. Others in Leonidas had breastworks three feet high when first discovered, with circular entrenchments, and pathways leading into the same, and sally-ports, showing method and skill in their construction. Some of these fortifications had three breastworks or circles, the gateway being at a different place in each, so that an enemy forcing an entrance, must still fight the besieged behind his entrenchments before he could force the second or third entrance. On these breastworks, trees are, or were, growing four feet in diameter, of the same character as those of the surrounding forest in which the entrenchments are now found. Mr. Crane opened a mound on the banks of Sturgeon lake, which he calls a "sacrificial fire-place," in which he found the bones of all the animals and fish now known to St. Joseph county, besides some of the extinct animals. He, however, believes this deposit was made by the modern Indians, who in former times used to offer such sacrifices, by building a fire-place and a fire therein, and throw on their offerings of flesh, fish and fowl, and immediately cover the whole with earth, and the charred remains would preserve the bones. Mr. Crane also found in a mound he excavated in Burr Oak, copper utensils and the usual flints. These relics are found all over the county, and are to be seen in every cabinet the people have taken the trouble to gather. Dr. Nelson I. Packard, of Sturgis, has some very fine flints, but Mr. Crane has the finest selection, he having paid more attention to the subject.

### THE NORTHWESTERN INDIANS.

The home of the bands of the Pottawatomie, Ottawa and Chippewa Indians, comprising the bands known as the Nottawa-seepe Indians, was in the St. Joseph valley. At the treaty of Chicago, in 1821, when the territory of Southwestern Michigan was ceded to the United States, several reservations were excepted from the general sale of lands, among them one called the Nottawa-seepe reservation, which embraced one hundred and fifteen sections of government surveys, and included all of what is now known as the township of Mendon, a portion of the western part of Leonidas, eastern part of Park, and the townships and parts of townships lying directly north of these in Kalamazoo county. On this reservation the Nottawa Indians resided, having their different villages scattered throughout its area. One was in Leonidas, another in Mendon, near the trading-post on the opposite side of the river from the present site of Mendon village. The reservation comprised some of the choicest lands in St. Joseph county, taking in a portion of Nottawa prairie, the oak-openings of Mendon, Leonidas and Park, and the heavy-timbered lands to the north; and the settlers looked with longing eyes upon the Indians' home, and desired to possess it for themselves. The Indians of Nottawa-seepe were principally Pottawatomies, with a few Ottawas—commonly called Tawas—and fewer Chippewas.

At the settlement of St. Joseph county the Pottawatomie nation was scattered over a vast territory—a portion remained in Canada, a portion in what is now known as the Upper Peninsula, a portion along the Miami of the lakes, and a portion in the State of Illinois, besides the small branch which remained on the Nottawa reservation. These separate branches or sub-divisions were governed by their respective head and subordinate chiefs, agreeably to their national policy, and the usages, customs and traditions by which they had always been governed; no national measures could be adopted, nor transfer of their hunting-grounds be made, without the sanction of a majority of the head-chiefs of all the several departments or tribes. The Nottawa Indians at this time acknowledged the sway of Pierre Morreau, once an accomplished and educated Frenchman, a native of France or a descendant of one of the old French families of Canada. "In early life he commenced his fortunes in Detroit, but meeting with ill success, sought a secluded spot on the banks of the St. Joseph, and remained till he exhausted the remnant of his stock of goods, and then married an Indian woman, adopted the Indian habits and costume, and into his character of savage seemed to have merged every reminiscence of civilization, and to have lost the last vestige of its manners and habits. By his wisdom in council and prowess in war he won the position of chief-sachem or head-chief in this tribe or branch of the Pottawatomies. When the settlements began to gather around the Nottawa prairie he was a superannuated old man, decrepid, infirm and disfigured." He was a man of powerful frame, about six feet in height, notwithstanding, and conversed fluently in the French tongue, but was ignorant of the English. Morreau, by his Indian wife, had seven children, who attained to adult age—Sau-au-quett, the oldest of four sons, Monice, Isadore, Wan-be-ga and three daughters, Betsy, Win-ne-wis and Min-nah. "Cush-ee-wees was the legitimate chieftain of the tribe, who was supplanted by Morreau, and after the latter became so dissipated and imbecile as to be no longer able to exert his power as chief, his son Sau-au-quett disputed the right to govern with the supplanted chief. Sau-au-quett was a wily, shrewd man, and possessed great powers as an orator, while the latter was modest and unassuming; and both parties had their adherents, but the warmest friends of Sau-au-quett admitted he had no just claims to the chieftainship, and yet were unwilling to submit to the government of Cush-ee-wees. Sau-au-quett was six feet three inches in height, straight and well-proportioned, of a commanding presence and an imposing and winning address, which was the secret of his great power over the tribe, and which being improperly used, precipitated the whole tribe into ruin." The settlers, or some of them, supplied the Indians with strong drink, which served to increase their dissensions, and sank them into the most abject poverty and dissipation. They ceased to hunt for game and furs, traded their horses and guns, and even their blankets, for whisky, and left their children to starve in the wigwams. In this crisis of their wretchedness they were constantly plied by the settlers and the agents of the government with overtures for the cession of their reservation to the United States. And in the then condition of the Indians, their removal from the vicinity of the settlers was indeed a consummation devoutly to be wished, for the echoes of their midnight revels and drunken orgies were borne on every breeze to the quiet threshold of the settler's cabin, and when in their drunken fits, which were neither few nor far between, they were inconveniently familiar and insolent, although when they were sober they were quiet, inoffensive and neighborly. A few only of the settlers had contributed to the degradation of the red man, but many were sufferers in consequence thereof, and the government was unceasing in its efforts to procure the cession of the territory and the removal of its occupants. But the acquisition of the title to the reservation was no easy matter to compass. The immediate occupants were ready enough to surrender their rights, but their consent could pass no title to the land, nor could any title be had to the land except with the assent of a majority of the chiefs of the whole nation, who were scattered over an area of nearly five hundred miles.

This was the condition of this branch of the nation at the time the Indian war, known as the Black Hawk war, broke out in 1832, and sounded an alarm throughout the length and breadth of the whole northwestern frontier. The southern line of the Nottawa reserve traversed Nottawa prairie from east to west, near its centre, between north and south, and that portion of the prairie south of the Nottawa reserve line was among the first lands to be located in the northern part of the county. Along the southern margin of the reservation, and in the shadows of the beautiful groves and islands in this portion of the prairie, the cabins of the emigrants were scattered, when the news came to them that Black Hawk, at the head of his fierce and relentless warriors, was sweeping onward through Illinois, laying waste the settlers' possessions, murdering their wives and little ones, and declaring he would drive every pale face from the ancient possession of his people.

It is not to be wondered at that the settlers felt sensations of alarm, and that the mother drew her child closer to her bosom, as they were aroused from their slumbers by the wild shriek of the besotted Pottawatomie, in his midnight carousals across the prairie. A panic of fear seized the whole settlement; some families fled in haste, while others prepared for defence. Goods and valuables were concealed, cattle sold for a trifle or abandoned,

and all farming operations for a time suspended. Several anecdotes are told of those days that exhibit the humorous side of the excitement, but it was no laughing matter then. We give place to one. A family on Sturgis prairie gathered their china-ware and other valuables in that line, and for a place of safe deposit for them, selected the well. The articles were gathered into a tub, and the tub attached to the well-rope and lifted over the curb—the windlass receiving an extra amount of soft-soap as a lubricator. But alas!

"The best laid schemes o' mice and men,
Aft gang aglee."

and just as the receptacle and its precious contents swung clear, the rope parted, and the treasures of the good wife, which she had carefully preserved in a journey of hundreds of miles in a Pennsylvania wagon, over corduroys and through swamps, without the loss of a single cherished saucer, dropped down, down into the depths with a crash and a jingle that told too well that devastation had come to them, whatever might be the final outcome in the future.

But there were some who knew no fear, and did not believe the settlements were in any danger, and did much to reassure the fainting and trembling hearts of their neighbors. They penetrated the Indian camp and found there was as much fear among the Indians of an attack by the whites, as there was on the other side of the reservation line of an attack from the Indians; and the preparations of each party to ward off an attack gave rise to misapprehension, which, had it not been for such men as the Schellhous brothers, Col. Ben. Sherman and others, who felt no fear, a crisis would have been precipitated which would, probably, have caused more or less bloodshed; as it was, however, the excitement passed away a little, and calmer counsels prevailed, and finally peace returned.

The militia, however, were called out (that is, Captain Power's company), on Nottawa prairie, and a draft ordered from its ranks of fifty men, and a fortification decided upon, to be located on the land of Daniel H. Hogan, in the northwest corner of Colon township as now limited, and adjoining the reservation; a majority of a committee of "ways and means for the public safety," consisting of Martin G. Schellhous, Jonathan Engle, Sr., Benjamin Sherman, Amos Howe and Alvin Alvord, Sr., having reported in favor thereof, Schellhous and Engle dissenting. The report was received at four o'clock P. M., and the captain ordered his chosen corps of fifty men to repair at once to the site of the proposed fortification and commence operations. The order was promptly obeyed, and before nightfall several furrows had been plowed the whole length of the western traverse or outwork—the plan embracing an area of about five acres—and a ridge of earth two feet high and three feet at its base, seventeen feet long, picketed with divers grubs varying from one to three inches in diameter, loomed up formidably and was named Fort Hogan. Night brought repose, and the drafted soldiery repaired to their homes to rest, under orders to report at dawn of the next day to mount guard, while the remainder of the company should take their places at the works. Morning came, but with it none of the enthusiasm of the day before. About nine o'clock a few only of the original draft appeared at the redoubt, and went away again. Thus Fort Hogan was ingloriously abandoned, and visions of glory that might have clustered around and over its ramparts were incontinently brushed aside and dissipated.

Through personal assurances of safety from the Schellhouses, Martin G. and Cyrus, Cush-ee-wees, and two or three of the principal men of the Indians, were induced to meet the settlers for a "big talk" or council, and at this interview all misunderstandings between the settlers and Indians were explained and removed. The interview was held at Captain Power's house, and it transpired that the Indians, instead of being desirous of assisting the Sacs against the whites, were willing and anxious to do the very reverse, and a few of the tribe had actually gone with Captain Hatch, a trader, some days before to join General Atkinson's forces at Chicago. The day after the interview, the news came of the capture of Black Hawk, and "grim visaged war smoothed his wrinkled front" at once, and the military returned to the arts of peace.

But the fright this "rumor of war" gave the people made them more determined to possess the Indian reservation, and the government agents were more active than ever to get a session of it from some one, even if but a semblance of title could be acquired.

Soon after the Black Hawk troubles were quieted, Cush-ee-wees died of pulmonary consumption, and Pee-quoit-ah-kis-see, a lineal descendant of the Pottawatomie sachems, succeeded him. While his authority as head-chief was not questioned, the tribe or band had become so debased that little or no respect was paid by them to their national usages, and other aspirants disputed with the new chief the tribal authority. Among these was Muck-amoot, who, without any right to power, assumed the chieftainship, and drew to him certain followers. Sau-au-quett, however, continued to be the master-spirit of the tribe, and exerted a controlling influence over his people, which set at defiance all the pretensions of others.

In September, 1833, Governor Porter met Sau-au-quett and others of the tribe—inferior men—and by blandishments which won their hearts, in the way of gay trappings and military accoutrements, induced them to sign a treaty, ceding to the United States the Nottawa-seepe reservation. The treaty signed, a day for the first payment for the cession was appointed in December following, at Marantette's near Mendon village. In the conditions of the treaty was one that the Indians should retain quiet and peaceable possession of their reservation for two years before they were removed to a new reservation to be set off for them west of the Mississippi, to which they were to be taken by land, with their ponies and dogs, prepared to provide for themselves as best they could. The day of the "big payment" came, but in the meantime the Indians had been consulting among themselves, and the Nottawa band repudiated the treaty, holding that Sau-au-quett and the men who signed it, had no authority to sell the land, and they would not confirm the sale by receiving the payment offered. Governor Porter had issued his proclamation forbidding the sale of liquors on or near the reservation, but, notwithstanding, parties did bring it, and sold it, thereby getting the Indians drunk. For some days the negotiations went on without success, and in the midst of them Sau-au-quett came, dressed in his gayest apparel, blue military coat, regulation buttons, an immense chapeau with tall plumes, sword, sash and pistols, and mounted upon his horse caparisoned in grand style. Swinging his sword above his head, he exclaimed, "I have sold the land! and I would sell it again for two gallons of whisky." Quau-sett stood by his side, and as the chief uttered his last declaration, he sprang forward, and, seizing one of the pistols, aimed it full at the chief's breast, and pulled the trigger. The weapon missed fire, and before Quau-sett could recover himself, Sau-au-quett aimed a sweeping blow with the sword, which, striking on the shoulder of his foe, cut through the blanket which was around him, and a heavy plug of navy tobacco rolled up inside, and so saved Quau-sett's head. Mr. Marantette, who had great influence with the Indians, immediately took Quau-sett in charge, and kept him out of the way. After much delay, the Indians were finally induced, largely by Sau-au-quett, to receive their pay, about ten thousand dollars' worth of calico, trinkets, blankets, knives, tobacco, pipes, saddles, bridles, guns, hatchets, etc., which were distributed to them under the supervision of Governor Porter, by Messrs. Marantette, La Borde and Navarre. The Indians were dissatisfied at the payment, claiming that partiality was shown, but they finally took what was given them, and, as soon as it was possible to do so, squandered it all for drink, or were robbed of it by unprincipled men.

During the deliberations of the Indians, certain persons brought their whisky, not only up to the reservation, but immediately on it, where the council was being held, and, refusing to withdraw, Governor Porter ordered Mr. Marantette to break in the heads of the barrels, which was accordingly done, the Indians falling down on the ground and drinking as much as they could before the earth swallowed it up. Even the heads of the tribe did this worse than beastly thing, much to the disgust of the Governor, who had not been intimately acquainted with the red man on his "native heath." Mr. Marantette was subsequently sued by the owner of the liquor, and a judgment obtained against him, which went to the circuit court, and, notwithstanding the facts of the case—the orders of Governor Porter—the judgment was affirmed, which, with his attorney's fees, amounted to several hundred dollars, and Mr. Marantette was forced to pay the sum.

In 1835, the time set for the Indians' removal, they showed signs of rebellion and reluctance to remove according to the terms of the treaty, claiming that the same had been violated on the part of the government, in that, though they (the Indians) were to have peaceable and undisturbed possession of their lands for two years, yet the settlers had begun locating their lands immediately after they was true. As soon as it was ascertained that the United States had acquired title to the reservation, the settlers, disregarding the treaty stipulation to the contrary, began at once to make claims of choice locations, and it was but a short time before the better part of the lands were located. This movement closed up the trails of the Indians, circumscribed their hunting privileges, and drove off the game; and the cattle of the settlers trespassed on the fields and gardens of the Indians, which were unfenced, and bad blood was engendered on both sides. Negotiations were entered into to get the Indians together, to consent to remove, but no master-spirit was now among them to control them, or rouse their pride. Morreau was dead, Isadore had been poisoned, Sau-au-quett, warned by the death of his brother and of the chief, Sag-a-mo, of Chicago,

was not able to command the people as before, and it was not until the spring of 1840 that the Indians were finally induced to leave their homes, and then only by the appearance on the scene of General Brady and a troop of United States dragoons.

Sau-au-quett, in 1839, had fallen a victim to the never-dying sentiment and desire for revenge, which filled the hearts of some of his tribe. Pamp-te-pe and John Maguago were in hiding, and it was only after the appearance of the cavalry, that the Indians saw it was useless to resist longer, and thereupon submitted to the inevitable, and went away from the home of their people for hundreds of years, for ought we know, to a new one in the west. The women and children, the infirm and unhorsed, were carried in wagons, while those who had horses rode them, and thus passed the remnant of a great nation, which was once the lord of every foot of territory they traversed, to their halting-place in Holdeman's grove, La Salle county, Illinois. Here Maguago and his family, fearing assassination at the hands of some of his tribe, for his acts in securing their removal, secreted themselves until the search for them was given up, when they retraced their way to the reservation, and his descendants are now living in the township of Athens, in Calhoun county.

At Peoria the faith of the government agents with the Indians was again broken, and, contrary to the agreement that they were to be taken by land to the new reservation, with their ponies and dogs, they were cajoled and driven, at the point of the bayonet, on board of a steamboat, their ponies sold for a trifle, or confiscated, and then down the Illinois to the Mississippi, thence to the Arkansas, up the Arkansas to the border of Kansas territory, the powerless and impoverished people were taken, and disembarked under the superintendence of Buel Holcomb, now of Athens, the agents not daring to put in their appearance. The lands of the Indians proved to be valuable in after years, and they sold them and removed to the Indian territory, where they still reside.

The death of Isadore or Setone Morreau has been mentioned. He was poisoned by a squaw of a neighboring family, who offered him a drink of whisky, which he refused to take after smelling of it; but, on being taunted by her of cowardice, he drank, and soon after died. Isadore was as cruel as a savage could well be. He killed his own sister, who was known to the settlers as Betts, her family calling her Nem-oc-na-oe—stabbing her to the heart in a drunken frenzy, about two years after the "big payment" in Colon township.

Sau-au-quett had a little squaw, who was quite a favorite with the old chief, who, when everything was pleasant, and she was not under the influence of liquor, was comparatively amiable, but at other times was a fiend incarnate. She killed Quau-sett in 1835, the same who attempted to kill Sau-au-quett on the reservation in December, 1833. This murder, however, was condoned by the presentation of a horse, saddle and bridle to the son of the dead man, by Sau-au-quett, in accordance with the Indian custom and laws.

Sau-au-quett was killed at Coldwater in 1839, by one of the tribe who was opposed to the sale of the lands. The old chief was sleeping in his tent, when the murderer crept stealthily into the apartment, and, with one blow, drove his knife through the old man's belt and leather shirt, into his bosom to the handle. The chief sprang to his feet, gave one whoop, and fell to the ground dead. The murderer was arrested by the authorities of the county of Branch, and held in custody. The friends of the murdered chief demanded the murderer, to be dealt with according to their laws and customs, but were refused. After some negotiation they were appeased by the present of blankets, a pony and equipments, whereupon the friends of the prisoner came and demanded his release, the offence having been condoned. But they, too, were refused, unless they would consent to remove, with the tribe, at once from the reservation. This they declined to do; but in the spring of 1840, when the Indians were finally removed, the prisoner was released, and went away with them.

An incident occurred, in 1835, on the Nottawa reservation, near Nottawa creek, which is worth repeating. Daniel H. Hogan had employed George Benedict and Isaac Lenstobaco to cut and get out timber for a barn. Early one morning, as they were falling trees, they saw John Maguago, accompanied by an Indian named Johnson, approaching them, and who rode up and dismounted. Maguago stepped in before the axe of Lenstobaco, wrenched it, from him, and threw it into the woods. He then stepped between the tree and the axe of Benedict, but the latter stepped around to the other side of the tree and commenced chopping again. Maguago made a second attempt to step in, but Benedict looked him in the eye, and said "if you do I will cut you in two. Move your horses, the tree is going to fall." Maguago shook his head and would not stir, but a limb falling from the trunk frightened the ponies, and Maguago, in hot wrath, mounted and galloped back to the village, and in a few minutes the camp was alive with Indians, squaws, and pappooses, going in all directions, and trouble seemed to be brewing. Hogan saw at once he must treat with Maguago for the timber, and therefore he went at once to the village, where he negotiated with the irate Indians for the privilege to cut what timber he wanted, for one gallon of whisky, and two dozen of eggs, which Maguago insisted Hogan must go at once with him and get, and off they went, both on one horse, Hogan embracing the Indian for dear life, lest he should be unseated in the ride, which was made *à la* Gilpin. The bargain was finally and fully consummated only after Hogan had imbibed with the Indians for friendship's sake.

A similar interference with Hogan and Benedict when plowing, resulted differently. A party of drunken Indians attempted to drive them off, and frightened their oxen with their blankets. After bearing the interruption so long as they could, the plowmen cut some cudgels and so belabored the drunken fellows that those who were sober enough to run or walk, got out of the way, and the rest, who were lying in the furrows, were rolled out, and the plowing went on.

### THE DEATH OF WISNER

was the last Indian murder in St. Joseph County, and occurred in the winter of 1839.

Joseph Sin-ben-nim, known by the name of Joseph Muskrat, with his squaw and two children, came to the house of Mr. Wisner, and asked to stay all night; consent was freely given, and a good fire built up in the huge fire-place, in order that all might get warm, they being thoroughly chilled. The Indian was intoxicated, and wanted to wrestle with Wisner, but the latter declined. The Indian held a low conversation, in his own language, with his squaw, after which she seemed much excited, and took the gun and hatchet of her husband, and set them out of doors. The Indians laid down before the fire to sleep. Wisner and his wife did not undress themselves, as though apprehensive of danger. The Indian and the squaw were both restless, and rose several times, and at last the former seized Wisner, who threw him on the bed, and stepped back to the fire. The Indian then rose up from the bed, and before Wisner was aware of his intention, stabbed him (Wisner) in the temple, and he fell dead upon the hearth, with one hand in the fire. Mrs. Wisner pulled her husband out of the fire, but the wretch who had murdered him, interfered and cut one of her hands severely, crippling it for life. Mrs. Wisner called to her son, a boy of twelve years, to run and alarm the neighbors. He immediately darted out of doors, and around the house, pursued by the Indian, but escaped him, and gave the alarm. While the Indian was out, Mrs. Wisner closed the door and barred it against him, whereupon he started with his family for the settlement, stopping at the house of John DeYannaund, in the extreme northwest corner of the town of Mendon, where they got refreshments, and stayed about two hours, and then went east on the town line, and were overtaken between Bear Creek and the Portage, by Thomas P. Nolan, who was in advance of his comrades. On discovering Nolan, the Indian tried to shoot him, but his gun missed fire, by reason of the priming being covered to keep it dry. Nolan fired, but missed the Indian, and they then clenched each other, and a severe struggle ensued; but the Indian fell, and was held fast by Nolan until his comrades came up, who tied his legs and hands, and placed him in a "pung" they had brought along with them, covered him with a blanket, and started for Schoolcraft. Meeting a party of other pursuers, they went back to look at the ground where the struggle had occurred, leaving DeYannaund and O. Clark, who were driving the horse and walking behind the sleigh. The latter had proceeded but a short distance, when the Indian, who had succeeded in biting off the rope with which he was bound, sprang from the cutter, and raised the war-whoop, but DeYannond caught him by his wrists, and held him fast. The Indian seized DeYannaund's arm with his teeth, and bit through the coat and shirts, wounding the arm severely. He was thrown upon his face, his arms tied behind him, and so conveyed to Schoolcraft, where he was tried and sentenced to be hung; but his sentence was subsequently commuted to imprisonment for life. He died about two years afterwards.

We are indebted for the material in this chapter to P. Marantette, Hon. S. C. Coffinberry, and H. W. Laird, principally.

---

## CHAPTER IV.

THE FIRST PROSPECTING PARTY OF PIONEERS—PIONEERS AND THEIR JOURNEYS—INCIDENTS—EARLY MARKETS, PRIMITIVE DWELLINGS AND FURNITURE—SICKNESS—DISTRESS—INCIDENTS—FAIR DEALING—PERSONAL SKETCHES OF EARLY PIONEERS.

"I hear the tread of pioneers
Of nations yet to be,
The first low wash of waves where yet
Shall roll a human sea."

When the government officials returned to Detroit in the fall of 1825, after their survey of the great national road from that city to Chicago, they painted with glowing colors the landscape of the St. Joseph valley, dwelling on its magnificent openings and beautiful prairies, its noble river and the eligible water-power of the numerous streams tributary thereto. Their enthusiastic utterances fell upon the willing ears of the pioneers of Wayne county, who were dwelling in that heavy-timbered country and by the widespreading marshes of the Raisin; and many of them at once resolved to see for themselves this "land of delights" so rapturously described by the surveyors who had passed through its borders.

Among these prospecting parties were John W. Fletcher, Captain Moore Allen and George Hubbard. They followed the Chicago trail as it was then and had been for years called, to Bertrand's, on the St. Joseph river, near McCoy's missionary station, in the spring or early summer of 1826, when there was not a white man's cabin on the trail west of Ypsilanti or north of it, except at Ann Arbor and Dexter on the Huron. They traversed southwestern Michigan, finding no spot that pleased them so well as Nottawa prairie, but the land being unsurveyed and the Indians numerous, the party returned without making any location—Mr. Fletcher, however, determining in his own mind, to come back and locate at some future time.

In the following spring of 1827, quite early, another one of Wayne's pioneers took his household treasures and his cattle and came to seek a more favorable homestead, and found one to his liking at the western edge of White Pigeon prairie, within the present limits of the township of Mottville, on which he rolled up a rude log cabin, into which he gathered his family. But a few weeks afterwards, in May following, Leonard Cutler and his family of boys came in through the Hog Creek woods and settled on the eastern edge of the same prairie, and Arba Heald soon afterward came, and it is said these three men made a tripartite division of the prairie between themselves, their lines being determined by two furrows struck across the prairie from north to south. Not long after Heald, Dr. Page, the first physician in the county, a young and unmarried man, came and located on or near the present site of White Pigeon village, and was followed by Joseph Olds, the same year.

In August, John Sturgis, afterwards the first judge of the county court, and George Thurston, then a young man, came to that lovely gem of nature which bears the judge's name, and located a claim on the eastern edge of the prairie, in what is known now as the township of Fawn River, and "broke up" ten acres of land, sowed it to wheat and returned for the judge's family, who came on in the following spring, accompanied by Mr. Thurston's father and his family, the latter locating, however, on Oxbow prairie, just south of the territorial line.

Late in the year 1827 or very early in 1826, John Bear came in and settled still farther west than Winchell, in the timber, but lived there only a short time, removing to Klinger's lake, and finally to Bear lake in Cass county, where he died.

Early in 1828 Luther Newton, afterwards judge of the county court with Judge Sturgis, came to White Pigeon and located on Crooked creek, where he built the first mill in the county the same year, but lost it by high water, and rebuilt it the year following. Judge Newton sought and found a most estimable wife in the person of Miss Grisella Gardner, on Pokagon prairie, in Cass county, but which was then known as St. Joseph township, Lenawee county; this was probably the first marriage celebrated between white people in southwestern Michigan, and which was consummated in the spring of 1828. Judge Newton was followed by Asahel Savery, the first landlord in the county, and by Neal McGaffey, who was the first lawyer to be admitted to practice in the St. Joseph county court in 1830. Klinger came into the settlement on White Pigeon prairie the same year, and located on the creek where he built his mill soon after, and removed subsequently to the shores of the beautiful lake that bears his name. Judge William Meek came in and selected his location, known for years as Meek's Mill, and now the site of the flourishing village of Constantine, in the fall of 1828, removing thither with his family in the latter part of the following winter. A Mr. Quimby settled in the present town of Mottville, on the river, in this year, 1828, and Elias Taylor, the first sheriff of St. Joseph county, came to the grand traverse of the St. Joseph, as the crossing of the Chicago trail at Mottville was called, with a stock of goods, late in the fall of 1828 or early in 1829. Niles F. Smith took up his abode in White Pigeon in 1828, and opened a stock of goods for trade. Hart L. and Alanson C. Stewart, and Duncan Clark all came to "Pigeon" late in 1828 or early in the winter following. In the spring or early summer of 1828 George Buck and his family came to Sturgis prairie and located their home in the present city of Sturgis, living in their wagons in Hog Creek woods, six weeks. John B. Clarke and family soon followed, and putting up a substantial log-house on the present site of the Elliott House, opened the first hotel on Sturgis prairie. That same year Ephraim Bearss came in, or early the next year.

In 1829 Nottawa prairie received its first settlers—William Connor, afterwards judge of probate, and a most prominent citizen of the county, coming first and making his selection in May, and returning to Adrian, where he taught school that summer and came back to his location the first of September following.

In the meantime, however, Judge Sturgis had tired of his location on Sturgis prairie, and had selected one on section four in Nottawa township, and built a house or log cabin in August, which is still standing, the oldest house in the county. In August, too, Mr. Fletcher had carried out his intentions, and secured his present location on the prairie, and in October put up a house and brought his father and family, consisting of his mother and two sisters, to it, Christmas Eve, 1829, and on this homestead Mr. Fletcher has since lived. This Christmas party included also William Hazzard, Sr., and H. A. Hecox, with their families, Mr. Hazzard being the sole survivor of the parental heads of these families at the present time. Amos Howe, Henry Powers, Russell Post and Dr. Alexander McMillan, all came in 1829 to Nottawa prairie, the latter living with his family all winter in his house, the boys bringing in a living by their labor. Captain Alvin Calhoun came to White Pigeon prairie in 1829, locating within the present limits of Florence, and Jacob Bonebright to Constantine. Mottville gained Aaron Brooks, Abraham Reichert and John Hartman in 1829, and Levi Beckwith and his family in 1828. Jacob McInterfer pitched his tent on the shores of Rocky river, at Three Rivers, in the same year, and Buck came into Lockport the year after.

1830 gave Flowerfield her first settler in the person of Mishael Beadle, and Thomas Cade to Sherman, and Garrett Sickles to Fabius, and Roswell Schellhous to Colon, where he was followed by his brothers, Cyrus, Lorenzi, Martin G. and George, the year afterwards. Leonidas received its first settlers in 1831, in the persons of George Mathews and family; and Mendon, in the family of Francis Mouton. Burr Oak began to march towards civilization the same year, Samuel Haslett and family being the first white settlers within its present limits. John G. Cathcart took up his residence in Constantine this same year, Judge C. B. Fitch being there before him, and removing to Lockport township on Mr. Cathcart's coming. John S. Barry came to White Pigeon in 1831, Dr. Elliott in 1832, and James Eastman Johnston in 1836. In 1829 the Kelloggs, noble men, came to White Pigeon, and, in connection with Mr. Bull, opened the first stock of goods of any pretensions whatever for retail in the county. John W. Anderson came as early as 1829, if not earlier, and was the first register of probate. Dr. Hubbel Loomis came in 1828, and began his rival town of Newville, east of "Pigeon," but, though he had a blacksmith-shop, and school-house and cemetery there, the attractions were not strong enough to detach the growing population of White Pigeon from their first love, and soon the worthy Doctor and the first judge of probate in the county, ceased to cherish further hopes of his incipient city, and it passed into oblivion, "like the baseless fabric of a vision, leaving not a wreck behind." Hon. Joseph R. Williams made Constantine his home in 1836. The Tolls, Talbots and Langleys, of Centreville, came in between 1832 and 1836; John H. Bowman, in 1834, to Three Rivers; the Wolfs and Majors into Lockport about the same time. Joseph B. Millard, and Elisha, the old ark captain, the former in 1833 and the latter in 1835, to Three Rivers; the Farrands into Colon in 1836; Marantette into Mendon in 1833, whither he was followed in 1835 by Moses Taft—between the last two of the line. The Wakemans coming to Nottawa prairie, just south of the reservation line. The Lelands, John M. and Andrew, came for settlement in 1834, the former locating in the northeast corner of Lockport township, and the latter near by in Mendon. I. F. Ulrich came into Park in 1834, and the Fishers, Leonard and Jonas, settled the same year on the shores of the lake, to which their name was given. The Wheelers, Challenge S. and William, came to Flowerfield in 1831, Mishael Beadle selling to the former his mill privi-

lege, and going to Three Rivers to complete the McInterfer mill. Captain Levi Watkins began his pioneer life in Leonidas in 1832, and in the same year Norman Roys took up his residence in Florence, a young unmarried man, but where he soon afterwards found a faithful mate in one of the daughters of John Peck, who came into Florence afterwards. Elisha Dimmick and George Pashby, Sr., came into Florence in 1833 and 1834 respectively, and John Howard in 1833. William F. Arnold, with his father and family, came into Fabius in 1832; Hiram Harwood, Heman Harvey and Samuel Newell, and their families, preceding him by a year. David Petty came to Sherman in 1831.

To tell the story of the sufferings, privations, sorrows, toils, and successes of the old pioneers, would fill a volume, and make an intensely interesting narrative. The trials of all are but duplicates of any one of them, in kind, if not degree; and but a few incidents can be given, for want of space, which, however, will serve to illustrate briefly the days that "tried men's souls," and brought out their sterling qualities of manhood, that have triumphed at last over every obstacle, and made the old county the pride of the State.

The journeyings of the earlier pioneers to reach the goal of their hopes, a home in the west, were tedious, and severely tested, oftentimes, their perseverance and courage. Many of them came from Pennsylvania and New York with ox-teams, slowly toiling along the roads with their household goods and wearied little ones, for months; others, more fortunate in possessing the swifter-footed horses, came through the wilderness of forest in a few weeks; but all were rejoiced when the last corduroy was passed, the last swollen stream crossed, the last oozy marsh floundered through, the Black swamp and the Hog creek woods—terrors to the emigrant in the early day—left behind, and the openings and prairies of St. Joseph burst on their wearied vision, as the home-plat came into view.

John S. Newhall, of Sturgis, tells of crossing Swan creek when it was "bank-full," with a load of household goods piled upon poles laid upon the top of the wagon-box, the whole cargo being surmounted by a blooming young lady, who afterwards became the worthy wife of John Hull, of Florence, formerly sheriff of the county. Mr. Newhall swam his oxen across and kept the wagon upright by steadying it (by means of bracing) by the party in company with him.

Judge Nathan Osborn recounts the passage of the Maumee on a frail bridge of ice, by detaching one team and leading it behind the wagon, the family also walking, the other team drawing the goods, and preceded by guides, who with poles ascertained and kept the track, the ice on either side being so soft and porous the poles pushed through it. In the morning after the crossing, the ice was all broken up and rushing to the lake. Leonard Cutler came to a little stream at the close of the day, where, unable to proceed further, having been suffering with fever for several days before, he was laid under a tree to die. His wife and sons gathered around him, in the forest, amid the gathering darkness of an early spring-time evening, to receive his instructions as to what disposition they should make of his remains when the inevitable change, which seemed fast approaching, should come. The old pioneer said to the awe stricken group, "If I die, put me in the wagon, and bury me on the prairie of White Pigeon; but I am not going to die here;" and he did not, but is still living at an advanced age (over 90) in Decorah, Iowa.

There were sorer troubles which came to some, on their journeys to the west, and the most grievous of any which have come to our knowledge is that which befel the family of John Parker, who settled on Sturgis prairie, in 1830. They came to Buffalo and took a steamer for Detroit, and when but a short distance from the city, the boiler of the boat exploded, scalding to death no less than fifteen children, among them three of Mr. Parker's. They were taken back to Buffalo, where, though strangers, their great griefs made them sympathizing friends, who assisted in burying the little ones, when the balance of the family came on to Sturgis.

The difficulties and discomforts of the journeys of the pioneers to their new homes were but a prelude to greater ones during the early years of the country's settlement. No mills were nearer than fifty to seventy-five miles distant; no crops were raised, generally, the first year after their arrival; and though there was game in the woods, fowls in the air, and fish in the rivers and lakes, yet there were times when the hand was unsteadied, the eye dimmed by disease, and the game passed unscathed by the wildly-flying bullet. The supplies of a neighborhood would frequently run short, and a load of corn or wheat would be gathered, and sent off in charge of some one to Niles, Tecumseh, or Fort Wayne; "short commons" would be enforced upon all until its return, in two or three weeks. Salt, a most necessary article of diet, rose in the winter of 1831–32 to twenty dollars per barrel, and

2

forty bushels of beautiful wheat were considered its just equivalent. Money was not thought of, except as a positive good, beyond the reach of the most aspiring.

Pork, after it began to be raised in sufficient quantities to become an article of commerce, frequently sold for a dollar and a-quarter per hundred, and the finest trimmed hams brought but two and three cents per pound. This was one side of the picture; the other side was seen in 1836, when the great tide of immigration set in, and exhausted the supply of bread-stuffs and provisions, and wheat rose to two and a-half and three dollars per bushel. Amos Howe brought a load of wheat to Captain P. R. Toll's store at Centreville, for sale, in 1836, and when told the price, two dollars and a-half per bushel, refused to take it, saying it was more than it was worth, and more than the people could pay for it.

The first houses were poorly finished, and very poorly furnished as a general thing, in the early days. Many of them had no floors but the bare ground, which in dry weather may have been passably comfortable, but in wet or snowy weather was cold, damp, clammy, or uncomfortable. The roofs were "shakes," split out of logs, which laying lengthwise to the pitch of the roof, warped, and the snow sifted in over the beds and floors, so that the sleeper on arising or stepping out upon the strip of bark, placed alongside the rude "bunk" for a carpet, frequently found he was stepping into a colder, although a whiter carpet, than he anticipated. The chairs were frequently nothing but logs of wood, or rude benches, the table an improvised counter, and the bedsteads, sticks driven into holes bored in the logs, of which the house was built, the outer ends supported by posts driven into the ground, and shakes laid across for a platform, on which the bed-clothing was spread. But these were discomforts only, and had there been no other sufferings for the pioneers to endure, their history would be "stale, flat, and unprofitable" indeed. Sickness came to the dwellings of the settlers, and proved many times to be but the avant courier of its grim follower, Death. Almost every person who came to the county, from the first settler in 1827, until 1840, passed through the ordeal of the malarial fevers of the country; and owing to the lack of knowledge of the proper treatment, and the want of proper medicines, a great per-centage of the victims died. In 1834, and again in 1837-8, the sickness was terrible. There were not well men enough to care for the sick, or bury the dead respectfully. Relays of men, many of them scarcely able to be about, went from house to house to administer the remedies the physicians left, who rode day and night to minister to the people. One doctor who had no horse, had traveled on foot until worn out, when he went to his neighbor, a well-to-do farmer in those days, and told him his needs. He was told to call the next morning, and he, the farmer, would see what could be done. On the next morning the doctor found a snug built pony, and a new saddle and bridle awaiting him, and was greeted as follows, by the farmer: "This horse cost me thirty dollars, which you can pay at your convenience; the saddle and bridle you are welcome to." The doctor gratefully accepted the new mode of conveyance, and at once increased his practice and sphere of usefulness. Not alone were the men unselfish and assiduous in their brotherly kindness, but the women were untiring also in their heroic deeds of mercy. Not forgetting their own households, their hearts went out unto all. They gathered the children of the sick into their own houses, and cared for them tenderly, as for their own offspring, until they themselves fell victims to their own unselfishness and devotion; and were in turn cared for by their sisters, who ofttimes rose from beds of languishing to minister to others more dangerously ill than themselves. The dead were everywhere in 1837, and frequently not a single member of the family was able to stand by the grave in which their loved ones were laid to rest by the hands of neighbors. Levi Mathews came to Colon in August, 1833, and before the close of November following, five members of the family, including the father and mother, were buried. Where every one was kind, it would be invidious to specify individual instances, but we must relate one instance of devotion and neighborly solicitude, which has come to our knowledge among many others.

The Cowen brothers, unmarried young men in Leonidas, while engaged in building their mill, were both stricken down with the fever, and were sick some days before the news of their condition got abroad. Upon hearing it, Mrs. Wm. Fletcher, then nearly, or quite, seventy years of age, gathered together such things as she had, and which her motherly experience suggested would be beneficial for poor, distressed, and fever-stricken boys, and mounting the "buck-board," behind a pair of oxen, rode ten miles to carry cheer and healthful influence to her neighbors. This lady stayed with those boys until the next afternoon, washing their clothing, cooking provisions for them, and doing more for their recovery, by her cheerful and health-giving presence, than all the formulas of materia medica combined, and then rode

back to her own home on the top of a load of lumber. Verily she hath her reward, for there is not a pioneer in whose heart her memory is not enshrined, and her deeds remembered.

Mr. I. F. Ulrich relates the following touching incident of his pioneer life in Park township. Himself and his family were all stricken down, and the neighbors, being at great distances, and all having more or less sickness in their own families, no assistance came to them until the day a daughter died; the mother lying very ill at the time, and Mr. Ulrich but just able to get out of bed. The neighbors came in, and found the family's condition, and assisted in burying the daughter, none of the family being able to be present at the funeral. The night following the burial was a fearful one. Mr. Ulrich, left alone with his apparently dying wife, imperative necessity calling the neighbors elsewhere, passed the hours in agonizing suspense. In his extremity he fell on his knees and prayed to the All-Merciful One, for help in this his greatest time of need. The hours passed slowly by, and about midnight the fever-flush began to abate, and soon after a gentle perspiration bedewed the hot cheeks and parched lips of the sufferer, and she fell into a quiet, restful slumber. The crisis was safely passed, and she gradually recovered her health and strength, and the aged couple are still living on the same farm that witnessed their terrible sorrow.

Such experiences as these gave good grounds for the orator of the Pioneer Society of the county, to base the assertion he made in his historical address delivered in June, 1876, in which he characterizes the pioneer as being

"Men like the unmoved rock,
Washed white, but not shaken by the shock."

They were indeed true men and women when sorrow called, and by their deeds showed that in those days they were truly

"Such as could feel a brother's sigh
And with him bear a part,
When sorrow flowed from eye to eye,
And joy from heart to heart."

But not only were they brotherly and generous in times of sorrow and grief, but as a general thing they were just to one another. An instance of this kind will serve to show how the majority of the settlers were disposed to deal with one another. When the first entry of lands was made on White Pigeon prairie, Asahel Savery and Hiram Powers wished to enter the same tract, and rather than bid against one another, or take any undue advantage to get the precedence, they agreed to submit to a proposition to give or take a certain sum for the privilege of entering the tract. Powers offered to give or take fifty dollars for the chance, not having money sufficient to pay any "bonus" and purchase the land too, and Savery, to his great relief, accepted the offer, and Powers entered other lands on Nottawa prairie afterwards. This was not always the case, but, to the credit of the pioneers, it was seldom that any one had his location entered over his head after he had begun to improve it, though there were many lively races to the land-office to get a certain tract before another should advance a claim.

A few personal items of the earliest pioneers will not be amiss here. John Winchell was appointed a justice of the peace of Lenawee county by Governor Cass in 1827, and his jurisdiction from July of that year until November, 1829, co-extensive with the territory acquired by the Chicago treaty of 1821, which included all of southwestern Michigan, south of Grand river and west of the principal meridian. He held this position until the adoption of the State Constitution in 1835, at which time he removed to Door prairie, now La Porte, Indiana, where he lived many years, and proved to be a most useful man in his day.

Leonard Cutler removed to Door prairie in 1831, where he lived for some years, and then removed to Decorah, Iowa, where he is still living at an advanced age. His sons became somewhat noted in La Porte and Waukesha, Wisconsin—the son, Morris, being one of the original proprietors of the latter city. Arba Heald was the first actual settler to feel constrained by the increasing settlement of the county, and sold out his farm to Dr. Isaac O. Adams in 1830, and removed to Door prairie, where land was plentier.

Asahel Savery was a unique character. He was born in Vermont, but was a true borderer; he drifted away from the Green Mountain State early in his life, and Cass found him as a teamster in his army in 1812. He vibrated back and forth on the border until the Chicago road was surveyed, when he struck the trail for "Pigeon" and brought up there in 1828, and put up his log-hostelry, known for years as the "Old Diggins," where he provided good entertainment for man and beast; and in 1832 went to Washington to solicit the contract for carrying the mail from Tecumseh to Chicago, which he procured through the assistance of General Cass, then at Washington, who introduced him as "Colonel Savery, of Michigan." The title preceded the contractor to White Pigeon, and on his arrival he was greeted as "Colonel" Savery, and the title adhered to him ever afterwards. He left St. Joseph county and went to Texas, and fought under Houston all through the struggle for independence, and was at the capture of Santa Anna. He joined the United States army under Taylor, and was General Scott's wagon-master in his campaign against the city of Mexico, and returned to Texas, where he resided until the rebellion broke out, when he was ostracised and driven out on account of his Union sentiments, escaping with his life. After peace was declared he returned from St. Joseph county, where he had been staying among his old friends for a few years, to Texas, where he still resides, if living. He led companies to California, Montana, Colorado, Nevada and Idaho. Wherever the discoveries of gold or silver lured men to delve for them, there the old pioneer and soldier led the way; his skill in wood-craft, and experience in mountain and border life, making him an invaluable guide.

Amos Howe was a pioneer of Michigan in 1817. He came from Chautauqua county, New York, in the winter season, walking all the way, following the lake-shore, and carrying his knapsack and axe on his shoulder. On his last day out from Monroe, he met about noon a party of men going back, connected with the government business, who gave him a good dinner from their own commissariat, and a "swig" of good brandy to wash it down with, which Mr. Howe often said was the best meal and drink he ever had, and did him most effective service, as on the strength of it he made over twenty-five miles of travel, getting into Monroe before night. He located on Huron river, in Wayne county, in 1817, and was a tenant of Governor Cass for several years. He was the first purchaser at the land sale in 1819, in Detroit, and the register made him pay four dollars per acre for his location, because it joined the school section ! Mr. Howe, after his family joined him, and the supply of clothing began to wear out, having some flax on hand which he had managed to get swingled by a contrivance of his own, also set about making a spinning-wheel, which he completed—the wheel being one he found on Grosse Isle. He then had his thread woven at Ecorse, and had thirty-seven yards of cloth, enough for clothing, towels and sheets. Mr. Howe removed to Nottawa prairie in 1829, and was soon afterwards appointed a justice of the peace by Governor Cass. He was the second president of the Pioneer Society, and died in 1875.

Alvin Calhoun came to Michigan when he was but five years old, in the year 1807, his father settling on the Raisin, where he remained until after Hull's surrender in 1812, when the family removed, he returned to Monroe again in 1817. In 1829 Mr. Calhoun came to St. Joseph county and engaged in farming, though after the arking began on the St. Joseph, he followed the river for a while, where he gained his title of captain, by which he is familiarly greeted by his old friends, his brother pioneers. He was the third president of the Pioneer Society.

<hr>

## CHAPTER V.

CIVIL ORGANIZATION OF COUNTY AND TOWNSHIPS—FIRST LEGAL DOCUMENTS EXECUTED AND RECORDED—VILLAGE PLATS—FIRST TAX SALE.

On the 20th of November, 1826, the legislative council of the territory of Michigan attached to Lenawee county all of the territory the Indian title to which was extinguished by the treaty of Chicago in 1821, and on April 12th following, constituted and organized the township of St. Joseph's, with boundaries including the same territory, and ordered the first town-meeting to be held at the house of Timothy S. Smith. This house was in the present vicinity of the present location of Niles.

On September 22, 1826, the lands ceded by the treaty at Cary's Mission the same year, was attached to Lenawee county, and made a part of St. Joseph's township. On October 29, 1829, the council constituted the territory within the lines of townships 5, 6, 7 and fractional 8, south of the base line in ranges 9, 10, 11 and 12, west of the principal meridian, into the county of St. Joseph, and on the 4th of November following organized the county judicially, by ordering a circuit court to be held within the county, at the house of Asahel Savery, on the White Pigeon prairie, and also by establishing a county court with the same powers as given by the general act of the Assembly to such courts. On the day following the council attached to St. Joseph county the counties of Kalamazoo, Barry, Branch, Eaton and Calhoun, and all of the country lying north of townships numbered 4, west of the principal meridian, and south of the county of Michilimackinac, and east of the lines between ranges 12 and 13 and Lake Michigan—where said line intersects with the lake—and proceeded to divide the territory into townships. Government townships 6 and 7, and fractional

township 8, in ranges 11 and 12 west, now known as Lockport, Florence, Fabius, Constantine, Mottville and White Pigeon, were constituted the town of White Pigeon, and the first town-meeting ordered to be held at the house of A. Savery; townships 6 and 7, and fractional township 8 south, in ranges 9 and 10 west, now known as Colon, Nottawa, Burr Oak, Sherman, Fawn River and Sturgis, were constituted the town of Sherman, and the first town-meeting called at the house of John B. Clarke; townships numbered 5 south, in ranges 9, 10, 11 and 12 west, now known as Leonidas, Mendon, Park and Flowerfield, were constituted the town of Flowerfield, and the first town-meeting called at the house of John Sturgis. The counties of Kalamazoo and Barry, and the country north of the same attached to St. Joseph county, were called Brady township; and the counties of Branch, Calhoun and Eaton, and the same country north of Eaton, were called Greene township. July 26, 1830, the township of Nottawa was constituted, and included the present towns of Nottawa and Colon, and the first town-meeting was ordered to be held at the house of Hiram Powers, and the second one in Sherman, at Samuel M. Stewart's.

On March 3, 1831, the legislative council attached to St. Joseph county all that part of Cass county lying east of the St. Joseph river, and west of the township line—being the southwest triangular corner of Mottville—and made it part of White Pigeon township.

In 1833 several changes were made in the civil status of the county. March 21, the present towns of Leonidas and Colon were constituted into the township of Colon, and the present town of Mendon was given to Nottawa. Fabius and Lockport were taken from White Pigeon, and formed into the town of Bucks, reducing Flowerfield to its present limits, and those of Park. The first town-meetings in the new sovereignties were ordered to be held at the house of Roswell Schellhous, in Colon; at the house of George Buck, in Buck's, and at Joshua Barnum's, in Flowerfield.

The next change in the county kaleidoscope, was in 1836, when Leonidas came into the circle.

Its example was contagious, and in 1837, Constantine, Mottville and Florence all struck out for popular sovereignty. Constantine and Florence were unshorn of any of their full territorial rights, but White Pigeon retained the eastern tier of sections of township eight south in range twelve west, and in lieu of this loss Mottville was compensated by receiving the triangle of township eight, range thirteen west, which lies east of the St. Joseph river.

The first town-meetings were held in Mottville and Constantine, at the school-houses in the respective villages of those names, and in Florence, at the house of Giles Thompson.

In 1838, another trio, to wit: Burr Oak, Park and Fawn River, concluded they were equal to the responsibility of self-government, and made a successful venture of the same, and the first opportunity for tasting the delights of independent sovereignty was given the people of the respective towns by town-meetings in April of that year, in the mansions of Julius A. Thompson, of the first named town, James Hutchinson of the second, and Freeman A. Tisdel of the third. Leonidas came into the sisterhood of organized towns in 1840, leaving Bucks a single government township. But a change was imminent in Bucks, and as a territorial one was not advisable, the people determined on a case of nomenclature, and so in 1841 the Legislature was invoked, and, per consequence, the title of Bucks disappeared from the map of the county, and the more classical one of Fabius took its place. The first town-meeting of Lockport was held at the house of Solomon Cummings, and that of Fabius at Alfred Foss.

In 1843 township 5, south, range 10 west, gently knocked at the door of the Legislature for admission into the county counsels, and the request was granted it under the corporate name of Wakeman, with which name, however, the people were not long satisfied, and in 1844 sought and obtained relief from their dissatisfaction under the present name of Mendon. Sturgis was the tardiest of all the family circle to make claim for a separate corporate existence, and not until 1845 did she come into the county legislature as the last of sixteen splendid, independent sovereignties, which conduct their own domestic affairs inside their own geographical limits without interference or discord, levying and collecting their own taxes for state, county and local purposes, and sending their supervisors up to the capitol of the county to act as the managing head for the next higher grade of municipal existence.

The towns still retain the geographical limits assigned them in the final organization of all, with the exception of Lockport and Florence, the former suffering a diminution of her territory in the east halves of sections 25 and 36, which were added to Nottawa by the board of supervisors in 1856, and the latter giving up the three full sections 34, 35 and 36, in the southeast corner of the township, to White Pigeon, for the convenience of the inhabitants of both localities.

The first movement of the legal machinery of the county was made when John W. Anderson, register of probate, (appointed by Governor Cass) filed for record in his office in White Pigeon, a deed conveying lands, on the 15th day of February, 1830. Deeds and other instruments, conveying real or personal property absolutely, or for security, were recorded in the office of the register of probate from the first beginning of the territorial government until January 29, 1835, when the legislative council abolished that office, and provided for the election of registers of deeds, since which time all such instruments have been recorded in the offices of the latter officials.

The first deed above mentioned was a warranty deed from Allen Tibbits and Nancy his wife, of the town of White Pigeon, to Hubbel Loomis of the same place, dated February 11, 1830, and which, for a consideration of one hundred dollars, conveyed twenty-three and a-half acres off of the west side of the southeast quarter of section 5, township 8 south, range 11 west. The execution thereof was witnessed by John Winchell and E. Taylor, and acknowledged before John Winchell, justice of the peace, the same day of its date, and it is recorded in liber A, page 1.

The second deed *recorded* was one from John Foreman and Elizabeth his wife, to H. L. and Alanson C. Stewart, dated April 6, 1830, which, for a consideration of two hundred dollars, conveys the west half of the northeast quarter of section 1, township 8 south, range 12 west, the execution whereof is witnessed by Duncan R. Clark and Avery Brown, and acknowledged before Luther Newton, a justice of the county court, and was filed for record on the day of the date thereof, and recorded in liber A, page 2.

The *earliest dated* deed on record in St. Joseph county, is probably one recorded in liber A, page 204, which is dated May 4, 1829, and acknowledged ten days later before John Winchell, justice of the peace. It was given by Robert Clark, Jr., of the "township of Frenchtown, county of Monroe," to Leonard Cutler of the "township of St. Joseph, county of Lenawee," and for the expressed consideration of one hundred and fifty dollars therein, conveys the east half of the southeast quarter of section 6, township 8 south, range 11 west. It is witnessed by John and Lyman P. Winchell. The next earliest dated deed recorded is one executed October 12, 1829, whereby the same Robert Clark, Jr., of Monroe township, conveys to Arba Heald of "the township of St. Joseph, in the county of Lenawee," the north half of the southwest quarter of section 5, township 8 south, range 11 west, which deed is recorded in liber A, page 20. The next oldest three are all dated November 4, 1829, the very day the county was organized, and were from John Winchell and Amy, his wife, to Luther Newton; Luther Newton and Anna, his wife, to Hart L. and Alanson C. Stewart; and from Hart L. and Alanson C. Stewart and their wives to John Winchell, and convey lands on sections 9 and 10, township 8, range 11, and on section 2, township 8 range 12 west. These deeds are recorded in liber A, pages 5, 6 and 38, respectively.

The earliest dated mortgage is recorded in liber A of mortgages, page 2, and was dated January 18, 1830, by which Niles F. Smith conveys to Joshua Gale, to secure the payment of one thousand two hundred dollars, ten and a-half acres of land on the southeast quarter of section 1, township 8 south, range 12 west, in White Pigeon village. It was acknowledged before Neal McGaffey, justice of the peace; recorded May 8, 1830, and discharged September 13, 1833, as per record in liber A, page 183. The first mortgage recorded is one from Arba Heald to Nehemiah Coldria, dated May 7, 1830, executed to secure the payment of a note for one hundred dollars, due August 1, 1830, and conveying the east half of the southwest quarter of section 5, township 8 south, range 11 west, and recorded in liber A of mortgages, page 1. The first release recorded was one to discharge this last-named mortgage, and which was executed September 18, 1830, by Coldria to Heald, and recorded on page 6 of the same book.

The first village plat recorded was that of White Pigeon, located on the east half of the southeast quarter of section 1, township 8 south, range 12, and the west half of the southwest quarter of section 6, township 8 south, range 11 west, the proprietors being Robert Clark, Jr., Asahel Savery, Niles F. Smith and Neal McGaffey, who acknowledged the plat before Luther Newton, justice of the county court, May 6, 1830. It was recorded the next day in liber A of deeds, pages 15 and 16. The plat is variously shaded to show the interest of each proprietor.

Mottville was the second plat recorded, and was surveyed and platted by Orange Risdon, surveyor, May 31, 1830. John R. Williams, proprietor, acknowledged the same plat before Esquire Winchell.

Centreville was platted and recorded November 7, 1831.

The first sale of lands in the county for delinquent and unpaid taxes, commenced the 18th day of February, 1840, and was continued till the 28th of the same month, under the direction of W. W. Brown, county treasurer. The amount of taxes realized by this sale was four hundred and twenty-two dollars and fifty-two cents, and were of those levied for the years 1832 to 1836 inclusive. There were twenty-three different purchasers; but Messrs. Moore and Coffinberry were the heaviest buyers. The first five sales were made to L. S. Slater, of lands in Coldwater, for the delinquent taxes of 1832. The first sale of lands in St. Joseph county was of the northeast quarter of section 5, township 7 south, range 11 west, for two dollars and fifty-five cents—taxes of 1832—to C. T. Gilbert, but these taxes, as it appeared subsequently, had been previously paid, as shown by the receipt of the collector for 1834. Mr. Gilbert's next venture, on the southeast quarter of the southwest quarter of section 19, in the same township (Florence), wherein he invested two dollars and six cents, netted him better results, as he received a tax-deed for the said premises on the 8th day of April, 1842. The earliest dated tax-deed was one to Henry Gilbert, the purchaser, for the whole of section 17, township 5 south, range 11 west, executed by John W. Talbot, county treasurer, February 22, 1842.

---

## CHAPTER VI.

FIRST FARMS OPENED—LAND ENTRIES—A TRAGEDY—FIRST ORCHARD—NURSERY — IMPROVEMENT OF LIVE STOCK — AGRICULTURAL IMPLEMENTS—MINT-OIL DISTILLATION—AGRICULTURAL STATISTICS.

The first farms opened in St. Joseph county were those of John Winchell, Leonard Cutler and Arba Heald, on White Pigeon prairie, and John Sturgis, on Sturgis prairie, all in the year 1827. Mr. Winchell located on the western end of the prairie, in the spring of that year, and Cutler and Heald on the eastern edge of the same prairie, later in the same season, but still early enough to get in corn and buckwheat, from which they harvested a good crop. Mr. Sturgis broke up ten acres on his location, on the eastern side of Sturgis' prairie, in August, 1827, sowed the same to wheat, and reaped a good harvest therefrom the year following.

The first farms opened on Nottawa prairie were those of Judge William Connor, John W. Fletcher and Aaron McMillan, who broke up a portion of their locations in the spring of 1830. The first farms were located on the edge of the prairies, with the timber for a shelter, in which the cabins and sheds of the settlers were built, and it was not until such locations were all appropriated that the pioneers ventured out upon the prairies to build their homes.

The lands in St. Joseph county were surveyed into townships in the years 1825-6, and subdivided into sections in 1827. The only settlers who occupied their land before its subdivision into sections, were Winchell, Cutler and Heald. The land came into market in 1828, the first entry being made by Ezekiel Metcalf, of Cattaraugus county, N. Y., on the 14th day of June of that year, of the east half of the northeast quarter of section one, township eight south of range ten, west of the principal meridian, in what is now known as the town of Sturgis. Metcalf sold this tract to DeGarmo Jones, of Detroit, November 3, 1830. A portion of this tract is included in the corporate limits of the village of Sturgis.

The other entries made in 1828, were in the following order: John Sturgis, October 22, southwest quarter of section 8, in Fawn River township; on October 24, Arba Heald, east half of the southwest quarter of section 5; Robert Clark, Jr., west half of the southwest quarter of section 5, and east half of the southeast quarter of section 6; John W. Anderson and Duncan R. Clark, west half of the southeast quarter of section 6; Asahel Savery, southwest quarter of section 6—all in the township of White Pigeon, as at present constituted. On November 24, George Buck entered the west half of the southeast quarter of section 1, in Sturgis, and on the 29th of the same month Luther Newton and John Winchell entered the east half of the southeast quarter of section 8; and December 11, Leonard Cutler bought the east half of the northeast quarter of section 6, in White Pigeon. December 18, Ruth A. Clarke entered the east half of the southwest quarter of section 1, and Hart L. Stewart entered the west half of the southwest quarter of same section, in Sturgis. Alanson C. Stewart on the same day entered the west half of the northeast quarter and the east half of the northeast quarter of section 7, in Fawn River, which closed the entries for the year.

There were one hundred and sixty distinct entries made of lands in the year 1829, among them Judge Meeks' location in Constantine, and the locations of Henry Powers, Henry and Russel Post, William Connor, William

Hazzard and John W. Fletcher, on Nottawa prairie; Jacob McInterfer at Lockport and Three Rivers, and Joseph R. Williams and Robert Clark, Jr. and the Stewarts, at Mottville.

From their first settlement until June 1, 1831, the settlers were obliged to go to Monroe to enter their lands; but at the last named date a land-office was established at White Pigeon, of which Abram S. Edwards was the register, and T. P. Sheldon the receiver. In 1834 the office was removed to Kalamazoo, then called Bronson.

During the location of the land-office at White Pigeon, a tragic ending of a journey thither, befel Jacob Knox, the father of David, Charles H. and Lewis Knox, so well and favorably known to the St. Joseph citizens. Mr., (or, as he was familiarly known and called), "Squire" Knox, accompanied by Lewis, had been, June 6, 1831, to the land-office to enter his land, and having finished his business, came to the "Old Diggins," where some land-hunters were shooting at a target. Lewis, being a good shot, loaded one of the rifles, to try his skill, but the day being a damp, misty one, the gun missed fire, and after two or three unsuccessful attempts to discharge the piece, he threw it across his arm, and his attention being attracted by an advertisement posted up against the house, he began to read it, at the same time lightly snapping the trigger of the rifle, which unexpectedly exploded the priming and discharged the piece, the bullet entering the father's breast, killing him almost instantly.

After the office was removed to Bronson, a Miss Van Patten, of Centreville, having a desire for a certain eighty acres of land in Nottawa, started off on foot one summer morning for the office, to purchase the tract, and after fording the St. Joe near the present farm of W. B. Langley, was passed by a gentleman on horseback. Miss Van Patten kept on the even tenor of her way, and on coming out of the land-office met the same horseman going in, who, as it appeared in a few minutes, was after the same tract of land the lady had just secured by her superior powers of locomotion.

A party once went to White Pigeon to enter his location, and his boys, who were with him, proposed us go to the hotel first, but the old gentleman, a German, said, "No, poys, yust hitch the horses, and I will go and get the lant," and he did, and as he came out he met a neighbor who had just came in for the same land. "Dere poys, you see vat would have been the matter, off you had gone to der hotel! Remember to do to-day yust what you can't do to-morrow," said the old gentleman.

The United States surveyors took advantage of their knowledge of the lands they had surveyed, and entered for themselves and their friends some of the best sections in the county. Among them were Robert Clark, Jr., Orange Risdon, Musgrove Evans, and John Mullett.

The first orchard in the county was set out in the spring of 1829, by a Mr. Murray, on White Pigeon prairie, on the farm now known as the Tracy farm. The trees came from Fort Wayne, and are still bearing. Russell Post, who located on the Nottawa prairie in the year 1829, was a good horticulturist, and had an orchard, and a good one, as soon as the one first named, though it was not set out so soon by a year or two.

Leonard Cutler planted the first apple-seeds for nursery purposes, in the spring of 1828. When three years old, the young trees were grafted by a Mr. Jones, who, on Cutler's removal in 1831, transplanted them on the farm now known as Disbrow's, five miles east of Pigeon. A great many of the first orchards in the county were supplied from this nursery.

The first improved live stock was introduced by Elisha White, from Connecticut, in 1835-36. He first brought some short-horn cattle, and an improved breed of hogs, to his farm on White Pigeon prairie. The hogs were known as White's breed. Adams Wakeman also brought into the county some thorough-bred short-horns, after 1850; and from that time considerable attention has been paid to the improvement of cattle.

In 1834 Henry Chapin, Jr., advertised Saxon sheep for sale, selected from General Wadsworth's flock, of New York. The American merinos were introduced after 1850. At the Centennial exhibition, at Philadelphia, St. Joseph county wool, prepared by Franklin Wells, of Constantine, carried off the first award among one hundred competitors.

The stock of horses began to be improved, generally, earlier than other stock, and it is difficult to say who should have the credit of first introducing blooded horses. The father of J. J. Davis, of White Pigeon, brought the first blooded horse on that prairie for stock purposes, from Ulster county, N. Y., in 1833, but it was not until after 1840, that general attention began to be paid to the business.

The first improved farm machinery was introduced in 1841 and later, though the settlers were constantly devising methods of putting in and harvesting their crops, in a more economical and expeditious manner. The plows first used were cast-iron implements, which were soon thrown aside as impracticable, and in 1841 A. C. Fisher invented a plow with heavy cast-

ings and timber, measuring some fifteen feet from the handles to the clevis, the motive power required to work it being ten yoke of the best oxen to be had. Roots and grubs from six to eight inches in diameter were cut off by its share, easily and smoothly. This plow was used for breaking the opening and prairie sod. The plows now made in the county are perfect models of strength and beauty, and are most efficient implements.

The grain was first cut with cradles, and it was not until 1842 that a reaper made its appearance in the harvest field. The first reaper was brought into the county on White Pigeon prairie in 1842, but it did not work well, and was thrown aside. It was an old Kirby machine. The next season a McCormick machine was brought on the prairie by J. J. Davis and C. C. Newkirk, and when it was first started, it frightened the horses and they ran away, breaking up the machine seriously, and the old, discarded Kirby was called into requisition to finish the job. The same season the machines made by John M. Leland, the inventor of the open guard and sickle-edged knives, were introduced on Nottawa prairie, and proved a great success, and the Hussey reaper also was introduced by the Johnsons on Nottawa prairie.

The pioneers tramped their wheat out of the straw with their horses, and winnowed it in the wind, at first, and later, in 1835, improved their condition somewhat by bringing in the open-cylinder thrashing-machine, which also was an invention of John M. Leland. The first machine he built in the county was a small one for his own use, which was worked by two men with crank-power. The old cylinder and concave are preserved by Mrs. Leland at the old homestead on the St. Joe, in the northeastern corner of Lockport.

In 1844 the first separator was introduced on White Pigeon prairie, the same being manufactured at Constantine. They were introduced throughout the county soon after. There was a separator brought to Nottawa in 1842.

An industry has grown up in St. Joseph county from small beginnings—which now almost equals the entire product in all the rest of the State—in the distillation of mint and other essential oils.

Peppermint, which is the chief article from which oil is distilled, began to be cultivated on White Pigeon prairie, but within the present limits of the township of Florence, in 1835, by a Mr. Sawyer, who brought the roots from Ohio. However, before he distilled any of the product, he sold his farm out to Glover and Earle in 1836, who continued the culture for a time, but the prairie soil proving unsuited to the best development of the herb, it was discontinued.

Marshall and Orrin Craw, about 1840, obtained roots of the plant of Glover and Earle, or elsewhere; they introduced its culture into the oak openings in the northern part of Florence, which proved to be eminently fitted for its production, and in which it is entirely cultivated at the present time. The Craw brothers continued the cultivation of the plant and the distillation of its essential oils for several years.

Ranney & Smith began the culture in 1843, and since then the industry has rapidly grown into prominence, at one period the county producing more peppermint oil than all of the United States besides.

The original mode of the distillation of the oil was a very simple and rude process. The plants were corked in an ordinary iron kettle, and the oil skimmed off the water. The process was not economical, neither was it very profitable, but as soon as the distillation became more generally introduced, distilleries were established as at present.

The following sketch of the oil of peppermint, to which the manufacture of essential oils in this county and State is almost exclusively confined, has been written by Albert M. Todd, of Nottawa, who, though but a young man, is an extensive dealer in essential oils, and exhibited specimens of the same at the Centennial exhibition in Philadelphia, for which he obtained several prizes and diplomas:

"In the cultivation and distillation of oil of peppermint our country is far in advance of all others, annually producing about four-fifths of all that is distilled in the world; and of this amount about one-fourth is produced in the county of St. Joseph and its immediate vicinity. Next to the United States in importance is England, then Germany. Quite recently this industry has also extended to China and Japan, the former of which nations exhibited their production in the form of crystals at the late international exhibition.

"For the quality of their production the English have formerly claimed superiority, especially for that distilled from a variety of plant known as the "white Mitcham," cultivated near a town of that name, about twenty miles southwest of London. This district the writer of this article visited in the summer of 1875, and was by the proprietor shown over the finest extensive estate in England devoted to the manufacture of essential oils. The growth of the plants was much inferior to that of our country, particularly the " white Mitcham," which was distinguished from the common variety by lighter-colored leaves. Though bringing a much higher price this variety is but little cultivated owing to its very inferior growth.

" In addition to peppermint, there are also other essential oils in our county, viz.: spearmint, wormwood, pennyroyal, tansy and fireweed, but the combined amount of all these is but a trifle when compared with peppermint; therefore this sketch will be devoted to this oil alone, especially as the process of distillation is the same in all.

" Soon as spring opens, the ground being duly prepared, is marked out in deep furrows thirty inches apart. The roots and creeping-tendrils (called " runners "), which have grown from the settings of the preceding season, being taken from the ground and separated, are packed into large sacks These are thrown over the shoulders of the workmen in such a manner that there shall be at least one living root or " runner " the entire length of the row, and these, as they are thrown down, are covered by the feet of the workman to the depth of an inch.

" Cultivation commences as soon as the rows can be distinguished above ground. As the plants advance in growth a complete net-work of roots is formed beneath the surface; they also send forth " runners " above ground in every direction. These, sometimes attaining a length of over three feet, completely envelope the ground. As the runners also throw down roots a second crop will also be obtained from one setting, and sometimes a third should they escape the frosts of the succeeding winters. The height obtained by the plants is usually not over twenty-four inches, although sometimes it reaches forty-eight inches.

" Distillation commences in August when the plants begin to bloom. The effect produced by a large field of peppermint with its beautiful purple blossoms and rich fragrance is quite enchanting.

" The process of distillation is as follows:

" The plants having been cut, and having lain in the hot sun for six or eight hours, are taken to the distillery and tightly packed in large vats capable of holding from two thousand to two thousand five hundred pounds each. The vat, when filled, is closed over by a steam-tight cover. The steam being generated in a large engine-boiler, is conveyed through a pipe to the plants by means of an opening in the bottom of the vat. The oil, in the form of globules, is contained in minute vesicles on the lower side of the leaves and in the blossoms.

" As the steam is forced through the plants, the globules, being expanded by the intense heat, burst from their prison-cells, and are carried off in steam, which escapes from an opening in the top into a pipe called the " condenser," and from thence into its continuation, the " worm."

" Cold water being constantly pumped over these pipes, the steam inside is re-converted into fluid form. This having reached the terminus of the worm, flows out into the " receiver," a deep vessel, from near the bottom of which a spout runs up on the outside to within a few inches of the top. As the fluid flows in, the water and oil separate of their own accord; the oil being lighter, rises to the surface, and is dipped off; the water continually sinking to the bottom, is forced by the weight above to flow out through the spout.

" This water holds a certain per centum of the oil in solution still, yet is thoughtlessly allowed to go to waste, but should be retained for re-conversion into steam, as fresh water converted into steam will continue to absorb the oil; whereas that already impregnated would throw off the entire amount taken from the plants of successive charges. The importance of calling attention to this will be readily appreciated when it is stated that the amount of " peppermint water " which was formerly sold in England, but is here wasted, is over eight thousand barrels annually. The time required for steaming the plants, is, if they are well dried, not over forty minutes, with a high pressure of steam; but the time varies with the steam capacity of the distillery.

" The amount of oil obtained from a given amount of the plants varies greatly. If they are fine and well covered with leaves, and are distilled during warm, dry weather, and well dried, ten pounds of oil can be obtained from two thousand pounds of the plants; but from coarse, undried plants, less than one-third that amount has been obtained.

" After the charge is sufficiently steamed, it is lifted from the vat by pulleys attached to a crane, and being dropped upon a car or wagon is run off, and used for fertilizing the fields.

" Our average crop in this county will not exceed twenty pounds per acre, although in other localities double this amount has been occasionally produced upon low-lands."

Among the heavy manufacturers of and dealers in essential oils in the county, are the Wolf Brothers & Keech (George, Jr.), of Centreville; A.

P. Emery, of Mendon; William Roys, of Florence, and Charles W. Jones, of Sherman. Henry Hall, of Three Rivers, is an extensive dealer, and in former days Daniel Francisco, now of the latter place, has been a very extensive grower of the herb, and manufacturer of the oil of peppermint. Wolf Bros. & Keech are the heaviest producers of oils, aside from peppermint, they having probably the largest field of wormwood in the world—twenty-two acres; and the only fields of spearmint in the county, fifty acres. They also cultivate tansy and pennyroyal. The product of mint-oils in 1865, in the county, amounted to about 40,000 pounds, which was valued at $100,000. In 1870 there were 23,000 pounds produced, valued at $58,000. In 1876 there were about 30,000 pounds produced, and its average price per pound was $2.25, aggregating about $78,000. The price of the article varies according to the supply and demand, and being an entirely fancy product in the market, cannot be " pushed " when once the present demand is supplied. Peppermint oil is used mostly in confectionery and in pharmacy, and somewhat in perfumery.

The following agricultural statistics are taken from the census of 1874: Of taxable lands there were that year 305,532 acres, 197,404 of which were improved; 55,233 acres of wheat were harvested, yielding 593,241 bushels, the county ranking No. 7 in the State in that respect. There was a gain of 30,000 acres, and 228,000 bushels since 1854. In 1874 there were sown 67,000 acres of wheat. There were 29,771 acres of corn harvested in 1873, which produced 843,670 bushels, the county ranking No. 9 in the State. There were harvested also in 1873, 110,423 bushels of potatoes, and 20,639 tons of hay cut. The wool-clip was 161,190 pounds, and the pork crop was 2,294,276 pounds. There were made 642,900 pounds of butter and cheese, 9,306 barrels of cider, and 7,785 pounds of maple sugar; 1864 produced more " sweetenin'" by nearly 14,000 pounds. The cheese fell off largely from 1864, but the butter nearly doubled. There were 5,575 acres in orchards, 18 acres in vineyards and small fruits, and 54 in gardens, which produced in 1873, 186,485 barrels of apples, 5,841 bushels of other fruits and vegetables, the value of the whole product being $76,026; 100,000 pounds of fruit were dried. There were 2,450 farms in the county, averaging 113 47-100 acres each. There were 7,736 horses, 104 mules, 103 oxen, 7,078 milch cows, and 6,027 other neat cattle, over one year old, and 16,847 hogs and 32,683 sheep, in 1874.

## CHAPTER VII.

The old adage, " necessity is the mother of invention," was amply illustrated in the early pioneer-life in St. Joseph county. The early settlers brought in, generally, but small supplies of breadstuffs; and there being no mills to grind the raw material—which, too, was wanting for the first two or three years, in sufficient quantities to supply the demand—the first thing the man of the family set about doing, after providing a shelter for his charge, was to enlarge the bill-of-fare of the household. Notwithstanding the fact that wild game covered the prairies and filled the openings, and fish sported in the rivers and lakes in abundance, and the wild bees had been storing their honey for years uncounted in the hollow trees, thus affording a plentiful supply of such articles of diet for any one who chose to take them, " without money and without price:" yet with all this array of nature's bountiful provision before them (which would be considered by epicures of to-day, luxuries), the settler was not satisfied; but he and his family's appetites craved bread, whether of corn or wheat, it did not so much matter, but bread of some sort must be had; and therefore the inventive genius of the pioneer was at once actively exercised to produce something to reduce the raw material, whenever it should be got, into meal, trusting the good wife to get it baked in some shape fit for eating. Various devices were employed to get meal and flour; and graham, which is called for by many now-a-days as an article of diet was then well worth, was then the main-stay of breadstuffs.

Mrs. Judge Sturgis says the first bread she made in the county was prepared from corn meal, produced by rubbing the ears on the bottom of a tin pan perforated with holes, the rough edges of the perforations forming a grater surface, and the meal moistened with water, and baked on a board before the fire in an enormous fire-place. The corn was bought of the Indians, who were her nearest neighbors. The first buckwheat pan-cakes she made was from flour made by grinding the grain in her coffee-mill, and sifting the hulls out in her sieve. The coffee-mill was of common use among the earlier settlers.

The next device was called the *pioneer mill*, and consisted of a block of wood or stump of a tree, with a hole rounded and smoothed out therein, into which the grain was poured, and reduced to meal by means of a pestle attached to a spring-pole. The Indians had the pestle or mortar before the settlers came, but Yankee ingenuity invented the labor-saving part—the spring-pole—and, what is more wonderful, never patented the improvement.

In the summer of 1828, Arba Heald, living then near the east end of White Pigeon prairie, put up against a large tree near his house a large pepper mill, with double cranks for two persons working; which would grind about half a bushel of grain in a half-hour. This was for common use throughout the neighborhood, and served its purpose during the years 1828–29, as occasion required, until better facilities were offered. Samuel Pratt went to Cutler's to board in June, 1829, and a part of the consideration for his accommodation was that he should assist in grinding half a bushel of shelled corn in Heald's mill every other day.

In 1828 the nearest water-mill was at Fort Wayne, and the settlers of that year were compelled to go to that place, or Tecumseh, or use the expedients above described to procure their breadstuffs. In 1829 there was a mill on the Dowagiac. In the summer of 1828 Judge Luther Newton built a saw-mill one mile south of the Chicago road, on Fawn river—then called Crooked creek—but the dam went out, and the mill was undermined and thrown down before any work was done.

The mill was rebuilt in 1829, and the first sawing done in the fall of that year. The mill was built double for the purpose of putting in a run of stones for gristing, but no grinding was done in it for some time afterwards.

The first grist-mill put in operation in the county, was one built by Judge William Meek, on Crooked creek, near the present site of the railroad bridge, in Constantine. The judge located the water-power and mill site, June 15, 1829, and in the spring of 1830 built a small mill after this wise, as is related by Hugh Wood, the millwright who built the same. The dam thrown across the creek was as primitive as the mill. The mud sills were large logs sunk to the bottom of the stream, and puncheons split or hewed out of other large logs, pinned upon them; then a large log was placed on either side of the stream, one of them forming the foundation of the mill, and upon these two logs was hung the water-wheel, which was about eighteen feet long, and six feet in diameter. Brush and straw were thrown in above the mud-sills, and the water raised about eighteen inches, forming a current which carried the wheel. The wheel-shaft was a hewed log, with arms mortised into it, upon which the floats, or buckets, were withed. The gudgeons were made of wood, banded with iron that had once performed a similar service for wagon-wheel hubs. The bed-stone was made of a flat boulder found in the river, about two feet in diameter, and the runner was made of a similar one, found about three miles up the river. The wheels by which the stones were driven were entirely of wood. The wheel was stopped by floating a log under it, and when motion was again required, the log was drawn out. The mill was a log building, eighteen feet square, one and a-half stories high.

This mill was begun and completed (so states the millwright, Woods,) in twenty days, in the spring of 1830. William Hazzard says he carried his grists to this mill in 1830, and Lewis Rhodes, who was then living on White Pigeon prairie, and but a short distance from the Newton mill, says he went to Meek's mill in the fall of 1830, before Newton's mill did any grinding. This mill of Judge Meek's had no bolt at first, but afterwards he made one, the chest being made of flattened poles, and covered with ash bark, no iron being in the bolt, except the spindle. The meal was carried by hand from the stones to the bolt, which was turned by the hands of the owners of the grists—male or female.

Judge Meek the next season began a permanent improvement of his water-power, putting in a more substantial dam, just above the first mill, across Fawn river, digging a race and taking the water to the bank of the St. Joseph, where he built a saw-mill; into one end of it he put the mill stones of the primitive mill for a short time. He then built a small building, into which he put a run of good burr stones, and subsequently enlarged the building and put in two runs. The second mill (the saw-mill) went into operation in the summer of 1831.

In the summer of 1830 Michael Beadle built a small mill, very similar in construction to that of Judge Meek's, which went into operation in the fall of 1830, or winter of 1831.

In the summer of 1831 Weston W. Bliss built a carding and cloth dressing-mill, into which he also put a run of burr stones, for gristing.

The winter of 1831-2 set in early and severely, and the water in Judge

Meek's race froze solid in December, and his mills were stopped all winter; Beadle, Bliss and Newton supplying the people in the meantime with flour and meal.

In 1832 Judge Fitch built his saw-mill at the mouth of Hog creek, in his little village of Eschol, where he did an extensive business until 1840; but his mills have rotted down, the dam no longer obstructs the current of the stream, and Eschol is scarcely remembered by the "oldest inhabitant."

Mishael Beadle sold his Flowerfield mill to Challenge S. Wheeler, who settled there in December, 1831—Mr. Beadle coming to Three Rivers, and putting up, in 1832, a little mill on the east side of the Portage.

In 1832 Robert and James Cowen built a saw-mill on Nottawa creek, in Leonidas, now known as Kidd's mill. During its erection they wanted a small hook for some purpose, and as the nearest blacksmith-shop was at White Pigeon, twenty-five miles distant, James went there on foot to get it made. On his arrival, he found several parties waiting to be served at the only shop in the village and the smith drunk. After spending four dollars for board and consuming five days' time, he got the work he wanted done, paying fifty cents for it. The Schellhous saw-mill was built nearly as early in Colon, as Cowen's.

Merchant flouring began in the summer of 1834. In the *Michigan Statesman and St. Joseph Chronicle*, published in White Pigeon that year, Clark & Williams at White Pigeon, offer "fifty cents per bushel, in trade, for any quantity of good merchantable wheat delivered at the Constantine mills before the 1st of August," next ensuing, dating their offer May 27. After the 1st of August they offered only forty-three cents per bushel in the same kind of payment. But the immigration of 1835-36 made a demand on the mills sufficient to consume the entire product, and no shipments were made of any moment until the fall of 1837, at which time the old mills had been enlarged and improved and saw-mills built. The saw-mills were driven to their utmost capacity to supply the home demand.

The first wool-carding and cloth-dressing factory was built by W. W. Bliss, on Pigeon creek, as before stated, in 1831. The first brick made in the county were burned by Samuel Pratt and Philander A. Paine, in the months of August and September, 1829, at Mottville. They put up a kiln of 40,000, embracing both chimney and well brick. The well at Savery's "Old Diggins," was curbed with them. In 1830 Mr. Pratt and George Thurston made brick at the mouth of Crooked creek (Fawn river).

The first shoemaker in the county who brought his "kit" for regular trade, was Edwin Kellogg, at White Pigeon. In 1830 Savery built a large stabling barn near his hotel with an ample loft, in one end of which Kellogg made the first shoes manufactured in the county, and, at the same time, in the other end of the loft, two down-east Yankees, as Mr. K. says, "were doing a *smashing* business in the fanning-mill line."

A Mr. Weed built the first distillery in the county on Crooked creek, near Newton's mill, in 1832, and the Newtons having sold out their mill to W. W. & Elisha Miller, they rebuilt it, and soon after Weed's distillery went into operation they also built one. Some of the Nottawa Indians played a practical joke on one of the Millers to get some whisky. Going through the woods one day the Indians found some dead honey-bees on the ground, and marking the tree under which they were lying, they took the bees along with them toward the distillery, and when in its vicinity, scattered the insects on the ground under a sturdy old oak and went into the still-house, and told Mr. Miller they would show him a bee-tree if he would give them two gallons of whisky (squibby), and offered to show it to him first if he doubted their statement. Mr. Miller went out with the jokers, who led him to the tree where they had scattered the dead bees; on seeing which, Miller said he would give them the whiskey, which he did, and the Indians went away with it. As soon as a convenient opportunity offered, Mr. Miller cut down the tree and found not what he had sought, but that he had been badly "sold" by the "poor Indian." A Mr. Wilson once bartered three hundred bushels of fine white wheat to Miller for whisky, and drew the liquor to Detroit and sold it for twenty-five cents per gallon to get cash to buy necessaries with.

The first wagon-shop in the county was opened on White Pigeon prairie, at Newville, in 1830, but not much business was done. John Masterman was the first one to do a good business, and he located in White Pigeon about the year 1831-2. The first foundries were put in operation in Constantine, Sturgis and Flowerfield, in the year 1836, and plows and other castings were made. The first flour-barrels in the county, were made in 1834, at Centreville, for Johnston and Stewart.

The foregoing is substantially the history of the beginnings of manufactures, in outline, in St. Joseph county.

By the census of 1874 the following pleasing exhibit is made of the manufacturing business of the county, for the year ending May 4, 1874. There were eighteen flour mills (water), with fifty-eight runs of stone, employing $261,000 capital, and fifty employees, which made 103,381 barrels of flour, valued at $675,054. Sixteen saw-mills (four steam, twelve water power), employed $40,300 capital, and forty-one persons, and made 3,494,682 feet of lumber, valued at $37,949. Four planing-mills, five foundries and machine-shops, three agricultural-implement works, eight carriage-factories, five chair-factories, three pump, two stave-head and hoop, two barrel and churn factories, one tannery, two trunk-factories, one canning establishment, two woolen-factories, two boot and shoe factories, three brick and tile yards, two stone-yards, and one knitting and batten-factory, employed 475 persons and $543,450, and the value of their products was $607,364, making a total of eighty-two establishments, giving employment to 574 persons, and $844,750 capital, and producing products of commerce valued at $1,320,367.

The first merchants to bring a stock of goods for sale into the county were Hart L. and Alanson C. Stewart, which were brought to White Pigeon in the fall of 1829, but not opened for sale there, being transferred in bulk to Mottville, where the Stewarts afterwards located in the early part of 1830. Messrs. Bull & Kellogg brought the next stock of goods into White Pigeon, the summer of 1830, and they also opened a store at Sturgis soon after Elias Taylor, the old Indian trader at the "grand traverse" of the St. Joe, Mottville, located there in the year of 1828, but his supplies were principally whisky and tobacco. Judge Wm. H. Cross transferred a load of supplies to Taylor from Monroe in 1830, and he says the bulk of it was whisky. Taylor was the conservator of the public peace and morals in all that region of country for some years, and he made it his duty to see that the United States laws were not infringed by the sale of whisky to the Indians, except such as went over his counter. A Mr. Clements brought the first stock of goods to Sturgis prairie. Elias S. Swan followed Bull and Kellogg in 1831, and Barry & Willard opened up a heavy stock of general merchandize in the latter part of 1831. The first stock of drugs and medicines was kept by Bull & Kellogg. A man one day came into the store and inquired for quinine, and on being asked how much he wanted, replied, "Oh, two or three pounds, I suppose!" He was somewhat nonplussed when he was told it would take his best horse to pay for that amount. Niles F. Smith had a little stock of goods in White Pigeon in the spring of 1830.

The business of the pioneer merchant was almost exclusively conducted by barter and exchange. Money was scarce, and constantly grew scarcer as the emigrants used up their surplus, and could get no more for their produce. The dealers took wheat and had it floured, and shipped the flour to their eastern creditors, as the only medium of exchange within their reach. Men had wheat, pork, and the products of their dairy, but could get no cash for them, and so the merchants were forced to take their produce and run the risk of replenishing their stock on credit.

One day a well-to-do farmer came into the store of N. E. Massey, in Constantine, and asked to see some boots; he was shown some, and after examining two or three pairs, put a pair on, which seemed to fit him, and he inquired the price, and being told, he immediately asked Massey how many bushels of wheat he must bring to his store for the articles. Massey replied, "I cannot sell my boots for wheat, I must have the cash for them." The farmer repeated his inquiry more earnestly than before, and Massey reiterated his refusal to take wheat for the boots, adding that he could not refill his stock unless he had cash for such articles. But all to no purpose—the farmer persisted in knowing how many bushels of wheat would satisfy the merchant. Finding him inexorable, he said, "Well Mr. Massey, I have got these boots on, and I am not going to take them off, neither do I think you can take them off; now say just what I must bring you, in wheat, to make it square; I am not particular how much, set your own figures, but the boots I must and will have." Massey was forced to submit and state the number of bushels of wheat he considered an equivalent (which was some fifteen), and the same was at once brought, and the score settled.

FIRST BANKS.

A system of banking was inaugurated by the first Legislature that convened under the constitution of 1835, the same being based on what was known as the "safety fund," and several banks were chartered, and some of them did a fair, honest and legitimate business. But in 1837 the panic was so disastrous, that the financiers of the State thought unlimited banking facilities would mitigate the commercial distress and prostration, if, indeed, they did not prove a veritable Hercules, and lift the wheels of trade entirely out of the rut of stagnation and disaster, and, therefore, a general banking

law was passed, whereby an unlimited issue of paper could be put out as money, secured by real estate.

At the same time the State began to build her railroads, loaning $500,000 therefor, and being terribly swindled before she found her citizens could do such work better than herself, and wisely left internal improvements thereafter to private individuals and corporations. The general government extended aid, and also the State, generously, by donations of land, and while the money lasted, times were easy; but the crisis came at last, and the banks whose circulation was secured so slightly, collapsed at once, and swept away all the means the people had invested in them.

The first and only safety fund bank in St. Joseph county, was the Bank of Constantine, which was chartered July 23, 1836, with an authorized capital of $250,000. It was the only charter granted at the session of 1836, among many applications. The stock-books were opened, and the entire capital subscribed, and four hundred and forty-seven surplus shares besides, the first week. Among the heavy subscribers were: Isaac J. Ullman, two hundred and ten shares; Wm. E. Boardman, fifteen hundred shares; J. S. Barry, two hundred shares; Wm. H. Adams, two hundred shares. The first board of directors were W. T. House, President, N. E. Boardman, John A. Welles, I. J. Ullman, E. S. Swan, W. H. Adams and John S. Barry. The first instalment of capital was paid in, in specie, February 24, 1837, and the doors were opened for business March 3 following, with Chas. Augustus Hopkins, of Buffalo, for cashier. Business flourished with the new institution; the people gave it their confidence, and business began to feel its new factor's power. The first statement of the bank commissioner, Thomas Fitzgerald, made March 6, 1838, showed the following condition of the bank and its business: capital stock $250,000; paid in $27,025; circulation $29,430; specie on hand $15,465.49; bills of other banks $9,821.50. The bank continued its operations until 1841, when it closed its doors and suspended payment.

Under the general banking law the banks were designated in common parlance " wild cat " and " red dog," according to the facts of the case. If the notes the bank issued were printed directly for its location, that is with the name of the place where the bank was doing business, in the same colored ink, and at the same time the rest of the note was engraved, the bank was a " wild cat "; but if the notes were left blank, to be filled up with the place of business whenever that unimportant locality might be found, which filling up was done by stamping with red ink, then the bank belonged to the Canidæ instead of the Felidæ, and was denominated " red dog." Both were of the same genus, however, and scratched or bit the dear people who gave them their claws and fangs, indiscriminately.

There were two of the latter class of banks established in the county, which issued their promises to pay, and commenced to do business; one of each denomination, and both located at Centreville. There were two others attempted, one at White Pigeon, which went so far as to get the notes all ready for issue, but before they were put forth the supreme court of the State decided some important point against the law, and they all collapsed at once, and the White Pigeon men preserved their purity in that respect, per force. The other bank was to be located at Lockport, but no further progress was ever made than to subscribe for the stock and elect directors.

The charter for the St. Joseph County Bank at Centreville was granted in the summer of 1837, with an authorized capital of $100,000, ten per cent. of which was paid in specie, November 21 following, the same having been subscribed for by farmers chiefly. Columbia Lancaster was the first president, and W. E. Boardman, cashier. This was a " wild cat," and its condition on March 6, 1838, as shown by the bank commissioner's statement, was as follows: Capital, $100,000; paid in, not known; circulation, $18,095; specie on hand and on deposit with Bank of Constantine, for redemption, $1,038.50; bills of other banks, $734.

The Farmers' and Merchants' bank was a " red dog," and designed for St. Josephs, in Berrien county, but began business in Centreville. It was chartered February 1, 1838, and on the 6th of the same month the stockholders elected a board of directors and officers, but had difficulty in getting them to serve. Finally the men most interested in the bank gave bonds to T. W. Langley for the prompt redemption of the notes issued, and he published a notice warning the people against selling the notes at a discount, as they would be redeemed at par in twenty days. But the parties who gave the bonds failed to fulfil their agreements, and the bank " went the way of all the earth" early in the spring of 1838. W. C. Posse, of Constantine, was the first president, then William Foster, with A. C. Hubbard and Charles S. Adams, cashiers, but all resigned, and Mr. Langley acted as before stated. The first statement of the bank commissioner did not show a very healthy condition of the finances of the bank. The capital was $50,000, as authorized, but it was not known how much, if any, was paid in. Circulation was bad, too, there being $19,860 out, and no specie to keep the currents good ; but there were other bank bills, probably as good as those the bank had itself issued, that figured upon their face $1,113.

The bad odor of these banks did not prevent the counterfeiter from indulging his peculiar faculties, for before the St. Joseph County Bank had been presented with a single note of its own for redemption, counterfeits were passed over its counters, and into its "till." However, in a very short time afterwards, the counterfeit was as good as the genuine, both being equally worthless.

It was the custom of the parties who owned or controlled the last class of banks to join in getting a certain amount of specie, sufficient to comply with the law so far as any one bank in the arrangement was concerned, and make that deposit serve for all, which device was executed by loading up the specie as soon as the commissioner had inspected a bank, and sending it on to the next bank in the round of inspection, and so keeping the specie in circulation.

There were no other banks of issue established in the county, besides those above mentioned, until the national bank law was passed by Congress, when the First National Bank of Three Rivers was organized, in December, 1864, with $100,000 capital, and Edward S. Moore as President.

There are at the present time six national banks in the county, with an aggregate paid-up capital, surplus and undivided profits, of $610,866.49 ; whose discounts and loans, on December 31, 1876, amounted to $617,394.65. There were deposits in those banks, subject to call, or at a specified time, $342,669.05, and their outstanding circulation amounted to $264,800. These institutions owned real estate, furniture and fixtures, valued at $43,043.29, and other banks and the United States treasury and its agents owed them $152,315.09. Their circulation is secured by the deposit with the United States Treasurer of United States bonds, amounting to $295,000 ; and in their vaults they had $90,000 in cash, consisting of legal-tender notes principally.

CHAPTER VIII.

ROADS—CHICAGO TRAIL—THE VALUE OF COST-MARK AND ECONOMICAL SURVEY, BUT A CROOKED ROAD—A PIONEER TOLL-GATE—THE WASHTENAW TRAIL—ROADS LIMITING JURISDICTION—QUICK PASSAGE FROM NEW YORK—FIRST POSTAL ROUTE—STAGE-LINE—FIRST TAVERN—FIRST POST-OFFICE—COMMERCE ON THE ST. JOSEPH RIVER—ARKING—A "CLOSE SHAVE"—STEAMBOATING—TRAGEDY—DAMMING THE ST. JOE—RAILROADS—BUSINESS OF 1876.

Sociability is a prominent characteristic of the human family. The recluse in society is an exception, tolerated because he is in nobody's way, but of little use to those around him, whatever he may accomplish for the future. The desire in man's nature to communicate with his fellows lends him to make the means of such communication easily accessible, and therefore roads are laid out, streams are bridged, marshes causewayed, railroads built, telegraphs constructed, and the telephone invented.

The first roads were the trails of the aborigines followed for ages between distant points, but always in a direct line—"as the crow flies"—between the fords of the streams to where hard ground could be found to enter the same. There were two important and principal trails passing through the St. Joseph territory when the first settlers came to it, one of which they followed in their journeyings thither. This was the Chicago trail, between that point and Detroit, along which every year the Western Indians, led by Black Hawk and other less-noted warriors of the Sac nation, rode in immense cavalcade to Malden to receive from the British government their annuities. When the procession began to approach the settlements, runners would be sent out to notify the inhabitants along the trail that the main body were coming, and to assure them of the pacific intentions of their people. It was rarely that any trouble arose between the whites and these Indians, in fact no disturbance ever was made unless the Indians were intoxicated. Mr. Marantette, of Mendon, mentioned an incident that occurred at the trading-post at Coldwater in 1825 while he had charge of it, although he was then a boy about eighteen years old. Black Hawk and his people had been to Malden and received their annuity, and were returning home, and stopped at the post to trade, that being the last one before reaching Chicago. They dismounted, and soon the room where he sold his goods was filled with the braves and squaws indiscriminately,—all wanting to buy something—Black Hawk, armed with a long lance, among the number.

3

While the bartering was going on, a squaw offered Marantette a very fine smoked deer-skin in exchange for something she saw on the shelves, and at a glance he saw it was one he had bought but a few days before, and which bore his cost or price mark ("sixteen shillings") on one corner. He immediately seized it and claimed his property. The squaw retained her hold upon it, also, and vehemently disputed his title thereto, and amidst the wrangle Black Hawk came up, and laying his lance upon the skin, proposed to settle the difficulty by taking it himself. The boy persistently refused to be imposed upon by the woman or bullied by the chief, and he immediately took another skin he had just purchased, and laying his pen he made a similar mark on the corner of it and laid it down beside the skin in dispute, and pointed to the two marks as evidence of his title, and was greeted with the loud "How!" "How!" "How!" of the Indians, who at once relinquished the skin and drove the squaw out of the room, and patronized the boy-merchant more than ever, buying some five or six hundred dollars worth of goods.

The Chicago trail entered St. Joseph county on the east on the line of the southeast quarter of section 55, in Burr Oak township, thence ran southwesterly to Fawn River township, passing between Honey and Sweet lakes, thence westerly through Sturgis, White Pigeon and Mottville townships, crossing the St. Joseph at the village of Mottville, which was designated the "grand traverse of the St. Joseph."

The second important trail was called the Washtenaw trail, and entered the county from Calhoun county, in the northeast corner of the township of Leonidas, thence running in a southwesterly direction to Nottawa prairie, thence via Centreville to White Pigeon.

In 1825 the National Congress ordered the survey of a highway one hundred feet wide, for military purposes, between Detroit and Chicago, and appropriated ten thousand dollars to complete the same. The surveyor began an elaborate work, but after a few miles' progress discovered that if he pursued his original plans the appropriation would be exhausted before the work would be completed, and he at once began to make the survey and the money run parallel to each other. The result was, the road was laid out with the Chicago trail for a center-line, and is so traveled to this day, with the exception of a single mile in Washtenaw county, which was straightened by the first settlers and fenced out. Otherwise than this one change, the road follows the trail of the Sacs in every angle, bend and turn from Tecumseh to Chicago. The flagmen were sent in advance as far as they could be seen, the bearings taken by the compass, and the distance chained and marked ; then the flag was advanced as before, the trees being blazed fifty feet on either side of the trail. The road was not worked by the government through St. Joseph until after the Black Hawk war, but the emigrants cut their way through and filled up the marshes sufficiently to pass, each one adding a little, and bridging the smaller streams as occasion required. The stage-companies also worked the roads sufficiently to get their coaches through, and built more bridges, but it was not until 1833 that the government made systematic and thorough work of building the road through Branch, and 1834 in St. Joseph county. Then for thirty feet the road was grubbed out and leveled, for thirty feet more the trees were cut low, and the balance of the width the trees were cut ordinary height.

FIRST BRIDGE.

The bridge at Mottville, over the St. Joseph, was built in the summer of 1833-4, by Hart I. Stewart as contractor. It was a very strong and well built structure, sixteen thousand feet of timber being used ; some of it the very best the country afforded. Some of the "stringers" were sixty feet in length, and eighteen inches square. It cost about five thousand dollars, and stood till 1845, when it was taken down to make place for a pile-bridge.

One of the Nottawa Indians, called "Shavehead," once established a tolling station on the trail, and demanded and obtained tribute from the passers along the same. The demands generally being light, the travelers paid it rather than have any trouble with the old fellow, who claimed the land as his own. One day, as Asahel Savery was riding along the trail, Shavehead appeared and demanded his usual toll, and Savery stopped his team. The Indian coming up to the wagon dropped his chin down upon the edge of the box, leaned his rifle against the body and looked up at Savery, wickedly peering at him, as was the custom of the Indians whenever they gathered about a wagon. Savery, instead of handing out the demanded fee, reached over and grasped the would-be exactor by his scalp-lock with his left hand, and with his right held his black whip about the bare shoulders of the struggling victim until he had punished him severely, when taking up the rifle he discharged it and threw it to the ground, and drove on. That toll station was discontinued, and never again re-opened.

The Washtenaw trail was made the basis of a territorial road from Jack-sonburg (now the city of Jackson) via Spring Arbor, the north bend of the St. Joseph river, through Nottawa prairie and Centreville to White Pigeon, in April, 1833, and Edgar McCawly, Hiram Thompson and Milton Barn were the commissioners who laid it out. It is a beautiful avenue, and in Leonidas, from the village to Dry Prairie in Calhoun county, follows a "bee-line" for some seven miles.

A territorial road was laid out and surveyed through White Pigeon prairie, north to Grand Rapids, in June, 1832, John S. Barry, Isaac N. Hurd and E. B. Sherman being the commissioners; and at the same time one was laid out from the county-seat of Branch county, running west through the county-seats of St. Joseph and Cass counties, to the mouth of the St. Joseph, and Squire Thompson, C. K. Green and Alex. Redfield were the commissioners. The year following there was a territorial road laid out, running from the Indiana line, north through Sturgis and Nottawa prairies, Toland's and Gull prairies, in Kalamazoo county, to Grand Rapids; and Rix Robin-son, H. L. Stewart and Stephen Vickery were the commissioners. The Chicago road was the main thoroughfare between the east and west, from the first influx of immigration into the county, until the railroads were built and completed in 1851, when travel on it ceased, except for local traffic. However, it still remains as originally laid out, and forms the main business street of every city and village through which it passes, from east to west. It is a grand avenue of one hundred feet in width, shaded in many places by the original forest trees left standing by the roadside when the adjoining farms were "cleared up."

Though roads are the lines of communication between the people, there is an instance on record in St. Joseph county of a road being a bar to judicial proceedings between the people of neighboring townships, which we here relate. When the Talbots, of Centreville, conducted their branch store in Burr Oak, they were sued by some party on account of a wood contract, the suit being brought before a magistrate in Burr Oak, under the statute giving justices of the peace jurisdiction over defendants residing in an adjoining town. The plaintiff engaged E. B. Turner to prosecute his suit, and the defendants employed Chas. Upson, Esq., to defend their interests, both of the attorneys living in Centreville at the time. When the return-day came around Mr. Upson could not go, and so engaged Esquire Chipman to go and get a continuance. It was good sleighing, and Turner and Chipman rode over together in a cutter. On arriving at the house of the magistrate, the suit was called, and Mr. Chipman filed his declaration and moved for a hear-ing; whereupon Esquire Chipman rose, and in his peculiar manner said he had a motion to make, and electrified the counsel for the plaintiff by moving for a non-suit. "What for?" asked Turner. "For want of jurisdiction," responded "Chip." "I guess not!" responded Turner. "Not much!" said Chipman, and addressing the court continued, "You see, judge, that when these towns were first laid out they did join, but afterwards the highway commissioners of the two towns came and laid a road on the town line, and now they don't join by four rods!" and exemplified the point by placing two books in a similar position. The argument and proof struck the magistrate (who was a great admirer of his brother magistrate, Esquire Chipman) very forcibly, and he pulled at his fore-top a moment, finally deciding that Chipman's position was cor-rect, that he had no jurisdiction in the case, and so non-suited the plaintiff, much to the disgust of his attorney at first, but who, as he took in the broad farce, laughed at his discomfiture as heartily as Upson did when Chipman reported the conduct of the case to him on his return to Centreville.

In the Michigan Statesman, published in White Pigeon in 1834, it is gravely stated that the trip from New York to Buffalo was then made in the unprecedented time of three days, and that one and a half days only are consumed between Buffalo and Detroit, while passengers can go from Detroit to Chicago in four days, and by daylight at that! Chicago and St. Louis were only six days apart. In July of that year, the trip from New York to White Pigeon was made in six and a half days—longer than it takes to go across the continent now. Traveling was sometimes as cheap in those days as it was devoid of pleasure, as witnessed by an instance recorded of a party who paid forty-five dollars for the conveyance of fourteen persons in a lum-ber wagon, without springs, from Detroit to Constantine.

In 1829 the first mail route was established on the Chicago trail from Te-cumseh to White Pigeon, the contractor being John Winchell, of the latter place, and by his contract he was required to carry the mail over the route once a week each way in the summer time, and once in two weeks in the winter. He performed his service on horseback.

In 1830 two-horse stages were run over the route to Niles, by Asahel Savery and the Stewarts, twice each week, increasing to tri-weekly trips in

1832, but the Black Hawk troubles stopped all immigration to the country, and for weeks the wagons ran over the road without a single passenger. This broke up Savery's business, but a new line was, immediately after the troubles ceased, put on by General Brown, of Tecumseh, and De Garmo Jones, of Detroit, who ran a fine outfit of horses and Concord coaches—four and six horses to each—between Detroit and Chicago. In 1836, when the tide of emigration was at its flood, the company ran extras every day, every one of them being literally jammed with passengers. The stage com-panies flourished and grew rich for several years, until the railroads began to creep along across the State, making the distances between points less and less, until, in 1851, the shriek of the engine drowned out the "toot" "toot" of the driver's horn, and the lumbering coach passed away from the Chicago trail forever. Where once it "dragged its slow length along" over cor-duroy and marsh, or rattled noisily over the prairie with crowded inmates suffocated with dust and heat, or frozen with cold and snow, now heavily-laden trains, luxuriously upholstered and ventilated thoroughly, dash across the landscape at thirty miles an hour. Such magic has progress wrought!

The first hotel, or tavern as it was called then, opened in the county, was the "Old Diggins," on White Pigeon prairie, on the present site of the Union school-house, in the village of White Pigeon. It was a large and substan-tially built log house, erected in 1828 by A. Savery, for the purpose of a tavern, and kept by him as long as he lived in the county; Dr. Rowley suc-ceeding him in 1830. The second tavern was opened the same year on Sturgis prairie, by John B. Clarke, in a double log house situated on the present site of the Elliott House, in Sturgis. Captain Henry Powers opened his log tavern on Nottawa prairie in 1830.

These primitive hotels were great places of resort for all purposes, politi-cal, educational or religious. Town-meetings were invariably held at the tavern until school-houses were built, which were conveniently located. They were well kept, too, considering the facilities for supplying the larder and the sleeping apartments. The route between Sturgis and White Pigeon, a distance of twelve miles, at one time had no less than six places of entertain-ment of all kinds and sizes, from the quiet home of the settler to the rough roistering grocery of the vender of bad whisky.

The first post-office was established on White Pigeon prairie in 1828, with John Winchell as postmaster; the second one was established on Sturgis prairie, on the eastern edge of the same, in 1829, and Samuel Stewart was the first postmaster. The postmasters were authorized to retain the re-ceipts of their offices, provided they supplied the postal matter at their own charges. For some years the mails received at White Pigeon and Sturgis, were kept in candle boxes. The business of the Sturgis post-office for the quarter ending December 31, 1876, was as follows: seven hundred dollars' worth of stamps were sold, four hundred letters were received and dis-patched daily, and one thousand five hundred papers distributed weekly; seven mails per day were received and dispatched.

Although the Chicago road was the great artery along which had the pulses of travel, the St. Joseph river was the channel by which the people brought their goods into the county in the early days, and by which they forwarded their produce until 1850. Merchandise was shipped from New York by the Erie canal to Buffalo, thence by sail or steam around the lakes to the mouth of the St. Joseph, where it was transferred to keel-boats, pi-rogues, flat-boats, and finally steamboats, and run up to Mottville, Constan-tine, and Three Rivers, as occasion required. No freight was forwarded until after 1837, as previously there were no mills of sufficient capacity to flour wheat suitable for the eastern markets. There was one exception, however, to the above statement, there being a single shipment of wheat made in 1834 from Three Rivers.

The first keel-boat ever launched on the St. Joseph river was one that was built on the banks of the Pigeon creek, just opposite the present farm of White, in 1829, and was floated down the creek into the river. Previous to this, "pirogues" (large canoes cut through lengthwise and widened by in-serting boards and having a gunwale along the sides) had been used. ⟨

The navigation of the upper St. Joseph was first attempted in the spring of 1830, by John W. Fletcher and John Allen, the latter at work for Fletcher, who wanted seed potatoes and oats, and, with Allen, went to Allen's prairie, Hillsdale county, where he found and purchased ten bushels of the first, and fifteen bushels of the last named article, and then went to work and built two white-wool canoes, launched them in Bend creek, loaded in their purchase, and floated down a few miles to the St. Joseph river, finding navigation very difficult by reason of shallows, ripples, dams of floodwood, and snags, until past the entrance of the Coldwater, after which the stream was clear and the water high. They slid their boats over the dams on peeled basswood skids, cut off snags with axe and saw, and lightened over sandbars and shallows. They missed the game they shot at, the motion of the canoe disturbing their aim, and lived on baked potatoes and wild honey, having found a bee-tree along the bank of the river. The return trip occupied ten days.

Washington Gascon built keel-boats at Three Rivers, beginning in 1835, and continuing the business for several years. His first one he named the "Kitty Kiddungo," which he sold, and next built the "Three Rivers," running it himself. The Willards built a scow in 1838, and loaded it with flour, ran it down to the mouth of river, and pushed the "Three Rivers" back. In 1833 Burroughs Moore originated the idea of building what were afterwards called "arks," for the transportation of produce. After the first one was made and loaded, it was found that nothing but flour could be profitably or safely carried in them.

They were simply two cribs, forty by sixteen feet, made as follows: Bottom timbers, six to seven inches square, and posts at corners and along sides same dimensions, spiked firmly together, and the whole covered with the very best white-wood plank, two inches thick, and calked with tow and slippery elm bark. The first ones had sharp bows, but they were afterwards built with square fronts and were sometimes called "square-toed packets." They were brought to anchor by what was called in the river parlance "growlers," which were small stakes large enough when stuck down before the cribs to retard the motion, but not so strong as to break the bottom or cause the ark to swing around. The first ark which went down the river was loaded with wheat, and, of course, as no one knew the strength of the current or the condition of the channel, the voyage turned out disastrously. The first stopping place was made at Constantine, and the Knapps and James Smith, who were in command, cast the lines ashore and "snubbed" the craft so short that the tail-board was pulled off and some wheat ran out into the river. They refitted and went on, and at Elkhart met with the same misfortune again, and lower down the river they stove a hole through the bottom of one of the cribs, and had to unload and refit again, and then were finally wrecked totally on the "Granddad," a ripple at Niles, and the whole cargo was lost.

This ended arking until 1838, during which time, from 1834, the freighting was done by pirogues and keel-boats. The arks, however, when first begun to be shipped, became quite popular. The next ones were built in 1838, and officered by the Millards; Reuben Freeman and Isaiah Smalley being in the first crew. The Bolles family also were good pilots, and ran the river for years. The arks were coupled in two sections, and had rafting oars before and behind to guide them by. They were never brought back up the stream, but sold for whatever they would bring, or allowed to float out into the lake after being unloaded.

When the dams began to be constructed across the river, much trouble was experienced in passing the chutes or getting through the locks. Captain Elisha Millard relates an incident of getting a heavily-loaded ark through the lock at Mishawauka, by unloading the first section and putting it on the second, when the water lifted it through and then carried the load of the second forward to the first, when it passed partly through and stuck between the posts of the lock, but by considerable pushing it was finally safely floating in the river again. He once ran a very narrow chance for his life at the Elkhart bridge. The water was at a very high stage in the river, and a temporary bent was put in, leaving but a thirty-feet span over the main channel. Captain Millard saw it, but it was too late to stop in the swift current, and the craft struck the bent and knocked it out, and was caught by the rope guy supporting the derrick and nearly capsized, but slipping, cleared everything that lay on the top of the ark—the captain and his mate, James Thaus, jumping for their lives. Thaus said if he had been six inches taller he would have lost his head.

The navigation of the river was difficult when the water was low, and dangerous when it was high, and it was only by careful observation and experience the arks could be safely delivered at their port of destination. Captain Millard had a narrow escape from serious disaster in the harbor of St. Joseph. There was a stiff current in the bay or mouth of the river, and miscalculating the velocity of the current, the lines parted when he tried to "snub" at the wharf, and the ark went on towards the lake. As it floated past a ship in the harbor, lines were thrown to the captain, which were made fast, when a new and more serious difficulty arose; the momentum of the ark being stopped, the current began to act upon the square surface exposed to it, and the first section exhibited symptoms of going below the surface of the tide, and it was only by hastily unloading the first or front crib and transferring it to the rear section, that the cargo was saved, if not the men.

Captain Alvin Calhoun constructed a fleet of small arks which would carry about twenty barrels of flour each, and after unloading them brought

them back by land in wagons. An ordinary ark would carry from four hundred to six hundred barrels. The millers would ship their flour in the spring and fall of the year, and frequently would not get advices or returns from it for six months. The first arks that ran from Colon were built in 1841 or 1842 by Captain Millard, and loaded by John H. Bowman at his mill on Swan creek. The very best white-wood timber in St. Joseph county was used up in building arks, and but little can now be cut in the county. Steamboats were built to navigate the St. Joseph, and ran regularly from 1842 till 1850, as far as Constantine; but a few trips only were made to Three Rivers, owing to the shallow water on a certain ripple known as "Knapps." A steamboat was built in Union City, and floated down the river to Mishawauka, where the machinery was put into it, and it ran on the river until 1845, when, while owned by the Kelloggs of White Pigeon, it was broken up on the piers of the Mishawauka bridge, Mr. Charles Kellogg being drowned. The passengers, of whom there were a large number, were all on the bow of the boat, which lifted the stern out of water and the rudder could not act, and before the danger could be averted the boat swung broadside on against one of the piers and broke in two. Mr. Kellogg fell into the water and could have saved himself, but thinking more of others' safety than his own, he devoted himself to a boy, whom he handed up out of the water, and as he was taken Mr. Kellogg disappeared, and when recovered was dead.

The first dam built across the St. Joseph in Michigan, was one constructed by Judge Cross, in Leonidas, in 1847, which was at first a great bugbear to navigators, but when completed was found to be no serious obstacle to arks in running the shute in any stage of water suitable for them to navigate the river with. The dam is not now in existence, but there are three others on the river in the county.

In 1833, the furore which seized the people of Michigan for internal improvements found the citizens of St. Joseph county ready to cast themselves headlong upon the wave of popular sentiment, and they held conventions, wherein high-sounding resolutions were passed, portraying in vivid colors and in "words that burn" the advantages of St. Joseph county, and the appreciation of values when railroad or canal communication should be had with the rest of the world.

On the 13th of November, 1834, a convention was held at Niles to take action on the improvement of the St. Joseph river, and Congress was petitioned to aid in the matter. Captain Philip R. Toll was the delegate from St. Joseph county. On the 1st of January following, a convention was held at Savery's to devise ways and means to get a railroad connecting Lakes Erie and Michigan, of which body Neal McGaffey was chairman, and Joseph Jernegan secretary. There were delegates present from White Pigeon, Constantine, Mottville, Michigan City, Toledo, Lagrange and Bristol, who resolved that a railroad was absolutely necessary between the lakes above named, and appointed a committee to memorialize Congress, the Secretary of War, or anybody else who would be likely to give aid and comfort to the much-desired object. They petitioned Congress to order a survey via White Pigeon, "believing it to be the best route, and more advantageous, etc., than one already made."

On February 2, 1836, a meeting was held at Edwardsburg, Cass county, to deliberate on the project of a canal from Niles to Constantine. H. L. Stewart, Duncan Clark and Dr. Watson Sumner were the delegates. The convention discouraged the canal project, but indorsed a similar proposition for a railroad between the same points. The crash of 1837, however, dissipated all the visions of the sanguine, enterprising people of St. Joseph county, as well as their neighbors in other parts of the State, and nothing further was done to build railroads until the State sold its interest in the Michigan Central and Southern, and those companies began to push their tracks westward, when the usual struggle for their passage through, or near, certain localities began, in 1849—the south part of the county getting the first prize.

A charter was granted in 1836 for a railroad or a canal, as might be deemed best by the stockholders, from Constantine to Niles, but the stock was never subscribed and the scheme failed.

The first railroad in the county was the Michigan Southern and Lake Shore, known then as the Michigan Southern, which was completed through Sturgis and White Pigeon in 1851. The terms of the charter of this road forbade the company going out of the State with their track, and also compelled the road to make the St. Joseph river a point on its line. This seemed to fix the line through the centre of St. Joseph county, touching the St. Joseph at Constantine, and the people of that place, not supposing any particular effort necessary to induce the company to take this route, were caught "napping," White Pigeon being made a point, and the road run up to Constantine as a mere matter of form to comply with the provisions of the charter. The road was afterwards, by township aid largely given, extended north to Grand Rapids, touching Three Rivers.

The Grand Rapids and Indiana road was built through the county from Sturgis, north through Nottawa and Mendon, in 1867; and the Michigan Air-Line—now the Michigan Central Air-Line—was built in 1871, passing through Colon, Centreville and Three Rivers, those towns giving heavy donations in aid of the same. The Michigan Southern, by securing a charter of a new road from Three Rivers south, was enabled to make connections with Chicago, and subsequent legislation secured to it the present franchise. Hon. I. D. Toll was chiefly instrumental in preventing the deduction of the road south of Coldwater, while in the State Senate in 1847, he opposing the sale of it to Toledo parties, though they offered one hundred thousand dollars more to the State, which then owned it, than the Detroit parties offered. He favored Detroit from a feeling of State pride, and so vigorously advocated the sale of the same to her own people, that it was thus disposed of.

The business of the railroads in the year ending December 31, 1876, exhibits the following grand aggregate: There were one hundred and nineteen millions and fifty thousand (119,050,000) pounds, or 59,525 tons of freight forwarded, and 104,640,000 pounds, or 52,320 tons of freight received at the several stations in the county; and the ticket sales in the same time amounted to $100,000. The shipments were largely of wheat and other grain.

## CHAPTER IX.

The judicial system under which the people of St. Joseph county are now living prosperously has reached its present excellence by and through a tortuous way, beginning with the "coutume de Paris," introduced by the French in their first settlement at Detroit, and running through the various systems of judication of France, England, the laws of the Congress of the United States, territorial enactments, constitutional provisions and State legislation, to the present time.

On the 27th day of April, 1827, the legislative council of the territory re-enacted the law previously passed, establishing the probate courts, and the day following re-enacted the law establishing the supreme and circuit courts, the territory now included in the limits of St. Joseph county being then attached to Lenawee county for judicial purposes. October 29, 1829, the council formed St. Joseph county and the territory attached thereto into the ninth judicial district, and on the 4th day of November following, ordered a circuit court to be held at the house of Asahel Savery, on White Pigeon prairie, on the third Tuesday of August following. The council also established a county court for the county under the act establishing such courts, and directed its session to be held on the first Tuesday of June and December.

The county court was abolished in April, 1833, the "circuit courts of the territory of Michigan" taking their business and jurisdiction. The latter courts were held by one circuit judge and two associated judges, two of whom must be present in order to open and hold the court.

The constitution of 1835 vested the judicial powers of the State in one supreme court and as many other courts as the legislature might establish, providing, however, in that instrument, for the establishment of a probate court, and the election of four justices of the peace in each township. The legislature provided for circuit courts to be held by the judges of the supreme court, and a chancery court with one chancellor, the latter being abolished in 1847, and its business transferred to the circuit courts. The county courts were the same year re-established with one county judge and a second judge, who officiated in the absence of the first one. The court was again abolished in 1853. St. Joseph county was in the third circuit, and third chancery district.

The constitution of 1850 vested the judicial power in one supreme court, circuit court, probate courts and justices of the peace.

Municipal courts can be provided by the legislature. For six years the supreme court was to be composed of the circuit judges of the State, after which the legislature was to provide for its organization with one chief and three associated justices, to be elected by the people for a term of eight years. The term of one judge expires every two years. The legislature obeyed this injunction in January, 1859. The circuit judges are elected for six years,

and their courts have original jurisdiction in all matters, civil or criminal, not excepted in the constitution nor prohibited by law, and appellate jurisdiction from all inferior tribunals, and supervisory control of the same, and terms of this court are to be held in each organized county in the State. The probate courts have jurisdiction exclusive of all matters of wills, intestacies, minors, etc., and the judge thereof is elected for a term of four years. Justices of the peace have the same jurisdiction as under the old constitution, and each township is entitled to elect four of them to a constitutional term of four years, one term expiring each year.

In 1873 the legislature provided for a salary, not exceeding one thousand five hundred dollars per annum (in St. Joseph county it is one thousand two hundred dollars), to be paid out of the county treasury to the probate judges, in lieu of all fees, except such as are charged for exemplification of records and papers, and the draftlog of petitions and bonds, thus making the most liberal provision for the settlement of estates of decedents of any of the sister States, for now, in Michigan, the poor can have their estates settled without the payment of costs of court, and the rich pay the salary of the judge by their taxes. Litigants, however, like all other luxurious livers, have to pay for their own pleasures.

The courts which now exercise jurisdiction over the people of St. Joseph county are as follows:

THE SUPREME COURT OF THE UNITED STATES.—Hon. Morrison R. Waite, Ohio, Chief Justice, with terms at Washington for each year.

THE UNITED STATES CIRCUIT COURT.—Hon. Halmer H. Emmons, Judge, Detroit.

THE UNITED STATES DISTRICT COURT FOR THE WESTERN DISTRICT OF MICHIGAN.—Hon. Solomon L. Withey, Judge; John H. Standish, United States Attorney; John Parker, United States Marshal; J. Davidson Burns, Kalamazoo, and H. E. Thompson, Grand Rapids, Registers in Bankruptcy. The terms of this court are held on the third Mondays in May and October, at Grand Rapids.

Samuel Post, United States Pension Agent, Detroit; Levi T. Hull, Collector of Internal Revenue, second district, Constantine.

THE SUPREME COURT OF MICHIGAN.—Hon. Benjamin F. Graves, Chief Justice; Thomas M. Cooley, James V. Campbell, and Isaac Martin, Associate Justices; Andrew J. Smith, Attorney General.

The terms of this court are held at Lansing and Detroit.

THE CIRCUIT COURT OF ST. JOSEPH COUNTY is at present constituted as follows: Hon. E. W. Keightly, of Constantine, Judge; John C. Joss, Clerk; D. H. Hawley, Sheriff.

THE PROBATE COURT OF ST. JOSEPH COUNTY is held by Hon. W. H. Cross, Probate Judge, on the first Monday of every month; but he is present in his office every other of the six working days in every week, so that the people are sure of a hearing whenever they may come.

The gentlemen who have been the presiding judges of the circuit court of St. Joseph county since the adoption of the constitution in 1835, are as follows: Epaphroditus Ransom, from 1836 to 1848; Charles W. Whipple, from 1848 to 1864; Nathaniel Bacon, 1856 to 1864; Perrin M. Smith, 1864 to 1866; R. W. Melendy, 1867 to 1869; Charles Upson, 1869 to 1873; Henry H. Coolidge, 1873; Edwin W. Keightley, from January, 1874, to the present time.

The judges of the county court and associate justices of the circuit court, from 1829 to 1853, when the new constitution abolished the office, were as follows: Luther Newton and John Sturgis were the first two, and received their appointment in 1829—Judge Wm. Meek taking Judge Newton's place in 1831. Hart L. Stewart took his seat on the bench with judges Meek and Sturgis at the December term, 1832; and in 1836 Judge Sturgis and Charles B. Fitch were elected. In 1840 Melancthon Judson and Isaac B. Dunkin were elected to preside with the circuit judge, and Judge Judson and James Parker were his side supports in 1844. In 1845 Nathan Osborn was chosen to fill a vacancy, and in 1846 Judge Osborn was elected county judge of the new county court, and Chauncey May second judge. In 1847 Cyrus Schellhous was elected second judge, and again in 1850, Wm. Savier being at the last date chosen as county judge. This was the last election of associate judges, the circuit-court commissioners taking their place, so far as their powers in vacation were concerned.

The judges of the probate court have been as follows: Dr. Hubbel Loomis the first one from January, 1830, to May, 1833, at which last date John S. Barry assumed the direction of mortuary settlements, and gave way to Digby V. Bell, May, 1835. Wm. Connor succeeded Judge Bell, September, 1836, and surrendered the dignity to Dr. Cyrus Ingerson in a year thereafter. Judge Ingerson held the position till his death in 1844,

COPY OF ORIGINAL-LETTER of GUARDIANSHIP to ISAAC TYLER over LUCY CODNER.

Territory of Michigan }
County of St Joseph } ss

By the Honorable
Hubbel Loomis Esq Judge of Probate
of Wills and for granting letters of Administration on the estate of persons dec'd
having goods & chattles rights or credits
in the county of St Joseph & Territory
aforesaid and for appr guardians to minors &c
To Isaac Tyler of the county afor
greeting. Whereas application hath been
made to have a guardian appointed for a
minor of the age of Ten years by the name
of Lucy Codner and whereas it so appears that
the same was necessary Trusting therefore in your
care and fidelity I do by these presents appo
you guardian to sd Lucy Codner

April 12th 1830 Hubbel Loomis
Recorded Lib A pag 7th Judge of Probate

Territory of Michigan } ss
County of St Joseph }

By the Hon Hubbel Loomis
Esq Judge of the Probate of Wills
and for granting Letters of Admin-
stration on the estate of persons
deceased, having goods, chattels,

[PLAIN WATER SEAL] rights or credits in the county of
St Joseph within the Territory aforesaid
To Elizabeth Thurston
of the county aforesaid Greeting
Whereas Amos Codour of said county deceased had
while he lived & at the time of his decease
goods, chattles, rights, or credits, in the county
aforesaid lately died intestate whereby the power
of committing administration and full
disposition of all and singular the goods
challtes & credits of the said deceased and also
the hearing examining & allowing the
account of such administration doth appertain unto me

Trusting therefore in your care
and fidelity I do by these presents, commit
unto you full power to administer all and
singular the goods chattles rights and credits
of the said deceased, and well and faithfully to

dispose of the same according to Law, &
also to ask gather Levy recover & receive
all and whatsoever, credits of the D Dcd
which to him while he lived and at the
time of his death did appertain and to
pay all Debts unto which the D Dcd
stood bound so far as his goods, chattels
rights & credits did extend according to the
value thereof

And to make a true and perfect
inventory of all and singular the goods
chattles, rights & credits and to exibit the same
into the Registry of the court of probate
for the county aforesaid at or before the
twentysixth day of Jun next ensuing and to render
an a plain and true account of your
D Administration upon Oath at or
before the twentysixth day of March which will be
in the year of our Lord one Thousand
eight Hundred Thirty one

And I do hereby Ordain, constitute
and appoint you Administratrix of all
and singular the goods. chattles rights
and credits aforesaid

In Testimony whereof I have hereunto
set my hand and seal of the P Court
of Probate Dated at White Pigeon
the twenty six day of March in the year
of our Lord one Thousand eight hundred
and Thirty

Attest. Regur of Probate

Jno. W. Anderson

Hubbel Loomis
Judge of Probate

---

Territory of Michigan }
County of St. Joseph } SS

Office of the Register of
Probate White Pigeon
March 28th 1830

Received for Record March 26th 1830
at 11 oclock A.M. and Recorded in Libro A
Page

Jno. W. Anderson Regr
of Probate
County of St. Joseph Mich.

and Benjamin Osgood was elected to fill the vacancy, as well as for the constitutional term. Judge Osgood was honored by the people's suffrages for three successive terms of four years each; and then, January 1, 1857, Charles L. Miller came in for a single term, and was succeeded by Judge J. Eastman Johnson, who was also favored with three terms. Judge Johnson doffed the ermine in 1872, and Wm. H. Cross put it on, and still wears it most acceptably to the people, who testified their appreciation of his labors at the election of 1876, re-electing him by the largest majority of any candidate on the successful ticket. The business has largely increased in this court during the last few years, until it has averaged during Judge Cross's present term over one hundred new estates per annum.

The first court of record ever held in St. Joseph county was a session of the probate court, held at the office of the register of probate, John W. Anderson, in White Pigeon village, on Friday, March 26, 1830, just five months after the county was organized. It was held by Dr. Hubbel Loomis, probate judge. The business transacted was the granting of letters of administration to Elizabeth Thurston, on the estate of Amos Codnor, deceased, of which decedent the said administratrix was formerly the widow. Arba Heald and William Hunter were her security, under bonds of one thousand dollars. On Monday, April 12, Isaac Tyler was appointed guardian of Lucy Codnor, a minor heir of said Amos Codnor, deceased, under bonds of five hundred dollars. June 2, Samuel Hopkins, John Sturgis and Isaac J. Ulman were appointed commissioners to assign the dower of Elizabeth Thurston in the estate of said Codnor.

August 23, the first will was presented for probate in the county, which was that of John Baumdee, and a hearing set for September 6, at which time the same was proven and admitted to record, and Hart L. Stewart, Abraham Reichart and John Baer were appointed appraisers of the estate.

Judge John S. Barry was inducted into office in May, 1833, and his first order, entered on the 22d of the month, was relative to the appointment of Adna A. Hecox guardian of William Hecox.

The first probate court held in Centreville was on October 24, 1834, and orders were entered in the estates of William Johnson, Robinson S. Hazard, Amos Codnor, Rufus Downing and Ambrose S. Wocks, deceased. During Judge Barry's incumbency, courts were held alternately at Centreville and White Pigeon.

April 30, 1835, the official signature of Judge Barry is appended to the records of the court for the last time, on page 20, liber 1, and on the next page appears the bold sign-manual of Digby V. Bell. It was this position of judge of probate that gave Judge Bell his title, by which he was ever afterwards known.

THE CIRCUIT COURT OF ST. JOSEPH COUNTY held its first term, according to the order of the legislative council, August 17, 1830, at Savery's, in White Pigeon, with the following presence: Hon. William Woodbrige, circuit judge; Henry Chipman, associate; E. B. Sherman, district attorney; D. Page, clerk; Daniel Murray, crier, and David Winchell, bailiff.

Neal McGaffey was admitted to practice before the court as an attorney, and a grand jury was impaneled as follows: Duncan R. Clark, foreman; Edward A. Trumbull, Niles F. Smith, James Knapp, Asahel Savery, Reed Page, Leonard Cutler, Arba Heald, John Robbe, Orrin Rhoades, Jacob Lane, Leon Martin, Alfred Martin, Joseph Martin, Anderson Martin, Laban Keyes, Jeremiah Lawrence, Jr., and John W. Anderson. John Winchell, postmaster, and Dr. Loomis were excused from service. The grand jury returned a presentment of the southern boundary, which the circle was ordered to copy for publication and presentation to the legislative council.

William Johnson, of Berwickshire, England, declared his intentions to become a citizen of the republic, and renounced his fealty to William IV. "by the grace of God" King of England. This was the first foreign-born resident admitted to citizenship in the county. The grand jury also found indictments against John Knapp and Thomas Bendure, but the indicted were not tried at this term.

The next term of court was held at the same place, August 16, 1831, by Judges Woodbridge and Sibley. A grand jury was impaneled, with John Winchell as foreman; and a petit jury was also called, but there being no business for them to do, they were discharged. Several defaulting jurors were ordered to be respectfully cited to appear and show cause at next term why they were not in contempt. Knapp, who was indicted at the last term for an assault and battery, was fined twenty dollars and costs, and Bendure was discharged from his recognizance. The grand jury also found two indictments, and the court, after two days' session, adjourned, Isaac W. Willard being the clerk.

The third term of the court was held at the academy in White Pigeon, August 21, 1832, by Judges Sibley and Morell. Solomon McInterfer,

having assaulted a fellow-citizen, was indicted therefor, but, having satisfied the punishee, the punisher was allowed to depart the court on payment of costs; and Phineas Driskell, for the same offense and satisfaction, was treated similarly. Columbia Lancaster came into court as district attorney, and swore, by high heaven, to do his duty by the county in his official capacity. Cyrus Lovell, John S. Barry, Cogswell K. Green and Alexander H. Redfield were examined by Wm. H. Welch, L. I. Daniels and E. B. Sherman, touching their legal attainments, and, on the recommendation of the committee, the quartette were admitted to practice as attorneys. John Winchell, justice of the peace, returned a writ of certiorari not entirely to the satisfaction of the court, and was directed to try again, and be more explicit in his answers and complete in his records, and fail not so to do on the first day of the next term of the court.

The next term of the court was held in Centreville, in the court-house, October 24, 1833, by Hon. W. A. Fletcher, circuit judge, and Wm. Meek and Hart L. Stewart, associates, with Isaac W. Willard, clerk, Isaac I. Ulman, foreman of grand jury, E. Taylor, sheriff. Five suits were dismissed, one continued, one indictment quashed and one not. pros'd. Rules of practice and pleadings were adopted, and George Woodward, a Yorkshireman, shook off the chains of kingly authority, and declared himself ready to become a republican. Two judgments were rendered by default for three hundred and eighty-four dollars and fifty-eight cents, and Isaac O. Adams obtained an order of sale on attachment against Frederick Tobey, levied on certain live-stock and produce.

At the next term, held April 29, 1834, there were judgments to the amount of fifty-five hundred dollars rendered, and nine jury-trials, one confession and ten defaults were had; and the first divorce-case made its appearance on the docket, wherein Catharine Hecox complained plaintively of Adney A. Hecox, and the court ruled Adney to plead answer or demur to Catharine's complaint at the next term. Some infants—certain Phelps' heirs—were defaulted, and the bill of complaint filed against them taken as confessed.

At the October term Aurora Amulet Gilbert complained most bitterly of the cruel desertion of her by her lawfully-wedded husband and lord, David B. Gilbert, and meekly said if the court did not wish to take her unsupported statements they might inquire for themselves; but the court evidently believed Aurora Amulet, for at the April term, 1835, they decreed that David should have Aurora as an "Amulet" no longer to charm away sorrow, and bade her resume her maiden name and single blessedness. At this last term Oliver Raymond, being found guilty under an indictment for selling liquor to Indians, moved an arrest of judgment because the indictment was indefinite—the name of the particular Mr. Lo not being given, nor the particular locality where the alleged infringement of the law had taken place. At the October term the plea was allowed. Three more subjects of William IV. refused longer to obey his mandate, and came into the fold of the republic. Five white men pleaded guilty to selling liquor to the Pottawatomies, and were fined five dollars and costs, and bid to go and sin no more, at the same price of condonement.

The October term of the circuit court was held by Hon. Epaphroditus Ransom, and Judge Connor, Judge Sturgis and Isaac G. Bailey were on the grand jury, and Columbia Lancaster was prosecuting attorney. The indictments which had hitherto-before ran in the name of the United States now appeared "in the name and by the authority of the good people of the State of Michigan." J. Eastman Johnson was admitted to practice.

In the October term, 1837, the first of the bank-suits appeared on the docket, and was brought to a hearing on a promissory note against Ralph Akers, wherein the interlocutory judgment, for want of a plea, was rendered absolute, and the damages assessed at six hundred and ten dollars and thirteen cents. There was a little breeze of discord at this term which rippled the usually placid surface of the court. The prosecuting attorney, Lancaster, moved the court for a rule on the sheriff, E. H. Trumbull, to produce the bodies of Charles E. Harrison and Jonathan Vickers, indicted for larceny and having counterfeit money in possession, respectively, before the bar of the court instanter; or in default, to be amerced in the sum of one hundred and two hundred dollars respectively; and further, that the rule be made absolute. But the court did not wish to act peremptorily, and declined to enter the rule, whereupon the prosecutor declined any further service for the term, and J. Eastman Johnston was appointed in his stead, and at the next term he appeared as the regular appointee.

At the September term, 1838, Daniel Fulton, Jr., was indicted for exercising secular labor on the Sabbath, and also for resisting an officer who interfered with his exercise, but a jury of his neighbors said he was not guilty of either charge.

THE COUNTY COURT

held its first term at Savery's, in White Pigeon, December 7, 1830, Luther Newton and John Sturgis, judges; D. Page, clerk; Daniel Murray, crier; Jesse Baum, bailiff. A grand jury was impaneled of noted pioneers, as follows: Hart L. Stewart, foreman, Ephraim Bearss, Sylvester Brockway, W. W. Bliss, Jason Thurston, Blakely Thurston, Alanson C. Stewart, I. J. Ullman, Wm. Hunter, Philander A. Paine, Nathaniel Syas, Joshua Gale, William Thomas, John McNeal, William Meek, Daniel Lyon, Jr., William G. Knaggs, William Stevens and Henry M. Paine.

The jury indicted John Knapp for shooting a mare, and after one day in session the court adjourned. June 7, 1831, the court convened again at Savery's, Judges Meek and Sturgis presiding, and adjourned to the schoolhouse (academy). Columbia Lancaster was admitted to practice as an attorney, Judge Meek's commission read, and the docket called. The United States vs. John Knapp, indictment for shooting "one mare, the property of Frederick Sedorus," was called, and the defendant pleaded not guilty, filed his affidavit of the absence of a material witness, and moved for a continuance. The court gave him postponement, conditional upon his furnishing bail in the sum of three hundred and fifty dollars in twenty minutes, and took a recess for that time; but on re-assembling, the defendant had failed to find any one sufficiently desirous to pay the forfeiture, or trust the honor of the prisoner, and therefore a jury of twelve good and lawful men was called to try the case, among them Arannah Phelps, Dr. Loomis, J. W. Coffinbury, and three of the Martin family. The prosecution called an array of witnesses, and the jury brought in a verdict of guilty as charged in the indictment, and the court sentenced the shooter to pay a fine of twenty dollars and costs into the county treasury, and one hundred and eighty dollars damages to the owner of the mare, being treble the animal's value, and to stand committed till the whole amount was paid, or he was otherwise discharged. The court established rates of ferriage at the grand traverse of the St. Joseph river (Mottville), and ordered a seal for the county, with the following device and inscription: "A sheaf of wheat, a merino sheep and a pair of scales;" and inscribed, "St. Joseph county seal."

The third term was held by the same judges, at the same place, in December, 1831, with John W. Anderson as foreman of the grand jury; David Clark, John S. Barry and Elias S. Swan were members also. The Rev. Reuben Sears produced his credentials as a Presbyterian minister in good standing, and was allowed to celebrate marriages according to the laws of the territory. Owing to the severity of the weather, the defaulting jurors were excused.

The first civil suit on the docket of the court, Joshua Gale versus George Whited, on appeal was "stricken from the docket, and the judgment below affirmed."

At the June term, 1832, Robert Wade, John Coats, William Barnard and Thomas Hobson made application for naturalization, but the same was continued.

In December, 1832, Hart S. Stewart took his seat with Judges Meek and Sturgis, and constituted a full bench. Eight delinquent jurors were ordered to purge themselves of their contempt at the next term of the court, but never had the opportunity to clear their reputations on that particular point, as the court was abolished that same winter. No jury trial was ever had in the court.

CHAPTER X.

LOCATION OF SEAT OF JUSTICE — BUILDING OF COUNTY JAIL — COURTHOUSE — OFFICES — COUNTY POOR-FARM — ABSTRACT OF PROCEEDINGS BOARD OF SUPERVISORS AND COUNTY COMMISSIONERS — CHAIRMEN OF THE BOARD — PRESENT MEMBERS — REVENUE SYSTEM — ASSESSMENTS AND TAXES — STATE AND COUNTY EQUALIZATIONS — TREASURY RECEIPTS EARLY, AND LAST — POPULATION STATISTICS.

The temporary seat of justice for St. Joseph county was located at White Pigeon when the county was organized, November 4, 1829. In 1830, commissioners were appointed by the governor to locate the county-seat, who reported in favor of its location on the plat of George Buck's village, on the present site of Lockport village—the proprietors, Mr. Buck and Jacob McEusterfer, donating certain lots on the public square and elsewhere to the county, in consideration of such location. This location was not satisfactory to many people of the county, and therefore, on March 4, 1831, before the governor issued his proclamation locating the county-seat in accordance with

the report of the commissioners, the legislative council set aside the report, and appointed a new commission to re-examine the proceedings in the premises. The new commissioners were Thomas Rowland, Henry Desbrow and George A. O'Keefe, and they reported in favor of locating the county-seat at or near the geographical centre of the county, on the plat of Centreville, the proprietors of that village offering more liberal inducements in aid of the erection of public buildings than were offered elsewhere. On the 22d day of November, 1831, the governor issued his proclamation, in pursuance of the statute in such case made and provided, locating the county-seat at Centreville.

On May 24, 1832, the legislative council ordered the courts of the county to be held at the academy in White Pigeon, or such other suitable place in said village as could be procured by the sheriff, until such time as suitable accommodations should be procured at the new county-seat. The county authorities at once bestirred themselves, and on January 23, 1833, Governor Porter issued his proclamation directing the courts to be held at the court-house at the county-seat, and the county officials to take up their residence there. The first accommodations for the courts and officials at the county-seat were provided by the board of supervisors, by leasing an upper room in the first frame building erected in Centreville, the same being twenty by thirty feet long, and two stories high, located on the northwest corner of Main and Clark streets. The same building, enlarged, is still standing on the same spot, and is occupied by Mr. Gregory for a harness shop, below, and a Grange hall above. The building was put up in the fall of 1832 by Thomas W. Langley, who bought out the original proprietors of Centreville, and the building was subsequently bought from him by the county.

At the May meeting, 1832, of the board of supervisors in White Pigeon, they voted to build a county jail at Centreville, after the following plans and specifications: The said jail to be made of hewn or sawed timber one foot square and dovetailed at the corners, and laid close; to be built in two square blocks, with a space of eight feet between—the whole to be covered with one shingle roof. The buildings to be of two stories of seven feet each in height, and the lower floors of the same thickness and materials as the framework; the second floor eight inches thick, and the third floor six inches. The doors to be of four-inch plank, and grated windows.

In July, 1833, the jail was accepted from the contractor, A. H. Murray, upon his making the floors and windows more secure.

The first man incarcerated in this jail was committed without formality or warrant; he had committed an assault on Mr. Langley, the landlord of the town at the time, and was "collared" by Sheriff Taylor and thrust into an apartment of the jail, and the door closed, but not locked, upon him. He was considerably more than "half seas over," and, finding a good supply of shavings on the floor, at once lay down and fell asleep. The jailor, Walter G. Stevens, forgot all about his boarder till nearly noon the next day, when he went over to the jail and found his tenant gone. At night the fellow came round and offered Stevens a quarter of a dollar to let him sleep there again.

This jail did service for twenty-one years, and when at last it was condemned, and the supervisors absolutely refused to make any further repairs on it, one summer midnight, in 1854 (August 14), the old relic went heavenward in smoke, except such portions of it as had sufficient aeirduposis to remain on terra firma. There were three prisoners confined in it at the time, one of whom, named De Forest, set it on fire, as supposed, the incendiary losing his life thereby, and the others escaping from the burning building, but not from custody. The old lock, weighing some twenty-five pounds, is now in the possession of Orlando J. Fast, Esq., prosecuting attorney of the county, who bought it of some boys who had fished it out of the St. Joseph, near Mendon. How the relic came there is a question yet to be answered. The lock was a most ingeniously-wrought combination of wards and bolts, made by E. C. White, the gunsmith of the village, and none but an expert locksmith could pick it, even with the key, when the combination was once fully set, being as fully proof against a rapid entrance into, as a sudden exit from, the jail. White drew the plans and combination mostly, and, Judge Connor supervised the work. The jail was built by a few persons mostly, notwithstanding the order of the supervisors for its erection, and, when first occupied, would not keep prisoners inside of its walls only so long as they chose to stay. It was afterwards refitted thoroughly, and was a secure fortress for the keeping of criminals. A certain criminal who had broken out of every jail in the country in which he had been confined, and had been outlawed in Missouri, and came back to the county and was re-arrested, was safely kept after the old lock was put on the jail, and was convicted and sent to the Jackson penitentiary, from which he soon afterwards made his escape. He kept clear of St. Joseph county after that.

In October, 1851, the first move was made for a new jail, when the supervisors refused to make further appropriations for repairs on the old building, but the people declining to second the motion, the subject was not broached again until 1853, when a committee was appointed to draft plans and specifications for a suitable building for jail purposes. In 1854, on the burning of the old jail, a temporary affair was ordered and built, but the present edifice was not completed until 1856-7. Mark Wakeman, Edward S. Moore, George W. Beisel and Judge Connor were appointed a building committee, and limited to an expenditure of not less than four thousand dollars, nor more than five thousand dollars. The jail is located opposite the court-house, on the east, and cost five thousand dollars. It is built of brick, and the main building is thirty-two by forty-five feet on the ground, two stories high, with an extension to the south, one story high, twenty by forty-eight feet. It has ten cells, and contains nine rooms for the use of the sheriff and his family, who usually reside in it.

On February 22, 1841, the county commissioners resolved to build a court-house, of wood (the present one), in the centre of the public square of the village plat of Centreville, which was to be completed in three years, or sooner, if practicable. Judge Connor was appointed to draft plans and specifications, and furnish a bill of materials for the proposed building. On March 12, Judge Connor having reported favorably on his work, the commissioners ordered contracts for one hundred thousand feet of lumber, sold to the lowest bidder, and ordered notices posted about the county calling for sealed proposals. The expense was to be met by the appropriation of all money on hand from the sale of lots, and the balance to be raised by direct taxation on the taxable property of the people of the county. Judge Connor was appointed superintendent of the work, with liberal discretionary powers.

The materials were generally purchased by the county, and the labor done by contract. John Bryan was awarded the contract for the work on the superstructure, at three thousand two hundred dollars. The board of supervisors came into power again before the building was completed, and Judge Connor was continued in the superintendency of the work. The building was completed and accepted in the fall of 1842, and cost about seven thousand dollars. Some alterations have been made since, but substantially the building stands unchanged at the present time.

At the April town-meetings in 1846, a proposition to raise one thousand dollars for the erection of the fire-proof buildings for the county offices, and the preservation of the records, was submitted to the people, who voted against it. On December 28, 1859, the supervisors voted to build the present brick offices, standing on the north side of the public square, occupied for the purpose above named. They appointed William Allman, Comfort Tyler and William H. Cross, a building committee, who contracted with William Laffey and Isaac R. Delote to build offices, according to the plans and specifications adopted by the board, for three thousand two hundred dollars. They are forty-four by twenty-four feet on the ground, with walls fourteen and a half feet high and thirteen inches thick, with tin roof and stone foundations, with stone-and-brick floors. A fire-proof vault was added subsequently to the register's office after the robbery of the records, described more fully elsewhere.

On January 1, 1848, the board of supervisors ordered the superintendents of the county poor to purchase a farm of one hundred or one hundred and sixty acres for a county poor farm; and one was bought the same year of Cyrus Schellhous for two thousand eight hundred dollars, in the township of Colon, which was subsequently sold, and another one, the old Latta farm and tavern-stand in Fawn River, obtained in 1857 by the forfeiture of Latta's recognizance under an indictment for counterfeiting, and which the county now owns. The farm consists of two hundred and forty acres or more, and is located on sections three in Fawn River and thirty-four in Burr Oak. The house on the premises is a large and comfortable building of about seventy by seventy feet on the ground, two stories in height, and will accommodate about fifty persons comfortably. The unfortunate poor are here cared for humanely while living, and when dead are buried in the Fawn River cemetery, and at their graves neat marble headstones, bearing inscriptions which give the name, age and demise of each, are erected by the county authorities. This last act of humanity is the result of Hon. Isaac D. Toll's efforts, while on the board of supervisors.

Under the ordinance of 1787, the governor and judges of the territory provided for the management of the fiscal concerns of the counties by courts of general quarter sessions, composed of the justices of the county courts and the justices of the peace, and gave them power to audit bills for the expenses of the county, and levy taxes to liquidate the same; to manage the pauper support, open and regulate roads, build bridges, divide their

counties into townships, and report their action to the governor for confirmation. On May 30, 1818, the same authority abolished these courts, and constituted in their stead boards of commissioners, who succeeded to the same powers as held by the courts, which boards continued till April 12, 1827, when the legislative council, which had, on the 30th of March preceding, provided for the election, by the towns, of supervisors, authorized these latter officers to meet at the county-seats, as a county board, with substantially the same powers as the commissioners had, which latter body was abolished. The legislature under the constitution did not seem to admire the operation of the supervisor system in the management of county affairs, and on December 31, 1837,—the first opportunity that offered,—that body remanded the counties to the commissioners' rule, and re-invested them with the power pertaining to the board of supervisors. But three commissioners from a whole county, all of whom might be in adjoining townships, did not suit the ideas of the people of the several towns, after having tasted the sweets of joint participation in the government of the county and the levy of its taxes, and the pressure was renewed for a change, which the legislature granted. February 10, 1842, by bidding, the commissioners surrendered their authority to the board of supervisors, which was reconstituted and re-invested with the charge of the strong chest of the treasury, and the replenishment and disbursement of the contents thereof. The legislature, under the new constitution, continued the regime, and it is still in force, with power sufficient to keep the wheels of government of the county well lubricated and in good repair, and therefore making satisfactory progress.

The first meeting of the board of supervisors of St. Joseph county was held at White Pigeon, on the 19th day of April, 1830. Luther Newton, supervisor of White Pigeon township, and Henry Powers, supervisor of Sherman township, met, but not being advised whether two members were a majority of the board, they agreed to meet on the 23d instant. On that day the two above named, and William Duncan, supervisor of Brady township (Kalamazoo county), met at A. Savery's house and organized the board, and appointed Neal McGaffey clerk, to hold his office during the pleasure of the board. They proceeded at once to give the people a slight taste of the cost of independent government, by levying a tax of fifty dollars for county purposes; fifty dollars in White Pigeon, thirty dollars in Brady, thirty-five in Sherman, and fifteen dollars in the township of Greene, for township purposes. They instructed the assessors in the several townships, for the year 1830, to return horses at thirty dollars each, oxen at forty dollars per yoke, and cows at ten dollars; all of which animals should be over three years old. They valued land at one dollar and twenty-five cents per acre, and fixed the compensation of the clerk at one dollar per day, and adjourned after a single day's session.

On the 5th day of October, the same year, the board held its second meeting, at which supervisors Newton, Powers, and Seth Dunham, of Greene township, were present. They met at Savery's again, and allowed Dunham four dollars for his services, and, as the record says, "transacted sundry other business relative to the tax lists in pursuance to the statute," and adjourned without day.

On March 17, 1831, the board met again, with Newton and Powers only present, but they were equal to the task before them. Believing in just weights and measures, they directed the clerk to procure sundry measures of the bushel and its aliquot parts, of wood and tin, and divers weights, or sixty pounds and less, terminating with a half-ounce avoirdupois, and furnish the county scaler with the same, and also with a stamp marked M. T., and ordered the county treasurer to pay the clerk ten dollars to make the purchase with. The bills of Powers and Newton for services, ten dollars and forty cents and eight dollars and thirty-seven cents and a half cents, respectively, and six dollars and fifty cents for the clerk, were allowed, and the board adjourned.

On June 7, 1831, the new board elected at the previous April town-meetings met at Savery's, at which William Connor, of Nottawa, and Weston W. Bliss, of White Pigeon, were present. They directed the assessment of all lands in the county, with the improvements thereon—except houses not worth one hundred dollars, and school-houses—and horses and cattle over three years of age, to be made at their actual value.

In October of the same year the board met again, and supervisors Bliss, Connor, Dunham of Greene, and Jason Thurston, 2d, of Sherman, were present; accounts to the amount of seventy-one dollars and six cents were audited, three-fourths of which were for attorneys' fees; showing that the privilege accorded the county of "suing and being sued, impleading and being impleaded," was not an unmixed blessing. They offered a bounty of one dollar for each wolf-scalp taken in the county, and elected Seth Dunham chairman of the board, whose signature is appended to the record of that meeting.

On March 5, 1832, the board met, with supervisors Bliss, Conner and Dunham present. Robert Clark, Jr., was appointed the clerk for that meeting. The board audited the following accounts: Supervisors' services, thirty-two dollars and twenty-nine cents; sheriff's accounts, twenty-four dollars and forty-six cents; wolf-scalps, four dollars; clerk, for stationery and services, four dollars and fifty cents, and three per cent. commission to the county treasurer on what he had received for the county, amounting to nine dollars, making a total audit of seventy-four dollars and ten cents. The treasurer had a balance on hand of one hundred and eighty-four dollars and sixty-nine and a half cents.

The next meeting was held at the academy, in White Pigeon, on May 12, 1832, with the same town represented as at the last meeting, and Albert E. Ball acted as clerk. Values were increasing, or stock was getting better in quality, for stallions kept for stock purposes, were listed at one hundred dollars each; first-rate team-horses sixty dollars, and second-rate ones at thirty dollars; oxen, forty-five dollars per yoke, and cows, thirteen dollars. Improved lands were valued at two dollars and fifty cents per acre, and unimproved at one dollar and twenty-five cents; wagons at forty-five dollars; carts, twenty-five dollars; stage-coaches and pleasure wagons, and houses worth more than one hundred dollars, at their actual value.

At the October meeting the same year, the same members being present, the first allowance for a pauper was made—one hundred and seventy-one dollars and thirteen cents for the support of Tim Shields. The sheriff drew out of the county treasury two hundred and seventy dollars, and the supervisors and their clerk sixty-three dollars and ninety-seven cents more. Havoc had been made among the genus canis, twenty-five of the gaunt and hungry fellows having fallen victims to the price set on their heads.

The next meeting—the first one held at Centreville—was a special one, convened March 30, 1833, but no business of moment was done. At the June meeting following, John S. Barry, a justice of the peace, appears on record by a report of fines collected by the county court justices. The sale of six of the best lots in Centreville, belonging to the county, was ordered, and the clerk directed to advertise the sale by posting notices in every post-office in the county. Digby V. Bell was appointed clerk of the board at the May meeting, 1835, and S. W. Truesdell was elected in 1836—the first clerk elected in the county. At the October meeting, 1837, Columbia Lancaster, county treasurer, having received "in the line of his duty" a counterfeit ten-dollar bank-note of some collector whom he could not designate, was allowed the amount in his account, and the worthless "rag" solemnly burned to prevent further mischief on its behalf.

The October meeting, 1838, is notable as being the last one before the re-entrance of the county commissioners, and also for being the first meeting to equalize the assessment of real-estate.

On December 28, 1838, the county commissioners met and organized the board, with John G. Cathcart, of Constantine, John Sturgis, of Sherman, and James Hutchinson, of Park, as members, and elected William Hutchinson chairman, and adjourned until January 9, 1839, when they re-assembled and appointed Neal McGaffey, Edward S. Moore and Hiram Jacobs county superintendents of the poor, these being the first of those officers that appear on the record. In May, 1839, the board licensed Asher Bonham to run his wares as an auctioneer, and gave Smith & Bowman the right to run a ferry across the St. Joe at Three Rivers. In September, 1839, the demand for wolf-scalps largely exceeded the supply, as would appear by the price paid by the commissioners for them—thirty dollars for two, which probably were no better than those offered to the board of supervisors in early days for a dollar apiece. But the price fell off in October, and the board paid but ten dollars for each. The first two were Sherman wolves, and the latter were White Pigeon stock. On April 9, 1842, the commissioners directed Judge Connor to continue his superintendency over the court-house, then in process of erection, until relieved by competent authority, and then gracefully bowed themselves off the stage, and the curtain fell upon the final act. It rose again as the new board of supervisors made their début before a critical audience, amid the rejoicings of the anniversary of the natal day of the republic—July 4, 1842. George G. De Puy, of White Pigeon, was elected chairman of the new board, which was composed of fourteen members. The board appointed a committee to examine the county jail, which subsequently reported the same in a destitute condition, not a prisoner being then confined within its walls. The board, in 1844, abolished the distinction between county and township poor, and assumed them all as a county charge.

The following gentlemen officiated as chairmen of the board since the first one was chosen in 1831, the board of 1830 acting without any legal head: Seth Dunham served for the year 1831; Benjamin Sherman, 1832; W. W. Bliss, 1833–34; William Connor, 1835–37; Isaac G. Bailey, 1838; George G. De Puy, 1842; C. B. Fitch, 1843; James L. Bishop, 1844; A. E. Massey, 1845; William Savier, 1846–49; W. C. Pease, 1850; Hon. Isaac D. Toll, 1851; William McCormick, 1852; Comfort Tyler, 1853–59 and 1867; William G. Woodworth, 1860 and 1868; William H. Cross, 1861 and 1866; John Harrison, 1862–65; Hiram Lindsley, 1869; Norman Roys, 1870; William F. Arnold, 1871 and 1873; J. C. Bishop, 1872; S. M. Nash, 1874; G. W. Osborn, 1875.

The present board is composed of the following supervisors, to wit: Andrew Climie, chairman, Leonidas; A. P. Emery, Mendon; Daniel Pfleger, Park; Ira Starkweather, Flowerfield; Henry Stoltz, Fabius; William F. Arnold, Lockport; John C. McKercher, Nottawa; Ansel Tyler, Colon; J. C. Bishop, Burr Oak; H. C. Hopkins, Sherman; Norman Roys, Florence; Aaron Howard, Constantine; J. C. Hattler, Mottville; G. B. Markham, White Pigeon; L. E. White, Sturgis; Isaac D. Toll, Fawn River.

A necessary and unavoidable concomitant of government is a system of taxation, by and through which revenues may be derived for the payment of the expenses incurred in the direction of the public affairs of a community; and the more perfect and simple that system is, the less friction it involves in its exercise or administration. The system at present in vogue in Michigan is a very simple one, the townships being the fountains from whence all the streams of revenue flow. The machinery, too, is simple, and easily worked. The supervisor in each town lists the taxable property in the township, and takes this list up with him to the board of supervisors, who, as an equalizing board between the several townships of the county, equalize the same, and once in five years the State board of equalization equalizes the assessments of the counties between the several counties in the State, for a basis whereon to levy each county's just proportion of the State taxes. After the equalization is made by the supervisors, the estimate of the county requirements for the year is made, and the percentage necessary to be raised on the equalization assessment for State and county purposes determined, the amount for State purposes being reported from the auditor-general. The amount to be raised for town, school and road purposes, is regarded by the people in the towns and districts themselves, and the county authorities have no cognizance of it.

The supervisor casts and extends the taxes, makes up the tax-roll of his town, and certifies the same to the township treasurer, who proceeds to the collection of the taxes thereon, under penalty of double the amount thereof, making his returns to the county treasurer for the State and county taxes, and to the proper town official for the township and other taxes.

Sales of land for delinquent taxes are made by the county treasurer on the first Monday of October succeeding the return of the same to that official, the owner of the land retaining the right of redemption from such sale for one year thereafter, upon the payment of the amount for which the same was sold, together with an added penalty of twenty-five per cent., graduated into equal quarterly portions at the option of the redemptor. At the expiration of the year after the sale, the unredeemed lands are certified to the auditor-general, who executes all tax-deeds therefor.

The amount of the assessed valuation of property in the county is not shown by the records for the year 1830, but the amount of county taxes levied was $110.24, the county treasurer receiving the net amount of $95.05; $130.00 was raised for town purposes, each town having the privilege (?) of paying its respective amount on its own assessment. The assessment of 1831 is not given either, but the levy of one-fifth of one per cent. on the same, ordered by the supervisors, produced $228.95, and therefore the assessment must have amounted to $114,475. In 1832 the assessment of the real and personal property in the county amounted to $119,228, and the county tax levied thereon at the rate of one-half of one per cent. produced $620.93, the county netting the sum of $516.70, the balance being swallowed up by the commissions of the collectors and the non-resident taxes. The latter, however, were paid, or made, at the tax sale in 1840.

The foregoing assessments included the taxable property of Branch county. The first assessment in St. Joseph county, as at present limited, was made in 1833, and amounted to $200,173, and one-sixth of one per cent. was levied on it for county purposes, producing $478.44. $235.00 were levied for township purposes. The assessment of 1834 amounted to $347,194, and the tax charged against it, $1,455.56, for county use. There were $1,804 also raised in the different townships for their own use, $895 being for White Pigeon alone. The assessment of 1835 was returned at $386,085, with a county levy of $1,931.73, and a township tax of $528.19 additional.

In order that Colon might not be totally neglected in the township levy, it was assessed a single dollar only. In 1836 the county paid her first tribute to "the powers that be" over her, and her assigned quota of the State taxes amounted to "$1,529.18.10," as the record reads. The county needs amounted to $2,012.98, and therefore the sum of $3,542.16 was levied on the assessment that year, which amounted to $611,672.

The first equalization of the assessment of real estate between the townships of the county, was made by the board of supervisors in 1830. Improved lands in Florence were raised to fifteen dollars per acre, and unimproved to five dollars. Unimproved lands in Park were valued at four dollars per acre, and twenty-five per cent added to the valuation of real estate in Colon. Unimproved lands in Leonidas and Fawn River were placed at four dollars per acre, and the assessments of the other towns were unchanged from the valuation of the assessors.

The assessment of 1840 is not given in the records, but the State and county taxes for the year amount to $5,800. In 1850 the assessment footed up $997,133, and $8,813.57 covered the State and county levy.

In 1851 the first equalization by the State board of the assessment of the county was made. The assessment, as equalized by the supervisors, amounted to $1,094,920. The State board placed the entire assessment of the State at $30,976,270, and on that basis fixed the assessment of St. Joseph county at $1,088,920, for State purposes of taxation. The taxes of 1851 were $3,726.25 for the State, and $6,569.52 for the county.

In 1856 the county equalized the assessment at $5,412,958, and the State board reduced it for their purpose to $4,450,000. The State taxes that year amounted to $2,101.39, and the county's to $11,502.53.

In 1861 the county equalization was $5,825,565, and it was left unchanged by the State board. The State levy for revenue was $15,716.02, and that of the county, $18,705.

In 1866 the county equalized its assessment at $6,343,536, and the State board added nearly three millions to it, making it $9,229,741.66. The State claimed $17,440.24, and got it, and the county levied $17,200 for its needs.

In 1871 the county returned the assessment as equalized at $12,753,118, and the State board added nearly one hundred per cent., placing it at $24,300,000. The State taxes amounted to $29,730.27 that year, and those of the county to the same sum.

In 1876 the assessment, as equalized by the board of supervisors, amounted to $8,074,871, and the State board equalized it at $18,025,000, on the basis of $539,000,000 for the entire State. This was a better rate than the equalization of 1871, by some $6,275,000, and, as it stands for five years before any alteration can be made in it, the county will save the taxes on that excess for that period of time. This reduction was effected by the arguments of Hon. Isaac D. Toll, the representative of the board of supervisors of the county to the State board of equalization. Mr. Toll argued from the statistics, furnished by the census of 1884, that St. Joseph county was about equal in wealth to the counties of Branch, Calhoun, Kalamazoo and Cass, while it had been assessed several millions of dollars higher than either one of them. Andrew Climie, Esq., chairman of the board of supervisors, also presented the argument before the board that ten thousand population in the older counties represented about the same wealth that double that population did in the new ones, and on that basis St. Joseph county had been placed too high in the valuation of the State board, by some millions of dollars.

The State and county taxes for 1876 amounted to $41,250, the same being equally divided between the two powers. There were 317,267 acres of land assessed in 1876, at an average value of $21.10 per acre. The present property valuation, as equalized, amounts to $1,607,606, which averages $62.06 per capita, on the census of 1874, which places the population of the county at 25,906.

The values reported in the census are a more faithful index of the real wealth of the county than the assessments made for taxation, which vary from one-half to one-third of the actual value of the property assessed. In 1870 the property was assessed at one-half its estimated cash value, which places the latter at $50,990,256. It is estimated by competent judges that the assessment, as equalized by the State board of equalization in 1876, is scarcely more than one-quarter of the actual value of the property liable to taxation in the county, which, according to that estimate, would be worth at least $70,000,000.

The total receipts into the county treasury, from 1830 to 1835 inclusive, from all sources, aggregated the sum of $4,778.53, which included $80, docket fees and fines, and $150 received on sale of county lots in Centreville. The receipts, from all sources, into the treasury for the year ending

4

December 31, 1876, aggregate the sum of $70,801.93. This amount includes the State taxes of 1875, $20,108.56; the primary-school fund from the State, $4,451; fines, to the library fund, $800.50; costs, docket, jury and reporters' fees from circuit court, $803.09; the liquor tax, $6,452.74; the county taxes, $34,703.47; redemptions from drain assessments, $206.78, and sundry receipts from other sources, $913.53. Among the disbursements were the following: For the support of the poor in the county and at the insane asylum, $10,478.95; to the supervisors, for sundry services, $1,432.92; for jurors and witnesses and the house of correction, $3,137.81; salaries of county officers, $4,950; incidentals and sundry other items, $562.16, and but $30 for attorneys' fees. The amount of the delinquent land-tax for the year 1875 was $1,469.40, and $538.10 was charged back to the township for collection on the rolls of 1876.

In the fall of 1827 there were not more than five families of actual white settlers within the limits of the county of St. Joseph, composed of perhaps thirty individuals. Ten years later the population had increased to 6,337. In 1850 there were 12,717, divided among 2,318 families, and dwelling in 2,303 houses. In 1860 the population had increased to 21,111, composing 5,362 families, who dwelt in 5,347 houses. In 1870, 26,272 people called the county "home" at the time the census was taken, and the number of families had increased but ten, and the dwellings sixty-two in the decade. In 1874 the population, as shown by the State census, had fallen off somewhat, there being but 25,906 persons returned. Counting Wayne county, with 144,903 inhabitants, as the first in rank, St. Joseph would rank in respect to population as twenty-two; of these 25,906 people, 13,267 were males, and 12,689 females. Ten years later the population had increased to 6,337. Of the latter were of marriageable age; 2,417 men were between forty-five and seventy-five years of age, and 2,563 women between forty and seventy-five; 115 men were between seventy-five and ninety years, and one between ninety and one hundred—Thomas Cade, of Sturgis; 122 females were over seventy-five years. There were 3,188 boys between ten and twenty-one, and 2,373 girls between ten and eighteen. There were 3,176 boys and 2,967 girls under ten years. There were of the widowed and divorced, 1,018; of males over twenty-one years, 1,411 were bachelors, and of females over eighteen, 1,383 had eschewed matrimony. The married were nearly evenly matched, there being 5,199 men and 5,201 women in the list. Of the unfortunate there were sixteen blind, ten deaf and dumb, eight insane, and twenty idiotic; and there were 158 colored persons throughout the county, and not a single one of the former lords of the soil, the followers of Sau-au-quet.

## CHAPTER XI.

ELECTIONS—POLITICAL STATUS—OFFICIALS AND TERMS OF OFFICE.

The first election ever held within the present limits of St. Joseph county, was in the year 1827. Austin E. Wing and John Biddle were opposing candidates for the office of delegate to Congress, and the election being conducted on personal grounds rather than political ones, it was very closely contested. Major Calvin Brittain, afterwards a State senator from the district of which St. Joseph county formed a part, came to White Pigeon and organized a poll, at which fourteen votes were cast, which were sealed up, and the gallant major took them as the messenger of the election board, and posted away to Detroit, where the returns were to be canvassed. At the final canvass it was found that Wing had just seven more votes than his opponent, Biddle, had. Biddle's friends were furious, and charged that there were not fourteen white people west of Lenawee county to Lake Michigan. Major Brittain claimed the votes to have been cast by actual residents, who had most undoubtedly lived long enough in the country to gain a legal residence therein; but when pressed for other qualifications required by the law of elections, admitted that some of the voters bore a striking resemblance in color and physiognomy to certain of the dusky clansmen of White Pigeon, the chief of the Pottawatomies. At this election there was also chosen a member of the legislative council.

The next election was held in the summer of 1829, at which Messrs. Biddle and Wing were contestants for the same position, Biddle being the successful candidate.

The next election held in the county was the annual town-meeting in April, 1830, held in the townships of Sherman and White Pigeon, and which was the first election ever held in St. Joseph county proper. At this election, besides the township officers, there were a county treasurer and coroner elected, John Winchell being the first-named official and ———— ———— the second. Greene township (Branch county) and Brady township (Kalamazoo county) voted with the St. Joseph county townships at this election.

At the election of 1835, on the adoption of the constitution, there were 216 votes polled. There were no contests which developed the strength of political parties in the county until the Presidential election of 1840. That year the Whigs carried the county by 39 majority, Harrison receiving 800 and Van Buren 761 votes. The contests on local officers have always been conducted more on personal than on partisan grounds, and the tickets have been "scratched" liberally, both parties electing candidates frequently at the same election. Edmund Stearn, a Democrat, and Charles H. Knox and William Laird, Whigs, were so popular in the early days that whenever they were nominated their election was a foregone conclusion.

In 1844, in the Polk and Clay campaigns, the Whigs carried the county again by 40 plurality over the Democrats, the liberty men polling 84 votes. The total vote was 976 for Clay, 936 for Polk, and 84 for Birney—1,996 in all. The liberty vote for governor in 1843 was 103.

In 1848 the total vote was 2,392, and the Democratic party carried the county by 48 plurality over the Whigs—the free-soil party, then organized, drawing its adherents more largely from the latter than the former party. The vote was for Cass, 1,011; Taylor, 963; Van Buren, 418. One man was determined to know whom he voted for, and having no confidence in the electors, cast his ballot direct for Martin Van Buren for president. Judge I. P. Christiancy, at present United States senator from Michigan, was one of the free-soil electors.

In the campaign of 1852 the Democrats carried the county again by an even 100 plurality over the Whigs, the total vote being 2,678. Pierce received 1,263; Scott, 1,163, and the liberty vote was 252.

In the Fremont campaign of 1856, the first appearance of the Republican party, the new actor made his début with a majority of 837 votes, in a total poll of 3,811.

The Republicans polled 2,324 votes, the Democrats, 1,475, and the prohibition ticket had a round dozen supporters. In 1860 the relative strength of parties remained about the same, the Republican majority over all being 831. There were 4,832 votes cast, of which the Republicans had 2,832; the Democrats, 1,980, and the prohibitionists cast just as many votes as there are years which must elapse before the native American can exercise what ought to be his proudest right, the elective franchise. In 1864 the Republican majority was increased a trifle, there being no third party in the field. In a total vote of 4,477, the Republicans cast 2,681, and the Democrats, 1,796. In 1868 General Grant received 3,562, and Seymour, 2,490 votes, the total poll being 6,052. In 1872 Grant received 3,154 votes; Greeley, 1,791; O'Conor, 90, and Black (the prohibition vote), 6, making a total vote of 5,041. In 1876 Governor Hayes received 3,165 votes; Governor Tilden, 2,490, and Peter Cooper, the "Greenback" candidate, 748.

In 1848 the congressional race was between Charles E. Stewart, Democrat, and William Sprague, Whig. Notwithstanding the Democratic vote on presidential electors was the largest, yet Sprague claimed the county by 267 majority. The secret of Sprague's success lay partly in the fact that he was a presiding elder of the Methodist church, and his brethren supported him, irrespective of party ties, to a considerable extent. He was stronger in the county even than Governor Barry, who was one of the Democratic electors, and carried the county by forty-eight votes only. In 1849 the election for representatives to the State legislature was somewhat noticeable in its results. William H. Cross and Edwin Kellogg were the only Whig candidates, and Norman Roys and Asher Bonham, the Democratic nominees. Mr. Kellogg received 989 votes; Messrs. Roys and Bonham, 979 each, and Mr. Cross, 978. The two Democrats having tied on the vote, drew lots, and the prize fell to Mr. Bonham. One of Judge Cross' personal friends, by a little "tiff" just before the day of election, lost the judge his election by staying at home, and keeping half a dozen others from attending the polls, all of whom were friends of the unlucky candidate.

There were one hundred and seventy-seven men in the county, in 1849, who expressed themselves satisfied with the constitution of 1835, and twelve hundred and twenty-two who wished for a change. It was a close race for the county offices in 1850, under the new constitution, John Hull getting the sheriff's place by a bare majority of eight votes; C. D. Bennett taking the clerk's by thirty-one majority, and William Laird securing the county treasury plum by sixty-seven. Edmund Stearn held the Democratic vote and some of his Whig friends, and came smiling into the register's office, backed by two hundred and sixty-one more votes than his competitor.

In 1853 a special election was held to determine the sense of the people on the question of prohibiting the manufacture and sale of intoxicating liquors in the State, which resulted in showing that one thousand two hundred and

ten of the persons voting on the question were in favor of prohibition, and eight hundred and eighty opposed to it. There was not a third of the votes of the county cast. Burr Oak, Mendon, Nottawa, Florence, Sherman, Sturgis, Lockport, White Pigeon and Constantine gave majorities for the proposed law, the last four townships quite notable ones; the remaining towns gave majorities against prohibition.

In 1870 Governor Blair received just seven hundred more votes for governor than Governor Barry, the former receiving 2,777, and the latter 2,077 votes.

The county officers under the governors' and judges' administration in the territory, were appointed by the governor, and were the following: justices of the county courts, clerks of the courts, sheriffs, judges of probate, coroners, county commissioners, justices of the peace and constables. On the 30th day of March, 1825, the legislative council terminated the official terms of all of the above offices on December 31, 1825, and fixed the new terms at four years, except those of sheriffs and justices of the peace, which officials were given but three years at the public crib.

In April, 1825, the council gave the people the right to elect the county commissioners, treasurers, coroners and constables. The judges of probate, from 1809 till 1827, appointed their own clerks or registers, but in the latter year the council gave the power of the appointment to the governor. January 29, 1835, the council abolished the office, and charged the judge of probate with the execution of the duties theretofore performed by the register, and provided for the election of register of deeds.

The governor had the power of appointment of the judges and clerks of the several courts of record, the sheriffs and justices of the peace during the continuance of the territorial government, but under the constitution of 1835 the people had the power of electing their officials, with the exception of the circuit or chief judges of the circuit court, and the prosecuting attorneys, who were still appointed by the governor.

The county officials, under the first constitution, were associate judges of the circuit court, judges of the county courts, judge of probate, sheriff, two or more coroners, county clerk, who was ex-officio clerk of the courts (circuit and county), register of deeds, county surveyor, county treasurer, and three county commissioners, who afterwards gave place to the board of supervisors. Under the constitution of 1850, the same officers were provided for, except the associate judges of the circuit court, judges of the county court, and county commissioners; prosecuting attorneys were to be elected. The official terms of all were fixed at two years, except that of the judge of probate, who had a lease of power for four years, with the privilege of an indefinite extension thereof, at the option of the people assembled at the polls.

The township government, under the territorial authority, was vested by the act of the legislative council of March 30, 1827, in a supervisor, town clerk, collector of taxes, three or five assessors, at the option of the supervisors, three commissioners of highways, two overseers of the poor, and as many constables, fence-viewers, pound-masters and overseers of highways as the people might think could be kept at work to advantage, and care-their pay—on which none of them ever became wealthy, and all of which officials were elected by the people, their masters.

Under the first constitution the people in each township elected a supervisor, town clerk, treasurer, three assessors, one collector, three school-inspectors, two directors of the poor, three commissioners of highways, and as many justices of the peace and constables as the town was entitled to, which could not exceed four of each at any one time, and as many overseers of highways and pound-masters as were necessary to keep the roads in good order, and the fields secure from the depredations of four-legged animals.

Under the new constitution the list of town officials was cut down somewhat. The town clerk and inspector now do the work of three inspectors of schools formerly; and one commissioner of highways holds the honor alone of a position, wherein, under the old organic law, the "honors were easy," as well as the work, between three.

The first officers in the county were Dr. Hubbel Loomis, probate judge; John W. Anderson, register of probate; John Sturgis and Luther Newton, county judges; and E. Taylor, sheriff; all of whom were appointed by Governor Cass in 1829–30.

The list of judges appears elsewhere in connection with the history of the courts.

Mr. Anderson held the custody of the probate records until March 21, 1834. Dr. S. W. Truesdell being his deputy after the office was removed to Centreville. On March 27, 1834, T. W. Langley appends his signature to the foot of the records of deeds, and continues to do so until April 22, 1835, when his sign-manual disappears with the office of register of probate, and Jacob W. Coffinbury's flowing chirography meets the eye, he being the first incumbent of the new office of register of deeds just then created, to be filled by election by the people. His services extended to December 31, 1838, and Allen Goodridge came in with the new year, and remained in possession of the office till December 31, 1846, having had four successive elections. Edmund Stears succeeded to the position January 1, 1847, and held its emoluments for eight years also, when in January, 1855, Asahel Clapp took his position at the register's desk, and held it ten years, and then only gave way to his son, Leverett A. Clapp, who held it for a single term only because he would not be a candidate against Captain Myron A. Benedict, a brave soldier, who lost his right arm before Atlanta, in the defense of his country. This gallant officer was elected 1866, and has held it to the present time, voluntarily standing aside for another—Thomas G. Greene—who was elected in November, 1876.

David Page was the first clerk of the county of St. Joseph and of the courts therein, and was appointed in 1830, and appears as the first county-court term. Isaac W. Willard succeeded Page, and was the first clerk of the circuit court, at its first term held in the county. Willard held the position until September 6, 1834, when Dr. Trussdell took it, and kept it till the latter part of 1838, and was succeeded by Albert E. Massey, who was elected at the November election of 1838, and was master of the situation two years, when Asher Bonham succeeded him two terms, Massey again coming in for two years, ending December 31, 1848. Charles Upson then held the office for a single term, and C. D. Bennett kept it for two, his lease expiring with the year 1854. Hiram Lindsley was then the " coming man," and he came in and remained for ten years, and stepped aside for the present popular incumbent, Captain John C. Joss, who gave a leg for the old flag, and all it symbolizes, in the Wilderness. Captain Joss was elected and re-elected for six successive terms. He went to the rear to give Hon. R. W. Melendy a place in the front, who was elected in November, 1876.

The first county treasurer was elected in April, 1830, John Winchell being the favored individual, and he received the taxes of 1830–32. In 1833 Major Isaac I. Ulman succeeded to the keys of the treasury vault, and accounted for the revenue of 1833–4–5. In 1836 Columbia Lancaster was elected, and held the position one term. Alexander V. Sill succeeded Lancaster in 1838, but did not fill out the full years of his term, by reason of removal to Illinois. John W. Talbot filled the position for a portion of 1839, and then W. B. Brown was elected to fill the remainder of the term. In 1840 John W. Talbot was elected, and disbursed the funds of the public for four years, surrendering the county cash-book in 1844 to Jacob W. Coffinbury, who posted its accounts for a single term, and then stepped down for William Laird, who stepped up and remained on guard over the county funds for six years. William McCormick came to the front in 1852, and fell to the rear in 1856, and William Hutchinson took the vacated place for four years, and then gave way in 1860 for David Oakes, who, after discharging his duties in the office for eighteen months, resigned the position to go in the support of the government as captain of Company A, 11th Michigan Infantry, and died in the service. William Allison filled the vacancy, and was re-elected in 1862, and again in 1864. William L. Worthington then held the keys of the strong box four years, the present incumbent, James Hill, coming in January 1, 1871, and has been re-elected for a term ending with 1878.

The first sheriff was E. Taylor, as previously stated ; he was the old Indian trader, at the grand traverse of the St. Joseph river, and held the position until the first sheriff was elected by the people in 1836, who was Edward A. Trumbull ; Trumbull was succeeded in 1838 by Charles H. Knox, who held the position for five terms ; Horace Metcalf coming for one term during the years 1842–3, because a man could not be elected for three successive terms. Horace M. Vesey secured the sheriffalty for a single term, and then John Hull came in with the new constitution, and exercised the authority of the State against evil-doers for four years. William Harrington was elected in 1854, and was re-elected two years afterwards, and then William K. Haynes secured the prize for two terms. William L. Worthington then sold the people's effects on execution and final judgment for four years, and William M. Watkins succeeded to the business for a like term, which ended with 1870. Elva F. Pierce, John A. J. Metzger and Daniel H. Hawley were each given but a single term in the brick hotel opposite the court house, and then Charles M. Lampman was elected in 1876.

The coroners who have served in St. Joseph county since 1833 are as follows : Benjamin Sherman was elected in the last-named year and served till 1837, and Samuel Pratt and Isaac G. Bailey to 1839 ; John V. Overfield, 1840 ; William Thackery and Joseph Pharaon to 1842, filled the position. From that time to 1853, the incumbents were, respectively, Peter F. Putnam, Charles McNair, Joseph Miller, John Aiken and Lyman Bean. In 1852 A. D. Sprague and William Morrison were given the doubtful

honor of inquiring into the sudden and violent taking off of their fellow-mortals for two years, and then Fordyce Johnson and Orrin F. Howard, John S. Williams and Elisha Foote, and H. Brazee and William Arney succeeded to the cheerful duty for a single term each. Charles E. Simons and Isaac Howard were elected in 1860, and the latter filled the position for two terms—Nathan Mitchell being his coadjutor during his last term. Joseph W. Pike and James W. Mandigo came in, in 1864, and in 1866 Mitchell and Dr. Mandigo took the honors again. William Harrington and Nicholas J. Sibley held the office for two years together, and then Isaac Howard came in for four years, J. A. Rogers being his companion the first term, and A. C. Williams the second. The present incumbents, L. W. Weinberg and Charles W. Boerstecher, were elected in 1874.

The first county surveyor elected was James Cowen, in November, 1836. There had been other surveyors previously ; among them Robert Clark, Jr., Orange Risdon, Musgrove Evans and W. H. Adams, but no regularly appointed county surveyors till Mr. Cowen's election. The next one was Hiram Dresser in 1838, who was succeeded in 1840 by Hiram Draper. Simeon Gilbert carried the compass for two years, and James Hutchinson and Josiah Knauer each for four years, Mr. Knauer being sandwiched between Hutchinson's first and second terms. A. F. Watkins then shouldered the "Jacob's staff" for one term, and was succeeded by Norman L. Andrews, who set the bounds of the people for the period of six years, ending December 31, 1861. Hiram Hutchinson held the office from 1862 to 1864, and James H. Gardner followed in his footsteps among the ancient land-marks till 1870, when he surrendered the position to John S. Rose for a single term, and re-entered it again for two years more. In 1874 Norman L. Andrews was elected again, and still holds the position, in 1876.

Prosecuting attorneys were appointed by the governor until the constitution of 1850 was adopted, and the first appointee was E. B. Sherman in 1830. He was succeeded by Columbia Lancaster in 1833, and Lancaster by J. Eastman Johnson in 1838. Judge Johnson attended to the pleas of the people until the March term of the circuit court in 1838, at which term Neal McGaffey appeared for the people, and E. B. Mitchell at the September term the same year. From and after this term of the court, until the March term, 1846, Chester Gurney and Judge Johnson prosecuted criminals for the State, the larger portion of that time falling to the judge. Hon. H. H. Riley appeared for the people from and including the March term, 1846, to November, 1849, when W. C. Pease filled the situation till the first election under the new constitution.

The first prosecuting attorney elected in the county was E. B. Turner, in 1850, Charles Upson succeeding him in 1852. From 1854 to 1858 William L. Stoughton drew the indictments against evil-doers, and William Saddler followed suit for a like term of four years. After him came Henry F. Severens for a single term, and then Germain H. Mason led the attack on male-factors for two terms. Talcott H. Carpenter continued the warfare against the same class who were so unfortunate as to fall into his clutches, until 1872, and then E. W. Keightley and R. R. Pealer held a tight reign on the violators of the public morals and peace for a single term each, Orlando J. Fast being elected in 1876.

In 1852 the county judges' office being defunct, their place was taken by the circuit court commissioners, who had the same power as the judges in vacation, and also of the masters in chancery, who were also prohibited in the new constitution. The first commissioner was William L. Stoughton, who was elected in 1852, and was succeeded by Chester Gurney in 1854. Gurney held the position till 1858, and was succeeded by James M. Lyon, who in turn gave way to G. H. Mason in 1860. Two commissioners were elected in 1862, namely, Paul James Eaton and Talcott H. Carpenter. The latter held the position six years, James H. Lyon being his associate during his second term, and Mr. Eaton again in his last one. In 1868 R. W. Melendy and Samuel Chadwick were elected, and Mr. Melendy being re-elected in 1870 with R. R. Pealer. Mr. Pealer held the position four years, O. J. Fast serving with him during his second term. The present incumbents are Daniel E. Thomas and David Knox, Jr., who were re-elected in 1876.

The county commissioners, who had charge of the financial affairs during their short lease of power, from April, 1838, to July 4, 1842, were as follows : The first ones elected were Enos G. Cathcart, of Constantine ; James Hutchinson, of Park, and John Sturgis, of Sherman (Sturgis now) ; those gentlemen drawing terms of one, three and two years, respectively. Judge Conner, of Nottawa, was elected for three years to take the place vacated by Mr. Cathcart in 1839. In 1840 Giles Thompson came on the board in place of Judge Sturgis, from Bucks, and Mr. Hutchinson was re-elected in 1841, which was the last election of commissioners, the board of supervisors taking the reins of government again in 1842.

The people of St. Joseph township, while yet under the jurisdiction of Lenawee county, were first represented in the councils of the territory by delegates, who were elected in 1829 as members of the legislative council. St. Joseph county, with the counties of Cass and Kalamazoo, sent their first delegate to the council in 1831, which was the fifth council, and met in Detroit, May, 1832. In 1833 Calvin Brittain was elected to the council from St. Joseph, Kalamazoo, Berrien, Calhoun and Branch counties—732 votes being polled in the district. In 1835 Isaac I. Ullman was elected to represent the county in the State legislature, and in 1836 Neal McGaffey and Martin G. Schellhous were chosen. In 1838 Samuel A. Chafin and Frederick Shurtz were elected, and in 1839 Isaac G. Bailey and John G. Cathcart succeeded to the dignity. In 1840 Comfort Tyler and A. R. Metcalf lifted up their voices in the general assembly, and gave way in 1841 for Otis Preston and John L. Chipman. In 1843 P. E. Runyan and Frederick Shurtz went to the capitol to legislate for the people, and in 1844 Washington Pitcher and John H. Bowman made the same journey for the same purpose. From 1845 to 1851 inclusive, the county was represented successively by Earn S. Cole and Isaac D. Toll, Alfred S. Driggs and Patrick Marantette, William Morris and Levi Patchin, L. C. Mathews and P. H. Buck, Edwin Kellogg and Asher Bonham, and Alexander H. Moore and J. G. Wait. In 1852 Charles L. Miller and John Frey were elected, Judge Miller being re-elected in 1854 with John Lomison. William Allman and Hezekiah Weatherbee, Harrison Kelley and Thomas Mitchell, and Edward Stewart and William Wheeler were sent successively to make laws from 1856 to 1862 inclusive. In 1863 there were three members sent from the county, to wit: Edward Stewart from the first district, William Wheeler from the second, and Charles Betts from the third. In 1864 Mr. Stewart was re-elected in his district, and Orrin F. Howard and W. T. Smith went from the second and third, respectively.

In 1866 Messrs. Wm. R. Eck, O. F. Howard and Lafayette Parsons were the tribunes of the people, whose terms of office were extended to two years; and in 1868, William R. Eck, Charles Millington and James W. Mandigo spoke among the rulers.

In 1870 Andrew Climie, Millington and Bracey were elected.

In 1872 the representation of the county was reduced and the county re-districted, and Parsons and Climie were sent as legislators.

In 1874 Frank S. Packard and William Hull were elected, and William Allman and G. B. Markham in 1876. The present districts divide the county north and south, each district taking eight townships.

John S. Barry, Calvin Brittain and William H. Comstock represented, in the first State Senate, the counties of St. Joseph, Berrien, Branch, Hillsdale, Kalamazoo, Cass and Calhoun, composing the third district, the election being held in the fall of 1836, at which 1,875 votes were cast.

In 1838 Samuel Etheridge, of Coldwater, was the senator for Branch, Hillsdale and St. Joseph; and in 1840 John S. Barry, of Constantine, again succeeded to the senatorial toga for St. Joseph, VanBuren, Cass and Branch.

In 1841, Mr. Barry having been elected governor, Digby V. Bell was elected to fill the vacancy. George Redfield was elected in 1843, and Wm. H. Richmond and George Martin in 1844; Joseph N. Chipman and Flavius I. Littlejohn in 1845, and Rix Robinson in 1846. Isaac D. Toll and Jerome R. Fitzgerald were in the Senate in 1847, Alex. H. Redfield in 1848, John McKinney and Philetus Hayden in 1849, and H. H. Riley, of Constantine, in 1850. William McCumber and Philetus Haydon were elected in 1852, Edward S. Moore, of Three Rivers, in 1854, and Charles Upson, of Centreville, in 1856; Comfort Tyler, of Sherman, in 1858; J. R. Williams, of Constantine, in 1860.

In 1862 J. G. Wait, of Sturgis, was elected, and held the position for six years, giving way, in 1868, to D. D. Three Rivers, who also held the office for six years. In 1874 Matthew T. Garvey, of Branch county, was elected for the district composed of St. Joseph and Branch counties, and still occupies the honorable position.

In 1867 county superintendents of schools were provided for by the legislature, and Charles M. Temple was the first incumbent of the office in St. Joseph county. In 1869 L. B. Antisdale was elected, and again in 1871. In 1873 J. W. Beardslee was elected, after which the office was abolished, and town superintendents substituted.

In 1860 the office of drain commissioner was established, and Jeremiah H. Gardner was the first commissioner. He was succeeded by A. C. Van Vlack in 1871, when the office was vacated, and town commissioners substituted therefor.

In 1835 the county of St. Joseph and the territory south of it to the boundary line, as established by the ordinance of 1787, was, by the legislative council of Michigan, constituted the thirteenth district, and authorized

to elect three delegates to the convention called to frame a constitution, and John S. Barry, Hubbel Loomis and Martin G. Schellhous were elected.

In September, 1836, the people of the county sent Columbia Lancaster and Dr. Watson Sumner as delegates to the convention at Ann Arbor, called to accept the terms of admission into the Union, imposed by Congress upon the people of Michigan, but which acceptance or assent was not given. Of the four hundred and fifteen votes cast for the delegates, two hundred and twenty-one were in favor of giving assent to the conditions, one hundred and eighty were opposed to it, and fourteen did not care enough about the matter to express their desire either way.

The people sent to the second convention, held in December, 1836, for the same purpose as the first one, Aaron B. Watkins, Philip R. Toll, Stephen W. Truesdell and W. H. Adams, one hundred and twenty-six votes only being cast, and all for the above-named delegates.

The delegates to the constitutional convention of 1850, were Judge William Connor, Hon. Joseph R. Williams and Edward S. Moore.

Hon. Henry H. Riley, of Constantine, was selected by the governor to represent St. Joseph county in the constitutional convention of 1867, the labors of which came to naught when submitted to the people for ratification.

St. Joseph county has been represented in the United States Congress by her own citizens, as follows: Hon. John S. Chipman, for the term of 1845–47; Charles Upson, from 1863 to 1869; General William L. Stoughton, for two terms, 1869–73. Hon. E. W. Keightley was elected in 1876 for a term of two years, beginning March 4, 1877.

The old county has also furnished a fair proportion of the State officers since its organization. Governor Barry was elected, while yet a resident of the county, for two successive terms, 1842–44, and again in 1850. Governor Bagley, though not a St. Joseph citizen at the time of his election, began his business life in Constantine. He has held the position of chief magistrate of the State for four years, ending with 1876.

Leverett A. Clapp was elected commissioner of the land-office in 1872, and re-elected in the year 1874, his term just expiring. He has been the most efficient officer the State has ever had in that position, and by his energy and watchfulness has saved the school fund thousands of dollars by a vigorous prosecution of trespasses on the public domain of the State school and university lands.

Hon. J. Eastman Johnson was a regent of the university at Ann Arbor from 1858 to 1870, and Andrew Climie, Esq., is on the board of regents at present. Frank Wells, of Constantine, is one of the directors of the agricultural college. Charles H. Knox was United States marshal for the western district of Michigan, under President Taylor.

---

## CHAPTER XII.

Not only does "love laugh at locksmiths," but no vicissitudes of time or place debar the rosy little god from leading willing captives amid the privations of the border, as well as in the centres of affluence and ease. The first parties who sought the aid of St. Joseph officials to launch their bark upon the untried sea of matrimony, were James Knapp and Martha Winchell, both residents of the then township of St. Josephs, Lenawee county, now the township of Mottville, St. Joseph county. The groom located the tract of land on which tradition says the old Indian chief, White Pigeon, was buried, and the bride was a daughter of Judge John Winchell, the only magistrate in all southwestern Michigan at the time—1828, during the summer or fall —the ceremony was celebrated by him. This couple resided on White Pigeon prairie several years, having several children born to them, and removed thence to Indiana, and subsequently to Texas, where they both died.

The next wedding was that of Abel Olds and Ann Thurston, who rode from Jonesville, Hillsdale county, to White Pigeon, fifty miles, to find a magistrate to ratify the contract for a life partnership they themselves had previously made. Judge Winchell was the official the contracting parties found, for the very good reason there was no other to find. He soon made the twain one flesh, without much ceremony, in the month of May, 1829. The newly-wedded pair rode back to Jonesville, via Oxbow prairie, where the relatives of the bride had made ready the nuptial feast. In after-years they returned and took up their residence in St. Joseph county.

On the 15th day of August following, William Locke, who came on horse-back from Wayne county, Ohio, and Rachel Gardner, who had preceded him from the same place a few weeks before, came to Judge Luther Newton's cabin, on Crooked creek, the judge having married a sister of Miss Gardner, on Pokagon prairie, the spring before—and sending for the second magis-trate in the township, Neal McGaffey, were by him united in the holy bonds of wedlock. The horse which had brought the groom to the bride was now required to carry both groom and bride back to the Ohio home of the former, which he did safely, in about two weeks' time, which journey is the first extended wedding-tour recorded in the county. It was unattended with luxury or display, and love was the sole attendant. From Oxbow to Fort Defi-ance, with the exception of a single night, when they had the hospitalities of a wayside cabin extended to them, the wedded pair couched in the woods, canopied by the stars alone and the blue ether.

In October, 1829, Valentine Shultz and Susan Hartman, the latter a daugh-ter of Solomon Hartman, who settled in Mottville township a short time previously, were married. This couple settled on section five in that town-ship, at first, and afterwards removed to Coldwater, in Branch county, and finally went to Iowa, where the lady died in 1870.

The Winchell family furnished one of the parties to the next marriage in the county—David, the eldest son, who married Mary Ann McEnterfer, a daughter of the first white settler in Lockport township. The wedding was celebrated in the first house built north of White Pigeon and Sturgis prairies, with one exception, that of Judge Week's, at Constantine; the happy affair being consummated in the month of February, 1830—Rev. Erastus Felton probably officiating. Mr. Winchell is dead, but his widow still survives, and resides in Indiana, near Laporte.

The next bride came from the same family, and was Sarah McEnterfer, who surrendered her legal individuality to William McIntosh in November following. McIntosh lived on Young's prairie, and on his journey for his bride lost his way and became bewildered, and did not arrive until long after the hour appointed for the ceremony, which was not performed till midnight. This couple are still living on Young's prairie, in Cass county, whither they went the next day after their marriage. The next marriage was probably that of John W. Fletcher, of Nottawa prairie, and Sarah Knox, a daughter of Jacob Knox and sister of David Knox, of Sturgis prairie, which was celebrated by Samuel Stewart, a justice of the peace, on the 18th day of September, 1831. After the wedding festivities were over, Mr. Fletcher brought his bride to his home, where they have ever since re-sided. The original house has of course given way to one more ample and elegant, and in which their children and children's children—a goodly num-ber—are wont to gather, and listen to the tales of the long ago, as they fall from the lips of the first white man who fixed upon Nottawa prairie for a home. About the same time, William Stewart and Mary Cade, a daughter of the oldest man now living in the county, Thomas Cade, of Sturgis, were married, but whether before or after Mr. Fletcher, we have been unable defi-nitely to determine. It was in the same fall, however, and not far from the same day.

The bridal costume of the pioneer times was not so elaborate as that of the brides of 1877. We give a description of one of the former, which was neat but not gaudy, nor could it be said to be inexpensive, if rated at the price of wheat at the time. The dress was of calico, and the only attempt at ornament was a long pink silk sash, tied around the waist, the ends of which depended to the hem of the skirt, which was somewhat scant in the pattern, both longitudinally and latitudinally. The groom was gor-geously arrayed in yellow pantaloons, crimson vest and blue coat with shining buttons, and had an immense brazen chain about his neck, at the lower extremity of which a "bull's-eye" watch was concealed by his vest pocket.

Probably Mrs. Dr. Isaac Adams, of White Pigeon, had the least fastidi-ous company of wedding-guests that ever sat down to a nuptial feast in the settler's cabin in old St. Joe. The doctor bought the farm of Arba Heeld, who, in 1830, finding that neighbors were getting too near to be comfortable, sold out his fine location on Pigeon prairie, and moved west. One day, in the summer of 1833, a young Pottawatomie Indian, from the Nottawa-seepe reservation, on his way to Indian prairie, in Indiana, to claim a bride, stopped at the doctor's place, and one of the younger Adams' getting in con-versation with him found out his business, and, with the consent of Mrs. Adams, invited him to call with his wife on his way back and take dinner. The invitation was accepted, and a few days afterwards the young brave and his dusky mate rode up to the door, but not alone. The invitation had been amplified in its transmission to the bride, and a numerous, numbering some dozens or more, of the young male and female friends of the parties, were es-corting the newly-wedded pair to their home on the reservation. They were

all trinketed out in a fine array of calicos, beads and buckskin leggings and breeches, and were a jolly, rollicking crowd. Mrs. Adams, though a little taken aback at the array of guests before her, was not dismayed, and hid-ding them dismount and take themselves comfortable, she set about getting up a dinner for the party, and soon had it smoking-hot before them. The menu was not as elaborate and varied, doubtless, as that of many a wedding-feast in St. Joe since, but it was plentiful and wholesome, and was most thoroughly enjoyed by the partakers thereof, who showed their appreciation of it by dispatching the entire bill of fare in a wonderfully short period of time. After profuse thanks from the groom and protestations of undying gratitude from the bride, the gayly-bedecked party mounted their ponies, and galloped off over the prairie towards the home of the Nottawa.

EARLY BIRTHS.

To whom the honor attaches of being the first white person "to the manor born," in St. Joseph county, has not been definitely ascertained, but it lies between two individuals, Selinda Reichert, a daughter of Abraham Reichert, who was born in what is now known as Mottville township, in May, 1829; and a child which was born the same year in Leonard Cutler's family; on the eastern side of the prairie of White Pigeon, the probabilities lying with the latter.

On the 10th day of August, the same year, Eleanor Heald, a daughter of Arba Heald, was born, and the same season the first child of the first mar-ried couple of the actual settlers in the county, James and Mary Knapp, was born. In the fall of the same year Leonard Rickart had a son born to him, but which did not survive many months. The first-named child is still living. Constantine next came into notice, Henry Bonebright, a son of Jacob Bone-bright deceased, being born February 8, 1830. Nottawa prairie came next, John Foreman, now of Leonidas, being born thereon on the 6th day of February. Sturgis prairie next followed with its work, David Sturgis being the representative, who was born February 11, and then Nottawa came again to the front, in the person of William Hazzard, Jr., who was born March 10, 1830. In "the merry month of May," a little daughter came to gladden the hearts of John B. Clarke and his worthy spouse, in Sherman village—now Sturgis. The little lady made it extremely lively for the neighbors to attend to her requirements, and at an unseasonable hour in the morning, too. Peter Buck and his gray mare were forced into requisition to go for nurses five miles off, and another neighbor was sent for Doctor Loomis, at White Pigeon, twelve miles away. In June Joseph C. Meek was announced at Constantine, and made his début while the roses were blooming. Mottville closed the record of the year with the birth of Sophronia Burns, on the 30th day of October.

DEATH'S RECORD.

"Man has but a summer's dawn,
And from the cradle to the tomb
A common destiny."

Long before a permanent burial-place had been selected, or a cemetery laid off, the reaper—death—had begun his harvest, and tender buds, opening flowers, and ripened fruit had been garnered beneath the flowery sod of prairie and opening, and moistened by the tears of affection of mourners who dropped the thread of busy life for a moment to lay their treasures in the dust, and to prepare to resume their duties under the imperious demands of the active present in which they lived.

White Pigeon prairie leads the column in the joy of matrimony and the gladness of childhood, and Sturgis stands first on the brink of the grave.

Death came suddenly and without warning in his first assault on the set-tlers of St. Joseph; George Buck and Levi Waterman being the first vic-tims, August 8, 1829. They were buried in a well they were digging in the village of Sherman (then composed of about three houses), on the east side of Nottawa street, as now laid out. The funeral services held for their ob-sequies was the first religious service ever held on Sturgis prairie by the settlers.

In the winter of 1829–30, a man named Sawyer, who was at work for George W. Dille, of Nottawa, was killed by a tree falling upon him. He was buried in the school section, on which a cemetery has since been laid out. Also in that year, 1830, a Mr. Hartman died in Mottville. In 1832 Oliver Raymond buried two little girls in Sturgis prairie.

THE DIVORCE COURTS

are almost as insatiable, in these days, as death himself, but in the early days of the pioneers they had little business. It was not until there had been five terms of the court held, that a married couple in St. Joseph county resorted to the law to do what death had alone done previous thereto.

The first party who applied for a legal separation evidently "kissed and made up," for no decree was ever entered.

The first decree of divorce was entered in the circuit court, at the October term thereof, 1835, on the petition of Aurora Amulet Gilbert, filed against her husband, David Gilbert, on a plea of cruelty and desertion, most piteously expressed by Neal McGaffey, Esq.

The following incident, related by Hon. E. H. Lothrop, late of Three Rivers, now deceased, is apropos here. One day a lady came to Mr. Lothrop complaining bitterly of the cruel treatment of, and desiring Mr. Lothrop to effect a legal separation from, her tyrannical lord. Mr. Lothrop expostulated with her, declaring it would scandalize the community if such an old and worthy couple should, after so long a wedded life as theirs, separate; but the lady was immovable in her determination. Thinking to conciliate the parties, Mr. Lothrop went to the house occupied by them, accompanied by the lady, where they found the husband fortifying his position with an array of scriptural texts, and the upshot of the matter was that a separation was agreed upon. The wife was to retain the farm for her support, and the husband was to take the team and wagon, and go out from the homestead and begin anew. The arrangement was consummated, but after the clean linen was soiled which the old gentleman took with him, he came to the lady and engaged her to do his washing. Not long afterwards he came and engaged board with her, and the result was soon manifest in her taking him back altogether, and no further mention was made of disagreements or separations.

Notwithstanding the havoc made by death's artillery and the smaller arms of the courts, there are notable instances of long years of marital felicity that place the county of St. Joseph well towards the front rank in that respect. Eight venerable couples were living in St. Joseph county at the annual meeting of the pioneer society in June, 1876, who had celebrated their golden wedding, but three of them were broken before the year closed.

Ezra Cole and wife were married before they were nineteen years old, in January, 1816, and have lived together fifty-nine years. They have reared a family of seven children, are seventy-seven years old, and have never had any severe illness. They came to Three Rivers in 1839, and have lived there ever since.

Samuel Van Dorston and his wife, seventy-seven and seventy-eight years old respectively, have lived together as man and wife over fifty-six years. They lived in Three Rivers, and have reared a large family of sons and daughters.

Isaac Major and wife, of Lockport township, were married in Montgomery county, N. Y., February 22, 1821, and at the time of Mrs. Major's death in October, 1875, they had lived together by the family hearthstone nearly fifty-six years. Mr. Major is eighty-four years old. His brother, William Major, of the same town, who died in December, 1876, aged eighty years, was married to the wife who survives him, in the last-named county, February 19, 1824, their wedded life covering nearly fifty-three years.

Zerah Benjamin and Asenath Adams started out together on life's journey in Durham, Greene county, N. Y., on January 17, 1824, and have not yet parted company, though fifty-three years of the lights and shades inseparable from human existence have passed over their heads. They came to Florence in 1833, and located on the farm where they have ever since resided. In 1874 they celebrated their golden wedding, having present with them five of their six children and twelve of their fourteen grandchildren. Forty-one relatives in all were present, among them a brother and sister who had witnessed the wedding fifty years before. There were five others living at the time, who also were witnesses of the old-time wedding.

Isaac F. Ulrich and his wife were married December 16, 1824, and at the end of fifty-two years are serenely passing down life's western declivity together, till the "gates shall stand ajar" for them by and by. Their golden wedding was a notable occasion, made so by the assembling of twenty-nine of their thirty-six descendants, spanning three generations, the aged couple making the fourth. M. J. Ulrich, a son, and the first child born in Park township, delivered an eloquent address, and presented the patriarch with a gold-headed cane, and the venerable mother with an easy-chair. Cyrus Ulrich, another son, read an original poem. Mr. Ulrich is seventy-six years old and lives on his original location in Park, whither he came in 1834.

George Keech, Sr., and Mary M. Hunt were married in New York city on the 10th day of September, 1826. They are aged seventy-eight and seventy-three years respectively, and have lived together for half a century, and are now hale and hearty, kind and hospitable as old pioneers are usually. Mr. Keech has died since the above was written. In this family are three Georges: George I, George II. and George III.; and though their blood may not be as "blue" as that which was accorded to the Brunswick Georges of

old colony and Revolutionary times, it is better, if there is any truth in the history of the titled Georges, *Rex dei gratia*. Mr. and Mrs. Keech lived in St. Joseph thirty years.

Hon. Edward S. Moore, of Three Rivers, had lived with the wife of his youth for fifty years, when she was called to go before him to that haven of rest where, when he shall follow, old friendships shall be renewed never more to be broken. Inman Arnold and Narcissa Morey, of Constantine, married in Oxford, Chenango county, N. Y., January 19, 1815, and that union, declared when the treaty of peace between the United States and Great Britain was signed, was for sixty years undissolved, and then only death was powerful enough to loose the bands thereof. Mr. and Mrs. Charles Macomber, of Park, and latterly of Three Rivers, had passed fifty-two years of wedded life together, when the husband was called hence in 1875.

The ten couples here named have spent in the aggregate over five hundred and forty years of wedded life together, and their aggregate ages span fourteen hundred years! The survivors can sing with "the spirit, and with the understanding also," Burns' touching lines:

"John Anderson, my Jo, John, we clamb the hill thegither;
And mony a canty day, John, we've had wi' ane anither.
Now we maun totter down, John, but hand in hand we'll go,
And sleep thegither at the foot, John Anderson, my Jo"

There were registered in the county, in 1876, two hundred and seventy-five marriages, four hundred and forty-two births, and one hundred and sixty-three deaths.

CEMETERIES.

The first permanent cemetery was laid out in White Pigeon, in or about the year 1831, where it is still located, in the northwestern part of the village. One place a burial-place laid off by J. W. Coffinberry, on a tract of land named by him "Carlton," but which existed as a village only in the airy castles of Mr. Coffinberry's fancy. One Chidester, a carpenter, and a man named Day, died in the year 1831, and were buried in this plat, and so, also, were several persons who died about the same time, one of them a son-in-law of Colonel Selden Martin.

The old cemetery of Sturgis was laid off for burial purposes in 1833, and about that time the one on section sixteen in Nottawa was laid off. There are at Sturgis and Three Rivers most eligibly situated grounds, now being beautified and adorned by art and affection, nature having been especially lavish in her never-to-be-excelled work in the Riverside cemetery of the latter city. Descriptions of these grounds in detail appear in the respective histories of the townships.

---

CHAPTER XIII.

FIRST RELIGIOUS SERVICES—MISSIONARIES—FIRST CHURCHES ORGANIZED—
SUNDAY-SCHOOLS—PRESENT STATISTICS—EDUCATION—EARLY SCHOOLS
AND SCHOOL-HOUSES—WHITE PIGEON ACADEMY—BRANCH OF UNIVER-
SITY—PRESENT SCHOOL STATISTICS.

The first religious services held by Europeans in the territory once included in the boundaries of St. Joseph township, as a part of Lenawee county, and whose principal and only magistrate was John Winchell, of White Pigeon prairie, was the service held by the Jesuit missionary, Claude Allouez, on the St. Joseph river, near its mouth, where he had, in 1675, followed the footsteps of Père Marquette, and gathered around him a little village of the Pottawatomies, organized a school, and taught his wild pupils the tenets of salvation through the merits of a risen Saviour, as he understood them. One hundred and fifty-four years later, Lyman B. Gurley and Erastus Felton, missionaries from the field of the Methodist Episcopal church, proclaimed to the pioneer settlers, the successors of Allouez' pupils in the St. Joseph valley, the news of salvation as they understood it. A few years later, Cory and Jones, missionaries of the Presbyterian faith, Gershom B. Day and William Brown, of the Baptist persuasion, and Isaac Ketchum, of the Dutch Reformed views, proclaimed the "very same Jesus" to the same people, as they understood it. Thus the followers of Loyola and those of Wesley, Knox, Roger Williams and others, but all disciples of the lowly Nazarene, proclaimed his doctrines of peace and good will to man, from their different stand-points, but with good intent to better the condition of their fellows.

The early missionaries endured hardships that would appal the stoutest hearts to-day; not only the Jesuits, who literally went through fire and blood to fulfil their self-appointed missions, but those who followed them, when the white men were their hearers. The itinerants of Wesley penetrated forests, waded marshes, swam rivers, crossed prairies, sleeping wherever night overtook them, frequently canopied only by the blue vault over their heads, with the stars for watchers. They braved storms of rain and snow, and the pitiless pelting of the sleet and hail, and ate with thankfulness the meagre fare set before them by the pioneer, knowing that, though scanty, it was of the best, and oftentimes, the last the hospitable host had to give. One of these brave souls, named Walker, had a circuit of twelve hundred miles to ride, into Ohio, Indiana and Michigan; and he traveled it on horseback every six weeks, fording all the streams, and swimming the Miamee twice every trip.

Gershom B. Day, the pioneer Baptist, was a useful man in his time. He not only preached to the people, but he sang to them in church meetings, and at home in their houses; and at their celebrations on the 4th of July he was their chorister.

He left this country and went to California, where he gained some considerable more of this world's goods than he was likely to do by following his clerical calling here, but he lost his life thereby, being killed and scalped by the Indians on his return.

John Armstrong, a presiding elder of the Methodist conference having jurisdiction over the churches of that creed in St. Joseph valley, was a muscular Christian, and, when need demanded, led the Michigan volunteers against Black Hawk, as a scout, and was with General Atkinson at the capture of that redoubtable chieftain. His knowledge of the country, gained in the years of his itinercy, proved of inestimable value to the commander of the United States troops.

He conducted the first camp-meeting ever held in western Michigan, on Prairie Ronde, in 1834.

Reverends William Jones and Christopher Cory were the earliest Presbyterian ministers, and preached in southern Michigan and northern Indiana in 1829, and later, and organized all of the earlier churches of that denomination in that region of the country. P. W. Warrimer succeeded them, and was for years a noted man among the people.

Among the other missionaries and early proclaimers of the gospel were Baconi Harris, whose appointment as an elder in the Methodist Episcopal church was granted by Bishop McKendrie, July 24, 1810, at Lyons, New York. Sprague received his appointment from Bishop Hedding in 1831. Thomas Odell was an early Methodist minister, and so, also, was Erastus Kellogg. Reverend George B. Brown appears to be the first liberal minister who came into the county, and was here in 1835.

### METHODIST EPISCOPAL CHURCH.

The whole territory of Michigan was included in the Detroit district of the Ohio conference of the Methodist Episcopal church until 1832, at which time the southwestern part of the territory was set off into the Indiana conference, under which jurisdiction it remained until 1840. In 1833 southwest Michigan was included in the northwest district, but in 1834 it was changed to the Laporte district, and Newell E. Smith was in charge. The new conference was designated "Wood's Raft." In 1840 the State line was made the southern boundary of the Michigan conference, which body was organized in 1835 or 1836. In 1834 the St. Joseph mission, as the charge in St. Joseph valley had been previously designated, was changed to the St. Joseph circuit of the Laporte district, and in 1837 the circuit was divided, and that part of it included in Michigan named the White Pigeon circuit, and embraced White Pigeon, Constantine, Centreville, Nottawa, Sturgis, Edwardsburg, Three Rivers, Florence, Prairie Ronde and other small societies. It was a four weeks' circuit, with two preachers. In 1839 the circuit was again divided into the White Pigeon and Centreville circuits, with a single preacher in each; John Erchanbnrck was the presiding elder of the district. In 1847 the circuit was changed to the Constantine circuit, and the preacher "lived in a hired house" in the village of Constantine, on the corner of Washington and Centreville streets.

The following presiding elders have held authority in the St. Joseph district: John Armstrong, previous to 1840; John Erchenbrnck, 1840; J. P. Davidson, 1841-4; William Sprague, 1845-8; Francis D. Bangs, 1849-51-56; John K. Gillett, 1852-5; David Burns, 1856-9; Thomas H. Jacokes, 1860-3; Riley C. Crawford, 1864-7; Resin Sapp, 1868-71; Andrew J. Eldred, 1872-5; J. W. Robinson, 1876-9.

The first Methodist society organized (which was also the first church organization of any kind in the county) was a class formed at Newville, about two miles east of White Pigeon, in the fall of 1829, of which David Crawford was the leader. This class was the first results of the preaching of Mr. Felton. In February following a class was organized in White Pigeon village, with Captain Alvin Calhoun as leader. Among the members of this last class were Alanson C. Stewart and wife, John Bowers and wife, Mr. and Mrs. John Coates and David Rollins. The first church edifice in the county was erected by this society in the village of White Pigeon in the year 1832, and which was a small frame building. Mr. Stewart was a local preacher, and went to Chicago in after-years, where he and his wife died.

In the spring of 1830 Messrs. Felton and Gurley organized a class on Nottawa prairie, at the house of William Hazzard, Sr., the first members of the same being Mr. Hazzard and his wife Cassandra, and William Fletcher and Hannah his wife, with the preacher in charge as leader. Amos Howe was the first regularly appointed leader. Services were held fortnightly, at first at private houses, and afterwards, when school-houses were built, the meetings were held in them, and for some time after 1833 in the county court-house in Centreville. The only surviving member of the Nottawa class is William Hazzard, Sr., in whose house the same was formed. He is now about eighty years old.

### PRESBYTERIAN CHURCH.

The first Presbyterian church organized was of White Pigeon, on the 8th day of August, 1830. The organization was effected by Rev. William Jones. Benjamin Blair, David Clarke, Neal McGaffey, James Mathews and James Blair were appointed and ordained ruling elders, and beside them the following were the first members of the church: Mrs. Elizabeth Blair, Mrs. David Clarke, Mrs. McKibbon, Martha Waterman, Mrs. Sarah Mathews, Mr. and Mrs. Abijah C. Seeley, Alexander McMillan and his wife Susanna, John and Rebecca Gardner, Mrs. Hannah McGaffey, Mrs. Mahala Gale, Mrs. Hannah Stewart, Mrs. Benjamin Blair, James Anderson, Patience McNeil, Francis Jones and Sarah Bronson. These came from all parts of the country roundabout, as far north as Prairie Ronde, and as far east, west and south, and many of them entered into the organization of the early churches, in after-years, in Elkhart, Constantine, Prairie Ronde and other places. The first preachers to this congregation were not local pastors, but the missionaries before named, Jones and Cory, the first regularly installed pastor being Rev. P. W. Warrimer, in 1834. The first church of that denomination was built by this society in 1834. It cost about one thousand nine hundred dollars, and had the first steeple and church-bell west of Ann Arbor. The same building, though remodeled and enlarged somewhat, remains still in use by this society.

### THE FIRST BAPTIST SOCIETY

was organized in Constantine in October, 1832, and the first Dutch Reformed—now known as the Reformed church of North America—in Centreville, in April, 1839, though Rev. Isaac L. Ketchum preached there as early as 1835-6. The detailed history of these churches may be found in the respective township histories.

The first Sunday-school organized in the county was one in White Pigeon, in the early days of the Presbyterian and Methodist churches, but the precise date is not known. It was a union school, and was well attended. Mrs. Jane Cowen, of Leonidas, organized a class in her own house, quite early, at least as soon as there were children to go to such a school, and taught them orally, her husband, Robert Cowen, taking his class—the older individuals—out of doors in seasonable and pleasant weather.

### THE EVANGELICAL ASSOCIATION.

The first society of the above-named church was formed in the township of Park, about the year 1849, under the labors of Rev. George Dell, a missionary sent out by the Ohio conference of the Evangelical association, who also organized a class in Flowerfield township, four miles northwest of Three Rivers, about the same time. He served the mission (then called the St. Joseph mission) two years, and was followed by two missionaries named M. Hoehn and George Kissel, who likewise served two years. The St. Joseph circuit of Michigan conference, under which the classes and churches of this denomination have been organized and erected, was constituted out of the St. Joseph mission, which was discontinued in 1849 or 1850, since which time the following ministers have been the presiding elders of the district: Rev. A. E. Driesbach, 1853-54; Rev. A. B. Schafer, 1855; Rev. G. G. Platz, 1856-59; Rev. Joseph Fisher, 1860-63; Rev. George Steffey, 1863-64; Rev. Andrew Nicolai, 1865-68; Rev. M. J. Miller, 1869-74; Rev. L. Scheuermann, 1875; Rev. S. Copley, 1876-77.

Under the labors of Rev. G. S. Brown there were one hundred persons added to the church in the St. Joseph circuit, and from seventy-five to eighty were added as members under the ministrations of Revs. E. B. Miller and T. N. Davis. Under the present pastor, Rev. J. H. Keeler, who has supplied us with the history of the churches of this denomination, there have been one hundred and sixty-five persons added to the church, and a revival is now in progress at this writing (January, 1877).

The religious sentiment in those days was as well-defined and aggressive as it has been since, as far as opportunity offered.

The present statistics make the following exhibit of the religious affiliations and church property in the county in 1876:

The Methodist Episcopal denomination has fourteen hundred and ninety-six members; thirteen churches, which, with their parsonages, are valued at one hundred and eleven thousand six hundred dollars. There are enrolled in its Sunday-schools seventeen hundred and thirty scholars, and its libraries aggregate thirty-six hundred and eighty-two volumes. The Presbyterians have about five hundred members; five churches, valued at fifty thousand dollars. The Reformed Church (Dutch) have about the same membership, and the same number of church edifices are valued at forty thousand dollars. The Baptists have about four hundred members, and three churches valued at twenty thousand dollars. All other denominations, including Episcopalians, Catholics, Lutherans and the Evangelical Association, number some nine hundred members, and their thirteen churches are valued at fifty thousand dollars. The total of church membership in the county exceeds thirty-eight hundred, and thirty-nine churches are valued at the sum of two hundred and seventy-one thousand six hundred dollars.

EDUCATION.

A government " for the people, by the people and of the people," to be successful and just and progressive, must be based on intelligence. Native wit and ability, to be broad and liberal, must be cultivated. The rich few must give of their plenty for the education of the less unfortunate many, if a free and independent Republic is to be maintained, for if " the fountain send forth bitter waters, how shall the stream be sweet?" Michigan, recognizing the principle that on intelligence the State is most surely founded, made ample and liberal provision in her constitution for the education of her people, and alone, of all her sister States in the great northwest, has reaped, and is still gathering, abundant harvests from the munificent donations of the general government to them in aid of the instruction of the masses. She alone of all her sisters has founded and maintained, from the proceeds of the generous benefaction, an institution for the classical, professional and scientific education of not only her own sons and daughters, but of all others who may come, without distinction of race, sex, condition or color, and substantially without money or price. The fame of the Michigan University is national, and it stands in the front rank of educational institutions in the land, not only for the erudition of its instructors, but also for the excellence of its system of instruction and the extent of its appointments.

The State not only stands foremost among her sisters of the northwest, in regard to her provision for the higher education of her people, but she leads them in her system of common schools. Her excellence is shown in this respect by her successful competition in the grand gathering of the world's evidences of progress, at Philadelphia, in the centennial year of the republic, whereat she was awarded eight prizes in the educational department on her exhibit of the attainments of her children in her free public schools, and for her unsurpassed system of instruction therein. Under the first constitution there were no absolutely free schools, and only those persons sent their children to the schools which were established but such as paid the small per capita tax laid on each scholar; yet it was optional with the people to vote a general tax on the property of the district, and dispense with the per capita tax whenever they chose so to do. Some districts adopted the latter course from the outset, and others continued the first until after the adoption of the new constitution, which provided for free schools without payment of tuition. In 1859 the legislature provided for the establishment of graded or union schools, whenever the people of a district saw fit to adopt that system.

The settlements on White Pigeon and Sturgis prairies, and in the openings of Constantine and Mottville, were " neck and neck " in the first establishment of schools in the county, each one having a term taught in 1830; but White Pigeon has the honor of building the first school-house. In the summer of 1830, a log school-house was built at Newville (east of White Pigeon village), and a Mr. Allen—afterwards postmaster in White Pigeon —taught the first school in it, in the winter of 1830–31.

The same year a school was taught in the upper room of the double log house of Philip H. Buck, in the village of Sherman (Sturgis), by Doctor Henry, which was attended by all the young men and maidens of the region round about. The schools were taught in this room until 1832, when a log house was built on the east side of Nottawa street as now laid out. From this beginning has arisen the truly admirable Union school of Sturgis.

In the fall of the same year a school was taught in Mottville township, in Solomon Hartman's neighborhood, in a log house formerly occupied as a residence by John Bear, but the name of the person who taught the school is forgotten by the old residents. Mr. Hartman's children and three or four of the Davidsons attended the school.

The first school taught in Constantine was presided over by Thomas Chariton, at the time a clerk in Niles F. Smith's store, in the basement of which store, fronting on the river, the children were confined. This was in the winter of 1830–31. The room was dark and gloomy, one small window admitting the sunlight, to cheer and gladden and lighten the tasks of the pupils; the door was on the river bank; the benches were split logs with sticks for legs, and the desks were rough counters nailed against the walls. If the young prisoners longed more for liberty than they did for that intelligence that makes liberty more desirable, it is not to be wondered at. Joseph Bonebright and his sister, Mrs. A. B. George, are still living in Constantine, the only representatives of this pioneer school. The master treated his pupils to a Christmas dinner of " sweet-cake," during his term of authority. But from these crude and forbidding beginnings has been developed that which is a just pride and ornament of old St. Joe, the superb Union school and its magnificent house and appointments of Constantine.

In 1832 a school-house of logs was built on Nottawa prairie, near the present house of the late Thomas Engle, deceased, and Miss Delia Brooks was the first teacher therein, the same year. The teacher afterwards married Colonel Jonathan Engle, but has since died. This old building is still standing, but it is fast settling to mother earth, from whence it came. It has been the nursery of many who are now gray-headed; and within its rude walls and on its ruder benches, the young idea in Nottawa, in pioneer days, received its " bent," to " shoot" in later times for the increased benefit of later shoots from the old parental stem.

Within sight, almost, of its fast disappearing outlines, stands the commodious Union school building of Centreville, where the sons and daughters of the pioneer boys and girls, who thumbed their dog-eared " elementaries," and " Dilworth's," and worried over their "Colburn's," and glibly analyzed —but never declined—the verb " to love," and blushingly said, " I love, you love, he loves," and in after-years practically added the plural " we love," are now learning to take the places of these same pioneers, whom they are fast pushing out of the way. May they fill the places vacated, not only as well, but better than they were filled of yore!

In 1831 the White Pigeon Academy Association was incorporated—Don Cathcart, Dr. Isaac Adams, Hart L. Stewart and Neal McGaffey being leading incorporators of the same. A building was erected in 1832, and a school taught for several years. The old building is now doing service as Louis Rhoade's stable. " To what base uses has it come at last."

In 1836–7 the State educational authorities established a branch of the University of Michigan at White Pigeon, as was the plan of the State at that time. This school was for several years partially sustained by appropriations from the State, but the plan having changed to one main institution at Ann Arbor, the appropriations ceased in 1845, after which it was conducted for a time as a private institution, but was finally abandoned, and was taken down a few years ago, and is at the present writing used as a barn, on a farm near the village of White Pigeon.

The first teacher employed in the Branch was Rev. Charles Newberry, assisted by Wilson Gray, a graduate of Dublin University. Mr. Gray was a finished classical scholar. He was the brother, and afterwards, associate, of the editor of the Dublin Freeman. In later years he was appointed to a position on the Queen's bench, and went to New Zealand as a member of the supreme bench of that province, and died in 1875. The Branch, under the management of such men as Newberry and Gray, achieved an excellent reputation, and for some years maintained it successfully; and its true successor, which gathers to itself all the honors its predecessor gained, is the Union school of White Pigeon, under the able supervision and management of Professor Ploughman.

The school facilities, and what they cost the people to maintain them in 1876, are shown from the following summary taken from the official returns of the township school superintendents, on file in the county clerk's office at Centreville. There are one hundred and twenty-three school-houses, eighty-eight being of wood, thirty-four of brick, and one of stone, valued at $280,690. The houses have a seating capacity of nine thousand five hundred and twenty-eight. There were in the county eight thousand seven hundred and six children between the school ages of five and twenty years, of whom seven thousand six hundred and sixty-six attended school during the year. There were seventy-six male teachers employed, who were paid $19,857 for their services, and two hundred and thirteen females, who received $24,873 for their services. The schools were in session eight months, on an average, except the Union schools—of which there were eight —which had their terms for ten months. The total income of the schools for the year ending September 4, 1876, from all sources, amounted to $96,582.88, and the total expenditures, including $20,000 paid on indebtedness and buildings, amounted to $89,032.86. The cost of the graded schools, exclusive of payments on indebtedness and tuition fees received from non-resident scholars (which last amounted to $1,529), aggregated the sum of $27,615. The indebtedness of the Union school districts amounts to $42,000. There are three thousand six hundred and forty-five volumes in the school libraries.

The first public school money received from the State was in the year 1839, and amounted to six hundred and ninety-four dollars, which was distributed among the several townships according to law.

CHAPTER XIV.

THE LEARNED PROFESSIONS—THE BAR OF ST. JOSEPH, PAST AND PRESENT —THE MEDICAL STAFF, THEN AND NOW—LOBELIA AS A REMEDIAL AGENT FOR CORNS.

The whole universe is under law, and from the beginning all nature has moved forward in obedience thereto, and in the very constitution of things must continue to do so indefinitely. Society is not exempt from the all-pervading principle, but progresses obedient to the unaltered and unalterable decree of Omnipotence, pronounced in the very outset of time; consequently, courts of justice organized under law, schools of medicine founded in law, and educational institutions fostered by the law, have arisen, which testify in the strongest terms to the wisdom of the axiom, "Lex suprema est!" Enthusiasts and visionaries look forward to a time when the race of man shall have attained to perfection, morally, physically and mentally, but long ages have rolled by since order began to emerge from chaos, and society was begun, and longer ages may perhaps intervene before such a much to be desired state shall come; and until that Utopia shall become a reality, the learned professions must continue to be what they ever have been in the past, not only honorable, but most useful components of the body politic.

In St. Joseph county these professions have and are ably represented, the bench and bar standing in high repute in the State, the medical staff being second to none in point of knowledge, skill and experience, and the county is noted for its admirable corps of teachers and instructors.

THE BAR.

The first resident attorney to be admitted to the practice of his profession in the courts of St. Joseph county, was Neal McGaffey, Esq., of White Pigeon, whose name was entered upon the roll of the bar on the 17th day of August, 1830, the same being the first day of the first term of the circuit court of St. Joseph county, held in the county at White Pigeon, in Savery's tavern. He was admitted on motion of E. B. Sherman, prosecuting attorney of the circuit, and sworn to duly and justly perform the duties required of an honorable attorney at law and solicitor in chancery by Hon. William Woodbridge, the presiding judge of the circuit and court.

On the 7th day June, 1831, Columbia Lancaster was admitted to practice in the courts of the county on motion of Mr. McGaffey, made before judges Meek and Sturgis of the county court, the same being the first day of the second term of that court held in the county, in the White Pigeon academy. Lancaster appeared at the August term of the circuit court in 1832 as district attorney.

Both of these attorneys remained in the practice in the county for more than a quarter of a century, when McGaffey went to Texas, and Lancaster to Oregon. The latter attained to a high eminence in the west, being at one time attorney-general of the State.

At the August term of 1832 of the circuit court, Judges Sibley and Morell presiding, Cyrus Lovell, John S. Barry, Cogswell K. Green and Alexander H. Redfield were examined, touching their knowledge of law, by W. H. Welch, L. J. Daniels and E. B. Sherman, and on the committee's recommendation were admitted to the bar. At the April term of the circuit court of 1837, Judge Ransom presiding, J. Eastman Johnson was added to the roll of attorneys, and is still practicing in the courts, a venerable white-haired old gentleman, but still vigorous, and in his capacity of magistrate is a terror to evil-doers. At the September term, 1838, of the same court, W. C. Montrose was admitted to the bar, and at the March term following Chester Gurney received his first circuit-court fee in the county. In Septem-

ber of the same year Nathan Osborn, who was a practicing lawyer in Steuben county, N. Y., before his removal to St. Joseph, was admitted. Judge Osborn now resides in Marcellus, Cass county. At the March term, 1840, Horace Mower and Nathaniel A. Balch were admitted, on the recommendation of Abner Pratt, John S. Chipman and Columbia Lancaster, and in September following, Aaron E. Wait. Mr. Balch is an eminent attorney of the Kalamazoo bar, and Mr. Wait is in Oregon. In 1814 William C. Pease and Edward Flint were admitted as attorneys. Hiram Draper and James C. Wood received permission to plead for others in the courts of the county, in March, 1844, and Elisha Stevens in 1845. Perrin M. Smith, afterwards judge of the circuit, was admitted in 1849, and George W. Haddon and William L. Stoughton in 1850.

Mr. Stoughton became famous in the annals of the nation as the colonel of the 11th Michigan infantry and general of a brigade, losing a leg before Atlanta, and after his discharge was elected to Congress for two terms from the St. Joseph district.

In November, 1851, Orange Jacobs, John C. Bishop and J. W. Flanders were admitted. Mr. Jacobs afterwards went to Washington territory as chief justice of the United States court, and has served the territory two terms as delegate in Congress. Mr. Flanders is a prominent member of the bar in Sturgis.

John B. Shipman, Edward P. Wait, James H. Lyon, John H. Baker and William Sadler were admitted during the year 1856. Mr. Shipman is a member of the Coldwater bar, and is prominently named as a candidate for the vacant judgeship. Mr. Lyon and Mr. Sadler are members of the St. Joseph county bar at present. A. E. Hewit and Gilbert R. Shays were admitted in 1857, and also Hiram S. Taylor. Charles R. Millington and Asher Bonham were admitted in the year 1845. In 1858 Paul J. Eaton, William Allison and Samuel Chadwick were admitted, and Alson Bailey, Oscar Waters and Germain H. Mason in 1859. Henry F. Severens was the only one added to the list of barristers in 1857, but the year following, Geron Brown, Talcott C. Carpenter, and a Mr. Dennis were added.

1862 seems to have passed without adding any new candidates for forensic honors, and 1863 gave but a solitary one, Comfort T. Chaffee. 1864 added two, J. J. Crandall and Alfred A. Key, and 1865 increased the list with the addition of Gersham P. Doan. 1866 gave three new competitors for legal fees and practice, two of whom afterwards became judges in the circuit court, to wit: Edwin W. Keightley and R. W. Melendy; Frank H. Guion making up the trio. Judge Keightley was elected to Congress in November, 1866, and Judge Melendy had the same favor extended to him as county clerk.

R. R. Pealer was admitted in 1867, and was the prosecuting attorney in 1875 and '76. In 1868 Philip Pudgham and W. H. H. Wilcox; 1869; Walter Littlefield and Oscar L. Cowles; 1870, Alfred D. Deming, Benton S. Hewe and D. Clayton Page were admitted. Charles W. W. Clarke and William H. Howe in 1873; G. W. Lyster and Bishop E. Andrews in 1874; Stillman L. Taylor in 1865, and James W. Welch and Seymour McG. Sadler in 1876, complete the roll as admitted by the circuit court.

Besides these, have been others eminent in the profession who have resided in the county, or still reside there. Hon. John S. Chipman, familiarly known as "Black Chip," was a leading attorney and a member of Congress. He flourished as early as 1838, and later, Hon. Charles Upson, who began his life in St. Joseph county as a school-teacher in Constantine in 1845–6, read law with Chester Gurney, and practiced in Centreville, was afterwards elected judge of the circuit; still later he served three terms in Congress. He now resides in Coldwater, and is a leading member of the Branch county bar. Hon. H. H. Riley, of Constantine, has been for at least thirty-five years a member of the bar, and an ornament to the profession, ranking very high for legal ability. Judge S. C. Coffinberry, also of Constantine, began to practice in the St. Joseph courts before 1844, being an old practitioner before he came to the county. He is a fine, fluent speaker, eloquent and forcible.

William Savier began his practice in the county about 1845, at White Pigeon, and for many years was the only attorney of the place. He died just before or during the war of the rebellion. A Mr. Ames and E. V. Mitchell preceded him. E. B. Turner located at Centreville in 1847, or thereabouts, and was the first prosecuting attorney elected in the county— the election being under the constitution of 1850. He subsequently went to Texas, and was elected to the position of attorney-general of that State. Hon. John S. Barry attained to a high rank in the councils of the nation, being elected three times to the office of governor, 1841, 1843 and 1847. He had previously held the position of State senator, and was in that station when first called to the higher and more important trust of governor. He came to the gubernatorial office when the State was suffering severely in

5

the loss of her credit, and by his able and economical administration of the public affairs, raised the credit of the Commonwealth to the first rank, which has ever since been maintained. He was the only man in the State who has held the position of governor three terms. He lived in Constantine since 1835, where he died January 14, 1870. He never followed the profession of the law, however, but engaged in mercantile pursuits.

Charles Henry Stewart was also a very prominent lawyer, residing at Centreville, in 1834 and later. He was celebrated in the chancery practice, and removed to Detroit, where he became one of the leading members of the bar of that city. George H. Palmer was an attorney in Constantine in 1835.

The present bar of the county includes the following attorneys: Hon. H. H. Riley, Judge S. C. Coffinberry, Hon. E. W. Keightley, L. B. French, Constantine; J. W. Flanders, D. E. Thomas, T. C. Carpenter, A. B. Dunning and C. W. W. Clarke, Sturgis; James H. Lyon, O. F. Bean, David Knox, Jr., R. R. Pealer, Bishop E. Andrews, Henry McClory and N. H. Barnard, Three Rivers; Judge J. Eastman Johnson, William Sadler, S. M. Sadler, Alfred Akey, P. J. Eaton, Hon. R. W. Meloudy, Stillman L. Taylor and Charles J. Beerstecher, Centreville; D. Clayton Page, White Pigeon; O. J. Fast and G. P. Dunn, Mendon; W. W. Howe and O. L. Cowles, Burr Oak.

PHYSICIANS.

The first man who came to the county of St. Joseph to minister professionally to the ills that flesh is heir to, was Dr. Page, a youth of some twenty-five summers, who rode on to White Pigeon prairie late in the fall of 1827. He was fresh from his matriculation, and thought his eastern *Alma Mater* had given him a theoretical knowledge of pharmacy and the human anatomy; nature, and contact with her alone, could fit him for the work he was destined to perform in the West. His knowledge of the practical realities of life was all to be gained by actual experience, but it is said he became a skillful physician and surgeon in after years. It is told of him that on his way to White Pigeon, he stopped one night at a cabin and asked for accommodations for himself and horse, and being assured of the same, asked where he could find water for his steed, and was directed to a spring a short distance from the house, which he was advised he could easily find by the "blazed" trees around it. He started off, and after being gone for nearly half an hour came back and reported he could not see any tree *blazing* in the woods, and could find no spring. He was laughed at heartily, and the term explained to him. He was well posted in the border vernacular before he left St. Joseph county. He performed, probably, the first surgical operation in the county on a white person, in the summer of 1828, for Peter Klinger, who was injured in falling down a well he was digging for Judge Sturgis, on his first location on Sturgis prairie.

In 1828 Dr. Hubbel Loomis came to White Pigeon and located at Newville for a time, but subsequently went to White Pigeon, and was appointed the first judge of probate of the county. His official duties did not interfere much with his professional calls, as there were but four days of court from March 26 to September 6, 1830.

Dr. Henry came to Sturgis prairie in 1829, and Dr. Alexander McMillan to Nottawa the same year. The latter gave more attention to the elucidation of philosophical and chemical problems, than he did to the practice of medicine, and seemed, in his own mind, to be very near the realization of his hopes, but, like an *ignis fatuus*, the solution of his problems ever eluded his mental grasp, and he died still pursuing them; but, nevertheless, he was a kind neighbor and the very soul of honor.

Dr. W. N. Elliott located in White Pigeon in 1832, and is still hale and hearty, and the leading member of the profession in the county. He is a very skillful surgeon, and was appointed to that position in the 11th Michigan Infantry, and served therein during the whole term of service of the regiment with great credit.

Dr. Rowley came to White Pigeon in 1835, and to his professional duties added those of boniface, and kept the "Old Diggins" for several years.

Dr. Watson Sumner came to Constantine in 1834, and was a noted physician for several years, but his own health failed and he left the county. The doctor was prominent in politics also, being a delegate to the convention that rejected the terms imposed by Congress on the admission of Michigan into the Union.

Dr. Mottram came to Nottawa prairie in 1834, and had for years a most extensive ride throughout the country. He declined to locate in Centreville because he was poor, and could not get so good an outfit as Dr. Johnson had, but he did not long have that for an excuse, as his practice grew rapidly, and he accumulated a handsome property. He is now a prominent

physician in Kalamazoo, whither he went after 1850, and before the close of that decade.

Dr. Cyrus Ingerson, Dr. Johnson and Dr. S. W. Truesdall practiced in Centreville from and after 1834, Dr. Ingerson dying in 1844, while holding the position of judge of probate. He was a skillful physician, and a very genial gentleman.

Dr. Ira F. Packard has been one of the ablest physicians in the county, and successfully followed his profession from 1839 till 1850, when his health failed, and he surrendered his extensive practice to his son, Nelson I. Packard, who still continues it in Sturgis. The old doctor went to California for a year, but on his return did not resume his profession, and never has done so. He resides in Sturgis, in his old homestead.

Dr. Nelson I. Packard went out with the 11th regiment as assistant surgeon, and served with ability during the war.

Dr. Edwin Stewart, of Mendon, Dr. Isaac Sides, Dr. A. J. Kinne and Dr. Mitchell, of Colon, all belong to the early list of physicians, though forming a part of the medical staff of the present. Dr. Mitchell had, in an early day, an extensive ride.

Dr. Hyatt, of Mendon, was formerly a partner of Dr. Mottram, in Nottawa, and removed to Mendon in 1859.

Dr. Parker came to White Pigeon in 1830, and Dr. Marshall to Constantine in 1837.

Dr. Baldy was a partner of Dr. Sumner, in the latter place, in 1836, and afterwards. Dr. Eagery came to Three Rivers in 1836, and Dr. Hurd about the same time.

Elias Boulton Smith, M. D., located at Sturgis in 1834-5, and was well known throughout that section of country; but he subsequently abandoned the practice of medicine, and entered the legal profession at Lima, Indiana.

The names of the present physicians of the county will be found in the respective township histories.

Dr. Elliott once performed a surgical operation upon a lady for a dropsical affection, by which, at one operation, he drew one hundred and thirty pounds of water from her body.

Amariah Bennett was a botanic physician, who located on the Indian reservation at an early day. He attended a council of physicians at Schoolcraft at one time, at which some of the regular-school doctors, thinking to quiz the old man, asked him what he would prescribe for a severe case of corns. The old man gravely replied: "I would give the patient, first, a dose of lobelia, and repeat it at the end of an hour. At the end of the second hour, I would give him—lobelia; and at the end of the third hour, I would administer a very large dose of——lobelia, when, doubtless, the corns would be cast off!"

Dr. VanBuren was probably the first homœopathic physician who practiced in the county—settling in Centreville in 1836. Dr. A. T. Woodward died in the latter place after a practice of a few years.

CLERGYMEN.

The prominent ministers of the Gospel, past and present, are named in connection with the church-history in the several townships; and so, also, are the leading teachers and professors of the early days and the present, in the school-history of the townships.

---

CHAPTER XV.

ASSOCIATIONS—AGRICULTURAL SOCIETY—FIRST FAIR AND ADDRESS—TOTAL PREMIUMS PAID IN TWENTY-SIX YEARS—INSURANCE AGAINST THIEVES AND FIRE—PIONEER SOCIETY—TEMPERANCE SOCIETY OF 1835—MEDICAL SOCIETY—TEACHERS' ASSOCIATION—MASONIC—ODD FELLOWS—THE GRANGE.

Recognizing the fact that in association there is strength to execute what there should be wisdom to contrive, the people of St. Joseph county have not been backward to avail themselves of the joint and mutual efforts of each other in the various departments of life, social, professional, religious and reformatory, as well as in point of the various business callings they follow, and insurance against fire and depredators. The association now in existence, which dates its organization the earliest in the county, and in which all the people are interested, is

THE ST. JOSEPH COUNTY AGRICULTURAL SOCIETY,

which was organized November 27, 1849, by several citizens of the county, who met in the court-house hall in Centerville, and elected Mark H. Wakeman, chairman, Henry K. Farrand and J. Eastman Johnson, secretaries. The meeting adopted a constitution, and elected the following board of officers, to hold their positions until the next spring: Mark H. Wakeman, president; Nathan Osborn, vice-president; Samuel Chipman, treasurer; J. Eastman Johnson, recording secretary; Levi Patchen, H. K. Farrand, J. A. Thompson, Moses Taft and H. M. Vesey, managers. These gentlemen and twelve others signed the constitution, and were the first members of the association.

On April 9, 1850, the same officers were re-elected, and also George Talbot, corresponding secretary, and on the 29th day of June following, the society adopted a code of by-laws for the government of the exhibitions of the association. On the 20th of September, 1851, the executive committee called the first fair or exhibition, and offered ninety-three dollars in premiums on live stock, on farms and farm products. The fair was held October 22 following, at which George Boyes received the first premium, five dollars, for the best stallion, W. D. Oviatt the first on matched horses, M. H. Wakeman for the best work-horses, William Armitage for the best breeding mare, and F. Wallace for the best roadster. C. L. Wheeler had the best bull, H. K. Farrand the best working oxen, and Mark H. Wakeman the best cow. Joseph Horton took the blue ribbon for the best buck sheep, Norman Harvey for the best ewes, Peter F. Putnam for the best boar, and George Carman's breeding sow was similarly decorated. Moses Taft, L. H. Bishop, Asher Bonham and J. M. Leland carried off the first prizes on cheese, butter, apples and wheat, respectively. The ladies received eight first prizes for patchwork, all of which were discretionary and meritorious. Fellows & Townsend had the best plows, and W. D. Pettit the best carriages.

Hon. Joseph R. Williams, of Constantine, a member of the society, delivered the first address, in which he discussed the problems that are still occupying the attention of the people, of how to farm lands properly and to the best advantage, and urged the people to give their careful attention to the improvement of stock and intelligent culture of the soil. On these points he said: "There are times in the progress of every art and science when one man is right, and all the world besides is wrong. The world tests him and guided by a beacon light far in advance of his generation. If conservatism is right anywhere, it is wrong in agricultural inquiry. The first man who took the first wild plants and roots, and began to mature them into rice and wheat and potatoes, was a visionary. The first man who took the wild crab-apple and the bitter almond, to mature them into delicious fruit, was doubtless a laughing stock. The first man who put salt upon his provisions, in order to save his family from starvation, was regarded as throwing away positive labor for possible good. The first fence was doubtless viewed with indignation, as an encroachment on the common rights of mankind. The first man who had the audacity to shut up a pig, under the silly idea that he would fatten faster and cheaper, was as big a fool as a member of a modern agricultural society.

"In the science of agriculture we know little or nothing. The most profound inquirer is superficial. The earth is a vast chemical laboratory, few of whose operations we comprehend. Every time we tread the grass beneath our feet, we trample on an operation of nature as wonderful and more inexplicable than that of the magnetic telegraph. After the surface of the earth has been for months sealed up and congealed, the genial influences of the the same sun whose power in impressing the Daguerrean plate we deem so potent and magical, entices from the dreary waste—not pictures—but realities of wonderful beauty and variety, and causes to thrive and flourish and mature, the sustenance for hundreds of millions of men, and the countless swarms of animal life. To cause the growth of a single spire of grass, elements far more numerous are called into requisition—chemical action far more inscrutable is going on. Do you understand the occult attractions, affinities, combinations, which enter into the germination and growth of a single seed or plant of tiniest shoot of vegetation? Do you understand the delicate, yet potent, influences of light, heat, water and electricity? 'Can't' thou measure the sweet influences of the pleiades?' No! you are as ignorant of most of the influences which affect your crops as the clod you tread upon! Of some of the appliances which stimulate, of some of the acts which destroy, you know something, but know little. Yet, strange as it may appear, we hear men often exclaim, 'I understand my business well enough; I want none of the instructions of your books!'

"When the world had not yet recovered from astonishment at the discoveries of Newton, he declared that he felt like a man picking up pebbles on the sea-shore, while the great ocean of truth lay unexplored before him. If you understand farming 'well enough,' I mean as a science, you have fathomed all the processes encased and hidden beneath the surface of the earth.

You are a wiser, if not a humbler man than Newton, and to the question so significantly asked, 'Canst thou, by searching, find out God?' you can triumphantly answer 'yea.'"

Mr. Williams exhibited some little crabbed, wrinkled apples, grown on a seedling, stunted in its growth by neglect, which he labelled "Good enough," and alongside of them fine specimens of grafted fruit, as a practical illustration of the theme of his eloquent oration.

At the next fair, held October 14, 1852, Hon. Isaac D. Crary delivered the address to the largest assemblage of people ever before convened in the county. One hundred and forty dollars was distributed in premiums, George Carman taking the first one on farms, T. B. Millard the second. The society has held twenty-six annual fairs, besides two sheep-shearing festivals in 1865 and 1866, and spring exhibitions in 1874 and 1876. The society has paid in premiums since its first organization over seventeen thousand dollars in cash, besides valuable prizes distributed in silver-ware and other articles. The report of the committee on farms in 1857 is exhaustive and interesting. Michael Kline carried off the first prize, and William Major the second. Mr. Major's farm of two hundred and forty acres produced in 1856 one thousand five hundred and sixteen dollars, and Mr. Kline's, of two hundred acres, produced two thousand one hundred and fifty-four dollars.

The fair in 1863 was said to be the best one that had then been held. Professor Tenney, of Williams College, Massachusetts, was the orator. The exhibition of 1876 was noticeable for the eminent speakers present, who were M. M. (Brick) Pomeroy, who delivered a practical address of "How to make money, and how to spend it;" General H. C. Carey, candidate for vice-president on the "Greenback" ticket, and ex-Postmaster General J. A. J. Cresswell—these two gentlemen discussing the finance question; and H. H. Chamberlain, candidate for Congress from the St. Joseph district on the combined Democratic and Greenback ticket, and a prominent lawyer of the district of the Republican party—the two latter speakers discussing the general political issue. The receipts at the gates were over three thousand dollars, and one thousand, two hundred and twenty-four dollars and seventy-five cents were paid in premiums.

The society owns some eighteen acres of land joining the village of Centreville, eligibly located, on which they have erected commodious buildings and sheds, the whole valued at several thousand dollars.

The present officers of the society are David D. Antes, president; James Hill, secretary; John C. Joss, treasurer; O. P. Brush, H. K. Farrand, James Hutchinson, Isaac Runyan, Nelson Spalsbury and Thomas Cuddy, directors.

THE ST. JOSEPH COUNTY MUTUAL PROTECTION ASSOCIATION

was organized March 28, 1854, for protection against the depredations of horse-thieves, and the whole power of the society is pledged and exerted to recover the property and catch the thief, whenever a member of the association has a horse stolen. The first officers were P. M. Smith, president; John Hull, secretary; C. H. Starr, treasurer; and Joseph Horton and Jehial B. Dimmick, directors. There are now five hundred members in the society, all residents of the county, to whom the membership is confined. There are two thousand dollars now at interest of the available funds of the society, but no assessments have been made for several years. The entrance fee is now five dollars, having been steadily increased since the first organization of the society, when it was but one dollar. This association has, in its practical operation, proven to be the most perfect insurance company ever organized, as it has been for several years as absolute preventive of crime. Not a horse has been molested, belonging to members, for years, and instances have been frequently known where horses have been stolen just alongside of others belonging to members, which much more valuable, were left untouched. The society issue each year a list of the members thereof, which is printed on cloth and posted up in the barns of the members, or other public places, and criminals have been captured in other parts of the country with these lists on their persons. There has been but one horse taken, since the society was organized, from a member, and that was turned loose, by reason of the sharp pursuit that was at once organized and most vigorously pushed forward. The present officers are William B. Langley, president; Edmund Stears, secretary; J. H. Gardner, treasurer; and A. M. Leland and Joseph Stadden, directors.

THE ST. JOSEPH COUNTY VILLAGE FIRE INSURANCE COMPANY

was organized in 1863, under the mutual plan of insurance against loss by fire in the villages of the county, as provided for by the general insurance law of the State. The incorporators were scattered all through this and adjacent counties, among whom were William Allison, D. F. Wolf, C. H.

Barr, John W. Talbot, J. W. Spitzer, of Centreville, J. W. Flanders and Bracy Tobey, of Sturgis. The capital is represented by the policies issued, and has amounted to eight hundred and fifty thousand dollars. The legislature in 1873 confined the business exclusively to dwellings and buildings connected therewith, cutting off the business risks the company had theretofore taken, and the income of the company is consequently much less than formerly. The first officers were C. H. Starr, president; William Allison, secretary, and D. F. Wolf, treasurer. The present officers are J. W. Spitzer, president; Charles Cummings, treasurer; J. Eastman Johnson, secretary. Directors: John Hutchinson, E. B. Thomas, J. W. Lovett, S. P. Davis, T. E. Clapp and John Dice.

THE FARMERS' MUTUAL FIRE INSURANCE COMPANY

of St. Joseph county, was organized March 10, 1863, with A. R. Metcalf, president, and A. W. Parkhurst, secretary. Its risks are confined to farm-buildings and stock only. There are now one thousand and sixty-two members in the company, and the capital liable to assessment—which is the property insured—amounts to two million three hundred and eighty-one thousand eight hundred and fifty-five dollars. The present officers of the company are Daniel Shurtz, president and treasurer; L. A. Clapp, secretary. Directors: Andrew Perrin, H. K. Farrand, Isaac Runyan, Thomas Stears and John W. Fletcher.

THE PIONEER SOCIETY OF ST. JOSEPH COUNTY

was organized October 16, 1873, at Centreville, of citizens of the county who had settled therein previous to 1840. Its first officers, with the dates of their settlement, and their location, were as follows: President, Asahel Savery, 1828, White Pigeon, and who was, at the time of his election, the earliest living settler in the county. Vice-presidents: William M. Watkins, 1833, Leonidas; Ransom Schellhous, 1830, Colon; Samuel Needham, Burr Oak; I. D. Toll, 1834, Centreville (now of Fawn River); P. Marantette, 1833, Mendon; Amos Howe, Sr., 1829, Nottawa; Stephen Cade, 1830, Sherman; Hiram Jacobs, 1831, Sturgis; E. H. Lothrop, Lockport; I. F. Ulrich, 1834, Park; Alvin Calhoon, 1829, Florence; George W. Beisel, 1832, White Pigeon; Challenge S. Wheeler, 1831, Flowerfield; William Arney, 1833, Fabius; William Hamilton, 1832, Constantine, and James Barnes, 1830, Mottville. Hon. J. Eastman Johnson, treasurer, 1836, White Pigeon, but now of Centreville; and Hon. William H. Cross, secretary—the latter a pioneer in Lenawee county in 1826, and a settler in St. Joseph county in 1846, in Leonidas, and in Centreville in 1872.

Messrs. A. R. Metcalf, who came to Constantine in 1836–7, John Hull who came to Florence in 1837, and Judge Johnson, as a committee for the purpose, reported a constitution defining the objects of the association, and providing for its government and future usefulness, which was adopted and signed by one hundred and fifty pioneers.

This society has done much to awaken an interest in the pioneer history of the county, which is fast passing into forgetfulness, and its honored secretary, the Hon. William H. Cross, has been indefatigable in recovering the lost threads of the old story of the past, and placing them on record; and to him we owe much for the able and generous assistance he has most cheerfully rendered us in the prosecution of our present work.

The society adopted a rule to make the oldest living resident of the county the President of the society for a year, and its second one was Amos Howe, Senior, of Nottawa, for the year 1874; Captain Alvin Calhoon, of Florence, was the third president, in 1875, and at the annual meeting in 1876, John W. Fletcher, who came to Nottawa in 1829, was elected.

At the last annual meeting, June 17, 1876, Hon. Isaac D. Toll delivered an able and eloquent address before the society, which we have taken the liberty of quoting largely from in other parts of our work.

In dropping the tear of remembrance for those of the society who had passed away from earth since the organization of the society, he pays them this tribute: " A Leland, a Lothrop, Tyler, Mrs. Douglass, Talbot, Parker, Hutchinson, Mrs. McKinley, Daniel Stewart and Amos Howe, our lamented president, among the earliest pioneers, not only of St. Joseph, but also in the State in 1818. The latter was borne to the tomb on the 26th day of last August, by the friendly hands of his fellow pioneers, leaving a memory without reproach; around which, with those of others who had preceded, and some who have followed, cling many pleasing recollections."

The orator paid the following justly merited tribute to the secretary of the society, which was greeted with rapturous applause: " Thrice fortunate are we, Mr. President, that the pioneer in this State, of fifty years, then in Monroe, now Lenawee county, is with us to-day, the man to whom, more than any other, (I might add, than all others,) we are indebted for the incep-

tion, advancement and flourishing condition of our society. Truant though he was, for a time, coquetting with the El Dorado of the west, he has found that St. Joseph was the better land. Ireland, the land of Emmett, Curran, Burke and Moore, gave him birth; California could not hold him; St. Joseph claims him! I mean, Sir, the Hon. William H. Cross, our secretary." He urged the society to gather the records preparatory to the compilation of a history, commemorating by name the dead and living pioneers of the county, and added: " We look with feelings akin to veneration upon the birth-places of conquerors. We make pilgrimages to the shrines of poets and philosophers; and we might well be deemed insensible, nay, ungrateful,—more, unfilial—if we not record in lines that immortally save, the toils, the sacrifices, the virtues of our fathers.

"By gradual growth of centuries the character of our founders had been formed. From the throes of civil war in England, from Runnymede, from which came Magna Charta, to the abnegation of divine right, for which Hampden bled; through the heroic struggle of the Hollanders against Spain, developing almost the grandest character in history—William the Silent,—to Washington,—' the tyrant tamer,' and his coadjutors,

'The stole Franklin's energetic shade,
Calming the lightnings which his soul hath made,
And Henry—forest-born Demosthenes—
Whose thunders shook the Philip of the seas'

" Nor have I forgotten the pilgrims of Maryland, who, under Calvert, founded their colony to enjoy religious freedom. From precedent to precedent, by sure steps, adding strength to strength for the great work: the hardy middle class, with muscles of steel, and will of adamant, mostly of the yeomanry, were our fathers fitted for the subjugation of wild nature and wilder men, and their descendants, our pioneers were acting up to the laws of blood, of race, they could not shame, and would not if they could. " In this Centennial of the Republic, ambassadors of the old world have come hither to view the power, the progress, the arts and productions of the young giant of the new continent, the offshoot of their own loins. Let them come hither to the ampenam peninsulam, made so by your strong arms. Let them visit our schools, the hope and pride of our young State; our asylums for the unfortunate; if a bigot to aristocratic institutions—to the law of force—we will point to the decorated graves of our dead patriots, illustrating that the citizen—the maker and executor of the laws—while living the peer of any, dead, is crowned by the affections of his countrymen, and a candidate for Heaven's nobility, the only recognized divine right."

The address was closed with an earnest appeal to the sons of the pioneers to make good use of the examples set before them; and especially to remember their duty to their country, in view of what the fathers had suffered and sacrificed for them; and those who should follow; and the orator then added, " Your patriotism can have no doubtful ring with a charity as broad as the heavens; your whole country, your Mecca and the precious legacy so dearly bought, will be worthily bestowed. To you is left the guardianship of 'Time's last and noblest empire.' Ever cherish the love of the fathers, and may yours be as unselfish."

THE ST. JOSEPH COUNTY TEMPERANCE SOCIETY

was the outgrowth of the first agitation of the temperance-reform movement in St. Joseph county. It was organized March 25, 1835. Erastus Kellogg was the chairman of the convention, which proceeded to the election of officers as follows: Digby V. Dell, president; Dr. W. N. Elliott, James Cowen, Elias True and Martin Hazzard, vice presidents; Dr. Cyrus Ingerson, secretary. Executive Committee: Otis Preston, S. A. Chapin, J. W. Fletcher, William Simpson, Erastus Thurber, Guy H. Leonard, Isaac G. Bailey and Martin Watkins. Committee to organize township societies: Neal McGaffey and Duncan Clark, of White Pigeon; Jonn Bryan and Elias True, of Constantine; Dr. S. W. Truesdell and Ingerson, of Centreville, and Messrs. Cowen and Bailey, of Leonidas.

The society flourished for a time and went down, its place being occupied in after years by Washingtonians, Sons of Temperance, Good Templars, and lastly, in this present year of grace the " Red Ribbon League " have begun the agitation of the question of teetotalism.

Apropos of the early times in the temperance movement is a story of one of the McCoy missionary Indians, who had, despite his teaching, been led astray, and was reeling towards the mission, when he was met by one of his friends who expressed his sorrow at seeing him in his present condition, and inquired how it was he had so far forgotten himself as to get drunk. The young man looked up at his interrogator with a drunken leer, and said, " Me only half missionary and half Injun, and Injun good deal biggest half," and staggered on.

### THE ST. JOSEPH MEDICAL SOCIETY

was an association of the physicians of the county for mutual benefit, and was organized July 27, 1835, with the following officers: Dr. Hubbel Loomis, president; Dr. Watson Sumner, vice president; Dr. S. W. Truesdell, secretary; Dr. W. N. Elliott, treasurer, and Drs. Sumner, Elliott and Ingerson, censors.

The society held annual meetings until 1845 or thereabouts, when it was abandoned, and afterwards succeeded by the St. Joseph Valley Medical Society, including a large area of territory in its membership. Dr. Edwin Stewart, of Mendon, was the president, and Dr. C. H. Backus, of Three Rivers, secretary, in 1876. The county society, as well as the present one, represented the regular school of practice, commonly called the "allopathic."

### THE ST. JOSEPH COUNTY TEACHERS' ASSOCIATION

was organized in 1860 at Constantine, where, in February, a session was held for three days, at which the best methods of teaching were discussed and illustrated by actual class-work, which is the business the association was organized to perform. It meets annually in the different towns of the county where there are union schools, the members being nearly, if not quite, exclusively confined to teachers in those schools. The present officers are: Professor S. B. Kingsbury, of the Constantine high-school, president; and Professor L. B. Antisdale, of the Centreville Union school, secretary.

### SECRET SOCIETIES.

FREE-MASONS.—Mt. Hermon lodge, No. 24, A. F. and A. M., at Centreville, was the first Masonic lodge instituted in the county. It worked under a dispensation during the year 1848, and was chartered January 10, 1849, with the following members: Benjamin Osgood, W. M.; Ezra Cole, S. W.; S. C. Coffinberry, J. W.; Charles Thome, treasurer; J. Eastman Johnson, secretary; John R. Belote, Dr. Sol. Cummings, Glover Laird, John Carr, Francis Flanders, Benjamin Sherman, John H. Clewes, John Gascon and Joel Redway. Hon. S. C. Coffinberry, now of Constantine, filled the office of Grand Master of the State of Michigan, during the years 1866–7–8, and during the first year of his incumbency assisted in the burial obsequies of Governor Cass, upon which topic he dwelt most eloquently in his annual address in 1867. There are, at the present time, ten subordinate or "blue" lodges in the county, numbering nine hundred members. There are also five chapters of Royal-arch Masons, the first one of which, established in the county, was Centreville chapter, No. 11, under dispensation in 1852 and chartered in 1853, the history of which, in detail, will be found in the history of Centreville. There are about four hundred members of the chapter in the county. There is also a council of Royal and Select Masters in Constantine, and two commanderies of Knights Templar, the latter numbering some two hundred rank and file. There are also two Eastern Star lodges in the county.

ODD FELLOWS.—There was at an early day, as early at least as 1845, an Odd Fellows' lodge instituted in Centreville, which was known as the St. Joseph County lodge, but which ceased work some years ago. There is one there at present whose history will be found elsewhere.

An Odd Fellows' lodge was instituted at Constantine, February 17, 1847, called Constantine lodge, No. 22, but it suspended work for several years, until 1870, when it was revived, and is still in good working order. The old charter-members were W. C. Pease, William Savier, Dr. Elliott, L. C. Laird, George Brown and Elisha Stevens. There are about five hundred members of the subordinate lodges in the county, which number ten. There are also five encampments of Patriarchs in the county, and three Rebekah degree lodges.

PATRONS OF HUSBANDRY.—The St. Joseph County Grange, No. 4, was organized July 29, 1875, with thirty-seven members, Richard Dougherty of Park, being the first master, and J. H. Gardner of Lockport, the first secretary. The county grange meets at Centreville unusually on the first Thursday in January, and quarterly thereafter. The present officers (1876) are as follows: W. G. Leland, master; W. B. Langley, overseer; H. Collins, lecturer; S. G. Leland, steward; J. Freeman, assistant steward; Richard Dougherty, chaplain; G. Schoch, treasurer; J. H. Gardner, secretary; C. Schellhart, gatekeeper; Mrs. W. B. Langley, Pomona; Mrs. W. G. Leland, Ceres; Mrs. L. Schellhart, Flora; Mrs. S. Leland, stewardess. The present membership is sixty-six.

J. H. Gardner has been for the past two years the purchasing agent for the State grange, and his contracts, for the time he has served as such, for different materials used by the members of the grange, have amounted to one hundred thousand dollars—all of which purchases have been made either directly with the manufacturer and producer or the wholesale jobber, at first figures.

### ABSTRACTS OF TITLE.

An institution of importance to the people of St. Joseph is abstracts of title to the real-estate in St. Joseph county, compiled and issued by Leverett A. Clapp, Esq., of Centreville, formerly land commissioner of Michigan for four years. He has thirty-two books devoted to the title to farm property, and eight volumes devoted to the title to village property, all of which have been compiled under Mr. Clapp's personal supervision, who has had twenty years' experience in the titles of St. Joseph county. The books were begun by Edmund Stears in 1853, who compiled the farm titles from the original entries, up to 1855, when Mr. Clapp succeeded to the proprietorship of the business, and completed the work as it now stands. These abstracts are reliable, and of great convenience to the people.

---

## CHAPTER XVI.

THE PRESS OF ST. JOSEPH, PAST AND PRESENT—MICHIGAN STATESMAN—
EARLY "ADS"—CENSUS OF CHICAGO, 1836—OLDEST EDITOR.

"—— Take away the sword:
States can be preserved without it.
The pen is mightier than the sword."

The power of the press of the United States is almost unlimited. It "makes or it mars" politicians and their schemes, and leads a community forward in the march of progress, or follows, cur-like, in the rear, as its standard of morality, ability and intelligence, is high or low, aggressive or defensive. The press of St. Joseph county compares favorably, both past and present, with that of the sister interior counties of the State in point of ability, dignity of character and influence; and its history is not an uninteresting or an unprofitable one.

The first newspaper published in St. Joseph county was called the Michigan Statesman and St. Joseph Chronicle, and was edited and owned by John D. Defrees, now public printer of the government at Washington, which position he has held for many years. The first number was issued about December 10, 1833, and was the first paper published between Detroit and Chicago, and the first in the territory of Michigan. It was a twenty-four column sheet, radically Democratic, supporting President Jackson ably, and as ardently afterwards, in 1836, Martin Van Buren for the same office. Mr. Defrees published the paper but a few months, selling out his interest, eighth) June 28.

Mr. Gilbert, who has been a resident of Kalamazoo for many years, since September, 1835, and latterly the warden of the State penitentiary, very kindly has placed the files of the paper, from June 28, 1834, to December, 1836, in our hands, which act we greatly appreciate, as it has enabled us to get exact and reliable data for our work, which it would have been impossible to have otherwise secured. The Statesman was a fearless and uncompromising advocate of the Democratic party and its principles, and Mr. Gilbert, yielding a trenchant pen, handled his Whig opponents without mercy or favor. Its columns, too, were devoted to the prosperity and advancement of the county, and White Pigeon particularly. The temperance movement, and all moral and religious works, found in the paper an able and willing assistant. It was quite liberally patronized, as its advertising columns fully show, and was the recognized organ for the publication of the government contracts and congressional laws—the column being headed with a spread eagle and the national blazonry. In the first number issued by Mr. Gilbert, a Fourth-of-July celebration at White Pigeon was advertised, and the programme of exercises given, John D. Defrees being the orator. John Carlin advertised his brewery on the Chicago road for sale, and Mishawaka advertised for proposals for building a dam, with a canal one hundred feet long and a lock. M. Seydle, first hatter in the county, gave notice to the people of the county that he could fit their customers with the latest styles of New York, on short notice, at his manufactory, in Lockport. Elias S. Swan offered one cent reward for Nathan T. Lucas, a bound boy, who had run away from him. John W. Anderson offered his hotel for sale, in White Pigeon, and Ezekiel Case posted his wife, Olive, for having deserted him. In the number of September 10, Wallace & Stewart advertised for one hundred laborers to work on the Wabash and Erie canal, the firm being located at Mottville. Three prisoners escaped from the county jail, at Centreville, August 15, and two more September 22, and fifty dollars reward was offered for their recapture. Thanksgiving day was appointed for November 27. In the papers in February and March, 1835, the local campaign for county offices was hotly discussed. J. W. Coffinberry was a candidate against T. W. Langley, for the register's office, and he put his advertisement into the paper in advocacy of his—Coffinberry's—claims.

> "I make not the public good my plea,
> The end of all my wishes;
> With half an eye a man can see
> I need the 'loaves and fishes.'"

The "*morus multicaulis*" fever, it appears, attacked the pioneer settlements of the west, as well as the older States on the seaboard. A party on Prairie Ronde offered mulberry trees for sale in the spring of 1835, which he guaranteed had been tested for silk-cocoons and not "found wanting." The plant was also recommended for "hedge-fences."

At the spring election of 1835 Selden Martin was elected colonel of the 11th regiment of Michigan militia, Benjamin Sherman, lieutenant-colonel, and S. A. Chapin, major. Hart L. Stewart, at the time, was general of the 6th brigade.

In October, 1835, the *Statesman's* office of publication was removed to Bronson (now Kalamazoo), the editor setting forth, in the issue of October 2, his reasons for the removal, which he thought ought to convince all of his reasonable patrons of the wisdom of his action. The paper was conducted for twenty-five years and more, as a Democratic sheet, by Mr. Gilbert, who changed the name to the *Gazette*, in January, 1837, under which name it is still published in the interest of the same party, at Kalamazoo, but by another publisher, Mr. Gilbert having retired from the editorial tripod some years ago.

The next papers established in the county, were the *Peninsular*, at Centreville, the first number of which was issued July 2, 1836, and the *Republican*, at Constantine, July 6th. The former was published by E. Van Buren, who issued it until December following, when it was suspended until April, 1837, when its publication was resumed by a Mr. Knappen for a short time, and then abandoned. It was an advocate of the interests of Centreville particularly, and its political principles were Democratic under Van Buren's control. In number thirty-two, May 4, 1837, it is gravely stated that "Chicago already contains eight thousand inhabitants, has from forty to fifty lawyers, thirty to forty physicians, twelve public-houses, three newspapers, one hundred and twenty-eight stores, and there were twenty-eight thousand tons of merchandise taken in the port the last season." The announcement was made of the presentation of a fine battery of six guns, with ammunition and equipments, by Major J. T. Chambers, of Kentucky, to the Republic of Texas for service against Mexico. The *Republican* was published by Daniel Munger and Mr. Cowdery, and was issued during the years 1836, 1837 and 1838. It was fiercely Democratic in its politics, and waxed furious in its denunciation of the Whigs of the county, who "stole a march" on the Democratic convention in August, 1836, and compassed the nomination of Neal McGaffey for the legislature. It hoisted the name of Dr. Sumner at the head of its columns, but McGaffey was elected in spite of its bitter warfare. E. Van Buren began the publication of the White Pigeon *Gazette* in August, 1837, and continued for a short time, when he was succeeded by Daniel Munger, who was subsequently joined by A. W. Adams, the paper being published until 1841–42. It was also Democratic in politics. January 13, 1843, J. Eastman Johnson and W. B. Josslyn issued the initial number of the Centreville *Republican*, a twenty-four column paper, devoted to the prosperity of the county, and Centreville especially, being Democratic in politics. Josslyn was associated in the paper but a few months, and upon his retiring, Judge Johnson conducted the editorial and business management of the sheet alone. He published it until the year 1845. In 1841–42 James R. Adams published a paper in White Pigeon. In February, 1845, Albert E. Massey and Horace Metcalf began the publication of a paper in Centreville, called the St. Joseph county *Advertiser*, advocating the principles of the Whig party. The publication of the paper was continued until 1848, and being succeeded previous to 1848, and being succeeded by Williams, who died about 1850, and was succeeded by S. B. McCracken; he, however, retained his interest but a short time, closing his course with the paper in June, 1850. In February, 1851, Massey disposed of the office to Levi T. Hull and John M. Farquhar, and in June following it was removed by the new publishers to Constantine, where it appeared under the new name of

CONSTANTINE MERCURY AND ST. JOSEPH COUNTY ADVERTISER.

In August Mr. Farquhar withdrew from the paper, since which date it has been published continuously by Mr. Hull, the only intermission being that occasioned by the burning of the office, March 1, 1874, when the regular issues were suspended for a few weeks.

The *Mercury* is a staunch and determined advocate of the views of the Republican party, and has been since that party was organized. It is an outspoken and fearless in its opinions, and seeks to lead, rather than follow, public sentiment. A well-equipped job-office is connected with the paper, and, with power presses, very neat typography is executed with despatch.

Mr. Hull is the oldest publisher in the State who has been continuously in the same office. His labors have met with just recognition from the "powers that be," by his appointment to the office of assistant assessor of internal revenue, which position he held from September, 1862, until May, 1873, with the exception of six months, from November 15, 1866, to April 1, 1867. The office was abolished in May, 1873, and on August 1, following, Mr. Hull received the appointment of collector of internal revenue, which position he held until September 20, 1876, at which date the district was consolidated. January 1, 1877, Mr. Hull received the appointment of deputy collector for the fourth division of the third district, which division comprises Cass, Berrien, Van Buren and St. Joseph counties. From 1863–6 St. Joseph county returned the heaviest revenue in the district—forty thousand dollars per annum, ten thousand dollars of which were for the tax on peppermint oil alone, and twenty thousand dollars for income tax.

In 1867 Mr. Hull was a member of the constitutional convention.

About 1843–4, C. E. Simonds began the publication of a paper in Sturgis called the Sturgis *Republican*, which he continued for a short time only, being succeeded by Hackstaff, who published the paper (or another one) as a Democratic organ. This last effort, however, was spasmodic only, and was succeeded by Joseph Willis, who continued the publication of the *Republican*. Willis was succeeded by Easton & Sawdy, who changed the name of the paper to the Sturgis *Journal*, and not long afterwards (1860) sold the office to J. G. Waite, who conducted the paper very ably for twelve years, when he retired from its publication, and was succeeded by his son, Arthur E. Waite, for two years, who then disposed of the paper and office to Dr. T. F. Thornton, in the year 1874. Messrs. Alleman & Sweet published, for a short time, the Sturgis *Times*, but in the year 1876 Dr. Thornton purchased the latter paper and consolidated the two offices, and issued the new paper under the name of the *Journal-Times*, and its publication is still continued under the management of the Doctor and Mr. Mattingly, a practical printer, formerly of Rochester, New York.

The *Journal-Times* office is the best-equipped office in the county. Its stock of type and presses are surpassed by none in the State, in quality, and but by few, outside of Detroit, in it equaled in amount. The job-work is remarkably neat in execution, the catalogue of the high-school of Sturgis, for 1878, being a notable specimen of its mechanical ability.

The *Journal-Times* is ardently and vigorously Republican in sentiment and teaching. It has defended the Republican party in its covert attacks of weak-kneed followers. It is high-toned and dignified in its editorials, enterprising and liberal in its advocacy of local matters, devoted to the interests of Sturgis, and backs "Old St. Joe" against the world, in point of general excellence.

THE WESTERN CHRONICLE

was published by Harvey Crossette, in Centreville, its first issue appearing some time in October, 1850. It was subsequently published by Newton S. Bouton, who removed the office, in 1854, to Three Rivers, where the publication was continued until after 1861, when it was discontinued. It was violently Democratic in its partizanship, but was very fairly edited, and gained considerable influence throughout the county.

THE ST. JOSEPH COUNTY REPUBLICAN

was established by D. S. Weston, in 1845, at Centreville, and was published for about two years, when it suspended. The present paper of that name and location appeared in April, 1869, H. Egabroad being the publisher of the present time. It is a thirty-two column paper, Republican in politics, but pays more attention to matters of local interest than to national affairs. The local editor (a son of the proprietor) makes a newsy sheet of the issue.

Dr. Welper published a little sheet a short time in Three Rivers, but its name, even, has escaped the memory of the inhabitants.

Messrs. Reynolds & Curtis published a paper for a short time in Sturgis. Messrs. Hackstaff & Paine published a paper in White Pigeon some years after the one published in 1842 by Adams, and several proprietors succeeded one another, until 1866, when Sweet & Hackstaff published the *Democratic Union*, with a tremendous spread-eagle for a head. It was Democratic in politics, and was removed to Elkhart by Sweet, where it is still published as the Elkhart *Union*.

The present paper of White Pigeon is

#### THE ARGUS,

published by J. J. O'Brien, which was established by E. H. Graves, in 1875, who conducted it for a short time—E. O'Brien succeeding to the office and conducting the paper to the end of the first volume, at which date the present proprietor succeeded to the paper. It is an interesting local paper, independent in politics, and its editor and proprietor is doing his best to make it useful to the town.

#### THE MENDONIAN

was published in 1871–73, by a Mr. Sweet, and was independent in politics; and A. C. Miles published a paper during the war; both of these latter publications being issued in Mendon. H. Egabroad issued an edition of his *Republican* for Colon, which is known as the *Colon Enterprise.*

#### THE MENDON WEEKLY TIMES

was established in the fall of 1874, by A. Rindge, the first number appearing October 2. It is a seven-column folio, brought out in good style, and presents a neat and clean appearance. It is devoted principally to local interests, and is independent in politics. Its office contains the first job press brought to the town of Mendon, and is well stocked with materials for job work, for which it is rapidly gaining an excellent reputation.

#### THE WEEKLY JOURNAL

is published by W. A. DeGroodt and George C. Everding, at Constantine, who issued the first number November 4, 1876. The proprietors are young practical printers, and are striving to build up their paper to an honorable position in the ranks of the press in the county. The *Journal* is independent in its political views.

Doctor Amariah Bennett issued the *Vegetable Herald* for a short time at White Pigeon, in the interest of a botanical pharmacy, and he also published in Centreville for a short time the *Michigan Farmer.*

#### THE ST. JOSEPH COUNTY DEMOCRAT

is published by the Democratic publishing company, in Sturgis, L. E. Jacobs editing the same. It is Democratic in sentiment, and was established in 1876.

#### THE THREE RIVERS HERALD

is published, as its name indicates, at Three Rivers, by Doctor O. Arnold and Son; is a quarto sheet; Democratic in politics, and is now (1877) in its ninth volume. The original press and material of this establishment were purchased in Chattanooga, Tennessee, by a Mr. Reynolds, of Sturgis, and moved to that place, wherewith Mr. Reynolds published for a short time the *Sturgis Star.* Subsequently the office was bought and removed to Burr Oak by a Mr. Dewey, who commenced there the publication of the *St. Joseph County Democrat,* which he continued for about a year, and then sold his interest to Messrs. Smith & Newton, who continued the publication of the paper for about the same time, when Smith sold his interest to his partner, Newton, in July, 1872, Newton continuing the publication another year in Burr Oak, and in June, 1873, removed to Three Rivers, where, after issuing five or six numbers, the publication was discontinued. In September, 1873, the present proprietors purchased the presses and materials of Mr. Newton and revived the *Democrat,* and continued the publication of the paper under that name until August, 1875, when the form was changed from a folio to a quarto, and the name to the *Herald,* since which time it has flourished and attained a good circulation. It is ably edited and conducted, and possesses among its readers a leading influence.

The Three Rivers *Reporter* was established previous to 1860 by Wilbur H. Clute, the present editor and proprietor. It has been a fearless and uncompromising supporter of the Republican party up to 1874–75, when it as radically assumed the greenback theory, and has ably defended that cause, being largely instrumental in moulding the greenback sentiment in St. Joseph county, and making an agressive campaign in 1876. The mechanical appearance of the paper is very neat, and the job work executed at the *Reporter* office is second to none in the county.

## CHAPTER XVII.

AMUSEMENTS—PLEASURES OF THE CHASE—BEAR-STEAK—MILITIA COURT, MARTIALS—A TRANSFORMATION SCENE—NATIONAL HOLIDAYS—PIONEER BALL AND COSTUMES—GOVERNOR PORTER AND TAILOR O'BRIEN—DAMS WITHOUT WHISKY—A PIONEER DUEL AND ITS RESULT—CONTEMPTIBLE CONDUCT—HOW TO ROB AN INDIAN SAFELY—CRIMINAL CALENDAR—COUNTERFEITING BROKEN UP—MURDER OF ESTERBROOKS—ROBBERY OF THE COUNTY RECORDS.

Amid the most severe trials and privations, which often brought sadness to the heart, the pioneers of St. Joseph toiled for many years before they were justified in seeking needed relaxation, to "knit up the raveled sleeve of care," and enjoy the works their own hands had made. Yet their lives were not necessarily gloomy ones—devoid of all sunshine and pleasure—but, acting on the sentiment, " catch the sunshine when you can," they had their holiday gatherings and neighborhood frolics, that lightened their burdens, shortened the shadows imposed by continuous labor, and discounted the future ease—hypothecating the renewed strength of the then present, as security for the loan. And it was a wise investment, as scores of old, white-headed pioneers, who are now living in comfort and happiness on the homesteads of " auld lang syne," fully attest.

The early pioneers made pleasure contribute largely to the physical needs of the family, thus blending the useful with the agreeable most happily and judiciously. The keenest sense of pleasure realized by the old men who came, was that which came to them across the sights of their trusty rifles, as a full-antlered stag bounded out of some little dell or sequestered spot, and the next moment sprang into the air and fell a victim to the unerring bullet; or, as a gray wolf, sauntering along the edge of the prairie, suddenly sniffed the air, and the next instant lay on the grass, rolling in the agonies of death. The feathered game, such as turkey, duck, geese and grouse, were "small fry," but at times were an acceptable addition to the settler's bill-of-fare, and the finny tribes which roamed through and enlivened the rivers and lakes, furnished rare sport to the pioneer, and gave variety to the daily diet, palatable and desirable. The wild bees stored their treasures in the hollow trees, and the bee-hunter in his quest for the same, on a spicy October morning, when the woods were putting on the royal livery of crimson and gold, and the squirrel chirped and filled his whisk with a saucy, impertinent air, found a zest hardly to be appreciated by those whose " bee knowledge" is confined to the apiary on their own premises, or the brilliant essays found in the various publications on the Italian queens and their production.

Isaac F. Ulrich, it is averred, was a good hunter, and one hundred and fifteen deer fell before the deadly aim of his rifle during the first three years of his residence in the county; but Columbia Lancaster has a record that puts the 'squire into the shade. Legal fees were scarce in the first years of Lancaster's practice, and the most of his time was spent in the chase. It is said that his memorandum showed, on the morning of a certain 31st day of December, that he had killed three hundred and sixty-four deer during the year, and thinking to add another to the list, and thus making his average one per day, he sallied forth, and before noon brought down two, and now the query is, was that year a leap-year? It was a poor hunter who could not get his venison steak fresh for breakfast, from the prairie or woods, for they were there by hundreds, with black and gray, and some prairie wolves.

A jolly time was had on Sturgis prairie in August, 1828, on the occasion of Governor Cass' passage through the settlement, on his way to Niles, to purchase the reserves of the Chicago treaty. He was accompanied by Joseph Parks, a white man once captured by the Wyandots, as interpreter, and eight others from Detroit. A large bear had been killed the day previous, while crossing the prairie, by one of the earliest settlers, and a proposition was immediately made to the governor to tarry and partake of a feast of bear's flesh, to which his excellency readily assented. The arrangements were soon made, and Bruin was on the spit, from which he was transferred—when cooked to a turn—to the table, and his juicy carcass was highly relished by all. Fun reigned supreme, the Governor forgetting his judicial dignity for the time, joining in the sport as zealously as any of his staff. He had in his train eight ponies, four loaded with two hundred pounds each, of good calicos, ginghams, and notions, for presents after the bargain was made, and four loaded with silver to pay for the lands.

Another opportunity for amusement for a time, until it became uninteresting, was the trainings and muster of the militia, who were organized as early as 1831. The first general training was held in June, 1831, Colonel

H. L. Stewart, commanding, and General Brown and Major Hoag, of Tecumseh, as inspectors. There were present on dress parade three companies, commanded by Captain Hunter, of Sturgis; Captain Stewart, of White Pigeon, and Captain Powers, of Nottawa; the rank and file, staff and line, numbering not to exceed one hundred men. The males in each township capable of bearing arms, were required to turn out two or three times each year for drill, inspection and review, and after the Black Hawk scare had subsided and no alarm was felt of war, it became irksome to the settlers to be dragged out for the "pomp and circumstance of glorious war," which was in no likelihood ever to be needed, and so were frequently in default when the roll was called; and as dereliction in duty, which was suffered to pass without notice, was fatal to military discipline, courts martial were assembled, and the delinquents summarily tried and fined in sums sufficient, at least, to liquidate the expenses of the court. Up to this point it is difficult to see where the pleasure came in, but it began immediately on the attempt to enforce the collection of the fines. All sorts of devices were resorted to to avoid payments, sometimes with most ludicrous results. One instance will give the tribulations the collectors were frequently exposed to, in their tours of tithing among the militia. One of the delinquents was fined for default, and the collector sent from Centreville, where the court martial was held, to enforce the sentence of the tribunal, which sentence, it is needless to say, was, soon after its promulgation, announced to the delinquent, with a warning to look sharp for the collector. One day, about eleven o'clock in the morning, the latter individual entered the front door of E. S. Swan's store in White Pigeon, in which the young man was engaged, and who, having been notified by some one on the watch, slipped out of the back door as the collector entered the front, and, mounting a horse, rode off as the collector emerged from the back door in search of him.

The collector hailed the fugitive, but to no use, he was apparently as deaf as a post and kept on his way, but stopped at a store a moment, when the collector sprang forward and was eluded again by the defendant in the warrant. Thus the pursuit went on for two or more hours, when the collector gave up the pursuit in disgust and returned to the stable of a friend where he had left his horse, when a transformation met his eyes which he could scarcely credit. His horse, which was of a bay color when he left it, was now a bright green, alternating with stripes of another color. His neck and tail, which had been adorned with long, flowing, glossy, black hair, were guiltless of anything but the stiff stubbs of the same. In short, his steed of the morning, which pawed the air and smelled the battle afar off, was a sorry nondescript, unfit for anything but a crack-brained Don Quixote to bestride. Nevertheless, the collector made a virtue of necessity, mounted his beast and rode back a madder if not a richer man than when he came. Such were the expedients taken to evade the burden men felt to be as needlessly imposed as it was onerous to bear, and the militia system fell into disuse and was finally abandoned, independent companies in after years taking its place.

The great holidays were the natal days of American Independence, the observance of which were begun by the pioneers as soon as there were enough of them in the county to be sociable, and make a gathering pleasurable. The first observance of the

NATIONAL BIRTH-DAY

in the county was at White Pigeon, in 1829, which, however, was an informal affair, and no attempt was made to celebrate, but the day was used by some forty of the settlers to get together and have a social time. Savery provided dinner for them at the " Old Diggins."

THE FIRST CELEBRATION

on the 4th of July, or the anniversary of the declaration of Independence, held in the county, was had at Mottville, in 1820. Messrs A. C. and H. L. Stewart, then in that village, had erected a large warehouse just above the bridge, the upper floor of which building furnished an ample auditorium. There was a general gathering of the settlers from all parts of the county and vicinity. John Morse, of Coldwater, a skillful performer on the clarionet, came to regale the people with his rare music. Neal McGaffey, Esq., was the orator of the occasion, and among the distinguished guests who graced the assemblage with their presence, were Major General Brown and Inspector General Hoag, who were on a tour of inspection. After the oration was delivered, Edwin Kellogg and a companion, a fanning-mill maker in White Pigeon, sang, to the delight of the audience, the " Ode to Science," and were congratulated in flattering terms at their success by Hoag. The next celebration of the natal day of the Union, was held at White Pigeon in 1832, at which Colonel Seiden Martin was the president of the

day. There were people present from Niles, Coldwater, Jonesville and elsewhere, and the music was also from Coldwater. About one hundred persons were present.

In 1834 a celebration was held on the 4th of July, in White Pigeon, at which John W. Anderson was marshal, Reverend P. W. Warriner, chaplain, Charles Kellogg, chorister, David Clark, Jr., reader, and J. D. Defrees, orator. The procession was formed at Savery's, and filed through the streets to the music of an improvised band, and toasts were offered and responded to, and patriotism ruled the hour.

In 1835 the glorious " Fourth" was celebrated in grander style than ever before in the county, at White Pigeon, Sturgis and Constantine, the orators being W. Loomis, Esq., Dr. Elias Boulton Smith and Dr. Sumner, respectively. The Statesman reported the proceedings at length, and reproduced the orations in full in its subsequent issues. We give below a few only of the toasts drank on the occasion at the different places.

The seventh sentiment, offered by Vice-President Gilbert, at White Pigeon, was as follows : " Michigan—the queen of the West ; nature's choicest provisions for the husbandman ; may the spirit of enterprise connect her navigable waters by canals, and transform her Indian trails into railroads."

At Constantine the twelfth regular toast was this : " John Quincy Adams—the able and eloquent advocate of justice ; he fearlessly raised his voice in defence of the friendless ; Michigan owes him a debt of gratitude." Three cheers and music ' Logan Water '.

At Sturgis the orator's toast was the following sentiment : Michigan—destined by Nature to excel all her sisters in wealth and importance, her fair lakes, fanned by the breezes of pure freedom, break into dimples and laugh in the sunshine of inimitable prosperity."

At Constantine a celebration of the Fourth was held in 1833, the festivities closing with a grand ball; the dancing commencing before night and lasting till daylight the next morning. The music was a fiddle and a clarionet, principally the latter, which was manipulated by the fingers of Daniel Arnold. The fiddler was from Elkhart, and could play but two tunes, and Arnold had to play without relief all night. The costumes were more varied than elegant, and would bring a Parisian modiste to dispair, so mal apropos would they seem to her. The ladies, and they were ladies, wore their winter and summer dresses of every pattern and shade, which to be appreciated must needs have been seen. The gentlemen wore home-spun pants, heavy boots, high shirt-collars, and danced in their shirt-sleeves, the weather being too warm for coats.

In 1836, at a celebration of the national day, in Constantine, the following toasts were drank, among others, with uproarous applause. By Daniel Munger—" Michigan: though oppressed in her infancy, she will soon become the tallest toad in the puddle." By John A. Appleton (now a member of the great publishing house of Appleton Bros.)—" Uncle Sam's youngest child : fat, rugged and saucy."

The Christmas and New Year's festivities were not forgotten, but the presents of a whole community would not, oftentimes, equal those of a single petted darling of to-day ; but the happiness was unbounded, and hilarity and fun pervaded the entire settlement. Wild turkies, browned to a turn ; venison saddles, juicy and savory ; mallards and canvas-backs, dripping in fatness, graced the boards of the hospitable pioneer, around which the whole neighborhood gathered, and, after some patriarch of the settlement had offered hearty thanks for the bounties given to their hands by the Giver of all good, fell to and discussed the good things with a relish that was aught else than spiritual.

Were we to record all the interesting and noteworthy incidents with which the lives of the early pioneers abounded, volumes would be required to show forth the entertaining story, and, therefore, from the reliable data we cull a few of the more striking and prominent, to illustrate somewhat the life we are endeavoring to picture.

There were no aristocrats in those days, who looked down from a higher plane upon lower beings of their race, trudging along in common dust, but all were equal, or at least considered themselves so, and any attempt to show superiority or " lord it" over another, was sure to meet with condign and immediate consequences.

One O'Brien was among the first tailors of White Pigeon, and a great lover of shooting ; he had his shot-gun always by his board in his shop, which fronted on the main street of that village, and near by the entrance to the hotel. One day a covey of prairie chickens flew over the village, which, being espied by O'Brien, that worthy grasped his gun, and rushing to the door of his shop " let fly" at the birds, missing them but most severely startling Governor Porter, who had just arrived in town and was at that moment entering the hotel. The magisterial dignity of his excellency was considerably ruffled, and when O'Brien came in to look at the distinguished arrivals, he was taken to task by the governor and lectured roundly, which O'Brien resented, whereupon the chief magistrate, to impress his auditor with the importance of more care, said, "I would have you know, sir, that I am the Governor of Michigan!" to which O'Brien tartly replied, "and I would have you know that I am the tailor of White Pigeon!" and walked off to his shop.

In 1838-9 immigration ceased to a great extent, and the surplus crops were worth little or nothing in the market, wheat being sold at thirty-one cents per bushel. During that winter, a mother wanting some flannel for her baby, asked the father what they should do in the emergency. After studying a while over the situation, he quietly took his knife and ripped the lining from a camlet cloak he had, and gave it to his wife to make the needed garment of.

When William H. Cross built the Leonidas dam across the St. Joseph, he announced that he should furnish no whisky, and in consequence thereof it was confidently predicted and asserted by the men themselves that there would be a "strike" before forty-eight hours after the timbers were ready to put into the water. But, contrary to the prediction and expectation, the work was accomplished after many vexatious and expensive obstacles, delays were overcome and passed, and not a penny had been spent by the proprietor for whisky. After the hard work was done, Mr. Cross asked one of the most talkative men of crowd, who had said the most against the course adopted, how it was he had not kept his word and refused to work in the water without liquor. The man replied, "Well, I did not mean to do so, because I supposed you would stand on the bank in dry clothes and 'boss' the job, but when I saw you jump into the water the first of all, and stay there till all the rest were out, I was ashamed, and said I would not be boat by a little fellow like you, and now I don't care for whisky. Besides, you gave us good coffee five times a day, and treated us like gentlemen."

Dr. Hanchett, who was located at Coldwater, but practiced somewhat in St. Joseph county, getting out of medicine, went to Detroit, one hundred and ten miles, on horseback, to get a new supply—having but ten dollars in his purse, four dollars of which he used up for his expenses. He went to old Dr. Chapin's drug store and stated his needs, and was urged to take all he wanted, but declined to take more than his cash—six dollars—would buy, which was put up, and it is fair to presume there was a very small margin of profit charged in the bill for the same. Dr. Chapin said to Dr. Hanchett as he tied the little package up, "When this is gone send for more, money or no money!"

An incident in the lives of George Mathews and his estimable wife Margaretha, of Leonidas, will not be amiss here to show of what stuff some of the pioneers were made. One day, soon after Mathews had built his cabin on his location which joined the reservation, some Indians, who were drunk, rude up and wanted to see him, but he was sick on the bed and would not go out; but finally, they made so much noise and disturbance about the house, he did get up and went out doors, pulled one of the Indians off his horse and slapped his face smartly, whereupon the rioters went off. A few days afterwards the Indian whom Mathews had thus treated, came back and said to him, "You abused me the other day when I was drunk, and now you must fight me when I sober." Mathews was a tall, broad-shouldered fellow, lithe as a panther, and brave as courage itself, and he at once assented to the proposition; he accompanied the Indian to the woods, followed by Mrs. Mathews, who, fearing treachery, carried an enormous butcher-knife under her apron. Arriving at a little open space, a short distance from the house, Mathews found several Indians and their squaws sitting on the ground in a circle, silent and moody.

The Indian told his story, and Mathews related his version of the affair, and said he was ready to fight, and asked what the manner of the contest should be. The Indian chose rifles, and Mathews sent his wife back to the house for his gun, sitting down on the log beside his antagonist the meanwhile. Mrs. Mathews returned with the rifle, and then the challenger wanted to substitute knives, and Mrs. Mathews was desired to go for a knife, whereupon she took from beneath her apron the huge, glittering carver of her kitchen, at sight of which, in the hands of the tall borderer, the braggart showed the white feather, and, at the repeated demands of Mathews to "come on," stood silent, with downcast head. Mathews stepped to one side, and cutting a stout hickory whip, laid it vengefully over the bare shoulders of the coward, amid the grunts of satisfaction of the other Indians, who called the man a squaw, which was resented also by the squaws, who cut switches and whipped the fellow back to camp. Mathews and his wife were ever after regarded as friends by their tawny neighbors.

6

When the "big payment," as it is called, was made to the Indians for the Nottawa reservation, in the fall of 1833, or rather early winter (the same being in December), and the weather quite cold, there were depredations committed upon the Indians, after they had received the goods, by citizens of St. Joseph county and others, that ought, if the perpetrators thereof are still living, cause the blush of shame to mantle their brows with crimson, for it was nothing short of downright robbery. Not content with selling them whisky, and taking heavy pay therefor in silver, the miscreants, after the Indians were made drunk, began and executed a system of robbery that should condemn them for all time to infamy and contempt.

An eye-witness thus describes the theft: The Indians, having received their blankets and cloths, would take their cash at once to the venders of whisky, buy a bottle or jug full, and then, seating themselves upon their blankets in a circle, and putting the bottle in the centre of the ring, would begin to drink, passing it round from mouth to mouth. By the time the jug had passed twice around the circle, the drinker would begin to "hitch" along, and soon after, as he made another hitch, the blanket would begin to disappear from beneath his person, and finally would be withdrawn entirely, by some one who held one corner of the same, as the occupant changed his position; and so the robbery was completed. When the Indians were in their drunken sleep, they would be unceremoniously rolled out of their blankets, and then left unprotected by anything but their scant wardrobe. It is but justice to say that this treatment of the Indians was frowned upon and condemned by the majority of the people of St. Joseph, and the most of the thievery was done by renegades from other parts, but there were a few outcasts who were ulcers on society in St. Joseph, who were in after years sloughed off, as in all other new settlements.

## CRIMINAL RECORD.

A gang of counterfeiters infested the southern border of the county, from 1850 to 1857, where they could conveniently slip across the State line into Indiana, when the officers of the law in Michigan came after them, and vice versa. E. W. Pendleton, of Sturgis, then and now, followed their trail like a sleuth-hound, in season and out of season, despite of warnings of personal danger and the loss of property, he having twelve horses poisoned by the gang or their accomplices, and finally ran the game to earth and captured three of them—"old man" Latta, N. B. Latta, his son, and one McDougall, and twenty-five thousand dollars of the "queer," and the paraphernalia for manufacturing and printing, except the dies, which one of them, another McDougall, took and ran across the border with, and into the arms of the Indiana regulators, who gave him a short shrift and a shorter rope.

Through the confessions of McDougall, when closeted in Pendleton's hotel, the latter was enabled to make the seizure, which was done in broad daylight at Latta's hotel, on the Chicago road in the little village of Freedom. Latta, senior, had caused the several parts of the press to be made at different blacksmith-shops about the country—in Lima, Sturgis, Freedom, Burr Oak and White Pigeon—to avoid suspicion, but this very precaution worked his ruin, and Pendleton's procuring the identification of every part of the work, and Latta's connection with the same. The latter gave his fine farm as security, and was allowed his liberty on bail. N. B. Latta was discharged by the examining magistrate, on representations being made and substantiated to that official's satisfaction that he (Latta) was one of Pinkerton's detectives, and had been working up the case when arrested. The jail was broken open, and McDougall escaped, and when the old man saw the array of testimony piling up against him, he decamped, and left his bondsmen to pay the forfeiture of the recognizance, which they did by turning over to the county Latta's farm of two hundred and forty acres in Fawn River, which the board of supervisors immediately proceeded to utilize by selling the farm the county then owned, and transferring the indigent thereon to the new acquisition, where they are now cared for. The farm-property belongs, however, to the school-fund of the county under the law of forfeitures and fines. Mr. Pendleton "bluffed" the gang for five years by putting several insurance-plates on his house, the Exchange hotel, though he carried no insurance whatever for the time.

In 1846-47 Gamaliel Fanning was murdered by a horse-thief, whom he was endeavoring to arrest near Latta's, an account of which in full, from the pen of Hon. I. D. Toll, who afterwards captured the murderer, will be found in the history of Fawn River.

On June 10, 1854, Amos White and Samuel Ulum were arrested for the murder of Thomas B. Esterbrook on the 13th day of November, 1853. They were indicted, tried, convicted and sentenced to penitentiary for life—White dying soon after their incarceration. The testimony was circumstantial, except that given by witness Giles Harding, an accomplice, who was impeached by the defence, but a part of whose testimony was corroborated by other witnesses. He, though a proven villian, gave the thread of the story which, being skilfully followed, unraveled the tale of blood, and fastened the crime, to the entire satisfaction of the jury, upon the prisoners. The testimony, though voluminous, was consistent, and the case was most ably prepared for trial by Hon. Charles Upson, then prosecuting attorney of the county, assisted and seconded efficiently by John Hull, then sheriff of the county. Hon. Nathaniel Balch, of Kalamazoo, assisted in the prosecution, and complimented the two officials highly for their conduct of the case. The murdered man was last seen at the Leonidas hotel, on Sunday, the day of the murder, and his presence there was fixed by a train of circumstances that did not speak very highly of the respect for that day by several of the residents of that hamlet.

Harding testified he was there and saw Esterbrook, and Harding's presence was proven by several other witnesses who testified what they were doing, thus corroborating Harding's testimony. Such circumstances as these, and there many of them testified to by Harding, being corroborated, gave his direct testimony, bearing on the alleged details of the murder, more weight than it otherwise would have received, and though the prisoners denied all participation in the crime, and averred their innocence, yet the fact that they were the last persons seen in his (Esterbrook's) company, gave further weight to Harding's statement, and although the body of the unfortunate man was never found, the verdict of the jury was murder in the first degree.

Harding testified that the prisoners were overheard by him planning the murder, being discovered by them, they threatened to kill him if he did not join them; and if he would do so, they would share the plunder together; and Harding consenting, was posted as a spy on the movements of Esterbrook, who was supposed to possess considerable ready money, which he carried about his person, and was expected to be in Leonidas soon, on a matrimonial quest.

Esterbrook appeared in the village on the fatal Sunday, and White was immediately notified by Harding, who notified Ulum, and during the afternoon, or early evening, was taken in charge by White, who proposed to conduct him to the house of his intended, on the road to Mendon, which was the last ever seen of him by any person in the village.

Harding testified further that on arriving near the Cowen mill, the party met Ulum in a wagon, or were overtaken by him, and were asked to get in and ride, as he was going directly past the house they wished to reach. The invitation was accepted, and soon after the wagon turned abruptly to the right, which being observed by Esterbrook, he asked why they were taking that course, and was quieted by an explanation that it was a nearer route.

Soon after, while riding along in the shade of the woods, White struck Esterbrook with a wagon-stake, felling him to the bottom of the wagon-box, and then finished his horrible work by beating his victim on the head till life was extinct. The two men, White and Ulum, then rifled the pockets of the murdered man, not finding what they expected—the money, as it appeared afterwards, being found by the supposed dead man's relatives in a tin trunk, which was forwarded to the lady whom he came to marry.

The murderers then, as Harding testified, buried the body of Esterbrook in the woods, where it remained until after the search, which was instituted for it afterwards, was over, they joining in the same with evident alacrity and zeal; and then they removed the remains and disposed of them elsewhere, unbeknown to Harding.

Harding was arrested for some offence in the spring of 1854, and confined in the county jail; from some words and hints dropped in the hearing of Sheriff Hull, he was suspected of knowing something about the affair, and was placed under a judicious, but searching examination; he finally confessed to what has been detailed above, and gave dates, names and circumstances which enabled the officers to ferret out the facts testified to on the trial.

It is but just to say that there are some worthy citizens of the county who are very skeptical regarding the whole thing, and do not believe the man was ever killed, but went away at once from the country.

One of the remarkable crimes recorded in the criminal history of the country was committed in St. Joseph county in the year 1872, the same being a successful theft of several of the records of deeds and original documents of title from the register's office at Centreville. Captain Benedict was register at the time, and Elva F. Peirce the sheriff of the county. One A. P. Fonda and Richard Lane were indicted for the crime, and Lane convicted and sent to the penitentiary for five years, Fonda being acquitted.

The robbery was committed on the night of the 28th of June, 1872, forty-four volumes, twenty-two of deeds, and as many of mortgages, three index books,

and about one hundred deeds and mortgages not recorded, being taken away. The board of supervisors were called together July 1, who took measures to bring the guilty parties to justice and recover the records, if possible. Anthony P. Fonda (a member of Captain B. C. Yates' private detective force, of Chicago) and his brother, John Fonda, of Three Rivers, were arrested, and on the examination held by Samuel W. Platt, Esq., of Centreville, John was discharged, and Anthony held to bail under two thousand dollars' bonds to appear before the circuit court. The notorious Charles C. Hildebrand put in appearance, and was shadowed by under-sheriff C. E. Peirce to Indianapolis, and was there arrested, brought back and held in durance two months, and then discharged.

A P. Fonda had the notorious Dick Lane arrested in Chicago, under a fictitious name, for the robbery, and by a writ of habeas corpus issued by Judge Williams, of Chicago, he was discharged. Lane claimed to know all about the robbery, and was subsequently arrested and brought to St. Joseph county for trial in February, 1873, by Sheriff Peirce. Soon after this Fonda had his trial, and was acquitted before Judge Cooley, presiding. In March Lane was tried before Judge Brown, and convicted and sentenced, as previously stated. Fonda was defended by Allen of Chicago, Sadler of Centreville, and Judge Upson of Coldwater. Lane was defended by T. C. Carpenter of Sturgis, and prosecuted by E. W. Keightley, prosecuting attorney, and Hon. H. H. Riley of Constantine.

About the 15th of August, 1872, Sheriff Peirce was informed that a party had received a letter from Chicago, saying the books would be turned over for five thousand dollars. The sheriff sent a person to Chicago to ascertain what reliance could be placed on the representation, with directions to telegraph the result of the conference. On receipt of the telegram, Sheriff Peirce and William M. Watkins, Esq., one of the supervisors, went to Chicago, and to Eldredge & Tourtellotte's law-office, where the information came from. Five thousand dollars were demanded for the surrender of the books, and it was agreed to lay the matter before the board of supervisors. This was done, and the board offered three thousand dollars for the return of the books, and privately instructed the sheriff to act on his own discretion, but to get the records at all hazards.

About the 1st of September, Sheriff Peirce went to Chicago, where he met Mancel Talcott, and made an arrangement with Eldredge & Tourtellotte for the delivery of the records for three thousand five hundred dollars, and on the 5th of September the sheriff, James Hill, county treasurer, and William M. Watkins, in behalf of the county, and Eldredge & Tourtellotte, attorneys for the thieves, entered into an agreement for the delivery of the records, and deposited with Eldredge & Tourtellotte three thousand five hundred dollars. Mancel Talcott being surety for the attorneys. The records were to be delivered by the 12th instant. They were dug from the earth, where they had been buried since the 28th of June, on the 6th of September, at night, in a badly-damaged condition, and Winslow Hatch notified at 11 o'clock P. M. The sheriff and Mr. Watkins were at the Hatch House, in Three Rivers, on their return from Chicago; Mr. Hatch immediately informed them of the exhumation of the records, and the sheriff at once ordered the books taken to the court house. This was done at 2 o'clock A. M., and when the sheriff discovered the terrible condition the records were in, he at once telegraphed to the attorneys, and took the cars at 4 o'clock for Chicago, where, on his arrival at 10 o'clock, he immediately notified Eldredge & Tourtellotte of the damaged state in which the records had been delivered, and demanded a return of the money deposited; but the attorneys claimed it had already been paid over. Suit was commenced against the attorneys for the recovery of the money deposited, and Tourtellotte came to Centreville, November 22, 1872, and registered as Tuttle. Sheriff Peirce happened to see him about 4 o'clock P. M., and drove to Sturgis, saw General Stoughton, the county's attorney, came back to Centreville and procured a writ, drove to Three Rivers, and procured the services of the same by under-sheriff C. E. Peirce, who had been but a short time from Centreville with Tourtellotte, the latter having lots of sport with him about the old sheriff and the records. The writ was served about 12 o'clock at night, Tourtellotte querying, "Who the h—l are you?" Peirce replied, "I was your hostler coming over; I am under-sheriff now!"

The suit was transferred to the District Court of the United States, at Grand Rapids, March 19, 1873, and tried in September, 1874, judgment being rendered for three thousand five hundred dollars and interest, by a jury before the United States Judge, Withey presiding. General Stoughton and Hon. H. H. Riley were the attorneys for the county, and Eldredge & Tourtellotte appeared in person, and also by J. B. Church of Grand Rapids. A motion for a new trial was argued and over-ruled, and an appeal taken to the United State Supreme Court, where it has as yet been undisposed of.

The total cost of the nefarious transaction to the county thus far is as follows:

Paid for the recovery of the records, - - - - - $3,500
Cost of new records, and copying and comparing same, 3,500
Paid for attorneys' fees, - - - - - - 1,000
Paid for incidental expenses, - - - - - 1,500

Total, - $9,500

## CHAPTER XVIII.

Never did a palm-shaded oasis, cooled and refreshed by its bubbling spring of pure cold water in the midst of a parched and scorching Sahara, look more inviting to the weary, dust-begrimed Arab, than did the flower bedecked prairies and openings from St. Joseph, when in the full glory of their summer foliage, to the pilgrims from the heavy-timbered and mountainous regions of New York and Pennsylvania, in the pioneer days of the county. Sturgis, White Pigeon and Nottawa prairies were gems of beauty wrought by that incomparable artist and limner, Nature, into a multitude of forms of loveliness. The oak openings of Florence, Burr Oak and Flowerfield were parks of unsurpassed extent and woodrous elegance. All undergrowth obliterated as though a gardener had passed through with axe, spade and rake; the view in the openings was unobstructed for miles, and the whole surface was carpeted with a rank growth of rich grasses and beautified with myriads of flowers of various hues and forms. Lakes glittered in the openings, rivulets meandered through the woods, and a noble river, entering the county in the northeast, wound its serpentine way through the entire length and width of its territory, passing out at its extreme southwestern corner. Its surface was a general level, in some parts rolling, running up into knobs in Fabius and Sherman. The prairies and openings were gently undulating, but in many places as level, apparently, as a house floor.

The area of the surface of the county contains about 329,619 acres, of which 319,895 acres are land, and 9,724 acres are water surface. The prairie surface in the early days included about 12,535 acres, the balance of the land area being oak openings and heavy timber. The latter feature of the surface was confined principally to the towns of Mendon and Leonidas, although there was more or less heavy timber on all of the river and creek bottoms.

The heavy timber consists of oak, beech, maple, hickory, whitewood, ash, black walnut, butternut, cherry, sycamore and elm, principally. The white-wood is nearly extinct, it being used largely in the manufacture of "arks" in the ante-railroad days, for transporting flour to the lake down the St. Joseph.

The woods harbored deer in countless herds when the settlers first came in, and for several years afterwards it was no difficult matter to bring in a saddle of venison any day in a few minutes. Black, grey and prairie wolves, and bears were plentiful at first, but the larger of those animals early gave way before the advancing tide of civilization, which poured into the county in 1835-6.

Feathered game was abundant, of all descriptions common to the west. Wild turkey, geese, duck and grouse of several varieties, and quail, made most excellent sport for the hunter, and even at the present time these fowl may all be met with, sparingly, in the county. Woodcock, plover and snipe are, in certain localities, yet plentiful.

The lakes and rivers were literally filled with fish, and do not appear to have suffered much diminution at the present time. Sturgeon, pike, bass, red-horse, perch, suckers, sun-fish and a variety of smaller fry were the natural stock of the lakes, but later efforts at pisiculture have introduced white-fish, trout, graylings and other varieties into some of the lakes, but sufficient time has not yet elapsed to show how successful the attempt will be.

The present geographical situation of St. Joseph county is defined thus: It is bounded on the north by Kalamazoo county, on the east by Branch, on the south by the counties of Lagrange and Elkhart, in the State of Indiana, and west by Cass county, Michigan—the south line of the county being also the boundary line between Indiana and Michigan. The county-seat, Centreville, is very nearly the geographical centre of the county, and

is distant from Detroit about one hundred and fifty-eight miles, and from Chicago one hundred and twenty-six miles. The climate is mild and not usually subject to sudden changes, though violent extremes have occurred in a short period of time very noticeable. The Michigan Statesman, published at White Pigeon, 1834-36, records the summer of 1834 as very hot—the range of the mercury for two months being between ninety and one hundred degrees above zero. The wheat and corn crop that year in the county was short, no surplus being left for marketing, outside the wants of the people themselves, and much sickness was experienced throughout the county. This was the second season of the cholera—the first season (1832) the plague passing over without attacking any one in the county. Several victims were carried off by it in 1834, and the people were very much frightened and disturbed by its visitation, as they well might be, when it exhibited such virulence in the pure atmosphere of the new country, so far away from city and town. George Keech, Sr., of Centreville, kept a diary of the atmospheric changes for twenty-four years, from which we cull a few of the more extreme registers of the weather: January 8, 1836, was a very cold day, the mercury standing at twenty-eight degrees below zero at nine A. M. January 1, 1864, the fluid fell fifty-eight degrees in sixteen hours, standing twenty-four degrees in the morning, and twenty degrees below on the morning of the 2d. February 3, 1866, the mercury stood twenty-five degrees below, and on March 4 of the same year it marked ten degrees below. The following summer was extremely hot, the thermometer marking on June 14 ninety-two degrees, below which it did not fall for four days—till the 18th—when it rose to one hundred degrees. On the 30th it was at ninety-six degrees. July 1 the fluid stood at ninety-four degrees; 3d, ninety-five degrees; 4th, ninety-nine degrees; 11th, ninety-eight degrees; 12th, one hundred degrees; from the 13th to the 15th, both inclusive, one hundred and three degrees; 16th, ninety-eight degrees; 17th and 18th, one hundred and two degrees, and 19th, one hundred and one degrees; while the average from the 20th to the 28th inclusive was ninety-four degrees. On the 17th of January, 1870, a terrible gale of wind arose about one o'clock A. M. in Centreville, whereby buildings were blown down and one man, Charles Boyer, killed, and Mrs. Newark fatally injured by the falling buildings. In March of that year, on the 15th day of the month, the mercury fell seventeen degrees between twelve and two o'clock P. M., standing thirty-three degrees above at noon and only three degrees at six o'clock; and on the morning of the 16th was at zero. From May 19 to June 3, 1871, the weather was very severe—the mercury ranging from eighty-eight to ninety-three degrees. In May, 1874, there were some remarkable elevations of the mercury, showing as high as ninety-six degrees on the 26th, ninety-four degrees 27th, ninety-two degrees 29th, and ninety-three degrees the 30th. July 8 it registered at ninety-eight degrees, and on the 27th at one hundred degrees. In 1875 a severe ice-storm passed over the county, by which fruit and forest trees were severely broken up and injured. The winter of 1876-77 was remarkable for the excellent sleighing, which commenced in the early part of December and lasted for more than six weeks, and which was followed by about the same length of time in which the sun was visible the whole day long. The weather was bracing, but not severe, during the time the snow remained on the ground, and the fine weather which followed was simply superb. The temperature was so mild the ground was not frozen, except in exposed situations, the whole winter. The month of March was ushered in by a famous snow-storm, which continued more or less severely for some days, the snow remaining on the ground, and the sleighing being excellent until after the 22d of the month.

The soil of the county is, for the most part, a rich, sandy loam, light and warm, changing on White Pigeon and Sturgis prairies to a heavier loam, but none the less fertile. On Nottawa prairie the soil in some parts—notably so in Mendon—is a black, sandy loam of remarkable depth and richness, and in this peculiarity differs from the other prairie-soil. Wheat is the staple product of the county, though large amounts of corn are successfully raised. All cereals thrive well in the soil, the openings being better adapted to the mint-culture than the prairie. The St. Joseph country seems to be a natural habitat of the apple, which produces enormous quantities of most delicious fruit.

Peaches have, in former years, thriven generously, but after 1850 a series of severe winters killed the trees, since which time the culture of the peach has not revived to but a limited extent. Cherries are productive, and a certain crop; but plums, once abundant, not fair a native in the country, but also cultivated, have disappeared by reason of the ravage of the curculio.

The geological feature of the county are not striking to the ordinary eye, untrained to look for "sermons in stones, in brooks and in trees," but the soil is, nevertheless, eloquent of past ages and early forms of life. There are no stones *in situ*, no quarries showing the gradations of their deposition, but such as lie buried hundreds of feet beneath the *debris* of the glacial action, which is most abundantly testified to by the coralline deposits in the soil, and the presence of innumerable bowlders and drift-stone all over certain parts of the county. No stone are found on the prairies, and in but a portion of the openings. On the west side of the township of Constantine there are large quantities of bowlder-stone, as also in Nottawa, Leonidas and Fawn River townships, but they are less heavily scattered in other parts. These stone are valuable for cellar and foundation walls, and so used almost exclusively. Occasionally a building is constructed of them, but it is not often such use is made of them. The Union school-house, at Centreville, is so built, and presents an appearance of solidity that would defy the frosts and storms of ages. When selected with taste, and wrought with care, the appearance of a foundation has a pleasing effect as the variegated surface sparkles in the sunlight. They are composed of the usual varieties of the bowlder-drift—flint, granite, gneiss, trap, lime, pudding-stones, quartz, etc. Some very fine garnets are found imbedded in the bowlders at times, upon breaking them up for use.

An amateur but enthusiastic geologist gives us the following list of fossils he has found in the soil of Fawn River, which are identical with those found in other parts of the county, the soil of which is very rich in fossiliferous deposits:

"Fossils of the Lower Silurian age, Trenton period: RADIATES—polyp corals, the petraia corniculum, columnaria alveolata, taeniaste spinosa; MOLLUSKS—chaetetes lycoperdon or costalis leptaena plicifera, ptilodictya fenestrata, retepora incepta, a trilobite, calymene senaria.

"Hudson period: RADIATES—favistella stellata.

"Upper Silurian, Niagara period: RADIATES—chaetetes-corals, chonophyllum Niagarense, favosites Niag.; MOLLUSKS—fenestella; RADIATES—several crinoids, caryocrinus ornatus; BRACHIOPODS—atrypa nodostriata; spirifer sulcatus occidentalis; O. testudinaria.

"Carboniferous: trigonocarpum, tricuspidatum and lepidodendron. Some very perfectly preserved crinoid stems, by the St. Joseph river and in distinctly.

"Devonian, carniferous period: RADIATES—zaphrentis gigantes, Z. Rafinesquii, Phillipsastrea verneuili; cyathophyllum rugosum; favosites Goldfussi; syringopora Maclurii; aulopora coronta."

The bottoms of many of the lakes and marshes are marl-beds formed of crinoids and shells, the marl being used, in the days before transportation became as easily effected as now, as lime, large quantities having been burned in the county. It is not as strong as limestone, but makes a very white wall.

The county is well watered and drained by the St. Joseph river and its tributaries, the Portage, Rocky, Fawn and Pigeon rivers, and Nottawa, Hog and Swan creeks, and the several lakes included in its borders.

The St. Joseph, as before stated, enters the county in the northeast, and runs diagonally through it to the southwest. The Portage and Rocky enter the St. Joseph at Three Rivers, from the north; the Fawn enters the county from Indiana, and runs northerly, and enters the St. Joseph above Constantine; the Pigeon rises in Indiana and the southern lakes of the county, and enters the St. Joseph below Mottville, running through the townships of White Pigeon and Mottville in a westerly direction; Nottawa creek enters the St. Joseph near southwest corner of Leonidas, entering the same township on section one, from Branch county; Hog creek rises in Branch county, and runs through Burr Oak and Nottawa township, and enters the St. Joseph on section thirty of Lockport; Swan creek empties into Sturgeon lake near the entrance of the St. Joseph, rising in Branch county, and enters the township of Burr Oak on section twelve, and thence through Colon to its outlet. The principal lake surface is confined to Colon and Fabius in the aggregate. The larger ones are Sturgeon and Palmer, in Colon; Pickerel and Klinger's, in White Pigeon; Fisher's, in Lockport and Park; Fish in Sherman, and Sand in Nottawa. The lakes in Fabius are noted more for their number than their area.

The early settlers experienced many hardships, but none were so severe as those endured by reason of the malarial diseases that were prevalent until after the land had become generally broken up. As long as the fires ran through the woods and over the prairies, there was but little or no sickness, as there was no vegetation left to decay and taint the air with its miasm. But as soon as the fires were kept out, and the grass and leaves left to decay, although the soil was enriched thereby, a miasmatic exhalation arose from the mass, that poisoned the air, and fever and ague, bilious and typhoid fevers were prevalent. Every person coming into the county in the earlier days of its settlement, before getting acclimated had to pass through what they called a "seasoning," the fall after locating.

One of the early physicians, who was an extensive practitioner, says that the fatality of the diseases, which in 1837–38 was fearful, was the result, largely, of want of proper care and medicines. Calomel was considered a specific by many, but it killed more than it cured, according to his testimony, and he was a regular-school physician, notwithstanding.

Since those early days the mortality has been no greater than ordinary, and is much lower than in many other localities, equally situated, in the west. Clear, pure water can be obtained by digging from twenty to fifty feet, in almost any part of the county, and the air is fresh and pure except in certain localities where stagnant mill-ponds or marshes gather decaying vegetation.

## CHAPTER XIX.

PATRIOTISM OF ST. JOSEPH COUNTY—AN ELOQUENT AND WELL MERITED TRIBUTE—THE FIRST VOLUNTEERS OF MICHIGAN—BLACK HAWK WAR—MEXICAN WAR—REBELLION RECORD—HISTORY OF REGIMENTS.

In tracing the history of the patriotism of the people of St. Joseph county, no more fitting prelude to the brilliant record can be made than the eloquent tribute paid to them by Hon. Isaac D. Toll in his exhaustive and able address delivered before the St. Joseph pioneer society at its annual meeting, June 9, 1876, at Centreville. After alluding to the marvelous development and progress of the State of Michigan, in agriculture, mining, manufacture and education, he classes its patriotism as the grandest record of all, and claims the same as a just reason for congratulation—and the more, that the people of St. Joseph county had done their full share in accomplishing the grand results. He then adds: "From the Black Hawk war, of which there are survivors here present, to the present time,—in the war with Mexico, when this county sent out its representatives, to the great war which closed in 1865, have we ever been wanting in our full duty? Your national colors were upheld at Contreras and Churubusco by sinews hardened for the work on your own soil. Also at Molino del Rey and Chepultepec,

> "There fought the Greek of old,—
> How well he might again ;
> Shall not the self-same mould,
> Produce the self-same men ?"

"There your braves sleep in unknown graves, the cloud-capped Popocatapetl, the pedregal of Contreras, the mute witnesses of their valor, as of their rest. The cypresses of Montezuma

> "Wave above them their green leaves,
> Grieving, if aught inanimate e'er grieves,
> O'er the unreturning braves."

"From Bull Run, 'beside their cannon, conquered not, though slain,' to Malvern ; at Shiloh ; in the march to the sea, at Chantilly, Gettysburg, to the surrender at Appomattox, everywhere, where the stars and stripes were unfurled—the emblems of unity—there were your sons.

"Upon your Bennett, Oakes, Hazzard, Stevens, Newberry, Starr, Bishop, Wilcox, Washburn, Thurston, and alas! too many others, your eyes may not again rest here ; soldiers for the unity, for the nation, for the State, neither for centralization, nor sovereignties independent of the aggregate, but for country from shore to shore ; 'a republic, whose beneath the sway of mild and equal laws, framed by themselves, one people dwell, and own no lord save God !'"

> "By fairy hands their knell is rung,
> By forms unseen their dirge is sung ;—
> There honor comes, a pilgrim gray,
> To bless the turf that wraps their clay ;
> And Freedom shall a while repair
> To dwell, a weeping hermit, there."

The first evidence of Michigan patriotism was given to the world when the gallant Major Antoine De Quindre, and his company of French volunteers from Detroit, joined the American forces at the battle of Monguagon, or Brownston, August 9, 1812.

The Indian allies of the British forces began the attack, whereupon the French riflemen delivered so effectual a fire the savages were thrown into confusion ; the riflemen then charged bayonets and routed the Indians, throwing them back upon the British lines, which in turn were broken and thrown into confusion, and the advantage thus gained being pressed by the commander of the American troops, the enemy were routed, the Indians scattering through the woods, and the British compelled to take refuge in their ships in the Detroit river.

This Detroit company were the first volunteers of Michigan.

In May, 1832, the news of the advance of Black Hawk at the head of his painted warriors on the settlements in Illinois, of his avowed intention to march to Detroit and slay every pale-face who was trespassing on the red man's land, startled the sparse settlements in St. Joseph county, and filled the hearts of the settlers, with fear and uncertainty. Two military companies were mustered, Captain Stewart's of White Pigeon, and Captain Henry Powers' of Nottawa Prairie, and drafts of fifty men from each company ordered and made.

Captain Powers' men were to act as a corps of observation on the borders of the Nottawa-seepe reservation, which was occupied by a large band of Pottawatomies, and Captain Stewart's men were to advance to the relief of Chicago and the frontier; but the day after the draft for the fifty men was made, (one for forty having been made previously and revoked), and before the soldiers had left White Pigeon, the news was brought that Black Hawk had been captured, his warriors defeated, and the war over; then the men returned home to their wives and little ones, and took up the works of peace again. The drafted men, however, drew a month's pay (eight dollars) from the United States, and forty acres of land, for their services. A company of men from Coldwater and vicinity, went as far as Niles, and a portion of them, with some volunteers from Sturgis prairie, as far as Door prairie, but met no enemy. However they made a charge on the commissary department and succeeded in capturing sufficient supplies to get at least one good supper, while they were on the way back. The excitement lasted about two weeks and passed away, and quietness again reigned throughout the settlements; but its effect was felt for nearly a year in the falling off of emigration, which almost entirely ceased till the next season.

When the United States declared war against Mexico, St. Joseph county was not behind in responding to the call for volunteers. Hon. Isaac D. Toll, then a member of the State senate, received a commission from the government, as captain in the 15th United States infantry, in March, 1847, and at once came to Fawn River and began to recruit a company. With the assistance of Lieutenants Goodman, Titus and Freelon, the ranks were filled in April, and the company (E) left Detroit for its destination, Vera Cruz, the same month. The company was engaged at Riconada Pass, June 24; Contreras and Churubusco, August 19 and 20; Molino del Rey, September 8, and Chepultepec, September 13, Captain Toll commanding in every engagement, except Chepultepec, which latter he reached from the hospital at Mexcone, in ambulance, towards its close. The greatest loss by far was at Churubusco, and this, too, on the St. Joseph county men, Captain Toll having command of the caroline. The regiment, under command of Colonel Morgan, was thrown into disorder by the overwhelming fire of the foe, (eight to one), Colonel Morgan severely wounded, First Lieutenant Goodman of Company E killed, and Orderly Sergeant Cunningham desperately wounded. The Captain rallied the men on the colors, leaving Company E unsupported, but in good order. This left the company the apex of an inverted V (thus ⋀), and made the severest loss in the regiment fall on that company. They would not desert their leader, who himself rallied the regiment with the aid of Adjutant Brudhead, (who was killed at Chantilly in the war of the rebellion), and pressed and overcame the enemy, who, besides their great number, were protected by a wide, deep ditch, and a fence of large magney.

The company was enlisted in the counties of St. Joseph, Kalamazoo, Kent, Cass and Jackson.

The St. Joseph county men were as follows:

Isaac D. Toll, captain.

John Cunningham, first sergeant, mortally wounded at Churubusco.

Francis Flanders, Jr., sergeant, afterwards drum major of the regiment.

William S. Smith, sergeant, a most brave man, participating in every engagement, died of chronic diarrhœa on the way home.

Daniel P. Hanks, corporal, mortally wounded at Churubusco.

Fitch Cornell, a half brother of Hanks, shot through the head, the ball entering left eye, now alive and well. Surgeon Slade said he would die and Hanks would recover, but the reverse was the case.

Horace Bartholomew, corporal, Theron Bartholomew, Levi Bartholomew, (three brothers, of Fawn River), Abraham Bers, Ludlow Cox, Richard W. Corbus. The last named died of wounds received at Churubusco. Samuel B. Corbus, Nathaniel Crofoot, wounded at Churubusco; James H. Davis, Solomon Gilman, Wesley Gordon, wounded in same battle; Daniel W. Hamblin, Sylvester Holiday, John Ladd, Clark Munson, died from wounds in same battle; William J. Norton, Isaac A. Smith, wounded in same battle.

The Michigan "Contingent" in the war of the rebellion was largely made up of men who enlisted for three years, and were mainly from the more respectable and industrious classes. Leaving the peaceful avocations of civil life, these men were disciplined into soldiers and converted into heroes, sometimes even during the operations and emergencies of a single campaign. Patient and obedient under the most rigid discipline, persistent and enduring on the long and tedious march, cheerful and untiring in the trenches, apt in experiment, and most ingenious in construction, they added to all these qualifications and merits, true courage in the field, while almost every important action has illustrated their heroism, and almost every battle-field is consecrated with their blood.

Of these heroic men St. Joseph sent to the field twenty-six hundred and ninety-two, and they were not only prompt and prominent at the outset of the rebellion, but were also in at its death. They were among those who, under Wilcox, first crossed the Long Bridge into Virginia, and participated in the capture of Alexandria. They were in the command of the brave and lamented Richardson, who first opened fire upon the rebels at Blackburn's Ford, on July 18, 1861, in the vicinity of Bull Run. They were with General McClellan in West Virginia in the first year of the war, and were in South Carolina and Georgia in 1862, and during that year served with the army of the Potomac on the peninsula and in Maryland, with General Banks in the Shenandoah valley, in Virginia with Burnside, in Louisiana with Butler, and in Missouri with General Pope and Colonel Mulligan.

In 1863 they bore a gallant and conspicuous part in the ever memorable campaigns under General Hooker in Virginia, and General Meade in Pennsylvania; at the defence of Knoxville by General Burnside, at the capture of Vicksburg by General Grant, and on the celebrated Kilpatrick raid against Richmond. They were also engaged in the grand campaigns of General Rosecrans against Chattanooga.

In 1864-5 they were with General Grant on his great march against Richmond, and bravely participated in most of the hard-fought battles of the eventful campaign. They were also with General Sherman when he "marched down to the sea," and were prominently engaged in most of his memorable and successful battles, and with General Sheridan in his matchless encounters with the enemy in the valley of the Shenandoah, where, in command of the gallant and intrepid—and now lamented—Custer, their sabres flashed in every battle. They took part in the gallant defense of Nashville by General Thomas, and were with Generals Stoneman and Wilson on their raids into North Carolina and Georgia; and St. Joseph veterans were at the capture of Jefferson Davis in his inglorious flight to escape deserved punishment for his infamous treason and rebellion.

Not only were the men of the county heroic, but so too were the women. As the places filled by their husbands, fathers, sons and brothers, at the plow and in the harvest, in the shop and at the counter, were vacated, the wives, daughters and sisters stepped into the empty places, and took up the implements of toil their loved ones had laid down for the musket and sabre, and all through the bloody struggle performed the tasks intended for stronger arms, many of them, alas! never more to return. The sanitary commission never issued an appeal in vain to the women of St. Joseph county, who vied with their sisters all through the North in their deeds of love and mercy for the soldiers of the Union. This discipline, though a stern one, was not without its benefits, for it taught the women self-reliance, and gave them new ideas of power and new fields of usefulness.

Michigan sent out thirty regiments of infantry, eleven regiments of cavalry, fourteen batteries of artillery, one regiment of mechanics and engineers, one regiment of sharp-shooters, besides several companies who went into organizations of other States; and, with the exception of the 18th, 21st and 22d regiments of infantry, St. Joseph county was represented in them all; consequently the history of the St. Joseph heroes is co-extensive with the history of every regiment and battery the State sent out in her noble army of ninety thousand seven hundred and forty-seven veterans, to the defence of a common country imperilled by treason.

We give in the following summary a brief history only of those regiments and batteries, of which organized companies from St. Joseph county formed a part, and must refer the reader for the entire interesting record to the complete and exhaustive reports of the adjutant-general of the State of Michigan, from whose official records the summary has been compiled, as well as the names of the gallant men which appear under the respective township histories, in another part of our work.

### THE FIRST INFANTRY.

The 1st Michigan—the regiment which, under Colonel Wilcox, led the advance of Michigan troops to the front—although hurriedly organized and hastily equipped, left the State a pattern regiment in every respect, none better having proceded it to the National capital from any State; arriving there at a critical time when that place was in great and immediate danger of being attacked and captured by the rebels, whose troops then picketed the Potomac. Its presence aided much in establishing confidence among those in authority, that the capital was safe, and its appearance on Pennsylvania avenue was hailed with the cheers of loyal thousands. As it passed in review before the lamented Lincoln, it received his highest praise, and through them thanked the State for their prompt appearance in Washington.

The regiment was assigned to Heintzelman's division, and, under Colonel Wilcox, led the advance of the Union troops across Long Bridge into Virginia, on the 24th of May, driving in the rebel pickets, and entering Alexandria via the road, simultaneously with the regiment of Ellsworth's Zouaves that entered it by steamer.

At the battle of Bull Run the regiment belonged to the brigade commanded by Colonel Wilcox, and was in the hottest of the fight, eagerly pressing forward on the enemy, losing heavily but fighting stubbornly and gallantly. On that disastrous field the 1st established the highest standard for Michigan troops, so uniformly and so remarkably maintained throughout the entire war. Its dead were found nearest the enemy's works. In the engagement Captain Butterworth, Lieutenants Mauch and Casey were wounded and taken prisoners, and afterwards died of their wounds in rebel custody. Colonel Wilcox was also wounded, and falling into the hands of the enemy, was exchanged after fifteen months captivity.

The regiment on the expiration of its three months' term of service returned to the State, and was mustered out August 7, 1861, but was soon after reorganized as a three years' regiment, and left for the army of the Potomac August 16, commanded by Colonel John C. Robinson, then captain in the regular service, who continued to command it till April 28, 1862, when he was appointed a brigadier-general of volunteers, and was succeeded in the command of the regiment by Colonel H. S. Roberts, promoted from lieutenant-colonel. It went to the Peninsula with McClellan, and was in the engagements at Mechanicsville, June 26; at Gaines' Mills, June 27; at Malvern Hill, July 1, and at Gainsville, August 29.

It rendered most gallant and valuable service during the war, and suffered severe losses in killed and wounded. Among its numerous engagements, none perhaps will be more vividly remembered by the regiment than the disastrous charge so bravely made, but with such fearful loss, upon the enemy's position along the Warrenton and Centreville pike, on August 30, 1862, during the series of engagements near Manassas, now known as the second battle of Bull Run.

The regiment, under command of Colonel Roberts, was in General Fitz John Porter's corps, and had during the day been posted in the woods fronting the enemy's lines, and near one of his most important batteries. At 4 P. M. the order was given to advance and dislodge the enemy. The 1st Michigan, with the 18th Massachusetts and the 13th New York regiments of infantry deployed column and with cheers charged. They instantly found themselves the target of a terrific fire from ambushed infantry of the enemy and five batteries, four of which had been masked, and hitherto unseen. The charge was a murderous one, and within a few moments eight officers and fifty per cent. of the regiment fell. The men stood their ground bravely, with veteran coolness under these trying circumstances, and when the impossibility of success became a certainty, and the order to retreat was given, fell back in good order to the woods and reformed their division. Had victory been possible, their courage and persistency would have won it. Their demeanor, amid disaster and defeat, affords one of the greatest examples of true courage. Colonel Roberts was killed, shot through the breast with a minie ball, and Captains Charles E. Wendell, Russell H. Alcott, Eben T. Whittlesey, Edward Pomeroy, and Lieutenants H. Clay Arnold, J. S. Garrison and W. Bloodgood, also met their death.

After the death of Colonel Roberts, Lieutenant-Colonel Franklin W. Whittlesey was promoted to the command of the regiment, but was absent from the field on account of injuries received in the Peninsular campaign. The regiment was engaged at Antietam, September 17; at Shepherdstown Ford, September 20, and at Fredericksburg, December 13 and 14, at which latter place it was commanded by Lieutenant-Colonel Ira C. Abbott, of Burr Oak, who went out in August of 1861 as captain of Company B, and was promoted to the position of major, April 28, 1862. It was heavily engaged at Fredericksburg, and lost one officer—Captain J. B. Kennedy—and seven men killed, together with seven officers and thirty-three men wounded.

At Chancellorsville, April 30, 1863, it went into action under command of Colonel Abbott, who had been promoted a short time before, with twenty-three officers and two hundred and forty muskets, and was in the various engagements in that vicinity. From the 28th of May to the 2d of July, it skirmished nearly every day with the enemy's cavalry, and after severe and laborious marches, it reached Gettysburg at 1:30 A. M. of the last day above named, and entered into battle with twenty officers and one hundred and twenty-five men, sustaining a loss during the engagement of Captain Amos Ladd and four men killed, with six officers and twenty-five men wounded, among whom was Colonel Abbott, disabled early in the action, the command devolving upon Lieutenant-Colonel W. A. Throop. It joined in the pursuit of the enemy on the 5th, and on the 18th recrossed the Potomac into Virginia, and aided in driving the foe through Manassas Gap, and went into camp at Warrenton.

In the battles of the Wilderness, commencing May 5, 1864, the regiment, in command of Lieutenant-Colonel Throop, especially distinguished itself. It was in Bartlett's (3d) brigade of Griffin's (1st) division, 5th corps, in the van of General Grant's celebrated movement on Richmond, which ultimately culminated in the fall of the rebel capital and the surrender of Lee's army. It fired the first musket of that glorious campaign, and its brigade checked the rebel advance on the road leading to Orange Court House, and thus opened the last act of the great drama. In the opening engagements of the campaign, so constantly was it under fire, and so perilous were the duties to which it was assigned, that on the evening of the 8th of May, after a brilliant and successful charge at Alsop's farm, its gallant commander was able to muster but twenty-three men fit for active service. But this handful still pressed forward, undaunted and fearless, and participated in the battles of Spottsylvania, Jericho Mills and the engagements near Cold Harbor, and on the 17th of June sat down before Petersburg and went into the trenches. On September 30, was in the desperate fighting at Poplar Grove church, and, unaided, stormed and carried the strong fortifications and a portion of one line of works. During this action its commander, Captain James H. Wheaton, was killed. On December 6 it raided the Weldon railroad, and February 6, 1865, was at Hatcher's Run, and lost three killed and three taken prisoners. March 25 it was engaged again at Hatcher's Run, having several wounded. On the 29th it engaged the enemy on the White Oak road, and also on April 1, at Five Forks; the 5th at Amelia Court House; at High Bridge on the 6th, and at Appomattox on the 9th.

The total losses of the regiment during the war were one hundred and forty-six men and fifteen commissioned officers, killed or died of wounds received in battle, and ninety-six men and one officer died of disease.

### THE SECOND INFANTRY.

The 2d regiment, under command of Colonel J. B. Richardson, was also in the first engagement, and opened fire on the enemy at Blackburn's Ford, July 18, 1861, in Richardson's division, which covered the retreat of the army from Bull Run on the 21st.

The regiment, under command of Colonel O. M. Poe, participated in all the engagements on the Peninsula, first meeting the enemy in that campaign at Williamsburg May 5, 1862, and lost seventeen killed, thirty-eight wounded, and four missing. It was at Fair Oaks on the 27th, at Charles City cross-roads on the 30th, and at Malvern Hill July 1st. At Fair Oaks it lost ten killed and forty-seven wounded, while its bravery was so marked as to receive the following notice in the published history of the time:

"Meantime Heintzelman had sent forward Kearney to recover Casey's lost ground, and a desperate fight was going on at the extreme left. The enemy had been successfully held in front of Couch's old entrenched camp until Kearney's division arrived, when he stayed the torrent of battle. Here another his gallant regiments pushed forward, and pressed back the fiery rebels with more daring than their own. Here the 55th New York won new laurels, and Poe's 2d Michigan was bathed in blood. Five hundred of them charged across the open field against ten times their number, and stopped them in mid career, losing seventeen brave fellows in that one desperate essay."

Immediately following the battles of the Peninsula, it entered on the campaign of General Pope, and was engaged with the enemy at Bull Run August 28, 29 and 30, at Chantilly on September 1, and at Fredericksburg December 12, following. In 1863 the 2d was transferred to another field of operations with the 9th corps, and served with distinction on the Grant campaign in Mississippi, terminating with the fall of Vicksburg, and the defeat and route of Johnston at Jackson. It was also with Burnside in East Tennessee, actively engaged in the defense of Knoxville against Longstreet, and in the various battles with his forces in that vicinity.

Among the numerous battles of the regiment none will hold a more prominent place in the memories of its survivors than Jackson and Knoxville. Colonel Humphrey was in command in the former fight, and thus reports:

"At 7 A. M., the order came down the line from the right to 'forward, double-quick!' The men at once advanced with a cheer, drove in the enemy's skirmishers through their camps and into their reserves strongly posted in a deep ravine; charged and broke the reserve, and drove it up out of the ravine into its main support, drawn up in line of battle on the top of the south bank of the ravine; charged under a hot fire of musketry and artillery, up the steep bank against the main body, broke this line and drove the enemy within its works. We now waited for our support to come up, but on sending for it, were surprised to find we had none."

Finding it impossible to hold the ground they had won without support, and the enemy being reinforced, Colonel Humphrey ordered the regiment under cover of the bank of the ravine, and held the position until the wounded were carried to the rear, and then following the movement of the regiment on the right, fell back to the line from which he had advanced an hour before.

"By some mistake," Colonel Humphrey reports, "the three companies (C, F and H) on the left, did not advance with the rest of the regiment in this charge, which was made with about one hundred and seventy men. Fifty of these had fallen."

In this charge nine were killed, thirty-nine wounded, and eight taken prisoners. On the 24th of November, 1863, the regiment, under command of Major Cornelius Byington, (Colonel Humphrey being in command of the brigade) at the siege of Knoxville gallantly charged a strong force of the enemy protected by entrenchments and a house they occupied, driving them from the position and leveling the house and works to the ground. In the charge the regiment lost in killed and wounded out of one hundred and sixty-one officers and men engaged, eighty-six. Among the killed were Lieutenants William Noble (adjutant) and Charles R. Galpin, and Major Byington and Lieutenant Frank Zoellner mortally wounded. This charge is handed down in the history of the day as among the most brilliant of the war.

In 1864 the 2d returned with its corps to the army of the Potomac, and on the 5th of May crossed the Rapidan, and on the 6th, under Colonel Humphrey, participated in the battles of the Wilderness, losing six killed and thirty-two wounded. Among the latter was Captain John C. Joss, in command of Company G, who lost his right leg. On the 10th, 11th and 12th, it was in the battle of Spottsylvania Court House, where Captain James Farrand was killed. On the 3d of June it was at Bethesda Church, June 17 and 18 it was in the engagements before Petersburg, losing twenty-two killed, one hundred and forty-three wounded, and six missing. On the 30th of July, in the attack following the springing of the mine, it lost six killed, fourteen wounded, and thirty-seven missing, Captain John S. Young and Lieutenant John O. Bosch being among the killed. March 25, 1865, the 2d suffered heavy loss at Fort Steadman, and on the 3d of April was engaged in the capture of Petersburg. The 2d was in the battle of Williamsburg, of which the New York *Tribune* thus spoke:

"The 2d Michigan took into action only sixty men, the rest being left behind, exhausted with the quick march through mud and rain. Yet they lost one out of every five engaged. The regiment was in the hottest of the fight. By the confessions of prisoners eight hundred of Berry's men (mostly Michigan) drove back, at the point of the bayonet, sixteen hundred rebels." The loss was seventeen killed, thirty-eight wounded, and four missing. The total losses of the regiment during the service were eleven officers and one hundred and ninety-two men killed or died of wounds, and three officers and one hundred and twenty-eight men died of disease. Company G was recruited largely from Constantine, and was commanded by Captain John A. Lawson.

### THE FOURTH INFANTRY.

This regiment went to the field with great dispatch, in command of the lamented Colonel Woodbury, who recruited and raised it at Adrian. Captain A. R. Wood recruited a company (C) at Sturgis, and joined it.

The regiment was in the first Bull Run engagement, and retired from the field in good order, covering the retreat of the Union army from that disastrous affair. It went to the peninsula with McClellan, and was the first regiment to open fire on the enemy at New Bridge, May 24, 1862, the commencement of the seven days' battle, when five companies of the regiment crossed the Chickahominy a short distance above New Bridge, under the stream under a heavy fire. The gallantry of the regiment was made at the time the subject of a dispatch to the War Department, from General McClellan, which mentioned the matter thus: "Three skirmishers to-day; we drove the rebels from Mechanicsville, seven miles from New Bridge. The

4th Michigan about finished the Louisana Tigers,—fifty prisoners and fifty killed and wounded,"

The 4th gained imperishable honor in the Peninsular campaign, being in all of the engagements, and conspicuously and specially noticeable in the sanguinary conflict of Malvern Hill, in resisting the numerous and desperate charges of the rebels on its lines, the men fighting until all their cartridges were exhausted, then using those taken from the boxes of their fallen comrades.

Colonel Woodbury fell on this field at the head of his regiment, and Captains Du Puy and Rose were also killed. From June 26, to July 1, both inclusive, the loss of the regiment was fifty-three killed, one hundred and forty-four wounded and forty-nine missing.

The 4th at Shepherdstown Ford, September 21, forded the Potomac in face of a battery, killed and drove off the enemy, and captured the guns; and December 13 and 14 was at Fredericksburg, suffering severe loss. May 4, 1863, it participated in the battle of Chancellorsville, losing thirty in killed, wounded and missing. At Gettysburg its loss was most severe, twenty-six being killed, sixty-six wounded and seventy-nine missing. Among the former was its noble commander, Colonel H. H. Jeffords, who was killed by a bayonet-thrust while rescuing the colors of his regiment from traitorous hands; and among the wounded were Captain French of company C, of Sturgis, and Lieutenant Sage of White Pigeon.

In the battles of the Wilderness, the 4th was heavily engaged, and suffered severely; losing another commander, Colonel Lombard, also Captain W. H. Loveland.

On July 8 and 9, 1864, it was engaged with the enemy at Laurel Hill, and on the 24th at Jericho Mills, and at Bethesda Church, August 3; on the 19th it was in the engagement before Petersburg.

General Meade at Chancellorsville directed General Griffin to send two regiments to hold an important point. The General reported to him that he had sent them. General Meade asked, "Can they hold it?" Griffin replied, "They are Michigan men"; Meade insisting on being assured, said emphatically, "Can they *hold* it?" Griffin quickly and emphatically answered, "General, they can hold it against hell!" They were the 4th and 16th Michigan.

Its total losses in the war were one hundred and sixty-eight men, and twelve officers killed, or died of wounds; and one hundred and five men, and one officer died of disease.

### THE SIXTH INFANTRY.

The 6th regiment of infantry, afterwards organized as heavy artillery, was the peculiar regiment of Michigan, by reason of its entire isolation,almost amounting to exile, from the rest of the Michigan troops during the whole term of its faithful service.

It left the State in August, 1861, commanded by Colonel F. W. Curtenius, under whose direction it was raised and organized, to join the army in the field; but was detained at Baltimore, where it remained on duty most of the following winter; thence sailed to Ship Island, Mississippi, and in April, 1862, left that place for New Orleans, and was one of the first regiments to occupy that city on its surrender to General Butler. Serving during its whole term of service in the extreme south, it lost more men by disease than any other regiment from the State.

The 6th was engaged at Sewell's Point, Virginia, March 5; at Port Jackson, Louisiana, April 25; at Vicksburg, Mississippi, May 20; at Grand Gulf, Mississippi, May 27, and at Amity River, Mississippi, June 20. The battles of Baton Rouge and Port Hudson, prominent in the history of the rebellion, are among the most conspicuous in which the 6th was engaged.

At Baton Rouge, August 5, 1862, when that place was being heavily attacked by the rebel forces in very superior numbers under Breckenridge, the regiment, then in command of Captain Charles E. Clark, received and repulsed the principal attack made on that day by the troops led by General Clark of Mississippi, against the right wing of the Union forces. The attacking forces of the rebels were fully six thousand, while the Union forces engaged were not over two thousand.

The importance of the repulse was acknowledged by General Butler, in a congratulatory order issued soon after the engagement, in which the regiment was highly complimented for its gallant and valuable services, conspicuous bravery and most determined fighting.

At Port Hudson, with General Banks, the 6th fought with the most determined coolness and desperate intrepidity, being, during the whole siege, in the most advanced position. In the assault of May 27, 1863, the regiment, commanded by Colonel Clark, led the division of General T. W. Sherman, and lost more than one-third of the men it had engaged, including

Lieutenant Fred. T. Clark, who fell while gallantly leading Company D to the charge. Captain Montgomery also led a forlorn hope of two hundred volunteers from the regiment. An assault was made June 14, when the 6th, then commanded by Lieutenant-Colonel Bacon, advanced by three detachments. June 29, the regiment, commanded by Captain Cordon, again advanced to the assault, when thirty-five of the regiment, composing a forlorn hope, assailed the enemy's works at the point known as the citadel. The party gained the ditch, but were overpowered and driven back with a loss of eight killed and nine wounded, among the former Sergeant M. O. Walker, who led the detachment. General Banks thanked the regiment for its gallant and meritorious conduct during the siege.

The 6th was at the reduction of Mobile, and did most gallant and efficient service as heavy artillerists, doing very fine execution with batteries of ten-inch mortars at a range of fourteen hundred yards. After Spanish Fort was taken, companies A and K manned and turned the heavy captured guns of the rebels, consisting of seven inch Brooks' rifled and one hundred pound Parrott's, on the rebel forts Huger and Tracy, and did excellent service on all the works within range. The losses of the regiment during the war were sixty-three men and two officers killed or died of wounds, and four hundred and fifty-two men and five officers died of disease. Company C was raised in St. Joseph county; Lester Fox, of Flowerfield, going out as corporal, and being mustered out as first-lieutenant.

THE SEVENTH INFANTRY.

The 7th Michigan—the gallant forlorn-hope regiment at the battle of Fredericksburg—was recruited and organized under the direction of Colonel Ira R. Grosvenor, at Monroe. Leaving for the field September 5, 1861, first encountered the enemy at Ball's Bluff, Va., October 21st following, and gained credit even in that disastrous engagement. It passed through the peninsular campaign with McClellan, participating, in common, in its victories and defeats, and served as rear guard of the army on the retreat to Harrison's Landing.

At the battle of Antietam, it lost more than half its forces engaged, including Captain Allen H. Zacharias, who died of his wounds on January 1, following, and Lieutenant John P. Eberhard, Company K, of Colon, who was killed. "But one of the great feats of the war than which none will appear brighter in history, was reserved for the 7th at Fredericksburg, on December 11, 1862, when Burnside concluded to cross the Rappahannock and attack the rebels in their stronghold. The upper pontoon had been laid part of the way by the engineers during the night of the 10th. Daylight exposed them to the fire of the enemy's sharp-shooters, which drove them off. Volunteers were called for to cross the river and gain a position to protect the laying of the bridge. Immediately the 7th Michigan, under the gallant Baxter, rushed to the boats, crossed the stream in full view of both armies, under a most terrific fire from the enemy's sharp-shooters, losing heavily, but vigorously charging the rebels on the opposite bank, drove them from their rifle pits, taking a number of prisoners and holding the ground. Colonel Baxter having fallen severely wounded, recrossed the river while the regiment, with the 19th and 20th Massachusetts, which had crossed by the second trip of the boats, dashed up the hill into the city, driving the enemy from house to house, and from stronghold to stronghold, capturing nearly as many prisoners as the regiment numbered, and inflicting a severe loss in killed and wounded; their own loss also being heavy, including Lieutenant Franklin Emery of the 7th. The river thus protected, the laying of the pontoons was speedily accomplished and a portion of the army was crossed.

"At Gettysburg the regiment arrived, after fatiguing marches, July 2d, and was immediately sent to the front on Cemetery hill, having fourteen officers and one hundred and fifty-one men. It occupied the same position until the close of the battle on the 3d, losing twenty-one killed and forty-four wounded. Among the killed were Lieutenant-Colonel Amos E. Steele, commanding the regiment.

"On May 5, 1864, the 7th was engaged, under Major S. W. Curtis, at the Wilderness, and from thence to Petersburg was engaged in all the battles and skirmishes which distinguished that great campaign. Its services were arduous and most gallantly performed from the time it arrived at Petersburg, July 15, to October 26, when at Hatcher's Run, in the hottest of the fight, the 7th, only eighty-five strong, took twenty officers and four hundred and eighty men prisoners, and Sergeant Alonzo Smith (afterwards first-lieutenant), captured the colors of the 26th North Carolina infantry, for which he was presented a medal of honor by the Secretary of War.

"Through some misunderstanding, the 7th was left on the line after the Union forces were withdrawn, and remained in that condition until the morning of the 26th, when Colonel Lapointe, then in command, finding his

regiment had been left alone on the field, formed his men and explained to them their perilous situation, telling them to stand by him and they could find their way out. They commenced at once their dangerous undertaking, marching twelve miles through the country held by the enemy, gallantly fighting their way at almost every step, pursued and harassed constantly by cavalry threatening to cut them off, but they arrived safely within the Union lines at sundown of the same day. General Hancock, their corps commander, complimented the regiment highly on the occasion, and characterized the undertaking as one of the most praiseworthy and daring of the war. The regiment participated in the closing battles of the war, doing most excellent service and maintaining its high standard won on many hard-fought fields. The total losses of the regiment during its entire service were one hundred and seventy men and eleven officers killed and died of wounds, and one hundred and fifty men and four officers died of disease. Company K was the St. Joseph company in the 7th."

THE ELEVENTH INFANTRY.

The 11th Michigan was pre-eminently a St. Joseph county organization, it being recruited at White Pigeon, and its ranks principally filled by citizens of St. Joseph county, the several townships sending six hundred and ten men and officers into the field under its colors. The staff officers at its organization, and during the whole of its long and honorable service were nearly all St. Joseph men, and there were four full companies recruited in the county, as follows: A, Captain David Oakes, Jr., Nottawa, who died at Murfreesboro; C, Captain Calvin C. Hood, Sturgis; D, Captain Benjamin G. Bennett, Burr Oak, promoted to major, and killed at Missionary Ridge; E, Captain Henry N. Spencer, Lockport, resigned, and Lieutenant Thomas Flynn promoted to vacancy, and killed at Stone River, and Second-Lieutenant Charles W. Newberry, of Burr Oaks, promoted to captaincy, and killed at Chickamauga. Besides these companies, Company G, officered by Captain Mosse and Lieutenant Comstock of Branch county, had over fifty men from St. Joseph county in its ranks, and Company F, commanded latterly by Captain Myron C. Benedict of Leonidas, had nearly as many more. Company I had a squad of about fifteen, recruited by Lieutenant Henry S. Platt, of Sturgis.

The great and important battles of Stone River and Chickamauga will always be referred to by the 11th as among the most desperate in which it was engaged during its gallant career, and in which it was most eminently distinguished, and lost heavily. Few regiments on those fields were harder pressed or defended themselves more heroically, and the surviving members of the regiment refer to their services on these occasions with justifiable pride.

At Stone River the regiment, commanded by Colonel William L. Stoughton, of Sturgis, was hotly engaged during the entire battle, being in Negley's division of Thomas' corps, which, on December 31, held the ground near the centre of the Union lines, where it received and checked the onset of the rebel forces, which came sweeping on in column of divisions, after having driven the corps of McCook from its position, and is acknowledged to have been one of the fiercest assaults of the day, in which the enemy was dreadfully punished. The 11th Michigan, with the 19th Illinois, charged in advance, and drove back an entire rebel division; and after the retrograde movement of their own division, these regiments made another dash to the front, driving the enemy. In the engagement the 11th lost thirty-two killed, seventy-nine wounded, and twenty-nine missing.

The gallant commander, Colonel Stoughton, thus writes officially of the part taken by his regiment in the engagement:

"On the morning of the 31st of December, 1862, heavy firing was heard to our right and front, and apparently rapidly approaching the position occupied by the 2d brigade. The regiment was immediately formed and marched to the brow of the hill, near brigade headquarters. The skirmishing soon after indicated the approach of the enemy to the right of this position, and my regiment was formed in line of battle, under cover of a ledge of rocks about one hundred yards in this direction. The skirmishing continued with much spirit for nearly an hour, when a heavy roar of musketry and artillery announced that the principal attack of the enemy was being made on our left and rear. I immediately gave orders to change front on first company, which was promptly executed under a heavy fire, and the regiment advanced in line of battle to the crest of the hill from which Shoult's battery had first been driven, and poured a well-directed and effective fire into the advancing columns of the enemy. The firing continued with spirit and energy until orders came to retire. The fire of the enemy was apparently concentrated upon this point, and was terrific. Men and officers fell on every side. The regiment fell back about eighty yards, was again formed, and then delivered its fire upon the enemy as he advanced over the hill, then retiring to the cover of the cedar woods in our rear. Here some confusion was at first manifest. A large number of regiments had fallen back to this place for shelter, and the enemy's infantry and artillery opened upon us from all sides, except from the left towards Murfreesboro pike. Order, however, was promptly restored by our division and brigade commanders, and my regiment, with others, moved slowly to the rear, keeping up a steady fire upon the enemy. When nearer the cleared field to the right of the Murfreesboro pike, the regiment was rallied, and held the ground for twenty or thirty minutes; it was then marched about half way across the open field, when orders came to charge back into the cedars. My regiment promptly obeyed my orders, rallied on the colors, and charged into the woods with great gallantry, checking the enemy by the sudden and impetuous attack. After delivering one volley, orders came to retire, and the regiment fell back in good order to the left of Murfreesboro pike. Here closed the active operations of that day.

"On the 2d of January we were again called into action. In the afternoon of that day we were posted, as a reserve, in an open field in the rear of our batteries, on the right of the left wing of our army. Between three and four o'clock the enemy made a heavy attack with artillery and infantry on our front. My command was kept lying upon the ground, protected by a slight hill, for about half an hour.

"At the expiration of this time the enemy had driven back our forces on the opposite side of the river, one regiment crossing in great disorder and rushing through our ranks. As soon as the enemy came within range, my regiment, with the others of this brigade, rose up, delivered its fire and charged across the river. In passing the river my line of battle was necessarily broken, and I led the regiment forward to a fence on a line of ground, and re-formed the line. Here the firing continued for some time until the enemy was driven from his cover and retreated through the woods. My regiment was then promptly advanced to the edge of the woods, and continued to fire upon the enemy as he fled in disorder across the open field in front to his line of entrenchments. At this time the ammunition was nearly exhausted, and my regiment, with the others in advance, formed in line of battle, threw out skirmishers, and held our position until recalled across the river. The 11th was among the first to cross Stone river, and assisted in capturing four pieces of artillery abandoned by the enemy in his flight.

"I cannot speak too highly of the conduct of the troops under my command. They fought with the bravery and coolness of veterans, and obeyed my commands under the hottest fire with the precision of the parade-ground. The officers of my command behaved with great gallantry and firmness. Where all nobly discharged their duty, it would, perhaps, be unjust to discriminate. Lieutenants Wilson and Flynn were killed while gallantly leading their companies. Major Smith and Lieutenants Hall, Briggs and Howard were wounded, the two former severely, and Lieutenant Hall is a prisoner."

At Chickamauga the regiment, in command of Lieutenant-Colonel Melvin Mudge, was then in the brigade of Colonel Stoughton, being the 2d brigade, 2d division, 14th corps. This brigade constituted part of the command of General Thomas, and on the last day of that sanguinary conflict held one of the most important points on his line of defence against a largely superior force—the regiment fighting most persistently, successfully repelling charge after charge of the enemy, losing seven killed (including Captain Charles W. Newberry, of Burr Oak), seventy-six wounded and twenty-three missing—and was one of the last regiments to retire from the field in the darkness of that fearful night when the army fell back. Next morning Colonel Stoughton took up a position in front of Rossville, covering the approach to the battle-field, and held it during that day, and in the night fell back on Chattanooga, covering the rear of the retiring army. In the movement Colonel Stoughton drew off his artillery by hand to escape the notice of the enemy. He remained on his picket-line until past four A. M., when, hearing the enemy stirring, he successfully withdrew his pickets, and made a forced march to Chattanooga without the loss of a man, thus most successfully accomplishing a very dangerous and important duty, for which he was afterwards complimented personally by General Thomas.

After the battle of Mission Ridge, in November, 1863, where the regiment, under command of Major B. G. Bennett, participated in the decisive charge, losing its gallant commander and thirty-nine in killed and wounded, the 11th, being in the 2d brigade, 1st division, 14th corps, moved forward on the Atlanta campaign, engaging creditably in all of the important battles.

On July 4, following, it took part in the successful charge on the enemy's works near Marietta, losing thirteen in killed and wounded, including among the severely wounded Colonel Stoughton, who lost a leg, and Lieu-

7

tenant Myron Benedict of Company F, who lost his right arm. The regiment was engaged at Peach Tree Creek July 20, with a loss of eleven killed and wounded, and on August 7 it was in the charge on the enemy's works in front of Atlanta, losing Lieutenant Edward Catlin and fifteen men killed and wounded. The period for which the regiment enlisted having expired, it was ordered to Chattanooga, August 27. The rebel general Wheeler being then engaged in making a raid into Tennessee, the regiment, immediately after its arrival at Chattanooga on the 30th, was ordered to join the column in pursuit, and marched to Murfreesboro, and thence to Huntsville, Alabama, but without meeting the enemy. It returned to Chattanooga September 18. Leaving here two commissioned officers and one hundred and fifty men, (veterans and recruits whose terms had not expired,) the regiment started for Michigan on the 18th, arriving at Sturgis on the 25th. On the 30th it was mustered out of the service. Its total losses in the service were five officers and eighty-eight men killed or died of wounds, and two officers and one hundred and eighty-five men died of disease.

The original roster of the regiment, including the line officers of the St. Joseph companies, was as follows:

Colonel, William J. May, of White Pigeon, who resigned April 1, 1862.
Lieutenant-Colonel, William L. Stoughton, Sturgis.
Major, Benjamin F. Doughty, Sturgis, resigned August 18, 1862.
Surgeon, Dr. William N. Elliott, White Pigeon.
Assistant-Surgeon, Nelson I. Packard, Sturgis.
Chaplain, Holmes A. Pattison, Colon.
Quartermaster, Addison T. Drake, Sturgis.
Adjutant, Samuel Chadwick, Sturgis.
Sergeant-Major, James M. Whallen, Burr Oak.
Quartermaster's Sergeant, John Underwood, White Pigeon.
Commissary-Sergeant, Elva F. Peirce, Nottawa.
Captain Company A, David Oakes, Jr., Nottawa.
First Lieutenant Company A, Christian Haight, Leonidas.
Second Lieutenant Company A, Aaron B. Sturgis, Sturgis.
Captain Company C, Calvin C. Hood, Sturgis.
First Lieutenant Company C, Mathias M. Faulkner, Sturgis.
Second Lieutenant Company C, Loren H. Howard, Fawn River.
Captain Company D, Benjamin G. Bennett, Burr Oak.
First Lieutenant Company D, John R. Keeler, Burr Oak.
Captain Company E, Henry N. Spencer, Lockport.
First Lieutenant Company E, Thomas Flynn, Lockport.
Second Lieutenant Company E, Charles W. Newberry, Burr Oak.
Captain Company G, Charles Mouse, Branch county.
Second Lieutenant Company G, Silas G. Comstock, Branch county.
Second Lieutenant Company I, Henry S. Platt, Sturgis.

## THE THIRTEENTH INFANTRY.

The daring bravery of the 13th Infantry, raised and organized by Colonel Charles E. Stuart, of Kalamazoo, is attested by its persistent fighting and splendid achievements on many fields. It participated in the bloody engagements at Stone River, December 30 and 31, and January 1, 2, and 3, going into action with two hundred and twenty-four muskets, and losing out of this number twenty-five killed or died of wounds, sixty-two wounded, and eight missing. At Chickamauga, the noble regiment, under command of Colonel J. B. Culver, displayed again its brilliant fighting qualities in the efficient service rendered on the 18th of September, and the 19th also, when it rejoined its brigade and division some distance to the left of Lee and Gordon's mills, executing the movement under a heavy fire of the enemy, on the double-quick, with the mercury above ninety. Soon after the regiment charged in a handsome and gallant manner, checking the onset of the rebels, who were forcing back a part of the brigade; in which charge it lost heavily. The regiment went into the engagement with two hundred and seventeen men and officers, and lost fourteen killed, sixty-eight wounded, (of whom eleven died), and twenty-five missing. It joined Sherman's forces in the famous "march to the sea," and moved with them through the Carolinas, and was engaged with the enemy at Catawba river, South Carolina, February 29, 1864, at Averysboro, North Carolina, March 16, and at Bentonville, on the 19th, where it fought the enemy the entire day, sustaining a loss of one hundred and ten killed, wounded and missing, and among the killed was the commanding officer, Colonel W. G. Eaton. It participated in the grand review at Washington. Captain William McLaughlin, of Sturgis, and Captain Norman H. Hoisington, of Fabius, held commands in the 13th. Its total losses in the service were four officers and seventy-four men killed or died of wounds, and two officers and two hundred and sixty-six men died of disease.

## THE FIFTEENTH INFANTRY.

The 15th, in command of Colonel J. M. Oliver, by whom it was organized, first met the enemy at Shiloh, on the 6th and 7th of April, 1862. Arriving there only the day before the battle, it the next morning became hotly engaged, and was thus early initiated into the sad realities of war, and at a great sacrifice, losing in the engagements of both days two officers and thirty-one men killed, and one officer and sixty-three men wounded, and seven missing. The regiment was with Halleck before Corinth, and also with Rosecrans, when his position at the same place was assaulted by Price and his command, October, 1862. At that time the regiment, under command of Lieutenant-Colonel McDermott, held the outpost at Chewalla, on the Memphis and Charleston railroad, about ten miles from Corinth, where it met and checked the advance of Price, and most signally made its mark as a most reliable and brave regiment. On the morning of the 1st of October the pickets of the 15th were driven in, the regiment holding the enemy in check during the day; and in the evening was reinforced by the 14th Wisconsin and a section of a twelve-pound battery, the whole force being under command of Colonel Oliver, of the 15th Michigan. The command fought during the 2d and 3d against overwhelming numbers, contesting every inch of ground, but falling back gradually upon Corinth,—several times being completely flanked and obliged to return on the double-quick, with the enemy on both flanks. It is claimed that the admirable disposition made by Colonel Oliver of his force, and the steadiness and gallantry of the men engaged, delayed an army of forty thousand men (or thereabout) at least twenty-four hours in making their main and final attack upon Corinth, thus enabling General Rosecrans to make the disposition of his forces which most successfully secured the repulse of the enemy, and compelled him to make a most disastrous retreat. The regiment was at Vicksburg in June, 1863, and participated in the advance on Jackson, leading at the crossing of the Big Black river on the 6th of July. It veteranized and participated in the Georgia campaign in 1864, taking part in the engagements that occurred during the movement on Resaca. On the 21st of July, the 15th, under command of Lieutenant-Colonel F. S. Hutchinson, eminently distinguished itself, rendering most gallant and valuable service.

Early on the morning of that day the enemy attacked, in flank and rear, the 17th corps, which was on the left of the 15th corps, driving it back with much loss. About one o'clock the 15th Michigan was ordered to fill a gap on the extreme left of its corps, about one mile distant from the position it then occupied. The regiment moved on the double-quick, and upon coming into line near the position indicated, found it in possession of the enemy; it, however, moved gallantly forward in line, striking the enemy on the flank, driving him from his position, taking seventeen officers and one hundred and sixty-seven men as prisoners, and capturing the colors of the 5th Confederate Infantry, and also the colors of the 17th and 18th Texas, and suffering a loss of four killed and six wounded. This was the advance of two rebel divisions which were massed in a wood but a short distance in the rear. The promptitude with which the movement was executed by the 15th deterred the remainder of the rebel force from making a forward movement, and thus prevented the enemy from breaking the Union lines, and probably averted disaster from that part of the field.

The regiment participated in the campaign before Atlanta, and marched with Sherman from Atlanta to Savannah, maintaining its glorious record to the last. Its losses during the war foot up seventy-five officers and men killed or died of wounds, and one hundred and thirty-two died of disease. Captain John A. Waterman, of Burr Oak, commanded a company in the 15th, recruited largely from St. Joseph county.

## THE NINETEENTH INFANTRY.

The 19th was organized by Colonel Henry C. Gilbert, who was killed at Resaca while leading his regiment upon a rebel battery. There were two full companies from St. Joseph county in its ranks: D, Captain Hazen W. Brown, and afterwards commanded by Captain Frank D. Baldwin, who also was promoted to the lieutenant-colonelcy of the regiment; and Company E, Captain John J. Baker, who was also the lieutenant-colonel of the regiment when discharged—Lieutenant David J. Easton of the same company holding the commission and rank of major at his discharge. The last two were Sturgis men, and the former of Constantine. The 19th won great celebrity in many important battles and campaigns, but in none more prominently than the following:

On the 5th of March, 1863, the 4th brigade of General Baird's division of the army of Kentucky, composed of the 33d and 85th Indiana, 22d Wisconsin, and 19th Michigan, numbering in all about one thousand five hundred and eighty-seven men, strengthened by two hundred of the 124th Ohio, with de-

tachments of three regiments of cavalry about six hundred strong, and one battery of six guns, met the enemy in force at Thompson's station, Tennessee, and at the point where the railroad joins the pike the rebels opened fire upon the Union forces, who were under the command of Colonel Coburn, and who immediately formed his line and ordered a section of the battery to occupy a hill on the left of the pike, sending the 19th Michigan and 22d Wisconsin to support it. The 33d and 85th Indiana, with the other guns of the battery, took position on a hill on the right. The enemy had two batteries on a range of hills three quarters of a mile in front, and south of the position of the Union troops. The 33d and 85th Indiana made a demonstration on the left of the enemy to draw him out or charge his batteries according to circumstances. This was commenced and continued under a most galling fire from the enemy's batteries. Upon reaching the station the skirmishers unmasked two whole brigades of dismounted rebel cavalry posted behind stone walls and other defenses.

It being impossible to advance farther under the incessant and severe fire, the regiments were ordered to retire to their former position on the hill, supported by two companies of cavalry, but for some reason or other the cavalry did not accompany them. No sooner had the two regiments commenced to fall back than they were pursued by two regiments, one from Arkansas and one from Texas, both firing rapid volleys into the retiring ranks, which were at the same time under fire from the rebel batteries. As soon as they reached the hill, the Indiana regiments faced about and drove the enemy in turn in double-quick, killing Colonel Earle, of Arkansas. The enemy again rallied and charged desperately, but were driven back. It then became evident that Colonel Coburn had encountered the entire cavalry of Bragg's army, commanded by General Van Dorn, about eighteen thousand strong, in six brigades, under the command of Generals Forrest, Wheeler, French, Armstrong, Jackson, Martin, and Crosby. The rebels then advanced upon the left, where were posted the 19th Michigan and 22d Wisconsin. These regiments opened fire upon the enemy, and held him in check for about twenty minutes.

At the time the left was first attacked, that portion of the battery there stationed hurriedly left that part of the field without orders, leaving the two regiments without artillery to assist them in repelling the enemy then charging desperately. At the same time Lieutenant-Colonel Bloodgood, of the 22d Wisconsin, with three companies of that regiment, left the field without orders, moving off by the left flank and joining the retreating cavalry and artillery. Forrest, checked in his advance, made a circuit with his whole force beyond the ground occupied by Coburn, to the east, with the intention to turn his left flank. The 19th and 22d were then moved on the west side of the pike, leaving the 33d and 85th to protect the hill on its south face. The four regiments had scarcely formed line, lying behind the crest of the hill, when Armstrong's brigade charged from the east, and the fighting became terrific. Three times the enemy charged gallantly up the hill from the east, and thrice were they forced back.

In one of their charges the 19th Michigan captured the colors of the 4th Mississippi, and four prisoners. The fighting was close and desperate. The enemy, having gained possession of the hill on the east of the road, were hurling grape and canister into the ranks like hail, and the battle raged furiously. But it was a hopeless struggle; defeat was only a question of time. The ammunition was getting short, and Forrest getting between them and Franklin, who was approaching from the north. A new line was formed, by Coburn's force facing north, to meet the new line of advance. Forrest was met and held in check until the last round of ammunition was fired. The gallant and brave little band then fixed bayonets to charge and break the enemy's lines and escape; but just as they were about to charge, it was discovered that the enemy had still another line in reserve, and a battery began to open and take a new position. Escape was hopeless, and to avoid useless loss of life the command surrendered, having lost one hundred and thirteen in killed and wounded. Colonel Gilbert had his horse shot under him in the early part of the engagement, and behaved most gallantly. When he offered his sword to the Confederate commander, the latter declined to receive it, saying "that an officer who was so brave in battle, and commanded so gallant a regiment, deserved to retain his arms."

In Sherman's advance upon Atlanta, the 19th was in the 1st brigade, 4th division, 20th corps, and at Resaca, May 15, 1864, became conspicuously and desperately engaged, when, with the brigade, it gallantly charged a four-gun battery, captured the artillery, and held the position. In this charge Colonel Gilbert, commanding the regiment, was mortally wounded, while leading and urging on his men, and died at Chattanooga on the 24th of that month.

At Peach Tree creek the regiment, under command of Major John J. Baker, participated in the repulse of the fierce attack of the enemy on the Union lines July 20, in which Major Baker was wounded and thirty-five of his men, four being killed.

The 19th "marched down to the sea" with Sherman, participating in the numerous engagements of its corps with credit and distinction. At Averysboro, North Carolina, on March 16, 1865, it bore a brilliant part in the assault on the enemy's works, which were captured, with the artillery therein. The 19th lost in the assault two brave officers, Captain Leonard Gibbon and Lieutenant Charles G. Purcell, and four men killed and fifteen wounded, several severely.

Lieutenant Baldwin, of Company D, was the hero of a brave defense, though short and hopeless; with fifty men of the company, he was stationed at a stockade on the Nashville and Chattanooga railroad at Stone river, and was attacked, October 5, by a large force of rebel cavalry and artillery under Major General Wheeler, who, after sending forward one hundred and fifty men in the Federal uniform as a decoy, quietly surrounded the company and demanded its surrender. Lieutenant Baldwin returned answer that "he must fight before he got him," on the receipt of which a battery immediately opened on the stockade, and was responded to by a fire of musketry; the firing was continued for an hour and a half, throwing nearly forty charges of grape, canister, solid shot, and shell; the shot passing through the stockade, knocking the logs to pieces, and causing more damage from the splinters than from shot. Lieutenant Baldwin, deeming it useless to attempt to hold his position any longer against such odds, and expecting no assistance, surrendered his command,—having six wounded, while the attacking force lost two killed and eight wounded.

The enemy's force consisted of two divisions of cavalry and twelve pieces of artillery. Lieutenant Baldwin's men were disarmed, and plundered of their overcoats, money, and all articles of value, and unconditionally released, and under a pass from General Wheeler returned to its encampment at the stockade, and next morning marched from Murfreesboro.

The loss of the regiment during its term of service was seven officers and ninety-one men killed or died of wounds, and one hundred and thirty-five men died of disease.

THE TWENTY-FIFTH INFANTRY.

The 25th was recruited and organized at Kalamazoo, under the superintendence of Hon. H. G. Wells, commandant of camp, and was commanded by Colonel O. H. Moore, and was a splendid and well-disciplined regiment. Two companies went out under its colors from St. Joseph county: D, Captain Julius C. Cross, of Three Rivers, afterwards succeeded by Lieutenant Henry McCrary, of Leonidas; and Company G, Captain William Fulkerson, of Lockport, who was succeeded by Lieutenant John B. Handy, of Three Rivers. The 25th first tasted the realities of war December 27, 1862, three months after leaving Kalamazoo, at Munfordsville, Kentucky, where they engaged the rebels under General Pegram. On July 4, 1863, the regiment was especially distinguished at Tebbs', near Green River bridge, Kentucky, where it most gallantly repulsed an overwhelming rebel force with heavy loss.

"About July 1, Colonel Moore was stationed with five companies of his regiment on the north side of Green river, ten miles north of Columbia, on the main road running from Columbia to Lebanon, Kentucky, and on the 2d of July was advised of the fact that the rebel general, John H. Morgan, was about crossing the Cumberland river to invade the State with a cavalry force of from three to four thousand men. Being left to exercise his own discretion, and there being no Union troops nearer than at a post thirty miles distant, Colonel Moore felt it to be his duty to retard the progress of the great raider, if but for a few hours, as they might prove precious hours to the country. He might have retreated with entire success, but from patriotic motives chose to fight when he could scarcely entertain the hope that he and many others would ever live to tell the story of that terrible battle. After surveying the surrounding country, he selected a strong position for a battle-ground, on the south side of Green river, about two miles from the encampment, in a horse-shoe bend of the river, through which the road ran on which the rebel forces were advancing. This chosen battle-ground, which was at the narrows entering the bend of the river, afforded high bluff-banks, which protected the flanks of the command and also compelled the enemy to fight him upon his own front. * * * On the evening of July 3, General Morgan encamped with his entire command about five miles south of Green river, and Colonel Moore after dark advanced with his command of five companies, numbering less than four hundred men, about two miles toward the enemy, leaving the river in his rear, and occupied the

ground which he had previously selected, and prepared for the battle. The defense which had been completed that night consisted of some felled trees on the battle-line, which was in the rear of an open field, and was intended more particularly as an obstruction to the advance of cavalry, while to the front, about one hundred yards in the open field, was thrown up a temporary earth-work, which was intended to check the advance of the enemy, and more especially to command a position where he would evidently plant a battery. This work was not intended to be held against charges of a superior force, on account of the flanks not being strong, and was occupied by only about seventy-five men, who were instructed that when it became necessary to abandon the work, it should be done by flanking to the right and left from the centre, so as to unmask the reserve force on the battle-line and expose the enemy to their fire. This work was located, in anticipation of its capture by the rebels, a little down the slope of the field, so that when it was in possession of the enemy it would be useless, and leave him exposed to a deadly fire. At the gray of the morning the fire of the enemy upon the pickets resounded through the woods, and the entire rebel division, under Morgan, was pressing upon the front. The fire was returned with spirit as the pickets retired to the breastwork, where they joined about seventy-five of their comrades already in the advance work, and there, with their united fire as sharp-shooters, held the enemy in check, without exhibiting their numbers and the real object of the work. The rebel artillery of four pieces had gained the anticipated position, and at once opened fire with some effect, when Morgan suspended firing, and, under a flag of truce, demanded an immediate and unconditional surrender of the entire force and stockade. Colonel Moore replied to the demand: 'Present my compliments to General Morgan, and say to him that this being the Fourth of July, I cannot entertain the proposition to surrender.' Colonel Alliston, Morgan's chief of staff, said, 'I hope you will not consider me as dictatorial on this occasion. I will be frank: you see the breach we have made upon your work with our battery; you cannot expect to repulse General Morgan's whole division with your little command; you have resisted us gallantly and deserve credit for it, and now I hope you will reconsider your reply by reconsidering your reply to General Morgan."

"To this Colonel Moore replied: 'Sir, when you assume to know my strength you assume too much. I have a duty to perform to my country, and therefore cannot reconsider my reply to General Morgan.' The rebel officer, seemingly moved by these remarks, extended his hand, and said, 'Good-bye, colonel; God only knows which of us may fall first.' They turned their horses and galloped in opposite directions, and at once renewed the conflict. No sooner had the rebel battery re-opened fire than Colonel Moore commanded the force to 'rise up and pick off those gunners at the battery.' At the word, a deliberate and deadly fire by rank was delivered, which silenced the battery. Colonel Johnson's brigade then charged the work, and the little command abandoned it as previously instructed; and when the rebels reached it they found that it availed them nothing against the deadly fire which was poured into them from the main force on the battle-line in the timber. The foe, with hideous yells, charged across the open field a number of times in the face of a terrific fire, which repulsed them on each occasion with severe loss. The conflict was almost a hand-to-hand struggle, with nothing but a line of felled trees separating the combatants. At the same time the rebels were engaged in cutting out a gorge leading through the precipitous bluff into the river bottom, which had been obstructed with felled timber. The entrance was finally effected, and a regiment commanded by Colonel Chevault opened fire on the right flank of the line of Union troops. This was a most critical and trying moment: the enemy had gained an important point; to defeat it was of the utmost importance; a company had been held in reserve for any emergency which might arise during the battle, and it was now brought forward; deployed as skirmishers across the river bottom, with the right flank extending beyond the rebel line, and presented the appearance of being the advance line of reinforcements.

"The strength of Colonel Moore's command was a matter of doubt with the enemy, rendered more so by his instructions to his men to keep quiet and pour in a rapid and deadly a fire as possible. As cheering was suppressed, nothing but the efficacy of the firing afforded ground for estimating their strength; and when Colonel Moore brought forward and manœuvered the reserve company with the shrill noise of his bugle, it had the desired effect of impressing the rebels with the idea that reinforcements of cavalry or artillery were advancing; and by the bold front and deliberate firing of the line of skirmishers the rebel command in the river bottom was routed, its colonel killed, and it driven back through the gorge through which they entered, disheartened and defeated. New courage inspired the heroic little hand, who had sustained eight determined charges upon their front when the attack upon their right flank was defeated:

"The enemy, having met with a heavy loss after a battle of four hours' duration, retreated, leaving a number of killed and wounded upon the field greater than the entire number of the patriotic little band that opposed them. Among the number of killed and wounded were twenty-two commissioned officers.

"It was the intention of Morgan, as he declared, to capture the city of Louisville; but this unexpected and terrible repulse cost him more than twelve hours' delay, and caused him—which fact he stated—to change his plans and abandon his attack on Louisville. By this brilliantly fought battle the city was saved from sack and pillage, and the government from the loss of an immense amount of property, consisting of munitions of war, and army supplies amounting to the value of many millions of dollars. Major-General Hartsuff acknowledged the victory in a general order recounting the heroic deed. The legislature of Kentucky also acknowledged the services of Colonel Moore and his command on that occasion in complimentary resolutions. Morgan himself admired Colonel Moore's generalship so much in the conduct of the battle that he too sent him complimentary messages, and announced that he promoted him to the rank of brigadier-general.

"Colonel Allston, who was captured a few days after the battle, and with him his private journal, which was published, in a memorandum of the battle of the Fourth of July quotes Morgan's demand for the surrender of the Union command, and Colonel Moore's reply, and adds: 'The colonel is a gallant man, and the entire arrangement of his defense entitles him to the highest credit for military skill. We would mark such a man in our army for promotion.'"

The regiment in 1864, in the Georgia campaign, was identified with the movements of the army of the Ohio, and participated in the various engagements at Rocky Face Ridge, May 19; Resaca, May 14; Altoona, May 26, 29; Pine Mountain, June 15; Culp's Farm, June 22; and Nickajack Creek, July 1. On the 22d it was before Atlanta, and was actively engaged in the siege of that place.

At Resaca the 25th was most conspicuously distinguished, where, in command of Lieutenant-Colonel B. F. Orcutt, it participated in the desperate charge made by Judah's division, of the 23d corps, and Newton's, of the 4th corps, driving the enemy from a strong and well-fortified position, and although not held, enabled General Sherman to advance his lines and get his artillery in such a position as to render it impossible for the enemy to again occupy the place. This charge was made under a most murderous fire of musketry and artillery, first across an open field and then over a stream with the water nearly waist-deep, and bordered with thick bushes and vines, cut and lopped in such a manner as to entangle the troops. In the charge the regiment lost about fifty men in a very few minutes, among the killed being Adjutant E. M. Prutzman, of Three Rivers. At Nickajack creek, near Kenesaw, on July 1, the 25th again most signally maintained its fighting qualities while making a flank movement with its division (Hascall's) to the extreme right of General Sherman's army,—the regiment advancing seven miles during an intensely hot day, continually under fire of musketry and artillery from early in the forenoon until dark, and being engaged in two brilliant and successful charges during the day, driving the enemy from every position, and securing the desired point, known as the cross-roads, near Nickajack creek. The result of the movement was the evacuation by General Johnson of his strong position on Kenesaw mountain, and the abandonment of all his works between that point and the Chattahoochee. The regiment was also at the defense of Nashville, under General Thomas, and was in the pursuit organized that grim old warrior after Hood. From this campaign it was transferred to Schofield's command, and participated in its movements in North Carolina. The losses of the regiment during the war foot up thirty-five men and one officer killed or died of wounds, and one hundred and twenty-three men and two officers died of disease.

### BATTERY D (BIDWELL'S), FIRST LIGHT ARTILLERY.

The 1st regiment of Michigan light artillery was composed of twelve six-gun batteries, but it was never brought together as a regiment. Battery D was largely filled up with St. Joseph men, though officered by Branch county men. It left the State in 1861, proceeded to Kentucky, and first encountered the enemy, damaging them much, at Hoover's Gap, Tennessee, June 26, 1862, when Rosecrans was advancing on Tullahoma and Chattanooga. Its most prominent fight, as appears from its record, was at the great battle of Chickamauga,—September 19 and 20, 1863,—where, in command of Captain J. W. Church, it became closely and hotly engaged,

behaving in splendid style, but losing heavily, having nine wounded and three missing, among the wounded its commander. It was also in the assault on Mission Ridge, November 25 following, and on the preceding day aided in covering Hooker's advance up Lookout mountain. On both occasions it proved a serviceable battery, and its splendid firing and valuable services attracted much attention.

### BATTERY F.

Captain John S. Andrews raised and organized Battery F, and Norman S. Andrews, of White Pigeon, took some thirty or more men into it from St. Joseph county, and went into service with the organization as junior first lieutenant. Its first engagement with the enemy was at Henderson, Ky., in 1864. In 1864 it was with General Sherman in the Atlanta campaign, and passed through numerous engagements, maintaining a high reputation for promptness and efficiency. Among its principal encounters with the enemy may be classed its severe fight at Utoy Creek, Georgia, August 4, where, in command of Lieutenant Miller, it vigorously engaged the enemy with some loss, and had the equipments and wheels of two guns literally shot to pieces, but bravely held its position, and finally silenced two rebel batteries. On this occasion the battery attracted much attention and favorable comment on account of its stubborn and effective fighting. The battery was transferred to General Schofield's command on the North Carolina coast early in 1865. In the engagement at Wise Forks, March 10, the battery maintained its previous high reputation for gallant service and daring courage.

### BATTERY G

was raised by Captain C. H. Lamphere in 1862, in connection with the 13th regiment of infantry, and was stationed at West Point, Ky., in February, 1863. It first engaged the enemy at Tazewell in May following. In November of the same year it was ordered to Memphis, and from thence to the Yazoo river, Miss., and, in command of Captain Lamphere, was actively engaged in the battle of Chickasaw Bayou, December 28 and 29, losing ten wounded (two mortally), with eight horses killed or disabled. The loss of the battery at this point indicates its gallant and valuable service. It participated in the Vicksburg campaign, and was engaged in the fight near Port Gibson on May 1, 1863, where is acquired much distinction, and was mentioned in the report of General McClernand, as follows: "The splendid practice of Lamphere's and Foster's batteries disabled two of the enemy's guns, and contributed largely to our success." Corporal Jonathan G. Waltham, of Constantine, and thirty-four others from St. Joseph county, were members of Battery G.

In gathering the names of the men who went from St. Joseph county into the war for the Union, we have taken them from the records of the adjutant-general's office, and have been unable to locate some, who have made honorable records of suffering and death, in any township in the county; and in order that these men may have at least an honorable mention at our hands, and a place in our work, the history of the county,—whose quotas, under the imperative calls of the government for help they contributed to fill,—we give their names and record here:

### SECOND REGIMENT INFANTRY.

Private Charles Atwood, Company I; died of wounds received in Wilderness.

### FOURTH INFANTRY.

Corporal James Pierson, Company C; discharged for disability.
Corporal Constantine Pease, Company C; died of wounds received at Gettysburg.
Private Samuel Clay, Company C; discharged for disability.
Private George M. Lee, Company C; discharged for disability.
Private L. A. Shaeffer, Company C; died in brigade hospital, November 20, 1861.
Private Wilson Becker, Company C; killed at Fredericksburg, December 14, 1862.
Private John Thomas, Company C; discharged for disability.
Private William Havens, Company E; died at Victoria, Tenn., of disease.
Private Philo O. Parker, Company C; killed at Gaines' Mills, June 27, 1862.

### FIFTH INFANTRY.

Private James Roots, Company F; died at Chancellorsville.

### SIXTH INFANTRY.

Musician Freeland W. Brice, Company C; died at Carrollton, Louisiana, May 11, 1863.
Private Joseph E. Howe, Company C; died at New Orleans, August 15, 1862.
Private John McAllen, Company C; died at New Orleans, May 30, 1862.

Private William A. Porter, re-enlisted, and killed on cars en route to Louisiana.

Private J. C. Stone, died at Port Hudson, Louisiana, September 30, 1863.

SEVENTH INFANTRY.

Private John A. Howe, Company I; killed at Antietam.

Private Tillman Dammond, Company I; killed at Spottsylvania.

Private Wesley Fenton, Company K; died at Washington.

Private Alfred Turk, Company A; killed at Antietam.

Private Albert M. Ferrill, Company K; wounded at Fair Oaks, and discharged.

Private John Griffin, Company K; lost a leg at Antietam, and discharged.

Private Charles L. Hill, Company K; died October 14, 1862, of wounds received at Antietam.

Private John Malone, Company K; died at Harrison's Landing, Virginia, July 22, 1864.

Private James E. Ward, Company K; wounded at Bristoe Station, Virginia, and discharged.

Private William H. White, Company K; died of measles, at Camp Benton, Maryland.

Private James D. Barnhisel, Company K; wounded at Spottsylvania, and mustered out.

Private Lemuel Leak, Company K; wounded at Wilderness, and not seen since.

ELEVENTH REGIMENT INFANTRY.

Musician Foreman Burke, died July 11, 1862.

Private George F. Grather, Company A; died at White Pigeon, October 19, 1861.

Private Wilson Hinds, Company A; died at Bardstown, Kentucky.

Private Edward Perrett, Company A; died at Nashville, September, 1863.

Private Thomas Naughton, Company A; died at Belmont, Kentucky, April 17, 1862.

Private Jerome Allen, Company C; died April 18, 1862.

Private John Goodle, Company C; died at Nashville.

Private Daniel C. Leonard, Company C; killed at Stone River, December 31, 1862.

Private George H. Norton, Company C; died of small-pox, June 3, 1862.

Private Thomas Rapp, Company C; died January 29, 1862.

Private William Schochenberger, Company C; killed at Marietta, Georgia, July 4, 1864.

Private Arthur W. Miller, Company D; died February 10, 1862.

Private Henry Burleson, Company D; killed at Stone River, December 31, 1862.

Corporal Washington I. Snyder, Company E; promoted and died at Chattanooga.

Private Thomas Manning, Company E; killed at Stone River, December 21, 1862.

Private Joseph Spranger, Company E; died at Stevenson, Alabama, August 29, 1863.

Private William M. Sherman, Company E; died at Nashville, March 2, 1863.

Private Silas Burleson, Company F; died March 26, 1862.

Private John Vale, Company F; died June 22, 1864.

Private Oscar E. Fuller, Company F; died at Chattanooga.

Private Cosmore E. Mannigold, Company G; killed at Chattanooga.

Private Francis E. Stanton, Company G; died March, 1862.

TWELFTH INFANTRY.

Private Augustus Miller, Company F; died at Duvall's Bluff, Arkansas.

Private Richard Armitage, Company H; died at Washington, Arkansas.

Private Albert Evans, Company I; died at Washington, Arkansas.

Private Silas S. Ford, Company I; died at Duvall's Bluff, Arkansas.

THIRTEENTH INFANTRY.

Private Wellington Cook, Company B; died October 17, 1862.

Private Jacob E. Reis, Company E; died at Savannah, Georgia.

Private James M. Howard, Company G; died at Tullahoma, May 17, 1864.

Private Joseph L. Bogardus, Company G; killed at Bentonville, North Carolina.

Private Hiram W. Eldred, Company G; died at Newark.

Private Cortes F. Foote, Company H; killed at Bentonville, North Carolina.

Private George F. Miller, Company K; killed at Lookout Mountain.

FOURTEENTH INFANTRY.

Private Charles Hero, Company C; died at Kingston, Georgia.

Private Frank Murray, Company C; killed at Bentonville, North Carolina.

FIFTEENTH INFANTRY.

Private Benjamin Booth, Company A; died at Keokuk, Iowa.

Private Dwight Duncan, Company A; re-enlisted, and killed before Atlanta.

Private David Fowler, Company A; killed at Shiloh, April 6, 1862.

Private John R. Martin, Company A; died at Monterey, Tennessee, June 10, 1862.

Private Walter O'Brien, Company A; died April 18, 1862, of wounds received at Shiloh.

Private William Denater, Company A; died May 8, 1862.

SIXTEENTH INFANTRY.

Private George Hall, Company D; killed at Gaines' Mills, Virginia.

Private William D. D. Gilson, Company G; died on transport, August, 1862.

NINETEENTH INFANTRY.

Private Henry R. Sharp, Company E; killed at Cassville, Georgia, May 19, 1864.

TWENTY-FIFTH INFANTRY.

Private William H. Baughner, Company D; died of wounds received at Chattanooga.

Private William Robins, Company A; died at Mumfordsville, Kentucky, January 16, 1863.

Private William Young, Company D; killed at Resaca, Georgia.

Private Jerry Hopeman, Company D; killed at Resaca, Georgia.

Private Roswell Beebe, Company D; killed at Tebbs' Bend, Kentucky, July 4, 1863.

Private Edward O'Herran, Company G; died September 7, 1863.

TWENTY-SIXTH INFANTRY.

Private Charles H. Bryant, Company A; died at Detroit.

Private Warren V. Easton, Company I; killed at Deep Bottom, Virginia.

TWENTY-SEVENTH INFANTRY.

Benjamin F. Ward, 2d Independent company sharp-shooters; killed at Petersburg.

Lafayette Young, 2d Independent company sharp-shooters; killed at Litchfield, Virginia.

TWENTY-EIGHTH INFANTRY.

Private Horatio C. Failing, Company C; died at Murfreesboro.

Private Warren Ellis, Company E; discharged for wounds.

Private Frederick Blackman, Company H; died at Alexandria.

Private Charles W. Hutchins, Company H; died at Newbern, North Carolina.

Private Lawrence Gassnel, Company H; died at Detroit.

Private Samuel T. Lindley, Company A; drowned at Jackson, Michigan.

FIRST MECHANICS AND ENGINEERS.

Private Charles Spalding, Company H; died February 8, 1864.

FIRST CAVALRY.

Private Albert Chittenden, Company G; killed at Gettysburg, July 3, 1863.

THIRD CAVALRY.

Private George B. Williams, Company A; died at St. Louis, October 16, 1864.

Private Edward M. Richardson, Company F; died at Duvall's Bluff, Arkansas.

Private Lorenzo Seger, Company M; died.

SEVENTH CAVALRY.

Private Charles C. Knapp, Company A; died in Salisbury prison-pen.

NINTH CAVALRY.

Private W. H. Van Brunt, Company E; died in Andersonville.

Private Augustus Butler, Company K; killed at Stone Mountain, Georgia, October 2, 1864.

Private John Kemple, Company K; killed at Stone Mountain, Georgia, October 2, 1864.

BATTERY D—FIRST LIGHT ARTILLERY.

Private Geo. W. Swift; died at Camp Gilbert, Kentucky, June 20, 1862.

Private Floran Aufrance; died at Murfreesboro.

BATTERY M.

Private Edward D. Rowley; died of wounds received August 10, 1863.

Private John Sensibe, Battery L; died at Knoxville, September 18, 1863.

Private Edgar A. Sherwood; died at Knoxville.

FIRST MICHIGAN SHARP-SHOOTERS.

Private Emanuel J. Stiffler, Company F; died at Washington.

FIRST UNITED STATES SHARP-SHOOTERS.

Private Edward S. Hamblin, Company I; died near Falmouth, Virginia, January 27, 1863.

Private Warner Houghtaling; died near Suffolk, Virginia, May 12, 1863.

## CONCLUSION.

And now, dear reader, our pleasant task is done. We have rambled with you by the stream of history as for fifty years it has meandered through the superb county of St. Joseph. We have seen the fleet deer bounding through the glades or over the billowy prairies, followed by the scarcely less agile red man, or the no less untiring pale-faced borderer. We have looked upon the pioneer as, with the slow and toilsome pace of the patient oxen, he has moved his household goods into the Indian's country, and with brawny arms has rolled up the rude logs for a shelter for his domestic treasures. We have joined the merry throng and congratulated the newly-wedded bride on her new-found happiness; have rejoiced with the mother when she has felt the dewy breath of the babe upon her breast; and we have stood by the open grave and shed tears of sympathy with the stricken ones as they laid their treasures in the dust, and no healer was nigh but Him who has ordered all things for the best. We have seen the old Pennsylvania wagon, with its broad tires and broader-backed horses toiling through the marshes and swimming rivers, give way to the "coach and four" as it rattled over the Chicago trail and up to the door of the old log hostelry, at the crack of the driver's whip and the echoing notes of his horn. We have seen the awkward flat-boat and clumsy ark, carrying the produce of the sturdy yeomanry of old St. Joe to a market, as they floated lazily down the noble river that for twenty years and more was the main artery of commerce in the county; and we have seen, at length, the ark and the flat-boat, together with the rumbling, swaying "Concord," give way to that steed whose iron stomach craves no lighter diet than coal and water, and under whose tireless impetus the world has been revolutionized. We have seen, as the result of these changes, the beautiful lawns, open vistas, and free wild prairies transformed from their unexcelled natural loveliness to broad well-tilled farms; the log cabins disappear and elegant mansions come into view; and the dotted landscape become villages; and the villages, thriving cities. We have seen the rude mills of the pioneers with their primitive wheels and imperfect boulder stones, whose product, like the figs of the prophet's vision, was so bad it could scarcely be eaten for badness, fall away, and on their sites rise the three-storied structures of the present, with their Leffels and polished and ironed "burrs," whose product ("prime super extra white winter") commands the markets of the world. We have beheld, and the log school-houses, with their rough benches and simple elements of education, have faded, and in their places magnificent buildings rise, wherein reign the best systems of instruction in literature and science. We have worshiped in the settler's cabin and in the groves—"God's first temples"—when the Boanerges of the early days launched the judgments of Heaven at our defenseless heads, or melted us to tears as they told of the love of a merciful Father; and we have seated ourselves on the luxuriously upholstered sofas in the costly and capacious tabernacles that now lift their towers to the skies, and have listened to the swelling tones of the organ and the story of the Man of Nazareth delivered to us in the well-turned periods of rhetoric and display. And—prouder sight than these—we have seen, when the banner of treason floated the air and the armed hosts beneath its folds struck at the nation, the old, the middle-aged, and the young leave the homestead garlanded with love and affection, and with brave hearts and determined wills go forth to beat back the foes of freedom and union; and we have seen—a grander, nobler sight than all—the shattered regiments come back with colors proudly flying, though tattered by shot and shell, and the veteran soldiers—heroes all—settle back into their accustomed places, and take up again the arts of peace without disturbance or unusual commotion.

And now, standing face to face with all these evidences before us, shall we not say that, link by link, here and there over the whole earth, the testimony accumulates that the march of progress is ever onward and upward? Over the gory trail of war, it may be, as well as by the pleasant paths of peace, the Divine purpose is being developed—a pledge, though much tribulation, toil and pain may intervene before the grand consummation shall be reached, that humanity shall yet attain unto god-like perfection and knowledge, and "the wilderness shall blossom like the rose."

RESIDENCE OF J. BROWN, FLORENCE TP, ST JOSEPH CO, MICH.

RESIDENCE OF A.C. ZIMMER, FAWN RIVER TP, ST JOSEPH CO, MICH.

# TOWNSHIP HISTORIES.

## WHITE PIGEON.

In a county so rich in Indian reminiscence as is St. Joseph, it is somewhat singular that but two towns in its borders should commemorate its aboriginal inhabitants, and especially when the Pottawatomie dialect abounds with characteristic nomenclature, liquid in accent, and beautiful in signification. Nottawa perpetuates the band of warriors who lived thereon, and White Pigeon a noted chief of the nation. Tradition says the old chief, who died before any white man ever lived on the prairie, was buried on a knoll just outside the village boundaries, on a farm once owned by James Knapp, and now owned by Martin L. Gortner. Tradition goes on to say that a cabin was once built over the chief's remains, against the earnest remonstrance of his clansmen, who believed such an act was a desecration of the (to them) sacred spot, and that they told the builder of the cabin that it would not stand there long,—and it did not, being burned shortly afterwards; since which time the site has been respected. Trees have been planted thereon several times, but they have hitherto failed to thrive, and have finally died. There has been some talk about erecting a monument on the spot to commemorate the old-time warrior and sachem of the red men, but nothing has as yet been done towards such a reasonable and commendable work. But his name is preserved, and has been spread throughout the land by the fame of the settlement of white men, who could find no more appropriate or beautiful name for their colony (and, afterwards, township) than that of the leading war-chief, of his day, of the Pottawatomie nation. Long before the settlement around Fort Dearborn became a fact generally known, White Pigeon prairie was a noted spot in New England, New York and Pennsylvania. White Pigeon was for years the distributing point of emigration into the west, and all southwestern Michigan and northwestern Indiana was settled by emigrants who made their first stop at this point.

### TOPOGRAPHY.

The surface of the township of White Pigeon is a level plain, slightly undulating in portions, and originally covered with light burr- and white-oak openings, with the exception of about one thousand acres of its area, which was a portion of the far-famed White Pigeon prairie. Its entire area includes, as at present limited, about eighteen thousand acres, of which some twelve hundred and sixty-five are water surface. The soil is of the same general character of that throughout the county, and is very fertile and productive.

### THE DRAINAGE

of the township is ample, and it is watered by the Pigeon and Fawn rivers, and Pickerel, Klinger's, Aldrich, Marl and Fish lakes. The Pigeon enters the township from Indiana, on the south line of the southwest quarter of the northwest quarter of section twenty-two, and runs northerly and westerly, passing out on the west line of the southwest quarter of the northwest quarter of section twelve, township eight, range twelve. The Fawn enters the township by Aldridge lake, on sections thirteen and twenty-four, and passes through Pickerel lake, running thence nearly due north, passing out of the township on the northwest quarter of the northwest quarter of section twenty-seven, township seven, range eleven west. Klinger's lake —so named from a pioneer who settled on its shores in 1829—is the largest body of water in the township, having an area of about seven hundred acres, and lies on sections one and two, township eight, and thirty-five and thirty-six, township seven, range eleven. Marl lake, a long, narrow sheet of water, lies on the southwest quarter of section seventeen, and has an area of about eighty acres. A portion of Fish lake, about eighty acres, covers a part of the southwest quarter of section nineteen.

in White Pigeon were made in the spring of 1827, the first one by John Winchell, from Wayne county, Michigan, on the 10th of April. He located with his family on the west end of the prairie. The second location was by Leonard Cutler, from Indiana, who came with his family to the east end of the prairie in May of that year. After these two pioneers came a third, Arba Heald, from Wayne county, who also located at the eastern end of the prairie.

Winchell and Heald came first to the prairie in the fall or winter of 1826, and made their selections, and returned to Monroe for Winchell's family,—Heald returning with Winchell in April, and remaining a portion of the summer, bringing on his own family in January, 1828.

The land was not then in the market, not having as yet, previous to the arrival of Winchell and Cutler, been subdivided into sections,—the townships and ranges only being determined. The subdivision into sections was perfected during the summer of 1827.

These three pioneers divided the prairie between them, or a certain portion thereof, by striking two furrows across the same, to mark the respective bounds of their claims. Winchell built himself a cabin, as did also the other two as soon after their arrival as it was possible to do so, the same being in the edge of the timber which flanked their prairie land.

The families of these first pioneers of St. Joseph county were as follows: Mr. Winchell had nine children, viz.: Elizabeth, who afterwards married Samuel Markham; David Winchell, who married Mary Ann McInterfar, the daughter of the first settler in Lockport township; Lyman Winchell, William Winchell, Martha, who married James Knapp in 1828, the first marriage in the county; John, Cynthia, Angelina, and James. In the fall of 1833 Judge Winchell removed to Door prairie, in Laporte county, where he died December 20, 1836. Of his children but three are living,—Mrs. Markham and John in California, and Mrs. G. W. Reynolds (Cynthia) in Kingsbury, Indiana, within half a mile of the mill her father built after leaving St. Joseph county, and where he died. Mr. Winchell was the first postmaster in the county, and also first justice of the peace, being appointed while all of southwestern Michigan was but one township (St. Joseph) in Lenawee county. The post-office was called Millville, and was established in 1828. Mr. Winchell was also the first mail contractor on the Chicago road between Coldwater and Niles, and carried the mail once a week each way in summer, and once in two weeks in winter, on horseback. His log cabin was built on the north side of the Chicago trail, and his blacksmith-shop on the south side, just in the edge of the timber. He was an Eastern man, his wife being a native of the same section of the country. He was very accurate and prompt in his business transactions, and was a "Christian in precept and example," as is testified to by those who knew him best.

Leonard Cutler was a native of Bennington, Vermont, and shortly after his marriage, in 1811, emigrated to Canada; but when the war broke out between Great Britain and the United States he left the Canadas and moved into New York, joining an artillery company in the United States army, and doing good service therein. He moved into Jennings county, Indiana, after the close of the war, then an unbroken wilderness, where he remained five or six years, in the mean time clearing up, mostly with his own hands, a heavily timbered farm. In May, 1827, as before stated, he came to St. Joseph county, arriving on White Pigeon prairie on the 18th day of that month. His family consisted of his wife Mercy and several children, three only of whom are living: Merice D., the oldest son, at Waukesha, Wisconsin, of which he was and is one of the principal proprietors; John, a physician, who emigrated to California in 1849, where he served with distinction in the

State legislature, and held the position of county judge for several years; Alonzo R., who now resides at Laporte, Indiana.

Mr. Cutler left St. Joseph county in the spring of 1831, and settled on Door prairie, in Indiana, selling the lands he had bought at one dollar and twenty-five cents per acre at a large advance,—the entire sale bringing three thousand dollars. He lived on his second location for several years, and then moved again "into the west," and settled at Decorah, Iowa, where he still resides, at the advanced age of ninety-seven years. A single incident in the journey of Mr. Cutler to White Pigeon prairie will illustrate his tenacity of purpose. He was stricken down with fever on the road, and, after journeying as long as possible, the wagon was drawn up beside the trail and the sick man lifted out and laid upon an improvised bed to die, as his family feared. As soon as the sons could command their feelings sufficiently to ask the question, they inquired what they should do with him in the event of his death,—where they should bury him? He replied, "Not here, but on White Pigeon prairie; there is where I started to go, and there I am going, dead or alive. If I die, put me in the wagon and take me to that prairie and there bury me. But I'm not going to die now,"—and he did not. They came to the spot they afterwards selected for a home, and Mr. Cutler was soon himself again. He was ministered to by an Indian, who gave him some medicament he had himself prepared after the Indian formula, preceding its administration by an offering of tobacco to the Great Spirit by burning the same in the fire, and praying to the Manitou. A Dutchman named Kimball, who was sick at Cutler's cabin, and was cared for by him and his wife, loaned Cutler the money to enter his claim, and shared with the latter in the purchase. He bought eight hundred acres.

While on the trail from Tecumseh they were mired-down in the marshes several times, and had to cut down the banks of the streams to get in and out of the same, and cut the trees down sometimes to get through the thicker part of the woods. One night, just before sunset, the wagon, which was drawn by two yoke of oxen and two yoke of cows, mired in the middle of a wet marsh, and there was not time enough to drag it out before dark, and therefore the boys unhooked the cattle from the wagon, and putting their mother and father on one team—the children taking such things as were needed for camping-out and supper—rode the other yoke of oxen, and, with St. Paul and his companions at Melita, "so they all got safely to (dry) land." The boys, however, concluded to get the wagon out that night, and not have the disagreeable job disturbing their dreams, and so, cutting poles, they pried up the wheels out of the mud, and the team dragged the wagon out ready for a fresh start in the morning. The Cutlers' daughter Mary was the first white child born in the county.

Arba Heald was a native of Maine, and came to White Pigeon in 1828, as before stated, with his family, consisting of his wife and five children, viz.: Sarepta E., William, John V., Jane C., and Norris McK., of whom but two are living at the present time,—Jane, now Mrs. D. Kimball, of Door village, Laporte county, Indiana, and Sarepta, now Mrs. Samuel D. Hall, of Roxbury, McPherson county, Kansas. Two children were born in White Pigeon to him,—Eleanor, August 10, 1829, now Mrs. Griffin Drone, of Roxbury, Kansas, and Eldredge, December 30, 1831, now deceased.

The only son now living, Edwin C., of Roxbury, Kansas, was born in Laporte county, Indiana. Mrs. Heald was a native of Essex county, New York, where she and Mr. Heald were married in 1818. In 1820 they removed to Pennsylvania, thence to Ohio, and from thence, in 1825, to Monroe, Michigan, and from thence to White Pigeon.

Mr. Heald removed to Door prairie in June, 1832, having disposed of his location to Dr. Isaac O. Adams. He built a saw-mill, and was a most useful man in his day, dying in 1853.

Mrs. Heald died in Door village in 1869. When Winchell and Heald had reached the western edge of the White Pigeon prairie, in the latter part of the year 1826, Heald said, "Winchell, right about face! We have gone far enough! This location is good enough for anybody!" And thereupon the two retraced their way to Monroe, Winchell coming back in April of 1827, accompanied by Heald, and Heald returning for his family, whom he brought back with him in January, 1828, arriving near the last days of the month.

The next comer to the prairie after the tripartite division of the land was Dr. David Page, who was the first physician in the county. He was an unmarried man, of an extremely youthful appearance, and was accompanied by a brother, Reed Page; they built themselves a house of logs, not far from the present site of the village of White Pigeon, westerly therefrom.

Joseph Olds came in the same fall (1827), and located on the north bank of the Pigeon, on what is now included in the White farm.

Asahel Savery came to the prairie in December of that year, and built the east wing of the "Old Diggins," as it was afterwards known, in 1828, and opened the first house for public entertainment in the county.

From that time onward the settlement increased rapidly. Including the little village, the following were among the early settlers on the prairie: James Knapp, Beckwith and family, Luther Newton, and Peter Klinger and family, and Billy Naggs, a trader on Indian prairie, one mile south and west from the village,—all came in 1828. The three brothers Phelps, who first began Nottville, came in 1828-9.

Samuel Pratt and Philander A. Paine came in May, 1829, and when they came they found, besides those before mentioned, the following here before them: John W. Anderson, register of probate and deeds; Duncan and David Clark, brothers; and Robert Clark, Jr., United States surveyor. Orrin Rhoades and his family came in September of the same year; when they arrived, Lewis Rhoades, who has resided in the same township nearly fifty years, says there were, besides those already mentioned, Hart L. and Alanson C. Stewart, D. Keyes, —— Crawford, —— Selden, and Joseph Martin, William Rowen, —— Lawrence. Robb and Murray were on the prairie or vicinity, and John Coates came in the same fall, as did Neal McGaffey, the first lawyer, who was soon after followed by his brother-in-law, Joshua Gale. Dr. Hubbel Loomis, the first probate judge of the county, came in the summer of 1829. Between Rhoades' advent and Kellogg, April 30, 1830, the following came in: Robert Weale, a Yorkshireman,—as were Coates and Rowen,—Orrin Thompson, a brother-in-law of Savery; Benjamin, or as he was sometimes facetiously called, "Dr." Franklin, and Mr. Neal, father of McGaffey's and Gale's wives. Samuel A. Chapin, C. B. Fitch, Erastus Thurber, Daniel Robinson, Lewis B. Judson, J. W. Coffinberry, Rev. William Jones,—the latter the first Presbyterian minister in the county,—Thomas, and his nephew Armstrong, a tanner; Crippen, a shoemaker, and Roberts, a blacksmith, all came in 1830. Dr. Isaac O. Adams and his family of boys, Isaac, Wm. H., George, and Washington, came in 1831, and the doctor bought out Arba Heald, who went to Indiana. Mr. Bull also came in 1830, and went into trade with the Kelloggs, and was followed in 1831 by Elias S. Swan, John S. Barry, and I. W. Willard in the mercantile line—Niles F. Smith having had the precedence over all in that line, and was in trade when Kellogg came in April, 1830, and had, as Kellogg writes, "a one-horse store with a wheelbarrow full of goods;" but Mr. K. probably speaks satirically as to the quantity of stock on hand, for P. A. Paine, in 1830, finds it valuable enough to trade land for it. & P. Williams, now of Lima, Indiana, was a resident-merchant of White Pigeon in 1831-2, and subsequently formed a co-partnership with David or Duncan Clark. Dr. W. N. Elliott came to the village in 1832, in the spring of the year, and Peter and George W. Beisel in 1831.

Of these old pioneers but two are still living in White Pigeon,—Dr. Elliott and George Beisel. Mr. Willard, who was subsequently the clerk of the courts until they were held in Centreville, is now residing at Pawpaw, Van Buren county. A. Savery, when last heard from, was in Texas; Robert Clark, Jr., died in Monroe in March, 1837, aged only twenty-eight years, and David Clark died at White Pigeon the 19th of the same month. Lewis B. Judson resides in Oswego, Kendall county, Illinois, and the sons of Dr. Adams are in Chicago. Whether any of the others are living we do not know, while on the contrary we do know that the greater portion of them are dead. The first emigrants previous to 1830 were mostly from Wayne county, Michigan.

### THE FIRST FARMS

opened on the prairie were those of Winchell and Cutler, who broke up the new sod and planted corn, potatoes and buckwheat, sowing wheat in the fall. Cutler had a strong team—three yoke of oxen and two of cows—and he broke up several acres.

The first entries of public lands in the present limits of the township were as follows: The east half of the southwest quarter of section five, Arba Heald; the west half of the southwest quarter of section five, and the east half of the southeast quarter of section six, Robert Clark, Jr.; the west half of the southeast quarter of section six, John W. Anderson and Duncan R. Clark; the southwest quarter of section six, and the northwest fractional quarter of section seven,—three hundred and seventy-one acres,—Asahel Savery; all on the 24th day of October, 1828. The east half of the southeast quarter of section nine, Luther Newton and John Winchell, November 29; and the east half of the northeast quarter of section six, Leonard Cutler, December 11, 1828; which were all there were in 1828, there being nineteen made in 1829. Judge Winchell's entries at the west end of the prairie were made on January 25, 1829, and were the east half of the southeast quarter of section three, township eight, range twelve—those first named being in township eight, range eleven.

In 1873 three thousand and thirty-three acres in wheat produced twenty-four thousand six hundred and sixty-eight bushels, and two thousand one hundred and eleven acres of corn, forty-nine thousand six hundred and eighty bushels. The crop of 1873 also yielded one thousand six hundred and five bushels of other grain, six thousand one hundred and sixty-one bushels of potatoes, one thousand four hundred and thirty-three tons hay, five thousand six hundred and sixty-six pounds wool, fourteen thousand four hundred and eighty-five pounds pork, thirty-two thousand four hundred and twenty pounds butter, three thousand four hundred and eighty-six pounds dried fruit, six hundred and ninety-nine barrels cider, and ten thousand six hundred and sixty-five bushels of apples and other fruit. There were owned in the township at the same time three hundred and sixty-nine horses, four mules, three hundred and thirty-six cows, two hundred and ninety-three head of other cattle, eight hundred and seventy-two hogs, and one thousand one hundred and eighty-five sheep. One flour-mill employed three persons, twenty thousand dollars capital, four run of stone, and made eight thousand two hundred and ninety-three barrels of flour, valued at sixty thousand five hundred and thirty-eight dollars.

In 1876 there were fifteen thousand eight hundred and seventy-six acres of land assessed at four hundred and twenty-eight thousand and sixty dollars, by G. B. Markham, the supervisor of the township, which is held to be from one-fourth to one-third of the real value.

The leading farmers of the township at the present time are Peter Putnam, Daniel Shurtz, Henry E. Root, Giles B. Markham, Cornelius Cooper, Welgamwood brothers, Lewis White, an old settler of 1832, Eleazar Tracy, A. W. Huff, and John Catton. Mr. Shurtz came with his three brothers, Frederick, John, and James, in 1836. Frederick served as State senator in 1856. They were from Pennsylvania.

### THE FIRST HOUSE

built on the prairie, as before stated, was that of John Winchell, a log-cabin at the west end of the same. The first frame buildings were erected in White Pigeon village by Samuel Pratt, Hosmer Kellogg, and A. Savery in 1830. Pratt's probably was the first one, as Niles F. Smith had his little stock of goods in it, on the corner where the American hotel now stands, in April, 1830.

The first brick house in the township was built by Dr. Elliott in 1843, and is still his residence. It was one of the earliest, if not the very earliest one, in the county. It was twenty-four by forty-six feet, and two stories.

Neal McGaffey also built a frame house in the latter part of 1830 or 1831, and planted the first fruit-tree in the village—an apple—in 1830; it was next west of W. O. Austin's house and store.

### THE FIRST ORCHARD

was set out by Murray, in the spring of 1829, one and a half miles east, on what is now known as the Tracy farm. The trees were brought from Fort Wayne, and are still bearing.

Cutler planted the first fruit-seeds for nursery purposes in the spring of 1828, occupying three acres. When they were three years old Jones grafted them, and moved them five miles east of Pigeon, on the Dishrow farm, from which nearly all of the early orchards of the county were taken. W. W. Bliss had an orchard in bearing in 1836, at New Lowell, which he set out in 1834. Dr. Isaac Adams sold two thousand apple-trees in 1834, five years old.

### IMPROVED LIVE STOCK

were first introduced into the township by "Father" Elisha White in 1835, being a fine breed of swine, known throughout the county as "White's breed," and some thorough-bred short-horns from Connecticut. Giles B. Markham is a breeder of Alderney cattle at the present time.

The first blooded horse brought to the prairie was a Messenger mare, imported by the father of J. J. Davis, from Ulster county, New York, in 1834.

### IMPROVED FARM MACHINERY

was first introduced on the prairie in 1835, in the form of open-cylinder threshers; fanning-mills coming into use in 1832, and of White Pigeon manufacture too.

The first separator-thresher was brought in, in 1844, by McBaul from New York. The Constantine separators were introduced in 1845–6.

The first reaper introduced was a Kirby, in 1841–2; but it did not do good work, and the next season J. J. Davis and C. C. Newkirk brought in a McCormick, and the first time they hitched the team to it, the novel, noisy thing frightened the horses, and they ran away, breaking up the machine,

8

and the Kirby was brought in to finish the job, while its gay rival was laid up for repairs.

### THE FIRST WHITE CHILD

born on the prairie, and within the present limits of White Pigeon township, was a daughter of Leonard Cutler, who opened her eyes to the light of day in the early part of the year 1828, and was also the first white child born in St. Joseph county. Her name was Mary, and she married a Mr. Hunt, and died near Laporte some years ago.

### THE FIRST MARRIAGE

on the prairie was that of James Knapp and Martha Winchell, in the year 1828, and was the first marriage in the county. This wedding occurred at Judge Winchell's residence on section three, township eight, range twelve.

### THE FIRST DEATHS

that occurred in the township were in 1830; among them were several of the old citizens, who were buried in the little plat laid off by J. W. Coffinberry, and named "Carlton." One of these was a son-in-law of Colonel Selden Martin. Others were buried in the cemetery at Newville in 1831, and before.

### THE FIRST SCHOOL-HOUSE

was built on the prairie—or, rather, near the same—at Newville in the summer of 1830, and was the first building erected in the county for that especial purpose. It was a log house, with primitive seats and desks; and the first school taught in it was in the winter of 1830–1, by a Mr. Allen, who was afterwards the postmaster at the village. Hon. John B. Howe, of Lima, Indiana, taught school in the township at one time; and so too did Columbia Lancaster, in the village, in the spring of 1832.

The school statistics of 1876 make the following excellent showing for the educational enterprise of the township. There are seven school districts in the township, each having a school-house, one of which, the union school-house of the village, is of brick, and the others being frames; and all valued at twenty-four thousand seven hundred dollars.

There are six hundred and three children in the township between the ages of five and twenty years, and four hundred and ninety-three attended the schools, which were in session an average of eight months and over, during the year ending September 1, 1876.

Three male teachers were employed and paid one thousand five hundred and forty dollars for their services, and thirteen females received two thousand and three hundred and sixty-three dollars and sixty cents. The total income of the districts for the year was six thousand seven hundred and eight dollars and seventy-seven cents.

### THE FIRST RELIGIOUS SERVICES

were held at Newville, in the school-house and at private houses, a Methodist class being formed there in the fall of 1829, with David Crawford as class-leader. It was organized by the Rev. Erastus Felton, Rev. Stoddard preaching afterwards. The Baptist church was also first commenced here, and afterwards re-organized and built up in White Pigeon village. A Free-will Baptist minister named Holmes, who came in 1828, lived on Winchell's farm.

### THE FIRST MANUFACTURES

in the township, at least by power other than that derived from human muscle, was the sawing of lumber by Judge Luther Newton, in the fall of 1829, in his mill on Crooked creek, or Fawn river, as now called. This mill was also the first in the county. Newton began its erection in 1828, and built a dam across the creek, but it went out, and with it the foundation of the mill, the superstructure falling to the ground. Nothing daunted, Mr. Newton set about rebuilding it the next season, and completed it, and went to sawing before the close of the year. He afterwards put in a run of small stones, and grinded wheat and corn. Subsequently he sold his property to the Miller brothers, who added a distillery to their manufacturing interests, after 1832, and operated the same for several years.

Weed built the first distillery in the township in 1832, near Miller's. None are now in existence in the township, and have not been for many years. W. W. Bliss built a cloth-dressing and wool-carding factory on the Pigeon, calling his establishment "New Lowell," in 1832. He also, as was the custom in those days wherever there was a water-power in use, put in a run of stones and gristed for the neighborhood.

The first blacksmith-shop built in the township was that of Winchell's, in 1827, at the west end of the prairie. There was one also in Newville in 1829–30, and a shoemaker plied his trade at the latter place at the same time. The first means of getting meal, aside from the ordinary Indian, or pioneer mill, the stump and pestle, was a huge pepper-mill put up against a tree by Arba Heald at the east end of the neighborhood, where, with diligence and a good expenditure of man-power, a half bushel of corn could be reduced in circumference sufficiently to make johnny-cake and samp. Samuel Pratt paid for his board at Cutler's, for a time, in labor at the mill in the summer of 1829.

### CIVIL ORGANIZATION.

White Pigeon township dates its organization coeval with that of the county, on the 29th day of October, 1829, it being one of the three original townships into which the county was divided at its organization. The township, as then organized, included, besides its present limits, the townships of Florence, Lockport, Fabius, Constantine and Mottville, except that portion of Mottville included in township eight, range thirteen, which was subsequently added to the township of White Pigeon, March 3, 1831. In 1833, March 21, the present townships of Lockport and Fabius were set off from White Pigeon, under the name of Bucks, and in 1837, Florence, Constantine and Mottville were set off and constituted into separate townships, circumscribing White Pigeon to little more than a half township.

The first tier of sections in township eight, range twelve (Mottville) was retained by the original township, as a part of the village plat of White Pigeon was located thereon. Subsequently, also, three of the south tier of sections of Florence, (thirty-four, thirty-five and thirty-six, lying east and south of an extensive and impassable marsh, compelling a detour nearly to White Pigeon whenever township business demanded the presence of the inhabitants of those sections at the town-meetings,) were set off to White Pigeon, and are now included in the township.

On the public surveys the township is known as township eight, range eleven west, including sections one, twelve, thirteen, twenty-four, and one-half of twenty-five, township eight, range twelve, and sections thirty-four, thirty-five and thirty-six, township seven, range eleven.

### THE FIRST TOWN-MEETING

was held in April, 1830, at the "Old Diggins"—Savery's hotel—but the township records were destroyed by fire in 1851, and a full list of officers then elected cannot be obtained at the present time. Luther Newton was chosen supervisor, and Neal McGaffey, town-clerk. The position of supervisor has been held since by the following gentlemen: W. W. Bliss, 1831–4 and 1837; H. L. Stewart, 1835; John G. Cathcart, 1836; Daniel Howell, 1838; Washington Pitcher, 1842; R. M. Conover, 1843; Philip E. Runyan, 1844; Edwin Kellogg, 1845 and 1850; William Savier, 1846–9 and 1860; G. G. Depuy, 1851–2 and 1855–6; J. W. Mandigo, 1853 and 1857–9 and 1862, 1865–6 and 1871; J. S. Hamilton, 1854; L. C. Laird, 1861; J. B. Cook, 1863 and 1869; G. W. Beisel, 1864; Peter Putnam, 1867–8 and 1873; E. Blackman, 1870–4; G. B. Markham, 1875–6.

Town Clerks—Neal McGaffey, 1830–31; J. H. Barry, 1832–35; Thomas Charlton, 1836; C. C. Woodbury was town clerk in 1851 when the records were destroyed in his office, which was also burned. Since then the office has been filled one term by each of the following named gentlemen: George Brown, W. O. Austin, W. B. May, G. W. Beisel, J. E. Johnson, John S. Hamilton, J. B. Cook, P. E. Runyan, J. M. Stott, and Edson Blanchard. John Hotchin held the position for seven years, 1859–62, 1865–66 and 1871; L. A. Labadie, 1869–70; J. C. Page, the present incumbent, 1874–1877.

The following named gentlemen have held the position of justice of the peace for more than one term: John Winchell, 1827–33; Neal McGaffey, 1829–35; Albert Allen, 1830–35; J. S. Barry, 1831–33; William Savier, 1840–48; Peter Cook, 1842–56; George G. Depuy, 1863, and still in office; C. C. Woodbury, 1852–60; Lewis Rhoades, 1852–56; George W. Beisel, 1853–57 and 1868 and still in office; Edwin Kellogg, 1853–57; Isaac Runyan, 1860–72; W. O. Austin, 1861–73; J. E. Johnson, 1855–60; John Hotchin, 1869, and still in office.

### THE FIRST ROAD

surveyed through the township was the National military road between Detroit and Chicago, commonly known and called to this day the Chicago road, which passes directly through the township from east to west, forming a magnificent boulevard the entire length thereof, on either side of which lie splendid farms, and elegant farm dwellings and capacious barns rise, giving an idea of wealth and comfort second to no other thoroughfare in the county. Along this broad avenue sprang hostelries in the pioneer days, numerous and in close proximity to each other, running through all the grades of excellence, inferiority and positive badness. There were no less than five of those places of entertainment for the traveling public and the immigrant between White Pigeon and Sturgis, a distance of twelve miles, in the palmy days of stage coaches, in 1836 and onward. Chief among them all, and first on the great trail in the county, was

SAVERY'S "OLD DIGGINS,"

the first instalment of whose afterward extensive proportions, the east wing, was built in the winter of 1827–8. It was a log building, and the resort of all the important personages of early days. Here the electors assembled and met in motion the wheels of government of the new county in the fall of 1829, when the first caucus was held in the county, and Elias Taylor was recommended to Governor Cass as a fit person to take charge of the courts and keep the peace in the sheriff's office; John W. Anderson received a similar recommendation for the position of register of probate and of deeds, and John Sturgis and William Meek were nominated for county judges. Here, too, in this pioneer hotel the first town-meeting was held the spring following, and the election of the fall previous. In 1830 the proprietor added a very respectable frame addition to his log building—the new building becoming the main part of the house. Here the first court held in the county was convened in August, 1830—Hon. William Woodbridge and Henry Chipman, judges, presiding. Here in the shadow of its porch Jacob Knox met his death at the hands of his unfortunate son, who, though entirely innocent of all intentional wrong, has become wretched indeed from the terrible accident that occurred nearly forty-five years ago. In this old hostelry the merry laugh and jocund song have resounded in the olden days, and a motley throng has found entertainment at its generous tables, and rest beneath its wide-spreading roof. Its proprietor owned and operated the

FIRST STAGE-COACHES

on the Chicago road, in 1831–2, and drove them himself, cutting out the roads and building the bridges to get through from Tecumseh to Niles. "Colonel" Savery was a distinguished character, noted for years on the Michigan frontier, on which he was found when it was bounded by Monroe and Brownstown. He picketed the line as it advanced, and in 1835–6 went to Texas and joined the armies of that new republic, fighting under Houston at San Jacinto, when the hero of many legs (Santa Anna) was captured. When the advance moved into Mexico the old borderer was in the front, and never left it until the army of Scott marched back to Vera Cruz carrying their trophies of victory. When the tide of emigration rolled into California, he was on its foremost crest, and as it recoiled and lapped back on Colorado, Nevada and Idaho, the tough old pioneer was the first to "touch bottom" on the ebbs. He drifted back into Texas, from whence he was forced to flee by the rampant secessionists, who would not tolerate the sound unionism of the old fighter for their independence, and he came back to his old love—changed indeed, in feature, but not in spirit, to him—where he was welcomed by the pioneers in their society, and made their first president. He remained in the county until after the war was over, when he returned to his adopted State where he had fought for freedom, and fled from before the wrath of those for whom he helped to achieve it, because he advocated it for all men, white or black, rich or poor—and they would not receive him or his doctrine. If living, he is still a resident of Texas.

The old tavern occupied the present site of the union school-house, and in 1837 was occupied by Rev. Charles Newberry, temporarily, for the purpose of the branch of the University of Michigan, while the branch building was being erected.

The first keel boat ever launched on the St. Joseph river, was built in 1829 just opposite Old's cabin on the Pigeon, and floated down the creek into the St. Joe.

### THE FIRST POST-OFFICE

on the prairie was at Winchell's at the west end of the same, and was called Millville, Winchell being the postmaster, and receiving his appointment in 1828. He also was

### THE FIRST MAIL-CARRIER,

or at least contractor, in the county, carrying the same on horseback between Coldwater and Niles; Savery succeeding him with his stage line. The land office of southwestern Michigan was established here in 1831, and remained until 1834, when it was removed to Bronson, now Kalamazoo. The register was Major Abraham Edwards, and the receiver, Thomas E. Sheldon.

### POPULATION.

In 1838, the inhabitants of White Pigeon, limited then as now, except the three sections from Florence, which were not then set off to the former township, mustered eight hundred and seventy-two souls. In 1850, the township had fallen off in population, seven hundred and ninety-five only being returned as the numerical force of her people. In 1870 the census returns footed up eighteen hundred and thirty-three persons, of whom nine hundred and ten were males and nine hundred and twenty-three females. In 1874 the census-marshal reported but seventeen hundred and thirteen individuals, eight hundred and seventy-nine being males and eight hundred and thirty-four females; four hundred and seventy-six of the males were over twenty-one—one hundred and eighty-four of these last being between forty-five and seventy-five, and ten between seventy-five and ninety years. Two hundred and eighty-five females were between eighteen and forty years, one hundred and ninety between forty and seventy-five, and eleven over seventy-five years of age. Four hundred and three boys under twenty-one, and three hundred and forty-eight girls under the age of eighteen years, constituted the young folks of the township.

### THE POLITICAL DIVISIONS

of the towns-people are evidenced by the way they have cast their ballots at the Presidential elections. In 1840 the Whig electors received sixty-nine votes; the Democratic electors, seventy-one votes. The same relative strength of parties was exhibited in 1844, when the Whigs polled seventy-eight and the Democrats eighty votes, the Liberty men giving James G. Birney two votes. In 1848 the Whigs cast fifty-nine votes, the Democrats seventy-one, and the Free Soilers eighteen. In 1852 the Whigs polled ninety-nine, the Democrats one hundred, and the Abolitionists fifteen. In 1856 the Republicans cast one hundred and forty-nine votes, the Democrats one hundred and forty-six, and the Prohibitionists had a trio. In 1860 the Republicans cast one hundred and eighty-eight votes, the Democrats one hundred and ninety-two. In 1864, Lincoln received one hundred and seventy-three, McClellan one hundred and thirty-two. In 1868 the Republicans polled two hundred and forty-four votes, and the Democrats two hundred and twelve. In 1872 the Republican party cast two hundred and eight, the Greeley men numbered one hundred and eighty-three, and O'Connor and Black paired on two votes each. In 1876 the Republicans gave Hayes two hundred and one votes, Tilden received two hundred and thirty-eight votes, and Peter Cooper had a half dozen. This last vote would indicate a population in the township of over two thousand.

### THE TAXES OF 1830

were fifty dollars for township purposes and a modicum of fifty dollars more assessed on the whole county for its needs. The assessment of 1834 amounted to two hundred and fifteen thousand three hundred and fifty-nine dollars, and the taxes were two hundred and twelve dollars for county, and eight hundred and ninety five dollars for town purposes. In 1836, when the first State tax was levied, the assessment of the township was placed at two hundred and forty-five thousand and thirty-six dollars,—and its taxes were for State purposes, six hundred and twelve dollars and fifty-nine cents; for county and town, seven hundred and sixty-five dollars and fifty-nine cents. In 1876 the assessment stood at three hundred and ninety-nine thousand and ninety-eight dollars on real-estate, as fixed by the county board of equalizers; one hundred and twelve thousand five hundred dollars on personal property—a total of five hundred and eleven thousand five hundred and ninety-eight dollars, and on this amount taxes were levied for State and county purposes two thousand and six hundred and thirteen dollars and forty-six cents—equally divided between the two powers; the township taxes, including schools, being more than double that amount.

### THE VILLAGE OF WHITE PIGEON.

The first house built within the present limits of the village of White Pigeon, was Savery's log tavern in the winter of 1827-8, Savery coming to the prairie in December. The original plat was laid out by Robert Clark, Jr., Asahel Savery, Niles F. Smith and Neal McGaffey, proprietors of the land on which the plat was located, viz: the east half of the southeast quarter of section one, township eight, range twelve, and the west half of the southwest quarter of section six, township eight, range eleven. The plat was surveyed and mapped May 6, 1830, and was the first village plat recorded in the county. McGaffey built a frame house that summer, and Samuel Pratt had one up and occupied by Niles F. Smith as a store before the village had been surveyed—being the advance guard of the trade that flowed subsequently through the streets of the village. John W. Anderson, Duncan and David Clark (brothers), and Robert Clark, Jr., were residents of the village previous to May, 1829, and between that time and September following. Hart L. and Alanson Stewart came. McGaffey came in during the fall, and was followed by Orrin Thompson, Lewis B. Judson, J. W. Coffinberry and Rev. William Jones in 1830, and also by Mr. Bull, who, with Edwin Kellogg, opened the first stock of goods really worthy the name. In 1831, Elias S. Swan opened a heavy stock of goods, bringing them in by the way of the St. Joseph to Constantine, where they were unloaded and left upon the bank of the river in the woods over night, without

watchers and were untouched! Barry & Willard came the same year and opened a general stock of merchandise; shortly after them Clark & Williams opened another heavy stock, with drugs included. Bull & Kellogg kept the first stock of drugs in the town. The Stewarts brought a remnant of a stock of goods from Detroit, and stored them during the winter of 1829-30; they were not opened for sale, but were removed in the spring to Mottville. Isaac Adams and Whitaker had a stock of goods, but closed out in the summer of 1832, and were succeeded by Peter Beisel and Melancthon Judson, who came in 1830. Bowman succeeded the last-named firm, and finally G. W. Beisel came into the business, and the firm continued for some years. Washington Pitcher came in 1834, and was with E. S. Swan, and in 1842 went to Constantine.

### MANUFACTURES.

The first manufacturing, aside from blacksmithing, was the making of fanning-mills in the village by Hunt, in 1831-2.

In the spring of 1832 Hunt & Grover also manufactured mills, ten men being employed in both establishments.

Edwin Kellogg made shoes in the end of Savery's stable-loft in 1830, and says that "two down-East Yankees at the same time were doing a *smashing* business in the fanning-mill line." Mr. Kellogg also says that "Lewis B. (?) Judson came to Pigeon with a peddler's wagon well-stocked with goods, and at once built a long low house on the southwest corner of Chicago and Kalamazoo streets, in 1830, and remained there for three or four years, and married Miss Paine and built a house," which was afterwards converted into Kellogg's building.

John Masterman was the first wagon-maker, and Leonard Tainter the second. They operated about 1833 and afterwards.

Woodworth was the first blacksmith, and worked in a shop opposite Savery's.

Augustine Austin was the first jeweler; John I. Brien the first merchant tailor, and Otis Preston the second, the latter in 1833-4.

Lonson F. Dewey was a hatter in 1834, the *Statesman* of September 3, of that year, having his first "ad."

In the early days of the village there was a beet-sugar manufactory established, and stock subscribed, and machinery bought and operations commenced, but it did not prove a success and was abandoned. Dixon was the agent; Chapman Yates, secretary, and S. W. Chapin, treasurer.

In 1838 McGaffey, Chapin and Kellogg dug a race on the Pigeon, and sold power to Levi Baxter, who built the first flouring-mill in White Pigeon village, and Hosmer Kellogg built a saw-mill at the same time. The flouring mill was burned down in 1860 and rebuilt by D. P. Hamilton in 1862. It is now owned and operated by Hamilton, and known as the White Pigeon mills. Mr. Hamilton floured forty-one thousand bushels of wheat in 1876. The mill is forty by fifty feet on the ground and three and a half stories in height, and has four run of stone. The capital invested in the mill and stock to operate it is thirty thousand dollars, and the value of its yearly product about sixty thousand dollars.

Hotchiss & Cooper built a foundry in 1858 and employed eighteen men. It passed through several changes of ownership and finally ceased to be.

Thomas Brown was a blacksmith and bell-maker in 1833.

### THE POST-OFFICE

was first established in the village in 1830, and Albert Allen was postmaster after Mr. Winchell, whose office terminated in 1832. Chapman Yates succeeded Allen, and George W. Beisel was in a short time in 1842, and then W. O. Austin until 1852. Justin Elliott, W. B. May and C. C. Woodbury filled the years till 1861, when Theodore E. Clapp came in for five years and stepped out till 1868, and is still in the possession of the office—Harwood, Sage and Hackstaff dividing the three years that Mr. Clapp was out. The post-office under Allen, Yates and Austin was kept in the building now occupied by Mr. Austin, west of Hotchins' harness-shop.

The business of the post-office for 1876, was as follows: Stamps sold, one thousand nine hundred and eighty-six dollars and sixty cents; money orders drawn, one hundred and eighty-five dollars and seventy-three cents; money orders paid, two thousand eight hundred and twenty dollars and seventy-one cents; two hundred and twelve letters are received and dispatched daily, and eight hundred and fifty papers distributed weekly; twelve mails are received and dispatched daily, two of the office was first established there were two mails per week—one each way over the Chicago road.

C. C. Woodbury committed suicide, while in the position of postmaster, by poisoning, in August, 1860.

HOTELS.

John W. Anderson kept a hotel, and wanted to sell it in 1834. Pratt kept the American some years, and Dr. Rowley opened the "Old Diggins" after Savery left it.

William Watson, father of the Watson brothers, now in trade in that village, built a hotel in 1835-6, and kept it for a time.

Daniel Howell succeeded Rowley in the "Old Diggins," and the Sickels' succeeded Anderson in the Anderson house.

The present hotels are the American hotel, Christman & Bisbee, proprietors; the Railroad eating-ouse, by Jacob Bebee, and the Union house, by Charles Schuler, which can accommodate about one hundred and fifty guests.

BANKS.

In 1838, the people of the village had a very narrow escape from a "wild cat" of formidable proportions, but it collapsed before the final "scratch" came, and was a dead, cold corpse in April of that year. The bills were all prepared, but no cashier had the hardihood, at that stage of the proceedings, to affix his signature thereto, and so pussy had no claws wherewith to tear the people who had been charmed with soft purring and velvety paws. The first corporation of the village, in 1837, issued "shinplasters," but they did not become sufficiently numerous to be either advantageous or otherwise.

The only banking institution in the village is the Exchange bank of A. Clapp & Son, which sold the amount of one hundred and fifty-one thousand four hundred and forty-one dollars and sixty-seven cents of exchange in 1876.

THE RAILROADS.

The Michigan Southern railroad was completed to White Pigeon by the energy and determination of its inhabitants, the same having been located thereto in 1851. Dr. Elliott was one of the most forward citizens in securing the road, and built the eating-house the same year, under fair promises and agreements of the railroad officials, that, if kept, would have secured to the Doctor a competency, but the promises seemed to have been made simply to be broken, and the enterprise resulted badly.

The road ran up to Constantine in 1852, and soon after a connection was made with the Northern Indiana, as detailed in the Lockport history, and the traffic, which for a time increased, passed on and was distributed all along the route.

The business done at the station in White Pigeon in 1876, was as follows: Freight forwarded, twelve millions six hundred and forty-nine thousand seven hundred and eight pounds, including eleven thousand six hundred and fifteen barrels of flour, and one hundred and twenty-five thousand two hundred and twenty-five bushels of grain. Freight received, five millions eighty-seven thousand and sixty-four pounds. Ticket sales, thirteen thousand three hundred and seventy-two dollars and twenty cents. J. W. Sanderson, Esq., the agent of the road, kindly furnishes the above information.

The United States express company has an office at the station, H. J. Davis, agent, and the earnings of the company for 1876, on transportation and collections, amounted to over three thousand dollars.

J. J. Davis and J. L. Davis are engaged in buying grain, and their purchases aggregated for the crop of 1876, up to December 31, 1876, one hundred and twenty-five thousand bushels.

THE PROFESSIONS.

The first physician in the village was Dr. W. N. Elliott, who located therein in the spring of 1832. Dr. Page and Dr. Hubbel Loomis were on the prairie before Dr. Elliott, and are as named in the township history. Dr. Loomis came to the village after Dr. Elliott, and they formed a co-partnership for some years. Dr. Parker was a resident in the town in 1831. Dr. Rowley came in 1834, Dr. Josiah A. Cook next. Dr. James W. Mandigo, a student of Dr. Elliott in 1840, is one of the resident physicians, as is also Dr. Elliott. Doctors Ellis P. Fraser and Robert A. Green, homeopathists, are also of the present resident physicians of the village.

The first lawyer to give counsel and advice for a fee, and to practice before the courts of the county, was Neal McGaffey. He was the first resident lawyer of the county, and Columbia Lancaster was the second legal limb. James Eastman Johnson came in 1836, and was followed by Aines, G. V. Mitchell and William Savier, the latter being a resident in the village from 1840 until 1872, when he died. In 1865 Hon. E. W. Keightley opened an office (his first one), in the village, and continued there until 1867, when he removed to Constantine, and was succeeded by D. C. Page, the present lawyer of the village.

The first minister to be settled over a congregation was the Rev. P. W. Warriner, the Presbyterian pastor of 1834, though Revs. Messrs. Jones and

Corey, of the same denomination, had preached in 1830 and before, and Felton and Gurney in 1829.

The first professor of instruction was Rev. Samuel Newberry, principal of the branch of the University in 1837.

BUSINESS OF 1876.

Trade.

Dry Goods—H. E. Fisher.
General Stock—A. W. Murray & Co., S. W. Reynolds, A. Clapp & Son.
Hardware—John Murray, Watson Brothers.
Clothing—R. F. Jarrett.
Drugs and Clothing—Cooper & Mandigo.
Drugs—George C. Brown.
Groceries and Provisions—George E. Salmon & Co., Frederick Buzzell, Frederick Saxe, Jacob Whiteman.
Boots and Shoes—C. Rosenhour, M. Cole.
Millinery—Mrs. McGowen, Mrs. H. Dunwell.
Tobacconists—King & Whitmore.
Agricultural Implements—Loring & Kittle.
Merchant Tailor—John H. McGuire.
Markets—Wimple & Sheaf, William Foster, George Baker.
Lumber—O. P. Arnold.
Grain and Produce—J. J. Davis, J. L. Davis, D. P. Hamilton.
Livery—Thomas Cooper, John Driesbach.
Restaurant—Lewis A. Labadie.
Furniture—J. M. Stott.
Harness—John Hotchins—been in business over thirty years; William Boyer.

Manufactures.

White Pigeon Mills—D. P. Hamilton.
Sash, Doors and Blinds—S. T. Wilson.
Carriages and Wagons—A. W. Wilson, A. J. Fox.
White Pigeon Woolen Mills, established in 1872 by J. A. Rogers—building the first frame school-house, donated by the district to Rogers—George McMilly present proprietor; two-set mill; knitting work done; no weaving, though have looms; twenty horse-power, steam.

Artisans.

Shoemakers—P. O. Bronson, Frederick Kanzeler, James B. Crain.
Blacksmiths—George Jackson, Hugh Folger, Isaac Bourne.
United States Express—H. J. Davis, agent.
M. S. and L. S. Railroad—J. W. Sanderson, agent.
Printing Office—J. O'Brien (history of paper elsewhere).

A fair estimate by different and impartial men, citizens of the village, places the capital invested in business in the village at about one hundred and fifty thousand dollars.

THE SCHOOLS.

White Pigeon made an early move for a superior order of schools. The first one was an ordinary district school taught in the winter of 1830-1, by Neal McGaffey, over Pratt's store, and had a large number of scholars. In 1831 the White Pigeon Academy was chartered, Dr. Isaac Adams, Charles B. Fitch, Albert E. Ball, David Page and Neal McGaffey being the incorporators named in the bill. The house was built in that year—a small, frame building, and the schools taught therein for a time, and also for church purposes, and the early courts were held there in 1832. The building is now used for a stable by Lewis Rhoades.

In 1837 the branch of the State University was established in the village, and a building erected soon after, the school in the meantime being taught in the "Old Diggins" by Rev. Samuel Newberry. When the building was completed, Wilson Grey, an Irishman and a brother and afterwards associate of the editor of the Dublin Freeman, was an assistant.

The school was supported by the State for a time, but the appropriations grew less and less, and finally, about 1846, ceased altogether; and then the building was repaired and fitted up, and a private institution conducted by Rev. C. M. Temple, from 1855-58, and finally abandoned altogether. The town built the house and gave it to the State, but some years ago it was taken down and removed out on the prairie, where the walls that once echoed to the conjugation of Greek and Latin verbs, and the explanations of Euclid's theorems, are mute witnesses of the pailing of the "milky mothers of the herds," and redolent with the smell of clover blossoms and apple blooms. The first district school-house was built in 1844, of brick, Dr. Elliott being the director at the time. Some opposition had been manifested to the building, but the people elected the Doctor, and empowered

HISTORY OF ST. JOSEPH COUNTY, MICHIGAN. 67

him to build a school-house, and he did so forthwith. The Doctor has ever been a warm friend of the public school, and a zealous and efficient advocate of them. The brick school house is now used for a dwelling. Dr. J. W. Mandigo taught a school in Dr. Elliott's office in 1843, during the winter. The first frame house was built by the district in 1857. The old Branch was used for barracks during the war. The frame school-house was used until 1872, when the present elegant structure of red brick was erected and the wooden building was donated to J. A. Rogers for a woolen factory, and is so used at the present time. The new school-house is a model for ventilation, convenience and capacity. A hollow chamber, of some two or three feet wide, passes up from the basement to the floor of the upper story—the third—with grates opening into it on every floor, the foul air thus finding exit through the chimney-stack, with which the chamber connects; the cold air comes into the same from the basement. The house is heated with furnaces, is fifty-three by fifty-six feet on the ground, of three stories and basement, and has five school and one recitation rooms. It has been in use since 1872, and yet there is not a scratch or stain on the walls, but they are as clean and fresh as when the building was first opened.

The first vote for a union school district was carried September 1, 1866, J. S. Hamilton, John Murray, George G. Depuy, Philip Drake, J. W. Mandigo and John Hotchkiss being elected trustees. In 1870 the question of a new school-house began to be agitated, and operations were begun in 1872, and the building completed at a cost of sixteen thousand five hundred dollars; John M. Stott and C. C. Newkirk, building committee.

The school is divided into six departments and eleven grades, as follows: The first primary, grades one and two; second primary, grades three and four; first intermediate, grades five and six; second intermediate, grades seven and eight; grammar and high-school department, grades nine to twelve. The course of study comprises two years in each department, promotions being made on merit. Professor Ploughman, the present principal, has invented a very simple and effective record of attendance, which is kept by the pupil himself, and shows at any hour of the day the standing of every pupil in that particular respect. Professor Ploughman came to the school in 1870, teaching in the old building for a time previous to the building of the new one, and is as popular and thorough as an instructor as he is courteous and modest as a gentleman. His popularity is attested by the fact that every tax-payer in the district signed a petition for his retention as principal, two years ago, when it was feared that the non-action of the school-board was likely to cause his engagement elsewhere.

The cost of the school for the year 1876 is here shown. The school was in session ten months, and three hundred and ten pupils attended it. One male teacher was paid one thousand two hundred dollars, and four females one thousand three hundred and eighty dollars. The total income of the district was five thousand seventy-three dollars and sixty-six cents, including two hundred and sixty-eight dollars tuition fees from foreign pupils, and one thousand five hundred dollars was paid on indebtedness. The total expenses covered the income. The house and grounds are valued at twenty thousand dollars, four hundred sittings are furnished, five hundred and fifty-three volumes are in the library, and the school has some apparatus.

The graduates of the high school are Katie Millar and John G. Shurtz in 1874, and Hattie Arnold, Livonia Beard and Ella Putnam in 1875. The present corps of teachers are Professor J. G. Ploughman, principal; Miss Anna West, assistant in grammar school; Miss Libbie Cairnes, second intermediate; Mrs. S. E. Ferguson, first intermediate; Miss Cora E. Folwell, second primary; Miss Lina Cairnes, first primary.

School-board, 1876–7—Robert A. Greene, moderator; J. M. Stott, director; T. E. Clapp, assessor; J. J. Davis, J. L. Davis and Peter Putnam.

A lyceum connected with the school meets every Friday evening in the upper hall, where a social time is had from seven to eight o'clock, and music and literary exercises from then till nine o'clock, under the supervision of the professor.

THE CHURCHES.

Not only was White Pigeon the beginning of civilization in southwestern Michigan, but the beautiful prairie witnessed the commencement of all the arts, amenities and advantages that follow in its train. Trade, manufactures, the church, the school, the State—all had their inception here for the large tract of country ceded by the aborigines in 1821 to the general government. The first merchant, manufacturer, school-teacher, minister and politician, who plied his calling in that section of the territory acquired as above, commenced on White Pigeon prairie, and that between 1827 and 1830. The first religious society formed in that territory was a Methodist class, at Newville, in 1829, as before stated. The second one was also a similar class, formed in White Pigeon village, in February, 1830, with Captain

Alvin Calhoon as leader. The detailed history of early Methodism will be found in the general history of the churches in the county. This class, which was the beginning of the

METHODIST EPISCOPAL CHURCH,

of White Pigeon, of to-day, was composed of the following members: Alvin Calhoon, leader; Alanson Stewart, local-preacher, and his wife; John Bowers and wife, John Coates and wife, and David Rollins. The first church was built in 1832, and was a small frame building. The Methodist conference was held in it in 1841—Bishop R. R. Roberts presiding; H. Colclasa, secretary. In October, 1839, James V. Watson was appointed to this charge, and when his appointment was announced in the conference, he jumped upon a seat and inquired who could show him where his "Pigeon" was. He succeeded in finding not only what he sought, but was instrumental in leading many other anxious inquirers to the Heavenly Dove, before his charge was completed over this church. He became distinguished as a preacher, and was the first editor of the *Northwestern Christian Advocate*, of Chicago, and died in that city October 17, 1856.

White Pigeon, in the early days, was the headquarters of Methodism in Southwestern Michigan, and in 1833 the society there was a flourishing one. The historical records of this society have been very meagerly kept, and what facts we have gained of interest have been gathered from other sources than itself. The record of ministers is simply *nil*. M. H. Dougherty was over the charge since 1855; S. P. Ferguson, 1875–76, and James Webster, the present incumbent, came in October, 1876. The church, which has been re-built once or twice, is now valued at forty-five hundred dollars, and contains two hundred and fifty sittings. There are fifty-nine members on the church-roll. The Sunday-school, which was organized several years ago, has enrolled one hundred and eighty scholars, Professor Ploughman being its superintendent. The society was first incorporated February 1, 1839, and Robert Wade, Alvin Calhoon, John Coates, Alanson Stewart, Alfred Allen and Peter Beisel elected trustees.

THE PRESBYTERIAN CHURCH

of White Pigeon was organized August 8, 1830, by the Rev. William Jones, and was the first church of that denomination in western Michigan. The ruling elders of the church were Benjamin Blair, David Clark, Neal McGaffey, James Mathers and James Blair; and besides these were the following members: Mrs. Elizabeth Blair, Mrs. David Clark, Mrs. McKibben, Martha Waterman, Mrs. Sarah Mathers, Abijah C. Seeley and wife (Jane), Alexander McMillen and Susannah his wife, John and Rebecca Gardner, Hannah McGaffey, Mahala Gale, Hannah Stewart, Mrs. Benjamin Blair, James S. Anderson, Patience McNiel, Francis Jones and Sarah Bronson. These persons came from all parts of the country—as far away as Prairie Ronde, and east, west and south for an equal distance; and many of them afterwards entered into the organization of the early churches in the localities of Elkhart, Constantine, Prairie Ronde and other more distant points.

The first church edifice was built in 1834, and though re-modeled, it has remained ever since the place of worship of this society. The cost when first built, in 1834, was nineteen hundred dollars. It had the first steeple ever erected west of Ann Arbor, and its bell was the first one to call to prayers the pioneers, and whose titillating tones reverberated in western Michigan. The society was organized under the statute, January 16, 1833, when Elijah White, Nicholas B. Chapin, Hubbel Loomis, Charles Kellogg, Lewis B. Judson and William Rowen were elected its first trustees. The certificate was sworn to before W. H. Welch, justice of the peace, by David Clark and Mr. Chapin. The regular pastors of the church have been as follows: The first two preachers, Revs. William Jones and Christopher Corey, were not regularly installed, but, as were others in after years, stated supplies; P. W. Warriner, 1834–39; H. H. Northup, 1841–45; William Fuller, 1845–47; Rev. C. M. Temple, 1858–68; L. M. Gilliland came early in 1871, and still occupies the desk. Julius Steel supplied the desk from 1839 to 1841; Mr. Lantz, a German Reformed minister, for a time between Mr. Fuller and Mr. Temple, and J. B. Hubbard between Mr. Temple and the present pastor.

A Sunday-school was organized soon after the church was built, but no record exists of its early history or membership. In 1866, and again in 1867, interesting meetings were maintained, and several united with the church. In 1873 there were twenty-five admissions, and in April, 1876, fifty joined the church upon confession of faith. The latter work commenced in the Sunday-school in Christmas week, 1875. By request of Superintendent Loring, the teachers in the school made a personal written appeal to each of their scholars in regard to religious matters, which awakened an interest, and meetings were held all through the winter with the above-named gratifying results. The present membership of the church is about sixty, and the Sunday-school has enrolled one hundred and fifty scholars, and has two hundred volumes in the library.

The present church edifice has three hundred sittings, and is valued at five thousand dollars. The present officers of the church and society are as follows: Ruling elders, Isaac Blue, George K. Loring, J. K. Bothorf, and John Blue; Trustees, George K. Loring, J. L. Davis, Francis Putnam, J. K. Bothorf and Isaac Blue; Superintendent of Sunday-school, George K. Loring. The first church was dedicated January 1, 1835—Reverends Humphrey, Warriner and Brown officiating; Rev. Warriner was installed as pastor at the same time. A large audience was present.

### THE BAPTIST CHURCH

of White Pigeon dates its organization in 1843, at Crooked creek, when P. O. Bronson was the superintendent of a union Sunday-school, in which he was engaged for eight years. Debates arose on the question of baptism; and several discussions were had pro and con, and sermons preached on the subject by Methodist, Episcopal and Baptist divines. When Mr. Bronson came to that village, Dr. Elliott, Mr. Cooper, Dr. Mandigo and others told him if he would get Elder John Sage to preach, they would help to build a church for him; and thereupon arrangements were made and the Elder came at a salary of eight hundred dollars; five-eighths to be paid by the society, and the balance by the church aid association, of Brooklyn, New York. The salary was raised and the church mostly built by the parties outside of the membership of the church, in 1857, under Elder Sage's pastorate.

The society was first organized in 1854, by Elder Sage, with the following members: Elder Johnson, wife and wife's sister, Mr. Wright (clerk) and wife, Justin Elliott (deacon) wife and mother, P. O. Bronson (deacon) and wife, Mrs. Raymond, Mrs. Kelley, and one other whose name is not remembered. Of these members, P. O. Bronson and wife only remain in White Pigeon. At the next covenant meeting, held four weeks afterwards, as many more united with the church.

The meeting to raise Elder Sage's salary and take subscriptions for the building of the church, was held in the office of the American hotel. The society was first incorporated on March 8, 1864; J. W. Mandigo, Charles Cooper, and P. O. Bronson, trustees. The old church was sold to the Lutheran and German Reformed churches in 1867, during which year the present spacious and elegant brick structure was erected, costing twelve thousand dollars, with three hundred sittings, and which is at the present writing (1876) entirely free from debt. The bell weighs one thousand two hundred and thirty pounds net, and cost five hundred dollars. The church numbers one hundred and seventy-six members. A Sunday-school was organized in 1857, under Elder Sage's pastorate, and Charles Cooper was the first superintendent, there being twenty scholars. Edwin Sage, Daniels, Stevenson, Fieldhouse, and Douglas Smith succeeded Cooper; George E. Salmon being the present superintendent. The school now numbers two hundred and twenty-five scholars, and has three hundred and fifty books in its library. Under Elder Emery's preaching, a large number of the scholars united with the church, and in 1875, under Mr. Palmer's preaching, thirty-one joined the church. The pastors of the church have been as follows: Elder Johnson was the first one in 1854, and he was succeeded by Elders Cook, Sage, Fish, Emery, Olney, Hill, Davis, Shanafelt, Reis, Russell, Adams, and Hendricks, the present pastor.

### THE CATHOLIC CHURCH

in White Pigeon was first organized under the mission of Notre Dame, at South Bend, in 1850, and the early members were Mrs. Dickey, John Welch and family, Widow Queenan, Thomas Hogan and family, George Argos and family, Fenton Hogan, John Hogan, Thomas Kelly, Michael Carty, Judith McGuire and family, John Propst and family, and others. Previous to 1850 services had been held occasionally by Fathers Quentin and Shortus, from 1848 to 1850. Father Rickert was the first priest in charge, but located at Coldwater.

In 1856 the church came under the jurisdiction of the diocese of Detroit. Fathers Schilling and Carley began the collection of money for a building-fund, and in 1871 the present edifice was erected at a cost of one thousand three hundred dollars, and will seat about three hundred persons. Father McKinney succeeded Carley, and Father McKerni, the present priest in charge, succeeded McKinney. The station is still located at Coldwater. There are two hundred members in the church. A Sunday-school was or-

ganized at the same time as the church, and now numbers fifty scholars, and is under the direct charge of the priest.

### THE GERMAN REFORMED CHURCH

of White Pigeon was organized June 19, 1865, by Rev. Henry Weigand, in a school-house two miles west of the village. Mr. Weigand remained as pastor of the church until 1872, and the desk was supplied as opportunity offered until May 10, 1874, when Rev. E. B. Willard, the present pastor, was settled over the church. Since Mr. Willard's settlement with this church, there have been thirty-five members received into its communion, the present membership being eighty. Their Sunday-school was organized September 12, 1875, and numbers ninety scholars. The old Baptist church is occupied jointly with the Lutheran church by this society, they having purchased the same in 1867, the two societies alternating on succeeding Sundays.

### THE EVANGELICAL LUTHERAN CHURCH

of White Pigeon was organized September 29, 1866, by Rev. P. Bergstresser.

The following were the constituent members: George Gortner, Evan C. Bittenbender, Mary Gortun, James S. Gortner, Mary E. Gortner, Elizabeth Antis, Christian Rosenbauer, Jacob Gentzer, T. H. Ocker and I. E. Ocker. Mr. Bergstresser was succeeded in the pastorate by Rev. J. N. Barnett, in 1867, who in turn was succeeded March 1, 1874, by Rev. Alexander McLaughlin, the present pastor.

The present number of members is thirty-eight. Since its organization one hundred and nineteen members have been received into the church, from which twenty-two were called away to form a church at Van Buren, and twelve or fifteen have gone to Constantine. A Sunday-school was organized by Mr. McLaughlin, December, 1875, which now numbers eighty scholars. The society occupy, on alternate Sundays, the old Baptist church, which was purchased jointly with the German Reformed church, December 19, 1867.

### THE CEMETERY

in the village was primarily laid out in 1830, by the original proprietors of the village, and has since been enlarged to its present area—ten acres. The ornamentation is that which has been done by private parties. The first interment was a child of Duncan or David Clark, and the second a child of John G. Cathcart, the latter in 1832. Mr. Cathcart's whole family, save himself and two children (the only survivors), are all buried in this plat. Many persons have been brought from long distances for sepulture in this cemetery, being either old settlers or their children. In the fall of 1830, a child of Dr. Loomis was buried here.

### ASSOCIATIONS.

Among the pioneer societies of White Pigeon was a female benevolent society, which was in operation in 1834, and which held a fair in December of that year. The Statesman, in a very flattering notice of its exhibition, mentions the various articles exposed for sale in the ornamental and useful line, among which were "cuffs, socks, bosoms for gentlemen, handkerchiefs, mufflers," etc.

A lyceum was organized in 1836, and on December 9 met at the academy and discussed the momentous question whether or not Brutus was justifiable in killing Cæsar. The Constantine Republican, which announced the debate, did not state whether Brutus received absolution for the wound from which "great Cæsar's soul gushed out," and whose fall brought down the house of Marc Anthony and the Roman rabble with it.

In 1830 a lyceum was also in operation, and a more interesting question was discussed, which was, whether the then existing military system of the United States should not be abolished. A. R. Cutler, a non-commissioned officer in the Michigan militia, took the affirmative, and clinched his argument by saying, if the system was abolished he, being an officer, would be personally a loser thereby; but, nevertheless, he was willing to sacrifice the chance of "seeking glory at the deadly, imminent breach," and forego the renown there might accrue in the Michigan militia for the general good of the country.

In 1838 the farmers of the surrounding country met at White Pigeon, on January 27, to consult relative to the formation of an agricultural society, and adjourned till February 7, to hear the report of their committee, but the report was never made public.

In February, 1838, there was a movement made for a manual-labor school, under Presbyterian auspices, and a committee was appointed to take the matter under advisement, but the school was never established.

A Young Men's Christian Association was formed that year in the village, and existed for some time, in connection with the churches, and afterwards with the University.

White Pigeon lodge, No. 104, Accepted Free Masons, was instituted under dispensation November 11, 1857, and chartered the following January. Hon. J. Eastman Johnson was the master from 1857 to 1860, inclusive; George O. Depuy, 1861–6; Robert A. Greene, 1867–9; J. W. Mandigo, 1870; George K. Loring, 1871–2; George E. Salmon, 1873–5. Hon. J. Eastman Johnson was the D. G. M. of the State in 1862, and G. M. in 1863.

In 1867 the lodge, in conjunction with sister lodges of Sturgis, Constantine and other places, celebrated with *éclat* St. John's Day, Hon. S. C. Coffinberry being the orator. The ladies of the Presbyterian church realized a handsome sum from their refreshment stands.

The present officers are Robert A. Greene, W. M.; W. S. Dow, S. W.; W. T. Bycroft, J. W.; T. E. Clapp, treasurer; George K. Loring, secretary; D. C. Page, S. D.; George Pike, J. D.; N. H. Lenhan, tiler. The craft number eighty workmen.

WHITE PIGEON CHAPTER NO. 82, ROYAL ARCH MASONS, was instituted under dispensation in 1868, and chartered in 1869; Thomas A. Shansfelt was the first H. P.; George G. Depuy, K.; Jacob S. Fox, S. The office of H. P. has been filled as follows: Thomas A. Shansfelt, 1868–70; R. A. Green, 1871–4; David A. Wilson, 1875–6. The present officers are: David A. Wilson, H. P.; George E. Salmon. K.; Hughes Folwell, S.; A. C. French, C. H.; A. Tweedale, P. S.; E. R. Willard, R. A. C.; R. A. Greene, G. W. Pike and A. J. Webster, M. of V.; H. J. Davis, treasurer, and George G. Depuy, secretary. The craftsmen number one hundred and ten.

INDEPENDENT ORDER OF ODD FELLOWS.

White Pigeon Lodge No. 78, was chartered in 1859, and has now ten members. The office of N. G. has been filled by the following gentlemen: T. E. Clapp and L. C. Laird, 1859; Chauncey Garbor and G. W. Beisel, 1860; William H. Bock, 1861; N. H. Garter and J. B. Cook, 1862; David Johnson and J. W. Mandigo, 1863; J. M. Stoit in 1864. George W. Beisel was the grand master of the State in 1865, and representative to the grand lodge of the United States. The present officers are John Murray, N. G.; A. W. Murray, V. G.; David Johnson, R. S.; J. W. Mandigo, P. S., and John Hotchins, treasurer.

White Pigeon Eastern Star Lodge was organized in 1868 with Mrs. William Hackenburg as president, but it soon ceased to work, and was suspended. Good Templars' lodges and divisions of Sons of Temperance have arisen and flourished for a time, and died the usual deaths from non-support, and none are now in existence in the village.

PATRONS OF HUSBANDRY.

White Pigeon Grange No. —, was organized in the fall of 1874, with Daniel Shurts as the first master. The grange now has eighty members, and its present officers are Daniel Shurts, master; C. C. Newell, overseer; F. E. Ferguson, secretary; Thomas J. Hopkins, treasurer; Mrs. Garter, Ceres, Miss Line, Pomona, and Miss Smith, Flora.

THE MUNICIPALITY.

The village of White Pigeon was first incorporated in March, 1837. On May 3 the election of trustees and officers was held, and resulted as follows: Neal McGaffey, president; Melancthon Judson, recorder; trustees: Elias S. Swan, Daniel Howell, W. N. Elliott, Otis Preston, Samuel Pratt and Joseph Skerrett. This corporation lapsed after two or three years, and the village was not again incorporated until April 4, 1865, when the following officers were elected: William O. Austin, president; Joseph Yost, treasurer; William Savier, John S. Hamilton, Charles Cooper, James W. Mandigo, George K. Loring and Oliver P. Arnold, trustees, and Leonard Tainter, marshal.

In 1866 Austin and Depuy were re-elected, and Depuy held the office of recorder until 1872, when G. W. Beisel was elected and is the present incumbent.

The position of president has been filled as follows: 1865–6, W. O. Austin; 1867, J. W. Mandigo; 1868–71, W. N. Elliott; 1872, Edson Blacklin. The present city officials are: J. W. Mandigo, president; G. W. Beisel, recorder; Theodore E. Clapp, treasurer; W. O. Austin, assessor; Thomas Cooper, marshal. Edson Blackman, John Hotchins, John Murray, Giles Markham, Robert F. Jarrett and Samuel Dreisbach, trustees. The *Statesman* of July 19, 1834, says the village then contained five dry goods stores, two churches, one silversmith, three public houses, one shoe and leather store, one chair and two cabinet shops, one tailor and one harness-shop, one tin and one hatter's shop, three doctors and one lawyer, and that a good harvest had been gathered by the farmers by the aid of a little whiskey.

AMUSEMENTS.

The first observance of the Fourth of July in White Pigeon was in the year 1829, which was an informal affair, and consisted simply of a social gathering of about forty persons at Savery's for a dinner. There were no orations, toasts, music, burnt gunpowder, or the other usual accompaniments of the glorious day, but a simple gathering of the pioneers for a visit and friendly chat. In 1832 there was a regularly appointed celebration of the day, to which Coldwater, Niles, Jonesville and other places sent delegations, the former sending also the music. Colonel Selden Martin was the president of the day, and there were about one hundred persons present.

The Fourth was commemorated in fine style in 1835; Robert Clark, Jr., was the president of the day, Henry Gilbert, editor of the *Statesman*, vice-president; Colonel Martin and Major S. P. Williams, marshals; W. Loomis, orator; David Clark, reader; Reverend P. W. Warriner, chaplain; and Charles Kellogg, chorister. The procession moved through the streets to the academy for the oration, and thence to Rowley's—formerly Savery's—for dinner, where toasts and songs were in order after the bill of fare was discussed. In 1837 the White Pigeons celebrated again with Neal McGaffey in the chair, and Dr. Thomas B. Kerr, orator. In 1834 John D. Defrees, at the time editor of the *Statesman*, was the orator of the day, and John W. Anderson, marshal.

On the 22d of February, 1838, there was a grand fox-hunt at Lima, to which place a large sleigh-ride was organized.

INCIDENTS.

During the summer of 1829 Samuel Pratt and P. H. Paine explored Nottawa prairie, not meeting a white man in the two days' expedition, nor an Indian, of whom they could get anything to eat. Their rations were a little corn bread and three or four pounds of smoked shoulder. The nearest mill then was at Fort Defiance, and Paine went that summer with two yoke of oxen to that mill, to procure a load of corn meal and flour and sold it out among the settlers. But, though provisions were scarce, no families were allowed to suffer for necessaries—daintics, of course, were out of the question. Venison hams could be bought at almost any time of the Indians for twenty-five cents, and fish were plenty in the streams and lakes, and were easily caught.

Temptation was as potent in bringing men into disgrace in the pioneer days as now, as will be seen by the following incident: Breadstuffs becoming scarce in 1829, the neighbors on the prairie clubbed together and made up a load of grists, and sent a hired man of Orrin Rhodes' to Niles to get them ground. He arrived safely, but alas! for the weakness of poor human nature and the sin of idleness, the meal-chest of the community was emptied, drunk, he kept up his debauch until the proceeds of the load of grists were nearly consumed; then he returned to the settlement with the pitiful remnant, which was not enough to go around among the senders thereof, and ten days having passed, the meal-chest of the community was emptied, and while a new cargo was being transported and returned, Cutler's pepper-mill was kept in constant use.

Mr. Rhodes was a pioneer in Michigan, in 1795, in Monroe, or French-town, as it was then called. He was a soldier in the war of 1812, and with a brother-in-law fought through the war. Lewis Rhodes, his son, now residing in the village, was born in Monroe in 1820. When Rhodes came to White Pigeon, he brought along two very fine black-walnut boards, with which he made the door to his cabin, and with a shake roof, puncheon floor, mud chinks and brick chimney, he had quite an aristocratic home.

The Kellogg family consisted of five brothers, Edwin, Hommer, Charles, Albert and George, and were noted for all good and public works. Charles was drowned on the little steamer that was built in Union City, and which ran on the lower St. Joseph, on account of which may be found elsewhere. Edwin went to Kansas, and in the famine caused by the grasshoppers he was in the direst distress; no shoes, his feet on the ground, except such protection as an old boot leg could afford. In this extremity his White Pigeon friends sent him money and stores for relief, and he came with an ox-team to Topeka to get the money, and defeated an outrageous attempt to rob him by presenting a determined front,—the trip occupying three weeks.

Peter Beisel and his family, consisting of his wife and five children, traveled from Gettysburg, Pennsylvania, in a wagon with five horses, being six weeks on the road, in the spring of 1831. He came the year before and selected his location, and afterwards opened a large farm in Kalamazoo county, which his son, George W., now a prominent citizen of White Pigeon, managed for him, after trying his hand at harness-making at four dollars per month and board himself. Mr. Beisel, Dr. Elliott and A. T. Drake married three sisters, daughters of James McKinney, a former citizen of Sturgis, who came with his family of six daughters to that village in 1836, from Bing-hamton, New York. He died in 1838.

J. Eastman Johnson, while in White Pigeon, compiled an *Analytical Abridgment of Kent's Commentaries on American Law*, which has run through several editions from the press of New York. Chancellor Kent commended it very highly, as also did Daniel D. Barnard, an eminent jurist of that city. Judge Johnson was one of the regents of the University of Michigan from 1858 to 1870.

In 1828-9 Governor Cass passed through the settlement on his way to Chicago to treat with the Indians for their lands, and stopped over night with Cutler. The governor accepted the luxury of a bed, but his suite camped under the trees. The Indians used to pass through the settlement by hundreds from the west on their way to Malden to receive their annuities from the British government.

Peter Klinger built a large log house near his mill, and the fire-place therein was so huge he used to draw the back-logs into it with his oxen, they standing on the side of the house opposite the door, and the chain running through the house.

### THE MILITARY RECORD

of White Pigeon began to be early written; in the very infancy of the colony it achieved a renown quite equal to any community in the State. Colonel Stewart, Colonel Martin, Colonel McGaffey, Major Williams, and a dozen more were a constellation of stars of no inconsiderable magnitude in the military history of the territory. Colonel Stewart was the commander of the forces sent against Black Hawk in 1832, but did not leave the State, or territory, more properly speaking. He commanded the regiment known as "the Eleventh," and was then elected brigadier of the 6th brigade. Augustus Chapin was the major of the 11th in 1835. The details of the Black Hawk war, and the part borne by the township of White Pigeon, are related elsewhere.

In the war of the rebellion White Pigeon responded to the whole extent of her duty, and filled her quotas with alacrity, paying twenty thousand dollars to encourage enlistments. The 11th infantry, the St. Joseph county regiment, was recruited at White Pigeon, the old Branch building being used as barracks.

We give a brief list of the citizens of White Pigeon who shouldered the musket, or drew their swords in defense of the national government against the assaults of the traitors in arms.

#### SECOND MICHIGAN INFANTRY.

Private John Dale, Company F; missing in action.
Private Henry C. Myers, Company F; mustered out.
Private Thomas G. Olmstead, Company I; died of wounds, in Wilderness, May 6, 1864.

#### FOURTH INFANTRY.

Charles McCollister, quarter-master's sergeant; discharged for disability.
Private William Blanchard, Company C; discharged, expiration service.
Private James S. Greene, Company C; discharged, expiration service.
Private Richard Sage, Company C; discharged, expiration service.
Chaplain John Sage; resigned.

#### SIXTH INFANTRY.

Private Chauncey Miller, Company B; mustered out.

#### SEVENTH INFANTRY.

Private Martin Eighmig, Company K; died June 3, 1862, of wounds received at Fair Oaks.

#### ELEVENTH INFANTRY.

Colonel William J. May; resigned April 1, 1862.
Surgeon W. N. Elliott; mustered-out with regiment.
Quarter-master's sergeant John Underwood; first lieutenant and quarter-master, and mustered-out.
Musician Henry H. Hackenburg; mustered out August 22, 1862.
Musician Henry F. Cliffell; mustered-out August 22, 1862.
Private Martin V. B. Clark, Company A; discharged, expiration service.
Private James F. Bicklin, Company C; discharged, expiration service.
Private Charles E. Barnes, Company C; died at Chattanooga, December, 1863.
Private Warren F. Barnes, Company C; discharged, expiration service.
Private John Fisher, Company C; killed at Stone River, December, 1862.
Private Lorenzo H. Griffith, Company C; discharged, expiration service.
Private Perry Letson, Company C; discharged for disability.
Sergeant William Robinson, Company D; discharged.
Private Thomas R. Hodgkins, Company D; killed near Dallas, Georgia.
Private Charles H. Dalton, Company E; mustered out.

Private William E. Raymond, Company E; promoted and mustered out, 1864.
Private Christ Welgamwood, Company E; mustered out.
Private Peter O. Dowd, Company G; discharged, expiration service.

#### TWELFTH INFANTRY.

Private Henry Heightsman, Company F; mustered out.
Private William R. Kinkead, Company F; mustered out.
Private Orlando Mack, Company F; mustered out.
Private John Ralphsnider, Company F; mustered out.
Private George Schotters, Company F; discharged for disability.
Private Samuel Winslow, Company F; mustered out.
Private Joseph Nichols, Company H; mustered out.

#### SIXTEENTH INFANTRY.

Private Charles Wygant, Company C; died at Alexandria.

#### SEVENTEENTH INFANTRY.

Private Fayette Olmstead, Company H; died November 2, 1863, of wounds received at Campbell's Station, Virginia.
Private Delavan Smith, Company H; mustered out.

#### NINETEENTH INFANTRY.

Private William Eastwood, Company D; mustered out.
Private Thomas Franklin, Company D; mustered out.
Private George Hudson, Company D; mustered out.
Corporal William Haines, Company E; mustered out.
Private George W. Antis, Company E; discharged.
Private William Bachman, Company E; mustered out.
Private Adam Bear, Company E; died at Columbia, Tennessee, March 24, 1863, of wounds received at Thompson's Station.
Private Mathew Daniels, Company E; mustered out.
Private Charles L. Ellis, Company E; mustered out.
Private James Griffith, Company E; discharged.
Private Isaac Green, Company E; died at Columbia, Tennessee, March 24, 1863, of wounds received at Thompson's Station.
Private Burnett B. Harris, Company E; discharged.
Private Henry Holderman, Company E; died at Atlanta, Georgia.
Private Lewis A. Labadie, Company E; promoted to first-lieutenant and mustered out.
Private John Pratt, Company E; mustered out.
Private James A. Prouty, Company E; mustered out.
Private John H. Peirce, Company E; mustered out.
Private William Snooks, Company E; mustered out.
Private Sol. B. Stephenson, Company E; mustered out.
Private George Shultice, Company E; discharged.
Private Moses B. Tice, Company E; discharged for disability.
Private George Willander, Company E; discharged.
Private William F. Whitcomb, Company E; mustered out.
Private George Wagner, Company E; mustered out.

#### TWENTY-THIRD INFANTRY.

Private John G. Greene, Company F; veteran reserve corps.

#### TWENTY-FIFTH INFANTRY.

Private W. M. Kane, Company G.

#### TWENTY-EIGHTH INFANTRY.

Private Theodore Yost, Company H; mustered out.

#### SECOND CAVALRY.

Private Timothy Cloonan, Company D; mustered out.
Private Charles Gardiner, Company D; mustered out.
Private Adam Heightsman, Company D; killed at Lyonsville, Tennessee, December, 1864.

#### THIRD CAVALRY.

Private Daniel J. Weston, Company D; mustered out.
Private Richard Weston, Company D; mustered out.
Private John Jarrett, Company I; mustered out.
Private William Jarrett, Company I; mustered out.

#### FOURTH CAVALRY.

Private Adam Kline, Company F; at capture of Jeff. Davis, and mustered out.

#### EIGHTH CAVALRY.

Private Josiah Flumerfelt, Company E; mustered out.
Private Samuel McGaffey, Company H; mustered out.
Private John M. VanVleet, Company H; enlisted at Camp Nelson, Kentucky, January 8, 1863.

STURGIS
UNION SCHOOL BUILDING AND GROUNDS,
St Joseph County, Michigan

Private J. M. Weatherwax, Company H ; mustered out.
Private Delos B. Freeman, Company L ; mustered out.
Private Silas Billmeyer, Company A ; mustered out.

NINTH CAVALRY.

Private William R. Gillett, Company E ; discharged for disability.
Private Philo H. Drake, Company E ; mustered out.
Private James Isabel, Company L ; mustered out.
Private Albert E. Ellis, Company L ; died at Camp Nelson.
Private Alexander Phillps, Company E ; discharged for disability.

TENTH CAVALRY.

Private James H. Davis, Company G ; mustered out.

ELEVENTH CAVALRY.

Private Stephen J. Myres, Company I ; mustered out.

FIRST LIGHT ARTILLERY.

Corporal Josiah Flumerfelt, Battery D ; discharged, expiration service.
Private Peter H. Stitzell, Battery D ; mustered out.
Private William Conner, Battery D ; mustered out.
Private Jacob Mosier, Battery D ; mustered out.
Private Daniel Saunter, Battery D ; mustered out.
Private John W. Swartz, Battery D ; mustered out.
Private Benjamin Winslow, Battery D ; mustered out.
Junior First-Lieutenant Norman S. Andrews, Battery F ; mustered out.
Sergeant George W. Nash, Battery F ; mustered out.
Corporal Charles A. Sweet, Battery F ; re-enlisted and mustered out.
Private John Miller, Battery F ; re-enlisted and mustered out.
Private L. S. Ellis, Battery F ; mustered out.
Private Charles Stevenson, Battery F ; mustered out.
Corporal Adam V. Thompson, Battery G ; mustered out.
Corporal James McElroy, Battery G ; re-enlisted in regular army.
Private George W. Brown, Battery G ; mustered out.
Private John Kietlin, Battery G ; mustered out.

Private Fred. Kleifish, Battery G ; mustered out.
Private John Myer, Battery G ; mustered out.
Private James Clemson, Battery G ; mustered out.
Private John Huff, Battery G ; mustered out.
Private Peter Snook, Battery G ; mustered out.
Private Charles Swan, Battery F ; died of disease.

FOURTEENTH BATTERY.

Private Charles Ackerman ; mustered-out.
Private Lorenzo C. Cooper ; mustered-out.
Private Henry M. Ellis ; mustered-out.
Private Henry Fitch ; mustered-out.
Private John Hill ; mustered-out.
Private Daniel Swarts ; mustered-out.
Private George A. Shoefelter ; mustered-out.
Private John G. Bronson, 78th New York infantry ; veteran reserve corps.

TWENTY-THIRD ILLINOIS VOLUNTEERS.

Private Samuel Dickey, Company B ; mustered-out.
Private John Bisbey, Company B ; mustered-out ; four years in service.
Private Robert Foster, Company B ; mustered-out.
Private Peter Smith, Company B ; killed at Kernstown, Virginia.
Private —— Conger, Company B ; killed at Opaquie Creek, Virginia.
Private Martin Simmons, Company B ; mustered-out.
Private —— Wade, Company B ; mustered-out.
Private —— Carter, Company B ; mustered-out.
All of the above squad in Company B, 23d Illinois, were with Mulligan, at Lexington, Missouri.

We are under obligations, and tender our acknowledgments therefor, to Dr. W. N. Elliot, George W. Beisel, Dr. J. W. Mandigo, Lewis Rhoades, W. O. Austin, Rev. L. M. Gilliland, Rev. Mr. Hendricks, P. O. Bronson, George G. Depuy and Lewis A. Labadie, for information received and assistance rendered in the compilation of the foregoing history of White Pigeon.

---

# STURGIS.

AMID the unexcelled natural beauty of St. Joseph county, Sturgis prairie stands pre-eminent. Nearly or quite oval in shape, it is, for the greater part of its area, level, although in some portions it is slightly undulating. The original area contained about three thousand acres, a portion of which is now included in the townships of Sherman and Fawn River. Sturgis prairie originally included in the township of Sherman, was not set off therefrom into a distinct sovereignty until 1845, being the last constituted in the county. The township was named from the prairie which is mostly included within its limits, and which received its name from the first settler thereon, Judge John Sturgis. Its area is but a trifle in excess of half a government township, and contains thirteen thousand three hundred and ninety-seven acres of land, and about twenty-five acres of water surface. Its soil is the same fertile, sandy loam common to the St. Joseph valley, and produces abundantly the cereals, fruits and vegetables also common thereto. It is situated high and dry, and is as healthily located as any point in the county, and much more so than some. It is watered but slightly, Fawn river coming in near the southeast corner of the township in the northeast quarter of section twenty-four, and bending like a bow through the northwest quarter of the same section and the northwest and northwest quarters of section 20, retires into Indiana for a new advance into the county further west, in White Pigeon. A little creek rises near the east line of the southwest quarter of section thirteen, and runs westerly, entering the Fawn on the southeast quarter of the northwest quarter of section 21. Green Lake lies on the northwest quarter of the northwest quarter of section 3, and the southern extremity of Johnson's lake hangs over the verge of the township line on the north, with just hard land enough between it and Green lake to make a highway. On the government surveys the township is described as "township eight, south of range ten, west of the principal meridian."

FIRST SETTLERS.

On August 20, 1827, the first ripple of civilization broke upon Sturgis prairie, and left its impression on that beautiful gem of nature. Judge John Sturgis and George Thurston were the advance of the host that was to fol-

low. They broke up ten acres on the eastern edge of the prairie (which is now included in the limits of Fawn River township,) and sowed it to wheat; then returned to Monroe, Michigan, whither Sturgis came, in 1816, from Canada. In the spring of 1828 Mr. Sturgis and his family and Mr. Thurston, who was an unmarried man accompanied by his father's family, arrived on Sturgis prairie, with ox teams, having been twenty days on the road from Brownstown. The weather was rainy, roads bad, and the Hog creek marshes were terrible. They were all of one day in getting a mile through the mire to hard ground, having to unload their goods frequently and carry them to a little dryer—or, more correctly speaking, a little less moist—spot, and reload. Mr. Thurston's family located on Oxbow prairie, a few miles south of Sturgis, in Indiana.

Mr. Sturgis at once proceeded to put up a house on his location, which was the first human habitation for white people built on the prairie. He broke up thirty acres more that summer, and sowed it to wheat. Thus the settlement of Sturgis prairie began. The first settler on the prairie included in the present limits of Sturgis township, was George Buck, who, with his family, came to the present site of the village of Sturgis in the summer of 1828. He was a native of New York State, but removed to Canada in 1812, and from thence to Michigan in 1828, traveling with horses to Detroit, and from Brownstown with oxen. They tented in the Hog creek woods for six weeks while building their house, which was located on the east side of Nottawa street, and north of the Chicago road, (now Chicago street in Sturgis.) Their house was made of rough logs, and had no windows.

The next settlers were: John B. Clarke, Truman Bears and Jacob Hopkins and their families—all of whom came, in the order named, in 1828. David Petty came in 1829, and settled on the prairie, and Ephraim Bears came in the same year. John Parker came in 1830.

PROMINENT SETTLERS.

Beside those already named, among the first settlers were Hiram Jacobs, who came in 1831 ; John S. Newhall and David Knox, in 1832 ; Oliver Raymond, in 1830 ; J. G. Wait, in 1834 ; Major Isaac J. Ulmann, in 1830 ;

9

Luther Douglass, 1833; Rev. J. E. Parker, 1830, now at Washington, D. C. His father, John Parker, and family came in the same time, meeting with a terrible loss of three children by the explosion of the boiler of the steamboat on which they were embarked for Detroit. On arrival at Sturgis the family of Mr. Parker were admitted into the house of Ephraim Bearss, and in the single room which it contained the two families resided until the following spring.

Jacob Pearsoll came in 1831. He and Jacobs, Nathaniel Rathbun, Aaron Gillham, Parker, Washington and Edw. Osborn, Philip Aurner, Michael Welliver, the Newhalls, and Ransom and Henry Mumford, all came from Livingston county, New York—of whom Mr. Parker was the pioneer, he having walked from that county and back on his visit to St. Joseph county.

### THE PRIVATIONS

of the pioneers were such as were incident to the lives of those who are brave enough to tempt the dangers of the wilderness and the loss of the luxury and ease of the older settlements in the eastern States, where their home mostly were. As a general thing the early settlers were young people, seeking to build a home, with little or no surplus means, and must, perforce, wrest the same from nature with steady and vigorous strokes. The border was no place for laggards or cowards, and none but brave, persistent natures would and did succeed in gaining their hearts' desires—a home of their own, around whose hearth-stones have gathered their children in many happy days after the toils and struggles of earlier life were over. The worst trials and most severe sufferings were such as were consequent upon sickness, which could not be avoided in the early days, with any knowledge or skill the people then possessed. John S. Newhall says he had thirty-two ague "shakes" in as many days, and many times has lain down in the furrow, while plowing, until the paroxysm passed its climax, and then resumed his work. In 1847 he helped to bury fourteen persons on the prairie. When the father of Rev. Gershom Day died, the son preached the sermon or conducted the exercises, Mr. Newhall and his hired man being the only persons, besides the son, present. So many people were sick, Newhall could not get a single meal of victuals on a journey from Lima to Coldwater, in September of that year. J. G. Wait also bears testimony to the distress occasioned by the terrible sickness which pervaded the whole country in those years. The convalescent ministered to those less fortunate, while those who escaped the sickness altogether were angels of mercy, untiring in their efforts to ameliorate the condition of their neighbors.

### FIRST LAND ENTRIES.

The first entry of public lands in St. Joseph county was made within the present limits of the township of Sturgis by Ezekiel Metcalf, of Cattaraugus county, New York, June 14, 1828, and was the tract known as the east half of the northeast quarter of section one, township eight south, range ten west. Metcalf sold the tract subsequently to De Garmo Jones, of Detroit, who still owns it. On November 28, in the same year, George Buck entered the west half of the southeast quarter of section one, and on the 18th of December, Ruth A. Clarke, of Fairfield, Conn., entered the east half of the southwest quarter, and Hart L. Stewart, of Pennsylvania, the west half of the southwest quarter of same section. The above named were all the entries made in 1828, and there were but four the year following. The Stewarts came and settled in the county in 1829.

### THE FIRST FARMING OPERATIONS

in Sturgis were those begun by George Buck and Ephraim Bearss, who, in 1829, broke up and fenced a field of seventy-five acres in the eastern part of the town. The plows in those days were run with from four to ten yoke of oxen. Newhall operated one on his farm with four yoke, with a wooden mould-board four feet long. Corn was dropped in the furrow, or chopped through the sod with an axe, and a good crop secured if the season was not too dry.

### THE FIRST HOUSE

in Sturgis was built in 1828 by George Buck, and was made of rough unhewed logs, without doors or windows.

This was afterwards succeeded by a double log house, built by Philip H. Buck, son of George Buck, in 1830, after the latter's death. The upper room of this house was used for some years for church-meetings and schools.

### THE FIRST FRAME HOUSE

was built by Oliver Raymond in 1831, and used by him for a hotel. Clarke's log house was the third house and first hotel on Sturgis prairie.

### THE FIRST MARRIAGE

on Sturgis prairie was that of William Stewart and Mary Cade, in the fall of 1831.

### THE FIRST BIRTH

in the township was that of a little daughter of John B. Clarke, in May, 1830.

The first male child born on the prairie, was David Sturgis, on February 11, 1830; but the farm on which he was cradled is now included in Fawn River township.

### THE FIRST DEATH

which occurred in the township, and which, too, was the first in the county, was a dual one, two victims being taken at once, and suddenly, without previous warning.

On the 9th of August, 1829, about a year after his location on the prairie, George Buck was killed, together with a man named Levi Waterman, by the caving in of a well in which they were at work. The alarm was given, and the people from White Pigeon and Sturgis came to the rescue, but it was too late, death had intervened before they could be extricated. The funeral obsequies of these men were probably the first religious meeting held on the Sturgis prairie.

### THE FIRST SCHOOL

taught in the township, held its session in the upper room of Philip H. Buck's house, in the village, in the fall of 1830. Dr. Henry, who was the first physician on the prairie, was the first teacher, and had for his pupils a large number of young men and women from the region around. The

### FIRST SCHOOL-HOUSE

was built in the village, on the east side of Nottawa and south of Chicago street, as now laid out, in 1833, and was a small log building. This was replaced by a frame building in 1838. The full history of district No. three, in which these school-houses were built, will be found in the history of the village of Sturgis.

### THE FIRST CHURCH

built in the township, was the Methodist Episcopal church, in 1843, a full and complete history of that society, and all others, appearing elsewhere.

### THE FIRST CEMETERY

laid out was the old one in the rear of the Lutheran Church, and west of the railroad. The ground was given to the town by the proprietor of the land, Hiram Jacobs, and the first burial in it was that of a stranger who died suddenly in the summer of 1833. The grave was dug with the hand of it to the north, and the party having the burial in charge insisted on having the direction changed to east and west, which was done. The old cemetery is not used at present, the new one being substituted therefor, a description of which will appear elsewhere.

### THE FIRST IMPROVED FARM MACHINERY

was introduced on Sturgis prairie in 1843-4, by Judge Sturgis, the same being a McCormick reaper, which he brought from Hillsdale. Separator threshers were introduced a little later, open-cylinder threshers being brought in in 1833; previous to which date the farmers trampled out their grain with horses, and winnowed it in the wind.

In 1831 the seed-corn in the country was not good, and seed was obtained in Ohio, for which one shilling per quart was paid. The crop was planted three times, the last time in June, but nevertheless a good crop was harvested. Wheat that year was worth twenty cents per pound, and salt twenty dollars per barrel, and its equivalent in corn was eighty bushels of the latter. The neighbors "clubbed" and obtained a barrel or two, and divided it up.

### IMPROVED LIVE STOCK.

The stock of horses began to be improved about 1840, though the efforts in that direction were confined to good working material, fast "steppers" not receiving much attention for some years later. The interest was general, and no one person can claim particular priority in the first advance. Cattle did not receive much attention until after 1860. Isaac Runyan introduced thoroughbred short-horns from some noted herds in the Eastern States, in 1870. Mr. Runyan has a fine herd now of that stock, and has disposed of several very fine specimens.

### THE FIRST ROAD

surveyed through the township was the great national military road from Detroit to Chicago, described in the general history of the county.

The second one was the territorial road surveyed from the Indiana line north through the county to Grand Rapids, which was laid out in 1833, Rix Robinson, H. L. Stewart and Stephen Vickery being the commissioners. The Chicago road was worked through Sturgis in 1834, James Johnson, a heavy business man now in Sturgis, being the contractor.

### CIVIL ORGANIZATION.

In 1845 the legislature of the State, at its winter session, set off the township numbered eight of range ten west, hitherto included in Sherman township, and called it Sturgis, it being bounded on the north by Sherman, on the west by White Pigeon, on the east by Fawn River, townships, and on the south by the State of Indiana. The first town-meeting was held at the school-house in the village, and John Parker was elected the first supervisor; J. G. Wait, town clerk; William Morris, justice of the peace, and Dr. J. M. Taft, school inspector. The town records previous to 1860 were burned in one of several conflagrations which have devastated the business portion of the village, and a full list of the first officials who set the wheels of the government in motion cannot be given.

The supervisors of the township since then have been as follows: Philip H. Buck, 1846-8 and 1851; William Allman, 1847, 1853, 1855, 1859, 1860-2, and 1866; William K. Haynes, 1849, 1856 and 1858; A. T. Drake, 1850; D. Knox, 1852; William Henry, 1854; Hiram Jacobs, 1863-4; Bracey Tobey, 1865; S. B. Follett, 1867-8, 1870-2; J. G. Wait, 1869; Frank S. Packard, 1873-4; L. E. White, 1875-6.

Among the town clerks, William Allman has held the position two years; Benjamin Fairchild, two years; William L. Stoughton, one year; Henry Leavett, one year; M. Vandusen, one year; Homer Packard, four years; J. B. Jacobs, two years; C. Jacobs, two years; Bracey Tobey, six years; L. E. White, five years; Henry L. Anthony, the present incumbent, two years.

Among the justices of the peace the following have held more than one term of four years: David Knox from 1866 to 1876, inclusive; Bracey Tobey from 1857 to 1877. A. F. Patch is at present holding the position. The town superintendents of schools since the creation of the office, have been P. S. Packard, 1875, and G. D. G. Thurston, 1876.

### THE FIRST ASSESSMENT

of property for taxation in the new township was made in 1845, the same being placed at fifty-five thousand and sixty-eight dollars on real-estate, which the county board of equalization reduced ten per cent., the total assessment standing at sixty-nine thousand one hundred and fifty dollars, on which State and county taxes were levied and paid amounting to six hundred and fifty-six dollars and eighty-eight cents.

### THE LAST ASSESSMENT,

that of 1876, as returned by the supervisor was five hundred and eighteen thousand one hundred and fifty dollars, which was reduced by the county board to five hundred and four thousand four hundred and eighty-eight dollars on real-estate; the personal assessment amounted to one hundred and seventy-seven thousand one hundred and forty-five dollars, the whole aggregating the sum of six hundred and eighty-one thousand six hundred and thirty-three dollars. The State and county levy of taxes amounted to one thousand seven hundred and forty-one dollars and four cents each, and the town taxes, including schools, to eleven thousand and seventeen dollars and ninety-two cents, the whole aggregating fourteen thousand five hundred dollars.

### THE COST OF SCHOOLS

for the year ending September 1, 1876, including the fine union school of the village, will be seen by the following exhibit: There were four schools taught in the township, averaging nine months in each session, which seven hundred and sixteen scholars attended. Five male teachers were employed and paid two thousand two hundred and sixty dollars, and fourteen females who were paid three thousand one hundred and sixty-eight dollars. The total expenses, including eight thousand dollars paid on bonded indebtedness, amounted to fifteen thousand three hundred and fourteen dollars and seventy-eight cents, the total resources of the districts being fifteen thousand seven hundred and thirty dollars and sixteen cents, including tuition received from foreign scholars. The township has four school houses—three brick and one of wood—valued at forty-five thousand dollars, capable of seating nine hundred and fifty pupils, and has eight hundred and one children of suitable age to attend school.

### THE CENSUS OF 1874

shows a population of two thousand two hundred and forty-eight, one thousand and seventy-six being males, and one thousand one hundred and seventy-six females. Three hundred and eighty-four males were of the military age—between twenty-one and forty-five years, and two hundred

and twenty-six were beyond the fear of a draft in case of war, being under seventy-five years of age; twelve males were between seventy-five and ninety years. Four hundred and eighteen females were of marriageable age—between eighteen and forty years, and two hundred and sixty were past the heyday of life, and under seventy-five years, while nineteen were in the "sere and yellow leaf," beyond the three-quarter stake of the century.

Ninety-two farms contained twelve thousand eight hundred and twenty-three acres, three thousand two hundred and sixty of which were sown to wheat, and one thousand one hundred and ninety-six planted to corn. The season of 1873 produced twenty-three thousand nine hundred and eighty bushels of wheat, and thirty-four thousand three hundred and nineteen bushels of corn; other grain, six thousand and forty bushels; potatoes, eleven thousand six hundred bushels; hay, eight hundred and forty-three tons; wool, one thousand nine hundred and nine pounds; pork, seventy-eight thousand six hundred and thirty pounds; butter, twenty-five thousand five hundred and sixty-five pounds; dried fruit, two thousand one hundred and twenty-five pounds; cider, six hundred and seventy barrels. One hundred and eighty-nine acres in orchards produced nine thousand and thirty bushels of apples, and twenty-three and a half acres produced one thousand five hundred and fifty bushels of other fruits and vegetables.

There were owned by the people of the township in 1874 three hundred and fifty-nine horses, a single mule, one pair and a half of oxen, three hundred and six cows, one hundred and eighty-seven other cattle, four hundred and fifty-four hogs, and three hundred and ninety-three sheep, against four hundred and twenty-four of the latter in 1873.

Two planing-mills, one foundry or machine-shop, three carriage-factories, two chair and furniture factories, one broom factory, one pump factory, two churn and barrel factories, two trunk and harness-shops, one canning establishment, two boot and shoe factories, and two stone-yards, employed one hundred and twenty-three persons, with a capital of sixty-three thousand dollars, and the value of their productions were one hundred and twenty-two thousand and two hundred dollars.

### THE POLITICAL BIAS

of the township on the national issues may be seen by the manner in which the people have cast their votes for presidential candidates. In 1848 the Whig candidate received eighty-one, the Democratic fifty-nine, and the Free Soil candidate twenty-six votes. In 1852 the Whigs polled one hundred and thirty-four votes, the Democrats ninety-five, and the Abolitionists nine, there being just enough of the "Old Guards" to make a single tailor. Four years later they grew to a majority of one hundred and thirty-three, the Republicans polling two hundred and thirty-four, and the Democrats one hundred and one votes. In 1860 the Republicans gained twenty votes, and the Democrats seven on the vote of four years before. In 1864 there was a falling off in the Democratic vote, and a corresponding gain in the Republican, the former casting but eighty-one, and the latter two hundred and eighty votes. In 1868 both parties gained heavily, the Republicans polling three hundred and seventy-four, and their opponents one hundred and fifty-five. In 1872 the Republicans polled three hundred and one, and the Democrats one hundred and thirty-six votes; Charles O'Connor received fifteen straight votes, and Jeremiah Black a single one. In 1876 Hayes received three hundred and sixty-seven, Tilden two hundred and forty-six, and Peter Cooper fifty.

This last vote, allowing seven persons to each vote cast, would give a population in Sturgis at the present time of four thousand six hundred and forty-one, or at five persons to each voter, would give three thousand three hundred and fifteen.

### THE LEADING AGRICULTURISTS

in the township have been and are as follows: Judge John Sturgis owned at the time of his death, which occurred in 1874, one thousand four hundred and fifty acres, lying in a body partially in Sturgis and Sherman. His sons, Amos, Thomas and David, succeeded to the greater portion of the estate, and are residents thereon at the present time. David Knox has been for over forty years a leading farmer on Sturgis prairie. John S. Newhall owns a fine farm, on which he located in 1832. Hiram Jacobs, Rice Peavoll, John Lasrick and Isaac Bunyan are all representative men among the farmers, and well-to-do in that line. Mrs. Sturgis, the venerable widow of Judge Sturgis, resides on the old homestead, now in her eightieth year, with Amos her son, who was but a few weeks old when he came to the prairie.

### AMUSEMENTS.

The good folks of Sturgis prairie enjoyed life in the early days despite the sorrow, afflictions and trials incident thereto, and entered into the pleasures

of festive occasions with a freedom that gave zest to the humdrum of every-
day toil for days to come.  "Tommy" Jones, an artistic fiddler, contributed
largely to the enjoyment of the gatherings in the settlement, and his own
house was a resort for the old and young for an evening's entertainment.
His worthy and hospitable wife always gave a party for the young people on
Christmas, and "Tommy"—a brother of Hon. De Garmo Jones, of Detroit—
followed suit on New Years with an assembly of the older people.  Roast
turkey and "chicken fixins" were plentiful and free on those occasions.
At one of the first gatherings Judge Sturgis and his daughter led off the first
dance, and soon the old people were tripping the "light fantastic" to Tommy's merry measures in full glee.  This was before 1832.
  The first celebration of the Fourth of July of any note was held in 1835, and
Elias Boulton Smith, M. D., was the orator of the day.  Among the toasts
drank on the occasion was the following: "Sturgis prairie—her farmers
grow wealthy by their industry, and her pure air preserves the red checks
of her fair daughters."
  In 1839 the day was celebrated with great éclat, fifteen hundred persons
being present.  The States were represented by young ladies dressed in the
national colors.  Hon. John S. Chipman delivered an eloquent oration; Hon.
J. G. Wait was the president, Dr. John F. Packard, vice-president; Mr.
Holmes, reader; Horace Vesey, marshal; Captain Harry McArthur, aid,
and Elder Day, chorister.  A Mr. Webb had his arm blown off by the prema-
ture discharge of a cannon.
  The celebration of the day in 1852 was noted for the distinguished officers
and guests of the occasion, and the number of people (two thousand) in
attendance.  General Isaac D. Toll was marshal of the day, Hon. William
L. Stoughton, orator.  The drummer was Tommy Jones before named.
Several soldiers of the war of 1812 were present, among them Edward
Evans, a Baptist clergyman, then eighty-nine years of age, who declined to
ride to Jacob's grove where the oration was delivered, preferring to walk,
though the mercury stood ninety-three degrees at 5 o'clock P. M.  Two
Revolutionary soldiers were present—Arzunah Hibbard, grandfather of
Frank Hibbard, druggist in Sturgis at the present writing; and another one
whose name is not remembered.  Mr. Evans' grandfather lived to the age of
one hundred and ten years.
  An incident in the pioneer-life of John S. Newhall, worth preserving, is
the fact that when he came to Michigan in 1832 to find a location, he left
his horse at the Maumee, and traveled two thousand miles on foot that
summer, from May to July, before he was satisfied that his present location
was the best one he could find.  He went from Ullmann's to Bronson's for
breakfast, shooting a turkey on the way, which was served up for a wedding-
supper at Benson's, on the Kalamazoo.  Mr. Newhall once owned two thousand acres of land in Nebraska, and broke up one season seven hundred and
fifty acres.
  Dr. Packard used to take wheat of his patients in payment for his services, haul it to Monroe and sell it for cash to buy medicine with.  He once
floured one hundred and sixty barrels of best white wheat, and sold the same
to R. & J. Williams for two dollars and sixty-two cents per barrel, which
was the first money he received from sales in the county.  The military
parades, musters and courts-martial were a never-failing fund for amusement while they lasted—Captain Harry McArthur being the inspiring genius
of these occasions.

                              THE VILLAGE OF STURGIS.

  The first beginning of the present village of Sturgis was the house of
George Buck, built on the south side of the Chicago road, which was then
surveyed and staked-out across the prairie, in the summer of 1828.  He was
followed the same season by John B. Clark, who built a log house of somewhat more generous dimensions, and put out his sign for entertainment of
travelers, and the village was au fair accompli.  It had, however, no name
but Sturgis prairie until 1832, when Philip H. Buck surveyed and platted
forty lots, sixty by one hundred and sixty-five feet, equally disposed on
either side of the Chicago road, on the east half of the southeast quarter of
section one, township eight, south range of ten west, and named it the village
of Sherman—the same being the name of the township at the time, and
until 1845.  These lots were all east of the present Nottawa street.  In
April, 1834, Mr. Buck laid out an addition, on the south side of the same
road, of forty lots, and in May following, Andrew Backus, who had succeeded to the ownership of the original purchase of Clarke, laid off a plat
on the west side of the present Nottawa street, embracing the tract bounded
west by the line of the present Grand Rapids and Indiana railroad, on both
sides of the Chicago road, and called his village (in deference to his daughters' wishes), Ivanhoe.  The young ladies were admirers of the "Black
Knight," as immortalized by Sir Walter, and to their poetic feelings Sher-

man seemed too plain and unromantic, and therefore they gave to their city
the name of the most distinguished character of the great novelist.  From
that time onward the several additions of Drake, Hatch, Harvey and
Allman were named and described as, and conveyances executed for lots in,
the several additions to the villages of Sherman or Ivanhoe, as the case
might be, until February, 1857, an act was passed by the legislature for the
replatting of the original villages and additions thereto, under the name of
Sturgis; and William K. Haynes, William L. Stoughton and E. H. Wallace,
commissioners, made such plat, and recorded the same February 5, 1858.
But the confusion has been rendered rather worse than before by the apparent lapses in title, which occurred by not identifying the original descriptions closely with the new plat.

                              THE FIRST HOTEL

in the village was that of John B. Clarke, situated on the present site of
the Elliott house.  He was succeeded in the same building by Major Isaac
J. Ullmann, who was a well-known character in the county for years.  He
was a staunch Democrat, and it is told of him that being at a convention
he was called to the chair to preside, which position he accepted, and as soon
as seated, a member presented a set of resolutions, and began to read them.
They were fiercely denunciatory of the Democratic party, and by the time
the preamble had been read and the second resolution well begun, the major
rapped the reader to order vigorously, and rising, delivered himself of the
following: "I taught men I accepted dis chair I vas in a Democratic convention, but I believe it ish noting put all tam Whiggery, und I vill not
shtay here."  And he didn't, but vacated the place and withdrew from the
room.  He sold his interest in the village to Backus—who was an eastern
man—in the fall of 1833, but the new proprietor did not at once assume the
role of Boniface, Mr. Luther Douglass succeeding Major Ullmann in that
line.
  Mr. Douglass came to White Pigeon in the fall of 1832, with his family
of five boys and one girl,—Alonzo, Orson and Oremus (twins), Orley,
William H, and Lucinda,—the latter being now deceased.  In the winter of
1833 Mr. Douglass leased the hotel of Ullmann, and, May 14, was lost on
Lake Erie in a sail-boat, while going out to take a steamer in the offing at
Erie during a snow-squall.  In 1835 Backus succeeded the Douglasses in the
hotel business, and the family removed to their farm near Douglass station,
on the Michigan, Southern and Lake Shore railroad, in White Pigeon township.  Mrs. Douglass was one of the untiring Florence Nightingales of the
prairie, who went everywhere, in season and out of season, to care for the sick
in the years of distress.
  Oliver Raymond built, in 1831, on the corner where Wallace's block now
stands, opposite the Sturgis hotel, the

                              FIRST FRAME BUILDING

in the village, as well as on the prairie, and kept a hotel in opposition to
Ullmann.  The

                              FIRST BRICK BUILDING

was probably the block on the southeast corner of Nottawa and Chicago
streets, built by Peck and Wallace in 1854.  The bricks were made in
White Pigeon, in 1851, and when the building was rebuilt in 1874, the
material was apparently as good as the day it was burned.

                              THE FIRST POST-OFFICE

on the prairie was kept on the Stewart location, on section seven, in Town
River township, by Samuel Stewart, the first postmaster; it was established
in 1829, and the mail was brought from Coldwater to White Pigeon via
Sturgis prairie, by John Winchell, postmaster and contractor.  Afterwards
the Stewarts carried the mail and passengers in a democrat wagon until
Savery put on his coaches in 1832.
  Oliver Raymond was the first postmaster in the village, and he kept the
mail of the entire settlement in a single pigeon-hole, which constituted an
entire candle-box.  The mails came irregularly, sometimes every week, then
once in two weeks, again semi-weekly, tri-weekly, and finally every day in
each direction, east and west.
  Mr. Raymond was succeeded by Judge Sturgis, and he by Philip H. Buck,
the latter by Major C. C. Hood, and the major by Captain William Mc-
Laughlin, under President Johnson; the captain was in turn succeeded by
Major Hood, who gave way to the present incumbent, Hon. J. G. Wait.
  The business of 1876 affords a fine contrast to that of the pioneer days.
The sales of stamps averaged seven hundred dollars per quarter; four hundred letters were received and dispatched daily, and one thousand five hundred papers were distributed weekly.  Seven mails were received and dis-
patched daily; postal orders were sold to the amount of eighteen thou-

CYRUS W. RICH.

MRS CYRUS W. RICH.

RESIDENCE OF CYRUS W. RICH,
Sturgis Tp. St Joseph Co., Mich

sand eight hundred and sixty-seven dollars and one cent ; and orders to the amount of nine thousand seven hundred and twenty-five dollars and eighteen cents were paid ; during the same time two hundred and fifty-seven registered letters were dispatched.

The office has been under the entire management, for the past three years, of Miss Nettie P. Plympton, by whose efficiency and promptness the large business of the office is most satisfactorily and admirably conducted.

### THE FIRST STAGE LINE

on which coaches were used was Savery's, which began to carry passengers and mails in 1831-2 ; but the Black Hawk scare broke him up by stopping emigration, and for weeks his coaches went over the road with nothing but the mails, not a single passenger being in the same.

The second line was owned by General Brown, De Garmo Jones, and Forsyth, and began to operate in 1833. This line ran four-horse coaches daily over the route between Detroit and Chicago. John Lanrick, now a resident of the village, was driver for the line many years, commencing in May, 1833. From 1836 to 1840 the rush of travel westward was immense ; extras were run every day at times, and sometimes two or three each day ; and heavy mails were transported. In 1839-40, as high as one thousand three hundred pounds of postal-matter have been carried frequently. Passengers were transported at seven cents per mile, and carried rails to help the coaches through the marshes. They were probably transported with anything but feelings of gratitude toward the stage company, notwithstanding the liberal charge for transports.

### THE FIRST RAILROAD

which gave rapid communication with the outside world to Sturgis was the Michigan Southern, now known as the Michigan Southern and Lake Shore railroad. The energetic efforts of this company and the people to make Sturgis a point are described in the general history of the county. Hon. J. G. Wait was a contractor on this line, and built the depots of the company from Coldwater to Niles, as well as the fencing-in of the right of way. He was also engaged largely in securing the right of way in Branch and St. Joseph counties. All of the liberal-souled people of Sturgis and White Pigeon moved with alacrity and vigor to accomplish the passage of the line of the road as it now is traveled, and succeeded, much to the chagrin of the more northern towns of the county, who, expecting that the line was fixed unalterably through the centre of the county, gave themselves no uneasiness relative thereto, and let the first road of the county slip through their fingers.

However, in after years they made the most heroic struggles and generous offerings to gain the Central, and were successful. The subscriptions to get the railroad south of the centre of the county were thirty thousand dollars. In 1866 the township voted fifteen thousand dollars in aid of the Grand Rapids and Indiana railroad, passing north through the county, which was subsequently built ; Mr. Wait being largely interested in its success, as also were all of the citizens, it being a competing road and opening up a shorter connection north.

The business of the railroads in 1876 aggregate the following amounts : The Michigan Southern and Lake Shore forwarded twenty-nine millions seven hundred and fifty-two thousand six hundred and eighty-four pounds of freight, and received ten millions three hundred and seventy-one thousand three hundred and ninety-four pounds, making an aggregate of freight carried during the year of forty millions one hundred and twenty-four thousand and seventy-eight pounds, or twenty thousand and sixty-two tons. Of the shipments thirteen millions eight hundred and thirty-one thousand and twenty-five pounds were grain ; eleven millions thirteen thousand two hundred and seventy pounds were of lumber and other forest products, and one million three hundred and ninety-two thousand pounds of live animals. The wheat amounted to two hundred and thirteen thousand one hundred and ninety-five bushels. The earnings of the road were for freight forwarded, twenty-eight thousand five hundred and three dollars and sixty cents ; for freight received, ten thousand eight hundred and ninety-five dollars and eighty-eight cents ; for ticket sales, fifteen thousand six hundred and twenty-one dollars and five cents ; the total earnings amounting to fifty-five thousand and twenty-one dollars and forty-three cents—an excess of three thousand four hundred and sixty-five dollars and thirty cents over those of 1875. J. K. McKee, the freight and station agent, and T. J. Collins, ticket agent, very courteously furnished the above information concerning the business of the road.

During the same year the Grand Rapids and Indiana railroad received forty-four millions thirty-one thousand six hundred and sixty pounds of freight, and forwarded three millions eight hundred and fifty-five thousand

nine hundred pounds, the receipts being largely of lumber. The ticket sales amounted to sixteen thousand one hundred and seventy dollars. Arthur Wait, the agent at Sturgis, gave us the above figures from his books.

The grand aggregate of the shipment and receipt of freight and passenger traffic of the railroads in the village is as follows : Total freight forwarded in 1876, thirty-three millions six hundred and eight thousand five hundred and eighty-four pounds ; received, fifty-four millions four hundred and three thousand and fifty-four pounds, or a grand total of forty-three thousand seven hundred and seventeen tons of freight carried during the year. The passenger traffic paid into the coffers of the companies the handsome sum of thirty-one thousand seven hundred and ninety-one dollars and ninety-five cents.

### THE PROFESSIONS

have been ably represented, and still are, in Sturgis, both lay and clerical. The bar of Sturgis are named in the general history of the county. The first physician, as before stated, was Dr. Henry. Dr. Griffith, Dr. Ira F. Packard and Dr. James H. Taft, the latter now deceased, were successors, in the order named, to Dr. Henry. The present medical staff of the village are Dr. Nelson I. Packard and Dr. Putnam, of the regular school ; P. H. Van Vlock, homeopathic ; Ira S. King, eclectic, and Drs. Hurlbut and Eastman. The first dentist was Dr. Hutchinson. The present professors and operators in dental surgery are W. G. Cummins, D.D.S., who has a most admirably arranged and equipped suite of rooms, in the first brick building built in the village, as before named, in which he employs all of the modern appliances for the rapid and painless execution of his professional duties ; J. W. Beck, D.D.S., also has a pleasant suite of rooms.

The teachers of note are named in the history of the union school, and the clerical profession have honorable mention in the history of the churches. The history of the press will also be found in the general history of the county.

The pride and ornament of Sturgis, to which the people may justly point visitors with commendable self-congratulation for their own efforts, is the

### UNION SCHOOL OF STURGIS,

which had its beginning in the pioneer class gathered in the upper room of Mrs. George Buck's log-house, in the winter of 1830, to learn what they could from good old Dr. Henry's teaching. The district (No. 3) was first organized February 10, 1836, while yet the township was called Sherman. Philip Buck was the first moderator, Jacob French the first director, and Jeremiah Dewel the first assessor.

The school taught in the district was not a free school—an assessment more or less heavy being laid per capita on all who sent their children to the school. Nor was it an absolutely free school until September, 1859, when a general tax was levied for all expenses. The first school-house was built in 1833, as before stated, before any district was organized, and while the State was in territorial tutelage.

On the 26th of February, 1838, the people of the district voted to build a new school-house, and changed the site to block forty-three, giving seventeen dollars and fifty cents for the site, and building the house for two hundred and ninety-eight dollars—the same being a frame structure. The first public money received from the State was in 1839, and amounted to thirty-seven dollars and twelve cents, at which date there were in the district seventy-one children between the ages of five and seven years ; and seventy-nine dollars and seventy-one cents were the total expenditure for the year. Oliver Raymond taught the school the winter term of 1839-40, for twenty-six dollars per month, and boarded himself, but being taken sick, Angus McKerlie filled his contract.

The first teacher in the old log-house could not solve the mathematical problems his pupils presented him, and after a single month he was dismissed, and a Mr. Depue was engaged and "filled the bill." He is now the postmaster at Lima, Indiana. Mr. Raymond had for one of his pupils a lad who was called the "long-haired boy," who is now President Graham, of Hillsdale college. In 1849 the school-house site was changed again to a half-acre lot in B. C. Buck's field, the old house sold for one hundred dollars, and one thousand dollars voted for a new one.

In 1852 the school board adopted a series of text-books, including, among the higher studies, Davies' Algebra, Olmstead's Natural Philosophy and Astronomy, Beck's Chemistry, and Cutler's Anatomy and Physiology. The first movement for a union school was made in 1855, under the act of that year, but it was not successful. On the 1st of September, 1859, the people voted to make the school free to all scholars in the district, and raised a general tax of two hundred dollars for that purpose. On the 26th day of the same month, the district was organized under the statute of 1859 as a union school district, and the following board of education elected: William Allman, Philip H. Buck, J. D. Cook, W. A. Wright, Jacob Sidner and William L. Stoughton. Seven hundred dollars were voted for school purposes and one thousand dollars for a building fund. The basement of the Presbyterian church was temporarily leased, and the higher classes removed thereto.

In 1860, the first year of the union school, the receipts from all sources were one thousand four hundred and forty-four dollars and seventy-seven cents, including one hundred and seventy-three dollars and sixty-six cents received for tuition from scholars outside the district. Eight hundred and sixty-four dollars were paid for teachers' salaries, and three hundred and fifty-two scholars drew public money. The same year (1860) the site for a school-house was changed again to block sixteen, the present beautiful location—two thousand dollars being paid for the same. A brick school-house was contracted for with Z. H. Wallace, for eight thousand dollars, the same when completed and furnished costing ten thousand seven hundred and eighteen dollars. The seating cost four hundred dollars, and the old building was sold for five hundred and twenty-five dollars. The building was completed in the fall of 1861, and occupied the first week of January following. On September 7, 1873, a committee, consisting of Z. H. Wallace, E. W. Pendleton and A. T. Drake, was appointed by the regular meeting of the district, and reported October 10, 1875, recommending an addition to the school-house, which report was accepted, and eight thousand dollars voted to carry out the recommendations, and operations at once begun, which were completed in the summer following, resulting in the elegant and commodious structure, a view of which we present to our readers on another page of our work. It was occupied the fall term of 1876. In November following the city council contracted with A. Howard & Co., of Boston, for placing a tower-clock in the main tower of the building, having a dial on each face of the same; and which clock the company guaranteed would not vary fifteen seconds in any single month for five years. The cost was seven hundred dollars. The building is furnished with modern apparatus for heating and ventilation, and its sittings are easy and roomy.

The course of instruction comprises the primary department, including the eighth, seventh and sixth grades—one year of time is to be passed in each grade; the junior department, which includes the fifth, fourth and third grades—the same time being occupied in each grade; the senior department, which includes the second and first grades, and one year in each grade; the high-school department, which has a classic and scientific and academic course. The school has a valuable though not extensive library, and has the beginning of what it needs, good and proper apparatus, philosophical and otherwise.

The first graduating class received their diplomas in 1874, the members being William P. Stoughton, scientific course; Virena Morrison, Anna Barrows and Huldah Seeley, English course. The class of 1875 were: Cora M. Wright. Albert M. Todd, classics; Stella Sturgis, scientific; Kittie Buck, Frankie Wilson, Albert Chandler, Wallace Weatherby, English literature. The class of 1876, Frederick Buck, Charles Wilson, classics; Lillie Hamilton, scientific; Charles Barrows, English literature.

The present corps of teachers are: J. D. Williams, A.M., principal; Mrs. M. A. Hackstaff, preceptress; senior school, W. H. Wheeler, Laura M. Page; junior school, Etta Sheperdson, Lillie B. Edmonston and Miss Whitney; primary, Meda E. Lester, Sophia A. Coye and Kittie Buck. Mrs. Hackstaff has been connected with the school for several years.

The present school board are: Levant E. White, director; Charles B. Peck, treasurer; E. S. Mundon, moderator; Dr. N. I. Packard, D. E. Thomas and G. D. G. Thurston, trustees.

What this institution costs the people may be seen from the following exhibit for the year ending September 1, 1876: Five hundred and eighty-six scholars attended the school, which was ten months in session, and was taught by two male teachers, who were paid one thousand seven hundred and fifty-five dollars for their services, and nine females, who received two thousand nine hundred dollars for their wages. Two hundred and one dollars and twenty-five cents were received as tuition fees from non-resident pupils—the total resources of the district being fourteen thousand five hundred and sixty-two dollars and forty-one cents, of which fourteen thousand four hundred and fifteen dollars and fifty-eight cents were expended, including eight thousand seven hundred and forty dollars and sixty-six cents for building and repairs. The district board value their property at forty thousand dollars, on which they owe eight thousand dollars.

#### THE CHURCHES.

The first preacher was Rev. Erastus Felton, the Methodist missionary from Ohio. The first religious service was held in Mrs. Buck's "upper

chamber," a resort for all denominations, orthodox or liberal, who desired to use it. It was free to all, without money or price, and the family always helped to make up the audience. The first church society established in Sturgis prairie was

#### THE METHODIST EPISCOPAL CHURCH,

which was organized in 1832 by Rev. Mr. Robinson, of the Indiana conference. The class was composed of one man and seven women, the solitary male member, David Knox, being the class-leader. Five of the females were Mrs. David Knox, Mrs. Rachel Knox (David's mother), Mrs. Betsey Buck (widow), Harriet Brooks and Mrs. Thomas Cade. In 1843 the first church was built on public ground, in front of the old cemetery, where the present Lutheran church is situated, and was afterwards moved across the street and used as a factory. The present edifice was built in 1863, is valued at twelve thousand dollars, has four hundred sittings, and is a neat, comfortable brick structure. The builder of the first church was a man named Nickerson. In 1845 a Sunday-school was organized, Mr. Knox, Hiram Jacobs and A. T. Drake drafting the constitution. Mr. French was the first superintendent, and then Truman Bateman, who was succeeded by William Allman, who has held the position ever since—nearly thirty years. There are now enrolled three hundred and sixty-five scholars, and there are seven hundred and thirty-four volumes in the library. There are two hundred members now in the church. The pastors who have ministered unto this flock have been, since Robinson, who served another year (1834), Babcock, Young, Peter Sabin, Newell, Beswick, Erastus Kellogg, Todd, John Ercanbrack, Richard Meek, the two Boyingtons, Lee, Lyon, McAllister, John L. Brockway, N. A. Knappen, Welch, Sherman and Worthington. The present pastor is John Graham, a pleasant but firm Scotch gentleman, who has just a spice of the accent of " auld Scotia" on his tongue, and who is an acceptable preacher to the community of church-going people generally. The presiding elders of the Sturgis district have been John Armstrong (named elsewhere for his ability and patriotism), Richard Hargreaves, Aaron Woods, John Ercanbrack, James T. Davidson, William Sprague, David Burns and —— Gillett.

#### THE BAPTIST CHURCH

of Sturgis was organized October 6, 1836, as a conference, composed of Elder Gershom B. Day, moderator; Abel Crossman, clerk; Wear Drake, Mordecai Leighton, Thomas Davis, and sisters Elizabeth Day, Roxana Crossman and Lydia and Catharine Drake. January 26, 1837, an ecclesiastical council was held, constituted of Elder William Brown, moderator; Elder H. J. Hall, clerk; William Taylor and L. M. Choat; and the conference was formally organized as a church, with the same members as first named, and also Polly S. Ellis and Eunice B. Raymond. The services of dedication were participated in by Elder Brown, who preached the sermon from Luke xii. 32, and gave the right hand of fellowship; William Taylor, who gave the charge to the new church, and Choat, who invoked the Divine blessing upon them. The first and present church edifice was erected in 1846, in conjunction with the people at large, and was held several years in common with other denominations; but in 1858 the church bought out the partnership with the world, and now own it exclusively. It is valued at seven thousand dollars, and will seat two hundred and fifty persons comfortably. There are ninety members in the church society at present. October 31, 1846, a Sunday-school was organized, and a large class formed, with P. H. Evans as superintendent. The present membership of the school is ninety; G. D. G. Thurston is the superintendent, and there are one hundred and forty volumes in the library. The first pastor was Elder Day, the first Baptist preacher in the county, and who was afterwards killed by the Indians in California. He was succeeded by Reverends R. Graham, L. H. Stocker, R. H. Cook, P. Forbes, P. H. Evans, U. B. Miller, E. Curtis, G. L. Stephens, E. J. Fish, A. L. Vail, George A. Amos and L. F. Compton, the present pastor.

#### THE PRESBYTERIAN CHURCH

of Sturgis was organized in 1836-7, by Rev. W. Corey, of Lima, Indiana, among the first members being the following: Mr. Wilbur and wife, Elder James L. Bishop and wife, Rice Pearsoll and wife, Mrs. Ransom and Ahira Brooks. The first church edifice was erected in 1858, and is valued at six thousand dollars. It is built of brick, has three hundred sittings, and the society has seventy-five members on its roll. A Sunday-school was organized about the same time as the church, jointly with the Baptists, in whose house the new denomination worshiped for a time. John Taylor and Harvey H. Breese were early superintendents of the school. There are one

DAN. R. PARKER.

## D. R. PARKER.

D. R. PARKER comes of old and respectable Pennsylvania families, his father, John Parker, having been born in Chester county, Pennsylvania, July 3, 1793, and his mother, Elizabeth Seisar, in the township of Linn, Northampton county, February 9, 1800. He was born in Nancy Creek township, Lycoming county, Pennsylvania, October 27, 1818. At the age of seven his parents removed to Livingston county, New York, where they remained about five years, and in 1830 removed to Michigan, and settled on Sturgis' Prairie, in the County of St. Joseph. They embarked at Buffalo, in the steamer Peacock, and when but three miles out an accident occurred—the bursting of the steam-pipe—by which fifteen persons were scalded, fourteen fatally, among whom were Margaret, Lovina, and Samuel, two sisters and a brother of Mr. Parker's. This catastrophe cast a deep gloom over the family, the accident being regarded as an ill omen, fraught with disagreeable consequences for the future; which, however, never transpired, for we find the residue of the family comfortably settled on a fine farm in Section 11, Sturgis township, where they remained for many years, enjoying that peace and happiness, contentment and prosperity, which are the inseparable concomitants of the farmer's life. On the 13th of April, 1848, Mr. Parker took unto himself a wife in the person of Miss Mary J. Aikin, and the same year settled on his present farm, in Section 12. Four children were born unto them, of whom three survive. Olive L. was born November 8, 1849; Henry R., born January 9, 1852; Franklin L., born April 4, 1853—died September 4, 1856; John H., born March 16, 1855. On the 5th of September, 1856, Mrs. Parker died, after a happy wedded life of less than a decade. This great bereavement was keenly felt by Mr. Parker and his young family, and left a void in his heart which has never been filled. She was a woman of rare qualities; beloved by all her acquaintances and friends; worshiped by her husband and fondly loved by her children, by all of whom her memory is affectionately cherished.

In character, Mr. Parker is industrious, economical, and genial. By hard work and prudential management he has become possessed of two hundred and forty acres of improved and finely cultivated land. In politics, he is a Republican; in religious belief, a Spiritualist. He is generally esteemed as a shrewd business man, a good, practical farmer, and an intelligent and worthy citizen. (See Illustrations.)

RESIDENCE OF D. R. PARKER,
STURGIS, ST JOSEPH CO, MICHIGAN.

hundred scholars on the roll of the school, two hundred volumes constitute the library, and John Q. Wilson is the present superintendent.

The church was reorganized in 1853 (August 13), and incorporated, and J. L. Bishop, William Kyle and P. H. Buck were elected trustees. The pastors settled over the church have been, since Mr. Covey's pastorate, Rev. Charles Newberry, Rev. Mr. Fuller, who was with the church ten years; Mr. Clarke, three years; Knapp, two years; C. M. Temple, three and a half years, and Mr. Stevens, the present pastor. During the pastorates of Mr. Fuller and Mr. Temple very interesting meetings were held, and noted accessions were made to the church.

### THE FIRST LUTHERAN CHURCH

was organized January 1, 1864, the first members of the same being Henry Lohrman, Charles Froh, Fred Pasel, Christ. Froh, Charles Witt, William Witt, Fred Zedawaten and Christin Wagoner. The church edifice, which is of wood, was built in 1871, and is valued at fifteen hundred dollars, and has one hundred sittings. The church at present consists of twenty members. The first pastor was Rev. Mr. Evers, and the second, and present, Rev. Albert Henkel.

### THE FIRST GERMAN LUTHERAN CHURCH

was organized in 1869 (September), by the Rev. Mr. Ellis, as pastor, with John G. Seeb, John Kreger, John Schroeder, George Siropegal, Jacob Underkirk and other members. The present next brick edifice, on the site of the old Methodist Episcopal church, was built in 1869–70, and cost four thousand dollars, and has two hundred sittings. The present membership of the church is seventy-five. A Sunday-school was organized in 1872, with forty scholars, and Mr. Seeb as superintendent, who still holds the position. The pastors have been, since Mr. Ellis, Rev. Mr. Gera, Mr. Henake, Mr. Eippersoll, and Mr. Rein, the present one.

St. John's Mission of the Episcopal Church was organized in 1873. Rev. W. Forgus is the missionary in charge. There are nine members of the church, twenty Sunday-school scholars, and four teachers.

### THE HARMONIAL SOCIETY

of Sturgis was organized September 2, 1858, with J. G. Wait, Harrison Kelly, James Johnson, B. B. Gardener, William Osborn and Nathaniel Hutchinson as an executive committee. The church walls were put up that season, and inclosed and finished the next summer. It is of brick, has a round tower, and is located east of Nottawa and south of Chicago streets, next adjoining the Baptist church. It was dedicated June 16, 1859, by Rev. J. M. Peebles, to "humanity and free thought," a large audience being in attendance. December 18, 1870, the constitution was revised and adopted, and signed by fifty-seven members.

A lyceum is connected with the society, which holds its session at twelve o'clock each Sunday. John B. Jacobs was conductor when it was first organized, Mrs. Vance being the present one. The present officers of the society are J. G. Wait, president; Nellie M. Smith, secretary; Joel A. Fox, treasurer; B. C. Buck, Joel A. Fox, Mary J. Peck, B. B. Gardner and Mrs. J. T. Graham, executive committee.

### SOCIETIES.—MASONIC.

Meridian Sun Lodge, No. 49, A. F. M., was organized under dispensation in 1851, and chartered in the year following. James S. Bishop was its first secretary, and served four years in that station. W. H. Kent was the worshipful master in 1853, and Dr. Nelson I. Packard filled that position eleven years, at different times. The other masters have been: B. F. Doughty, Homer Dunne, S. Valentine and C. Jacobs, who is the present incumbent. The lodge has one hundred and nineteen members on its books, in good standing.

### STURGIS CHAPTER, NO. 26, ROYAL ARCH MASONS,

was organized by charter, January 8, 1864, with B. F. Doughty as first high priest; N. I. Packard, scribe, and Charles H. Putnam, king. The office of high priest has been filled since the organization to present date by Charles H. Putnam, W. H. Kent, Homer Dunn, C. Jacobs and C. B. Peck.

### COLUMBIA COMMANDERY, NO. 18, KNIGHTS TEMPLAR,

was organized by charter, May 15, 1867, with W. A. Kent, eminent commander; H. H. Wallace, generalissimo, and R. H. Morrison, captain-general. The position of commander has been filled since its organization by H. H. Wallace, R. H. Morrison, Lyman Nelton, W. G. Cummins, N. J. Packard, Z. H. Wallace and Edwin Kelley. The present membership numbers eighty rank and file. The present officers are E. W. Kelly, E. C.; W. W. Stone, Gen'o; W. G. Cummins, C. G.; Rev. Wellington Forgus, pre-

late; R. H. Morrison, recorder, and Ira F. Packard, treasurer. The commandery attended the triennial conclave of the grand encampment of Knights Templar of the United States, in 1874, held at New Orleans, with forty Sir Knights, under command of Dr. N. I. Packard, E. C.; W. G. Cummins, Gen'o; H. L. Anthony, C. G. The command was highly commended by the press of the city for its soldierly bearing and excellent drill. Many of the wives of the knights accompanied them. R. H. Morrison was with the grand commandery of Michigan as grand captain-general.

### EASTERN STAR LODGE, NO. —,

was organized in 1866, with Mrs. Alexander, M.D., as first worthy president. Mrs. C. B. Peck, Mrs. E. W. Pendleton, Mrs. N. I. Packard, Mrs. E. Willetts, Mrs. D. H. Hawley, Mrs. Elizabeth Ayers, and Mrs. Thomas Hill have held the position, some of them two years, and the latter is holding the third term at present. H. L. Anthony is the present vice-president (1876), and Mrs. Vial is the secretary. The lodge has about forty members.

### ODD-FELLOWS.

#### STURGIS PRAIRIE LODGE, NO. 37, I. O. O. F.,

was chartered in 185–. On July 27, 1860, a new hall was dedicated by the Grand Master —— Dennis, Hon. Henry Waldron, member of Congress, being the orator for the occasion. The lodge was highly complimented in the grand master's address at the next session of the grand lodge, as one of the best working lodges in the State. Among its presiding officers (N. G.) may be named Rice Pearsoll, William Allman, Z. H. Wallace, L. S. Ensign, David Knox, R. H. Morrison and P. A. Hubbard. The present officers are B. F. Duntee, N. G.; A. A. Wilbur, V. G.; L. J. Twichell, treasurer, and Thaddens P. Wait, secretary. There are fifty-seven members on the lodge-books, in good standing. One of its members, R. H. Morrison, has honored the lodge by holding the position as representative to the grand lodge of the United States from the grand lodge of Michigan, in 1870, and that of treasurer of the latter body since that date to the present.

#### SCHILLER LODGE, NO. 137, I. O. O. F.,

was instituted January 8, 1870, to work in the German language. Its present officers are John A. Dice, N. G.; Thomas Collins, V. G.; Alvah Hawley, secretary, and has twenty-five members on its roll.

#### MORRISON ENCAMPMENT, NO. 41,

was instituted April 23, 1871. Its present officers are John A. Banker, C. P.; John C. Merry, H. P.; E. F. Duntee, S. W.; A. A. Wilbur, scribe; O. D. Colwell, J. W.; L. J. Twichell, treasurer. There are twenty-seven members on the roll of encampment.

#### DAUGHTERS OF REBEKAH.

Jacobs Lodge, No. 9, was instituted ——, and C. Jacobs holds the position of N. G., and Mrs. A. A. Wilbur that of V. G. There are about twenty-five members.

#### PATRONS OF HUSBANDRY.

Sturgis Grange, No. 332, was organized in the spring of 1874. Its present officers are J. W. Parker, master; Isaac Runyan, overseer; Robert Hamilton, secretary; Mrs. Otho Moe, Ceres. There are one hundred and fifty members in the grange.

#### GOOD TEMPLARS.

Sturgis Lodge, No. 955, I. O. G. T., was organized in March, 1876, with James Elliott as W. C. T.; H. O. Tuttle, W. V. T., and Ada Kent, secretary. The present officers are John C. Drake, W. C. T.; J. B. Phillips, W. V. T.; Miss Elma Adams, secretary. There are fifty-six members at present in the lodge. There have been other temperance organizations effected, but they have been ephemeral, although they were productive of some good while they were in operation.

#### STURGIS SACRED TEMPLE, NO. 2,

is an organization the second of its genus in the State, and which exists in no other State, Hillsdale and Sturgis monopolizing the order, which was founded in the former city. Its object is the elevation of women, and no man is allowed to enter the sacred precincts dedicated to his better, though later half, except as an honorary member. The Sturgis society was organized October, 1867, Mrs. General Stoughton being its first mistress. Mrs. Ira F. Packard, Mrs. Thomas Hill, Mrs. C. B. Peck, Mrs. Mary Stowe and Mrs. John McKerlie have each filled the position for two years, the latter being the present incumbent. Mrs. Stowe, Mrs. Hill and Mrs. Robert Hamilton are officers of the society, which has forty-three members.

## A LIBRARY AND LECTURE ASSOCIATION

was organized in 1871, with C. M. Temple as president and Mrs. General Stoughton as secretary, and secured lectures by "Nasby," Du Chaillu and Mrs. Livermore. The society has paid five hundred and fifty-five dollars for books, which circulate among its members, of whom there are at present eighty-six, the membership fee being one dollar per year. The association is organized under the statute, and its present officers are E. S. Amidore, president; L. E. White, treasurer; Dr. P. H. VanVleck, secretary; Laura Page, vice-president; Mrs. S. Hirsh, librarian.

A former society, called the "Eclectic Literary Association," was organized in 1852, but did not get so far as a lecture-course; but one formed in 1867 accomplished that object, securing lectures from Wendell Phillips, Charles Sumner, Fred Douglass, Professor E. O. Haven and John G. Saxe.

In 1846 a township library was established, and books bought by the school inspector, amounting to sixty-six dollars and seventy-four cents, were distributed among the several districts of the township, pro rata to the scholars therein.

In this connection it is proper to say that Major C. C. Hood, who was an enthusiast in conchology, gathered together a very fine cabinet of shells, minerals and fossils; and when he removed, Dr. Cummins and Dr. N. I. Packard became the purchasers thereof, and have the same, well displayed, in their respective offices.

## THE STURGIS AGRICULTURAL AND HORSE-BREEDERS' ASSOCIATION,

for the improvement of horses, principally, was organized January 4, 1867, Luther Savery and Major C. C. Hood being the first president and secretary thereof. The association held four exhibitions, at which some good horses were entered and good time made.

A sheep-shearing festival was held in June, 1868, and some fine equine specimens and their foals exhibited. The last meeting of the association was held June, 1870, and the society is now defunct.

## THE STURGIS CORNET BAND,

of twelve pieces, was organized in 1870. The present leader is R. Dye, and A. A. Wilbur is the director. The band performs very creditably, and produces some fine music. During the campaign of 1876 they were called out several times, putting money in their treasury thereby, as well as gaining a good reputation.

## TRADE.

The first merchant on Sturgis prairie was a Mr. Clements, who brought a stock of dry-goods for sale as early as 1829. Edwin Kellogg, who came to White Pigeon in 1829, opened a store at Sturgis in 1830 or 1831; and E. S. Swan followed with another not long afterwards.

J. G. Wait went into the mercantile business in 1842, and continued in it until 1857. Wasson & Greene were merchants in the village in 1839, and Major Ullmann kept a little stock, of wet-groceries principally, in 1832.

C. B. Peck, at present in the dry-goods line, has been in trade in Sturgis since 1850. L. E. White, in the same line, has been in the trade since 1859, has a fine assorted stock, and is a heavy and successful dealer.

J. C. Herbert has been in the trade since 1860, and has built from his profits the fine brick block he occupies, thirty by one hundred feet, three stories in height. There are over two hundred and twenty-five thousand dollars, by fair estimates, employed in the mercantile trade in Sturgis at the present date.

The produce-buyers, James Thornton and Messrs. Sebring & Co., bought, from July 1 to December 1, 1876, one hundred and thirty thousand seven hundred and seventy-six bushels of grain, against one hundred and thirteen thousand two hundred and twenty bushels of the crop of 1875. The value of the amount they bought in 1876, at the average price the market has shown, figures up one hundred and thirty-five thousand three hundred and ninety-five dollars. The First National Bank of Sturgis paid out in one day five thousand five hundred dollars for wheat alone. Their average during the season of 1876 was five thousand dollars per day.

One of the institutions without which the business men of Sturgis would be sorely troubled to conduct their extensive trade and manufacturing interests, is

## THE FIRST NATIONAL BANK OF STURGIS,

which was organized in 1865 with a capital of one hundred thousand dollars, with the following board of directors: William Allman, S. P. Williams, Z. H. Wallace, Ira F. Packard, N. I. Packard, B. Bursell, Jonathan Holmes and J. J. Beck. The same board of directors are in office at the present time, Mr. Allman being the president; S. P. Williams, of Lima, Indiana, vice-president; and Mr. Beck, cashier, which last position has been held by

Mr. Beck since the first year of the organization of the bank. Mr. Allman, an old-time resident of Sturgis, and a man identified with every interest of the town in its inception or completion, in some way, financially or otherwise, has held the position of president for some years.

The quarterly statement of the bank, dated October 2, 1875, makes the following exhibit: The capital stock paid in, surplus and undivided profits, amount to one hundred and thirty-one thousand six hundred and sixty-six dollars and sixty-seven cents; its circulation outstanding amounts to forty-five thousand dollars; its deposits, subject to draft or on time, were seventy-eight thousand three hundred and eight dollars and four cents; its loans and discounts amounted to one hundred and twenty-three thousand two hundred and fifty dollars and seventy-three cents; United States bonds, to secure circulation, fifty thousand dollars. There were due the bank from other banks, agents, and the redemption fund in United States treasury, forty thousand two hundred and ninety-seven dollars and thirty-six cents. It owned real estate, furniture, etc., valued at eleven thousand nine hundred and six dollars and forty-nine cents, and had in its vaults in cash, principally legal-tender notes, twenty-five thousand three hundred and sixty-one dollars and forty-eight cents.

## R. H. MORRISON & CO.,

in the insurance and real-estate business, conduct a heavy foreign exchange business, in which the firm has been engaged since 1850. Mr. Morrison's father resides in London, and gives personal attention to business in that city, and elsewhere on the Continent, having business connections in all parts of the commercial world.

## THE HOTELS

of Sturgis, the successors of Clarke, Ullmann, Raymond and Backus, of the pioneer days, are

The Elliott House, on the site of the old "Exchange," kept by the first two and last-named individuals, and by E. W. Pendleton later (or after 1850), and in the charge of "Pap" Elliott when it was burned, January 1, 1876. It was opened to the public on Christmas following the fire. It is a fine brick building, three stories in height, and will accommodate one hundred guests in first-class style and comfort. The hosts are E. W. Elliott & Sons.

The Berridge House is a neat new structure near the Michigan Southern and Lake Shore depot, kept by P. W. Berridge, and will accommodate from forty to fifty guests comfortably.

The Central Hotel and Dining Room, on the corner opposite the "Elliott," is kept by T. M. Sheriff, a most courteous and accommodating gentleman, who is ever actively engaged in looking after the comfort of his guests, of whom he can entertain some thirty or forty.

The old Sturgis House, leased by Elliott & Sons, and occupied while they were building the "Elliott," is now vacant. In front of this house, on the stone flagging which forms the sidewalk on either front, a tablet tells the passer-by that "Judge John Sturgis was the first settler on Sturgis prairie, in 1827."

## MANUFACTURES.

The first thing done in the manufacturing line on Sturgis prairie was blacksmithing, and that was confined principally to mending plows, sharpening their points and shares, and shoeing horses.

The first blacksmith-shop was built by Philip H. Buck, and one Filkins was the first smith to work at the anvil.

J. G. Wait begun, really, the first manufacturing of any moment in the village, in the year 1835-6, at which time he employed five or six shoemakers in the work of shoemaking. In 1837 he opened the first cabinet and furniture shop, employing in both lines fifteen men. He was largely engaged at the time, and later, in building, and in 1836 built the first barn ever erected on the prairie.

Previous to 1840, William Morris built a large mill and distillery, which afterwards burned down.

In 1843 Lester & Rolfe begun blacksmithing, and the same business, with carriage and wagon-making added soon after, has been carried on to the present, under different names—Mr. Lester closing out his interest in the business the latter part of 1876. Other firms and establishments have grown out from this original shop, some of whom are still in business, and some are not. The present firm, who succeed to the original Lester, is Lester & Kinzie.

C Burroughs has been in the wagon-making line in Sturgis twenty-five years.

In 1837 D. Page established the first foundry in Sturgis, and one of the first in the county, which was run, through various changes of name and

MISS MILLIE MAY MORRISON

ROBERT H. MORRISON

MISS ANNA K. MORRISON

MRS. MILLIE L. MORRISON

RES. OF ROBERT H. MORRISON, STURGIS, ST. JOSEPH CO., MICH.

firms, until now it is known as A. T. Drake & Co., and has been so known since 1870. Ten to twelve men are employed.

The first steam-mill was built by Morris & Vesey, in 1847, on the present site of the Methodist Episcopal church. It was burned to the ground some years afterwards.

The second mill was built by A. T. Drake & Co., in 1858, on the present site of Wallace's planing-mill, and was burned also about 1867.

The present flouring-mill was built, in 1865–6, for a warehouse and elevator, and in 1873 was fitted up for flouring wheat, and three run of stone put in, with a capacity of eighty barrels per day, besides custom work. Fisher & Mulford are the owners of the property, and Alexander Beach lessee.

The most perfect manufacturing establishment in Sturgis, and which, for equipment and convenience for handling the product in course of manufacture, as well as in the rough, is the

SASH, DOOR AND BLIND FACTORY

of Z. H. Wallace. It was built by Mr. Wallace in 1869; is a frame building, with brick boiler-house detached, the main building being forty by one hundred feet, two stories, situated on the corner of Clay and Hatch streets. Twenty-five to forty men are employed. The latest-improved machinery—for all kinds of work, from the rough-sawing to the polishing of the finished work—is employed, and every thing goes *forward*. The lumber comes in from the yard to the surfacer or saw, and never goes backward a foot, but is carried steadily forward until completed, when it is delivered on the opposite side of the building from where it entered. The amount of capital employed by Mr. Wallace in his business amounts to eighteen thousand dollars. Mr. Wallace has also been one of Sturgis' prominent merchants.

THE STURGIS MANUFACTURING COMPANY

was organized in 1873, with a capital of twenty thousand dollars, for the manufacture of furniture; and while it was operating its works, until September, 1876, from fifty to seventy-five men were employed. Its factory is a brick building, forty by one hundred and twenty feet, three stories, and equipped with the most complete and improved machinery that could be had.

We give these two manufactories thus fully, to show the progress that has been made in the county since the first rude mills were made in 1830.

Johnson, Packard & Austin (James Johnson and Frank S. Packard) are heavy lumber manufacturers and dealers, their wholesale and manufacturing yards being at Lockwood. They handle in Sturgis one and a half million feet of lumber and eight millions of shingles and lath.

The Packard Drying Company operate F. S. Packard's patent dryer, for drying fruits and vegetables. The factory has a capacity of about two hundred bushels per day, and twenty persons are usually employed in the season.

The Alden Drying Company have a finely-equipped factory for the purpose of fruit-drying by the Alden process, but it is unfortunately in the meshes of the law, and standing idle.

Jones Brothers are manufacturers of Jones' patent portable and factory dryer; they sold one of their machines at the Centennial to go to Australia.

E. H. Funk, patentee and manufacturer of the champion churn, has a factory of two stories, forty by forty feet, operated by steam, in and about which business he employs thirty-five men, shipping seven hundred to eight hundred of his churns per month to all parts of the country. He has been engaged in the business eight years, and has built his trade up to the present status from a beginning of nothing but his "dash."

The following is the

BUSINESS OF THE PRESENT.

*Trade.*

Dry Goods and General Merchandise—L. E. White, C. B. Peck, D. Naylor, J. G. Seeb, Hirshfield & Dembuffsky, J. C. Herbert.

Hardware—O. Shepardson, W. E. Rundell.

Groceries and Crockery—Olmstead Brothers, S. Valentine, H. B. Champlin, J. Alexander, W. A. Wight, Lester & Merrick, A. W. Dice, L. J. Twichell, A. Rommel, A. V. Merrill (thirteen years).

Produce and Live Stock—James Thornton, Sebring & Co. (of Kalamazoo), Charles B. Buck, Buck & Stowe.

Clothing and Furnishing Goods—Cahn & Somers, Hirsh & Frank.

Boots and Shoes—S. D. Flowers, H. Ely, S. Homan.

Books and Stationery—William Harrison, E. M. Roberts.

Furniture and Undertakers—E. S. Barnes, A. S. Munger, M. H. Warren & Co.

Musical Instruments—A. S. Munger, E. A. Jones.

10

Jewelry and Watches—G. N. Fairbanks, George Harris.

Drugs and Medicines—Henry L. Anthony, Frank Hibbard, Henry S. Church. Mr. Anthony has some very fine ornamental carving in black-walnut in bracket-work, in the form of wreaths and fruit—hand-work of a young artist in the town—displayed on his panels and medicine cases.

Photographers—William Reiterman, eleven years in the business, and a first-class artist in all the departments of his business; his studio is fitted-up with the latest improvements in the art, and he himself is an enthusiastic artist. Frank Barrow.

Upholstery and Mattresses—Caldwell Brothers.

Markets—George Rogers, Lewis Zent, A. C. Russell.

Millinery and Ladies' Furnishing Goods—Mrs. Bennett, Mesdames Miller and Bagg.

Livery—E. T. Parker, "Exchange Livery."

Agricultural Implements—Sidener Brothers.

Insurance and Real-Estate—R. H. Morrison & Co., A. F. Patch.

Confectionery—C. A. Palmer.

United States Express—Henry S. Church, agent.

*Manufactures.*

Sash, Doors and Blinds—Z. H. Wallace.

Saw and Planing-mill—Jacobs & Sons.

Flouring-mill—Alexander Beach.

Churns—E. H. Funk.

Wagons and Carriages—Lester & Kinzie, Lester Brothers, John Shepherd, C. Burroughs, Thomas Collar.

Fruit-dryers—Jones Brothers, Packard Dryer Company.

Pumps—Merry & Kennedy, T. I. Booth. The former make windmills, and the latter a device of endless-chain buckets.

Harness—William Lockwood, P. A. Smith, William McMichael.

Marble-cutting and Stone-yards—Kane & Bath, Thomas M. Perrin.

Cigars—B. Housinger, A. A. Wilbur.

Brewery—John Wagner.

Blacksmith—John Jones. The wagon-makers have shops for smith-work.

Carriage-trimmer—George W. Beebe.

There is a capital of about one hundred thousand dollars invested in the manufacturing business of Sturgis, which employs two hundred persons the greater part of the year.

The business prosperity of the village may be gathered somewhat by the building of dwellings and other edifices in 1875 and 1876. In the former year seventy-five dwellings were erected, and all are now occupied, together with twenty-five additional ones put up in 1876. During the latter year there were also erected the new school-house, the Elliott House (and a block of several stores adjoining), all of which are now completed and occupied. There has been a steady, healthy growth of the village during the panic times, since 1873—the railroad business, a pretty sure indicator, showing a regular increase in 1875 and 1876 over the previous years.

A *fiasco* in the manufacturing line occurred in the history of the village a few years ago, which it may not be amiss to mention, lest posterity may think that the business road of Sturgis has been a "royal" one, covered with roses, and redolent with the bloom of continuous success. One Jean H. Broadus, an energetic, active man, came into the village and contracted for the fine farm of John S. Newhall, and erected a fine foundry on the railroad for the manufacture of a patent heat-multiplier. He laid off the farm into a handsome addition to the town; advertised an auction sale of the lots, gave a barbecue, and with plenty of music and feasting the sale began, and amounted to nine thousand dollars the first day. He procured a charter for a street railroad from his works through the principal street of the town, the council granting permission for the laying of the tracks; but just before his visions became realities, his airy castles, which in time might have become solid stone, brick and mortar, were dissipated by the sheriff, who had an unromantic attachment for Broadus and his iron, and the whole fabric faded away, except the very completely built and equipped foundry, which has never been soiled with a single blast. Broadus retired and began operations elsewhere, and is said to have been more successful. Sturgis derived some benefit from the matter by being most extensively advertised.

CONFLAGRATIONS.

There have been several destructive fires in Sturgis since its beginning three of which, more noted than others, we mention. In 1859 a fire broke out which swept off all of the business portion of the village on the south side of Chicago street, from Nottawa to North street.

In 1867, the Herbert block and Sturgis hotel were burned ; and January 1, 1876, the Exchange hotel was destroyed.

### CITY ORGANIZATION.

The village was first incorporated as Sturgis February 12, 1855, by act of the legislature. William K. Haynes was elected the first president, and William L. Stoughton the first recorder.

The first code of ordinances was adopted by the common council—whose names we cannot obtain, the earliest records being destroyed in the fire of 1859. The code under which the village is at present governed was revised and adopted August 16, 1876, and is very complete and stringent for the protection of the morals of the people and the preservance of order, inflicting severe penalties for the breach and violation of the same.

The general act of incorporation passed by the legislature, March 15, 1865, was adopted by the council in April following ; and in March, 1875, the people voted to re-incorporate, under the general act of 1873, and are now so governed.

### THE FIRE DEPARTMENT.

On June 20, 1859, the council passed an order to buy a fire-engine, and one was accordingly bought, with a hose-cart and two hundred feet of hose ; and a fire-company organized, called the "Watchword Fire-Company," with William Hammond as foreman ; Daniel Flynn, first assistant ; Henry McAfee, secretary ; C. B. Peck, treasurer ; John P. Gilmer, company engineer, and forty-three other members. David Page was the second foreman. This machine is familiarly known as the "Old Tub," and has been under the ban of the council, they having ordered its sale several times, but notwithstanding it has done some effective "washings" of more modern engines at firemen's tournaments in different parts of the State. The last order concerning it was to put it in order for emergencies, and the "Old Tub" is still officered and manned by the "Deluge Fire-Company," Charles Fairbanks foreman, and forty men.

In 1863, December 14, Extinguisher Fire-Engine No. 2, with hose-cart and hose, was purchased for three hundred and fifty dollars, and soon afterwards additional hose to the amount of one hundred and thirty-seven dollars was purchased.

In 1864 the council bought a site for an engine-house and erected the present firemen's hall, at an expense of seventeen hundred dollars, William Allman and W. A. Kent being the building committee.

In 1865 the fire-company was re-organized and uniformed at the expense of the corporation.

In 1873 the council dug the public well and built the water-tank at a cost of seven hundred dollars ; and the next year enlarged the tank to eighteen feet diameter and twelve feet high and twelve feet from the ground, at a cost of four hundred and ninety-six dollars. The Extinguisher Fire-Company has forty men ; A. A. Wilbur, foreman.

The receipts into the corporation treasury in 1857 amounted to three hundred and fifty-nine dollars and sixty-four cents ; in 1866, they were two thousand seven hundred and fifty-eight dollars ; in 1876, three thousand four hundred and seventy-eight dollars. The expenses of the year ending March 1, 1876, were as follows : fire department, seven hundred and twenty-seven dollars and eighteen cents ; streets, one thousand and thirty-one dollars and eighteen cents ; old indebtedness, seven hundred and fifty-one dollars and thirty-two cents ; salaries, four hundred and seventy-six dollars and twenty cents ; miscellaneous, two hundred and sixty-four dollars.

### CITY OFFICIALS.

Presidents—Hiram Jacobs, 1859 ; P. H. Buck, 1860–2 ; S. B. Follette, 1865–7 ; L. E. White, 1868–76.

Recorders—Edward Dawes, 1859 ; Henry McAfee, 1860–2 ; Ira F. Packard, 1863–5 ; William McLaughlin, 1866–7 ; Bracey Tobey, 1868 ; J. B. Foley, 1869 ; M. D. Kirk, 1870 ; S. B. Follette, 1871 ; M. R. Lester, 1872 ; Ed. S. Amidon, 1873–4 ; H. L. Anthony, 1875–6.

Treasurers—C. B. Peck, 1859 ; Z. H. Wallace, 1860–1 ; E. Dawes, 1862 ; William Allman, 1863–4 ; Joel A. Fox, 1865–7 ; J. J. Beck, 1868–76.

Marshals—Samuel Valentine, 1864 ; William L. Race, 1865 ; Joseph T. Graham, 1866 ; S. S. Phelps, 1867 ; J. S. Swan, 1868 ; James Sprague, 1869–74 ; Horace Hinkley, 1875–6.

### PRESENT CITY GOVERNMENT, 1876.

Levant E. White, president ; trustees, Ambrose M. Littlefield, John G. Seeh, T. Franklin Thornton, Marcus D. Kirk, Frank S. Packard, R. H. Morrison ; J. J. Beck, treasurer ; Harry L. Anthony, clerk ; C. Jacobs, street commissioner ; Horace Hinkley, marshal ; Samuel B. Follette, assessor ; chief engineer, William McLaughlin ; fire wardens, Thomas Keats, John Wallace, James Kennedy, Daniel Burger ; pound-master, David Fitch.

### OAK LAWN CEMETERY,

containing twelve acres, and lying just south of the village, on the southwest corner of the southwest quarter of the northeast quarter of section twelve, is a beautiful and eligible location, bought by the board of health of the township of Sturgis in 1867, which board proceeded to lay it out and order a sale of the lots the same year. One-half of the receipts from the sales were invested in a vault, and for the grading and adornment of the grounds, and the other half of the receipts were invested, and the interest accumulated thereon to be expended in the future adornment of the naturally beautiful place. The present building was put up in 1876. The ornamentation is principally private work, though the grading is all done by the board of health. The selection of the location, and the evident care bestowed upon its preparation and preservation, reflect great credit upon the board, which cannot fail to be appreciated by the people and all who visit the beautiful city of the dead so liberally provided from the public purse. There are some beautiful and elegant monuments and marbles in the grounds, among which the massive Scotch granite shaft placed on Judge Sturgis' lot first attracts the attention, and detains the passer-by.

Jacob Laurick has erected a most beautiful fluted and draped column to the memory of an only daughter, a most lovely girl. The McKerlie, White, Anthony, Pendleton and Wallace marbles are elegant and massive.

THE SOLDIERS' CEMETERY occupies a little rounded summit to the south of the main grounds, and is decorated with a flag-staff, with a howitzer (the gift of the State in 1875) mounted at the base of the staff. Four soldiers are there buried, and on decoration-day services are usually held there.

### PATRIOTISM OF STURGIS.

The patriotism of Sturgis prairie was severely tested in 1832, when the messengers from Fort Dearborn brought the news of Black Hawk's advance on the outlying settlements in Illinois, and their appeal for help to stay the anticipated tide of devastation was not unheeded by the hardy pioneer of the infant settlement, itself in the midst of what they might well deem, under the circumstance, implacable and blood-thirsty foes ; and though the very next messenger which arrived from General Atkinson brought news of the capture of the leader of the hostile array, yet it did not militate against the feelings inspired in the breasts of the settler of giving aid to their distressed brethren in the west, as well as protection for their firesides.

An independent rifle-company was raised and sent to White Pigeon, and thence to Niles, and a few of the Sturgis men went to Door prairie. They were a jolly lot, and had, as Hiram Jacobs, who was one of the volunteers, says, "a big time." Besides Mr. Jacobs there were Asa W. Miller, P. H. Buck, Captain Hunter, who commanded the company, John Parker, Moses Roberts, Edward Mortimore, Baumgartner, and several others, who volunteered to serve out a sixteen days' campaign, making their principal raid on the commissary supplies, there being no other enemy on whom to forage.

The records of the township in the war of the rebellion is a glorious one, not only for the numbers of its citizens who volunteered in the defense of the old flag, but for the distinguished part they held in upholding the integrity of the Union, and making it in deed and in truth the "land of the free" as it has ever been "the home of the brave."

The following are the names of those citizens, as far as we have been able to designate them from the records and by the memories of the citizens of the town. If any names do not appear in this list, they may possibly be found in the other township lists, as it was impossible that some errors should not occur with the means we had by which to locate them by township.

### FOURTH REGIMENT MICHIGAN INFANTRY.

#### Company C.

Captain Abraham R. Wood ; shot on picket near Yorktown, April 18, 1862.

First Lieutenant Ebenezer French ; wounded at Gettysburg ; promoted to captain September 1, 1862, and mustered out at end of service.

Sergeant Gordon Bates ; discharged for disability.

Sergeant John McAfee ; discharged at expiration of service.

Private George A. Chandler ; discharged at expiration of service.

Private David F. Dudley ; discharged at expiration of service.

Private Nelson Field ; discharged for disability, June 1, 1861.

Private Fayette Howk ; discharged for disability.

Private Joseph Humphries ; discharged for disability.

Private Thomas B. Whittlesy ; discharged at expiration of service.

Sergeant James W. Vesey ; second-lieutenant, November 1862 ; died of wounds near Richmond, June 30, 1864.

**SEVENTH REGIMENT INFANTRY.**

**Company K.**

Private Orson D. Lampman; killed at Cold Harbor, Va., May 31, 1864.

Musician James M. Vesey; re-enlisted and mustered-out at end of war.

Private Cornelius Bixby; killed at Antietam.

Private Alonzo Chambers; discharged for disability.

Private Thomas Crampton; re-enlisted; sergeant, January 1, 1863; first sergeant, September 1, 1864; wounded at Petersburg, June 18 and October 13, 1864; second lieutenant, and mustered-out at end of war.

Private John B. Denny; transferred veteran reserve corps and mustered-out.

Private John A. Hooker; wounded; discharged November, 1862.

Private George Pedler; re-enlisted and mustered-out at end of war.

Private Oscar Wilson; discharged for disability, 1862.

**ELEVENTH REGIMENT INFANTRY.**

Colonel William L. Stoughton; lost a leg before Atlanta; entered service as lieutenant-colonel, and promoted to brigadier-general on the field and mustered out.

Major Benjamin F. Doughty; resigned August, 1862.

Assistant-Surgeon N. I. Packard; mustered out with regiment.

Quartermaster A. T. Drake; mustered out with regiment.

**Company A.**

Second Lieutenant Aaron B. Sturgis; resigned.

Private John D. Billings; discharged for disability.

**Company C.**

Captain Calvin C. Hood; resigned.

First Lieutenant Matthias M. Faulkner; promoted to captain and resigned.

Sergeant Charles W. Bishop; died of typhoid fever, January 30, 1862.

Sergeant Enos M. Twichell; discharged at expiration of service.

Sergeant Nelson B. Engle; discharged at expiration of service.

Corporal Jasper D. Ladow; discharged for disability.

Corporal Courtland W. Doughty; discharged for disability.

Private Ira M. B. Gillaspie; discharged at expiration of service.

Private Enoch I. Gillaspie; deserted at Bardstown, Ky., December 26, 1861.

Private Martin V. Gillaspie; discharged at expiration of service.

Private Charles Leonard; died at Sturgis.

Private Henry V. Russell; discharged.

Private Matthew H. Warren; discharged at expiration of service.

Private John C. Drake; mustered out at end of war.

Private Earom J. Weigle; mustered out at end of war.

**Company E.**

Private Henry J. Booth; mustered out at end of war.

Private Perry Sprague; mustered out at end of war.

Private George H. Schimpa; mustered out at end of war.

Private John R. Tyler; mustered out at end of war.

Private Frank H. Church; mustered out at end of war.

**Company F.**

Private Sidney A. Munger; mustered out at end of war.

**Company G.**

Private James Curns; discharged at expiration of service.

**Company I.**

Second Lieutenant Henry S. Platt; promoted to first lieutenant and mustered-out.

**TWELFTH INFANTRY.**

**Company F.**

Private Daniel J. Tompkins; drowned in Arkansas river, at Little Rock.

**THIRTEENTH INFANTRY.**

**Company B.**

Captain William McLaughlin; resigned.

**SIXTEENTH INFANTRY.**

**Company K.**

Private George Remmel; mustered out at end of war.

**NINETEENTH INFANTRY.**

**Company A.**

Private Martin Stuckman; mustered out at end of war.

Private George Stuckman; mustered out at end of war.

Private Peter Nash; discharged at expiration of service.

**Company D.**

Peter Dyer; mustered out at end of war.

William Poppins; mustered out at end of war.

**Company E.**

Captain John J. Baker; major, June 27, 1864; lieutenant-colonel, October 28, 1864; wounded at Lookout Mountain, and discharged.

First Lieutenant David J. Easton; captain, May 2, 1864; major and mustered-out.

Second Lieutenant John F. Clarke; first lieutenant, May 1, 1863; captain and mustered-out.

Sergeant Edmund S. Amidon; discharged for disability.

Sergeant John J. Coblentz; second lieutenant and resigned.

Sergeant William J. Smith; killed at Resaca, Ga., May 14, 1864.

Sergeant Wesley Locke; second lieutenant and mustered out.

Sergeant Andrew J. Lamb; mustered-out.

Corporal C. B. Rodabaugh; mustered-out.

Corporal George Dawes; died at Annapolis, April 20, 1863.

Corporal John H. Popino; mustered-out.

Corporal Isaac B. Turner; mustered-out.

Musician John W. Hawk; mustered-out.

Wagoner John C. Davis; mustered-out.

Private William H. Allen; discharged.

Private Thomas Adams; mustered-out.

Private Lyman S. Allen; discharged.

Private Alonzo I. Bacon; killed at Thompson's station, Tenn., March 5, 1863.

Private Thomas W. Barr; killed at Resaca, Ga., May 14, 1864.

Private Pulaski C. Crapo; mustered-out.

Private William A. Culver; mustered-out.

Private George C. Cole; wounded at Thompson's station, Tenn., March 5, 1863, and discharged.

Private Clinton S. Compton; mustered-out.

Private George H. Chandler; discharged, disabled.

Private William H. Ashley; died at Annapolis, April 11, 1863.

Private Frederick Doss; veteran reserve corps and mustered-out.

Private Robert Fox; discharged.

Private Charles B. Ford; mustered-out.

Private DeWitt C. Greenman; killed at Thompson's station, Tenn., March 5, 1863.

Private Elon C. Greenman; mustered-out.

Private Charles S. Harper; mustered-out.

Private Franklin Hause; mustered-out.

Private Henry D. Lester; mustered-out.

Private Valentine Mustack; died at Nashville, February 25, 1863.

Private Charles B. McAboy; deserted at Dowagiac.

Private Daniel H. Morrison; mustered-out.

Private Aaron D. McConnell; wounded and discharged.

Private Franklin G. Rice; mustered-out.

Private Edmund S. Smith; discharged.

Private Charles E. Stowe; mustered-out.

Private Thomas A. Shirts; wounded in hand; mustered-out.

Private Daniel Thurston; mustered-out.

Private John Walker; died at Annapolis, May 8, 1863.

Private William G. Mugg; died of wounds, May 30, 1864.

Private John W. Anderson; died at McMinnville.

Private John Thurston; transferred to 10th regiment, and mustered-out.

Private Elial J. Mugg; mustered-out.

Private Hamilton A. Coe; mustered-out.

Private John R. Miller; mustered-out.

Private Oliver P. Hanks; mustered-out.

Private Delos Lake; mustered-out.

Private Henry H. Pullman; mustered-out.

Private Ephraim Werner; mustered-out.

Private James Hofftador; died at Annapolis, April 24, 1863.

**TWENTY-SEVENTH INFANTRY.**

**Company G.**

Private Byron Greenman; mustered-out.

**FIRST MECHANICS AND ENGINEERS.**

**Company E.**

Private Albert Allen; discharged at expiration of service.

# BIOGRAPHICAL SKETCHES.

HON. J. G. WAIT,
STURGIS.

MRS. J. G. WAIT,
STURGIS.

## HON. JONATHAN G. WAIT.

Jonathan G. Wait was born in the town of York, Livingston county, New York, November 11, 1811. His parents, Josiah and Martha Ann (Graham) Wait, were natives of the town of Alstead, State of New Hampshire, but in early life moved to the town of Ovid, New York, and from thence to York, before named, and thence to Perry, Lake county, Ohio. The family name has been variously spelled at different periods, as follows: Waite, Wayte, Wayght, Waight, Wait, Waitt, Wate, Weight and Waiet. It has been traced back as far as A.D. 1075. William the Conqueror gave the earl-dom, city and castle of Norwich in England, to Rolf De Waiet, son of Rolf, an Englishman by a Welsh woman, who married Emma, sister to Roger, earl of Hereford, cousin of the conqueror. Records show that Wayte, of county Warwick, A.D. 1315, was escheator of the counties of Wilts, Oxford, Berkshire, Bedford and Bucks. Thomas Wayte was a member of parliament, and one of the judges who signed a warrant in 1649 for the execution of King Charles the First. Their descendants, Richard, John and Thomas, were among the earliest settlers of New England. Thomas Wait was the father of Josiah Wait, the father of Jonathan G. Wait, the subject of our sketch. Josiah Waite, the father of Jonathan G. Wait, was a farmer, and

the son was instructed in that business until the age of fourteen years, at which time the family removed to Lake county, Ohio. At the age of sev-enteen Jonathan G. Wait commenced teaching district schools, which occu-pation, for portions of the time, he followed for several years. In the fall of 1834 Mr. Wait left Ohio for the State or Territory of Michigan, traveling through the southern part of the same, and as far west as Laporte, Indiana, and thence returned to Ohio, and in the spring of 1815 removed to St. Jo-seph county, Michigan, and made a permanent location on Sturgis prairie, in what was then known as the village of Sherman, but now is the city of Sturgis. Here he has remained to the present time. For two win-ters, succeeding his first location on the prairie, he taught the village school in the old log school-house that was first erected in the place for that purpose.

In the year 1836 he began to build in the village, and that season erected four dwelling-houses. He also began the manufacture of boots and shoes, and cabinet and chair-making, employing from ten to fifteen men, the work being all done by hand. In 1841 Mr. Wait commenced business in the mercantile line, and was engaged therein fifteen years, and was also engaged in the manufacture and sale of lumber in Bronson, Branch county, where he owned and operated two saw-mills during the same period. In 1849 and 1850 he was the agent of the Michigan Southern Railroad Company, to procure the right of way and otherwise aid in the construction of the road. He also had heavy contracts on the road for building depots and fences, culverts and bridges, and furnishing ties. He built all of the buildings from Bronson to Sturgis on the road, furnished the ties from the former place to White Pigeon, and fenced the road the same distance. In the fall of 1850 he was elected to the legislature of Michigan as a Whig, during Governor Barry's administration. Hon. T. W. Ferry, now United States senator, was a member of the house that same session, and Hon. I. P. Christiancy, also United States senator, was in the senate. At this session occurred the greatest and last struggle between the Michigan Central and Michigan Southern railroads, in which the Southern came off victorious.

In 1857 Mr. Wait assisted to organize the Grand Rapids and Indiana Railroad Company, and was elected a director thereof, which position he has held continuously to the present. During this year he graded and bridged twelve miles of the road between Sturgis and La Grange. In 1850 he was elected to the State senate, and re-elected for two succeeding terms—six years consecutively. During this time he had charge in the senate of the bills providing for an extension of time limited for the construction of the Grand Rapids and Indiana road, by which the land-grant was to be saved to the road, the bills being successfully passed through both houses, and becoming laws. This action was the foundation of the final success of the road, as, if the land-grant had lapsed, the road would never have been built. Mr. Wait was for several years engaged in the location and construction of the road, and was amply rewarded by meeting with full success.

In all things pertaining to the prosperity of Sturgis, Mr. Wait has ever taken and still does take the liveliest interest, and is among the foremost to secure advantages for the town that seem to prophesy or promise well for its advancement in material wealth, or social improvement, or educational progress. In the early days of his residence in the township, then called Sherman, and including Sherman, Burr Oak, Fawn River and Sturgis, he was the town clerk, supervisor, and justice of the peace for several years. In politics he is a staunch and uncompromising Republican, being elected to the house of representatives of Michigan in 1850 as a Whig, and to the senate in 1860, 1862 and 1864 as a Republican. In 1860 he commenced the publication of the Sturgis Journal, a radical Republican paper, in which he discussed the political issues of the day with marked ability and vigor. He continued to edit and publish the Journal for fourteen years, when he disposed of it to his son, who succeeded to the editorial tripod for a time. In 1872, as an acknowledgment of the faithful service rendered by the Journal to the Republican cause, Mr. Wait received the appointment of postmaster of Sturgis, which position he holds at the present time.

On the 20th day of October, 1839, Mr. Wait was united in marriage to Miss Susan S. Buck, a daughter of George Buck, of Erie county, New York, and the second family to settle on Sturgis prairie in 1828. Mrs. Wait was born in Erie county, New York, June 8, 1821, and removed with her father and his family to Michigan, as before stated, where she has ever since resided. Twelve children have gathered around the family hearthstone of Mr. and Mrs. Wait—nine sons and three daughters, of whom five sons remain, the others having passed beyond this present state of existence. One son, Arthur, is the agent of the Grand Rapids and Indiana Railroad at Sturgis.

DR. IRA F. PACKARD,
STURGIS.

MRS. IRA F. PACKARD,
STURGIS.

## DR. IRA F. PACKARD.

Among the citizens of Sturgis, none have a more creditable position in its society than has Dr. Ira Fobes Packard. By his own endeavors and integrity he has made himself a place among his fellows, honorable to himself and the community in which he lives. He comes, too, of a sterling ancestry, who have made a record for themselves upon which their descendants may reflect with just and commendable pride. His grandfather, Elijah Packard, was a native of England, where he followed the profession of a dissenting clergyman, provoking thereby such fierce persecution from the State church authorities, that he was forced to flee to America, and leave a fine estate, which was confiscated to the British crown. On his arrival in America in the earlier part of the eighteenth century, he adopted the business of a civil engineer, and entered the service of the Bristol Company of the Massachusetts colony, for whom he surveyed large tracts of the country, receiving, in 1765, as part payment for his labors, a fine tract of land cover-

ing the site of a manufacturing city on the Kennebec, in the State of Maine. While engaged in the survey of the Company's possessions within the present limits of the State of Maine, he was murdered and robbed.

He was the father of seven children, of whom Benjamin Packard, the father of Dr. Ira F. Packard, was the youngest son, and who was born in Bridgewater, Massachusetts, June 7, 1760. At the age of fifteen years, Benjamin rallied with the minute-men of the colony to the defense of Lexington, and behind the stone walls, hedges and fences that lined the road, hung upon the retreating red-coats, pouring into their disordered ranks charge after charge of buck-shot, from the tube of an old "queen's arm" he carried. At the end of that bloody day he entered the ranks of the colonial army, and never returned to his home until after the long and sanguinary war was gloriously ended for the colonies, by the surrender of Cornwallis, at Yorktown, and the Republic was born. He was at

Bunker Hill, and in most of the important battles of the Revolution. He received four wounds, but fortunately none of them were very serious. He was promoted to a lieutenancy for gallantry and meritorious action on the field. He was married in 1784, to Mehitable Fobes, of Bridgewater, Massachusetts, and removed from thence to Royalton, Vermont, where he died September 19, 1823. Like his fathers before him, his family also consisted of seven children, of whom Dr. Ira F. Packard was also the youngest son, and who was born on the forty-eighth anniversary of his father's birthday, June 7, 1808, in Royalton, Vermont, where the son went to school for nine years, until he was fifteen years of age, when, the father dying, the lad was thrown upon his own resources for his maintenance and education. In 1824, Ira went to Boston and entered the service of Kittredge & Wyman, as a clerk in their mercantile establishment, where he remained until the following winter, when he returned to Vermont to attend school. The next year he shipped for a whaling voyage, sailing from Newburyport, in the ship "Alexander," September, 1826, which voyage was completed successfully by filling the ship with oil and bone, and returning safely to port in July following. He made several other shorter voyages, bringing up at last in Philadelphia, in the fall of 1828, when he engaged to assist in drifting coal for Adam Burr, in Pottsville, the work being managed by a nephew— George Burr. In February, 1829, he went to Pike, Allegheny county, New York, where his brother Benjamin resided, and from thence to Yorkshire, Cataraugus county, in the same State, where he engaged in the mercantile business; but the same not proving successful, he closed it out and removed to Erie, Pennsylvania, in the spring of 1832, and began the business of a merchant again in the grocery and provision line; but disappointment again overtook him. The cholera broke out that summer, and all business was temporarily suspended, and he therefore sold out his interests in Erie, and returned to Yorkshire and engaged as a clerk for Messrs. A. & W. Hibbard, merchants. In the spring of 1836, he commenced the study of medicine and surgery with Dr. Bela H. Colegrove, of Sardinia, Erie county, New York, and continued his readings for three years, attending lectures at the Western College of Physicians and Surgeons at Fairfield, Herkimer county, New York. In 1839 he made a tour in the west, seeking a location to settle for the practice of his profession, and selecting Sturgis prairie, in the then village of Sherman, returned and brought his family to his new home in St. Joseph county, Michigan, in the fall of the same year, where he has ever since resided. He was elected to the honorary degree of doctor of medicine in the Western College of Physicians and Surgeons, of Laporte, Indiana, a short time after he took up his residence in the county. He followed his profession until the spring of 1850, when his health failed, and he made a tour to California, returning the spring following, since which time he has not practiced except in emergencies.

On the 27th day of April, 1829, he was united in marriage to Miss Emily M., a daughter of Colonel Araunah Hibbard, a lieutenant in the war of 1812,

who was at Lundy's Lane with General Scott, and was severely wounded at Queenstown Heights. Colonel Hibbard was one of the earliest settlers on the Holland purchase, in the vicinity of the present site of Clarence, Niagara county, New York, where Emily was born April 23, 1812. She is said to have been the first white female born in that township, when it was a wilderness, with neighbors no nearer than three miles, and but very few at that. She was the daughter of a pioneer, and fitted for the trials and deprivations of the pioneer-life to which she succeeded in Michigan.

Dr. and Mrs. Packard have never lost a member of their family by death, though three sons and two daughters have gone out from their fireside to make firesides of their own, around which now cluster the fifth generation since the stout old dissenter sacrificed his property and fled from his native land, rather than relinquish his faith and his right to proclaim it. These sons and daughters are Dr. Nelson I. Packard, who succeeded to his father's extensive practice in 1850, and still pursues it; Homer H., who now resides in Ashland, Nebraska; Emily N., now the wife of Henry S. Church, of Sturgis; Franklin S., a member of the firm of Johnson, Packard & Co., heavy lumber dealers of Sturgis, and formerly a member of the legislature from St. Joseph county; and Lucina M., now Mrs. Thomas J. Acheson, of Emporia, Kansas.

Dr. Packard was for many years connected with the official relations of schools in Sherman, and afterwards Sturgis village, and has been a firm and zealous advocate for the maintenance and support of the public schools and their advancement to the highest grade of excellence possible. In public improvements and expenditures for the common good of all her citizens, Sturgis has had no wiser head or more liberal hand than his. Prudent and well regulated in his habits, his example has been such as to bring him the esteem of his fellow-citizens, and the regard of all who have the pleasure of his acquaintance, and the Packard homestead is a place at which every comer is made welcome by its master and mistress, with an unstinted hospitality.

Dr. Packard was originally a Whig in politics, and cordially embraced the principles of the Republican party at its organization, and has been an active supporter of its general policy up to the present time. In religious sentiment Dr. and Mrs. Packard are liberal, broad and catholic, and while holding to their own convictions, accord the same liberty to others without comment or reflection; and at an age when the silver which crowns their heads admonishes them of the inevitable change that must ere many years come to them, are serenely awaiting the summons, with naught of fear or dread to becloud or dim the vision of the future that slowly unfolds before them.

Dr. Packard was one of the original members of Sturgis Prairie Lodge, I. O. O. F., and erected the hall of the same. He is also a member of the Masonic bodies in Sturgis, from the blue lodge to the commandery of Knights Templar.

---

## JOHN R. HARRIS.

This gentleman was born in Livingston county, New York, December 28, 1817. His parents were in moderate circumstances, and having a family of ten children, it was necessary that the sons should commence at an early age to contribute to the support of the family; hence the advantages of education were poor. The subject of our sketch bought his time of his father by giving him all he earned, except enough to buy his every-day clothes. In 1836 he had a chance of emigrating to Michigan, which he embraced, coming with a man by the name of Abel Crossman, who agreed to give him fourteen dollars a month for a year, paying him in advance, out of which he bought of his father the balance of the time remaining before his majority. He arrived in Michigan, and purchased eighty acres of land. He fulfilled his contract with Mr. Crossman, and then went to work on his own land.

He had no experience and no education, procuring what knowledge he now possesses after his marriage. His capital was his health, his industry and his ambition. He was industrious and temperate, having been brought up to work, and having joined the Washingtonian society when but twelve years of age. These characteristics as success was required in a new country, and by their practical application his success was insured. He first settled on section twenty-four in Sherman township, St. Joseph county, Michigan, and afterwards, in 1846, removed to his present home on section fourteen, in Sturgis township.

On the 3d of April, 1842, he married Sarah Parker, a native of Pennsylvania, by whom he had six children, namely:

HENRIETTA E., born April 26, 1844.

ALBERT E., born June 23, 1846; died March 28, 1848.

WILLIAM E., born May 12, 1848.

ELLEN R., born August 22, 1850.

CLAYTON J., born January 19, 1854.

CARRIE A., born December 24, 1855.

Mr. Harris has always devoted his attention to agriculture, and is generally considered a sound, practical farmer. In politics he is a Republican. In religious sentiment he is liberal, never having affiliated with any particular religious denomination. He adheres to the grand principle of human justice, unbiased by religious prejudice and unharassed by dogmatic theology. In his every-day life he is actuated by strict integrity, has comported himself with rectitude, has been an affectionate husband, a fond parent, a good neighbor and a firm friend,—in manners genial and courteous, in disposition affable and kind, and in public career an honest and upright citizen. Having thus lived, a retrospection of his past has no conscientious defects, and his future no disagreeable apprehensions.

John R. Harris.                    Mrs. John R. Harris.

RESIDENCE of JOHN R. HARRIS,
Sturgis Tp. St. Joseph Co. Mich.

and a journey to Three Rivers before him. But a friend, who heard the young man's story, furnished him a breakfast and paid his fare to the latter place. He then went to Fulton county, Illinois, where he taught school for three years, accumulating during the time eight hundred dollars in gold. In the fall of 1860 Mr. Carpenter entered the law department of the Michigan University, where he remained for the fall and winter terms, and was admitted to the bar of St. Joseph county in the spring of 1861, entering the law-office of Henry Severns, of Three Rivers (now of Kalamazoo), where he remained until August of that year, and then removed to Sturgis, where he entered the law-office of Hon. William I. Stoughton, and, upon that gentleman's entering the army, succeeded to his practice, and has ever since been located there.

Mr. Carpenter has an extensive and lucrative practice, which he conducts with success to himself and his clients. He is courteous and affable, and the amenities of the legal profession suffer no diminution at his hands, or by his manner. In the fall of 1862 he was elected to the position of circuit court commissioner of St. Joseph county, which position he held for six years. In 1868 he was chosen prosecuting attorney for the county, and held the office four years. In politics he is a Republican.

On the 3d of January, 1863, he was united in marriage with Miss Helen M. Whitney, a daughter of Nathan B. Whitney, of Fulton county, Illinois, but a native of Massachusetts. Three children have blessed this union,—John H., Ella L. and Carrie L., all now living with their parents in the beautiful and cozy cottage erected by Mr. Carpenter, in Sturgis.

The mother of Mr. Carpenter died at his residence in Sturgis, in December, 1864.

Among the self-made men of St. Joseph county, Talcott C. Carpenter, one of the foremost members of the St. Joseph bar, stands eminently. Thrown upon his own unaided efforts at the early age of seventeen years, he gained an education at the common-schools of the county and the University at Ann Arbor, undergoing the severest privations in order to fit himself for his profession without incurring pecuniary obligations to any person, asking and receiving no assistance from a single individual, and paying his way by the labor of his own hands, performed after the hours of the day devoted to study had passed by. Such self-denial and determination have been amply rewarded in the success which has followed Mr. Carpenter thus far in his honorable career. He was born in Delhi, Delaware county, New York, February 19, 1835. His parents, Younglove C. and Rhoda (Sabin) Carpenter, were natives of Connecticut and Massachusetts respectively, and with them he migrated to Mendon, St. Joseph county, when but two years of age. Here, on a farm, in the log-house of the pioneer, the boy lived until the father died in 1852. The hardships endured by the family can scarcely be appreciated by the present rising generation, but a slight idea may be gained of them when it is stated that until the subject of our sketch had attained the age of fourteen years he had never enjoyed the luxury of a pair of shoes for his feet, but had worn cloth moccasins made by his mother. The cabin, like others in those days, scarcely kept out the snow, which sifted in under the shakes, upon the beds and over the floor, through which the children, of whom there were seven,—five girls and two boys,—left their tracks when they rose in the winter mornings, and went to the big fire-place to perform their toilets.

Upon the death of the father, Talcott told his brother that if he would stay on the farm and take care of the family, he (Talcott) would give him his (Talcott's) interest in the estate, and, upon arrival at his majority, Talcott quitclaimed his interest accordingly. From that date (1852) onward, the boy took up the thread of life for himself. He attended the district school at Centreville for two terms, and was also two terms at the normal school at Ypsilanti, after which he spent two years at the Michigan University at Ann Arbor, in the literary department, supporting himself by sawing wood after school-hours, cutting and splitting one hundred cords of the same during his stay in Ann Arbor. His needs were so pressing and his determination so great to finish his two years' course with honor, that he lived, for four months on nineteen cents per week, and when he arrived at Kalamazoo at the end of his term, he had but a quarter of a dollar in his pocket,

DAVID KNOX, SR.,
STURGIS.

David Knox was born in Cayuga county, New York, August 30, 1806, and in the spring of 1822 came with his father and mother, Jacob and Rachel Knox, to Michigan, locating in Wayne county, near Detroit. Ten years later, in 1832, he removed to St. Joseph county, and settled at Sturgis. Here his life has been spent principally in the occupation of farming, and having endured the hardships of pioneer-life and the labor incident to the development of a new country, he is one of the few early settlers who yet remain strong and vigorous to enjoy the harvest of their toil.

Mr. Knox has raised a family of eight children, all but one being the children of his second wife, Thirza Knox, who was the daughter of Benjamin Jacobs, one of the early settlers on Sturgis prairie, to whom he was married in 1835, and who died in 1871. Of his children only five are now living, being Henry, David, Charles, Mary and Gurnet.

His sons Henry and Charles are farmers. David is in business at Three Rivers, as a lawyer. In political belief and action Mr. Knox is Republican, being one of the original Abolitionists of that party. His religious tendencies led him early to connect himself with the Methodist church, and he has been one of its strongest and most faithful supporters from the first organization in this county to the present time. A man physically strong, with a liberal, cultivated mind, and an earnest, true nature, he has always been prominently identified with every good work about him, and the whole influence of his life has been on the *right side*

# MOTTVILLE.

AMONG the earliest settlements in the county of St. Joseph we find Mott-ville takes its place. Originally a portion of White Pigeon township, of which it remained an integral community until 1837, its history is intimately connected with that of the latter township. Its present area includes thirteen thousand and eighteen acres of land surface, of which sixteen hundred acres were of the original White Pigeon prairie, the rest of the area being covered with burr and white oak, principally the "openings" of the country. The soil possesses the usual characteristics of that of the openings, and is, as else-elsewhere in the county, very fertile and productive.

The township is well drained by the St. Joseph and Pigeon rivers, the former entering the township on sections five and six, and, passing to the southwest quarter of the section, forms from thence the western boundary of the township and county as well. The Pigeon enters the township on the east line of the northeast quarter of section eleven, and runs westwardly and southwest to the St. Joseph, which it enters on the northeast quarter of section twenty-three, township eight, range thirteen. The township is known on the maps of the United States surveys as township eight, range twelve, and a fraction of township eight, range thirteen, which lies east of the St. Joseph river, which was formerly a portion of Cass county. The eastern tier of sections in the township were retained by White Pigeon in its limits when Mottville was constituted a separate township. The surface is a general level.

## THE FIRST SETTLER

within the present limits of the township, other than Quimby, who located on the present site of the village, was Levi Beckwith, who, with his family of wife and four children, came to the west end of White Pigeon prairie in August, 1828, at which time there were but three families living in houses at that end of the prairie—Winchell, Page and Paine; and Beckwith's and another family lived in their wagons for a time, until they could build houses. Henry E. Root, of Constantine, and a large land-owner in White Pigeon, married one of Mr. Beckwith's daughters. The next settler was John Bear, who came in late the same year and built a cabin, and subse-quently sold his location and moved into Constantine, and from thence to the lake in Cass county, to which he gave his name.

## OTHER EARLY SETTLERS

were Aaron Brooks, of Ohio, who came with his family in 1829, and located on his present farm on section twenty-four, and was accompanied by Nathan, Thomas and James Odell. Solomon Hartman and his family came in from Ohio in August of the same year. Thomas Burns, of Pennsylvania, settled in the township in 1830, on the farm now occupied by Jonathan Hartzler, on section twelve. Benjamin Carr came in 1831, and located on section thirteen, and Andrew Thompson located in 1832 on section thirteen, where he still resides. He came from Ohio. William Cook came in from New York, and located on a farm two and a half miles east of the village, and now resides in the village. Elizabeth Rathbone, an English lady, came into the township and settled in 1831. In 1834 C. P. May came in from New York and located, and in the spring of 1835 a man by the name of Adams came in, and died the following August. The sickness of 1835 in this locality was quite as severe as in 1838. A family of Davidsons came in and settled in 1830.

## THE FIRST FARM

was opened in the present-limited township by Levi Beckwith, in the year 1829. Aaron Brooks, however, opened one the same year, and raised the first wheat cultivated in the township, harvesting the same in 1830. Elias Taylor, the oldest Indian trader at the crossing of the St. Joseph, planted the first nursery from which the first orchard grew in 1829.

## THE FIRST ENTRIES OF PUBLIC LANDS

in the government township were made in 1829, and numbered fifty-one, of which the first three were as follows:

East half of the southeast quarter of section one, Robert Clark, Jr.; west half of the southeast quarter of section two, Daniel Reed, of Tompkins county, N. Y.; and east half of the southeast quarter of section three, John Winchell, all on January 15, 1829. Seventeen entries were made June 15. The three first-named entries are now included in White Pigeon township. In 1876 there were twelve thousand and sixty-one acres assessed for taxa-

tion, and valued by the supervisor at two hundred and seventy-seven thou-sand two hundred and twenty dollars,—about one-quarter to one-third of its actual value.

## THE ASSESSMENT OF THE PROPERTY

in the township in 1837 for taxation was fixed at one hundred and fifty-four thousand five hundred and forty-six dollars, and the taxes amounted to five hundred and fifty dollars. In 1876 the total assessment of property was fixed by the board of supervisors at two hundred and sixty-seven thousand three hundred and eight dollars on real estate, and fifty-four thousand and twenty hundred and sixty dollars on personal property; and the tax levied thereon amounted to one thousand six hundred and forty-two dollars and twenty cents for State and county purposes—one-half to each—and one thousand three hundred and sixty-three dollars and six cents for township purposes, including schools, making an aggregate of three thousand and five dollars and twenty-six cents.

## THE CROP STATISTICS

of 1874 show that the harvest of 1873 produced seventeen thousand six hun-dred and fifty-seven acres sown of wheat from two thousand five hundred and twenty-one acres sown, thirty-eight thousand four hundred and sixty-five bushels of corn from one thousand four hundred and fifty-five acres planted, and two thousand eight hundred and eighty-two bushels of other grain, three thousand five hundred and thirty-two bushels potatoes, nine hundred and seventy-three tons of hay, seven thousand seven hundred and fifty-three pounds of wool, one hundred and seven thousand eight hundred and seventy pounds of pork, twenty-two thousand six hundred and fifty pounds of butter, four thousand and seven hundred and thirty-four pounds of dried fruit, four hun-dred and eighty-seven barrels of cider, eight thousand six hundred and eleven bushels of apples, and seven hundred and eighteen bushels of other fruit and vegetables. There were owned in the township in 1874 three hundred and three horses, two mules, five hundred and twenty one cows, two hundred and fifty-five other cattle, nine hundred and eleven hogs, and one thousand two hundred and ninety-seven sheep.

## THE FIRST HOUSE

built in the township now included within its borders, was the cabin of Levi Beckwith in the early fall of 1828, and the second one was that of John Bear, both of which were primitive log-cabins. The first frame and brick houses were built in the village subsequently.

## THE FIRST WHITE CHILD

born in the township was Selinda Rickart, who was a babe-in-arms when Solomon Hartman came to the township on August 10, 1829, and was some two or three months old then. The second one was a son of Leonard Rickart, and was born in the fall of the same year. A daughter of James Odell was born the same year also, and Sophronia Burns was born October 30, 1830.

## THE FIRST MARRIAGE

of white persons in the township was that of Valentine Shultz and Susan Hartman, in October, 1829. They first settled on a farm on section five, and then removed to Coldwater, and finally to Iowa, where Mr. Shultz died in 1870. Benjamin Montgomery and Rebecca Davidson were married in 1830.

## THE FIRST DEATH

which occurred in the township was that of the child of Leonard Rickart before named, which lived but a few months. The first adult who died was Solomon Hartman, his death occurring August 4, 1830. His coffin was made of the side-boards of a wagon with which he had come into the coun-try. He was the first person buried in

## THE CEMETERY

which was laid out in the village of Mottville, in 1830, being donated by the proprietors of the plat. · Baum died in 1831, and was buried therein also.

## THE FIRST PREACHERS

were the Methodist missionaries, Felton and Gurley, in 1829 and 1830, and Elder Holmes, a Free-will Baptist, who came to the settlement in 1831, Judge Winchell building him and his wife a snug cabin on his, Winchell's, farm. He continued his labors for some years, preaching in the settlers' cabins and under the trees as occasion offered or weather permitted.

RESIDENCE OF **ISAAC RUNYAN**, STURGIS TP, ST JOSEPH CO, MICH.

RESIDENCE OF **JOHN WALTHAM**, MOTTVILLE TP, ST JOSEPH CO, MICH.

MANUFACTURES.

Jonas Hartman built a brewery in an early day, 1833–34, and ran it a year, by which time Jacob Lintz had fathomed the mysteries of beer-making, and operated for some time, and was said to have made a most excellent article of "home-brewed" ale. Peter Burgett built a tannery near Mottville village, and finished his leather as often as he killed a 'coon which was fat and juicy. This tannery was built before 1836. Isaac Benham, of Constantine, bought his first stock of leather of Burgett, trading a rifle for the same, for which Burgett was to allow seventeen dollars, provided Benham could hit Burgett's hat at fifteen rods with it. Burgett rolled his head covering up into as small a compass as possible and stuck it up on a stump, much to the chagrin of Benham, who thought anybody could hit as big an object as Burgett's "slouch;" still by a lucky shot Benham hit the mark, and then it was his turn to laugh, for he had ventilated the sombrero handsomely, the ball perforating every fold. John Carlin operated a brewery in 1834, on the Chicago road, in the township. In August, 1829, Samuel Pratt and P. A. Paine made brick in the township—burnt forty thousand.

THE FIRST ROAD

was surveyed through what was afterwards the township, in 1825, and was the national military road between Detroit and Chicago, being the first ripple of the incoming tide of civilization, ante-dating by two years the first settlement in the county. The first road surveyed by township authority was the Bristol and Mottville river road, surveyed July 7, 1831, by Mathew Rowen.

THE FIRST STAGE LINE

was run over the Chicago road by Savery, in 1831–32, ten miles. An accident occurred in 1852, by which Dr. Joseph M. Chase, an eminent physician and estimable citizen, met his death, being killed instantly by being thrown from his buggy.

EDUCATIONAL.

The primitive educational facilities of Mottville were limited. A school was taught in the log-house of John Bear as early as 1830, at which the Hartman and Davidson children were attendants. Some two or three years subsequent a school-house was erected at Mottville, but regular school districts were not organized until 1837. We quote the subjoined extract from the first records of the proceedings, as defining the locality of the five original school districts:

"At a meeting of the inspectors of schools of the township of Mottville, in the school-house at the village of Mottville, May 1, 1837, the township was divided and numbered into school districts as follows:

"District No. 1 to commence at the northeast corner of said township, and running from thence west on the township line to the southeast corner of section four, from thence south on the section line to the north side of Pigeon creek, from thence following up said creek to the township line, thence north to the place of beginning.

"District No. 2 to commence at the northeast corner of section four, thence running west on the township line to the river St. Joseph, thence down the river to the line of section six, thence south to the north side of Pigeon creek, thence up the creek to the west line of section ten, thence north to the place of beginning.

"District No. 3 to commence on the township line on the northwest side of the river St. Joseph, thence running west on said line to the line of Cass county, thence running south on said county line to the south side of the river St. Joseph, thence down the river to the north side of Pigeon creek, thence up the creek to the southwest corner of section eight, thence south following the section line to the river, thence up said river to the place of beginning.

"District No. 4 to commence on the south side of Pigeon creek, thence south to the south line of the State of Michigan, thence running east on said line to the quarter-post of section twenty-one, thence north to Pigeon creek, thence following down the creek to beginning.

"District No. 5 commencing at the quarter-post of section twenty-one, on the State line, and running thence east on said line to the east line of the township of Mottville, thence north on the township line to Pigeon creek, thence down the creek to the centre of section sixteen, thence south to the place of beginning. To which is added all that part of District No. 4, of the township of White Pigeon, south of the Pigeon creek, and west of section sixteen."

John F. Johnston, W. A. Sanger and Francis Nixon are the present school inspectors.

In 1876, there were taught five schools in as many school-houses in the township, which were in session an average of eight and three-tenths

11

months each during the year ending September 1. There were two hundred children in the township of the requisite school-age, between five and twenty years; and one hundred and eighty-one of them attended the schools. Four male teachers were employed, and paid five hundred and seventy-two dollars and fifty cents for their services, and five females, who received four hundred and eighty-seven dollars for their work. There are two hundred and fourteen volumes in the district libraries; and the school-houses, which can supply two hundred and eighty-nine sittings, were valued at four thousand five hundred dollars. The total expenses of the districts were one thousand one hundred and seventy-eight dollars and thirty cents, and a balance was left on hand, for the current year, of three hundred and twenty-three dollars and forty-eight cents.

THE FIRST TOWNSHIP MEETING.

At a meeting of the electors of the township of Mottville, convened at the school-house in the village of Mottville on the 3d of April, 1837, the organization was effected by choosing Thomas Odell moderator and Lot Gage clerk—Chauncey May, William Barnes and John Sixby inspectors of said meeting.

After the board had declared the polls open, they proceeded to ballot, and the following officers were elected:

Supervisor, Andrew Thompson, 1837; Town Clerk, Joseph F. Johnston; Justices of the Peace, John Sixby, Chauncey May, Peter Buck and Daniel Osborn; Collector, James Hartman; Constables, James Knapp, John C. G. Roach and Henry Kurten; Assessors, Daniel Osborne, Thomas Finney and William Barnes; Highway Commissioners, Nicholas I. Sixby, Thomas Finney and Abraham Rickart; Inspectors of Schools, William A. Sawyer, Joseph F. Johnston and Francis Nixon; Overseers of the Poor, Charles McCollister and Calvin P. May.

"Voted, That seed-horses over eighteen months old should not be free commoners." (?)

"Voted, That twenty-five hundred dollars be raised for the support of the poor." Adjourned.

The township officers have been as follows:

Supervisors.—Andrew Thompson, 1837; Daniel Osborne, Harvey Cook, two years; Hiram Holabird, S. C. Abbott, two years; Asahel Clapp, three years; George G. Gilbert, Daniel Roush, two years; Nicholas I. Sixby, two years; William Ferguson, Joseph M. Chase, Edward Gray, fifteen years; John Waltham, Aaron Nash, twelve years; Stephen N. Nash, four years; J. A. Hertzler, present incumbent, 1876.

Clerks.—Joseph F. Johnston, 1837; O. E. Thompson, two years; Lyman Loomis, Rufus Ingersoll, two years; Hiram Holabird, James G. Smith, four years; James H. Voorbies, two years; A. H. Moore, Warren Miller, William Ferguson, three years; Jacob L. Rathbun, six years; Rufus Ingersoll, George B. Kapp, William Waltham, Samuel Taylor, four years; John P. Madden, D. C. Fuller, present incumbent, 1876, and three years previously.

Justices of the Peace.—Edmund Davis, John Sixby, Chauncey May, eight years; Harvey Cook, six years; E. C. Abbott, Hiram Holabird, Abraham Goble, James Hutchinson, O. E. Thompson, Aaron Brooks, Ralph Markham, A. H. Moore, A. Markham, John Chase, sixteen years; James Kellogg, Stephen Walter, Jacob Gortner, eight years; Joseph M. Chase, F. A. Long, William Ferguson, eight years; Samuel R. Wiley, J. C. Caul, Solomon Rote, John Rickart, John Smith, eight years; Edward Gray, ten years, and present incumbent, 1877; John P. Hackenburg, Stephen N. Nash, eight years; Dr. D. L. I. Flanders, Perry S. Bower, George Smith, Eleazar Crouch, seven years (and present incumbent); John P. Madden, William Wolfinger, J. L. Rathbun, twenty years (and present incumbent); Daniel Klockner, Joseph Clouse, 1876 (and present incumbent).

POPULATION.

In 1838 the inhabitants of Mottville township numbered four hundred and ninety-seven souls. In 1850 they had increased to six hundred and eleven, and in 1860 to seven hundred and thirty-five. The next decade showed a loss of fourteen, there being three hundred and fifty males and three hundred and seventy-one females. They lived in one hundred and fifty-three houses, and there was not a vacant one in the township, each family having one to themselves. During the next four years the township gained three inhabitants, having seven hundred and twenty-four in all; of these three hundred and forty-seven were males and three hundred and seventy-seven females—the ladies still retaining the numerical superiority, if they could not vote. Of the males one hundred and eleven were of the military age—over twenty-one and under forty-five. Seventy-one were beyond any fear of a draft, but not over seventy-five years, and nine had passed the three-quarter score and were coming down the "home-stretch," but had not marked the ninth decade of the century. Of the females one hundred and forty-four were over eighteen and under forty years; seventy-six had passed the heyday of life, but had not reached the threescore and fifteen—as six of their sisters had done, and passed it. One hundred and fifty-six boys were under twenty-one years, and one hundred and fifty-one girls were under eighteen years of age.

### THE POLITICAL SENTIMENT

of the township has been Democratic by a fair majority ever since the first presidential election in 1840, with the exception of 1860. In 1840 the Whigs polled sixty-one votes, and the Democrats forty-two. In 1844 the Whig vote was forty-nine, and the Democrats sixty-three, with a single, solitary Liberty man. In 1848 the Whig candidates received fifty-four votes, the Democratic ones sixty-four, and the Free Soilers ten. In 1852 the Whigs polled forty-one votes, the Democrats sixty-seven, and the Abolitionists, though they had a remarkable increase in percentage, cast but eleven votes. In 1856 the Republicans cast seventy-five votes, and the Democrats eighty-eight, but in 1860 "old Abe" found more friends than his fellow-citizen of Illinois (Douglas), receiving ninety-five votes to eighty-six for the latter. In 1864 the pendulum swung back across the whole arc and the Democrats polled one hundred and one, while the Republicans cast but sixty-three votes. In 1868 each party increased their votes by sixteen tallies, leaving their relative strength the same. In 1872 there was a loss on both sides, the Democrats polling eighty-two votes, and their opponents fifty-three—O'Connor and Black each having a single friend. In 1876 Mr. Tilden received eighty-eight votes, Mr. Hayes sixty-seven, and Mr. Cooper twenty-six, which would indicate a population in the township of about nine hundred.

### MOTTVILLE VILLAGE.

This village, at one time the most important village in the county, is situated on the south side of the St. Joseph river, and was first settled by Joseph Quimby, who took up his permanent residence on its present site in the year 1828. He remained for some months the only white resident of the place, until Joel Stevenson and Elias Taylor came in the spring of the following year (1829). The village, or rather the site of the village, was visited by several, of whom some subsequently became settlers of the adjoining country,—before the settlement of any one except Quimby,—notably Mr. Aaron Brooks and James Odell, who passed through there by stage in the summer of 1828, their business being to select a good location for settlement. The site of the village was known for years as the grand traverse of the St. Joseph river, the Chicago trail crossing the river at this point. The plat was first surveyed May 31, 1830, by Orange Risdon and John R. Williams, proprietors of section six of township eight, range twelve, on which the original plat is located.

### THE FIRST HOUSE

erected here was a log-hut, built by Quimby immediately after his arrival. In 1830 this solitary habitation was followed by one of a more pretentious kind—a frame house, built by Elias Taylor, which served as the *first store* in the place, also as the *first tavern*, and likewise as the *first post-office*, of which various conglomerated establishments Taylor was the first proprietor. The store answered the purposes for which it was intended for some years, while the tavern was succeeded by the present structure in 1833. It was built by Hart L. Stewart, and has been kept by various persons—notably Joseph Knorr, who was a genial host, and a very successful tavern-keeper. The present proprietor is Samuel Earley, No. 2.

### THE FIRST FRAME HOUSE

was erected by Elias Taylor as above stated. He was the old Indian trader at the grand traverse, and also the first sheriff of the county, receiving his appointment from Governor Cass in 1829.

### THE FIRST BRICK HOUSE

was built by Abraham Goble in 1844, of brick furnished by Messrs. John Hartman and Thomas Burns—the former now a resident of Cass county (living about a mile from the county line); the latter a resident of Mottville. It is now owned and occupied by George Bostock.

One of the principal features which led to the early importance of Mottville, was the erection of a bridge spanning the St. Joseph river there. The first structure was built in 1833, by Hart L. Stewart, as a military crossing, under the territorial laws. The timber was furnished by Solomon and John Hartman, of which sixteen thousand feet were required, including some of the best

ever used for the purpose. There were some pieces used in its construction sixty feet in length, and eighteen inches square. It cost about five thousand dollars. It stood until 1845, when a piled bridge was built, Thomas Burns driving the piles. This bridge was built at a cost of about three thousand dollars, and lasted until superseded by the present structure in 1867. The latter is an arched bridge, built of wood, and stands on stone abutments, with a central pier, also of stone. The contractors were Mahlon Thompson and Joseph Miller, and the cost of construction was about seven thousand dollars.

The original owners of the site of the village were John R. Williams, of Detroit, and Hart L. Stewart, the former retarding the growth of the village by asking an exorbitant price for his part of it. At one time he offered to sell his interest for three thousand dollars, but when Messrs. Hart L. and A. C. Stewart offered that sum, he declined to accept, and also refused two successive advances, each of one thousand dollars—asking six thousand where he had formerly agreed to take three. The self-same property was subsequently sold for taxes.

A great and creditable feature of the former prosperity of the village was its facilities for transportation, it being the depot for freight dispatched by water. The keel-boats used to run up to the village from its mouth; they were propelled by poles, manual labor being the force used. Finally small steam-boats were employed, and then it looked as though, with the stage route between Detroit and Chicago passing through the village, and its increased advantages for transportation, the prosperity of the place was assured.

At one time, it is stated on excellent authority, there accumulated at Mottville fourteen thousand barrels of flour, to be shipped on the opening of navigation in the spring. The chief era of its prosperity was from 1840 to 1850; from the latter date gradually declining from the most important village in the county to one of comparatively no commercial account.

In 1851 a tannery was erected at Mottville by Messrs. Hoag & Buck, and was continued by them till 1841, when it ceased operations. A second enterprise of a similar nature was started by Horace Reynolds in 1855, which underwent many changes of proprietors, and finally wound up in 1874.

One of the earliest enterprises in the village was a distillery, which was established by Henry Heywood in 1829. He conducted it for about fifteen years, when it passed into the possession of Reuben M. Daniels. It was discontinued in 1849.

The man Daniels, above-mentioned, was attacked with *mania a potu* during the Mexican war, and while laboring under that disease, he became possessed of the hallucination that the Mexicans were pursuing him. He was out in the woods, and having his rifle with him, he discharged it at his phantom foes, and then ran and hid, not showing himself for several days. The rifle was subsequently found by Messrs. Burns and Field.

The father of Governor Bagley, of Michigan, was a tanner at Mottville at an early day, going from thence to Constantine to follow his trade.

The Stewarts built the first warehouse in the village, and the second store, and brought in the second stock of goods.

Kellogg & Paine also were in trade in the flush days before 1835, and Stewart kept the hotel in 1835, and John Newells after 1840.

Jacob Lutz built a woolen factory in Mottville after 1860.

### THE FIRST PHYSICIAN

in the township was Dr. L. S. Lillibridge, who settled there in 1836. Previous to that date Dr. Loomis, of White Pigeon, served the people medicinally. Dr. Joseph M. Chase succeeded Dr. Lillibridge, and was killed accidentally in 1852, as related elsewhere.

A post-office was established in Mottville in 1830, Hart L. Stewart postmaster. The greater part of the people are accommodated at the present time at White Pigeon and Constantine, although there is yet a post-office at Mottville.

### METHODIST EPISCOPAL CHURCH OF MOTTVILLE.

The first preaching in Mottville was according to the doctrine of the Methodist Episcopal church, by the Rev. Erastus Felton, in 1829. Brother Thomas Burns, who still resides in the village, heard him preach in 1830. The first preaching was in Conrad Cook's dwelling-house and in Stewart's hotel. Rev. Thomas Odell, a local preacher, came from Ohio in the spring of 1820, and settled here; he was among the first to preach the Gospel to the scattered settlers in this vicinity. He had been an itinerant minister in Ohio for eighteen years. He subsequently moved to Fort Scott, Kansas, where he died in 1872.

JOHN HARTMAN

MARY HARTMAN

RESIDENCE OF JOHN HARTMAN, POWTER TP, CASS CO, MICH. ONE MILE WEST OF MOTTVILLE, S.T JOE C.º

The first class was organized at Mottville, in the summer of 1832, by Rev. L. B. Gurley. The members were George B. Gilbert, who was the leader, and his wife, Conrad Cook and wife, Mrs. Caskey, Mrs. Hull, Mrs. A. Globe, Rev. Thomas Odell and wife, Orin E. Thompson and wife, William Cook and wife, both of whom are still residing in the village. Mrs. Hull is in California; Mr. Gilbert is supposed to be still living. Conrad Cook died in 1836; Rev. Erastus Kellogg preached his funeral sermon. Meetings were held in dwellings, hotels and school-houses until 1846, when a church edifice was built. The dedication was conducted by Rev. William Sprague, during the pastorate of Rev. Franklin Gage, now located at North Adams, Michigan. The old building is still doing service, but, in the words of Brother Robinson, of the *Niles District Record:* "It ought to be released. A new house is greatly needed. And we mistake greatly if there are not ample means in that old and wealthy community to build one. Shall it be done?"

The present membership of the church is twenty; the pastor is Rev. Z. G. Boynton. The church officers are Hiram Hutton, class-leader; Lavinia Burns and Mary Ann Cook, stewards; William Cook, Hiram Hutton, William Shoemaker, Harvey Field and Joseph Knorr, trustees.

### TRINITY EVANGELICAL LUTHERAN CHURCH OF MOTTVILLE

was organized on the 5th day of July, 1857. At the first church-meeting, on the day and date above mentioned, a committee was appointed to prepare a suitable constitution for the government and discipline of the church. The following members of the committee were present: Pastor *pro tem.,* Rev. A. S. Bartholomew, Joseph Bittenbender, J. R. Jones, Conrad Bittenbender, Jacob Doctor.

At a second meeting, on the 10th day of August, 1857, the committee reported that they had framed a constitution, and presented the same, which was unanimously adopted, and signed by a number of brethren. And they proceeded immediately to the election of church-officers, which resulted in choosing J. R. Jones, deacon (for two years); Jacob Doctor, elder (for two years). On the 11th day of October following, a second election was held, at which James Kleckner was chosen elder (for one year), and Joseph Bittenbender, deacon (for one year). The council being thus elected, according to the constitution, chose out of their number Joseph Doctor, president; James Kleckner, secretary; Joseph Bittenbender, treasurer; and the church council was inducted into office on the 19th day of November, 1857.

The first regular congregational meeting after organization was held at the Methodist Episcopal church at Mottville, on the 5th day of March, 1858, for the purpose of calling a pastor, and the Rev. A. S. Bartholomew received and accepted the call.

The meetings of the church organization were held in the Methodist Episcopal church edifice until 1869, when they erected their present church building at Mottville. The succession of pastors has been: A. S. Bartholomew, Peter Bergstrasser, J. N. Barnett and Alexander McLaughlin, the present incumbent.

The present church officers are: Jacob Bittenbender and William E. Cook, elders; Jacob L. Rathfon, William G. Bittenbender and Amos Clark, deacons; Charles Schall, Ellis Artley and Joseph Clouse, trustees; J. L. Rathfon, secretary; Joseph Bittenbender, treasurer.

The original roll of membership contained the names of seventy-four persons, among whom were all the above-named first officers and their families. The present membership is about eighty. The church is in a generally flourishing condition.

### INDEPENDENT ORDER OF ODD-FELLOWS.

St. Joseph Valley Lodge, No. 56, I. O. O. F., was instituted about 1857-58, with F. Gruneway, N. G.; A. C. Williams, V. G.; William Cook, P. S.; L. W. Schall, R. S.; but it ceased to work several years ago.

### AMUSEMENTS.

The first celebration of the Fourth of July, of any pretensions, in the county, was held in Mottville in 1830, the same being held in the upper room of the Stewart warehouse, just above the bridge. Neal McGaffey was the orator of the occasion. John Morse, of Coldwater, furnished the music with his clarionet. Edwin Kellogg and Hunt, of White Pigeon, sang the "Ode to Science," and the distinguished guests were Major-General Brown, and Inspector-General Hoag of the Michigan militia.

Near Sheriff Taylor's residence there was a sapling that used to serve as a "lock-up" for his prisoners while *in transitu* to the county jail, and the sheriff had more pressing duties to attend to at his hostelry. The sheriff was the only legalized trader with the Indians, and, being conservator of the peace, he saw to it that no whisky was sold to his customers except what

went over his counters. He was an efficient executive in that respect, at least.

### THE RECORD OF PATRIOTISM,

written up by the citizens thereof, reflects credit upon the township. They cheerfully bore the burdens imposed by war, when secession madly referred its cause to the arbitrament of the sword, and filled the quotas of the township with alacrity,—maintaining its honor and that of the State and nation on many well-fought fields. We here append a list of the names of those who, forsaking home and its endearments, shouldered their muskets in defense of the government, by whose upholding against treason such homes as are found in St. Joseph county only are possible to acquire.

#### FOURTH MICHIGAN INFANTRY.

Private Jacob M. Gragg, Company F; mustered-out.

#### FIFTH INFANTRY.

Private James Luft, Company D; missing near Southside railroad, Virginia.

Private William Avery, Company D; mustered-out.

Private James Ketchum, Company D; mustered-out.

Private Asher D. Artley, Company F; killed at Gettysburg, July 2, 1863.

Private Cyrus Luft, Company F; died at Camp Pitcher, Virginia, January 11, 1863.

Private Wilson Gibson, Company F; discharged.

#### EIGHTH INFANTRY.

Private Adam Snook, Company D; mustered-out.

#### ELEVENTH INFANTRY.

Private W. H. Smith, Company C; discharged at expiration of service.

Private Jacob Rathbun, Company C; discharged at expiration of service.

Private Henry B. Smith, Company E; died at Murfreesboro, January 19, 1862.

Corporal Samuel Haas, Company G; died at Grayville, April 4, 1864.

Private James P. Haas, Company G; discharged at expiration of service.

Private George M. Nash, Company G; died of wounds received at Stone River, January 4, 1863.

#### SIXTEENTH INFANTRY.

Private John Haas, Company D; killed at Gaines' Mill, Virginia.

Private Jesse N. Brooks, Company E; mustered-out.

Private David B. Perry, Company E; mustered-out.

#### NINETEENTH INFANTRY.

Private John Gee, Company D; mustered-out.

Private Edward Gear, Company D; mustered-out.

Private William Hendrickson, Company D; mustered-out.

Private David Sadorius, Company D; discharged.

Private Michael Voltz, Company D; mustered-out.

Private William H. Huff, Company E; enlisted in regular army.

Private Robert Watterson, Company E; died at Annapolis, Maryland, April 25, 1863.

#### TWENTY-FIFTH INFANTRY.

Private Charles Smith, Company G; died October 19, 1863.

Private George B. Harker, Company G; mustered-out.

Private Wellington Smith, Company G; mustered-out.

#### SECOND CAVALRY.

Private Charles W. Baker, Company A; mustered-out.

#### THIRD CAVALRY.

Private Thomas Leinbach, Company I; mustered-out.

#### EIGHTH CAVALRY.

Private William H. Wagner, Company G; mustered-out.

Private Allen F. Chase, Company H; mustered-out.

#### FIRST LIGHT ARTILLERY.

Private Hiram L. Hartman, Battery G; died November 20, 1864.

Private John Koon, Battery G.

Private Thomas B. Parks, Battery M; mustered-out.

#### FIRST MICHIGAN SHARP-SHOOTERS.

Private Albert H. Knorr, Company F; mustered-out.

Private Perry Machemer, Company F; mustered-out.

Private David H. Early, Company F; mustered-out.

#### SEVENTEENTH INFANTRY.

Private Charles Smith, Company C; mustered-out.

Private Silas C. Smith, Company C; died in Andersonville.

We tender our acknowledgments, for assistance received in the compilation of this history of Mottville, to Messrs. Aaron Brooks, Thompson, John and Solomon Hartman, and Lewis Rhoades, of White Pigeon.

## BIOGRAPHICAL SKETCHES.

ANDREW THOMPSON.

There is always something of peculiar interest surrounding the life and labors of the pioneer; he who fearlessly leaves the home of his childhood—perchance a home of comparative ease and comfort, situated perhaps in some richly-settled eastern State, or amid the green hills of New England—and who submits cheerfully and manfully to the privations and hardships incident to new settlements, till his steady and earnest toil is rewarded with the blessings commensurate with his laborious struggles, and crowned with the many bounties of Providence. Great changes grow out of unwearied and constant strokes; the sturdy forest is laid low, and there in time is reared the pleasant home with all its cherished adornments, the quiet hamlet and the wondrous city.

Oftentimes the whole of one's allotted span of life is spent amid the beauteous scenes of the country; and to agricultural pursuits alone does he devote his earliest and his latest labors. To this latter class belongs, pre-eminently, the subject of this sketch. Born away back beyond the present century, the only time he ever left the plow was to take up the musket in order to defend the flag his father fought to sustain.

Mr. Thompson first saw the light on the morning of March 25, in the year 1790. His native element was the farm, and on a farm he was born, within sixteen miles of the city of Leesburg, Virginia. When but four years old he removed with his parents to Piqua Plains, in the State of Ohio, and five years afterwards they again removed, this time settling on and clearing up the present site of the town of Circleville, Ohio. In 1812 he enlisted in a regiment of reserves, went to the front, and did good service for his country.

After the cessation of hostilities he married Mary Davis, a native of Kentucky, and his house became the home of a dozen young olive-branches, lacking one. This sketch having been designed as a family record, we annex a brief genealogy of this branch of the house of Thompson:

THOMAS D., born November 17, 1813; married April 15, 1841.
MORRIS, born December 27, 1814.
CYNTHIA, born July 6, 1816.
PHŒBE, born August 17, 1818.
ELLEN, born August 25, 1820; married David Kurshner, February 6, 1840.
ISAAC, born May 14, 1822; married Susan Davis.
JEMIMA, born February 7, 1825; married George Kerstater, April 16, 1843.

JAMES, born June 18, 1827; married Jane L. Davis, February 16, 1850.
ELIZABETH, born February 15, 1829; married Joseph Kleckner, June 5, 1853.
LEWIS, born June 5, 1831; married Margaret Connor, January 14, 1857.
MARY ANN, born January 1, 1835; married William Milner, January 10, 1860.

It was in 1832 that Mr. Thompson first took up his abode in Mottville township. He then settled on a farm of one hundred and seventy-five acres, pleasantly situated on both sides of Pigeon creek. He subsequently purchased thirty-seven acres more, but has since sold some small parcels, leaving him now one hundred and ninety-seven acres of well-cultivated land. In 1837 Mr. Thompson assisted in the organization of the township, and was chosen its first supervisor. He never sought political preferment, and positively refused to serve after the expiration of his term.

In 1866 he sustained the deep-felt loss of his estimable wife, who had shared his struggles for more than half a century, having been married in 1813. In religion he is a Mormon of the Joseph Smith branch of that faith—not believing in plurality of wives, but having a lasting faith in the creed promulgated by the founder of this peculiar sect. In politics he is Republican, having cast his first vote for the Whig candidate, Monroe, in 1816. On the regular organization of the Republican party he allied himself with it, and has stood firmly by it, especially through the perilous times of 1861-1865. Socially, he is a genial, whole-souled gentleman; honest in all his dealings, and enjoying the friendship of all with whom he comes in contact. By industry and frugality, coupled with a certain degree of shrewdness, he has managed to secure a comfortable competency, which, after his four-score and six years, he enjoys, with a fair prospect of continuing thus to reap the benefits of a good career yet for many years.

AARON BROOKS,

the oldest living settler in Mottville township,—in point of settlement, and the third oldest in point of age,—was born in Fayette county, Pennsylvania, on the 7th of February, 1798. He was reared on a farm, and has spent all his life in agricultural pursuits. In 1808 he removed to Licking county, Ohio, and settled within seven miles of the present site of the city of Newark. In 1829 he removed to Mottville township, St. Joseph county, Michigan, and settled on the farm he now occupies, located on section twenty-four. It was then included in Cass county, but in 1830 the citizens residing thereon petitioned the legislature to have all the land on that side of the St. Joseph river annexed to St. Joseph county, which was accordingly done. On the 19th of July, 1819, he married Cassy Newell, a native of Tuscarawas county, Ohio, by whom he had six children. January 7, 1838, he sustained the loss of his wife, and after remaining single for about four years, he married, in 1842, Ann Bell, a native of Monroe county, New York. By this union he has three children, namely:

JANE ANN, born December 29, 1843; married Robert Corner, April 20, 1863.
AMY JEANETTE, born August 4, 1849; married Frank M. Anderson, January 1, 1866.
ELLEN, born June 13, 1854, and married Amos J. Yoder, December 30, 1875.

In 1844 the people of his township evinced their appreciation of his integrity and general good character by electing him to the office of justice of the peace, which he filled with general acceptability.

In 1849 Mr. Brooks "took up his tent and silently stole away," so to speak, to California, the then newly-discovered Eldorado, where he remained for about one year. He returned with about two thousand dollars, the result of hard and constant toil in the diggings. He made the overland journey, occupying five months and twenty days in its accomplishment. He returned by Panama, New Orleans, St. Louis, Peru, and thence by rail to Chicago, and from there by stage to his destination.

In religion he has always entertained liberal views, and has never assimilated with any particular denomination. In politics a Democrat, he polled his first vote for Andrew Jackson in 1832. He has always adhered firmly to the principles of Jacksonian Democracy, and has refused to recognize any of the many political innovations that have been made upon the old-time Democratic principles.

AARON BROOKS.

MRS. AARON BROOKS.

## JOHN HARTMAN.

John Hartman, for many years a resident of Mottville township, but now a resident of Cass county, Michigan, was born in Schuylkill county, Pennsylvania, on the 20th of August, 1811. When but four years old he moved with his parents to Wayne county, Ohio, and from thence, in 1819, to Crawford county, in the same State.

After remaining in Crawford county ten years, his father (Solomon Hartman) concluded to come still farther west, and in 1829 came to St. Joseph county, Michigan, and settled on the south side of the St. Joseph river, about two miles east of the village of Mottville. There they entered eighty acres, and proceeded at once to erect their log-cabin, which was then the only kind of habitation in all this region.

On the 4th of August, 1830, Solomon Hartman died, leaving the family under the protection of his sons, Solomon, and the subject of this sketch. Solomon soon removed, and John subsequently bought eighty acres more land, which he developed into a fine, well-cultivated farm. In 1859 he removed to Cass county, and settled on his present farm. They endured similar hardships to those of other pioneers, and Mr. Hartman relates, among other things, that when they first came into the country they camped out fifteen nights before they could make the necessary arrangements to erect their log-house.

In 1837 he married Mary, daughter of Armstrong Davidson, Esq., an old pioneer and prominent citizen of Cass county. They have reared a family of six children, of whom five are still living. Levi, the second son, died in California, and the rest are all married, and are respected citizens of Cass county, living within five miles of the paternal roof. Through hard work and sound, practical economy, Mr. H. has increased his possessions until he now has a farm of two hundred and forty acres, where he resides, and a smaller one of eighty acres a few miles distant.

In politics he is a Democrat of the "Old Hickory" school. His religious sentiments embrace an extensive liberality. Having joined no particular church, he yet rightfully assumes the character of a good citizen and a respected neighbor. His estimable wife, the partner of his early struggles, and faithful helpmate for forty years, enjoys, by virtue of her many excellent traits of character, the respect and esteem of a large circle of friends. A portrait of this worthy couple, together with an illustration of their pleasant home, will be found elsewhere in this work, where it will remain as an monument to their industry, economy and good sense.

## HALSEY CASKEY.

Among the many prominent settlers of Mottville township, none occupied a more worthy place in the esteem and confidence of his fellow-townsmen than he of whom we write. Halsey Caskey was born in New Jersey, on the 8th of February, 1811, and, when but a child, accompanied his parents to Ontario county, New York.

April 30, 1835, he married Mary Hoagland, a native of Canadice, New York, and a family of four children blessed the union.

On the 6th of September, 1844, Mr. Caskey and his family came to St. Joseph county, and in the year following took up their permanent residence on the farm now owned by his heirs. He was brought up to agricultural pursuits, and was in every respect a good, practical farmer. His homestead bears the imprint of his careful management, and is considered as fine a property as exists in the township.

He was for many years a working member of the Methodist Episcopal church of White Pigeon, with which organization he united soon after his settlement in this county. His piety was one of his most prominent characteristics, and he always maintained a leading position in all matters relating to the growth and prosperity of the religious body to which he belonged. In all his business transactions he was actuated by a stern integrity, and he was never known to defalcate in any financial engagement, his word always being considered as good as his bond. In politics he was a Republican, and, while he never took an active part in the political movements of his day, he ever evinced a deep interest in what he considered the country's good demanded, and this by rendering intelligent support rather than by affiliating with the political machinery in vogue.

After a useful, though not a long life, on the 11th of September, 1869, he died, leaving behind him a record that will long survive. By his death his family lost a kind and affectionate husband and father, the community an honest and upright citizen, and the church a useful and earnest member. His widow still resides in the old home, enjoying the comforts which the industry of her husband, coupled with her own economical household management, enabled them to accumulate.

The portrait of Mr. Caskey, which adorns our pages, was inserted by his widow as a token of affectionate regard, and we feel assured that it will always be to her and her children a source of reverential remembrance of the dear departed one.

## JOSEPH MILLER.

Among the many old gentlemen whose biographies grace the pages of this history, none deserve a better mention than he whose name stands at the head of this sketch. The facts of his history are furnished us by members of the family, and are somewhat incomplete.

Joseph Miller was a native of Heidelberg, Lehigh county, Pa., and was born September 13, 1793; here he lived, following the occupation of a farmer. In 1817 he was married to Miss Mary Hill, of Pennsylvania; she was born December 5, 1797. As a result of this union four sons and three daughters were born to them, viz.: Charles F., Samuel, Stephen P., Joseph, Esther, Mary, and Rachel A.

In 1836 Mr. Miller and family removed to St. Joseph county, Michigan, and located one and a half miles east of Mottville, on the old Chicago road; here he followed farming, in connection with keeping a public-house, till the spring of 1864, when he settled a half-mile farther east, where he resided until his death.

During the early days—before the era of railroads—he was engaged in carrying goods for merchants in Constantine and White Pigeon from Detroit and other places.

His faithful wife died May 9, 1851, leaving a large circle of friends to mourn her loss.

Mr. Miller was again married to Miss Effie Barclay, of Northumberland county, Pennsylvania, January 5, 1854. She was born December 3, 1819. Five children were born to bless this union, viz.: Hattie L., Emma A., Carrie M., Frank L., and Dellie,—all of whom are living except Carrie M.

Mr. Miller has lived a quiet, unassuming life, and enjoyed the confidence of his fellow-citizens. He was for more than thirty years a worthy member of the Masonic order.

On the 14th of August, 1876, Death came and claimed him for his own. Mr. Miller lived respected and died regretted by those who knew him.

Mrs. Effie Miller is still living at the old home, surrounded by many of her children. She is the generous donor of this sketch and portrait.

JACOB S. SMITH.

B. J. WILEY.

## JACOB S. SMITH.

Jacob S. Smith, son of Jacob and Catharine Smith, was born in Bucks county, Pa., October 22, 1800. He continued to reside with his parents while they lived, working on the farm, and having a general supervision of the old Pennsylvania homestead,—he being the only surviving member of the family.

He began life very poor, but by hard and persistent industry and frugality he has succeeded in securing a fair competency. When in his twentieth year he had saved enough to warrant him in taking a wife, which he did by marrying Elizabeth Wyant, a native of Union county, Pa. The event transpired in October, 1820. Ten children, six sons and four daughters, have been born to them, of which number nine are still living; their names are Julia Ann, Peter, John, Kate, Isaac, Maria, Aaron, Susan, Joseph and Robert; and they were born in the succession as their names appear.

In May, 1857, Mr. Smith and his family removed to Mottville township, St. Joseph county, Michigan, and settled on the farm they now occupy, located within a convenient distance of the village of Mottville. He owns one hundred and sixty acres of well-cultivated and highly-productive land, while he is also accredited with possessing one of the finest barns in the township.

In politics Mr. Smith has always been a Republican since the organization of that party. Most of his children are married, and reside in different parts of the county,—possessing many of the excellent traits of character which their father endeavored to instil into their minds before they left the parental roof.

Mr. Smith very rightly enjoys the confidence and respect of the community in which he lives. He is a quiet, unassuming man of very prudent habits, but always willing to patronize a laudable enterprise. A portrait of Mr. Smith is placed in this work as a tribute to his general worth, and as a monument for his family and friends to cherish.

Samuel R. Wiley, of Mottville, St. Joseph county, Michigan, was born at Naples, Ontario county, New York, August 31, 1796, and is therefore past fourscore. He was educated at the common-schools of his native town, and, at an early age, was apprenticed to the shoemaking trade, which, with tanning and currying, he followed until he reached his thirty-fifth year. At this time, namely, in 1831, he purchased a farm of fifty acres in Ontario county, where he remained until his removal to St. Joseph county, Michigan, in 1850. He settled on his present farm, which then contained one hundred and forty-five acres, but now, through a subsequent purchase, increased to one hundred and eighty-five acres. For the former he paid eight dollars per acre, and for the latter ten dollars. His farm is now a model of neatness, and his land in a high state of cultivation.

In 1856 he built his present neat dwelling-house, and added, by various improvements, to the value and beauty of his adopted home.

In 1821 Mr. Wiley took unto himself a wife in the person of Patience Clark, who was born at Naples, Ontario county, New York, June 14, 1801. This marriage was productive of much happiness and eleven children, of which number eight reached the age of maturity and are now comfortably settled in various States, and are respectable members of society, evincing in their lives the admirable lessons of self-reliance and rectitude taught them by their parents.

On the 24th of September, 1852, Mr. Wiley lost, by death, his wife, who had been his faithful companion for more than thirty years. It was to him and his family a sorrowful bereavement, but with the fortitude born of his Spiritualistic faith he feels her essential presence always with him, and humbly abides the time when they shall be again united.

Mr. Wiley was elected to several offices of trust in his native township, and has also served as school-director in the township of Mottville one term. In politics he is a Democrat, priding himself in having voted for "Old Hickory" away back more than half a century ago. In religious belief he is liberal, as before intimated, holding fast to the doctrines of Spiritualism of the higher and nobler nature, and discountenancing its charlatanism. He carries his four-score years well,—the result of an abstemious and industrious course of life; and possessing the use of all his faculties unimpaired, he has fair prospects of living yet to see the dawn of another decade. In character, he is positive; in business, honest; in the discharge of duty, prompt and fearless. A good citizen and a desirable neighbor, he enjoys the respect of all who know him.

DAVID EBI.

MRS. DAVID EBI.

## DAVID EBI.

The subject of our sketch comes of an old and respectable family, his grandfather, David Ebi, having served as a soldier in the Revolution, in a Virginia regiment of volunteers, through the entire war, when he was honorably discharged, but never claimed the pension allowed the old veterans of 1776. He of whom we write was born near Canton, Stark county, Ohio, December 19, 1813, and was one of a family of seventeen children, of whom fourteen survive.

The first nineteen years of his life he remained at home, assisting his father on the farm. At this time, however, he evinced a desire to learn the carpenter trade, and stipulated with his father for the remaining years of his minority, agreeing to pay the old gentlemen fifty dollars therefor, which contract he faithfully fulfilled, much to the satisfaction of the father.

In 1831 he shouldered his knapsack and left his father's roof to begin life for himself, and was domiciled for that year with his uncle, David Ebi; during which time he attended school.

In 1832, with his brother Michael, he was apprenticed to a carpenter, but worked so hard that at the end of the second year he was obliged to return to his uncle's house to recuperate, availing himself of the opportunity, in the meantime, to again attend school; and resumed his apprenticeship in the spring.

On the 30th of August, 1835, he engaged in a business expedition to Michigan for a brother, and walked to Akron, Ohio, the first day. He arrived at Mottville on the 6th of September, walking from Detroit since the 2d of the month. On arriving at Mottville he found his brother, Daniel Ebi, living with his father-in-law, Daniel Shellhammer. Here he met his future wife, Catharina Shellhammer, to whom he was married March 30, 1837.

Mrs. Ebi was born in Schuylkill county, Pennsylvania, November 11, 1817, and died September 26, 1858.

Eight children were born to them, of whom five still survive. Among the greatest trials of the married life of Mr. and Mrs. Ebi was the loss of three of their older sons, who died at a time when they were just developing into interesting youths. An unfortunate financial transaction, caused by the delinquency of another, cost Mr. Ebi the loss of all of his hard-earned property, at a time when he was laying the foundation for future competence.

The life-history of Mr. Ebi is a chequered one, experiencing all of the vicissitudes of a pioneer existence. He has at last, after many wanderings and changes, returned to the township where he made his first stay in Michigan of more than a single night.

He went to York township in Indiana (Elkhart county) the day after he was married, a one-horse wagon sufficing to transport his wife and all of his household effects. He bought forty acres of land and built a small board-house, without doors, windows or chimney. The cooking was done out of doors, a stump being utilized for a stove, and thus passed the honey-moon; it would scarcely come under the head of "love in a cottage," and yet love was not wanting, though the cottage was yet to be built. It came in good time, however, and was all the better for being the sole handiwork of the master of the house himself.

He resided here twelve years, when, his wife's health failing, he changed his location to the village of Bristol, in which place he built two cottages for his own use, residing there many years.

On the 10th of April, 1860, in company with one A. P. Wright, he went to Colorado, where, after prospecting for a time, he settled in Gilpin county, and engaged in mining. At intervals he worked at building himself a house, which, on completion, he converted into a provision-store, and succeeded well in the business of merchandizing in that line.

In 1866 he returned to Bristol, where he met Mrs. Barbara Koehler, a widowed lady whom he had known for twenty years, and on the 15th of April following they were married. He subsequently purchased the farm of his wife's former husband, on which they resided two years, and then sold the same and moved to Oshkosh, Wisconsin, where they resided five years.

In 1873 Mr. and Mrs. Ebi paid a visit to his sons living in California, where they remained nearly a year and returned to Elkhart July 6, 1874, and on the 18th of the same month fixed their residence, as at present, in Mottville.

Mr. Ebi, while in Colorado, assisted in framing the territorial laws and regulations, and was a delegate to the first territorial convention, in 1860, from Gilpin county.

Mr. Ebi is a member of the Methodist Episcopal church, which he joined, with his wife Catharine, in 1838; and it was only by the consolation of their religious belief they were enabled to bear their great griefs in the loss of their sons.

The present wife of Mr. Ebi has two children by her former husband, Conrad Koehler (a native of Germany), a son and a daughter.

Mrs. Ebi was born in Lancaster county, Pennsylvania, in the year 1821, her maiden name being Barbara Whitman. She was first married when nineteen years of age. We present the portraits of Mr. and Mrs. Ebi in this connection, which will be gladly recognized by the many friends of the originals.

## STEPHEN M. NASH.

Sampson C. Nash, father of the subject of our sketch, was born in Maryland, and Lovina Allerton, his wife, was born in Pennsylvania. Stephen M. was born in Stark county, Ohio, January 26, 1823. In the fall of 1843 Mr. S. M. Nash, in company with his father's family, emigrated to St. Joseph county, Michigan, and located some four miles south of White Pigeon. Here Stephen continued to live till the spring of 1848, when he settled in Mottville township. In September, 1852, he purchased some eighty acres of land of Joseph Miller; this, together with what he previously owned, constitutes his present home. In April, 1853, he was married to Miss Caroline Voorhees, daughter of Christopher Voorhees. November 26, 1854, their only child, Ada A., was born. Mr. Nash has filled various positions of trust and honor in the town, with credit to himself and general satisfaction to his constituents,—has served as justice of the peace, supervisor of the town, and chairman of said board. In politics Mr. Nash affiliates with the Democratic party; and in religion his sympathies are with the Disciple church.

# NOTTAWA.

Nottawa-seepe, "a prairie by a river," was the Indian cognomen given to the prairie partially included in the limits of the present township of Nottawa, Colon, Mendon and Leonidas—the little stream being called, by the dusky dwellers along its banks, by the same term. The prairie was irregularly shaped; points of wood-land jutting out like capes into the sea, at some points entirely cut off, and thus forming islands. At one point the opposing wood-lands—oak openings—would almost meet, as it were reaching out their sinewy hands to throttle the wavy sinuous plain, devoid of forest growth, but luxuriating in the richest grasses, and adorned with the most beautiful flowers. Again the forest would retreat on either side, and the waving grass would sweep to the right and left, until its billowy outlines were miles in extent, and then the oaks would gather steadily for a grand charge on either flank, and the plain would recoil under the shock until but a narrow pass was left between the monarchs of a thousand years and the survivors of tempest and fire for nearly as long.

Such was the outline Nottawa prairie presented to the eyes of John W. Fletcher, Captain Moses Allen and George Hubbard, as, in the summer of 1826, they followed the trail of Black Hawk and his fierce Sac warriors on their annual pilgrimage to Malden, and made the tour of southwestern Michigan in search of a place to build homes for future families to rest in. Theirs were the first views of this prairie vouchsafed to a white man, in whose breast arose a feeling that there he would make his home; there he would build a roof-tree, and gather around him a family in time to come. But one of this trio ever executed his then formed design, and realized his aspirations.

### AREA.

Nottawa is a full government township, known and designated on the public surveys as township six, south of range ten west, principal meridian, and its area contains twenty-three thousand two hundred and thirty-eight acres, three hundred and eighty of which are water surface. Two thousand six hundred acres of the original prairie are included in the present bounds of the township, the rest of the acreage being covered with oak openings principally, the bottoms along the creek and the St. Joseph being covered with heavy timber of various kinds, common to the county.

### TOPOGRAPHY.

The surface is generally level, undulating, more or less, in some portions of the openings. The soil is of the general characteristics of that of the whole county, and in the southern and western parts of the township there is a considerable deposit of bowlder-stone, which are of great use for building purposes.

### DRAINAGE.

The township is watered and drained by the St. Joseph river, which crosses the northwest corner of the township diagonally, through sections five and six. Hog creek, or Prairie river, enters the township from the south, on the southeast quarter of the southwest quarter of section thirty-six; runs northerly into the southeast quarter of section twenty-six, and thence west and south, passing out on the southeast quarter of the southwest quarter of section thirty-four, and re-entering on the southeast quarter of the southwest quarter of section thirty-three, and, running northwesterly, makes its final exit from the township on southwest quarter of section nineteen. Evans' lake on the southwest quarter of section twenty-one, and Sand lake on the southeast quarter of section twenty-seven, are the principal lakes, though a little one on section thirty-four rejoices in the highly-perfumed name of Skunk lake. A little creek comes into the township on section thirteen, which rises in Colon, and runs through the centre of the township, west, and enters Hog creek near the centre of section nineteen.

FIRST SETTLERS.

The first white man to select a location for a home on Nottawa prairie, was Judge William Connor, still a worthy and honored resident of the township, whither he came forty-eight years ago, in the freshness and elasticity of early manhood, to hew out for himself and those who should follow, a home amid the oak parks and flowery lawns designed and wrought by that deft landscape gardener—Nature. He came to the prairie in May, 1829, and, against the protests of the Indians,—who claimed all of Nottawa prairie, arguing that the line of their reservation, as drawn upon the surveys as the southern limit of the same, was in fact the centre line of the reservation,—made his selection and returned to Monroe to enter the same; after which he remained at Ypsilanti and taught school one term—returning to his location and settling thereon permanently, September 1, 1829. Other parties followed Judge Connor in looking for locations, among them Judge John Sturgis, who had, in 1827, made a settlement on Sturgis prairie, but having sold the same, came to Nottawa and made a new location on section four, against the same earnest and angry protests of the Indians that were made to Connor. Judge Sturgis tried to show them that their line was not so far south as his location; failing in which, he persuaded them to go to Lima or Mon-go-qui-nong prairie, as it was then known, and lay the matter before a friend of theirs—a white man—in whom they reposed the utmost confidence; agreeing, if he should say the line of the reservation included his location, he would at once abandon it. They repaired at once to the referee, who showed them, by the terms of the treaty, that the surveyed line of the reservation was correctly drawn, and the Indians withdrew their claims for the land south of it, but ever strongly insisted that the government, by its agents, over-reached their chiefs in the treaty, and took from them the best of what they meant to reserve. Mr. Sturgis came to his location in August, a few days before Judge Connor arrived upon his.

THE FIRST LAND-ENTRIES

made in Nottawa township, then unnamed and unorganized, were the following: June 12, 1829, the northeast quarter of section four, by John Sturgis; the west half of the southeast quarter of section ten, and the west half of the northeast quarter of section fifteen, Henry Powers; the west half of the southwest quarter of section ten, Henry Post; the east half of the southwest quarter and the east half of the northwest quarter, December 15th, Russell Post; the west half of the northwest quarter of section fifteen, William Connor. On August 28, 1829, John W. Fletcher came again to his first selection in 1828, and secured the west half of the northeast quarter and the west half of the southeast quarter of section seventeen; and, on the 10th of October following, William Hazzard entered the other half of the same quarter sections, which were the only entries made that year.

THE FIRST HOUSE

in the township, or on the prairie, was a log cabin erected by John Sturgis, on his location, section four, in August, 1829, and which is still standing on the original site, but fast sinking in the embrace of mother earth, from whose loving breast it came forty-eight years ago.

Other cabins soon followed the Sturgis house; Mr. Fletcher returning in October, and putting up one and securing some marsh hay, and then returning to Wayne county, Michigan, whence he came, and taking his father's family (himself being an unmarried man), consisting of father, mother and two sisters, and their household goods, into a wagon drawn by oxen, in company with William Hazzard and his family and Hiram A. Hecox and family, similarly transported, made their way through the forest, following the Chicago trail, to White Pigeon, and thence to the cabin on section seventeen, at which they arrived on the evening of Christmas, 1829. The party drove their cattle and hogs through, and had a rough journey. The weather was cold and bad, the streams difficult to ford, and eighteen days were consumed in making the trip from Brownstown. This cabin, which was a duplicate of the early ones, was built by Mr. Fletcher in October, he having come to make his selection about the 1st of August; after entering it, he procured a yoke of oxen and a wagon, and returned in October, rolled up the logs, covered it with a "shake" roof, and floored it with "punch-

12

eons." It was a good house for those days. Mr. Powers built a cabin the following winter, but a Mr. Lane, Judge Connor, Judge Sturgis and Mr. Fletcher, were the only ones to get into their own cabins in 1829. Connor's first cabin was rolled up on Spring creek, east of the present road, on the north and south line of section sixteen. Amos Howe made his selection of a location in 1829, but did not occupy it with his family until 1830. Among other early settlers were Dr. McMillan and his family, who came late in the year 1829, living all winter in their wagons. The good old Doctor took his time to build his house, as to his precise, mechanical eye, the slightest deviation from a right line to the cardinal points of a compass, would have been a perpetual annoyance to him. Connor's cabin had a hole cut in it for ingress and egress, and the door to close the aperture was made when time and money were less pressing. Benjamin Sherman, Jonathan Engle, Sr. and Jr., George W. Dille, John Foreman, Glover Laird Gardner, Hiram Gates and Henry Powers, came in the spring or early part of 1830. Russell and Henry Post, John and Samuel Cuddy, Samuel McKee, James and Adney Hecox came to the prairie in 1829, during the fall; most of them were from Smooth Rock, Michigan, Judge Connor's former school district, but originally from the Eastern States.

The trials of these pioneers were the same, in kind, as those described elsewhere in the general history of the pioneers of the county, and a rehearsal of them here would be but a recapitulation of what has already been told. Suffice it then to say, that the privations which befell them, the sorrows and afflictions which at times encompassed their pathways, were as bravely, unflinchingly and cheerfully borne by them as by any of their fellow-pioneers in the county elsewhere. Their charities and works of mercy for their fellows were no whit behind the most charitable; and their record of kindness and sympathy in times of distress is colored by the same radiance of love and brotherly affection that casts its halo around and over all of those unselfish and helpful men and women of "auld lang syne." Mrs. Fletcher's deed of mercy to the Cowens is preserved in the general history of the county.

THE FIRST FARMS

were opened in 1830, simultaneously by the above-named settlers of 1829, and early comers of 1830, no one having a pre-eminence in that direction. Nottawa was an exception to every other township in the county, by receiving a colony instead of a single settler in the beginning. The seeding for the first crop was brought in from other points,—Mr. Fletcher getting his oats and potatoes from Allen's prairie, now in Branch county, in the manner described in the history of the navigation of the St. Joseph river. Corn, potatoes, and oats were grown and harvested in 1830, and wheat sown in the fall of that year and harvested the year following.

FIRST ORCHARD.

Mr. Fletcher brought thirteen hundred small apple-trees, currant and grape cuttings in the fall of 1829, from Wayne county, and preserved them during the winter by putting them in a bee-hive, which was buried in the earth; in the spring of 1830 he transplanted them into a nursery. Benjamin Sherman brought in larger apple-trees in the spring of 1830, from Ohio, when he came, and set them out, which bore the first fruit grown on the prairie, which is now noted for its fine orchards and their productions. Judge Connor and H. A. Hecox planted their orchards the same year.

EARLY CROPS.

A fact, which is as yet unexplained, is stated by Judge Connor and borne out by the records, that up to 1844 smut in wheat was a terrible pest, but it then disappeared from that cereal and has never since re-appeared. The theory that cutting off the timber affects the rain-fall of a given district does not appear to hold good in St. Joseph, as the old settlers say when they first came to the county it was drier than it has been since. The greatest snow-fall since the first settlement were those of the winters of 1831–32–33. The sickly season of 1837–38 was preceded by a series of wet, cold ones, the two named being excessively hot and dry. In June, 1835, a frost killed the crops to the ground, and it was three or four weeks before suckers re-formed. The early wheat was destroyed, the later sown escaping, and the next year the price of wheat was very high, Judge Connor had ninety acres of the latter sown, and did not save enough from the frost to live on.

THE FIRST FRAME BUILDING

erected on Nottawa prairie was a barn by John and Samuel Cuddy, on their farm, in 1832. The first frame house erected in the present township of Nottawa, outside of Centreville, was that of John W. Fletcher, on his location on section seventeen, whereon he still resides. He built the same in 1835, and William Hazzard built one the same year.

#### THE FIRST BRICK HOUSE

outside of the village of Centreville, was the present one of Colonel Jonathan Engle, built by himself.

#### THE FIRST CHURCH SOCIETY

in Nottawa appeared before the schoolma'am did, contrary to the usual rule of precedence. In the spring of 1830 a class was formed by the Rev. Erastus Felton and Rev. Lyman B. Gurley, missionaries of the Ohio conference of the Methodist Episcopal church. William Fletcher and wife (parents of John W.) and William Hazzard and his wife being the members. A history in detail of this class, and the subsequent flourishing society which grew therefrom, will be found in the history of Centreville.

#### THE FIRST SCHOOL-HOUSE

was built in the spring or early summer of 1831, on section sixteen. It was a rude log-house, and is still standing a short distance from Thomas Engle's residence, though fast crumbling to dust to mingle again with the earth whence it came, to re-appear in living forms again at the bidding of that unalterable law that makes no mistakes. Miss Delia Brooks taught the first school therein, in the summer of 1831; she had among her pupils Hamilton A. Hecox and David Hazzard, both of whom are now residents of Nottawa, and Amanda Fletcher, afterwards Mrs. Ira Thurston, now of Iowa. Miss Brooks married Colonel Jonathan—familiarly called "Jock"—Engle, Jr., but has been deceased several years.

The school statistics of the township for 1876 are as follows: There were nine school-houses, including the fine union school-building of Centreville, (which is of stone,) three of them being brick and five frame-buildings; the whole valued at twenty-nine thousand and five hundred dollars. They have six hundred and thirty sittings. There were seven hundred children in the township between the ages of five and twenty years, six hundred of whom attended the different schools, which were in session, not including the union school of Centreville, an average of eight months during the year. Six male teachers taught twenty-nine months, and were paid one thousand six hundred and one dollars; and thirteen females taught eighty-six months, and received two thousand five hundred and twelve dollars therefor. The total resources of the districts amounted to twelve thousand four hundred and twenty-seven dollars and forty-six cents, of which was expended eleven thousand four hundred and thirty-six dollars and sixty-three cents,—including one thousand dollars on bonded indebtedness, and one thousand and eighty-five dollars and forty-three cents for repairs.

#### THE FIRST IMPROVED FARM MACHINERY

was introduced in 1832–3, in the shape of fanning-mills. One of the latter was owned by four neighbors, Mr. Fletcher being one of the stockholders. It was agreed that whoever used it last should keep it till it was called for by some other of the quartette, when, if it was not actually in use, no matter if so little time as ten minutes only intervened before the party in whose possession it was intended to use it, the party who came for it had the preference and took it away.

Previous to the advent of this mill they had harnessed zephyr to the work, and by her gentle, or more hurried breathings had winnowed their grain. In 1836 the open-cylinder threshers came in use—the first ones, manufactured by Sprague, being rude, clumsy, clattering affairs; these, in 1837, were superseded by others made by Daniel Johnson, which were a great improvement over the flail and tramping-process by horses. The "shaker" was added to the open cylinder next, then the "straw carrier," and finally, in 1842, the great separators were introduced with their eight and ten-horse powers.

The reapers came in also about this time, the Johnsons bringing the first one, a Hussey—the J. M. Leland machines coming in for trial the year previous, or thereabouts. There was no reel on the first reaper, a man drawing the standing grain to the platform by a rake or other device. This was not so difficult a feat to accomplish as it would seem in the presence of the automatic machines of the present, as the machines were then drawn by four horses, and at a high rate of speed.

In the season of 1842, one of the neighbors on the prairie fell sick, just as his harvest was ready for the sickle, and Mr. Johnson, with his "Hussey," followed by a large concourse of neighbors, appeared early one Sunday morning before the sick man's door and asked to be shown into the wheat-field. The request was complied with, and by night the whole field of thirty acres was covered with shocks of golden grain. The next Sunday the same was stacked, and the Sunday following it was threshed with a Con-

stantine separator, the thirty acres yielding six hundred and forty bushels. This was the largest day's work done by any reaper, before or since, in the county. The Sunday work, too, was on the the principle of the Master, that the "Sabbath was made for man, and not man for the Sabbath."

The McCormick reapers were first introduced by the Wakemans and John Bowers; Judge Connor introduced the first combined machine in 1854—a "Manny."

John M. Leland was the first to introduce the reel on reapers, but never received any benefit from its invention, and also invented the open guards, both of which improvements are as inseparable and essential to all reapers and mowers as the needle with an eye in its point is to a sewing machine, and yet Mr. L. never gained a penny of profit from either invention.

#### IMPROVED LIVE-STOCK

began to be introduced early, but no attention was paid to cattle until the Wakemans brought their thorough-bred short-horns from Ohio, in 1850. Judge Connor bought a Devon bull-calf in Rochester, New York, paying forty dollars for it, in 1836, and kept it several years, but nothing else of moment was done in that line previous to the date before given.

James Stadden has raised several very fine farm-horses, and Mr. Brown, of Sand Lake, once had an excellent stallion, from whose viciousness Brown lost his life. The horse was then taken to Kalamazoo, where he killed two other men, and was shot to prevent further mischief.

Sheep have been raised to a considerable extent, the American merino seeming to take the preference. Cultivation of the soil, however, is the branch of agriculture which chiefly occupies the attention of the Nottawa farmers, and in that they are unexcelled.

#### MANUFACTURES.

The first manufacturing done in Nottawa was by Asa Belote, in his blacksmith shop on section fifteen, in 1831.

Henry Powers and Russell Post were the first carpenters in the settlement, and John V. Overfield, a Virginian, burnt the first brick on the prairie in 1832. He was a mason by trade, and it is said of him that for forty-two years he never failed to cast his vote at any election where he was entitled to do so except once, and was then only prevented by a storm so fierce that he could not reach the polls before they closed,—he being at Mottville and the election at Nottawa. He made the attempt, but failed to reach the polling-station until after the election was closed.

Glover Laird built the first distillery on the northeast corner of section one in 1831–2, and Hopper built another near the corner of the townships of Burr Oak, Colon, Sherman and Nottawa in the years 1836–7. The location is now known as Hopper's corners. The Johnsons had one subsequently.

The first and only flouring-mill ever built in the township, outside of Centreville, was started by Mr. Langley, who brought his mill-irons with him from Philadelphia, in October, 1832. He had, in June of that year, purchased the site and building in process of erection on the present farm of George Kline, deceased,—whose widow is a grand-daughter of Mr. Langley,—which site was owned by a Mr. Foster, who had begun the erection of a saw-mill. The saw-mill was put into operation in December following, the dam being thirty-two rods long, with a heavy embankment of gravel on Hog creek.

The grist-mill was pushed to completion after many obstacles were overcome, and commenced operations with a single run of small burr-stones in April, 1833. The mill was a three-story building and was completely equipped the following fall by Johnston & Stewart, who succeeded to its ownership with three run of larger stone, and flouring wheat for merchant-work was carried on. Mr. Langley regained possession of the mill and run it himself, and it was also leased by Philip R. Toll and operated by him. It was burned some years afterwards and the site of the dam removed to Centreville, where the mill was rebuilt by the Talbots. As an instance of what practical knowledge and genius can accomplish in the face of obstacles, before which simple skill is powerless, the following incident, transpiring at this mill, is given: When Johnston & Stewart took possession of the establishment, according to their agreement, they at once set about refitting it, and for the purpose procured the services of two skillful mill-wrights from Rochester, who came on and began their work. They were exact and careful workmen, but met difficulties to which they were unaccustomed in their experience in the east. At last they came to the large cogged wheel, and were brought to a stand for want of properly seasoned timber out of which to make the cogs, and could do nothing. After some delay Messrs. Johnston & Stewart sent to John M. Leland, who came, and, learning the difficulty, set at once about supplying the needed material. The

SARAH FLETCHER

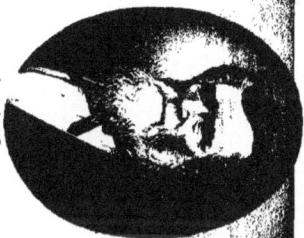

JOHN W. FLETCHER

RESIDENCE OF JOHN W. FLETCHER, NOTTAWA TP. ST. JOSEPH CO., MICH

young men, though skilled mechanics, knew of no way of making what they wanted out of unseasoned timber, always having had a supply of seasoned lumber on hand. Mr. Leland chose his lumber and boiled it first thoroughly, and transferred it to the oven and baked it as "well done" and proceeded with the work.

Cornelius Kline built a tannery in 1836–8 on the west side of Saud lake, and the building is now Mr. West's barn.

Elisha Strong built another tannery on the north side of the lake, about 1840.

### THE FIRST MERCHANT

outside of Centreville, in Nottawa, was O. B. Harmon, who sold goods in 1830, on section one to the Indians and white people.

### THE FIRST ROAD

was surveyed in the summer of 1830, from the Indiana State line through Sturgis prairie to Sand lake, to the corner of sections fifteen, sixteen, twenty-one and twenty-two, at which point the survey ended, and every section-line in the township was declared to be a public highway. The commissioners of the town of Sherman, Truman Bearse and Amos Howe, laid it out. Alfred L. Driggs built a saw-mill in Branch county soon after the Schellhous mill was built in Colon, and Judge Conner went to Driggs' for lumber, cutting and blazing his way through, whereupon the commissioners laid out the trail as a highway direct from Sand lake. The angles have been straightened since, until there is but a small portion of the original road left,—which is near the present school-house on the prairie.

### THE FIRST HOTEL

on Nottawa prairie was kept, in 1830, by Captain Henry Powers, on the west half of the northeast quarter of section fifteen. The building was a log-house twenty-two by twenty-eight feet, one and a half stories high, with a wing fifteen by fifteen feet. It had a double fire-place and a brick chimney. It was a great resort for dancing-parties, and also political gatherings before Centreville became the centre of the latter movements. It was the head-quarters for some days of Governor Porter at the time of the "big payment" in December, 1833. It was also the location of the

### FIRST POST-OFFICE

on the prairie, Captain Powers being the first postmaster. James Powers carried the mail twice a week to and from White Pigeon, and the captain had the profits of the office for transacting the business. It was a small affair, but answered its purpose. Judge Conner was the deputy, and transacted the business during Powers' incumbency, which continued until the fall of 1835, when he was succeeded by Dr. Mottram, who removed the office to his own house, and was succeeded in after years by his partner, Dr. Hyatt, who held the position until the office was transferred to Mendon.

### THE FIRST BIRTH

in the township of a white child was that of John Foreman,—now of Leonidas,—who was born February 6, 1830. William Hazzard, Jr., was born in March following, on the 12th day of the month. The first white female child born in the township is said to be Clarissa Buel, the wife of Cyrus Buel, of Centreville. She was the daughter of Mr. and Mrs. John W. Fletcher, and was born December 18, 1832.

### THE FIRST MARRIAGE

in the township of white people was that of John Potter, of Green, Branch county, and Mary McKee, of Nottawa, or "Shearman," as the record reads. William Fletcher, town clerk of Sherman, granted the license December 25, 1830, and it is fair to presume that the merry Christmas time was made all the merrier by the wedding of the parties on that day.

### THE FIRST DEATH

occurred suddenly in this township, as it did in Sturgis. The victim was Asahel Sawyer, who was killed by a falling tree in February, 1831. He was an intelligent, practical man, a machinist, farmer, business man, or schoolmaster, as occasioned required. He seemed to have a presentiment that he would be killed in the manner in which he did meet his death, and was fearful when in the woods, and that very fear precipitated his death. The tree he was engaged in cutting, in falling brought down two others with it, and he became frightened, and in his confusion ran directly into the danger he could most easily have avoided had he kept his presence of mind. He was buried on the school section, on which the

### FIRST CEMETERY

was afterwards laid out, in 1833 or thereabouts.

### THE FIRST PHYSICIAN

who made his residence in Nottawa, outside of Centreville, was Dr. Mottram, who settled on the prairie in 1832. He was poor, not having even a horse to ride, and Judge Connor very generously furnished him with one the first summer. Dr. Mottram lived on the prairie while he remained in the county. He is now an eminent and wealthy physician of Kalamazoo. Dr. Merritt came after Mottram first located, and practiced a while, and Dr. McMillan used to ply his vocation in emergencies; but his chemical studies usually engrossed his attention, and he gave but little heed to his profession, passing his time almost exclusively among his retorts and crucibles, sand-baths and furnaces, with which his premises were supplied. Dr. Hyatt came later, and formed a co-partnership with Dr. Mottram, which continued some years, the latter removing to Mendon in 1859, where he now resides and follows his profession. Dr. McMillan died in 1874, at the age of eighty-five years.

### THE LEADING FARMERS.

Since the settlement of the township there have been Judge Connor, who enclosed his first purchase,—eighty acres,—the first year, and the next year (1831) had the largest area under cultivation of any one on the prairie; Benjamin Sherman, who had seventy acres under cultivation in 1830, the first year of his coming; John W. Fletcher, William Hazzard, Sr., William Hazzard, Jr. (succeeding to the paternal acres, and adding largely to them), the Johnsons, Glover Laird and his son Harry W., the Wakeman brothers (represented now by Hiram Wakeman), W. B. Langley, Samuel Kline, Henry Powers, and Russell Post. Fletcher, William Hazzard, Jr., Harry Laird, Kline, and Langley are residents at the present time on their original locations.

James Culbertson came to Nottawa in 1835, stopped about a week, became home-sick, and went back to Union county, Pa., where he remained about two weeks, thoroughly disgusted with the rough mountainous country, which he was continually contrasting with the beautiful land he had just left; whereupon he took his family and returned to Nottawa, and buying the location of Richard Calvin, settled there and remained until his death. His son John occupies the old homestead, and James, another son, is a leading mint-producer in the township, having a fine farm on the bank of the St. Joseph. He has one of the best mint-distilleries in the county, and received one year, from the production of twenty-one acres, three thousand pounds of oil. He has the first hydraulic cider-press erected in Michigan.

Colonel Isaac Wampole was a noted man among the early residents of Nottawa, coming in 1833 from Pennsylvania and locating the present fine farm of W. B. Langley. He was an energetic, stirring man, and died very much respected.

Judge Connor was unmarried when he made Nottawa his home, but in 1835 married the widow of Ambrose S. Wicks (deceased), of New York, who survived her wedding day but seven months. The Judge mourned for his lost one until 1838, when he found consolation by marrying a daughter of Captain Powers, with whom he lived most happily nearly a generation, she passing to her rest in 1870. He is now seventy-four years of age, but a hale, hearty man notwithstanding, whose perceptions are clear and mind vigorous, as in younger days. He added farm to farm until his acreage was equal to any in the township, and more than the most of his neighbors. Since the death of his companion he has distributed his property among his children, and, as he quaintly puts it, "is living now on borrowed time." He is one of St. Joseph's worthiest citizens.

### INCIDENTS.

During the excitement of the Black Hawk war, some of the settlers became very much alarmed, and loaded a few necessaries and their families into their wagons, and moved eastward as fast as their teams could travel. One day a man, driving across the prairie, broke the king-bolt to his wagon, and offered a new and good plow for another, that he might not be detained. The fording of the streams was never a pleasant task in high-water, and sometimes was positively dangerous.

Judge Connor relates an incident of a ford once attempted by him, which partook of neither of the above mentioned characteristics. It happened to him in the winter of 1829–30. He was going to White Pigeon with a team of steers, and Hog creek, which he had to cross, was frozen for about one-third of the breadth on either side, leaving an open space in the centre of the stream. The usual ford was made by going into the stream, and then ascend it about ten rods and go out on the opposite side, where the exit was favorable. Connor 'stripped to the buff' and urged his cattle in, walking by their side, the ice cutting his skin badly, and the cold wind piercing his 'upper works' no less severely. The steers refused to make the exit, when he mounted one of them and began to belabor them a little, but it made matters worse and they bolted out on the side they came in on, and shook off the unlucky rider and ran into the woods. The judge put on his clothes and regained his cattle and his seating, and made the ford successfully at last.

The first theft committed in the settlement was at the expense of Judge Connor, and was as follows: In 1830, when Connor went to purchase his second lot, it was known he was to have the money for its purchase sent to him from the eastward; and the day before he was to go to Monroe, he left his cabin alone during the day, as he had frequently done before. The nearest cabin to Connor's was Lane's about half a mile off. When Mr. Connor returned at night he found his trunk broken open, and his money gone, but fortunately not that which he was to enter his land with, that having been sent to him at Ypsilanti, which he received when he arrived there on his way to Monroe. But what he did have, twenty dollars, was a large sum to lose in those days, and besides it was every dime he had, and he had to work his passage to and from Monroe, with his friend John W. Fletcher, who paid the bills out and back.

Lane's reputation was not of the best when he came to the settlement, and it improved none after the burglary was committed.

A CHRISTMAS GATHERING

of the surviving pioneers of Nottawa was held in 1876 at Colonel "Jock" Engle's by his express invitation, which stated "that the toughest specimen in his flock of turkeys would be sacrificed on the occasion," in order to carry out the "eternal fitness of things." There was a noted assembly of the old men and women, who had come to the prairie and vicinity in the days when the red man disputed their way; among them, William Hazzard, aged seventy-eight years; Judge William Connor, seventy-three; John W. Fletcher, seventy; Mrs. H. W. Hampton (Fletcher's sister), sixty-three; and H. A. Hecox, fifty years. Five of them came to Nottawa on the eve of Christmas, 1829, settled on land in sight of the house of their host, and reside thereon ever since.

Connor, Hazzard, Fletcher and Engle were present at the first political meeting held in the northeast part of the county, June, 1830, to recommend Amos Howe for justice of the peace, and these four are all who are living of the seventy-five who attended the meeting. Mr. Hazzard is the sole survivor of the first Methodist class organized north of White Pigeon, in western Michigan.

Judge Cross was present, a pioneer in Monroe county, in 1826. Hecox and his father (now deceased), were both natives of Michigan, the grandfather coming to Grosse Isle, in the Detroit river, in 1797, where the father was born in 1800.

CIVIL ORGANIZATION.

Nottawa was originally included in the township of Sherman, the organization of the latter being coincident with that of the county, October 29, 1829, and being one of the three original townships into which the county was first divided.

It was first set off into a separate township, July 28, 1830, and included the present township of Colon within its geographical limits.

The first movement for a new township was made in June, 1830, at William Connor's cabin, and there were present at the meeting, William Connor, Amos Howe, Benjamin Sherman, Jonathan Engle, Senior and Junior, Dr. A. McMillan, George W. Dille, Russell Post, Henry Post, John Foreman, John and Samuel Cuddy, ——— Gardiner, Hiram Gates, Hiram, James and Adney Hecox, Samuel McKee, William and John W. Fletcher, William Hazzard, Joseph Lane and Henry Powers, who agreed to call the new township Nottawa, and signed a petition to the legislature to that effect, recommending Amos Howe to Governor Cass as a proper person to appoint as justice of the peace. William Connor and Asahel Sawyer were subsequently appointed a committee to get the act of legislature passed to carry the wishes of the people into effect.

The needed legislation was had, as before stated, in the following session of the legislature, and the first town-meeting directed to be held at the house of Henry Powers, Mr. Howe receiving the appointment of justice from Governor Cass, whose tenant he had previously been. The

FIRST TOWN-MEETING

was held April 4, 1831, and was organized by Amos Howe, justice of the peace, administering the oath of office to Benjamin Sherman, moderator, and William Connor, clerk, wherein they pledged themselves to perform the duties of judges of election, according to the best of their abilities, and endeavor to prevent deceit and fraud or abuse in conducting the same. The

electors resolved to choose their officials by a separate ballot, and proceeded to elect the following list of

TOWN OFFICERS FOR 1831.

William Connor, supervisor; William Fletcher, town clerk; Benjamin Sherman, George W. Dille, William Hazzard, assessors; Henry Powers, J. W. Fletcher, William Connor, commissioners of highways; Hiram A. Hecox, constable and collector; Russell Post, Amos Howe, J. W. Fletcher, William Connor, Samuel McKee, directors of the poor; Shellhous' mill, on treasurer; William Connor, Henry Powers, Benjamin Newman, William Fletcher, Amos Howe, Alex. McMillan, school commissioners and inspectors; Russell Post, pathmaster; Russell Post, William Hazzard and John Foreman, fence-viewers; William Hazzard, poundmaster; Jonathan Engle, overseer of highways.

The electors prohibited stallions from running at large, under a penalty of ten dollars, and offered fifty cents bounty for wolf-scalps.

In September the town auditors allowed fifty-two dollars and fifty cents for township expenses.

The first roads laid out by Nottawa authority, were ordered August 31, 1831; the first beginning on the line between sections four and nine, running southwest to the corner of sections nineteen and thirty, township six, range four miles. The second was from Shellhous' mill, on Swan creek, to Coldwater road, one mile; and the third was from the same mill, northwest, to Nottawa-seepe prairie,—surveyed September 1; the fourth, from the north line of section fourteen, township six, range ten, to west line of section six, two and one-fourth miles: and the fifth, from west line of section six, township six, range ten, to corner of sections two and three.

The second town-meeting was held at the house of George W. Dille, April 2, 1832, and Benjamin Sherman was chosen supervisor, and Amos Howe, town clerk.

March 21, 1833, the boundaries of the township were changed, township six, range nine being taken off, and with township five, range nine, formed into the township of Colon, and township five, range ten, attached to Nottawa.

The third town-meeting was held at the school-house near Engle's, Mr. Connor being re-elected supervisor, and James H. Clowes, clerk, and the township divided into four road districts.

At a special town-meeting, June 1, 1833, Benjamin Sherman, William Connor and George W. Dille were appointed a committee to prevent Indian traders from selling whisky to the Indians.

June 28, 1831, the first school district (number one) was defined and bounded, and contained sections four and seven, township six, range nine, and sections one and twelve, and east half of sections two and eleven, township six, range ten.

At the April meeting, 1834, twenty dollars were appropriated for the poor, and a lawful fence declared to be four and a half feet high, with four inches space between first four rails.

At the April meeting in 1836, the first justices of the peace were elected, and were Digby V. Bell, Benjamin Sherman, Elisha Strong and Luther B. Goodrich.

At the September election for delegates to the Ann Arbor convention, to act upon the Congressional conditions for the admission of Michigan into the Union, thirty-seven voted to accept, and fourteen to reject, the conditions.

In 1841 the strife waxed hot between the Mendonians and the Nottawas, and the former carried the scalps of the latter at their belt by a "scratch," Mark H. Wakeman being elected supervisor by a vote of ninety-four, over his competitor, Judge Connor, who received ninety-three votes. Sam Brown took the war-look of Lentulus Huntley by a vote of ninety-four to ninety-one, and Samuel McKee performed the same feat for John W. Fletcher, ninety-four to ninety-three, and George W. Dille by the same vote smoked the pipe of peace with J. C. Goodrich.

In 1842 the clans rallied again, and victory perched upon the tufts of the Nottawas, who gave the Mendonian chief a severe defeat, Connor being chosen leader of the tribe by one hundred and eighteen votes to seventy-four for Wakeman. Samuel Brown was re-elected clerk, and Joseph Jewett, treasurer,—the latter a Mendonian.

Peace reigned in 1843, the Nottawas having everything their own way.

In 1844, township five, range ten, was set off and organized into a new township, called Wakeman, but changed the next year to Mendon, and Nottawa shrunk to her present proportions.

In 1846 the electors offered ten dollars bounty for wolf-scalps.

In 1849 they voted one hundred and seven against, and seventy-eight for, license to sell liquor.

In 1864 the electors voted at four different times to raise bounties for volunteers, the total amount appropriated being fourteen thousand six hundred and thirty-two dollars and fifty cents.

In August, 1864, after two trials, the township voted to raise fourteen thousand dollars to aid the Grand Rapids and Indiana railroad in its construction through the township, and subsequently increased the amount to fifteen thousand dollars.

On June 22, 1869, twenty-five thousand dollars were voted in aid of the Michigan Air Line railroad, now the Michigan Central Air Line.

OFFICIAL ROSTER.

Supervisors.—William Connor, 1831–33–37–40–42–43–53; Benjamin Sherman, 1832; James B. Dunkin, 1838; Samuel Brown, 1839; M. H. Wakeman, 1841; Charles H. Knox, 1844–49; N. E. Massey, 1845–46; William McCormick, 1847–48, 1850–52–57; Cyrus Foreman, 1854; John Rutherford, 1855–56–61–66; Horatio N. Wilson, 1858; William G. Woodworth, 1859–60–67–69; Robert Alexander, 1870; William L. Worthington, 1871; George B. Mathewson, 1872; John McKercher, 1873–76.

Town Clerks.—William Fletcher, 1831; Amos Howe, 1832–34–48–51; James H. Clowes, 1833; Cyrus Ingerson, 1835; William Mottram, 1836; A. Bonham, 1836–37; J. C. Goodrich, 1838–39–44; Samuel Brown, 1840–43; William McCormick, 1845–46; Lewis Harris, 1847; Hampden A. Hecox, 1852–54; Leonard Stillson, 1855; Isaac R. Belote, 1855–64; Oscar Waters, 1865–67; P. J. Eaton, 1866; L. A. Clapp, 1868–69; William Ennis, 1870–74; Charles R. Talbot, 1871; James Hill, 1872–73; Alfred A. Key, 1875; C. O. Gregory, 1876.

Justices of the Peace.—Amos Howe, 1830–36; L. B. Goodrich, 1836–44; Benjamin Sherman, 1836–46; Asher Bonham, 1837–48; John Pattee, 1838 –46; L. E. Thompson, 1839–47; George W. Dille, 1841–47; Samuel Chipman, 1844–1869; Lewis Harris, 1845–53; John Rutherford, 1849–57 and 1873–77; Lentulus Huntley, 1854–1870; Chester Gurney, 1855–59; John S. Weeks, 1857–66; Samuel W. Platt, 1858–9 and 1870–77; Charles A. Palmer, 1868–77; W. G. Woodworth, one term, 1869; Rufus Currier, 1871–76; Charles E. Sabin, 1873–77; J. Eastman Johnson, 1875–77; J. W. Coffinberry, 1833–5 and 1844.

MARRIAGE RECORDS.

The register of the town clerk shows the first license issued by a Nottawa clerk, to have been November 15, 1832, to Justin Cooper and Lovilla Hazzard; December 12, he granted a permit to marry to George W. Dille and Miss Lydia Martin; January 21, he consented to the nuptials of James Hecox and Miss Ida Shellhous; and January 26th, said Jacob Williamson might take a bale of dry goods, provided Miss Eliza was willing. In May, Mr. Clerk Clowes granted absolution to Ira Thurston and Amanda Fletcher; and in November granted the same indulgence to John B. Harmon and Eunice McMillen. On January 1, 1834, one John Wetherhogg was allowed to inflict his name upon Emeretta Trasel. In 1834, Esquire Howe, as the clerk, gave his permission to William Cline and Mary Ships, James Powers and Diadema Ferris, and Joshua B. Cory and Melissa Harwood, to enter into the state of wedlock; and to make his consent more binding, ratified the contract in the name of the people of the territory of Michigan.

Asher Bonham, as clerk, March 3, 1838, made the following entry on the township records: "I, Asher Bonham, clerk of the township of Nottawa, do hereby certify, that I have granted license to John R——, to embrace the rites of matrimony with Betsy A——."

BRANDS AND MARKS.

Hiram A. Hecox, half-penny, underside of both ears.
William Hazzard, right ear split, and half-penny underside of left.
J. W. Fletcher, square crop right ear, and left ear split.
Amos Howe, square crop of left ear.

POPULATION.

In 1838, Nottawa township, then including Mendon, had a population of seven hundred and thirteen. In 1850 it had increased in Nottawa, as now limited, to one thousand one hundred and sixty-five. In 1870 it had gained seven hundred and three, standing at eighteen hundred and sixty-eight, divided among three hundred and seventy-two families, and with three hundred and eighty-seven dwellings. Nine hundred and fifty-nine were males and nine hundred and nine of the opposite sex. The State census of 1874 gives but fourteen additional population to that of 1870, placing it at one thousand eight hundred and eighty-two, increasing the males to nine hundred and seventy-five, and reducing the females to nine hundred and seven. Three hundred and eleven masculines were of the age reckoned fit to go to war, one hundred

and seventy-nine were exempt, being over forty-five and under seventy-five, and eight were between the three-quarter post and the last decade of the century. Three hundred and thirty-nine of the feminine gender were marriageable, two hundred and nine were under seventy-five, but beyond the age of forty-five, and twelve had passed the point of three score and fifteen. There were two hundred and thirty-eight boys and one hundred and seventy-one girls between ten and twenty-one, and four hundred and fifteen children of both sexes under ten years of age. The married men were three hundred and sixty-seven, and the single ones, who ought to have been married, were one hundred and eleven—and there were twenty widowed ones. There were three hundred and seventy-four married females, seven of whom were under eighteen years of age, and one hundred and eighteen yet looking for mates; while sixty-eight were mourning for companions had and lost, two of them being under eighteen years of age.

THE POLITICAL SENTIMENT

of Nottawa may be seen by the tally-sheets of the presidential elections. In 1840 "Tippecanoe and Tyler too" had one hundred and fifty-nine and the "Kinderhook fox" one hundred and eleven votes. In 1844 Harry Clay received ninety-five votes, Polk ninety-five, and the "old Liberty guard" polled eleven votes. In 1848 "old Zach" Taylor had ninety-nine votes, Governor Cass one hundred and five, and the "free soilers" thirty-two. In 1852 General Scott polled eighty-one, General Pierce one hundred and four, and the Abolitionists "got away" with twenty votes. In 1856 Fremont Republicans cast one hundred and sixty to the Buchanan Democrats ninety-six. In 1860 Lincoln received one hundred and thirty-nine votes, and the Democracy cast one hundred and thirty-eight for the "Little Giant," S. A. Douglas. In 1864 the Republican vote fell off twenty-seven, standing at two hundred and twelve, but the Democratic vote remained unchanged, one hundred and thirty-eight. In 1868 the General of the army, Grant, received two hundred and eighty-three votes, and the General of the Potomac, McClellan, one hundred and fifty-five. In 1872 Grant received an indorsement of two hundred and fifty-six votes, the philosopher, Horace Greeley, ninety-six, and Charles O'Connor, the straight Democrat, twenty-two. In 1876, the present President of the United States, Rutherford B. Hayes, received three hundred and ten votes, Mr. Tilden one hundred and forty-seven and Peter Cooper twenty-eight.

ASSESSMENTS AND TAXES.

The first tax paid by Nottawa as an independent sovereignty, amounted to fifty dollars, and was levied in 1831 by the county authorities for her own use, besides one-fifth of one per cent. on her assessment for county purposes. The assessment of property in 1834 amounted to thirty-six thousand six hundred and fifty-three dollars in the township, and the amount of county taxes was fifty-four dollars, and town taxes one hundred and fifty-two dollars.

In 1876 the assessment was fixed on real-estate by the supervisors at five hundred and eighty-one thousand three hundred and sixty-four dollars, and reduced to five hundred and forty thousand three hundred and forty dollars by the county equalizing board. The personal assessment was returned at one hundred and fifty-three thousand four hundred and sixty-eight dollars, making a grand total of six hundred and ninety-eight thousand five hundred and eight dollars. On this amount the following taxes were levied: State and county, three thousand five hundred and sixty-eight dollars and twenty-eight cents, divided equally between the two departments; schools, seven thousand two hundred and fifty-five dollars and fifteen cents; township, two thousand six hundred and twenty-eight dollars and twenty-eight cents; charged back, ninety-six dollars and ninety-six cents; total thirteen thousand five hundred and forty-nine dollars and thirty-one cents. In 1870 the total taxes raised in the township were: State, one thousand seven hundred and sixty dollars and forty-nine cents; county, three thousand two hundred and five dollars; school, seven thousand and ninety-two dollars; cemetery, one thousand nine hundred dollars; miscellaneous, one million one hundred and forty dollars; a grand total of fifteen thousand five hundred and thirty-two dollars. In 1872 the entire costs, on an assessment of one million one hundred and forty-two thousand four hundred and forty dollars. In 1876 there were twenty-two thousand two hundred and seventy-two dollars of land assessed.

CROP STATISTICS.

In 1874 there were sown five thousand one hundred and eighty-five acres of wheat, against four thousand two hundred and fifteen in 1873, and there were two thousand three hundred and nine acres of corn planted in 1874. The crop of 1874 yielded forty-one thousand one hundred and seventy-seven bushels of wheat, seventy-one thousand two hundred and thirty-three bushels of corn, nineteen thousand three hundred and forty-two bushels other grain, five thousand and forty-eight bushels potatoes, one thousand three hundred and eighty-four tons of hay, fourteen thousand and thirteen pounds of wool, two hundred and two thousand seven hundred and sixty-two pounds pork, forty-one thousand two hundred and forty pounds butter and cheese, nine thousand five hundred and eighty-two pounds dried fruit, and eight hundred and eighty barrels cider. Three hundred and thirty acres in orchards and gardens produced nineteen thousand one hundred and eighty bushels of apples and five hundred and sixty-four bushels of other "truck," valued at seven thousand five hundred and fifty-four dollars. There were owned in the township six hundred and seven horses, seven mules, four oxen, four hundred and eighty cows, four hundred and eighty-four other cattle, one thousand two hundred and sixty-six hogs and two thousand five hundred sheep—three hundred and twelve less than in 1873.

### THE VILLAGE OF CENTREVILLE.

The original plat of Centreville was surveyed and laid out, acknowledged and recorded, November 7, 1831, by the proprietors—Robert Clark, Jr. (a government surveyor), Electus W. Deane, Daniel B. Miller and Charles Noble. It was located on the east half of the northeast quarter of section twenty-five, and east half of the southeast quarter of section twenty-four, township six, range eleven, and on west half of the northwest quarter of section thirty, and west half of the southwest quarter of section nineteen, township six, range ten. In consideration of the location of the county-seat on the plat, the proprietors of the village donated to the county, in aid of the county buildings, fifty-six lots and the public square,—the court-house, when built, to be located on the latter. Clark was the real man in the proprietorship, and acted as attorney in fact for his coadjutors, by virtue of a document recorded in Liber A, page two hundred and thirty, in the register's office at Centreville.

### THE FIRST HOUSE

was built by Columbia Lancaster on a lot just north of the public square, which the original proprietors had given him for services rendered. It was not much of a house, and only served as a shelter for him while out on his frequent hunting expeditions. It was made of rough logs, the site of the village being originally heavy oak openings, and had neither door, window, nor floor.

In June, 1832, Thomas W. Langley, a gentleman in the manufacturing line in Philadelphia, but on a tour westward in quest of his health, came to White Pigeon with a party from Detroit, who were on a prospecting tour. Hearing of the location of the county-seat at Centreville, he inquired where it was, and was informed by Lancaster, who was at the time teaching school in White Pigeon, and who also offered to pilot him to the site on the next day or two, when his school ended for the week, which he accordingly did. After viewing the location he returned to White Pigeon, and on Monday came back alone and looked the ground over again; he returned direct to Monroe and bought the interest of the proprietors, Clark and Deane, and also the location of H. W. Foster, who was engaged in putting up a saw-mill one-half mile east of the village plat, the whole purchase covering three-fourths of section thirty, in Nottawa township. Making arrangements for the continuance of the work on the mill, Mr. Langley returned to Philadelphia for his family, consisting of his wife; Mrs. Hartley, afterwards Mrs. Adams Wakeman; five sons, William B., Joseph L. F., De Witt C., Thomas C. and Washington E., and one daughter, Susan B.; a nephew, William L. Hirst, and two colored servants, William Bell and Anne Williams,—the first of their race to find in St. Joseph county a home. Buying a stock of goods well assorted for the pioneer trade, in New York, he shipped them via the Erie canal and the lakes to the mouth of the St. Joseph, and, together with a set of mill-irons and his household goods, took passage from Troy, New York, on a line-boat for Buffalo, and from the latter point to Detroit by steamer, bringing also from Buffalo horses and wagon, with such household goods as were necessary. The mill-irons, the nephew and the servants were transported to Centreville,—Mr. Langley and the rest of the family coming through to White Pigeon in one of Forsyth's coaches, chartered-expressly for the party. The roads had to be cleared in many places, the limbs of trees cut off, Hog creek made fordable, to let the coach through the woods and marshes, and in and out of the creeks and rivers.

The party arrived without broken bones, though badly used up, at White Pigeon, September 25, 1832, and at Centreville, October 3, William B. Langley,—then a boy of some fourteen years or thereabouts,—piloting the caravan of goods, servants, proprietor, family and carpenters from White Pigeon, mounted on the pony which had been over the ground several times before. When the party arrived in view of Lancaster's cabin, the grass,

which had been growing rankly therein all summer, was plainly visible to its future inmates, and gave them a sudden and uncomfortable idea of pioneer trials and privations in the very outset. The ladies were given full and exclusive possession of the cabin, after the grass was mown down, and the men and boys camped under the trees. The next day business began in earnest in the village of a single family; a door was put in the cabin, a frame building began for a court-house, and also a frame blacksmith-shop. A double log-house, with seven rooms, was begun on the 4th and finished with floors, doors, windows and a chimney, and occupied on the 13th of October. The court-house building, twenty by thirty feet, now standing on the corner diagonally northwest from the public square, and lengthened out somewhat, was the

### FIRST FRAME HOUSE

in the village. On the 19th of February, 1833, there were in the village eight good frame buildings, one small and one large log-house, comprising the frame blacksmith-shop (twenty by thirty), the court-house, and six private dwellings. The double log-house was afterwards sold to A. C. Stewart for hotel purposes, and the frame blacksmith-shop fitted up and enlarged for Mr. Langley's family residence, and which he subsequently opened as a hotel, for which purpose it was used many years. A new blacksmith-shop was put up on the corner of the block next north of Dr. Trowbridge's present residence, being the second block north of the main street running east and west through the village, and north of the street leading to the railroad depot.

This shop was erected with marvelous celerity. On Tuesday morning the materials were growing in the woods, and Thursday night the shop was done and shingled, the forge up, and a horse had been shod. On April 1, two blacksmiths were at work in the village; the mill, one-half mile east, was in operation, sawing and gristing; and mail twice a week was received.

Three couples had been married in the village, of its residents, before April 8, and a month later the capital of the county had a population of one hundred souls—eleven families besides the unmarried men; and thirty-six lots had been sold to parties who were under contract to put up a good framehouse on each purchase, under penalty of forfeiting half of the purchase money.

In 1833 the courts were held in Centreville, and the board of supervisors held their meetings there; the county jail had been erected; hotel accommodations were fair; a school had been taught (a private one), public worship had been maintained for several months, and the village was assured of both a "local habitation and a name," to go down to posterity with whatever of honor or disgrace the future might bring. The first important thing in the history of a county-seat, aside from a place to hold courts, was a decent place to feed and rest the attendants on the sessions of the same, and Mr. Langley set about providing for that important functionary, the landlord, who was Alanson C. Stewart. He leased and opened the double log-house as

### THE FIRST HOTEL

in Centreville. It was built near the present site of C. H. Starr's barn, and opened to the public in December, 1832; but Mr. Stewart did not remain in it, and Mr. Langley opened his own residence in April, 1833, as a hotel, with Julius A. Thompson as landlord, who remained but a short time, finding he did not know how "to keep a hotel." Mr. Langley himself then took the helm of affairs and managed the hotel until about 1836, when he sold the property to Alexander V. Sill, now, and for seventeen years, the postmaster at St. Charles, Kane county, Illinois. Mr. Sill kept the house in a very satisfactory style until 1840, when he sold his interest, and removed to Illinois, where he has since remained. This building stood on the site of the fruit-canning and batten-factory, which burned down in December, 1876. One Mr. Fish built the St. Joseph House, and was bought out by Langley & Talbot, who began, in 1837, the erection of the "Exchange," which was completed by Langley, Talbot retiring. It was not until along the road between Detroit and Chicago for its architecture, its balconies being supported by pillars formed of burr oak logs, unbarked. E. J. Van Buren was the first landlord, and kept the house in 1837-9, and Charles H. Knox kept it in 1840, or later. Mr. Langley kept the Sill house at different times. Dr. Cyrus Ingersoll kept the Mansion House previous to 1840. The only hotel now opened in the village is a brick building, built by I. A. J. Hatch, and leased by W. S. Beardsley, who is a popular host with the legal fraternity and traveling public generally. Mr. Beardsley pays close attention to the comforts of his guests, keeps a quiet, orderly house and is well patronized.

WILLIAM B. LANGLEY.

MRS. WILLIAM B. LANGLEY.

VIEW LOOKING NORTH.

VIEW LOOKING EAST.

RESIDENCE OF WILLIAM B. LANGLEY, NOTTAWA, ST. JOE CO., MICH.

## THE FIRST MERCHANT

in Centreville was Niles F. Smith, who bought the stock of goods forwarded by Mr. Langley from New York, while the same were in transit, Smith obligating himself to sell the same at retail in Centreville. The transfer was made to Smith November 28, 1832, and the goods opened for sale about Christmas, between which time and the 20th of February one thousand six hundred dollars worth of them passed over the counter in legitimate trade.

Dr. Johnston and C. H. Stewart opened a large stock of goods in 1833, and afterwards leased or bought the mills at the east of the village, and removed their stock there in 1834. A hotel was also kept at the mills, and Harvey Cady, who came to the village in 1836, was the host thereof in 1837. In 1834 Captain Philip R. Toll, of Schenectady, N. Y., and his family, consisting of his wife and sons, Isaac D., and Alfred, and three daughters and two nephews, Philip R. Toll and Charles H. Toll, came to Centreville and began an extensive mercantile and manufacturing business, which he continued until 1838, when he removed to Pawn river, and continued his flouring and milling operations there for many years. Charles H. Toll was a partner in Centreville, and he and Philip R. Toll were most able and efficient aids in the various business enterprises carried on by the firm. They leased the mills, and operated them in 1836–8. They sold a large amount of goods; they brought shoemakers and tinsmiths, and kept them busy, too. G. Lansing Outhout, of the best blood of the Knickerbockers, a graduate of Union College, and a man of high culture, was also associated with Captain Toll. Isaac D. Toll was then a boy of seventeen to twenty years old, and a gay lad. He is credited with getting up the first dance in Centreville, in 1836, and it is not a difficult thing to believe that the statement is true, for he was the leader of the young men of his day in the village.

Langley and Talbot were in trade in 1837, and the Talbots—the heads of the house being John W. Talbot and George—have been in trade there in various lines ever since. The old house bears an honorable record for justice and integrity, and its mantle has descended on worthy shoulders—its representatives of to-day. Three of the family emigrated to Texas some years ago, and one of them was elected to the position of State superintendent of schools.

Henry C. Campbell was a merchant in the place, and has been postmaster for the last sixteen years. Calvin H. Starr came to the village in 1835 or 1836, and has been closely identified with its interests from that time to the present. He was a young unmarried man, but has built himself a fine residence, married a St. Joseph wife, and has been one of its trusted citizens for years. His taste ran counter to that of many of the villagers in regard to the condition of the public square, he desiring it to remain in its natural state so far as the large oaks were concerned,—while the others desired to "clear" it off. This they did, and now frequently admit the correctness of Mr. Starr's views. The day was hot when the "clearing" began, and before all the larger trees were sacrificed the laborers were worried out, and so here and there on the square stands a remnant of the forest, very tantalizing to one in a hot day, when he remembers that once the square was an elegant park of just such growth.

C. D. Bennett and J. W. Spitzer are both merchants of several years' standing, and now engaged in trade in the village.

## MANUFACTURES

The first manufacturing done in the village was blacksmithing, Mr. Langley bringing in the "kit," and furnishing the shop and hiring the smith, in 1832. E. C. White was the first resident smith to own and operate his own shop in 1833. De Mott, a blacksmith, was noted for his skill in hardening mill-picks. Mr. Day was the first tinsmith, and Combs & Son the first shoemakers, and came in and worked for Captain Toll in 1834–7. A. E. Massey had a tin-shop afterwards in 1840. John P. Van Patten and George Stone came in with the Tolls also, and were carpenters. Melvin Brown, still a resident of the village, with his son Eldridge, was the first cabinet-maker, and opened a shop in 1834. Thomas Studley was a shoemaker, and settled on the prairie in 1832, and Morris Early and A. Murray were early carpenters in the village in 1832–3. Munger and Ruggles were the millwrights of the village at the same time. William Russell, a brother-in-law of A. V. Sill, was the first gunsmith. Deacon Henry W. Hampson was one of the leading builders of the village for years. He came in 1833 with Willett Disbrow, who was also a carpenter. Dunbar & Clarke were the first wagon-makers, though Mr. White worked at the trade before their advent into the village, in 1839. Tyler & Bryfogle succeeded the first-named firm. James and Frank Dressler were the first harness-makers, and were succeeded by Thomas and William Case. Lazarus Eberhart was the first tailor to ply his trade in the village. Harvey Cady made the first barrel in 1837, the first church-

bell in 1842, and the first drum in 1837, in the village. The bell he forged from a steel bar. Mr. Cady also kept the first livery-stock for hire, beginning with a single horse and buggy in 1837–8,—continuing the business twenty years, and ending with ten fine horses and "rigs."

Joseph L. Buel and his family came to Centreville in 1834, and he followed his trade of a carpenter for years, his son Cyrus (whose wife is a daughter of John W. Fletcher, and the first white female born on Nottawa prairie), succeeding to the business.

Walter G. Stephens was probably the earliest carpenter in the village, and came permanently in 1832, being married on Christmas of that year. He built the first brick house in the village. He was the first jailor, too, of the county after the jail was built at Centreville,—previous to that time a sapling, near Sheriff Taylor's house at the grand traverse of the St. Joseph, doing duty oftentimes for a lock-up.

In 1847 Gibbs, Dille & George E. Gurnsey built and operated a pottery, and made good ware for two or three years.

The first flouring-mill in the village was built by George Talbot and Henry D. Cushman in 1851, the dam being built by Mr. Langley, and the power sold to the firm. The mill was furnished with three run of stone, was burned in 1856, and rebuilt soon after by Brokaw & Hoffman, and is now owned by D. D. Antes and Samuel Kline. Its work, in 1876, was twenty thousand bushels of wheat floured, beside the custom work of one hundred bushels of grain per day. The sales of the firm, in flour and wheat shipped, aggregated ninety thousand dollars and over.

The foundry of William Allison was built in 1868, and has been operated by him ever since.

The Centreville Knit Goods Manufacturing Company organized for active operations in 1873, on January 4, with Harvey Cady, president; Edward Talbot, secretary, and Daniel Stewart, treasurer. John C. Joss and Henry C. Campbell were chosen to the latter positions soon after, and have occupied them ever since. The company built their extensive works in the north part of the village, and furnished them with the most complete and latest-improved machinery, and operated them successfully for two years; but unfortunate litigation has intervened, and the splendid and valuable property has lain idle for more than a year. It is, however, kept in good condition, and whenever the lawyers get through with it, it will be ready to start up immediately. The investment amounts to about seventy-five thousand dollars, and is held by stockholders.

The Centreville Fruit-Preserving Company organized January, 1874, with David D. Antes, president; J. C. Joss, secretary; L. A. Clapp succeeding to the latter position subsequently. In June, 1875, after running the season of 1874 on its original business, machinery for the manufacture of cotton-batting was put into the building also, and was operated a portion of the time in that line; and was so operating (and successfully) when it was totally destroyed by fire in the early part of December, 1876, entailing a loss of eighteen thousand dollars on the stockholders, without any insurance.

Messrs. Dockstader Brothers owned and operated a carriage manufactory adjoining the batting-works, which had been in existence some few years, and was also burned.

## THE FIRST NATIONAL BANK

of Centreville was organized January 22, 1873, with C. T. Chaffee, president; Edward Talbot, cashier, and Henry S. Platt, assistant cashier. L. B. Hess succeeded Mr. Platt as cashier, and is still in the position. D. F. Wolf succeeded Mr. Chaffee as president, and was himself succeeded by L. A. Clapp, who fills the position at the present time. The present board of directors are L. A. Clapp, George Keech, Jr., John C. Joss, E. D. Thomas, John I. Major, John Yauney, Wm. W. Jones. The last quarterly statement of the bank, dated January 20, 1877, shows the following condition: Its loans and discounts were seventy-two thousand nine hundred and sixty-six dollars and thirty-four cents. There were due from other national banks and reserve-agents twenty-three thousand eight hundred and forty-four dollars and fifty-nine cents. Its real estate, furniture, &c., were valued at fifteen hundred dollars, and there was cash on hand and in the United States treasury to redeem its circulation, ten thousand one hundred and seventy dollars and fifty-three cents. Its outstanding circulation amounted to forty-four thousand three hundred dollars, which was secured by fifty thousand dollars in United States bonds deposited with the United States treasurer. Its capital-stock paid in and surplus funds and undivided profits amounted to seventy thousand four hundred and fifty-six dollars and thirty cents. Its individual deposits, subject to draft or certificates, stood at forty-three thousand seven hundred and fifty-nine dollars and sixteen cents.

The American express company keep an office in that village, George Keech, Jr., being the agent. During the year two hundred and forty-three packages, aggregating sixteen thousand eight hundred and ninety-one pounds, and three hundred and seventy-four packages under twenty pounds each, were received and forwarded, and money-packages disposed of similarly, including collections, valued at forty-one thousand one hundred and fifty dollars.

### THE POST-OFFICE

was first established in the village, March 2, 1833, and Mr. T. W. Langley appointed the first postmaster, he providing for the transportation of the mail from White Pigeon out of his own pocket, if the receipts of the office did not cover its cost. The first mail was brought from White Pigeon, April 25, and was continued tri-weekly by Langley until July 5, when Savery, the contractor on the route from White Pigeon to Kalamazoo, left it and took it up. Mr. Langley held the position until 1840; C. Bronson, 1841–44; Samuel Chipman, 1845–48; A. E. Massey, 1849–52; Samuel Chipman (again), 1853–60; Henry C. Campbell, 1861–77.

The business of the office has trebled since 1860. It was as follows during the year 1876: Fourteen hundred dollars in stamps were sold; one hundred and twenty-five letters per day received and dispatched; eight hundred and fifty-three registered letters dispatched; six mails received and dispatched per day; and seven hundred newspapers distributed per week, including one hundred dailies and three hundred and fifty county papers.

### THE RAILROADS

of the township do not touch the village,—the Grand Rapids and Indiana running through the eastern part of the township, and the Michigan Central Air Line running nearly a mile north, but the latter is the station for the village, and where all its business is done.

The Grand Rapids and Indiana was the first road to enter the township and received fifteen thousand dollars therefrom to aid in its construction, besides the individual assistance rendered.

The Michigan Central railroad was built through the township in 1870–1, and received a donation from the town of twenty-five thousand dollars, besides other assistance from the village residents.

Oscar Waters, a young lawyer of Centreville, was the first agent, and is now holding the same position on the road at Battle Creek. The present agent and telegraph operator is R. W. Hayes, who has very kindly furnished the following statement of the business of the station for the year 1876: There were forwarded four millions four hundred and eighteen thousand five hundred and forty-two pounds of freight, and one million four hundred and twenty-seven thousand seven hundred and thirty-six pounds of the same received.

There is employed in business in the village at the present time about two hundred thousand dollars capital.

### THE BUSINESS OF THE PRESENT

is as follows:

Dry Goods—J. W. Spitzer.
General Merchandise—C. D. Bennett.
Hardware—Talbot & Worthington, R. N. Avery.
Groceries—H. C. Campbell, E. W. Talbot, John Lucas, Chris. Elser & Co.
Drugs, Stationery, &c.—Geo. Keech, Jr., E. D. Thomas.
Essential Oils—Wolf Brothers and Keech.
Harness and Trunks—Charles O. Gregory, H. D. Westcott.
Millinery and Ladies' Furnishing Goods—Mrs. H. M. Davis, Mrs. S. E. Blanchard.
Boots and Shoes—Louis Klesner, Louis Booth, C. H. Thomas,—one of the oldest in the county.
Tailors—D. D. Ashley, E. Davis.
Markets—Holt & Hasbrouck, Lyman Putney.
Jewelry and Watches—George Richards.
Live Stock—John S. Major.
Nottawa Hack-line—B. A. Wells.
Livery—Joseph P. Dockstader.
Eggs and Butter—J. B. Quivey.
Agricultural Implements—D. D. Antes, H. A. Hecox.
Insurance—L. A. Clapp, C. H. Starr, John D. Antes, James Eastman Johnson.
Drayman—John Wilson.
Steam-Threshers—Samuel P. Kline, John W. Schermerhorn—both in the township.
Hotel—W. S. Beardsley.

### MANUFACTURES.

Flouring-Mills—Kline & Antes.
Foundry—William Allison.
Book-bindery—A. Beerstecher.
Furniture, &c.—C. Cummins.
Gunsmiths—F. Beerstecher, Isaac Platt.
Carpenter-shops—Thomas R. Shaffer, C. R. Buel, Charles F. Beerstecher, Platt & Emmons, J. D. Bonner, George Yauney, David Overfield, James Belote.
Wagon-shops and Blacksmiths—George Thoms, Clarence Culver, Charles Loop, George H. Dexter, George H. Knapp, Daniel Drescher.
Cooper—George Morrison.
Barber—Professor Jennings Hyatt.
Masons—A. O. Bishop, W. G. Bishop, James Wilson, W. H. Keeney, (in township).
Dressmaker—Mrs. Haight.

### THE FIRST ROAD

that was laid into Centreville was one from the Branch county line in 1832, William Connor, Henry Powers and J. W. Fletcher laying the same out on the line since adopted by the State road. Hog creek was then very high, and the line of the road has been changed somewhat since.

The road to Constantine was surveyed by Robert Clark, Jr., on horseback, and Captain Alvin Calhoon followed Clark as axeman, also mounted, and blazed the road through among the higher limbs, and the line has never been changed to the present time.

### THE FIRST STAGE LINE

that was operated through Centreville, was under the management of Harvey Hunt, of Constantine, and Moses Austin, of Kalamazoo; in 1836 they ran their wagons between these points. Langley & Stockwell carried the mail and passengers between Coldwater and Centreville afterwards, but the first coaches that came into Centreville were those of Amos Spafford, in 1840, on his line from Bronson to Mottville. Louis A. Leland carried the mail on horseback from Centreville to Niles in 1838; it being taken by another party from the last point, and carried to the mouth of the St. Joseph.

### THE FIRST LAWYER

was Columbia Lancaster, who was also the first man to build a human habitation on the village plat; his clients at the time being skipping over the prairies and through the woods in droves. He emphatically made their interests his own, as many a fine pair of antlers which graced his cabin testified. Subsequently his brother Elizur (now a resident of Burr Oak), and two sisters came to Centreville and resided with him; the latter subsequently marrying Merlin Hazzard and Jacob Kline. The attorneys who subsequently located in the village were L. F. Stevens, —— Crary, G. H. Mason, D. V. Bell, S. C. Coffinberry, J. Eastman Johnson, William Sadler, George A. Key, S. J. Mills, —— Hammond, —— Dresser, P. M. Smith, William Allison, John S. Chipman, Aaron E. Wait, Chester Gurney, Charles Upson, Alfred A. Key and S. M. Sadler. The present bar of the village is named in the general history of the bar, elsewhere in the work.

### THE FIRST PHYSICIAN

who located in the village was Dr. S. W. Truesdell, who also kept the first drug-store opened in the place. He came to the village in January, 1833. Soon after he came, Dr. Johnston, the mercantile partner of Charles H. Stewart, located in 1833, and next came Dr. Cyrus Ingerson, the same year, who was afterwards elected judge of probate, and died in office in 1844. Dr. A. T. Woodworth located in the village in 1837, and Dr. Richardson about 1839 or 1840. John Bennett read medicine with Dr. R., and subsequently practiced his profession in the village. Dr. Greene came in 1840. Dr. Van Buren, of the homœopathic school, came in 1836, and Dr. Anthony, a botanic physician, was an early-comer to the village. The present medical staff of the village is as follows: Drs. F. C. Bateman, G. M. Trowbridge and —— Sabin, allopathic; Dr. E. Clarke, homœopathic, and Dr. Whitman. The first doctor of dental surgery was J. A. Russell, who was succeeded by his brother, Dean Russell, the present practitioner in that line. William Fitzsimmons is a skilful veterinary surgeon, and the only one of his profession in the vicinity.

### THE FIRST CEMETERY

was laid out in the village in 1833, the lots for the same being donated by the county on the condition that the people of the town, or village, put up a picket-fence around them. The first burial in the same was that of Mr.

OLIVER W. WILCOX

MRS OLIVER W. WILCOX

RESIDENCE OF OLIVER W. WILCOX, NOTTAWA TP. ST JOSEPH CO. MICH.

Cooley, father-in-law of H. W. Foster. The second burial was the child of Peter Cox, which died in January, 1834. A new cemetery was purchased by the board of health, in 1869–70, northeast of the village, which is very eligibly located, and susceptible of very fine adornment, being elevated and undulating. Several monuments and slabs attest its occupancy.

#### THE FIRST SCHOOL

taught in Centreville was a private one, by Mrs. Hartley, in the family of Mr. Langley, in 1832. In the winter of 1833–34, H. R. Lamb taught the first public school in the court-house building, a Mr. Stoddard succeeding to the birch the winter following. Dr. Cyrus Ingerson taught the school in its early days. Rev. W. B. Brown, a Baptist minister, taught in 1838, and his daughter also; and a Mrs. Briar taught a school in the Trowbridge house.

#### THE FIRST SCHOOL-HOUSE

was built in 1841. Harvey Cady made the shingles for the same. It was in district No. 1, fractional, Lockport and Nottawa. Deacon H. W. Hampson, one of the Centreville early settlers, built the house for about five hundred dollars. The size, lot eight, block twenty-nine, cost fifty dollars. There was no school taught in it the winter of 1841–42, but a select school was taught the following winter, by a Mr. Pople. The first public school was taught in it by Mrs. Mary Chapin, the summer of 1843,—she receiving two dollars per week for her services. There were eighty-three pupils in the district at the time. H. L. Hare taught the winter of 1844–45. In 1848, a new school-house was built on the same location, two other lots being added. The house cost one thousand two hundred and ten dollars, eight hundred dollars cash, and lot ten and the old building for the balance. The contractors were Deacon Hampson and William Laffty. Four hundred dollars were paid for the additional lots. The building was thirty-four by fifty-six feet on the ground, two stories, the lower one eleven feet in the clear, and upper one thirteen feet.

Hon. Charles Upson was the last teacher in the old building, and Hiram Hamilton the first in the new one, and he received four hundred dollars for ten months' work. His wife, Guinevra Hinsdell, and Mrs. McMarter were his assistants. In 1850 the district elected four additional trustees, the board being Charles Upson, C. H. Starr, Samuel Chipman, Alexander Stewart, A. E. Massey, moderator, P. M. Smith, director, and H. W. Hampson, assessor. John W. McMath was the first principal under the new regime, and teachers' wages amounted to five hundred and thirty-two dollars. In 1853 the school was graded into senior and junior classes.

In 1870, at the annual meeting of the district, September 5, the question of a new site for a school-house began to be agitated, and after much balloting the lots owned by C. H. Starr, known as "the Grove," were purchased for one thousand dollars. It is a beautiful location, none more so in the village. The annual meeting of 1873 decided to build a new house, and one was completed in 1874, and dedicated formally with interesting exercises, Judge J. Eastman Johnson officiating as orator on the occasion.

The building is constructed most substantially of stone, and is commodious and comfortable and conveniently arranged. It cost twenty-two thousand dollars. L. B. Antisdale has been the principal since 1875,—George C. Bannon holding that position in 1870–71, and Frank A. Minor in 1872. The board of education for 1876 is as follows: D. D. Antes, moderator, G. M. Trowbridge, director, Marder Sabine, Edward Talbot, F. Beerstecher and John C. Joss.

The cost of the school and the resources of the district for the year ending September 1, 1876, were as follows: There were ten months of school taught, two hundred and seventy-four pupils being in attendance. One male teacher was paid one thousand dollars, and four female—one thousand four hundred dollars for their services; two thousand nine hundred and fifty-four dollars were paid on bonded indebtedness, and one thousand and one hundred and twenty-seven dollars and thirty-seven cents on repairs, insurance, &c. The total resources of the district amounted to eight thousand one hundred and thirty-six dollars and sixty-six cents, including one hundred and fifty-three dollars and fifty-two cents tuition fees received from non-resident pupils. The school property is valued at twenty-four thousand five hundred dollars, and the house contains three hundred and eight sittings, and has a small library and some apparatus.

#### THE PEOPLE'S SEMINARY.

In 1836–37 the Centrevillians struck for a higher institution of learning than they had previously possessed, and issued a prospectus to the people of the county of a proposed People's seminary, to be governed by twenty-four trustees, six to go out of office each year, who were to be elected by the patrons of the school. To keep the school out of the control of any one

13

man or set of men, no person could have more than three votes, no matter how much he subscribed and did for the school. Everything was pictured out in roseate hues of the advantage to the people the proposed school would be; the cheapness of board being particularly enlarged upon; the same to be furnished by the parents of the prospective pupils to a common boarding-house; by which co-operative arrangement, it was declared, solemnly, that a saving of expense would be effected "sufficient to offer inducements to bring a professor from London to them."

The proposers expressed themselves forcibly on this point. "There is no fiction in this," says the prospectus, and proceeds to eliminate the theory: "The farmers' boys could work in the summer and eat up in the winter, at their own school, a portion only of what they had raised, the ware and tare of clothing would be less by sending their own bedding," &c., &c. But the branch of the University was located at White Pigeon, and the proposed People's seminary became a thing of naught.

#### RELIGIOUS SERVICES

were held regularly during the summer of 1833, and as early as January of that year, by the ministers of the different denominations who passed that way on their missionary tours. The early itinerants of the Methodist Episcopal church, Gurley and Kellogg, came, and others; and Bishops Chase, of Ohio, McCrusky, of Detroit, of the Episcopal church, Reverends Whitesides of the same church, from Philadelphia, and Schuyler and Rev. P. W. Warriner, of White Pigeon, a Presbyterian, and Rev. Mr. Sweet, a Universalist, occupied the court-house at different times up to 1837. The first religious society organized in the village was

#### THE MORAL AND RELIGIOUS SOCIETY,

an association formed June 7, 1835; its first officers being Philip R. Toll, president; Peter Cox, vice-president; Charles H. Stewart, secretary; Cyrus Ingerson, treasurer; Digby V. Bell, Thomas W. Langley and Henry W. Hampson, trustees.

The preamble to the original constitution adopted by the society (in the handwriting of Digby D. Bell) sets forth that "believing an association for religious and moral purposes will tend to the general promotion of individual happiness by securing more permanently to the public the regular means of religious worship, with all its invaluable privileges; the better adoption and practice of genuine moral virtues, and the consequent beneficent influence on public morals;" and therefore the members did form an association in accordance with the spirit of the preamble, and adopted the constitution which provided for the membership of "any male or female person over fourteen years of age, who should be of good moral habits, and believe in a Supreme Being, in a future state of rewards and punishments, and in the forgiveness of sins through the great Redeemer alone." The male members only had the right of voting for the officers; the women—and they were worthy mates—being silent partners. The trustees and president fixed times of meeting, and invited ministers of the Gospel to preach, and were to "make arrangements for worship on all Sabbaths,"—the expenses to be liquidated by voluntary subscriptions alone. The members of this society, at its organization, were Peter Cox, John Cruden, C. H. Stewart, Michael Hewes, Dr. Ingerson, Lloyd Childs, William Major, H. W. Hampson, D. V. Bell, Columbia Lancaster, T. W. Langley, Philip R. Toll, Mrs. C. H. Stewart, Miss Van Patten, Mrs. Childs, Miss Lancaster, Miss N. O. Van Patten and Mrs. Cox. The sum of sixteen dollars was subscribed for a donation to Rev. P. W. Warriner for his services as preacher previous to the organization of society, and fifteen dollars of the amount paid over to him,—Charles H. Stewart, Philip R. Toll, Thomas W. Langley and James and Robert Cowen paying twelve dollars of the same.

#### THE FIRST SUNDAY-SCHOOL

was organized at the same time as the above-named society, though a movement for one began a year before. Four dollars and seventy-eight cents were subscribed for books, and the school began, but suspended until June 7, 1835, when it was permanently organized in connection with the society, with the following officers and corps of teachers: Peter Cox, president; C. H. Stewart, secretary; T. W. Langley, treasurer; H. W. Hampson, librarian. Teachers: Dr. Ingerson, William Hazzard, Columbia Lancaster, Mrs. Stewart, Mrs. Hartley, Miss Van Patten and Miss Vrinon. There were twenty-three pupils. Twenty dollars and sixty-one cents were expended for books, the same being selected and purchased by Mrs. Stewart, from the Michigan Sunday-school Union, of which the school was made an auxiliary. Among the books were "Lives" of Daniel, David and Moses, at "three shillings" each; two short discourses were listed at fifteen cents each; "An Only

Son" was bought for forty cents, and "Frankie's Memoirs" were rated at the same figure. One "story" book was valued at fifteen cents, and "Belemuel, or a Visit to Jerusalem," was marked "three shillings." "Leigh Richmond" was invoiced at thirty cents.

THE FIRST CHURCH EDIFICE .

built in the village was that of the Methodist Episcopal society in 1841. The society or class was first organized in the spring of 1830 at the house of William Hazzard, on the prairie, by Revs. Erastus Felton and Lyman B. Gurly,—Mr. Hazzard and his wife Cassandra and William Fletcher and his wife Hannah being the only members. Amos Howe joined the class afterwards, and was the first regularly-appointed class-leader. Preaching services were held fortnightly,—first at private houses, afterwards in school-houses, and afterwards in the court-house in Centreville.

In 1836 Erastus Kellogg was the preacher in charge, and movements were soon after made towards the erection of a church building. The timber was prepared and the building framed in 1837 or 8, but was not raised and completed until 1841, and was dedicated by Mr. Kellogg.

The present church edifice of this society was built in 1856, during the pastorate of Reverend J. Buell, the dedicatory services being conducted by Reverend J. K. Gillett, September 20 of the last-named year.

In 1871 the building received material improvements with the addition of lecture and class-rooms, and has four hundred and twenty sittings. The present membership is two hundred and twenty-five; its Sabbath-school, which was organized soon after the church-edifice was erected in 1841, has one hundred and ninety-six scholars on its roll, and its present pastor is Reverend G. W. Tuthill.

The church property is valued at twelve thousand dollars, and there are four hundred books in the Sunday-school library. The old church-building is now Dr. Bateman's barn, and was twenty-four by forty feet on the ground.

THE REFORMED CHURCH OF NORTH AMERICA,

or as it was originally, and until within a few years called, "The Dutch Reformed Church," was first organized April 8, 1839; though services had been held by Reverend Isaac S. Ketchum as early as the winter of 1835-6. Mr. Ketchum was a missionary sent out by the New York missionary society of the Reformed Dutch church, and after his family removed to Centreville from the Mohawk valley in 1836, he continued to preach to the people until 1839, when the society was organized, as before stated, by electing a board of trustees, consisting of Philip R. Toll, Isaac S. Ketchum, John W. Talbot, Jacob D. Kline and Solomon Cummings.

On the 25th of May a consistory was held at the court-house, composed of Reverend Asa Bennett, president ; Dr. S. Cummings, Peter Cox and Jacob D. Kline, elders ; and Alfred Todd and William Van Deusen, deacons ; who formed the church as the "First Protestant Reformed Dutch Church of Centreville," and admitted to membership therein the following persons : William Van Deusen and Matilda his wife, Alfred Todd and Mary his wife, John Pierce, Jacob D. Kline and Elizabeth his wife, Solomon Cummings, Sally Bennett, P. R. Toll and Nancy D. his wife, Peter Cox and Mary his wife, and Mrs. Huldah Dunbar ; and, on confession, Miss Mary Eliza Dorchester and Miss Sarah M. Cox.

Mr. Ketchum was subsequently the Indian agent for a time, and his widow now resides in Centreville with her daughter, Mrs. Talbot, a hale, hearty, active and intelligent old lady, with whom it is a rare pleasure to converse of the olden time,

"When life seemed sweet as the poet's rhyme."

On October 5, 1841, it was resolved by the consistory to build a church, and Harvey Cady, J. A. Clarke and Cyrus Ingerson were appointed a building committee. Joseph I. Dunbar drew the plans and made the estimates for the building, which was erected at a cost of about one thousand one hundred dollars,—of which amount six hundred and fifty dollars was given by eastern parties.

Mr. Bennett's pastorate ended September, 1843,—B. C. Taylor succeeding him on the 30th of the month, and remaining but a year, when he resigned, and David McNeish succeeded to the desk.

The church was finished in 1845. Mr. McNeish continued his pastorate until January, 1847, and was succeeded then by Reverend Safrenus Seeber. Since then the following pastors have cared for this desk : Reverend John Minor, 1848-52 ; Reverend J. N. Shults, June 28, 1852, to October 27, 1855; Reverend J. H. Kershaw, 1855-1865; Reverend A. H. Van Vrauken, 1865 until the present time.

The bell was bought for the church in 1853, for one hundred and seventy-five dollars, and the parsonage in 1850, in the spring of that year.

The church has been greatly improved and enlarged, having an area on the ground of fifty-four by seventy-two feet, with lecture-room and dining-hall in lower or basement story. The building is warmed by furnaces, and its sheds for the accommodation and comfortable housing of the horses of those who attend upon the worship are conveniently and amply arranged, and the presence of one or more occupants of each stall, on almost every Sunday, evinces the interest of the people in the preaching they hear in the church.

There are, at the present writing (December, 1876), one hundred and sixty-six members of the church, and one hundred and fifteen scholars in its Sunday-school, which was organized early in the history of the society. There are five hundred volumes in the library, and Alexander Sharpe is the present superintendent. The church has six hundred sittings, and is valued, together with the parsonage, at eight thousand dollars.

In 1867 the name was changed to its present one, the Reformed Church of North America. During that year a noted revival was conducted by the present pastor, forty-three uniting with the church by confession and baptism. There have been three hundred and twenty-five members on its roll since its organization.

Reverend Asa Bennett was a settler in the county, near Centreville, in 1839-40. He was the pastor of the Reformed church at Constantine after his pastorate at Centreville ceased, and was a good man and highly respected. John Bennett, one of his sons, became an eminent physician ; and Cornelius D. Bennett, a successful merchant in Centreville for several years, and previously a clerk of the courts of St. Joseph for some years, is also a son. Mr. Bennett died January 16, 1858.

THE BAPTIST CHURCH

of Centreville was not organized until 1852, though preaching had been secured as early as 1838, by Rev. W. B. Brown. In February, 1852, Perrin M. Smith, Henry W. Hampson and Henry J. Cushman, in behalf of several communicants of the Baptist faith, addressed a letter of invitation to Rev. G. N. TenBrook to settle with them as pastor, which was accepted by the latter, who began his labors among them July 1, 1852.

On the 28th of August following, there met at the house of Mr. Smith, and formed the Baptist church of Centreville, the following-named persons, all communicants : Rev. G. N. TenBrook and wife, Joel Redway and wife, Henry J. Cushman and wife, Norman Rawson, S. G. Antes, P. M. Smith and wife, H. W. Hampson, Frederick Sailer and wife, Mrs. Flowers and Maria Weld. Mr. TenBrook acted as chairman ; P. M. Smith, secretary, and Joel Redway was appointed deacon. During 1852, Mrs. Chester Gurney, Mrs. John Major, Mrs. Norman Rawson, Mrs. Dwight Stebbins, Oliver Wilcox and Warren Collins were received into the church.

On November 27, 1852, the society voted to build a church, and appointed brethren Wilcox, Redway and Hampson a building committee. The society met in the court-house for worship. P. M. Smith, the secretary, entered on the records the following explanation : " In the reception of members up to January 1, 1853, the brethren and sisters of the church, consisting of a few scattered and homeless wanderers, have fellowshipped one another as Christians of the Baptist denomination, known to each other, some with and some without letters, but of good Christian character."

The church was erected in 1853, of brick, on the spot where it now stands, east of the public square. The first communion was observed on the Sunday succeeding the last Saturday in December, 1852. The first missionary-collection was taken up April 30, 1853, and amounted to two dollars and sixty-eight cents.

In May, 1853, the church was admitted to the St. Joseph Baptist association, which met at Niles that year, but which held its session in June, 1854, at Centreville. Rev. Mr. TenBrook died in the service of his church, April 3, 1857, and was buried the following day, Rev. Mr. Fish and Elder Sage officiating.

Rev. Aaron Potter succeeded Mr. TenBrook in August, 1857, remaining till October, 1858, and Elder Stanwood supplied the desk from that date until November 27, 1859, when Rev. C. R. Nichols was installed as pastor, and remained till March 27, 1862, when he resigned on account of ill-health. March 30, 1861, one of the members, John Barnes, was commended for his " piety and ability to preach, and authorized to improve upon his gift."

The desk was supplied by different ministers, a stated pastor occasionally coming to the charge and remaining but a short time, until March 31, 1867, when Rev. William Pack began the supply of the desk, which he continued until February 22, 1860, and was then installed as pastor, and remained thus until April 1, 1870. From that date to April 1, 1876, Elder Dunnett, Rev. C. T. Chaffee and Rev. C. A. Clarke, respectively, were pastors ; at

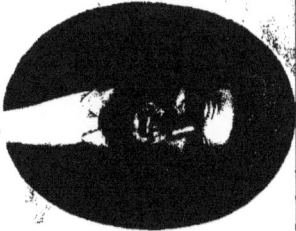

RESIDENCE OF THOMAS CUDDY, Nottawa Tp. St Joseph Co, Mich.

which last-named date Rev. J. C. Burkholder, the present pastor, assumed charge of the flock on the call of the same.

Deacon Henry W. Hampson, long and actively a member of the church, died April 14, 1873, sincerely regretted. Hon. P. M. Smith was the clerk of the church from its organization till his death, which occurred in March, 1866. Dr. Marden Sabin was elected clerk June 27, 1866, and is still in the position. Chester Gurney and John Bennett were the first baptisms in the church, April 25, 1855. One hundred and forty-six members have been enrolled on the church-records, eighty-three of whom have been baptized, and sixty-three received by letter and experience; ten have died, thirty-five have been dismissed by letter, and nine dropped from church-membership or excluded, leaving the present number eighty-seven. The baptistry was built under the church in May, 1872, and the bell bought in October, weighing one thousand one hundred pounds. The parsonage was built in 1867. The church has three hundred sittings, is heated with furnaces, and, with the parsonage, is valued at eight thousand dollars.

A Sunday-school was organized about the time the church was built, and has been continued ever since. It numbers now one hundred and ten scholars; has one hundred and twenty-five volumes in library, and Dr. Trowbridge is the superintendent.

THE ASSOCIATE REFORMED SOCIETY

(Scotch) of Centreville was organized March 9, 1839, by electing the following trustees: John McKee, William Gilchrist and Robert Campbell. The first pastor was the Rev. Mr. Hotchkiss; the second, the Rev. Mr. Baldridge, and the third, and last, Rev. Mr. Blair. The society built a church in 1846, or thereabout, but it has been closed for several years.

SOCIETIES.—MASONIC.

Mount Hermon Lodge, No. 24, A. F. M., was instituted under dispensation in 1848, and chartered January 10, 1849. The first master was Benjamin Osgood; Ezra Cole, S. W.; S. C. Coffinberry, J. W. The charter-members are given in the county history. The office of worthy master has been filled as follows: S. C. Coffinberry, 1852; F. C. Bateman, 1857-8; Nathan S. Johnson, 1859; James J. Dresler, 1860-61 and '65; Peter M. Gray, 1862-4; L. A. Clapp, 1866-70; William Fitzsimmons, 1871-3; William M. Antes, 1874-6.

The present officers are W. M. Antes, W. M.; J. B. Quivey, S. W.; George Frankish, J. W.; Charles Cummings, treasurer; William Frankish, secretary; H. W. Hayes, S. D.; C. F. Yauney, J. D.; Rev. A. H. Van Vrauken, chaplain; James Yauney and John F. Wolf, stewards; D. Westcott, tyler. There are seventy-six members on the roll of craftsmen, in good standing. The lodge is the oldest one in the county, and was the first one instituted. It meets in its own hall, in Wolf's block, and which has been neatly furnished and prettily adorned with portraits of the presiding officers of the lodge.

CENTREVILLE CHAPTER, NO. 11, R. A. M.,

was instituted under dispensation, July, 1852, and received its charter February 1, 1853,—Solomon Cummings being the first H. P., Benjamin Sherman the first scribe, and John Belote the first king. The other charter-members were Nathan Gurney, John Richards, Edwin Perry, Samuel Tyler, Benjamin Osgood, Asahel Huntley, James L. Bishop and F. A. Kent. Hon. J. Eastman Johnson, Hon. S. C. Coffinberry and Louis A. Leland, Esq., were the first "team" to receive the R. A. degree in the chapter. Judge Coffinberry was elected G. H. P. in 1857, and re-elected for the next two succeeding terms. His address before the annual convocation of the G. C., in January, 1858, was a very able and exhaustive document on Masonic jurisprudence.

Another of the members of this chapter has reflected honor upon it,— Hon. J. Eastman Johnson, who was appointed grand secretary by G. H. P. Coffinberry in 1859, to fill a vacancy, and was elected to the same position every year thereafter up to 1874.

In 1856 the chapter was removed to Constantine, where it remained until 1858, when it was returned to its original location.

The office of H. P. has been filled as follows: S. C. Coffinberry, 1854-6; John Belote, 1857-8; B. F. Doughty, 1859-60; Hiram Lindsley, 1861-6; J. E. Johnson, 1867; Peter M. Gray, 1868-9; L. A. Clapp, 1870-71; Charles A. Palmer, 1872-5. The officers of 1876 are: William Fitzsimmons, H. P.; William L. Antes, K.; John F. Wolf, S.; William Frankish, P. S.; J. B. Quivey, C. H.; Charles Yauney, R. A. C.; H. D. Westcott, J. O. Childs and J. P. Dockstader, M. of V.; George Yauney, sentinel; J. W. Spitzer, secretary; James Yauney, treasurer; Rev. A. H. Van Vrauken, chaplain. The roll numbers ninety-three craftsmen.

ODD-FELLOWS.

There was a lodge of Odd-Fellows instituted at one time in Centreville (one of the first, if not the first in the county), but it ceased working several years ago. It was known as the St. Joseph County Lodge, No. —, I. O. O. F.

PATRONS OF HUSBANDRY.

Centreville Grange, No. 76, was organized September 23, 1873, with thirty members, William Hazzard being the first master, and John C. Joss the first secretary. The officers of 1876 were as follows: William Hull, master; James Yauney, overseer; J. Mosher, lecturer; Samuel Blair, secretary; George Hazzard, treasurer; Mrs. Benjamin, Pomona; Mrs. M. A. Kline, Ceres; Mrs. James Yauney, Flora. There are, at present, seventy-one members in the grange, which meets in the old court-house, which has been the scene of the organization of nearly every church and society in the village.

THE MUNICIPALITY.

Centreville was first incorporated as a village in 1837, and, at an election held May 1, in that year, the following trustees were elected to manage the corporation: Captain Philip R. Toll, J. W. Coffinberry, Alexander V. Sill, Cyrus Ingerson, Edmund White, E. J. VanBuren and John Graham. The first action of the board was to express their gratitude to their constituents, and invite them to partake of a collation at the Centreville Hotel on the Monday evening following.

This government was sustained but a short time,—not later than 1840,— and the village was not again incorporated until February 23, 1877, when the citizens voted to re-incorporate under the general statute for such purposes.

The election for trustees and officers was held March 13, and resulted in the choice of William Fadler, president; Alfred A. Key, clerk; Giles F. Dockstader, treasurer; William Fitzsimmons, marshal; Daniel F. Wolf, street commissioner; Edward Talbot, assessor; William Fitzsimmons, constable. Trustees, Marden Sabin, Henry C. Campbell and Israel B. Quivey, one year; J. W. Spitzer, John C. Joss and D. D. Antes, two years.

AMUSEMENTS AND INCIDENTS.

The first party of young people gathered in Centreville for a dance assembled under the leadership of Hon. Isaac D. Toll, in 1836, at the Centreville Hotel, kept then by A. V. Sill.

In 1840 a dancing-school was taught at the "Exchange" by Griswold and Arnold, during Knox's administration, at which, besides dancing, there was considerable good manners taught, the conductors of the assemblies being thorough masters of their business. So their old pupils say.

The national birthday was celebrated in 1837 in grand style. Harvey Cady built the drums, both bass and snare, with which, and a fife, keg-bugle and fiddle, the procession marched through the streets to the ground prepared for their exercises. The drums and fife would play until out of wind, and then the bugle and fiddle would take up the strain, and prolong the harmony until the bugler was red in the face and the fiddler's arm was wearied, and then the martial music would relieve the orchestral part of the arrangement, and thus the melody was continuous through the entire route. The committee of arrangements, consisting of Philip R. Toll, D. H. Johnson, Dr. Motiram. Oliver Raymond, and ten others of the early citizens, issued an announcement of the programme, which read as follows: "Sixty-first Anniversary; Independence Day, 1837;" and a huge spread-eagle overshadowed what followed; star-spangled banner hoisted in the public square, and a salute of thirteen guns fired; procession, oration at the court-house, and dinner at the Centreville Hotel, kept by A. V. Sill; balloon ascension in afternoon, and fire-works and ball in the evening. Officers of the day: E. J. Vanburen, marshal; J. W. Coffinberry, reader; Dr. Motiram, orator; Revs. W. W. Brown and I. S. Ketchum, chaplains; Rev. G. S. Day, chorister.

Mrs. Charles Henry Stewart's home was a resort of the citizens for pleasant and agreeable entertainment, and the hostess being an excellent pianist, dancing was always in order, and much enjoyed.

In later days the private theatricals of amateur comedy and tragedy have claimed attention somewhat, and some very creditable presentations have been made by the young people of the village.

One day an Irishman named R. B. Osborn came to Philip R. Toll and asked for a job of work, and was set to chopping timber in the woods. After a day or two the chopper came into Mr. Toll's store, and showed young Isaac D., then a clerk for his father, a sketch of a landscape, which, on inquiry, was found to be the work of the wood-chopper himself. It was well executed, and a faithful representation. The young man immediately set about raising a class for instruction in the art, and soon got up one, and Osborn quit chopping; and after a while he and his companion, also a fine sketcher, found work in civil engineering in Chicago, from whence they returned to Ireland, from which they had been sent to "tone" them down somewhat in their ways.

The first juries, after leaving their business for a week, would be called up and thanked by the judge for their labors, and then allowed, graciously, to pay their hotel bills and go home. There were no fees allowed jurors for some years. One of the St. Joseph juries were somewhat tenacious on what they considered their rights, and once upon a time, when a judge from another circuit was holding the court in St. Joseph, a jury brought in a verdict directly contrary to the instructions of the court, and, when afterwards questioned why they so acted, the foreman replied: "Do you suppose we were going to have a foreigner come in here and tell us what we shall and what we shan't do? No, sir: not much!"

### NOTTAWA STATION,

on the Grand Rapids and Indiana railroad, occupies the former site of the village of Oporto, which once boasted of an existence among the villages of St. Joseph county. Its proprietor, Whitney, who settled early on Sand lake, sold a few village lots which were taxed as such,—which act of oppression was too burdensome upon the embryo city, and it incontinently relapsed into its original element of farming lands. A store was kept by one Thompson for a time, and a post-office was established thereat, of which W. D. Ovid was postmaster for a while, and then R. A. Cutler for fifteen years, a part of the time the office being at his place. The office was removed to Hopper's corners, where it remained for a few years. The present hamlet rose when the railroad was built through the township.

The business of the village is conducted by J. W. Schermerhorn, who is the station and U. S. Express agent, and deals in produce and lumber; Drake and Todd, dealers in general merchandise; Albert M. Todd, dealer in essential oils; C. E. Sabin, in general merchandise; William Willington, hardware; J. W. Hagelgans, furniture; T. D. Atkinson, manufacturer of carriages and wagons, and blacksmithing; and J. B. Howard, lessee of the hotel. The post-office was re-established when the station was located, Samuel Klady being the postmaster, who was succeeded by the present incumbent, C. E. Sabin, in 1870. Robert Schermerhorn has a mint-oil distillery near the village. There were shipped from the station during the year 1876, sixty-seven thousand seven hundred and one bushels of grain, and three hundred and sixty-six thousand two hundred and seventy-six pounds of other merchandise.

### WASEPI

has a recorded existence on the surveys of St. Joseph, the plat of the village having been recorded in December, 1874. Messrs. Barnard, Gee, Connor et al. were the original proprietors. They located their city at the crossing of the Michigan Central Air Line Railroad and Grand Rapids and Indiana road. It contains a post-office, which accommodates about thirty families; C. A. Ensign is the present postmaster,—Frank M. Tuttle, as deputy, doing the business. D. C. Gee was the first postmaster. The business is done at the station principally. Messrs. Connor & Ensign have a fruit-drying factory (Jones' process), and about one hundred and fifty barrels of apples, twenty-five barrels of dried apples and one hundred barrels of cider were shipped from the station during the fall. Mark Connor is the station agent, but Mr. Tuttle does all of the business connected with the station.

### PATRIOTISM OF NOTTAWA.

Nottawa prairie bore a conspicuous part in the troublous times of Black Hawk, by reason of its proximity to the Nottawa-seepe reservation, occupied by some hundreds of supposed implacable warriors. A company of one hundred men was organized, officered by Captain Henry Powers, Lieutenant Jonathan Engle, Jr., Hiram Gates, ensign, and Frank McMillan, orderly sergeant. The company, composed of boys and gray-headed men, turned out to a man, but were detailed as a corps of observation on the line of the reservation, and began the erection of Fort Hogan, as described elsewhere. A draft of twenty men started for the west, but went as far as White Pigeon only, the war having ended before proceeding farther. The organization of the company was kept up for a time, but no further call was made upon the citizens until the great war of the Rebellion, except such as might have volunteered in the Mexican war. During the war for the Union (1861–5) Nottawa filled her quotas with commendable alacrity, and her citizens covered themselves with undying glory on the field as well as at home, in helping forward the cause of freedom and nationality. The old

flag had no braver or more able defenders than those Nottawa sent to the front, and the record they made for her is imperishable.

The following is a list of the men who sustained her honor untarnished amid gloom and defeat, as well as when flushed with victorious success. If any names are missing from the roll of honor, the reader may find them recorded elsewhere in the other township histories, where they may have been erroneously located:

#### FOURTH MICHIGAN INFANTRY.

Sergeant Eli Starr, Company C; killed at Malvern Hill, Va., July 1, 1862.
Private George Ackers, Company C; discharged for disability.

#### FIFTH MICHIGAN INFANTRY.

Private John E. Culbertson, Company C; mustered out at close of war.

#### SIXTH INFANTRY.

Wagoner Mortimer J. Barkman, Company C; discharged.
Private Isaac Gince, Company C; re-enlisted; mustered-out.
Private Albert A. Jones, Company C; enlisted in regular service.
Private Andrew W. Morrison, Company C; died in Michigan, March 1, 1864.
Private William E. Morrison, Company C; re-enlisted; died in Centreville.
Private Jason B. Taylor, Company C; discharged for disability.
Private Henry C. Walters, Company C; re-enlisted; mustered-out.
Private George W. Walters, Company C; died in regimental hospital, October 3, 1862.
Musician Nelson Wells, Company C; discharged for disability.
Private Hiram Hill, Company C; mustered-out.
Private Joseph W. Rolfe, Company C; mustered-out.
Private Francis Douglass, Company C; mustered-out.

#### SEVENTH INFANTRY.

Private W. R. Gifford, Company I.

#### TENTH INFANTRY.

Private William A. Knapp, Company K; mustered-out.

#### ELEVENTH INFANTRY.

Commissary Sergeant Elva F. Peirce; veteran reserve corps.
Musician George D. Clarke; mustered out August 22, 1862.
Captain David Oakes, Jr., Company A; died at Murfreesboro, January, 1862.
Sergeant Walter A. Johnson, Company A; died at Centreville, January 12, 1862.
Sergeant James F. Lovett, Company A; killed at Chickamauga.
Sergeant Hiram G. Platt, Company A; discharged at expiration of service.
Corporal John W. Hall, Company A; discharged for disability.
Corporal Abner V. Wilcox, Company A; killed at Chattanooga, October 24, 1863.
Musician George W. Kent, Company A; discharged for disability.
Musician W. H. H. Platt, Company A; sergeant-major; discharged at expiration of service.
Private Robert Baker, Company A; discharged for disability.
Private George W. Dickinson, Company A; discharged at expiration of service.
Private Charles W. Donkin, Company A; discharged at expiration of service.
Private Rollin O. Eaton, Company A; discharged at expiration of service.
Private Charles Fisher, Company A; discharged at expiration of service.
Private Henry Hall, Company A; discharged at expiration of service.
First Lieutenant Henry S. Fisher, Company A; captain, January 30, 1863; resigned.
Private William C. Iddings, Company A; discharged at expiration of service.
Private Francisco Klady, Company A; discharged at expiration of service.
Private Cyrus E. Peirce, Company A; discharged for disability.
Private William R. Thrasher, Company A; discharged for disability.
Private James A. Todd; discharged for disability.
Private Martin V. Wilcox; promoted and mustered-out.
Private Hiram D. Westcott; discharged at expiration of service.
Private Jay Dickinson; died at Louisville, Ky.
Private Festus E. Eaton; mustered-out.
Private James Ennis; mustered-out.

MRS. WILLIAM HAZZARD.

WILLIAM HAZZARD.

OLD HOMESTEAD OF WILLIAM HAZZARD, SEN. (BUILT IN 1837.)
NOTTAWA TP. ST. JOSEPH CO. MICH.

Corporal Melvin D. Hazzard, Company C; discharged at expiration of service.

Private Cyrus A. Bowers, Company C; discharged at expiration of service.

Private James Findlay, Company C; enlisted in the regular army and never heard from.

Private John Fisher, Company C; discharged at expiration of service.

Private David Shafer, Company C; mustered out at close of war.

Private George L. Clark, Company E; discharged at expiration of service.

Private William Frankish, Company E; promoted and mustered-out.

Private Andrew Knapp, Company E; discharged at expiration of service.

Private Duncan Stewart, Company E; died at Columbia, Tenn., June 30, 1862.

Private John Dickinson, Company E; mustered-out.

Private Almerna O. Currier, Company G; discharged at expiration of service.

Private John Savage, Company G; discharged at expiration of service.

Private George Savage, Company G; discharged at expiration of service.

Private Robert D. Ennis, Company G; died of wounds before Atlanta.

Private Jacob Gruber, Company G; mustered-out.

Private Aristus O. Bishop, Company G; discharged for disability.

Private John Salmon, Company G; mustered-out.

Ephraim A. Austin, Company G; died at Nashville, Tenn.

Private Edward Smith, Company G; mustered-out.

TWELFTH INFANTRY.

Private Eugene Bacon, Company F; died at Little Rock, Arkansas.

THIRTEENTH INFANTRY.

Private Lewis West, Company D; mustered-out.

FIFTEENTH INFANTRY.

Private Orlando B. Boughton, Company A; re-enlisted.

Private John E. Butler, Company A; re-enlisted and mustered-out.

SEVENTEENTH INFANTRY.

Private W. H. Baker, Company C; mustered-out.

Private Francis M. Wright, Company I; mustered-out.

NINETEENTH INFANTRY.

Assistant Surgeon John Bennett; surgeon July 18, 1863, and mustered-out.

Sergeant Ira S. Carpenter, Company D; mustered-out.

Sergeant E. E. E. Bacon, Company D; mustered-out.

Corporal Henry Vivian, Company D; mustered-out.

Corporal Charles H. Connor, Company D; mustered-out.

Wagoner William B. English, Company D; mustered-out.

Private George W. Adams, Company D; died at Annapolis, July 22, 1863.

Private Charles Adams, Company D; mustered-out.

Private Pembroke S. Beckwith, Company D; mustered-out.

Private Oliver Craft, Company D; mustered-out.

Private Joseph Goodwin, Company D; mustered-out.

Private Chauncey Rose, Company D; died at Danville, Kentucky, January 22, 1863.

Private John A. Sutton, Company D; died at McMinnville, Tennessee.

Private Andrew Shaver, Company D; mustered-out.

Private John L. Thomas, Company D; mustered-out.

Private Frederick A. Thienbeaud, Company D; mustered-out.

Private William R. Washburne, Company D; discharged.

Private George W. Wynkoop, Company D; mustered-out.

Private John C. Whitaker, Company D; mustered-out.

Private George Grubber, Company G; transferred to Tenth, and mustered-out.

Private George Henry Clark, Company H; mustered-out.

TWENTY-FIFTH INFANTRY.

Private Jason Saylor, Company D; discharged for disability.

Private Francis Bell, Company G; mustered-out.

TWENTY-EIGHTH INFANTRY.

Private Wilbur F. Hazzard, Company H; mustered-out.

FOURTH MICHIGAN CAVALRY.

Private Irwin H. Emory, Company E; at capture of Jeff. Davis; mustered-out.

EIGHTH CAVALRY.

Private H. B. Brown, Company A; mustered-out.

Private Alva J. Carson, Company G; mustered-out.

NINTH CAVALRY.

Private George W. Fletcher, Company E; mustered-out.

FIRST REGIMENT LIGHT ARTILLERY.

Wagoner David Hazzard, Battery D; mustered-out.

Sergeant Frederick C. Knox, Battery D; mustered-out.

Private Samuel Cady, Battery D; mustered-out.

Private Justin Sinclair, Battery D; mustered-out.

Private Andrew Shafer, Battery D; discharged at White Pigeon, December 6.

Private Elias B. Shummel, Battery D; died at Gallatin, Tennessee.

Private Burton S. Howe, Battery D; discharged for disability.

Private Chauncey Veder, Battery D; mustered-out.

Private Daniel W. Williams, Battery D; mustered-out.

Private Nathan Adams, Battery D; mustered-out.

Private Horatio Allen, Battery D; mustered-out.

Private Samuel Mansfield, Battery D; mustered-out.

Private Abel L. Russell, Battery D; mustered-out.

Private William Waters, Battery D; mustered-out.

Private Daniel Williams, Battery D; mustered-out.

Private Joshua C. Goodrich, Battery G; discharged for disability.

Private Julius A. Goodrich, Battery G; mustered-out.

Private Robert M. Hazzard, Battery L; mustered-out.

PROVOST-GUARD.

Augustus Kahn; mustered-out.

Joseph E. Thrasher; mustered-out.

David W. Eaton; mustered-out.

FORTY-FOURTH ILLINOIS INFANTRY.

Private Abner M. Tuttle, Company B; mustered-out.

The publishers hereby tender their acknowledgments to John W. Fletcher, W. B. Langley, C. H. Starr, H. C. Campbell, H. A. Hecox, Harvey Cady, Edmund Stears, Daniel T. Wolf, George Keech, Jr., Hon. J. Eastman Johnson, William Sadler, Esq., Mrs. Isaac S. Ketchum, and Cyrus Buel, for information given us in compiling the history of Nottawa.

---

# BIOGRAPHICAL SKETCHES.

## WILLIAM HAZZARD.

James Hazzard, the father of our subject, was born in Massachusetts in 1769; was married in 1791 to Miss Sally Andrus of the same State. The fruits of this union were five sons and five daughters. William, the fourth child, was born February 10, 1798, at Berkshire, Massachusetts. When he was thirteen years of age his father died. The family were at that time living in the State of New York. After the death of his father the family removed to Vermont, where they remained a short time, and then removed to Oneida county, N. Y., and from thence, in 1817, to the territory of Michigan. They settled on the Huron river, near Detroit, where they remained until 1829. In the spring of that year Mr. William Hazzard penetrated the wilderness as far as the present town of Centreville, in St. Joseph county, in quest of a location for a home. He selected a government lot about two miles east of the county-seat, which has ever since been the home of himself and family. He made a little improvement and put in some crops on his new purchase, and returned in the fall to the family in Wayne county, and in the month of December, in company with the Fletchers and others,

came out to St. Joseph county. They arrived on Christmas day, 1829. He was married at the age of twenty-five to Miss Casandra Coan, of Monroe, Michigan, by whom he became the father of fourteen children, named respectively James, Augustus, David, William, Melvin, Electa, Emily, Huldah, Sarah, George, Elvira, Lovilley, and two infants not named. Eleven of these children are now living, and all married. Mrs. Hazzard, the mother, died at the old homestead in 1871, aged sixty-four years, universally regretted and mourned by her husband and friends.

The old gentleman, having all his life enjoyed the loving care of a wife and companion, felt his loss keenly, and finding an opportunity of repairing his loss, he married a second time. This was consummated in 1875. His second wife was a worthy widow lady of Mendon, with whom he leads a peaceful, happy life in his old age.

Mr. Hazzard is to-day the only surviving member of the first Methodist class formed in St. Joseph county in 1830, and has been all his life an honored member and a zealous advocate of the claims of the Methodist Episcopal church. The children were all educated in the tenets of that church, and two of the sons became ministers, and another is an exhorter and licensed preacher.

We present in this work a fine view of the old homestead, and portraits of the old pioneer and his deceased wife.

JUDGE WM. H. CROSS.                                    MRS. WM. H. CROSS.

## JUDGE WILLIAM H. CROSS.

On the banks of the upper Delaware, in the hilly country of Sullivan county, New York, in the town of Bethel, on the 6th day of March, 1807, William Hanna Cross was born. His father, John Cross, was an only son of Joseph Cross, of county Londonderry, Ireland, who, soon after the birth of John, left his wife and child and came to America. The Revolution of the colonies soon after commenced, and the wife never again met her husband, nor heard from him but a few times, but learned that he had joined the armies of the colonies, and was wounded at Charleston, South Carolina, and so concluded that he died from this cause. Left alone, the mother struggled to provide for herself and child, and soon after he arrived at an age sufficient to do somewhat for his own support, she too left him, then, alone in the world. By dint of hard work and self-denial the lad obtained a limited education, and before he attained his majority became a convert to Methodism, and was licensed as one of Wesley's earliest itinerants in his native land. In his travels he met Margaret, the young widow of Bernard Conolly, of Armagh, a daughter of the aristocratic Hannas, of Newry, and, contrary to their wishes, the young itinerant and the blooming widow were married. The opposition of the wife's family continuing, the young couple removed to Sligo, where they resided for several years, and until after the Emmett rebellion in 1798.

Mr. Cross protected some of the implicated parties, and in consequence fell under the suspicion of the government as being in sympathy with the rebels; and his business as a grocer, which he had taken up some time after his removal to Sligo, was so much disturbed, that in 1803 he determined to remove to America. Fearing annoyance and possible arrest, the mother took the family and crossed the Atlantic alone with the children, leaving the father to close up his business and follow her two months later—when they were again united in New York city, and, after a short stay, settled in Newburg, Orange county, New York, where Robert J., the brother of the subject of this sketch, was born, in 1804. In 1806 the family removed to Bethel, Sullivan county, where Mr. Cross engaged in the mercantile business. Here, in the rude school-houses of that day, under the government of the birch-rod and maple-ruler, the ideas of school education instilled into the youthful minds of Robert J. and William H. were wrought out.

The second war with Great Britain, in 1812, so disturbed all business relations, that Mr. Cross found himself at its close financially crushed; and the mother having some means in Ireland, and hoping for some aid from her family there to check the tide of misfortune, left her home to again cross the ocean in 1815, going and returning alone, but bringing means with her sufficient only to stay the rush downward for a time. After struggling on between hope and fear for a few years, they at last gave up all, and in 1822 removed to Bloomfield, Ontario county, where the father gave up the un-

equal contest in July, 1824, and sank to his rest. The sisters being married, and the two remaining sons being aged twenty-one and eighteen respectively, the family-home was broken up in the spring of 1825, Robert J. coming in June of that year to Tecumseh, Lenawee county, Michigan, and locating a farm, whither, in September, 1826, he and William removed and began their pioneer-life as bachelors—being their own cooks, housekeepers and washerwomen; sick at times and no one to care for them but the sympathizing settler miles away, perhaps, yet gaining a self-reliance that no school but that of bitter experience could give. For a year and a half theirs was the nearest market. He hauled one thousand five hundred pounds of merchandise (mostly whisky), with two yoke of oxen, and was three weeks on the round trip. The view of Sturgis prairie so pleased the young man, that the brothers sold their lands on the Raisin, in June, 1830, and in the month of September following selected their farms at Coldwater (then the town of Greene, county of St. Joseph), being the east three quarters of section twenty-two.

In November following they built their second cabin, twelve by fourteen feet inside, with a sloping roof to the north, leaving the roof inside at the rear but six feet high. Here they spent two winters and one summer, hauling their supplies the first year from Tecumseh and Detroit. In the fall and winter of 1831-32, William built a log-house on his own farm, on the same ground now occupied by the mansion of Judge Loveridge, of Coldwater.

But a bachelor's freedom could not always compensate for its other disadvantages, and the pioneer met his fate at Tecumseh, where, on the 12th day of March, 1832, he surrendered his single-blessedness unconditionally to find a "more perfect union," and was united in marriage to Nancy, a daughter of John and Lydia Landon, of Ithaca, New York.

Scarcely six weeks had passed when the Black Hawk war, which had been raging in Illinois, reached Michigan in its effects, and the colonists were called to the defense of their own borders and to assist their brethren farther west, and the young bride was left with two others who had just passed the honeymoon with her (Mrs. Judge Harvey Warner and Mrs. James B. Tompkins), to alternate fears and hopes, while the young husband shouldered his rifle in obedience to the command of the State and the instincts of self-preservation.

But the cloud of war was soon dissipated by the capture of Black Hawk, and the young people were reunited in about three weeks; and business, though seriously interfered with, recommenced again on the farm.

In June, 1835, Mr. Cross and his brother Robert sold their farms to an eastern company; Robert going to Winnebago county, Illinois, and settling

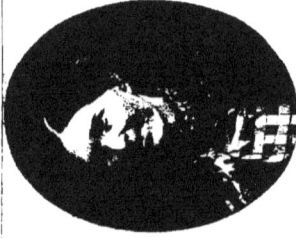

GLOVER LAIRD

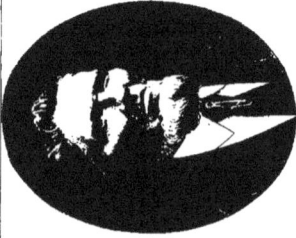

H. W. LAIRD

MRS H. W. LAIRD

RESIDENCE OF H. W. LAIRD, NOTTAWA & MENDON TP, ST. JOSEPH CO., MICH.

on Rock River, where he died in 1873. Owing to the poor health of Mrs. Cross and her child, William, instead of going into a new country for a new beginning, concluded a partnership with Judge Silas A. Holbrook in the mercantile trade; but the crash of 1837 and "wild-cat" banking overwhelmed the new merchant and operator, and the means he had gathered as a farmer were scattered to the winds of heaven,—and the pioneer, penniless, but still undaunted, began again at the foot of the toilsome ascent, and pushed bravely onward, encouraged by the companion of his choice and nerved by the dependency of his little ones. But disappointments were yet in store for him, and many a promising golden apple of Hesperides turned to ashes in his grasp,—as contractor on the Michigan Central railroad, and the Fort Wayne and Michigan City canal, and as a forwarding and commission merchant in Hillsdale.

In 1845 he removed to Leonidas, St. Joseph county, and engaged in the mercantile trade again; and in 1847 constructed the first dam across the St. Joseph river ever built in Michigan, but at a loss, for want of funds to complete the additional improvements necessary to utilize the really excellent water-power he had secured.

In 1851, the allurements of California proving too great to be resisted, Mr. Cross left his family for the new El Dorado, where for seven years he delved in the mines, led on by fickle fortune's flattering promises, which at times seemed just ready to become solid realities, only to be dissipated the next moment into nothing tangible.

In 1858 he returned to Leonidas, and was within a short time thereafter elected to the office of supervisor, a position he had held for the five years preceding his departure to California, and in which he continued until he secured an appointment, which was deemed inconsistent to be held with his former one.

Since that time, to 1872, he served the public in the various positions of assistant assessor of internal revenue, assistant United States provost-marshal, and postal clerk on the Michigan Southern and Lake Shore railroad.

In 1872 he was elected judge of probate of St. Joseph county, while a resident of Sturgis, but removed to Centreville the following summer, where he still resides.

In 1876 the Republicans renominated him unanimously to the same position, and he was re-elected, by the largest majority given to any candidate on the ticket, over his opponents on the Democratic and Greenback tickets. In fact it was difficult to find a man in those parties to run against him, several declaring they would not, but should vote for Judge Cross.

The tender and sympathizing nature of Judge Cross eminently fit him for the discharge of the delicate and arduous duties of his position, which brings him in contact with the widow and orphan, and charges him with the settlement of their estates and interests; and it is currently stated that Judge Cross' tribunal is less a court for legal adjudications than an arbitration for the reconcilement of differences and difficulties between heirs. His success in that direction is most satisfactory to the parties who appear before him, as well as to himself.

A single incident will illustrate his manner of dealing with questions which, by a technical construction, there is no warrant for in the law.

"A lady dying, expressed a wish that a small portion of her estate might be appropriated by her administrator for a certain object, but left no will or written instrument to that effect. When the estate was settled the administrator asked Judge Cross what he ought to do in the premises. The judge quietly said, ' What would you wish to have done if you were in her position, and she in yours?' ' Why, I should want my wishes carried out,' replied the administrator. 'Then as you would have others do for you, so do you do for her,' responded the judge, and the matter was ended."

His decisions, however, are good, for, with a single exception, not one of them has ever been reversed on appeal to the circuit or supreme court.

Judge Cross' political fealty was first pledged to the Whig party, and to it he remained true and steadfast till it disappeared, and then he gave in his adhesion to the new opponent of the Democratic party which rose in 1856, the Republican party, and has been a staunch, unbending partisan in its ranks to the present time.

Judge Cross united with the Presbyterian church in Coldwater in 1837, his wife joining a church of the same faith in Ithaca ten years before, and they have continued as members of kindred churches wherever their lot has been cast since that time, Mr. Cross having been an elder from the second year of his membership in Coldwater.

When Judge Cross resigned his position as postal-clerk, he was recalled to Toledo by the superintendent of that division of the service, and on his arrival found his fellow-clerks assembled in the superintendent's room, who proceeded, through that official, to present the judge with a gold-headed cane, accompanied with a very complimentary expression of confidence and esteem.

Mrs. Cross was born in Ithaca, New York, on the 7th day of November, 1812, and removed to Tecumseh in 1828.

Five children gathered around the family hearthstone of Mr. and Mrs. Cross,—one, the oldest, a son, and four daughters,—who, with the exception of one who is deceased, reside at and near the present homestead.

Mr. and Mrs. Cross have traveled life's pathway together forty-five years, mutually sharing its sorrows and its joys, and their heads are now silvered with the snows of nearly seventy winters, but with hearts so full of human kindness they ne'er grow old, and their eyes undimmed by naught save time, they are confidently walking in that "light which shineth more and more unto the perfect day."

---

## GLOVER LAIRD.

The "gem of the sea," Ireland, sent one of her children to St. Joseph county among her early settlers, and his name was Glover Laird. He was proud of his name and his financial honor, and when the crash of 1837 hurled thousands into bankruptcy, and pinched fearfully thousands of others, he among the rest felt the stringency of the times deeply, and was most keenly alive to the mortification consequent upon his inability to meet his business engagements promptly and fully. One day a stranger accosted him, inquiring if he was Glover Laird; Mr. Laird responded quickly, " My name was Glover Laird, but since these hard time have come on, and I am unable to meet the just demands against me, I think it will not be Glover Laird any longer."

Mr. Laird emigrated from his native land when a young man, and came to New York, and married a native of Connecticut, Samatha Walcott by name. In 1820 he removed to Ohio to fix upon a site for business, having seven hundred dollars of the notes of the Mansfield Bank of that State on hand. He settled in southern Ohio, in Butler county, and after reaching his destination found his money was worthless, the bank having failed. Ten years afterward he came to Michigan, arriving on Nottawa prairie in October, 1830, and located on section two in Nottawa township, adjoining the reservation on the south. In the spring of 1831 he built his cabin, and broke forty acres and fenced eighty.

In 1852 he sold his farm to his son, Henry W. Laird, and soon afterward lost his companion. He then returned to the east to visit his old friends at South Briton, Connecticut, where he met and married Miss Olive Hinman. He died in South Briton, March 22, 1872. His Irish nature made him a warm friend or an open opponent, and a cordial welcome was extended to all who came to his log-cabin home, at which the latch-string hung ever on the outside of the door. He was liberal to those in need, and his sympathies went out to all in difficulty and distress.

---

## HENRY W. LAIRD.

The subject of this sketch, Henry W. Laird, or as he is familiarly called, " Harry " Laird, is a son of Glover Laird, a native of Ireland. He was born in Greene county, New York, October 14, 1812, and with his father migrated to Ohio in 1820, and from thence to Michigan in October, 1830. After assisting his father in breaking up forty acres and fencing eighty on section two in Nottawa township, in June, 1831, he returned to Ohio to attend school. In 1833 he came again to Nottawa, where he remained through the winter and returned to Ohio,—making similar journeys in 1835-36.

In 1837 Mr. Laird was married, and in 1852 he purchased his father's old homestead, whereon he still resides, a view of which we present to our readers on another page of our work. Since he purchased the old homestead he has made many improvements thereon, and has given his time mostly to agricultural pursuits. He is public-spirited and enterprising, and was efficient in securing the location of the Grand Rapids and Indiana railroad through the township, giving much time and considerable money in aid of its construction. He is an active member of the pioneer society, and has been zealously engaged in gathering and writing a history of the Nottawa Indians for the same, much of which we have quoted largely in our work elsewhere. Mr. Laird is a Republican in politics, but was formerly a Whig. He has held the office of county treasurer several terms, and was, in the old

Whig days, the most popular candidate of that party. His creed is embodied in his motto, "No man should live for himself alone, but also for others." Mrs. Laird is a native of Harford county, Maryland, and was born February 10, 1817, and has borne to her husband six boys and one girl, all now living.

## ROBERT McKINLAY.

At the close of a long and useful life it must be a pleasure to be able to transmit to our children and friends a comfortable fortune, more especially if it is accompanied by the fact that it has been acquired in an honorable manner, and if with it is connected the history of a long line of ancestry of honorable name and noble character.

As an instance of this we present the subject of this sketch,—Mr. Robert McKinlay,—who was born at Killern, in Sterlingshire, Scotland, on the 27th day of October, 1797, and he is the descendant of a long line of the Saxon-Scotch race. His father, John McKinlay, was born and reared in the same town; was married, and reared a family of seven children,—three sons and four daughters,—of whom Robert was the youngest. Robert acquired the common English branches of an education at the parish-schools, and before he reached his majority had learned the trade of a stone-cutter. In the year 1820, at the age of twenty-two, he embarked for America in quest of a new home for himself and his father's family. He went to Quebec, and for the next four years worked at his trade in Canada and Vermont. During this time he located some land in Canada, which he afterwards disposed of. His mother died in 1822, and, two years after, his father's family, which consisted of his father, three sisters and a brother-in-law, embarked for the United States. They settled at Amsterdam, in the State of New York, where they continued to reside for many years. In the year 1837, at the home of his daughter in Jefferson county, the elder McKinlay died at the extremely advanced age of ninety-two years.

In the year 1837 Robert was united in marriage to Miss Catharine Campbell, of Amsterdam, New York, a very worthy Scotch lady, whose family had emigrated to this county in 1829. In the year 1835 Robert, in common with many others, was seized with what was termed the "western fever," and came out to the wilds of Michigan in quest of an investment in wild lands. He visited Wayne county, where he located, and purchased five government lots, and then going further west into St. Joseph county, he bought six government lots about three miles south of the county-seat. He then returned to New York, where he remained, engaged in the construction of bridges, locks and aqueducts on the Erie canal and its enlargement until 1843. In the fall of that year he removal with his family to St. Joseph county. In a few days after his arrival he had constructed a cheap frame house on his land in the forest, and moved his family into it, since which time he was engaged in clearing up his lands and farming. The family has continued to reside on the farm ever since, until 1871, when they removed into the village of Centreville, where they have since resided.

Mr. McKinlay is the father of six children,—two sons and four daughters, —whose names are Elizabeth, Mary C., Catharine, John, Archibald and Amanda. Only three of the children are living at this time. One of the daughters is married, and resides in Canada. John and Amanda are at home with the old gentleman.

A sad event occurred on the 26th day of January, 1875, in the death of Archibald McKinlay, whose mother was so overcome with grief that she only survived her untimely death two days, and mother and son were both buried on the 29th of January, 1875. This loved wife and life-long companion is still mourned by this venerable old gentleman and the bereaved children. She was born at Paisley, Scotland, on the 13th day of May, 1812. Mr. Robert McKinlay is a true type of an old Scotch gentleman, and enjoys the confidence and esteem of all his friends and acquaintances, and the love and devotion of his children and relatives.

In politics he is a Republican, in religious faith Presbyterian. In the pages of this work we present a fine view of his farm-residence, and portrait of himself and his deceased wife.

## JOHN W. FLETCHER.

In the year 1828, away out in the wilderness, far from the haunts of civilized life, could have been seen a few sturdy young men engaged in cutting the logs and building a house on the spot now occupied by the Fletcher family, of Nottawa township, St. Joseph county.

John W. Fletcher was the first white man, who is living at this time, that struck a blow as a settler in the forests of St. Joseph county. He had, at the age of twenty, in 1826, in company with Captain Allen and George Hubbard, made a trip through the wilderness as far as the present town of Niles, and again in 1829, in company with his brother, he made another trip into the wilds of southern Michigan,—this time in quest of a desirable location for a home for himself and his father's family. He selected a quarter-section of government land near the present county-seat, on which he has ever since resided.

After entering his land at Monroe, he returned to the home of the family at Flat Rock, in Wayne county, near Detroit, and procuring a yoke of oxen, wagon, tools and provisions, returned to his recent purchase, following the Indian trail all the way.

After building a log-house and cutting a stack of hay, he returned, with his oxen and wagon, to fetch the family to their new home. A number of families came in company with them, thus forming the nucleus of quite a settlement.

The little colony were seventeen days on their tedious journey, arriving at their destination in the month of December, 1829. The Fletcher family consisted of the parents, two daughters and John W., the subject of this sketch.

They all lived together as one family for the first few years, and the parents continued to live with John W. until the day of their death,—Mr. Fletcher, the elder, dying in 1832, and his widow in 1860.

On the 18th of September, 1831, John W. Fletcher and Miss Sarah Knox, the daughter of a settler on Sturgis prairie, were united in marriage, and it is conceded that this was the first marriage of a couple who became permanent residents of the county. The products of the farm for the first few years were floated down the St. Joseph river in arks to its mouth in Lake Michigan, and there found a market, and in after years Hillsdale and Kalamazoo became their market-towns.

Mr. Fletcher comes of the good old Revolutionary stock of the war for independence, being the son of William Fletcher, who was the son of William Fletcher who fought as a soldier all through the struggle that gave to the country liberty and independence, and to the world the Great Republic. John W. was born at Otsego, New York, in the year 1806, and was one of a family of six children,—four sons and two daughters.

When our subject was ten years old his father emigrated to Ohio, where they remained until 1824, when they again emigrated, this time to the territory of Michigan. They settled on the Huron river, near Detroit, from whence, as we have mentioned, they made a permanent settlement in St. Joseph.

Mr. Fletcher is the father of ten children, nine of whom are living,—five sons and four daughters. Three of the daughters and two sons are married. The other children are at home with the old gentleman.

Mr. Fletcher and his wife have for many years been honored members of the Methodist Episcopal church. In politics he is a staunch Democrat and a strong advocate of the constitution and the maxims of our fathers. He is at this time president of the Pioneer society, in which he takes a deep interest. We take much pleasure in presenting to the people of St. Joseph county a fine view of the Fletcher homestead, with portraits of this old pioneer and his excellent wife.

## THOMAS CUDDY.

As an example of what a life of industry and patient perseverance will do in the face of difficulties and discouragements in the building up of a comfortable fortune and the formation of reputation and character in the individual, we will mention the name of Mr. Thomas Cuddy, who was born in county Ulster, Ireland. His father died when he was eight years of age, and his mother when he was ten years of age, leaving him and an only sister to the care of his mother's sister, by whom the children were brought up on a farm, assisting in the farm-work and in a tannery, and, at intervals, attending the national school, where he obtained the rudiments of the common English branches.

At the age of twenty, by advice from his relatives in the United States, he, with his sister, embarked in June, 1849, for this country. They came direct to New York, and from thence to Nottawa prairie in St. Joseph county, where he had four uncles, who were among the early settlers of this region. He commenced for himself by working the farm of Mr. John Cuddy, his uncle. His sister kept house for him about ten years. She

Thos. W. Langley.

then married Mr. John Brown, of Allegan county, where she has since resided.

A short time previous Mr. Thomas Cuddy was married to Miss Catharine McKinlay, daughter of Robert McKinlay, an old settler near Centreville. This was in the spring of 1850. By this marriage he was the father of four children,—three sons and one daughter. One son and one daughter are living. The daughter is married; the son is at home with his father.

In 1869 Mrs. Cuddy died, and thus created a vacancy in the home and a void in the heart of Mr. Cuddy.

In 1871 he was united to Miss Catharine Culbertson, of the same town, a worthy lady with whom he had been long acquainted. In religious faith he is Presbyterian, although not a member of any church organization. In politics, Democratic; in social intercourse, kind and affable; and in all matters of public improvement, liberal and public-spirited; in business dealings, shrewd and clear-headed,—and he is known as an honorable gentleman in all the relations of life. He is the owner of three hundred and sixty acres of the finest farming lands on Nottawa prairie, and three hundred and sixty acres also in the county of Allegan. He has a fine residence on the prairie, a view of which we present in this work, accompanied by the portraits of himself and wife.

---

### WILLIAM B. LANGLEY.

The subject of this sketch comes of a long line of English ancestry. His grandfather emigrated to New York city at an early day in its history, where he became a distinguished architect and builder. He built the theatre known for many years as the Old Bowery, the first City Bank in New York city and the first State capitol buildings at Albany, and many others of lesser note. He left at his death three children,—one son and two daughters. Thomas W. Langley, the son, served an apprenticeship in the woolen-manufacturing business, and at the age of twenty-one went into partnership with his brother-in-law at Germantown, near Philadelphia, and at the same time was connected with his mother in the mercantile trade, in the city of Philadelphia. He was married, in 1822, to Miss Margaret Stigman, of the same city, by whom he had seven children,—six sons and one daughter,—of whom William B. Langley is the eldest. He was born at Germantown on the 9th day of June, 1823.

In the year 1832 Mr. Thomas W. Langley came to the territory of Michigan in quest of a location. He selected the site of the present town of Centreville, as the town had already been platted, and was owned by two or three individuals, of whom Mr. Langley purchased the entire prospective village. He also entered seven government lots, lying contiguous. He then returned to Philadelphia and closed up his business, and, with his family, which consisted of himself and wife, six children, a nephew, and a couple of colored servants, started for the "far west."

At the same time he brought on the machinery and irons for a saw- and grist-mill, also a stock of dry-goods and groceries. He was for many years actively engaged in a variety of enterprises, such as farming, milling, distilling, hotel-keeping and selling goods,—in all of which William B. Langley, our subject, actively assisted his father, attending the common-schools for the first years, and afterwards the academy at Canandaigua, New York; also, for a short time, a military school at Bristol, Pennsylvania. When not at school he was at home, occupied with the varied duties of clerk in the store and post-office, and as a help upon the farm and in the mills.

At the age of twenty-three he became acquainted with and married Miss Julia V. R. Woodworth, of Centreville. They were married July 25, 1847, and soon after established themselves on a new farm, three miles north of Centreville, where they have since resided, engaged in the quiet occupation of farming and rearing their family, which consists of four children,—two sons and two daughters. The two daughters are married, and one of them has lost her husband, and is left a young widow with a young child. She is at this time living at home with her parents.

Mr. Langley has a fine farm of two hundred and sixteen acres, situated on the south bank of the St. Joseph river, well adapted to the production of the various kinds of grain for which this region is so justly celebrated. In religious sentiment he is liberal in his views, without any decided preference of denominational fellowship.

In politics he is more pronounced, cherishing very decided Democratic views. A kind husband and father, generous and honorable in his dealings, he commands universal respect and esteem from his neighbors and acquaint-

14

ances, and love and devotion from his friends and relatives. He has, in the pages of this work, bequeathed to his friends and the citizens of St. Joseph county a fine view of the homestead, with portraits of himself and his estimable wife, which will remain as a monument to the memory of that truest and noblest type of manhood, an American gentleman.

---

### OLIVER W. WILCOX,

whose portrait and that of his excellent wife, with a fine view of his farm residence, may be found elsewhere in the pages of this work, was born in the town of Westerly, Rhode Island, in 1803, on the old Wilcox farm, he being one of the fifth generation of that family since its first settlement on this side of the Atlantic.

He was the son of Oliver, who was the son of Isaiah, a Baptist minister, who was the son of Stephen, who was the son of Edward Wilcox, who emigrated from England and settled in Rhode Island at an early period in the history of the English colonies.

Oliver W. is the eldest son in a family of twelve children, and received but limited advantages from the common-schools of that day, remaining with and assisting his father on the farm until he attained his majority; he then left home and commenced work for himself. He was engaged in ship-building about ten years at New Bedford and other places.

He then came west to Rochester, New York, where he remained six months, and then went to Michigan in quest of a farm. He selected and made a purchase of one hundred and ten acres in the present town of Nottawa, St. Joseph county, and the same fall built the house in which he now resides. He then returned to Massachusetts in quest of a wife to preside in it.

On his return, he, with his usual business promptness, made an offer of matrimonial partnership to Miss Harriet Vincent, which was as promptly accepted; and in February following he returned, bringing his wife to their new home in the wilds of Michigan, since which time Mr. Wilcox has been engaged in the quiet occupation of farming, never mixing in the strifes and turmoils of political or public life.

In the year 1842 he met with a great loss in the death of his beloved wife, which left him alone with his three little ones, one son and two daughters. The two daughters are living, both married. The son died in the Union army, at Chattanooga. After four years of dreary mourning, Mr. Wilcox decided to fill the vacancy in his heart and home by taking another companion, which he did by marrying Miss Lucy A. Kent, of Kalamazoo, a native of Rutland, Vermont. The fruits of this union are three sons and two daughters; one son and one daughter are married,—the other three children are living at home with the old gentleman. A member of the Baptist church for the last forty-seven years; a consistent Christian; temperate in all things, and a Republican in politics. He is to-day, at the age of seventy-three years, a hale and hearty old gentleman, universally respected by his acquaintances, and loved by his friends.

---

### THOMAS W. LANGLEY.

Foremost among the enterprising pioneers of St. Joseph county, Thomas W. Langley, the first actual settler on the site of the present village of Centreville, stood pre-eminent. Energetic and untiring, he achieved fully as much, if not more, with the means at his disposal, than any other man in the early days of the settlement of the county. Buying the bare site of the county seat, he pushed to completion in the incredible space of three months, a frame court-house, twenty-four by thirty, the largest log-house in the county, for hotel purposes, a blacksmith-shop, store-building, flouring and saw-mill, and had a post-office, a school, and religious services in regular and successful operation. He was constantly doing something to aid in the prosperity of the village and enhance the value of the property therein. He brought in the first stock of goods sold in the village, and engaged, at various times, in mercantile, manufacturing and agricultural pursuits, and, as occasion required, kept the hotel of the village. He was the first postmaster of the village, and held the position from 1833 to 1840.

Mr. Langley was born in Murray street, New York, in the year 1801. His father, William Langley, was a native of England; he was a mason by trade, and assisted in the building of the Drury Lane theatre, in London, the old Bowery and the old City Bank in New York, and the first capitol buildings at Albany.

The mother of Mr. Langley, the subject of this sketch, Susan Elliott, was a native of Ireland, and came with her parents therefrom to Philadelphia when she was ten years of age.

Mr. William Langley, the father, also landed first at Philadelphia, where it is supposed he was married to Miss Elliott. During the building of the old capitol buildings at Albany, in 1812, Mr. Langley left his wife and children at old Fort Stanwix for safety, during the war then being waged between the mother country and the United States.

Three children were the fruits of this marriage, viz.:

SARAH, born in New York city, and who afterwards married W. G. Hirst, who emigrated from Wakefield, England, and was a manufacturer of woolen goods; he owned and operated a factory known as the Branchtown mills, near Germantown, Pennsylvania.

THOMAS W., the subject of our sketch; and

SUSAN, born in New York also, and who married Lawrence Butler, a sea-captain, with whom and a son, she was lost at sea about the year 1831, leaving two daughters surviving her.

At the age of fourteen years Thomas W. Langley was apprenticed to the trade of a woolen manufacturer, with his brother-in-law, Hirst, and at seventeen years was promoted to the position of foreman of the mills, with fifty operatives under his charge. At twenty-one years of age he was admitted into the business as a partner with Mr. Hirst.

About the year 1822 Mr. Langley rented the Black Rock mills near Germantown, and operated them in connection with the Branchtown mills, conducting also, at the same time, two dry-goods stores in Philadelphia, on Market and Second streets, in company with his mother, Mrs. Susan Langley. In 1825 he purchased a farm and mill in Treydiffen township, Chester county, Pa., twenty-one miles from Philadelphia, and changed the mill into a woolen factory, which he conducted under the name of the "Clintonville factory;" he also operated a store, limestone quarries and kilns, and continued his connection with Hirst in the Branchtown mills, having over one hundred operatives on his pay-rolls. He sold his Chester county property in 1831, and removed again to Branchtown mills. In May, 1832, he suffered from a severe attack of fever, and, upon the peremptory advice of Doctors Physic and B. Franklin Bache, of Philadelphia, traveled over the Alleghenies in a carriage, accompanied by his son, William B., then a boy of nine years, to regain, if possible, his usual robust health. He traveled as far as Rochester, New York, where he stopped with his cousin, Judge E. Smith Lee, his health being much improved.

Receiving letters from home informing him of the mills' suspension by reason of the cholera then raging, he took a packet on the Erie canal for Buffalo, where he met an old friend, who commanded one of the three steamers then afloat on Lake Erie, who persuaded the invalid to try the virtue of the lake breeze, at least as far as Ashtabula, but landed him in Detroit, where, meeting with old friends,—Colonel Macks, Desnoyers and others,—was persuaded to stay over one trip and look at the country. He bought a section of land where the site of Flint, in Genesee county, is situated, and, hearing Thomas Sheldon, the receiver of the land-office at White Pigeon, discourse in glowing terms of the St. Joseph county, Mr. Langley, on receipt of further news from home, concluded to take a look at the beautiful prairies and oak-openings of St. Joseph; and so, buying an Indian pony, saddle and outfit, the whole costing fifty dollars, he went, in company with Sheldon, General Brown, Colonel Anderson, and other officers who were going to the Black Hawk war, to White Pigeon, where he arrived in

June, and proceeded to explore the county and buy the site of the county seat, as fully detailed in the Centreville history, as is also his settlement and operations thereon, and his emigration with his family from Philadelphia thereto. On his return to the latter place, his friends said he had left the city a sick man, and had returned a crazy one, so enthusiastic was he in his praises and description of his new purchase in St. Joseph county.

On the 22d of March, 1822, Mr. Langley was married to Margaret Stigman, the ceremony being performed by Rev. Dr. Broadhead, in Philadelphia. She was a native of Maryland, and her parents dying when she was at a tender age, she became a member of the family of her uncle, Thomas Badaraque, a Frenchman, engaged in the East India trade with one Lewis Clapier, in Philadelphia, and by her said uncle was nurtured in affluence, with everything at her command, and illy fitted to fill the position she subsequently so worthily and uncomplainingly occupied, amid the privations of border life.

The children which were the fruits of this union were:

WILLIAM BADARAQUE LANGLEY, born in Germantown, June 9, 1823; now a farmer in Nottawa.

JOSEPH LAFAYETTE LANGLEY, born in Philadelphia, September 28, 1854, the same day the great and good Lafayette was received with hearty welcome to that city; now a wholesale tea-merchant in New York.

DEWITT CLINTON LANGLEY, born in Treydiffen township, Chester county, Pa., July 28, 1826; now a real-estate broker in New York city.

THOMAS CHESTER LANGLEY, born in Treydiffen township, September 23, 1828; now a merchant in Constantine, St. Joseph county.

WASHINGTON ELLIOTT LANGLEY, born in Treydiffen township, February 21, 1830.

SUSAN B. LANGLEY, born at Branchtown Mills, April 28, 1832; now Mrs. J. Austin Sperry, of Little Silver, N. J.

LAWRENCE BUTLER LANGLEY, born in Centreville, St. Joseph county, Michigan, April 19, 1835; now engaged in stock-raising at Rio Frio, Uvalde county, Texas; and

HENRY STIGMAN LANGLEY, born in Centreville, September 6, 1837, and died September 21 following.

Joseph L. married Antoinette Hale, in Detroit, in 1851, and Thomas C. married Susanna J. Proudfit, of Constantine, November 24, 1852.

Mrs. Langley died August 21, 1850, after a short illness, aged a little more than forty-six years.

In 1851 or 1852 Mr. Langley closed out his interests in St. Joseph county, and returned to Philadelphia, where he formed a mercantile agency, traveling through the South for several of the jobbing-houses of that city; he was thus engaged at the time of his decease, at Paducah, Ky., January 9, 1855.

Mr. Langley "possessed a noble and generous nature, a mild and amiable disposition, and a kind, benevolent heart, and, as a consequence, enjoyed the confidence of many devoted and affectionate friends." About a month before his death (November 9, 1854), he was married to Mrs. C. R. Moore, of Philadelphia, and started immediately to the West in her company. Upon landing at Paducah he was injured by a fall, which he survived but thirteen days, and was cared for most kindly, and buried by the Masonic fraternity, of which he was a member. In politics he was a Democrat.

RESIDENCE OF GEO. I. CROSSETTE Constantine, S.T Joseph Co. Mich.

RESIDENCE OF JACOB S. GENTZLER, Two Miles North of White Pigeon & Two Miles South East of Constantine, Constantine Tp. S.T Joe Co. Mich.

# CONSTANTINE.

The settlement of the territory included in the present limits of the township of Constantine, began in the year 1829,—William Meek, of Wayne county, Ohio, being the advance-guard of the host to follow. He came in the winter of 1828-9,—possibly in the summer of 1828,—and made his selection of a location at the intersection of the Fawn and St. Joseph rivers, where the present village of Constantine is situated; but his family did not come until the spring of 1829, when he built a cabin for them, (the first in the settlement,) then went to Monroe and bought his land. In the following winter he began the erection of a saw-mill,—from which time onward, until long after the plat of the village was laid out, the settlement was known as "Meek's Mill."

The second family to come into the settlement was Jacob Bonebright's, which settled on the farm at present owned and occupied by A. Hagenbuch on section twenty-six. Mr. Bonebright, from Pennsylvania, originally came and located in May, 1829, and built the second house in the settlement. Nathan Syas and family came in the same spring or summer after Mr. Bonebright. He located a farm which covered the site of the present dwelling of Hon. H. H. Riley.

C. B. Fitch, afterwards judge of the county-court, came in from Ohio in 1830 and located on the prairie, and built the first frame house outside of the village, but in 1831 sold the same to John G. and William Cathcart, who, with their families, came in the fall of 1831.

William Hamilton, from Ohio, came to the prairie in 1827 to look at the country, but returned to Ohio, and again came in 1830, and returned without purchasing. In 1827 he went to Beardsley's prairie, in Cass county, and worked through harvest. In 1832 Mr. Hamilton came with his family of four sons, a married daughter and her husband, Alfred Poe, and their child, and settled in the openings on what is now known as Broad street, on the farm now owned by Adam Gentzler. Heman Harwood came in 1832 to Broad street, and located a portion of the farm now owned by the Gibsons. Mr. Hamilton built two log-houses in the summer and fall of 1832. John Garrison came in 1833 to Broad street.

Mr. Bonebright, who came to look for a location in 1828, stopped with Klinger on the shores of Klinger lake, making his location the following year, as before stated. He sold his first location in 1836-7, and removed to the one now occupied by his widow and son Henry, where they have lived over forty years.

Caleb Arnold and family moved into Constantine in 1833,—having previously (1832) bought a location in Fabius,—and located on the opposite side of the river from the then settlement. Deacon William Churchill had settled on the edge of the prairie in 1831. Mr. Arnold's family consisted of his son, William F., now of Three Rivers; Daniel, now of Constantine; Dr. O. F., of Three Rivers, and Lyman, who is now dead, and a daughter, Mrs. Tracy. William F. Arnold located on Broad street in 1836, and remained some years, removing to Lockport in 1854. Aaron Hagenbuch came into the township in 1837, and Norman Harvey in 1833, both of whom were of the leading citizens of the township.

Joshua Gale settled on the prairie in 1830, and afterwards sold his claim to William Welbourne, an Englishman, in 1835. It is said Gale moved his barn once, or was about to move it, when Mr. Welbourne bought him out, to get rid of the manure that had accumulated about his yards, but Mr. Welbourne moved the latter instead.

Alfred L. Driggs came to Constantine in 1831 and bought land on Broad street, but went to Branch county and built a saw-mill, where he remained until 1836, when he returned to Constantine and went to clearing-up and cultivating his land. He was supervisor of the township for eleven years, and representative from the county to the legislature in 1846. John Harrison was a leading citizen, too, of the township, holding the position of supervisor, continuously for ten years, from 1857 to 1866 inclusive. Hiram Lindsley is an old and well-known resident of the township, having held the position of county clerk for ten years. Deacon William George and family, of whom A. B. George, one of Constantine's foremost men of to-day, was a member, came into the settlement in 1834.

## TOPOGRAPHY.

The surface of the township is, generally speaking, a level, though somewhat broken as it approaches the St. Joseph, which passes through the township. Its area includes within its limits twenty-two thousand seven hundred and fifteen acres of land-surface, sixteen hundred acres of the same being a portion of White Pigeon prairie. The balance of the area was originally covered with burr-oak and white-oak openings, some of it very heavy, and other portions light and scattering. The river-bottoms are heavily-timbered (or were so originally) with various kinds of wood common to the country. There are about four hundred and sixty acres of water-surface, the drainage of the township being as follows: The St. Joseph river enters the township on the north line of the northeast quarter of the northeast quarter of section one, and runs southerly through sections one, twelve and thirteen, and southwestwardly through sections twenty, twenty-three, twenty-seven and thirty, making its final exit (after two attempts) on the southeast quarter of section thirty-one. Mill creek rises in two forks,—one on the northeast quarter of section three, the other in the northeast half of section six, and, uniting on the southwest quarter of section seven, runs nearly south to the St. Joseph, which it enters just south of the south line of the southwest quarter of section thirty-two. Fawn river or Crooked creek enters the township near the southeast corner of section twenty-four, and passes through the corporate limits of the village of Constantine to the east bank of the St. Joseph, which it enters through the elaborate works of the Hydraulic Company. Black run is a little creek, which rises on section sixteen, runs mostly due south, and enters the St. Joseph on the southeast quarter of section thirty-two.

The soil is the same fertile, sandy loam of the openings that characterizes the other portions of the county, and the prairie soil is similar in constituent elements to that of Nottawa prairie, the whole township being a highly-productive one in the cereals, corn, and agricultural products. The bowlder-drift passed by this township generally, except in the western portion, along the Cass county line, where a heavy deposit of stone is found, which has supplied the needs of the township up to the present time, and will continue to do so for some time to come.

## THE FIRST FARMS

opened were those of Judge William Meek, in 1829, Jacob Bonebright and Nathan Syas the same year, and Joshua A. Gale on the prairie, in 1830. The first house was built by Judge Meek in 1829,—a log cabin on the south bank of the St. Joe. The following were among the entries of public lands in 1829, the first year any were made in the township: On the 15th of June William Meek entered the southeast quarter of the northeast quarter and the southeast quarter of section twenty-three, the west half of the southwest quarter and the southeast quarter of the southwest quarter of section twenty-four, and the west half of the southwest quarter of section twenty-five. The same day John Coleman entered the west half of the southeast quarter of section thirty-four; H. L. and A. C. Stewart the east half of the southeast quarter of section thirty-one and the southwest quarter of section twenty-five, and Johnson Meek the east half of the southwest quarter of section twenty-five. On the 16th, William Meek entered the west half of the northwest quarter of section thirty-six, and on the 29th, Aaron Brooks, of Richland county, Ohio, entered the west half of the southwest quarter of section thirty. July 13, Jacob Bonebright entered the south fraction of the northwest fraction-quarter of section twenty-six. There were twenty-five other entries the same year. In 1874 there were one hundred and thirty-four farms in the township, averaging one hundred and forty-three acres each. There were sown in 1874 four thousand two hundred and forty-seven acres of wheat, and two thousand acres of corn planted. The crop of 1873 yielded forty thousand five hundred and fifty-three bushels of wheat from three thousand eight hundred and two acres sown; forty-nine thousand one hundred and seventy-three bushels of corn from one thousand eight hundred and eighty acres; three thousand four hundred and seventy bushels of other grain, three thousand five hundred and seven bushels of potatoes, one thousand one hundred and twenty-five tons of hay, fifteen thousand two hundred and thirty-seven pounds of wool, ninety-three thousand three hundred and twenty-five pounds of pork, twenty-nine thousand and twenty pounds of butter, and two hundred and forty-one barrels of cider. One hundred and eighty-one acres in orchards produced ten thousand three hundred and forty-seven bushels of apples, valued at six thousand four hundred and fifteen dollars. There were owned in the township, in 1874, three hundred and seventy-five horses, fifteen mules, three hundred and seventy-two cows, two hundred and fifty-three head of other cattle, one thousand two hundred and eighty-eight hogs, two thousand five hundred and ninety-eight sheep against three thousand two hundred and seventeen of the latter in 1873.

The leading farmers are: Samuel Gibson, who owns four hundred and thirty-three acres on Broad street in a body, a view of whose elegant farm-house and buildings, and a bird's view of his well-tilled acres, is given on another page of our work. Mr. Gibson is justly credited by his towns-people as being the most successful farmer in the county. The farm, for the most part, is under cultivation, and lies on both sides of Broad street, and two hundred rods on the St. Joseph, about two and a half miles from Constantine. Also Jacob Gentzler, John Hamilton, O. C. M. Bates, the Tracy brothers, Adam Gentzler, and Aaron Hagenbuch,—the latter being one of the heaviest land owners in the county, having eight hundred acres under cultivation.

The first frame and brick houses in the township were built in the village, and are especially named in the history thereof. The first fruit-trees planted were on the farm of Joshua Gale, in 1830. John G. Cathcart also set out an orchard in 1832, and Judge Meek, in 1829, planted apple-seeds and peach-pits.

### THE FIRST IMPROVED FARM MACHINERY

was introduced into the township as follows: Fanning-mills, 1831; cylinder-threshers, 1835; reapers, 1842-43, and separators, 1842,—the prairie farmers leading the way in each instance.

### IMPROVED LIVE-STOCK

were introduced by Erastus Tracy, who dealt in short-horn stock, and raised the same for several years after 1850; but no one now makes a specialty of either fine-blooded cattle or sheep, cultivation of the soil engaging the attention of the majority of the farmers of the township almost exclusively. Milo Powers brought in some cattle from Wadsworth's herds, New York.

### THE FIRST WHITE CHILD

born in the township was Henry Bonebright, a son of Jacob Bonebright, who was born February 3, 1830, on the present farm of A. Hagenbuch, near Constantine village. Joseph C. Merk, son of Judge Meek, was born the following summer.

### THE FIRST MARRIAGE

was that of Elliott Woods and Eliza Meek, who were married in 1830 or 1831. Thomas and Nancy Armstrong were married about the same time, and Hiram Kell and Malinda Syas soon after.

### THE FIRST DEATH

that occurred in the township was that of a child in the village, in 1830. Mr. Sixbury's child, and a child of a Mr. Pendleton were buried during the year. Nathan Syas buried a daughter in the winter of 1830-31, and Mr. Bush buried a child soon after, near the mill-pond. The wife of Thomas Williams was the first adult who died. She was buried in

### THE FIRST CEMETERY

laid off in the township, the site for which was given to the town by Judge Meek, in 1831, when the plat of the village was laid out. The present cemetery was bought by the board of health of the township, in 1853, and contains ten acres. It lies about a mile east of the village. Mr. Abner Thurber was the first person to be buried in it, but was first buried in the old cemetery, and removed subsequently to the new one. The most notable monument in the grounds is that of Governor Barry and his wife. It is a double-fluted column, joined at the top by drapery, and is very unique and beautifully wrought. The governor died January 14, 1870, and his wife in March, 1869.

### THE FIRST SCHOOL

taught in the township was in the winter of 1830-31, by Thomas Charlton, in the basement of Niles F. Smith's store.

The first "school ma'am" in the township was probably Miss Rhoda Churchill, a daughter of Dr. William Churchill, and afterwards the wife of William F. Arnold. She taught school on the edge of the prairie, about one mile from the village, in the summer of 1832.

The first school on Broad street was taught in 1830, in a school-house built that year. A lady taught the school, and had ten pupils.

The statistics of schools in 1870 were as follows: There were schools taught in ten different districts, one of them being the union school of the village. There were seven hundred and ninety-three children in the township between

five and twenty years of age, and eight hundred and twenty-one scholars attended the schools, which were taught on an average of eight months during the year. Seven male teachers were employed, and paid two thousand four hundred and ninety dollars; and twenty females, who received two thousand six hundred and twenty-five dollars and fifty cents. The total income of the districts for the year ending September 1, 1876, was eleven thousand four hundred and fifteen dollars and six cents, and the total expended was ten thousand three hundred and sixty-three dollars and four cents, including three thousand six hundred dollars on bonded indebtedness. There are eight hundred and seventy-five volumes in the library of the town. The township owns ten school-houses, valued at forty-four thousand five hundred dollars, with nine hundred and fifty sittings.

### THE FIRST RELIGIOUS SOCIETY

organized in the township, outside of the village, was a Methodist class, on Broad street, consisting of eight members, with O. F. French as leader. Reverends Erensbrack and Todd formed the class.

Another class was formed in 1840, or thereabouts, at North Constantine, and a log chapel built soon after on the present site of the brick chapel, and meetings were held therein until 1849-50, when the brick chapel was begun, under the pastorate of Rev. N. L. Brockway, but was not completed until November 10, 1863, during the pastorate of D. K. Latham. It cost twelve hundred dollars.

The Broad street class and its appointments were discontinued on the organization of the North Constantine class, the members of the former going to the latter class, and to the village. This brick church is the only church-edifice erected in the township, outside of the village.

### CIVIL ORGANIZATION.

The present constituted township of Constantine was organized in 1837, having been previously included in the township of White Pigeon. Its geographical limits were confined to that township, numbered seven south, of range twelve west of the principal meridian, on maps of the government surveys. The township took its name from the village, which was laid out in 1831, and so named at the suggestion of Niles F. Smith, the first merchant to locate in its precincts.

### THE FIRST TOWN-MEETING

was held April 3, 1837, at the school-house in the village. Dr. Watson Sumner was the moderator, and Thomas Charlton the clerk thereof. The following officials were chosen for the discharge of the various municipal trusts growing out of the new sovereignty, to-wit: John G. Cathcart, supervisor; W. C. Pease, clerk; justices of the peace, Heman Harwood, four years; W. C. Pease, three years; William Cathcart, two years; Horace Metcalf, one year; Norman Harvey, A. R. Metcalf and William H. Adams, assessors; John Bryant, Ozias F. French, Alex. S. Shepherd, commissioners of highways; Erastus Thurber, constable and collector; Heman Harwood, John A. Appleton, overseers of the poor; Watson Sumner, Heman Harvey, Allan Goodridge, school inspectors; Lyman R. Lowell, constable; Heman Harwood, John S. Kano, fence-viewers; Erastus Hart, poundmaster.

The meeting voted in favor of the county borrowing money to erect public buildings, and appropriated one hundred dollars for the poor, and levied a bounty of five dollars on wolf-scalps taken from large wolves, and three on prairie wolves, and declared a rail-fence five feet high of "good sound rails," or a board fence four and a half feet high, were lawful fences. On May 15th day, the highway commissioners laid off five road districts and agreed with the Florence commissioners for the separate jurisdiction of specific portions of the town-line road. In 1838 the bill for 1837 were audited for town expenses, and amounted to one hundred and eighteen dollars and sixty-five cents. In 1842 the town raised three hundred dollars to repair the bridge over the St. Joseph at Constantine. This bridge was built in 1835, the building committee, Isaac J. Ulmann, secretary, advertising in the Michigan Statesman, issued at White Pigeon, under the date of December 1, 1834, for proposals to build the same for a sum not exceeding fifteen hundred dollars, and to be completed in one year. In 1843, the taxes of the Bank of Constantine were returned unpaid forty-three dollars, and no property could be found whereon to levy to make the same, and the board of town auditors instructed a committee to inquire into the reason of such return by the collector.

In 1848 Governor Barry was commissioner of highways, and Hon. Joseph R. Williams inspector of schools. In 1849 the people voted ninety-eight against, and fifty for license, and in 1850 voted eighty-two for license and fifty-eight against.

MRS. O.C.M.BATES.

O. C. M. BATES.

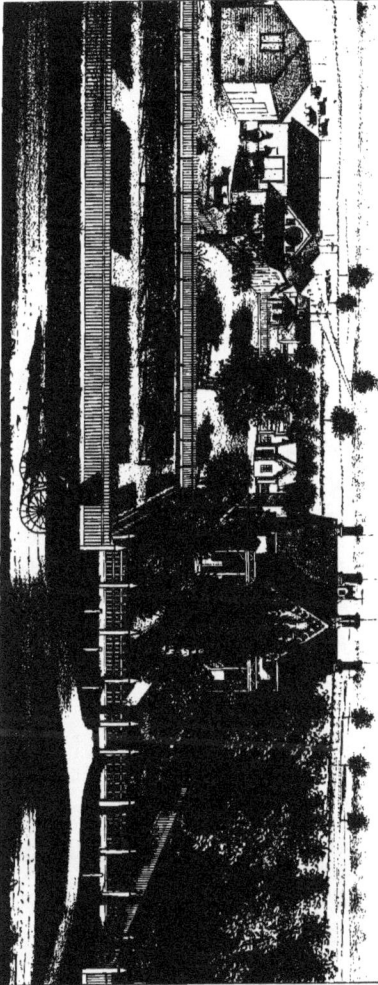

RESIDENCE OF O. C. M. BATES, CONSTANTINE TP., ST. JOSEPH CO. MICH.

In 1854 hogs, cattle, sheep, horses and mules were restrained from running at large, and in 1855 somebody had a grievance, and so influenced the vote of the people that they prohibited hens and chickens from scratching in anybody's lettuce-beds except their masters. In 1863 the town assumed the bounty raised by individuals for volunteers. In 1869 the

was voted for, and thirteen thousand dollars appropriated to build the same. It was built that year, and fell, in December into the river and, was rebuilt the following winter or spring with a double-chain support, two arches and a single span. May 27, 1869, the people of township offered the Michigan Air Line railroad company fifty thousand dollars as a loan if they would build their track through the township, but the company declined the tempting offer and went through Fabius.

The town officials, since the organization of the township, have been as follows: Thomas Charlton was appointed justice of the peace for "Meek's Mills" in 1831, and held the position until May or June, 1836.

Supervisors—John G. Cathcart, 1837–39; A. L. Driggs, 1840-44-1846-48-49-54-56; John Bryan, 1845; Charles H. Hopkins, 1847; W. C. Pease, 1850; Henry T. Steele, 1851-53; C. S. Engle, 1852; Thomas Mitchell, 1855; John Harrison, 1857-1866; Hiram Lindsley, 1867-69; Aaron Howard, 1870, 1872-76; E. H. Sheldon, 1871.

Town Clerks—W. C. Pease, 1837-1844; Franklin Wells, 1845; Washington Pitcher, 1846; Albert Miller, 1847-49; Clinton Doolittle, 1856-58, 1862-63-65-69, 1871-72; David E. Wilson, 1873-76; George Palmer, T. T. Gurney, And. I. Palmer, T. C. Langley, Millard F. Thayer, L. T. Hull, Lyman Harvey, German Brown, John C. Joss, Charles M. Morton and John W. Stevens have each held the office one year only.

Justices of the Peace—W. C. Pease, 1837-1852; Heman Harwood, 1837-41; William Cathcart, 1837-42; Horace Metcalf, 1837 and 1856-60; J. Eastman Johnson, 1838-42; A. R. Metcalf, 1840-1855; Peter F. Putnam, 1841-1853; Henry T. Steele, 1851-59; Charles R. Millington, 1852-56-1864-72; Hiram H. Harwood, 1857-1865; Levi T. Hull, 1857-63; E. H. Sheldon, 1863-77; Hiram Lindsley, 1866-73; Samuel P. Rockwell, 1870-77; Theo. Rumbach, 1875-77; Robert M. Flack, 1876-77; Thomas Harrison, 1873-77.

Thomas Charlton was the first justice of the peace in the township, having received his appointment from Governor Porter in 1831. For five years he never kept a docket, but kept his record of cases on slips of paper, and for convenience sake (?) put the slips into a barrel promiscuously, and when a particular paper was wanted, turned the contents of his one "pigeon-hole" upon the floor, and, "pawing" them over until he found the paper he wanted, put the rest all back again as before, into the barrel, whither the one wanted went as soon as it was used. The first entry made on the docket by him is dated April 25, 1836, but there is no hint, from beginning to end in the entry, that the matter treated of was heard before him, or for that matter before anybody. The only case on the docket tried before him which shows, of itself, that it was tried by him, is a criminal examination—which incidentally states that the parties appeared before "Esquire Charlton" for examination. His signature does not appear once on the record, and but once in connection with it, and that is on the inside of the front-cover where he assigns his costs, and on the docket, to E. Thurber, and has attached his signature.

The first suit entered is one wherein Elias True was plaintiff and Samuel H. Abbott defendant, summons issued April 25, 1836, returnable May 2. The account filed by the plaintiff amounted to thirteen dollars, and after deducting ten dollars and thirty-eight cents for "drag-teeth, beatle-wedges and rings, and also for horse-shewing, hay and oats for horses," the court rendered judgment for the balance of the account and one dollar and seventy-five cents costs, and the judgment was subsequently paid.

On the 7th of May, 1836, a suit is docketed, The United States vs. Richard Pearson, and Mrs. Pearson his wife,—and, on complaint of Johnson Patrick, made against the defendants for larceny, a search-warrant was issued and returned on the 9th, and, with the body of Mrs. Pearson, brought into court. The writ was endorsed: "Search made May 7, 1836, nothing found secreated—ten dollars delivered to me by Mrs. Pearson, which she said Mr. Pearson sent to her—further served, May 9, by searching the person of Mrs. Pearson and her daughter Susan Pearson,—not any money found except a poccl piece of Susan's—bro't the body of Mrs. Pearson before Thomas Charlton, Esq. for examination." There were six witnesses sworn, and Mrs. Pearson was discharged.

On the 9th of March, 1839, the Bank of Constantine brought eleven suits against as many different parties on notes, mostly Sturgis men, on which Esquire Pease rendered judgments, and the same were subsequently paid.

surveyed and laid out in the township, were done by the White Pigeon authorities.

On September 4, 1830, a road was surveyed by Robert Clark, Jr., from White Pigeon north to McInterfer's prairie, which begun at the north border of the Chicago road, township eight, between ranges eleven and twelve. On the 7th there was another road surveyed by Clark, commencing at the corners of sections thirty-two and thirty-three, township seven, range eleven, on township line between townships seven and eight, range eleven, and running to Chicago road west of St. Joseph river, and near the crossing at Mottville, and running past Klinger's "old mill," nine miles.

On July 6, 1831, a road was surveyed by Mathew Rowen under the direction of Alvin Calhoon and Daniel Read, highway commissioners, "beginning on the northwest border of the St. Joseph river, nearly opposite Meeks' mill, at a thorn tree," and from thence runs north and northwest to west boundary of St. Joseph county, six miles, fifty chains and thirteen links."

July 12 a road from Mottville to Meeks' mill was surveyed, and September 10, 1832, the road from Young's prairie to Mottville was laid out.

May 5, 1833, a road was surveyed from the north boundary of White Pigeon township south to Meek's mill, beginning at the corner of sections one and two, township six, and sections thirty-five and thirty-six, township seven, range twelve, west, thence south to the river opposite the mill. Broad street, so named in 1840, and ever since known by that title, was first worked in 1832, but partially, however. It is now three miles long, a perfect air line, four rods wide, and in the summer season a most lovely and charming boulevard. It is much frequented by the town-people of Constantine on pleasant Sunday-evenings. Most excellent farms lie on either side of this avenue, and some of the best farm-houses in the township are found here, notably those of O. C. M. Bacon and Samuel Gibson.

In 1838 Constantine township had a population of eight hundred and forty-two souls; in 1850, the souls had multiplied and increased until they numbered one thousand four hundred and ninety-six. In 1870 the increase had brought up the population to two thousand four hundred and four persons, forming five hundred and twenty families, with but five hundred and nineteen houses to live in. One thousand two hundred and one of them were males, and one thousand two hundred and three females. In 1874 the State census showed the population to be but seventeen more than four years before, and one thousand two hundred and fifty-eight were males, and one thousand one hundred and sixty-three females. Just what kind of logordumain was used to transform twenty-three females into males appears does not clearly appear—accepting the trite saying that "figures won't lie"; four hundred and fifty-two of the gentlemen were married, and one hundred and sixty-one were not, and never had been, who were over twenty-one years of age; four hundred and fifty females were "keeping house" for their lords, and two hundred and eight of their sisters were enjoying their independence of husbands' cares and responsibilities. Twenty-five males and sixty-nine females were widowed or divorced. Four hundred and thirty-six men were subject to military duty, and one hundred and ninety-nine exempt by age, six of them being over seventy-five and under ninety years of age. Five hundred and three ladies were of the marriageable age, and two hundred and twelve were over forty years, and eleven were over seventy-five years of age. There were six hundred and twenty-three boys under twenty-one years of age, one hundred and fifty-one of them too young to go to school; and four hundred and thirty-seven girls under eighteen years, one hundred and twenty-two of them being under ten.

of the people may be gathered from the way they deposited their ballots at the presidential elections: in 1840, Harrison polled eighty votes, and Van Buren eighty-four; in 1844, the Whigs cast one hundred and six ballots, the Democrats one hundred and five, and the Liberty men seven; in 1848 the Whigs cast ninety-nine, General Cass, Michigan's "favorite son," received one hundred and twenty-one votes and the Free Soilers drew into their net sixty-nine; in 1852 the Whigs gave General Scott one hundred and fifty-three votes, the Democrats one hundred and thirty-nine votes and the Abolitionists numbered twenty-two; in 1856 the Republicans cast two hundred and fifteen votes, and the Democrats one hundred and thirty-three ; in

1860 the Republicans gave Lincoln two hundred and sixty-nine, and Douglas received one hundred and eighty-one votes ; in 1864, Lincoln received two hundred and sixty-seven, and McClellan one hundred and ninety ; in 1868 the Republican vote was three hundred and forty-three, and the Democratic two hundred and fifty-seven ; in 1872 Grant received three hundred and twenty-eight, Greeley one hundred and forty, and O'Connor "a few, that is, eight" ; in 1876 Hayes received three hundred and thirty-two votes, Tilden two hundred and sixty-seven, Cooper five and Mr. " Scattering " two.

What the people paid for the privilege of self-government in 1837 and 1876 is here shown : The assessment of property in the township for the year 1837 amounted to one hundred and seventy-four thousand nine hundred and thirty-nine dollars, on which the sum of seven hundred and twenty-eight dollars was levied for taxes for State and county purposes, besides the expenses of the township for schools and otherwise.

In 1876 the assessment of real-estate for taxation amounted, as fixed by the supervisor, to six hundred and fifty-three thousand dollars, which amount was reduced to six hundred and thirty-five thousand and seventy-six dollars by the county-board. The personal assessment stood at one hundred and seventy-five thousand six hundred dollars; total eight hundred and ten thousand six hundred and seventy-six dollars. On this assessment an amount of four thousand one hundred and forty-one dollars and twenty-six cents was levied for State and county purposes, divided equally between the two objects. The township taxes, including schools and the corporation taxes, would swell the grand aggregate to fifteen thousand dollars probably.

THE VILLAGE OF CONSTANTINE.

The first and original plat of the village of Constantine was surveyed and laid out in August, 1831 (at which date there were five families only on the site), by Judge William Meek, who settled on the site of the plat, the east half of section twenty-three, township seventy south, range twelve west, in 1829, and built the first house thereon, a log-cabin of the usual primitive style of construction, and cleared off and plowed a few acres the first year. Mr. Meek was attracted to the spot by its advantages for a manufacturing point, being shown the location by Leonard Cutler, then, in 1828, living on White Pigeon prairie.

Judge Meek began the erection of a saw-mill in the winter of 1829-30, on Fawn river, or Crooked creek, just below junction with the St. Joseph, and in the spring, before he had completed the saw-mill, he constructed a rude dam, and a ruder wheel and stones, and commenced to grind grists, the same having been entirely completed in twenty days.—Hugh Woods, who came in with Judge Meek, being the mill-wright. This pioneer mill is described at length in the county history in the chapter on manufactures.

These mills gave the little hamlet a name abroad, throughout the settlements of Cass and St. Joseph counties, and it was known for years afterwards as "Meek's mills," the more romantic and high-sounding name of Constantine, given to it at the suggestion of Niles F. Smith, being ignored by the early settlers, especially those of the sister and rival colony at White Pigeon, who, occasionally, when asked by emigrants of the whereabouts of Constantine, were totally oblivious of any such place, but one minute description being given of the desired point, at once brightened up, said, "Oh! you must mean Meek's mills!" The traveler in search of Constantine, in the flush days of 1836, had an elaborate, lithographic ground-plan of the village, which, on bond paper, appeared to be "no mean city," like Tarsus of Apostolic days ; but when the looker for corner lots and speculative investments arrived in the centre of the city of his dreams, he was still in the woods, and its greatness was still in the keeping of its inhabitants, and its life lay all before it.

Niles F. Smith was the first man who opened a store in the place, and he built a little frame building on the banks of the river, on or near the present site of the store of Barry & Eacker, at the south end of the bridge, in 1830. He built also his dwelling at the corner of Washington and Water streets, and afterwards opened it for hotel purposes.

Isaac J. Ulmann came to Constantine in 1832-3, and entered into partnership with Smith, but the firm dissolved April 27, 1834, as appears by the notice to that effect in the Statesman of that date.

John S. Barry engaged in the mercantile business in Constantine in 1834-5, dissolving his connection with J. B. Willard, in the same line in White Pigeon, in July, 1834. Mr. Barry remained a citizen of, and engaged in trade, in Constantine, until his death in 1870, having been in the meantime elected to the State senate for three terms, and as governor three times, the latter distinction of three terms having been conferred upon no other citizen of Michigan. Governor Barry's whole life was identified, as it were, with Constantine's prosperity, and his integrity and financial ability were great and

important factors in the development of the Constantine of to-day. He was largely interested in the Michigan Southern railroad, and entered into the management of the company when its stock was quoted at a nominal figure, and by his economical and judicious management of its affairs, raised the commercial value to such a point that he and many others amassed great wealth thereby.

The Statesman of August 1, 1834, says Constantine had "three stores, a good grist- and saw- and shingle mill and several mechanics." W. A. & W. T. House, twin brothers, were one of the mercantile houses, and advertised to buy wheat at the Constantine mills at fifty cents per bushel, but a few days later changed their " ad," knocking down the price three cents. Mr. Meek built a second saw-mill in 1835, and improved his water-power, and the village was assuming a thriving, hustling aspect. Major Ulmann brought in several large stocks of goods prior to 1840, when he removed to Wisconsin, where the old veteran is still living.

Albert E. Massey came to the village in 1834, and opened trade ; he remained until 1840, when he was elected county clerk, and removed to Centreville, engaging in trade and publishing until 1852, when he removed from the county. Elias True, a carpenter, came in 1831 ; he was a highly-esteemed citizen and useful man in the community. Samuel Teesdale and Abraham Miller came in 1835 from White Pigeon, and began wagon-making, the first in the village, Miller doing the blacksmithing. H. and A. R. Metcalf came in 1834, and were prominent among the early citizens for many years.

There were, in 1835, about three hundred inhabitants in the village. In 1836 three large stores were built by the House brothers, Major Ulmann and William H. Adams, and filled to their utmost capacity with finely-assorted stocks of general merchandise and groceries. Adams & Appleton occupied one of them with groceries and a fine stock of liquors and cigars. The Appleton of this firm, John A., became afterwards a member of the famed publishing-house of Appleton Bros. In 1836, also, came Charles L. and Albert Miller and opened a fine stock of dry-goods, next west of Barry's store, the latter still standing near the original site thereof. The Millers remained in trade for some two years, and then removed to Colon, where a son is still engaged in business. Charles L. Miller was elected probate judge in 1856, for a term of four years.

Allen Goodridge and A. E. Massey were in trade that year, the former advertising in the Republican, published then in Constantine, thus : " One thousand pounds codfish, and one hundred pounds high-scented Maccaboy snuff." Whether the thousand pounds were high or low scent does not appear. This year Constantine indulged in great expectations and built many fairy " castles in Spain."

The Republican was edited by Daniel Munger, and he advertised the village extensively. The steamboat Constantine began to be projected, and her stock was offered for sale. W. T. House & Co. had two shares they would sell if any desired to purchase, and their keel-boat Constantine was busy carrying away produce and bringing back merchandise.

The manufacturers were busily engaged, and were : William Reid & Co., carriages and wagons ; A. & W. Pentland and Henry Gibler, blacksmiths ; P. E. Grover, fanning-mills ; Denham, Doolittle & Co., saddlery ; Samuel Abbott, same line ; Christian Kuch, furniture ; and Reed, Teesdale & Co. (Benham), plows. The merchants were as before named. W. T. House & Co. advertised for hide to build a mill with six run of stone.

Railroad and canal meetings were held and the advantages of inter-communication with the rest of the world glowingly set forth ; Congress and the Secretary of War were memorialized, and the domestic legislature invoked to extend a helping hand to the development of untold wealth and prosperity lying dormant, but ready to spring forth at the slightest provocation.

Meek, Sumner, Hoffman, House and Cathcart were moving spirits in the commercial conventions that discussed, to the Constantine of 1836-37, the important measures of rapid and easy transportation by lake, river and canal. Massey wanted two hundred thousand feet of lumber at once, and House wanted one hundred and fifty thousand feet more, sooner.

Munger & Cowdry catered to the intellect in books and stationery, and Drs. Sumner and Baldy ministered to the ills of the body in drugs and medicines. Harvey Hunt added to his American hotel, dining- and ball-rooms forty feet long, in time for the national holiday, and his hotel then occupied sixty-six feet on Water and forty-four feet on Washington street.

The Constantine North Addition Land Company began the grading of their tract and raised the first building November 10, 1836 ; and the Republican discoursed most eloquently on the water-privileges already wanted at the village, for an oil-mill, edge-tool manufactory, paper-mill, and last though by no means the least, a blast-furnace, the material to keep the latter in ope-

MANUFACTORY OF

GEORGE AND TWEEDALE,

FOUNDERS & MACHINISTS.

AGRICULTURAL IMPLEMENTS, SASH, DOORS & BLINDS.

CONSTANTINE, MICH.

ration being declared to exist as bog-ore "in inexhaustible quantities near by."

A relic of the mound-builders was found while grading the north addition, eight feet below the surface, which caused a learned discussion by the editor, who confessed his ignorance and asked of the future archæologist "more light." Necessaries having become plentier or more easy to acquire, luxuries began to appear and find demand.

J. P. Gladding opened the first jewelry stock in the village, in 1838, and is in trade at the present time. A. Austin also competed with Mr. Gladding, coming from White Pigeon to worship the rising star of Constantine. Robert Shilcook, the first cooper, also began this year.

In the Constantine marine list, Mosely & Massey advertised for information concerning the schooner "John E. Hunt," then long over-due from Buffalo. A poem by the lawyer of the place, published in the *Republican* of February 22, 1837, was parodied by a leading merchant in the next number, creating considerable merriment. The new store of Albert Andrus was opened in September, 1837, the St. Joseph river was surveyed from Mottville to Constantine for canal purposes, and the house of W. T. House & Co. was merged into that of Adams, Appleton & Co.

The Bank of Constantine commenced business March 3, 1837, and bird suppers in the director's parlor added zest to the era of good feeling that pervaded the community generally. The state of bliss was too ecstatic to last, and the crash of 1837, and the depression of 1838 toppled over many artistically-wrought castles of ærial foundation and superstructure; and when "bottom facts" were reached a revulsion was experienced that swept many fine-built schemes into oblivion. But commerce revived, and the St. Joseph remained a natural channel to take the products of the country to the seaboard, and for years, until the railroads came in 1851–52, Constantine was a busy point.

In 1839 Hon. Joseph R. Williams & Co. erected a fine large flouring-mill, having previously bought the water-power of Judge Meek, in 1836. The parties interested in this purchase were: George Howland of New Bedford, one-half interest, Hon. Daniel Webster,—the great expounder,—one quarter, which was afterwards assumed by Thomas H. Perkins of Boston, and quarter interest of Mr. Williams, who subsequently acquired Howland's interest for a brother-in-law and his (Williams') father. The mill was completed in 1841, and put in operation, with six run of stone; Mr. Williams being the manager of the same, and conducting besides an extensive mercantile trade, employing in and about his business twenty men or more. Twenty-five thousand barrels of flour were made per year for many years, which were sold in New York; from four to six months being occupied in the transit, frequently by the later cargoes in laying over winter at St. Joseph or Buffalo. The receipts for the sales of flour were frequently received a year after the wheat was purchased. The mill was destroyed by incendiarism, and the dams damaged through malice.

In 1843 the first steamboat arrived at the wharves of Constantine, and from thence to 1851 their principal business was towing keel- and flat-boats from St. Joseph to Constantine, and carrying light boats back. In 1845 Governor Barry built his warehouse on piles over the river, so that the steamers and other boats could unload directly therein without extra hauling. After the railroad came, and navigation in the river ceased, the warehouse was moved to the bank, where it now stands, occupied by Barry & Eacker.

Lima shipped all of her produce and received all of her merchandize at Constantine until the railroads came. The "Mishawaka" was the first steamboat that came to Constantine, and the "Algona" was a large one which also ran on the lakes as far as Grand Haven. The little "Ruby" made several trips to Three Rivers. The "Red Foxes" were lively little craft, and did a large service in transportation by towing and passenger traffic.

The bridge was built on piles, first with a swing in the centre, and then changed to a high curving arch, sufficient to admit of the passage of steamboats. The first one was built in 1834, and rebuilt in 1841, and again rebuilt in 1849, by Nettleton, for one thousand dollars; individual subscriptions, three hundred seventy-six dollars and fifty-nine cents, and the balance raised by tax. It was razed in 1852, before which time it was on the same level as the second-story of Barry's warehouse. The village was

### FIRST INCORPORATED

in the spring of 1837, the first board of trustees being elected in May, who were as follows: Dr. Watson Sumner, president; Allen E. Massey, Willis T. House, James M. Hunt, Allen Goodridge, Pierpont E. Grover and Erastus Thurber. Albert Chandler was elected clerk.

The report of the trustees, in May, 1838, showed that three hundred and twenty-eight dollars and seventy-seven cents in taxes had been levied, of which one hundred and twenty-three dollars and ninety-three cents were delinquent and unpaid, thirty-six dollars were consumed in fees of collection, fifty dollars had been paid for repairs on the bridge, the indebtedness of the corporation amounted to one hundred and ten dollars and fifty cents, and there were fifty-six dollars and seventy-one cents in the treasury.

This corporation lasted until 1839, when it lapsed, and the village was not again incorporated until March 15, 1861, the first election occurring in April, when the following officials were elected : H. H. Riley, president; John B. Shipman, recorder; Ephraim H. Sheldon, treasurer; Almeron Bristol, Thomas C. Langley, John G. Miller, Levi T. Hull and Joseph Horton, trustees. Isaac T. Mozier and Cyrus Schellhous, assessors.

### THE FIRST FRAME HOUSE

built in the village was Niles F. Smith's store, in 1830, and the first brick building erected was the store now occupied by A. Kahn on Water street, east of Washington. It was built by Charles R. Millington in 1856–7. Mrs. David T. Holmes was one of the earliest adults to die in the village, her death occurring in 1833. Mrs. Doctor Sumner and Mrs. Hart died in 1834. Alexander Woods' child died in 1833, and a child of Mrs. True died about the same time.

There are no public buildings other than a calaboose, which was built in 1861, at a cost of one hundred dollars. Planked sidewalks are laid down on all the principal streets. There is no fire-engine provided as yet. The balance of cash remaining on hand at the end of the municipal year, in April, 1876, was seven hundred and sixty dollars. The present officials are as follows: Charles H. Barry, Jr., president; William B. Pierson, recorder. Trustees, Silas Kline, Edward George, Henry E. Moore, Jacob Strohm and James M. Harvey.

### MANUFACTURES.

The beginning of Constantine's somewhat extended manufacturing history dates with the erection of Judge Meek's rude pioneer grist-mill, in the spring of 1830. He completed his saw-mill the same season, and also erected a building in which he put his milling stores, and continued his gristing operations. Josiah Fisher, father-in-law of John Hull, of Florence, in November, 1831, put up a shingle-mill adjoining the saw-mill, but before he could complete it and get it into operation, the water froze solid in the race, and not a wheel turned in Meek's mill until spring. Mr. Fisher went to Eschol, and put up his machinery for a time. In 1835 Judge Meek built his second saw-mill. Isaac Benham built the first foundry in 1837. It was a small affair, the power for "blowing" being furnished by a horse, and Mr. and Mrs. Benham pouring out the hot iron into the moulds. They made andirons, and such like goods. In 1836 there was a great influx of manufactures as before named. Benham put up a foundry on the east side for manufacturing plows. A ship-yard was in operation three-fourths of a mile above the village, by John McMillan, where one steamboat—the "Constantine"—was built in the course of some three years, and her engines put in. She was a poor investment, except to advertise the village. Clinton Doolittle, in 1835, and Samuel Abbott, in 1832, were both harness-makers, and Mr. Doolittle is still engaged in the same line in the village. Hawkins was the first blacksmith, but the shop and tools were furnished by Judge Meek in 1830. Henry Gibler came in October, 1832, and went into the same shop, and bought his first lot of steel and iron at White Pigeon with an order of the judge for seven dollars. Armstrong built a tannery one mile up the creek in 1836, and, subsequently, the father of Governor Bagley built and operated one in the village. House & Ulmann made a few plows in 1836, and Hunt & Grover made fanning-mills in 1834, and Grover continued the business in 1836–7. Mr. Carter built sleighs in 1837, and Beaufait made cabinet and furniture work in 1833, and Gould manufactured chairs about the same time. R. M. Welch built a carding-machine in 1844–5, which was subsequently moved to the present site of the commercial mills, and fitted up for milling purposes by Gardner. After passing through different changes of owners, August 1, 1876, it became the property of Mr. D. Frazier, the present proprietor. Samuel Teesdale was the first wagonmaker, and continued in the business until June, 1875, when he was succeeded by S. Cothermon & Co., who began the manufacture of fine carriages. Their new works are on Water street. Stafford & Mitchell manufactured separators in 1846, and carried on for several years an extensive business. Chamberlain at one time manufactured pumps in the village.

In 1841–2 a joint-stock company, composed of mechanics, of which Brush Sutherland, Jason Shepherd, L. L. Richardson and James E. Proudfit were the leading and controlling members, built a foundry, and put it into operation, to which Stafford and Mitchell afterwards succeeded. David Stafford first bought and enlarged it, and made separator-threshing machines in 1844; in 1859 Mitchell & Stafford, who then owned the works, added the manufacture of reapers and mowers, water-wheels and steam-engines. George & Tweedale own and operate the works at the present time,—Mr. George learning the foundry and machinist trade of Mr. Stafford in the same shop he now owns.

The joint-stock company built a distillery after they sold the foundry, which was afterwards occupied by John Bostwick, and was run until closed by the revenue officers.

Pease & Denis built a foundry in 1851, and operated it by steam. It is now owned and occupied by Rosman, as an oil and soap manufactory.

In 1837 Almeron Bristol, carpenter and cabinet maker, carried on a thriving business, and afterwards extended his line to the manufacture of hay-rakes, doing an extensive trade in that business.

In 1864 Cyrus Schellhous and the Schoofields built a woolen-mill at a cost of twenty thousand dollars, wherein they manufactured good cassimeres and cloths, and employed twenty persons. It was burned November 19, 1872, while Hedges was operating it, entailing a loss of twenty-four thousand dollars on stock and building.

In 1868 Peter Lintz built an extensive brick brewery and operated it until 1871, and, failing in the business, it has not been in operation since. He had a small brewery about three miles below the village plat, and ran it successfully for many years, achieving a fine reputation on his "home-brewed ale."

Klinger built a saw-mill on Mill creek, on section 19, in 1830-1.

### PRESENT MANUFACTURES.

The Williams mill was burned in June, 1856, and rebuilt in 1860, by Miller, Hagenbuch & Harvey, and is operated by Edwards & Harwood, who now own it. It has always been known as the "Fawn River mill," has four run of stone, is sixty by seventy feet on the ground, three stories, manufactured twenty-five thousand barrels of flour in 1876, and is exclusively a merchant mill.

The Commercial mill, now owned and operated by D. Frazier, has three run of stone, is sixty by seventy feet on the ground, two stories, and made seven thousand barrels of flour between August 1, 1876, and the close of the year, besides a heavy custom business.

Samuel Frankish, a well-known gentleman of Centreville was head-miller in the Williams mill for many years, coming to Constantine in 1837.

The foundry of George & Tweedale make heavy castings and machines. They bought Mitchell & Stafford out in 1861, and starting then with merely nothing but energy, determination and industrious habits, they have wrought out of the business the present fine establishment and extensive patronage. They employ sixteen persons.

The saw-mill of Bonebright & French was built in 1848 by Joseph R. Williams, and, passing through the hands of different owners, came into possession of the present proprietors in 1866. It has a capacity of four hundred thousand feet per year.

The furniture factory of Heywood & Francisco began in the present wareroom with steam-power in 1836. They now employ five men.

A. Bristol manufactured chairs in 1836, and built the present factory of H. E. Eldridge in 1848. He was the first chair-manufacturer in Constantine to use power. The shop is thirty by seventy feet, and seven men are generally employed.

One of the most, if not the most, important improvements projected in Constantine is that of the Hydraulic Company, which was organized February 10, 1868, the corporators being Franklin Wells, Thomas Mitchell, S. P. Davis, Aaron Hagenbuch and H. H. Riley, who organized the company by choosing Dr. Edward Thorne, president; Mr. Wells, secretary, and George I. Crossett, treasurer, the rest holding the same positions. Their works were built in 1873, and are as follows: Two race-ways or canals; one on each side of the river, eighty feet wide, with seven feet depth of water, having a fall of nine feet. The power can be displayed or used on a frontage of more than four thousand lineal feet, embracing sixty acres. Buildings of brick, two stories, thirty-four by sixty feet, and one twenty by twenty feet, of three stories, with frame structures, all covering an area of five thousand two hundred and twenty-seven square feet. The dam across the St. Joseph is an admirable structure, safely and substantially built. The cost of constructing the works and acquiring the necessary lands amounted to the sum of thirty-five thousand five hundred dollars, and, with one hundred

and sixty-one acres of adjacent lands for overflow, the property is valued at fifty-three thousand dollars. It has never been utilized yet.

### HOTELS.

The first hotel kept in Constantine was by Harvey Hunt, in 1833, if not before. He was located on the corner of Water and Washington streets, and the old building, after being used many years, was abandoned for hotel uses, and converted into a tenement-house and known as the "Beehive," and after endangering the business houses for years, it was finally bought by Mr. Langley and moved away. This house was the stage-house, and Hunt and a landlord (Austin) at Kalamazoo, run a line of stages between Constantine, Kalamazoo and White Pigeon, breakfasting at Hunt's, taking tea at Austin's, and lodging at Hunt's, at the south end of the route, and reversing the same at the north end thereof. This was in 1836. The same year there was a stage line established from Lima, Ind., to Constantine via White Pigeon, W. M. Carey being the proprietor.

The present hotels are the Wells hotel, kept by Henry Root for twenty years, an old resident of Constantine and the second tailor of the village, in 1836; and the Constantine House, Chester Fields, proprietor.

John M. Wells, a son of Joseph Wells, kept the American hotel 1841-6, then built and opened the Wells hotel, managing it until 1850, when he went to California.

### THE POST-OFFICE

was first established in the village in 1831, and Thomas Charlton was the first postmaster and held the office until 1835, and was then succeeded by John S. Barry, who held the position until 1840; he was succeeded for a short time by Cogswell, under Harrison, who gave way to John K. Briggs, who was in the office until 1849. J. R. Williams held the appointment in 1849-52, during the Whig administration, and then Briggs came in again in 1853, and did not retire until March, 1861. Then R. E. Case, for the years 1861-5, held the office, and was succeeded for a short time by Nicholas Hill, under Johnson, and then Thomas Calam came in, in 1865, and has still the charge of the mail bags. He was the deputy-postmaster under Case from 1861 to 1865.

The present business of the office is as follows: Stamps sold during the last quarter of 1876, five hundred and ten dollars and thirty-six cents; money orders issued last six months of 1876, two thousand three hundred and sixty-six dollars, and paid three thousand seven hundred and forty-three dollars and fifty-five cents. There are five hundred and fifty letters received and dispatched daily, and eleven hundred and forty-nine newspapers distributed weekly, and six daily mails received and dispatched.

### THE BANKS.

The First National Bank of Constantine was organized under the United States banking law in 1865, with a capital of fifty thousand dollars. E. H. Sheldon was chosen the first president, and Peter Haslett the cashier; Aaron Hagenbuch succeeded Mr. Sheldon as president, and held the position two years, and was succeeded by George I. Crossett, who is the present incumbent, and has been since that time. Mr. Haslett has been the cashier from the first organization. In 1871 the present fine brick building was erected on the corner of Washington and Second streets by the bank for its own offices, which occupy the first floor, and the upper floor for professional offices for rental. Nothing has been neglected to insure the safe-keeping of the funds of the bank and of its patrons, Sargent's chronometer-lock being affixed to a burglar-proof safe, enclosed by a fire-proof vault. The present board of directors are George I. Crossett, president; Peter Haslett, cashier; Aaron Hagenbuch, Jonas Wolf, J. Mark Harvey, F. A. Hagenbuch, T. J. Morse and Thomas Mitchell. The last published statement, dated December 20, 1876, makes the following exhibit of its condition: Loans and discounts, eighty-five thousand seven hundred and one dollars and ninety-seven cents; United States bonds to secure circulation, sixty-five thousand dollars; other securities, seven thousand nine hundred and seventy-nine dollars and fifty-six cents; due from national banks, reserve agents and redemption fund, twenty-three thousand one hundred and twenty-three dollars and twenty cents; real-estate and fixtures, five thousand two hundred and sixty-two dollars and fifty cents; cash on hand, eighteen thousand three hundred and eight dollars and sixty-one cents; liabilities, capital stock, surplus and undivided profits, one hundred and four thousand seven hundred and sixty-nine dollars and fifty-three cents; circulation, fifty-eight thousand dollars; individual deposits, forty-five thousand one hundred and sixty-five dollars and thirty-one cents.

RESIDENCE OF A. L. DRIGGS,
CONSTANTINE,
MICH

WELLS AND GALAM'S BLOCK,
CONSTANTINE, ST JOE CO, MICH.

FIRST NATIONAL BANK,
CONSTANTINE, MICH

## THE FARMERS' NATIONAL BANK

was organized December 4, 1874. Directors: Milo Powers, president; Charles H. Barry, Jr., cashier; Charles W. Cond, Edward Thorne, A. M. Beardslee, Daniel Shurtz and John H. Eacker, who own all the stock, and are the present board of directors. The statement published in December, 1876, shows the following as the financial condition of the bank: Assets,—loans and discounts, sixty-nine thousand two hundred and eighty-nine dollars and thirty-four cents; United States bonds to secure circulation, thirty thousand dollars; due from other national banks, reserve agents, redemption-fund and cash on hand, thirty-two thousand seven hundred and seventy-seven dollars and sixty-six cents; liabilities,—capital stock paid in, surplus and undivided profits, seventy-seven thousand four hundred and sixty-seven dollars and forty-one cents; circulation, twenty-seven thousand dollars; deposits, twenty-seven thousand five hundred and ninety-nine dollars. The history of the old Bank of Constantine will be found in the general history of the county.

## THE RAILROAD

history of the township and village is given in the general history of the county. The Michigan Southern and Lake Shore is the only road running through the village, and its business for the year 1876 was as follows: Total shipments of freight, eleven millions eighty-three thousand three hundred pounds, including forty-three thousand five hundred and seventy barrels of flour. Freight received six millions twenty-six thousand two hundred and forty-six pounds. Ticket sales, six thousand seven hundred and forty-nine dollars and sixty-five cents. By the courtesy of J. W. McKinney, station agent, we have been furnished with the above information. The Western Union Telegraph company have an office in the station-house of the railroad, and W. P. Hibbard is the operator.

## THE MINERAL SPRING COMPANY

was organized February 4, 1865, under the name of the "Constantine Petroleum Company," to develop an oil-well. The company leased grounds and began operations, going down eight hundred feet, at which depth the drill got fast and could not be removed. Some oil was found, but not in quantity sufficient to warrant further proceedings on its behalf. The water was tested and found to contain mineral and medicinal qualities, and therefore the name of the company was changed to the one it now bears, December 20, 1870. The "Ladies' Town Hall Enterprise Association" loaned the company three hundred and seventy dollars, on condition that the water should be free to the people of Constantine, the money to be refunded out of the first profits, and paid to the Reformed, Presbyterian, Methodist and Lutheran churches, equally, with interest at ten per cent. Bath houses were built, and for a time used, but no one occupies them now. The first officers were H. H. Riley, president; J. B. Shipman, secretary, and T. C. Langley, treasurer. R. C. Kedzie, professor of chemistry of the Micigan Agricultural College, gave the following analysis of the water of the well: Total number of grains of solid matter in the imperial gallon, 283.34, consisting of

| | | | | |
|---|---|---|---|---|
| Bi-carbonate of lime, | - | 40.00 | Bromide of sodium, - - | 3.15 |
| Sulphate of lime, | - | 1.67 | Bi-carbonate of soda, - - | 41.86 |
| Bi-carbonate of magnesia, | | 18.92 | Bi-carbonate of iron, - | 1.74 |
| Phosphate of lime, | - | 2.10 | Silics, - - - - | 2.10 |
| Chloride of potassium, | - | 66.50 | Free carbonic acid, 13 cubic inches. | |
| Chloride of sodium, | - | 105.30 | Nitrate of ammonia, traces. | |

## THE PROFESSIONS.

The first lawyer to locate in Constantine, was George N. Palmer, in 1835, who advertised his profession in the *Statesman* that year. James Eastman Johnson came next, in 1837; W. C. Pease in 1841, and Hon. H. H. Riley about the same time. Judge Coffinberry came later, having first located at Centreville in 1844, or thereabouts. Judge E. W. Keightley came in 1867, having practiced two years previously in White Pigeon.

The present members of the bar are named in the general history thereof in the county. James P. Langley is the official stenographer of the St. Joseph and Branch county circuit.

## THE FIRST PHYSICIAN

in the village was Dr. Tye, an Englishman, who came and opened the first drug-store in the town, in 1831. He was followed by Dr. Peter L. Baldy, in 1833, and Dr. Watson Sumner in 1834, they forming a co-partnership in 1835, and opening a fine drug store. Dr. Sumner continued his practice so long as his health permitted, and died in 1844. He was one of Constantine's noted citizens.

15

This firm was succeeded by Dr. Edward Thorne, still a resident of the village; Doctors Montrose, Marshall, Morse, Force, Chase, Keebles, Kelly, Hibbard, Culp, Thomas and Radley.

The present medical and surgical staff is: Doctors Thorne, Morse, Force, Hibbard, Young, Thomas, Culp and Radley.

The first operator in dental surgery, aside from the regular physicians, was Dr. Galord, who operated in 1836-7, a short time at Dr. Montrose's office. The present dental surgeons are: B. H. Kingsbury and L. T. Dryer. Dr. Eagery practiced some in 1838, and Dr. Butler later.

### BUSINESS OF 1876.

General Merchandise—Eacker & Barry, Wells & Calam, F. C. Langley, John W. Simons, A. W. Luther.

Groceries, Crockery, etc.—D. E. Wilson.

Boots and Shoes—Easterbrook & Thomas.

Clothing and Gentlemen's Furnishing Goods—E. Howser, —— Melcher, Roberts & Davy, Nathan B. Kahn.

Lumber—Oliver Harwood.

Millinery and Ladies' Furnishing Goods—Mrs. Betsey E. Thomas, Mrs. M. J. Cox, Mrs. Bancker, R. L. Dunlap, —— Karchner.

Newsdealer—J. P. Gladding.

Drugs, Medicines, Paints, Oils, etc.—Haslett & Gladding, Young & Morrison, F. M. Crossette.

Hardware—Jones & Harvey, Hoselton & George.

Tinsmith—John Roy.

Agricultural Implements, etc.—Castle Brothers.

Fruit and Vegetables—Garnett & Kline.

Watches and Jewelry—William Henry, G. W. O'Harra, O. M. Bates.

Dressmaking and Family Sewing—Mrs. Huff, Mrs. Cross, Mrs. A. J. David, Mrs. Buchanan.

Livery—John Barnard, Levi Root.

Meat Markets—J. P. Drake, Fred. Welborn, Pidgeon & Harvey.

Draymen—George Davis, H. Scribner.

#### Artisans.

Designers and Contractors—C. F. Greene, M. L. Ernst.

Painters—Malie Bandholtz, W. E. Bandholtz, J. Russell, D. Rider, J. Teeswale, George Driggs.

Carpenters and Joiners—Israel Diefenderfer, Henry Holmes, J. P. Hummer, Harry Hutchinson (miller and millwright), W. W. Clement, Nathan Crudit, John Melvin, Silas Walker, G. C. Sayles, G. H. Jacobs, W. Engelmann, S. Whitmore, I. Curtis.

Stone and Brick Masons, &c.—Daniel Paul, Lewis Cross, J. C. Tague, D. W. Smith, E. Force, M. L. Ward, —— Butler, John Cannada, Oscar Cannada, E. Shaw, Charles Otis, —— Syler.

#### Manufacturers.

Merchant Millers, and Produce Dealers—Edwards & Harwood, D. Frazier.

Saw-Mill and Lumber—Bonebright & French.

Foundry and Machine-Shop—George & Tweedale, William Patterson.

Carriages and Wagons—S. Cothermon & Co., Samuel Teesdale, Robert C. London and W. W. Modie.

Blacksmithing—Thomas Hawkin, George Dutch.

Pumps—Levi Machemer, A. L. Hatfield.

Furniture—Charles N. Barnum.

Harness—Clinton Doolittle, E. B. Easterbrook.

Harness-Oil and Soaps—Marden & Rossman.

Cigars—D. J. Harrison, A. M. Butler.

Cooperage—John Daniels, C. A. Borst, Russell Reddy, Alonzo Evans.

Bakery—George Offinger.

Fair and competent business men estimate the amount of capital employed in business in Constantine at the present time (January, 1877), at from one-half million to six hundred thousand dollars.

The press is represented by the *Mercury*, Levi T. Hull, editor and proprietor, and the *Journal*, the detailed history of which will be found in the general history of the press of the county.

### THE SCHOOLS.

The first school taught in Constantine was kept by Thomas Charlton in the winter of 1830-1, in the basement or cellar of Niles F. Smith's store, the master interspersing his pedagogical duties with those of salesman. The seats were hewed-logs, with saplings for legs, and the desks rough-board counters nailed against the walls of the cellar. One door gave ingress and egress for the prisoners, and one small window gave them a "pale, ineffectual light," more dim than religious. Charlton gave his pupils a Christmas dinner of sweet-cake and "goodies," to make their confinement less irksome. Joseph Bonebright and his sister, now Mrs. A. B. George, were among those first pupils; they are still residents of Constantine, and look daily upon the magnificent outgrowth from such insignificant seeding, the union school of Constantine, where their children are gaining an education forty-five years afterward. Luther Lowell taught the next school in a little building on the corner opposite, eastward of the First National Bank, and was the pedagogue of Constantine for several years.

The first school-house was built in 1832, and was a small frame-building, built jointly by the towns-people and the Baptist church-society, Deacon William Churchill giving the hewed timber therefor. It was used for religious meetings by all parties until the Presbyterian session-house was built in 1839, when it became the general meeting-house until other churches were built some years later. The first school in the school-house was taught by a Mr. Laflin, in the winter of 1832–33, and after him Mr. Lowell came in again. The old school-house is now doing duty as a residence for a Mr. James, in a nursery near town.

In 1847 the second house was built on the same ground as the first, to wit, near the present Reformed church. The school-house was completed and a school taught in it the winter of 1847–48, William B. Patch being the first teacher. Governor John S. Barry was the moderator; Hon. Joseph R. Williams, director, and Franklin Wells, assessor of the district. Mr. Patch taught three months at twenty-five dollars per month, and the rate-bill for teachers' wages was fifty-four dollars and fifty cents, the balance being paid out of the primary school-fund received from the State. Mr. Patch taught two quarters additional, and the whole income of the district for the year 1847 –48 was three hundred and sixty-six dollars and ninety-three cents, and there were one hundred and ninety-five children in the district between four and eighteen years of age. In September, 1848, the board employed two teachers, a male and female, and classified the scholars according to their scholastic attainments; Miss Elizabeth Ellsworth being the assistant and teacher of the second grade, at sixteen dollars per month, Mr. Patch receiving thirty dollars for the first grade. In 1849, Miss Ellsworth and her sister Almira were engaged for five months to teach the school, at sixteen dollars per month each; and twelve months school voted for in 1840–50.

In October, 1852, Hon. H. H. Riley, Charles G. Wait and Thomas Mitchell were appointed a building-committee, and, on their report, the annual meeting of the district in September, 1853, voted to build a brick school-house on the same site, thirty by sixty feet on the ground, of two stories. A contract was made with Almeron Bristol to build the same for three thousand dollars. The cost of hall and blinds and seating was seven hundred dollars, and the building was completed and ready for occupancy in 1853. Eight hundred and twenty-one dollars and eighty-one cents were paid for teachers the first year of the new school-house, 1855–56.

On the 28th of September, 1859, the district voted to incorporate the same under the law of 1859, for union school purposes, and elected the following board of trustees: Levi T. Hull and George W. Waterson, one year; George M. Clark and Franklin Wells, two years; Francis J. Morse and Thomas Mitchell, three years. Twenty-five dollars raised by the people by entertainments, were donated to the new régime for apparatus. The first teachers in the union school were Daniel Lautz, principal; Nancy Hull, James H. Thurber, German Brown, D. H. Davis, Willard P. Straight and Sarah Straight, assistants.

The total receipts for 1859–60, the first free school taught in Constantine, were one thousand three hundred and forty-one dollars and ninety-three cents, and teachers' wages amounted to one thousand one hundred and forty-seven dollars and ninety-two cents. In 1862, two hundred and eighteen dollars and fifty-three cents were received from non-resident pupils as tuition fees. In 1866 the school was graded into four departments, primary, intermediate, grammar and high-school, E. G. Reynolds, principal.

In 1867 a new school-house was voted, and twenty thousand dollars appropriated therefor—a new site was selected on block forty-two of the original village plat, and the plans of the house, drawn by Leon C. Welch, adopted. The new house was completed in 1869, at a cost, including site and furnishing, of thirty-two thousand five hundred and forty-five dollars and twelve cents, which was raised in installments of three thousand dollars per annum, except the first five thousand dollars, which was provided for the first year, 1867. W. H. H. Miller was the contractor. The old school-building and lot were sold for two thousand six hundred dollars, and the additional twelve thousand dollars was voted in 1869. The last bond was provided for in the tax of 1878, and the district is now out of debt.

The house is situated on the crown of the rising ground in the southwestern part of the village, and overlooks the country for miles around. It is in the form of a Greek cross, and has an area equal to eighty by eighty feet. It has three stories and a basement, with Mansard roof. The material is white brick, with a most solidly constructed foundation and basement of bowlder-stone. It is heated with furnaces, most thoroughly ventilated, and cared for with scrupulous neatness by the janitor, who has his residence in the basement.

The house furnishes six hundred and fifty sittings, aside from the hall. There are ten school-rooms, ten ante-rooms, one library-room, one laboratory, one cabinet and one janitor's-room, above the basement. The hall on the upper floor contains four hundred sittings, and is fitted-up with a very tasteful and roomy stage and scenery,—the donation of the pupils. Beautiful pictures adorn the walls,—the gifts of friends or the purchases of the scholars. One charming landscape (an oil-painting) of a scene on the Cataskill, is the gift of Mrs. Judge Keightley. The school is equipped with philosophical and chemical apparatus valued at twenty-five hundred dollars, the scholars, by their exhibitions and entertainments, purchasing one thousand dollars worth. One student's microscope, of four hundred diameters in power, with full attachments; three object and eye-pieces, and one hundred mounted objects; one thousand specimens in the mineralogical and geological cabinet; Holt's electrical machine, of Boston manufacture; a Rumpkauff coil for galvanic experiments; Geisler-tubes in profusion for electrical effects, to demonstrate the generation of light by friction, are among the most costly and important apparatus possessed by this school, which is supported by the public purse drawn from the property of the people, to educate the masses, rich and poor.

No other public-school in the State is so well provided for the instruction of children in the higher branches of education. The library contains six hundred volumes of standard works on history, travels, cyclopedias, essays, fiction, etc., and a full supply of geological maps of the State survey of Michigan, and charts of its fauna and flora.

Lieutenant Frank D. Baldwin, a Constantine boy, now in the regular army, has sent several valuable mineralogical and Indian relics to his alma mater, which are displayed in the cabinet. House-plants in generous profusion adorn and cheer the school-rooms and hall,—the gifts of teachers and scholars,—charming the eye with their beauty and gratifying the sense of smell with their delicate fragrance.

The income and expenditures for teachers' wages since the school was graded, in 1866, are as follows: 1866–67, income, two thousand and seventy-five dollars and twenty-four cents; wages, one thousand six hundred and forty dollars. 1867–68, income, one thousand seven hundred and fifty-nine dollars and eighty-one cents; wages, one thousand seven hundred and fifty-two dollars and fifty cents. 1868–69, income, two thousand one hundred and sixty-one dollars and eighty-nine cents; wages, one thousand eight hundred and eighty-nine dollars and fifty cents. 1869–70, income, three thousand seven hundred and eighty-one dollars and seventy-one cents; wages, two thousand five hundred and forty-nine dollars and fifty-six cents. 1870–71, income, nine thousand six hundred and eighteen dollars and thirty-five cents; wages, two thousand seven hundred and sixty-three dollars. 1871–72, income, eight thousand eight hundred and sixteen dollars and fifty-four cents; wages, three thousand two hundred dollars. 1872–73, income, ten thousand and seventy-three dollars and fifty-eight cents; wages, three thousand four hundred and sixty-five dollars. 1873–74, income, eight thousand two hundred and eighty-seven dollars and forty-five cents; wages, three thousand three hundred and forty-seven dollars and fifty-six cents. 1874–75, income, eight thousand six hundred and seventy-seven dollars and fifty-two cents; wages, three thousand four hundred and sixty dollars. 1875–76, income, nine thousand five hundred and ninety-nine dollars and seventy-seven cents (including three hundred and eighty-three dollars and fifty cents tuition fees); wages, three thousand four hundred and ninety dollars.

The following gentlemen have held the position of principal since the school was graded: E. G. Reynolds, 1866–67; J. M. P. Bachelder, 1867–68; Edgar H. Tallman, 1868–69; J. N. Jones, 1869; Professor S. B. Kingsbury, 1869–77.

The graduates of the high-school department (three years' course) are as follows: The class of 1872, David K. Broucher, M. D., Frederick W. Knowles (law student). Class of 1874, Misses Cora F. Titus, Flora C. Titus, and Elma R. Sixby; teachers, Misses Ella M. Jackson and Clara Roys (the two latter now married), Munroe Stebbins (farmer), and Albert C. Titus (law student). Class of 1875, Misses Ella Barnard, Loea Calhoon, Adaline Easterbrook (teacher), Nellie M. Harwood, Lucy Hagerman, Francis Horner (teacher), Mary Ridelle (teacher), and Mary J. Titus

COMMERCIAL MILLS,

D. FRAZIER, Proprietor, AND DEALER IN GRAIN, FLOUR AND FEED,

CONSTANTINE,
MICHIGAN.

(teacher); Charles F. Bates, Arthur Bliss, John M. Calam, and John W. Gentzler. The roll of honor of 1875–76 has the names inscribed thereon of three pupils in the high-school who were neither tardy nor absent during the entire school-year of ten months, and they were Ida V. Benham, Motta Cothermon, and Joseph Horner.

The corps of teachers for 1876–77 are Professor S. B. Kingsbury, A.M. (superintendent and principal of the high-school), Mrs. L. P. Bryson (preceptress), Theodore Rumbaugh and Frederick W. Knowlen (grammar-school), Miss Frances Horner (second intermediate department), Mrs. Electa Harwood (first intermediate department), Miss Hettie Joss (second primary), Miss Louie S. Wells (first primary).

The school-board for 1876–77 are as follows: Hon. Henry H. Riley (moderator), L. T. Hull (director), George J. Crossette (assessor), A. Tweedale, T. C. Langley, and J. W. Jackson; Aaron B. Avery (janitor).

of Constantine are the Methodist Episcopal, Baptist, Reformed, Lutheran and Presbyterian, the first one and last named having houses of worship. An Episcopal society formerly existed in the village, but has not been in existence for some years.

The first religious services were held by the Methodist missionary Felton in 1830, and by his colleague, Lyman D. Gurley, in 1831, who formed the first class of that denomination. The class numbered but twenty members in 1840, and Seeley Goodrich was the first, or at least the earliest known leader of the same. The class met in the school-house until the Presbyterian session-house was built in 1839, when it met therein until 1848, at which time the present church-edifice was erected and dedicated. Franklin Gage was the pastor, who began the building in 1847, and completed it under great embarrassment and discouragement—Richard Pengilly—the succeeding pastor, in 1848, dedicating the building. In 1848 the society bought a lot on the Three Rivers road, and built a parsonage in 1849–50, which was occupied as such until 1855, when it was sold, and the nucleus of the present building bought on Pigeon street for five hundred and twenty-five dollars. It has been enlarged and greatly improved, and is now valued at twelve thousand dollars.

In the summer of 1856 a great revival occurred under the ministration of S. C. Adams, local evangelist, and the pastor, Horace Hall. The pastors who have had charge of this church are as follows: Erastus Felton, Lyman B. Gurley, Benjamin Cooper, William Sprague, R. S. Robinson, George M. Berwick, Newell E. Smith, Erastus Kellogg, Richard C. Meek, William Todd, John Erenabruack, J. V. Watson, W. H. Sampson, Henry Hudson, Peter Sabin, W. H. Collins, R. Parker, A. J. Eldred, Franklin Gauge, Richard Pengilly, S. A. Osborne, Peter Sharp and Elijah Crane, all of whom served but one year from 1830 to 1852 in the order they are named, except R. S. Robinson, who served in 1832–3, and 1835–6. Since 1851 the following have been settled over the church from one to four years each: Frank May, Horace Hall, four years—1854–6 and 1875–6; Thomas B. Granger, S. W. Earle, B. F. Doughty, three years; N. L. Brockway, Stephen C. Woodward, D. R. Latham, W. B. Cambrus, David Thomas, A. A. Knappan, H. H. Parker, James N. Dayton, A. A. Dunton, L. M. Edmunds, and George D. Lee, the present pastor.

Rev. Mr. Thomas died in 1870, after thirty years of itinerancy in the church. The record says of him: "His remains are buried in Constantine cemetery; his record and his rest are on high."

Rev. L. M. Edmunds, by his careful and persistent research, has laid us under heavy obligations for the history of the Methodist Episcopal church in Constantine and the county at large. Dr. Thomas is the present superintendent of the Sunday-school. The present membership of the Church is one hundred and seventy-two, and the church property is valued at seven thousand five hundred dollars, including the brick chapel at North Constantine. The Sunday-school numbers one hundred and seventy-two scholars, and has four hundred and fifty books in its library.

THE BAPTIST CHURCH

of Constantine was organized at the house of William Churchill, situated just outside of the present village, September 29, 1832.

On September 15, several Baptist communicants there assembled, with Elder Clark as chairman and Deacon Churchill as clerk,—unanimously agreed to call a council to organize a church; the council convened on the 29th at Mr. Churchill's house, being composed of Elders Clark, Alford and Miller, Deacon Grubb, and a brother Norton, Oliver Alford acting as moderator and D. A. Grubb as clerk, organized the church, and the communion was celebrated the following Sunday. Elder Alford was en-

gaged to preach on the first Sabbath in each month for one year. On the 1st of December, 1832, the covenant-meeting was held in the new school-house, and Elder Alford preached there the next day. The second communion was celebrated April 2, 1833.

July 1, 1834, the society had a house, thirty by twenty-four feet, to meet in, and five ministers were present. May 30, 1835, the first messengers were appointed to the Baptist association, viz.: Deacon William Churchill, Benjamin Swany, Joseph Olds and Jacob Virgil. July 6, the rite of baptism was first administered, the candidate being Mrs. Brooks. August 1, the record says, "we met at our church," and the second baptism was had—Mrs. Sanford—Elder Hall being the preacher.

On May 21, 1836, Francis Bungay and wife were received, and on the 6th of July Mr. Bungay was elected deacon and clerk of the church, and remained as such until his death in 1838. He and his family, wife and two sons—Francis, Jr., now a citizen of Constantine, and George W. Bungay, a poet and writer in New York—came to Constantine in 1833. He was a carpenter and cabinet-maker.

On June 17, 1836, Bungay, Allen Goodridge and Woodworth were appointed a committee to buy a lot and procure subscriptions to build a church, and the society was incorporated by electing trustees, viz.: Francis Bungay, William Churchill, Daniel Woodworth, William F. Arnold, Allen Goodridge and Erastus Tracy; but the church was never built, though a lot was partially paid for, the title remaining in the name of one of the brethren.

Owing to the number of congregations who occupied the school-house jointly, some inconvenience was experienced in point of time for using the same, one congregation frequently waiting on the steps, or in the yard, for the close of the service of another, which were protracted somewhat beyond the usual length. Therefore arrangements were made by the different congregations, in 1838, during the winter season, whereby the inconvenience was afterwards avoided.

In the summer of 1838 meetings were suspended by reason of the general sickness which prevailed. In October and November, 1841, a series of interesting meetings were held; a large number uniting with the church. The Sabbath-school was organized July 19, 1842, Daniel Woodworth superintendent, and Isaac Crum secretary. Previous to this time a union school had been in operation, which was first organized, in 1833, in Mr. Beaufait's cabinet-shop, by Messrs. Dickinson and Gibler. The later meetings of the society were held in the Presbyterian session-house, but there has been no regular preaching since 1800.

The ministers who have preached to this society, more or less regularly, are as follows: Rev. Oliver Alford, Elders Hall, Taylor, G. B. Day, W. B. Brown, J. Gilbert, Barnes, M. Clark, John Wright, E. J. Corey and John Sage. Elder T. M. Shacafelt, of White Pigeon, and the pastors at Three Rivers, have supplied what preaching has been had since 1860.

THE PRESBYTERIAN CHURCH SOCIETY

was organized October 27, 1836, by Rev. P. W. Warriner, of White Pigeon, with nine members, six males and three females. John Howard and Franklin Cowdery were the first elders installed, and the latter was ordained soon after. In May, 1837, the church called Rev. Thomas B. Bradford, of Philadelphia, to be its pastor, but he declined, yet supplied the desk for a year. April, 1839, William Cathcart was chosen and ordained a ruling elder, and remained thus until his death, January 18, 1861, aged sixty-seven years. In April, 1843, Isaac Bonham and John McMillen were chosen elders. In November, 1853, John Gibson and R. B. Shannon were chosen elders, and John G. Cathcart, G. Hopkins and D. A. Watt, deacons.

In 1839 the session-house was built on the site of the present church, which latter was built in 1854, for three thousand and four hundred dollars, and dedicated November 23 of that year. Rev. A. Y. Moore, of South Bend, Indiana, preaching the sermon, and installing, the next day, Samuel C. Logan as pastor of the church. Rev. Jonathan Edwards, of Fort Wayne, preached the installation sermon, and Revs. A. Y. Moore, H. L. Vannuys, of Goshen, and T. P. Cummins, of Laporte, officiated in the other ceremonies. This church was then the only one of the denomination in all of southern Michigan. It was forty by fifty-six feet on the ground, and was a great credit to its projectors and builders at the time, and was free from debt. In 1874 the house was remodeled and renovated throughout, and on December 16, Rev. T. Parry, the present pastor, was ordained and installed—Rev. Alfred Eddy, of Niles; Rev. Addison K. Strong, of Kalamazoo; Rev. L. M. Gillisland, of White Pigeon, and Rev. William A. Masker, of Three Rivers, officiating and assisting in the ceremonies. The remodeling of the church cost three thousand dollars.

The ministers who have supplied the desk, or acted as pastors, are as follows: Revs. Thomas B. Bradford, 1837; Benjamin Ogden, 1839; Charles Nichol, 1843; James Geer, 1843-4; R. R. Wells, 1846; S. C. Logan, 1850-7; P. F. Taylor, 1857; John W. Major, 1858; —— James, 1858; Daniel Lantz, 1859; I. S. Killen, 1860-5; T. E. Hughes, 1866-9; Joseph Swindt, 1870-2; VanNess, 1873; T. Parry, 1874-7, and, at present, the incumbent.

The present elders of the church are: G. W. Cook, N. H. Townsend, E. Leimbach, T. Putman and H. Servison. The present membership of the church is ninety-four; the sittings in the church-building, two hundred and fifty; Sunday-school pupils, one hundred and twenty; and two hundred books are in the library.

### THE REFORMED CHURCH OF NORTH AMERICA,

formerly known as the Dutch Reformed church of Constantine, was organized March 11, 1843, with Joseph Wells, John Sixbey, elders; and Nicholas I. Sixbey and John Harrison, deacons,—the latter being the clerk of the consistory. The formal organization was effected April 23, by Reverend Asa Bennett, who ordained the above named officers.

On May 20 the following were received as members of the church: Darius D. Evans, Asahel Slote, Eleanor Harrison, Lucy Wells, Rachel Hagenbuch, Elizabeth Sixbey, Catharine Sixbey, Christiana Sixbey, Frances Slote and Peter F. Putman, deacons,—the latter two by confession of faith, of whom all are deceased but three.

The legal organization of the church was effected March 11,—the elders and deacons being elected trustees, and in June recertified to the county clerk.

The first children baptized were Jane, daughter of John and Margaret Pearce, and Reuben, son of Asahel and Frances Slote, September 13, 1843, and that same day the second communion was celebrated.

The first marriage, on the register of the church, was that of Franklin Wells and Helen M. Briggs, October 31, 1844, by Reverend Asa Bennett. The first death that occurred among the members was that of Mrs. Lucy Wells, wife of elder Joseph Wells, March 13, 1843.

The first pastor was Reverend Asa Bennett, 1843-6, and preached first in the school-house,—the first one built in 1832. There were nineteen members in the church at the close of his ministry.

The first church-building was begun and nearly completed under Mr. Bennett, and was thirty-one by fifty feet on the ground, eighteen feet clear in height, flat ceiling, vestibule nine feet wide, seats fronting the door; the two rear ones raised for the occupancy of the choir. Two aisles had twenty-two seats opening into each, with doors of much superior finish to any church before attempted in Constantine. The building cost two thousand two hundred dollars; some five or six hundred being contributed cost.

The second pastor Reverend David McNeish, dedicated the house on New Year's day, 1846, and preached the sermon,—Reverend Benjamin Ogden, of Three Rivers, Presbyterian; Reverend Mr. Steel, Congregational, and the Presbyterian minister from White Pigeon assisting.

The first bell was bought in 1847, but cracked; in 1848 the present bell of one thousand pounds weight, and costing five hundred dollars, was bought —Meneely discounting handsomely.

The ladies sewing-society added the blinds to the church. Reverend McNeish stayed with the church until December, 1849; then went to South Bend, and Reverend David A. Jones came as pastor, August 1, 1850, three hundred dollars of his salary being paid by the church, and the balance from the domestic mission fund.

The number of members had increased to forty-three, and the Sunday-school had enrolled fifty scholars. Mr. Jones stayed till October 1, 1852, and then Mr. McNeish came again and stayed until his death, September 3, 1854. Reverend William Bailey came as next pastor, April 29, 1856; his salary of six hundred dollars being raised jointly between the church, the Mottville congregation and the domestic missions; the former paying three hundred and fifty dollars, the second one hundred dollars, and the balance from the latter fund; but in 1857 the church shouldered the whole burden. Bailey stayed till August 5, 1863, during which period he attended sixty-seven weddings, baptized eleven adults and thirteen children, and received into the church forty-eight members, thirty-seven by certificate, and eleven by certificate; twenty members were lost by death and removals, leaving the membership at sixty-seven at the time of his pastorate.

Reverend J. W. Beardslee, the present pastor, commenced his ministry to the church January 31, 1864.

In the spring of 1865 the interior arrangements of the church-building were remodeled, seats reversed, a recess made in the rear for the choir and desk, a porch added, and the old vestibule thrown into the audience-room.

In 1876, the present elegant structure was erected; Christopher F. Greene, architect; John Wolf, T. H. Calam and the pastor, building committee. It is a frame veneered with white brick, has a basement for Sunday-school and other purposes, and is eighty-one by sixty feet on the ground; a tower fourteen by fourteen feet surmounts the southwest corner, commanding a view of the whole country. There are transepts on the sides from front to rear, ten by twenty-two feet, with recess for desk six by twenty feet.

The first operations on the building began April 11, 1876, the frame was raised June 17, the first brick laid June 27, and the corner-stone July 24; the building was completed the same year, and dedicated December 31, 1876, by the pastor, assisted by Reverend A. H. Van Vranken, of Centreville; Reverend A. T. Stewart, D. D., of Holland College; Reverend G. D. Lee, of Methodist Episcopal Church, and Reverend T. Parry, of Presbyterian Church of Constantine, and Reverend N. D. Williamson, of South Bend Reformed Church.

The subscription for the new church was headed, "The ladies-fund, seven hundred dollars," being secured by them in 1871, in contributions of five cents per week for a year.

Since Mr. Beardslee came in 1864, he has received into the membership of the church one hundred and seventy-seven persons, one hundred and twenty-seven of them on confession, and fifty on certificate. There have been eighteen deaths during the time; and forty-one adults and twenty-one infants have been baptized. He has attended one hundred and ninety-one funerals, solemnized one hundred and thirty-two weddings, and preached one thousand seven hundred and eighty sermons. There are now enrolled in the church one hundred and forty-five members, one hundred and thirty-six being active ones, and two hundred and twenty Sunday-school scholars, and three hundred books in the library; Mr. Beardslee, superintendent, and J. P. Drake, the active assistant.

Mr. Beardslee preached a Centennial sermon in July, 1876, from which the foregoing facts, relating to the church, have been mostly gathered.—Mr. Beardslee adding, personally, such as have become matters of record since the delivery of the sermon.

### THE FIRST EVANGELICAL LUTHERAN CHURCH

of Constantine was organized March 3, 1866, by Rev. P. Bergstresser, pastor of the Mottville and Park Grove churches, and who had preached for six months previously in Constantine, once each month. He was assisted in effecting the organization by Rev. H. Weigand, a German Reformed preacher, and Rev. J. W. Beardslee, of the Dutch Reformed Church of Constantine. The members of the church, at its organization, were William and Sarah Fox, William A. and Martha M. Wagner, Mary Klapp, Abraham and Elizabeth Strohm, George and Mary A. Bergtorff, Henry and Susannah Bittenbender, Christian Klapper, Aaron, Margaret and Sarah C. Heckman, John Leiser, Sarah A. Roe, Jacob Krum, Catharine Klapp and David Wagner, and fourteen others were admitted after the constitution was adopted. The officers were: Elders, William Fox and Aaron Heckman; Deacons, Henry Bittenbender, treasurer, and Abraham Strohm, secretary; trustees, George Bergtorff, Andrew Laverty and Solomon Dentler,—and there were thirty-eight members in all. The first baptism of an infant was that of Minnie Irene Bittenbender, and of an adult,—that of John Riddelle; both occurring June 28, 1868.

In 1867 the church society, in conjunction with the German Reformed Church at White Pigeon, bought the old Baptist Church building at the latter place for joint occupancy, and on December 1 of that year, Rev. J. N. Barnett was installed as pastor over the churches at Constantine, White Pigeon and Mottville. The church-society was incorporated under the statute, March 19, 1870, the trustees elected being Daniel Klackner, Aaron Heckman and Andrew Laverty, and William Fox and Jacob Gentzler were appointed a building-committee to act with the trustees. On April 22, 1872, a lot was bought on the corner of Canaris and Fifth streets for a church site. In relating the efforts to get a church-edifice erected, the secretary writes upon the records thus: "Much delay and indecision having arisen in proceeding to build a church, it was determined by some of the members to commence work, and by a coup d' etat precipitate action, and therefore, on August 29, 1872, the ladies were called out to dig the basement and foundation trenches. Rev. R. F. Delo and wife and many others came down from Three Rivers to aid in the initiatory movement." This brought matters to a crisis of enthusiasm, and, on October 5, 1872, the corner-stone was laid with solemn ceremonies and great eclat. Rev. Delo preached the sermon, and, the day being the anniversary of the birth of the pastor, the occasion was a doubly interesting one. Rev. J. W. Beardslee also assisted, making an address,—Crossette's cornet band adding to the

RESIDENCE OF **SAMUEL GIBSON**, BROAD STREET,
CONSTANTINE TP. ST JOSEPH COUNTY. MICH.

RESIDENCE OF **P. B. BATES**,
CONSTANTINE TP. ST JOSEPH CO. MICH.

pleasure of the day, and leading the singing. The records give an elaborate description of the articles placed in the corner-stone, and the manner of their deposition therein. The church-edifice is seventy-two feet on Canaris street, by forty-two feet on Fifth street; fronts south, and is built of red brick, with a basement, and a round tower with castellated ramparts, and is furnished with excellent stained-glass windows.

Miss Helen S. and Charles H. Barry, Jr. gave the bell, costing over five hundred dollars—Miss Helen being also a generous donor to the church. The bell is inscribed, "Messiah Lutheran church, 1873, C. H. and H. L. Barry." It was hung in the tower August 26, 1873, and none but the pastor knew of the gift until it arrived in town. Mr. Eacker gave the carpets, and B. O. Gladding the chandeliers. The church was dedicated September 7, 1873, the Rev. F. W. Conrad, D.D., of Philadelphia, preaching the dedicatory sermon; the other ceremonies being performed by the pastor, assisted by the Revs. Delo, of Three Rivers; J. Shafer, of Butler, Indiana; J. Steisinger, St. Joseph county, Indiana; L. M. Gilliland, of Presbyterian church at White Pigeon, and J. W. Beardslee, of the Dutch Reformed church of Constantine. The church was finished in 1874, and is valued at ten thousand five hundred dollars. October 1, 1873, the Constantine church separated from the Melancthon pastorate, and is now known as the Messiah pastorate, of the Synod of Northern Indiana. Mr. Barnett resigned his pastorate January 2, 1876, and the Rev. G. P. Raup, the present pastor, was called thereto June 11, and installed November 9, 1876, by Rev. J. Stuckenburg, of Wittenburg College, and Rev. A. McLaughlin.

The first funeral service in the church was that performed at the burial of Elizabeth Lintz, a native of Alsace, France, August 16, 1874, Deacon Henry Bittenbender, died in his seat in the Sunday-school, February 20, 1876, the day the pastor (Mr. Barnett) preached his farewell sermon. The present officers of the church are Elders Aaron Heckman, treasurer; Deacon Theodore Rumbaugh, secretary; Trustees, Adam Gentzler and Martin L. Ernst; Mrs. Maria Bradley, organist. The church edifice contains three hundred sittings; there are one hundred and twenty members on the roll of the society; and the Sunday-school, which was organized in 1873, has enrolled one hundred and thirty-four scholars, has three hundred books in its library, and the pastor is the superintendent, Mr. Barnett preceding him in the position.

St. James Protestant Episcopal church was organized and a vestry chosen and wardens elected, in October, 1836,—Bishop McCrosky, of Detroit, preaching on the 12th of that month, and initiating the movement. Mr. Whitesides, of Philadelphia, preached in September previous, and continued his ministrations over the societies at Constantine, White Pigeon and Centreville, for a year or more. There was no church edifice ever built in Constantine, and the society is now dissolved. A frame was put up for a church, but never enclosed, and after standing some time was sold to the Methodists, who took it down and worked it into their building.

SOCIETIES—MASONIC.

Siloam Lodge, No. 35, A. F. M., was instituted under dispensation, in 1849, and chartered the year following, J. J. Mason was the first worshipful master. He was succeeded in the office by C. S. Engle, 1854; Benjamin Merrill, 1855–56; S. C. Coffinberry, 1857–59; Thomas Wass, Jr., 1860–61; Thomas M. Greene, 1862–66; Rev. D. Lantz, 1867; David E. Wilson, 1868–72; A. C. French, 1873–76. Hon. S. C. Coffinberry was the grand master in 1866–68, of the State, and, during the first year of his incumbency, performed the masonic burial-service at the funeral obsequies of Governor and Senator Cass, and delivered an able address at the next session of the grand lodge. The present membership of the lodge is one hundred and twenty-one.

Centreville Chapter, No. 11, R. A. M., once was moved to Constantine and remained two years, but was again removed to Centreville, and no chapter is located here at present.

Nebuzar-adan Council, No. 37, R. and S. M., was organized and instituted May 29, 1872. Its present officers are Hiram Lindsley, T. I. M.; A. C. French, D. I. M.; A. J. Knapp, P. C. W.; A. B. George, recorder; E. George, treasurer. Number of members, forty-four.

The Masons own their hall. In 1852 they bought and fitted up nicely the hall which was burned in the spring of 1871. They bought the present one in the Davis building, fitting it up in good style, and dedicated it on Christmas, 1871.

INDEPENDENT ORDER OF ODD FELLOWS.

Constantine Lodge No. 22, I. O. O. F., was instituted February 17, 1847, its charter-members being W. C. Pease, W. Savier, Dr. Elliott, L. C. Laird, George Brown, and Elisha Stevens. March 3, 1848, the fraternity formed

an Odd Fellows' Hall Association, and bought H. H. Riley's property on Water street (fifty by eighty feet), the same being the original American hotel. The association, of which Washington Pitcher was president, and W. C. Pease secretary, moved the building, finished and furnished the dancing-hall for a lodge-room, and the bed-rooms for ante-rooms, etc. After the lodge had worked a few years prosperously, it fell into a collapse, and discontinued its meetings; and the property of the association was sold to John K. Briggs, and he turned it into a tenement-house,—known as the "Bee-hive,"—and it was afterwards sold and removed. In 1870 the lodge resumed its labors, under Levi T. Hull as N. G., and has been prospering to the present time. Its present officers are D. H. Raup, N. G.; William Drummonds, V. G.; C. Clappee, treasurer; J. J. Strong, recording secretary; Ambrose Williams, permanent secretary, and has thirty-eight members.

Dennis Encampment, No. 14, of Patriarchs (so named in honor of Grand Master Dennis), was first instituted at Sturgis in 1860 or thereabouts. In 1866 it was removed to White Pigeon, where, in 1869, it had the largest membership of any encampment in the State. February 22, 1872, it was removed to Constantine, where it still remains. L. L. Ensign and George W. Beisel were its first chief-patriarchs, and David Knox was one of the early ones in 1862. George W. Beisel was elected G. S. W. in the grand lodge in 1861; G. H. P., 1862, and G. P., 1863. David Knox was elected G. S. W. in 1864–65, and G. H. P. in 1866; and another of its C. P.'s (R. H. Morrison) has held the office of grand-treasurer in the Grand lodge of the State since 1866. The present officers are J. J. Strong, C. P.; Theodore Rumbaugh, H. P.; Frank Hagerman, S. W.; D. H. Raup, scribe; C. Clappee, treasurer,—and has thirty members.

PATRONS OF HUSBANDRY.

Constantine Grange, No. 236, was instituted January 29, 1875, J. S. Richards being the first master, and L. T. Hull secretary. It numbers one hundred members, and its present official list is J. S. Richards, master; J. A. Marsh, secretary; Miss Ardelle Richards, Ceres; Miss Mary Stears, Flora; Miss Sarah O'Hara, Pomona.

The first temperance society was organized January 7, 1838, and L. R. Lowell was the secretary.

A Good Templars' lodge was organized and worked in 1871, meeting in the Davis building, but it was suspended, and none is in existence at the present time.

December 10, 1836, Constantine had a debating-society, at which grave questions affecting the fate of empires were discussed and determined to the satisfaction, doubtless, of the disputants.

Among the most noted associations of Constantine, and one which has been the herald of her fame all over the State, is her unrivaled musical association,

CROSSETTE'S CORNET BAND.

It includes sixteen instruments, every one in the hands of an accomplished artist. It was organized by its present leader, F. M. Crossette, in 1871, from fragments of other bands, many of the members having previously achieved meritorious distinction as expert performers. A musical critic thus writes of its leader and organizer: "Mr. Crossette, although still a young man, has served in the capacity of a leader of bands for twenty years. At the age of sixteen he became the leader of one of the first bands in Vermont, of which State he was a native. At the breaking out of the war he, with his band, accompanied the 2d Vermont Infantry to the army of the Potomac, where they acquired meritorious distinction." Crossette's band was selected to attend the governor of Michigan at the laying of the corner-stone of the State-house, in 1874, and during the forming of the line of procession, occupied a conspicuous position on the platform, and executed in admirable style a choice selection of music. They also won many warm encomiums from the press for their gallant bearing in the march and most exquisite melody at the grand-stand. In 1873, at the State fair, and at Grand Rapids at the encampment of the Knights Templar of the State, they carried off the palm, —at the former competing with thirty-one other bands. C. E. Rogers, the B-flat cornet, is the finest soloist in the State, as is generally acknowledged. The band furnished music one day at the county fair at Centreville, in 1876, and were most highly complimented by Hon. J. A. J. Cresswell, of Maryland, for their exquisite rendering of classical music. The members of the band, who are all engaged in other business, are as follows: F. M. Crossette (E-flat cornet), Daniel Arnold and Augustus Arnold (E-flat clarionet), C. E. Rogers solo, (B-flat cornet), William Gregey (B-flat cornet), E. Schellhous (E-flat tenor), J. H. Wells (E-flat tenor), S. W. Kline (slide-trombone, solo), Charles H. Arnold (B-flat trombone), R. M. Flack (B-flat bass), H. Hutchinson (E-flat bass), H. Drake (drum), F. Knapp (cymbals,,

George Simmons (tenor-drum), C. Cutherman (tenor-drum), C. Rumsey (piccalo).

Another favorite musical organization of Constantine, and the oldest in the West, is

HULL AND ARNOLD'S QUADRILLE BAND,

organized in 1837 by John Hull and Daniel Arnold, their first appearance before the public being in Constantine, in December, 1837; Mr. Hull playing the violin, and Mr. Arnold the clarionet, which instruments they have continued to perform upon to the present time.

In 1839 Oliver P. Arnold came into the organization with a cornet, and was a member of the same until 1869. Morris I. Arnold joined as basso in 1844, and remained until 1862, and was succeeded by the present basso, Charles H. Arnold; Charles E. Rogers, the present cornet, came into the band in 1872.

Mr. Rogers is the superior soloist in Crossette's band, and in his velvety tones and staccato movements, most exquisely executed, he is a fair rival of Arbuckle, Levy and Henry.

This band plays all over southern Michigan and northern Indiana, from Monroe to Laporte, and from Grand Rapids and Lansing to Fort Wayne. Mr. Hull is an excellent director of terpsichorean assemblies, and will have, and does command the most decorous and courteous behavior in the hall while the festivities are in progress, under penalty of suspension of the music.

AMUSEMENTS.

The first celebration of the Fourth of July was had in 1831. The ladies made a flag which was run up on the tallest tree in the village, and the men made howitzers of stumps and blew them up; altogether the hubbub was sufficient to draw in the people of the vicinity for some miles around, to see what the fun was, there being nearly one hundred present. The ladies got up a dinner in a bower in the centre of what was afterwards Washington street, near the site of the south end of the present bridge. No orations were delivered but such as were inspired by "John Barleycorn," a stray waif that had found its way into Constantine the spring previous, without an owner, and was appropriated as contraband, and brought into requisition for the purposes of the day.

The Fourth, in 1836, was celebrated with great pomp and circumstance, the route of the procession being " down Third street to Canaris, up Canaris to Fourth, down Fourth to Mottville, up Mottville to Canaris, down Canaris to Water, up Water to the American hotel, where a dinner will be in readiness for those who may wish to participate."

There were at the time not to exceed two houses on each of the streets named, except Water street.

P. E. Grover, marshal of the day, toasted the village thus : "The village of Constantine ; like the hickory, rapid in growth ; may its citizens evince as much liberality in the support of the arts and sciences, as they have in building up our beautiful village." (Grover made fanning-mills, whose sole office is to blow.)

Norman Roys toasted the ladies thus : "The fair daughters of Michigan ; the cherished objects of our affection and regard,—whilst they give to life its present joys, they afford the strongest proofs of the blessings of union."

The next March Mr. Roys married one of the fair daughters he toasted so loyally and gallantly. The ladies did not lack for homage that day, for the orator, Dr. Sumner, and an old Revolutionary soldier, Lemuel Butler, toasted them in gallant phrase; Esquire Charlton drank to the starry flag right loyally, and Charles S. Adams offered this sentiment to the St. Joseph river: "Our noble and beautiful St. Joseph,—may we use her, and not abuse her; and may we ever be as pure, though not quite so crooked."

The steamboat Constantine, then on the stocks, was toasted; and about everything else. Columbia Lancaster giving the last : "To your tents, Oh! Israel ;" which, being interpreted, meant, to the dancing-hall, Oh! ye sons and daughters of Constantine, and they "toed and heeled" until daylight in the morning, at Hunt's Hall.

The officers of the day were : Dr. Sumner, orator ; Major Ulmann, marshal ; Captain Grover and Lieutenant Kenn, aids ; Nelson Bryant, reader ; Reverend Mr. Stanley, chaplain ; Mr. Thatcher, chorister ; W. H. Adams, president ; A. E. Massey, vice-president.

In 1835 the day was celebrated, Judge Meek being the president ; W. T. House, vice ; Dr. Sumner, orator ; Major Ulmann, marshal ; Captains Grover and Thomas, aids ; Edwin A. King, reader ; Reverend Mr. Wolf, chaplain. They dined at Hunt's, and toasts were drank.

On December 20, 1837, a grand ball was given at the American hotel by Charles Hopkins, David Munger, Gilbert Miller, W. T. House, and Major

Ulmann,—Hull and Arnold furnishing the music. James Hunt was given carte blanche, and told to get up the supper regardless of expense; and the boys thought he did so, when they were presented with their bills after the supper was over, for it took a ten dollar note to settle the score.

Mr. Albert Chandler brought the first piano into the village in 1837-8.

INCIDENTS.

John Bryan, the builder of the court-house in Centreville, laid out the frame of the Williams mill in 1839, with an old square, the corners of which were all worn off, because it had never failed him, and so accurately was the measurement done that not a tenon had to be changed when the frame was raised. The wheels were breast-wheels, powerful but costly, one thousand dollars being expended in their construction. Bryan built a large barn in 1836, and furnished no whisky at the raising of it, contrary to the usual custom ; but Mrs. Bryan instead prepared coffee, cakes and pies, and the work was well done and no accidents happened to interfere with the harmony of the proceeding.

A Scotchman named Clark, having been rejected in his suit for a lady in the village, jumped off the bridge one cold night in the early days, with the intention of drowning himself and putting an end to his woes ; but the water being cold and its chilliness influencing his better judgment, he scrambled out again upon the ice and was nearly frozen before he was rescued. However, he was warmed up and recovered, not only his spirits, but his passion for the object of his addresses, and the next evening repaired to her residence and called on the lady ; but she, perceiving a butcher knife slily concealed about his person, screamed and ran out of the room, and the father came upon the scene, whereupon "Sandy" concluded it was not best to "bide a wee," and left at once, and was not seen afterwards.

In October, 1832, Robert Clark, Jr., the United States surveyor, informed Hugh Woods, Judge Meek's millwright, and Robert Cassaday that a good mill-site existed on Pawpaw river, ten miles from its mouth, and gave them the lines of the sections and told them how to find the location, but on attempting to discover the place were lost in the woods. A fearful snow-storm came on and their rations ran short, and they lost their reckoning, but finally wandered on through woods, keeping as near to a west course as they could, and came out on the shore of Lake Michigan, fifteen miles north of Kalamazoo river. They took their back track to St. Joseph, along the lake shore, and thence to Constantine, being gone twelve days.

An incident in the gubernatorial life of Governor Barry is given by Hon. H. H. Riley, which will serve to illustrate the startling character of the man. A somewhat notorious character infested the St. Joseph country in the governor's official days, and, having committed some crime in Pennsylvania, was overpersuaded by some party, whose manner was too "child-like and bland" to be resisted, and the first intimation the fellow had that all was not right, was when he found himself en route for Erie, the scene of his exploit, where, on arriving, he was incarcerated in the common jail of the county. He at once began to take measures to effect his release, and taking a lawyer into his counsel, the latter at once suggested his client was kidnapped and must be released by application of the Governor of Michigan upon the like executive of Pennsylvania, and immediately repaired to Constantine to get the necessary requisition. He came into Mr. Riley's office, made his business known, and inquiring where he could find the governor, was directed to his office. He seemed to think it would be no difficult matter for him to influence his excellency to resent the infringement and invasion of the rights of his people by a sister commonwealth, but in half an hour afterwards Mr. Riley saw him and asked him what success he had with the governor, and received for a reply, "That governor is a ⸻ of a fellow." The Erie attorney went back to his client to lay out another line of attack. Mr. Riley meeting the governor soon after, asked him about the interview, and was informed thereof by his excellency, who said, "Do we want such men as this fellow was ! I don't think we need them. If the Pennsylvanians can make anything out of him, let them try ! I won't interfere. I'm glad he is gone."

It is on record that when the governor first assumed the executive function, applications were made to him for the grass in the State-house grounds, as had been the custom under previous administrations backward to the time "whence the memory of man runneth not to the contrary ;" but the governor thought there was money in the same for the State, and so, at the haying season, had the grass cut and the hay sold, and the proceeds covered into the State treasury, which at that time was very much depleted. This was a new departure, and served as a good "roorback" for his Whig opponents at the next election ; but his prudence pleased the people, who re-elected him, and again, after one term intervening, called him to their highest gift in the State in 1847.

Governor Barry was born in Amherst, N. H., January 29, 1802, and was married to Mary Kidder, in Grafton, Vt., in October, 1824. They left no children. He was a self-educated man, working on his father's farm before marriage, and lived six years in Georgia, and practiced law there one year.

### THE ORIGINAL PROPRIETOR

of the village of Constantine, Judge William Meek, sold his interest in the village, at least his interest in the water-power, to Joseph R. Williams and others, and moved with his family to Des Moines, Iowa, where he located a mill-site, and then traveled some in Texas, but returned to Des Moines and settled there. His son, William Meek, Jr., went to Oregon in company with Jackson Poe and Columbia Lancaster, became a heavy dealer in lumber, and is now very wealthy. Thomas Chariton married one of Judge Meek's daughters and went west with him. Alexander Woods married the other daughter, and removed at the same time.

Among the leading citizens of the past and present history of Constantine, not before especially named as such, may be mentioned Hon. Joseph R. Williams, who came to the village in 1836, Franklin Wells in 1837-8, Thomas C. Langley in 1842, John K. Briggs in 1838-40, Norman Harvey in 1833, Thomas Mitchell in 1840 or thereabouts, David Stafford in 1840, and J. P. Gladding in 1836.

Mr. Williams was born in Taunton, Mass., November 14, 1808, and graduated at Harvard college in 1831; studied law under "honest" John Davis of Worcester, Mass., was admitted to the bar and practiced in New Bedford, and came to Constantine to reside in 1839. Mr. Williams was one of nature's noblemen, of an enthusiastic nature, far-seeing and enterprising; he was zealous in all things pertaining to the advancement of the township and county, and served the latter in the State legislature, in the upper-house thereof, with great ability and acceptance to all, in 1880-1. He was a man of kindly feelings and generous disposition, a good neighbor and honorable citizen, and was sincerely mourned by his fellow-citizens when death took him from their midst. He was also a member of the constitutional convention of 1850, and died June 15, 1861, while holding the position of president of the State senate.

Mr. Wells has been, and still is, closely identified with the material prosperity of the village,—was a merchant in the earlier days, and is still interested in that line. He is at present a member of the board of control of the State Agricultural College. Mr. Langley entered the mercantile trade in 1842, on his first coming to the village, and is at present one of the leading men in that line. Mr. Briggs was connected with Governor Barry in business for several years, and managed his mercantile trade after State affairs devolved upon the latter. Mr. Harvey's history will be found at large at the end of this township history.

Mr. Mitchell was one of Constantine's early and long-time manufacturers, and a prominent and worthy citizen throughout its history to the present. He is still a resident of that village, living at his case on his well-earned competency. Mr. Stafford was, for many years, connected with Mr. Mitchell in manufacturing. George I. Crossette is also a prominent banker, has been a resident of the village for many years, and has a most beautiful mansion on Washington street. His wife is a daughter of one of Constantine's earlier residents, Joseph Bonebright, one of the second family to make the township their home; is still an honorable and respected resident and manufacturer of the village, and his partner, Mr. French, is an early-comer and long-time worthy citizen of the village.

Mr. Gladding was the first jewelry-dealer and watchmaker in the village, and he has been continuously in trade from 1836 to the present time. He preserved a file of the first paper published in Constantine,—the *Republican*,—from July 1, 1836, to the close of 1838, and presented it to the union school library, where it is subject to perusal, and gives a correct history of Constantine at that time.

### THE MILITARY RECORD

of Constantine is no whit less glorious and honorable than that of any of her sister towns in the county. Her citizens in the rebellion were just as brave and self-sacrificing as those of other towns, and volunteered in the nation's defence with alacrity, filled her quotas whenever they were levied, cheerfully and uncomplainingly, and bore their burdens as steadily and persistently as any. Where all are heroes, who is *le chevalier?*

An incident of the Black Hawk war is related by John Hamilton, which we give place to. When his father's family were coming in the county, they arrived at Adrian just as the news came through of the advance of Black Hawk into Illinois, and Roberts, who was traveling in company with Hamilton, having considerable cattle and several small children, decided to return to Monroe county and wait until the war should be over. Hamilton submitted the question of advance or retreat to his son John, then about eighteen years old, and his son-in-law, Alfred Roe, who, with the father, decided to go on, and did so, arriving in Constantine in due time. The very day after their arrival, Roe and young Hamilton were enrolled in the militia, making as even one hundred in White Pigeon township, as the territory was then called. The draft for forty men was made, and Poe drew a prize to go to the west. This order for a draft was revoked, and another one for fifty men was ordered and made, and Poe drew the prize again, Hamilton drawing a blank each time. The next day the news of Black Hawk's capture came, and the men were sent home, or never got together, but drew eight dollars in cash and forty acres of land, and so Mr. Poe, as Mr. Hamilton says, "did draw a prize after all."

Lieutenant Frank D. Baldwin, who distinguished himself in the war of the rebellion, the details of which are recorded in the general military history of the county in the account of the service of the 19th infantry, after rising from the ranks to the position of lieutenant-colonel, entered the regular army as second lieutenant, and distinguished himself in Texas while in command of a detachment of Company D, 6th United States cavalry, December 7, 1874, which he led against two hundred Indians, in a rough and broken country, attacking and driving off the savages, capturing all their property, and rescuing from a loathsome captivity two little girls who had long been held prisoners, and whose father, mother and brother were murdered, and two other sisters also captured. The sufferings of these captives were most horrible.

In 1876 Lieutenant Baldwin, while with Crook's command, attacked Sitting Bull, the famous Sioux warrior and chieftain, captured his camp and all of his ponies and property, and drove the Indians out, barely covered with clothing sufficient to prevent their freezing. The weather was terrible, but the campaign was a successful one. Lieutenant Baldwin was all through the campaign with Crook, and performed much gallant and effective service. He was a Constantine boy.

We here append a list of the citizens of Constantine who went into the war of the rebellion, in defence of the flag, and fought against treason and its cohorts:

#### SECOND MICHIGAN INFANTRY.

Addison R. Conkling, regimental band; mustered out August 1, 1862.

Abner Thurber, regimental band; mustered out August 1, 1862.

Captain John A. Lawson, Company G; enlisted September 10, 1861.

First Lieutenant Richard T. Morton, Company G; resigned March 6, 1862.

Sergeant John C. Joss, Company G; first lieutenant and captain; lost a leg in the battle of the Wilderness, May, 1864.

Sergeant Peter S. Bell, Company G; re-enlisted December 30, 1863; died of wounds, June 25, 1864.

Sergeant David M. Rumbaugh, Company G; re-enlisted December 31, 1863, and died of wounds near Petersburg, July 20, 1864.

Sergeant Elisha P. Clark, Company G; discharged at expiration of service.

Corporal Jesse A. Gaines, Company G; re-enlisted and reported missing near Petersburg, Va.

Corporal Theodore Rumbaugh, Company G; discharged for disability.

Corporal Charles W. Dryer, Company G.

Corporal Clinton Snyder, Company G; discharged at expiration of service.

Corporal Marcus D. L. Train, Company G; died of typhoid fever at Yorktown, Va., May 28, 1862.

Corporal William H. Woolworth, Company G; discharged for disability.

Private Silas T. J. Abbott, Company G; discharged at expiration of service.

Private John M. Adams, Company G; killed at Knoxville, Tennessee, November 24, 1863.

Private William H. Chase, Company G; died January 13, 1864.

Private Forrest Doolittle, Company G; discharged.

Private George Darlison, Company G; discharged at expiration of service.

Private O. F. French, Company G; enlisted in regular army.

Private George Green, Company G; discharged for disability.

Private Washington Georgia, Company G; re-enlisted December, 1863; mustered out, lost knapsack at Bull Run and found it again at Petersburg.

Private Albert Harwood, Company G; lost right arm in Peninsula campaign; discharged for disability.

Private Charles Henderson, Company G; discharged at expiration of service.

Private David H. Knipple, Company G; shot accidentally at Camp Arlington, Va.

Private Cyrus Knight, Company G; killed at Knoxville, November 24, 1863.

Private Fred Lang, Company G; killed at Knoxville, November 24, 1863.

Private Daniel F. Motley, Company G; discharged at expiration of service.

Private Charles Morton, Company G; lost right arm at Williamsburg, Va.; discharged for disability.

Private Benjamin F. Morton, Company G; enlisted in regular service.

Private Philo R. Stewart, Company G; discharged at expiration of service.

Private Ernst Schinke, Company G; re-enlisted and mustered-out.

Private Benjamin Stell, Company G; discharged at expiration of service.

Private John L. Taylor, Company G; discharged for disability.

Private Francis E. Thurber, Company G; killed at Campbell's Station, Tenn., November 16, 1863.

Private Jacob Welches, Company G; discharged at expiration of service.

Private Arthur Williamson, Company G; discharged.

FOURTH INFANTRY.

Private Merritt Enos, Company C; discharged at expiration of service.

FIFTH INFANTRY.

Private Nicholas O. Brown, Company G; mustered-out.

SIXTH INFANTRY.

Private Hiram Driscoll, Company A; died of disease, at Fort Gaines, Alabama.

Private Ezra Florence, Company C; re-enlisted and mustered-out.

Private Charles H. Knight, Company C; discharged at expiration of service.

Private Garrett E. Moyer, Company C; died at Baton Rouge, June 21, 1862.

Private James Syas, Company C; mustered-out; died since from disease contracted in service.

Private Thomas B. Hill, Company C; mustered-out.

Private David H. Simonds, Company C; discharged for disability.

SEVENTH INFANTRY.

Private Joseph R. Smith, Company B; died in Salisbury prison-pen.

NINTH INFANTRY.

Private Alfred Peck, Company A; died at Chattanooga, of disease.

Private John Mater, Company B; mustered-out.

Private Reuben Harvey, Company F; mustered-out.

Private Henry M. Patchan, Company G; mustered-out.

TENTH INFANTRY.

Private James P. Cole, Company A; mustered-out.

Private John Holmes, Company K; mustered-out.

Private Jeremiah Holmes, Company K; mustered-out.

ELEVENTH INFANTRY.

Musician Edwin Higgins; mustered out August 22, 1862.

Private Orville A. Chittenden, Company A; discharged for disability.

Private John H. Bennett, Company A; mustered-out.

Private Lester Bennett, Company A; mustered-out.

Private George Vandewalker, Company A; mustered-out.

Private Robert W. Thomas, Company B; died.

Private Luzerue G. Brooks, Company C.

Private Isaac Hogaboom, Company C; discharged at expiration of service.

Private Benjamin J. Tuttle, Company D; discharged for disability.

Private John H. Knevils, Company E; mustered-out.

Private Richard H. Darling, Company E; mustered-out.

Private Charles W. Ferguson, Company E; mustered-out.

Private Charles Hate, Company E; mustered-out.

Private David Hate, Company E; mustered-out.

Private John Knowlan, Company E; mustered-out.

Private Austin Mereness, Company E; mustered-out.

Private Jesse Roberts, Company E; mustered-out.

Private Henry Roach, Company E; mustered-out.

Private Thomas Williamson, Company E; mustered-out; died of consumption, 1876.

Private W. H. Harrington, Company E; mustered-out.

Private Daniel Moyer, Company E; mustered-out.

TWELFTH INFANTRY.

Private Caleb I. Brown, Company A; mustered-out.

Private John H. Hunt, Company A; mustered-out.

Private William S. Dota, Company A; mustered-out.

Private Andrew Ularich, Company E; killed at Duvall's Bluff, Arkansas.

Private Charles A. Salyer, Company E; mustered-out.

Private Charles A. Whaley, Company E; mustered-out.

Private James S. Folett, Company F; mustered-out.

Private DeWitt S. C. Church, Company F; mustered-out.

Private John Shawl, Company F; mustered-out.

Private Melvin Shawl, Company F; mustered-out.

Private Alfred B. Sweet, Company F; mustered-out.

Private Royal Mason, Company F; died at Little Rock.

Private Isaac H. Fuller, Company H; died at Little Rock.

Private George W. Sarno, Company H; mustered-out.

Private Bruce Knapp, Company I; discharged for disability.

Private Chauncey Osborne, Company K; died at Duvall's Bluff, Ark.

Private Allen P. Jordan, Company K; mustered-out.

Private John R. Blackmer, Company K; discharged for disability.

Private Henry Kemberling, Company K; mustered-out.

THIRTEENTH INFANTRY.

Private John McEnterfer, Company A; mustered-out.

Private William Olmstead, Company D; mustered-out.

Private Alfred Breninger, Company E; mustered-out.

Private Allen E. Wheeler, Company G; mustered-out.

Private Augustus Day, Company I; died on division train, Ga.

Private Robert N. Breninger, Company E; mustered-out.

FIFTEENTH INFANTRY.

Private William Chadwick, Company A; mustered-out.

Private W. B. Pierson, Company A; mustered-out.

SIXTEENTH INFANTRY.

Private John Dickson, Company C; mustered-out.

NINETEENTH INFANTRY.

Private Francis C. Doty, Company C; mustered-out.

First Lieutenant Frank D. Baldwin, Company D; captain, January 22, 1864; lieutenant-colonel, and mustered-out.

Sergeant Charles W. Mandeville, Company D; died in action at Dallas' woods.

Sergeant James Harris, Company D; mustered-out; died since.

Private John B. McLeod, Company D; died at Nashville, March 8, 1863.

Private Samuel Keasey, Company D; mustered-out.

Private Thomas E. Bouner, Company D; mustered-out.

Musician Charles M. Chittenden, Company D; discharged for disability.

Musician Charles Whiting, Company D; died at Nashville, May 9, 1863.

Private Timothy Bailey, Company D; discharged.

Private Leman W. Bristol, Company D; mustered-out.

Private Samuel Curtis, Company D; mustered-out.

Private Shepherd Curtis, Company D; mustered-out.

Private Charles H. Caswell, Company D; mustered-out.

Private George Hate, Company D; mustered-out.

Private David D. Knapp, Company D; mustered-out.

Private John Lawler, Company D; veteran reserve corps.

Private Jacob Lintz, Company D; mustered-out.

Private William Melvin, Company D; discharged.

Private John Melvin, Company D; mustered-out.

Private Peter Moyer, Company D; died at Gravel Pit, Ohio, October 5, 1862.

Private Benoni Simons, Company D; discharged for disability.

Private Benjamin F. Thomas, Company D; mustered-out.

Private Aaron Thomas, Company D; mustered-out.

Private C. F. Thomas, Company D; mustered-out.

Private William J. Thomas, Company D; mustered-out.

Private George D. Ward, Company D; mustered-out.

Private Martin L. Ward, Company D; mustered-out.

Private Marvin C. Hutchins, Company D; mustered-out.

Private Obadiah M. Ward, Company D; died at Lexington, Ky.

Private Almon Woodworth, Company D; mustered-out.

Private Eben Odell, Company D; mustered-out.

Private Joseph Shival, Company D; mustered-out.

Private John Draper, Company D; mustered-out.

Private Hiram Ray, Company D; discharged.

MRS JACOB LINTZ.

JACOB LINTZ.

RESIDENCE OF JACOB LINTZ, CONSTANTINE TP. ST. JOSEPH CO. MICH.

Private Austin Mereness, Company E; mustered-out.
Private Matthias Hullen, Company E; mustered-out.
Private Daniel Christman, Company F; died at Chattanooga.
Private Marion Braden, Company F; mustered-out.
Private Perry Holmes, Company C; mustered-out.

TWENTY-FIFTH INFANTRY.

Private W. W. Olmstead, Company D.
Private Jasper N. Shaw, Company D.
Private Jacob Appleman, Company G; mustered-out.

TWENTY-EIGHTH INFANTRY.

Private George Davis, Company I; mustered-out.

FIRST MECHANICS AND ENGINEERS.

Private Asa Sheldon, Company B; discharged at expiration of service.

FIRST CAVALRY.

Private Henry Crosby, Company E; died of wounds at Washington.
Private George Marlott, Company M; died at Philadelphia, July 9, 1864.
Private Albert Cobb, Company M; mustered-out.
Private Manasses Haslin, Company H; mustered-out.
Private Charles Thatcher, Company L; missing at Beaver Dam, Va.

THIRD CAVALRY.

Private James W. Kent, Company A; mustered-out.

FOURTH CAVALRY.

Private Ezra Thomas; died at Nashville, May, 1864.

EIGHTH CAVALRY.

Private Henry S. Brown, Company F; died in Andersonville prison.

NINTH CAVALRY.

Private T. Leinbach, Company E; discharged for disability.
Private Hilton Springstedt, Company E; mustered-out.

FIRST LIGHT ARTILLERY.

Private Adelbert Chittenden, Battery D; mustered-out.
Private William Draper, Battery D; mustered-out.
Private Spencer King, Battery D; mustered-out.
Wagoner Lyman Irwin, Battery F; mustered-out.
Private Andrew Almy, Battery F; re-enlisted and mustered-out.
Private Samuel Brandall, Battery F; re-enlisted and mustered-out.
Private James Cook, Battery F; re-enlisted and mustered-out.
Private Justus Miller, Battery F; re-enlisted and mustered-out.
Private Frederick Smith, Battery F; re-enlisted and mustered-out.
Private Andrew Weatherwax, Battery F; mustered-out.
Corporal Jonathan G. Waltham, Battery G; discharged.

Corporal Elisha Moyer, Battery G; discharged, and enlisted in regular service.
Corporal James S. Briggs, Battery G; mustered-out.
Private Jacob R. Ackerman, Battery G; transferred to regular army.
Private Thomas M. Curtis, Battery G; discharged for disability.
Private Michael Loughran, Battery G; discharged for disability.
Private Henry L. Beecher, Battery F; discharged for disability.
Private Martin G. Stowell, Battery L; mustered-out.
Private Jacob Renz, 5th United States Artillery.

FIRST MICHIGAN SHARP-SHOOTERS.

Benjamin Huskell, Company D; mustered-out.
Abner Thurber, Company G; mustered-out.

ONE HUNDRED AND SECOND UNITED STATES COLORED TROOPS.

Private Ashberry Ash, Company B; mustered-out.
Private Calvin M. Copley, Company B; mustered-out.
Private Hamilton Saunders, Company B; mustered-out.
Private Thomas Mitchell, Company B; mustered-out.
Private Robert Smith, Company F; mustered-out.
Private Oliver Griffin, Company B; mustered-out.
Private George H. Smith, Company F; mustered-out.
Private Elijah Saunders, Company H; mustered-out.
Private Achilles McMullen, Company K; mustered-out.
Private William Silas Copley, Company K; mustered-out.

PROVOST GUARD.

Urias Shellenbarger; died April 21, 1863.
James S. Briggs; mustered-out.
Joseph Gepford; mustered-out.
Martin Hayden; mustered-out.
George W. Robinson; mustered-out.
Frank Wertz; mustered-out.

SIXTY-SIXTH ILLINOIS VOLUNTEER INFANTRY.

Private Francis McKinley, Company D; mustered-out.
Private Leander Sanborn, Company D; mustered-out.

We hereby tender our acknowledgments for information and assistance given us in compiling the history of Constantine, to Hon. Franklin Wells, Thomas C. Langley, Esq., Hon. H. H. Riley, John Hamilton, Esq., John Hull, Esq., A. B. George, Esq., Joseph Bonebright, Esq., J. P. Gladding, Esq., Thomas Calam, postmaster, A. Hagenbuch, Esq., Rev. J. M. Beardslee, Prof. S. B. Kingsbury, Deacon J. G. Cathcart, Isaac Benham, Henry Gibler, Mrs. Barbara Bonebright.

# BIOGRAPHICAL SKETCHES.

## JACOB LINTZ

was born in Griesbach, Alsace, France, October 26, 1812. He received a good education in the German language. His chief occupation in the land of his birth was brewing. In the spring of 1834 he emigrated to America, and, after a brief stay in New York, where he followed the coopering business, he came to Constantine, where he engaged in any business that presented itself, until the fall of the year, when he accepted an engagement with Jonas Hartman, in his brewery at Mottville. He remained here until Mr. Hartman sold to Joseph Knorr, who, being comparatively unacquainted with the business, took Mr. Lintz into partnership with him, and found that his practical experience compensated for his lack of capital.

On the 26th of September, 1843, he married Christiana Mallow, who was also born in Griesbach, May 26, 1820. They had four children, of whom all survive except Sarah Alice, who died when but two years old, September 2, 1856. In 1845 Mr. Lintz's residence, together with all his personal property was destroyed by fire, but, by perseverance and energy, he was enabled within two years of the accident, to erect his present commodi-

16

ous house, an illustration of which, with its surrounding, can be seen on another page in this work.

When he first arrived at his new home in the west, his possessions consisted of his wearing apparel, and two five-franc pieces. By hard work and sound practical economy, he has become possessed of four hundred and fifty-three and a half acres of land, all in one body. Besides farming, he has been engaged in brewing; both enterprises having been successful.

Mr. Lintz has always been a Democrat, but has never been induced to accept any office. He was brought up under the teachings of the Lutheran church, of which his wife is a devoted member. He is one of the pioneers of Constantine, and has seen the place grow from a mere straggling settlement to a populous and wealthy township, himself materially assisting in its development.

He is now, at the age of three and a half score years, enjoying good health, and all the comforts which an industrious and moral life is sure to bring. He bears an admirable reputation for good judgment and probity, and is generally looked upon as an upright and substantial citizen.

MR JOHN G. CATHCART.

MRS. JOHN G. CATHCART.

## JOHN G. CATHCART.

John Gilford Cathcart was born in Watsontown (formerly called Tobey township, Northumberland county, Pennsylvania, on the first day of January, 1799. He is a son of John and Mary Cathcart, who passed away to their final rest many years ago. His father and grandfather were both Revolutionary soldiers in the stirring times of '76, and gave to their children, little else than a sterling patriotism and sound religious views. Mr. Cathcart, on the first day of May, 1823, married Jane Hutchinson Welch, who was born in the same township, December 5 of the same year—1799—and with whom he lived most happily over forty-six years, she having died December 1, 1869. The fruits of this marriage were: James W., John G., Jr., Mary A., Joseph W., Sarah J., Martha J. and Caroline H., all of whom are now sleeping beside their mother in the White Pigeon cemetery, except Martha, now the wife of John Woodward, of Plymouth, Indiana, and Mary, now the wife of William D. Anderson, of Constantine.

In the spring of 1841 Mr. Cathcart came to White Pigeon prairie, to look for a location; and finding one that suited him, purchased it of Judge C. B. Fitch, in the southeastern corner of the present limits of Constantine township. He returned to Pennsylvania for his family, with whom he came to St. Joseph county and settled on his purchase, where he remained until 1860, at which time he sold the land (which he had brought from a wild, uncultivated tract to a well-tilled and productive farm, by his own efforts and those of his children and partner) and removed to the village of Constantine, where he has ever since resided. He also bought other lands in Constantine township, of the United States, the same fall he came in with his family. In

1835 he was elected supervisor of the township of White Pigeon, then comprising the present township of White Pigeon, Florence, Constantine and Mottville, and was re-elected in the year 1836. In the spring of 1839 he was also elected one of the three county commissioners, who took the place of the board of supervisors, and drew the two years' term; at the end of which the office was abolished, the supervisors coming in again. In the fall of 1839 he was elected to represent the county in the lower house of the General Assembly of the State.

In politics Mr. Cathcart is, and has always been, a Democrat. His religious views are in consonance with those of the Presbyterian faith, of which church he has been a consistent and zealous member for fifty-four years. He was a member of the Presbyterian church at White Pigeon, from his first coming to the county until 1840, since which time he has been a deacon in the church of that denomination in Constantine.

He was again married on the 19th of September, 1871, to Sarah J. Baldy, who died September 9, 1875. By her no children were born to him, and she now rests in the cemetery of White Pigeon, whither this old farmer of St. Joseph county of forty-six years, is looking serenely and calmly—to be gathered by and by, like a sheaf of corn fully ripe, beside the loved ones of his own home, who have gone before him.

Mrs. Cathcart, the former wife of Deacon Cathcart, united with the Presbyterian church in Pennsylvania in 1822, her husband uniting therewith the year following.

## NORMAN HARVEY.

## GEORGE BLANSHARD.

George Blanshard was born at Barlow, in the parish of Brayton, Yorkshire, England, on the 4th day of August, 1790. In early life he followed agricultural pursuits, his father having been a respectable English yeoman. On May 8, 1820, he married Mary Gale, daughter of Rev. Henry Gale, D.D., vicar of the parish of Escrick, near the city of York. This union was blessed with issue, three sons and one daughter, namely:

JOHN, born February 8, 1821.

ELIZABETH, born December 7, 1823.

CONYERS, born July 21, 1824; and

HENRY GALE, born December 2, 1828.

These were all born in England, and accompanied their father to America, whither he emigrated in the year 1836. He first temporarily settled on the east end of Pigeon prairie, in Constantine township, and afterwards permanently, on the west end of the prairie in the same township. Here he remained for almost fifteen years, when he removed to the village of Constantine, where he continued to reside until his death, which occurred suddenly on the 17th day of February, 1876.

Mr. Blanshard is described by those who knew him well, as an honest, quiet and unobtrusive gentleman, who always discharged, with unfaltering fidelity, every obligation he incurred. By careful investment of his savings and great frugality he accumulated considerable fortune, which at his death, amounted to eighteen thousand dollars, in money and securities. He was sorely afflicted with deafness, and in consequence, possessed some peculiar characteristics, which to strangers oftentimes assumed the aspect of eccentricities. To his family he was kind and indulgent; and though having a strong preference for solitude, yet his house was ever open to his friends.

This sketch, with the accompanying portrait of the deceased, was inserted in our work by Mrs. Elizabeth Miller, wife of Stephen P. Miller, of Mottville township, and only daughter of the late George Blanshard.

Among the foremost men of Constantine, Norman Harvey stood, for a generation. Coming to the township in 1833, when it was an unbroken wilderness, he lived to see it change to a region of finely-cultivated farms, and where, when he first came, a few straggling log-houses played hide-and-seek amidst the woods, he helped largely to build a thriving, bustling village. Mr. Harvey was born in Rupert, Bennington county, Vermont, June 23, 1807. His father (Ephraim Harvey) was a farmer, and a native of the same State. His mother was Pamelia Harwood (of a well-known Vermont family), who still survives, and is now residing in Constantine, in the ninety-fourth year of her age. Mr. Harvey's opportunities for an education were something more than common-school privileges, he having attended the academy at Salem, New York; and in his younger days taught school during the winter months of several years. In 1828 he was united in marriage to Rhoda, daughter of Seth and Rhoda Moore, of Rupert, and, in 1833, with his wife and two children, removed to St. Joseph county, Michigan, where he began the life of a pioneer, and cleared up a farm of four hundred acres, about two and a half miles north of Constantine, on which he resided for twenty-two years. His political sentiments were those of the Whig and Republican parties, and though not an office-seeker, he filled acceptably to the people the positions of supervisor, justice of the peace and other minor offices, for several years. Probably there were but few who felt more interested in the settlement and prosperity of the county than himself. He removed to Constantine village, in 1855, where he was actively engaged in business of various kinds,—such as farming, milling, manufacturing, real-estate, and mercantile operations. He was also one of the founders of the First National Bank of Constantine, of which he was a director until the time of his death, which occurred April 17, 1866.

Mr. Harvey united with the Congregational church at Rupert, Vermont, and after his removal to Michigan, was an attendant and supporter of the Reformed church of Constantine.

The children of Mr. and Mrs. Harvey were as follows: Charles Merritt, Seth Moore, Lyman Reuel, Delia Salome, William Sheldon, Norman Henry, Rhoda Pamelia, Daniel Martin, Seth Moore, James Mark, William Wallace, and Cephas, of whom four sons and a daughter survive,—Norman Henry, Daniel Martin, James Mark, William Wallace, and Delia Salome (now Mrs. George I. Crossette).

Mr. Harvey was emphatically domestic in his habits, and devotedly attached to his family. His genial disposition secured him a large circle of friends, while his readiness to assist those less favored by fortune than himself, is well known.

## HON. EDWIN W. KEIGHTLEY.

Edwin William Keightley was born in the township of Van Buren, county of La Grange, and State of Indiana, on the 7th day of August, 1843. His parents, Peter L. and Elizabeth (Winter) Keightley, emigrated from Lincolnshire, England; the former in the year 1831, and the latter in 1828, and in 1836, soon after they were married, located on the farm in Van Buren township where the subject of this sketch was born, and where they have since resided.

Edwin received the rudiments of a common-school education in the district where his parents still reside, from whence he entered the Valparaiso Collegiate Institute, and from thence entered the law department of the University of Michigan at Ann Arbor; graduating therefrom in March, 1865, at the age of twenty-one years.

On April 24, following, he opened a law-office in White Pigeon, St. Joseph county, Michigan, where he remained for two years, laying the foundation of an excellent future practice. During his residence in White Pigeon he interspersed his legal duties with those of the editorial function, ably conducting for two years the publication of the White Pigeon *Republican*, a staunch advocate of Republican views and policy.

In 1867 he removed to Constantine, and entered into a law partnership with Judge S. C. Coffinberry, which terminated in 1869, mutually and pleasantly. At the close of this partnership Mr. Keightly opened an office in Constantine for the prosecution of his increasing practice, and at the election of 1872 the people called him to the position of prosecuting-attorney for the county of St. Joseph, which position he filled with signal ability until January 21, 1874, when he was appointed by Governor Bagley, judge of the fifteenth judicial circuit, comprising the counties of St. Joseph and Branch, to fill the vacancy occasioned by the resignation of Hon. R. W. Melendy. In the spring of 1875 both political parties—Republican and Democratic—united in the nomination of Judge Keightley, and elected him to the same honorable position for a full constitutional term of six years.

In the campaign of 1876, the Republican party in the fourth congressional district of Michigan made the Judge their candidate for the lower house of Congress, nominating him on the first formal ballot by a handsome majority in the convention, and afterwards making it unanimous. The wisdom of their choice was clear by the gratifying majority of two thousand three hundred and eighty-six votes the Judge received in the district, over the vote for the candidate of the combined Democratic and Greenback parties.

On the 14th day of July, 1868, Judge Keightley married Mary Mitchell, an estimable lady, and the daughter of Thomas Mitchell, a long-time resident of Constantine, and closely identified with its manufacturing and material interests.

The fruits of this union have been two bright and active children, a daughter, who died at the age of little more than a year, and a son, George, now three years old.

Judge Keightley has been an ardent Republican in politics, and his speeches in the canvass of 1876 were of no small moment in working up the splendid majority he himself, and the general State and National ticket received throughout the fourth district.

The estimation in which Judge Keightley is held, by the people where he is best known, is shown by their calling him to the various positions above named; and the following resolution, passed by the bar of the fifteenth circuit, at Coldwater, January 22, 1877, will tell how kindly the legal fraternity bear him in memory:

"Resolved, That the honesty, ability and impartiality with which Judge Keightley has uniformly performed the difficult and perplexing duties devolving upon him as circuit judge, reflect the highest honor upon himself, and merit our entire confidence and hearty approbation."

Judge Keightley's congressional term will commence March 4, 1877.

## HEMAN HARWOOD

Heman Harwood was born in Delaware county, New York, June 21, 1810. Emigrated to Ontario county, New York, in company with his parents in 1822. He had fair common-school advantages for those days. In the spring of 1831 he emigrated to Constantine, St. Joseph county, Michigan, and in the following year served in the Black Hawk war. In the summer of 1835 he returned to Ontario county, New York, and in the month of September, 1835, he was married to Miss Rebecca Fisher, of Gorham, Ontario county, New York, and the following spring (1836) returned to Constantine and settled on Broad street.

His family consists of his wife and three sons, all of whom are good, respectable citizens. Mr. Harwood's occupation has been principally farming, although at present he is somewhat occupied with one of his sons in the milling business. In politics, he is found among the Republicans, and has been a worthy and efficient member of the Methodist Episcopal church, for more than forty years. The portraits of himself and wife may be found in another part of this work.

# FLORENCE.

If the eye of man ever looked upon nature in more beautiful mood and aspect than she exhibited to the first settlers in the territory now included in the township of Florence, it hath not been revealed to the historian, to what portion of the earth he must go, to find the record of such vision. The original burr-oak plains, which comprised the greater portion of the area of the township, were in the summer, indescribably lovely. Level, and devoid of undergrowth, the plains covered with a sparse growth of old oaks, the grasses most luxurant, the flowers most brilliant and fragrant—the scene was enchanting beyond the present conception of those whose eyes never rested upon the charming landscape.

Neal McGaffey, Esq., who was the member of the lower house of the General Assembly, in 1837, from St. Joseph county, was so delighted with the pleasing prospect afforded by a drive in the elegant park, that he gave the most appropriate name then to be found, to the new township, and named it after the queen of the sea, Florence.

Even now, when the old oaks have given way before the axe of the pioneer, and the flowers have disappeared before the waving cereals, one gets glimpses of the old-time beauty and loveliness, with which nature arrayed herself in the days of the pioneer, when the wild deer in herds fed upon the plains, and wild turkies strutted and called to their broods, when the partridges drummed in their coverts, and the wild bees stored the sweets of thousands of flowers, of varied hue and beauty.

The soil is a rich sandy loam, free from stone, and highly productive; adapted to the successful culture of the cereals, corn, mint and fruit. Its drainage is effected by the Fawn river, the only stream within the limits of the township, which rises to the dignity of a river, and which enters the same on the south line of the southeast quarter of section twenty-seven, and runs north and northwest, passing out near the southwest quarter of section nineteen. A little creek rises near the west line of the southwest quarter of section twelve, and meanders southward, losing itself in the Fawn, near the west line of the northwest quarter of section twenty-seven. Klinger's lake lies partly on sections thirty-five and thirty-six, and partly on adjoining sections in White Pigeon township.

THE PRESENT AREA

of the township comprises about twenty-two thousand five hundred acres; three full sections (thirty-four, thirty-five and thirty-six) being set off to White Pigeon, by reason of a large and impassable marsh lying between the south-

HEMAN HARWOOD      CONSTANTINE, ST JOSEPH CO. MICH      MRS HEMAN HARWOOD

HALSEY CASKEY.             EDMUND BEAM.

MOTTVILLE.             FLOWERFIELD

east corner of the township and the balance of the township, compelling a detour nearly to White Pigeon village, by any one desiring to go to the centre of Florence from those sections. The original prairie formerly included in the township boundaries, was about twelve hundred acres.

#### THE ENTRIES OF PUBLIC LANDS

were first made in the township, in the year 1829, seventeen being made in that year, and ten in the year following. The first three entries were as follows: the southeast quarter of section thirty-two, by John Martin, of Monroe county, Michigan, August 20; the east half of the southwest quarter of section thirty-two, by John Croy, of Marion county, Ohio, August 24; the west half of the southwest quarter of section thirty-two, by Leonard Cutler, September 7. In 1876 there were twenty-one thousand four hundred and nine acres assessed in the township for taxation, valued by Norman Roys, the supervisor of the township, at three hundred and seventy thousand and sixty-five dollars; about one-third, or one-quarter, of its real value. The farms, in 1874, averaged one hundred and twenty-seven acres each.

#### EARLY SETTLERS.

David Crawford, and a man by the name of Martin, came from Monroe, Michigan, and took up a permanent settlement some time in the spring of 1829.

In October of the same year, Alvin Calhoon came in with his wife and one child, and settled on section thirty-two. Jeremiah Lawrence took up a transient residence in Newville, then a small settlement located two miles east of White Pigeon, in 1829, and removed to Florence in 1830, where he afterwards resided for many years.

In 1832 Norman Roys settled on his present farm, on sections five and six, where he has remained for forty-five years. John Howard came into the township in the spring of 1832, and settled with his family on section six. He lived with his wife fifty-seven years, and died in 1875, at the age of ninety-three years.

Elisha Dimick arrived in 1833, and took up his permanent residence on section seven. He was also accompanied by his family.

George Pashby, Sr., with his wife and two children, first settled on section twenty, in 1834, and subsequently moved to the farm now occupied by his son, George Pashby, Jr.

John Hagerman settled on the farm now occupied by his son, William Hagerman, on section eighteen, in 1836.

Among other early settlers were William H. Roys, John Peek, William Geible (now of Constantine), the Stears family, Giles Thompson, John Hull, Oliver P. Arnold and others. Henry Levison is a heavy farmer, owning seven hundred and seventy-four acres, six hundred of which lies in a body.

#### THE FIRST WHEAT SOWN

in the township was by David Crawford, in the fall of 1829; Alvin Calhoon, and Jeremiah Lawrence, each sowed twenty acres the following year.

#### THE FIRST CORN

was planted by the same parties in the spring of 1830.

#### THE FIRST ORCHARD

was planted by John Coats on the southwest quarter of section thirty-one, in the spring of 1831.

#### THE FIRST LOG HOUSE

erected within the present limits of Florence township, was by David Crawford, on Pigeon prairie, in the spring of 1829. It was similar, in general, to all the primitive habitations of the pioneers.

#### THE FIRST FRAME HOUSE.

As to who erected the first frame house, considerable doubt exists; we are of the opinion, from what information we were able to glean on the subject, that the frame of the present residence of Norman Roys, was among the first regular frame erected. John Peek had a small wooden structure erected by one A. C. Fisher, who is said to have been the

#### FIRST CARPENTER

who made his home in the township. The house was put up between sunrise and sunset, one fine day in the year 1837.

#### THE FIRST BRICK HOUSE

in the township, was the one erected by Stockton Anderson in the year 1845. It stood on the farm now owned by Moses Walters, on section seventeen.

#### THE FIRST TAVERN

was kept in the log house of Elisha Dimick as early as 1833, on the homestead farm. He kept it until almost 1840. William Telfer, with his father and sister, located on the Centreville road, and kept a hotel known as "Providence Green."

#### THE FIRST BLACKSMITH

in the township was John Peek, who erected a smithy in 1836. The shop consisted of a board building, and stood a little north of the present residence of David Boyer.

#### THE FIRST PHYSICIAN

who practiced in the township was Hubbel Loomis, M. D., of White Pigeon, and his partner, Dr. Elliott, who still practices, being one of the oldest practitioners in the county.

#### THE FIRST POST-OFFICE

established in Florence township was kept at the tavern of Lyman Bean, in 1840; it was, on the completion of the Kalamazoo division of the Lake Shore and Michigan Southern railroad, removed to Florence station, where it has since been kept by John Ruggles. Bean drove into the county the entire distance from Maine, with four horses, in 1834.

#### PEPPERMINT STILLS.

For many years the manufacture of peppermint has been a leading enterprise of Florence township. The first distillery erected in the township, was by Reuben and Otis Matthews in 1837. In the spring of that year they procured of Calvin Sawyer, who had just arrived from Ohio, a few roots, which they planted on the farm now owned by Joseph Brown.

They commenced distilling early in the year 1838. This was the nucleus around which subsequently developed a great and lucrative business.

In 1876 the entire product of the township amounted to four thousand pounds of oil; to make which, required the yield of almost three hundred acres.

Among the heaviest operators are William H. Roys, William Hagerman, George and Frank Roys.

#### BURYING-GROUNDS.

The first regularly used burying-ground in Florence township, was that now adjoining the Methodist Church, which was first used for the interment of Rev. Edward E. Adams, October 31, 1836. Mr. Adams was a local preacher of the Methodist Episcopal persuasion. Among the early settlers buried in it were, Mrs. Minerva Wilson (daughter of Rev. Adams), December 9, 1838; Rebecca Thompson, October 28, 1839; Jeremiah Lawrence, October 28, 1840.

There was another burying-ground located on the farm of John Peek, and first used as early in 1841 for the interment of Elsie Peek, daughter of the donor of the land. It is situated on section fifteen.

#### FIRST MARRIAGE.

This question, not being definitely answered by any of the old pioneers now residing in the township, was referred to Mrs. Altha Lawrence (widow of Jeremiah Lawrence, one of the earliest settlers of Florence), who is now residing with a daughter at Ypsilanti, from whom we received the following reply:

"My first recollection of a wedding in Florence township is of one which occurred in a log school-house, as there were no churches then. The parties were John Phelps, and Leafy Wilder; and the ceremony was performed by Rev. Leonard B. Gurley. This was about the year 1831."

#### FIRST BIRTH.

The first birth in the township, was that of Wolcott H. Lawrence, fourth son of Jeremiah and Altha Lawrence, who was born November 27, 1830.

#### THE FIRST DEATH

was that of an Englishman by the name of Burnham, who came in the early part of 1831, and died during that year.

#### FIRST SCHOOL-HOUSE.

The first school-house erected in the township, was a log structure which stood near the present school-house belonging to district No. 1, and was built in 1836, and known as the Roys' school-house. A frame house was built about the same time on the prairie in what is now district No. 2. Among the early pupils who attended the former, were the Peeks, Dimicks, Lawrences, Calhoons, Loomises, Fitches, and the son and daughter of George Pashby, Sr. Jeremiah Lawrence was the first director, who procured Parmelia Whited as teacher.

The above-mentioned houses were both erected while Florence yet constituted a part of the original township of White Pigeon. The former was designated district No. 11, under the old organization.

On the 17th day of October, 1837, a meeting of "the board of school directors for the township of Florence, town seven south, range eleven west," was held, at which it was

"*Ordered*, that a school district be laid off, containing the west half of section number four, and sections five, six, seven and eight, to be known as district No. 1.

"*Ordered* further, that sections fourteen, fifteen, sixteen, and the east half of section seventeen, and the northeast quarter of section twenty, the north half of section twenty-one, the north half of section twenty-two, and the northwest quarter of section twenty-three, be known as district No. 2.

"*Ordered* further, that sections twenty-eight, twenty-nine, thirty, thirty-one, thirty-two and thirty-three, be known as district No. 3.

"*Ordered*, that the board adjourn the meeting.

"Signed: Giles Thompson, Mathew Rowan, Norman Roys, school inspectors. Florence, October 17, 1837."

The following is from the report of the school inspectors, dated October 18, 1842, and shows the number of scholars in each district organized as above, with the number, also, of district No. 4, which was formed in 1840:

District No. 1, whole number of scholars between five and seventeen years, thirty-nine; district No. 2, whole number of scholars between five and seventeen years, fifty-eight; district No. 3, whole number of scholars between five and seventeen years, forty-three; district No. 4, whole number of scholars between five and seventeen years, thirty-two,—making a total of one hundred and seventy-two scholars.

The amount received from the superintendent of public instruction for the year 1841 was forty-eight dollars and two cents.

In 1876 there were seven schools taught in the township in as many school-houses, four of the latter being built of brick and three of wood, and valued at seventy-five hundred dollars. The houses afford three hundred and sixty-six sittings, and there were three hundred and forty-three children in the township of the requisite school-age, three hundred and thirty of whom attended the schools, which were in session an average of eight months during the year ending September 1. There are two hundred and thirty-six books in the district libraries. Seven male teachers were employed, and paid one thousand one hundred and forty dollars for their services, and nine female teachers received three hundred and fifty-four dollars and eighty cents for their work. The total expenditures for the year were two thousand five hundred and ninety-one dollars and eighty-five cents.

### RELIGIOUS.

The first religious service, according to the rites of the Methodist Episcopal church, was at a class-meeting, held in 1834. The first class-leader was Calvin Calhoon. Among the early members were Jeremiah Lawrence, Benjamin Ball and wife, Giles Thompson, Hiram Bidwell, Alvin Calhoon, and their wives. The meetings were held in the dwelling-house of Benjamin Ball until 1835, when the school-house was erected on the site of the present school-house in district No. 2, in which the meetings were subsequently carried on, until the erection of the brick school-house, in which they conducted their religious services until the erection of the present church-edifice in 1868. The first minister who preached in the school-house was the Rev. Erastus Kellogg, who was also the original pastor in the dwelling-house meetings. The regularly installed pastors who have officiated since the building of the church, were: Reverends H. H. Parker, J. N. Dayton, —— Dunton, L. George (to fill vacancy caused by the sickness of Rev. Dunton), L. M. Edmunds, H. Hall, and the present incumbent, Rev. G. D. Lee. The church-edifice was dedicated by Rev. H. M. Joy, of Kalamazoo. The present officers are Absalom Roberts, Alvin Calhoon, George Pashby, 2nd, John Pashby, Jacob Moony, Robinson Pashby and Markus F. Bailey, trustees; William Pashby and William B. Stathers, stewards. The present membership is sixty-three; members in the Sunday-school, fifty; superintendent, Markus F. Bailey.

### THE REFORMED CHURCH

of Florence was organized in 1868 by Rev. William Weigand. The first elders were Samuel Moyer and B. N. Shafer, for two years; deacons, B. F. Rengler and George Coonfer, for the same period. The church organization laid passive, having no pastor for almost two years. Then, in 1874, the Rev. E. R. Willard, of Tiffin, Ohio, was installed pastor. The present elders are Samuel Moyer and George Rengler; deacons, B. F. Rengler and Allen Moyer. The present church-edifice, a fine brick structure, was erected in

1876, and dedicated on the 5th of November, of the same year. It cost about three thousand five hundred dollars, which is all paid. The building committee was composed of Samuel Haas, B. F. Rengler and James S. Richards. The present membership is forty; Sunday-school members, sixty, under the superintendence of the pastor.

### THE CIVIL ORGANIZATION.

Florence—which is known on the maps of the surveys of public lands of the United States as township seven, south of range eleven west—originally formed an integral part of the township of White Pigeon, and remained a portion thereof, until 1837, when it was erected into a separate and independent township.

The first meeting held in Florence township, convened at the house of Giles Thompson, in pursuance of the act regulating township meetings, whereat John Howard was appointed moderator; Matthew Rowen, clerk; Edward E. Adams, Jeremiah Lawrence and Allen Calhoon, judges of the election then to be held; who were qualified according to law, and whereat Giles Thompson was elected supervisor of Florence township; John Howard, Giles Thompson, Matthew Rowen and Jeremiah Lawrence, justices of the peace; John Yauney, clerk; Matthew Rowen, Orin F. Howard and George T. Gray, assessors; Solomon Wallace, collector; Alvin Calhoon, M. G. Craw and Solomon Wallace, commissioners of highways; Edward E. Adams and Albert H. Strong, directors of the poor; Norman Roys, Matthew Rowen and Giles Thompson, inspectors of schools. All these were elected by ballot. The following were elected *viva voce*: John Yauney and Smith Hunt, fence viewers, and the same persons were also chosen pound masters. On motion of Mr. Adams it was voted that twelve overseers of highways be appointed,—whereat Samuel S. Hart, John Peck, John Jackson, Orin E. Craw, John Yauney, David Cole, Giles Thompson, Joseph Garton, George I. Gray, William Garnet, Gardner Pitts and Jeremiah Lawrence were accordingly appointed; and it was further voted that a fence shall be five feet high and well filled; and further, no seed-horse, two years old, shall be suffered to run at large under penalty of ten dollars; and further, that two dollars be paid for every wolf-scalp taken within the limits of the township; and further, that fifty dollars be raised for the support of the township paupers; and further, that our supervisor vote against money to erect public buildings; and be it further enacted that the first township meeting be held in the school-house in district No. 11, in the township of Florence.

We do hereby certify that the above is a correct record of the township meeting, and that the above officers were duly elected according to law.

JOHN HOWARD, Moderator.
EDWARD E. ADAMS,  ⎫
JEREMIAH LAWRENCE,  ⎬ Judges.
ALVIN CALHOON,  ⎭

### THE PRINCIPAL TOWNSHIP OFFICERS,

from 1837 to 1876, have been: Supervisors—Giles Thompson, 1837; Nelson Church and William Laird, four years; George G. De Puy, three years; Thomas Stears, Jr., four years; John W. Harrison and Norman Roys, from 1857 to 1877, or twenty consecutive years, and six years previously.

Clerks—Matthew Rowen, 1837; A. H. Strong, two years; Nathan Osborn, two years; Giles Thompson, two years; John Hull, seven years; George G. De Puy and L. O. Howard, three years; Thomas Stears, Jr., and O. P. Arnold, two years; Henry Stears and Joseph Hall, two years; Morris I. Arnold, six years; Thomas Stears, two years; Charles B. Kellogg, two years; Benjamin Rengler (present incumbent) six years.

Justices of the Peace—John Howard and Giles Thompson, 1837–44; Matthew Rowen, Jeremiah Lawrence, John Coats, Nelson Church, Norman Roys, C. G. Waite and George G. Depuy, eight years; Orrin F. Howard, twelve years; Calvin Johnson, H. G. Dockstarter, Marshall G. Craw and David Cole, three years; Lyman Bean, eight years; Jehiel B. Dimmick, twenty-one years; John Putnam, six years; Hiram A. Pitts, twenty years; Thomas Stears, fourteen years, and present incumbent; Reuben Troxell, ten years; George W. Titus and Jacob Shaver, twelve years; Daniel Sparks and William H. Roys, eighteen years, and present incumbent; John H. Gray, Jasper King, John Greensides, R. L. Waters, Ephraim Adams and George E. Roys, six years, and present incumbent; John Stebbins, present incumbent.

### THE FIRST ROAD.

The subjoined is the earliest record now in existence of a road having been surveyed in Florence township:

"Survey of a road beginning at the east line of the township, on the section-line between sections twelve and thirteen, eighteen degrees west

ROBERT McKINLAY.

MRS ROBERT McKINLAY

THE FARM RESIDENCE OF ROBERT McKINLAY, FLEMING TP. ST. JOE CO. MICH.

RESIDENCE OF **NORMAN ROYS.**
TOWNSHIP 74, ST JOSEPH CO. MICH.

NORMAN H. ROYS.

from white-oak tree twenty-seven links; also north seventeen degrees, and west from white-oak tree twenty-seven and a-half links west to road running from White Pigeon to Prairie Round.

| Sections. | | Sections. | | West. | | Chains. |
|---|---|---|---|---|---|---|
| 12 | . | 13 | . | 80° | . | 80 |
| 11 | . | 14 | . | 80° | . | 80 Crossing point of marsh. |
| 10 | . | 15 | . | 80° | . | 80 |
| 9 | . | 16 | . | 80° | . | 80 Crossing Centreville road. |
| 8 | . | 17 | . | 80° | . | 80 |
| 7 | . | 18 | . | 80° | . | 60 |

"Whole length five and three-quarters miles—four hundred and sixty chains.

"JOSEPH J. PRENTICE, Surveyor.
(Signed.)        JOHN JACKSON,
                GARDNER PITTS,
"May 25, 1838.        Highway Commissioners."

### THE CROPS.

The census of 1874 gives the following exhibit of the crop of 1873: There were four thousand two hundred and forty-five acres of wheat harvested, which produced thirty-seven thousand four hundred and two bushels, and two thousand three hundred and five acres, which yielded ninety thousand seven hundred and fifty bushels. There were also produced two thousand two hundred and fifty-six bushels of other grain, seven thousand six hundred and thirty-six bushels potatoes, one thousand one hundred and forty-four tons hay, seven thousand and twenty pounds wool, one hundred and ninety-eight thousand three hundred and eighty pounds pork, forty-three thousand one hundred pounds butter and cheese, and six hundred and fifty barrels cider, while three hundred and fifty-seven acres in orchards, produced eleven thousand eight hundred and eighty-one bushels of apples and cherries, valued at two thousand three hundred and fifty dollars. There were owned in 1874, in the township, four hundred and seventy-nine horses, eight mules, eight oxen, four hundred and fifty-three cows, three hundred and forty-one other cattle, one thousand two hundred and forty-five hogs, and one thousand two hundred and eighty-nine sheep. The clip of 1873 was taken from one thousand five hundred and sixty sheep.

### THE TAX-GATHERER

has had the following rate-bills against the property owned in the township since its organization: In 1837 the assessment for taxation was fixed at one hundred and one thousand eight hundred and forty-seven dollars, and the tax-levy amounted to four hundred and twenty-two dollars for State and county purposes alone. In 1852 the assessment was returned at seventy-four thousand three hundred and forty-six dollars, and the taxes levied amounted to one thousand five hundred and eighty-three dollars and eleven cents for all purposes. In 1860 the assessment was fixed at three hundred and forty-six thousand five hundred and sixty-six dollars, and the taxes aggregated two thousand six hundred and eleven dollars and sixty-three cents. In 1870 the assessment reached almost three-quarters of a million, being placed at seven hundred and thirty-seven thousand three hundred and fifty-two dollars, and the taxes amounted to four thousand three hundred and sixteen dollars and sixty-eight cents. In 1876 the assessment, as equalized by the county board of equalization, was placed at three hundred and seventy-seven thousand eight hundred and twenty-nine dollars on real estate, and fifty-eight thousand five hundred and twenty dollars on personal property,—making a total assessment of four hundred and thirty-six thousand three hundred and forty-nine dollars. On this amount, taxes were levied for State and county purposes, amounting to two thousand two hundred and twenty-nine dollars and eighteen cents, one-half thereof to each object; and two thousand one hundred and thirty dollars and sixty cents for township purposes, including schools,—making the total tax-list four thousand three hundred and fifty-nine dollars and seventy-eight cents.

### POPULATION.

In 1838, there were four hundred and forty inhabitants in Florence, and in 1850 there were seven hundred and thirty-one. In 1860 they had increased to nine hundred and eighty-one, and in 1870 they numbered nine hundred and seventy, of whom four hundred and ninety-one were males, and four hundred and seventy-nine females. In 1874, the State census returned nine hundred and fifteen persons in the township; four hundred and seventy-five males and four hundred and forty females. Of two hundred and forty-seven males over twenty-one years, one hundred and fifty-six of them were of the military age, eighty-six were over forty-five, four were

between seventy-five and ninety years, and one old veteran had passed the ninth decade of his century, and was coming down slowly home. Of two hundred and fifty-five females over eighteen years, one hundred and seventy were under forty years, eighty-one were between that age and seventy-five years, and four were past the three-quarter post of the century. Two hundred and twenty-seven boys had not attained their majority, and one hundred and eighty-five of the girls were "over young to marry yet" without the consent of pater familias. The married men numbered one hundred and eighty-six, and the women one hundred and eighty; the single ones were still nearer matched in numbers, there being fifty-five, and fifty-seven, respectively of each. Six widowed husbands were just one-third the number of the widowed wives.

### THE POLITICAL BAROMETER

has fluctuated somewhat since 1856, as will be seen by an examination of the tally-lists of the presidential elections, which we here give. In 1840 the Whigs polled for "Harrison and hard-cider" forty-nine votes, and the Democrats gave Van Buren, seventy. In 1844 the Whig vote was thirty-eight, the Democratic eighty-three, and the Liberty-men cast eleven votes. In 1848 the Whigs cast fifty-two votes, the Democrats eighty-nine, and the Free-Soilers twelve. In 1852 the Whigs polled fifty-three votes, the Democrats eighty, and the Abolitionists three. In 1856 the Republicans cast one hundred and six ballots, to ninety-three by the Democrats; but in 1860 the two parties tied, on one hundred and sixteen votes. In 1864 the balance was broken, the Democrats polling one hundred and ten votes, to ninety by the Republicans. In 1808 the pendulum had swung to the opposite side of the arc, where it has remained ever since,—the Republican vote that year being one hundred and thirty-one, and the Democratic, one hundred and eleven. In 1872 Grant received one hundred and thirteen votes, Greeley eighty-one, and O'Conor, two. In 1876 Governor Hayes received one hundred and one votes, Governor Tilden ninety-two, and Mr. Cooper thirty-three. This last vote indicates a population in the township of over one thousand.

### THE MILITARY RECORD.

In the rebellion, Florence filled her quotas, whenever called upon by the government, with dispatch and promptitude; and we append the list of such of her soldiers as we have been able to locate in the township. In the general county history will be found a list of such of the soldiers of the county as we were unable to locate by townships, but whose records we were desirous should not be omitted from the history of the county; and so it we refer the reader, as well as to the other township histories of the county, where any missing names of Florence may be found.

SEVENTH INFANTRY.

Private Lemuel Sweezy, Company K; discharged at expiration of service.

TENTH INFANTRY.

Private Isaac Thompson, Company B; mustered-out.

ELEVENTH INFANTRY.

Private Luther W. Straight, Company A; died October 27, 1862.
Private Dwight V. Denio, Company C; re-enlisted and mustered-out.
Private Henry E. Mood, Company C; discharged at expiration of service.
Private James Armstrong, Company G; discharged at expiration of service.
Private Byron A. Williamson, Company E; mustered-out.

NINETEENTH INFANTRY.

Corporal William Lefler, Company D; killed at Altoona, Ga., May 25, 1864.
Private Eli W. Atland, Company D; mustered-out.
Private James Blair, Company D; mustered-out.
Private Marcus Daniels, Company D; mustered-out.
Private Warren Daniels, Company D; mustered-out.
Private Harvey M. Lindsley, Company D; mustered-out.
Private James Thompson, Company D; promoted and mustered-out.
Private George W. Waters, Company D; mustered-out.
Private John Miller, Company K; discharged.

NINTH CAVALRY.

Private William Rusling, Company L; mustered-out.

TENTH CAVALRY.

Private Frank Pitts, Company F; mustered-out.

FIRST LIGHT ARTILLERY.

Corporal Edward L. Armstrong, Battery D; died at Louisville, April 7, 1863.

Private Nelson F. Baird, Battery E; mustered-out.
Private Charles Anthony, Battery F; died at Louisville, March 27, 1862.
Private Philip Lang, Battery II; mustered-out.

FIRST MICHIGAN SHARP-SHOOTERS.

Private George Hollenbeck, Company H; mustered-out.

SIXTY-SIXTH ILLINOIS VOLUNTEER INFANTRY.

Private Gilbert E. Mead, Company D; mustered-out.

We tender our acknowledgments for assistance and information received in the compilation of the history of Florence, to Captain Alvin Calhoon. Norman Roys, Esq., William Roys, George Pashby and John Hull, Esq.

# BIOGRAPHICAL SKETCHES.

MR. ALVIN CALHOON.

MRS. ALVIN CALHOON.

## ALVIN CALHOON,

of Florence township, St. Joseph county, Michigan, was born at Pittsford, Monroe county, New York, September 17, 1802. When four years of age his father removed his family to Frenchtown (now Monroe), Michigan, where they remained until 1812. At the surrender of Hull to the British, consternation and dismay took possession of the frontier settlements, and Mr. Calhoon was compelled to flee with his family at midnight, bareheaded, and without shoes, in order to escape the Indians. They went to Ohio, where they remained for about five years, and then returned to Monroe, Michigan, again. Here they stayed until 1823, when the subject of our sketch, being about twenty years old, returned to his native place and took up his residence on the Ridge road, forty miles from the city of Rochester. On the 6th of September, 1829, he left there for White Pigeon prairie, where he arrived in October following. He settled on section thirty-two of the present township of Florence.

April 22, 1837, he married Eliza L. Hunt, a native of Monroe county, New York, by whom he had nine children, of whom five reached maturity. His elder son, Oscar A., married Alvina Gray, and his elder daughter, Cynthia, married Edmund O. Cromwell. Mrs. Calhoon died December 25, 1841, in the thirty-third year of her age.

On the 30th of March, 1842, Mr. Calhoon married Lois J. Bean, by whom he had eight children,—six of whom, two daughters and four sons, are now

residing in Polk county, Nebraska. The other two (twins) reside at home with their parents.

He has a farm of one hundred and seventy-five acres, of which, all but twenty acres of timber and the same extent of meadow land, is under excellent cultivation.

For forty-six years Mr. Calhoon has been a member of the Methodist Episcopal church, and has frequently held offices in the church government. He has been a bitter anti-mason ever since the mysterious disappearance of Morgan, in 1826. He positively refuses to support any candidate for whatever office he may be seeking, who is a mason; neither will he tolerate them even in religious matters. He is true to his principles in this respect; whether right or not, it is not our province to discuss.

In politics he is Republican, having first been a Whig, voting for John Quincy Adams in 1824. He voted for the Democratic candidate in 1848, and from then, on to 1860, supported the Democratic ticket. In 1860 he voted for Lincoln, and for Grant in 1868 and 1872.

Mr. Calhoon is a man of very positive character, and when once he assumes a stand on any question, he never wavers, but sticks to the principles he advocates through thick and thin. Socially, he is genial and pleasant, a good husband and a fond father, honest and upright in his dealings with his fellow-men,—possessing, in fine, the many attributes of a good citizen.

## JOSEPH JEWETT, of Florence.

JOSEPH JEWETT was born in the town of Dudley, Worcester county, Massachusetts, January 29, 1803, where he lived with his parents till 1828, when he removed to Delhi, Delaware county, New York, when he engaged in the manufacture of woolen goods. In 1830 he purchased a farm, and in the fall of the same year married Miss Mary Farrington, daughter of March Farrington, Esq., of Delhi. In 1835 Mr. Jewett came to the West on a prospecting tour, and after a thorough examination of the country resolved to locate in St. Joseph County, near Mendon, which he did in 1836. He removed to the town of Florence, in the same county, in 1847, where he died July 26, 1876. at the ripe age of seventy-three years. He was of a strong physical frame, and, until within a few years of his death, in robust health. He gave close attention to the cultivation and improvement of his lands, and prospered accordingly, accumulating a handsome property, while he lavished upon his family every comfort and luxury that reasonable hearts could desire. For forty years he was a resident of St. Joseph County, twenty-nine of them being happily and prosperously spent in the fine and comfortable homestead where he died.

In politics, Mr. Jewett was what was known as a Jackson Democrat, and then an old-line Whig, of the Clay school, up to the organization of the Republican party, since which time he was always true to its principle, but never taking any very active part in its meetings and conventions. He was the first supervisor of the town of Mendon, and though from time to time solicited to accept places of trust in his neighborhood by those who knew his excellent judgment and his strict honor and integrity, he preferred the quiet of home to the noisy atmosphere of the political arena, and was satisfied to know that good, honest, and trustworthy men were selected to fill the offices and administer the laws of the land.

He and his estimable wife (who still survives him) lived to see grow up around them four daughters, to whom were given the liberal advantages of education at home, and the most popular seminaries in the Western States and Canada.

He died regretted by a host of warm friends, and his memory and good deeds will long remain green in the hearts of the people of St. Joseph County.

JOSEPH JEWETT.

MRS. JOSEPH JEWETT.

RESIDENCE OF MRS. JOSEPH JEWETT, Florence Tp, St Joe Co, Mich.

MR. MORGAN L. KETCHAM.

MRS. MORGAN L. KETCHAM.

## MORGAN L. KETCHAM,

son of Joseph and Alida Ketcham, was born in Pottstown, Rensselaer county, New York, November 2, 1804. He remained with his parents on the farm, until his majority, and then commenced as an apprentice at the carpenter's trade, which he continued to follow for several years. In company with his father's family, in 1830, he settled in Perrinton, Monroe county, New York, and there became the owner of one hundred and twenty acres of land, which he sold for one thousand eight hundred dollars. He also lived in Wayne county, New York, for some time.

In the fall of 1834 he and his brother Daniel came to Michigan, and spent the winter near Ypsilanti; his brother returned in the spring, and he came to Constantine. During the summer of 1835 he purchased, in company with one Samuel Francisco, a saw-mill located at Shipeewannie Indiana, which they sold the following year. In the fall of 1835 he returned to Monroe county, New York. In 1837 he again came to Michigan; remained some little time, returned the second time to Monroe county, New York,—and was married to Miss Laura Jenks, of Farmington, Ontario county, New York, May 1, 1839.

Mrs. Ketcham was born July 26, 1812, in Farmington. To bless this union, six children have been born, some of whom, with their mother, have passed to the other shore. The names of the children were as follows:

GEORGE J., born March 16, 1840, and died September 10, 1876.

ISAAC, born January 24, 1842; died August 6, 1842.

EDWARD M. was born March 7, 1844, and is now living in Marcellus, Michigan.

EMELINE J., born August 22, 1846, and is married to Samuel Wolf, of this county.

HANNAH J., born October 16, 1848, and married to D. M. Castle, of Constantine.

MARY L. was born May 16, 1851, and is at home with her father.

Mr. Ketcham lived in Rochester, New York, for nearly two years after his marriage, and carried on the hardware business; removed to Hannibal, Oswego county, New York, and remained some three years. During the month of May, 1846, he emigrated to Michigan with his family, and settled in Florence, St. Joseph county, on the farm where he now resides. At one time he was the owner of some three hundred acres of land, but has sold out so that he now owns but one hundred and forty acres. In politics he was at first a Democrat, then a Whig, and now a Republican.

Mrs. Ketcham was a faithful wife and an affectionate mother; religiously, she was a Friend, but was a constant attendant at the Methodist Episcopal church. She died May 18, 1875, and was buried in the Florence cemetery. Mr. Ketcham is living on the old homestead, with his daughter Mary.

## NOHMAN ROYS,

one of the few remaining pioneers of Florence township, was born in Sheffield, Berkshire county, Massachusetts, on the 22d of February, 1807. When in his twenty-fifth year, he left his home with the intention of trying his fortune in the west. Starting from Sheffield in May, 1832, it was not until the following June that he arrived at his destination in White Pigeon, now Florence, township. The journey occupied about a month, and was made first by private conveyance to Hudson, thence up the river to Albany, and from there by stage, to the depot of the Albany and Schenectady railroad (one of the first in the country). From the latter place, he traveled on the Erie canal to Buffalo, thence by lake to Detroit, and from there to the end of his journey, in the first of Asahel Savery's stage-coaches. It must be a peculiar retrospection to him, to consider that the same journey which occupied him a month can now be accomplished in twenty-four hours! On his arrival in the new settlement he was domiciled with Deacon Howard, and went to work on the land he had entered, succeeding in breaking up fifteen acres during the first month of his settlement, and the following fall sowed it with wheat. He first entered but one hundred and twenty acres, not possessing the necessary funds to take the quarter-section. Nothing daunted, however, he went up to Grand Rapids, and there hired out to assist in the erection of a dam and saw-mill, which was then in course of construction on Buck creek. Here he earned and saved enough to complete the purchase of the wished-for one hundred and sixty acres.

March 16, 1837, he married Caroline, daughter of John Peck, who had come into the township two years previously. This union was blessed with three children, namely: George E., born April 17, 1838, who married Sophia Hull, and resides in the township; Annie E., born November 17, 1839, married Frederick A. Austin, and resides in Aurora, Illinois; Frank, born July 16, 1849, married Alice Ennes, and resides with his parents.

For twenty-six years Mr. Roys faithfully served his township as supervisor,—first in 1839 and 1840, then in 1843, from 1846 to 1849, and from 1857 to 1877. This is a record of long continued fidelity to the interests of the people of his township, not surpassed in the State. For two terms he also served as a justice of the peace, and four years as school-inspector, with a like acceptability that has characterized his other office. Politically, Mr. Roys is a Democrat, though strongly adhering to the principles advocated by the Greenback party. A generous liberality governs his religious sentiments; he belongs to no sect, yet possesses the necessary Christian qualifications of a good citizen. By his industry and economy he has accumulated a fair competence. He now owns two hundred and ten acres of well cultivated land in Florence township, and also eighty acres of heavy timber in Fabius. His home is among the neatest and best in the township, as can be seen by examination of the illustration, elsewhere in this work.

Mrs. Roys, the estimable wife of Norman Roys, was born in Gorham, Ontario county, New York, May 2, 1821. She moved with her parents to Florence township, in 1835. Her father, John Peck, was a respectable mechanic and farmer, and her mother a daughter of John Garrison, one of the pioneers of Constantine township. For forty years Mrs. Roys has been a faithful and loving wife and a fond mother, which we believe constitutes the prudest and best record a woman can leave to her posterity and friends. The portraits of Mr. and Mrs. Roys, grace the pages of our work elsewhere.

## GEORGE PASHBY, Sr.,

was born in the village of Brantingham, Yorkshire, England, on the 10th day of September, 1802, and is consequently now in his seventy-fifth year. He attended school for a very brief period only, in his native place, and laid the foundation of a common education, which future years of travel and observation have developed into sound, practical knowledge. After attaining his majority, he left home and proceeded to Sunderland, where he embarked as a sailor, and, after a fair voyage, landed in the city of New York, on the 16th day of June, 1824, where he remained until the spring of 1828. On the 9th day of February of that year, he was united in marriage with Mary Watson, who had but recently arrived from the shores of "merry England." This union was blessed with two children, Elizabeth, born March 24, 1829, and now the wife of Samuel Stears, of Florence township, and Robert, born May 19, 1831, who died November 18, 1854, soon after returning from California, whither he went in 1851.

On the 6th day of May, 1834, Mr. Pashby sustained the greatest misfortune of his life, the loss of the partner of his early struggles, joys and sorrows. In August of the same year, he removed from New York state,

with the intention of making a permanent settlement in the west. He journeyed with teams, and at the expiration of seventeen days arrived at White Pigeon, on the morning of the 11th day of September, 1834. He proceeded at once to Kalamazoo, and entered eighty acres of land, located on section twenty of Florence township, paying the nominal sum of one dollar and twenty-five cents per acre. On this he erected his log cabin, which he subsequently disposed of. By prudence and economy, coupled with an untiring industry, he has been able to add, by subsequent purchases to his possessions, until he now owns three hundred and sixty-four acres of improved land in the same township.

On the 25th day of July, 1835, Mr. Pashby married Jane Cook, a niece of Rev. George Cook, M. A., Fellow of St. John's College. Cambridge, England, a well known and eloquent divine of the Episcopal church, who preached the funeral sermon over the remains of Lord Nelson, in 1806. By this marriage he had nine children, of which number, five—two sons and three daughters—are living. On the 9th day of October, 1865, after a second term of conjugal happiness, extending over a period of thirty years, death again visited his household and took from him his wife, leaving him with a growing family; and, looking at the event in a Christian light, he thought of the Scriptural injunction, "It is not good for man to be alone," and on the 19th day of July, 1865, he married Mrs. E. C. Scholey, a sister of his deceased wife, who had been before in his household, and to whom his children had become greatly attached. He had the rare felicity of getting an admirable wife, a second mother to his children, a good housekeeper, and an excellent lady in every particular.

Mr. Pashby has never sought political preferment of any kind, but, notwithstanding this fact, he has been elected to fill several township offices. He was also chosen a director in the Farmers' Mutual Fire Insurance Company, of St. Joseph county, at its organization, and held that office for eleven years. He finally resigned, finding the duties of the office too arduous for his advanced age.

In religion Mr. Pashby is allied to no particular creed. He was brought up and confirmed in the church of England, but has never actually joined any denomination. He has, however, always generously supported every movement of a religious or benevolent nature. His donations towards the equipment of the soldiers who went from his township to the war, are a fair criterion of his philanthropy.

Mr. Pashby has, by judicious financial management, accumulated a goodly fortune, and is now calmly enjoying the fruits of his industrious and well-spent life. His residence is among the finest in the county, and is alike an ornament to the township in which he resides, and an honor to its possessor. Perhaps there could be no fitter evidence of the benefit which Mr. Pashby's settlement has brought to the township, than the fact that there are now seven families who bear his name in Florence township, and in Black Hawk county, Iowa. He has twenty-seven grandchildren and two great-grandchildren. Portraits of Mr. and Mrs. Pashby adorn our pages, together with an illustration of their beautiful home.

## JACOB GENTZLER,

son of George and Margaret Gentzler, was born in York county, Pennsylvania, December 16, 1798. He always followed farming for a living; he was married to Miss Elizabeth Speck, of Lancaster, Pennsylvania, in 1819; she was born January 14, 1800. Ten children have been born to them, eight of whom are still living.

October 10, 1849, he emigrated to Michigan, and settled in Florence, and in a few years he was the owner of sixteen hundred acres of as good land as there is in the county, most of which is still owned by members of the family. In politics he was a Democrat; in religion he was a worthy member of the Evangelical Lutheran church, and for more than twenty-five years previous to his coming to Michigan, was a leader of a choir. He died May 16, 1871, and was buried in the White Pigeon cemetery. The widow is seventy-seven years of age, and is living with her son William, in Florence.

Jacob S. Gentzler, son of Jacob, Sr., was born in York county, Pennsylvania, September 29, 1833, and came to St. Joseph with his father. While in Pennsylvania he assisted his father in the carding and woolen business, and since, has been principally engaged in farming and dealing in live-stock; is the owner of a fine farm of four hundred and sixty acres, a view of which may be seen elsewhere. He married Miss Elizabeth Lehmer, of York county, Pennsylvania, April 27, 1854; she was born March 12, 1835; five children have been born to them, two of whom are still living. In politics Mr. Gentzler is a Democrat, and is an advocate of good schools and churches.

MRS GEO PASHBY JR.

GEORGE PASHBY

MRS GEO PASHBY (1ST)

RESIDENCE OF GEORGE PASHBY, FLORENCE TP, ST JOSEPH CO, MICH

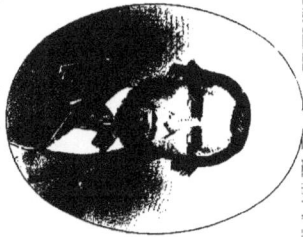

RESIDENCE OF THE LATE HIRAM A. PITTS, Florence Tp, St. Joseph Co., Mich.

HIRAM PITTS

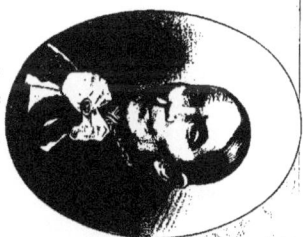

MRS. HIRAM PITTS

## HIRAM AMASA PITTS.

Hiram Amasa Pitts was born in the township of Onondaga, Onondaga county, in the State of New York, November 11, 1818. He moved with his parents to Monroe, in this State, in October, 1832, and in August, 1835, they came to St. Joseph county and settled in the township of Florence, where the subject of this biography resided until his death, which occured December 25, 1874, at the age of fifty-six.

He was married, December 14, 1848, to Eliza Thompson, a native of the State of Vermont, but at the time of their marriage, a resident of Sherman, in this county.

He purchased the farm upon which he resided, in 1846, on section twelve, township seven south, range eleven west, where he erected a fine brick dwelling with good and substantial out-buildings, the present residence of Mrs. Pitts, his widow.

Mr. Pitts enjoyed the confidence of the people in his township, having been elected to responsible offices frequently during his life-time. He exhibited an interest in education, and was untiring in his efforts to establish schools in his township, having been a school-officer in the district where he lived continuously until his death. He was kind and obliging to his neighbors, and always ready to lend a helping hand to the needy and worthy poor. Being an early pioneer in Florence,—even before the township was organized,—he assisted in forming school-districts, laying out highways and all other important work in the interest of the township. As a citizen of the county he was a useful man, and rendered the people many important services.

## WILLIAM MACHIN.

It is a pleasure to record the experience, and incidents in the life of a worthy and successful man, who, unassisted, began its battles in days and amid surroundings, that afforded no opportunities to secure even the rudiments of an education, and whose boyhood and youth were spent amid deprivations that are strangers to our day.

Mr. Machin, the subject of this sketch, was born at Basby, England, April 7, 1813, and by industry and economy was enabled, at the age of twenty-five, to provide a home for himself and wife. He was married in Walcott, England, to Elizabeth Girton, May 15, 1838, she being his playmate in childhood, friend in youth, and advisor in early manhood. Children blessed their union :

MARY, born February 12, 1839.

JOHN, October 7, 1842.

WILLIAM, May 27, 1844.

ANN M. and JOSEPH, January 31, 1847.

Desiring to better the condition of his family, and give them an opportunity to secure homes not attainable with their small capital in England, he emigrated in 1851 to America. Delayed by a year's sickness, at Brockport, New York, he arrived in Florence township, St. Joseph county, his capital exhausted; and, with only one dollar, with which to begin again, commenced to labor for a home. Assisted by a kind friend—George Pashby, an honor to mankind!—he was enabled soon to realize his expectations. By diligence and economy, assisted by his noble wife, he secured for himself a fine home, and lived to see his children comfortably located.

In early life he became a member of the Wesleyn Methodist church. His adopted country found in him a faithful citizen, and his chosen Republican party, an earnest supporter.

He died February 23, 1871, and we do simple justice to the memory of the man by showing his portrait in connection with this history, believing that in his record many things may be learned, of practical value to those who follow after.

# LOCKPORT.

The surface of the township of Lockport (so called from the extensive water-power projected on the St. Joseph river in that township), was originally covered with heavy burr-oak and white-oak openings, with heavy-timbered lands along the river St. Joseph, which passes through the township from northeast to southwest. Its area includes twenty-two thousand eight hundred and ninety-seven acres of land, and one hundred and twenty acres of water surface. It is known on the government survey as township six south of range eleven west, and is bounded north by Park, east by Nottawa, south by Florence, and west by Fabius townships. Its soil is the same that characterizes the oak-openings in other parts of the county,—a fertile, sandy loam capable of producing large crops of the cereals, corn, fruit, and vegetables. Its drainage is superb, being watered favorably by streams bordered by high bluffs; and very little or no marsh lands are found within its limits. The surface is a general level, rolling more or less as it lies contiguous to the St. Joseph. The St. Joseph river enters the township on the southeast quarter of section one, and meanders very eccentrically through the township, passing out therefrom on the southwest quarter of section thirty. The Portage, a very considerable stream, enters the township from Park on the north line of the northeast quarter of section four, and, running southwestward, forms a junction with the St. Joseph at the city of Three Rivers. The Rocky river enters the township within the corporate limits of Three Rivers, and unites with the St. Joseph just below the junction of the Portage. Hog creek enters the township on the east line of the southwest quarter of section twenty-four, and runs southwest and westwardly, emptying into the St. Joseph on the southwest quarter of section thirty. A portion of Fisher's lake lies within the township, on the northeast quarter of section three.

The first settlement made within the present limits of the township was that of Jacob McInterfer and his family, in the spring of 1829. He came first to look for a location, in 1828, and selected a square mile of land on the west side of Rocky river, on a portion of which the third ward of Three Rivers is located, and returning to his home in Wayne county, Ohio, came back in the spring following, in company with the Rowens, Armstrongs, and Davies, his neighbors, all of whom settled in Mottville township but himself. He had no shelter for his family, which consisted of several children and his wife (two or more daughters being among the number), save his wagons, and in them they lived, cooking in an improvised shanty, put up between two trees, until he could build a house, which he proceeded immediately to do, erecting a substantial hewed-log house on the present site of Elisha Millard's barn. Mr. McInterfer died in 1831. The next settlers who came into the township were George Buck and his family, who located in the spring of 1830 on the present site of the second ward of Three Rivers, north of the prairies of White Pigeon and Sturgis, where he put up a double log house, and opened the first tavern in the township. This house was the resort of the people of the county in their political gatherings, and the first convention ever held in the county was convened in this house, and Mrs. Buck, unaided by other female help, prepared a bountiful dinner for seventy-five guests.

Charles B. Fitch, afterwards judge of the county court, located in the township in 1831, coming in from his first location on White Pigeon prairie a year before. His location was made on section thirty-one, where he entered two hundred acres, including a valuable mill-privilege on Hog creek, which he immediately proceeded to utilize. His son (Samuel Fitch) is still a resident of the township.

Michael Beadle located on the west side of the Rocky, buying McInterfer's mill-privilege thereon, in 1831 (the latter part of the year), and completed the mill, the erection of which was begun by McInterfer, and suspended by reason of his death. In 1833 John H. Bowman came to look at the mill-privileges at the junction of the three rivers, but did not finally bring his family until 1834, though he made his location, during his first visit, between the rivers, and proceeded to enter other lands, which he cultivated. Philip H. Hoffman, with his family of seven children, located in the township, in September, 1833, on the present site of the first ward of Three Rivers; Borden Hicks located about the same time, on the river. Mr. Hoffman was an extensive farmer, and came from Pennsylvania; as did also Mr. Bowman. Eli Bristol came in 1834–35, and located; and Burroughs Moore in 1833. William Arney came in 1833. Mr. John Hoffman (a son of P. H. Hoffman) is a heavy manufacturer in Three Rivers. The Wolf brothers came in with their father, from Pennsylvania, in 1834; he located three hundred and twenty acres on section twenty-seven. Joseph P. Sterling came in 1835, and A. C. Prutzman in 1834, but the latter, with Edward S. Moore, first located on Prairie Ronde. Joseph B. Millard came in 1836, and Elisha Millard in 1835. John M. Leland first came in 1833; made his location in the northeast corner of the township, and brought his family thereto in the summer of 1834. His purchase was made on sections two and eleven. The family lived in their wagons during the summer of 1834, the beds thereof, with the covers, being taken from the running-gear and set on logs, and a shanty built (supported by two trees for posts) to cook in. Soon after the shanty was occupied, a furious storm arose, and the trees were so rudely shaken that the shanty had to be re-built and the tree-tops cut off to reduce their swaying. Hezekiah Weatherbee was an early comer to the township. Jonas and Leonard Fisher came from Pennsylvania in 1834, in the spring, and located on the shore of the lake that subsequently took their name. William Armitage came in 1836, and Charles F. Thoms, a Swiss soldier in the first Napoleon's army, with his two sons, now living in the township, came in in 1834. George W. Gardner came in 1835, and J. H. Gardner in 1836. Andrew Goode came in 1834–35, and is still a resident on his first location. George Leland and Washington Gascon came in with John M. Leland and his family in 1834. The Majors (William and John I.) came in 1834.

The foregoing were prominent among the earlier settlers in the township, and their representatives (with the exception of, perhaps, the McInterfer family,) are living in the township to-day, and many of the very individuals themselves. McInterfer, Buck, Fitch, Beadle, Bowman, Hoffman, Arney, Burroughs, Moore, John M. Leland, Armitage, and Thoms have gone to rest beneath the turf they once trod upon in vigorous stride, but their descendants still live, on their old homesteads mostly, treasuring up the memories of those sturdy old pioneers, and building upon the foundations they laid.

### THE FIRST FARM

opened was that of Jacob McInterfer, who put in a crop of corn and potatoes in the spring of 1829. George Buck followed with a crop in 1830. Small tracts of these first fields were cleared from the forest growth by hard labor. Philip H. Hoffman cleared and broke up five acres only, in 1833, and planted corn, potatoes, and buckwheat, and the second year cleared and plowed ten acres more.

The first entries of public lands in the township were made in the year 1829, and were as follows: June 13, southwest quarter and west half of the northwest quarter of section eighteen, two hundred and thirty-eight acres, by Jacob McInterfer; southeast quarter fraction of section eighteen by Robert Clark, Jr., C. Noble, H. L. and A. C. Stewart; north fraction of the northwest quarter of section nineteen by William Rowen; southwest quarter and south half of the northwest quarter of section nineteen by Abraham Reichert. These include all of the entries of 1829. There were assessed in 1876 twenty thousand and thirty-three acres of land.

The crop of 1873 yielded: wheat, forty thousand seven hundred and fifteen bushels; corn, sixty thousand nine hundred and forty-five bushels; other grain, two thousand and ninety bushels; potatoes, seven thousand and twenty-six bushels; hay, one thousand four hundred and twelve tons; wool, eight thousand five hundred and eleven pounds; pork, one hundred and twenty-five thousand eight hundred and ten pounds; butter, twenty-eight thousand nine hundred and fifty pounds; dried fruit, one thousand two hundred pounds; cider, four hundred and ninety barrels. The acreage of 1873 in wheat was four thousand two hundred and ninety-eight acres, and corn two thousand three hundred and nineteen. Four hundred and eight acres in

orchards and gardens produced nine thousand seven hundred bushels of apples, and forty-five bushels of other fruit, valued at five thousand three hundred and ninety-seven dollars.

There were owned in the township five hundred and thirty-one horses, nine mules, six oxen, four hundred and eleven cows, two hundred and seventy-nine other cattle, eleven hundred and ninety hogs, and two thousand and fifty-six sheep.

### THE FIRST FRUIT-TREES

were planted by George Buck, the same being apple-trees. Hoffman planted peach-stones in 1833, and a few years later he gathered an abundance of delicious fruit from the trees which they produced. They froze down, however, several years afterwards, and though they sprouted again and bore for a short time, were finally winter-killed and destroyed.

William Arney set out an orchard in 1834, on the farm now owned by D. Francisco.

### THE FIRST IMPROVED FARM MACHINERY

was introduced in 1835, in the form of fanning-mills and open cylinders, the latter being made by John M. Leland. Mr. Leland subsequently manufactured reapers, and introduced them into the township in 1843–4.

### LIVE STOCK

began to be improved but little until after 1860, though sheep and horses had received attention before, to some extent. The cultivation of the soil is the main business of the farmers of this township; but little attention is paid to stock-raising, that is, of the improved breeds. A great feature of the farming in this township is the

### MINT-OIL PRODUCTION,

which is fast rivaling that of Florence. D. Francisco, now a resident of Three Rivers, was for many years a heavy producer and dealer in essential oils. He began the cultivation of peppermint in 1848, and has had one hundred to one hundred and ten acres of the herb in a season. He has sold the oil from five dollars per pound down to one dollar and fifty cents for the same quantity, and thinks oil at two dollars per pound a better crop than wheat at one dollar per bushel. His sales amounted to eighteen thousand dollars in one term of three years.

Wolf Brothers are the leading producers of the present day, and have, besides peppermint, the largest field of wormwood in the world, and the largest field of spearmint in the county.

### THE MANUFACTURES,

outside of Three Rivers, of moment, were the mills of Judge Fitch at his little city of Eschol, where, in 1831, he began the erection of a saw-mill, completing the same in 1832, and afterwards putting in a small pair of stones for gristing purposes. Subsequently, in 1838, a carding-machine was added by R. M. Welch, and a shingle-mill, and for a time Eschol was a promising hamlet, but the tide of trade set towards Three Rivers, and ebbed slowly away from Eschol, and after 1840 the dam went out of the creek, the buildings fell into decay and were never rebuilt, and Eschol village-plat reverted to farming-lands, and the town was no more.

John M. Leland built a saw-mill in the year 1834 on his farm; a natural embankment being formed by the bluff banks of the stream on which it was built, sweeping around and almost meeting at the lower end of a swale which he flooded for his mill-pond.

His dam went out two or three times before he built it in its present situation. The log carriage in this mill is run by friction and not by cogs or gearing.

A large cedar was cut down by the side of the mill and taken to the Centennial Exhibition as a specimen of the red-cedar of Michigan. It was the largest tree of the variety, that could be found in the State, and measured over three feet across the stump.

Mr. Leland built his reapers and threshing-machines here, and a fine mansion has succeeded to the pioneer-cabin. He died a few years ago.

### THE FIRST HOUSE

built in the township was the hewed-log house of Jacob McInterfer, erected in 1829. Michael Beadle built the first frame house on the west side of the Rocky in 1832, and a frame store-house near the present bridge in Three Rivers, on the St. Joseph, in 1833.

### THE FIRST BRICK HOUSE

was built in Three Rivers by John Young, and is now a portion of the store-building of Mr. Bennett.

RESIDENCE OF J. B. MILLARD, SEC 19 THREE RIVERS, MICHIGAN.

#### THE FIRST WHITE CHILD

born in the township, was a little daughter of Solomon McInterfer, who was born in November, 1829, and died soon after, being also

#### THE FIRST DEATH

in the township. The first death of an adult person that occurred in the township was that of this little child's grandfather, Jacob McInterfer, the first settler, which event took place in 1831.

This family also furnished the bride of the first marriage in the township; she being Mary McInterfer, and the groom David Winchell, a son of the first settler in the county. This marriage was celebrated in February, 1830.

In November of the same year another bride from the same family, Sarah by name, formed the "better half" of the second wedded pair in the township, the groom being William McIntosh, of Young's prairie, in Cass county.

The first white male child born in the township was Asa Bear, a son of John Bear, in 1830, while the parents were on a journey to Prairie Ronde, or on their return therefrom.

#### THE FIRST RELIGIOUS SERVICES

held in the township were at the funeral obsequies of Mr. McInterfer, which were held in his own house in 1831; but who officiated is not known. It was probably one of the Methodist missionaries of those days.

#### THE FIRST SCHOOL

in the township, was taught in the winter of 1834–5, in "Canada," in the old McInterfer cabin, by "Father" Arny, who had thirty pupils under his charge.

There are (in 1876) six school-houses, two of brick and four of wood, containing one thousand and forty-eight seatings, and valued at twenty-three thousand eight hundred and fifty dollars. Two of the schools taught therein are graded schools. There are one thousand one hundred and twenty-nine children between five and twenty years of age, and nine hundred and eighty-two attended school during the year. There was an average of eight and two-thirds months school, taught in the different districts, and five male teachers were employed, who were paid two thousand six hundred and fifty dollars for their services, and eighteen females, who received four thousand two hundred and sixty-one dollars. The total expenditures of the year ending September 1, 1876, were twelve thousand six hundred and three dollars and sixty-one cents, including payments on bonded indebtedness and repairs.

#### THE ONLY CHURCH-EDIFICE

in the township, outside of Three Rivers, is that of the Lockport society of the Evangelical Association, which was built in 1875. It is situated three and a half miles east of the city of Three Rivers, and is a neat frame structure, thirty-four by forty-eight feet on the ground, seating from two hundred and fifty to three hundred persons, and cost two thousand dollars.

The society was organized in 1871, under the pastorate of Rev. Peter Weist. The first members were Jacob Godshalk and wife, Emanuel Walz and wife, and Edward Walz and wife. Jacob Godshalk, Emanuel Walz and Roland Hinebach were the building-committee to erect the church, and Jacob Godshalk, Edward Walz and James Engel were the first, and are the present, trustees. The church was named the "First Evangelical Church of Lockport," and was formally dedicated to the service and worship of the Triune God, by the Rev. Bishop J. J. Escher, December 23, 1875, the following ministers officiating also in the services: Rev. S. Copley, presiding elder; Rev. D. F. Wade, preacher in Chicago, and Rev. J. H. Keeler, missionary in Jackson, Michigan. A union Sunday-school was organized in 1876, with Edward Walz as superintendent. The school numbered about seventy-five scholars. The present membership of the church is twenty-six. The names of the ministers who have had charge of this, as well as the other societies of the association in St. Joseph county, since the date of the organization of this society, are as follows: Reverends Peter Weist, S. Copley, J. W. Loose, Alonzo Russell, P. Swille, E. B. Miller, B. F. Wade and J. H. Keeler, the present pastor of the circuit.

#### CIVIL ORGANIZATION.

The first organization for township government, which included the present territory of the township of Lockport within its jurisdiction, was that of White Pigeon, October 29, 1829, which said township included the entire western half of the county, except its two northern townships.

On March 29, 1833, township six of ranges eleven and twelve, were set off from White Pigeon township, and constituted a separate and distinct township under the name of Bucks, in honor of the first, and only hotel-keeper in the township.

The first town-meeting was called at Buck's tavern, which was known and advertised as the "Half-Way House," between White Pigeon and Prairie Ronde, but the meeting was not organized until the 11th of April, and then only by special act of the legislature; sufficient time not having elapsed between the passage of the act constituting the township, and the regular day of holding town-meetings in the territory. George Buck, Esq., a justice of the peace, appointed by Governor Porter, April 3, 1833, was the conductor of the election; Columbia Lancaster was moderator, and J. W. Coffinberry, clerk. Both of the latter gentlemen were citizens of Centreville, but resided in the Lockport part thereof. The electors decided that no person should vote or hold office but such only as were legally entitled to do so, and then proceeded to cast seventeen votes as the entire poll of the day. The following officers were elected: Michael Beadle, supervisor; Heman Harvey, clerk; C. B. Fitch, James Whited, Alanson C. Stewart, assessors; David Beadle, Jr., constable and collector; Elizur Lancaster, constable; Garrett Sickles, James Whited, Thomas H. Fitch, commissioners of highways; C. B. Fitch, poormaster; Thomas Knapp and George Buck, fence-viewers; Gideon Bail, Hiram Harwood, Levi Griswold and J. W. Coffinberry, pathmasters.

Rams and stallions were prohibited from running at large, and one dollar was offered for each wolf's scalp taken in the township.

Thirty dollars in 1835 was raised to pay town officials in 1834, and one hundred and twenty-two dollars and fourteen cents audited for the year's expenses.

The town-meeting in 1835 was held in the school-house near Schnable's mills, the old McInterfer cabin. This meeting appropriated ten dollars for pauper relief.

In 1840 the government townships number six, south of range eleven and twelve west, forming the township of Bucks, were divided, and the latter was constituted the township of Lockport, the former retaining the original name of Bucks,—for a short time only.

The settlement with the township treasurer in March, 1842, was recorded on the township books in this manner: "Settled with Henry W. Hampson, treasurer of Lockport township, and find that we come out square and even, March 26, 1842." This entry was signed by the town board, and the deacon was re-elected.

May 6, 1871, the people of the township voted seven thousand five hundred dollars to build a bridge over the St. Joseph at Three Rivers.

#### THE OFFICIAL ROSTER

of the township since its organization in 1833, is as follows:

Supervisors—Michael Beadle, 1833–4; C. B. Fitch, 1835–1843; John Arney, 1836–8; John Baum, 1842, and 1846–8, 1852–3, 1855–7; Eli H. Bristol, 1844–5; Ezra Cole, 1854; W. F. Arnold, 1858–62, 1864–71, 1873–6; William Hutchinson, 1849–50; Charles H. Thoms, 1851.

Town Clerks—Heman Harvey, 1833–4; Burroughs Moore, 1835–6; B. Osgood, 1836–9–44; Solomon Cummings, 1845, 1849–51; Harvey Cady, 1852–4; H. H. Cole, 1855–62; E. H. Lothrop, 1865–6; John S. Mowry, 1868–9; J. M. Kirby, 1876.

Justices of the Peace—George Buck, 1833–40; Cyrus Ingerson, 1836–44; B. Osgood, 1840–51; Ezra Cole, 1840–49, and 1857–61; J. E. Johnson, 1846–54; H. N. Spencer, 1846–1856; W. D. Pettis, 1849–58; Charles H. Thoms, 1855–66; W. F. Arnold, 1856–67; Samuel Chadwick, 1863–70; E. H. Lothrop, 1864–74; Joseph W. French, 1874–7; J. M. Kirby, 1875–7; John W. Schnaylor, 1876–7. These justices and clerks who have served but a single term, or part of a term, are not named in the above list.

#### THE FIRST ROAD

laid out in the township by township authority, was one from the north boundary of White Pigeon township, to the north boundary of Bucks, six miles, which was surveyed by Mathew Rowen, June 7, 1833. Another was surveyed from the St. Joseph river, opposite Eschol, to the one-quarter post between sections twenty-six and thirty-five.

#### THE FIRST TAVERN,

or hotel, was kept by Mr. George Buck, as before stated, in what is now known as the second ward of Three Rivers. Here, too, was the

#### FIRST POST-OFFICE,

established and kept by Mr. Buck, postmaster, for some years. The first stage-line that traveled through on the route from White Pigeon to Kalamazoo, or, as it was then called, Bronson, was Harvey Hunt's, of Constantine.

## THE FIRST BRIDGE

built over the St. Joseph in the township, was at Three Rivers, on or near the site of the present one. It was built in 1838 by Asa Weatherbee, who lately died in the State Insane Asylum of Michigan. The present bridge was built in 1875, and cost seven thousand five hundred dollars.

## THE HEAVIEST LAND-OWNERS,

who cultivate the soil in the township, are J. H. Gardner, who owns four hundred and seventy-seven acres; the Major brothers, six hundred, and the Wolf Brothers, who own together seven hundred acres. The senior Majors came to Lockport township, settling on the eastern side of the same, near Centreville, where they have lived side by side until last December (1876), when William departed from the busy scenes of this life and passed to his rest. The John M. Leland tract remains intact in the family, the widow and two sons succeeding to the estate. The sons inherit the genius of their father for mechanics, and are both practical workmen. The younger one, Samuel G., is agent for the manufacturers of the Leffel water-wheels, his mechanical ingenuity making him a competent person to set the wheels, or show what the trouble is when improperly set.

## POPULATION.

In 1838 the population of Bucks township, as then organized, numbered seven hundred and eighty-two. In 1850 Lockport township contained one thousand one hundred and forty-two inhabitants. In 1870 the population had increased to three thousand four hundred and fifty-five—six hundred and eighty-three families—one thousand seven hundred and eighty males and one thousand six hundred and seventy-five females. In 1874 the State census showed the population to be three thousand eight hundred and ninety-two—males, one thousand nine hundred and forty-seven; females, one thousand nine hundred and forty-five. There were seven hundred and sixty-seven males between the ages of twenty-one and forty-five; three hundred and twenty-two between forty-five and seventy-five, and fourteen who had passed three-fourths of a century and had not turned the last decade stake. Seven hundred and ninety-three female females were between eighteen and forty years; three hundred and thirty-six between forty and seventy-five, and twelve over the latter age. There were eight hundred and forty-four boys under twenty-one years of age, and eight hundred and four girls under the age of eighteen years. The married females exceeded by a single individual the males in that condition, they numbering eight hundred and sixteen and eight hundred and fifteen respectively.

The single men over twenty-one years were two hundred and fifty-six, and the females with whom they could properly mate were two hundred and ten; thirty-two of the gentlemen were widowed or divorced, and one hundred and sixteen of the ladies were in the same sad and solitary condition.

## THE WAY THE PEOPLE VOTED

on the national issues, since 1840, will be seen by the following exhibit of the tally-lists of the Presidential elections:

In 1840 Bucks township gave the Democratic ticket one hundred and two votes, and that of the Whigs seventy-two. In 1844 Lockport township voted eighty-five Democratic; eighty-two Whig, and seven Liberty. In 1848 the Whigs had ninety-three votes; the Democrats eighty-three, and the Free-soilers thirty-two. In 1852 the Whigs polled one hundred and ten; the Democrats one hundred and forty-one, and the Abolitionists thirteen. In 1856 the Republicans gave Fremont two hundred and twenty-nine votes; the Democrats gave Buchanan one hundred and eighteen, and the Prohibitionists had not enough votes to make a plural, there being but one cast. In 1860 Lincoln received two hundred and seventy-four votes, and Douglas two hundred and seventy-one. In 1864 Lincoln received two hundred and seventy-five, and McClellan two hundred and forty-three votes. In 1868 Grant polled three hundred and ninety, and Seymour three hundred and forty-two. In 1872 Grant received four hundred and eight votes; Greeley two hundred and sixty-six; O'Conor twelve, and Jeremiah Black one. 1876 Peter Cooper, the greenbacker, received three hundred and seven votes; Hayes two hundred and sixty-nine, and Tilden two hundred and fifty-eight.

## THE TAXES THE PEOPLE PAID

in 1834 were as follows: The assessment of the property owned in the township of Bucks amounted to thirty-three thousand one hundred and thirty-three dollars, and on this amount there was levied one hundred and thirty seven dollars for county and town taxes. The first State tax amounted to one hundred and ninety-one dollars and forty-six cents, and was levied, in 1876, on an assessment of seventy-six thousand five hundred and eighty-four

dollars, the total taxes of that year amounting to four hundred and eighty dollars and forty-six cents. The first assessment of Lockport was that of 1841, and amounted to seventy-nine thousand two hundred and thirty-five dollars, and the taxes of the year aggregated one thousand and sixty-eight dollars. The assessment of 1876 of real estate was returned by the supervisor at one million nineteen thousand one hundred and thirty dollars, and reduced by the county equalizing-board to one million fourteen thousand two hundred and twenty-nine dollars. The personal assessment was two hundred and eighty-six thousand four hundred and forty dollars, making a total of one million three hundred thousand six hundred and sixty-nine dollars on which was levied for State and county purposes six thousand six hundred and forty-four dollars and thirty-eight cents, equally divided between the two governments.

## THE CITY OF THREE RIVERS.

The present city of Three Rivers covers no less than three original plats whose names have passed away, two of them being of a very brief existence. July 28, 1830, Christopher Shinnaman laid out a village plat on the south half of the northwest quarter of section nineteen, township six, range eleven, and named it Moab, and recorded his plat as such. On the 30th of June following, George Buck and Jacob McInterfer laid out a village plat in the northeast corner of the northeast fraction quarter section nineteen, township six, range eleven, and called it St. Joseph.

There was a strife between the several parts of the county as to the location of the county-seat at that time, and several parties who owned land at or near the village plat of St. Joseph, were anxious to offer inducements to the county authorities sufficiently convincing to effect the location of the county-seat at that place; but the proprietor could not see the wisdom of giving away so much for so little in return, as nature had done so much for a court-house site; but nevertheless the proprietors did enter into bonds to give the commissioners for the county, eight lots adjoining the public square on the east side, and two other lots if they would locate the county seat on the square.

The seat of justice was first located on the plat of St. Joseph, but subsequently the action was reconsidered, and the county-seat finally located at Centreville, the proprietors of which offered more liberal inducements in aid of the erection of county buildings. The relocation of the county-seat gave the quietus to Moab's aspirations, and it became, not a waste howling wilderness like its ancient prototype, but smiling corn-fields occupied its site.

In December, 1836, George Buck, Jonathan Brown, Benjamin Sherman, Edward Pierson, and L. D. Brown laid out a new plat on sections nineteen and twenty, township six, range eleven, and named the village Lockport, and projected a canal and immense water-power. They had been preceded a month by John H. Bowman, who laid out the plat of Three Rivers on section eighteen, on the 25th of November.

In 1871 the corporation limits of Three Rivers were extended and embraced Lockport as the second ward, "Canada" as the third ward, lying on the west side of the Rocky river, and a tract on the east side of the Portage lying between it and the St. Joseph, as the fourth ward,—the original village being the first ward.

## FIRST SETTLEMENTS.

The first settlers of the territory included in the second and third wards of the city, were as before stated: Jacob McInterfer, in 1829, and George Buck, in 1830. The first settler on the original site of the first ward was John H. Bowman, who came in 1833, and located between the Portage and the Rocky. He was followed that year by Burroughs Moore. In the summer of 1834 the village contained six families, Burroughs Moore's, Mr. Dawley's, Mr. Weatherbee's, John H. Bowman's, Lewis Frost's and John M. Leland's. Moore, Dawley and Weatherbee (Asa) were the only ones who had houses. Bowman's and Leland's family lived in their wagons, as described elsewhere, and Frost's in a shanty of boards. On the Lockport side Mr. Buck's log-house was the only one, and on the "Canada" side Mr. Beadle had a small saw- and grist-mill, and there were one frame and two log-houses there.

## THE FIRST FRAME HOUSE

built in what is now the city of Three Rivers, was erected by Mishael Beadle, in 1832, in "Canada," now the third ward of the city. There, too, was the first log-house built by McInterfer, in 1829. The first house built in the original village of Three Rivers was that of Burroughs Moore, who afterwards kept a hotel therein.

Elisha and Thomas Millard came to the village in 1835, but took up a farm soon after and moved upon it. The Captain, Elisha, however returned in 1837. Joseph A. Smith came to the place in 1836, and entered into part-

RESIDENCE of J. W. HOFFMAN,
THREE RIVERS, MICH.

"HOFFMAN MILLS", PROPERTY of J. W. HOFFMAN, THREE RIVERS, MICH.

nership with J. H. Bowman in manufacturing and mercantile lines. William R. Eck came to the village in 1833, and remained there several years, removing finally to Colon where he now resides. Joseph Sterling came to Lockport in 1834. C. B. Hoffman came to the village in 1833–34, and returned to Colon, 1863, where he died in 1875. Ezra Cole came to the place in 1838, and lives there yet with the wife he married in Benton, Yates county, New York, January 14, 1818. The first frame house of any pretensions was built by John H. Bowman, in 1834, and is still a well-preserved mansion.

### MANUFACTURES.

Jacob McInterfar began the erection of a saw-mill in 1830, on the west side of the Rocky, but before completing it he died, and the property passed into the hands of Michael Beadle, who completed the mill and put in a pair of rude bowlder stones, and ground grists. It was a simple affair; but, like Mercutio's wound, it served its purpose. Beadle afterwards disposed of his mill and privilege to Schnabel, who sold the same to Smith & Bowman in the spring of 1836, who proceeded to make more extensive use of their power, and the present Three Rivers mill was raised in July following, and flouring began in February, 1837.

Moore & Prutzman succeeded to the mill, as lessees, in 1838–9, and bought it a short time afterwards, operating the same for twenty years. Since then (1850) it has passed through several changes, being at present owned by Lewis Emery, of Titusville, Pennsylvania, and operated by Griffiths & Dunham, lessees. It had at first but two run of stones, but has now six, with first-class appointments. Its product in 1876 was forty thousand barrels of flour. These lessees also bought and shipped a surplus of one hundred thousand bushels of wheat, besides the amount floured. In the Lockport mills, also leased and operated by these gentlemen, the product from August to December 31, 1876, was eight thousand barrels of flour and one hundred car-loads of feed. The Lockport mills are owned by Milo Powell, and were built by William Fulkerson and —— Shaler, after 1837, and have three run of stones.

George Buck built a saw-mill on the Lockport side in 1836. Himself, S. B. Brown, Edward Pierson, and Benjamin Sherman formed the St. Joseph Canal and Lockport Manufacturing Company, and began an extensive improvement of the water-power of the St. Joseph, at their village. In the *Peninsular*, published at Centreville, May 4, 1837, Sherman, as the agent of the company, advertised for proposals for the construction of a tree dam, a bridge, a canal, and a lock; and would accommodate parties with large or small contracts. But the panic and crash of 1837 came, and all their schemes for the building up of their village and putting money in their pockets, vanished, leaving a wreck behind; Sherman being cleaned out of everything he had. The land reverted to Mr. Buck, who had sold it to the company for sixty-six dollars per acre, in 1836, and J. B. Millard bought some of it in 1843 for six dollars per acre.

In 1836–7 Michael Beadle built another saw-mill, farther up the Rocky, which passed successively through the hands of Samuel Salsig, Philip Lantz and C. S. Wheeler, and the latter-built a large distillery near it. In 1850, which burned down in 1853–4, when he built a smaller affair, but was not successful in operating it.

Luther Carlton built, in 1839–40, a woolen factory, where wool-carding and cloth-dressing were also done by Carlton & Bonfoy, which Cox & Throp bought finally, raised up the building for a furnace, and built a brick building for a moulding-shop. They stand on the west side of the Rocky, at the end of the bridge, on either side of the street. The frame building is now used by John Hutchinson in the manufacture of corn-shellers.

Joseph B. Millard commenced the first wagon manufacturing in the village in 1837, which he continued one year, having a widely-extended patronage, but which brought him little money, and more experience. He sold out his shop to W. D. Pettit, who was succeeded by Z. Ruggles, the present owner and manufacturer.

Brigham & Warren have been twenty years in the carriage-making line, in the village.

In 1845 Luther Carlton and Mrs. Hoskins began the erection of a flouring-mill on the Portage, on the corner of the Hoffman mill, which passed to J. B. Millard and William Hutchinson, who completed it and commenced flouring. They subsequently disposed of it to Philip H. Hoffman and John H. Bowman, in whose possession it was burned in the fall of 1851, and rebuilt by them the year following.

They continued to operate it till Bowman's death. John Hoffman, son of Philip H., is the present owner. It has seven run of stones, is forty by sixty-five feet on the ground, three stories in height, with a warehouse twenty-

eight by forty-eight feet. Its product in 1876 was twenty thousand barrels of flour, besides doing an extensive custom work of fifty bushels per day.

Mr. John Hoffman has been thirty-one years in the business of milling, beginning, as he tersely puts it, " when mill-picks were like grubbing-hoes, and living to see all work about a mill done with neatness and dispatch, by machinery."

In the spring of 1851 the Lockport Hydraulic Company, composed of Joseph H. Mather, of Deep River, Connecticut; Stephen R. Weeden, Providence, Rhode Island, and George Merriam, of Springfield, Massachusetts, with Joseph B. Millard as superintendent and manager, began its operations. That year the dam across the St. Joseph was put in, and the race dug. The first use of the water-power created by this improvement was made by J. B. Millard and George Troy, who built a furnace on the present site of Robert & Throp's extensive works, which was operated by the builders for two years, then by Troy alone, and was finally bought by Roberts & Cox, in 1855.

The next manufactory on the canal was an axe-handle and spoke-factory, built by one Clark, who operated it a few years, and sold it to J. W. French, and he, to the Three Rivers Pulp Company, who now operate it in the manufacture of pulp for the making of paper,—J. W. French being the president; J. B. Millard, treasurer, and Charles W. Millard, secretary and superintendent. Its capital stock is seventy-two thousand dollars, of which thirty-five thousand dollars are paid in. The company ships pulp to Massachusetts, and elsewhere largely.

The Rosette paper-mill was built in 1853–4, by Shaler, Becker & White, and is now manufacturing a very fine quality of stock. The president of the company, which is known as the J. W. French Manufacturing Company, is J. W. French.

The saw-mill now owned by George A. Jackson & Co. was built by Charles Twichell, in 1853. A sash, blind and planing factory was built by George Troy, 1853–54, and sold by him in 1855 to Caldwell & Co., who enlarged the same to its present dimensions and business, and sold to Shurts, Greene & Co., and they to Judge Dikeman, of Schoolcraft, who is the present owner,—C. E. Dexter being the lessee and present thereof. Wilcox, Arnold & Co., built in 1863 the sash and blind factory now owned and operated by Arnold & Caldwell. Smith, Lafferty & Bliss built the large brick pump-works in 1871–72, and manufactured wooden pumps for two and a half years, and did a good business; but nothing is being done in it now—the same parties still owning it.

In 1866 the Three Rivers Manufacturing Company built their furnace and machine shops, L. B. Swarthout, general manager, and William Swarthout, treasurer. The works are still in operation. The soap-factory of Arnold & Smith was built in 1876. In the fall of 1865 E. P. Smith began the manufacture of pumps in a small way, and was subsequently joined by Orrin Gifford, and the business increased, Gifford retiring January, 1867, and J. E. & J. P. Prutzman, sons of Hon. A. C. Prutzman, came into the business and manufactured for the jobbing-trade entirely; their sales amounting to twenty-six thousand dollars the first year. The Prutzmans were with Smith two years and then retired, and Munson came in a short time and gave way to Lafferty, and the year following the firm was merged into the Northwestern Pump Company and continued in business till removed to Toledo. This company own the brick manufactory in the second ward before mentioned. J. E. & J. P. Prutzman built their present works on the Portage, near the bridge, and soon after adopted the name of the " Michigan Pump Company," and manufactured the so-called Michigan pump, adding in 1876 the manufacture of plows, under the name of the " Three Rivers Plow Company," being Prutzman Brothers & McIntyre. Their sales here steadily increased, reaching, in 1874, the sum of forty-three thousand dollars. They employed thirty-five men in 1876.

The extensive manufactory of Roberts, Throp & Co. has arisen from a single small furnace built by J. D. Millard and George Troy, the same passing into the hands of Roberts & Cox, in 1855— Mr. John A. Throp succeeding Cox soon afterward. The company was incorporated in 1853, as Roberts, Throp & Co., Cyrus Roberts, president; John A. Throp, vice-president; George A. Roberts, treasurer, and S. J. Throp, secretary. The capital stock is two hundred and fifty thousand dollars, eighty thousand dollars of which is paid in. They manufacture threshing-machines, the "Invincible Vibrating Thresher," the original vibrating machine, and cultivators. The president built his first vibrator in 1848, and patented the present style of his machines in 1860. The company employ fifty persons on an average during the year. The main shop is fifty by one hundred and eighty feet on the ground, two stories; the blacksmith-shop thirty by sixty five feet, same height, and both of brick; the wood-work shop is forty-four by sixty-five feet, and the warehouse forty by sixty-nine feet. A fine flowing well, covered by a neat, tasteful summer-house, furnishes an abundance of pure, cold water for the operatives.

The first blacksmith-shop was built by Ellis Troy, in "Canada," in 1833. He came with Philip H. Hoffman in September of that year. J. H. Bowman built one also in 1834 near his residence, and another was put up the same year on the corner, diagonally opposite from the Three Rivers House.

J. L. Spellman began the manufacture of cigars, July 16, 1874, and employs eleven men. His sales amounted in 1876 to forty thousand cigars per month. The Bellman Cigar Company was incorporated January 1, 1876; President, G. H. Bellman; Secretary, Frederick A. Bellman; Treasurer, W. H. Lothrop. Capital, twenty thousand dollars. George H. Bellman began the business of cigar-making in 1866, with a single man. In 1876 the company employed thirty men, and sold nine hundred thousand cigars, doing a jobbing trade only.

M. H. Flynn has been in the carriage-making line fourteen years—he employs eight men. M. Seville manufactured hats in 1834, in Lockport, and advertised in the *Michigan Statesman* to give patrons fits in style or finish. In 1837 G. H. & T. H. Prindle were blacksmiths in Lockport.

The census of 1874 returns three flour-mills with fourteen run of stones, one saw-mill, one planing-mill, two foundries, two agricultural-implement works and two pump factories, employing one hundred and fifty-eight persons, and three hundred and eleven thousand dollars capital; the value of whose product was placed at five hundred and eighty thousand dollars.

### TRADE.

The first stock of goods brought to Three Rivers for retailing was opened by Smith & Bowman in a little building, sixteen by thirty-two feet, on the present site of the Three Rivers House. Smith was his own clerk when present, and in his absence J. B. Millard officiated and weighed out the groceries, or measured the tape and calico for the farmers' wives and girls.

In the spring of 1837, J. & B. Eddy opened a store, and Moseley came in June of the same year.

In the *Constantine Republican* of February 3, 1837, it is stated that there were then in Three Rivers three stores in operation and another one building.

In July, J. Gregory advertised his business as a tailor, and Dr. E. A. Eagery was announced as the physician of the place, having his office in Smith & Bowman's building, opposite Moore's hotel.

The keel-boat, Three Rivers, was announced in the marine list as having arrived at Constantine with merchandise for Moseley's stores at that place and Three Rivers.

Moore & Prutzman opened a branch store at Three Rivers, in October, 1836, and came themselves personally, in the year 1838, at which time they began shipping flour down the river on the arks. Their first stock of goods was hauled to Prairie Ronde from the mouth of the St. Joseph, in the spring of 1835, at a cost of seven shillings per hundred weight.

These gentlemen came to Three Rivers in the fall of 1834, expecting their stock of goods to arrive at the mouth of the river soon after their own arrival, but the winter set in early and the mouth of the river froze over and the vessel on which the goods were shipped could not make the landing and had to return to Grand Haven, where she lay all winter, the owners of the goods passing the time meanwhile on the east end of Prairie Ronde, whither they took their goods for sale. Moseley opened his store in "Canada."

### HOTELS.

The first hotel was built by Burroughs Moore in the fall of 1833. It was a little one, fourteen by fourteen feet, one and a half story, but he kept guests when they came. He added to it in 1834, and from time to time afterwards until it had the appearance of a little village of itself, and was yclept "Shanty Row." But it was a home for many a weary traveler in its day, and had a long lease of usefulness. It was situated on the present site of the brick block opposite the First National Bank. The building itself was moved back from the street and is now owned by Mr. Hutchinson, and occupied as a tenant house.

Luther Carlton built, in 1838, a frame hotel, which is now the front part of the Three Rivers House.

The present hotels are the Three Rivers House, kept by Leonard Fisher & Sons, to the old frame of which, enlarged and refitted, a large and commodious brick building has been added, affording a comfortable home for its patrons; the Hatch House, a fine brick building, just north of the *Reporter* building, kept by A. S. Bradt; and the Central House, also a commodious brick building, near the bridge over the St. Joseph, kept by D. S. Hale.

### BANKS.

Since the attempt to start the "wild-cat" bank in Lockport, in 1837, which only got so far as a subscription of the capital stock of one hundred thousand dollars and an election of directors, (the projectors being saved the sin of issuing its promises to pay), no attempts for a bank of issue were made in Three Rivers until the national banking law was passed.

In December, 1864, the First National Bank was organized with Hon. Edward S. Moore, president; C. C. Warren, cashier. Mr. Moore has continued to fill the position of president to the present time. Mr. C. L. Blood is the present cashier, and the present board of directors are as follows: E. S. Moore, D. Francisco, N. Pierson, J. W. Hoffman, A. C. Prutzman, S. A. Walton, Stephen Kelsey, E. L. Brown, W. M. Thomas, C. L. Blood, J. P. McKoy.

Mr. Moore was largely instrumental in founding the bank, and Charles Macomber, now deceased, was also prominent in its organization. Its last quarterly statement, published January 22, 1877, shows its loans and discounts amounted at that date to one hundred thousand one hundred and ninety-six dollars and ninety-eight cents; United States bonds to secure its circulation, fifty thousand dollars; other bonds and mortgages, twenty-three thousand seven hundred dollars; due from other national banks, approved reserve agents and redemption fund, fourteen thousand and ninety-seven dollars and seventy-nine cents; real-estate, furniture and fixtures, twenty thousand four hundred and thirty-eight dollars and fifty-eight cents; cash on hand, fifteen thousand one hundred and thirty-three dollars and eighty-two cents. Its capital stock, surplus and undivided profits amounted to one hundred and thirty thousand nine hundred and seventeen dollars and forty-five cents; its circulation to forty-five thousand dollars, and its deposits, subject to check or on certificates, were forty-seven thousand six hundred and forty-nine dollars and seventy-two cents.

The present bank-building of this bank is one of the finest and most convenient offices in the State. The bank has divided among the stockholders five per cent. semi-annually from its organization in 1864. It divided its surplus earnings in 1876, being forty per cent. of its capital.

### THE MANUFACTURERS' NATIONAL BANK,

of Three Rivers, was organized in 1872, with Joseph B. Millard, president, and William E. Wheeler, cashier. Mr. Millard has remained the president to the present time, but E. H. Lothrop succeeded Mr. Wheeler as cashier, and held the position till his death, which occurred September 10, 1874. The vacancy was filled nominally for a short time by W. H. Lothrop, who was succeeded by William E. Wheeler, until January 1, 1876, when the present cashier, O. F. Millard, came to the desk. The present board of directors are J. B. Millard, J. W. French (vice president), O. F. Millard, Henry Hall, W. H. Lothrop, Cyrus Roberts, W. S. Millard, L. T. Wilcox, E. F. Thomas.

The stockholders never withdrew any dividend until January 1, 1877, when a dividend of ten per cent. was declared and drawn.

The statement of the bank, published January 22, 1877, shows its condition financially. Its loans and discounts amounted to one hundred and seventeen thousand five hundred and fifty-seven dollars and ninety-seven cents; United States bonds to secure circulation fifty thousand dollars; due from other national banks and approved reserve agents and redemption fund fifty-five thousand seven hundred and fifty-one dollars and ninety-eight cents; furniture and fixtures, expense and taxes, six thousand five hundred and twenty-eight dollars and ninety-one cents; cash on hand nine thousand eight hundred and fifteen dollars and thirty-eight cents. Its liabilities were: capital stock, surplus and undivided profits, one hundred and nine thousand one hundred and two dollars and twenty-one cents; circulation outstanding, forty-four thousand nine hundred dollars; deposits eighty-five thousand seven hundred and fifty-two dollars and three cents.

### POST-OFFICE.

The first post-office established for the accommodation of the people of Lockport and vicinity was in 1830–1, and was kept by George Buck as postmaster, at his tavern, the "Half-way House." He was succeeded by Burroughs Moore, who kept the office in his tavern in Three Rivers. Moore was succeeded by John McKee in 1839. H. H. Cole was postmaster in 1846, and the mail was brought daily by stage from Kalamazoo and White Pigeon, and could be kept in "a quart cup." Isaac Crossette succeeded Cole, and was in turn succeeded by J. E. Kelsey. S. Allen Smith came behind the boxes after Kelsey, and held the position until his death, when Kelsey came in again for the balance of Smith's term, and generously gave the proceeds of the office to the widow of his predecessor. Isaac Crossette came in again

RESIDENCE of D.D.TENNYSON,
THREE RIVERS, MICH

RESIDENCE of H.BURCH,
THREE RIVERS, MICH.

PRESIDENT                          CASHIER.
E. S. MOORE.                       C. L. BLOOD.

FIRST NATIONAL BANK.
OF
THREE RIVERS, MICHIGAN.

CAPITAL ................................................ $100,000.

DIRECTORS
E. S. MOORE,        N. PIERSON,        A. C. FRUTZMAN,    STEPHEN KELSEY,
D. FRANCISCO,       J. W. HOFFMAN,     S. A. WALTON,      J. P. McKEY,
        E. L. BROWN           N. M. THOMAS         C. L. BLOOD.

after 1852 to 1860; then A. B. Ranny was in for a time,—W. H. Clute coming in from 1861 to 1865; Charles Fonda, 1865–8, and Clute again 1869–72; John B. Handy, the present very efficient incumbent and courteous gentleman receiving the appointment in 1872.

Mr. Handy very kindly furnished the following abstract of business of the office for 1876: amount of money-orders issued, nineteen thousand five hundred and ninety-four dollars and seven cents; amount of money orders paid, sixteen thousand two hundred and ninety dollars and seven cents; number of stamps, stamped envelopes and postal cards sold, four thousand and eighty-seven dollars and fifty-five cents; letters dispatched and received daily one thousand; papers distributed weekly, about two thousand two hundred.

### EARLY METHODS OF TRANSPORTATION.

The transportation of merchandise in the ante-railroad days, was all effected, or nearly so, by the river communication afforded by the St. Joseph. A ship-yard was once established in Lockport, near the present foundry. Washington Gascon built keel-boats and ran them on the river as early as 1836–7; and Burroughs Moore originated the idea of the arks which were built largely at Three Rivers, by Elisha Millard and others; Captain Millard being the most experienced and successful pilot and captain on the river. The first ark ran down from Three Rivers in 1834, as fully described in the general history of the county, as is also the manner of building the arks and navigating the river with them.

The first keel-boat, built by Washington Gascon, ran down the river from Three Rivers in the spring of 1837. Its first cargo was the first flour made in the Smith & Bowman mill; J. B. Miller had one hundred barrels on the boat—the Kitty Kiddungo—and went down himself as super-cargo; he took it to Chicago, receiving nine hundred dollars for his venture in that city, the freight being two dollars per barrel.

In June flour was thirteen dollars per barrel at home. He invested three hundred dollars in wheat, at ten shillings per bushel as the first move.

Moore and Prutzman shipped first in the spring of 1838, and extensively after 1840,—building their own arks. They shipped in this way to the mouth of the river which reached Niles in 1849, then intercepted the road at that point, until 1853, when the Michigan Southern reached Constantine; then the arks disappeared, and flat-boats were used between Three Rivers and Constantine,—teams on the road hauling the flour to the latter place and sometimes towing the boats back.

The steamer Ruby, a small boat, made several trips to Three Rivers.

Calvin Brittain manufactured keel-boats in Three Rivers in 1839, and Gascon before and after.

Out of the first arks sent to Constantine in 1852, wharves were made on which to unload the future cargoes of the keel-boats, the depot being a mile distant from the landing.

Five hundred barrels was the usual load of an ordinary sized ark, forty by sixteen, of two sections or cribs, but as high as six hundred barrels have been carried. The transportation cost from one hundred and twenty dollars to one hundred and seventy-five dollars per trip. The lumber for the keel-boats was whip-sawed.

### RAILROADS.

In 1853, Hon. Edward S. Moore, as president of the St. Joseph Valley railroad company; S. H. Wheeden, secretary; made an arrangement with the Michigan Southern railroad company to build a railroad to Three Rivers under the charter of the former company, which charter was then owned by that company, and the stock subscribed.

The St. Joseph Valley charter allowed a railroad to be built to the State line of Indiana; whereas the charter of the Michigan Southern, denied that company the right to lay their track nearer than three miles from the State line. By this arrangement Three Rivers got a railroad, and the Michigan Southern a connection with the Northern Indians, and thus formed a continuous line to Chicago,—avoiding a law-suit brought for violation of charter.

This railroad to Three Rivers was first laid with strap-rail, and when the superstructure was worn out the road ceased to be operated for a time, thereby causing another effort to re-construct the same and lay it with T rail. The effort was made successful by extending the road north to Schoolcraft, Kalamazoo and Grand Rapids, by the combined enterprise and assistance of the people along the line, and which they paid heavily for. It is now one of the best and safest roads in the State. The township of Lockport aided the re-construction of the road in 1864 by a donation of thirty-five thousand dollars besides the most liberal donations by individuals. In the first building of the road, Moore & Prutzman contributed heavily to get it through to Three Rivers, giving the extensive depot-grounds and grading the same.

There was no lack among the public-spirited citizens in supplying the needed inducements to make the road a success, but Moore & Prutzman were notably zealous and liberal in the work. When the road was extended north, the bridge was built mostly by extra subscriptions of the people. The right of way, half-way to Constantine, was given by citizens.

The business of this road in 1876 is shown by the following exhibit kindly furnished by H. L. Chadwick, station and ticket agent of the Michigan Southern railroad company, as the road is now called: There were seventeen millions four hundred and fifty-two thousand two hundred and ninety-eight pounds of freight received during the year at the station in Three Rivers, and seventeen millions one hundred and fifty-eight thousand eight hundred and forty-two pounds forwarded; the latter including seven millions one hundred and sixty-three thousand six hundred and forty-two pounds of flour, and six millions seven hundred and thirty-seven thousand five hundred and eighty-five pounds of grain, representing thirty-five thousand eight hundred and eighteen barrels of the former and one hundred and twelve thousand two hundred and ninety-three bushels of the latter article. The ticket-sales amounted to nineteen thousand two hundred and eighty-one dollars. William A. Davis is the operator of the Western Union Telegraph company, whose lines run along the company's right of way.

The township also voted to aid the contemplated road from Port Huron to Chicago, an outlet for the Grand Trunk of Canada to get to Chicago, to the amount of sixty-thousand dollars, November 6, 1866, but the road was never built. On May 3, 1869, a donation of forty thousand dollars was made by the township to aid the Michigan Air-Line railroad, which was subsequently built and is now in operation, being "gathered in" after the donations of the township were secure, by the Michigan Central, and by which name it is now known. Mr. J. N. Besson, the station agent, has courteously furnished the following exhibit of the business of the road transacted at the Three Rivers station during 1876: Freight forwarded, twelve millions four hundred and eighty-six thousand four hundred and sixty-two pounds, which includes twenty-nine thousand four hundred barrels of flour, and twenty-eight thousand bushels of wheat. The freight received amounted to twelve million four hundred and forty thousand two hundred and fifty pounds. The ticket sales were fourteen thousand seven hundred and sixty-five dollars and fifty-five cents. The Western Union Telegraph lines also run over the Central's right of way, and O. P. Slote is the operator at its station.

### THE AMERICAN EXPRESS COMPANY

have done during the year 1876, according to the statement kindly furnished by D. M. Bateman, their agent in the city, an amount of transportation and collection business which earned the company four thousand eight hundred and ninety-seven dollars and fifty-seven cents, very nearly equally divided between shipments and receipts.

### THE FIRST PHYSICIAN

was Dr. Eagery, before named. Dr. Hurd came about the same time, in 1836–37. Dr. Pickering and Dr. Choate were also early physicians. The present medical staff of the city are: Dr. C. W. Backus, Dr. L. S. Stevens, Dr. Ion Vernon, Dr. Ikeler, Dr. Adams, Dr. Corbin, Dr. Macomber, Dr. Luke and Dr. Hatch. Dentists—Messrs. S. B. Sill & Son and C. M. Wheeler.

### THE FIRST LAWYER

in the village was a Mr. Hewitt, and next J. H. Lyon, who is still a resident attorney of the place; H. F. Severns, Samuel Chadwick, Seth Bean, R. Grosvenor, W. H. H. Wilcox and Clarence E. Wilbur were located in the village in times past, but left to practice elsewhere. The present legal lights of the community will be found enumerated in the general history of the bar of the county.

### THE BUSINESS OF THE PRESENT

in the city is distributed and conducted as follows:

*Trade.*

Dry Goods and General Merchandise—S. M. Ashby, Johnson Bennett, A. B. Clark, J. L. Shively, S. Kelsey & Son.

Groceries—Edward Armitage, W. W. Burrows, J. J. Dikeman, Dunham & Thoms, Frederick Frey, Hale & McMurtrie, Hummell & Co., E. F. Peirce, James Odell, J. A. Ranney, Jr., J. A. Morton, Tucker & Bickel, Frank Fetaner.

Hardware—H. Penfield, N. Pierson, Griffiths & Dunham.

Boots and Shoes—F. B. Greene, C. Shaad, J. F. Slenker.

Clothing and Furnishing Goods—George C. Brissette, M. Eisig.

18

Drugs—H. D. Cushman, Henry Hall, Snyder & Lindsley, Leidcy & Corbin.
Flour and Feed—G. W. Gillespie, J. J. Kline.
Agricultural Implements—Griffiths & Dunham, N. S. Johnson.
Lumber—Arnold & Caldwell, S. Pugh, C. E. Dexter.
Jewelry—T. L. Arnold, T. B. Snyder, A. B. Ranney.
Books and Stationery—J. H. Pitzel, A. B. Ranney.
Harness—John George Ott, W. W. Rea.
Furniture—Geoge Neidhardt, W. F. Bartlett.
Markets and Butchers—H. Maxfield, A. R. Close, Creighton Brothers.
Butter and Eggs, "Creamery"—McMurtrie & Gibbs.
Photographs—A. Udell, a first-class studio, appointed in the best style of the art.
General Commission—E. M. George.
Marble Works—Robert Hill.
Essential Oils—S. Johnson & Co.
Livery—Hosea Burch.
Merchant-Tailoring—George C. Brissette, M. A. Gamby.
Michigan Southern Railroad—H. J. Chadwick, agent.
Michigan Central Air Line Railroad—J. N. Beeson, agent.
American Express Company—D. M. Bateman, agent.
Western Union Telegraph Company—W. A. Davis and O. P. Slote, operators.
Real-Estate and Insurance—Tennyson & Booth, E. L. Brown, R. E. Case.
Millinery and Ladies' Furnishing Goods—Mrs. L. J. Ayres, Mrs. W. Daniels, Mrs. A. E. Harris, Mrs. N. D. Hunt, Mrs. J. L. Spellman.
Sewing Machines—D. W. Johnson, A. J. Hiles, Mowrey Brothers, J. M. Gilchrist.
Confectionery—Francis Apted.
Restaurant—J. N. Richards.
Musical Instruments—George N. Wright.
Hotels—Leonard Fisher, A. S. Bradt, D. S. Hale.
Newspapers and Job Offices—W. H. Clute, Reporter; Arnold & Son, Herald.
Magnetic Springs Cure—Thomas Silliman.

Manufacturers.

Threshing Machines and Cultivators—Roberts, Throp & Co.
Millers—Griffiths & Dunham, Three Rivers mill; J. W. Hoffman, Hoffman mill.
Paper, Handles and Spokes—J. W. French Manufacturing Company, (Rosette paper-mill.)
Foundry and Machine Shop—Three Rivers Manufacturing Company.
Plows and Pumps—Three Rivers Plow Company; Michigan Pump Company; Protzman Brothers & McIntyre.
Pulp—Three Rivers Pulp Company.
Carriages and Wagons—Brigham & Warren, Z. B. Ruggles, M. H. Flynn.
Mill-Hoppers and Corn-Shellers—John Hutchinson.
Saw-Mill—George Jackson & Co.
Pumps—Jonathan Willetts & Sons.
Soap Manufacturers—Arnold & Smith.
Cigars—Bellman Cigar Company, J. L. Spellman & Co.
Picture-Frames and Mouldings—J. H. Bowen.
Sash, Doors and Blinds—C. E. Dexter, Arnold and Caldwell.
Blacksmiths—John J. Foster, Arthur Silliman, Peter Everett.
Coopers—Fesse & Stillman, — Hill.
Gunsmith—F. E. Brown.
Painters—Kline & Ellison, G. W. Seeley, D. S. Shoemaker.
Shoemakers—P. Bingham, A. Vanderheyden, F. Pulver, Jacob A. Reed.
The capital employed in business in Three Rivers, according to the estimate of competent and impartial men, aggregates seven hundred and ninety-one thousand seven hundred and nineteen dollars in trade, manufactures and banking.

THE FIRST SCHOOL-HOUSE

built in Three Rivers was a plank building, twenty-four by thirty feet on the ground, situated just south, and opposite the present dwelling of John W. Hoffman, in the eastern part of the city. It was then in district number one, of Bucks; but now in Lockport, and was built in the fall of 1837; being completed December 1. The posts were ten feet high.
The district was organized July 1, 1837, by electing Philip H. Hoffman, moderator; Joseph Sterling, director, and Thomas Millard, assessor. There were eight persons present at the meeting. They voted also to raise one

hundred dollars to built a school-house; and, July 15, selected the site before named, and voted an additional tax, not to exceed five hundred dollars, to complete the building, and adopted the plan of the same. The school-district included sections four and nine, and that part of sections sixteen, seventeen and eighteen lying north of the St. Joseph, and east of the Rocky.
The annual meeting was called to order, October 21, at "early candle light," the record says, and the electors proceeded to vote to have the studding of the new school-house filled in with wood, laid in clay mortar, "if any one would do it reasonably." The price was probably meant to be limited, and not the manner in which the work should be done.
There were forty-six children in the district, between five and seventeen years of age.
Five dollars was appropriated for a library, and a sum sufficient to get a suitable case, and H. Bowman was appointed librarian.
In 1840 the school-house was removed to the public square, west of the school-house lot. It was subsequently sold and moved again, and is now occupied as a residence.
A brick school-house, the rear portion of the present building, was built in 1851, and cost one thousand two hundred dollars. The district adopted the union school system September 26, 1859, and graded the school; the first board of education being as follows: Dr. Richardson, S. P. Adams, D. Francisco, I. Crossette, John Cowling and J. C. Bassett. The present school-house was built, except the rear portion, in 1858–59. The total amount of funds raised for the year 1859–60, was two thousand seven hundred and thirty-five dollars and fifty-five cents, six hundred dollars being paid for teachers' wages. The district is free from all debt at the present time, and has a comfortable and capacious house, well lighted and ventilated, though not so pretentious as many of the sister towns in the county, possess. The first principal in the union school was W. H. Paine, who received four hundred dollars and taught one hundred and thirty-five pupils, with two assistants. He continued to teach seven years, from 1857—commencing in the old building—until 1863. He is now in Adrian. He was succeeded by Prof. Simpkins, two years, Prof. Clark, three years, Prof. Stone, six years, and Prof. Baker, the present principal. The board of education for 1876–77 is as follows: D. M. Bateman, moderator; R. R. Dealer, assessor; D. Francisco, director; Thomas M. Clark, J. H. Lyon, Joseph M. Kirby.
School district number four has its school-house in the second ward of the city, and was organized separately and independently, September 10, 1855, by electing William Fulkerson, moderator; W. F. Arnold, director, and Frederick O. White, assessor. At the annual meeting that year, J. W. French was elected moderator, and the people voted to build a school-house twenty-six by thirty feet, one story, ten feet high. Three hundred dollars was appropriated to purchase a site and build the house on the southwest corner of Mr. Arnold's farm. The house was built the same fall and cost five hundred dollars. The teacher's wages for the first year amounted to two hundred and nineteen dollars and ninety-seven cents. September 3, 1866, the people voted to raise one thousand dollars for a new building, and one thousand dollars in 1867, and in the latter year, voted to build the house on a plan of thirty by seventy feet on the ground, two stories, eleven and twelve feet in the clear respectively; and the site was changed to the northwest corner of the west half of the southwest quarter of section twenty, containing two acres. The building was erected in 1868, and cost about four thousand five hundred dollars. It is of brick, and very pleasantly located, is capacious and well lighted, and built more for convenience than architectural display. The school was graded in 1869, but the district has never adopted the union school system.
The statistics of the schools of Three Rivers for the year ending September 1, 1876, are as follows: there were two brick school-houses with eight hundred and sixteen sittings, valued at twenty-one thousand dollars; eight hundred and twenty-four pupils attended the schools, which were in session ten months. Two male teachers were employed and paid two thousand and fifty dollars for their services, and twelve female teachers received three thousand nine hundred and twelve dollars. The total income for the year amounted to eleven thousand five hundred and ten dollars and sixty-seven cents, including three hundred dollars received for tuition from non-resident pupils. Total expenditures, including thirteen hundred dollars on bonded indebtedness—the last installment—ten thousand seven hundred and five dollars and sixty-five cents. There are six hundred and fifteen volumes in the town library.

THE CHURCHES.

The first church organized in Three Rivers was the First Presbyterian church of that place; its formation dating from August 12, 1838. This society was organized by Rev. Mr. Stanley, of Mottville, with nineteen

SAMUEL A. FITCH.                    MRS. SAMUEL A. FITCH.

RESIDENCE OF SAMUEL A. FITCH, LOCKPORT, ST JOSEPH CO, MICH.

RESIDENCE of JOHN BAUM, Lockport Tp. St Joseph Co, Mich.

RESIDENCE of E. R. WILLEMIN,
Lockport Tp, St Joseph Co, Mich.

members, viz.: James Slote, Hannah his wife, and Mrs. Sarah Snyder, their daughter; John Boodman, Catherine Mowrey, John Sickler and Anoa his wife, Edward S. Moore and Mary P. his wife, Mrs. Elizabeth Moore, Dr. Edward S. Eagery, Mrs. Louisa Manning, John Troy, and Robecca his wife, Samuel L. Sterling, Miles Bristol, and Celestia his wife. On the same day James Slote, McDonald Campbell and Edward S. Moore were ordained as elders. Mr. Moore filled the position of elder until January 2, 1876, when he resigned, from his own choice, to make way for younger men. The first session-meeting was held at the house of Dr. Eagery, March 4, 1839, at which were present Rev. Benjamin Ogden, of the Presbytery of New Brunswick, and Edward S. Moore, elder; the other elders being deceased—Mr. Campbell dying within a month of his ordination, and Mr. Slote in February, 1839. After a lapse of thirty-eight years, on July 2, 1876, six only of the original members were living in the communion of the church, viz.: Edward S. Moore and wife, (the latter since deceased), John Sickler and wife, Samuel L. Sterling and Dr. Edward S. Eagery; while of ten others who united with the church during the first year of its history, eight remain: Jonathan Hoats and Mary his wife, Mrs. Sabina McKey, Mrs. Mary L. Prutzman, Mrs. Martha Fengler, Mrs. Maria P. Kelsey, Miss Bondman, now Mrs. John Armitage, and Miss Mary Kepler.

The total membership of the church since its organization has been five hundred and twenty-four, of whom one hundred and sixty-three were (July 2, 1876), known to be living and in good regular standing in the church. From the time of its organization until the beginning of the year 1876, twelve ruling elders had served the church,—besides the three before named, they were John Troy, John Sickler, Eli H. Bristol, Lomison, Abram C. Prutzman, Alexander H. Hicks, Henry N. Spencer, John Armitage and Robert M. Lafferty. Of these, Messrs. Bristol, Hicks and Spencer have died, Troy, Lomison and Lafferty have been dismissed to other congregations, and the others remain with the church. Mr. Moore and Mr. Sickler served the church, respectively, thirty-eight and thirty-seven years.

On January 6, 1876, the following board of elders were elected on the term system,—a portion to retire each year; William Sickler, John P. Prutzman, John Dunham, George W. Gillespie, Borden M. Hicks, Charles B. Tucker and Albert B. Ranney. Ten ministers have served the church, as follows: Rev. Benjamin Ogden, from November 1, 1838 to 1843; Rev. Albert H. Gaston, from October 29, 1843, to May, 1846; Rev. Robert McMath, from August, 1846 to 1850; Rev. William Page, from 1850 to 1854; Rev. William Blackburn, from May, 1854, to 1856; Rev. Almon G. Martin, from August, 1856 to January, 1859; Rev. Joseph A. Ranney, from 1859 to 1872; Rev. George Barnes, from 1872 to 1873; Rev. John D. McCord, from November, 1873 to 1874; Rev. William A. Masker, who preached three Sabbaths, as supply, in November and December, 1874, and has served as acting pastor since January 1, 1875, to the present writing—1877. During an existence of thirty-nine years, the church has had but one installed pastor,—Joseph A. Ranney,—who was installed September 21, 1850, his pastorate extending until September, 1872. Mr. Ogden and Mr. Page are dead, and the others are actively engaged in the work of the ministry. In 1850, under Mr. McMath, a time of refreshing was had in the church, Rev. Calvin Clark assisting the pastor some weeks, at the end of which (in March) twenty-six persons united with the church,—twenty of them by profession of faith. In 1855, during Mr. Martin's charge, thirteen were received. In 1860, the first year of Mr. Ranney's pastorate, thirty-four were received into the church,—twenty-seven on profession of faith, and one year after fifteen more were added. The most memorable communion-season, in the history of the church, occurred in 1866. Mr. Moody was with the church a few days, and at the April communion sixty-three were received into the church on profession, and five by letter,—thirty-three being baptized. In 1859 seventeen were added to the church. During Mr. Ranney's pastorate two hundred and sixty-six united with the church, being an average accession of more than twenty in each year,—one hundred and fifty-eight joined on profession of faith, and one hundred and eight by letter. There have been thirty-eight added since,—by Mr. Barnes, eight; Mr. McCord, fifteen, and Mr. Masker, fifteen.

During the first ten years, the society had no house of its own to worship in, but met in private residences and in school-houses. On February 14, 1849, the first church was completed and dedicated,—Rev. O. P. Hoyt, of Kalamazoo, and Rev. Mr. Steele, of Constantine, officiating. This building was supposed, by most of the congregation, to be large enough to accommodate the congregation for many years to come, but, ten years later, it was enlarged at least one-third, bringing it to its present size. It now stands by the side of the beautiful and capacious temple which this society erected in 1868-70,

at a cost of about thirty thousand dollars,—the same being nearly paid up at the present time. It was dedicated May 11, 1870, the sermon being preached by Rev. William Hogarth, D. D.

The church was represented in the armies of the Union, during the war of the rebellion, by eight members,—one being the son of the pastor, and another, Captain Henry N. Spencer, the superintendent of the Sunday-school. Besides these eight, there were three husbands of members, twenty-seven sons, and twenty-two brothers, of members, and ten members of the congregation,—eighty in all. Of these the following gave their lives in defense of the country:

Members of the church—Ariel Lamb, killed in battle in West Virginia; William Woodruff, died of fever at Helena, Arkansas; Jacob Fengler, husband of Mrs. Martha Buck Fengler, died in New Orleans; Ray Hicks, son of Mrs. Sophia Hicks, died in Louisiana; William P. Baum, son of John Baum, died of fever at Helena, Arkansas; Edward W. Prutzman, son of A. C. and Mary Prutzman, (adjutant 25th Michigan Infantry,) killed at Resaca, Georgia, in an assault upon the enemy's works; John Gilbert, an attendant upon the church service, died at Louisville.

The following brothers of members also gave their lives for the old flag: Yeager Baum, Charles H. Horton, Joseph M. Marsh, Lorenzo M. Petit, John Troy, George Westover and David T. Whitney. Frank Smitley, whose mother was a member of the church, was killed by a sharp-shooter during the Atlanta campaign. Thus the roll of the church slain numbers fifteen.

The above historical record of the Presbyterian Church we have condensed from an exhaustive Centennial sermon, delivered by the present pastor, Rev. William A. Masker, July 22, 1876, a copy of which the reverend gentleman most kindly furnished us, and for which he has our thanks.

The first class of the Methodist Episcopal church of Three Rivers was formed in 1836, by the circuit preacher in charge; Joseph Sterling and wife, John Carpenter and wife, Mrs. Grant Brown and Mrs. Catharine Hoffman being the original members. The class numbered fourteen in May, 1839, Ezra Cole, his wife and brother, joining it at that time. Mr. Sterling was the leader of the class until Mr. Cole came, when he was chosen, and preached also to them every two weeks, from June, 1839, until December of that year. Rev. John Ercanbrack was the circuit preacher in charge, from 1837 to 1839, but Reverends Beecher and Stanley preached occasionally during the former part of the latter year. The society was not organized as a church until April 11, 1842, when Ezra Cole, John Arney, Philip H. Hoffman, Joseph Sterling and George Hardy were elected trustees.

In 1846 the first church-edifice was erected on the site of the present one, at a cost of one thousand five hundred dollars. It was built of brick, and was thirty by forty feet on the ground. The building-committee was Warren D. Pettit and Z. B. Ruggles. The society had met previously in the school-house. The present edifice was erected in 1863-5, and dedicated by Reverends A. T. Hatfield and Thomas Eddy, of Chicago. It is a fine building, large, roomy and comfortable, and cost about thirty thousand dollars. In the winter of 1840-1, Rev. Erastus Kellogg, assisted by Mr. Cole, created an enthusiasm in the community, and one hundred joined the church during the year.

The following ministers have had charge of the class and church from the organization of the former, until the present time. Reverends John Ercanbrack, 1837-9 and 1844-6; Erastus Kellogg, 1839-41, and Father McCoole about this time; Richard Meek, —— Worthington. Samuel Osborne, 1849-51; H. Penfield, 1851-2 and 1859-60; A. J. Eldred, Salmon Steel, Enoch Holstock, 1854-6; Thomas Granger, 1856-8; David Burns, 1860-2; A. A. Dunton, 1862-4; D. G. Gillett, 1865-7; Thomas Jacokes, 1867-9; W. H. Pierce, 1869-71; Levi Tarr, 1871-3; Israel Coggshall, 1873-5; J. W. Miller, 1875-7.

A Sunday-school is in full and successful operation in connection with the society.

THE FIRST BAPTIST CHURCH

of Three Rivers was organized as a society, April 6, 1861, the council for the purpose being composed of Rev. J. L. McCloud, of Schoolcraft; Rev. Samuel Haskell, of Kalamazoo, and Rev. S. F. Faxon. The roll of members at the time the organization was effected was William F. Arnold and wife, William M. Griffin, wife and two daughters, Cornelius Young, William Churchill and his son Adney, Mrs. Sally Woodhull, Mrs. Frost and Samuel Ludwig. William Churchill and Ludwig were the deacons, and Griffin the first clerk. The only church edifice ever built by the society, was erected, in 1864, at a cost of seven thousand dollars. It was of wood, its dimensions on the ground were thirty-eight by sixty feet, and it afforded three hundred sittings. It was burned in 1871. The number of members, when last reported, was one hundred and seventy. There have been no meetings for two years.

The first pastor of the church was Luther H. Trowbridge, who was a licentiate when he first came, in 1861, but was ordained in Three Rivers, and remained with the church until the close of 1869. J. S. Goodall succeeded Mr. Trowbridge in 1870–3, the congregation meeting in Kelsey's Hall after the church was burned. E. Curtis succeeded Mr. Goodall for six months, and Mr. Pack came next, for one year, since which time there has been no shepherd over the flock. The church was dedicated December 27, 1864.

A Sunday-school was organized before the church was built, and was kept up until the meetings were suspended; J. W. French being the superintendent.

### THE FIRST REFORMED CHURCH OF THE UNITED STATES

of Three Rivers was organized February 1, 1863, by Rev. D. Kroh. Among the first members of the church were John G. Ott, John Buss, Lucas Thurer, F. Burgin, and John Steininger, with their wives; Henry Stotz, George Schneidhart, Charles Ettelman and F. Keiser.

The present church-edifice was built in the third ward of the city, in 1870 –71, at a cost of eleven thousand dollars. It has three hundred and fifty sittings. The society numbers one hundred and seventy-five members, and its Sunday-school, eighty scholars, and has one hundred and fifty books in its library, the pastor being the superintendent. The pastors of the church have been Rev. H. Wiegand, J. L. Schlosser and L. Grossenburg, the present incumbent.

### TRINITY CHURCH (EPISCOPAL)

of Three Rivers was organized September 14, 1863, with the following members: William H. Warren, John Cowling, John M. Bailey, Isaac Crossette, L. L. Herrick, S. Chadwick, C. Robertson, L. A. Selleck, William Demott, Thomas M. Clark. The first vestry were, John Cowling, S. W.; Edwin Warren, J. W.; W. E. Wheeler, treasurer; Calvin Robertson, secretary; Thomas M. Clark, Edward Murphy, Isaac Crossette and Samuel Chadwick.

October 26, 1863, a call was extended to Rev. V. Spalding to settle with the church as rector, at a salary of five hundred dollars, and was accepted the same day.

May 12, 1864, Thomas M. Clark, Edward Murphy, Wardens, and W. E. Wheeler, treasurer, as delegates, attended the Diocesan convention at Grand Rapids, and changed the name of the church to St. Joseph's church, but it was subsequently changed back to "Trinity." The rector resigned April 20, 1866, and was succeded in July following, by Rev. William Charles, from Stevens Point, Wisconsin.

The present church-edifice was built in 1866–7; it is valued at six thousand dollars, and will seat three hundred persons. The Sunday-school was organized under Mr. Charles' rectorship. The Trinity Church Aid Society, formed of the ladies of the church, has been a most efficient aid in the building of the church and in supporting a rector. They have a library of one hundred and fifty volumes. Mrs. N. S. Andrews is the president, and Miss Cora Shiveley, secretary.

The rectors who have been settled over the church since Mr. Charles resigned, March 2, 1868, were Reverends Alexander H. Rogers, 1868–70; M. J. Hyde, December, 1870, to November, 1871; Henry McClory, 1872–3; M. E. Buck, 1874–6. There is no rector with the church at the present time. The present vestry are: Thomas M. Clark, S. W.; John Cowling, J. W.; E. L. Brown, treasurer; D. M. Bateman, secretary; W. W. Rea, C. W. Harvey and J. F. Lake. There are seventy members on the roll of the church, and thirty-five scholars in the Sunday-school.

### ST. JOHN'S EVANGELICAL LUTHERAN CHURCH

of Three Rivers, was organized April 3, 1870, and adopted a constitution and elected trustees, viz.: Aaron Schall, Samuel Weinberg, Levi Van Dorsten and the pastor, Rev. Delo. Among the first members, of whom there were twenty-nine, were Samuel Fees (now dead), S. H. Acker and wife, James King and wife, Lanson G. Reichart and wife, Samuel Bobb and wife, Mrs. M. C. Delo, Mrs. Mary M. Schall, Mrs. Levi Van Dorsten, Samuel Van Dorsten and wife, Jacob and Matilda Swartz, and Josiah Steininger.

The first pastor was Rev. Delo, who remained with the church six years; the present one, Rev. A. J. Cromer, coming to it in the early part of 1876. *

The society erected in the second ward of the city, in 1872–3, a fine brick edifice, which will seat from three hundred to three hundred and fifty persons, and is valued at ten thousand dollars. A Sunday-school connected with the church has seventy-five scholars. There are fifty-five members in the church, and the elders at present are Aaron Schall and Gideon Boyers.

### THE PROTESTANT METHODIST CHURCH

of Three Rivers numbers eighty members. Its house of worship is situated in the eastern part of the second ward of the city, and is valued at five thousand dollars. It contains two hundred sittings, and is thirty-four by forty-eight feet on the ground. Rev. Mr. Becker was the pastor in 1873, Rev. William Tompkinson in 1875–6, and Rev. J. H. Webb is the present shepherd.

### SOCIETIES—MASONIC.

Three Rivers Lodge, No. 57, A. F. M., was instituted under dispensation in 1852 and chartered in 1853. Its first worshipful master was Ezra Cole, who served under the dispensation and two years under the charter. Since then the position has been filled as follows: H. H. Cole, 1855–9; John Cowling, 1860–2 and 1874; D. M. Bateman, 1863–6; W. H. Warren, 1867; Thomas M. Greene, 1868–73 and 1876, and L. T. Wilcox, 1875. The present officers are Thomas M. Greene, W. M.; Sylvester Troy, S. W.; B. F. Wells, J. W.; W. W. Rea, secretary. The lodge's roll of craftsmen numbers one hundred.

Friendship Lodge, No. 338, was instituted by charter in January, 1876, with John Cowling as master; C. W. Backus, S. W.; I. H. Greenwood, J. W.; L. T. Wilcox, secretary; James F. Thoma, treasurer, and thirty-four charter-members. It has added ten more craftsmen to its list since its organization.

Salathiel Chapter, No. 23, R. A. M., so named in honor of Judge S. C. Coffinberry, was instituted under dispensation in 1859 and chartered in January following. Its first officers were Ezra Cole, H. P.; John Cowling, K.; Joseph C. Morse, S. Since then the office of H. P. has been filled by John Cowling from 1861 to 1871 inclusive, and 1873–5; Thomas M. Greene, 1872. The present officers are D. D. Thorp, H. P.; Jacob F. Slenker, K.; William G. Caldwell, S.; John Cowling, secretary; James F. Thoma, treasurer. The roll of members numbers one hundred.

### THREE RIVERS COUNCIL, NO. 7, OF R. AND S. M.

was chartered February 2, 1860, with B. F. Doughty, T. I. M.; John Cowling, P. C. W., and H. H. Cole, recorder. John Cowling, I. C. Bassett and J. E. Prutzman have been the T. I. Masters. The present officers are Joseph E. Prutzman, T. I. M.; David Knox, Jr., S. W.; L. B. Hess, P. C. W.; John Cowling, recorder. There are eighty-five members engaged in the crypt.

Three Rivers Commandery, No. 29, K. T., was chartered June 20, 1872. L. S. Stevens, E. C.; S. B. Kingsbury, Gen'o; D. D. Thorp, C. G.; J. Eastman Johnson, prelate, and Thomas G. Greene, recorder, being its first officers. There were twenty-four charter-members. D. D. Thorp, W. E. Wheeler, J. E. Prutzman and C. W. Backus have been the commanders. The officers of 1876–7 are George C. Brissette, E. C.; C. W. Backus, Gen'o; D. D. Thorp, C. G.; Rev. A. H. Vanvranken, prelate; John Cowling, recorder, and L. T. Wilcox, treasurer. The commandery has on its muster-roll eighty six knights.

John Cowling was for fourteen years high priest of Salathiel Chapter, and has been secretary for most of the Masonic bodies during a great portion of their history. All the Masonic bodies meet in the same hall, which Three Rivers Lodge holds under a twenty years' lease. It is handsomely and neatly furnished. The dedication of the hall was a noted event in the history of the order in Three Rivers. The officers of the Grand Lodge of Michigan were present, and the editor of the *Michigan Freemason* delivered the oration.

### ODD-FELLOWSHIP.

Excelsior Lodge, No. 80, I. O. O. F., was chartered in 1860, Isaac C. Bassett and Cyrus Roberts filling the position of N. G. the first year, and John Cowling and T. E. Clapp, succeeding thereto during the second year. In 1860, the forty-first anniversary of the institution of the order was celebrated in Three Rivers with great *eclat*. The officers of the year 1876 are: Watson Gray, N. G.; Charles Sandberg, V. G.; W. P. Gibbs, permanent secretary; H. W. Whitman, recording secretary; Ion Vernon, treasurer. There are ninety-four members in good standing on the books of the lodge.

Golden Rule Lodge, No. 184, was chartered in 1872, Enoch Kline being the first N. G., and with twenty-two charter-members. Its present officers are: James Smitley, N. G.; William Sickles, V. G.; J. W. Ferguson, P. S.; William Woodward, R. S.; H. T. Arthur, treasurer; and its members number seventy-five.

Curtis Encampment, No. 39, of Patriarchs, was instituted February 1, 1871, and its present officers are: John Foster, C. P.; D. W. Johnson, H. P.; T. Troy, S. W.; O. P. Smith, J. W.; W. P. Gibbs, scribe; Ion Vernon, treasurer. It has thirty-eight members on its roll.

RESIDENCE OF L. B. SWARTWOUT, THREE RIVERS, MICH.

RESIDENCE OF DR. C. W. BACKUS, THREE RIVERS, MICH.

Rebekah Degree Lodge, No. —, was chartered in 1871, and suspended work the year following.

John Cowling is the oldest Odd-Fellow in western Michigan.

Three Rivers Lodge of Good Templars, No. —, was organized in 1866, with O. F. Bean, W. C. T. It awakened an interest in the temperance cause, having at one time two hundred members on its books. It worked well for several years, but has been suspended for some time.

### PATRONS OF HUSBANDRY.

Three Rivers Grange, No. 179, was organized December 27, 1873, with John E. Cook, master; William Fulkerson, overseer; W. D. Pettit, lecturer, J. W. Schuyler, secretary, and a goodly number of members.

The officers of 1877 are: W. D. Pettit, master; S. M. Snyder, overseer; Lucas Thurer, lecturer; J. W. Schuyler, secretary; Mrs. W. D. Pettit, Ceres; Mrs. C. W. Garrison, Pomona, and Mrs. J. E. Cook, Flora.

### ARNER'S SILVER CORNET BAND

was organized in 1874 as the Three Rivers Cornet Band, with six instruments; was reorganized in 1875 under the present name, and increased its equipment to sixteen of the best silver instruments manufactured by Hall & Quimby, eight of which are helicons, costing five hundred dollars. The uniforms of cadet-gray, and full equipments, cost one thousand dollars. W. J. Arner is the leader and director of the association.

### THREE RIVERS LIGHT GUARDS

were enlisted September, 1874, and mustered into the Michigan militia in 1875. The company numbers eighty-three muskets and three commissioned officers: Harlow E. McCarey, captain; —— Coup, first lieutenant; Charles W. Millard, second lieutenant. The company was in the encampment at Grand Rapids, a week, in 1876. The State furnished their arms and equipments, the former being the Springfield breech-loading rifles.

### THE ST. JOSEPH FIRE-COMPANY

was first organized October 1, 1859, with fifty members, and a hose-company on the 25th of the same month. The first engine-house was John Young's shop. The present engine-house was built in 1866, at a cost of over four thousand dollars. Cisterns were built in the city in 1860.

### THE MUNICIPALITY

of Three Rivers began its legal existence February 13, 1855, when it was incorporated by express action of the legislature. The first president was —— ; first recorder, George B. Reed, and first trustees, A. B. Moore, Thomas M. Clark, L. L. Herrick, Sylvester Troy, and W. F. Barton.

In 1860 the corporation thinking to add to the pleasure of its citizens, purchased some musical instruments, and a brass band was organized.

August 6, 1866, the board appointed D. Francisco, S. Kelsey, and A. C. Prutsman a building-committee for the erection of an engine-house.

In 1871 the corporation was extended over Lockport, which was designated as the second ward, and also to include "Canada," which was designated the third ward.

The assessments of property, and taxes thereon, for corporate purposes in the corporation, for the year 1876, are as follows: In the first ward, seven hundred and seventy-eight thousand two hundred dollars; taxes, nine hundred and fifty-six dollars and twenty cents. Second ward, two hundred and seventy-nine thousand nine hundred and eighty-five dollars; taxes, four hundred and seven dollars and ninety-eight cents. Third ward, one hundred and seventy-four thousand nine hundred and twenty dollars; taxes, two hundred and forty-five dollars and ninety-two cents. Fourth ward, fifty-five thousand three hundred and ninety-five dollars; taxes, eighty-five dollars and thirty-nine cents. Total assessment, one million two hundred and eighty-eight thousand three hundred and sixty-eight dollars; total taxes, one thousand six hundred and ninety-five dollars and forty-nine cents.

There are no debts outstanding against the township, corporation, school-districts, or churches, of any amount.

The position of president of the corporation has been filled since the first election as follows: Daniel Francisco, 1859, 1861, 1864-6, 1868-70; Thomas M. Clark, 1860; Stephen Kelsey, 1862, 1869, 1874; L. B. Rich, 1863; J. C. Morse, 1867; Henry Yauney, 1871-2; George A. Jackson, 1873; Henry Hall, 1875-6.

The recorders have been as follows: George B. Reed, 1855; D. M. Bateman, 1856; James H. Lyon, 1857-8; H. L. Dickinson, 1859-64-67-70; John Cowling, 1860-76; Norman S. Andrews, 1861; C. Robertson, 1862-63; L. N. Straw, 1865; W. H. Warren, 1866; Joseph E. Prutsman, 1868; R.

R. Pealer, 1869-72; Thomas G. Greene, 1871; David Knox, Jr., 1873-75; W. B. Pierson, 1874.

### THE MAGNETIC SPRINGS.

One of the prominent institutions of Three Rivers, which is advertising the place to a considerable extent, is the cure, established at the magnetic springs, by Thomas Silliman. There are several flowing springs in the city, which are said to contain magnetic properties; but the only one that has as yet been utilized for medicinal purposes, is the one owned by Mr. Silliman.

Mr. C. C. Flint owned the property at the time the spring was discovered, the land, on which a small house was erected, being occupied by Mrs. Greene, for whose benefit the owner drove a well in the lot, in 1869 or 1870, some forty-five feet in depth, when water flowed over the top. Mrs. Greene, being in ill health, used the water, and was cured by it. The suggestion was then made of its possible magnetic qualities, and upon applying a test, the steel in a very short time became highly charged with magnetism. The rumor spread, and people began to come, to use the water; whereupon Mr. Flint built some bathing-tubs, and began to utilize the water in a small way, and was soon overtaxed for want of room for his patients, who were rapidly increasing.

In the spring of 1873 Mr. Silliman bought the property, and enlarged the buildings, putting in a larger boiler and better facilities for using the water. He has had all the patients he could accommodate, besides shipping large quantities of the water to distant localities. The water has never been scientifically analyzed, and no exact statement can be made of its elements, but its magnetic qualities seem to be unquestioned.

### FIRST POULTRY EXHIBITION.

The Michigan Southern Poultry Association was organized in 1876, and held its first exhibition at Three Rivers, February 9, 1877, at which, some very fine fowls were exhibited. The present officers are: S. D. Hutchinson, Parkville, president; J. H. Clemont, Colon, first vice-president; Henry Yauney, second vice-president; Edward Armitage, Three Rivers, treasurer; E. G. Tucker, Three Rivers, secretary.

### RIVERSIDE CEMETERY

is located on the northeast quarter of the southwest quarter of section seventeen, township sixty-six range eleven west. The association was organized under the statute for such purposes provided, October 2, 1858, by individual corporators:—Edward S. Moore, president; E. H. Lothrop, vice-president; Adolphus E. Hewitt, secretary; A. C. Prutsman, treasurer; Henry N. Spencer, sexton; and nine trustees. The association adopted a code of ordinances, laid off a "Strangers' Home," and made their first purchase, paying one thousand dollars therefor. January 11, 1859, the name "Oak Dale" cemetery (under which the organization was effected) was changed to the name it now bears, and in April additional grounds were purchased,—the whole tract now containing thirty-three acres, most beautifully and eligibly located on the north bank of the St. Joseph,—and grading was begun. The association paid fifty dollars per acre for their land, have laid out a large sum in grading and beautifying the grounds, and have two thousand dollars in their treasury. The oaks of the original openings shade the grounds most invitingly, and no lovelier spot can be found in all the county, replete though it is with charming landscapes, for a city of the dead. Several elegant monuments attest the taste and affection of the living, who have laid their loved and lost to rest in the beautiful spot prepared for them by the liberality of the foremost citizens of Three Rivers. The present officers of the association are S. P. Adams, president; J. B. Millard, vice-president; Stephen Kelsey, treasurer; D. M. Bateman, secretary.

The first cemetery was given to the village by the original proprietors of the plat, and was used until the new cemetery was laid out; since which time the old ground has been abandoned, and the greater portion of the inmates removed to the new one. But the old grounds are unprotected by fences, and lie open as commons, presenting a forbidding aspect, to the stranger, at least.

### REMINISCENCE.

Littlejohn, in his legends of Michigan, makes the present site of the original village of Three Rivers, the scene of a desperately fought battle between the Ottawas and the Pottawatomies on the one side, and the Shawnees or Shawanese, of Indians and the south, under Elkhart, a noted chief in the later history of the west. The imaginative author, by a most skillfully-prepared campaign,—sketched out while surveying the public domain,—forces the Pottawatomies from White Pigeon prairie, and drives them back upon the Kalamazoo, where a confederation is formed with the renowned fighters (the Ottawas), and a grand assault is made under cover of the night, with a skillfully planned surprise upon the intrenched Elkhart, who, assailed in front and on both flanks, is driven from his fortifications, and his warriors slaughtered without mercy, until, broken and disheartened, they flee southward; their power to invade the fertile plains of Michigan, forever broken. However graphically the story is told, it rests on the merest thread of tradition. Such a thing might have been, but none but the most fervid imagination could weave so brilliant a web from so fragile a thread.

Where the city now rises in brick blocks and palatial residences, present citizens have seen herds of deer, numbering twenty and thirty fine animals. Turkers strutted in broods, bears lumbered lazily along, wolves howled, and sneaked wickedly by, and prairie-chickens drummed and uttered their musical and mournful notes, where now the daily bustle of the streets resounds, and commerce holds sway.

### LOCKPORT IN THE REBELLION

made a record upon which her citizens may look and reflect with pride. She sent more than two hundred of her men, the flower of her citizens, to the front; and when her wasted companies returned, their tattered ensigns testified but too plainly that they had been borne by brave men, and that, though

> "Stormed at by shot and shell,
> Bravely they charged, and well,
> Into the very jaws of hell,"

of the frightful, fratricidal strife precipitated upon the nation by traitorous men. Her citizens lie mouldering beneath the flowery sod of the sunny south, or bear about their persons the sad evidences of the sacrifices demanded of heroic men, by the bloody Moloch of war.

We here append a list of the citizens of Lockport, who went out from their homes at the call of the nation, to defend and uphold its integrity and its flag:

#### SECOND MICHIGAN INFANTRY.

Private Edwin P. Arnold, Company F; mustered-out.
Private Henry Henner, Company F; discharged for disability.
Private Martin V. Moore, Company F; mustered-out.
Corporal Samuel D. Southworth, Company G, lieutenant in regular army; dead.
Private William G. Bennett, Company G; discharged for disability.
Private Gilbert Blovelt, Company G; died of typhoid fever, Yorktown, Virginia, May 6, 1862.
Private Augustus Flint, Company G; discharged for disability.
Private Hiram Hutchinson, Company G; discharged for disability.
Private William S. Woodhead, Company G; discharged at expiration of service.
Private Alonzo Wescott, Company G; discharged for disability.

#### FOURTH INFANTRY.

Private Lewis L. Flint, Company G; discharged for disability.

#### SIXTH INFANTRY.

Private John R. Cowden, Company C; re-enlisted and mustered-out.
Private Jacob Feagles, Company C; died at New Orleans, August 14, 1863.
Private John P. Graham, Company C; re-enlisted and mustered-out.
Private Walter I. Hunter, Company C; died at Port Hudson, Louisiana, February 4, 1864.
Private Day Hicks, Company C; re-enlisted and mustered-out.
Private Ray Hicks, Company C; died at regiment hospital, October 2, 1862.
Private Jacob W. Monroe, Company C; discharged for disability.
Private Rudolph Mohney, Company C; died at Camp Williams, Louisiana, September 9, 1862.
Private George P. Sterling, Company C; mustered-out.
Private James M. Smithey, Company C; re-enlisted and mustered-out.
Private Solomon Sugars, Company C; re-enlisted and mustered-out.
Private Joseph Sargood, Company C; discharged at expiration of service.
Private Charles Tutton, Company C; discharged at expiration of service.
Private Samuel P. Babcock, Company C; died at Memphis, Tennessee.

#### SEVENTH INFANTRY.

Private John Kelly, Company B; killed near Petersburg, Virginia.

#### ELEVENTH INFANTRY.

Adjutant Samuel Chadwick; resigned.
Drum-major Charles E. Franklin; discharged, February 6, 1862.
Principal Musician Hiram M. Wheeler; mustered-out, August 22, 1862.
Musician Horatio G. Taggart; mustered-out, August 22, 1862.
Musician Jason Clarke; mustered-out, August 22, 1862.
Musician Charles Rice; mustered-out, August 22, 1862.
Musician James A. Knevels; mustered-out, August 22, 1862.
Musician Alfred Lantz; discharged for disability.
Musician John B. Silliman; discharged for disability.
Private Charles Francisco, Company A; discharged for disability.
Private Loriston Fulkerson, Company A; died at Bardstown, Ky.
Private Henry Hale, Company A; discharged at expiration of service.
Private John A. Mills, Company A; veteran reserve corps.
Private George S. Sheffield, Company A; discharged at expiration of service.
Private Anson Spencer, Company A; discharged at expiration of service.
Private Milo L. G. Wheeler, Company A; discharged at expiration of service.
Private Thomas V. Woodhouse, Company A; discharged at expiration of service.
Private Elias Ward, Company A; discharged for disability.
Private Dexter Avery, Company B; discharged.
Private Samuel Pugh, Company B; discharged.
Private Elliott S. Gray, Company C; discharged.
Captain Henry N. Spencer, Company E; resigned.
First Lieutenant Thomas Flynn, Company E; captain and killed at Stone River.
Sergeant John Graham, Company E.
Sergeant Edward M. Frost, Company E; discharged at expiration of service.
Sergeant George Nyce, Company E; discharged for disability.
Corporal John W. Banter, Company E; discharged at expiration of service.
Corporal Harvey Lockwood, Company E; discharged at expiration of service.
Corporal Lot T. Woodworth, Company E; discharged for disability.
Corporal Ezra Spencer, Company E; died at Stone River.
Corporal James T. Elliott, Company E; discharged for promotion.
Private George S. Baum, Company E; discharged at expiration of service.
Private Frank M. Bauter, Company E; discharged.
Private Arthur M. Bush, Company E; discharged for disability.
Private Hiram L. Brewster, Company E; discharged at White Pigeon.
Private Edwin Craig, Company E; discharged at White Pigeon.
Private George Drescher, Company E; discharged at expiration of service.
Private Charles David, Company E; discharged at expiration of service.
Private John Eggelshoffer, Company E; discharged at expiration of service.
Private Augustus Ennis, Company E; discharged at expiration of service.
Private Alexander Ennis, Company E; discharged at expiration of service.
Private Caleb W. Elmer, Company E; died at Louisville, August 10, 1862.
Private Cornelius J. Fonda, Company E; died at Nashville, August 10, 1862.
Private Michael Fellinger, Company E; discharged.
Private Henry Hix, Company E; discharged.
Private Philip Jones, Company E; discharged at expiration of service.
Private Joseph Malalivly, Company E; died at Tullahoma, Tennessee, July 12, 1863.
Private Samuel Quaco, Company E; discharged at expiration of service.
Private John Ramsey, Company E; discharged for disability.
Private George W. Spencer, Company E; discharged at expiration of service.
Private James Graham, Company E; died Charleston, Tennessee.
Private William S. Woodhead, Company E; mustered-out.
Private Dwight Cummings, Company E; mustered-out.
Private Edward W. Franklin, Company E; mustered-out.
Private William Oswalt, Company E; mustered-out.
Private Charles E. Quaco, Company E; mustered-out.
Private Adrian Van Ordstrand, Company E; mustered-out.
Private Reuben Truxler, Company E; mustered-out.
Private Alex. Detwiler, Company F; mustered-out.
Private Daniel Harwood, Company G; discharged at expiration of service.
Private Eli Mann, Company G; discharged at expiration of service.
Private Foster Drake, Company G; discharged at expiration of service.
Private Charles H. Stamp, Company H; mustered-out.
Private Adam Oswalt, Company H; mustered-out.
Private George W. Barton, Company K; discharged at expiration of service.

#### THIRTEENTH INFANTRY.

Private Samuel Stamp, Company E; missing at Bentonville, Arkansas.
Private Orlando J. Bradley, Company E; mustered-out.

RESIDENCE OF **JACOB GODSHALK**, LOCKPORT TP., ST. JOSEPH CO., MICH.

RESIDENCE OF **GEORGE SCHOCK**, LOCKPORT TP., ST. JOSEPH CO., MICH.

Private Herbert L. Chadwick, Company E; mustered-out.
Private Charles Jackson, Company E; mustered-out.
Private John Quake, Company E; mustered-out.
Private Joseph S. Stamp, Company E; mustered-out.
Private Conrad Wagner, Company E; mustered-out.
Private Daniel F. Stamp, Company E; mustered-out.
Private Garrett J. Wise, Company E; mustered-out.
Corporal George W. Buck, Company H; discharged, June 16, 1862.
Private Philo Arnold, Company H; re-enlisted and mustered-out.
Sergeant Charles C. Flint, Company K; mustered-out.

FIFTEENTH INFANTRY.

Private Robert Shiffard, Company A; re-enlisted and mustered-out.
Private John W. Hollowell, Company C; mustered-out.
Private Elias Ward, Company K; mustered-out.
Private Alfred McApted, first independent company; mustered-out.
Private Oscar Lockwood, Company H; died at City Point, Virginia.

NINETEENTH INFANTRY.

Private John J. Garrison, Company D; mustered-out.
Private John C. Jones, Company D; mustered-out.
Private Henry Ney, Company D; discharged.
Private James M. Duncan, Company D; mustered-out.
Second Lieutenant Charles W. Fonda, Company D; first lieutenant and adjutant; discharged for disability.

TWENTY-FIFTH INFANTRY.

Captain Julius C. Cross, Company D; resigned.
Corporal David H. Dunham, Company D; mustered-out.
Private Charles P. Buck, Company D; mustered-out.
Private Joseph Detwiler, Company D; mustered-out.
Private George W. Detwiler, Company D; discharged.
Private Levi E. Wing, Company D; mustered-out.
Private Daniel W. Fease, Company D; mustered-out.
Private Samuel S. Fease, Company D; died December 3, 1862.
Private George A. Garrison, Company D; veteran reserve corps.
Private Henry Hale, Company D; mustered-out.
Private William C. Hale, Company D; died August 7, 1864.
Private Smith Jones, Company D; mustered-out.
Private John E. Sickler, Company D; mustered-out.
Private Burton H. Wright, Company D; died at Louisville, Kentucky, January 19, 1863.
Private Jonathan Stuck, Company D; discharged at expiration of service.
Private Christie G. Walters, Company D; mustered-out.
Captain William Fulkerson, Company D; resigned.
First Lieutenant John B. Handy; Company G; captain, and mustered-out.
Second Lieutenant D. D. Thorp, Company G; discharged for disability.
Sergeant Romanso J. E. Bailey, Company G; died at Louisville, February 8, 1863.
Sergeant William L. Cole, Company G; first lieutenant, and mustered-out.
Sergeant John Gilbert, Company G; second lieutenant, and resigned.
Sergeant Philemon Bingham, Company G; discharged.
Corporal Ashbel W. Snyder, Company G; second lieutenant, and mustered-out.
Corporal Daniel O. Thorp, Company G; veteran reserve corps.
Corporal James K. Franklin, Company G; mustered-out.
Corporal Benjamin B. Cronk, Company G; mustered-out.
Corporal Hugh Wallace, Company G; died at Louisville, May 10, 1863.
Corporal Wilkinson C. Porter, Company G; discharged.
Musician Charles W. Hiles, Company G; mustered-out.
Musician William H. Lesner, Company G; mustered-out.
Private Edward T. Bolton, Company G; died at Louisville, December 17, 1862.
Private Robert H. Buck, Company G; mustered-out.
Private Charles W. Bassett, Company G; N. C. S.; mustered-out.
Private Hiram L. Brewster, Company G; mustered-out.
Private Joseph Collesi, Company G; mustered-out.
Private William H. Cummins, Company G; mustered-out.
Private John H. Cole, Company G; mustered-out.
Private Veual Dupuire, Company G; mustered-out.
Private Isaiah Dexsee, Company G; mustered-out.
Private Bernard Euckerott, Company G; mustered-out.
Private Charles S. Fitch, Company G; died at Bowling Green, Kentucky, March 8, 1863.

Private John Forste, Company G; died at Louisville, November 14, 1862.
Private William Ferry, Company G; mustered-out;
Private George Gearth, Company G; mustered-out.
Private Henry J. Horn, Company G; mustered-out.
Private William Jay, Company G; mustered-out.
Private Cyrus Judson, Company G; discharged.
Private Edwin Lantz, Company G; mustered-out.
Private Jefferson P. McKey, Company G; mustered-out.
Private Wesley Noe, Company G; mustered-out.
Private Benjamin Oswalt, Company G; mustered-out.
Private William F. Stivers, Company G; mustered-out.
Private James M. Snyder, Company G; died August 8, 1864.
Private Stephen M. Snyder, Company G; mustered-out.
Private Isaac M. VanOestraud, Company G; mustered-out.
Private George A. Westover, Company G; killed by guerillas.
Private Allan Westcott, Company G; discharged.
Private Aaron S. Wilhelm, Company G; mustered-out.
Private Edward Miller, Company G; mustered-out.
Sergeant-Major Edward M. Prutzman; adjutant June 17, 1863, and killed in action at Romeca, Georgia, May 17, 1864.
Quartermaster's Sergeant Edwin R. Wilbur; first-lieutenant, and mustered-out.

TWENTY-EIGHTH INFANTRY.

Private Joseph Lehr, Company I; died at Louisville.
Private Hosea Burch, Company K; mustered-out.

ELEVENTH CAVALRY.

Private Jacob K. Ennis, Company C; transferred to Eighth Cavalry, and mustered-out.
Private Stephen T. Woodhull, Company C; mustered-out.
Private Dwight Cummings, Company D; discharged for disability.
Private Charles E. Austin, Company H; transferred to Eighth Cavalry, and mustered-out.
Private John L. Taylor, Company K; mustered-out.
Private Augustus Flint, Company K; mustered-out.

FIRST MICHIGAN LIGHT ARTILLERY.

Artificer George C. Meade, Battery D; mustered-out.
Private Charles Crachy, Battery D; discharged for disability.
Private John H. Donahue, Battery D; discharged for disability.
Private Columbus Fulkerson, Battery D; mustered-out.
Private Sylvester C. Smith, Battery D; mustered-out.
Private Joseph H. Dunworth, Battery D; mustered-out.
Private John Taylor, Battery D; mustered-out.
Private Samuel Pugh, Battery D; mustered-out.
Private John McClymont, Battery D; mustered-out.
Private James Honts, Battery F; re-enlisted and mustered-out.
Private George Honts, Battery F; re-enlisted and mustered-out.
Private Adam Miller, Battery F; re-enlisted and mustered-out.
Private Hiram Millard, Battery F; re-enlisted and mustered-out.
Private James Wheeler, Battery F; discharged for disability.
Private Alonzo Westcott, Battery F; mustered-out.
Private Edgar W. Ensign, Battery F; mustered-out.
Private William A. Ensign, Battery F; mustered-out.
Private Joseph Adams, Battery G; mustered-out.
Private John Richards, Battery H; mustered-out.
Private C. C. Cummings, Battery M; mustered-out.
Private Austin E. Wing, fourteenth battery; mustered out.

FIRST MICHIGAN SHARP-SHOOTERS.

Private Henry Apted, Company H; killed in the Wilderness.
Private Michael Fellinger, Company H; killed near Petersburg.
Private Benjamin VanOrdstraud, Company H; mustered-out.
Private Charles E. Judson, Company H; mustered-out.
Private John Miller, Company H; mustered-out.
Private Sullivan Cook, Company H; mustered-out.

UNITED STATES NAVY.

Private William Baum; died at Helena, Arkansas, August, 1862.

We are under obligations to Hon. Edward S. Moore and J. B. Millard, the presidents of the national banks of Three Rivers; Hon. A. C. Prutsman, Captain Elisha Millard, Ezra Cole, Esq., John Cowling, Esq., Mrs. Sol. Hartman, Mrs. John M. Leland, John W. Hoffman, Esq., Captain John B. Handy, Rev. W. A. Maaker, W. F. Arnold, Esq., and D. M. Bateman, Esq., for valuable aid rendered in the compilation of the history of Lockport and Three Rivers.

## BIOGRAPHICAL SKETCHES.

MR. CHARLES MACOMBER.

MRS. CHARLES MACOMBER.

### CHARLES MACOMBER.

The subject of the following sketch was born July 16, 1800, in Johnstown, in the State of New York, where he lived with his parents, Rogers and Anna (Waterman) Macomber, until he was fourteen years of age, when he went to live with an older brother (John) in Scipio, in the same county. With him he remained until 1820, at which time he removed with his parents to Perry. Genesee (now Wyoming) county, New York. He received an ordinary English education at the district schools of the State, and assisted his elder brother on the farm until he removed to Perry. After a residence of seven years in Perry, Mr. Macomber removed to Alabama township, Genesee county, where for sixteen years he pursued the legal profession, being also a justice of the peace during the whole period of his stay in the place.

In September, 1843, he removed with his family to the township of Park, St. Joseph county, Michigan, and located a large tract of land (six hundred acres), which was wild and uncultivated, but which his sons, under his management, subdued and brought to a high state of productiveness. He built a fine brick residence on the old homestead,—the first one in the township, and at the time, and for many years afterwards, the best one on the Buckhorn road (so-called). He removed to Three Rivers in 1864, purchased a comfortable residence, in which he resided two years, and then went into the northern part of the State for about two years longer,—returning to Three Rivers in 1868, and remaining there until his decease, October 31, 1874. At the time of his death, Mr. Macomber was a director in the Manufacturers' National Bank of Three Rivers, which institution he contributed largely to organize. His business calling, for the last few years of his life, was principally that of a capitalist.

While he resided in Perry he met an estimable young lady (five years his junior), Miss Mary Burt, and won her for his bride,—leading her to the altar on the 16th day of May, 1822, from whence they journeyed together, under the lights and shades incident to human life, for a period of over fifty-two years. During this long pilgrimage, eleven children were born to them,—eight of whom are now living, viz: Reuben, of Three Rivers; Mrs. Caroline Roach, Mrs. Electa Wheeler and Mrs. Maria Smith, of Three Rivers; Mrs. Mary Sabin, Mrs. Nettie Wheeler, Mrs. Jennie Mather and Mrs. Ella Hewings. Mrs. Roach and Mrs. Electa Wheeler reside at Morley, and Mrs. Sabin, Mrs. Mather and Mrs. Hewings, at Howard, in Michigan; Mrs. Nettie Wheeler, at Reynolds, Indiana. Jerome, the eldest son,

died while en route to California, in 1849–50. He and Reuben, during the first six years of their residence in Park, broke up over eight hundred acres of wild land for their father and neighbors.

Mr. Macomber's religious views were those of the Baptist faith, to which church he joined himself in Alabama township, being baptized in 1830. When he came to Park,—there being no church of the Baptist denomination in that vicinity,—he united with the Wesleyan Methodist society, and remained in that communion until his death. In politics he was in early life a Whig,—joining the Republican party at its organization, and remaining a member thereof until his death. His decease was sudden, but not unexpected,—nor did the grim messenger find a fearful listener, for having already accomplished something more than the span of life allotted to man on the earth, he was ready for the summons which his failing health warned him might come at any moment, but which he might well anticipate with composure after a long life of strict integrity and uprightness. Peaceful as his life had been, his change came, and he passed from earth as the light of an autumn day fades into the twilight; going to the grave, crowned with years, and willing to be garnered to the everlasting rest.

Mary Burt, the daughter of Alpheus and Chloe Burt, was born in Huntington, Chittenden county, Vermont, March 10, 1805,—removing therefrom with her parents to Riga, New York, in 1809, and from thence, in 1818, to Perry, where she was married to Charles Macomber, May 16, 1822. In 1827 she removed with her husband and family to Alabama township, Genesee county, and from thence to Park township, St. Joseph county, Michigan, in 1843,—in which township, and at Three Rivers, she resided, except two years (1864–6) in Ionia county, up to the time of her husband's death, in 1874; since which event she has passed her time with her children at their homes, and among her relatives in the east, where she is ever a welcome and honored guest.

She joined the Baptist church with her husband in 1830, and with him also the Wesleyan Methodist society in Park; but on her removal to Three Rivers she worshiped with her children in the Presbyterian congregation,—of which they were members,—she herself joining it afterwards in 1870. She has been a help-meet indeed, and her husband appreciated and often acknowledged the fact. After seventy-two years of life's experience lighted with joy and shaded with sorrow, she is looking calmly forward to the time when she will pass through the same dark portals which her loved ones have passed before her, to the joy of the reunion beyond.

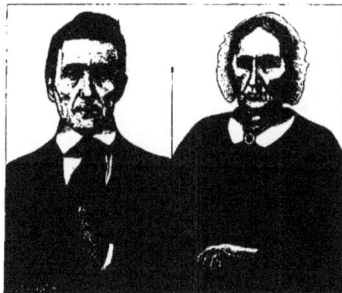

JOHN WOLF.

The paternal ancestor of the subject of this sketch, whose name was John Wolf, was born in Wittemberg, Germany, April 18, 1769, and emigrated to America with his parents, when he was but two years old, settling with them in Columbia county, Pennsylvania, where he died April 18, 1824. His maternal ancestor, whose name was Catharine Hoan, a daughter of David Hoan, was born in Pennsylvania, May 8, 1776, and died in Lockport township, Michigan, September 28, 1835.

He, of whose life we here present a brief sketch, was born November 17, 1794, in Columbia county, Pennsylvania, where he lived nearly forty years. He was educated in the German language; and the only knowledge he ever obtained of the English tongue was such as was communicated to him by his children in after years, and by intercourse with his neighbors who spoke that language. He learned the trade of miller, and followed it exclusively during the last nine or ten years of his residence in Pennsylvania.

In the spring of the year 1834 he removed from that State to St. Joseph county, Michigan, locating three hundred and twenty acres in section twenty-seven in the township of Lockport, on which he resided till his decease, October 16, 1851. He followed agriculture principally during his life in Michigan, but his practical knowledge in milling brought his services into requisition frequently to dress the stones in the different mills in the county, and to put them in operation.

In the year 1815 Mr. Wolf was united in marriage to Barbara Drescher, by whom the following children were born to him:

SAMUEL, who died August 17, 1839; STEPHEN, who died September 20, 1828, when but ten years old; JOSIAH; CATHARINE, afterwards Mrs. Isaac Fort of Lockport, but now deceased; DANIEL F.; JOHN F.; AARON, now dead; AMOS C.; MARY ANN, afterwards the wife of David D. Antes, of Centreville, but now deceased, and THOMAS B.

The living sons are all now located in the township of Lockport on fine farms of their own, and rank among the leading farmers of the county; Amos C. being on the old homestead purchased of the government forty-three years ago. John F. and Daniel F. have been, and still are among the very heaviest mint-oil producers of the county.

Mrs. Wolf was born in Pennsylvania, in August, 1790, where she was married. The family arrived at P. H. Hoffman's, in Lockport, May 28, 1834, after a wearisome journey of a month in wagons, which latter vehicles and a small board shanty furnished them their only shelter during the first summer. In the fall of the year they removed into a frame house Mr. Wolf had built himself, for though a miller by trade, his genius was not by any means confined to that branch of handiwork, but he was an adept at anything in mechanics necessary to be done in a new community.

Mrs. Wolf died on the 2d of April, 1866, in Centreville, at the residence of Daniel F. Wolf, with whom her home had been for eight years previously. Mr. and Mrs. Wolf were members of the Methodist church of Centreville, at the time of their death; Mr. Wolf being one of its stewards for many years. They united with the church in Pennsylvania some years before they removed west.

In politics Mr. Wolf was a Democrat, but not being a strict partisan, he voted for "Tippecanoe and Tyler too," in 1840. He filled offices of trust in the township, and assisted in laying many of its early roads, being one of the highway commissioners for several years.

This pioneer pair filled their station in life, well and quietly, without ostentation or parade, giving all who came to their house a hospitable welcome, unstinted in measure, and unalloyed in quality; and they have left behind them naught but pleasing memories.

19

CHARLES B. FITCH,

judge and farmer, came of English parentage, his grandfather having been one of the early governors of Connecticut, under British authority. He (Charles B.) was born in that State about the year 1774, and remained there until 1805, when he removed to Trumbull county, Ohio, and was one of the pioneers in that section of country.

In the war of 1812 he entered the American army, and was fought several engagements along Lake Erie, at Detroit, &c. He afterwards served in the Black Hawk war.

Removing to Lower Sandusky (now Fremont), Ohio, at an early day, he soon won the confidence and esteem of the people, and was elected county judge. Removing to Seneca county, Ohio, he was honored with the same office, which he filled, as before, most satisfactorily.

In 1830 he removed with his family to Michigan, and settled temporarily on Pigeon prairie, where he entered five eighties of government land. The following year he came to Lockport (then Buck) township, where he entered two hundred acres of land, and took up his residence upon it. He was afterwards chosen county judge of St. Joseph county, which office he continued to hold for several years.

In early life he sided with the Democrats, but in 1848 he joined the "Free Soilers," and acted and voted with the Republican party from its organization to the close of his life, believing its principles to be those most conducive to the preservation and perpetuity of our government. He always had the best interests of his township at heart, and had few equals, and perhaps no superior, in his efforts for its development. Thus, when past the confines of fourscore years, he could look back over an active and blameless life, conscious of having made diligent use of the talents committed to his care—displaying a character remarkable for its purity, for its extraordinary energy, its power of endurance, the warmth of its friendship, its social geniality, and its domestic affection. Thus he enjoyed to the last, a vigorous frame, and, when called upon to yield to the inevitable destiny of man, he met death calmly, and left his relatives and friends a reasonable consciousness that he "was not lost, but gone before."

SAMUEL A. FITCH,

fourth son of Judge Charles B. Fitch, was born in Trumbull (now Mahoning) county, Ohio, October 18, 1811. When in his nineteenth year, he accompanied his parents, and settled first on Pigeon prairie, and subsequently in what is now Lockport township. He remained on his father's farm until 1838, when he branched off for himself, purchasing eighty acres

on section thirty-one, being a part of his present farm. By subsequent purchases he has added to his original tract until he now has four hundred acres in a body, of which almost half is under excellent cultivation—the remainder mostly timber, with about forty acres of marsh.

March 23, 1837, he married Catharine Riemsnyder, a native of West Earl township, Lancaster county, Pennsylvania; by whom he had six children, two only surviving, namely:

MILTON B., born August 8, 1838; married Susan Caseman, and resides in a part of the homestead.

FRANLIN M., born May 21, 1852; married Alice Talkalberry, and resides with his parents. Of the others

CHARLES SAMUEL, born October 28, 1840, died of apoplexy, at Bowling Green, Kentucky, while serving in the war of the rebellion in 1863; and

EDWARD HENRY, born October 4, 1855, was accidentally drowned in the St. Joseph river, August 12, 1862.

In the troublous times of the Black Hawk outbreak, the Fitches, father and son, went to the front, doing active service in its suppression. The subject of our sketch served in Captain Alvin Calhoon's company.

Politically, Mr. Fitch is a Democrat, but liberal and non-partisan. He advocates the principles of the Greenback party, believing that the financial policy of our government is wanting in that security which it should have in order to insure its permanent prosperity. In character he is upright and honest, in his social relations, genial, and in his domestic circle kind and affectionate, a fond husband and father, and a good citizen. His admirable wife has been to him a help-meet indeed, these forty years, and to her good judgment and sound common sense he attributes a fair share of the success which has attended him through life.

This worthy couple rightfully enjoy the respect and esteem of the community in which they live, and we feel assured that their portraits, and that of Judge Fitch, as also the illustration of their residence, will be a source of genuine satisfaction to themselves, to their children and to their many friends.

WILLIAM F. ARNOLD.

William Foote Arnold, the son of Caleb and Rachel Arnold, was born in Unadilla, Otsego county, New York, August 6, 1812, removing with his parents in 1815 to Berkshire, Broome county (now known as Richford, Tioga county), in the same State, at which place he resided and received a common school education, assisting his father in a saw and grist-mill and carding-factory after he was of age sufficient to be useful, until he was twenty years old, when, with his father, he came to St. Joseph county in the year 1832. His father located a farm in Fabius township, and William went back for the family, returning with them in the following autumn.

On the 18th day of May, 1834, he married Rhoda Churchill, a daughter of Deacon William Churchill, of Constantine, and also the first female school teacher in Constantine township. The fruits of this union were eight children, five daughters, four of whom are married and now living, and three sons, one of whom died in infancy.

Mrs. Arnold died October 6, 1854, and Mr. Arnold finding it not good for man to be alone, took to himself another wife on the 17th day of March, 1856, in the person of Mrs. Margaret Greene, by whom one son, Ira, has been born to him.

Mr. Arnold bought lands on Broad street, in Constantine, and, until 1854, resided alternately on those, and the farm in Fabius. At that date he removed to Three Rivers, in what is now known as the second ward of the city, where he has since resided.

Mr. Arnold was elected town clerk of Fabius in 1844–45, and supervisor in 1846. He has held the office of justice of the peace in Lockport township for twelve years since 1856, and the office of supervisor of the township has been filled continuously by him from the fall of that year, to the present time, with the exception of the years 1863 and 1872.

Mr. Arnold, with his former wife, united with the Baptist church of Constantine, being baptized in 1838, and he and his present wife are members of the same church at Three Rivers.

Mr. Arnold's political views are, and ever have been, in sympathy with those of the Democratic party, but during the rebellion he was in favor of a vigorous prosecution of the war, and was represented in the Union army by his two sons, Philo and Edward P.

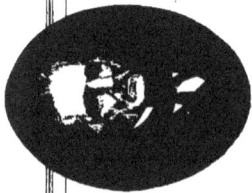

E. S. MOORE

"MOORE PARK" RES. OF E. S. MOORE, ST. JOSEPH CO., MICHIGAN    PARK TP.

## HON. ABRAHAM C. PRUTZMAN.

Among the public-spirited and enterprising citizens of the thriving city of Three Rivers, Abraham C. Prutzman stands in the front rank. Liberal towards all measures for the common good, and zealously active in their accomplishment, Mr. Prutzman has been, and still is, noted for his benefactions to churches, and to enterprises for the general prosperity and advancement of his town and city.

He was born in Columbia county, Pennsylvania, March 6, 1813, and from thence removed with his parents, Joseph and Maria Prutzman, to Danville in the same State, when but a lad.

Mr. Joseph Prutzman was the second sheriff of Columbia county, and also surveyor for some years.

When the subject of our sketch was but fourteen years old, he was indentured by his father, as an apprentice to Colb & Donaldson, to learn the business of a merchant; and with them he remained four years. He then went to Pottsville, Schuylkill county, Pennsylvania, where he followed the same business until the fall of 1834, when he formed a co-partnership with his brother-in-law, Hon. Edward S. Moore, and with him, removed to St. Joseph county, Michigan, sending their goods around the lakes to the mouth of the St. Joseph. On account of the lateness of the season, the vessel on which they were shipped was not able to get into the harbor, but lay all winter at Grand Haven.

Mr. Prutzman spent the winter of 1834-5 at Prairie Ronde, and in the spring of that year the firm of Moore & Prutzman opened a mercantile establishment, where they retailed goods of all kinds for two years, when they closed up the business there and removed their stock to Three Rivers, and a year afterwards leased the flouring-mills of Smith & Bowman, and purchased them in 1840. They continued the business of merchandizing and manufacturing until 1859, when the partnership, which had existed a quarter of a century, was dissolved by mutual consent.

Mr. Prutzman continued in the mercantile line alone, and subsequently with his sons, until 1867, when he retired from active business, and has never re-entered the lists of trade.

On the 14th day of July, 1836, Mr. Prutzman was united in marriage with Mary L., daughter of John Phillips, of Chester county, Pennsylvania. The children of this marriage were: Joseph E., John P., and Edward M. (who was adjutant of the 25th Michigan Infantry, and killed at Reseca); Maggie M. (now Mrs. C. B. Tucker of Three Rivers), and A. Clifford Prutzman.

The sons are extensively engaged in the manufacture of pumps and plows at Three Rivers, under the name of the Michigan Pump Company and the Three Rivers Plow Company.

In politics Mr. Prutzman was a Whig, and has been a staunch, unfaltering Republican since the organization of that party.

He held for ten years a position on the State board of agriculture of Michigan, and for six years represented St. Joseph county in the State Senate.

Mr. and Mrs. Prutzman are both members of the Presbyterian church— Mr. Prutzman an elder, at Three Rivers, for several years. He and E. S. Moore were the main pillars and support of the society, during all its infancy, and well nigh in its maturer years. His donations to the church-building have been munificent.

Mr. Prutzman was also efficient in securing the location of the railroads through the town, and not a scheme for the prosperity of the town or the advancement of its interests in any way, morally or financially, has been initiated, that does not bear his impress, and has not felt the aid of his vigor or his purse.

## HON. EDWARD S. MOORE.

On the banks of the historic Delaware, four miles above the city of Trenton, in the State of New Jersey, Edward S. Moore first opened his eyes to the light of day on the 4th day of June, 1805. His parents, Stephen and Parthenia Moore, had ten children born to them, eight sons and two daughters, of whom the subject of this sketch was the youngest.

When Edward was three years old his parents and their family removed to the county of Northumberland, Pennsylvania, to a tract of country that was then a wild tangle of woods, but is now known as Mooresburg. Five years afterwards the father died, leaving the family to struggle on alone, with but little means besides their own hands for support.

At ten years of age Edward was sent to Danville, Columbia county, as copyist in the register's office, and two years afterwards went to reside with Dr. Petrikin, where he remained one year, attending the district-schools. At the end of the year he was apprenticed to William Wyley to learn the tailor's trade, and served several years; but finding the business uncongenial to his tastes, he bought his time of his master, and commenced for himself.

His first independent act was a most happy and opportune one, and was the beginning, as he acknowledges, of all his success in after life. This act was consummated on the 6th day of July, in the year 1824, when he married Mary, daughter of Joseph Prutzman, with whom he lived most happily for more than half a century.

The youthful pair went immediately to Philadelphia, where they remained about a year, and then returned to Danville, whence, leaving his young wife in her father's care, Mr. Moore went to Detroit, Michigan, to look for a location for business. The outlook seeming favorable, he returned to Danville with the intention of an immediate removal to the West, but was persuaded to postpone his departure till a later period.

Pennsylvania was then just beginning her canals on the west and north branches of the Susquehanna river, and Mr. Moore became one of an organization of contractors, for building dams, locks, bridges, &c., on the new improvements.

After obtaining several contracts, he sold out his interest in them to his brother Andrew, and entered the mercantile trade, opening a store at Danville, in 1830, and another in Pottsville, in 1832, with his brother Burrows, with whom he remained till 1833, when the brother withdrew from the firm and removed to Three Rivers, St. Joseph county, Michigan, and A. C. Prutzman, a brother of Mrs. Moore, came into the partnership, which lasted for more than a quarter of a century.

In the fall of 1834 Moore & Prutzman packed their stock, and sent it via New York by the great lakes to the mouth of the St. Joseph river, and taking Mr. Moore's family, started on an overland journey for the west, with no definite idea of a permanent location.

After six weeks of hard travel they arrived October 29, at Three Rivers, which, however, then had not attained to the dignity of a name, being a hamlet of but three or four houses. One of these little dwellings was the home of Burroughs Moore, and under its roof, covering two rooms of twelve by fourteen feet, with outside stairs to reach the upper one, nineteen persons passed several days.

The stock of goods did not arrive until the next spring, on account of the early approach of winter and the harbor of St. Joseph closing up with ice. The family of Mr. Moore, and Mr. Prutzman, he being unmarried, passed the winter on the west side of Prairie Ronde, in Kalamazoo county, and in the spring, the firm built a store on the prairie, and opened their goods, remaining there for two years, when they removed to Three Rivers, having previously opened a branch store there.

Some two years afterwards they bought the Three Rivers flouring-mill, having rented and run it a year previously, and continued to operate it in connection with their extensive mercantile trade until 1859, when the partnership so long, pleasantly and profitably maintained, was mutually and agreeably dissolved.

Mr. Moore, however, did not long remain an idler in the community, with whose business interests he had been so closely and continuously identified; but in the year 1864 he helped to organize the First National Bank of Three Rivers, was chosen its first president, and has ever since held that position.

He also aided in the organization of the Riverside Cemetery Association; he was its first president, and was also largely instrumental in bringing the Michigan Southern railroad to Three Rivers, from Constantine, as appears more fully elsewhere.

In politics, Mr. Moore has always been called a Democrat, but he has never sought office, nor has he always supported the party nominations; but has "scratched" the ticket whenever a candidate thereon was believed by him to be immoral or intemperate.

When the great rebellion marshaled its legions against the national authority, he proclaimed himself free from all party affiliations till the country was restored to peace, and the laws of the land were once more supreme; and he faithfully kept the pledge throughout the struggle.

During the early part of the war he wrote a private letter to Hon. John Van Buren, of New York, setting forth his views on the situation; which the latter handed to the *New York Evening Post* for publication, with the endorsement that it contained "the hardest sense he had seen."

In 1850 Mr. Moore was elected a member of the convention of Michigan, to frame a new constitution, in which he took an active part, and claims to have been the means of introducing some of its most conservative articles.

In 1851 Mr. Moore was elected one of the regents of the University of Michigan, serving in that capacity for six years.

In 1852 he was elected to represent St. Joseph county in the upper house of the legislature, and was appointed chairman of the committee on education; which position he filled with great credit to himself and honor to his constituency. As such chairman he reported the bill requiring the State to replace to the credit of the University fund one hundred thousand dollars previously withdrawn therefrom for other purposes, in violation of the terms of the grant from the general government.

He also reported adversely to granting the prayer of numerous petitions from Detroit, backed by important influence, asking for a distribution of the public school-fund to sectarian schools, believing such a course detrimental to the true interests of the State, and opposed to the genius of the constitution.

Mr. Moore being thoroughly domestic in his tastes and habits, early provided a home for himself and family, by purchasing a fine tract of four hundred and fifty acres of burr-oak openings in Park township, some four and a half miles north of Three Rivers, on which he built, later, a spacious mansion, whose hospitable doors have always swung wide to admit troops of friends, whose voices and merry laughter have echoed through his elegant parlors and beautiful grounds, shaded by the oaks of the original forest, which once covered his entire tract.

From this homestead, Mr. Moore has gone daily to his business at Three Rivers, for nearly forty years, using now for the purpose the railroad, which has built a very neat station-house near his residence, and named it " Moore Park."

In their religious views, Mr. and Mrs. Moore conformed to those of the Presbyterian polity, and united with the church at Danville, Pennsylvania, in 1830, and also, with fifteen others, assisted in the organization of the Presbyterian church of Three Rivers, in 1837, Mr. Moore being chosen one of the elders thereof, which position he has actively held for thirty-seven years, rarely being absent from his accustomed seat in the sanctuary on the first day of the week.

In the work of building up society by Christian influence and moral rectitude, he has performed a full and honorable share, and having done much therein, only regrets he could not have done more. Holding to the principle that giving, enriches, while withholding brings poverty, his bounties and benefactions to public and private charities and enterprises, in religious and reformatory to public and private charities and enterprises, in religious and reformatory lines, and to the town, have been munificient.

Mr. and Mrs. Moore have had born to them two children only, a daughter, now Mrs. Kelsey, residing at Three Rivers, and a son, Armitage G. Moore, now, with his wife, residing with his father on the old homestead. But these two children, beloved though they are, could not monopolize the parental love, that swells such hearts as beat in the bosoms of the master and mistress of Moore Park, and it went out unto no less than fifteen father-less and motherless boys and girls from two to twelve years of age, who were from time to time gathered around the family hearthstone, to be nurtured, educated, and prepared for life's warfare, and when sent out into it, were fairly equipped for its successful maintenance. One only of those thus brought into the family has remained, and of her—a distant relative of Mrs. Moore, Mary Kepler, by name—Mr. Moore bears this testimony, " She has from a mere child identified herself with the family in every respect, socially and domestically, and has exhibited a self-sacrificing spirit, all the more noted because of its rarity.

Mr. and Mrs. Moore passed fifty-two years in the relation of wedded life, and her death, which occurred August 29, 1876, was the first visit the grim messenger ever made to their home.

Mr. Moore pays this tribute to the sharer of his early struggles for a living, his later efforts for a competency, and his successful achievement of an honorable reputation and worldly wealth in the days of the " sere and yellow leaf:" " She was truly a help-meet, and to her I attribute much of the prosperity of my later years. Her influence, in the kindness of her nature, sound judgment and strong common sense, combined with a patient, persevering Christian character, gave me a direction and aim in life, which I feel I could not have attained without her." And now, at the age of nearly seventy-two years, Mr. Moore daily seeks his lonely, though still beautiful home, the light of which, in his eyes, faded and went out, when its long-time mistress and dispenser of its hospitalities, was carried through its portals by the hands of sympathizing neighbors, and followed by her household and intimate friends, in sadness and tears. But though sadness and loneliness intrude where joy and domestic companionship once held undisputed sway, yet the husband remains attentive to business and to his church obligations, expectant of the summons not long to be withheld, and is

" Only waiting till the shadows
Be a little longer grown;
Only waiting till the Shepherd
Comes and calls and claims His own."

## LEWIS MILLER.

The subject of this brief sketch was born in Vermont, August 10, 1802. In 1829 he removed to Akron, Summit county, Ohio, where he engaged with his eldest brother, the latter being a carpenter, and the former a painter by trade. He remained in Akron till 1845, when he removed to Lockport township, taking a farm of eighty acres, which he cleared up and improved. He taught the " young idea how to shoot" for fourteen winters, in the States of Vermont, Ohio, and Michigan. Casting his first vote for John Q. Adams, in 1824, he aided in organizing the Democratic party in 1828, and became an Abolitionist in 1835, then casting the only vote of that complexion in Lockport township. He has also taken an active part in the temperance reform, and all public enterprises of his vicinity. His family consists of six children, five of whom (four sons and one daughter) are living.

## GEORGE SCHOCK.

George Schock, son of John and Elizabeth Schock, was born in Washington township, Union county, Pennsylvania, December 17, 1819. He remained under the paternal roof until 1840, when he removed with his parents to Thompson township, Seneca county, Ohio, where he worked first for his father at one hundred dollars per year, and subsequently for a stranger at one hundred and fifteen dollars a year. He learned the carpenter and joiner trade, at which he worked for about three years.

On the 20th day of September 1845, he married Lucy Ann Wehr, a native of Lehigh county, Pennsylvania. They reared a family of nine children, namely:

BENJAMIN F., born January 10, 1847.
JOHN, born September 25, 1849.
JOEL, born October 29, 1851.
POLLY, born October 28, 1853.
ELI, born May 14, 1856.
SARAH, born June 10, 1858.
HETTY A., born March 7, 1861.
LYDIA A., born May 2, 1863; and
EMMA A., born November 13, 1867.

Mr. Schock has been mostly engaged in farming, although he has devoted a considerable portion of his time to the manufacture of sorghum, and to the raising of poultry. In 1871 he removed to Michigan and purchased his present fine farm of one hundred and sixty acres in Lockport township, which he keeps in an excellent state of cultivation in addition to attending to his other business.

He is at present, treasurer of Grange No. 178, and also treasurer of Pomona Grange, No. 4, of St. Joseph county. In politics he is a Republican, though he has recently affiliated with the Greenback party. In religion, he is a member of the German Reformed church. For a late settler in his township no man enjoys more the confidence and esteem of the people than does he of whom we write. A view of his residence and buildings can be seen elsewhere in this work.

## J. F. THOMS.

J. F. Thoms, son of Charles and Julie Thoms, was born in the Canton of Neufchatel, Switzerland, July 28, 1813. His father, an honored soldier in the first Napoleon's army, brought with him into private life a pure and spotless reputation, and unsullied integrity, and he carefully instructed his son in lessons of loyalty, industry, benevolence, and the many virtues of which his life was a worthy illustration.

At the age of four years, his parents and himself, in company with friends, emigrated to America, and landed at Philadelphia, in August, 1817. He remained with them during their residence in Pennsylvania, attending school when the opportunity presented, and assisted his father in conducting the mercantile business at different points where he located.

In 1836, at the age of twenty-three, he came to St. Joseph county, Michigan, where he has made a home and many friends by his industry and honorable deportment. He commenced by clearing a tract of land entered by his father, which he subsequently purchased and improved.

March 23, 1838, he was married to Louisa Friedlein. Two years elapsed, and, with its experiences came the loss of his wife. March 23, 1843, he was again married to a worthy companion, Miss Eleanor Dougherty, of Mattison, Branch county, Michigan. A family of four children,

A. C. PRUTZMAN.
- THREE RIVERS -

WM. F. ARNOLD.
- THREE RIVERS -

D. KNOX, JR.
- THREE RIVERS -

I. F. THOMS
- THREE RIVERS -

MRS. I. F. THOMS
- THREE RIVERS -

LEWIS THOMS.
- THREE RIVERS -

MRS. LEWIS THOMS
- THREE RIVERS -

WM. HULL.
- LOCKPORT TP. -

LEWIS MILLER.
- LOCKPORT TP. -

DWIGHT STEBBINS.
- LOCKPORT TP. -

GARRETT SICKLES.
- LOCKPORT TP. -

carefully trained and pleasantly located, contribute to make his declining years his most pleasant ones. .

FRANK J., was born February 3, 1844, and resides in Sherwood, Branch county, Michigan.

ALICE was born December 2, 1847, and resides in Three Rivers with her husband, A. R. Close.

JOHN C. was born May 10, 1852; he also resides in Three Rivers, prosperous in his chosen vocation.

FANNIE M. was born November 4, 1855, and remains at home contributing to the comfort of her parents in their advanced years.

Mr. Thoms has held various offices of trust, being at different times elected assessor, justice, and commissioner of the corporation of Three Rivers; is also a member of Friendship Lodge No. 338 of Masons, and Salathiel Chapter No. 23. He is also a member of Three Rivers Commandery, and holds the office of treasurer in the three societies. He also served as treasurer in Mount Hermon lodge No. 24, for a period of twelve years.

Mr. and Mrs. Thoms are earnest, active Methodists, and largely contribute to the support of the church of their chosen profession. In politics a Democrat, he cast his first vote for Martin Van Buren. Mr. Thoms is in every sense a representative man, as his standing, both socially and financially plainly indicates.

In connection with this history is shown a portrait of himself and wife, and we take great pleasure in referring our readers to them, knowing that their pleasant expression is in perfect harmony with this plain record of their well spent lives.

## LEWIS F. THOMS.

Switzerland, the land of beautiful lakes, grand mountain scenery and the home of noted patriots, immortalized in song and story, was the birth-place of Lewis F. Thoms. It was here in the Canton of Neufchatel, August 11, 1806, where the dark blue waters of the Lemen reflect the rays of the meridian sun, amid the towering peaks of the everlasting Alps,—emblems of integrity —that the subject of our sketch was born, and was taught those lessons of truth and fidelity, sincerity and virtue, which characterize the man. Kind parents taught him early, lessons of self-reliance and industry,—and the record of his life proves that they have been well observed.

At the age of twenty-two, we find him actively engaged in the mercantile business at Lewisburg, Pennsylvania, in company with his father and brother. Time passes, and he becomes sole owner thereof, purchasing his father's and brother's interest. Commercial changes, a few years later, cause him to retire from trade with reduced means, owing to the failures of many patrons whom he had generously trusted. After honorably adjusting every account, he removed to St. Joseph county, Michigan, June 7, 1835, and entered land to the amount of twenty-seven acres, in Lockport township. This he cleared and improved, beginning with a log-house, table, chairs and furniture, made with his own hands, in pioneer fashion.

The log-house has been changed for a fine residence of modern style, shrubbery planted, buildings erected, acre added to acre, and the result is a fine farm, and a beautiful home.

On February 10, 1827, he was married to Miss Sarah Baker. A family of six children has been raised, namely:

ISAAC, born December 8, 1831.

GEORGE W., born February 22, 1832.

CHARLES F, born January 18, 1835.

MARY J., born February 19, 1838.

JOHN L., born May 6, 1842; and

JOSEPH, born October 2, 1844.

Two sons, Charles and Lewis, defended their country during the rebellion, enlisting early, and serving with credit in Sherman's army, and at the close of the war were honorably discharged.

Mr. Thoms held various offices in the Methodist church, of which he is a member, and he advocates his political views by voting as a Republican. Andrew Jackson, as candidate for president, received his first ballot. At the advanced age of seventy-one, in good health and mind, Mr. Thoms presents as example of longevity, attributable to his habits of abstinence and temperance; and his pleasant home and ample resources, are sufficient proofs of his industry and success. He is a true friend in the social circle, a kind neighbor in the community, a pious Christian in the church, an affectionate husband, and a kind father at the domestic hearth, and well merits the space that he occupies in this work, with his portrait, as being one of the successful representative men of St. Joseph county.

# COLON.

THIS township, which takes its name from the village within its limits near Sturgeon lake, has a generally level surface, but is somewhat broken up about the village, and has within its boundaries an eminence which is called Colon mountain; not remarkable for its elevation, though it is the highest point in the township—one hundred and twenty feet above the general level. The soil is a sandy loam, stony in portions of the township, but very fertile and productive. Its area includes twenty-one thousand four hundred and sixty-seven acres of land and one thousand five hundred and seventy-five acres of water surface. The land was originally of the oak openings, except in the northwest corner, where the Nottawa prairie comes into the township on section one, and also a small prairie near Levi Mathews' and M. G. Schellhous' locations, on section four.

On the river bottoms heavy timber is found, consisting of oak, walnut, hickory, soft maple, black and white ash, sycamore, etc. Its drainage is good, and it is watered as follows: The St. Joseph river enters the township on the east line of the southeast quarter of section one, and passes by Sturgeon lake, out of the township on the north line of section thirty. Swan creek enters the township from the south, near the village of section thirty-three, and runs northerly through Long lake and an arm of Palmer, and enters Sturgeon lake, near the entrance of the St. Joseph, on section two. A little creek rises on the southeast quarter of section twenty, and runs northwardly and westwardly, passing out of the township near the centre line of section

eighteen, and another small one enters the township on east line of southeast quarter of section thirty-six, and runs northwest to Swan creek, which it enters on the section line between the southwest quarter of section twenty-three and the southeast quarter of section twenty-two. Beaver lake, so called from a beaver dam that was once in it, lies on section twenty-eight, and contains one hundred and eighty acres. Lepley's lake lies on the southeast corner of section twenty-seven, and contains forty acres. Palmer lake, so called from a pioneer who settled on its banks, and Sturgeon lake, so named from the fish formerly caught in it, are the largest bodies of water in the township, having an area of about four hundred acres each. Washburn lake also lies within the township and takes its name from a settler on its banks. Ancient mounds and fortifications are numerously scattered throughout the area of the township, and are fully described in the general county history.

### FIRST SETTLEMENTS.

Roswell Schellhous came from Ohio in 1829 to Nottawa prairie, and located on what was afterwards included in Colon township. He built a log house, of two rooms, near the present elegant dwelling of William Bowers, which he kept as a hotel, his patrons being chiefly "land-lookers" for some years. His location was on section six.

In 1838 Mr. Schellhous went to Illinois and located near Nauvoo, and was afterwards in Missouri, where he made himself obnoxious by his advocacy of anti-slavery sentiments.

Lorauzi Schellhous, a brother of Roswell, came into the township in 1830, as did also George F. and Martin G., two other brothers, and bought land on sections three and six, Lorauzi buying, however, the mill-site on Swan creek, where the present flouring-mill is situated in the village. They returned to Ohio, and, during the winter, Lorauzi made mill-irons and breaking-plow irons, and in April, 1831, he with his family of five children, (Lorus, the youngest, being two years old), George and his family, Martin G. and his family, and George Brooks and his family, in all thirty-one persons, commenced their journey for their western home in St. Joseph county, and arrived May 16, 1831, at Roswell Schellhous' log-house, where they stopped one night. The next day, though it was Sunday, Lorauzi Schellhous took up his line of march again, and coming to his mill-site, built a tent of poles and crotches cut along the marsh, roofed it with bark and slept in it that night, preferring elbow room in such a shelter to the crowded apartments of his brother. He at once commenced the erection of a cabin, and completed it with a shake-roof and puncheon floor and a door made of one of his wagon boxes, ready for occupancy by the next Saturday night, and was living in his own house in a week's time after he arrived on his location. He came in with two wagons, five yoke of oxen, three cows and nine hogs, a sow and eight shoats.

The next week Mr. Schellhous made a breaking-plow, selecting a winding tree for the mould-board, and broke up a garden spot at his own house and six acres on the prairie at his brother Roswell's, on which latter breaking, he planted corn, harvesting a good crop in the fall, and his garden gave him vegetables, broom-corn and melons. His stock came home regularly, and his hogs thrave and fattened finely on the mast that had lain on the ground through the previous winter. These persons above named were the first settlers in the territory included in the present bounds of Colon.

Charles Palmer came in from Ohio in the fall of 1831, bought three hundred acres east of the creek, and lived with his family of six children with Mr. Schellhous, until the spring of 1832, when he moved into a cabin of his own.

Mr. Schellhous built a saw-mill in 1832 and got it in operation, bringing his plank from Adams & Kent's mill in Bronson, Branch county.

In 1832, all of the people who came in the year previous, except Lorauzi Schellhous, were sick with the fever and ague.

After sawing one thousand two hundred feet of lumber, the water undermined the dam, which went out, but was replaced, and again washed out during 1832. Then Lorauzi sold his location to Martin G., his brother, to raise funds to rebuild his dam again, and so well did he perform the work, that the foundation remains to this day.

In 1832 Cyrus Schellhous, another brother, came in, with their mother, who died the same year.

The neighbors in 1831 were Roswell and Martin G. Schellhous, and Dr. McMillan, on the west side of the township in Nottawa, and a trader named Hatch, on the river near Martin's, and George Brooks and George Schellhous.

In 1832, the people went to Coldwater for blacksmithing, to Bingham's on the east end of the prairie, it being a ten days' trip to go and come with oxen.

Mr. Schellhous sold his mill interest to George, with whom he was in partnership, and in 1835 went to his farm, where he now lives, and built a blacksmith-shop, put in it a turning-lathe and made chairs, spinning-wheels, flax-wheels and reels.

Palmer's daughter, a girl of seventeen years, died during the summer of 1833.

Mr. Schellhous is now eighty-four years of age, in the full possession of his faculties, and with his aged and beloved partner, one year his senior, has lived to see the township which he named, rise from an unbroken forest to one of the principal agricultural towns in the county.

Among the early settlers, we name Comfort and Job Tyler, who came in 1832; Alvin Hoyt and Hopper in 1832, and also Abel Belote, 1832–3. The early settlers came from various localities, but were mostly natives of the eastern states. The Schellhouses and Dr. Mitchell were natives of Vermont; the Tylers, Farrands, Henry K. (1836) with Phineas and their father (1838), Dr. A. J. Kline (1831), the Bowers, Adam, William and the father, John, William H. Castle (1835), Charles L. Miller (1841), and Dr. McMillen (1834) were New Yorkers; Hoyt, Stebbins, Brooks (1831), and Noyes (1831), and Chaffee (1835) were from Ohio; the Schoefields and Louis A. Leland (1833) were from old Massachusetts; the Eberhards, Wagners, Dr. Voorhis (1836) and John H. Bowman (1839) from Pennsylvania; the Bycus, Danburys and Tellers were Knickerbockers from the Mohawk valley, as

were also the Van Vorcis; Levi Mathews (1832) was from the land of steady habits—Connecticut; the Alfords (1830) and Palmers were Buckeyes; David King and family were English; the Clipfells (1839) came from Alsace, and the Borns and Engles were all from the south of the Rhine, near the French border.

## THE FIRST FARM

opened, was that of Roswell Schellhous, on section six, and the first crop raised was corn and potatoes. Wheat was not sown until 1830, and but a little patch then, though quite a handsome acreage was sown in 1831, and reaped in 1832.

The first entries of public lands in the township were made in 1830, as follows: The north half of the northwest quarter of section six, by John Foreman, June 4; south half of the northwest quarter of section six, by Roswell Schellhous, June 26; northeast quarter of section six, by George F. Schellhous, September 30; and north half of the northwest quarter of section three, by Martin G. Schellhous, October 27. No other entries were made until the next year.

In 1873 there were two thousand six hundred and thirty acres in wheat, which produced thirty-four thousand seven hundred and two bushels, and one thousand six hundred and seventy-six acres in corn, which yielded forty-nine thousand one hundred and fifty-five bushels. There were also produced that year in the township thirteen thousand nine hundred and seventy bushels of other grain, seven thousand two hundred and five bushels of potatoes, one thousand four hundred and fifty-three tons of hay, seventeen thousand four hundred and eighty-four pounds of wool, one hundred and fifty thousand six hundred and sixty-nine pounds of pork, sixty-one thousand seven hundred pounds of butter, fourteen thousand and forty-five pounds of dried fruit, and eight hundred and thirty-five barrels of cider. Three hundred and sixty-four acres in orchards yielded nine thousand four hundred and forty bushels of apples, and thirty-two bushels of pears, valued at four thousand seven hundred and twenty dollars. There were owned in the township six hundred and fifty horses, two mules, four oxen, five hundred and five cows, four hundred and eighty-seven head of other cattle, nine hundred and forty-two hogs, and four thousand one hundred and twenty sheep.

In 1876 there were twenty-one thousand one hundred and seventy-two acres of real estate assessed for taxation, which were valued by the supervisor of the township, Comfort Tyler, at three hundred and fifty-eight thousand two hundred and fifty dollars, but which the board of supervisors increased to three hundred and sixty-five thousand one hundred and thirty-eight dollars, in their equalization of the entire assessment of lands in the county. H. K. Farrand bought, in 1837, the last tract of government land left unsold, at ten dollars per acre.

## THE LEADING FARMERS

of the past and present, in Colon, have been, and are, as follows: Comfort Tyler, who was one of the tidiest of farmers, and whose old homestead is occupied by a worthy successor, his son Ausel; Adam Bower, who succeeds his father, John, on the homestead, to which he has added many broad acres; the farm now contains between four and five hundred acres, on which Mr. Bower has erected the most extensive and elegant farm-dwelling in the township; Gilbert Liddie, who owns four hundred acres; Martin G. Schellhous was an extensive land-owner and farmer in his day; Henry K. and Phineas Farrand,—the latter on the old homestead of his father, Joseph Farrand, who bought the original Brooks location on the bank of Sturgeon Lake; William H. Castle, James Scott, M. P. Thurston and William Tyler.

The heaviest mint-growers are George Teller, Bastian, Wagner, Lowder Brothers, and Coney; about four thousand pounds of peppermint oil being produced annually, at the different stills in the township. George Engle has been, in the past, the heaviest mint-producer in the township, but George W. Teller is the heaviest now. Mr. Teller presents to the reader a view of his fine dwelling, and farm of one hundred and twenty-four acres, on section twenty-two, on another page of our work.

## THE FIRST HOUSE

built in the township was by Roswell Schellhous, as before stated, on section six. It was a log house with two rooms, to which he afterwards made an addition; this was also the first frame house in the township.

Gilbert N. Liddle built the first brick house erected in the township, which was a fair dwelling for the time (1847).

Adam Bower has a most elegant stone dwelling, and commodious barns, a fine view of which we present on another page.

Henry K. Farrand also has a commodious and convenient dwelling,—a fine two-story frame,—surrounded by a grove of sugar-maples and chestnuts, in the midst of a well situated farm of several hundred acres, sloping to the east, a view of which may be seen elsewhere, as also the old homestead of Phineas Farrand.

Samuel Gorton built a snug mansion of stone in 1875, of which he presents a view on another page of our work.

Lorauri Schellhous built the first barn, in 1836.

### THE FIRST ORCHARD

planted out in the township, was by Martin G. Schellhous, but Roswell Schellhous planted the first nursery in 1829, it being of apple-trees. In 1838 H. K. Farrand bought some of the seedlings and set them out on his farm, where they are still in bearing.

Louis A. Leland produced the first peaches from peach pits, planted by Mrs. Noyes, in 1831, on their location on section ten, where she also set out apple-trees. Peaches were raised in 1835, and plentifully in 1837, when Leland bought the farm. He never was known to sell a bushel of the delicious fruit, but divided with his neighbors gratis. No peaches have been raised since 1852, on account of the severity of the winters, but apples are abundant and fine. Wild plums were also abundant in the woods, but the curculio has ruined the fruit, and none can now be found.

### IMPROVED LIVE-STOCK,

which is now a leading feature of the township, was first introduced in 1837, by Augustus Tyler, in a fine lot of hogs, which he brought from Albany, New York.

The first thoroughbred sheep were American Merinos, brought in by Henry K. Farrand, in 1846. Horses began to be improved earlier, but who owned the first horse of improved blood is not known.

Adam Bower, Joshua and Phineas Wagner, Willis G. Davis, Henry K. Farrand and Joseph Farrand are now engaged in breeding and training blooded horses that have made good records on the track, as trotters. One fine animal, brought in by Mr. Davis from Boston,—a magnificent black stallion with a fine record,—died in the fall of 1876.

A private driving-park is laid off on H. K. Farrand's farm, near the village, but no association has been formally organized yet.

Blooded cattle were first introduced by Henry K. Farrand in 1852-3, they being thoroughbreds from the noted herds of the blue-grass regions of Kentucky,—short horns. Phineas Farrand was also interested with this importation afterwards, and the two brothers have at present the best blooded stock in the county. Phineas Farrand has the finest sheep in the township, in which much attention is paid to wool-growing. Comfort Tyler has fine herds of cattle, sheep and swine. Comfort Tyler imported blooded cattle to some extent in his lifetime.

### IMPROVED FARM MACHINERY

was first introduced into the township in the form of open-cylinder threshers, in 1841. Separators were not brought into use until 1848, when Mr. Shuert introduced the first one.

About 1856 reapers and mowers were first introduced, Gilbert Liddle and William H. Castle being the first owners of machines of that class in the township. Mr. Castle bought a Ball combined machine.

Joseph Farrand owned the second open-cylinder thresher ever operated in New York, in 1828. Its teeth were cast-iron, which broke, and nearly burned the man in which the dangerous machine was used. John Moore, was the patentee, and rebuilt his machine with wrought-iron teeth.

### THE FIRST MERCHANT

in the township was Louis A. Leland, who settled, in 1836, on section ten (the old Noyes homestead) to which Samuel Noyes and his family of daughters came, from Ohio, in 1831. Mr. Leland married Mr. Noyes' daughter, Mary Ann, and bought the homestead after the father's death. Prior to his settlement in Colon, Mr. Leland, who came originally from Sherburne, Massachusetts, settled on Bronson's prairie in 1833, and passed back and forth through the country between Bronson's and Centreville, trading, carrying his goods in a wagon; and when he permanently located in Colon, in 1836, retailed his goods at his house. Cyrus Schellhous brought a small stock of goods into the township in 1834, and in 1838 J. D. Freeman opened a little store on the Roswell Shellhous farm.

### MANUFACTURES.

The manufacturing done outside the village of Colon, in the past and present, was and is as follows:

John D. Everhard built, in 1837, a saw-mill on the north branch of Swan creek; and in 1856, a grist-mill was added where custom-work is exclusively done. Both mills are now owned and operated by Philip Everhard, a son of the original proprietor.

In 1839-40 Samuel King built a distillery on Spring creek, on section seventeen, and operated it four years, when it was abandoned.

About one mile northeast of the village, at the Leland bridge, William R. Eck, L. C. Mathews, and S. S. Riley built a saw-mill on the St. Joseph in 1849. It passed into Hoffman's hands in 1872, and was sold by his administrators to George and Samuel Fredericks, who now operate it.

Bricks were first made by Cyrus Schellhous in 1837, and by Joel Dunc next, in 1844. The Seminary company hired a yard, in 1858-59, and made bricks for their building; the same yard is now run by a German.

Whitmore made fanning-mills when he first came to Colon.

In 1839 Jacob Clipfell, Sr., bought the farm of Roswell Schellhous, in the northwest corner of the township, and in 1841 built a brewery, which was operated by him until 1847, when the tragedy (related elsewhere) occurred, and the business of brewing was never resumed.

In 1873 there were two flour-mills, one foundry and planing-mill, two carriage-factories and one tannery, which were in operation in the township, and which employed twenty-nine persons and forty thousand dollars capital. The value of the product thereof was rated by the takers of the census at forty-three thousand dollars.

### THE FIRST WHITE CHILD

born in the township was a boy of Roswell Schellhous, and the second one, also a boy, a son of Martin G. Schellhous, both of whom died in a short time after their birth. The first one was born in the summer of 1830, and the second one in the summer of 1831.

### THE FIRST MARRIAGE

celebrated in the township was that of Jonathan Engle, Jr., and Delia Brooks, in 1832-33. The next one was that of Reuben Trease and Sally Rumsey, whose marriage license was issued August 15, 1834, by M. G. Schellhous, town clerk.

### THE FIRST DEATH

that occurred in the township was that of the first white child born therein (before-named), a son of Roswell Schellhous, in the summer of 1830. He was followed by a little cousin, born the next summer, who died shortly afterwards. The first adult person who died was the grandmother of these little boys (Mrs. Schellhous), in 1832. This same year Emily Noyes, aged eight years, was killed, and was the first burial in

### THE CEMETERY,

which lies west of the village, and which was first laid off in 1832, containing then but a single acre. In 1838 it was regularly laid out, and additional grounds bought. In 1876 more additions were made, and it now has an area of eight acres, pleasantly located on the west bank of Sturgeon lake. There is a burial-ground near the Everhard mill, also.

### THE FIRST SCHOOL-HOUSE

was built in 1833, on the Brooks (now Phineas Farrand's) farm, and Martin G. Schellhous was the first teacher therein,—the winter of 1833-4. Mrs. W. H. Castle was a pupil in that school, and Jerome Cobb, now a prominent citizen of Schoolcraft, also. Martha Schellhous was the first school-ma'am, and taught in that same house, the summer of 1834, and was followed the next winter by a Mr. Harwood. That teacher is now Mrs. Keyes.

The school-statistics of 1876 are as follows: Ten schools were taught in the township, in as many school-houses,—eight being frames, one brick and one stone,—capable of seating four hundred and eighty-four pupils. Three hundred and twenty-seven scholars, out of three hundred and forty-eight children in the township (of the legal school age) attended the schools, which were in session an average of eight months. There were two male teachers employed, who were paid two hundred and eighty-seven dollars and fifty cents for their services, and eighteen females who received one thousand three hundred and six dollars and sixty-five cents for their work. The total income of the districts was two thousand two hundred and fifteen dollars and seventy-seven cents, of which was expended one thousand nine hundred and ninety-one dollars and seventy-one cents. The school property is valued at six thousand nine hundred and seventy-five dollars. One private school was taught, having thirty-five pupils in attendance.

THE FIRST RELIGIOUS MEETING,

aside from the funerals of the persons before-named, was held in 1833 at the Brooks school-house, and was a Methodist service. Elder Alford, a Baptist minister, attended and officiated at the funerals. He was a very kind neighbor, and came into the township in 1830. In 1836 the meetings were held in Lorausi Schellhous' barn, near the present cemetery. A circuit-rider preached also in Glover Laird's barn, and in his exhortations was not choice in the selection of his language. He once exhorted his hearers to make a clean breast of the matter of religion, and "go the whole hog or nothing, and not be like Esquire Howe's oxen,—one a mooley, and the other having horns."

THE DUTCH REFORMED CHURCH,

which is located near Philip Everhard's mill, was built in 1874. It is a brick edifice, and cost three thousand dollars; it has three hundred sittings. The society was formed, in 1848–50, by Rev. Daniel Crow, in school district number five,—among the first members being, John Yelter, Michael Yolter, Peter Miller, John Ult, Adam Decker, Peter Wagner, George Decker, John D. Everhard and Daniel Rich. Rev. William Reed succeeded Mr. Crow, and Rev. Mr. Ellers followed Mr. Reed. Rev. Mr. Hackman was the next pastor, and was succeeded by the present one,—Mr. Lutzeinger. John D. Everhard was the leading spirit in the early history of this church, and was an early comer to his neighborhood, and gathered around him a large number of his Pennsylvania neighbors and acquaintance, among whom he was a leader in every good work and public enterprise. His record among them is that of a generous, benevolent, public-spirited citizen.

CIVIL ORGANIZATION.

The township of Colon was originally a portion of the township of Sherman, as primarily constituted in 1829. In 1830 it constituted a portion (the eastern half) of Nottawa township, from which it was set off, and with the present township of Leonidas, formed a separate township in 1833. The separation of the two townships (five and six, range nine,) occurred in 1836,—at which time Colon was limited to its present area, and is known on the government surveys as township six, south of range nine west. The township took its name from the village, which was projected in 1832.

THE FIRST TOWN MEETING

was held in the new township in 1833, Roswell Schellhous being elected supervisor, and M. G. Schellhous, clerk. The record of the meeting is incomplete, and the names of no other officers can be given who were then elected. In April, 1834, George F. Schellhous was chosen supervisor, Martin G. was re-elected clerk, and Aaron McMillan and George Brooks, highway commissioners. In 1835 Alexander McMillan, Levi Watkins and George Brooks were school-commissioners.

The office of supervisor has been filled in the township as follows: 1833, Roswell Schellhous; 1834–6, George F. Schellhous; 1837, Comfort Tyler, who also held the office from 1852 to 1859 inclusive, and from 1863 to 1870 inclusive; 1838, Joseph Farrand; 1839–41, Martin G. Schellhous; 1842–46, Levi C. Mathews; 1847, Cyrus Schellhous; 1848–51 and 1861–2, William R. Eck; 1860, William H. Castle; September, 1870–71 and 1874–76, inclusive, Ansel Tyler, who was appointed to succeed his father on the death of the latter, in 1870; in 1872–73 and 1875, Henry K. Farrand.

The position of town clerk has been filled by the following gentlemen: M. G. Schellhous, 1833–35; F. A. Mathews, 1836–38; Lorausi Schellhous, 1839–43; Louis A. Leland, 1844–1847; Charles L. Miller, 1845–46–1848–49 and 1851–57; Saud S. Riley, 1850; Loran W. Schellhous, 1858 and 1861–62; Alva L. Hoag, 1859; E. H. Hill, 1860; Charles M. Lumpman, 1863 and 1866–76; Charles Wilkinson, 1864; Daniel C. Richards, 1865.

The office of justice of the peace has been held principally by the following unnamed gentlemen: Martin G. Schellhous was appointed to the position by Governor Porter, April 3, 1833, on the recommendation of the citizens of the township, and M. W. Alford received a similar appointment, from the same source, and by the same endorsement, April 3, 1834. In 1836 the first election of justices was held, and at that election, Roswell Schellhous, Charles Palmer, M. G. Schellhous and Abel Belote were chosen, and drew the terms of one to four years, respectively, but Belote did not qualify, and the following year Comfort Tyler was elected to fill the vacancy, and Daniel Hogan was elected for the full term. Palmer held the office until 1843, and M. G. Schellhous, 1843; J. D. Clowes, 1840–48; J. D. Everhard, 1841–56 Abel Belote, 1843–1867; Louis A. Leland, 1845–49 and 1864 to the present time; Charles L. Miller, 1848–56 and 1861–65; Lorausi Schellhous, four years, 1840–53; William Tomlinson, 1855–1862; A. C. Chaffee, five years;

John W. Lovett, 1869–77; Edwin R. Hill, 1872–76; Nathan Mitchell, 1842–46 and 1869–71.

THE OLD RECORDS

of the township have some interesting entries, from which we cull a few only. Among the by-laws adopted by the annual town meeting of 1842, were the following: "All buck sheep are restrained from running at large, from July 15th to November 10th, and the owner of any animal so offending, shall pay five dollars or forfeit the buck, at his option," i. e., at the owner's option; "All boar hogs over three months old, may be changed by any one at the risk of the owner, that is found running at large."

In 1844 the town board directed the clerk (L. A. Leland), to buy a chest to preserve the township records in, provided it did not cost more than five dollars, and provided further, that the clerk would take it off the hands of the board and refund the money, if the people repudiated the appropriation at the next meeting. In 1845 the people voted eighty ballots for license, and seventy against the same. In 1864 the town voted one hundred dollars bounty to volunteers, in February, and in August, they voted another bounty of the same amount. The ear-marks, by which the people knew their own, were various. Oliver Alford, Jr. knew his cattle by a square crop of the left ear, and a slit in the end of the right. Charles Palmer made his mark on the left ear, by a square crop. M. G. Schellhous put a swallow-fork in the end of the left ear, and James Cowen gave notice to his neighbors in Leonidas and Colon, that any saw-logs marked with an "H" in the end thereof, were his property; and his cattle browsed the heather with a remnant of the right ear, the left, the major part thereof, having disappeared in a square crop of the end, a slit and a half-penny taken therefrom.

THE FIRST ROAD

was laid out through Colon, in 1836, from the village to the county-seat of Branch county, as then located,—Lorausi Schellhous was one of the chainmen, and marked every mile from Coldwater to Centreville. Two hundred dollars subscribed by individuals, and, with that amount and work donated, the road was cut through, the streams bridged and marshes causewayed to the town of Mattison, in Branch county.

THE FIRST BRIDGE

over the St. Joseph river, was built in 1839–40, and was known as the Farrand bridge,—it was the third one on the river. The Leland bridge was built in 1845. In 1868–69 the iron bridges were built over the St. Josephs, and in 1873 the iron bridge in the village over Swan creek was built, the whole cost being sixteen thousand dollars.

THE POST OFFICE

was first established in 1835, Lorausi Schellhous being the first postmaster, and carrying the mail between Colon and Kent's, and Adams' mill in Branch county, for the proceeds of the office, once a week. The office was kept at the postmaster's residence, where Mr. Schellhous now lives. Henry Goodwin, a boy eight years old, carried the mail a portion of the time, which was brought first, as before stated, from Adams' and Kent's mills, then from Thompson's; then from Samuel Needham's, and then from Leonidas, once a week.

In 1837 Louis A. Leland carried the mail from the Branch county-seat to Berrien, in Berrien county, maintaining the contract two years, making three trips per week between Branch and Centreville in a two-horse wagon, and weekly from Centreville to Berrien via Three Rivers, Cassopolis and Niles on horseback, there being nothing but a trail to follow. At that time Anson Burlingame's father lived in Branch, and the son was frequently at home.

The postmasters of Colon have been, besides Mr. Schellhous, who held the position for several years, J. H. Clowes, two years, Louis A. Leland, two years, Charles L. Miller, four years, Elisha Hill, seven years and E. C. Wellesley, sixteen years, from 1861, who is the present incumbent. The present business of the office is as follows: The amount of stamps sold during the year 1876 was seven hundred and twenty-eight dollars and eighty-eight cents; the number of registered letters forwarded, three hundred and twelve; the number of letters received and dispatched daily, one hundred and fifty; the number of newspapers distributed weekly, four hundred; the number of mails received and dispatched daily, six. During the war a daily mail was had and a reading-room and club established in the village.

THE FIRST HOTEL

kept in the township was Roswell Schellhous', in 1830 and later.

MRS. ADAM BOWER

ADAM BOWER

RESIDENCE OF ADAM BOWER, COLON TP., ST. JOSEPH COUNTY, MICHIGAN.

In 1838 Colon had a population of three hundred and sixty-eight souls. In 1850 the souls had increased and multiplied until they numbered eight hundred and forty-six. In 1870 they had still further increased and numbered one thousand five hundred and four; of whom seven hundred and eighty-eight were of the masculine, and seven hundred and sixteen of the feminine gender. Three hundred and eleven families had each a house to live in, with one to spare. In 1874 the census taker for the State could not find as many people as the United States marshal found four years before, and reported but one thousand three hundred and fifty-three; of these six hundred and eighty-one were males, and six hundred and seventy-two females. Of the former, three hundred and forty-seven were over twenty-one years of age, two hundred and fourteen of whom were liable to military duty, one hundred and twenty-six over forty-five, and seven were over seventy-five but under ninety. Of the females, three hundred and eighty-four were over eighteen years, two hundred and forty-five of them being under forty, and one hundred and thirty-three over forty and under seventy-five, and six over the latter age. Four hundred and sixty-one boys were under twenty-one years, and three hundred and seventy-nine girls were under eighteen years. There were two hundred and eighty-one married men and fifty single men, who were old enough to contract for such a condition legally, without asking "pa." Two hundred and eighty females were housekeepers at home, and seventy-two of their sisters had not referred the matter to the head of the family where they resided, and were still single. Nineteen males and thirty-three female females were widowed or divorced.

THE POLITICAL STANDING

of the people is shown by the result of the presidential balloting in the township. In 1840 the Whig vote was thirty and the Democratic fifty-nine. In 1844 the Whigs polled fifty-eight votes, and the Democrats seventy-five. In 1848 the Whigs cast sixty-nine, the Democrats seventy-four, and the Free Soilers seventeen votes. In 1852 the last Whig effort gave seventy-six votes, the Democrats gave sixty-four votes, and the Abolitionists polled sixteen votes. In 1856 the Republicans polled one hundred and forty-nine votes, the Democrats sixty-six, and the Prohibitionists numbered not enough to add a plural. In 1860 the Republicans cast one hundred and seventy-one votes, and the Democrats one hundred and thirteen. In 1864 the same parties cast one hundred and seventy-one, and eighty-four respectively, and in 1868 the Republicans cast two hundred and thirty-eight, to ninety-four by their opponents. In 1872 Grant received one hundred and twenty-nine votes, Greeley eighty-nine, O'Conor three and Jeremiah Black one. In 1876 Hayes received two hundred and thirty-three votes, Tilden one hundred and twenty-three, and Peter Cooper forty votes. This last vote would indicate a population of about two thousand in the township.

THE TAXES OF THE PEOPLE

have been as follows: In 1834 the assessment of property in the township for taxation amounted to fifteen thousand three hundred and ninety-one dollars, and the taxes levied thereon to seventy-nine dollars. In 1836, when the first State tax was paid, Colon's assessment was thirty thousand and eighty-eight dollars, and the levy of taxes one hundred and sixty-nine dollars and twenty-two cents, of which seventy-five dollars and twenty-two cents was for the State. In 1835 the town taxes were just a single dollar. It would be interesting to know what mathematical microscope the clerk used to cast the tax upon the individual assessments. In 1876 the assessment, as equalized by the county board, stood at four hundred and seventy-seven thousand one hundred and thirteen dollars, and the taxes levied thereon were, for State and county purposes two thousand four hundred and thirty-seven dollars and thirty cents, equally divided between the two treasuries; and township taxes, including schools, two thousand six hundred and fourteen dollars and fifty-six cents; making a grand total of five thousand and fifty-one dollars and eighty-six cents.

AMUSEMENTS.

The first celebration in Colon was in 1840, when the Whigs learned that "Tippecanoe, and Tyler too," had, in deed and in truth, "beat little Van;" Joseph Farrand gave a dinner to the Whigs of Colon and Leonidas, and they had a jolly time.

The sport which caused the keenest enjoyment in the early days was the capture of ducks and pigeons, with nets. L. A. Leland used to trap thousands of them, and ship them east to Boston and New York. Henry K. Farrand trapped them on his farm, and fed them by thousands. One season, over one hundred bushels of corn were fed to the ducks and pigeons, and

20

when taken they were fat and juicy, the rank flavor of the ducks, from feeding in the marshes, being entirely removed by their grain diet. Wild turkeys filled the woods, and afforded rare sport to the marksman.

INCIDENTS.

In the terrible sickness of 1833 and 1838 there were many sorrowful scenes and incidents, but none more touching and sad than the case of Levi Mathews' family. They arrived in Colon in August, 1833, and on the 9th of September Emeline died, and was followed by Mrs. Mathews, October 7; by Edward, October 23; by Mr. David Cobb (a son-in-law), November 2, and by Mr. Mathews himself, November 29. They all died on the Leland farm.

In 1838 the sickness was so general, and so severe, that there was no wheat sown that fall in the township. Corn stood in the field unhusked till after the winter set in and the sickness abated. Spring wheat was sown the next spring for family supplies. So protracted and fatal was the epidemic, malarial fevers that all hope was lost, all ambition crushed, all courage banished, and men and women were indifferent to all effort for the future. The dead and dying were in every house, and not a woman in the whole township could do anything more than the imperative demands of her own household made compulsory. Men, in relays, went from house to house to nurse the sick, minister to the dying, and bury the dead as well as their own feebleness and wretchedness would allow. The fatality arose quite as much for want of proper medicine and treatment as it did from the malaria which rose in exhalations from the soil, and made heavy the air with its baneful breath. From 1837 to 1841 the sickness continued more or less violent each summer, but the mortality and suffering were slight compared with those of 1838.

In 1847 a tragedy occurred which shocked the whole community, by bursting upon it unheralded, and filling it with horror and surprise. A family of Alsatians, named Clipfell (consisting of an old man and his son, and the wife and children of the latter), came into the township in 1839, bought the Roswell Schellhous place, and built a brewery. Jacob, senior (the son), had been back and forth to France once or twice to receive money from some unsettled estate in his native land, and was in comfortable circumstances; but one day in October, in the year first named, the son had some words about the money received from France with his father (the old man), and soon after went into the brewery, where the latter was, and struck him with a heavy Indian hoe, killing him almost instantly. He then shot himself, and died without a word or groan escaping his lips. He is supposed to have been insane, as a brother (Philip) some years afterwards committed suicide in Nottawa.

When the first white settlers came to Colon, a pair of bald-headed eagles had an eyrie in the tall trees on the river bottom or margin of the lake, on the land that was afterwards owned by L. A. Leland. These eagles came every year, built their nests, and hatched their young eaglets, until 1856–57, when some rascals cut down the tree, caught the young birds, and shot one of the old ones. This was deemed such an outrage by the people (Mr. Leland particularly, who looked upon the eagles as his especial pets, and had named his farm the "Eagles' Nest"), that if the vandals could have been caught they would have suffered for their malicious act, law or no law. Since then a single eagle has frequently been seen hovering about the lake, as though looking at the old home of twenty years ago and more.

Colon had its trials and tribulations, arising from bad neighbors, as well as other communities. A gang of sneak-thieves committed depredations on the farmers and merchants of the township, with impunity, for years,—stealing buffalo-robes, harnesses, clover-seed, wheat, corn, sleds, goods, blankets, whips, neck-yokes, etc., with a reckless indifference at once inconvenient and exasperating to the victims of their marauding operations. They were at last brought to grief, and large quantities of goods recovered. The rascals were sent to Jackson for a term of years. D. J. Pike and H. K. Farrand were chiefly instrumental in bringing them to justice. Justice Leland ably seconded their efforts by holding the prisoners under such heavy bonds that they could not furnish bail, and therefore were on hand when wanted, and received their deserts. Farrand had suffered from three raids, and on the third got on their track and ran the precious scoundrels to earth, the chief one getting ten years in the penitentiary, an accomplice being fined four hundred dollars, and sentence suspended over the youngest (Clayton Robinson), who left the State, went to Wisconsin, and entered the business of dealing in counterfeit greenbacks with N. B. Latta, was caught, turned State's evidence again, and sent Latta up for fifteen years, getting free himself. The goods found in the parties' barns and cribs were identified by persons from Indianapolis to Grand Rapids, the prisoners being members of a regular organization between the two places.

## THE VILLAGE OF COLON

was originally projected in 1832, by George Schellhous and the Indian-trader, Hatch, who surveyed and laid off the plat, which was not recorded. The first plat recorded of the village was that of the survey of John H. and William F. Bowman, January 5, 1844. The origin of the name of the village is somewhat singular. The first projectors were casting about for a name, when Lorausi Schellhous turned to the dictionary, which opening, his eye fell upon the word "Colon," and looking at its anatomical signification, said, "We will call it Colon; for the lake and the river correspond in their relations exactly to the position of the colon," and so it was named. The township on its organization retained the name. The village sank into somnolence, until the flouring-mill was built, and other manufactures sprung up after 1840. The first frame house built in the village was by Dr. Voorhis, in 1836.

## THE FIRST SETTLEMENT

on the present site of the village was made by Lorausi Schellhous and his family, in the spring of 1831, their cabin being the first house built thereon. Charles Palmer was the next settler, who came, with his family, the succeeding fall, and lived all winter with Schellhous in his one-roomed cabin, and in the spring removed into his own cabin, on the shore of the lake, which now bears his name.

Mr. Schellhous' brother, George, and family, were the next arrivals; they settled permanently, and George entered into partnership with his brother in a saw-mill on Swan creek, Lorausi subsequently selling out to him, and removing to his farm west of the village, in 1835. One Kirk, a millwright, was also a resident of the village at the time.

Dr. Isaac S. Voorhis came in 1836, and bought out the mill site and water power of the Schellhouses, and began the erection of a flouring-mill in 1838, which was completed in 1839, and sold to John H. Bowman. In 1841, the first stock of goods was opened for sale by Charles L. Miller, formerly of Constantine, and the village was assured of an existence, though it was for a time a sickly one.

## MANUFACTURING INTERESTS

were the vital force of the village, that which gave it life, and the first commencement of them was a saw-mill built in 1832, by Lorausi Schellhous, on the site occupied by the present saw-mill.

The second manufactory was the flouring-mill, above named, built by Dr. Voorhis in 1838-9. The mill was put into operation, in 1839, by William R. Eck, then of Three Rivers, who dressed the first stones and ground the first grist therein. Mr. Eck subsequently removed to the village in 1845, and is still an honored resident thereof. The mill had originally three run of stones, but another run was added a year ago, 1875. It is owned now by the C. B. Hoffman estate, and operated by John Hoffman and Sylvester Troy, lessees.

In 1845 David Barrows made wagons, the first vehicles of that class made in the village, but Erastus Mills put up the first regular wagon-shop in 1846, which is the present Davis house. C. A. Baxter succeeded to the business in 1850, and he, in turn, gave way to the present manufacturers of fine carriages and wagons, Anderson Brothers, in 1867. They employ nine men, and their sales in 1876 amounted to twenty thousand dollars.

The first foundry in the village was erected in 1847, by Shuert & Duel, and was burned down in 1852, and thus made the same year by Richards & Hazen, near the wagon-shop. D. C. and A. Richards succeeded to its ownership, and operated it for several years, when it was torn down and removed.

In 1858 Richards & Hughes built the present furnace, and commenced operations therein in 1859. The sales of 1876 amounted to two thousand dollars. Plows and other similar articles are manufactured, and three men employed. In 1854 William F. Bowman built a planing-mill, and ran it several years. It is now the wagon-shop of Anderson Brothers.

Prior to 1860 David Brownfield built the tannery, which is now owned by E. R. Hill, and operated by Hill & Doran. In 1858 W. F. Bowman built a machine-shop for repairs, etc., which is still operated by him. In 1860 Daniel S. Avery built a wagon-shop, which is now used for a cooper-shop by David R. Oliver, E. P. Wellesley and J. Moore.

Charles L. Miller, Jr., erected, in 1874, a large building for drying fruit by the Alden process, which has proved a great success, and is now in operation in the season. He made large quantities of vinegar in 1876.

The product of the factory in that year was sixty thousand pounds dried apples, two hundred and fifty barrels vinegar, and one thousand pounds dried pumpkin. Thirty-five persons were employed during the season of one hundred days.

Gorton was the first blacksmith, and had a shop in the village in 1837. Rockwell Hazen built a shop in 1844, and did an extensive business. Anderson Brothers are the present smiths. Ryan Williams built a cooper-shop in the spring of 1843, but there was one built in 1840, and was used in 1841 by the first merchant, as a retail store, while his building was being erected. Michael Keith was the first shoemaker, and was an itinerant, going from house to house to make up the stock the farmers bought. Ryan Williams was also a shoemaker in 1844. R. J. Hazen followed the trade of a cooper for ten years in the village, beginning in 1844. F. M. Bedford has been in the harness manufacturing line since 1866. He came to Michigan in 1861, and has followed his trade ever since.

## TRADE

began to find a channel in the village in 1841, Charles L. Miller being the first merchant to open a stock of goods for retailing in the village. He put his stock in a cooper-shop at first, until he built and completed his store. He was in trade twelve years,—a portion of the time in partnership with Williams. Mr. Miller was the leading merchant while he was in trade in that village, and had a large patronage. He was elected judge of probate in 1856, and was secretary of the committee on commerce of the United States senate, from 1861 until his death. The leading merchants, since his time, have been Don A. Watson and H. R. Hulbert, who are now out of the trade. E. Hill & Sons commenced in the mercantile trade in the village in 1851, and until 1868 were leading merchants, doing a heavy trade. They are now engaged in the produce and shipping line, and shipped forty thousand bushels of grain in 1876. They buy and ship also at Sherwood, in Branch county, the next station east of Colon, on the Air Line railroad. They also do an exchange business under the name and style of

## THE EXCHANGE BANK OF E. R. HILL & CO.,

having organized as such January 1, 1872. They sold in 1876 one hundred and twenty thousand dollars of exchange. Dr. Isaac Sides opened the first drug store January 14, 1859. W. B. Akey has a most elegant one at the present time, and Kimball & Bower are his competitors.

## THE PROFESSIONS.

Dr. Isaac S. Voorhis was the first physician; he located in the village in 1836 (as before stated), and died in 1838. Dr. Nathan Mitchell was the second physician; located in the village in 1839, and had an extensive ride, but received poor pay therefor; he is still in practice in the village. Dr. Romine was the next physician, and died in the village in 1855-6. Dr. Briggs came next, and was killed in 1856-7, at Toledo, in a burning building. Dr. Joyce came next, and practiced twenty years. Dr. Sampson came after Joyce, and then Dr. Isaac Sides came in 1859, and is still in practice, as is also Dr. Kimball, who located in 1870 in the village. Dr. Godfrey, homœopathist, was in the practice in the village for sixteen years, and is now succeeded by his son, the young Dr. Godfrey.

H. Austin is the only permanent dentist the village has ever had, and he is now in practice. Dr. A. J. Kinne came to Colon in 1846, having previously located in Leonidas in 1837, and practiced for a time, but does not follow his profession now.

The first doctor in the township was Dr. James Fisher, of New York, who located therein in 1832, on the prairie near the trader Hatch's place. A son of Dr. Fisher, born in Colon, distinguished himself in the United States navy. Dr. McMillan practiced some after he came into the township, in 1834, but was too much pre-occupied with his philosophical researches to give much attention to sublunary things.

## THE ONLY LAWYER

ever resident in Colon, was Hiram Draper; he never practiced his profession but once, and then was beaten, in his only law-suit, by Henry Farrand.

## THE RAILROAD

passing through the village was a great achievement for the people, and they are mainly indebted to Henry K. Farrand, Dr. A. J. Kinne, C. B. Hoffman and E. R. Hill for the accomplishment of the much-to-be-desired means of communication with the outside world. Mr. Farrand was especially zealous in securing the passage of the road through the town and village,—spending several hundred dollars, and the better part of two years, time in so doing. Dr. Kinne was also prominent in the work. Aid for the Grand Trunk road through Michigan, from Port Huron to Chicago, was moved for, first in 1863-4. It was the object of the Grand Trunk of Canada, to get a communication direct with Chicago. The first meeting of the citizens along its proposed line, from Jackson to Centreville, was held at the former place in 1865. The people of Colon saw that this was the time to get a railroad through the township to Centreville, and during that year the company was organized under the name of the Grand Trunk Railroad of Michigan, and subscriptions were obtained therefor, but no aid was rendered by the Grand Trunk of Canada, as had been promised.

Then the stockholders and subscribers changed the name to the Michigan Air Line Railroad, and a vote was taken in Colon to aid the same by town bonds to the amount of thirty-six thousand dollars, but the proposition was rejected.

Then Mr. Farrand, and the gentlemen before named, exerted themselves and procured subscriptions among the inhabitants of the township, amounting to forty-two thousand dollars, of which thirty-eight thousand dollars was paid in; and after the road was graded, the town again voted on a proposition to aid the road, and carried it through, loaning twenty-five thousand dollars, for which bonds were issued, and the road completed to Colon, July 3, 1871.

The bonds of the township were never paid, the company never fulfilling their contracts with the township on which the issuance of the loan was based.

The railroad company commenced suit on the bonds against the township, but were non-suited, and the bonds returned to the town authorities and cancelled.

The citizens who subscribed for the stock were swindled out of the same, by the consolidation of the company with the Michigan Central. Adam Bower, Peter Wagner and Comfort Tyler were generous subscribers to the stock of the road, from a sense of public duty to the township at large, rather than that of personal benefit, as all lived at a distance from the village, especially Bower and Tyler.

The entrance of the road was celebrated with great enthusiasm July 4, succeeding the day the track was completed to the village.

The present business of the station in the village will be seen by the following exhibit, furnished by F. L. Thompson, the agent of the road, for which he has our thanks. There were forwarded during the year 1876 from Colon station, seven million thirteen thousand eight hundred and ninety-two pounds of freight, including seven thousand four hundred and fifty barrels of flour, twenty-six cars of hogs, six cars of sheep, five cars of cattle and forty-six thousand four hundred and fifty bushels of grain.

The ticket sales amounted to three thousand eighty-two dollars and forty-five cents; five hundred and thirty-eight dollars and fifty cents being for Centennial tickets.

HOTELS.

The first hotel in the village was kept by M. H. Palmer and Rockwell Hazen in 1844, in the brown house on the east side, afterwards kept by Barney G. Everhard, and known as the Barney house.

Shuert kept the house now known as the Davis house, the same having been built by Erastus Mills for a wagon-shop, in 1846.

Everhard went to California in 1850 or thereabouts.

W. G. Davis, at the Davis house, now attends to the comfort of the traveling public, and looks after his fine blooded trotters, and seems to be making a success of both businesses, judging from common report.

THE BUSINESS OF THE PRESENT

is conducted as follows:

*Trade.*

General Merchandize—Clement Brothers, W. F. Patterson.
Boots and Shoes, etc.— —— Spencer.
Produce and Shippers—E. Hill & Sons, Hoffman & Troy.
Furniture—F. French.
Harness—F. M. Bedford, —— Dell.
Groceries and Crockery—Wilkinson & Co.
Drugs and Medicines—W. B. Akey, Kimball & Bower.
Hardware—Paul Wilson, C. M. Lampman.
Variety Store—C. H. Goodwin.
Merchant Tailor—E. C. Wellesley.
Cigars (manufactory)—F. Dickinson.
Millinery and Dressmaking—Mrs. S. Artridge and Mrs. M. Howe.
Markets—Henry Wanzcy, S. Lachman.

*Artisans.*

Shoemakers—W. T. Smith, A. Rogers, G. Deno, R. D. Wilder, S. Ensign.
Carpenters—Whitmore & Brother, J. P. Peters.
Blacksmiths—Anderson Brothers, Adams & Mellen.

*Manufactures.*

Flouring-Mills—Hoffman & Troy, Philip Everhard.
Saw-Mills—Fredericks Brothers, Hoffman & Troy.
Furnace—Dane Miles & Co., D. C. Richards.
Wagons and Carriages—Anderson Brothers, Adams & Mellen.
Plows—Daniel C. Richards.
Cooperage—David R. Oliver, E. P. Wellesley and J. Moore.
Alden Fruit Dryer—Charles L. Miller, Jr.
Tannery—Hill & Dorn.
Cider-Mill—Simons & Co.
Machine Shop—W. F. Bowman.
Newspapers—Colon *Enterprise*, H. Egabrod, proprietor. The Colon *Standard*, published in 1875, by L. E. Jacobs, was a Democratic sheet, and attained a fair circulation.
Taxidermist—E. H. Crain.

A fair estimate places the capital invested in business, in Colon village, at the present time, at one hundred thousand dollars.

THE SCHOOLS

of a village are of the first importance to the prosperity of the community, and the residents of Colon were not only not behind, but in advance of any other township in the county, in getting a superior school, excepting White Pigeon, although the same was a private enterprise. The village is included in district number four, and the first school-house built therein was in 1837, or thereabouts. The district was laid off in August of that year, and comprised within its boundaries sections twenty-three to twenty-six, inclusive, and thirty-five and thirty-six. This first school-house was built of logs, and was twenty-four feet square, standing on the corner of W. H. Castle's farm. The frame school-house in the village was built about 1847, and is now unoccupied.

In 1858 several of the citizens of the township, desirous of a higher grade of education than was to be obtained by their children at the public schools then taught in the township, formed and organized the Colon Seminary Company, under the statute, the leading stockholders and trustees being H. K. and Phineas Farrand, A. J. Kinne, Charles L. Miller, W. F. Bowman and Adam Bower, who remained its chief support during its ten years' existence. The company bought a frame building in 1858, fitted it up, and commenced their school,—Orlando Moffatt being the first teacher, and seventy to one hundred pupils being in attendance.

In 1862 the present fine brick structure, occupied by the union school, was erected at a cost of nine thousand dollars for the site and building completely furnished. It was dedicated with appropriate ceremonies, August 20, 1863, Judge J. Eastman Johnson delivering the address on the occasion before a large audience.

Elias Cooley, Jr., was the first teacher in the building. The school was conducted with great success until 1867, having a graded academic course of study, and had pupils from a considerable distance. Its reputation was good, and its discipline satisfactory, and ably maintained. H. K. Farrand and Dr. Kinne were constant visitors at the school, and gave their personal attention to its management,—a good example to be followed by the trustees of all union schools, or any other. Seth Moffatt, an eminent lawyer, and senator for two terms in the State senate of Michigan, was one of the pupils of this school, as was also John Downey, now a distinguished professor in Pennsylvania. More teachers went from this school during its existence than from any other of the same size in the State.

The seminary building is thirty-four by seventy-five feet on the ground, three stories high,—the upper story being a hall, used for religious and other purposes. It has two hundred sittings. After 1867 the school board rented the building of its present owner, William R. Eck, who was also a stockholder in the original company, and have occupied it ever since.

On September 4, 1871 the people voted to incorporate the district as a union school district, and elected H. K. Farrand, W. H. Castle, E. R. Hill, Orson Tomlinson, H. C. Kimball and C. M. Lampman, trustees. The first principal of the union school was D. W. Herman, 1871-72; the second, Robert W. Webb, 1874, and W. H. Day, the present incumbent, succeeded in 1875. Aurelia Carver, the first assistant, has been in that position eight years. The present school-board is as follows: T. Whitmore, moderator; W. H. Castle, assessor; J. W. Lovett, director; E. R. Hill, Thomas Howay and Joseph Grover.

THE CHURCHES.

The Baptist society, now worshiping in their own church edifice in Colon, was first organized in Leonidas, in 1837, by Elders Brown, of Centreville,

Taylor, from Prairie Ronde, and G. B. Day, of Sturgis. The preliminary meeting was held June 25th, and the council assembled and organized the church, August 13th, and ordained Elmore G. Terry as elder. The first members of the organization were E. G. Terry, David Franklin, Orrin W. Legg and wife, Sarah Legg, Mercy Vaughn, Experience Watkins, Enoch S. Gersline, Benjamin Blossom, Joseph Gilbert, Constant Vaughn, Armilla Terry, Justus W. Denton, Eli Denton, Lurelia Denton, Clarissa S. Denton, Mary Reynolds, Sally Reynolds, Clarissa Blossom and Anna Gilbert. Clarissa Blossom is the only one of those members now living.

The present church edifice was built in 1845, the society being incorporated January 20th of that year, the first trustees being Orrin W. Legg, Lorussi Schellhous and Seth Goodwin. The church is thirty-two by forty feet, and is free to all orthodox Christians when not occupied by the society which owns it. Elder Terry preached for the society until his death, and was succeeded by Elder Fuller; he by Philo Forbes, and he by Elder Southworth, in 1853. Elder Goodrich has also been the pastor, and was succeeded by Dr. E. J. Fish, who was succeeded by the present pastor, Elder William Park. Under the preaching of Elder Forbes, in 1845, there was a noted revival, thirty-five persons being baptized. The society held meetings previously to the building of the church in the building formerly occupied by Romine & Stoddard, for mercantile purposes. John Gray, Benjamin Blossom and Joseph Gilbert, were the first deacons, and Mr. Gray is now living in Lockport, New York, at the advanced age of ninety years and over. Joel Legg, William Grover and Mr. Rowe are the deacons at present. The church affords from two hundred and fifty to three hundred sittings, and is valued at two thousand dollars. There are eighty members on the church roll at the present time. A Sunday-school was organized in 1840, under Philo Forbes' ministry, with about twenty-four scholars. It now numbers fifty scholars, and is under the superintendency of J. W. Pike.

The first Methodist Episcopal society was organized in Colon township in the year 1844, by the formation of a class of sixteen members, by Ryan Williams and Aaron Bradley, (two local preachers, who moved into the township the previous year), with Ryan Williams as class-leader. Among the members of said class were Ryan Williams and wife, Aaron Bradley, Samuel Sheik, Mrs. Barber Mills, Mrs. James Palmer and Mr. Washburn, of which class not one member now remains. Colon, at that time was a part of the White Pigeon circuit.

The board of trustees for the society was elected August 18, 1856, with Phineas Farrand, William H. Harper, William F. Bowman, Solomon R. Salisbury, Ellis Hughes, Gilbert Liddle and Moses Blanchard as members of such board, duly appointed and elected under the statutes.

The society at this date (April, 1877), numbers seventy-two members. Brother Bowman was very enthusiastic in this work, and every Sunday sent teams all over the country within three or four miles of the village to bring the children together, and soon had a school of which any man would be proud. The school at this date (April, 1877), numbers fifty scholars, six officers and eight teachers, with John W. Lovell as superintendent.

Colon Lodge, No. 73, A. F. M., was instituted by charter in 1855, Martin Gloyd being its first W. M.; A. J. Kinne, S. W., and L. A. Leland, J. W., with fifteen charter members. The office of W. M. has been filled by the following gentlemen: Martin Gloyd, 1855 and 1860; A. J. Kinne, 1856-8, 1861-2, 1865-6; F. E. Mathews, 1859; M. W. Alford, 1863-4; W. E. Greene, 1867-9; J. W. Simons, 1870; Charles M. Lampman, 1871-6. The present officers are J. W. Simons, W. M.; George Engle, S. W.; Robert Fraser, J. W. The craftsmen number one hundred.

Colon Chapter, No. 81, R. A. M., was instituted under dispensation July 7, 1871, and chartered the following January. A. J. Kinne, H. P.; J. B. Peters, K.; M. Yentler, S., were the first council, who are still incumbents of the same positions. There were twelve charter members. There are now twenty-seven members.

Dennis Lodge, No. 96, so named in honor of Grand Master Dennis, of Michigan, was instituted by charter January, 1867, having been previously organized by dispensation April 10, 1866. The lodge met in Dennis' hall until 1867, when they removed to their hall in the post-office building, where they remained nine years, and removed to their old quarters at the incoming of the new year, 1877. The first principal officers were: Dr. Isaac Sides, N. G.; E. C. Wellesley, V. G.; E. Bathrick, R. S.; E. C. Bathrick, P. S.; W. Whitmore, treasurer.

In 1870 Dr. Sides was elected D. G. M. in the Grand Lodge; and 1871, grand master; and in 1872 representative to the G. L. U. S. Since its or-

ganization there have been initiated into the lodge one hundred members and five admitted by card. Eleven have withdrawn to assist in the formation of other lodges, and four have died. The lodge has now not far from thirty members; is out of debt; has a handsome little ' widows' and orphans' fund " of two hundred dollars, at interest; a well-furnished hall, and has held several social and literary entertainments. Dr. Sides, when grand master, officiated at the laying of the corner-stone of the odd fellows' temple in the city of Jackson, and that of the Odd Fellows' Institute at Lansing. E. C. Wellesley is at present a member of the Board of Commissioners of the Odd Fellows' Institute, and has served nine years as Representative of Dennis Lodge in the Grand Lodge of the State.

The present officers are O. Cline, N. G.; H. Snook, V. G.; M. Yentler, R. S.; W. Whitmore, P. S.; O. Deno, treasurer; M. Yentler, representative to G. L. W. Whitmore has held the office of permanent secretary and treasurer, alternately, since the organization of the lodge, continuously. Dr. Sides is an old veteran in the order, having joined it in Pennsylvania, November 29, 1843.

Elsie Lodge, No. 3, Daughters of Rebekah, was instituted May 18, 1869, by P. G. M. Sides, with fifty-two charter-members,—thirty males and twenty-two females—the lodge being named in honor of the wife of Grand Master Jay S. Curtis, who issued the dispensation for the organization thereof. The first officers were Dr. I. Sides, N. G.; Mrs. Kate Whitmore, V. G.; Mrs. Fanny Hill, R. S.; Mrs. E. Sides, F. S.; Mrs. E. Mellen, treasurer; W. Mellen, W.; and Mrs. M. E. Rogers, C. The past officers are E. F. Doty, J. W. Wyeant, R. W. Hafer, I. Sides, and E. C. Wellesley. The present officers are I. Sides, N. G.; Mrs. M. Deno, V. G.; W. Whitmore, R. S.; Mrs. Nellie Hill, F. S.; Mrs. Kate Whitmore, treasurer; Mrs. M. E. Rogers, C.; G. F. King, W.

The lodge has been an able auxiliary in the work of the order, and has been distinguished for its works of charity and true beneficence in the community in and outside of the lodge. There are thirty-five members in the lodge.

Riverside Lodge, No. 828, I. O. G. T., was organized February 5, 1875, by C. P. Russell, of Detroit, the organization being effected mainly through the earnest efforts of Mrs. J. Bowman and Mrs. M. E. Rogers. The first officers were C. B. Hoffman, W. C. T.; Mrs. Mary J. Bowman, W. V. T.; Isaac Sides, R. S.; Jesse Castle, T. S.; Mrs. Permelia Hill, treasurer. There were forty-eight charter-members. They meet at present in Wansey's Hall. The lodge membership is an active and zealous one, and much good has been effected by the organization.

Much credit for the success of the lodge is due to W. H. Castle, who has been untiring in his efforts to promote the efficiency of the same, and in which he has been ably seconded by St. Joseph Leland, G. Hill, Lamartine A. Leland, Mrs. Permelia Hill, Mrs. M. E. Rogers, Miss E. Bower, and many others. The present membership is fifty-five.

Several years ago Colon Lodge, No. 123, I. O. G. T., was organized with a large membership, Professor E. Cooley being the most active worker, and numbered at one time two hundred and twenty-five members. It flourished for a number of years, but finally became extinct.

Colon Grange, No. 215, was organized in December, 1873, H. K. Farrand, master, and O. Tomlinson, secretary. Mr. Farrand held the position of master during 1874, and W. H. Castle in 1875 and '76. There were fifty-six members in the grange, which is now suspended.

## THE MILITARY RECORD.

of Colon began to be written early in its history, George F. Schellhous and the millwright (Kirk) being drafted in the Black Hawk war. Cyrus Schellhous and Martin G. Schellhous were a bulwark between the Nottawa Indians and the settlers, and by their coolness and knowledge kept the hands of each off the throat of the other, as is fully shown in the general history of the county. Fort Hogan was commenced and ingloriously abandoned within the precincts of the present township of Colon, and the visions of glory faded as rapidly as they gathered about the unfinished ramparts and incomplete bastions. But when the tocsin of war sounded in 1861, and rebellious and bloody hands struck at the throat of the nation and fired upon its flag, the men of Colon, realizing it was to be no boy's play, but a struggle for supremacy between the forces of slavery and freedom, that would be like the fight of Roderick Dhu and James Fitz James,—a war to the death of one or the other,—rallied from the plow and shop, and filled the quotas of the township as often as they were called for during the long, weary, bitter strife.

RESIDENCE OF GEORGE W. TELLER, Colon Tp, St Joseph Co, Mich.

We give a list of those who went to the front, as they are recorded in the official records of the State:

SECOND MICHIGAN INFANTRY.

Private John Q. A. Thornton, Company F; mustered-out.

FOURTH INFANTRY.

Private James Burr, Company C; discharged at expiration of service.
Private Epaminondas P. Thurston, Company C; discharged at expiration of service.
Private John W. Wyant, Company C; killed at Chancellorsville.
Private Eugene Vaughn, Company C; discharged at expiration of service.
Private John W. Mosher, Company E; mustered-out.

SEVENTH INFANTRY.

Private Jonathan Shook, Company B; mustered-out.
Private Charles H. Trumbull, Company I; discharged, December, 1862.
First Lieutenant John P. Everhard, Company K; killed at Antietam, September 17, 1862.
Second Lieutenant George H. Laird, Company K; resigned, April, 1862.
Second Lieutenant Charles Hamilton, Company K; wounded at Fair Oaks; resigned, July 8, 1862.
Private Daniel D. Bennett, Company K; wounded at Spottsylvania; re-enlisted and promoted to lieutenant, captain, and major; mustered-out, 1865.
Private Lewis Frey, Company K; re-enlisted and mustered-out.
Private Elbert S. Schermerhorn, Company K; re-enlisted and mustered-out as sergeant.
Private Myron Howard, Company K; killed at Deep Bottom, Virginia, August 10, 1864.
Private William E. Romine, Company K; veteran reserve corps.
Private Orville Wood, Company K; wounded at Coal Harbor and mustered-out.
Private Philip Hofield, Company K; wounded in Wilderness severely and mustered-out.
Private Ezra Bell, Company K; mustered-out.
Private Truman E. Mason, Company K; transferred to United States cavalry.

TENTH INFANTRY.

Private W. C. Thornton, Company G; wounded in hand; mustered-out.

ELEVENTH REGIMENT INFANTRY.

Chaplain Holmes A. Pattison; mustered-out with regiment.
Corporal Philo Hoit, Company A; died at Nashville, December 24, 1862.
Private William Davis, Company A; discharged at expiration of service.
Private Bert Knickerbocker, Company A; discharged at expiration of service.
Private Hugh McCormick, Company A; discharged for disability.
Private Robert Renner, Company A; discharged at expiration of service.
Private Dudley C. Marvin, Company A; died at Murfreesboro, March 4, 1863.
Private Jared M. Taylor, Company A; missing at Chickamauga; died in Andersonville.
Private William T. Renner, Company A; discharged at expiration of service.
Private Wallace Washburn, Company A; died at Bardstown, Kentucky.
Private Charles E. Powers, Company A; wounded at Dallas; mustered-out.
Private Isaac Knapp, Company A; wounded and mustered-out.
Private Solomon Burchard, Company C; died of small-pox, February 6, 1862.
Sergeant Edwin P. Wellesley, Company D; discharged.
Sergeant John H. Montgomery, Company D; discharged.
Corporal Simeon D. Long, Company D; discharged at expiration of service.
Corporal Homer F. Romine, Company D; discharged for disability.
Corporal Marcenus A. Bronson, Company D; discharged for disability.
Private Daniel B. Adams, Company D; discharged for disability.
Private Ira R. Adams, Company D; lost arm at Lookout Mountain; discharged.
Private Byron C. Brunson, Company D; died May 16, 1862.
Private Stephen W. Chapman, Company D; discharged at Louisville, August 19, 1862.
Private James Everhard, Company D; discharged for disability.
Private George S. Gillott, Company D; killed at Chattanooga, November 25, 1863.

Private Byron I. Liddle, Company D; re-enlisted, and killed near Marietta, Georgia.
Private Martin V. Lytle, Company D; died January 13, 1862.
Private Stillman Robinson, Company D; died January 2, 1862.
Private Thomas Smith, Company D; discharged at expiration of service.
Private John H. Spitler, Company D; discharged at expiration of service.
Private William M. Wyant, Company D; discharged at Nashville.
Private Abram H. Wyant, Company D; discharged for disability.
Private Joseph Wixon, Company D; discharged at expiration of service.
Private Thomas A. White, Company D; discharged at expiration of service.
Private Charles A. White, Company D; died April 20, 1862.
Private William E. Thornton, Company D; mustered-out.
Private Isaac Lowder, Company D; mustered-out.
Private Isaac Kriberlin, Company D; mustered-out.
Private Joseph P. Farrand, Company D; mustered-out.
John Dewey, Non-commissioned Staff; mustered-out.
Private Jacob Bower, Company E; died at Bardstown, Kentucky, February 22, 1862.
Private George L. Bower, Company E; discharged at expiration of service.
Private Benjamin Clubine, Company E; discharged at expiration of service.
Private Henry M. Davis, Company F; died June 22, 1864.
Private John S. Taylor, Company F; mustered-out.
Private William H. Howard, Company F; mustered-out.
Private John Long, Company F; mustered-out.
Private James Kammerling, Company F; mustered-out.
Sergeant Thomas H. Smith, Company G; discharged at expiration of service.
Private Cyrus Gilbert, Company G; killed at Stone River, December 31, 1862.
Private Isaac B. Lyon, Company G; discharged at expiration of service.
Private William L. Thornton, Company I; mustered-out.
Private Emanuel Smith, Company D; discharged at expiration of service.

TWELFTH INFANTRY.

Private Charles Burbridge, Company F; died at Little Rock, Arkansas.
Private Ebenezer Decker, Company K; mustered-out.

THIRTEENTH INFANTRY.

Private George Voorhis, Company C; mustered-out.
Private William Yeatter, Company D; re-enlisted and mustered-out.

FIFTEENTH INFANTRY.

Second Lieutenant Jona. Snook, Company A; resigned.
Private Daniel E. Decker, Company A; discharged for disability.
Private Joseph Lepley, Company A; re-enlisted and mustered-out.
Private Abram Snook, Company A; died at Camp Sherman, August 25, 1863.
Private Charles Sixbury, Company A; veteran reserve corps, and mustered-out.
Private George B. Wilkinson, Company A; discharged for disability.
Private Edward E. Decker, Company A; discharged for disability.
Private Reuben Everhard, Company A; discharged at expiration of service.

SIXTEENTH INFANTRY.

Private Archie Wilkie, Company F; re-enlisted and mustered-out.

SEVENTEENTH INFANTRY.

First Lieutenant George H. Laird, Company C; captain, February 1, 1863; lieutenant-colonel of United States colored troops, One Hundred and Sixteenth regiment.
Wagoner William I. Calvert, Company C; died before Petersburg, Virginia.
Private Joseph Brandle, Company C; discharged for disability.
Private Myron H. Howard, Company C; discharged for disability.
Private Peter Moore, Company C; discharged for disability.
Private William C. Rumsey, Company C; discharged for disability.
Private Benjamin Vaughn, Company C; mustered-out.
Private John White, Company H; mustered-out.

NINETEENTH INFANTRY.

Private Arthur Belote, Company D; discharged.
Private Marshall Marvin, Company D; mustered-out.
Private James L. Belote, Company D; died at Nashville, April 28, 1863.

TWENTY-FIFTH INFANTRY.

Sergeant Warren E. Greene, Company D; discharged.
Corporal Horace Keys, Company D; mustered-out.
Wagoner Calvin J. Root, Company D; mustered-out.
Private Charles G. Liddle, Company D; mustered-out.
Private Henry M. Liddle, Company D; died at Bowling Green, Kentucky, March 1, 1863.
Private Frank Young, Company D; mustered-out.
Private Lester Taggart, Company D; veteran reserve corps.
Private Emory Blossom, Company D; mustered-out.
Private William Ward, Company E; mustered-out.

TWENTY-EIGHTH INFANTRY.

Private Abraham Crawford, Company C; mustered-out.
Private Peter G. Dehn, Company C; mustered-out.

FIFTH CAVALRY.

Private Leonard Leland, Company L; died at Frederick, Maryland, September 10, 1864.

FIRST LIGHT ARTILLERY.

Private Milton Ormsby, Battery B.
Private Edwin Negus, Battery E; mustered-out.
Private John J. Van Vorst, Battery F; discharged for disability.
Private John B. Winchell, Battery F; mustered-out.
Private Abner J. Van Vorst, Battery F; discharged for disability.
Nathan W. Doty, in an Iowa regiment, killed.

# BIOGRAPHICAL SKETCHES.

HENRY K. FARRAND.

Since society was first formed on the earth, the public burdens of a community have ever been borne by a few of its individual members. Is there a school-house to be built, a church to be erected, a railroad to be secured, or even a cemetery to be surveyed and laid off for the burial of the dead, the few free-hearted, unselfish, enterprising citizens of the community to be benefited must perform all the labor and sustain the greater portion of the financial responsibility.

The little village of Colon, though possessing as much enterprise among her citizens as many of her more pretentious sisters, is yet no exception to the general rule.

Foremost among the "bearers of burdens" for the public benefit stands Henry Kitchell Farrand, whose finely cultivated farm of eight hundred acres lies near the village. Thrown early upon his own resources he became thoroughly self-reliant, and with his native energy of character, disciplined by the trying ordeals of pioneer-life in Michigan, he was well fitted for the honorable position he occupied in his later years, and which has given him his well-earned title of a public benefactor. Though not an actual resident of the village of Colon, his residence being about a mile and a half distant therefrom, yet none of the residents have done more, and but a meagre few as much, for the prosperity of the village and to build up for it a good reputation than has Mr. Farrand.

Not one of her public institutions or conveniences but has felt the impetus of his energy and spirit, and drawn largely from his ever-open purse, from its inception to its accomplishment and successful operation, and it is the delight of the historian to do honor to such a truly representative man, and adorn the pages of this work with the records of his life.

Mr. Farrand was born in Mentz, Cayuga county, New York, on the 19th day of June, 1812, where he resided with his parents, Joseph and Julia Farrand, until 1834, attending the district-school in the neighborhood in his younger days, and assisting his father, on the the farm of the latter, later on in life.

In the spring of the last-named year Mr. Farrand made the first venture for himself in business, renting a farm near by his father's homestead for a cash rental higher than any tenant had ever paid before for it, every one of whom had made a losing operation of its management. His father, to test the young man, declined to assist him as he had his brothers before him, but this course, instead of discouraging the new beginner, served only as a stimulus for steady exertion on his part. His aunt, Maria Farrand, who was visiting at his father's at the time, admiring the spirit of her nephew, proposed to go to the farm with him and become his housekeeper, which proposition was quickly accepted, and on the 1st of April, 1834, young Farrand, with two good teams and one assistant, began his farming operations. He worked long and laboriously, taking no time or money for recreation or pleasure, but steadily pursued his business, and at the end of his first wheat-harvest, contrary to the expectations of his friends, freely expressed, he paid from the proceeds of his labor all of his rent, living expenses, the cost of his stock and implements, and had three or four hundred dollars to loan his prophetic friends whose predictions of failure had signally failed.

In the spring of 1836 the farm he had rented for a term of years having been sold, he surrendered his lease, to take effect after his next harvest, and went to Michigan to seek for a location of his own, and finding none that suited him as well as his present homestead, that he could buy at the government price, he bought two hundred acres on the east half of section fifteen in Colon and which was the very last tract in that township subject to entry in the general land-office.

He then returned to Mentz to harvest his wheat, which being done and disposed of, he, accompanied by his faithful aunt and judicious adviser, returned to his purchase in St. Joseph county, coming with a single pair of horses and wagon through Canada, a portion of the way with his brother Charles, whom he overtook on the road, and who settled near Burr Oak, but in Branch county.

Mr. Farrand arrived at Lorausi Schellhous' on the 12th day of October, where he and his aunt were provided for most kindly until a log-house was put up and made comfortable, into which the new-comers moved and passed the winter as pleasantly as circumstances would allow. This pioneer cabin was the home of Mr. Farrand for seventeen years, when it gave place to the present spacious mansion in 1854.

In the spring, when farming operations actively began again, Mr. Farrand found his means exhausted, but his will to do was as fixed and steadfast as ever, and so he began a steady march for a competency, which, despite sick-

RESIDENCE of HENRY K FARRAND,

COLON TP ST JOSEPH CO. MICH

ness and embarrassments incident to life in a new country, he has obtained, and has used no niggardly policy in his efforts therefor.

He has added to his original purchase some six hundred acres, having about four hundred acres under cultivation. His large and commodious barns and sheds are tenanted with some of the best blooded-stock in the country, both of cattle, sheep, horses and swine, to the breeding of which he has paid considerable attention for some years, buying his first sheep at public sale of Roswell Schellhous, in the spring of 1838. This small flock of sheep were the especial care of "Aunt Maria," who brought them home every night in the grazing season for some years.

Among the many schemes for the public good that Mr. Farrand has been engaged in since his first coming to Colon, none is more gratifying to him, by reason of the good results accomplished, than that of the Colon seminary, which was projected by himself, Dr. A. J. Kline and some few others, a detailed account of which will be found elsewhere in our work.

In securing the passage of the railroad through the village, and thereby making it a point on the same, Mr. Farrand's efforts were most persistently put forth, both in time and money, and it was largely due to his labors and zeal that the road was not diverted from Colon entirely. When the railroad company failed to fulfil their obligations under the contract for the township bonds voted in aid of the construction, Mr. Farrand, as supervisor, instituted and pushed the suit for the recovery of the bonds so vigorously that the whole amount, twenty-five thousand dollars and accrued interest, was cancelled and returned to the town authorities, and at a most insignificant expense.

Mr. Farrand has, for the most part of his busy life, pursued the quiet path of a private citizen, but during the years 1872–73–75 he held the office of supervisor of the township. In politics he was originally a Whig, and joined the ranks of the Republican party at its formation, being an active member thereof to the present.

He is an independent thinker on religion, and liberally inclined towards all creeds. He acknowledges with gratefulness the kind offices of his aunt, Maria Farrand, who was his housekeeper and adviser in the first business years of his life and until his marriage, and who, also, when death robbed him of a companion and his children of a mother, again assumed charge of his household, and gave herself unstintingly to the care thereof. He feels that to her, in a large measure, is due his early success in life, on which is based the prosperity of his later years. She died in the old homestead, February 2, 1869.

On the 7th day of December, 1837, Mr. Farrand was united in marriage with Maria, daughter of Levi and Eunice Mathews, and a sister of L. C. Mathews, of Colon. She was born in Plymouth, Litchfield county, Connecticut, on the 23d day of November, 1817. By this marriage Mr. and Mrs. Farrand had born to them the following-named children: ANN ELIZA, now Mrs. M. W. Price; HENRIETTA M., who died at the age of four years; MARGARET S., JULIA ELIZABETH, now Mrs. Oliver H. Todd; FRANCIS EUGENIA, and CHARLES H., the latter married, and with his wife and little boy and two sisters, "Maggie" and "Frank," living on the old homestead. Mrs. Farrand was an estimable woman and a helpmeet indeed for a pioneer. She was a member of the Protestant Episcopal church for several years previous to her death, which occurred on the 1st day of July, 1855. Mr. Farrand was again united in marriage on the 14th day of September, 1865, to Phebe M., daughter of Leonard and Mercy Blanchard, who was born in Marcellus, Onondaga county, New York, on the 26th day of November, 1827. A little girl, whom they called Louisa Kitchell, came to gladden their hearts for a few brief years only, and then her prattling tongue was stilled, and her active, winsome ways vanished from their sight. Mrs. Farrand is a woman of most amiable disposition, and has the love and respect of her household, among whom she moves quietly and trustingly. She is a member of the Methodist Episcopal church of Colon.

## WILLIAM R. ECK.

Not only have many of the citizens of St. Joseph county left honorable names to descend upon those who follow them, but many of them also can trace back their lineage to honorable names left by their ancestors for their inheritance. Such an individual is the subject of our article,—William Rittenhouse Eck, who, though he can as yet trace no descendants from him-

self, can and does go back in the line of his maternal ancestors to the first paper-makers of America,—the Rittenhouses of Philadelphia,—in the "good old colony times when we lived under the King."

Mr. Eck is the oldest son of Joseph and Mary (Rittenhouse) Eck, and was born in the township of Briar Creek, Columbia county, Pennsylvania, August 31, 1809, where he resided with his father, and obtained such an education as was imparted in the public-schools of that day. He assisted his father on the farm and in the clover and oil-mill until April 13, 1833, when he came west and located at what was then called the village of North Bend, but is now known as the second ward of Three Rivers. When he arrived at Buck's hotel he had only a French five-franc piece left in his pocket. He worked for Philip H. Hoffman and Christian B. Bowman two weeks, then for George Tuck for six weeks, after which he husked corn on Prairie Ronde, and put in the balance of the fall shaking with the ague. In the winter he split rails for Mr. Hoffman, and helped to raise the first frame-house in Three Rivers,—the store-house that stood near the site of the present bridge over the St. Joseph river. In the spring of 1834 he began

to learn the carpenter trade, and worked at it till May 31, when his master left the country, and the apprentice took his "kit" and knowledge (both very limited) and went into the service of John H. Bowman at farming, carpenter-work and milling, indifferently, and never left him until 1845. That year (on October 20) he came to Colon and bought an interest in the Colon mill,—the first stones of which he dressed,—and ground the first grist therein, in 1839. He operated the mill in company with John H. Bowman until 1848, and then with W. F. Bowman for three years longer, when he disposed of his interest to Joseph D. Millard, and in the summer of 1851, together with L. C. Mathews and S. S. Riley, built the saw-mill known as the Riley mill, and operated it two years, when he retired from the firm, and has not been engaged in any active business since.

He owns property at Three Rivers, and also the seminary building in Colon, and is quietly enjoying a well-earned competency. He has held the office of supervisor of Colon for six years, and represented the county two years in the legislature. Mr. Eck was a Whig in the days of that party, and has been a member of the Republican party since its organization to the present. He is not a member of any church, but from his good old Quaker mother imbibed principles of justice and mercy, which have actuated him in his dealings with his fellow-men through life.

For reasons satisfactory, doubtless, to himself he has never married, but he has not, therefore, ignored the just demands of society, but in all things that would serve to improve its standing has ever been a generous and hearty contributor. No subscription was ever circulated in the township for any charitable object or business enterprise that has not had his name thereon, with a liberal sum affixed thereto. He aided liberally in the building of the seminary, and also in securing the railroad, although at the time owning no real estate in the town. Mr. Eck is highly esteemed by his neighbors, and is passing through life's later stage with the serenity that a consciousness of a life of rectitude necessarily gives.

### ADAM BOWER.

One of the thriftiest farmers of the township of Colon is the subject of the present sketch, Adam Bower, who was born December 18, 1813, in Springport, Cayuga county, New York. His parents, John and Mary (Cline) Bower, were born in Schuylkill, Lancaster county, Pennsylvania, the former in 1764, and the latter in 1762, and were married in that place in 1795. They emigrated to Cayuga county in 1800, while it was a new and wild country, leading there the lives of pioneers—there Mrs. Bower died, August 10, 1817.

The senior Bower again married, and with his family removed to Colon, St. Joseph county, Michigan, in 1836, Adam accompanying them. He located a large tract of land on section six, on which the father and mother resided till their death in 1844. Mr. and Mrs. Bower are gratefully remembered by the older residents of Colon for their kindness and unbounded hospitality.

In the fall of 1836 Adam returned to the old home in Cayuga county, and brought back Hannah C. Richards as his wife. She was the daughter of Simeon and Mary Richards, and was born September 8, 1814, in Ballston Spa, Saratoga county, New York, and was married on the twenty-second anniversary of her birth.

The new housekeepers went to their own location on section eight in the spring of 1837, where they lived most happily together until December 6, 1848, when Mrs. Bower sank to her dreamless sleep, mourned sincerely by all who knew her. She was the mother of two sons, Simeon A. and John Francis Bower, of whom the latter alone survives.

Mr. Bower lived a life of loneliness until January 15, 1850, when he was united in marriage with Mary Elizabeth, daughter of Levi and Vilonda Pitts, who was born in Onondaga, Onondaga county, New York, November 3, 1827. Mr. Pitts was born in the same county, March 16, 1797, and his wife, Vilonda Deuel, in Washington, Dutchess county, New York, November 5, 1806.

They were married March 4, 1824, in Onondaga, whither Mrs. Pitts had removed seven years previously, and where Mr. Pitts died March 4, 1836.

Mrs. Pitts re-married July 18, 1840, and removed to Michigan in 1842 with her husband, Lewis Shuert, and her daughter, the present Mrs. Adam Bower.

By the second marriage Mr. Bower has had born to him six children: Augustus Levi, Hannah Elizabeth, now deceased; James Elliott, Lewis Adam (deceased); William Emery and Henry F. The two older sons are married and live on their own farms in Colon; one son is in business in Colon village, and the two younger ones are still members of the household on the old homestead of 1857.

Mr. Bower is an active member of the Republican party, and was formerly a Whig in his political affiliations.

Neither Mr. or Mrs. Bower are members of any church, but their preferences are towards the Methodist Episcopal organization.

Mr. Bower owns at the present time five hundred and fifty-seven acres of the choicest land in the township, and has given his son eighty acres besides.

In 1858 he built a most elegant mansion of stone, of which and his ample barns and beautiful grounds by which they are surrounded and connected, we present our readers a fine view on another page.

Mr. Bower is recognized by his neighbors as a man of liberal views, public-spirited and ready to assist generously with his purse and hands any object which bids fair to conduce to the public good; and hence he has been an able assistant in all of the enterprises which have advanced the prosperity of the town, and ministered to the progress of its society.

COMFORT TYLER.

Among the honored names of St. Joseph county, that of Comfort Tyler stands prominently out, as one who has done much to give the old county its proud position in the Peninsular State. His parents, Samuel and Deliverance (Whiting) Tyler, were natives of Connecticut, and removed therefrom in 1788, to Onondaga county, New York, where Mrs. Tyler lived nine months before seeing another white woman beside herself, and three months longer before she saw the second one. One of Mr. Samuel Tyler's brothers preceded him to Onondaga a short time before. They were of the very best and foremost of the families of that region, and gained a most enviable reputation as men of ability and straightforward business character.

Comfort Tyler was born in the town of Marcellus, in the above-named county, on the 7th day of March, 1801, where he received a limited education in the common-schools of the county, and assisted his father in the business of farming, milling and carding wool and dressing cloth, until he was twenty-four years of age, when he began life for himself in the business of his father before him.

In the year 1833 he traveled through Michigan and northern Indiana, and returned to Marcellus, and in the spring of 1834 removed with his family to the west, thinking to locate in Indiana; but on arriving at White Pigeon, those of the residents of St. Joseph county who had met him in the previous summer, were so favorably impressed with his bearing, they persuaded him to look further for a location in the county, and on doing so, he made his selection for a home in the southwest corner of the township of Colon, buying three hundred and thirty-three acres on sections nineteen and thirty-one, with the intention of making further purchases on the Nottawa prairie, when the Indian reservation should come into the market, but did not do so by reason of the particular tract he wanted being located by another party.

On this location on section thirty-one Mr. Tyler resided until his decease, bringing it from nature's dominion to the finely cultivated and productive fields of a thorough farmer.

The people of the township found in him an able and careful counsellor, and guardian of their public trusts, and they gave those trusts into his hands in the fullest measure. He was the supervisor of the township for twenty-five years, his last term ending in the year when his health would not permit of further service. He was also appreciated in the councils of the State, representing St. Joseph county in the lower house of the general assembly, in 1841, and in the upper house, as senator, in the year 1859. He was also

*Joseph Farrand*     *Phineas Farrand*     *B. M. Farrand*

RESIDENCE OF PHINEAS FARRAND, Cor. N. 2d. Jones County, Iowa

a member of the constitutional convention of 1867, from St. Joseph county. In politics Mr. Tyler was originally a member of the Whig party, joining the Republican party at its organization, of which he remained a staunch advocate till his death. He united with the Methodist Episcopal church at Centreville, in 1841, and was its recording-steward for twenty-five years, and died in its communion.

On the 16th day of January, 1823, Mr. Tyler married Desire, a daughter of Abel and Desire Belote, who was born in Onondaga county, New York, on the 11th day of March, 1803. The fruits of this union were the following children : JULIA ANN, now Mrs. O. H. Atchinson ; SAMUEL, now of Sherman; ANSEL, who succeeds to the old homestead in Colon; FIDELIA, now Mrs. A. C. Chaffee, of Colon; ASHER, now in California ; WILLIAM, now of Colon, and EDWARD, who died in infancy. The last two were born in Colon.

Mrs. Tyler was also a member of the Methodist church, and a lady of most estimable qualities. She died April 22, 1854. Mr. Tyler followed her on January 16, 1873.

Reverend Job Tyler, a brother of Comfort Tyler, preached to all classes of people without distinction of religious views, though a Sabbatarian himself. He was much esteemed by the people of St. Joseph county, among whom he dwelt and followed his calling until 1851, when he died at San Diego on his way to California.

Mr. Tyler was broad in his views, and liberal and enterprising in schemes for the public good. Though not particularly to be benefited by his act, he nevertheless aided generously in the construction of the railroad through Colon, believing it to be of general value to the people of the township.

In all matters of the public entrusted to his care he was scrupulously exact to see that his duties were promptly and fully performed, and he has left behind him a record as his monument, upon which his children may look with pride, and his fellow-citizens with admiration. His hospitality was unbounded, and he was generous to a fault.

JOHN H. BOWMAN.

The subject of the present sketch, John Henry Bowman, was born in Mount Bethel, Northumberland county, Pennsylvania, March 13, 1796. He was the oldest of ten children born to Jesse and Sally Bowman. He removed to Brier Creek, Columbia county, Pennsylvania, and resided in that county until 1834, when he removed, with his family, consisting of his wife and seven children, to Three Rivers, St. Joseph county, Michigan, where he built, the same year, the first frame-house of any pretensions erected in that city, and which was also, for many years, the best in the country around.

He bought one hundred and twenty acres of land on Johnnycake prairie and began farming ; and in 1835, with the Smiths of Prairie Ronde, bought the Beadle mill-property at Three Rivers, and with them erected the Three Rivers flouring-mill, and began the manufacture of flour in February, 1837,

21

which business the firm of Smith & Bowman carried on, together with merchandising, for about two years, when the mill was leased and afterwards bought by Moore & Prutzman ; and Mr. Bowman, in 1838, began the erection of another flouring-mill in Colon village with Dr. Voorhis, but the mill was not completed until after Voorhis' death.

The mill commenced operations in 1839, and soon after Mr. Bowman sold three-fourths of his interest to his son, William F. Bowman, and in 1845 removed from Three Rivers to Colon to reside.

He retained one-fourth interest in the Colon mills until his death, actively managing the property during the whole period.

On the 19th day of January, 1817, Mr. Bowman married Sophia, a daughter of John Freese, of Brier Creek, Pennsylvania, by whom he had four children : William F., Jesse, Sally and Martha, all of whom are now dead except the latter, who is the wife of Elisha B. Brown, of Columbia county, Pennsylvania.

Mrs. Bowman died in Brier Creek, October 12, 1823.

On the 15th day of December, 1826, Mr. Bowman was again united in marriage, to Mrs. Ann Millard, nee Rittenhouse, by whom he had born to him John Quincy, Andrew H. and Sarah Ann, all of whom are now dead; Amelia R., now Mrs. E. R. Hill, and Joseph E., both of Colon.

The second Mrs. Bowman died April 2, 1838 ; and July 6, 1844, Mr. Bowman took unto himself another companion,—Mary Ann Raymond, of Three Rivers, who still survives him. By this marriage one child was born, John Raymond Bowman, who is a practicing physician in Cheyenne, Colorado.

In the nullification times of 1832, Mr. Bowman was a major in the Pennsylvania State troops.

In his younger days he was a member of the Whig party, but joined the Republican organization at its inception, though he died before he cast a presidential vote therein. He was a member of the legislature of Michigan two terms.

He was a member of the Methodist Episcopal church in Pennsylvania, but never united with it in Michigan.

In May, 1855, he went west on a tour of observation, and was attacked by the cholera at Lexington, Missouri, and died after a short illness. Mr. Bowman was highly esteemed by his neighbors, and though sometimes despondent, was mostly of a cheerful frame of mind, and liberal to the extreme towards suffering and distress.

—

PHINEAS FARRAND.

One of the most successful farmers in Colon township is Phineas Farrand. His father, Joseph Farrand, was a success in the same line of business before him, beginning the same with the grandfather of Phineas, in Morris county, New Jersey. At the age of twenty-one Joseph Farrand married Julia, a daughter of Edward Campson.

Mr. Campson owned and operated the first mill for cutting iron into bars ever used in America. For fear of confiscation by the British forces during the Revolutionary war, he secretly operated his machinery in a cave, in the interests of the colonial armies.

In 1799 Mr. Farrand, immediately after his marriage, removed to Mentz, Cayuga county, New York, where he bought two hundred acres of land, wild and heavily timbered, subsequently adding two hundred acres more, clearing up three hundred and sixty acres of the tract, and bringing it to a high state of cultivation. Mr. Farrand owned and operated in his barn on this farm the second cylinder threshing-machine, which worked successfully, in the United States.

Of eight children,—five sons and three daughters,—Phineas, the subject of our sketch, was the youngest, and was born in Mentz, December 22, 1820. Here he attended the district-schools of the township, and assisted his father on the farm, until 1837, when he removed with his family, consisting of his father and mother and two sisters, Catharine A. and Abigail E., to Michigan, via Canada, by teams, arriving at Albion, in Calhoun county, in July of that year.

The family remained at Albion during the summer, Phineas occupying the time in driving a breaking-team of ten yoke of oxen, and the father making a tour of observation for a location, which he found in the township of Colon, wherein his son, Henry K., had located a year previous. He bought the location of George Brooks, one hundred and thirty acres, the last public land being entered by his son, Henry K., in 1836, in the township. This original purchase is the present homestead of the subject of this sketch. In the month of October the family removed to their new home, and occupied, for the winter of 1837–8, the small log-house on the premises built by Mr. Brooks.

There were about thirty acres partially broken-up on the location, and Phineas put eighteen of them into wheat that fall, which was the first crop raised by him in Michigan. One term at the district-school, in the Mathews school-house, during the first winter of his residence in Michigan, "finished" his education, and henceforth his "schooling" was that obtained in practical life.

To the original purchase the father and son added a large tract, the farms now numbering four hundred and ninety-one acres in a body, three hundred and nine-one of which are under cultivation, and upon which Mr. Farrand has erected fine, commodious barns and a comfortable dwelling—a view of which may be seen on another page of our work.

Orchards and good fences add to the sense of ease and comfort that pervades this old pioneer homestead, all of which has succeeded wild nature through the steady, persistent strokes of the original purchaser and his worthy successor, who now occupies it.

Mr. Farrand has also been engaged in the breeding of thorough-bred cattle and fine-wooled sheep, and has now upon his farm some of the best-blooded short-horns and American merinos in the county. He has also some very excellent horses, to the breeding of which he pays considerable attention.

During the terrible year of 1838, when death stalked abroad through the country, gathering his harvests with unrelenting hand, the two sisters died within a brief period of each other. In 1845, on the 8th day of January, the mother died, and on the 4th day of December, 1854, the father, too, sank to rest in the old homestead, and of the five persons who came to it in 1837 Phineas alone remains.

In politics Mr. Farrand is and has been a Republican since the rise of that party, and was a Whig previously. His religious sentiments are independent, and he is tolerant of all beliefs.

On the 23d day of October, 1845, Mr. Farrand was united in marriage to Betsey M., daughter of Elias B. and Martha Kinne, of St. Joseph county, Mrs. Farrand being a native of Naples, Ontario county, New York. She is a member of the Methodist Episcopal church of Colon. The children of

this household are Joseph K., Grant E. and Ella, all of whom remain at home. The second son, Theron G., died at the age of twenty-five years, leaving a wife, but no child.

## SAMUEL GORTON.

The subject of the following sketch, Samuel Gorton, was born in Lisbon, Connecticut, September 20, 1817, and is the second of eight children of John and Almira Gorton. At the age of about four years he removed with his parents to Henrietta, about six miles south of Rochester, N. Y., from whence, five years later, the family removed to Bergen, Genesee county, in the same State, where Samuel continued to reside with his father until 1840, when he came to St. Joseph county, Michigan, to look for a location for himself. In 1841 he finally located on section four in the township of Colon, but subsequently sold this location and made another on section ten in the same township, in 1842, where he still resides. His homestead contains eighty acres, besides which he owns sixty-five acres in the township of Leonidas. In 1874 he built an elegant house of the boulder stones found in the township,—a view of which we present to our readers in another part of this work.

Mr. Gorton's political faith in his early days accorded with the Whig policy, and when the Republican party came into existence he joined it, and remained a member thereof until 1872, when he voted for Horace Greeley for president, and in 1876 voted with the Democrats for Mr. Tilden. Though not a member of any church-organization, he acknowledges the force of a Christian line of conduct, marked out by the golden rule.

On the 8th day of April, 1844, he married Julia A., daughter of Samuel Noyes, late of Leonidas, but now deceased. The fruits of this marriage were: Charles James, who died in 1848, and Clarence Ernest, who is now living at home with his parents. Mrs. Gorton was born in Berlin, Ohio, in the year 1824, and came to Leonidas in the year 1832 with her father's family. She is a member of the Baptist church of Colon.

# LEONIDAS.

TAKING into consideration the variety of soil, prairie openings and heavily-timbered forests still remaining unbroken, the water privileges of its rivers and creeks, and Leonidas is justly entitled to her fame, as standing among the best townships in the county of St. Joseph. Its farmers are well-to-do, and their acres, broad and well-tilled, are second to none in the county. The area of the township contains twenty-three thousand and forty acres, of which, five hundred acres are water surface. The prairie originally contained about five hundred acres, and the balance of the land surface was covered with a growth of white and burr oak, more or less heavy, merging into heavily-timbered lands in the northern part of the township. About one half of the township was covered with a heavy growth of beech, maple, white-wood, ash, elm, walnut, hickory, etc. The very best quality of white-wood lumber was cut in the forests of Leonidas and made into arks, by which the transportation of the flour of the county was effected. Millions of feet were thus used, and the forests despoiled of their richest treasure almost entirely.

In some parts of the township stone abounds, the boulder drift having scattered its *debris* liberally throughout the heavy timber.

The surface is a general level, although the land is a little broken and undulating as it approaches the river. Its drainage is good, and but little swamp or marsh land that is unfit for use is found in the township. It is watered by the St. Joseph river, the Nottawa and Bear creeks, the Little Portage, and another small creek, and four small lakes.

The St. Joseph river enters the township on the southeast quarter of

section thirty-four, and runs northeast, passing out on the west line of the southwest quarter of the northwest quarter of section thirty.

The Nottawa enters the township on the southeast quarter of section one, and runs southwest through the same, entering the St. Joseph on the north bank, near the north line of the southeast quarter of the southeast quarter of section thirty.

The Little Portage runs diagonally across the west half of section six, into Mendon township.

A creek enters the township from the north on the northeast quarter of section three, and runs southerly and empties into the old Cowen mill-pond.

Three little lakes, Adams', Havens' and Mud, all lie on section thirty-six, and another small one, Benedict's, is situated on the southwest quarter of section thirty-two.

The township lies in the northeast corner of the county, being bounded north by Kalamazoo county, east by Branch county, south by Colon, and west by Mendon townships, in St. Joseph county.

All kinds of grain, fruit and vegetables can be and are successfully cultivated. Mint has been cultivated somewhat, but no considerable amount has been produced in later years. Maple sugar is manufactured more or less extensively in the northern part of the township.

### THE FIRST SETTLEMENT

of Leonidas was made in the year 1831. The first white man who had a cabin in the limits of the present township was a trader named Hatch, who

SAMUEL GORTON.

MRS. SAMUEL GORTON.

RESIDENCE OF SAMUEL GORTON, COLON TP. ST. JOSEPH Co. MICH.

came early in the spring of 1831, and subsequently married Marchee-o-no-qua, a sister of Magnago, a chief of one of the Nottawa bands of Indians. Hatch moved away or repudiated his Indian wife, when one Buel Holcomb married her according to the Indian fashion, but being brought to see the matter in a different light, Marchee desired Holcomb to marry her according to the rites of the church, and upon his declination, she sent him adrift and married a man of her own race, her descendants still residing in Athens, the adjoining township in Calhoun county. She was said to be a most beautiful woman in her younger days, and preserved traces of it long into old age.

The real settlers of Leonidas, however, in that year, were George Mathews and his remarkable wife and two children, who came from New York city, direct from that centre of luxury and wealth, into the timbered plains of Leonidas, to hew out for themselves a home. They arrived on the banks of the St. Joseph, where they selected their location near the present bridge, on section thirty-two, in May of 1831.

Alexander Foreman and his family of boys and girls came in a few days later, and settled near Mathews. Mr. Foreman came from Ohio, and his Buckeye girls used to run a ferry across the St. Joseph, and managed their craft as skilfully as their brothers or father could.

Of the first two named, Mr. and Mrs. Mathews, the following testimony to their worth and character is borne by their fellow-townsmen, who mourned their loss sincerely.

Mr. Mathews was born in affluence, and was truly a gentleman of the old school, courteous and affable in his deportment, ever ready to mete to all their just reward, with a hand ever open to relieve distress, which was not an infrequent applicant in the pioneer days. His memory abideth with his fellow pioneers imperishable. He died on the farm he located and cleared up, in 1845.

Mrs. Mathews was born in the city of New York, of wealthy parents. She was married in Ohio to an accomplished physician, Dr. Johnson, he surviving but a few years. On her marriage to Mr. Mathews she came with her two children to Michigan, locating as before stated, whereon she died May 11, 1874, she being the first white woman settling in the township, and the mother of the first white child born therein. Mrs. Mathews' abilities, both natural and acquired, were of a very high order, and her residence in a wild country, unaccustomed as she was to the backwoods, was at times as much as she could well bear, but she had indomitable courage and never-tiring patience, and these qualities, added to her unbounded charity and benevolence, carried her straight through all difficulties and vexations into the very citadel of the affections of her neighbors. These pioneers have gone to their rest and reward, and, it is safe to say, none were more sincerely mourned than were these friends and neighbors of the early days, in Leonidas.

In 1831 Leonidas received her next settlers, all of them prominent in her history.

James and Robert Cowen came from Pennsylvania to White Pigeon November 11, and to Leonidas, and bought their mill-site and commenced to raise their cabin, getting it part way up during the same month, when a storm came on, and they finished it the next April.

Isaac G. Bailey, from Connecticut, came in the same year and bought a large tract of land around the Cowen mill-site.

All three of these gentlemen were single men, but they all subsequently married and brought their wives to the settlement, Mr. Bailey in the fall of 1834, and Mr. Robert Cowen 1835, and James later. These pioneers were also noted men in the community.

Mr. Bailey and James Cowen were both educated as physicians, and the latter was an excellent surveyor. Mr. Bailey was elected to the legislature in 1838, at the November election, and died in Detroit the following March. He was postmaster of Leonidas from 1834 till his death, he having influenced the establishment of a postal route from Jackson to White Pigeon in 1835, the year following the establishment of the post-office at Cowen's mills. Mr. Cowen removed to Indiana in 1846.

In the fall of 1832 Leonidas received another citizen, whose name fills a most important place in her annals,—Captain Levi Watkins, who built his cabin on the banks of the Nottawa creek, in October or November, and stocked it with provisions, and went to work on the Cowen mill, which was then in process of construction, and waited for his family, who came in February, 1833, accompanied by his father, seventy years old; the latter, however, returning to the eastern home in Ontario county, New York, where he remained until the winter of 1834–5, when he, with his wife and son, Alex. H. Watkins, came on and made the township their home until their death.

In the spring of 1833, Arnold Hayward and family came in, and built a log-house just above Captain Watkins', adding a frame "lean to" the next summer, and beginning hotel-keeping as a business.

In 1835 George Benedict, who has never lived in any other township since, settled on the east side of the prairie, and the same year Ezra Roberts, Abraham Rhynearson and N. V. Truesdell and family settled on the Indian reservation in the western part of the township. Moses Whiting, Ira Millard and family, and Aaron B. Watkins,—a most useful citizen,—all came in 1835.

The Tylers, Augustus, Charles and Erastus, came in 1834–5, and settled in the western part of the township, and were extensive farmers and men of ability, energy and perseverance. Moses Taft came in with them from Massachusetts, but moved into Mendon in 1835.

In 1836 Edward K. Wilcox, a prominent and leading citizen from then until the present, and Joshua Lyon, a brother-in-law, came in the spring. In 1835–6, too, the Cowen brothers each brought a wife to the settlement, both intelligent, energetic women, who were a great accession to the community.

In 1837 William Bishop and a family of boys, two of whom, Lyman, Jr., and James, built the first brick houses in the township,—fine mansions,—came, as did also Addison Harvey and his father and family, and Elias Kinne and his family. Justus L. Vought,—a school-mate of Drew and Vanderbilts, and born in the same town,—came in 1836, with a very fine family of children, and the father is still living on the old homestead then selected, a much-valued citizen.

Stephen Van Rensselaer York came in 1840. W. M. Watkins came in with his father's family in February, 1833, and, with the exception of his residence in Centreville during his incumbency in the sheriff's office, has lived in the township ever since.

Jairus Peirce, originally from Berkshire county, Massachusetts, but later from Ontario county, New York, came in 1834, in the spring of that year, working at his trade of a carpenter. He helped to build the flouring-mill of the Cowens and many other buildings in the township. He removed with his family from Ontario to Leonidas in January, 1836, the latter comprising six children. In the fall of that year he settled on his present location. In 1834 he assisted to build the first saw-mill on Buck creek, seven miles from the present city of Grand Rapids.

Orrin M. and Martin C. Watkins, sons of Levi Watkins, came with his family in 1833, and were prominent citizens of the township till their death. In 1835 also came Elijah Purdy, two of whose sons are now resident in the township, and bought the location on which John H. Purdy, one of those sons, now resides, a fine view of whose elegant grounds and capacious dwelling and barns, on the old homestead, may be seen on another page.

Millard came in 1835, and located on the reservation. David Barker, also, came in 1835, and bought his land, and the families of Purdy and himself came on in the spring of 1836.

In 1840 William Minor came into the western part of the township, and Jonathan Galloway was also an early comer. In South Leonidas, a family of Gilberts, an old man and sons, and M. C. Keith and brother, and Levi and David Keyes, settled early. In 1840 also, James B. Dunkin came in and bought a location on Nottawa creek, and built a dam and saw-mill, which Andrew Climie now owns.

John Foreman, although a late comer to Leonidas, was an early one in the county, he being born on White Pigeon prairie, February 6, 1830. His brothers, Cyrus and William Foreman, both of whom were pupils in the first schools taught on Nottawa prairie in 1831, are now prominent lawyers in Osage, Iowa, and Cleveland, Ohio. John grafted and raised the first pear he ever saw or ate, grafting it in 1849, and eating the fruit in 1852, on Nottawa prairie.

### THE FIRST FARMS

opened were those of George Mathews and Alexander Foreman, in 1831, both of whom raised crops of corn that year, and the first wheat, also, the next year.

In 1873 there were three thousand three hundred and ninety-eight acres of wheat harvested, which produced thirty-four thousand six hundred and sixty-nine bushels, and one thousand seven hundred and thirty-seven acres of corn, which yielded forty-four thousand nine hundred and sixty bushels. The same year the productions also were, ten thousand eight hundred and four bushels of other grain, four thousand six hundred and twenty-five bushels potatoes, one thousand two hundred and fifty-five tons hay, ten thousand and ten pounds wool, one hundred and forty-seven thousand four hundred and seventy-nine pounds pork, fifty thousand seven hundred and fifteen pounds butter and cheese, sixteen thousand three hundred and forty-seven pounds dried fruit, five hundred and fifty-seven barrels cider and six thousand eight hundred and eighty-five pounds maple sugar. Three hundred and ninety-four acres in orchards produced twelve thousand seven hundred and ninety-nine bushels apples, valued at two thousand five hundred and seventy dollars.

The first land entry was made in 1830, in the southern part of the township, adjoining Colon, and by a Colon resident, and was as follows: The southwest fractional quarter of the southwest quarter of section thirty-four, Loran Schellhous, October 27, 1830. There were thirteen entries made in 1831, the first one being the north fraction and west half of the northeast quarter and the southeast quarter of section thirty-two, by Peter Beisel (then of White Pigeon), June 6, 1831. There were assessed in 1876, by Andrew Climie, supervisor of Leonidas, twenty-two thousand three hundred and thirty-two acres for taxation, which he valued at two hundred and eighty thousand seven hundred and three dollars, about one-fourth of its real value.

### THE LEADING FARMERS OF TO-DAY,

in the township, are John Leidy, Addison Harvey, John A. Purdy, Olney brothers, Richardson Coddington, William M. Watkins, Baxter Lewis, E. W. Davis, —— Rice, and Sylvester M. Clement.

### THE FIRST HOUSE

built by a white man in the township, was the shanty of Hatch the trader, in the winter of 1830-31. The next one was Mathews' log-cabin, and Foreman's the third. The first frame house was the "lean-to" added to Hayward's log-cabin, in which the first tavern was kept, in 1834. The first brick house was built by Lyman Bishop, Jr., and the second one by his brother (James), who now reside in them.

We show on other pages views of several of the fine residences of the present, all built up from pioneer cabins by the men who have succeeded thereto after years of toil and privation. The first frame barn in the township was built by Captain Watkins, in 1835.

### THE FIRST FRUIT-TREES

in the township, planted out by the hand of man, were standing on the river bank, just below the present site of the so-called Mathews bridge, when the first white settlers came, and were then in bearing (being old trees at the time). They were apples, and had been set out so long, the Indians then living in Leonidas had no tradition even concerning them, except a very vague one concerning some "Chenocoman great medicine, heap way off," who had planted them,—meaning missionaries. These trees were transplanted, at least some of them, by some of the settlers, but they never survived their removal.

The first orchard begun by the settlers was the nursery planted by Captain Watkins, in the spring of 1833, when he planted apple-seeds and peach and plum-pits, and in the fall of 1834 transplanted the young trees, from which nursery-orchards were grown from Niles to Ann Arbor, hundreds of trees being sold therefrom.

Mr. Mathews set out an orchard of larger trees, in the spring of 1835 (which he bought of Jones), on White Pigeon prairie, the same being from the Cutler nursery planted in 1826-29. Mr. Mathews raised the first apples in the township.

The first cider made in the township was manufactured by W. M. Watkins, in 1848.

Peaches were first produced in Leonidas in 1837, and for twelve years continued to be grown profusely, when the frost killed the trees to the ground, since which time the crop is an uncertain one.

Plums were first raised in 1845; and for eight years thereafter this delicious fruit was abundant, since which time the ravages of the curculio have absolutely banished it from the township,—not even the wild fruit, which once filled the woods, escaping the havoc of the insect.

### IMPROVED LIVE-STOCK

was first introduced into the township, in 1852, by Addison Harvey and E. L. Yaple, who bought "short-horn" bulls; but no special attention has been paid to that class of stock until within the last four or five years.

John A. Purdy, in 1873, began a systematic business in breeding thorough-bred cattle, of the short-horn or Durham variety, and has now a fine herd of them. He bought his half of Henry K. Farrand, of Colon, who brought his stock from the united herds of the blue-grass region of Kentucky.

Mr. Addison Harvey and the Olney brothers also have now good herds of these cattle, having just begun to pay attention to the breeding of the same. Olney brothers have also improved breeds of swine.

Mr. Purdy began to breed blooded horses in 1864, and sheep in 1867, and has some very fine stock in both varieties. His "Mambrino Chief" is of the thorough-bred stock of Kentucky.

There were owned, in 1874, in the township, four hundred and sixty-nine horses, six mules, twenty-four oxen, two hundred and eighty-nine cows, five hundred and sixty-five other cattle, six hundred and fifty-six hogs, and two thousand and fifty-nine sheep.

"Grandfather" Watkins brought the first team of horses into the township in 1835. One of them was a leopard-stallion, a very showy horse.

### IMPROVED FARM MACHINERY

was introduced into the township, in 1845, by Ruel Johnson (the same being a separator-threshing machine). Open-cylinders had been in vogue some years before.

E. K. Wilcox, in 1847-48, brought in a combined "Manny" reaper and mower; and Mr. Bishop, about the same time, introduced a "McCormick."

### THE MANUFACTURING INTERESTS

of Leonidas were early developed, the Cowens erecting, on Nottawa creek, a saw-mill in 1832, which was completed and operated in the winter of that and the succeeding year. A little incident, illustrating the old adage, "There's many a slip between the cup and the lip," attaches to this mill-site of the Cowens. In the fall of 1831, Isaac G. Bailey came into Leonidas looking for a location, and seeing the site in question selected it and returned to White Pigeon, and entered, as he supposed, the same at the land-office with several other contiguous tracts. Meeting Mr. James Cowen, he told the latter what he had found in Leonidas, and gave him a description of the neighborhood, Mr. Cowen taking the numbers of his entries and marking them on his map for reference, and soon after went to the location himself, where, after a careful examination, he found that the identical eighty acres on which the true site was located had not been entered at all by Bailey, whereupon Mr. Cowen returned to White Pigeon, and quietly entered the tract. Afterward, meeting Mr. Bailey, he told him that he, Cowen, also had found a good mill-site, and should immediately proceed to utilize it. When Mr. Bailey found that the cream of his location, by his own negligence, had been skimmed by another, his chagrin was great; but he swallowed his mortification, and afterwards, in 1833, built a saw-mill on Bear creek.

In 1836 the Cowens built their first flouring-mill, and the dam proving a treacherous structure, in 1840 they abandoned it and built a new one, and also a new saw-mill. There were thirteen men present at the raising of the frame of the grist-mill, which was a heavy job, the framed beats being very solidly constructed, and it was only by the most persistent and heroic struggles and lifting it was raised at all. One of the neighbors "enthused" the crowd by his words of command, which, like the bugle-blast of Roderick Dhu, was, just at that particular juncture, "worth a thousand men." The present saw-mill is the third one built on the site, and was erected by Kidd, who also repaired thoroughly the grist-mill and ran them for some years, and then sold to Robinson, and Robinson to Switzer, who tore down the old mill and flume and built the present one, which he now operates, in 1874. It has three run of stone, and does custom work exclusively.

In 1840 James B. Dunkin built a saw-mill on the Nottawa, above the Cowens, and owned and operated it until 1862, when Andrew Climie, the present owner, bought it, and added a grist-mill, which contains three run of stone. A. C. Fisher rebuilt the Bailey mill on Bear creek, and subsequently sold the same to the Hoags, who afterwards conveyed it to Addison Harvey, and the mill rotted down.

In 1839 Theodore Robinson and James Bishop built a saw-mill on Nottawa creek, on section one, which they ran four or five years, until the Branch county people enjoined the proprietors against raising their dam, when the mill was abandoned. In 1842-43 William, Charles and Nathan Scholfield built at the same place a woolen-factory, but in 1845 the machinery was taken into Park by Leonard Schellhous. The little hamlet that gathered around these mills and factory on section one, was called Factoryville, and a steam saw-mill was erected there in 1866, which is now owned by Mr. Beam. A steam saw-mill was built in 1856, in Kalamazoo county, and was removed to section four in 1874. It sawed out all of the timber in its vicinity some years ago, and since then has been itinerating, and, like the Methodist circuit-riders, has never been more than a single year in a place. It is now owned by Charles Woodworth. In 1873 a steam saw-mill was built on section five, by Millard brothers, and is at present owned by Nye, of Union city.

RESIDENCE OF JOHN A. PURDY, (SHERMAN TP, S⁰ JOSEPH CO., MICH.

The heaviest undertaking in the manufacturing line in Leonidas was the damming of the St. Joseph in 1847, by W. H. Cross, the present most worthy judge of probate of the county. He secured his charter in 1846, and began the construction of his dam in 1847. His first attempt was unsuccessful, and he saw the wild rush of waters take away the labor of weeks, and with it his hard earnings of years. But, nothing daunted, he began again, and triumphed over the obstacles of nature as well as the jeers of friends and prophecies of ill-omened wiseacres. The foundation was secured by trees with scraggy limbs, cut and placed in the stream with the tops down the current, and, as the water pressed against them, the limbs were driven deeper into the bottom, and so prevented from washing down the river. The ends of the logs were then fastened to stringers, and filled in with brush, stone and gravel, and the dam of logs built thereon securely. A shute was put in below the dam for the passage of arks and rafts, the first raft over being loaded with staves and piloted by Captain Elisha Millard. He next took over an ark loaded with flour, and proved the dam a success. In after years it became a great place of resort for the people, who used to run the shute for sport, in their boats. Judge Cross built a mill, but the expense was too great for him, and he sold out his interest to Peter Becker, and there is now no dam at the place.

James Cowen ran a raft of lumber from his mill, in June, 1833, down the St. Joseph, and shipped it to Chicago, and sold it for cash at sixteen dollars per thousand feet, the same being white-wood. This money assisted him greatly in the prosecution of his business, which, in after years, became a very extensive one. In the first voyage he was assisted by Puttle and Martin C. Watkins. He ran a raft every year for several years thereafter, making the first one in the creek, but the rest he laid up in the St. Joseph.

In the spring of 1843, the first ark went down the river from Leonidas, partially loaded with flour by the Cowens, completing its cargo at Three Rivers,—Elisha and Thomas Millard, pilots. There were a large number of arks built in Leonidas by Jonas and Alex. Newton, for different parties down the river, Dunkin's mill furnishing a large amount of the lumber therefor, the very choicest white-wood plank.

In South Leonidas, in 1842, and for some years afterwards, there were extensive cooper-shops. Philip Clipfell and Jerry McDonald began about that date, and carried on an extensive and lucrative business.

In 1864 West and Watkins brought into the township a sorghum-mill and pan, and induced the cultivation of cane. They made a few hundred gallons of syrup that year, and the year following two thousand eight hundred gallons of very fine syrup. In 1876 there was made considerable also.

Charles Farnam owns and operates a large cider-mill and boiling-works, for the manufacture of jellies from apples and cider, as well as other fruit. Tutewiler Brothers also operate a cider-mill, and are heavy manufacturers.

In 1873 there were in operation in the township one flour and three saw-mills, employing eleven men, and a capital of thirteen thousand five hundred dollars, which manufactured one thousand one hundred and fifty-eight barrels of flour, and nine hundred and ninety-five thousand five hundred and eighty-two feet of lumber, valued at seventeen thousand and forty-three dollars.

TRADE.

The first stock of goods brought to the township for sale was that of Justus L. Vought, in 1837. In 1843 Lester Buckley brought a larger stock, and was succeeded subsequently by his brother, Chester. Hewitt & Estes followed, and W. H. Cross had a stock on sale at Cowen's mills in 1847–8. Hewitt & Ramsdell, George Butler and William Little, Ladd & Galloway were all in trade after Cross, and E. L. Yaple made great deal of money in the same line, keeping a general stock, including hardware and leather. After Ladd & Galloway, Messrs. Duncan & Allen built a large store and filled it with goods, and—failed.

HOTELS.

Arnold Hayward, as before stated, opened the first tavern (in his log-cabin and frame addition) in 1834. In 1838 Captain Watkins built a new frame house on the Washtenaw trail, and kept the "Farmer's House." He also built a blacksmith-shop, into which Thomas King put a forge and tools in 1837, and worked therein.

THE FIRST WHITE CHILD

born in the township was a daughter of George and Margaretha Mathews, who first saw the light of day in the early part of the summer of 1833. She died in infancy.

THE FIRST MARRIAGE

of white persons in the township was that one celebrated between William Orcutt and Esther S. Watkins, a daughter of Captain Levi Watkins, in the fall of 1835.

THE FIRST DEATH

that occurred in the township was in the spring of 1834, the victim being Thomas Baldwin, from the city of Rochester, New York, who came to the settlement in the fall of 1833.

THE CEMETERY

is laid out on section sixteen, and is a short distance from the village, and was so set off in 1836, though burials had been made there previously. There are burial-grounds also in the southeast part and northwest part of the township, the latter lying partly in Waukeshma, Kalamazoo county.

SCHOOLS.

The first school-house in the township was built in the summer of 1836, in the limits of the present village. It was made of logs, roofed with slabs, had slab seats, and counters against the wall served for desks. It was sixteen by twenty feet on the ground. Miss Adaline Clark was the first teacher, and taught therein the same summer the house was built, which was also the first school taught in the township. Miss Clark subsequently married Alonzo Goodrich, and is now deceased. Lucina Watkins, now Mrs. Colvell, was one of the pupils of that school. The district—numbered one—was organized the same year.

Mehitable Bishop taught the first school in Factoryville, about 1842, in a log school-house built that year.

In 1839 there was a frame school-house built in the east part of the township, and a school taught therein by O. M. Beall the same winter.

The second school-house, built in district number two,—which was formerly district number one, and which includes the village of Leonidas in its limits,—was erected in 1841, and was a frame building twenty-seven by thirty feet, one-story. The building committee were Elias B. Kinne, Samuel Hanna and William Bishop, who were limited to an expenditure of two hundred and seventy-five dollars, of which fifty dollars only were to be paid in cash, the balance being lumber and grain,—the builders to allow eight dollars per thousand for the first commodity. In 1859 the present house was built by Andrew J. Graham and William B. Hemingway, for one thousand dollars. It is twenty-four by thirty-seven feet area, two stories in height, and built of wood.

The present officers of the district are John C. Kinne, moderator; W. M. Watkins, director, and James L. Farnam, assessor. The district has been constantly reduced in territory since its first organization, until but one-half of its area (when the house of the present was built) remains, and but sixty-one scholars draw public money.

In 1876 there were nine frame school-houses in the township, valued at twenty thousand eight hundred and twenty-five dollars, affording five hundred and twenty-four sittings. There were four hundred and thirty-six children, between the ages of five and twenty years, of whom three hundred and ninety-four attended the schools, which were in session an average of eight months during the year ending September 1. There were employed four male teachers, who were paid five hundred and fifty-five dollars for their services, and eighteen female, who received one thousand and sixteen dollars and eighty-six cents. The total income of the districts amounted to two thousand three hundred and ninety-five dollars and seventy-six cents, which was all expended except a balance of three hundred and forty-one dollars and ninety-six cents.

The school-house in district number three is a very neat affair, and is called the "Reserve school," being situated on the site of the permanent Indian village, in 1830–40, in Leonidas, on a plain as "level as a house-floor." There were thirty or forty huts there in 1840,—the same being Magusgo's village.

THE CHURCHES.

The first religious meeting held in the settlement was a Methodist gathering in May, 1833, at the house of Captain Watkins, whose house was open to everybody of any creed, though he was a Presbyterian himself, as well as his family. This meeting was held by the Rev. Mr. Dickinson, a missionary from the Ohio conference. His circuit extended from Monroe to Clinton, Jackson and Marshall, thence to a settlement on Climax prairie, thence to Leonidas, thence to a settlement in Branch county, and so back to Monroe. The Rev. Mr. Wiley succeeded him on the circuit, and meetings were held regularly (monthly) during the spring, summer and fall at Mr. Watkins' house, until the school-house was built in 1836, when the first meeting therein was held in July of that year, and before the roof was on the house. The meetings were held herein until the church was built.

The first Methodist Episcopal class was organized in the fall of the year 1835, by J. F. Davidson, with the following members: Aaron B. Watkins, leader, and his wife Polly, William Orcutt, Mrs. Eliza Hayward and Mrs. Mary Watkins; William Orcutt's wife Esther joined the class soon after its formation. The society built their present meeting-house, and only one, in the village of Leonidas, in the years 1854–6. It is thirty-two by fifty-four feet area, has a seating capacity of one hundred and fifty, and cost two thousand five hundred dollars. The house was dedicated June 5, 1858, by Rev. Mr. Joslyn,—late of Albion college, and now deceased,—assisted by the presiding elder, Dougherty.

A Sunday-school was organized in 1836, with a A. D. Watkins as superintendent. There are at present sixty members in the school, Mr. L. T. Clark being the superintendent. In South Leonidas a class was organized in 1847–8, with William Orcutt as leader,—Levi Keyes and wife, and William Parsons and wife, being among the members. It became a flourishing organization in after years, but is now extinct,—by reason of deaths and removals.

The ministers who have had charge of Leonidas Methodist Episcopal church since Mr. Wiley, are as follows: J. F. Davidson, who first came in 1835, and again afterwards; John Ercanbrack, 1837; R. C. Meek, Briar, Worthington, Tyler, Osborne H. Penfield, Hickey, Fawcett, Isaac Bennett, Gage, Jacokes, Mosier, G. W. Hoag, Gee, Edmunds and Kellogg, 1840, and the present incumbent, Rev. J. M. Smith.

In the winter of 1856–7, under Mr. Penfield's preaching, a revival was inaugurated, resulting in twenty accessions to the church.

A PRESBYTERIAN SOCIETY

was organized in the fall of 1837, at Cowen's mills,—among the early members being the following: Robert Cowen and wife, James Cowen's wife, Captain and Mrs. Levi Watkins, and his mother, Esther Watkins, Mrs. Haviland and Mrs. Martin Kellogg.

Rev. Benjamin Ogden, of Three Rivers, organized the society, and preached for the same statedly several years. He was succeeded by John H. Byrd for two years, who was followed by Rev. Holmes. William H. Cross and wife joined the society in 1847, on taking up their residence in the township. Captain Watkins was an elder of the church from its organization till his death in 1851, upon which occurrence the society soon after dissolved, there being but one meeting held afterward. Mr. Cross was an elder of the church also, and Robert Cowen was the deacon.

A Sunday-school was organized in connection with the church and conducted by Mrs. Robert Cowen and her husband. In 1841 a school-room was added to Mr. Cowen's house, and that used for the meetings afterwards, they having been held previously in dwellings and barns.

A CONGREGATIONAL SOCIETY

was also organized in the village in 1858–59, by Rev. Mr. Glidden, who was resident among the people, and who had preached alternate Sundays, previously, for a year or so. Among the first members of this society were Chandler Kingsley and wife, W. H. Cross and wife, and Mrs. Levi Watkins. The preaching was supplied outside of the church. Mr. Glidden was succeeded by Rev. Mr. Husted, who remained till 1868, when the organization suspended. The society occupied the Methodist Episcopal house.

A FREE-WILL BAPTIST CHURCH

was organized in South Leonidas, in 1838–39, and flourished about ten years, Rev. Mr. Fuller being the first and prominent minister thereof. Among the early church members were: Matthew and Joseph Gilbert and wives, and Daniel Adams, senior and junior, and wives. The society worshiped in the school-house in its neighborhood.

A BAPTIST CHURCH

was organized in the village in 1840, by Rev. Elmore G. Terry, and flourished until 1850, when Mr. Terry removed and it collapsed, though apparently in a prosperous condition when he left it. Among the early members were: E. G. Terry and wife, Levi Denton and wife, Mr. Carpenter and wife, the Jewetts and Van Brunts, who came from Dry prairie ten miles away. The members being so scattered caused the decline in the society.

A CHRISTIAN SOCIETY

was organized in 1847, by Rev. J. White, a very fluent speaker and excellent singer. There were a large number of members, among whom were: Mr. Wormley and wife, Mr. Galloway and wife, Ezra Roberts and wife, and

Mr. Covey and wife. Mr. White remained with the society three years, and then occasional preaching was had only until the Rev. Mr. Sackett came and preached a few times, when Mr. Wormley, the pillar of the society, sold out his farm and removed, and the society soon after died out.

THE FIRST PHYSICIAN

in the township was Dr. John Lee. The second one was Dr. Martin, then Doctors W. H. and Asaph Church, then Dr. Moore, who went to California, then Dr. G. W. Spalsbury who came in 1858, and is still the resident physician of the place.

THE POST-OFFICE

was first established in Leonidas in 1834, and Isaac B. Bailey, the postmaster, brought the mail from Nottawa post-office till the summer of 1835, when he influenced the establishment of a mail-route between Jacksonburg and Centreville, and the office, which had been kept at Bailey's house, was removed to the territorial road,—Washtenaw trail,—in 1836. A few years afterwards the route was changed to Marshall.

In 1842 the mail was carried between the latter point and Centreville on sleighs, from November 20 until the first week in April following, continuously, by Edward A. Trumbull, then elected sheriff in the county, and who is still living at Detroit with a sister. The post-office was kept by a deputy, Aaron B. Watkins, during Mr. Bailey's incumbency. On the latter's death in 1839, O. M. Watkins succeeded to the office and held it for several years, Martin C. Watkins succeeding thereto. Mahlon W. Hobart, Augustus Codman, James McCoy, N. Tompkins, successively held the office; E. W. Wilcox, the present incumbent, being appointed in 1875.

The first mail was established once in two weeks, then once a week, then once a day, either way, and now daily is received from Colon. The business of 1876 was as follows: Stamps sold, two hundred and forty dollars; fifty-one letters received and dispatched daily on an average, and four hundred newspapers, comprising eighty-six different issues, were distributed weekly. The first post-office was named Fort Pleasant.

In the early history of the office, before the stages brought the mail, N. Frank Peirce and Eber O. Peirce were mail-carriers, the former between Fort Pleasant (Cowen's mills) and Bronson's, or near there, on the Chicago pike, at Adams', and the latter between Sherwood and Nottawa, when but nine years old. Two trips, the water was so high, his horse swam the St. Joseph at Tyler's ford, and the boy stood on the horse's back and carried the bag over his shoulder. Lot Whitcomb brought the first mail into Sherwood, in 1834.

THE WASHTENAW TRAIL

ran from the east side of the township to the Indian village, and then through to Gourdneck prairie. It was afterwards laid out as a territorial road, and is at present one of the finest boulevards in the county. It was the first road laid out in the township. The first road laid out by the township authority of Leonidas was ordered June 28, 1836, commencing at a post ten chains north of quarter post of sections twenty-one and twenty-two, township five south, range nine west, thence west and northwest to the township. It was surveyed by James Cowen, and laid out by Levi Watkins and Ambrose Nichols, commissioners.

THE FIRST STAGE ROUTE

was established in 1838 from White Pigeon to Jacksonburg, E. A. Trumbull running the line from the former point to Leonidas and Arnold Hayward from Leonidas to Tekonsha, breakfasting and changing horses at Peirce's, now Foster's, place. Captain Watkins ran the line one summer, and when the mail route was changed to Marshall and Centreville in 1839, Trumbull drove at first, and was succeeded by Daniel Hogan, and he by Mr. Cox. The vehicles were open wagons drawn by two or four horses, according as the roads and travel were heavy or otherwise. The first bridge over the St. Joseph was built in the summer of 1835 by Captain Watkins, and was known as the Mathews bridge. This was the second one in the county thrown across that stream. It cost two hundred dollars, the contractor subscribing twenty dollars himself. It stood some ten or twelve years. The present one was built in 1856.

CIVIL ORGANIZATION.

In the first organization of townships in the county in 1829, township five south, range nine west, now known as Leonidas, was included in and formed a part of the township of Flowerfield. This constitution remained intact until 1833, when townships five and six, range nine, were set off and constituted into a new organization called Colon. The new organization remained unchanged until 1836, when township five was set off into a separate independency, and named Leonidas by mistake, which is thus explained: When

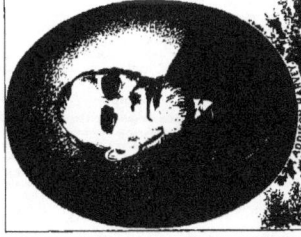

MRS. ADDISON HARVEY

ADDISON HARVEY

RESIDENCE of ADDISON HARVEY,
Leonidas Tp., St. Joseph Co., Mich.

the town was first settled, Captain Watkins desired to call it Fort Pleasant, from an ancient fortification in its limits, and the beautiful prospect the landscape afforded, and the post-office was so named at its first establishment in 1834. When the meeting for the separate organization of the township was held the people could not agree upon the name the post-office was known by, but adopted the name "Leoni" instead, and sent their petition to the legislature accordingly. Jackson county also sent up a petition for a new township to be named "Leonidas," and when the engrossing clerk copied the bill for the constitution of the two townships, he made a mistake and put the name Leonidas to the St. Joseph county town, and Leoni to the Jackson town, and the error was not discovered until the law was printed, and the names remain unchanged to this day.

### THE FIRST TOWN MEETING

was held at Martin C. Watkins' house April 4, 1836, James Cowen being the moderator; Aaron B. Watkins clerk, and Isaac G. Bailey and William Orcutt, inspectors. Mr. Bailey and Captain Watkins were both candidates for the office of supervisor, and each worked the best he knew how for his opponent's election, Mr. Watkins succeeding in electing his man and defeating himself, and Bailey vice versa, being, in his own estimation, successfully defeated in the man of his choice, and unsuccessfully elected by his opponent. Mr. Bailey had twelve votes and Mr. Watkins ten. The other officers elected at this meeting were as follows: Martin C. Watkins, town clerk; Joseph Gilbert, George Mathews, I. G. Bailey, and Aaron B. Watkins, justices of the peace; James Cowen, Levi Watkins, George Mathews, assessors; Charles Starkes, Ambrose Nichols, Levi Watkins, commissioners of highways; James Cowen, George Mathews, and M. C. Watkins, school commissioners; Arnold Hayward, Moses W. Whiting, overseers of the poor; Orrin M. Watkins, constable and collector. At this meeting it was voted to pay two dollars bounty for wolf scalps and fifty cents for foxes, and to raise twenty dollars bounty for contingent expenses; that the supervisor should purchase the requisite books and ballot-boxes for the town, and charge the same; that overseers of highways be fence-viewers, and that the school commissioners should lease the school section for a term of five years. Seven road districts were laid off March 30, 1837.

The second town meeting was held in the school-house, and the claims of 1836–37 against the town audited at the sum of eighty dollars and fifty cents. In 1838 the electors voted five dollars bounty on wolves, one dollar on foxes, fifty cents on wild-cats,—not of the banking genus,—and fifty dollars for panthers.

It seems that a settler going through a neck of woods in the township, just in the edge of the evening, was startled by his pony stopping short and snorting loudly, and refusing to go forward, but showing great readiness to turn about and go back. The rider, looking ahead, saw, at a short distance, an animal crouching in the trail, as if ready for a leap. It was now his turn to feel "backward about going forward," and he commenced shouting and thrashing the ground and bushes on either side of the trail, with a long gad he had in his hands. This he continued for some little time, when the animal, probably disgusted at the unsociability of the pony and his rider, gave a sudden leap into the air off to one side of the path, and disappeared. The rider and pony made the fastest time on their journey the next ten minutes, and burst into the first cabin,—that is, the rider did,—and in breathless accents told of his encounter with a terrible panther of enormous proportions. Hence the bounty that was laid on panthers' scalps the following spring. This bounty was never paid, the great cat moving to a region where his head-covering was less highly prized. Wolf-bounties increased however, to ten dollars a scalp, in 1839.

The report of the town auditors for 1836–39, showed fifty-two dollars paid for that kind of fur, and the people voted one hundred and sixteen dollars eighty-seven and a half cents for pauper relief, in 1839. In 1840 the board of auditors believed it was worth two dollars per week to board a lame Indian, and therefore allowed Captain Watkins at that rate, for such care of one of the Nottawas. In 1841 the town bought thirty dollars' worth of records, and a desk to put them in. In December, 1863, a bounty for volunteers was voted of one hundred dollars each, and on February 20, 1864, one thousand five hundred dollars were raised for the same purpose, and on January 24, 1865, two thousand five hundred dollars were offered for the encouragement of enlistments.

The position of supervisor has been held in the township as follows: Isaac G. Bailey, 1836–1838–39; Jairus Peirce, 1837 and 1842–44 and 1840; Elias B. Kinne, 1840; Thomas King, 1841; Charles Woodworth, 1845; W. H. Cross, 1847–1851 and 1850–61; William M. Watkins, 1852–54 and 1872; Albert M. Collins, 1855; James B. Dunkin, 1856; John E.

Moore, 1857–58; Justus L. Vought, 1862–63 and 1865; M. W. Hobart, 1864; David R. Beckley, 1866; Andrew Climie, 1867–68 and 1875–76; Josias Simpson, 1869 and 1871–73–74; William M. Haines, 1870.

The office of town clerk has been filled as follows: Martin C. Watkins, 1836–40; J. L. Vought, 1841–42; W. M. Watkins, 1843 and 1845–51; O. M. Watkins, 1844; W. H. Church, 1852; E. M. Roberts, 1853; A. T. Watkins, 1854; Samuel Cross, 1855 and 1863–64; Elisha M. Johnson, 1856–57 and 1861; S. L. Kinne, 1858; James McCoy, 1859–60; George A. Arnold, 1862 and 1865–66; N. Tompkins, 1867 and 1875–76; L. T. Clark, 1868; George K. Burch, 1869–71; Edgar Spalsbury, 1872–74.

The leading justices of the peace have been as follows, who have served more than a single term of four years: E. K. Wilcox, about twenty-three years; O. M. Watkins, sixteen years; Levi Keys, Nathan Scholfield, W. H. Church, Almon A. Fisher, James S. Lee, I. V. S. Banta, E. W. Foot, N. Tompkins, W. M. Watkins, present incumbent; H. N. Addison, James McCoy, present incumbent; John Foreman, present incumbent; Stephen I. Schott, Edgar Spalsbury, present incumbent.

### MARKS AND BRANDS.

D. W. Adams had, as it is recorded on the old record, for his mark, "a hole threw the wright ear and a crop of the left," and Michael C. Keith had "a hole threw both ears." Square crops and half pennies were divided between Hayward, Levi and A. W. Watkins and Jairus Peirce, with which they marked their cattle.

### POPULATION.

In 1836 the vote in November indicated a population of about one hundred and thirty-five in Leonidas; in 1837 the same gauge showed three hundred and five, and the census of 1838 revealed three hundred and seventy-five inhabitants, who, in 1840 had increased the number of fifty-five souls. In 1850 the census of that year showed eight hundred and fifty-seven inhabitants. In 1860 there were one thousand two hundred and fifty-nine inhabitants returned, and in 1870 the people numbered one thousand four hundred and sixty. In 1874 the State census returned one thousand four hundred and twenty-three only, of whom seven hundred and eighty-one were males and six hundred and forty-two females. Three hundred and seventy-nine of the males were over twenty-one; two hundred and twenty-four of them being subject to draft. Of the females, two hundred and thirty-three were between eighteen and forty years of age and one hundred and fifty-six above that age. There were four hundred and two boys under twenty-one, and their sisters, under eighteen years, numbered two hundred and fifty-three.

### THE POLITICAL CURRENT

sets strongly Republican in the township, as will be seen by the following exhibit, taken from the canvass of the several presidential elections held in the township: In 1840 the Whigs polled sixty-one votes, and the Democrats thirty; in 1844 the former cast ninety, and the latter fifty-two votes; in 1848 the same parties cast eighty-seven and forty-four respectively, and the Free Soilers cast twenty-four; in 1852 the Whigs tallied eighty-six, the Democrats sixty-one, and the Abolitionists two votes; in 1856 the Republicans cast one hundred and forty-nine, and the Democrats sixty-two votes; the same parties cast in 1860, one hundred and ninety-eight and one hundred and one votes, respectively; and in 1864, two hundred and ten and ninety-one; in 1868 two hundred and fifty-seven and one hundred and twenty-seven; and in 1872 two hundred and fourteen and fifty-six; in 1876 the balloting stood Hayes two hundred and thirty-one, Tilden one hundred and fourteen, Cooper twenty-two. This last vote would indicate a population of about one thousand eight hundred in the township.

In 1840, the campaign of Tippecanoe and hard cider, every legal voter in the township went to the polls and cast his vote; one old gentleman, named Gilbert, who was unable to walk or ride in a carriage even, was taken to the polls in his arm-chair by two stout and determined Whigs, that he might vote for "Tippecanoe and Tyler too," thereby pleasing the old veteran of ninety-three winters hugely.

### THE PRICE OF SOVEREIGNTY

to Leonidas will be seen in the taxes she paid to support the dignity she craved and received as a separate and independent township.

In 1836 the assessment of property in the township for taxation was placed at thirty-four thousand six hundred and twenty-seven dollars, and her State taxes were eighty-six dollars and fifty-six cents, her total levy being two hundred and thirty-five dollars and fifty-six cents. In 1838 the assessment was sixty-three thousand six hundred and fifty-seven dollars; the State and county taxes being two hundred and forty-six dollars, and her own township levy about one hundred dollars. In 1852 the assessment was sixty-one thousand eight hundred and seventy-four dollars, and the total taxes one thousand and twenty-six dollars and fifty-five cents. In 1860 the assessment was fixed at two hundred and seventy-one thousand two hundred and eighty-two dollars, and the levy of taxes one thousand eight hundred and six dollars and ninety-eight cents. In 1870 the assessment was returned at five hundred and sixty-nine thousand nine hundred and seventy-nine dollars, and the levy of the taxes thereon, eight thousand and eight dollars and forty-seven cents. In 1876 the assessment, as equalized by the supervisors, was two hundred and seventy-two thousand six hundred and sixty-seven dollars real-estate, and sixty-one thousand and twenty-eight dollars personal property; total three hundred and thirty-three thousand six hundred and ninety-five dollars,—about one-fourth value. On this amount the levy of taxes was State, eight hundred and fifty-two dollars and thirty-three cents; county, eight hundred and fifty-two dollars and thirty-two cents; township, including schools, two thousand five hundred and forty-one dollars and twenty-four cents; total four thousand two hundred and forty-five dollars and ninety cents.

### THE VILLAGE OF LEONIDAS.

The original plat of the village of Leonidas was laid off by E. G. Terry, December 30, 1846, on the northwest quarter of section twelve, township five, range nine west, at the intersection of the territorial road,—the Washtenaw trail,—which enters the village from the northeast, and passes diagonally through it to the southwest, and the road from Colon to Climax prairie, which passes through the village from south to north, and the road to Mendon village rÆ the old Cowen mills—now Switzer's.

The houses in the village began to be neighborly, and play " hide-and-seek " in the old oak openings, in 1835 ; a school-house being built in 1836, and a church in 1854-6.

The post-office was established on the territorial road, in 1836, and thus the village began.

A merchant came—Lester Buckley—in 1843, and opened his wares for sale, and others followed, until to-day

### THE BUSINESS OF THE PRESENT

is as follows :

Dry Goods, etc—Ferris, Wilcox and Schutt.

Drugs—Spalsbury Brothers, successors to E. Spalsbury, 1866, in dry goods and general merchandise, and 1870-5, drugs.

Groceries— —— Purdy.

Boots and Shoes, Dealer and Manufacturer—Charles Wentworth.

Harness— —— West.

Millinery—Mrs. Emma J. Watkins.

Tailor—Felix C. Baldery.

Blacksmith—C. L. Leach.

Wagons—William C. Davis.

Shoemaker— —— Pratt.

Steam Threshing—Watkins & Cleveland, Andrew Maxfield.

Hotel, " Leonidas House "—Lafayette Libhart.

Stage Line and Mail Carrier to Colon and Return—Seth West.

### SOCIETIES—I. O. O. F.

Blackman Lodge, No. 117, was instituted by charter April 2, 1868, with the following officers and members : P. B. Purchase, N. G. ; Loftus Hyatt, V. G. ; Clifton H. Clemens, R. S. ; N. T. Watkins, P. S. ; John Van Alstine, C. Wentworth, Leverett Beard, B. Orcutt and J. H. Beard. The lodge meets in its own hall, over West's harness-shop and Purdy's grocery. The officers of 1876 were Orson Orcutt, N. G. ; S. N. Clement, V. G. ; J. J. Bennett, R.S. ; N. Tompkins, P. S. (and for three years previously). The lodge has thirty-six members.

A division of Sons of Temperance was instituted in 1847, among the members being W. H. Cross, Seth West, Homer Ransom, O. M. Watkins, Cyrenus Whiting, P. Garrett, —— Clement, Gilbert Wing, and Mr. Burch. It suspended in 1849.

In 1856 a Good Templar lodge was instituted, and flourished for a time, and went down ; was reorganized in 1867-8, and lived for a few years longer, then suspended, and was again resuscitated in 1874, with Mrs. L. T. Clement, W. C. T. ; Mrs. Hannah West, W. V. T. It worked well until 1876, when something hindered, and it ceased to be.

Mrs. Clement, P. B. Purchase, H. G. Arnold and N. Tompkins, were prominent members of the second organization.

### PATRONS OF HUSBANDRY.

Leonidas Grange, No. 266, was organized February, 1873, John C. Kinne being the first master, and with sixty-five members. The present officers are W. M. Watkins, master ; David Purdy, overseer ; W. R. Addison, secretary. There are seventy members on the books.

On June 23, 1831, Peter Beisel and George Mathews laid off and surveyed a plat of a village, which they named, in honor of the former, " Beisel." It was located on the northeast quarter of section thirty-two, township five, range nine west, and was surveyed by C. Barnes ; but no village ever arose on the plat, and it relapsed into farming lands, if, indeed, it ever emerged therefrom.

### ANCIENT FORTIFICATIONS

abounded in the township of Leonidas, both in the openings and in the heavy timber, when the first settlers came thereto, the outlines of many of which are still distinctly discernible. One in the heavy timber has breastworks about three feet high, with gate-ways, sally-ports, and interior and exterior defences. A large cherry-tree has grown upon the intrenchments, and fallen and rotted thereon, since they were erected by a people, of whom the Indians, when first seen by white men, in the twelfth century, had no tradition.

On the north side of an old fort were found two wagon-boxes full of shells, about forty rods south of Nottawa creek. Many of the mounds have been opened, and bones of animals and man found ; in one three skeletons were found, of which the skulls, teeth, and large bones of the leg were well preserved, the smaller bones being gone.

W. M. Watkins, Esq., has several very fine relics taken from these mounds. Among them one celt, finely wrought, and a pipe, showing rude attempts at carving. A very exquisitely wrought stone, for some unknown purpose, with a perforation through its centre, proportioned accurately, was found, which shows consummate skill in the use of the rude implements the mound-builders possessed. Large quantities of pottery have been, from time to time, plowed up, but which fell to pieces on exposure to the air. On the bank of the St. Joseph, near the Mathews bridge, are the remains of an old trading-post or missionary station, which, when the first settlers came, were distinctly visible, and are sufficiently so at the present time to be outlined. The ruins of the stone fire-place and chimney are plainly distinguishable. Opposite these ruins, on the south bank of the river, the old apple-trees stood, mentioned before, which gave a name to the ford at that point, which was known as the "apple-tree ford."

### THE INDIANS,

who had their village in Leonidas, had for their chief John Maguago, who, after Sau-au-quet's death, aspired to the chieftancy of the Pottawattomie nation, or at least that portion of it remaining in Michigan. He was a very fine-looking man. Their main village was on the site of the Olney brothers' farm at the present day, their huts being made of poles, laid up like log-houses, with bark roofs, and a hole cut through the same for the escape of the smoke. These were their permanent residences ; their temporary ones, while on their hunting or marauding expeditions, being bark tepees.

They raised corn, potatoes and beans in a small way, but did not harvest very heavy crops, both on account of their method of cultivation and the trespassing of the cattle of their white neighbors. Their winter supplies of corn they buried in trenches, protected from dampness by flag-mats, shelling the same first. Sometimes they packed it in "mokucks," a kind of flag-basket. In the winter they went into the heavy timber for better protection against the severity of the climate, and to make maple-sugar, of which some was very fine. They usually stirred it until it was of the color of a fair article of muscovado, and put up but little in cakes. They made large quantities of it, packing it in mokucks of fifty to sixty pounds weight.

Their milling process was the pestle and wooden mortar, improved by the settlers by adding a spring-pole. In addition to their summer-houses they had sleeping platforms, raised several feet above the ground, which were reached by means of a ladder, which the occupants, usually females, drew up after them. These platforms served also as lookout-stations to guard against the trespass of stock on their gardens.

They were, both males and females, like the rest of their race, very fond of gay attire, and red and blue were their favorite colors. Their head-dresses of feathers and beads would draw tears of envy from many a hand-some belle of to-day.

In 1833, "Old " Moguago was a chief, an in distinction from his son John, was the second chief of the Michigan band, and a very old man, and was succeeded by John, as before stated. Old Setone was a quarrelsome

Res. of JOHN C. KINNE, Leonidas Tp., S<sup>t</sup> Joseph County, Mich.

SOLOMON PIER.

MRS. SOLOMON PIER.

RESIDENCE OF SOLOMON PIER, LEONIDAS TP., ST. JOSEPH CO., MICH.

character, and always in trouble. The band objected to the settlers plowing at first, but were disposed to be friendly. When Johnson settled in the south part of the township, he and some of his neighbors took the farmer's breaking teams and broke up several acres for Magungo, and fenced it for him, and continued to plow it every spring so long as he lived on the reservation. The old chief gave them two mokuks of sugar for their work, at first, and one or two each year, as the sugar was plentiful or short.

In 1838 and 1839, Grand Councils of the Indians were held in their village near the present "Reserve" school-house, Muk-moot being present. In 1839, there were five hundred of the tribe present, and negotiations were being carried on to induce them to leave for the west. W. M. Watkins performed a service for Magungo once, similar to the one performed by the younger son of Noah for that old patriarch, and provoked a similar acknowledgment for the commendable act from the wife of the drunken chief, who seized an oar and raised it to brain young Watkins, when Mandoka, her son, caught her and took her away.

At one time one of the Indians seemed to be changing his color, being considerably more than one-half white, and was much pleased at the idea that he was going to be a " Chemocoman " (white man).

The boys of the settlers and the Indian boys were great friends, and associated together as democratically as any fraternity ever did. Magungo's sons, Mandoka, Maqua and Memie, were good wrestlers, and the white boys used to test their skill and strength, and would trip them up, which was not according to the Indian rules of the ring, and brought forth the objurgation from the worsted boys, "No good! Chemocoman cheat!"

Old Setono once ordered Esther Watkins to catch his pony for him, and on her refusal pitched a block of wood at her, which happily missed its mark, but succeeded in getting the cross old fellow a sound thrashing from her brother, Marcus, who saw the act, and, with a hoop-pole in his hands, proceeded to lay it on the old man's bare shoulders unsparingly. Setono soon after got a dreadful scalp-cut with a knife in one of his frequent fights, and Watkins sewed it up and " plastered his nob," not " with vinegar and brown paper," but some healing medicament, and the old man was forever after the Watkins' sworn friend.

One day one of the Indians and one of the young settlers got into a quarrel, and the former made a murderous attack on the latter, when Eliza Hayward seized Mrs. Levi Watkins' pudding-stick, and laid it so heavily and unremittingly about the Indian's head that he was glad to forego his satisfaction until a more convenient season.

Captain Watkins used to make bitters of aloes and whisky, and, refusing to let an Indian have whisky who applied one day for "squiby," the bottle which contained the ill-flavored decoction fell beneath the gaze of the applicant, who immediately seized it and drank deeply therefrom, and recovering his breath as well as he could, with the puckering up of his throat and tongue, the victim sputtered out, " White man, one d——n lie!" He never asked Watkins for "squiby" again. Robert Cowen says that the treaty of 1833 for the reservation was prolonged so that the whisky all gave out, and was watered so thoroughly the Indians got sober drinking it, and made trouble in discovering, as they believed, the cheat practiced upon them. Mrs. Robert Cowen relates the following incident in relation to her experience with her Indian neighbors: One of them came to her house intoxicated, and ordered her to give him some dinner, which she did, after which he ordered her to fill and light his pipe, the first part of the order being promptly executed, but the latter part, the lighting of the pipe, owing to the extreme state of inebriation the fellow was in, was a feat difficult to accomplish. The coals would fall off the bowl, and he would swear; but finally, taking some paper she made a taper, and the sot managed to get up suction sufficient to light the tobacco, whereat he granted his thanks and staggered off. She usually was exempt from trouble from them when they were drunk, as she locked her gate, and they were unable to climb the fence.

In the sickly season of 1838, Mr. Cowen went to Pennsylvania, and while he was gone his wife was taken sick, her brother being the housekeeper. One day he was absent and the weather came on chilly, and she had no wood in the house and was too feeble to get it. Seeing some of the Indians go by, she crawled on her hands and knees to the door and beckoned to them, and went back to her bed. A dozen tall fellows came in, and she explained to them her situation and asked them to bring in some wood, and when the "chemocoman, who was gone, came back (paw maw), by and by, and make (man ponse) flour, she would give them some good bread (winett quiskin)." They brought in a large lot of wood, and when Cowen returned the pledge of his wife was redeemed in good measure. They offered her once two mokuks of maple sugar for her little girls, which proceeding, though it was "sweets for the sweet," was scarcely palatable to the mother.

22

Quite a scare was gotten up in 1838 by a party of fifteen of the Indians, equipped and painted for the war-path, appearing on the roads and about the dwellings of the settlers, who became much alarmed, and called out the militia to disperse the warlike fellows. The Mendon people went into garrison, but the scare passed over and all was quiet again.

## AN INCIDENT OF THE REBELLION,

in which A. T. Watkins, a former county surveyor of the county, was the principal and unfortunate actor, is related by his uncle W. M. Watkins, Esq. A. T. Watkins went south to Mississippi some years before the war and engaged in teaching, and soon after married a southern lady, by whom he had two children, a boy and a girl. He was a pronounced Republican at home, and did not conceal his sentiments in Mississippi, though he was not blatant about them; nor did he interfere with the "peculiar institution" of the South.

About the time of the breaking out of the war his father died, and his friends at once notified him of the fact, and of the necessity of his presence to take charge of the estate of the deceased, in order to save a home for his (A. T.'s) mother. He set about his return at once, and the feeling then in the south running very high, some of the people declared he should not leave, but he left nevertheless,—taking a train to make a connection with a railroad running north, which he missed, and chose rather to go on one hundred miles farther, and make another connection, than to stay over twenty-four hours at the first point. Soon after he was gone the parties who opposed his leaving heard of his departure, and immediately started in pursuit and telegraphed to a station on the road they supposed he would take,—and which he had expected to, and would have taken had he made his first connection,—asking his detention, but on arriving at that point the pursuers found he had taken a different route, and immediately sent another dispatch to a station on the other road for his detention, which point, fortunately, his train had passed before the receipt of the dispatch, and thus he escaped from rebeldom and arrived safely at home.

Almost immediately afterwards the Mississippi was closed, and the mail-service suspended, and so continued until after the surrender of Vicksburg,—during which period he could get no news from his family, whom he left in the south, nor they from him. Soon after Vicksburg fell he sent a letter through the lines to his wife's friends, and received a reply thereto informing him of her death, and that of his little boy, and that his girl was in the care of her relatives, who desired him to come and get her, which he proceeded to do against the remonstrance of his mother and friends, who feared the request was but a scheme to get him in the power of the southerners to make way with him.

He conveyed the estate of his father, which had passed into his possession, to his mother and little girl, and went to Vicksburg, where he deposited his surplus money, with instructions if it was not called for by him within a certain time to remit it to his mother, Mary C. Watkins, and wrote her to that effect. This was the last his friends ever heard from him direct, or received from his own hand; but after the war closed, and peace was declared, they learned the terrible sequel, which was as follows: After depositing his money, as before mentioned, he went in search of his little girl, whom he found as indicated, and immediately made arrangements to take her back to Leonidas; but the day before he was to leave for the north a squad of rebel cavalry, who were prowling about the neighborhood, arrested him as a spy, but released him upon the representations of his wife's brother. They came again, however, the same night, and said he must go with them to the headquarters of their colonel (a few miles away) and explain matters to him. He went with them, but found no colonel or headquarters, but was summarily tried and hung to a tree, and shot to death while hanging, behind the cabin of an old colored woman, who, after the murderers had departed, cut down the poor mangled body and buried it. The little girl, then grown to the age of seven or eight years, was, after the war closed, sent to her relatives in the north, and was an inmate of the family of W. M. Watkins for some years, where she was educated, and finally went to Nebraska to her grandmother,—both of them, however, at the present time, being members of Mr. Watkins' family in Leonidas. The money deposited by Mr. Watkins was received by his mother, according to his instructions.

## INCIDENTS.

A bear once, pursued fiercely by hunters and dogs, made his way into the village and was discovered by one of the brave pioneer women of Leonidas in her door-yard. She immediately seized the weapon to which her sex possesses an inalienable and indefeasible right, by right of conquest and possession, lo! these many years, and sallied forth to dispute possession with Bruin in her garden plat, which his huge plantigrades were demolishing.

Bruin looked at this new line of attack as it moved to the right, left and front in quick advance, seemingly puzzled to know where the main attack would be made, which was so skilfully masked and maneuvered. The baying of the hounds came floating, deep-mouthed and musical on the air; the hunters' quick tramp sounded painfully near; but nearer and more dreadful to the pursued beast was the reinforcement of calico and decision moving on his immediate works, and Bruin retreated to the fence, over which he scrambled, and "clum a tree," from which he was speedily brought by the rifles of the hunters who came up. This may not be "an over true tale," but we tell it as it was told to us, and our readers can put as much faith in it as seemeth good to them. We do not vouch for its entire accuracy, and yet, if it were true, Bruin would not be the only *bear* who has been brought to bay by a broom-stick in the hands of a determined woman.

In 1837–8 a military company was organized and drilled in the township, which produced a deal of merriment and sport for the people who were mustered into the ranks thereof. The first officers of the company were Levi Watkins, captain, and William Bishop, first lieutenant, who, being old men, the younger men elected, thinking their officers would not call them out to drill; but the young bloods reckoned without their host, for, though the captain and his lieutenant were along in years, yet they had both been good soldiers in the war of 1812, and were fully competent to drill their company, and they did, putting them through their facings, marching and countermarching by flank and file, *echelon* movements, change of front in battle, and all the movements of the old tactics, besides some according to the *standard* of the captain and lieutenant themselves, who enjoyed the manual of arms and military precision of their awkward squad immensely. The boys were glad to own themselves beat and accept younger drill-masters in the future, and therefore Edward K. Wilcox was elected captain; O. M. Watkins, first lieutenant; A. H. Watkins, second lieutenant, and the company organized as artillery; the only heavy ordnance they carried, however, were pocket-pistols. They maintained their organization for some time, and appeared at general parades at Centreville and Sturgis, and at the general trainings in June and September, and general muster in October of each year. There were some thirty or forty men, mostly from Leonidas, being all of the young men of the settlement not exempt from military duty.

### THE MILITARY RECORD

made by the men of Leonidas in the war for the Union, was an honorable one. They went forward at the call of the President to beat back treason in its foul and bloody attempt to pull down the temple of freedom, and whether they fought shoulder to shoulder, when the "elbow touch" sent its magnetic thrill through their serried columns, or fighting on the skirmish-line each one for himself, they were heroes all. They faltered not, nor gave back, though their numbers were thinned by the musketry of rebels and their comrades sank to rest, regardless alike of reveille and recall. The bugle sounds in vain for many of them, but they are not forgotten, nor have they, we trust, died in vain. Over each one of those who fell, whether in the camp, the field, the trench or the prison, future ages shall say, as did the young hero of Bunker Hill, "*Dulce et decorum est pro patria mori.*"

The following is a list of the soldiers who bore the honor of Leonidas upon their bayonets and her crest in their hearts, in the war of the great rebellion, as taken from the official records of the State:

#### FIRST MICHIGAN INFANTRY.

Sergeant Moses W. Hoffman, Company B; discharged.

#### SECOND INFANTRY.

Private James W. Wood, Company F; mustered-out.
Private Charles Van Vleck, Company K; mustered-out.
Private William Cooper, Company K; discharged at expiration of service.

#### FOURTH INFANTRY.

Private Michael McDonough, Company C; discharged for disability.
Private Don A. Rickett, Company C; discharged for disability.
Private Freeman P. Worden, Company C; killed at Gettysburg.

#### SIXTH INFANTRY.

Private Hiram D. P. Davis, Company F; re-enlisted and mustered-out.

#### SEVENTH INFANTRY.

Private Joshua Wilferton, Company B; mustered-out.
Private John Cramer, Company B; died while a prisoner.
Private George W. Foote, Company B; veteran reserve corps.
Private Henry B. Renner, Company B; discharged for disability.
Private Francis D. Lee, Company B; mustered-out.
Private George A. Collins, Company I; discharged for disability.

Private Chauncey G. Cole, Company I; re-enlisted.
Private Anthony Gerue, Company I; discharged for disability.
Private Thomas Hatch, Company I; discharged at expiration of service.
Private Charles Bishop, Company F; mustered-out.
Private Tower S. Benham, Company K; wounded at Antietam; re-enlisted and promoted to first lieutenant, captain and major, and mustered-out.
Private Thomas Foreman, Company K; discharged for disability; wounded at Fair Oaks.
Private John A. Ford, Company K; re-enlisted and discharged.
Private Festus V. Lyon, Company K; re-enlisted and discharged.
Private Mark W. Orcutt, Company K; discharged June, 1862.
Private Wilbur F. Studley, Company K; discharged for disability.
Private Meigs D. Wolf, Company K; wounded at Fair Oaks; veteran reserve corps.
Private Franklin Bills, Company K; accidentally shot, December 4, 1863.
Private Thomas Miles, Company K; missing at the battle of the Wilderness, and never heard of since.

#### ELEVENTH INFANTRY.

First Lieutenant Christ. Haight, Company A; died at Bardstown, Kentucky, February 5, 1862.
Sergeant Stephen P. Marsh, Company A; discharged at expiration of service.
Corporal Lemuel P. Pierce, Company A; discharged for disability.
Private Charles W. Baird, Company A; discharged.
Private Byron V. Barker, Company A; discharged; second lieutenant.
Private Olney Bishop, Company A; discharged for disability.
Private Eugene Carpenter, Company A; discharged for disability.
Private Henry C. Damon, Company A; escaped from Andersonville prison and chased by dogs; discharged at expiration of service.
Private Sidney A. Durfee, Company A; discharged at expiration of service.
Private Barzillai M. Earl, Company A; discharged at expiration of service.
Private James Everton, Company A; discharged at expiration of service.
Private John L. Gould, Company A; discharged at expiration of service.
Private Sylvanus Gould, Company A; died at Bardstown, Kentucky.
Private Richard F. Huxley, Company A; discharged.
Private William S. Lemunyon, Company A; died of wounds before Atlanta. His bowels were shot away by a cannon-ball. and he died in awful agony, but never complained, so his captain says.
Private Charles B. Purchase, Company A; died at Lavergne, Tennessee, September 15, 1862.
Private Elmer Surdam, Company A; discharged at expiration of service.
Private Royal M. Taylor, Company A; discharged at expiration of service.
Sergeant Charles Coddington, Company A; captain and mustered-out.
Private Byron Thomas, Company A; mustered-out.
Private Julius H. Tompkins, Company A; discharged at expiration of service.
Private W. P. Wood, Company A; discharged.
Private Smolloff H. Wood, Company A; mustered-out.
Private Albert O. Watkins, Company A; discharged at expiration of service.
Private Harrison Surdam, Company A; mustered-out.
Private Richard Hemingway, Company A; mustered-out.
Private James Benedict, Company A; mustered-out.
Private William P. Thomas, Company A; died at Rossville, Georgia.
Private William J. Barker, Company A; veteran reserve corps.
Private Jonas N. Barker, Company A; mustered-out.
Private Henry C. Barker, Company A; mustered-out.
Private A. E. Farnham, Company A; mustered-out.
Private George W. Cramer, Company A; mustered-out.
Private Joseph A. Franklin, Company A; mustered-out.
Private Charles Millard, Company A; mustered-out.
Private Hiram Vought, Company A; mustered-out.
Private W. W. Truelse, Company B; mustered-out.
Private Addison R. Noble, Company B; mustered-out.
Private Madison Watkins, Company B; mustered-out.
Private Charles Woods, Company B; mustered-out.
Corporal Martin W. Gilbert, Company C; discharged for disability.
Corporal Ezra Warren, Company C; died April 12, 1862.

MRS. SETH WEST.

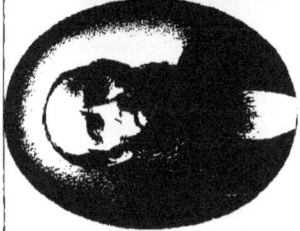

SETH WEST.

RESIDENCE OF SETH WEST,
LEONIDAS TP., ST. JOSEPH CO., MICH.

Private Daniel B. Watkins, Company C; discharged at expiration of service.

Private Levi Wilcox, Company C; died at Murfreesboro, June 28, 1863.

Private W. H. Everton, Company D; discharged.

Private Anson T. Gilbert, Company D; discharged.

Private Rawdon Keyes, Company D; discharged as captain.

Private Melvin J. Lyon, Company D; discharged.

Private W. H. Taylor, Company D; died, January 29, 1862.

Private Paul H. Orcutt, Company D; mustered-out.

Private William E. Morgan, Company A; mustered-out.

Private C. R. Lamson, Company E; mustered-out.

Private Edward White, Company F; killed before Atlanta.

Private Judson E. Hall, Company F; mustered-out.

Private Milton Greenwood, Company F; mustered-out.

Private Charles H. Farnham, Company F; mustered-out.

Private James C. Arnold, Company F; mustered-out.

Private James L. Haines, Company F; mustered-out.

Private Albert C. Lowther, Company F; mustered-out.

Private R. Barnes, Company F; mustered-out; wounded before Atlanta.

Private Felix Baldery; Company F; mustered-out.

Private John Etheridge, Company F; mustered-out.

Private Henry Etheridge, Company F; mustered-out.

Private Daniel Forbes, Company F; mustered-out.

Private E. J. Covey, Company F; mustered-out.

Private Wilson R. Lowther, Company F; mustered-out.

First Lieutenant Myron A. Benedict, Company F; lost his right arm before Atlanta; discharged.

Private C. A. Damon, Company F; discharged.

First Lieutenant J. L. Thomas, Company F; mustered-out.

Corporal Darius C. Dickenson, Company G; discharged at expiration of service.

Private Augustus Dickenson, Company G; discharged at expiration of service.

Private Henry Warren, Company G; discharged at expiration of service.

Private Samuel C. Dickenson, Company G; mustered-out.

Private Walter S. Terry, Company I; mustered-out.

Private William Miller, Company I; mustered-out.

Private Snyder Tutewiler, Company I; mustered-out.

Private A. C. Shafer, Company I; shot three times in as many charges upon rebel works before Atlanta, and still living; mustered-out.

Private M. Wilder, Company I; mustered-out.

Private D. Brockway, Company I; mustered-out.

Private Jacob Leginger, Company I; mustered-out.

Private Leander Porter, Company I; mustered-out.

Private Frederick Roberts, Company I; mustered-out.

Private Charles Smithe, Company I; mustered-out.

Private William Snooks, Company I; mustered-out.

Private Edward W. Watkins, Company K; discharged at the close of war.

TWELFTH INFANTRY.

Private Herbert L. Childs, Company K; mustered-out.

THIRTEENTH INFANTRY.

Sergeant William A. Noble, Company H; mustered-out.

Private Moses Halme, Company G; mustered-out.

FIFTEENTH INFANTRY.

Private John H. Kale, Company A; died at Detroit, May 27, 1862.

Private S. Lowell Bacheldor, Company I; mustered-out.

SIXTEENTH INFANTRY.

Private Elisha M. Johnson, Company H; mustered-out.

Private Orris S. Ferris, Company K; mustered-out.

SEVENTEENTH INFANTRY.

Corporal Anthony Gerue, Company C; discharged.

Corporal Theodore A. Hutchinson, Company C; mustered-out.

Private Charles M. Clement, Company C; mustered-out.

Private Clifton C. Clement, Company C; mustered-out.

Private Erastimus McDonald, Company C; mustered-out.

Private Henry C. Thomas, Company C; mustered-out.

Private Nathan C. Tenney, Company C; mustered-out.

Private Joshua C. Wolferton, Company C; mustered-out.

Private Morris C. Benham, Company C; mustered-out.

NINETEENTH INFANTRY.

Corporal Anthony C. Miles, Company D; mustered-out.

TWENTY-FIFTH INFANTRY.

First Lieutenant Henry McCrary, Company D; captain April 7, 1863, and mustered-out.

Sergeant William L. Thomas, Company D; veteran reserve corps.

Corporal Jubal Thomas, Company D; mustered-out.

Corporal Charles Clement, Company D; mustered-out.

Private Darius Gilbert, Company D; mustered-out.

Private Anson Lamport, Company D; discharged for disability.

Private Henry Lemm, Company D; discharged.

Private William Miers, Company D; veteran reserve corps.

Private Sylvester McDonald, Company D; mustered-out.

Private Andrew L. Pringle, Company D; mustered-out.

Private Thaddeus Rulinson, Company D; mustered-out.

Private Morgan Wallace, Company D; killed at Tibb's Bend, Kentucky, July 4, 1863.

Private Bruce C. Wilcox, Company D; mustered-out.

Private William Hoag, Company E; died September 17, 1864.

Private Nathan Schoefield, Company E; mustered-out.

TWENTY-EIGHTH INFANTRY.

Private William H. Jones, Company A; mustered-out.

FIFTH CAVALRY.

Private John E. Davis, Company L; mustered-out.

Private Edson E. Gould, Company M; mustered-out.

Private Richard Watkins, Company M; died at Annapolis, Maryland, August 21, 1864.

EIGHTH CAVALRY.

Private Albert Wilcox, Company G; mustered-out.

Private Ezra R. Harding, Company K; mustered-out.

Private George A. Collins, Company I; mustered-out.

NINTH CAVALRY.

Private Charles Harding, Company K; mustered-out.

Private Henry Miller, Company E; died at Coldwater, Michigan, April 6, 1863.

ELEVENTH CAVALRY.

Private James McDowell, Company A; mustered-out.

Private Emmett Elwell, Company F; mustered-out.

Private Benjamin Wilcox, Company I; discharged for disability.

FIRST ARTILLERY.

Private Wilbur F. Studley, Battery D; mustered-out.

Private Lewis E. Jacobs, Battery D; discharged for disability.

Private Freedom Randall, Battery F; mustered-out.

Private Benjamin F. Wilcox, Battery F; mustered-out.

Private Moses B. Baker, Battery 14; mustered-out.

Private Charles H. Haines, Battery 14; mustered-out.

PROVOST-GUARD.

Horace C. Hoag; discharged for disability.

THIRTY-SEVENTH ILLINOIS.

Private W. W. Ford, Company C; re-enlisted and mustered-out.

UNITED STATES NAVY.

Jacob Barron, mustered out; died in 1870 of disease contracted while in service.

We hereby tender our heartiest acknowledgments to W. M. Watkins, Esq., for valuable assistance rendered in the compilation of the history of Leonidas. We also acknowledge the receipt of information therefor from E. K. Wilcox, Esq., Addison Harvey, John Foreman, Esq., John A. Purdy, Mr. Millard, R. Coddington and Jairus Peirce.

# BIOGRAPHICAL SKETCHES.

## SOLOMON PIER.

Solomon Pier, of Leonidas township, St. Joseph county, Michigan, was born in Chenango county, New York, October 16, 1814. When he was but two years of age his father, Ethan Pier, moved with his family to Steuben county, where they remained until 1831, when they removed to Ontario county, and subsequently, in 1832, to Orleans county, New York, and finally, in 1838, to Washtenaw county, Michigan.

The facilities for education, as offered in early times, were few, so that Mr. Pier never enjoyed the advantages of extensive knowledge. Up to 1840 he worked on his father's farm, and then learned the trade of carpenter and joiner, at which he worked for the next sixteen years.

On the 3d of December, 1855, he married Frances, daughter of John and Frances Bird, of Morristown, New Jersey, by whom he had two sons, Nirum J. and Ethan B., who reside with their parents. In 1856 Mr. Pier went to farming on his own account, and, by industry and frugality, has become possessed of a well-cultivated farm of eight hundred acres, on which are neat and commodious buildings. He bought and paid for his place with his own savings, and feels proud of the fact that he owes no man anything, and has besides had to pay about one thousand dollars in endorsements for other people.

In politics he has always supported the Democratic party; in religion he believes in the grand old precept "do unto others as you would they should do unto you." A portrait of Mr. and Mrs. Pier grace our pages elsewhere in this work.

## JAMES BISHOP.

The name of James Bishop will be recognized as among those prominently identified with the history of Leonidas township, where a large portion of his life and energies were spent. Coming into that township in 1837, he was necessarily intimately connected with its growth, development and prosperity, and was always esteemed as one of its most substantial citizens.

James Bishop was born in Dryden, Tompkins county, New York, October 29, 1815. His parents, William and Sybil Bishop, were much-respected citizens of York State for many years, and retained in their new western home the character for industry and integrity which they formerly enjoyed in the place of their birth and early life.

In 1841 the subject of our sketch married Clara, daughter of David R. and Sarah Cooley, an old and respected citizen of Sherwood, Branch county, Michigan, by whom he had four children,—two sons and two daughters,—all of whom are living. They were married by L. C. Hobart, Esq., at the residence of the bride's parents, and subsequently removed to the pleasant little hamlet of Factoryville, Leonidas township, and from there to Albion, Calhoun county, Michigan, and thence to Leonidas township, where they permanently settled.

In 1849, during the gold furore, Mr. Bishop went to California, the journey thither occupying a year less five days. He had a desperate encounter with the Indians, in which he received a ball in his leg below the knee, which he carried with him to his grave. He remained in the land of gold and beautiful climate for one year and five months, and then returned to his farm in Leonidas, where he died on the 20th of January, 1867.

By industry and careful management he accumulated a fine property, consisting of two hundred and ninety acres of land, mostly under excellent cultivation.

As showing his general character we quote the following from an obituary which appeared in the *Spiritual Republic :*

" His was a grand triumph of the spirit over disorganized matter. Disease had long been insidiously undermining the system, and had preyed upon it until it had become a mere skeleton, seeming inadequate to hold a human spirit with all the force of former character teeming out through the senses which were retained perfect to the last. As his light became dim to material objects, his spiritual sight opened and he saw a father and brother; the father had been an inhabitant of the spirit realm twenty-one, and the brother four years.

" He leaves many sincere mourners, who will sadly miss him in the physical and material sense ; but they do not mourn as those without hope, for they have a knowledge that answers that oft-repeated question, ' What good does Spiritualism do?' that man is immortal, and his future home is not far removed from this, nor dissimilar and disconnected."

In politics Mr. Bishop was a Republican ; in religious belief a Spiritualist ; in character he was genial, kind and honest, and in his habits temperate ; a good citizen, a fond husband, and an affectionate father.

## MRS. CLARA BISHOP,

the widow of the above, and at present the wife of Mr. B. B. Gardner, of Sturgis, was born at Batavia, Genesee county, New York, March 10, 1818. She removed with her parents to Michigan in the spring of 1837, and settled in Sherwood, Branch county.

As above stated, she was a daughter of David R. and Sybil Cooley, the former six years later, aged seventy-four.

Soon after the death of her first husband, Mrs. Bishop removed to Sturgis, where she became acquainted with, and subsequently, on the the 27th day of May, 1869, married Mr. B. B. Gardner ; she now resides on Nottawa street in that city. She is a woman of very positive character, has always been a good wife and loving mother, and enjoys the respect of the community in which she lives.

At the dawn of modern Spiritualism, in 1848, she became a firm believer in it, and has since adhered to that belief. She possesses more than ordinary business tact, and transacts the affairs of her somewhat extensive property personally, and with creditable success.

## B. B. GARDNER,

one of the oldest and most prominent pioneers of Sturgis, was born in Montgomery county, Virginia, March 4, 1809. His parents were also natives of old Virginia, and were among its most reputable citizens.

In 1818 he accompanied them to Gallia county, Ohio, where he assisted in opening up and cultivating a large farm ; thus at an early age acquiring those habits of industry which have been so beneficial to him in after life.

After remaining in Gallia county twelve years, they removed to Williams county, Ohio, and in January, 1831, we find Mr. Gardner emigrating to Michigan and settling in Sturgis, where he has ever since remained. When he arrived his possessions consisted of a span of horses, an old wagon, a cow, a wife and child, a mother-in-law and seventy-five cents in money. He entered eighty acres of land, which by subsequent purchases he increased to two hundred and forty-seven acres of finely improved land, in Sturgis township, which he has since divided among his children.

On the 22d of January, 1828, he married Miss Nancy Thompson, a native of the same county as himself, which resulted in a family of eight children, of whom six survive, namely :

PHEBE B., born September 11, 1830.
PETER J. B., born July 5, 1832.
SARAH J. B., born October 26, 1838 ; died April 8, 1872.
MARIA E. B., born September 26, 1841 ; died January 12, 1871.
ADELINE B., born May 31, 1844.
LORETTA B., born October 16, 1846.
CALVIN B., born November 30, 1848.
SEPHRINIA B., born December 15, 1850.

Those remaining are all comfortably married and settled, enjoying the fruits of their father's munificence ; and are dutiful children, and respected members of society.

On the 15th of February, 1868, he sustained the loss of his wife, whose spirit took its flight to the "beauteous beyond," but still, he believes, hovers near him as of yore, holding sweet communion with his spirit, and awaiting the final reunion in the spirit-land.

In politics Mr. Gardner is a Republican ; in religious belief a Spiritualist, having, like his wife, embraced that belief at its birth, twenty-nine years ago. He possesses many marked characteristics, one being an aversion to all kinds of litigation. It is a fact worthy of note that he never sued nor was ever sued in his life, nor never defalcated in any business engagement, but while using all judicious economy, and priding himself on his powers of acquisition, he has never become parsimonious, but believing that charity ought to begin at home, he has lived up to that maxim, and having made his children comfortable, uses the proceeds of a neat competence, living in his quiet home surrounded by the comforts and pleasures of domestic life, and enjoying the fruits of his thrift and providence.

B. B. GARDNER.
(STURGIS.)

MRS. B. B. GARDNER.
(STURGIS.)

JAMES BISHOP.
(STURGIS.)

MRS. CLARA BISHOP.
(STURGIS.)

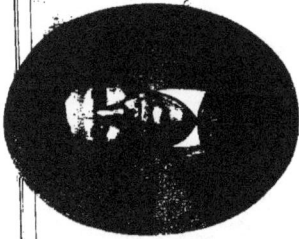

Levi Watkins

Wm. M. Watkins

Residence of WILLIAM M. WATKINS, Leonidas Tp. St Joseph Co. Mich.

## CAPTAIN LEVI WATKINS.

Among the staunch pioneers of St. Joseph county, who, in the burden and heat of the olden days bore their full share of labor, fearless in trial, undaunted in defeat, and modest and unassuming in final victory, stood Levi Watkins, one of the earliest settlers of Leonidas.

Captain Watkins came of sterling stock, his grandfather, Captain Nathan Watkins, commanded a company of soldiers in the Revolutionary war, his son, Mark Watkins, father of the subject of our sketch, entering the same company as a drummer boy at the age of fourteen years. The father and son were taken prisoners at the battle of Bennington, but the boy was soon released by General Burgoyne, and sent home to his mother as a present from that gallant officer. The father, Captain Nathan Watkins, was held, but re-captured by the colonial troops a few days afterwards.

When Boston was evacuated by the British troops, the small-pox was raging in the city, and Captain Watkins being the only officer of sufficient grade for the purpose, who had had the disease, was assigned to the command of the city.

The boy Mark went back into the service after his release by General Burgoyne, and served until he was honorably discharged.

Captain Levi Watkins also had the blood of Revolutionary ancestry on his mother's side. Her name was Esther Legg, and her father was also in the war for independence, serving with distinction.

He, of whom we write, was born in Partridgefield, Berkshire county, Massachusetts, August 5, 1785, and when eight years of age removed with his parents, who settled on a royal grant in Herkimer county, New York, near Little Falls, where they lived until Levi was sixteen years old, when the family removed to Naples, Ontario county, in the same State.

While living in Herkimer a hurricane passed over the house and prostrated a tree across the same, in such a manner as to imprison Levi until the tree was cut away. He fortunately escaped any serious injury.

He was the youngest of three sons, Elijah and Orrin being the other two besides himself. His father was a farmer, and Levi had no opportunity to attend school except for a single month, but gained his education in the hard school of experience. He always occupied the same farm with his father, but dwelt in a separate house, having everything produced on the farm in common.

He followed farming and cattle-droving for a business, driving to Philadelphia and Buffalo large herds.

He entered the army during the war of 1812, and was stationed on picket between Lewiston and Buffalo in command of a company, which gave him his rank and title of captain.

In 1820 he took contracts on the Erie canal, then in process of construction, which business he followed until 1824, but by the defalcation of the canal commissioner, and the fraudulent practices of a party for whom he was surety, he lost heavily, and was stripped of nearly all his property.

In the early part of the autumn of 1832, Captain Watkins came to Leonidas,—then known as Flowerfield—and selected a location on the Nottawa creek, near Dunkin's (now Climie's) mill, and built a log-house and put in nine acres of wheat. He brought in a horse with him, which he exchanged for a yoke of oxen, and bought some wheat and corn and had it ground for supplies for his family when they should arrive, and went to work for the Cowen brothers, who were building their mill. He had purchased another yoke of oxen of Judge Meek, of Constantine, and engaged to work two months for the Cowens for sixty dollars, just the price he had agreed to pay for his last yoke of cattle. When his time was up he took the Cowens' note for the amount due, and exchanged it for his own note, which he had given for his team, and so "squared" the account.

On the 20th day of February, 1833, the family arrived, bringing with them a span of horses and a wagon, which was an important addition to the pioneer's outfit. The location of Captain Watkins proving to be seminary lands, he relinquished it, and bought lands contiguous thereto, on what was afterwards known as the territorial road, in the summer and fall of 1836, and built another house thereon. This location he transferred to his son, William M., with whom he continued to reside until his death. Captain Watkins' father, Captain Mark Watkins, and his wife removed from Naples, in February, 1835, and resided with his son, as formerly, until his death, which occurred in June, 1836—his wife, Captain Levi's mother, surviving till October 24, 1847, when she too passed to her rest.

On the anniversary of our National Independence, in the year 1805, Captain Levi Watkins was united in marriage to Miss Silence Clark, a daughter of Major Clark, of Naples, New York, by whom there were born to him two children, Polly and Alexander H. The latter was born February 1,

1808, and his mother died on the 8th day of the following July. On the 29th day of April, 1809, Captain Watkins sought another companion in the person of Lucina D., daughter of Edward and Mary Kibbee, of Naples. The children of this marriage were Martin C., Orrin M., William M., Esther S., now the widow of William Orcutt, late of Leonidas, now deceased, and Lucina S., now Mrs. James Colwell. Of the seven children of Captain Watkins, but three survive, they being the last ones named above.

In politics Captain Watkins was in his early days a Democrat, but being possessed of strong anti-slavery instincts, he joined the Free-Soil movement in 1848, and died a thorough and absolute Abolitionist. He helped many a poor fugitive to freedom, when the underground railroad was in operation, even when a Democrat. He never held any superior position in official life, from choice. In his youth he united with the Presbyterian church, and was one of the founders of the first society of that denomination in Naples, New York, and was also the chief support of the society in Leonidas. His first wife was also a member of that church in Naples, and his second one was a member of both that society and the one in Leonidas.

Captain Watkins, after a life of untiring activity, passed to his final rest, October 12, 1851. His partner survived him a little more than ten years, when she fell asleep and was laid beside him, February 19, 1862. And thus passed from the sight of men one of the most active and energetic citizens of his day. His executive ability was remarkable, and the enterprises in which he was engaged while a resident of New York were monuments to his energy and determination, and that the State fulfilled its obligations, and its servants faithfully discharged their trusts, Captain Watkins would have been, notwithstanding his generosity, a wealthy man, living at his ease, long before his death. As it was, death found him with the harness on, every trace taut, and muscles strained for effective work, and he laid down "like a strong man taking his rest."

The second Mrs. Watkins was a pioneer of Ontario county, and set out the first apple-tree in Naples, which is still known as Mother Watkins' apple-tree.

## WILLIAM M. WATKINS.

The subject of our sketch is the foremost man of Leonidas, and one whom the people of his township have and still do delight to honor. Hospitable and generous, the ample dwelling of William M. Watkins is seldom without guests, who gather around his table to partake of his abundant cheer, freely set forth, and fill his rooms with laughter and merriment, that drives the demons of care and foreboding from every nook and cranny of the old homestead.

Mr. Watkins was born in Naples, Ontario county, New York, August 17, 1816, where he assisted his father, Captain Levi Watkins, and attended the district-school until he was sixteen years of age, attending the select school of Rev. John Morgan one year. In February, 1833, he came with his father's family to Leonidas, where he has ever since resided. In 1844 he bought his present location, and removed to it with his father and mother, with whom he has always resided. The father and son have ever been one in their aims and purposes, and held their farm in common, and had a common interest. The homestead now includes two hundred and seventy acres, and is one of the most beautifully situated farms in the county.

We present our readers a view of this rare landscape on another page, together with portraits of Captain Levi and William M. Watkins.

On the 26th day of October, 1841, Mr. Watkins was united in marriage to Barbara E., daughter of George and Amelia Hill, of Manchester, New York, and who was born in Manchester, Ontario county, New York. She came to St. Joseph county in 1839.

The fruits of this union were Edward W., Marcia A., Marcus L., Levi H., Emory O., Ida May, Eva and Sarah F., all of whom are living except Ida and Sarah. The sons are all married and living on farms of their own except Emory, who remains with his father on the old homestead. Edward entered the military service in the rebellion, in December, 1862, and served till the war was over. He was a member of the eleventh regiment of Michigan volunteer infantry. Mr. Watkins was active and untiring in his efforts in aid of the government to put down the rebellion, and gave time and money without stint to the enlistment of volunteers to fill the quotas of his township during the war.

In politics Mr. Watkins was originally a Whig, but joined the Republican party at its organization, and has been a staunch member thereof ever since. He has held the position of supervisor of his township for several years, and the position of sheriff of the county for two terms, from 1866 to 1870, inclusive.

Mr. and Mrs. Watkins are members of the Methodist church, of Leonidas, of which Mr. Watkins has been a trustee for many years.

## ADDISON HARVEY.

The subject of the present sketch, Addison Harvey, was the son of Thomas and Sabra Harvey, and was born in Oneida county, New York, August 21, 1814. He was one of a family of ten children, of whom he alone survives. He left Oneida county when but eight years old, in company with his father's family, removing to Cattaraugus county in the same State, where he resided until 1837, when he immigrated to Michigan in the month of September of that year, making the journey with an ox-team, and being twenty-seven days on the road. He purchased his present location on his arrival in Leonidas, St. Joseph county, on which there was a small log-house and about one acre enclosed. Mr. Harvey began life as a poor boy, but by industry and frugality is now, in his old age, the owner of one of the best farms in Leonidas, containing four hundred and thirty-six acres. The homestead of one hundred and fifty-six acres is finely improved, with large barns and a comfortable dwelling thereon, a view of which we present on another page of our work. In the spring of 1835 Mr. Harvey was united in marriage with Miss Anna Beadle, by whom two sons were born to him—James and Addison, Jr., the latter dying when about a year old. Mrs. Harvey died in the fall of 1837, and now sleeps in the cemetery near Leonidas village. In November, 1842, Mr. Harvey took to himself another companion—Miss Amer E. Hull, of Ashtabula, Ohio. Three children were the fruits of this union—Sophia, Elizabeth A. and Porter S., of whom Elizabeth only survives. On the 3d day of April Mrs. Harvey passed to her rest, leaving the husband once more alone. On the 8th day of September Mr. Harvey, finding a lonely life unendurable, brought a companion to share and brighten his desolate home. She was Miss Maria Teller, a daughter of Tobias Teller, of Saratoga county, New York, with whom she came to Michigan, November 10, 1843. Mr. Harvey was originally a member of the Whig party, and joined the Republican cause when that party was organized. He has been a prominent man in his younger days, and has held the offices of supervisor and justice of the peace for several years. Not having in his youth had very good advantages for an education, he has given his children all the advantages he was able to for a good one. Mr. Harvey's father was a Revolutionary soldier, and lived to a good old age.

## MR. ELIJAH PURDY,

son of Elijah, Sr., and Lovenia Purdy, was born in Bedford county, New York, November 26, 1805. At the age of nine he was put out as an apprentice at the shoemaking trade till he was twenty-one, which trade he followed for several years afterwards. He married Miss Martha Barker, January 7, 1830. Miss Barker, now Mrs. Purdy, was born in Scarsdale, Westchester county, New York, March 20, 1804. To bless this union five children were born,—Sarah L., died at the age of four; John A., now on the old homestead; Mary C., in Indiana; Martha A., died at the age of two years and a half; David B., owns the farm south of the old homestead. May 3, 1836, Mr. Purdy and family emigrated to Leonidas, St. Joseph county, Michigan, and settled where his sons John A. and David B. now reside. Mr. Purdy began life poor, but by industry and frugality, assisted by his faithful wife and family, became the owner of four hundred acres of good land. He was a worthy and consistent member of the Methodist Episcopal church for more than forty-six years, and did his part in building up society. In politics he affiliated with the Whigs and Republicans. As Mr. Purdy was unable to attend to his own affairs for several years before his death, he gave to his son John A. the charge, and John A. is a successful financier. Mr. Purdy died August 12, 1876. He lived respected by all, and died regretted by many.

Mrs. Purdy is now an old lady of seventy-two years, living on the old homestead with her son John A. She, too, is a member of the Methodist Episcopal church. She is one of the good mothers of Leonidas, and to-day, as ever, has a tender motherly care over her children, in whose hearts she occupies a warm place.

John A. was born in Westchester county, New York, October 15, 1833; came to Michigan with his parents in 1836; has followed farming for his living, and is to-day one of the best farmers and growers of fine stock in the county. He was married to Mary Galloway, November 10, 1862. She died June 20, 1864, and he was married the second time to Miss Emily C. Davis, Dec. 28, 1865. An idea of Mr. Purdy's fine farm-buildings and stock may be seen by looking at a fine double-page view found elsewhere in this work.

## IRA MILLARD.

The subject of our sketch, Ira Millard, son of Solomon and Anna Millard, was born in Lenox, Susquehanna county, Pennsylvania, September 5, 1798; followed farming, blacksmithing, and carpentering for a living, working with his father till he was twenty-four years of age, and before he left old Pennsylvania he had cleared up some fifty acres of heavy timber. July 29, 1822, he was married to Miss Emmila McDonald. She was born in Blakely, Luzerne county, Pennsylvania, September 10, 1803. As a result of this happy union twelve children have been born, namely:

William A., died at the age of nine.

Minerva, died at the age of twenty-five, leaving a son, Charles Woods.

Martha Ann, now in Oregon.

Noah Shaw, died at the age of two.

Ira Dolphus, living on the west half of the old homestead.

Jedoiada, with his parents at home, and the generous donor of this portrait and biography.

Asenath, now in California.

Louis Jane, in Cass county, Michigan.

Georie W., died at the age of two.

Huldah, died at the age of two.

Phebe Jane, died an infant.

Roby G., in California.

Mr. Millard settled in Leonidas, October 17, 1835; lived with Hamilton Watkins for a month or so; removed thence to Bailey's Mills, remained a year, thence on to the farm where he now resides. Mr. Millard commenced life a poor boy, but by industry and economy has gained a competency. September, 1858, Mr. Millard visited the "Golden State," remaining there nearly three years. On his return he came very near losing his life. His son Jedoiada was with him. They started on their homeward voyage in the steamboat "Moses Taylor," and after five days of terrible gale, the steamer became unseaworthy, and returned to San Francisco. They then took passage on the "Hermon" to Panama, then on the "America" to New York, being twenty-nine days on their way. Mr. Millard is a strong believer in the fundamental principles of the Democratic party as taught by Jefferson. In religion he is a believer in Universalism. Mr. Millard is now an old man of seventy-nine years, and still enjoys a fair degree of health. His faithful wife still lives. This noble couple have walked life's journey together for nearly fifty-five years. These years have brought sunshine, and sorrow to their home, but during them all no discordant sound has been heard, and to-day, more than ever, they enjoy each other's society. They have reared a large and intelligent family to industry and economy. They review the past with serene satisfaction, and look into the future with no apprehension.

## CHANDLER KINGSLEY.

CHANDLER KINGSLEY was born in Canaan, Columbia county, New York, in the year 1818, where he spent his earlier days and received his education.

He was married March 17, 1847, and moved to Bethany, Genesee county, in the spring of 1849, living there until December, 1853, when he and his family moved to St. Joseph County, Michigan, and located on Seminary land two miles south of Leonidas Centre. There, with axe in hand, a strong arm, and a purpose to hew out for himself a home, he felled the first trees to make room for a small house. The surroundings were then comparatively wild; the privations of the early settlers were fully realized, and the chill of the ague stood ready to greet him ere he had a few acres cleared to repay his toil.

But a kind Providence has smiled on his untiring efforts and years of hard labor, until he has lived to see the tall oaks give place to the fruit orchards, and fields of waving grain, which are seen in their season, yielding their increase to the husbandman. An humble home has been erected, which he and his family occupy at the date hereof.

CHANDLER KINGSLEY.

RESIDENCE OF CHANDLER KINGSLEY, LEONIDAS TP, ST JOE CO, MICH.

enlisted in the United States army, which was then quartered at Sault de St. Marie. He went with an expedition to explore the copper-mines, passing the picture-rocks, which the Indians held in great reverence, as being the home of the Great Spirit; went the entire length of Lake Superior; crossed to the Mississippi river, then back to Green Bay. His discharge was procured for him by an uncle, Levi Parish, who was an influential man at Washington, on account of minority, in 1831. He then returned to Naples, New York, and stayed all winter, telling wonderful stories of the western States, which caused many to sell their homes and emigrate to this part of Michigan.

1832 found him again here, working as a builder in Detroit, Monroe and Whiteford. He, the same year, bought at government price four eighty-acre lots, or three hundred and twenty acres of land, in the northeast portion of St. Joseph county. He worked at carpenter work in this and adjoining counties until 1836, when he went up the Missouri river to Chariton, Missouri, and spent one year.

In 1838 he was married in the village of Lima, Indiana, to Nancy Alexander, of Canandaigua, New York, and moved to Constantine, where they lived two years, then moved to Missouri, by the way of Illinois, living three months in Ottawa, and was in Missouri until 1840; then lived in Constantine until 1854, working as a carpenter and architect. He drafted the plan for the county buildings and did much nice work, as many buildings in the various towns of the county still show. In 1854 he moved on to his wild land and cleared a farm. Then, in 1862, he moved to the village of Leonidas and lived nine years, when he moved back to his farm, where he died after a distressing illness of five years, of a cancer in the stomach, the 11th of September, 1871.

GEORGE J. CLARK.

George Jefferson Clark was born August 18, 1810, in the town of Naples, county of Ontario, New York; was son of Calvin Clark and grandson of Elijah Clark; he lived in Naples until 1830, when he went to Albany and

# BURR OAK.

Almost half a century ago was erected the first white man's habitation,—a log cabin,—in the territory now comprised within the limits of Burr Oak township. In 1831 Samuel Haslet and family, together with George Miller, a bachelor, settled upon the land that afterwards became and has long familiarly been known as the Elder Farley farm. Haslet is not only accredited as being one of the first settlers, but he has also the honor of having

## THE FIRST WHITE CHILD

born in the now township of Burr Oak. This was in the year 1832. Towards the close of the year 1831, a man by the name of Snow came over from Snow prairie (from whom the prairie was named), in Branch county, and settled on the farm long since owned by Hiram Lockwood. Sometime afterwards Snow sold out and again settled within a stone's throw of the present village of Burr Oak. Haslet also sold out and settled near where Frank Williams now lives. Miller also settled on the banks of Prairie river, or Hog creek, as it is generally called, on the opposite corner, west of where Daniel Livermore now lives, and which land afterwards became the property of Marshall Livermore, now owned by John Ultz.

Hon. Wales Adams, a gentleman long and honorably known as one of the pioneers of Branch county,—from whence came Haslet and Snow,—gives the following brief description of these individuals:

"Haslet was an easy body, with whom the world in which he moved generally wagged well. His wife was the presiding genius, and the more positive character of the two."

Of the other original settler (Snow) Mr. Adams writes: "He was apparently forty or fifty years of age, of a taciturn cast of mind. His figure was

rather tall and spare. His sloping shoulders, compressed lips and black, evasive eye, gave to him a repulsive appearance. He was from one of the New England States,—had been married; but being a man possessed of keen sensibilities and a fondness for variety, he became disgusted with the restraints and annoyances of conjugal life, abruptly left his family to the mercy of the world, and sought repose for himself amid the wilds of the west."

About the year 1833, and thence onward, settlers of a more permanent character began to come in, some of whom remain to this day. In that year Reuben Trussell settled on the road leading to Centreville, where he lived and died, and his family long lived afterwards.

The premises are now owned by E. C. Campany. About cotemporary with him were the Eldreds, from Vermont, brothers and sisters, who settled on the farm where James Worden now lives. A man by the name of Spurgeon came about the year 1834, and settled where the descendants of John Start now reside. Cephas A. Smith settled on the farm afterwards the property of Isaac Slocum, now owned by his son-in-law, William Woodman. There came, also, about this time a negro by the name of Lewis, who settled on land a little east of where Henry S. Wheeler and his sons now reside. It was long known as Negro prairie.

We quote the subjoined incident from the oration delivered by S. Kibbe, Esq., on the Fourth of July, 1876:

"Smith became sick with the fever incident to the climate, his garden became overgrown with weeds, and the negro in passing by observed its forlorn condition, and offered to hoe it out. And consent being given, he went to work, hanging up his coat not far from the house. When the negro got well-nigh the farther end of the garden Smith goes out to talk with the negro awhile, and then returns to the house. In going back he halts near the coat, finally steps up to it, and passes on to the house. After the negro had finished his hoeing, and reaching for his coat, he discovered that his pocket-book, in which was about twenty dollars, was missing. Lewis did not know what to do; at length, seeing one of Haslet's sons passing along the road, he tells him the story and sends him for his father. Haslet, thinking it nothing but a joke, treated it as such. Lewis got tired of waiting and goes up to Haslet's; after consultation, it was thought too late to search Smith's house, so the negro waited till court-sitting, goes to Centreville before the Grand Jury, tells his story, and is unceremoniously ordered from the court-room. Lewis came home disgusted with the treatment he had received, and finally left the country, never coming back to claim his property."

About 1834 came Josiah and Marshall Livermore. The same year Gideon Sanburn settled on the farm where his family now reside. In 1835 James C. Stowell; the same year Henry S. Weaver and his father, Daniel, came and entered their land, taking up their permanent residence the year following. Soon after, in 1837, Ervin K. Weaver came in. In 1836 came James L. Bishop and Sidney Carpenter. In 1834 Reuben Trussell built the

#### FIRST FRAME HOUSE

in the now township of Burr Oak. He purchased his lumber at Dugg's saw-mill, located not far from where Jonathan Holmes' mill now stands. The lumber was rafted down Swan creek to a point at or near where Nathaniel Houston now lives, from whence it was taken by teams to the building site. Five dollars per thousand feet would command the best white-wood lumber, to-day worth from thirty to forty dollars per thousand. Nails were worth then thirteen cents per pound by the keg, to-day worth from three to four cents per pound. Salt only cost the small sum of ten dollars per barrel, —to-day worth a dollar and three-quarters.

#### THE FIRST BRICK HOUSE

was built by H. S. Williams in 1855, and now stands in the village of Burr Oak.

In 1838 the question of a new township began to be talked of, as the parent township, Sherman, was considered too large in extent for judicial and electoral purposes. Accordingly, in the spring of that year, we find the following legislative act recorded, viz.:

That "all that part of the county of St. Joseph designated in the United States survey as township number seven, south of range number nine west, be, and the same is hereby set off and organized into a separate township by the name of BURR OAK.

"And the first township meeting shall be held at the house of Julius A. Thompson, in said township.

"RANDOLPH MANNING, Secretary of State.

"Approved March 6, 1838."

Pursuant to the above-recited act of the legislature the meeting was held April 2, 1838, and organized by appointing Alvin Gates, Esq., moderator; Oliver Raymond, Esq., was present as acting justice of the peace; James L. Bishop and Hiram Draper were chosen clerks.

The following men were elected to fill the offices of the newly-made township: Supervisor, Marshall Livermore; Township Clerk, James L. Bishop; Assessors, Alvin Gates, Daniel Weaver and Hiram Draper; Commissioners of Highways, Oliver Raymond, Hiram Draper and Daniel Weaver; Supervisors of Primary Schools, Norman Allen, Oliver Raymond and Sidney Carpenter; Constables, John S. Sickles, Sidney Carpenter and Norman Allen; Collector, Norman Allen; Directors of the Poor, Cyrus Benedict, Phineas H. Sheldon; Justices of the Peace, Alvin Gates, Marshall Livermore, Hiram Draper and Oliver Raymond; Fence-Viewers and Pound-Masters, Julius A. Thompson, Warren Norton and Benjamin Stocking; Overseers of Highway: District No. 1, Josiah T. Livermore; District, No. 2, Samuel Needham; No. 3, Ervin K. Weaver; No. 4, Nathaniel Leavitt; No. 5, Casper Reed.

September 25, 1830, the township board audited the town accounts, amounting to seventy-seven dollars and twenty-five cents, of which sum the supervisors' account was two dollars. At the same meeting of the board it was resolved to raise the sum of twenty-two dollars and twenty-five cents as a contingent fund for the township.

The following have been elected to the offices over their names from 1839 to 1876, inclusive:

Supervisors—Marshall Livermore (three years), Josiah T. Livermore, James L. Bishop (seven years), Sidney Carpenter (seven years), William

Morris (two years), Samuel Needham, Harrison Kelley, Elizur Lancaster (three years), William C. Bryant, William H. Cross, J. Clinton Bishop, present incumbent (ten years).

Clerks—Sidney Carpenter, four years; William Clark, eight years; Charles E. Kibbe, two years; John H. Clewes, John S. Tyler, Hiram Betts, Allen C. Arnold, Lyman F. Hopkins, Charles Thornton, two years; Bliss N. Stone, two years; Walter W. Stone, Chester A. Ward, James Mills, two years; N. H. Soule, John H. Phelps, two years; N. G. Cooper, three years; L. S. Benjamin, F. F. Betts (present incumbent), three years.

Justices of the Peace—Norman Allen, four years; James L. Bishop, seven years; James P. Allen, two years; Alvin Gates, Richard Houston, eight years; Harrison Kelley, James Sickles, eight years; Samuel Needham, James H. Tisdell, twenty-eight years (and present incumbent, 1877); Hiram Betts, sixteen years; Sidney Carpenter, Ira C. Abbott, Bracy Toby, William Morris, Oscar L. Cowles, eight years; J. Clinton Bishop, Hiram Parker, William H. Cross, J. A. J. Metzer, Joseph Annis (to fill vacancy), Bliss N. Stone, eight years, 1877; B. B. Benedict, Elizur Lancaster, A. B. Mills, 1875-77, Reuben W. Trussell (present incumbent).

#### THE FIRST ROADS.

We quote the annexed extract from the Road Docket, on file in the township clerk's office:

"At a meeting of the commissioners of highways of the township of Sherman, in the county of St. Joseph, at the house of Julius A. Thompson (in said township), on the 27th day of March, 1837, it was ordered and determined by the said commissioners that a highway be laid out in the said township of the width of four rods, on the application and consent of Richard Houston and Phineas H. Sheldon, through whose improved land the highway is to pass a part of the distance, the residue being through lands not inclosed, improved, or cultivated. And the said commissioners have caused a survey thereof to be made as follows, viz.: The center line is to begin on the township line, between Colon and Sherman, at the corner of sections one and two, and running thence south on section-line sixty-seven chains; south thirty-seven degrees, east eleven chains; south five and a half degrees, east five chains and fifty-seven links; south sixty-six degrees, east eight chains; south on section-line thirty-three chains to quarter-post on east side of section eleven in township seven, south of range nine west.

"Also that another road be laid out as follows: The center line is to begin at a point on the east and west quarter-line of section twelve, in township seven, south range nine west, at twenty-nine chains and forty links east from quarter-post on the west side of said twelfth section, and to run thence south twenty-eight degrees, east seven chains and fifty links; south thirty-five and a half degrees, east thirty-seven chains and forty-four links; twenty-five and a half degrees, east eleven chains and seventy-five links; south eighty-four and a half degrees, east fourteen chains and forty links to the east line of section thirteen, in township seven south, range nine west, nine chains and fifty links south of the corner of sections twelve and thirteen, in the township aforesaid.
"HIRAM DRAPER, Surveyor.
"In witness whereof, we, the undersigned commissioners of highways, have hereunto subscribed our hands this 27th day of March, 1837.
"MARSHALL LIVERMORE,
"O. RAYMOND,
"Commissioners of Highways."

#### THE FIRST MARRIAGE

in the township was probably the one described by Hon. Wales Adams, of Branch county, thus:

"A man by the name of Miller, a chubby, grizzle-headed Dutchman, who had weathered the pelting storms of at least a half century, moved into the town of Burr Oak with the family of Mr. Haslet, in the year 1831. Mr. Miller had, from his infancy, lived upon the extreme borders of civilization, consequently had received no book education,—knew nothing about social enjoyments, except such as pertained to rugged prairie life. He had never been married. Soon after the advent of Mr. Miller into Burr Oak, two bachelor brothers, named Eldred, from Vermont, entered one hundred and sixty acres of land where Mr. Worden now lives, erected a log house, and commenced improvements. At length a maiden sister of theirs—probably forty years of age—came on to take charge of their domestic affairs; her plainness of countenance and form amounted to repulsiveness. Mr. Miller met Miss Eldred, and became violently enamored. He fancied that

" 'Plato himself had not surveyed unmoved
Such charms as she displayed.'

"After Miss Eldred had played the prude the usual time, she reciprocated his amatorial advances, and after a few months of billing and cooing, like younger lovers, these ancients were married."

### THE FIRST DEATH

that occurred was that of a Mr. Sheldon, from Vermont. He was a bachelor, about thirty-five years of age, well educated, and of high moral character. He purchased, at an early day, one hundred and sixty acres of land two miles north of Burr Oak village, now occupied by William Miller. He boarded with Mr. Smith, and commenced to work on his land, but in the fall of 1833 he died. Hon. Wales Adams supplied a rough coffin for his remains, and taking it to his residence with oxen,—the same being four miles distant,—Mr. Adams and two of the neighbors dug a grave, and buried the deceased on his own land.

### THE FIRST BURYING-GROUND

was located near the residence of Gideon Sanborn, on the farm now owned by his widow, the property of Joseph Graves, as early as 1838. Prior to this the pioneers buried their dead on their own premises; after the incorporation of the ground, these were taken up and re-interred in the present cemetery.

The first interment of an adult person was that of Mrs. Israel I. Stiles, who died in 1838. The first trustees of the cemetery were Cyrus Benedict, Israel I. Stiles and Samuel Needham.

### EDUCATION.

But all this time the educational facilities of the township were being developed. From the most authentic information obtained we learn that school-houses were erected and schools taught prior to the organization of the township. Julius A. Thompson's father is accredited with having taught the first school in what now constitutes the township of Burr Oak, in district number one.

In 1837 or 1838 Miss Sarah Washburn—since Mrs. Nathan Hackett—taught school in a new building with a loose floor above and below, a little east of the Thompson and Farley corners, in the same district.

On the 9th of May, 1838, the inspectors of primary schools organized the township into four school-districts. Number one was by the aforesaid corners, including sections numbers one, two, three, ten, eleven, twelve, thirteen, fourteen and fifteen; number two, by Esquire Needham's, comprising sections four, six, seven, eight, nine, sixteen, seventeen and eighteen; number three, long known as the Foley and Bishop district, composed of sections nineteen, twenty, twenty-one, twenty-eight, twenty-nine, thirty, thirty-one, thirty-two and thirty-three; number four, over south, near Harrison Plants', of sections twenty-two, twenty-three, twenty-four, twenty-five, twenty-six, twenty-seven, thirty-four, thirty-five and thirty-eight.

Mrs. Chapin taught the first summer term in district number three, and Sidney the first winter school in the same district.

Sidney Carpenter and Norman Allen were the first school-inspectors, by whom reports were received from districts one and three, and by them filed with the county clerk, October 5, 1838.

In 1876 there were seven school-houses, six frames and one brick,—the graded school of the village,—valued at twenty-one thousand four hundred dollars, which afforded six hundred and fifty sittings, and in which schools were taught on an average of seven and two-seventh months during the year ending September 1. There were five hundred and seven children in the township of the requisite school-age, between five and twenty years, and four hundred and forty-seven pupils attended the sessions of the schools. There were one hundred and thirty-eight volumes in the district libraries. Six male teachers were employed, who received for compensation one thousand seven hundred and thirty-five dollars, and twelve females, who received one thousand and thirty-two dollars. The total income of the districts footed up six thousand six hundred and sixty-six dollars and sixty-one cents, of which five thousand four hundred and twenty-seven dollars and sixty-four cents were expended, including payments on bonded and other indebtedness.

### THE RELIGIOUS HISTORY

of Burr Oak will be found in the history of the village, where it has been principally made, although, of course, meetings were held in various parts of the township prior to the settlement of the village.

### A DISTILLERY

was built in 1840, or thereabouts, by Hopper, in the northwest part of the township, and was operated by him for about five years, when it was abandoned.

23

### TOPOGRAPHY.

In the original constitution of the county, Burr Oak, which is known on the surveys of the public lands of the United States as township seven, south of range nine, west of the principal meridian, was included in the township of Sherman, which arrangement remained intact from November 5, 1829, until 1838, when Burr Oak was set off into a separate township, as recorded elsewhere.

The township is one of the best in the county, agriculturally considered. The surface, which is a general level, was originally covered with burr-oak timber—hence its name. The openings were superb, and only excelled, if at all, by Florence in its natural beauty. The soil is fertile and productive, yielding heavy crops of the cereals, corn and fruit. It is fairly watered and drained by Big Swan creek, Prairie river, and five small lakes.

The Big Swan creek enters the township on the east line of the southeast quarter of the southeast quarter of section twelve, and runs northeastwardly, passing out of the township near the northwest corner of the northeast quarter of section four. Prairie river makes its entry into the township near the southeast corner of section four, and runs northeast into the southwest quarter of section nine, then reverses its course, and runs southwesterly into Hog Creek lake, on the southeast quarter of section eighteen, and passing out therefrom, reverses its course again, as though loath to leave the beautiful township, and runs almost due north through the west half of sections seven and eighteen, making its exit on the east line of the southwest quarter of section six.

Eberhard's lake, so named from the good old man who settled near its banks, lies on section four. Bryant's, similarly named, reflects its waters on the southwestern quarter of section five. Fish, the name of which suggests its origin, shines in the summer sun on the west half of the northeast quarter of section nineteen; Sewart's on section thirty-two, and Adams' on the southeast quarter of section twenty-nine,—complete the table of the water system of Burr Oak.

### THE AREA

of the township contains twenty-three thousand and forty acres, of which four hundred and eighty acres are water-surface. In 1876 there were twenty-two thousand five hundred and sixty-one acres assessed for taxation, valued by J. Clinton Bishop, the supervisor of the township, at three hundred and eighty-six thousand six hundred and forty-five dollars, about one-third of its real value.

### THE FIRST LAND ENTRIES

in the township were made in the year 1831, and were as follows: The northwest quarter and west half of the southwest quarter of section eleven by Orman Coe, of Genesee county, New York, June 6; the east half of the northeast quarter of section twenty-four, by Lewis Austin, of St. Joseph county, Michigan, October 4. No other entries made that year.

### THE ASSESSMENTS FOR TAXATION

have been as follows: In 1838, the year of the organization of the township, the assessment was fixed at seventy-two thousand and eighty-five dollars, and the taxes levied thereon amounted to three hundred and three dollars. In 1862 the assessment was returned at fifty-five thousand four hundred and thirty-nine dollars, and the taxes levied footed up one thousand and nine dollars, of which amount four hundred and ninety-eight dollars and twenty-seven cents were for the State and county treasuries, and five hundred and one dollars and eighty-two cents for township uses. In 1860 the assessment stood at three hundred and sixty-eight thousand one hundred and eighty dollars, and the taxes (State and county) at one thousand one hundred and fourteen dollars and three cents; for township purposes one thousand six hundred and eight dollars and fifty-two cents. In 1870 the assessment was fixed at seven hundred and sixty-nine thousand seven hundred dollars, and the State and county taxes figured up three hundred and twenty-nine thousand three hundred and thirty-seven dollars, and the township levy to seven thousand seven hundred and ninety-three dollars and sixty-two cents. In 1876 the assessment, as equalized by the county board, amounted to three hundred and seventy-three thousand and ninety-two dollars on real estate, and eighty-two thousand seven hundred and ten dollars on personal property, making a total of four hundred and fifty-five thousand eight hundred and two dollars. On this amount there was levied the following sum of taxes: State and county, two thousand three hundred and twenty-eight dollars and forty-four cents, one-half to each; township, including schools, four thousand eight hundred and forty-five dollars and fifty-one cents, making a grand aggregate of seven thousand one hundred and seventy-three dollars and ninety-five cents.

## CROP STATISTICS.

The census of 1874 makes the following exhibits of the crop of 1873: There were three thousand eight hundred and ninety-two acres of wheat harvested in 1873, which yielded thirty-four thousand seven hundred and eighty-nine bushels, and two thousand two hundred and twenty-three acres of corn, which produced sixty-three thousand four hundred and eighty bushels. Besides these there were raised, gathered and produced fifteen thousand five hundred and thirty-one bushels of other grain, twelve thousand six hundred and ten bushels of potatoes, one thousand six hundred and ninety-three tons hay, eleven thousand nine hundred and eighty-four pounds of wool, two hundred and forty-eight thousand one hundred and seventy pounds of pork, sixty-one thousand four hundred and twenty-seven pounds of butter and cheese, eleven thousand one hundred and two pounds of dried fruit, and six hundred and sixty-eight barrels of cider.

Four hundred and thirty-seven acres in orchards produced sixteen thousand bushels of apples, and thirty-one acres in small fruit and vegetables yielded one thousand eight hundred bushels of that " truck," the same being valued at nine thousand nine hundred and forty dollars.

There were owned, in 1874, in the township six hundred and sixty-two horses over one year old; two mules, four oxen, five hundred and eighty-five cows, three hundred and eighty-five other cattle, one thousand and fifty-eight hogs, and two thousand four hundred and twenty-seven sheep—two thousand seven hundred and twelve of the latter giving the clip of 1873.

The manufacturing exhibit for the same date was as follows: One flour-mill, one saw-mill, one foundry, and one stave- and heading-factory, employed twenty-eight persons, and capital of seventeen thousand two hundred dollars, the value of whose product was returned at forty-six thousand dollars. Three thousand barrels of flour, and forty-eight thousand eight hundred feet of lumber were manufactured. The land was divided into two hundred and thirty-four farms, averaging ninety-one and forty-seven hundredth acres each.

## POPULATION.

In 1850 the township numbered its inhabitants, and found six hundred and fifty-eight individuals who claimed a residence therein. In 1860 there were one thousand seven hundred and seventy-three, the village yielding six hundred and sixty-six. In 1870 the population had increased to one thousand nine hundred and eleven souls—nine hundred and sixty-three being males, and nine hundred and forty-eight females. In 1874 there were one thousand nine hundred and forty-nine persons, of whom one thousand and six were males, and nine hundred and forty-three females. Of the former five hundred and forty-five were over twenty-one years, three hundred and thirty-nine being under forty-five, and two hundred and six above that age, the six being over seventy-five and under ninety. Of the females, five hundred and sixty-four were over eighteen years, three hundred and forty-three being under forty, two hundred and nine over that age and under seventy-five, and twelve beyond the threescore and fifteen. There were four hundred and sixty-one boys under twenty years of age, and three hundred and seventy-nine girls under eighteen years. The married and single males numbered four hundred and twenty-nine and one hundred and ten, all over twenty-one years, and the females in the like condition were four hundred and eighteen and eighty-seven respectively. The single ones were all over eighteen years of age, but ten of the wives were not so old. Twenty-six widowers and seventy widows wore their weeds of woe before the public.

## THE ELECTIONS

for president will show how the political barometer stands, and has stood, in the township. In 1840 the Whigs gave thirty-eight votes, and the Democrats twenty-nine. In 1844 the same parties polled forty-seven and twenty-five votes respectively, and the Liberty guard numbered eleven. In 1848 the Whigs polled forty-one votes, the Democrats twenty-two, and the Free Soilers thirty-eight. In 1852 the Abolitionists were in the majority, polling sixty-four votes to sixty-one for the Whigs, and forty-four for the Democrats. In 1856 the Republicans cast two hundred and one votes, the Democrats eighty-three, and the Prohibitionists six. In 1860 Lincoln received two hundred and seventeen votes, and Douglas one hundred and twenty-five. In 1864 Lincoln polled two hundred and forty-seven votes, and his opponent one hundred and twenty-three. In 1868 Grant received two hundred and ninety-one, and Seymour one hundred and sixty-two. In 1872 General Grant polled two hundred and fifty votes, Greeley one hundred and thirty-four, and O'Conor five. In 1876 Mr. Hayes had two hundred and ninety-three supporters, and Mr. Tilden one hundred and ninety-two. This last vote would indicate a population of about two thousand four hundred in the township.

## BURR OAK VILLAGE.

The village of Burr Oak was partly laid out on land owned by William Lock, in 1851, on the southeast quarter of section twenty-three, and in the year following an addition was made to it by Henry Weaver, who platted a part of the northeast quarter of the same section. It was surveyed by J. H. Gardner and Hiram Draper.

### THE FIRST FRAME HOUSE

was erected by Williams Betts in 1850, before the regular survey of the village had been made. The house is now owned by Adam Bower, of Colon township.

### THE FIRST STORE

was kept by John Talbot, on the corner now occupied by the post-office, in 1851. It was destroyed by fire December 14, 1865.

### THE FIRST TAVERN

was built by Julius A. Thompson in 1851. It is the same now kept by Isaac Green.

### THE FIRST CHURCH EDIFICE

was that erected by the Baptist society in 1858.

### THE FIRST POST-OFFICE

was removed to the village from Thompson's corners in 1852. The first postmaster, after the establishment of the office in the village, was John Clewes ; the present incumbent is Daniel F. Parsons.

### THE FIRST MILL

was erected by D. Page in the summer of 1853. It was run by steam until destroyed by fire in 1858. The present mill was built by Kibbe & Watson soon after the original one was burnt. The present proprietors are Messrs. Selby & Allen.

### THE GRIST-MILL

was built by Caleb J. Crane, in 1850, on Prairie river. It is now owned and run by Wilson & Hagenbaugh.

### THE FIRST PHYSICIAN

who settled in the village was Nathan Mitchell, M.D., who commenced practicing there in 1851. He stayed for two years, and was succeeded by Harvey Loomis, M.D., who came in 1853, and still remains there.

### THE FIRST LAWYER

was Hiram Tyler, who commenced the practice of law in the village in 1854.

### THE FIRST BLACKSMITH-SHOP

was built by James Tower, on the lot owned by Mrs. Gabriel Smith. He first commenced operations in 1852.

### THE INCORPORATION.

The village was regularly incorporated October 11, 1859, and the first annual meeting for the election of town officers was held on the first Monday in March, 1860. The following gentlemen were elected to fill the offices opposite their names : E. J. Goff, president; George Boardner, Henry P. Sweet, Ira C. Abbott, Chester A. Ward, William Fuller and Julius A. Thompson, trustees; Gilbert M. Lamb, clerk ; Allen C. Arnold, treasurer, and Henry T. Williams, assessor.

The present incumbents of the several offices are : A. B. Mills, president; Oliver Nichols, recorder; H. A. Howe, assessor ; V. C. Holcomb, treasurer; R. W. Trussell, Herman Hagenbaugh, John H. Stebbins, George Crawford, M.D., J. R. Keeler and J. N. Kneeland, trustees ; W. W. Stone, marshal.

### THE BUSINESS OF THE PRESENT.

The village now contains five dry-goods stores, one jewelry-store, two hardware-stores, two groceries, one boot and shoe store, two shoe-shops, one agricultural-store, three hotels, one saw- and one grist-mill, one foundry, one wagon-shop, three blacksmithies, one meat market, one exchange bank, three lawyers and five doctors, and five churches denominationally classified as follows: One Baptist, one Presbyterian, one Methodist Episcopal, one Evangelical Lutheran and one Episcopalian.

The annual amount of business done in the village is estimated at one hundred and seventy-five thousand dollars.

### THE MICHIGAN SOUTHERN AND LAKE SHORE RAILROAD

runs its trains through the village, and has done so since 1851,—at which time the village dates its birth. By the courtesy of J. Merle, agent of the

JOHN S. KIBBE

"LONE OAK COTTAGE," RESIDENCE OF J. S. KIBBE, BURR OAK TP. ST JOSEPH CO. MICH.

road at this point, we lay before our readers the following exhibit of business transacted at the Burr Oak station in 1876 : Freights forwarded, seven million four hundred and forty-nine thousand eight hundred and thirty-four pounds; and freight received, two million eighty-five thousand eight hundred and thirty pounds, on which the earnings were fourteen thousand one hundred and ninety-three dollars and three cents. The ticket sales were four thousand nine hundred and six dollars and sixty-five cents, making the handsome aggregate of earnings nineteen thousand ninety-nine dollars and sixty-eight cents.

#### THE BUSINESS OF THE POST-OFFICE

for 1876 was as follows: Stamps sold, one thousand dollars; letters received and dispatched daily, average one hundred and twenty-five; registered letters dispatched daily, one hundred and fifty, and four mails received and dispatched daily.

#### THE FIRST UNION-SCHOOL

was organized in 1863 from district number five, which was formed October 24, 1846. The organization was effected by electing a board of six trustees, viz.: A. F. Schmidt, H. Loomis, M.D., C. A. Ward, John S. Kibbe, P. S. Kilmar and George Boardner. The first principal was James J. Sadler, who was installed in the fall of 1863.

The first school, under the improved system, was held in the old frame-building in the village of Burr Oak,—now temporarily used by the Lutherans as a house of worship. A second story was added to it in 1863, in order to accommodate the two hundred and fifty scholars enrolled. A new fine and ample school-building was erected in 1868, and, including lot and furniture, cost the village twenty thousand dollars. The present principal is D. W. Herman, a gentleman who gives very general satisfaction to both parents and scholars. The assistant teachers are J. S. Stryker, grammar department; Miss Jessie Keeler, second primary; Miss Mary Atwell, first primary. The present enrollment of scholars is two hundred and seventy-eight. Present officers: Charles Betts, moderator; H. Loomis, M.D., director; Daniel Gillett, treasurer; Jeremiah Shane, George Crawford, M.D., and B. F. Sheldon.

During the year ending September, 1876, there were two hundred and thirty pupils in attendance, and two male teachers were employed and paid one thousand two hundred and fifty-eight dollars for their services; and three females, who received five hundred and sixty-two dollars. One thousand eight hundred and eighty dollars were paid on the bonded indebtedness, there being at that date seven thousand eight hundred dollars still outstanding. The total expenditure of the school, for the year, were four thousand one hundred and sixty-seven dollars and fifty-one cents, and eighty dollars were received as tuition fees from non-resident pupils.

#### THE BAPTIST CHURCH

was organized in February, 1855, under the pastoral ministrations of the Rev. John Southworth, and services were first held in his dwelling-house. Among the early members were: Solomon Brown, Patrick Burns and wife, George W. Moore, and others. The succession of the pastors has been: Reverends John Southworth, L. A. Alford, Daniel Pease, Philip R. Lodle, Elder Kelley, T. G. Lamb, Johnson Wyant, and the present incumbent, W. W. Smith. The church was reorganized April 11, 1876, and has now ninety members. Dr. George Crawford is the deacon, as is also J. R. Keeler. The church is self-supporting.

#### THE PRESBYTERIAN CHURCH

of Burr Oak was organized February 16, 1856, and legally incorporated July 7, 1858, both of which events occurred under the ministry of Rev. William Fuller, then a member of what was Coldwater Presbytery. Among the early members of the church were: James L. Bishop, J. H. Phelps, Giles B. Williams, Russel Rowley, Chester Ward, and their wives, Lorenzo Gates, Edward G. Major and Chauncey J. Parsons, M.D. The officers elected at the organization were: J. L. Bishop, G. L. Williams and J. H. Phelps, elders; J. L. Bishop, Samuel Needham and J. H. Phelps, trustees. Meetings were held in dwellings, school-houses and halls for many years before a regular organization existed. We find that the Rev. William Fuller officiated as pastor from 1851-59. The succession of pastors has been: Reverends William Ellere from 1859-64; Timothy B. Jervis from 1864-06; Samuel Flemming, LL.D., from 1866-69; H. H. Bridge from 1869-71; A. H. Gaston, present pastor, from 1871.

The first efforts to erect a church-edifice were made in 1867, but nothing definite was accomplished until 1868, when the present house of worship was commenced. The corner-stone was laid in June, 1870, and the sacred edifice was dedicated June 19, 1873. The services were conducted by Rev. H.

H. Northrop, of Grand Rapids. The structure is of brick, and cost about four thousand dollars, which is all paid. The present membership of the church is forty. The Sabbath-school, of which Mr. J. H. Phelps was superintendent for eighteen years, has a membership of sixty-five, and is now under the care of the pastor. The church is in a flourishing and prosperous condition.

#### THE METHODIST EPISCOPAL CHURCH

of Burr Oak was organized December 13, 1856, and the first quarterly meeting was held at Bronson, then a part of the circuit. The first official members were: Rev. J. Clubine, pastor; Gabriel Smith, local preacher; E. E. McWilliams, Charles E. Kibbe and George W. Foster, stewards; G. W. Foster and O. Atchison, class-leaders; Charles E. Kibbe, Gabriel Smith, O. Atchison and G. W. Foster, trustees. Among the early members were: Charles Gilchrist, Edgar Lampson, Ambrose Silverthorn and family. The present officers are: H. C. Peck, presiding elder; John S. Ross, J. E. Wright, D. W. Herman and G. E. Smith, stewards; D. W. Herman and Elliott Whitman, local preachers; J. E. Wright, Benjamin Lancaster, David D. Remar, Luther Graves and Edgar C. Lampson, trustees; Elliott Whitman, class-leader; Prof. D. W. Herman, superintendent of the Sunday-school; Present membership eighty-six. Teachers and scholars in Sunday-school, two hundred and two. The church property is valued at five thousand dollars.

#### EPISCOPAL CHURCH.

The Protestant Episcopal church of Burr Oak was organized in February, 1865, and admitted into the convention in June of the year following. The constituted members were: Rev. Levi C. Corson, missionary; A. F. Schmidt and wife, William Morris, Mrs. Richard Patrick and Henry Noe. The first officers were: A. F. Schmidt, senior warden; William Morris, junior warden; Otto Corn, Eugene Smith, Albert Morris and Charles Betts, vestry. From the time of the organization until the erection of the chapel in 1868, the services were held in the Presbyterian church-edifice. The present number of communicant members is ten. Present pastor, Reverend Henry Safford.

#### ST. JOHANNES' (EVANGELICAL LUTHERAN) CHURCH

of Burr Oak and Colon township was organized March 3, 1864. The society purchased the school-house in the village of Burr Oak in 1869, for the purpose of holding meetings and keeping school. Subsequently, a pleasant parsonage was built. Under the care of Rev. A. Henkel, this church has more than doubled its members since 1869. The instruction in the school of the society is given in the German language in all the branches which are taught in the union-school. The number of scholars at present exceeds forty. The preaching is in the German language also, as well as the instruction in the Sunday-schools, the latter at present being attended by upwards of fifty scholars.

#### SOCIETIES.

Eagle Lodge, No. 124, A. F. M., was organized under dispensation in 1859, and chartered in 1861. The worshipful masters of the lodge have been : O. L. Cowles, 1859-63 and 1865; William Shane, 1864; J. H. Waterman, 1866; A. Bordnor, 1867-9 and 1872-4; J. H. Stillman, 1870; Ira M. Allen, 1871; N. G. Cooper, 1875-6. The lodge has ninety-one craftsmen enrolled.

Whitney Lodge, No. 142, I. O. O. F., was instituted in 1870.

#### BURR OAK LODGE, NO. 849, GOOD TEMPLARS,

was organized on the 29th of April, 1875, by electing the following officers: Miss Jennie Hoyt, W. C. T.; Mrs. W. W. Howe, W. V. T.; Miss Mary Atwell, W. S.; J. Clinton Bishop, W. T.; C. Atchison, W. F. S.; W. W. Howe, W. M.; Carl Green, W. I. G.; N. G. Cooper, W. O. G.; Mrs. Passmoore, W. R. H. S.; Mrs. Cowls, W. L. H. S.; Rev. J. Hoyt, W. C.; Charles Morris, W. A. S.; Mrs. J. C. Bishop, W. D. M. These ladies and gentlemen were, for the most part, re-elected in 1876-7. The present membership of the lodge is one hundred and seven. Its condition is generally flourishing.

#### BURR OAK GRANGE, NO. 303, PATRONS OF HUSBANDRY,

was organized March 5, 1874, with B. F. Sheldon, as master; D. Himebaugh, overseer; J. R. Wallace, lecturer; D. Gillett, secretary; E. Himebaugh, treasurer; Mrs. L. Faulks, Ceres; Mrs. E. L. Himebaugh, Pomona, and Mrs. F. Gillett, Flora. The grange now has ninety-five members, and meets in Grange Hall, in the village of Burr Oak.

The present officers are: A. N. Russell, master; S. H. Bryant, overseer; J. R. Wallace, lecturer; E. Himebaugh, treasurer; H. Hawley, secretary; Mrs. H. Hawley, Ceres; Mrs. C. C. Needham, Pomona; Mrs. J. R. Wallace, Flora.

**BURR OAK IN THE REBELLION**

was prompt and efficient. She sent a company under Captain, afterwards Colonel, Ira C. Abbott, of the First Michigan Infantry, into the field to participate in Secretary Seward's ninety days' campaign, who were engaged in the first battle of Bull Run, the survivors of which re-enlisted for three years, when the First Regiment was reorganized after that bloody engagement. From that time forward her citizens rallied to every call made upon the township, filling its quotas promptly. They filled every position in the service, from the private soldier to the general in command of the brigade, and the eagles hovered on the shoulders of Abbott at the head of the First.

Bennett at Missionary Ridge and Newberry at Chickamauga, in the fighting Eleventh, paid the sacrifice of gallant officers who led where brave men dared to follow. Her soldiers fell by scores in the face of the foe, defending the flag they had sworn to uphold; and their ashes now give new lustre and sweeter fragrance to the flowers of the sweet sunny south, beneath whose bright petals brave men are sleeping, alike unconscious of reveille and recall. The bugle's blare or the stirring drum is alike unheeded, for beneath the leaden hail of traitors in arms they sank to their rest, that freedom and the Union might live and be perpetuated. These heroic men of Burr Oak are here named, as we have gathered their names and their history from the official records.

**FIRST MICHIGAN INFANTRY (three months' men).**

Captain Ira C. Abbott, Company G; promoted to colonel of regiment.
Private E. A. Cross, Company G; taken prisoner at Bull Run.
Private Charles H. Palmer, Company G; taken prisoner at Bull Run.
Private John Steitz, Company G; taken prisoner at Bull Run.
Private J. N. Trask, Company G; taken prisoner at Bull Run.
Private Andrew Craig, Company G; taken prisoner at Bull Run.
Private Jonas N. Barker, Company G; taken prisoner at Bull Run.
Private A. N. Russell, Company G; taken prisoner at Bull Run.
Private John Archer, Company G; taken prisoner at Bull Run.
Private C. S. Trimm, Company G; taken prisoner at Bull Run.

**FIRST INFANTRY (reorganized three years).**

Captain Ira C. Abbott, Company B; captain August 12, 1861; major, April 28, 1862; lieutenant-colonel, August 30, 1862; colonel, March 8, 1863.
Sergeant John Stepper, Company B; second and first lieutenant; captain, and mustered-out.
Corporal George Beaumeister, Company B; killed at Bull Run, August 30, 1862.
Corporal Benjamin F. Dow, Company B.
Private Henry Green, Company B; re-enlisted veteran; discharged for disability.
Private Daniel Heinbach, Company B; discharged at expiration of service.
Private Joshua Hawkins, Company B; discharged at expiration of service.
Private Willis H. Kibbe, Company B; first lieutenant, and mustered-out.
Private William Lowry, Company B; discharged at expiration of service.
Private Henry Lowry, Company B; discharged for disability.
Private Charles W. Patchen, Company B; discharged at expiration of service.
Private Levi Webb, Company B; re-enlisted veteran; died February 7, 1865.
Private Caspar Gamby, Company C; mustered-out.
Private Elias G. Hill, Company C; killed near Poplar Grove church, Virginia.
Private John R. Hoagland, Company I; mustered-out.
Private Theodore Watson, Company I; mustered-out.

**THIRD INFANTRY.**

Private Joel B. Mills, Company E; mustered-out.

**FOURTH INFANTRY.**

Private Charles F. Carnes, Company C; discharged for disability.
Private Mahlon Fry, Company C.
Private Alonzo Kilmer, Company C; discharged at expiration of service.
Private Henry Low, Company C.
Private James Livingstone, Company C; discharged for disability.
Private Charles M. Scirvin, Company C; mustered-out.

**SIXTH INFANTRY.**

Private Willard G. Needham, Company C; died at Cherry Stone, Virginia, December, 1861.

**SEVENTH INFANTRY.**

Private Joseph M. Stowell, Company I; killed at Petersburg.
Captain John H. Waterman, Company K; resigned January 2, 1862.
Sergeant Marc Abbott, Company K; wounded at Fair Oaks and Glendale; discharged October 15, 1862.
Sergeant Lorenzo D. Culver, Company K; wounded at Fair Oaks; discharged November 2, 1862.
Sergeant Edwin R. Green, Company K; discharged for disability.
Corporal Wellington Churchill, Company K; killed at Glendale.
Corporal John Clingan, Company K; died at Falmouth, Virginia.
Corporal Giles F. Williams, Company K; killed at Antietam.
Private George W. Austin, Company K; died at Alexandria.
Private Emory R. Belote, Company K; re-enlisted veteran; wounded at Spottsylvania.
Private Daniel Booth, Company K; discharged for disability.
Private Joseph G. Booth, Company K; veteran reserve corps.
Private John R. Booth, Company K; re-enlisted veteran, February 8, 1864; killed at South Anna River, Virginia, June 1, 1864.
Private William J. Church, Company K; discharged for disability.
Private James M. Green, Company K; discharged at expiration of service.
Private Leonard C. Green, Company K; discharged from veteran reserve corps.
Private Harry Kilmer, Company K; discharged for disability.
Private Nathan Kinsey, Company K; wounded May 31, 1862, and killed June 3, 1862, at Glendale.
Private Frank Lang, Company K; re-enlisted veteran; mustered-out.
Private James McDaniels, Company K; discharged.
Private Allison A. Mills, Company K; killed at Glendale, June 30, 1862.
Private Duane A. Mills, Company K; killed at Glendale, June 30, 1862.
Private Adolphus Neitzkee, Company K; discharged June, 1862.
Private James Pepper, Company K; re-enlisted veteran; discharged.
Private James Pepper, Jr., Company K; wounded at Fair Oaks and Gettysburg, promoted to sergeant, and mustered-out.
Private Marcus D. Richards, Company K; mustered-out.
Private Benjamin F. Smiley, Company K; discharged for disability.
Private John H. Story, Company K; discharged at expiration of service.
Private Alvah E. Stowell, Company K; wounded at Antietam; discharged.
Private Joseph B. Stowell, Company K; discharged.
Private Addison Wheaton, Company K; killed in action, September 17, 1862.
Private Alonzo Wheaton, Company K; discharged for disability.
Private George W. Whitman, Company K; died June 1, 1862, of wounds received at Fair Oaks.
Private Oscar G. Williams, Company K; discharged.
Private Frank G. Shaw, Company K; died in Audersonville prison.
Private John Alexander, Company K; shot by rebel guard at Salisbury prison, North Carolina, and died of the wound November 22, 1864.
Private John W. Steadman, Company K; killed at Cold Harbor, Virginia, May 30, 1864.
Private Henry Livermore, Company K; died at Stevensburg, Virginia, March 19, 1864.
Private Chester Terrell, Company K; died in hospital, September 10, 1862.
Private James Bellman, Company K; mustered-out.
Private Nelson Tyler, Company K; re-enlisted veteran and promoted sergeant.
Private Horace Calhoun, Company K; killed at Glendale, Virginia, June 30, 1862.
Private Oliver Green, Company K; re-enlisted veteran, taken prisoner December 15, 1864, and died January 1, 1865, at Annapolis.
Private Reason Green, Company K; re-enlisted; died February 1, 1865.
Private Levi R. Tuttle, Company K; wounded at Gettysburg; discharged.

**ELEVENTH INFANTRY.**

Sergeant-major James M. Whallon; resigned.
Private Edwin F. Plant, Company K; mustered-out.
Private James Lancaster, Company B; died at Nashville.
Private Simeon B. Gilkenson, Company C; discharged at expiration of service.
Private Samuel Hibberlee, Company C; discharged for disability, and re-enlisted.
Private Thomas D. Harding, Company C; discharged for disability.
Private Carlos Plumb, Company D; died of small-pox, February 5, 1862.
Private Hiram Sanburn, Company C; died of small-pox, March 2, 1862.

Private Charles E. Pomeroy, Company C; died at Cleveland, Tennessee.
Private Stuben Filkins, Company C.
Private George C. Gilkerson, Company C.
Captain Benjamin G. Bennett, Company D; major, January 7, 1863; killed at Missionary Ridge.
First Lieutenant John R. Keeler, Company D; resigned.
Corporal James W. Farrand, Company D; discharged.
Private Clarence E. Bennett, Company D; discharged for disability.
Private Benjamin F. Bordner, Company D; discharged at expiration of service.
Private Henry Bordner, Company D; discharged.
Private David L. Byrnes, Company D; died of wounds at Stone River, January 2, 1863.
Private Charles W. Eggleston, Company D.
Private Irving J. Metcalf, Company D; discharged.
Private Reuben Powers, Company D; discharged at expiration of service.
Private William W. Trusell, Company D; veteran reserve corps.
Private Henry Twiford, Company D; discharged for disability.
Private William E. Cary, Company D; mustered-out.
Private Leonard C. Cross, Company D; mustered-out.
Second Lieutenant Charles W. Newberry, Company E; captain; killed at Chickamauga, September 20, 1864.
Private Henry Plumb, Company F.
Private John A. Green, Company F; died of wounds, July 14, 1864.
Private Daniel Masters, Company G; mustered-out.
Private Miltiades Thurston, Company F; mustered-out.

TWELFTH INFANTRY.

Private Calvin Cowles, Company F; mustered-out.
Private Edwin R. Green, Company F; died at Duvall's Bluff, Arkansas.
Private Charles F. Carnes, Company F; mustered-out.

THIRTEENTH INFANTRY.

Private George Gorham, Company H; mustered-out.
Private Hiram B. Wait, Company H; mustered-out.
Private Samuel C. Plank, Company H; mustered-out.

FIFTEENTH INFANTRY.

Captain John A. Waterman, Company A; resigned September 21, 1862.
Private Samuel Betz, Company A; discharged for disability.

Private Joseph Z. Carnes, Company A; re-enlisted, and mustered-out.
Private John Floro, Company A; re-enlisted, and mustered-out.
Private David Tyler, Company A; re-enlisted, and mustered-out.
Private Stephen Upham, Company A; discharged for disability.
Private Stephen Whitney, Company A; re-enlisted, and mustered-out.
Private Joseph Watson, Company A; discharged for disability.
Private Chester Ward, Company A; discharged for disability.
Private Artemas Ward, Company A; re-enlisted, and mustered-out.
Private Crosby C. Whitney, Company A; re-enlisted, and mustered-out.
Private Calvin Marvin, Company A; veteran reserve corps.
Private Thomas Faulks, Company A; mustered-out.
Private Andrew L. Hogaboom, Company K; mustered-out.

SEVENTEENTH INFANTRY.

Private Richard Waite, Company A.

NINETEENTH INFANTRY.

Private Truman Green, Company D; mustered-out.

THIRD CAVALRY.

Private Robert M. Böyles, Company M; mustered-out.

EIGHTH CAVALRY.

Private Edward G. Faulks, Company G; mustered-out.
Private Freeman L. Miller, Company H; mustered-out.

NINTH CAVALRY.

Private Charles R. Monroe, Company E; mustered-out.

ELEVENTH CAVALRY.

Private Andrew J. Pepper, Company A; mustered-out.
Private David O. Caldwell, Company A; mustered-out.
Private Leonard Caldwell, Company A; mustered-out.

FIRST LIGHT ARTILLERY.

Private Noah Kerns, Battery D; mustered-out.
Private Cyrus W. Parker, Battery F; mustered-out.

NINETEENTH INFANTRY.

Private William J. Leah, Company E; died at Camp Denison.

We are under obligations, and tender our acknowledgments therefor, to J. S. Kibbe, Esq., J. Clinton Bishop and Elizur Lancaster, of Burr Oak, and to Hon. Wales Adams, of Bronson, for valuable assistance rendered in the compilation of the history of Burr Oak.

---

# BIOGRAPHICAL SKETCHES.

## JOHN S. KIBBE.

In another part of this work may be found a view of the home of John S. Kibbe, accompanied by the portraits of himself and wife.

The family-record shows that the paternal grandfather was born in Massachusetts, and that he died in 1818; that he was the father of three sons and three daughters.

JASON, the second child, was born October 20, 1783, and in 1811 was married to Miss Polly Eddy; she was born January 25, 1790. The issue of this marriage was three sons,—John S., Charles E., and Chester J. Charles E. died at Burr Oak, Michigan, in 1863, and Chester J. died at the same place in 1872.

John S. the only survivor of the family, was born October 25, 1812, at York, Livingston county, New York; was brought up on a farm, attending the common schools, and assisting in the farm labor until he reached his majority. He afterwards attended the academy at Lima, and the Clinton Liberal Institute.

In 1838 he entered the gospel ministry as a Universalist preacher, and in the succeeding years he was settled in various places in the State of New

York. In 1845 he was united in marriage to Miss Jerusha A. Coe, of West Turin, New York. In 1857 he removed with his family to Burr Oak, Michigan. His father had been a resident of Burr Oak since 1839. Here he became engaged in farming and preaching. At his father's death, which occurred December 14, 1872, he succeeded to the old homestead. His mother's death occurred July 6, 1862.

Mr. Kibbe is the possessor of two hundred and seventy-five acres of fine farming lands, one-half mile west of the village of Burr Oak. He has five children: Emma M., Edgar T., Alice G., Charlotte A., and Arthur B.

Mr. Kibbe enjoys an enviable reputation as an honorable man, a Christian gentleman of irreproachable character; Republican in politics, of liberal religious views, a generous husband and father, a kind and affable neighbor. His wife, Mrs. Jerusha A. Kibbe, is a descendant of the Pilgrim Fathers. Her paternal grandfather, Nathan Coe, was the father of two children,—a son and daughter. Sanford, the son, was born in Lewis county, New York, and he and his wife are still living on the same farm on which he was born. He was the father of Jerusha A., Nathan S., and Martin V. B., of whom Jerusha A. is the only surviving child. She was married at the age of twenty-four.

MR. SIDNEY CARPENTER.

MRS. SIDNEY CARPENTER.

## SIDNEY CARPENTER.

Among the many prominent men and pioneers whose portraits and biographies grace the pages of this book, none is more worthy of note than the subject of our sketch. Sidney Carpenter was born in Worcester county, Massachusetts, April 27, 1810. At the early age of ten he was put out to work on the farm summers, and attend school winters; at the age of fourteen went to Cattaraugus county, New York, to live with his brother-in-law till he should come of age; attended school winters, and worked on the farm summers.

The winter before he was twenty-one he taught school in his own district, and the following winter taught school in Lindon, and the following spring went down the Allegheny and Ohio rivers to Cincinnati with a load of lumber and shingles.

In 1833 was united in marriage to Miss Eunice Brown, and they carried on farming, on land purchased of the Holland Land Company.

Three years afterward, that company having sold out to the Devereux company of Utica, New York, this company immediately raised the price of said land. Mr. Carpenter sold out his improvements and emigrated to St. Joseph county, Michigan, in the fall of 1836, and settled on northwest quar-

ter of section twenty, town of Burr Oak. The following year he purchased eighty acres on section seventeen. During the winters of 1837 and 1838 Mr. Carpenter taught his district-school.

In 1850 he was married to his present wife, Miss Amanda Jane Worden, and to-day owns one of the productive farms of Burr Oak township.

From the very first Mr. Carpenter has been intimately connected with the political and material interests of his town, and from that time up to the present has held nearly all of its offices, and was a very efficient officer, and had as much influence in the board of supervisors as any other man in it.

His first vote was cast for General Jackson in 1832; in 1840 he voted for General Harrison, and from that time till 1865 he affiliated with the Whigs and Republicans, since then with the Democratic party.

Mr. Carpenter is a kind father, an affectionate husband and a good citizen. He seems to enjoy life, and is surrounded with all the comforts of a happy home.

HON. WILLIAM MORRIS,

son of William P. and Nellie Morris, was born in Surrey, England, September 25, 1804. While young he enjoyed fair advantages for education, which he improved. His principal business was farming. In 1823, he, in company with his parents and the family of eight children, emigrated to America and settled in New York city. Of the family, five of the children are still living. His father lived to be nearly ninety years of age and his mother died at the age of sixty. In 1834 he emigrated to Michigan and settled on Sturgis prairie, and remained there till the spring of 1852, then removed into the town of Burr Oak, and settled on the farm he now owns.

While Mr. Morris was living in New York he was engaged as a carpenter and joiner, and for some time a peddler of milk in the city; since coming west he has followed his trade while in Sturgis, and since coming to Burr Oak has followed farming. Mr. Morris possesses some four hundred acres of good land.

He has held various positions of trust and honor since coming to St. Joseph county. In 1842 was elected justice of the peace, which position he filled for several years; was postmaster in Sturgis from 1845 to 1840. In 1847 was chosen by the Democratic party to represent them in the legislature. Since coming to Burr Oak has served as justice of the peace four years, and supervisor for two terms, 1853 and 1854.

Mr. Morris was married to Miss Marcia M. St. John, of Chautauqua county, New York, December 30, 1840; she was born March 11, 1825. As a result of this union thirteen children have been born to them, nine of whom still live.

## WILLIAM CLARK.

William Clark was born in Farmington, Ontario county, New York, December 29, 1805, and was married to Margaret Whitney December 31, 1826. They had two children, both daughters, one of whom died in infancy. His wife died August 15, 1837. Mr. Clark married Sarah Mills February 9, 1841, and removed to Burr Oak, Michigan, and settled upon section fifteen in said township upon land which he had previously entered from the United States government, where he lived until the year 1865, when he sold his farm and removed to Eaton Rapids, Michigan, where he died June 19, 1874. He was converted in early life, and united with the Baptist church, of which he was ever after a consistent member. He was a man of strict integrity and honor, making it a rule to always fulfil promptly all engagements. In politics Mr. Clark was a Democrat till the formation of the Republican party, of which he was a member during life. He was elected township clerk of Burr Oak in 1843, which office he held several successive years. His widow and surviving daughter, the latter the wife of J. C. Bishop, of Burr Oak, still survive.

## JAMES L. BISHOP

was born in Lisbon, Connecticut, January 17, 1799. His parents were Samuel Bishop and Lucy Lord Bishop. His mother died when he was ten years of age, leaving five children. When at the age of fifteen, his father removed to the Genesee country, and settled at Attica, now Wyoming county, New York. In 1820 he went to Cattaraugus county, New York, which was then new, where he taught school, cleared land, etc., till 1826, when he was married to Mary Carpenter, who was born in Massachusetts August 5, 1799. He joined the Masonic fraternity about this time, to which he was a firm adherent during life. In 1829, at the age of thirty, he united with the Presbyterian church, and soon after was chosen ruling elder. In 1836 he, with his family, removed to St. Joseph county, Michigan, and settled in what is now the township of Burr Oak (then Sherman), and bought one hundred and sixty acres of land, which he cleared up, and upon which he lived till his death, December 13, 1859.

Soon after coming to Michigan he, with his wife, united with the Presbyterian church at Sturgis, which then consisted of nine members, and was soon after chosen ruling-elder, clerk, and was also Sabbath-school superintendent. In 1856 he and his wife helped to organize and became members of the First Presbyterian church in the village of Burr Oak, and both remained members till death.

Mr. Bishop was ever a strong advocate of religion, temperance, and education, always earnest in encouraging what he believed to be right, and discouraging what he thought was wrong; was kind in his family, and a good neighbor. In politics in his early manhood he was a Democrat, but upon the organization of the old Liberty party he was one of the first to join its ranks, always believing in equal rights to "all men," and still later was an active member of the Republican party from its formation till his death.

He held the office of justice of the peace several years in New York before he removed to Michigan, and when the township of Burr Oak was organized in 1838 he was elected township clerk, and kept the first records of the town. He afterwards held the offices of school inspector, justice of the peace, and supervisor, the latter office for several years. They had a family of eight children; two died young. Three sons died in the prime of early manhood in defense of their country. The widow survived her husband several years, and died the 4th of April, 1875. Three children,—J. C. Bishop, Mrs. Mary A. Johnson, of Burr Oak, and Mrs. Lucy L. Rowly, of Sturgis,—still survive.

# SHERMAN.

As originally constituted, November 5, 1829, the township of Sherman,—so named in honor of Colonel Benjamin Sherman, a pioneer of the county,—included the present townships of Sherman, Sturgis, Fawn River, Burr Oak, Nottawa, and Colon. In 1830 Nottawa and Colon were organized into a separate township, and in 1838 Burr Oak and Fawn River were set off into separate sovereignties, Sturgis following suit in 1845; reducing the once large territory to its present proportions, to wit: thirty-six square miles, including twenty-three thousand one hundred and seven acres, of which one thousand two hundred and twenty-five are water-surface. The township is at present known on the maps of the surveys of public lands of the United States as township seven, south of range ten west.

The township is watered by seven lakes,—Fish, Chapin, Thompson's, Middle, Johnson's, Crotch, and Crossman,—the last-named five of which are scattered in the south and southeast part of the township. Fish lake lies on section nine, and Chapin on sections eleven and fourteen. Hog creek deigns to cross the extreme northeast corner of the township, scarcely wetting anything but the northeast quarter of section one.

### DERIVATION OF NAMES OF LAKES IN SHERMAN TOWNSHIP.

Chapin lake was named after David Chapin, an old settler on its banks.

Crossman lake, from Abel Crossman, who settled on a farm in its vicinity, at an early day (about 1840).

Thompson's lake, from Elijah Thompson, who settled near it many years ago. Johnson's lake, from the fact of his settlement near it.

Fish lake, from the dual cause of its shape, and the abundance of the finny tribe it contains.

Crotch lake, from its peculiar crotch-like shape.

Middle lake, from its lying between Klinger's lake in White Pigeon township, and Thompson's lake in Sherman.

### TOPOGRAPHY.

Sherman township consisted principally of oak-openings, with a small extent of prairie land. Its surface is generally rolling, in some parts hilly. The soil is a rich clay loam, intermixed with sand and sandy loam. It is well adapted to wheat, corn, and clover, and is particularly productive of fruits, especially apples and peaches. Peppermint is a staple production of the township, many acres being annually cultivated.

### EARLY SETTLERS.

The first permanent white settler who took up his habitation within the present limits of the township of Sherman was Thomas Cade, Sr., a native of Yorkton, a small village about ten miles from the city of Hull, Yorkshire, England.

He arrived at the site of his future home on section thirty-six, in July, 1830, and proceeded at once to erect a log-house. He first went into the woods and selected some choice white-oak timber, with which he built, perhaps, the largest and best log-house ever before erected in St. Joseph county. It cost him just one hundred dollars in gold, no inconsiderable sum in those days. He entered five eighty-acre lots, or just five-eighths of the entire section (thirty-six).

In the fall of 1830 he planted twenty acres of wheat, having broken up the first farm in the township between the months of August and October of the same year.

Mr. Cade's family, on his arrival in the new settlement, consisted of his wife, four sons,—Thomas, Joseph, Samuel and Stephen W.,—and one daughter, Mary.

Stephen W. Cade now resides on part of the old homestead; Mr. Cade is still living at Sturgis, within sight of the four hundred acres he entered nearly a half-century ago. At the advanced age of ninety-one years he used to have to go to White Pigeon for groceries. Mr. S. W. Cade tells how his mother used to ride there on a pony, with himself behind her.

### OTHER EARLY SETTLERS.

Among those who came in immediately after Mr. Cade were: David Petty and wife, who settled on section thirty-six in the early part of the year 1831; a man by the name of Johnson, an old bachelor, who settled on section thirty-five the same year. Andrew and Benjamin Perrin settled on parts of sections fourteen and fifteen in 1835; Adonijah Foot and David Chapin settled on section ten during the same year.

Another of the early settlers was Mrs. John Gifford, who came to Sherman in 1838. She and her husband and family settled in Farmington, Oakland county, in 1827, going from thence to Adrian, Lenawee county, in 1828, where they kept a boarding-house for the workmen engaged in building the first saw-mill in that place, for Darius Comstock.

On the 17th day of July, the very day of their arrival, Mrs. Gifford prepared dinner for thirteen men, serving the same under a tree in lieu of a more sheltered spot. This was the first meal of victuals ever prepared by a white woman in Adrian, and the Gifford's cabin was the first house built therein, in 1828.

Mrs. Gifford after the death of her husband, came to Sherman and removed from thence to Sand lake in Nottawa.

### THE FIRST FARM OPENED

in the township was that of Thomas Cade, Sr., in 1830-31. The first lands were entered at the general land-office, in 1830, and were as follows: The southeast quarter of section thirty-five, William Johnston, of Scotland, June 7; the southwest quarter of section thirty-six, by Robert Storr, of England, July 15; the southwest quarter of section thirty-six, by Thomas Cade, of England, July 15; the west half of the northwest quarter of section thirty-six, by David Petty, of England, September 27, 1830. There were but four entries made the succeeding year.

In 1876 there were assessed for taxation in the township twenty-one thousand eight hundred and thirty-six acres of land, valued by H. C. Hopkins, the supervisor of the township, at two hundred and ninety-four thousand nine hundred and forty dollars, about one quarter of its real value. The assessment of property in the township as originally constituted in 1830, cannot be definitely ascertained, but the taxes of that year were thirty-five dollars for township purposes, and the just proportion of fifty dollars levied on the whole county for its uses. In 1852 the assessment of the township footed up thirty thousand nine hundred and fifty dollars on real-estate, and six thousand nine hundred and ninety dollars on personal property, and the taxes were, for State and county purposes, three hundred and sixty-five dollars and twenty-two cents, and for township purposes, including schools, three hundred and twenty-eight dollars and fifteen cents. In 1876 the assessment, as equalized by the county board of supervisors, was fixed at two hundred and forty-eight thousand five hundred and forty-three dollars on lands, and thirty-eight thousand five hundred dollars on personal property, making a total of two hundred and eighty-seven thousand and forty-three dollars, on which taxes were levied as follows: State and county purposes, one-half to each, one thousand four hundred and sixty-six dollars and thirty-four cents; and township purposes, including schools, three thousand nine hundred and seventeen dollars and four cents, an aggregate of five thousand three hundred and eighty-three dollars and thirty-eight cents.

There were harvested in 1875, thirty-six thousand five hundred and twenty bushels of wheat, from two thousand two hundred and eighty-nine acres sown; fifty two thousand six hundred and forty bushels of corn, from one thousand nine hundred and eighty-six acres planted; and also five thousand three hundred and thirty bushels of other grain, eleven thousand five hundred dred and seventy bushels of potatoes, eight hundred and eighty-three tons of hay, five thousand two hundred and fifty-nine pounds of wool, one hundred and eighty-four thousand five hundred and thirty-eight pounds of pork, forty-nine thousand six hundred and ten pounds of butter and cheese, six thousand one hundred and eighty pounds of dried fruit, and five hundred barrels of cider made. Four hundred and thirty-six acres in orchards and gardens produced twelve thousand seven hundred and ninety bushels of apples and sixty-one bushels of other fruit, valued at four thousand one hundred and seven dollars. There were owned in the township in 1874, four hundred and ninety horses, fifteen mules, four hundred and seventy cows, two hundred and ninety-nine head of other cattle, eight hundred and nine hogs and one thousand one hundred and fifty-five sheep.

One flour-mill and one grist-mill were in operation in the township in the year 1873, employing two persons and a capital of three thousand dollars, and produced four thousand barrels of flour and ninety thousand feet of lumber, valued at seven thousand three hundred and fifty dollars.

### THE CULTIVATION OF MINT

was first introduced into Sherman, in 1846–47, by Eric Jones, who settled in the township in 1838, coming thereto from the State of New York. His son, Charles W., now a resident, is the heaviest distiller, and has been in former years the chief and only buyer of the entire crop in the township. The roots of peppermint were first brought from a farm owned at that date, by William Jones, now of Centreville, and planted on the location of Mr. Eric Jones, which has been his residence since 1838, till his decease a short time since. The first peppermint-distillery in the township was built by Mr. Jones, two years later, 1848–49, and which has been the leading one therein from that time to the present. Mr. Jones and his son Charles W., have distilled in this distillery, from one to two thousand pounds of oil per year, for twenty years past. The crop of 1876 was about five thousand pounds. There are some seven or eight distilleries in the township.

### THE FIRST TOWNSHIP MEETING

was held at the house of John B. Clarke, in the village of Sherman, (now Sturgis), in April, 1830, Amos Howe being the moderator.

We quote the subjoined extract from the "township minutes," for the year 1841, as being explanatory of the reason why we are debarred from giving a complete list of the township officers from the organization of the township to the present, as is our custom:

"Also the clerk was then ordered to record the names of those persons who were elected on the 5th day of April, a.d. 1841, at the annual town-meeting held at the house of Betsy Douglass, in West Sherman, as township officers for the present year of 1841, there being no records of said township-meeting, in consequence of the loss of said records by fire, they having been destroyed on the night of the 7th day of May, 1841."

The supervisors have been as follows: John Sturgis, 1830; Jason Thurston, 1831–33; John Parker, 1834–41; Philip H. Buck, William Henry, Harry H. Breese, Levi E. Thompson, Salathiel C. Coffinbury, George Buck, George Keech, George W. Warren, David Oakes, Stephen W. Cade (seven years), Samuel Tyler, Beers Wilson, D. C. Gee, Samuel Tyler, H. C. Hopkins (five years), present incumbent.

Clerks—William Fletcher, 1830; John Parker, 1831–33; Philip N. Buck, 1834–36; Levi Holmes, 1841; J. G. Waite, Jeremiah H. Jones, Theodore A. Jones, Erastus Chapin, S. W. P. Hadden, George Taylor, George W. Warren, Thomas Wing, George W. Richards, A. C. Van Vleck, N. H. Gurney, Henry W. Pearsall, James Douglass, Thomas Perrin, Josiah Metzgar, John A. Bancker, James H. Fonda, Gaston Everett, J. A. P. Mason (three years), present incumbent.

John Sturgis, Amos Howe and William Hazzard were the first highway commissioners, 1830.

Justices of the Peace—James Rolfe, 1836 (six years), Andrew Perrin, Harry H. Breese (twelve years), Levi E. Thompson, Wilson D. Oviatt, Nathan H. Gurney (eight years), S. S. Johnson, George Keech (fourteen years), George Buck, Erastus Chapin, S. C. Coffinbury, David Oakes (eight years), Stephen W. Cade, A. C. Van Vleck (six years), John H. Millard, Joseph A. Millard, Daniel N. Thompson, Darius Gee (eight years), Gilson Everton, Harvey Avery, Thomas Wing, Floris Bancker, Warren Palmer, Joseph Weber, Julius E. Fenn, William T. North, James M. White, Josiah Metzgar, Theron Wilson (three years), John A. Bancker, Beers Wilson, Reuben J. Miller, John Kasdorf, Joseph Sweetland (three years), present incumbent. Philip H. Buck was elected a justice of the peace in 1837, and held his office in the village of Sturgis until that township was set off in 1845, and was the leading justice of his day in the township. In 1838 he had two hundred and sixty-three cases on his docket. His first suit, dated November 10, 1837, was one of Isaac Tyler vs. Elisha Bennett, which was called for trial November 20, and judgment entered by confession for thirty-four dollars and forty-four cents damages, and one dollar and seventy-seven and a half cents costs, on which execution was issued January 22, 1838, to C. H. Knox, deputy sheriff, and returned satisfied, with the plaintiff's receipt fully endorsed thereon April 6, 1838. Oliver Raymond and Hiram Humphrey were appointed justices by Governor Porter April 17, 1833, for Sherman township.

### THE FIRST ROAD LAID OUT

in the township was one ordered by the highway commissioners in 1830, from the Indiana line running north through Oxbow and Sturgis prairies to the

north line of township six, range ten, now Nottawa. This route was subsequently adopted by the commissioners for the territorial road from the same point to Grand Rapids, which was surveyed in 1833. Robert Clark, Jr., surveyed the first-named road, and received six dollars therefor, the road being over fifteen miles in length. On January 18, 1831, the town authorities granted a license to Benjamin Sherman to keep a tavern on this road.

### A POST-OFFICE

was established in the northeast part of the township in 1837, Julius A. Thompson being the first postmaster.

### A SIGNAL STATION

of the United States signal service has been established on the highest hill in Sherman for two or more years, and dispatches are sent daily to "Old Prob." of the state of the weather in that "neck o' woods," which help to swell the average from which the prognostications of the weather-bureau are made.

### RAILROAD.

The Grand Rapids and Indiana railroad, which traverses Sherman township north and south, was constructed in 1870. There is a small building, which the company substituted for a depot, on the farm of Amos Perrin, who gave the right of way through his premises, with the understanding that a respectable depot should be erected.

### FIRST FRAME HOUSE.

The first frame house erected in Sherman township was built by Thomas Cade on the present site of the residence of his son, Stephen W. Cade, in 1836.

### FIRST SAW-MILL

was erected in 1860 by David P. Robinson. It is located on section twenty-eight, and adjoins Mr. Robinson's farm of ninety-eight acres on the same section.

### FIRST GRIST-MILL

was also built by D. P. Robinson, and started in 1871. It is exclusively used for custom work. It is now owned by his son, Reuben Robinson.

### FIRST MARRIAGE.

The first marriage in Sherman township was that of William Stewart, Jr., to Mary Cade, in the fall of 1831. They removed to Madison, Wisconsin, immediately after getting married, and afterwards to Chicago, where Mrs. Stewart died in 1838.

### FIRST BIRTH.

was William, son of David and Fanny Petty, in 1833. He died quite young.

### FIRST DEATH.

of which we can glean any definite information was that of William Leonard, who died in 1838.

### THE FIRST BURYING-GROUND

was the one now in Sherman, which was used as a family burying-place as early as 1833, although not regularly surveyed and laid out as a cemetery until 1839. It was surveyed by John Kumer. The first interment in it was a Mr. Johnson, an early settler, who lived on the shore of the lake which now bears his name.

### FIRST PREACHER.

The first preaching in the township (and Sturgis) was in private houses by Rev. Christopher Corey, of the Presbyterian persuasion. Meetings were frequently held at the residence of George Buck.

### EDUCATIONAL.

The first school-house erected in Sherman township was in the present district number one. It was first taught by Harriet Foot in 1843, she having thirteen scholars and receiving thirteen dollars for her work.

The following records show the first division into school districts of the township of Sherman, as divided and numbered on the 29th day of May, 1841:

"District number one shall contain sections numbers eighteen, seventeen, seven, eight, six, five, and the west half of sections number four, nine, sixteen, in township eight, south of range ten west. Also, the southeast quarter of the southeast quarter, and the north half of the southeast quarter, and the east half of the southwest quarter of section thirty-two.

"District number two shall contain sections two, three, ten, eleven and the north half of section fifteen and the east half of sections four and nine, and the northeast quarter of section sixteen.

"District number three shall contain sections one and twelve in township eight, south of range ten west, and also the west half of section number six, township eight, south of range nine west.

24

"District number four shall contain sections thirteen, fourteen and the south half of section fifteen, and the southeast quarter of section sixteen, and the northeast quarter of section twenty-one, and the north half of sections twenty-two, twenty-three and twenty-four.

"District number five shall contain sections twenty-four, twenty-five, thirty-six and the northeast quarter of section twenty-six, in township seven, south of range ten west; also, sections nineteen, twenty, twenty-nine, thirty, thirty-one and the north half of the northeast quarter of section thirty-two, in the township of Burr Oak."

In 1876 there were four hundred and fifteen children of the requisite school-age—between five and twenty years—three hundred and twenty of whom attended the different schools taught in the township, eight in number, in as many school-houses, two being built of brick, and six of wood, and valued at six thousand one hundred and seventy-five dollars, and affording four hundred and seven sittings. The schools were in session an average of eight months during the year ending September 1, 1876, and cost two thousand four hundred and sixty-three dollars and forty-six cents, including three hundred and ninety dollars paid three male teachers, and one thousand three hundred and forty-four dollars to fifteen females. There are no graded schools in the township.

### TRAGEDIES.

In 1840 the suicidal mania first presented itself in Sherman township, since which time several have "shuffled off this mortal coil" by their own hands. The first instance was that of Babe Wells, who hung himself in a barn on the bank of Thompson's lake, section twenty-eight, in the above year.

John Carl hung himself in his barn on section twenty-one, in 1872. Mental derangement, superinduced by an excessive use of alcoholic stimulants, was the cause in both of the above cases.

In 1871 Florie Bancker, an old and highly respected farmer, committed suicide by poisoning. Domestic trouble was the incentive to the rash act.

On September 30, 1850, John Dice was found dead near a stump in a field. The justice's inquest showed that copious hemorrhage of the lungs led to his untimely death.

### POPULATION.

In 1838 the population of Sherman, which then included Sturgis only, numbered one thousand and forty-three souls. In 1850, in the present area of the township, there were three hundred and sixty-four people. In 1860 there were eight hundred and sixty-seven inhabitants, two of them "American citizens of African descent." In 1870 these people had increased to one thousand one hundred and sixty, comprising two hundred and thirty-seven families dwelling in as many houses,—five hundred and ninety-one of them (the people) being males, and five hundred and sixty-nine females. In 1874 the State census showed one thousand two hundred and fifteen inhabitants, of whom six hundred and six were males, and six hundred and nine of the opposite sex. Of two hundred and ninety-seven males over twenty-one years, one hundred and eighty-four were subject to military duty, and one hundred and thirteen exempted,—three of the latter being over seventy-five years of age, but less than ninety. Of three hundred and six females over eighteen years, one hundred and seventy-three were under forty years, and one hundred and thirty-three over that age,—three of the latter being over seventy-five years. There were three hundred and nine boys under twenty-one years, and three hundred and three girls under eighteen years.

### THE POLITICAL BIAS

of the public sentiment of the people will be readily seen by the following exhibit of the tally-lists of the presidential elections held in the township: In 1840 the Whigs voted one hundred ballots for "Tippecanoe and Tyler too," beating "Little Van" by forty-eight majority. In 1844 the party gave Harry Clay ("the Mill-boy of the Slashes") one hundred and three votes, the Democrats gave Polk and Dallas fifty-eight, and the Liberty men numbered five. In 1848, when Sherman was left to herself, she gave "Old Zach" twenty-five votes, Governor Cass thirty-two, and Van Buren, the Free-soiler, nine. In 1852 her people paired on the leading candidates, giving thirty-two to each,—the Abolitionists holding the balance of power with ten votes. In 1856 the Republicans drew to their candidate, "the Pathfinder," one hundred and three supporters, while the Sage of Wheatland had but thirty-three faithful followers. In 1860 the Republicans gave "Old Abe" one hundred and twenty-nine, and the "Little Giant" received fifty-three votes. In 1864 the Republican and Democratic votes were one hundred and thirteen and forty-four respectively. In 1868 the same votes stood one hundred and fifty-five and ninety-five, and in 1872 they were one hundred and four and sixty-seven. In 1876 Mr. Hayes received one hundred votes, Mr. Tilden one hundred and forty-two, and Mr. Cooper twelve.

This last vote would indicate a population of one thousand two hundred and seventy.

### SHERMAN IN THE REBELLION,

in proportion to her population, bore as conspicuous and honorable a part as any of her sister-towns. Her quotas were filled as promptly, and with as good material, and she has just cause for pride in the conduct of her heroic citizens. We here give a list of those who "rallied round the flag" once and again, as often as the calls were made, from the first seventy-five thousand to put down the rebellion in thirty days, to the last five hundred thousand men at the end of four years of bloody and relentless fratricidal strife.

**FOURTH REGIMENT MICHIGAN INFANTRY.**

Private William Cherry, Company C; discharged for disability.
Private James Persons, Company C; mustered-out; deceased.

**SIXTH INFANTRY.**

Corporal James G. Oakes, Company C; re-enlisted, and mustered-out.
Private Lewis Bawker, Company C; mustered-out.

**TENTH INFANTRY.**

Private Zenas H. Underwood, Company A; mustered-out.
Private Alonzo West, Company A; mustered-out.

**ELEVENTH INFANTRY.**

Private Royal M. Carlisle, Company A; died at Bardstown, Kentucky, January 2, 1862.
Private George W. Wetmore, Company B; mustered-out.
Private Charles V. Forbes, Company B; discharged at expiration of service.
Private Jerome Morehouse, Company B; discharged at expiration of service.
Private Eugene P. Willard, Company C; discharged at expiration of service.
Private Edward P. Willard, Company C; discharged at expiration of service.
Private W. H. Fress, Company E; mustered-out.
Private Peter Fress, Company E; mustered-out.
Private Robert H. Ives, Company E; mustered-out.
Private Reuben Walls, Company E; mustered-out.
Private Stephen Gilkerson, Company G; mustered-out.

**TWELFTH INFANTRY.**

Private Lewis H. Sackett, Company E; accidentally killed, at Duvall's Bluff, Arkansas.
Private John Rommell, Company E; mustered-out.

**THIRTEENTH INFANTRY.**

Private Stephen Cherry, Company B; died October 31, 1862.
Private Moses L. Jordan, Company B; mustered-out.
Private Ira S. Nickerson, Company D; discharged for disability.
Private Marcus Daniels, Company F; mustered-out.

**NINETEENTH INFANTRY.**

Private Julius N. Carlisle, Company D; veteran reserve corps, and mustered-out.
Private Isaac Driese, Company D; mustered-out.
Private Charles La Clear, Company D; killed at Chattanooga.
Private William G. Oakes, Company D; mustered-out.
Private Albert C. Wilson, Company D; mustered-out.
Private H. Hackstaff, Company E; mustered-out.
Private Moses Hibberlee, Company E; mustered-out.
Private Robert H. Hermance, Company E; discharged.
Private James Robertson, Company E; killed at Thompson's Station, Tennessee, March 24, 1863.
Private Washington Sprague, Company E; mustered-out.
Private James K. Sackett, Company E; mustered-out.

**NINTH CAVALRY.**

Private Purdy Hoard, Company E; died at Detroit, August 19, 1863.
Private Samuel Hibberlee, Company E; mustered-out.

**ELEVENTH CAVALRY.**

Private James A. Nickerson, Company I; mustered-out.

**FIRST LIGHT ARTILLERY.**

Private Michael Helwig, Battery F; mustered-out.

**FIRST UNITED STATES SHARP-SHOOTERS.**

Private Martin L. Wetmore, Company I; killed at Chancellorsville.
Private Reuben Walls, Company I; mustered-out.

**PROVOST GUARD.**

Private Myron Ingersoll; mustered-out.

S. W. CADE.

MRS. S. W. CADE.

RESIDENCE OF S. W. CADE, SHERMAN TP. ST. JOSEPH, CO. MICH.

The foregoing names are all we have been able to locate in Sherman, but would refer the reader to the other township histories, especially those of Sturgis, Burr Oak and Nottawa, where names of men properly belonging to Sherman may possibly be found.

We are under obligations, and tender our thanks therefor, to Dr. Ira Packard, of Sturgis, Stephen W. Cade, H. C. Hopkins and Mr. Bureb, of Sherman, for information given and assistance rendered in the compilation of the history of Sherman.

# BIOGRAPHICAL SKETCH.

### STEPHEN W. CADE.

Stephen W., son of Thomas and Elizabeth Cade, was born in Yorkshire, England, April 7, 1826. He emigrated to America with his parents in 1830, and came directly to the farm on which he now resides. There they erected their hewn-log-house, in which the first festivities in all that settlement were held, on the occasion of the marriage of his sister Mary in W. W. Stewart, when a good old-fashioned dance was indulged in, and the lively tune and the merry song were heard echoing in the neighboring forest.

Thomas Cade, the father of the subject of this sketch, still survives, being in his ninety-third year, and resides in Sturgis. He raised a family of five children, who were all more or less identified with the history of the neighborhood in which they first settled : MARY, who consummated the first marriage in Sherman township ; THOMAS, who now resides in Wisconsin ; JOSEPH, now a well-to-do resident of Sherman ; SAMUEL, who died June 3, 1876, in Indiana ; and he of whom we write, now residing within a few rods of where he arrived an infant nearly half a century ago. He received a limited education at the public-schools of Sturgis, attending them in the winter, and working on the farm during the summer months. He has followed agricultural pursuits all his life, and is generally considered a good practical farmer.

December 25, 1849, he married Phebe M., daughter of Charles Adams, a native of Cattaraugus county, New York, and for many years a much respected citizen of Burr Oak township, this county, where he settled in 1843. This union has been blessed with two children, namely :

ADELINE E., born November 1, 1851 ; married Edward S. Murdock, April 15, 1874.

CHARLES E., born December 7, 1874 ; married Miss Dillie Sturgis, August 10, 1876.

Mr. Cade has always taken a commendable interest in the affairs of his township, and has accomplished much towards its development and prosperity.

In 1862 he was elected supervisor, which office he filled satisfactorily during the greater part of the war. He also lent much of his time in assisting the cause of the government, by acting as a recruiter, at which he was eminently successful in helping to fill the quota of the township at various times. He also gave liberally of his means, having donated at different periods nearly one thousand dollars.

He was a justice of the peace seven years, and cheerfully converted a room in his house into a justice's court, thereby imperilling the furniture of said room, for the motley crowds that generally attend the trials before a justice, will smoke, you know, and consequently must expectorate, regardless of the consequences to carpets, etc. But this, and more in the cause of justice.

He also furnished a fair criterion of his enterprise by purchasing largely of the bonds of the railroad, which cannot be considered as a paying investment, at least to him. But if it assisted in the prosperity of the town, he is satisfied,—though minus the collateral that said bonds were supposed to represent.

It politics Mr. Cade is a Republican ; in religion a Methodist. He is genial and pleasant in manners ; an enterprising and intelligent farmer, and a good citizen. (See portrait and illustration.)

# FLOWERFIELD.

THE township of Flowerfield had but a single white inhabitant when it was first organized, or at least but a single family, Mishael Beadle, and then its territory was four times the area of the present township, comprising the four northern townships of St. Joseph county in November, 1829.

### ITS PRESENT AREA

includes twenty-two thousand six hundred and seventy-six acres of land, and about thirty-five acres of water-surface.

### ITS DRAINAGE

is effected principally by the Rocky river, which, rising in the township of Penn, Cass county, enters the township of Flowerfield on the east line of section nineteen, running eastward through sections nineteen, twenty, twenty-one and twenty-two, southwesterly through section twenty-three, and southerly through sections twenty-five and thirty-six, and passes out of the township at its south line. The north branch of the Rocky rises near the village of Flowerfield, and runs southerly through sections one, twelve, thirteen and twenty-four, entering the main stream on the south line of the last-named section. A little creek runs north through sections thirty-five and twenty-six, and empties into the Rocky near the north line of section twenty-six.

### TOPOGRAPHICAL AND DESCRIPTIVE.

Flowerfield originally consisted of what was known among the early settlers as "oak-openings," and "timbered lands." The southern and eastern portions of the township were of the former description, the northern and western parts of the latter. The central and southwestern parts of the township are hilly, and in some places also very stony. The rest of the township is level and slightly undulating. The soil is generally of a good sandy loam, and admirably adapted to the purposes of agriculture.

As indicated by its name, Flowerfield, the township oftentimes, in the days of its earlier settlement, presented a lovely appearance. Every fall the Indians were accustomed to burn the superfluous brush and scrub timber, and in the spring an abundance of wild flowers sprang up; hence the early surveyors gave the township and surrounding country the present name, which, on the erection of the township in 1829, was conferred upon it exclusively.

### EARLY SETTLERS.

The first white settler who took up a permanent residence in Flowerfield was Mishael Beadle, who settled near where the village of Flowerfield now stands, in 1829. He came from the State of Ohio, accompanied by his family. The year following James Valentine, Henry Whited and Henry Garver, also from Ohio. In 1831 Mr. John Nichols, William Mead and

Challenge S. Wheeler came in, followed, in 1832, by Aaron H. Foot and Robert Gill. All these, except Mead, came from the State of New York. The only one of these old pioneers now remaining is M. John Nichols, who, enjoying an excellent memory, has become a walking cyclopædia of historical information concerning local events.

An interesting episode in the history of one of the above-named pioneers, Robert Gill, is related by one who knows him well. Mr. Gill came from Canada as a British soldier in 1812. Not liking the principles involved in the struggle, he quietly moved to the State of New York, where he remained until 1832. He married a German woman of the Mohawk settlement, Naomi Angle by name, and with her removed to Flowerfield and first settled on the present site of Howardsville, and afterwards on the west half of the southwest quarter of section twenty-six. Their children were Jane, Eleanor, Eliza, John and William, the latter of whom now occupies the old homestead. He married Christiana Weinberg, a daughter of one of the earliest German settlers in the township. Robert Gill died in 1870 in the seventy-seventh year of his age.

H. Spaulding was also an early settler—the oldest now living—who settled in this part of the township. He came in with his wife and family in 1841, from Madison county, New York. He took up his permanent residence on section twenty-six, where he has lived for more than thirty years. In 1836 Horatio N. Monroe entered the southeast quarter of section twenty-six, but no evidence exists that he ever settled on it. R. F. Breese purchased it of him in 1858, while a resident of Kalamazoo. He did not take up his permanent residence until the spring of 1848. He has since lived on it, and now has a good farm.

Between 1840 and 1850 a continuous influx of Germans came into the township, and settled mostly on uncleared farms. They set to work in their steady, industrious way, and by hard work, coupled with thrifty management, soon became quite well-to-do. Prominent among these was the Weinberg family, which now represents an influential and wealthy element in the population of the township.

### THE FIRST FARM

opened in Flowerfield was by Michael Beadle in 1830. He planted the first crop in the spring of 1831, and raised the first crop the same year.

### THE FIRST ORCHARD

was set out by Daniel Wheeler in the spring of 1835, on a piece of land located on the east quarter of the south half of section eleven, purchased of M. John Nichols, and now owned by William E. Wheeler, of Three Rivers.

### THE FIRST HOUSE

erected in the township was a log structure, built by Michael Beadle in 1830. It stood on the present site of the dwelling of Joseph Johnson, on section one.

### FRAME HOUSE.

The first frame house was also built by Michael Beadle in 1831.

### FIRST BRICK HOUSE.

The first brick house in the township was erected by Aaron Harland on the present site of the residence of Samuel Weinberg, in 1847.

### BURYING-GROUND.

The first burying-ground (excepting the one in the village) was laid out on an acre of ground, donated by James Brown in 1838. The first burial was that of some member of the Arnold family, but no tomb-stones existing, we cannot give the precise name or date. There is another cemetery near the village of Flowerfield, first used in 1832, but not regularly surveyed until 1876. The first interment therein was Mrs. Gragg, wife of William E. Gragg, an early settler.

### THE FIRST MARRIAGE

of white persons in the township was that consummated between Justin Clark and Matilda Beadle, a daughter of Michael Beadle, which happy event came off in 1830. The second marriage was that of John M. Fellows and Olive Nichols, daughter of George Nichols, Esq., January 9, 1834, the Rev. Benjamin Taylor performing the ceremony.

### THE FIRST WHITE CHILD

born in the township was a son of William Wheeler, which died in infancy. The second one was Francis E., son of M. John Nichols, born November 19, 1833, and who is now a resident of the State of Missouri.

### THE FIRST DEATH

of a white person that occurred in the township was that of the wife of

William E. Gragg, who died in 1833, and was interred in the Flowerfield village burying-ground.

### THE FIRST PHYSICIAN

to take up his residence in the township was Dr. C. L. Clewes, who commenced the practice of medicine in 1832 at the village of Flowerfield, and had an extensive ride and a large list of patients.

### EDUCATIONAL.

The first school taught within the present limits of Flowerfield township was in 183-, by Malvina Nichols, in part of the residence of S. C. Wheeler. Among the first pupils were Oscar and John Smith, Hannah Wheeler, Lucinda Mead and sister, and others, in all about ten children.

### THE FIRST REGULARLY ORGANIZED SCHOOL-DISTRICT

was district number one, which was organized on the 6th of November, 1837, and included sections one, two, three, ten, eleven, twelve, thirteen, fourteen and fifteen,—just one-fourth of the entire township. We copy the annexed data from the records of the first meeting:

"Records of school-district number one of Flowerfield township, according to the division made by the inspector of primary schools.

"A meeting was held in pursuance of an order from the inspector of primary schools for the township of Flowerfield, directed to Henry Whited, Esq.

"Said notice directed the inhabitants of said district to meet at Asa Hicks', on Monday, the 6th day of November, 1837, at six o'clock P. M., in the village of Flowerfield, to organize said district.

"In pursuance of the aforesaid notice, the inhabitants of said district met at the place above designated and organized said school-district number one, by choosing its board of officers, viz.:

"Asa Hicks, moderator; William Wheeler, assessor; William Woodruff, director.

"On motion it was resolved that there be a school taught four months the ensuing season in said district."

The first regular teacher was Miss Ann Huckell, who taught two terms. She subsequently married Reuben Hepler; both of them are now deceased.

### THE FIRST SCHOOL-HOUSE

in the southeastern part of the township was built of logs, and stood on an acre of ground donated by James Brown, in 1839, in the centre of section twenty-six. It was used until 1849, when a frame school-house was built, and, after being used for about ten days of the winter term, it was destroyed by fire. Nothing is known as to who first taught in it.

The school statistics of 1876 are as follows: There are nine districts, each having a school-house, one of which is built of brick, the others being of wood, and which will afford five hundred and eighty-five sittings, and are valued at eight thousand dollars. Six hundred and four children between five and twenty years of age were returned by the school officials, five hundred and thirty of whom attended the schools, which were in session an average of eight months during the year ending September 1. Nine male teachers were employed, and paid one thousand three hundred and seven dollars for their services, and eleven females, who received five hundred and thirteen dollars and fifty cents. The total expenditures, including seven hundred and twenty-four dollars paid on indebtedness, amounted to two thousand nine hundred and nine dollars and thirteen cents.

### CIVIL ORGANIZATION.

In the original constitution of townships in the county, made November 5, 1829, the four townships numbered five south of ranges nine, ten, eleven, and twelve west, were constituted into one township, called Flowerfield. In 1833 the township numbered five south, range nine, now known as Leonidas, was set off, and, with Colon, constituted a new township, called Mendon, township five, range ten, was attached to Nottawa. In 1838 the township numbered five of range eleven was erected into a separate township, leaving Flowerfield with its original name but shorn of all its territory, except what its present area includes—one government township of six miles square.

### FIRST TOWNSHIP MEETING.

At a meeting of the voters of the township of Flowerfield, in the county of St. Joseph, held at the house of Joshua Barnum on the first day of April, A.D. 1833, A. H. Foot was nominated for chairman; C. L. Clewes, secretary. After they had been duly sworn, the meeting was called to order and proceeded to business, and on counting the ballots, they were found to stand as follows:

JANE J BEAM

RESIDENCE OF THE LATE JACOB Z. BEAM, FLOWERFIELD TP. ST. JOSEPH COUNTY, MICH.

"C. S. Wheeler, supervisor; Joshua Barnum, town-clerk; Samuel Valentine, George Nichols, Abraham Vandemark, assessors; Ira Stowel and Henry Whited, overseers of the poor; William E. Gragg, collector; Wm. Wheeler, M. John Nichols, C. L. Clewes, commissioners of highways; William E. Gragg, constable; Henry Garver, fence-viewer.

"After which the meeting was adjourned until the first Monday in April, 1834, to be held at the house of Joshua Barnum.

"William E. Gragg gave bail as constable, George Nichols and M. John Nichols becoming his sureties.

"Voted, That the town raise a tax of five dollars to pay for wolf-scalps caught in said township.

"Voted, That the town pay one dollar each for wolf-scalps caught within the limits of the township.

"Voted, That five dollars be raised for the support of the poor.

"Voted, That all hogs must weight forty pounds before they will be considered as trespassers.

"Voted, That the town raise two dollars and fifty cents to defray the contingent expenses of the term for the year 1835.

"Voted, That any boar (male pig?) running at large, weighing over twenty pounds, be liable to be castigated (castrated) by any person.

"April 18, 1837.—License granted to David L. Burson to be married to M. F. Arnold."

Clerks—Joshua Barnum, 1833-35; Aaron H. Foot, C. L. Clewes, Abner Moore, William Woodruff, Josiah Russell, John N. Wheeler, four years; George S. Bristol, five years; Abel Townsend, Nathaniel D. Thomas, three years; Stephen Whited, Milo Fellows, two years; F. A. Thurston, two years; Delos Breese, Henry Bowe, three years; Liberty N. Straw, Charles Williams, Jr., three years; Samuel Drumbiller, George Whited, Franklin W. Carlton, two years; C. L. Seekell, three years, and Hiram Weinberg, the present incumbent.

Supervisors—C. S. Wheeler, 1833, seven years; M. John Nichols, two years; William Wheeler, five years; Franklin Howard, Moses Stocking, John Kirby, six years; George G. Bristol, Aaron H. Foot, Wm. L. Worthington, six years; Daniel Bowe, two years; Joseph M. Kirby, two years; William Gill, two years; William D. Kirby, Grenville Kuevela, J. C. Munn, five years; Ira Starkweather, the present incumbent.

Justices of the peace—Isaac F. Ulrich, two years (1838, first record of regular election; prior to this, justices of the peace were appointed by the governor); Stephen P. Choat, Aaron H. Foot, Henry R. Moore, Henry Whited, Samuel Corry, sixteen years; James Brown, A. C. Parsons, T. P. Fellows, L. D. Wicks, Theodore Worthington, William L. Worthington, twelve years; John N. Angle, eleven years; Vivian Beck, R. P. Straw, Thomas J. Edwards, Delos T. Breese, Joseph Johnson, F. J. Chamberlain, John Q. Bears, R. T. Andrews (to fill vacancy), Ira Starkweather, eleven years, 1877; J. C. Johnson, H. M. Crout, James F. Atkinson, John Freeman, present incumbent.

The first person who acted in the capacity of a justice of the peace was George Nichols, who was appointed to the office by Governor Porter, in 1832, under the territorial laws.

THE FIRST ROAD.

The first record of a regularly-surveyed road in Flowerfield township is dated April 17, 1834. It was the main road running east and west through the centre of sections thirty-two, thirty-three, thirty-four, thirty-five and thirty-six.

The surveyor was a Mr. Briggs, who was assisted by M. John Nichols. The road commissioners were Henry Garver, George Nichols and Robert Gill. Prior to this the old settlers used to drive everywhere through clearings and over farms, making their courses lie between streams, generally following the Indian trails, which invariably led to the easiest fording-places. One of these trails started at an Indian rendezvous that formerly existed on Rocky run, on section twenty-three, on land now owned by George Foust, which meandered along the valleys towards Three Rivers. From constant and long use it became like a much worn-path, and was on an average about fifteen inches in depth. It avoided the hills, always either going to the east or west of them. In places this trail is still visible, notably on the farm of Mr. Spaulding, on section twenty-six.

THE FIRST LAND-ENTRIES

at the land-office of the government were made in 1830, and were as follows: The southwest quarter of section one, by Henry Whited, June 23, 1830; the north half of the northeast quarter, and the northwest quarter of section one, by Michael Beadle, September 14; the south half of the northwest quarter of section one, by David Beadle, October 30. There

were about the same number of entries in 1831, and also in 1832. There were assessed in 1878, twenty-two thousand four hundred and sixty acres, valued by Ira Starkweather, the supervisor of the township, at two hundred and sixty thousand one hundred and four dollars,—about one-third of its real value.

THE CROPS.

In 1873 there were harvested four thousand and sixty acres of wheat, which produced fifty-five thousand three hundred and seventy-four bushels, and one thousand eight hundred and sixty-nine acres of corn, which yielded thirty-four thousand four hundred and thirty-two bushels. There were also produced the same year, six thousand two hundred and seventy-one bushels of other grain, four thousand four hundred and seventy-nine bushels potatoes, one thousand five hundred and eighty-nine tons hay, nine thousand eight hundred and thirty-two pounds wool, one hundred and twenty-four thousand and six pounds pork, fifty-five thousand and sixty-three pounds butter, six thousand four hundred and eighty-four pounds dried fruit, five hundred and forty-four barrels cider, eighteen gallons wine, and one hundred pounds maple-sugar. Four hundred and seventy-three acres in orchards produced nine thousand nine hundred and ninety-two bushels of apples, and two hundred and ninety-seven bushels of other fruit, valued at three thousand five hundred and sixty dollars. Two flour-mills and two saw-mills employed nine men and a capital of twenty-six thousand seven hundred dollars, and manufactured nine thousand barrels of flour and three hundred and fifty thousand feet of lumber, valued at forty thousand dollars. There were owned in 1874, in the township, five hundred and fifty-five horses, six mules, twenty oxen, five hundred and seventy-eight cows, six hundred and thirty-two other cattle, one thousand five hundred and ninety hogs, two thousand four hundred and forty-nine sheep; two thousand and nineteen of the latter producing the clip of 1873.

ASSESSMENTS AND TAXES.

In 1834 the first assessment was reported at six thousand one hundred and seventy-seven dollars, on which the tax-levy was fifty-one dollars—twenty-six dollars for the county, and twenty-five for the township. In 1838 the assessment was returned at seventy-three thousand eight hundred and forty-two dollars, and the taxes were two hundred and eighty-eight dollars. In 1852 the assessment was fixed at forty-seven thousand five hundred and seventy-nine dollars, and the taxes amounted to one thousand two hundred and thirty-seven dollars and four cents, for all purposes. In 1860 the assessment was returned at two hundred and twenty-seven thousand seven hundred and fifteen dollars, and the taxes footed up one thousand eight hundred and forty-five dollars and five cents. In 1870 the assessment was fixed at four hundred and eighty thousand nine hundred and seventeen dollars, and the tax-levy at four thousand and twenty-three dollars and forty-three cents. In 1876 the assessment, as equalized by the board of supervisors, aggregated two hundred and fifty-seven thousand two hundred and forty-seven dollars on real estate, and forty thousand seven hundred and thirty dollars on personal property—a total of two hundred and ninety-seven thousand nine hundred and seventy-seven dollars, on which taxes were levied as follows: State and county purposes, one-half to each, one thousand five hundred and twenty-two dollars and twenty cents; for the township, including schools, five thousand five hundred and sixty-four dollars and eighty-seven cents—making the total tax seven thousand and eighty-seven dollars and six cents.

POPULATION.

In 1838 there was in the township a population of four hundred and six souls. In 1850 there were five hundred and sixty-four inhabitants, and in 1860 there were one thousand and ninety-seven returned. In 1870 the people were again numbered, and there were one thousand five hundred and thirty-eight of them—the males, who numbered eight hundred and nineteen, being one hundred in excess of the females. In 1874 the State census put one thousand four hundred and nineteen people in the township, of whom seven hundred and thirty-one were males, and six hundred and eighty-eight females. Of the males, two hundred and fourteen were between twenty-one and forty-five years; one hundred and forty-three between forty-five and seventy-five, and one over seventy-five and under ninety. Two hundred and seventeen of the females were between eighteen and forty years; one hundred and fifteen between that age and seventy-five, and eight over the last age. Three hundred and ninety-one girls were in the same category. The married females exceeded that class among the males by one individual, and there were two hundred and sixty-seven of them; while the single men were in a majority of fifteen, numbering fifty-seven—the ladies counting but forty-two. The widowed were seventeen males and thirty-two females.

## POLITICAL PARTIES

have cast their votes at the presidential elections as follows: In 1840 the Whig party polled twenty-six, and the Democratic party forty-four votes. In 1844 the Whigs cast thirty-four votes, the Democrats twenty-three, and the Liberty men twenty-two. In 1848 the Whigs cast twenty-four, and the Democrats eleven votes, and the Free Soilers gathered the balance, seventy-five. In 1852 the Democrats went back to their old love, and polled forty-four votes, the Whigs rallied a little and cast thirty-seven, but there were still forty-five genuine Abolitionists. In 1856 the Republicans polled one hundred and forty-nine votes, and the Democrats thirty-nine; and in 1860 the same parties polled one hundred and seventy-two and fifty-seven, respectively. In 1864 they polled one hundred and sixty-two and fifty-nine, and in 1868 two hundred and eight and ninety-seven, respectively. In 1872 the Republicans polled one hundred and eighty-three votes, the Democrats seventy-eight, and O'Conor received two. In 1876 Mr. Hayes received one hundred and forty-five votes, Mr. Tilden sixty, and Mr. Cooper, the "Greenback" candidate, seventy-eight votes. This last vote indicates a population of one thousand four hundred and fifteen in the township.

## INCIDENTS.

Ramsey Wheeler was killed by the explosion of a small cannon, at a Fourth of July celebration, about 1850, and two other young men by the names of Oscar Pershing and John Bouton, were somewhat severely injured by the same accident. The cannon was cast at a foundry that used to exist in the village; some defect, doubtless, being in the metal casting.

Three children of Robert Hicks, a former resident of the township, while left at home alone by their parents, wandered out to a pond adjacent to their home, to skate. The ice broke, and the three children were drowned. This accident occurred about the winter of 1850.

John Young was killed by being accidentally struck with a base-ball club, November 3, 1874. He survived the accident just a week, dying on the 10th of the same month.

## FLOWERFIELD VILLAGE.

The village of Flowerfield was surveyed and laid out in 1833, by Dr. David E. Brown, assisted by M. J. Nichols. The site was then owned by Challenge S. Wheeler, and was originally entered by James Valentine in 1830, and lies on section one, township five, range twelve.

The first saw-mill erected in Flowerfield township, was built by Michael Beadle, in 1830. The mill ran successfully until the spring of 1832, when it was destroyed by fire, and rebuilt the same year, and was operated steadily afterwards for more than thirty years, when it was abandoned.

In 1872 Messrs. Beam & Wheeler erected a vinegar manufactory and cider-mill on the site of the old mill. The business of this establishment for 1876 was two thousand dollars.

### A GRIST-MILL

was erected in 1831, also by Michael Beadle. It had one run of stones, which was made out of a natural boulder, almost two and a half feet in diameter. In the spring of 1832 the mill passed into the hands of C. S. Wheeler, who overhauled and repaired it, and put in a new set of burrs. The mechanical part of the work was done by Elisha Kirk. The mill ran steadily until 1851, when it was burned down; the fire was supposed to have been the work of an incendiary. At this time the mill was owned by Pershing & Bristol. It was rebuilt in 1855 by Lewis and Joseph Tubbs, with three run of stones. The present owners are the Heck brothers. It contains three run of stones, and did a business in 1876 as follows: Merchant, five thousand barrels; custom, twenty thousand bushels.

### THE FIRST DISTILLERY

was erected in the village, in 1830, by Abram Vandemark, Henry Kinney and David Hamilton, three unmarried youths, by whom it was continued for a few years. It was soon after abandoned.

### THE FIRST STORE

was erected by C. S. Wheeler, and kept by him in 1832. It was a general store, similar to those now in existence, only on a very modest scale.

### THE FIRST TAVERN

was opened by Joshua Barnum in the early part of 1833, and in it was held the first township-meeting. It stood near Wheeler's store, on the present site of Starkweather's store. The present tavern was built in 1839, by a Mr. Gillman.

### THE FIRST SMITHY.

The first blacksmith's shop in the village was kept by Samuel E. Foley, who came to the village in 1833, from Boston, the shop standing near the mill.

### GRAIN-CRADLE FACTORY.

This establishment was started on a small scale by Ami Palmer in 1843. At first it was devoted to the cooper business, and so mainly continued until bought out by Milo and Alvin Ingraham, in 1844. They began the manufacture of cradles on an extensive basis in 1847. Alvin only remained in partnership about a year, and since his retirement Milo has conducted it alone. In 1876 the factory turned out five hundred and thirty cradles, which, with repairing, made an aggregate business of about two thousand five hundred dollars.

### A FOUNDRY

was built in the village in 1837-8, and for a time a good business was done therein, and about the same time there was a carding-machine and cloth-dressing factory established there also.

### THE PRESENT BUSINESS

of the village is conducted as follows: The only general store is that of Ira Starkweather, an old settler of the neighborhood. There are also a drug-store and a hardware-store, which, with all other business enterprises, exclusive of the grist-mill, do a trade aggregating about twenty thousand dollars annually.

### THE POST-OFFICE,

which was established early, Challenge S. Wheeler being the first postmaster, has been presided over since his incumbency by the following persons: J. N. Wheeler, E. H. Keables, G. S. Bristol, William L. Worthington, J. M. Fellows, and Ira Starkweather, the present incumbent.

### RAILROAD.

The Kalamazoo branch of the Lake Shore and Michigan Southern railroad was constructed in 1863. In 1865, in accordance with a vote of the township, bonds to the amount of ten thousand dollars were issued in aid of the undertaking. Litigation ensued, and it was decided by the supreme court (Judge Christiancy presiding) that the vote of the township was illegal. In the interval between the issue of the bonds and the decision of the court, the railroad authorities had disposed of the bonds to third parties, and a subsequent decision of the court ordered the bonds to be paid. The people of the township are still paying them (with interest), although the road did not touch the township,—the nearest point being the Flowerfield depot, in the northwest corner of Park township, which refused any aid whatever to the enterprise. Opinion as to the benefits to Flowerfield township, derived from the road, are divided,—the contrary predominating.

### RELIGIOUS.

The first sermon preached in Flowerfield township was in the bar-room of the tavern kept by Joshua Barnum, in Flowerfield village, in 1831. It was preached by Rev. Benjamin Taylor, a very eloquent and earnest preacher of the Baptist persuasion. He was much respected and revered by the early settlers of all denominations. He subsequently removed to Boston, where he began a long and eminently useful career as the "sailors' preacher." A tender and interesting notice of this venerable divine is contained in "Fern Leaves," written by Fanny Fern, and published in 1854. The families of all the old pioneers attended the discourse, and were highly edified by its earnestness and truth.

### THE FIRST CHURCH-EDIFICE

was erected in 1853. It was intended for a school-house, but was purchased by the Baptist society of Flowerfield village, and converted into a church. Rev. John Kirby was the first pastor installed in 1858. He was followed successively by Revs. C. B. Macumber, in 1860; A. Buck, in 1862. John Kirby again served the church from 1863 to his removal to Cass county in 1867. Since that time there have been no regular services held. Among the original members were John, William, and Joseph Kirby and their wives, William Horr, Henry Ousterhout and wife, and F. Shutes and his wife.

### THE EVANGELICAL ASSOCIATION.

The Flowerfield class of this denomination was organized under the labors of Rev. George Doll, in 1849, with the following members: Leander Weinberg and wife, Peter Bloom and wife, Lourana Weinberg, and John Mohney. The church, which is called "Zion's Evangelical Church," was built, in 1866, on the farm of Leander Weinberg, four miles northwest of Three

RESIDENCE OF **JOSEPH JOHNSON,** FLOWERFIELD, ST. JOSEPH CO., MICH.

Rivers, and was dedicated November 25, 1866, by Rev. Bishop Joseph Long. It is a frame building, thirty-two by forty-eight feet on the ground, cost two thousand dollars, and will seat two hundred and fifty persons comfortably. The building-committee consisted of Leander Weinberg, Samuel Drumpeller, and Isaac Null. The present officers of the church are J. H. Null, Jacob Barnhardt, John Reimer, and J. W. Kline. Present membership, twenty-six. Besides the Rev. G. Doll, the following ministers have preached to this church since 1866: Reverends C. S. Brown, E. B. Miller, T. A. Davis, P. Wiest, S. Copley, J. W. Loose, Alonzo Russell, P. Swille, B. F. Wade, and J. H. Keeler (the present pastor of the circuit).

THE "KNOBS" CLASS,

so-called, was organized under the pastorate of Rev. Peter Both, in the year 1863, with twenty members, all Mecklenburg Germans. They worship in a school-house situated four miles west and half a mile north of the Flowerfield church, about one mile east of the Cass county line. A Sunday-school was organized there, in 1868, with Joachim Timm as superintendent. Adolph Buchoff is the present incumbent.

The present membership of the church is eighty-seven; and one thousand three hundred dollars have been subscribed towards the erection of a church which is projected, and to be built as soon as practicable. The present church-officers are Rev. J. Timm (local preacher), Fritz Tirks, and John Miller.

The preachers to this class have been the same as named in the Flowerfield class, since the organization of this class by Mr. Roth.

Organized religious meetings according to the usages of the Methodist Episcopal church, were held in the school-house which stood on section twenty-six, in 1843. The first circuit-preacher was Reverend Mr. Gage; and the first class-leader, Robert Gill. Among the early members were: Robert Gill, Sylvester Wood and John Stocking, with their wives. It was continued here until 1870, when the meetings were transferred to Howardsville, where the society was reorganized under the pastoral ministrations of Reverend John Pitezel. The present class-leader is Samuel Hice.

FLOWERFIELD GRANGE.

The grangers of Flowerfield organized themselves into a society in December, 1873. Their first annual meeting was held at the house of Leander Mohney, January 17, 1874, at which the following officers were elected: John Freeman, master; Clarence Somison, overseer; H. M. Crout, lecturer; Wesley Seekell, secretary; Leander Mohney, treasurer; Henry Moore, steward; Henry Weinberg, assistant-steward; —— Ebenezer, gate-keeper; Mrs. Ellen Seekell, Ceres; Mrs. Nancy Mohney, Pomona; Miss Hannah Weinberg, Flora; Mrs. Adelia Freeman, lady-assistant. The grange started with a membership of fifty-seven. The present executive officers are: Seymour Andrews, master; Clarence Somison, overseer; Hiram Weinberg, secretary; Ebenezer Thompson, treasurer.

HOWARDVILLE VILLAGE.

The present site of Howardville was formerly contained in the purchase of Robert Gill, who erected the first house there in 1833. He bought the land on account of the excellent water-power existing on it. He commenced building a dam, but sold the property to two brothers named Morse, who erected a saw-mill there in 1833. They conducted the mill until 1836, when Franklin Howard bought it and ran it until his death in the winter of 1845. It then came into the possession of D. K. Thurston, who sold it to Edmund Beam, the present owner, in 1862.

GRIST-MILL.

The grist-mill was built by Edmund Beam in 1864, and has been in continuous operation from that date. It has two run of stones, and is devoted exclusively to custom-work. Product for 1876, twenty thousand bushels. In the event of the construction of the long and fondly anticipated narrow-gauge railway running to the village, improvements will be made for merchant-work in the mill.

TAVERN.

The first tavern was built in 1856 by William Porter. It stood on the point of the hill, on land now owned by M. P. Yowells.

SCHOOL.

Franklin Howard donated six hundred dollars to build a school-house in 1845.

POST-OFFICE.

In 1856 a post-office was established at Howardville, and Chauncey Tinker was appointed postmaster. The settlement since then has been generally known by the name of Tinker Town.

FLOWERFIELD IN THE REBELLION

made a proud record. Her citizens were early in the field and came home late—those who came at all. She sent over fifty per cent. of her voting population in 1860, during the war, filling up the regiments first in the field, the Eleventh taking the larger number. The Sixth also had a goodly number and so also had the Twenty-fifth. One-third of her soldiers were killed, died or were discharged for disabilities. We give a list of the heroic men who went to the front in defense of the national unity and starry flag, as we have been able to locate them from the official records:

FIRST MICHIGAN INFANTRY.

Corporal William Fry, Company B; re-enlisted and mustered-out.

SIXTH INFANTRY.

Corporal Lester Fox, Company C; first lieutenant and mustered-out.
Private W. W. Bullock, Company C; discharged at expiration of service.
Private David R. Johnson, Company C; re-enlisted and mustered-out.
Private William McCumsey, Company C; discharged for disability.
Private James Oemer, Company C; discharged for disability.
Private John Reis, Company C; discharged at expiration of service.
Private Nelson Straw, Company C; died at Carrollton, Louisiana, March 4, 1863.
Private William J. Smith, Company C; re-enlisted and mustered-out.
Private John V. Thurston, Company C; died at Port Hudson, Louisiana.
Private Robert Johnson, Company C; mustered-out.
Private Jacob H. Hopkins, Company C; discharged.
Private Samuel H. Hepworth, Company C; discharged for disability.
Corporal George W. Hice, Company C; died at Ship Island, Mississippi, May 15, 1862.

SEVENTH INFANTRY.

Private George Beck, Company C; died in action in Wilderness.
Private William H. Eggleston, Company C; died at Andersonville.
Private Daniel Eggleston, Company K; died of disease, October 28, 1864.
Private Alonzo E. Butler, Company K; mustered-out.

ELEVENTH INFANTRY.

Musician John Ludwig, mustered-out, August 22, 1862.
Private Samuel P. Beck, Company B; mustered-out.
Private Henry Parker, Company B; mustered-out.
Private William Parker, Company B; mustered-out.
Private Samuel Spiegelmoyer, Company B; mustered-out.'
Private Oliver Stebbins, Company B; died at Chattanooga.
Private Aaron Hackenburgh, Company C; re-enlisted and mustered-out.
Corporal John I. Bloom, Company E; discharged at expiration of service.
Musician William H. Seekel, Company E; died at Nashville, October 20, 1862.
Musician James W. Seekel, Company E; discharged.
Private Richard Brayman, Company E; discharged at expiration of service.
Private James W. Beck, Company E; discharged at expiration of service.
Private Alva P. Hale, Company E; died at White Pigeon, December 10, 1861.
Private George Eggleston, Company E; discharged at expiration of service.
Private John T. Hale, Company E; died at Bardstown, Kentucky, January 26, 1862.
Private Bradley L. Lane, Company E; discharged at expiration of service.
Private John McKinzie, Company E.
Private Robert McIlvaine, Company E; died at Stone River, December 31, 1862.
Private Albert Oemer, Company E; discharged at expiration of service.
Private John C. Smith, Company E; discharged September 26, 1862.
Private Joseph E. Thompson, Company E; cut his throat while home on furlough.
Private Reuben G. Weinberg, Company E; re-enlisted in Company C, Fifteenth regiment.
Private William H. Weinberg, Company E; killed near Atlanta.
Private Edward Mosser, Company E; killed near Atlanta.
Private John B. Alcock, Company E; died at Nashville.
Private Daniel Frees, Company E; mustered-out.
Private Henry T. Frees, Company E; mustered-out.
Private John Lee, Company E; mustered-out.
Private Daniel Motter, Company E; mustered-out.
Private Horace Smith, Company E; mustered-out.
Private W. C. T. Sampsell, Company E; mustered-out.

Private Charles P. Ludwig, Company E; mustered-out.
Sergeant James Bouton, Company G; discharged at expiration of service.
Sergeant Orlando Williams, Company G; died January 30, 1862.
Corporal George Straw, Company G.
Corporal Laban Pierce, Company G; died February 5, 1862.
Private Oscar Angle, Company G; killed at Stone River, December 31, 1862.
Private Joel Pierce, Company G; died January 8, 1862.
Private Thomas Straw, Company G; died February 11, 1862.
Private Myron C. Palmer, Company G; died at Jeffersonville, Indiana, March, 1862.
Private James Walker, Company G; discharged at expiration of service.
Private Daniel Condick, Company G; mustered-out.
Private Charles D. Seckel, Company G; discharged.

TWELFTH REGIMENT INFANTRY.

Private George Williams, Company B; discharged for disability.
Private John Barnhart, Company E; mustered-out.
Private William B. Noyes, Company F; mustered-out.
Private David F. Plummer, Company K; died at Duvall's Bluff, Arkansas.
Private David N. Stocking, Company K; died at Duvall's Bluff, Arkansas.
Private Ross Knapp, Company K; mustered-out.
Private George W. Plummer, Company K; mustered-out.
Private John P. Plummer, Company K; mustered-out.
Private John Stebbins, Company K; mustered-out.

THIRTEENTH INFANTRY.

Private W. W. Bass, Company E; re-enlisted and mustered-out.
Private George Salter, Company G; died at Louisville.

FOURTEENTH INFANTRY.

Private Egbert B. Tubbs, Company C; died of wounds at Jonesboro, Georgia.

FIFTEENTH INFANTRY.

Private Reuben G. Weinberg, Company C; mustered-out.
Private A. G. Weinburg, Company C; mustered-out.
Private Harvey Tinker, Company C; mustered-out.

SIXTEENTH INFANTRY.

Private Bradley L. Lane, Company I; mustered-out.

NINETEENTH INFANTRY.

Private George W. Beebee, Company A; discharged for disability.
Corporal Charles F. Fuller, Company K; mustered-out.
Private John C. Kirby, Company K; mustered-out.

TWENTY-FIFTH INFANTRY.

Private George W. Bass, Company D; mustered-out.
Private Henry Beebe, Company D; died of wounds, August 22, 1863.
Private Thomas Crossman, Company D; discharged.
Private William Dewey, Company D; killed by guerillas.
Private Charles W. Hicks, Company D; mustered-out.
Private John S. Hard, Company D; died at Chattanooga.
Private Isaac J. Kline, Company D; mustered-out.
Private Clarence Lomison, Company D; mustered-out.

Private Ebenezer Rich, Company D; mustered-out.
Private Erastus H. Hicks, Company D; mustered-out.
Private Jacob N. Shocraft, Company D; mustered-out.
Private Roswell Beebe, Company D; killed at Tebb's Bend, Kentucky, July 4, 1863.
Private Lovinsky Beers, Company G; mustered-out.
Private George Barks, Company G; mustered-out.
Private Richard Cotherman, Company G; discharged.
Private Henry L. Cooper, Company G; veteran reserve corps.
Private Henry Stegeman, Company G; veteran reserve corps.
Private William Scott, Company G.
Private George F. Wheeler, Company G; mustered-out.
Private Abram V. Youells, Company G; mustered-out.
Private Burton Kirby, Company K; mustered-out.

TWENTY-EIGHTH INFANTRY.

Private Nehemiah E. Harris, Company D; mustered-out.
Private Nehemiah Harris, Company E; mustered-out.
Private Henry W. Osterhouse, Company H; mustered-out.
Private Daniel E. Decker, Company K; mustered-out.

FIRST MECHANICS AND ENGINEERS.

Private Peter Boner, Company B; discharged at expiration of service.
Private James Boner, Company B; discharged at expiration of service.
Private Ira Palmer, Company B; discharged at expiration of service.

SECOND CAVALRY.

Private Henry Parker, Company H; mustered-out.

EIGHTH CAVALRY.

Private Gideon Arnold, Company F; died at Camp Nelson.

ELEVENTH CAVALRY.

Private Christian Osterhout, Company I; mustered-out.

FIRST LIGHT ARTILLERY.

Private John S. Bullock, Battery F; mustered-out.
Private William Jones, Battery G; enlisted in the regular army.
Private Christian Motler, Battery 14; mustered-out.
Private William H. Fry, Battery 14; mustered-out.
Private Missouri Fetteral, Battery 14; mustered-out.
Private Thomas Hazen, Battery 14; mustered-out.
Private Aaron Hickenburg, Battery 14; mustered-out.
Private Farris Hickenburg, Battery 14; mustered-out.
Private Yost Kern, Battery 14; mustered-out.
Private Jacob Kern, Battery 14; mustered-out.
Private Emanuel Kline, Battery 14; mustered-out.
Private John Markle, Battery 14; mustered-out.
Private Reuben Shy, Battery 14; mustered-out.
Private Peter T. Youslls, Battery 14; mustered-out.

We return our thanks to M. John Nichols, Ira Starkweather, Mr. Johnson and William L. Worthington for valuable information received, and assistance rendered in the compilation of the history of Flowerfield.

# FAWN RIVER.

THE township of Fawn River, which takes its name from the beautiful little river which meanders through its southern area, is bounded on the north and west by the townships of Burr Oak and Sturgis respectively; on the east by Branch county, Michigan, and on the south by the county of La-Grange, in the State of Indiana. Its area is about twenty-four square miles, and includes within its limits thirteen thousand four hundred and forty acres,—being a little more than one-half of a full government township. It is known on the surveys of the United States as township eight, south of range nine, west of the principal meridian. With the exception of a portion of the northwestern sections, which include the eastern end of Sturgis prairie, the land was originally covered with timber,—the usual oak-open-

ings of the country; but many fine farms have been wrought out, on which not a stump now remains to tell of the forest growth of centuries, which once overspread the township.

THE SURFACE

of the township is diversified by hill and dale and gently rising slopes, dotted all over with comfortable farm-houses and barns, fields, orchards and meadows. A charming view is had from the summit of Kime's hill, just southwest of Fawn River village, where, overlooking the country for a circuit of twenty miles, the eye rests upon the village of Sturgis to the west and the splendid farms intervening; shut in at the north by the wooded ridge dividing the townships of Fawn River and Burr Oak, the line of

RESIDENCE OF J. C. MUNN, FLOWERFIELD, ST. JOSEPH CO. MICH.

vision sweeps around eastward to the heavy-timbered plains of Branch county, and, finally, rests with delight upon that gem of beauty, Pretty prairie, in LaGrange county, Indiana, bounded by the forest-crowned heights beyond.

### THE SOIL

is the same fertile, sandy loam, which gives St. Joseph county its excellent reputation as a wheat- and fruit-growing district.

The township is well watered and drained by Fawn river,—earlier known as Crooked creek,—which enters the township from Branch county, on the southeast quarter of section thirteen, and runs thence northwest to the west line of the southwest quarter of section ten, and thence southwestwardly till it passes across the southern line of the northeast quarter of section nineteen into Indiana, and also by a chain of four beautiful little lakes, running from the northwest corner of the township, through sections four, nine, eight, and northeast quarter of section seventeen, emptying into Fawn river near the west line of the northwest quarter of the southwest quarter of section sixteen. The two northern and larger ones have an area of about one hundred and sixty acres each. The northernmost one is named Sweet lake, in honor of the old landlord who built his log-hostelry on its southeastern bank, and the next one (south) is called Cade lake,—the nonagenarian, now living in Sturgis, having first settled on its northern shore.

There is also a little sheet of water of about forty acres area in the northwest quarter of the northeast quarter of section twenty-four, and also three little creeks which enter the river from the north, on sections thirteen, fourteen and nineteen. The bottom of nearly or quite all of these lakes have inexhaustible beds of marl within their limits, which make the finest kind of lime, and in the earlier history of the county were extensively worked for building-material. The healthiness of the township since the opening of the farms has been fair, and equals that of most of its sister-towns in the county.

### FIRST SETTLEMENTS.

The first settler within the present limits of Fawn River township was John Sturgis, who was also the first settler on Sturgis prairie. He and George Thurston (the latter then a young man) came first to the prairie in August, 1827, and broke up ten acres on the southwest quarter of section six, on the eastern edge of the prairie, and sowed the same to wheat, and returned to Brownstown, on the Detroit river, for the winter, and again came in the spring of 1828 with Judge Sturgis' family, and built a house on the tract above named, which was the first house built on Sturgis prairie. The tract was entered at the land-office in Monroe by Judge Sturgis, October 22, 1826, which date was one year before the organization of the county, and while the whole country south of Grand river and west of the principal meridian was known as the township of St. Joseph.

On December 18 of the same year, Alanson C. Stewart, of Westmoreland county, Pennsylvania, entered the west half of the northeast quarter and the east half of the northwest quarter of section seven, and these entries by Sturgis and Stewart were the only ones made that year, and were the first land-entries in the township. Three entries were made in 1829, and six in 1830. Judge Sturgis sold out his interest in 1829 to Richard Hopkins, and removed to Nottawa. The next settlers who came in were Mr. Hopkins, above named, Thomas Hall, Lemuel Graham and Samuel Stewart, all of whom came in 1829. Mr. Hopkins settled on Judge Sturgis' first location, Hall living with him at first, but locating land on another section; Stewart located on the purchase of Alanson C. Stewart, which is now a part of the farm of John McKerlie; Lemuel Graham entered a tract of land now included in the original farm of Sheldon Williams, walking to Monroe, a distance of one hundred and twelve miles, in two days, to do so. Jacob Knox came in 1830, a Mr. Sickels in 1832, and located on the Chicago road, and James Johnson the same year. George Thurston located on his present farm on the west half of the northwest quarter of section six in 1833. From that time to 1836, among the settlers there came Captain Charles Moe, a sturdy soldier of the war of 1812, and Joseph Bartholomew, who built the first house on the river, both of whom, with their families of boys and girls, came in 1835. Ebenezer Sweet, who built the first tavern, F. A. Tisdel, who laid out the little village of Freedom, Moses Roberts, William Amidon and James McKerlie, came in 1836; Captain Philip R. Toll came in 1836, and built the saw- and flouring-mills at Fawn River village, and became a permanent settler with his family in 1838. Later came W. F. Lee, who bought the lower mill, and Francis Flanders came in 1841.

In 1828 Judge Sturgis broke up thirty acres more of his first location, which, with the ten acres broken up the fall before, was the first farm opened

26

in Fawn River and on Sturgis prairie. The township was, until 1838, included in the township of Sherman.

There were times of sorrow which came to these early pioneers, like the waves of some great sea, which overwhelmed them with grief and dismay; and yet served to bind them one to another with cords of steel, as it were, by reason of the acts of unselfish devotion that shone out in the community like stars on a moonless night. Such a time were the years of 1837–38, when scarcely a family was exempt from the universal sickness which prevailed throughout the township. Relays of those well enough to be able to do any work went from house to house, to minister to the needs of the living, or pay the last hasty offices for the dead.

Among the many heroic women of the township, on whose heads, if living, or upon whose memories, if dead, there shine individual crowns, gemmed with acts of charity and humanity, stand out prominently Mrs. Philip R. Toll, Mrs. Richard Hopkins, Mrs. Charles Moe, and afterwards her daughter Mrs. James Johnson, and Mrs. James McKerlie, who, not forgetting the sick in their own household, went through the neighborhood, carrying cheer and a beneficent influence wherever they went on their errands of mercy. Mrs. Bartholomew fell an early victim to the general malady, and was the first to be buried in the old cemetery on the banks of Sweet lake in 1837. The summons of the grim messenger, death, which none, however loved, gifted or honored, can evade, successively brought many others to the little burial-place, who were laid to rest—often without a single relative with strength sufficient to look upon their sepulture—by kind and sympathizing friends, whose number was scarce sufficient to perform the sad service.

But the little community was not always sad. When at last the scourge of those sad years had passed away, returning health and increased prosperity and population brought increased activity and a zest for life's enjoyments, that even the memories of those sorrows could not always becloud with their pall.

The young people gathered at the log school-houses, which were few and far between, in the long winter evenings, which, however, passed rapidly away in the interest of spelling-jousts, forensic disputes and poetic effusions, in which beardless Lindley Murrays, incipient Henrys, and inglorious, though by no means mute Miltons, "vexed the ambient air," much to the merriment of these quondam youthful aspirants, but now gray-headed seigneurs.

Husking-bees and apple-parings, too, furnished a never-ceasing fund of fun and jollity for old and young. And those old-time joyous gatherings gave the opportunity, too, for many a bright-eyed lass to lead captive for life a sturdy knight sworn to her sole allegiance.

Esquire Flanders was once called upon to bind "the silken-tie" for a couple who had agreed to share life's toils and prizes together, and they appeared before his honor, arrayed, perhaps not like Solomon in all his glory, nor yet like the lilies of the field, but in the best they could afford for the auspicious occasion. The service performed, the gustatory pleasures commenced, for which ample provision had been made. During the repast the boys celebrated the nuptials by a discharge of artillery; not a whole park, indeed, but a single mill-gudgeon, which made no inconsiderable racket in the vicinity. The amateur artillerists then resolved themselves into a musical association and wound up the festivities in honor of the newly-wedded pair by a grand out-door concert, a la charivari, in which the melodious "kolink, kolunk, kolinkle, linkle" of the cow-bell, and the dulcet tones of the horse-fiddle mingled harmoniously and soothingly.(?)

A little incident which illustrates the sterling patriotism of old Captain Moe, occurred in the days of the northeastern boundary troubles between the United States and England. One Elder Farley, a minister of the Christian persuasion, and a non-resistant in doctrine and practice, was preaching in the school-house at Freedom one Sunday, and waxing eloquent over the gospel of peace and good-will to man; he adverted to the question then vexing the minds of the people, and giving a somewhat unfavorable description of the territory in dispute, claiming it to be a nearly, if not quite, worthless collection of rocks and sterile soil, he propounded to his auditors this query: "Now, my friends, don't you think it would be much better for us to give up our claim to this really valueless country instead of going to war about it, and killing people, and bringing so much misery and suffering on both countries?" The speaker, of course, did not expect an answer, and he was not a little disconcerted, and the audience electrified, to hear the sturdy old captain speak "right out in meeting" and say: "No! I would'nt give em a rock! not a rock! I'd give 'em the bayonet first!"

The early settlers were mostly from New York and Ohio, though some were from Kentucky. There are now about fifteen families of German residents in the town, who have come in during the later years.

## THE FIRST ROAD

surveyed in the township of Fawn River was the Chicago road from Detroit, in 1825, but it was not worked through the township until 1834, except such work as may have been done by Savery to get his early stages through, or perhaps the Stewarts, who carried the mails and passengers as early as 1830, before any stage-line was established.

The first roads laid out by the town authorities were as follows: On March 23, 1839, the commissioners of Fawn River and Bronson (in Branch county), jointly laid out the first one on the county line, running north one-half mile from the southeast corner of section one. The second was laid out by the commissioners of Fawn River, March 26, and commenced at the northwest corner of the southwest quarter of section eight, and ran eastwardly and northwardly through sections eight and four to intersect the Chicago road. The third was laid out the same day by the same authority, commencing at the southwest corner of section thirty-three, in Burr Oak, and ran south to the centre of section four, then west and south to the Chicago road. The fourth was laid out May 27, commencing at the southeast corner of section two, and ran west two miles to intersect the road running north and south at the southeast corner of section four, which latter road was laid out in 183-, by the authorities of Sherman township. The road leading north from Fawn River mills to the Chicago road, at Freedom, was laid out in 1839.

## SCHOOLS.

The first school in Fawn River was taught by Miss Jane Moe, a daughter of Captain Moe, and now the estimable wife of James Johnson, Esq. She held sway over her youthful subjects, numbering about fifteen, in a log cabin on the northern bank of Sweet lake, in the year 1835, and received for the instruction she imparted to the then rising generation a monetary compensation of about one dollar per week. The first school-house in the township was in district one at Freedom, in 1836, and was a log building, formerly used as a residence, but purchased by the school authorities for their use. The second was a frame building, erected in 1839, in district number three, at Fawn River village. The first meeting of the school inspectors of the township was held April 28, 1838, at which time they "set the bounds" of districts numbers one, two, and three. The first examination of teachers on record was held November 21, 1844, at which time D. L. I. Flanders received a certificate of competency to teach in district one. December 21, the same year, another examination was held, and Jonathan W. Flanders and Cyrus Lindsley received certificates. Lydia Flanders and Wealthy Greenman were the next who received authority to teach, which was given the next spring. The school statistics for 1876 are as follows: There are five school-houses in the township, one of brick and four of wood, which are valued at four thousand dollars, and which contain two hundred and eighty-five seatings; two hundred and seventy-five children between the ages of five and twenty years. One hundred and ninety-seven attended school an average of over eight months each during the year ending September 1. Three male and seven female teachers were employed and paid one thousand two hundred and fourteen dollars for their services. The total resources of the town for school purposes yielded an income of two thousand and fourteen dollars and ninety-one cents, out of which an expense account was liquidated aggregating one thousand nine hundred and eight dollars and sixty-eight cents, leaving a balance in the treasury of one hundred and six dollars and twenty-three cents. There is no union or graded school in the town, although in district number three, Fawn River village, sometimes two teachers are employed at one term. District number five has a bonded debt of six hundred dollars, which is the only school indebtedness in the town. The school taxes for 1877 amount to one thousand seven hundred and fifty-six dollars and sixty-one cents.

## A CEMETERY,

located on a little rounded summit on the bank of Sweet lake, a most charming spot, was the first burial-place for loved ones gone before, occupied in the town, and it is believed that Mrs. Bartholomew, the pioneer wife of Joseph Bartholomew, the mother of three brave sons in the war with Mexico, two of whom died there, was the first to be buried there. Mr. Sweet and several of the old citizens were also buried there, but no stone or other permanent mark has ever been put up at the graves, and they are now covered with a vigorous growth of young oaks, and not a vestige of the resting-places of the dead can now be seen.

## MANUFACTURES.

The first manufacturing done in the town was the burning of lime, by James Johnson, in the year 1835; the raw material being raised from the marl beds which underlie the waters of the small lake on the southeast

quarter, section eight. He built his kiln on the side of the bluff forming the eastern bank of the lake, and burned his lime after the marl was moulded into bricks and sun-dried. It was of a most excellent quality, and he supplied the country for miles round about with it, and did a prosperous business for many years. Many of the walls made or finished with this lime are in good preservation at the present writing. The manufacture of lime from this source has ceased since the introduction of railroads, as other points can furnish a cheaper article. Thomas Cade had a brewery on Cade's lake in 1836, the old malt-house standing on the bank of Sweet's lake. Leonard & Wasson succeeded Cade, and afterwards John Hiney purchased the establishment, and changed the business to the distillation of whisky. A good story is told in connection with Hiney's business, by Hon. J. G. Wait, of Sturgis. When one of the earlier churches was about to be built in that village, Mr. Wait was one of the solicitors for subscriptions, and he appealed to everybody for help, Hiney with the rest. Hiney, thinking to "bluff" the solicitor, said he would give a barrel of whisky. "All right! Put down your whisky," said the solicitor, at the same time presenting his list, and Hiney responded. The next day Mr. Wait drove up to the distillery and rolled the "ardent" into his wagon and brought it home and manufactured it into vinegar, turning the cash value of the article over to the building committee, much to the edification of the people.

A Mr. Freeman built a small flour-mill and distillery on Fawn river in 1840, on section sixteen, and afterwards sold it to Warren F. Lee and brothers, William and Nathaniel.

A large business was transacted there with mercantile accommodations by Mr. Lee (sometimes called the governor), his brother William, and afterwards by Messrs. Clark & Peck. The mill was subsequently burned to the ground, and the site remained vacant for several years until 1869, when Wells & Grinnell bought the site and rebuilt the mill, fitting it up with the best and latest improved machinery, and sold it to B. F. Trimmer, who sold it again, in 1874, to W. D. Johnston, the present proprietor and operator of it. It has three run of stones, and does custom work exclusively.

## THE FIRST TAVERN

was built by Ebenezer Sweet in 1835-6 on the southerly bank of the lake, to which the landlord gave his name, and on the Chicago road, at which time that trail was the great thoroughfare between Detroit and Chicago. It was built of logs, and was a place of resort for the men and boys of the whole country side. Justices' courts and sometimes town meetings were held there, and races and disputes without number were decided at times in a manner that sent the participants to their homes not a little worse for the encounter. These scenes were a natural outgrowth of society in a new country, and they passed away in time to give place to a higher and better civilization.

## THE FIRST POST-OFFICE

established on Sturgis prairie was located within the present limits of Fawn River in 1829, on the northeast quarter of section seven, and Samuel Stewart was the first postmaster. He and Hart L. Stewart had the contract for carrying the mails between Niles and Detroit, and they put on a democrat wagon, and conveyed passengers also, before the stage lines were put on the road. After the post-office was removed to the village of Sherman (Sturgis) an office was established at Freedom, and F. A. Tisdel was appointed postmaster. In 1844 the post-office was removed to Fawn River mills, and Isaac D. Toll appointed postmaster. He was succeeded by his brother Alfred Toll. His successors were C. F. Moore and Calvin Marble. The present incumbent is Mr. Derrick S. Buck, who was appointed by President Grant in 1873. The first mails were received at Freedom daily by stage. Afterwards, when the railroad brought them to Burr Oak, from which point Fawn River was supplied, they came irregularly, about twice a week. In 1874 Hon. I. D. Toll obtained a daily mail from Sturgis, which the town still enjoys. About one thousand letters pass through the office every quarter, and fifty-five newspapers are distributed per week.

## BIRTHS—MARRIAGES.

The first child born in St. Joseph county opened his eyes to the light of day in Fawn River township on the southwest quarter of section six. David Sturgis, a son of Judge John Sturgis, is the person who has the honor, and was born February 11, 1830. Solomon Hopkins, a son of Richard Hopkins, was born the next year and in the same house.

The first marriage in the township was that of John W. Fletcher and Sarah Knox, a daughter of Jacob Knox, the ceremony being performed by Samuel Stewart, Esq., a justice of the peace, on the 18th day of September, 1831. This was the first marriage in the county of actual residents.

JAMES JOHNSON.

MRS. JAMES JOHNSON

RESIDENCE OF JAMES JOHNSON, FAWN RIVER TP., ST. JOSEPH CO., MICH.

### CIVIL ORGANIZATION.

The township of Fawn River was organized and its boundaries assigned by the legislature at the session of 1838. The name struck the minds of the legislators as peculiarly charming, and more especially as the area was little more than half of the usual size of townships. Columbia Lancaster was in Detroit at the time, and took charge of the presentation of the application for the organization of the town, but the petition being delayed somehow, the committee reported for the organization before its reception, and Lancaster wrote Captain P. R. Toll that if the people did not wish to be organized, they could easily become *disorganized*. The first town-meeting was held by appointment of the legislature at the tavern of F. A. Tisdel at Freedom, April 2, 1838, Edward Swan being the judge, and Benjamin D. Goodrich the clerk thereof.

The following is a complete list of the officials then chosen to set the machinery of the new sovereignty in motion:

Edward Swan, John P. Van Patten, James McKerlie and Freeman A. Tisdel were elected justices of the peace for the terms of one, two, three and four years, respectively. James McKerlie was elected supervisor; Isaiah Sweet, clerk; Nicholas Goodrich, W. W. Plumb and Horace W. Fields, constables; Jonas Waters, John O. Swan and George McKerlie, assessors; Horace W. Fields, collector; Charles Moe, Jonas Waters and John P. Van-Patten, commissioners of highways; F. A. Tisdel, Isaiah Sweet and Jonas Waters, school inspectors; Charles Moe and Att Wood, overseers of the poor; Ebenezer Sweet and Isaac Culver, fence-viewers, and John O. Swan, Archer Mathews and John Haustin, overseers of highways for districts numbers one, two and three, respectively.

The record does not state how many votes were cast, but there being twenty-eight offices to distribute, and the electors drawing all of the prizes, it is pretty fair to presume that there were not many more voters than officers elected. Some of the recipients of the people's favor did not value it sufficiently to qualify for the performance of the duties of the offices to which they were elected, and, on May 3, a special election was held, and Edward Swan chosen assessor; Ebenezer Sweet, collector, and Thomas Cade, fence-viewer.

The town has been represented on the county board of supervisors from its organization to the close of the present year (1876) as follows: James Mc-Kerlie, 1838 to 1841; Att Wood, elected in 1839, but who did not serve; Freeman A. Tisdel, 1840. Heman Leonard was elected in 1842, after Knauer had declined to serve, but becoming restive under the weight of official cares, he resigned, and Isaac D. Toll, then a young man of twenty-three years, was appointed to fill the vacancy, in February, 1843. This, with the assessorship in 1840, was the commencement of the public life, since so full of honorable distinction of one whom the people of St. Joseph county, irrespective of party, have, and still do, delight to honor. Mr. Toll was elected in April, 1843, and was continued in the position until 1847, when he was absent in Mexico. After a single term held by John Iliney, he was again elected in 1848, 1850 and 1851, Josiah Knauer intervening in 1849. After his absence from the county, in the national service for eight years at Washington, in the United States Pension and Patent departments, he was again elected in 1863, and held the position continuously till 1860.

Sylvester Treat was elected in 1852, and was succeeded by Jonathan W. Flanders the next year, who gave place to Edward Osborn, who held the office five years. In 1859 Alfred Toll, a brother of Isaac D., was chosen, and again in 1860. In 1861 and 1862 Francis Green was the head official of the township, and Henry Driesbach succeeded I. D. Toll in 1869. William Rippey in 1870-71, and John Dunlap in 1872, held the position, and then Ozho Moe was called on to bear his share of the official burdens of the township, and did so worthily for three years, giving way to I. D. Toll in the centennial year, and for reasons that will be apparent by a reference to the action of the State board of equalization in reference to the assessment of St. Joseph county in 1876, and for five years to come, he representing the county before said board.

The justices of the peace who have held their courts in Fawn River since its organization are as follows: Tisdel, McKerlie, Van Patten and Swan were elected at the first town-meeting, as before stated. Tisdel held the position three years, and then was elected in 1842 and the year following. McKerlie held the office till 1845, and was elected again in 1846 for four years. Van Patten held but a single term of two years, and Swan but one year. In 1840 J. H. Hard was elected for a single term, and in 1841 Ebenezer Sweet was chosen for two years, but did not hold his commission for reasons hereafter given, and Isaiah Sweet was elected to fill the vacancy, and also W.W. Plumb was elected to fill a similar vacancy in Tisdel's office for a similar cause. The Sweet-Plumb dignity closed with the expiration of the term in

1843, and Philander Wilcox was elected that year, and again in 1846. In 1844 Francis Flanders was elected and held the magisterial scales in equipoise for sixteen years, from 1844-48 and from 1851-63. In 1845 David Knauer was elected for four years, and J. C. Richmond in 1847. In 1848 E. H. Pride secured the judicial ermine for four years, W. N. Lewis for three, and J. P. Wilson for two. In 1849 Sheldon Williams, familiarly known as "old Shell," was elected for a term of four years, and Francis Green began his judicial career, which only ended with the incoming of the present year; he having held the position twenty-seven consecutive years. In 1850 J. P. Wilson secured the prize for four years, and Sylvester Treat was treated to but a single year, it being the first town-meeting under the new constitution; but at the next town-meeting Mr. Treat was commanded for a full term of four years. In 1853 Warren F. Lee began a term which lasted till 1861, and in 1854 Harvey Hatch was given the chance of four years on the bench at Fawn River. In 1855 James Johnson was elected, and in 1858 Sellick St. John. Albert Scoville in 1859, David E. St. John and Thomas J. Grant in 1860, and Amos Fish in 1861, successively, were chosen to the position. In 1862 David St. John, R. I. Welch and Samuel Parker were elected, and Welch again in 1863, and Parker in 1865-66, and again in 1875. Daniel Stewart and Albert Moe were chosen in 1865, and J. W. Bedford in 1866. I. Eckerson in 1867 and John W. Mankin in 1870, successively, received the judicial baton, the latter being re-elected in 1874. In 1873 there were three successful competitors, Henry Driesbach, Amasa H. Johnson and Joseph Ziok. In 1874 Derrick S. Buck was elected, and Michael Rommel brought up the rear in 1876.

The office of town clerk has been filled as follows: Isaiah Sweet, 1838-39; Josiah Knauer, 1840-41. A perfect shower of the people's favors rained upon Mr. Knauer in 1842, he being elected supervisor, town clerk, school inspector, assessor, and overseer of highways; but the weight of honors thus thrust upon him was distasteful, and he declined them all but those of inspector and overseer, and James A. Hopkins was elected town clerk at a special election on April 26.

Eben Sweet was clerk in 1843, and Edmund Kean the year following. He was succeeded by John C. Richmond in 1845-6; and W. N. Lewis, Warren F. Lee, William Betts, H. Betts, John Oliver, Harvey Loomis, Sidney Marble and Isaiah Manes each had a single year in the office from 1847 to 1854 inclusive. Then Claudius Cæsar Cummins held the position two years; and during the years 1857-8-9, Dr. D. L. I. Flanders interspersed the official courtesies of the office throughout his researches and practice in materia medica, and compounded boluses and official notifications with equal zest. The doctor was succeeded in the clerk's office by his father, the old 'Squire, for two years, and then R. I. Welch came in for three years, and I. Eckerson and T. W. Selover each had two years' income from the emoluments of the office—Thomas W. Buck being sandwiched between them in 1867.

James A. McLauchlan was elected in 1870, and has held the position ever since, and it is to his courtesy that we are indebted for the means of gaining much of the foregoing official information. Colonel I. D. Toll has held the office of superintendent of schools for the past two years, that office having been created in 1875.

### EARLY RECORDS.

A few excerpts from the early records of the town will be of interest here to show how the pioneers were accustomed to discharge their official duties. At the first town-meeting the people laid a bounty of two dollars on all wolves killed in the town, and at the second, held at Captain P. R. Toll's house, in 1839, their charitable feelings found expression in the levy of twenty dollars for the relief of the poor. The next meeting was held at landlord Sweet's house, thus distributing the honor or profit which might accrue from the gathering of the people between the three most public places of the town.

In 1841 Esquires Sweet and Tisdel having taken out licenses to sell ardent spirits in their taverns, their commissions were held to be voided by the statute which forbid any court to be held in a bar-room or other place where intoxicating liquors were sold; and Isaiah Sweet and W. W. Plumb were elected to fill the vacancies, as before stated.

In an adjoining town in Branch county, Esquire Bronson, also a landlord, avoided such a decision in his case by an ingenious and convenient system of transference of his franchise to a nephew, one Bial Potter. When the justice had a case on the docket for trial he would transfer his interest in the "wet grocery" business to the nephew, who would immediately proceed to take the stock in the bar to another room in the house, which being done, the following colloquy would take place between the past and present retailer: The Court—"Bial Potter?" "Here, your honor." "Is this room a bar-room?" "No, your honor." "Then let the cause on the docket be called for a hearing;" and the cause was called and disposed of, whereupon a re-transfer of the franchise was effected, the "ardent" re-appeared in the accustomed place, the awful solemnity of the place of justice was swept out of doors, and Boniface, with his apron, took the place of Blackstone, with his wig.

Esquire Ebenezer Sweet, after the first voidance of his commission, adopted a similar expedient, and sold his fixtures and stock to Amos Mallory, and his brother Isaiah held his courts, whenever required, in the room thus vacated pro tem.

The town authorities had invested in five ballot-boxes, which were deemed by the electors to be superfluous by at least four of the number, and at a special election in June, 1841, they voted that four of them should be sold at public auction,—which being done, forty-eight cents net cash was received for them, which sum (as the clerk was careful to note) was paid over to the treasurer on the 13th day of November of that year.

In 1842 the people voted that the supervisor should have no assistants in assessing the property of the town for taxation, and in 1845 they voted that the county had no need of fire-proof county offices. In 1846 there were forty-eight votes for, and six against, granting licenses to sell liquor.

In 1844 they voted a bounty of half a dollar on red-fox scalps, and in 1845 they revoked both wolf and fox bounties, but in 1847 the "varmints" had become so troublesome that the bounty was not only restored, but increased to three dollars on wolves, and one dollar on foxes. In 1851 fox scalps were considered less valuable, and a quarter of a dollar was discounted from the price of 1847, but the market continued to decline, and in 1852 they were quoted at only fifty cents. In 1853 the market had improved, and seventy-five cents were freely offered for them, and a new article of commerce appeared,—the Mephitis Americana, for whose head-covering a York shilling was offered. Under this stimulus, before the "varmints" had eight of the "striped kittens" had ceased to taint the air, and commit depredations in the "gude" wife's poultry-yard. Whether the vote was one dollar for sly old foxes, and twenty-five cents for "little foxes." Whether this distinction was made by reason of the propensity of the "little foxes" to "spoil the tender vines," or because of the creation of a new industry in the farming of foxes, the record does not state. The market fluctuated for the next few years, running as low as one shilling only for a red-fox scalp,—after which there are no further quotations.

In 1852 but four persons thought a new jail was necessary in the county, and eleven thought not, and so voted.

In February, 1864, the question of offering bounties for volunteers was voted on and carried,—two hundred dollars being given for the quota of 1863, and one hundred dollars for that of 1864. It was carried sixty-nine for to one against. Similar votes were had in August, 1864, and January, 1865, and one hundred dollars offered for recruits, and the general expenses attendant upon the procurement of such recruits to fill the quotas of the town under the various calls for troops, were voted to be raised by a general tax. In 1865 three hundred dollars and over were, in some instances, paid.

### MARKS AND BRANDS.

Lemuel Graham's mark for his stock (which, with that of his neighbors, in 1838, ran at large and roamed where they would) was a "slit in the end of the right ear," and Tisdel had the same mark on the left ear. Jason Thurston and Orlando Griffith divided a "square-crop" between them, of the right and left ear, respectively, and David Knouer made a "square-crop" on both ears. W. W. Plumb's mark was "two slits in the left and one in the right ear;" John Houstin put a "V;" A. Worden a round "O," and C. Ballou "two slits" in the right ear.

### THE DOCKET

of Josiah Sweet, justice of the peace, exhibits the following entries, being the first three suits entered thereon: April 23, 1839, F. A. Tisdel confesses judgment on a note in favor of Lorenzo Griffith, for seventeen dollars and fifty cents, and Att Wood became security for a stay of execution. However, the execution was finally issued October 2d, the same year, and the amount thereof made March 2, 1840. On May 6, 1839, Philip R. Toll brought suit against Nicholas Goodridge on a charge of kleptomania, the immediate objects of his propensity being a clevis and pin, and a certain stick of timber, to which charge the defendant interposed his plea of "not guilty," and wanted a jury of his peers, whereupon came James McKerlie, Casper Reed, Isaac Culver, I. N. Barker, Minard Miller and Eben Foster, and they non-suited the plaintiff, from which verdict and the judgment of the court thereon, the said plaintiff then and there appealed to the circuit court. The

defendants seemed to be more in favor with juries than plaintiffs, for the next suit, George Foster versus Alvin Gates, for the right of property, was decided for the "under dog in the fight." On May 23, 1840, Gabriel Bradford complained of Joseph Sagar for an assault and battery. Sagar wanted a general assize, whereupon Justices Sweet, Tisdel and Bishop (the latter of Burr Oak) sat as a court and called a jury, who said the defendant was not guilty, "after hearing the evidence in a convenient position," as the entry of the court says.

The court of Esquire Sweet used to be the scene of many interesting forensic displays, in which Hon. John B. Howe, of Lima, Andrew Ellison, of La Grange, and other distinguished luminaries used to participate, and in order to make it still more interesting, the juries rarely agreed.

### VALUATION OF PROPERTY.

In 1840 there were assessed in Fawn River township eleven thousand eight hundred and seventy-seven acres of land, with the improvements, at thirty thousand two hundred and thirty-nine dollars. The best building was F. A. Tisdel's, valued at seven hundred and fifty dollars; the second, Isaac D. Tull's, five hundred dollars; then L. L. Graham at four hundred dollars, and Richard Hopkins next, at two hundred dollars. There were sixty-seven horses valued at one thousand eight hundred and ninety-five dollars; seventy-four oxen and steers at one thousand one hundred and eighty-four dollars; sixty-seven cows and heifers at five hundred and twenty-two dollars, and twenty-nine carriages and wagons at seven hundred and three dollars, making the total valuation of personal property four thousand six hundred and thirty-four dollars, and the total assessment of the town thirty-four thousand eight hundred and seventy-three dollars; the total taxes levied that year in the township amounted to two hundred and fifty-seven dollars and nineteen cents. There were forty-seven resident tax-payers that year in the town, and two liverymen and two taverns were rated for specific taxes.

In 1852 the assessment was as follows: real-estate, forty thousand four hundred and sixty-three dollars; personal property, eight thousand four hundred and nineteen dollars; total, forty-eight thousand eight hundred and eighty-two dollars. Total taxes levied seven hundred and seventy-one dollars and thirty-five cents.

In 1860 the property was assessed thus: real-estate, one hundred and forty-four thousand three hundred and thirty-eight dollars; personal property, fifteen thousand five hundred and ninety-five dollars; total, one hundred and fifty-nine thousand nine hundred and thirty-three dollars. Total taxes levied, eight hundred and forty-one dollars and thirty-nine cents.

In 1870 the assessment of real-estate was three hundred and six thousand three hundred and sixty-eight dollars, and personal property, thirty-three thousand six hundred and thirty dollars, making a total of three hundred and thirty-nine thousand nine hundred and ninety-eight dollars, on which the taxes levied amounted to two thousand nine hundred and sixty dollars and eighteen cents.

In 1876 the property was assessed as follows: Real-estate, twelve thousand nine hundred and eighty-four acres, one hundred and sixty-eight thousand two hundred and thirty-three dollars; personal property, thirty thousand five hundred and fifty dollars; total, one hundred and ninety-eight thousand seven hundred and eighty-three dollars. On this amount taxes were levied as follows: State and county, one thousand and twenty-seven dollars and eighty-six cents; township, two hundred and fifteen dollars; schools, one thousand seven hundred and fifty-six dollars and sixty-one cents, making a total of two thousand nine hundred and eighty-nine dollars and forty-seven cents. The valuation for taxation in 1876 is scarcely one-fourth, probably, of the real value of property, which would place the actual value at about four hundred thousand dollars.

### PRODUCTIONS.

The census of 1874 shows that in 1873 there were sown two thousand four hundred and forty-three acres of wheat, which produced twenty-two thousand four hundred and seven bushels; one thousand three hundred and ninety acres of corn produced forty-seven thousand four hundred and twenty-three bushels, and there were grown of other grain nine thousand and twenty-three bushels; of potatoes, nine thousand eight hundred and thirty-nine bushels; of hay, nine hundred and seventy-four tons; of wool, ten thousand seven hundred and thirteen pounds; of pork, one hundred and sixty-four thousand five hundred and fifteen pounds. Thirty-three thousand two hundred and eighty pounds of butter were made, five thousand six hundred and eighty-eight pounds of fruit dried, and four hundred and seventy barrels of cider made. One hundred and eighty-one acres in orchards, produced nine thousand eight hundred and seventy-five bushels of apples, and the gardens of the farmers' wives produced nearly three thousand dollars' worth of "sass." There were of live stock owned in the township, in 1874, three hundred and fourteen horses; mules and oxen, four each; two hundred and eighty-nine cows; two hundred and fifty-seven head of other horned cattle; six hundred and eleven hogs, and two thousand and seventy-three sheep. The two flouring-mills in town, with a capital of twenty-eight thousand dollars and six run of stones, made in 1873 twenty-three-thousand one hundred dollars' worth of flour.

POPULATION.

In 1840 there were forty-six votes cast at the annual town-meeting, indicating about two hundred and fifty inhabitants. In 1852 they had increased to four hundred and seventy-two, and in 1860 there were five hundred and seventy, comprising one hundred and twelve families. In 1870 there were six hundred and eighty inhabitants, three hundred and sixty-two of whom were males and three hundred and eighteen females. In 1874 there were six hundred and forty-seven inhabitants, three hundred and fifty-two being males and two hundred and ninety-five females. There were eight persons between the ages of seventy-five and ninety years, and eighty boys and seventy girls under ten years. Of the rural population one hundred and nineteen of them were happy benedicts, and forty-seven lone bachelors; while of the opposite sex one hundred and eighteen had eschewed single blessedness, and thirty-six of age suitable for wifehood continued to tread life's path alone. Death and the courts had separated thirteen husbands and fourteen wives from their lawful mates.

THE POLITICAL BIAS

of a majority of the inhabitants of the township has ever been Democratic since its organization. In 1840 the vote on the presidential question stood thus: For Harrison, twenty-three; Van Buren, twenty-three. In 1844 the vote was forty-nine for Polk and thirty for Henry Clay. In 1848 they voted Cass, sixty-three; Taylor, forty-two; Free Soil, four. In 1852 the Democrats polled sixty-five and the Whigs forty-nine votes. In 1856, the first year of the Republican party's history, there were sixty-three votes for Buchanan and thirty-nine for Fremont. In 1864 Lincoln received forty-five votes and McClellan sixty-one. In 1868 Seymour had seventy-six and Grant sixty-five votes. In 1872 Grant received seventy-two and Greeley seventy-six votes. In 1876 Tilden received ninety-five, Hayes sixty-nine and Cooper eight votes.

THE LEADING FARMERS

in the township have been, and are, James Johnson, the pioneer of 1832, who still lives in the township which he has seen change, under the steady persistent strokes and combined effort of himself and neighbors, from its wild beauty of flower-bedecked parks to perhaps a less beautiful though a vastly more valuable area of cultivated farms. Charles Moe, by whose judicious and intelligent culture of the soil, ably seconded by his sons Otho and Albert (the former of whom still lives on the old homestead), a most excellent farm has been made. James McKerlie and his son John, who has succeeded to the pioneer, and to the broad acres of the father has added fine herds of thoroughbred cattle, horses and sheep; Joseph Bartholomew, who came to the river in 1835; Sheldon Williams, who pitched his tent on the prairie in 1839, and his sons, Elias, Rawson, Miles and Spencer, who occupy splendid farms carved out of a magnificent stretch of prairie and opening owned by the father at his death; Richard Hopkins, in 1829, and for many years after; George Harrison and Peter A. Baker, comers here in 1840; Daniel Shaeffer, who owns an extensive and valuable tract of land in the southwest part of the township; A. C. Zimmer, whose fine commodious barn is the admiration of all who examine it, and Leonard Butz, who owns three hundred acres of the P. fl. Toll tract of one thousand three hundred acres on the river. John McKerlie has the only notable herd of blooded cattle, and he began to gather it together and improve his stock in 1858.

THE FIRST IMPROVED FARM-MACHINERY

was introduced on Sturgis prairie about 1844, when the McCormick reaper was brought there first. The separators were introduced later. Captain P. R. Toll had improved, previous to his removal to Monroe, several hundred acres of his large tract, besides carrying on his extensive manufacturing business.

FAWN RIVER IN THE REBELLION.

Fawn River furnished many men for the support of the old flag from her own citizens, besides recruits which were obtained outside of the county to fill the quota of the township under the several calls for troops made by the President for the support of the national honor and authority. The township paid in bounties, in aid of enlistments, four thousand five hundred

dollars, besides the relief granted the families of soldiers during their service. The names of citizens of Fawn River who went forward to the defense of a common country, are as follows:

FIRST INFANTRY.

Private W. H. Marble, Company G; enlisted in 1861; three months' men; mustered-out, August 7, 1861.

Private John Annis, Company B; enlisted in 1861; transferred to United States Second Cavalry.

Private Edward Dutcher, Company B; enlisted in 1861; died in hospital.

Private Daniel J. Gates, Company B; enlisted in 1864; mustered out at close of war.

Private Henry Seals, Company K; enlisted in 1861; discharged at expiration of service.

SEVENTH INFANTRY.

Private Martin V. Bowman, Company K; enlisted in 1861; died at Newark, October 12, 1862.

Private Benjamin E. Sanborn, Company K; mustered out at close of war.

Private Charles B. Wheeler, Company B; enlisted in regular service.

Private H. Harrison Harding, Company K; mustered out at close of war.

TENTH INFANTRY.

Private James Anderson, Company A; mustered out at close of war.

Private Philip E. Arver, Company B; mustered out at close of war.

Private George W. Atwood, Company B; mustered out at close of war.

Private Ashford D. Mankin, Company B; mustered out at close of war.

ELEVENTH INFANTRY.

Second Lieutenant Loren H. Howard, Company C; promoted to first lieutenant and captain, and mustered out at close of war.

Sergeant Smith A. Benedict, Company C; discharged.

Sergeant Alonzo H. Merrick, Company C; enlisted at Chattanooga.

Sergeant Harrison Graves, Company C; enlisted in 1862; mustered out at close of war.

Corporal Samuel L. Graves, Company C; enlisted in 1862; discharged for disability.

Private Lewis Wheeler, Company C; discharged at expiration of service, and died at home from disease incurred while in service.

Private Andrew Kershner, Company G; discharged at expiration of service.

TWELFTH INFANTRY.

Private Calvin Marble, Company A; enlisted in 1864; mustered out at close of war.

Private George A. Morgan, Company C; mustered out at close of war.

Private Willard A. Morgan, Company C; mustered out at close of war.

Private Harrison Moore, Company D; enlisted in 1864; mustered out at close of war.

Private Irwin Tisdel, Company D; mustered out at close of war.

Private Edward C. Graves, Company D; enlisted in 1864; died at Duvall's Bluff.

THIRTEENTH INFANTRY.

Private Lewis Carle, Company B; re-enlisted and mustered out at close of war.

SEVENTEENTH INFANTRY.

Private Andrew E. Brosee, Company D; discharged for disability.

NINETEENTH INFANTRY.

Private John C. Benedict, Company D; died at Danville, Kentucky, December 7, 1863.

Private Joseph D. Anderson, Company E; mustered out at close of war.

Private Hollis B. Haws, Company E; mustered out at close of war.

Private Martin E. Sanburn, Company E; discharged.

Private Samuel A. Wilson, Company E; mustered out at close of war.

Private Charles F. Dewater, Company E; mustered out at close of war.

TWENTY-SIXTH INFANTRY.

Private E. Henry Searls, Company D; died February 12, 1864.

SIXTH CAVALRY.

Private Levi H. Roberts, Company D; mustered out at close of war.

NINTH CAVALRY.

Private Edwin Cummins, Company E; mustered out at close of war.

Private Willard W. Morgan, Company A; discharged for disability.

Private Edmund A. Finn, Company K; mustered out at close of war, and afterwards ingrain in Tennessee cavalry, and died in Nebraska.

Private George Sellick, Company E; mustered out at close of war.

Private Sala Seymour, Company M; mustered out at New River, Tennessee, September 6, 1863.

Private Charles F. Donaldson, Company E; died at Coldwater, Michigan, April 6, 1863.

Private Robert Denman; died in service.

Private Albert S. Marble.

Private David Skinner.

Private Samuel Wheeler.

ELEVENTH CAVALRY.

Private O. C. Marble, Company I; mustered out at close of war.

ONE HUNDRED AND SECOND U. S. COLORED INFANTRY.

Private Frank Hatchell, Company K; mustered out at close of war.

Private Horace Roberts; mustered out at expiration of service.

Private James Baza; died in service.

Private Andrew Baza; mustered out at close of war.

Private Cornelius D. Kensey, died in service.

## VILLAGE OF FAWN RIVER.

The first location on the land afterwards laid out as the village of Fawn River, was made by Captain Philip R. Toll, in 1836. He put up a house, which is now standing on the north side of the river, which was first used as a boarding-house for the men employed by Captain Toll in building his mill-dam, race, etc. A saw-mill was completed the same year, and a flouring-mill the year following. The second dwelling-house was built a few months later by John P. Van Patten, who, with William Schermerhorn, both carpenters, were the first residents in the village. They did the wood-work on the mill.

In April, 1837, Captain Toll surveyed and laid out a village-plat on his location, covering a portion of sections number ten and fifteen, on the south side of the river, John Kromer being the surveyor; but the plat was not acknowledged or recorded until May 1, 1852. There were six full and two fractional blocks included in the plat, and the streets were named Tonipkine, Indiana, Centre, Cass, Water, Mohawk, and Jackson. This point was for many years a prominent one by reason of the scarcity of mills, and the most excellent reputation the Fawn River mills ever maintained, as well as for the mechanical and mercantile facilities afforded to the country round.

### SCHOOLS.

The district which includes the village in its boundaries was organized first as district number seven of Sherman township, June 7, 1837, at the house of Captain P. R. Toll. Benjamin D. Goodrich was chosen the first moderator, John P. Van Patten, director, and Nicholas Goodrich assessor for the new district. June 21st following, the people met again, and voted to raise four hundred dollars to build a school-house; and July 5th the same authority located the site for the house at the "southwest end of Fawn River village," and where the same building now stands—Captain Toll giving the site to the district. October 16, 1838, the district had become known as number three of Fawn River, and the people voted eighty dollars for school purposes. May 22, 1839, the school-board accepted the school-house from the contractor, Mr. John P. Van Patten, provided he would lath the same, and retained ten dollars to secure such provision. In December of that year the contractor was released from his contract, and the building finally accepted, and the next September one hundred dollars was voted to paint it and buy a stove. The first school taught in the house was in the year 1840 by Harriet Starr. She is now Mrs. Edward Montross, of Iowa. Brinkerhoff, Charles Belden, August M. Kinley, and his sister Catherine, and R. T. Cortright succeeded her. Jonathan W. Flanders taught the school in the winters of 1844–6.

### CHURCHES.

Reverend Gershom B. Day, a Baptist divine, preached in the Fawn River school-house as early as 1839. He was succeeded by Rev. John Skelly, of the Scotch Presbyterian church, who formed an organization,—Robert Hume, and several of his family, James McKerlie, John Grove, William Rippey, and others, uniting with the church at the time. In the winter of 1843–4 Reverend Benjamin Ogden took charge of the society, uniting La Grange, Indiana, with it, and preaching alternately in each place. Mr. and Mrs. P. R. Toll (though formerly of the Dutch Reformed church, united with the organization at that time. Rev. Sauvin E. Lane, of Lima, a son-in-law of Captain Toll (preaching there at the same time), and Rev. A. D. White succeeded Mr. Ogden. Rev. Aaron H. Kerr preached from 1848 to 1852, when he was succeeded by Rev. William Cathcart, who labored until 1861. Mr. Cathcart, with his wife and child, escaped from the burning steamer "Northern Indiana," on Lake Erie, through his own almost superhuman

exertions, in which he was badly burned. After 1861 to the present time, Methodist services have been for the most part held, but without any regular organization. There is at present, and has been for many years, a Sunday-school, which has its sessions every Sunday morning in the school-house (where all meetings are held), which is quite interesting in its exercises, and numbers sixty scholars. The good seed of practical living embodied in the golden rule is being sown there unsparingly by the son of the pioneer of the village, as well as encouragement given to obtain useful general knowledge of nature and her laws.

The house of Captain P. R. Toll was always the home of the clergymen who came that way, and to them he dispensed a lavish hospitality, no matter what their creeds or doctrines might have been. Though with his wife a member of the Dutch Reformed church, he was liberal towards all orthodox or evangelical denominations, and, desirous of preaching of some kind or other in the community, he actually paid the first preacher for his labors, out of his own pocket. There never was any church-edifice built in the township, the school-houses at Fawn River mills and Freedom being used for religious purposes.

### NO LAWYER

ever gained a "local habitation and a name" in this village, the neighboring villages of White Pigeon, Sturgis, Lima, and La Grange furnishing the legal exponents for those of its citizens who were litigiously inclined.

### GALEN AND ESCULAPIUS

had disciples who ministered to the ills of the bodies of the people, in the persons of Dr. Holbrook, who was the first to settle there, and who is now in California; Dr. Richardson, who came next, and then Dr. Bradley, who married a daughter of Esquire Flanders, and died while yet a young man, in the village; Dr. D. L. I. Flanders, a son of the old Squire, who diagnosed symptoms and prescribed for the cure of their causes, and went thence to Cass county, subsequently returning to Sturgis, where he is still located; and Edmund A. Finn, who went into the army, was a surgeon in a Tennessee regiment of cavalry, and on his return went to Nebraska, where he died a year or more ago. There is no resident physician in the village now—Colonel Toll gratuitously acting in emergencies.

### THE CEMETERY

(disclaiming any intention of being suggestive, by reason of following the record of the doctors) was laid off by Captain Toll in 1838, and is a beautiful little plat of about three acres, lying contiguous to the school-house site, and alongside of the highway, sloping easily down to the river and sheltered by large overspreading oaks, yet open to the free, bright sunlight from the west and south. The land was finally bought by the town authorities in 1847, when Captain Toll conveyed it to them and built a fence around it for the sum of thirty-six dollars and sixty cents.

The first burial in it, as far as is now known, was that of Mrs. Louisa R. Morse, wife of Amos Morse, the millwright of Fawn River mills. She died August 27, 1839, and a neat slab has been erected at her grave by Hon. I. D. Toll, as a mark of respect to her memory and the work of her husband. John P. Van Patten, the first carpenter of the village, was also buried here in 1840, or thereabouts.

A little daughter of I. D. Toll lies sleeping here, with the babbling of the water, the rustling of the leaves, and the singing of the birds making music, —a fit lullaby for little lives like hers, that shed their fragrance upon those who are left behind.

Here, too, just at the north end of the little plat, are lying the remains of the indigent who have died in the care of the county authorities; whose humanity is attested by neat headstones at each grave, bearing the name, age, and date of decease of the occupant. This, too, is the work of the broad-minded son and successor of the old proprietor of Fawn River village.

### MANUFACTURES.

The first manufacturing establishment in the village was the saw-mill built by P. R. Toll in 1836, which was followed the next year by a grist- and flouring-mill by the same party. The saw-mill has fallen into ruins, and the flouring-mill, after a busy existence of nearly forty years, was burned to the ground January 1, 1873, the work of an incendiary, and was rebuilt the same year by the present owners, Daniel Himebaugh & Sons, who commenced operations again October 28, 1874. The present building is thirty-eight by forty-four feet on the ground, three stories in height, and is furnished with three run of stones, and most completely equipped with all of the more modern improvements necessary to a first-class mill. The mill has always had a most excellent reputation, and during the early years of its history, the merchants of Lima and La Grange, and other points farther off even, sent large quantities of wheat to it to be floured for the purpose of remitting eastward, flour being a better medium of exchange than wheat in bulk. It still maintains its reputation, but does custom work almost exclusively. The mill-property was sold by the Tolls in 1865 to Stewart & Alexander, and they to Daniel Himebaugh. Captain Toll put up a blacksmith-shop and fitted it up with a set of tools soon after he began to build his flouring-mill, and the first regular smith who worked in it was George G. Gilbert, of Burr Oak, in 1839, who had a shop of his own at the same time on his farm in the latter place. Captain Toll also had a cooper-shop, and employed men for the manufacture of barrels, among them the following: William Smith, James Fuller, Roswell and David Cooper, James Hayes, Joseph Smith and Charles Bowman. Henry Sanders, E. H. Pride, J. Terwilliger, Albert Norton and Asa Hoard, all carried on blacksmithing on their own account from time to time; Pride extensively so in 1847 and later. A. D. Cross was a wheelwright there, and William Christian a tailor in 1846. John P. Van Patten and William Schermerhorn were the first carpenters, and did the work on the mills. Robert and Andrew Nelson succeeded them, and were in turn succeeded by L. Eckerson, T. W. Selover and James McLauchlin, which latter trio are still residents of the village. The artist who labored for the benefit of the *soles* of the people, to keep them in good condition for their understanding, was Charles McCue, who came in 1840, worked for several years, and was an excellent man. His successors were Henry Sweet and John Courtwright.

Francis Flanders, in the winter of 1841–2, rented the saw-mill of Captain Toll, and, engaging Doctor Isham Flanders, then a boy of seventeen years, to run it, went himself to getting out logs. Out of the lumber and timber made that winter the old fulling-mill and carding-factory was built the following summer, and the first work was done June 10, 1842. The old mill and its equipment cost two thousand dollars. There was no cloth made in it, wool being carded and cloth dressed only. A new woolen-mill was built in 1851 by the same proprietor, costing, completed, ten thousand five hundred dollars. There were in it one hundred and twenty spindles, two broad and.two narrow looms, three double carding-machines, one condenser, two sets of finishing machinery, and the fulling-mill apparatus complete. In this last mill all kinds of cloths, except broadcloth were made, and a large custom work done. Six men and five women were employed to operate its machinery. Mr. Flanders sold out his interest in 1858 to A. H. Johnson, and he disposed of it in 1861 to Daniel Stewart. Bristol Parham now owns it, but it is not in operation.

### THE MERCANTILE BUSINESS

of the village has been conducted by Captain P. R. Toll, the first merchant, the firm changing to Alfred Toll, and then to Tull & Brewster; Flanders & Sons, A. Toll & Co., F. Moore & Co., Derrick S. Buck and George Carr, the latter two being resident in the village now, Mr. Buck on the south side of the river and Mr. Carr in the old Toll store. They carry fair stocks of general merchandise, and are doing a good legitimate trade.

### THE ONLY SECRET SOCIETY

in the village is the Fawn River Grange, No. 56, Patrons of Husbandry, which was organized February 16, 1875, and now has forty-eight members. The present officers are Henry Driesbach, master; J. A. McLauchlin, secretary, and Lucy McLauchlin, assistant stewardess. The regular meetings of the grange are on the second and last Saturdays of each month, at the hall over the old Toll store.

### AN EXCITEMENT

rippled the usually placid surface of Fawn River society, in 1850, occasioned by the discovery of a floating corpse in the mill-pond by some fishermen. Esquire Flanders was notified, and a coroner's jury impaneled, who sat and solemnly viewed the "damp and unpleasant body," and returned a verdict, "Found drowned." The only property found on the person of the deceased man was an old pocket-knife and thirty-eight dollars in cash, and the latter was turned over to a man to make a box in which the body was buried.

As a story never travels without gaining some additions, so the news of this "crowner's quest" went abroad, and gathered to the original relations thereof a multitude of surmises, which grew into absolute statements, and murder and robbery were directly charged, and a coroner, accompanied by one hundred and fifty citizens of Sturgis and the surrounding country, one day invaded the peaceful precincts of the village, and demanded another jury, exhumed the body, and reviewed it again officially. No further developments were made, however, and the body was again buried, but not so with

the mystery. That, however, after a time was explained and quieted by the fact appearing that the body was that of an unfortunate lunatic who had escaped from his keepers, and had fallen into the river accidentally or otherwise.

## VILLAGE OF FREEDOM.

Judging from the elaborate geographical definition written on the plat of this little hamlet, it once indulged in "great expectations." Located on the Chicago road, the great artery along which beat the pulses of commerce in ante-railroad days, the proprietor wrought out exceedingly pretty aerial castles, but which, have all vanished, like the "baseless fabric of a vision," along with the rumbling stage-coaches on which this atmospheric joiner-work was based.

F. A. Tisdel built a handsome and commodious frame-tavern here in 1836, and caused a village to be laid out, the surveyor's plat of which, looking at it from the standpoint of to-day, is a curiosity worth preserving. One D. M. Cook, civil engineer, was the artist who drew the document, in September, 1836, and is thus historians: "The plat of the village of Freedom is located on section three, township eight, range south nine west; latitude forty-one degrees and forty-eight seconds, and longitude eight degrees and seventeen seconds, on the Chicago road, one hundred and thirty miles from Detroit, and situate on high-rolling burr-oak, white-oak and hickory land."

Its streets were named Maple, Pine, Hickory, Chestnut, Pearl, Branch, Minerva, Van Buren, Jefferson and Madison. The first post-office for the accommodation of Fawn River people was located here in 1836–7, and Mr. Tisdel was the first postmaster. The mails came as regularly as did the well-filled stage coaches which rattled up to the door at six miles an hour, heralded by the "tan-ta-ra" of the driver's horn,—at first once, then twice, then three times, and finally six times each week, each way between Detroit and Chicago.

Mr. Tisdel had a stock of goods here for a time, and was succeeded by Hewit & Randall, but no store or other business is carried on there now. Rev. Mr. Farley, a Christian minister, and J. H. Hard, a Baptist, preached occasionally at the school-house here, but no church was ever organized. Mr. Latta succeeded Tisdel; Latta's was as famous as a place of resort, and as well kept as Tisdel's or Sweet's,—Mrs. Latta being an excellent hostess.

Here, in the triangle formed by the intersection of the highways, Colonel I. D. Toll drilled his recruits for Mexico in March, 1847,—facing poor Terwilliger right, left and front, much to the discomposure of his own hundred and fifty pounds of adiposeté; demonstrating at last that his physical confirmation was an inseparable bar to the exercise of his patriotism, and remanding him to civic life to hammer glory out of the anvil rather than seek it in the "deadly imminent breach" on the plains of Mexico.

Here, too, was enacted the tragedy which cost poor Fanning his life, through the inefficiency of an Indiana sheriff. The following, clipped from a La Grange paper of November 2, 1840, will partly tell the story: "Last Saturday a horse-thief, with two valuable bay horses, having stopped at Latta's hotel, on the Chicago turnpike, in Fawn River, killed Ganaliel Fanning, a constable, who, with three others, was attempting to arrest him. He was, half an hour afterward, captured in the woods, one half mile north of the tavern, through the intrepidity of General I. D. Toll, who was a mile distant when Fanning was killed, and Sheriff Knox has him in jail. Toll has the knife now (an ugly-looking weapon) with which the bloody deed was done. The murderer proved to be a Mississippi desperado, named Ward, who was convicted and sentenced to fifteen years to the State prison at Jackson, and died there six years afterwards. His body was nearly covered with ███, from knife-wounds principally. Had the sheriff, who pursued the thief from Indiana, been possessed of the courage of a man fit for his position, the man could have been arrested without harm to any one; but he had not, and the pursuit being organized from the hotel in three parties (Fanning's being the largest party), he came up unsupported, closed in upon the thief, and lost his life by several desperate thrusts of the knife."

And here, too, in later years, fell the foul blot of disgrace upon the fair fame of Latta, which stripped him of his farm, and drove him forth a fugitive from deserved justice, and gave to the county their present farm and asylum for their indigent, which is the only point of interest now remaining in this once famous hamlet.

A little cemetery adjoins the school-house site, laid out in or about the year 1839. The stone bearing the oldest inscription is one standing at the grave of William Hoagland, who died August 20, 1839.

# BIOGRAPHICAL SKETCHES.

## CAPTAIN PHILIP R. TOLL.

The subject of this sketch was born May 10, 1793, in an ancient stone mansion on a farm, a part of an extensive tract of land which had belonged to his first ancestor in America, Carl H. Toll, two centuries ago, situated nearly three miles northwest of Schenectady, New York. It is now the property of his nephew of the same name, Philip Ryley Toll. (The family name is variously written in the old records, as Toll, Tol, Van Toll, Van Tholl and Tollius.)

Carl H. Toll, a very large land-owner, represented all of New York west of Albany in the colonial legislature, from 1715 to 1724. His son, Captain Daniel Toll, great-grandfather of Philip R. Toll, was born July 1, 1691, and was killed by the Indians in the Boekindale (Peach valley) battle, in August, 1748.

Heinrich Toll, surnamed in the original documents "the valiant," commanded the Dutch ship in which he bore the order for the surrender of New Netherlands to the English, July 7, 1674.

John, a son of Daniel Toll, and grandfather of Phillip R., was born August 13, 1719, and Charles H., his son, and the father of Philip R., was born February 10, 1745. He married Elizabeth Ryley, January 11, 1767. She was the daughter of Philip Ryley, who gave his name to her son Philip R. She was also a sister of Judge James V. S. Ryley, prominently known in the Mohawk valley.

Captain Toll was educated as a physician, but practiced as such only occasionally and gratuitously. He served in the war of 1812 in the United States army in its operations in Canada, as captain of a company of mounted artillery, which, owing to its fine discipline, was selected as guard at headquarters under General Wade Hampton, and was in several engagements.

In 1825 Captain Toll removed with his family to Ovid, Seneca county, New York, where he engaged in a general mercantile and produce business, and the manufacture of hats, boots and potash.

In 1834 he removed to Centreville, in St. Joseph county, Michigan, and engaged in a general mercantile business in company with a nephew, Charles H. Toll—Philip Ryley Toll, another nephew, being a clerk in the business. He also leased and operated the Centreville mills for a time.

In the fall of 1836 he built a saw-mill at Fawn River, and the next year a grist-mill, and removed to that place with his family in 1838. Afterwards he added facilities for flouring or merchant work, and had an extensive patronage. He held about thirteen hundred acres of land adjoining the mills, nearly all of it in a body, and much of it improved, besides large tracts in various parts of the State. In 1852 he removed to Monroe, Michigan, where he prepared a fine mansion and elegant grounds, and where he died August 17, 1862.

In 1817 he married Nancy, a daughter of Judge Isaac DeGraff, a citizen of Schenectady, and prominently known in the Mohawk valley. The fruits of this union, which was a most happy one and lasted forty-five years, were: Isaac D., Elizabeth (wife of Rev. E. S. Lane, and who died January 18, 1861, leaving three children), Susan D., Jane Anna, Charles, Alfred, and Sarah G., wife of Dr. A. I. Sawyer, of Monroe, Michigan, all of whom, except Elizabeth, are now living. Charles is a prominent citizen of Monroe, having in several ways received evidences of the partiality of the electors of the city and county of Monroe. Alfred is a successful lumber merchant of Hannibal, Missouri, and treasurer of the Lumberman's Bank of that city.

Captain Philip R. Toll was elected president of the village council of Ovid, and one of the trustees of the academy there while a resident of the place.

He united with the Dutch Reformed church in Schenectady previous to his marriage, and continued a member of that society until his residence in Fawn River, when, to assist in building up a church in that place, he, with his wife, united with the Presbyterian church, of which he was the chief pillar and main support. Notwithstanding his own predilections, he was liberally inclined toward all orthodox faiths, and assisted in maintaining the preaching of these doctrines, irrespective of creed. He was a man of simple tastes, pure life and most domestic in his habits; in short, a thorough gentleman of the old school. He was a man of great energy and decided convictions.

In politics a Democrat from early life. When President Jackson issued the famous specie circular, which threatened him with bankruptcy, he remarked, "This is ruinous, but it is right." The good that he did lives, and precious are the memories he has left behind him.

## NANCY DeGRAFF TOLL,

the wife of Captain Philip R. Toll, was born in Schenectady, New York, on the 18th day of September, 1798. Her father, Judge Isaac DeGraff, was a most zealous patriot, and served as major during the Revolutionary war. The oath of office prescribed by Congress in February, 1788, was administered to him by General LaFayette. His accounts of the Revolutionary times are embodied in history. After peace was declared, he served a long time as judge of the court of common pleas of the county of Schenectady, and died at the ripe age of eighty-eight years, preserving his faculties to the last. His son, John I. DeGraff, in the war of 1812,—as appears in a letter from Commodore McDonough,—when the government was out of funds and its credit impaired by the capture of Washington, furnished the commodore with means to prepare his fleet on Lake Champlain to meet the enemy; without which, the gallant old hero acknowledged he would have been powerless.

John I. DeGraff served two terms in Congress, was one of the proprietors and builders of the first railroad in the United States—the Mohawk and Hudson,—and declined the portfolio of the secretary of the treasury, offered him by President Van Buren, his own large estate (which he bequeathed at his death to his brothers and sister), requiring his whole attention.

The Dutch governor of the island of St. Eustatius, of the same name (John De Graff) and family, was the first foreign official who saluted the American flag. For this act he was recalled by his government, at the instance of Great Britain; but the liberty-loving Hollanders sympathized with him, and he grew in favor rather than diminished in their regard.

Mrs. Toll was ever characterized by great generosity. Her charities, like her vigilance over her household, like her industry and patience, were without stint or limit. The helpmeet of a pioneer in all the vicissitudes of a new country, in its sickness and wants, she was always ready for any demand, any emergency. Still residing at Monroe, at the head of her family, at a ripe age, and actively benevolent, she is gently and serenely passing down life's western declivity, to blend, by and by, in the full glories of its latest autumnal sunset. "Her children rise up and call her blessed."

---

HON. ISAAC D. TOLL.

Among the honored names of St. Joseph county, none stand higher on the roll thereof than that of the subject of our sketch, Isaac DeGraff Toll. Possessing the entire confidence of his fellow-citizens, without distinction of party or creed, he moves among them as one of the few public men upon whose garments clings no taint of corruption, and whose integrity runs parallel to his ability. Affable, courteous, hospitable, generous, his lines are bounded by no partisanship, and his charities know no sect.

Mr. Toll was the oldest son of Philip R. and Nancy D. Toll, who were of the first families of the old Knickerbockers of the Mohawk valley, and was born December 1, 1816, in Glenville, three miles from Schenectady, New York, on the family homestead of two centuries. With his parents he removed to Ovid, in the same State, in 1825, where he received an

academic education, and was admitted to the sophomore class of Union College (the school of his uncles on both sides of the family), but was immediately withdrawn from the college to accompany his father, who, in 1834, removed to St. Joseph county, and located in Centreville, and engaged in a mercantile and manufacturing business. Isaac assisted in the extensive business carried on by his father, both at Centreville, and subsequently at Fawn River, until 1846, and again, after the Mexican war, until 1853. He commenced his public life at the age of twenty-one years, as assessor of the township of Fawn River, and then as supervisor. This position he has held for fifteen years.

In 1846 he was elected to represent St. Joseph county in the lower house of the State legislature, by which body—of which he was the youngest member—he was made chairman of the committee on militia, he holding then a commission as major-general of the Michigan State troops. He was also on the committee of internal improvements, and was foremost in preventing the diversion of the Michigan Southern railroad, south of Coldwater, and its sale to Toledo parties, although a larger sum, by one hundred thousand dollars, was offered for it by such parties than by any in his own State. His State pride was aroused, and he worked successfully with it, as appears from newspapers of that day. As chairman of the former committee he framed what was said by the Detroit press to be the best bill for the organization of the State militia that Michigan ever had, by which bill—which subsequently became a law—the organization of the State forces was placed at once upon a sound financial basis by commutation fees in lieu of service, the commutation being applied for the benefit of independent companies. At a subsequent session of the assembly, the commutation clause was stricken out, and the law thereby shorn of its vital force. In the terse manner which characterizes his speeches, he lashed those who were opposed to the small commutation, as deserving of banishment to a "clime where patriotism is unknown, and Mammon is commander-in-chief."

In 1847 he was elected to the State senate, and while in that body was instrumental in promoting the educational interests of his county, and also the interests of his district and western part of the State, by obtaining an appropriation for the improvement of the navigation of the St. Joseph river.

At the close of the session he accepted a captaincy in the Fifteenth United States Infantry, in the war with Mexico, and returned home, and with the aid of Lieutenants Goodman, Titus, and Freelon raised a company, and went through the campaign with General Scott, in General (afterwards President) Pierce's brigade, from Vera Cruz to the city of Mexico, distinguishing himself at Riconada Pass, Contreras, Churubusco, and Molino del Rey, and with his regiment garrisoned Chepultepec. For the part taken by him at Churubusco, where he was wounded (and the loss was most severe), including his first lieutenant and sergeant, reference is made to the general history of the county.

In 1849, as a candidate for the constitutional convention of the State, he received every vote in his own township but three.

In 1854 he received the appointment of examiner of patents at Washington from President Pierce, between whom and himself there existed a strong personal friendship, engendered while campaigning together in Mexico. In this position he passed decisions upon applications in hydraulics, pneumatics, and electricity, with some minor subjects, some of which were published in the newspapers at that time. He held this position until 1861. As is well known, there was well-grounded cause for alarm at Washington in the early part of April of that year, and distrust was the rule. The departments of the government contained a large infusion of disloyal elements, and a number of officials resigned, went home, and took positions in the insurgent army. At a meeting held in the patent-office building, of which Mr. Toll was chairman, it was decided to enroll those of the interior department who might volunteer, for the purpose of defense, and, if occasion demanded, of offensive operations, as the city was deemed an object of attack. Mr. Toll was elected commandant of the volunteers, and meetings were held nightly for drill in the patent-office building square, and arms issued. This organization was kept up until the arrival of troops, and the military situation made Washington secure. He was elected at the time an honorary member of the National Rifles of Washington,—one of the best-drilled companies in the country.

His energetic course in the Union cause, no less than the promptness and ability with which he discharged the duties of examiner, caused a strong pressure for his retention in the department; but the demands of party were insatiable, and he was succeeded by one of the dominant party in the summer of 1861.

Since then he has been in the walks of private life from choice, except so far as to serve his township and county in the office of supervisor, where his efficiency and influence were ever apparent, guarding the interests of the people with watchfulness, and discharging his trusts with a liberal economy. He was once unanimously chosen chairman of the board of supervisors, though a majority of the members were of the opposite political party to himself,—and in 1876 was elected by a large non-partisan vote to represent the county before the State board of equalization, where, by his thorough knowledge of the values of property in his own and adjoining counties, he was able to convince the board that injustice had been done his county in the equalization of 1871, and therefore obtained a reduction of six million dollars on the valuation of the property of the county for State-levies of taxes, which, standing unchanged for five years to come, gives an aggregate reduction of thirty million dollars from the equalization of the five years previously.

On January 9, 1849, Mr. Toll was united in marriage to Julia V., daughter of Hon. Charles Moran, of Detroit. Judge Moran was for several terms a member of the old territorial council and of the State legislature. He shouldered a musket in the war of 1812, when scarcely fifteen years old, and was present in the army at Hull's surrender. He died October 13, 1876, at the ripe age of seventy-eight years, leaving an excellent reputation for uprightness and cardinal Christian virtues. His most kindly heart gave the unaffected cordial manners, characteristic of the old pioneer families of Detroit and of his race. He left a very large estate.

Three children were born to Mr. and Mrs. Toll: ANNA J., who died in infancy; CHARLES PHILIP, who is now a teller in the First National Bank of Detroit, and JULIA JOSEPHINE, now attending school in that city.

Mrs. Toll was a niece of the gallant Major Antoine DeQuindre of the war of 1812. She died at Fawn River, April 14, 1865, after a short illness of only three weeks, in the thirty-sixth year of her age, and in the communion of the Catholic church. The *Washington Chronicle*, in which city she had formerly resided, thus speaks of her: " The memory of Mrs. Toll will long be cherished in this community by the friends who so well knew the influence of her kind and gentle nature and the spirit of truth and devotion to duty that marked her brief pathway through life. Ardent in her friendship, unselfish in her purposes, and unostentatious in her charities, she unconsciously won the respect and affection of all who knew her."

Isaac D. Toll is as good a specimen of the old-school gentlemen as can be found in this present year of grace, and his prospects to hold his fair fame among his fellow-citizens for many years yet to come are flattering, as he carries his burdens lightly, and keeps his business most systematically in hand.

In politics Mr. Toll has ever been a Democrat, and his religious creed is the golden rule: " Whatsoever ye would that men should do unto you, do ye even so unto them."

### FRANCIS FLANDERS.

Francis Flanders was one of the early settlers of the town of Fawn River. He was the second son of Ezekiel Flanders, a soldier of the Revolution, and under the command of General Sullivan. He was born at Sutton, Vermont, April 5, 1792, and was a volunteer soldier in the war of 1812, and

was stationed at Portsmouth, New Hampshire. After receiving a common-school education he was apprenticed to Oliver Hunt, woolen manufacturer at Bath, New Hampshire.

After the war of 1812 he became associated in business with Captain John Smith, a trader to the West Indies, and they established a woolen-factory at Colebrook, New Hampshire.

He removed from Colebrook to Bristol, Ontario county, New York, in the winter of 1829, and afterwards settled in the town of Canandaigua, where he lived until September, 1841, and removed from there to Fawn River, in this county, where he arrived October 10 of that year. He immediately proceeded to the establishment of his business of wool-carding and cloth-dressing, which was a success and drew custom from a distance of forty miles. (I find upon examination of his books for June, 1842, wheat credited at thirty-seven and a half cents per bushel; butter, six cents; eggs, three cents; ham, five cents; pork, four cents. October, 1842, quarter of beef, one hundred and twelve pounds at one and a half cents.) The business grew into the manufacturing of woolen goods, which was established by F. Flanders & Sons in 1852. He retained his interest in this business until nearly the time of his death, September 14, 1861.

He held the office of justice of the peace for a long series of years, and his house was the "Gretna Green" for a large scope of country, situated just across the State line in Indiana. It was of frequent occurrence to see a strong-muscled Hoosier, dressed in blue jean, and leading a bronzed and blushing Hoosier girl, arrayed in bark-colored muslin and calico bonnet, inquiring the way to Esquire Flanders, where, they said, they were "*going to git spliced!*"

He was married January 18, 1818, to Elizabeth S. Chandler, of Colebrook, New Hampshire, who is still living at the age of seventy-nine. Their oldest son, FRANCIS FLANDERS, JR., was a school-teacher and medical student; but this being too tame a life for him, at the age of eighteen years he enlisted in the United States service. Three years of his term of enlistment was spent in the Florida war, and at the expiration of his term he returned. When war was declared against Mexico, and a call made for volunteers under the ten-regiment act, he enlisted under command of Captain I. D. Toll, but was transferred to the office of chief musician of a regiment, which gave him the title of major. Since the Mexican war he has resided in California and Mexico until the summer of 1876, when he returned to Sturgis, where his home is at present. He was the leading musician of the first brass-band organized in St. Joseph county, in 1845, organized at Sturgis, and called the St. Joseph County Democratic Brass Band, commanded by Captain A. S. Drake.

Their second son, JONATHAN W. FLANDERS, is a lawyer, located at Sturgis, St. Joseph county.

Their third son, DAVID L. I. FLANDERS, is a physician, located at the same place. They had four daughters, ANN B., ELIZABETH C., LYDIA L., and JENNIE, two of whom are living: Mrs. Ann B. Lewis, of Canaan, Wayne county, Ohio, and Mrs. Jennie Madden, of Champaign city, Illinois.

Mr. Flanders was made a Mason at Bath, New Hampshire, in 1813, and remained firmly attached to the order during his life. He was a charter-member of Mt. Hermon lodge, at Centreville, the first lodge established in the county, and was the first worshipful master of Meridian Sun lodge, of Sturgis.

# FABIUS.

FABIUS is noted for its lakes and knobs. The former lie scattered throughout its area, reflecting from their quiet limpid water the rays of light, like so many polished mirrors, or, rippled with the passing zephyr, break into a thousand silvery bars that scintillate in the moonbeams like the stars in the blue depths above them. The principal ones are named Corry, from a settler, —Joshua Corry,—who located near its shores; Mohney, from Abraham Mohney, upon whose farm it is situated; Boot, from its peculiar boot-like

shape. The remaining ones are smaller in area, and are named according to the suggestion of peculiar natural causes.

THE SOIL

is a sandy loam and clay, and susceptible of a high state of cultivation, to which state the greater portion thereof is brought at the present date. Its productions are similar to those of other parts of the county.

FRANCIS FLANDERS, SEN.R
— FAWN RIVER —

MRS. ELIZABETH S. FLANDERS
— FAWN RIVER. —

MAJOR FRANCIS FLANDERS, JUN.R
— FAWN RIVER. —

D. L. I. FLANDERS, M.D.
— FAWN RIVER. —

J. W. FLANDERS, ESQ.
— STURGIS. —

of the township includes twenty thousand nine hundred and forty-eight acres of land and twenty-one hundred acres of water surface, the latter being the most extensive of any other township in the county.

### THE SURFACE

is broken and diversified by prairie, timber, level plains, rolling and hilly land, and, with its numerous lakes, presents a picturesque prospect. Its timber consists of beech, maple, oak, walnut, elm and other varieties of wood, oak predominating. "Johnny-cake" prairie, so-called from its size and shape, lies in the eastern part of the township in the immediate vicinity of Three Rivers. The balance of the township was originally covered with timber ("oak openings"), and was heavily wooded.

### THE FIRST LAND-ENTRIES

were made in the township in the year 1829, and were as follows: The southeast quarter and northeast quarter of section thirteen, by Jacob McIntersfer, of Wayne county, Ohio, June 25, and the east half of the southeast quarter of section twenty-five, by William Meek, November 2. There were three entries only made in 1830.

In 1876 there were twenty thousand eight hundred and thirty-nine acres assessed for taxation, valued by Henry Stotz, the supervisor of the township, at two hundred and twenty thousand and fifty dollars, about one-third of its actual valuation.

### THE FIRST PERMANENT SETTLERS

in Fabius were Garrett Sickles, who came in together with his family, in the year 1830. They were followed about a year afterwards by Thiam Harwood, Heman Harvey and Samuel Newell, all of whom were also accompanied by their respective families. Of these original pioneers not one now remains to recount the story of their early trials and the hardships incident to the formation of a new settlement.

On the 9th of October, 1832, William F. Arnold, in company with his father's family, arrived and settled on the west half of the southeast quarter of section twenty-six, which had been entered by them in June the preceding year. At the time of their arrival there were only four families within the present limits of the township,—those whose names are given above. The mode of travel in vogue in those days was slow and tedious. Those coming in from the State of New York made the journey to Buffalo by the Erie canal, and then to Detroit by the lake, and from that point to their destination by ox or horse teams by the Chicago and Detroit road,—the journey generally occupying three weeks. There were no bridges in those days, so that all the streams on the line of travel had to be forded.

Those who came in from Ohio came with teams, and had to come through Black swamp, in the vicinity of the Maumee river, and the hardships endured by the adventurous pioneer were of the most trying character. The facilities for travel were miserable, while the miasmatic nature of the region through which they had to pass usually caused a serious sickness. And the region where they proposed making their permanent residence was cursed in those days with malarial diseases of a painful type.

These and other similar hardships they had to contend with, but, with a determination that has been pregnant with good results in the development of the township, they braved sickness and disease, and by dint of sheer determination, succeeded in bringing it from a vast forest to a fertile and prosperous settlement.

Those of the earlier settlers still remaining recall with painful vividness the sickly season of 1838. In that year the fever and ague and other malarial ailments were so general that it partook much of the the nature of an epidemic. In many families nearly all the members were stricken down, so that it was of frequent occurrence that there were more sick than there were well ones to take care of them.

A few years subsequent to the arrival of the old settlers above named, Deacon William Churchill and his sons Adna and Randall came into the township and settled on the west half of the southeast quarter of section twenty-six, now owned by Barak O. White. Cotemporaneous with them were: Mr. J. W. Coffinberry, Andrew Burritt, Benjamin Smith, Charles Rice (the latter dying at the advanced age of ninety-three), Alonzo R. Hunt, Michael Beadle, Alfred Poe, Solomon Hartman and B. M. King. Jacob McInterfer entered a large tract of land, partly in what is now Fabius, but he never settled in the township, dying in 1831.

### THE FIRST FARM OPENED

and improved in Fabius township was that of Garrett Sickles, located on section thirteen,—on what is now known as "Johnny-Cake prairie." The farm is now occupied by John G. Sickles, a son of the original owner.

### THE FIRST FRAME HOUSE

was erected by James Valentine, in the spring of 1836. The lumber used in its construction was sawed at the mill of Michael Beadle. It stood for than a quarter of a century, when it was torn down,—thus effacing a land-mark which might have attained a venerable antiquity. It stood on the farm now owned by William Hartman.

### THE FIRST BRICK HOUSE

in the township was erected by Stephen A. Rice, in 1849. It was built originally as an addition to his former residence, which was a frame building. The house yet stands on the site of the old Rice homestead, on section twenty-four. Its owner is Mr. S. A. Rice.

### MANUFACTURES

The first saw-mill in Fabius township was erected near the mouth of Lake run, about one mile from Three Rivers, by Michael Beadle, in the spring of 1835. The next one was built by Jasper and Barnabus Eddy, on the same stream, in the fall of 1837. This mill is still in operation, being carried on by Jasper Eddy, one of the original proprietors. The only other mill of any kind in Fabius, is the saw-mill of Sidney Johnson, which is located on the same stream. There is a mint-still operated by Charles W. Shall, at the head of Lake Four, on section five.

### BRICK-YARDS.

The first brick-yard in the township was established by Abishai Hoisington, on the farm now occupied by John E. Cook, on section thirteen, in 1844. He continued in the business for a number of years at the old place when it was abandoned, and the site thereof put under cultivation.

There are now three brick-yards in operation, all located on section twenty-three. They are owned, respectively, by Hoisington (a son of Abishai H.) & Wells, Simeon Dunn and Hiram Malone.

### A DISTILLERY

for the manufacture of high-wines was erected in the township by Challenge S. Wheeler in 1855, and, after continuing in operation for about two years, it was totally destroyed by fire in 1857.

### THE FIRST MOWER AND REAPER

was brought into the township by Garrett Sickles in 1842, who used to reap the grain for those who had no improved machinery. It was an old "Kirby."

### THE FIRST THOROUGH-BRED SHORT-HORNS

were introduced by Richard Illenden, about 1864. He did much towards improving the live-stock of the township, and the beneficial influence of his enterprise is now observable in the neat appearance of the cattle in the township.

There were owned in the township, in 1874, four hundred and ninety-four horses, seventeen mules, eight oxen, four hundred and ninety-five cows, four hundred and thirty-two other cattle, one thousand five hundred and thirteen hogs, and one thousand seven hundred and fifty-six sheep.

### THE CROPS

of 1873 were as follows: Wheat produced on three thousand five hundred and fifty-two acres, forty-nine thousand three hundred and fifty-one bushels; corn, on one thousand seven hundred and thirty-seven acres, fifty-four thousand three hundred and eighty-five bushels; other grain, ten thousand and seventy bushels; potatoes, six thousand two hundred bushels; hay, one thousand three hundred and sixty-one tons; wool, eight thousand and sixteen pounds; pork, one hundred and fifty thousand eight hundred and ninety-five pounds; butter, thirty-five thousand nine hundred and ninety pounds; dried fruit, four thousand nine hundred and fifty-nine pounds; cider, five hundred and eighteen barrels; maple-sugar, two hundred pounds; apples, thirteen thousand eight hundred and forty bushels from four hundred and forty-seven acres, and two hundred and three bushels of other fruit,—the apples and fruit being valued at four thousand seven hundred and sixty-four dollars.

### THE MANUFACTURING PRODUCT

in 1873 was as follows: Two saw-mills and three brick yards employed twenty persons and a capital of nine thousand dollars, and their product was valued at eleven thousand nine hundred dollars.

### CRANBERRIES.

Cranberries are raised extensively in the southwest corner of the township by William W. Johnson and others. An area of several hundred acres is used almost exclusively for the natural growth of this fruit. Sidney Johnson raised a large quantity of the berries by cultivation and artificial irrigation.

EARLY BIRTHS.

Who the first white child born in the township was has not been definitely ascertained. Lydia Arnold, a daughter of William F. Arnold, was born February 28, 1835, and four days afterward a boy cousin came to keep her company, named Thomas, a son of Randall Churchill. Mr. Samuel Newell had a new baby at his house about the same time also.

THE FIRST MARRIAGE

of white persons in the township was the one solemnized between William F. Arnold and Rose Churchill, the latter a daughter of Deacon William Churchill—both bride and groom being pioneers of Fabius.

THE FIRST DEATH

that occurred among the settlers of the township was that of Mrs. Ashley Rice, but the exact date thereof we did not learn.

THE FIRST BURYING-GROUND

regularly laid out was on land donated for the purpose by William Morrison, and called to this day "Morrison burying-ground," in honor of the donor, in 1838. The first interment therein was that of Mrs. Mehitable Harvey, wife of Heman Harvey, and second daughter of Charles Rice, who died in December, 1838. Prior to this the early settlers were accustomed to bury their dead on their farms, a plat being laid off for that purpose. Several of the old deceased pioneers were thus sepultured.

THE FIRST SCHOOL-HOUSE

in the township was built of logs in 1833, on the edge of the woods on the south line of section thirty-five, on lands now owned by Lewis K. Brodie. It was used as a meeting-house, and also for a Sunday-school. It only stood a few years, when it was destroyed by fire through the carelessness of some parties who were moving into the township, and stopped there over night and left the fire in such a way that it caught and burned the house. The next school-house was built on land of William Morrison, on section thirty-four, where the cemetery now stands. William F. Arnold (to whom we are indebted for valuable information touching the township history), taught school there in the winter of 1843-4 for the sum of fifty cents a day. The first school-teacher was Susan Tracy. John Arney also taught the first winter school therein, and Miss Arvilla Denio was an early teacher in it.

FIRST SCHOOL-DISTRICT.

The school records of Fabius do not antedate 1858. We learn on well-authenticated authority that the district was organized as early as 1838, but could find no one of the early settlers now living who could fix the date to a certainty. Joel Redway was the first school-director. The first school-house was a frame structure, and stood on the farm of Garrett Sickles, now occupied by his son, J. G. Sickles, almost thirty rods from the present building. The present site was purchased of Richard Fulcher in 1858, the consideration being fifty dollars. The officers elected in 1859 were Frederick A. Hoisington, director, and Stephen A. Rice, assessor. The statistics of 1876 show the following exhibit of the educational standing of the township at the close of the school year, September 1st: There were in the township ten school-houses, two of brick and eight of wood, affording five hundred and sixty sittings, and valued at six thousand nine hundred dollars. Schools were in session in these buildings an average of eight months during the year; four hundred and twenty-nine pupils attending the same out of four hundred and eighty-nine children in the township of the legal school age. Seven male teachers were employed and paid seven hundred and sixteen dollars, and fourteen females received eight hundred and seven dollars and fifty cents, the total expenditures being two thousand three hundred and five dollars and fifty-five cents.

RELIGIOUS.

The first religious services held in the township were, after the primitive fashion, in the houses of the old settlers. One of the first dwellings in which religious services were held was the house of Hiram Harwood, who was the first regular class-leader. The services were in accordance with the doctrines of the Methodist Episcopal denomination. Among the first preachers were Reverends Boyd, McCool, and Sutler. These were circuit-riders, and used to come around occasionally to enlighten the settlement with the teachings of the gospel.

TRAGEDIES.

About the year 1842 the citizens of Fabius township were thrown into a state of consternation by the discovery of the dead body of Mrs. Laura

Redway hanging from a beam in an out-house. It appears that the unfortunate woman was subject to attacks of temporary derangement, in one of which she committed the melancholy deed. The news was first circulated by a neighbor calling at the house of Mr. Solomon Hartman just as the family were about partaking of the evening meal. The women-folks observed that there was something more than the ordinary news to be imparted, and so became curious to know what had happened. The visitor was loath to tell them, and managed to keep his secret until after supper, when he took the people of the house with him to where the suicide lay in death.

The same year a Mrs. Casper suspended herself from the limb of a plum-tree; no reason ever having been assigned for the deed, except a morbid depression of spirits to which she was subject.

INCIDENTS.

Mr. Solomon Hartman relates how he used to shelter a destitute Indian in a shanty on his place. The aborigine was honest, and used always to pay for his lodging either with money or labor. The winter previous to the one during which Mr. Hartman sheltered him, he camped out on the prairie with nothing but his blanket to save him from the inclemency of the weather.

CIVIL ORGANIZATION.

Fabius was originally a part of White Pigeon township, but in the winter of 1832-33 the legislative council set off what is now Fabius and Lockport into a separate township and called it Bucks, after George Buck, one of the first settlers of Lockport township.

THE FIRST ELECTION

after the formation of the township of Bucks was held at the house of Hiram Harwood, on what is now known as "Johnny-cake" prairie, in the spring of 1833, for the purpose of designating who should be appointed justice of the peace. The justices were then appointed by the governor under the territorial law. The candidates were Hiram Harwood, Jacob W. Coffinberry, George Buck, and Charles B. Fitch. The township was only entitled to three, and there was a lively strife between Messrs. Buck and Fitch. The first three names were successful. There was no political machinery in those days, the only question being who was the best man and the fittest for the office for which he was a candidate. There were about twenty votes polled at the election; Charles Rice was chosen moderator, and he went around with his hat and gathered in the votes.

In 1840 the township of Bucks was divided, and township six, range eleven set off into a township called Lockport—township six, range twelve retaining the original name. In 1841 the name of the township was changed to Fabius.

FIRST TOWNSHIP-MEETING.

The first meeting for the election of township officers for the township of Fabius was held at the house of Alfred Poe, April 5, 1841, at which the following gentlemen were chosen to fill the offices opposite their respective names: Randal Churchill, Joel Redway and William Arney, assessors; Joel Redway, John Laughlin and Thomas Ward, school inspectors; William Arney, Joel Redway, and Garrett Sickles, road commissioners; Charles Rice, William Morrison, school directors; Charles J. Rice, collector; Charles J. Rice and Lewis K. Brodie, constables; Joel Redway, William Arney and Frederick Shurtz, justices of the peace.

LIST OF TOWNSHIP OFFICERS.

Clerks—Thomas Ward (1841), William Arney (two years), William F. Arnold (two years), Valentine P. Redway (four years), Alonzo R. Hunt (eleven years), Richard Fulcher, Hiram W. Wheeler, John Anable, Joseph W. McKee, Stacy B. Naylor, John Cowling (three years), Benjamin F. Wells, James P. Brodie, present incumbent (seven years).

Supervisors—Frederick Shurtz, Joel Redway, William Arney (two years), William F. Arnold, Hezekiah Wetherbee (fourteen years), Randal Churchill, William W. Johnson (two years), John Anable (eight years), Jasper Eddy, Henry Stotz, present incumbent (five years).

Justices of the Peace—William Arney (sixteen years), William Morrison (eleven years), Orrin Hicks, John White, Jonathan Reed, Stacy B. Naylor (eight years), Norman A. Cole, A. R. Hunt, George Reed, Samuel White, Charles Rice, Timothy Wyman, present incumbent.

KAISER LAKE HOUSE,
CHARLES F. KAISER, PROPRIETOR.
FABIUS TP. ST JOSEPH CO., MICH.

RESIDENCE OF A. P. SHEPHERDSON,
FABIUS TP. ST JOSEPH CO. MICH

RESIDENCE OF CHARLES G. VOORHEES,
MENDON, ST. JOSEPH CO., MICH

JOHN WATKINS.
- Fabius Tp. -

Wm. ARNEY.
- Fabius Tp -

A. R. HUNT.
Fabius Tp -

David Beadle
- Fabius Tp. -

Wm Mochin
- Fabius Tp -

## TAXATION.

The first assessment of property for taxation in the township of Fabius was made in 1841, and amounted to forty-three thousand four hundred and one dollars, and the taxes levied thereon to six hundred and three dollars. In 1852 the assessment was returned at forty-four thousand nine hundred and five dollars, and the tax-levy amounted to six hundred and fifty dollars and nine cents. In 1860 the assessment was placed at two hundred and twenty-seven thousand four hundred and ninety-three dollars, and the taxes at one thousand seven hundred and seventy dollars and twenty-one cents. In 1870 the assessment was fixed at four hundred and thirty-nine thousand eight hundred and forty dollars, and the taxes at three thousand seven hundred and eighteen dollars and forty-four cents. In 1876 the real-estate was assessed, as equalized by the board of supervisors, at two hundred and nineteen thousand four hundred and ten dollars, and the personal property at forty-three thousand four hundred dollars, making a total assessment of two hundred and sixty-two thousand eight hundred and ten dollars. On this amount taxes were levied as follows: For State and county purposes, one-half to each, one thousand three hundred and forty-two dollars and fifty-four cents; township purposes, including schools, two thousand four hundred and forty-three dollars and fourteen cents. Total tax, three thousand seven hundred and eighty-five dollars and sixty-eight cents.

## POPULATION.

In 1850 there were four hundred and ninety-seven persons dwelling in the township. In 1860 there were eight hundred and seventy-six, and in 1870 there were one thousand two hundred and seventy-seven, of whom six hundred and ninety-three were males and five hundred and eighty-four females. In 1874 the State census returned one thousand one hundred and thirty, five hundred and eighty-nine being males and five hundred and forty-one females; one hundred and sixty-eight of the males were of the military age, between twenty-one and forty-five years, ninety-five were between forty-five and seventy-five years, and three were between seventy-five and ninety. Of the females, one hundred and fifty were of the age called the "maternity age" on the census returns, between eighteen and forty-five years; ninety-eight were between forty and seventy-five years, and three were over seventy-five years. Three hundred and three boys and two hundred and ninety girls had not arrived at their respective legal majorities of twenty-one and eighteen years. The married males and females were equal, two hundred and seven each, but the single men exceeded the ladies in that condition, there being fifty-one of the former and thirty-four of the latter. The widowed were nine of the males and ten of the females.

## THE PRESIDENTIAL BALLOTING

in the township, since its organization as at present, has been as follows: In 1844 the Whigs cast thirty votes and the Democrats forty-six, and the Liberty ticket had three supporters. In 1848 the Whigs polled thirty-eight, the Democrats thirty-four, and the Free-Soilers eight votes. In 1852 the Whigs cast fifty-nine ballots, the Democrats forty-nine, and the Abolitionists five. In 1856 the Republicans polled one hundred and one votes, the Democrats fifty-six, and there was a solitary prohibitionist in the town. In 1860 the Republican vote was one hundred and nine and the Democratic ninety-six. In 1864 the Republicans polled sixty-six and the Democrats seventy-eight votes. In 1868 the Republicans polled ninety-nine and the Democrats one hundred and thirty-five votes. In 1872 the Republican vote was ninety-four, and the Democrats polled seventy votes for Mr. Greeley and two for Mr. O'Conor. In 1876 the Republicans cast one hundred and one votes for Mr. Hayes, and the Democrats gave Mr. Tilden ninety-nine, and the Greenback men gave Mr. Cooper fifty-six votes. This last vote would indicate a population of nearly one thousand three hundred in the township.

## FABIUS IN THE REBELLION,

won an enviable reputation. Her citizens rallied at the first tap of the drum and call of the bugle, and two of them fell at Bull Run,—their first engagement in the war. Her Hoisingtons, patriotic and brave, shouldered their muskets, and father and six sons (and sons-in-law) went to the front; a younger one was so small the officers would not take him, but left him at home with his mother, much against his inclination. Other families went, also,—the Keisers, five; Timms, three; McKees, three; Beadles, two; Bigles, two; Burnetts, two; Manleys, three; Eddys, three; Blodgetts, two; Reishs, two; Yagers, two; and so,

"By twos and threes, and single,
Up from the quiet dingle"

of the farm, they came, and into the horrid clamor and crash and carnage of war, before whose fierce assaults and laborious sieges those brave men, by

dozens, fell to rise no more. Others, maimed and mangled by shot and shell or enfeebled by disease, returned, and bear the painful evidences of their sacrifices about with them daily on their persons. One, David Beadle, has lost the precious legacy of sight, and now gropes in darkness unbroken by so much as a glimmer of the all-pervading sunlight, and must remain so throughout the balance of his days.

We here give a list of the men of Fabius who served their country in the hour of her extreme need, as we have gathered them from the official records:

**FIRST REGIMENT MICHIGAN INFANTRY** (three months' men).

Private David A. Jones, Company A; killed at Bull Run.

Private Calvin Colgrove, Company I; killed at Bull Run.

Private James W. Carpenter, Company A; re-enlisted in First Infantry.

Private James K. Fowler, Company K.

**FIRST INFANTRY** (three years' men).

Private James W. Carpenter, Company A; died at Harrison's Landing, April 5, 1862.

Private Gardner Eddy, Company B; discharged for disability.

**FOURTH INFANTRY.**

Private Andrew J. Keiser, Company C; discharged at expiration of service.

Private A. B. Parsons, Company C; died in hospital, July 7, 1861.

**SIXTH INFANTRY.**

Private Lucian J. Hoisington, Company C; discharged for disability.

Private Darius A. Babcock, Company C; mustered-out.

Private Sylvester Pierce, Company C; mustered-out.

Private Richard H. Walton, Company C; mustered-out.

**ELEVENTH INFANTRY.**

Drum-major Abishai Hoisington; discharged.

Corporal Benjamin F. Wells, Company A; discharged at expiration of service.

Private James W. King, Company A.

Private Edward Timm, Company A; died of wounds at Murfreesboro, January 7, 1863.

Private Lewis Timm, Company A; discharged at expiration of service.

Private Frederick Timm, Company A; discharged for disability.

Private August M. Wellman, Company A; mustered-out.

Sergeant Wallace W. Hoisington, Company E; died at Nashville, August 11, 1862.

Sergeant Borden M. Hicks, Company E; captain and mustered-out.

Private Henry Close, Company E; discharged at expiration of service.

Private Jason W. Manley, Company E; died at Nashville, September 21, 1861.

Private Reuben Manley, Company E; died at White Pigeon, December, 1862.

Private John Salter, Company E; discharged at expiration of service.

Private David Reish, Company E; mustered-out.

Private Nathan H. Legg, Company E; discharged.

**TWELFTH INFANTRY.**

Private Jay Whitaker, Company H; mustered-out.

Private B. W. Blodgett, Company E; mustered-out.

**THIRTEENTH INFANTRY.**

Private William Mabus, Company A; mustered-out.

Private George Phertanbaugh, Company D; mustered-out.

Private Jasper Eddy, Jr., Company E; died at Savannah, Georgia.

Private Edward R. Hutson, Company E; mustered-out.

Private Thomas P. Carr, Company E; mustered-out.

Private Josiah M. Hopkins, Company E; mustered-out.

Private John Harvey, Company E; mustered-out.

Private Solomon Keiser, Company E; mustered-out.

Private George Jackson, Company E; mustered-out.

Private Stephen P. Manley, Company E; mustered-out.

Private Miles A. Pulver, Company E; mustered-out.

Private George Shultice, Company E; discharged for disability.

Private Isaac W. Steininger, Company E; mustered-out.

Private William H. Tando, Company E; mustered-out.

Private James Avery, Company E; mustered-out.

Private John W. Blodgett, Company E; mustered-out.

Private William B. Eddy, Company E; mustered-out.

Private Solomon Reish, Company E; mustered-out.

Private Isaac E. Wing, Company E; mustered-out.

Private John Yager, Company E; mustered-out.
Private Peter Yager, Company E; mustered-out.
Private Omar W Hunt, Company H; mustered-out.
Captain Norman E. Hoisington, Company E; mustered-out.
Private Albert F. Keiser, Company E; mustered-out.

#### FIFTEENTH INFANTRY.

Private Byron Churchill, Company A; re-enlisted, and mustered-out.
Private Joseph W. Weatherbee, Company C; mustered-out.
Private John Houts, Company C; mustered-out.
Private John Nieman, Company E; mustered-out.
Private Samuel Cibben, Company G; mustered-out.

#### SEVENTEENTH INFANTRY.

Private John Arney, Company C; mustered-out.

#### NINETEENTH INFANTRY.

Private Alfred Clark, Company D; mustered-out.
Private Daniel P. Doty, Company D; mustered-out.
Private John S. Doty, Company D; mustered-out.
Private Henry E. Walls, Company G; discharged for disability.

#### TWENTY-FIFTH INFANTRY.

Sergeant Henry C. Lambert, Company D; promoted to second and first lieutenant, and mustered-out.
Corporal Orson Nelson, Company D; mustered-out.
Private Alonzo Burnett, Company D; mustered-out.
Private Benjamin J. Burnett, Company D; died at Bowling Green, March 28, 1863.
Private George J. Heckleman, Company G; discharged.
Private Eli Hartman, Company G; mustered-out.
Private Eli Houts, Company G; mustered-out.
Private Charles H. Howe, Company G; mustered-out.
Private Augustus Keiser, Company G; died at Bowling Green, March 12, 1863.
Private Augustavius Keiser, Company G; veteran reserve corps; mustered-out.
Private George H. Mohney, Company G; mustered-out.
Private Charles S. Newells, Company G; mustered-out.

Private James M. Walton, Company G; discharged.
Private Amos Dean, Company G; mustered-out.
Private John Bigle, Company G; mustered-out.
Private Peter Bigle, Company G; mustered-out.

#### TWENTY-EIGHTH INFANTRY.

Private And. L. Garrison, Company H; mustered-out.

#### FIRST MECHANICS AND ENGINEERS.

Private Duane Parsons, Company D; discharged at expiration of service.
Private Joseph Eggleston, Company H; discharged at expiration of service.

#### FOURTH CAVALRY.

Private Daniel E. Krumm, Company I; at the capture of Jeff. Davis.

#### ELEVENTH CAVALRY.

Private Stephen Corwin, Company K; discharged for disability.

#### FIRST MICHIGAN LIGHT ARTILLERY.

Sergeant Ira J. Beadle, Battery F; discharged for disability.
Sergeant David Beadle, Battery F; blind while in service—sight totally lost.
Private William Poe, Battery F; discharged for disability.
Private James M. Weatherbee, Battery M; mustered-out.
Private Charles W. Arney, Battery M; died at Cumberland Gap.
Private Joseph P. Deane, Battery 14; mustered-out.
Private Nathan Harwood, Battery 14; mustered-out.
Private Isaac Kimball, Battery 14; mustered-out.
Private Joseph W. McKee, Battery 14; mustered-out.
Private Daniel P. McKee, Battery 14; mustered-out.
Private Essington McKee, Battery 14; mustered-out.

#### FIRST MICHIGAN SHARP-SHOOTERS.

Thomas Crossman, Company G; mustered-out.

#### FIRST UNITED STATES SHARP-SHOOTERS.

William E. Close, Company I.

We tender our acknowledgments for information received and assistance rendered in the compilation of the history of Fabius, to William Arney, David and Ira Beadle, Solomon Hartman, Captain Hoisington and William F. Arnold.

---

# BIOGRAPHICAL SKETCHES.

### DAVID BEADLE,

son of Mishael and Ruth Beadle, old and respected citizens of St. Joseph county, was born in Crawford county, Ohio, December 18, 1823. Moved with his parents to Michigan, in October, 1827, and settled at Mottville. His father was connected with the early development of Mottville, Flowerfield, Three Rivers, and Fabius, in all of which places he erected mills at different times. He died on April 10, 1839, and the support of the family partially devolved upon the youthful David. He remained at home with his mother for the ensuing three years, and then purchased eighty acres of land from his sister, Catherine Stowell, and commenced paying for the same by work at the rate of ten dollars per month. Finding this method too slow for his ambition, at the commencement of the third summer he tried breaking-up land with six yoke of oxen, and found that by this means he could pay as much in ten days as he formerly did in as many months.

On the 10th day of April, 1847, he married Miss Lucy A. Wing, of Washtenaw county, Michigan, and settled on his farm in Fabius. In the spring of 1848 he was elected to the office of treasurer of the township, and served for two or three terms. On the 21st day of August, 1849, a son, Francis Marion, was born to him, who died at the age of twenty-three years from an accident caused by a threshing-machine.

On November 23, 1861, the subject of this sketch enlisted, and after serving the full term of three years, was honorably discharged January 11, 1865. From severe illness contracted in the army, he lost his eyesight, and has since drawn a full pension. After his discharge from the army he again took up his abode in his old home, where in his youth he hunted the wild deer and tilled the soil.

Here in 1872 he lost his wife, who had been to him a faithful partner in his early toils and cares. He was thus left with a family of six children, of whom three were quite small and dependent on their father for support.

Mr. Beadle is a gentleman very highly respected by all who know him, as a man of sterling integrity and great patriotism. (See illustration.)

### ABISHAI HOISINGTON.

Abishai Hoisington was born at Campton, East Canada, December 9, 1803, and is a man now seventy-four years of age, and the father of ten children, six sons and four daughters:

FREDERICK A., born March 13, 1830.
NORMAN H., born October 18, 1831.
JOHN M., born July 25, 1833.
LUCIAN J., born April 16, 1835.
WILLIAM, born December 12, 1837.
SUSAN M., born May 8, 1840.
EMILY A., born April 28, 1842.
MARY J., born August 23, 1844.
EDWARD A., born December 30, 1848.
FLORA M., born May 28, 1850.

His earlier ancestors were of English descent, his father being a native of Vermont, and his mother of New Hampshire. Two years after his birth his parents removed to Windsor, Vermont. Here he remained until the age of eighteen, attending school during the winter, and assisting at farming during the summer. He then, in company with his mother, returned to his former home in Canada, where he remained for a period of four years and then returned to Windsor, and served an apprenticeship in the office of the *Vermont Republican*. Here he remained until the age of twenty-five.

October 30, 1828, he was married to Miss Nancy Mason.

He was engaged in business at different periods at Castleton, Vermont; Fort Ann, New York, and Queensbury.

In 1843 he came to Jackson, Michigan, in company with his family, and engaged in manufacturing and building, laying the foundation for the first railroad depot in Jackson. Subsequent to this time he was seriously injured by the falling of rock in a well in which he was at work, from the effects of which he has never fully recovered.

Alisha Hoisington     J. M. Hoisington     N. H. Hoisington

S. J. Hoisington     Mrs. A. Hoisington     W. W. Hoisington

B. F. Wells     Daniel E. Brumm     H. C. Lambert

In May, 1844, he removed to Three Rivers, and later purchased a farm in Fabius township, and subsequently removed to the one on which he now resides in Flowerfield township.

The first gun fired upon Fort Sumter roused his patriotism, and, like the Spartans of old, he resolved to defend a liberty dearer to him than life itself. No bounty or office prompted him to forsake his home and friends at the first call of his country, but leaving the plow in the field, like the noble Putnam of old, he seized his drum and offered his services in any capacity that might be required.

He came to Three Rivers with his drum, being one of the best snare-drummers in the country, and volunteered to assist in raising troops to put down the rebellion in its incipient state, and avenge the outrage upon his country's honor. A company was raised by 'Squire Chadwick for the Twelfth, and also one for the Second regiment of volunteers, Hoisington assisting in furnishing the music.

On the 24th day of August, 1861, he volunteered in company G, of the Eleventh regiment, organized in St. Joseph county. After arriving in Kentucky he was appointed by the colonel, drum-major of the regiment, in which capacity he served until the next fall, when, on account of the extreme fatigue endured by the regiment, he was attacked by rheumatism, which assumed a chronic form. He was discharged on the surgeon's certificate, August 27, 1862.

No man evinced stronger devotion to his country than this aged patriarch, and no man deserves more credit than Abishai Hoisington, who tendered his time, his life, if necessary, and that of a family trained as he himself had been, to regard his freedom and liberty above all price.

Lucian J., his fourth son, was married March 3, 1859, to Susan Mohney, and now has a family of seven children, and resides at Marcellus Centre, Cass county, Michigan.

He enlisted in company C, of the 6th regiment, at Kalamazoo, on the 12th day of August, 1861, soon after the battle of Bull Run. This regiment went on board of transports at Baltimore for New Orleans. He was attacked with typhoid fever on the ocean, and arriving at New Orleans, was sent to the hospital. The disease finally settled in his eyes and rendered him unfit for duty. He was discharged on surgeon's certificate at Baton Rouge, August 12, 1862, one year from his enlistment, with the loss of one eye by the disease, and is now drawing a pension,—small compensation for a shattered constitution and a life having no hope of recovery from pain and suffering.

William W. Hoisington, the fifth son, enlisted in company E, of the 11th regiment, Michigan Volunteers, the 24th day of August, 1861. He was made sergeant of the company. A kinder, more devoted officer never volunteered. He possessed the confidence and esteem of all his officers and men, and his death, which occurred in Nashville, August 15, 1862, from typhoid fever, then prevalent in the regiment, created a loss felt by all. He left a wife and one child to mourn the loss of a kind, indulgent husband and father.

Captain Norman H. Hoisington, the second son, was born in Windsor, Vermont, and educated at Three Rivers, Michigan. He was married, March 10, 1858, to Miss Elizabeth Caul, who died February 8, 1866. He was again married, on the 25th of November, 1868, in Wayne county, New York, to Miss Mary Hamilton, daughter of David Hamilton. She was educated at the Oswego training-school, and in later years had charge as a critic-teacher of the Fort Wayne training-schools. Their family consists of two children, a son and daughter. He enlisted, on 15th of November, 1861, in Company G, of the Thirteenth Michigan infantry, and was immediately appointed orderly sergeant of the company. His company-books and papers were models for all other officers of the regiment. Kind to a fault with his men, he soon rose to the rank of second lieutenant, and was in the command of the company.

He was in the battle of Shiloh, and for his bravery was promoted to the rank of first lieutenant. He was with Sherman on his march to the sea, and promoted to captain, and discharged at Savannah on account of expiration of time of service.

He also served as engineer for a period of one year, detailed at Chattanooga. He served in battles and skirmishes without number, and received his commissions, not through favoritism, but because his courage, bravery and ability fully entitled him to the positions he was called to fill.

John M. Hoisington, third son, was married on the 2d of February, 1855, to Miss Elizabeth Haitmeux, daughter of one of the pioneers of St. Joseph county.

He merits the confidence of the community in which he lives, esteemed by all, and holds offices of trust for the people, accorded to him by his

chosen Republican party. He enlisted, August 17, 1864, in Company C, First Michigan Engineers and Mechanics; joined the regiment at Caterville, Georgia, some time in October, and was then attacked with diarrhœa, then prevailing among new recruits, and was sent to St. Mary's hospital at Detroit, and discharged in February, 1865. While fit for duty he was always ready and willing to obey orders, and strongly devoted to his country and the cause for which so many of his family had taken up arms.

Benjamin F. Wells, son-in-law, was born May 1, 1835, married August 27, 1861. He has a family of three children, and is pleasantly located in Fabius township. Three brothers manifested their patriotism by volunteering in the army at an early date. He enlisted in Company A, Eleventh Michigan volunteers, August 24, 1861, and was in all the battles from Stone River to Atlanta, and finally discharged as sergeant, with his regiment, on account of expiration of term of service. His record is that of a brave soldier, always ready for duty.

H. C. Lambert, son-in-law, was married February 16, 1861, and has a family of six children. He resides at Marcellus Centre, Cass county, Michigan. His father was killed in the army at an early date in the rebellion. He enlisted in Company D, Twenty-fifth Michigan Infantry, August 11, 1862, and was in the celebrated battle between General Morgan and Colonel Moore's forces, at Tibbs' Bend, in Kentucky, and was wounded in the arm. Was promoted to second lieutenant, February 23, 1864; again promoted to first lieutenant, January 1, 1865; was appointed orderly at enlistment. His record is that of a brave soldier, and merits the honor given him for his patriotism and bravery.

Daniel E. Krumm, son-in-law, was married April 24, 1862. It was his wish to volunteer at an early date in the rebellion, but was compelled to remain at home to care for his family and that of his brother, who had previously enlisted.

He joined Company I, Fifth Cavalry, and was one of the party who personally captured the leader of the rebellion, Jefferson Davis, in petticoats, and was discharged at the close of the war,—a brave and gallant soldier, holding rank as sergeant.

Frederick Hoisington, the eldest son, offered to enlist among the first, but on account of a stiff arm was rejected by the surgeon. He was drafted at the last draft, and was rejected when presented for muster, for the same reason.

The youngest son was only twelve years old when the war broke out, and the mustering-officer thought him too small or he would have gone with his father, Abishai.

A better army-record cannot be presented by any family in the country, and we take great pleasure in referring our readers to their portraits in a group, where will be seen father, mother, and the different members of the family, who so well merit the gratitude of their fellow-citizens for their loyalty and patriotism.

---

## JOHN WATKINS,

the subject of this sketch, was born in Kent county, England, March 10, 1814. His parents, John and Sarah Watkins, afforded him the advantages such an education as limited means and the primitive schools of that period would permit. He experienced the privations and hardships that were common to youths at that period, and early learned the lessons of industry, economy, and self-dependence which have been instrumental in making the successful man.

At the age of seventeen, in company with his brother William, he emigrated to America, and landed at New York, in 1832. He then served an apprenticeship of three years in learning a trade, and after fully mastering the details of his chosen avocation, embarked in business for himself at Albany, New York.

In September, 1836, he was married to Miss Maria Smith, and, after a brief residence at Albany, in 1846 removed to Three Rivers, St. Joseph county, then a town of but few houses. He entered a tract of eighty acres of land in Fabius township, which he cleared and improved, and subsequently removed to the farm on which he now resides.

In 1852, in company with friends, Mr. Watkins left to go to California via the Isthmus route; but owing to the want of steamers on the Pacific coast, his trip occupied a period of six months, it usually requiring but one month. He then engaged in mining at Coon Hollow, and after an experience of fifteen months, returned home, well repaid for the hardships of his mining experience.

Mr. Watkins has raised a family of six children, five of whom are now living in the State of Michigan. In politics Mr. Watkins is a Republican, casting his first vote for William H. Seward for governor of New York. For twenty years he has been a member of the Methodist church, and has always taken an active part in supporting the church of his chosen profession.

Faithful, true, and willing, a noble wife has shared his hardships, and always assisted in lessening the trying experiences of pioneer life. Together they have labored, and the result is a pleasant home and a fine farm of two hundred and ninety-four acres, free from encumbrance.

Upright and honorable in all business relations, an active supporter of every public measure that tends to better the condition of his fellow-men, kind and true to his family and friends, we have in the experience and life of Mr. Watkins a practical illustration of a successful man whose business and maturer life, commenced under adverse circumstances and unassisted, presents a copy worthy to be imitated and followed. We take pleasure in presenting the portrait of the subject of this sketch to our readers, in connection with this brief history of his life.

## A. R. HUNT.

Mr. A. R. Hunt, whose portrait appears in connection with this brief history, was born at Castleton, Vermont, July 16, 1810. A few years subsequent to his birth his parents removed to Montgomery county, New York, and two years later, removed to Clarkstown township, western New York. Here the subject of our sketch was educated in the common-schools of the county.

He remained at home, assisting his parents, until he was nineteen years of age; he then purchased his time from his father and commenced the battle of life for himself. Selecting a trade, he made himself master of it by serving an apprenticeship with Mr. Webster, of Brockport.

In 1834 he moved to St. Joseph county and entered a tract of eighty acres in Florence township. He here remained for a period of four years, and then removed to the farm on which he now resides, in Fabius township. Previous to his removal to Michigan, he was married to Miss Emma Beach, who shared with him the early experiences of a pioneer life.

A number of years elapsed, and with its changes the loss of his wife. In June, 1864, he was again married to Mrs. Bayn, of Three Rivers, the former wife of a pioneer minister of Jackson county.

Mr. Hunt has raised a family of six children. Two sons, in response to their country's call, nobly resolved to defend this Union, and enlisted as privates and served with distinction during the rebellion, and at its close were honorably discharged; one of them, on being mustered-out, held the commission and rank of captain.

The church, in Mr. Hunt, has an active, earnest member. During his twenty years in that relation he has held many offices of trust, being selected trustee and conference-steward; in all cases doing honor to the trust reposed in him. As a further mark of the esteem in which he is held and the confidence reposed in him, we need only to state that the people have at different times entrusted him with various township offices, all of which he has acceptably filled. He is Republican in politics.

Mr. Hunt has a pleasant home, and is the owner of a fine farm. He is evidently a self-made man. Beginning life with nothing but strong hands and a willing heart, he has by his own efforts made it a grand success. The pleasure of retrospection with him is the memory of time well spent.

In his declining years he proposes to earnestly continue to labor for the good of his fellow man, believing that in the near future he will realize large returns for his worthy and commendable efforts.

# PARK.

The township of Park was so named from its park-like appearance, when it was first visited by the settlers. The surface was originally covered with burr and white oak, the openings of which, being free from under-brush and small trees, gave the prospect an appearance of some lordly manor of the old world,—Nature herself being the exquisite landscape artist, and the Indians the means of keeping the forest free from obstruction by their annual fires.

### THE AREA

of the township is that of a full government township, and contains twenty-two thousand three hundred and ten acres of land and three hundred and thirteen acres of water-surface. Its surface is a general level, and the soil a gravelly, sandy loam, susceptible of high cultivation, and is admirably adapted to the production of the cereals, corn, clover and all kinds of fruit, the latter being an abundant crop.

### THE DRAINAGE

of the township is effected by the Portage river and Fisher's lake. The former enters the township on the east line of section nineteen, and runs southwest through that section and twenty-six, twenty-seven and thirty-one, passing out on the south line of the latter. Fisher's lake lies on section thirty-two.

### THE FIRST LAND ENTRIES

were made in the years 1830 and 1831, and were as follows: The northwest fractional quarter of section six, by Henry Garver, in 1830; the north half of the northeast quarter of section six, by Russell Peck, of Kalamazoo county, June 27, 1831; and the east half of the southwest quarter of section thirty-one, by Daniel Linn, Jr., the same day. There was one other entry in 1831 only.

### EARLY SETTLEMENT.

On the east bank of that beautiful sheet of water now designated by the name of Lake Fisher, (from Jonas and Leonard Fisher, the first settlers on its banks), partially located on the Pottawatomie reservation, in the fall of 1834 was erected a small log-cabin, which then constituted the grandest architectural monument of the township. It was built by Harvey Kinney, assisted by Jonas and Leonard Fisher and George Leland. It was then known by the settlers that the Indians were to yield up their possessions within two years, which put the land under squatter sovereignty. Under the treaty of Chicago the Indians agreed to surrender up their possessions within the time above stated. This treaty was made and confirmed in September, 1833; squatters commenced to locate claims in the eastern part of the reservation, but no claim was located on the western portion of it, especially on the two tiers of sections located in Park township, till late in the fall of 1834. Then Harvey Kinney located a claim on the southeast quarter of section twenty-four, upon which he erected the log-cabin above described, which he did not occupy until the spring following.

This conduct on the part of the settlers was regarded by the Indians as a violation of the treaty of Chicago. They argued that if the United States government was faithless, and allowed settlers to locate on the reservation before the time stipulated for them to give possession to the United States, that it was not only a trespass but a violation, and that they were not bound to fulfil their part of the contract, and had a right with physical force to resist any attempt on the part of the squatters. This view of the case by the aborigines caused deep apprehension of danger, and well might it be seriously entertained under the circumstances by those who were considered as trespassing upon the Indians' rights by locating pre-emptions. But these adventurous settlers—at least most of them—at all hazards continued on their claims, and others still located. Among the former was I. F. Ulrich,

RESIDENCE OF RICHARD DAUGHERTY, Park Tp. St. Joseph Co. Mich.

who erected his log-cabin in the fall of 1834, and made formal entry with his family as soon as the stick-chimney was finished.

Mr. Ulrich was born in Maiden Creek township, Berks county, Pennsylvania, in the year 1801. He removed from there to Columbia county, Pennsylvania, and there married Elizabeth Leech, a lady three years his junior, and who is still living, having raised twelve children in the fifty-two years which she has been his faithful wife. They started from Danville, Pennsylvania, with a double team, and at the expiration of seventy-two days, landed on the bank of the St. Joseph, on the present site of Three Rivers. They experienced the usual hardships and vicissitudes incident to an extended journey in those days. As an evidence of the tediousness of their traveling we may mention that on the occasion of their crossing the Black Swamp, in the Maumee region, it occupied the major part of a day to travel two miles, and cost them seven dollars to do it. Provisions were reasonably plentiful when they reached their destination in Park township, but in 1835, that complicated malady, the fever and ague, took possession of the settlement, and the provisions became less and less, until the settlers had to exist principally on barley bread while awaiting the annual crops. Mr. Ulrich relates how he paid thirty dollars for ten bushels of barley, which he had to procure at Prairie Ronde, then grown to be a considerable settlement. He took his barley to Three Rivers, where existed a miniature grist-mill, sarcastically yclept the "coffee-mill," the stones of which were only twenty-two inches in diameter. This mill was owned by Hezekiah Weatherbee. There, while waiting for his grist, a man from a distance offered him thirty dollars in gold for one half of his barley-meal, which liberal offer necessity compelled him to decline.

OTHER EARLY SETTLERS.

Among those who were contemporaneous in point of settlement with 'Squire Ulrich, were Jonas and Leonard Fisher, George Leland, Samuel Moore, (who is now the oldest living settler in the township, being in his ninetieth year; he settled on section nineteen near the present village of Moore Park); George Wilson settled on the east half of the southwest quarter of section twenty-five, in the year 1835, Michael Hower came in 1835, Isaac Mowrey settled on his present farm in 1836, Simeon L. Frost on the west quarter of section thirty-six, and John Boudeman on section thirty-four, in 1836. John Hutchison entered a large tract of land in section twenty-seven, —where his widow, a daughter of John Kneeder, a miller at an early day in Three Rivers, now resides,—in 1836; John Lomison settled parts of sections twenty-six and twenty-seven, entering a quarter of a section, and settled on the southwest quarter of section thirty-six; J. D. Brown also came in 1836; McDonald Campbell came into the township in 1837, and settled in section thirty-five. In 1836 Alexander Frazier,—the third oldest of the surviving pioneers—came in; also Jacob Bannon. Andrew Reed settled on his present farm on section thirty-five, in February, 1839.

GAME.

The early settlers depended largely on game for food, and Mr. Ulrich avers that he shot one hundred and five deers and three bears the first year of his settlement.

FIRST WHEAT SOWN.

The first wheat planted was a three-acre field, cleared and sowed by Mr. Ulrich in 1835; it turned out wonderfully smutty, being of almost equal parts of wheat and smut, so that before grinding it had to be washed.

THE FIRST ORCHARD

set out in the township was one by Isaac Mowrey, in 1836, on section thirty-five, his old homestead.

IMPROVED FARM-MACHINERY

was introduced as follows: Reaper and mower, first by Alexander Frazier, 1842(?). First threshing-machine, Hower & Stole. Separating-thresher brought in and used by Aaron Hagenbuck of Constantine. First seed-drill, Frederick Dentler.

FIRST IMPROVED STOCK.

The first blooded stock was introduced in Park township by Edward S. Moore, president of the First National Bank of Three Rivers, in 1850. It consisted of a Balco bull, cow, and calf, bought of the Ohio Shakers. Andrew Y. Moore was an extensive raiser of stock on Prairie Ronde also. The most extensive raiser of thoroughbred stock at present is Richard Dougherty, whose merino sheep and short-horn (Durham) cattle would reflect credit on any professional stock-raiser in the county.

27

THE FIRST FRAME HOUSE

was built by Michael Hower, on section twenty-seven, in 1835. The first brick dwelling was built in the township by Charles Macomber in 1851; Mr. Heinbach built one in 1853. The first blacksmith was Jacob Bannon.

THE FIRST SAW-MILL

was built on section twenty-four by Harvey Kinney in the fall of 1838. It was run successfully until the proposal to lay out the village of Parkville, which was first talked of in 1847, but not consummated until some five years afterwards. In that year (1847), however, the present saw-mill in Parkville was built.

FIRST BIRTH.

The first white child born within the present limits of Park township was Madison J. Ulrich, who was born December 6, 1835.

FIRST MARRIAGE.

There exist no records by which we can determine definitely the first marriage, but 'Squire Ulrich informs us that he married a man by the name of Fairchild, a non-resident, who came with his intended bride a distance of twenty miles to have the knot tied, and paid the 'Squire ten dimes as a marriage-fee. This was in 1835. Amos Reed and Ann Hower were married in 1837.

FIRST DEATH.

The first death occurred in the family of Harvey Kinney, and was that of one of his little sons. J. M. C. Ulrich died August 24, 1839.

FIRST CEMETERY.

The first regularly laid-out cemetery was the one now located on the northeast quarter of section thirty-five, on land donated by Isaac Mowrey and wife. It was organized under the name of the "Society of the Park Burying-Ground," on the 25th of August, 1852. The first officers were Isaac Mowrey, president; Isaac F. Ulrich, secretary; John Lomison, treasurer; Andrew Reed, sexton. The first interment in the ground was that of William Ballow, in 1845. This was prior to the organization of the cemetery-board, the ground having been used as a burying-place some years previous. Among the prominent citizens buried there are Amos Reed, Joseph Sterling, James Foster, John Weinberg, John Boudeman, George Leland and wife, and others.

FIRST PREACHER.

The first preacher who held forth in Park township was a circuit-rider of the Methodist persuasion, by the name of Kellogg, who flourished in the year 1837.

AN EARLY TAX-RECEIPT.

"Received from Isaac F. Ulrich, of Park township, three dollars and fifty cents, being his town, county, and State tax for the year 1839.
"F. HOWER, Collector."

BEAVER-DAM.

The remains of a beaver-dam exist on the farm of Philip Casper, on the northwest quarter of section twenty-five. Several skull-bones and pieces of timber have been found, at various depths, during excavations for ditches and other similar operations.

FIRST SCHOOL.

The first school taught in the township was held in a shoemaker's shop belonging to John Troy, in 1837, and was taught by a Miss Kimble, who resided near the Kalamazoo county-line.

THE FIRST SCHOOL-HOUSE

erected within the limits of the township was in the fall of 1838. It was built by contributions of labor and materials by the settlers. School was taught in it for the first time in the spring of 1839, by Isaac J. Ulrich. Among the first scholars were Robert Dougherty, Franklin Lomison, Findley Campbell, L. W. Ulrich, Andrew Leland, William Kimble, George Troy, Sarah Pelleti and others, in all about twenty-six. This old log-building answered the educational requirements of the southeastern part of the township until 1848, when a frame structure was erected about half a mile north of where the log-house stood. This remained until 1874, when the present neat and commodious brick building was erected, constituting the fractional school district number eight of Park and Lockport townships. It cost eighteen hundred dollars, and is noted as having furnished more scholars who have made their mark in the field of education and science than any school-district in this or neighboring townships.

The township was divided for school purposes in 1839, at which time five districts were made. There are now seven whole and three fractional districts in the township. No records of the early history of the schools exist. I. F. Ulrich was the first school-director.

### THE FIRST FRAME SCHOOL-HOUSE

in the township was built in district number one, and the first brick school-house was built in district number four on section two. in 1871. In 1876 there were eight school-houses, two of brick and six of wood, affording three hundred and seven sittings, and valued at eight thousand six hundred dollars. There were schools taught in them eight months during the year ending September 1, 1876. There were three hundred and ninety-eight children in the township of the legal school-age. Eight male teachers were employed twenty-five months, and received for their services one thousand two hundred and eighty-eight dollars, and eight female received four hundred and fifty-five dollars for thirty-seven months' work. The districts paid out in total expenses for the year two thousand eight hundred and forty-eight dollars and ninety-eight cents, including seven hundred and ninety-four dollars for repairs and indebtedness.

### THE EVANGELICAL ASSOCIATION.

The class of this association in Park was first organized about the year 1849, under the labors of Rev. George Doll, with the following members: Peter Bloom and wife, Leander Weinberg and wife, John Weinberg and wife, and Jacob Schraeger and wife. In 1853 the first Evangelical church was erected in Park, on Walter B. Love's farm, who donated a half acre of land for a site, on section twenty-one on the southeast quarter thereof. The church was twenty-four by thirty feet, a frame building, and cost four hundred dollars. In 1859 there was a parsonage built on Peter Bloom's farm, about thirty rods east of the church, sixteen by twenty feet, of wood, costing three hundred and twenty dollars, Mr. Bloom being the contractor. In 1869 the second church was built on the site of the old one, both the first and second one being known as "The Emmanuel Church" of the Evangelical Association. The second one was of brick, thirty-eight by sixty feet, on the ground, and cost five thousand dollars. It has a seating capacity of four hundred and fifty to five hundred. It was dedicated by Rev. Bishop J. J. Escher.

The first trustees of the old church were Peter Bloom, Leander Weinberg, and John Hulben. The present trustees are Peter Bloom, William Werner, and Samuel McCracken.

Sabbath-schools were organized and kept in both churches from their building until the present, during the year, except the winter, the congregation being scattered widely apart. William Schafer is the present superintendent, and the church numbers one hundred and thirty-one members.

The ministers who have had charge of the Park class and church are as follows: Reverends George Doll, M. Hoehn, George Kissell, Philip Porr, John Walz, G. M. Young, M. Alspach, G. Klopfer, Peter Burgener, P. Seille, Peter Roth, Reuben Riegel, C. S. Brown, E. B. Miller, T. N. Davis, P. Wiest, S. Copley, J. W. Loose, Alonzo Russell, B. F. Wade, and the present pastor, J. H. Keeler.

The Park class was the first one of the Association organized in the county, and its first church the first house of worship erected by the denomination therein.

### THE FIRST REVIVALS

of the Methodist Episcopal church were held in the log school-house built in 1838, and the beginning of the society now in Parkville was here in this house, Joure Fisher and Esquire Ulrich being the prominent converts.

### CIVIL ORGANIZATION.

In the original constitution of the townships of the county, Park formed a part of Flowerfield township, and remained such from November 5, 1829, until 1838, when township five south of range eleven west was set off and erected into an independent township named Park.

The first town-meeting was held at the house of Mr. Hutchinson, in April, 1838, and the new government set in motion by a full roster of officials, of which we give the important ones and those who have since filled these positions.

#### TOWNSHIP OFFICERS.

Clerks—Juba E. Day (1838), Robert Campbell, John Lomison (ten years), James Hutchison (three years), J. W. Childs (three years), George W. Hutton, Samuel B. Schrager (two years), A. H. Kester, Nathan Osborn, William M. Reed, Daniel Pfleegor (twelve years), George W. Osborn, Frank C. Dentler (five years), B. W. Cornell, George M. Campbell, present incumbent, appointed to fill vacancy.

Supervisors—Edward S. Moore (1838, two years), Juba E. Day, John Sickler, W. Woodruff (four years), George Wilson, Nathan Osborn, John

Lomison, James Boutewell, John Sigler, James Hutchison (fourteen years), A. J. Schoonmaker (two years), George W. Osborn (nine years), Daniel Frazier, Daniel Pfleegor to fill vacancy.

Justices of the Peace—Isaac F. Ulrich (1838, twenty years), Edward S. Moore, John Sickler, Juba E. Day (two years), Hiram Suyland, James Boutewell (eight years), Nathan Osborn (eight years), William Adams (twelve years), A. J. Schoonmaker (sixteen years), John Sickler (eight years), John Lomison, Jeremiah Smith, S. W. Ulrich, Adam Gentzler, Andrew Perrin, Hiram Schoonmaker, Jeremiah W. Bunn, Sterling F. Harding, to fill vacancy. George Dale, F. C. Schrauger, F. C. Dentler, L. H. Fort, J. W. Salisbury, L. W. Ulrich (two years), L. H. Fort (full term), George W. Osborn.

### THE FIRST ROAD

was surveyed in the township July 30, 1836. It ran through sections one, twelve, thirteen, twenty-four, twenty-five and thirty-six, and is now vacated, except that portion running through sections twelve and thirteen.

### ASSESSMENTS AND TAXES.

In 1838 the first assessment of the township was made for taxation, and returned fifty-five thousand eight hundred and twenty-three dollars, and the tax-levy thereon was two hundred and eighteen dollars for all purposes.

In 1852 the assessment amounted to sixty-four thousand four hundred and two cents, and the taxes to one thousand three hundred and forty dollars and two cents.

In 1860 the assessment was placed at four hundred and nine thousand four hundred and eighty-one dollars, and the taxes were two thousand six hundred and seventy-four dollars and ninety-two cents.

In 1870 the assessment was returned at eight hundred and twenty-two thousand four hundred and ten dollars amounted to eight thousand seven hundred and forty-eight dollars and twelve cents.

In 1876 the assessment, as returned by the county board of equalization, stood at four hundred and nine thousand nine hundred and seventeen dollars on real-estate and seventy-five thousand and ten dollars on personal property, and the tax-levy was as follows: State and county purposes, one-half to each, two thousand four hundred and seventy-seven dollars and twenty-two cents; township, including schools, two thousand seven hundred and thirty-nine dollars and sixty-one cents—a total tax of five thousand two hundred and sixteen dollars and eighty-three cents.

### THE CROPS.

In 1873 there were harvested three thousand nine hundred and twenty-two acres of wheat, which produced fifty-four thousand four hundred and thirty-six bushels, and one thousand eight hundred and ninety-two acres of corn, which yielded forty-seven thousand and fifty five bushels. There were also produced three thousand and sixty bushels of other grain, five thousand four hundred and seventy bushels potatoes, one thousand five hundred and seventy-five tons hay, twelve thousand one hundred and twenty-six pounds wool, one hundred and eighty thousand and ninety pounds pork, forty-three thousand one hundred and fifteen pounds butter, eight thousand two hundred and eighty pounds dried fruit, and seven hundred and nineteen barrels cider. Four hundred and seventy-five acres in orchards produced sixteen thousand and sixty bushels of apples and ten bushels of pears, valued at three thousand four hundred and seventy-two dollars.

### MANUFACTURE.

One flour-mill, one saw-mill and one woolen-mill employed ten persons and a capital of twenty-five thousand dollars, which manufactured two thousand barrels flour, two hundred thousand feet of lumber and other products,—all valued at fifteen thousand dollars.

There were owned in the township, in 1874, five hundred and thirty-two horses, two oxen, four hundred and eighty cows, four hundred and thirty-seven other cattle, one thousand five hundred and four hogs, and two thousand and thirty-six sheep. The clip of 1873 was taken from two thousand six hundred and fifty-five animals.

There were assessed in 1876 twenty-two thousand one hundred and seventy-two acres of land, valued by the supervisor of the township at four hundred and forty-two thousand six hundred and seventy-five dollars,—about one-third of its real value.

### POPULATION.

In 1850 there were eight hundred and twenty-five inhabitants in the township. In 1860 there were one thousand one hundred and twenty-one, and in 1870 there were one thousand two hundred and seventy-six, of whom

MRS. JOHN HUTCHINSON

JOHN HUTCHINSON

RESIDENCE OF JOHN HUTCHINSON, PARK TP., ST JOSEPH CO. MICH

JOHN LOMISON.

MRS JOHN LOMISON

RESIDENCE OF JOHN LOMISON, PARK TP. ST JOSEPH CO. MICH.

six hundred and fifty-three were males, and six hundred and twenty-three females.

In 1874 the State census returns show but one thousand two hundred and twenty-seven persons, of whom six hundred and forty-five were males, and five hundred and eighty-two females. Of the former three hundred and eighteen were over twenty-one years, one hundred and ninety-three being under forty-five years; one hundred and twenty-two did not exceed seventy-five years, and three were between seventy-five and ninety. Of the females three hundred and twenty were over eighteen years, two hundred and seven of them being forty years and under; one hundred and twenty-one under seventy-five years, and two over that age. Three hundred and twenty-seven boys and two hundred and fifty-two girls had not arrived at their respective majorities of twenty-one and eighteen years.

### THE POLITICAL BIAS

of the community of Park will be seen by the way they deposited their ballots at the presidential elections. In 1840 the Democrats cast forty-four votes, and the Whigs thirty-six. In 1844 the Democrats polled fifty-eight votes, the Whigs thirty-seven, and the Liberty men eight. In 1848 the Democrats polled sixty-eight votes, the Whigs twenty-six, and the Free Soilers thirty-six. In 1852 the Democratic vote was eighty-eight, the Whig thirty-nine, and the Abolition fourteen. In 1856 the Democrats cast one hundred and twenty-one votes, and the Republicans one hundred and fifteen. The vote of 1860 stood one hundred and thirty-five Democratic, and one hundred and thirty Republican; and in 1864 the same vote stood one hundred and forty-three and one hundred and fourteen respectively, and in 1868 one hundred and seventy-five and one hundred and thirty-eight respectively. In 1872 the Democratic vote for Mr. Greeley was ninety-two, and O'Conor five; and the Republicans polled one hundred and twenty votes. In 1876 the Democratic vote was one hundred and six, the Republican one hundred and eight, and Mr. Cooper, the Greenback candidate, had forty-nine votes.

## PARKVILLE VILLAGE.

The village of Parkville was laid out on a piece of land in section twenty-four, purchased by Luther Carlton of N. H. Taylor, in 1851. The village plat was surveyed by James Hutchison, and the first lot purchased by Mary King for ten dollars, in 1851. It is located on section twenty-four.

### THE FIRST POSTMASTER

was Samuel Schrauger; the present incumbent is George Dunham.

### THE FIRST STORE

was built and kept by Adam Kester in 1853. The same building is used as a store by Emanuel Boudeman.

### THE FIRST CHURCH

was the one erected by the Presbyterians in 1860. It is a frame-building, of a very neat appearance and commodious in extent.

The village now contains three stores, three churches—denominationally classified as follows: One Presbyterian, one Methodist Episcopal, and one Advent. (The latter was erected in 1861, the first members being Harvey Kinney and wife, Andrew Hafor, Oran Bovee, J. H. Alrich, Aaron H. Adams and Mary Sidler. No church organization now exists.) One grist-mill, one woolen factory, one saw-mill, one tavern, one common school, and two blacksmith's shops. The population of the village (by actual count) is one hundred and forty.

### BUSINESS TRANSACTED IN 1876.

The mill and factory, including the purchase of wool and grain, fifty thousand dollars (estimated); store business about fifteen thousand dollars.

### THE WOOLEN-MILL

was erected by Schellhous & Carlton in 1851. Mr. Carlton retired from the firm, however, before the actual business of the factory commenced. The amount of manufactured goods turned out in 1876 was about ten thousand dollars.

### THE GRIST-MILL

was built in 1853, by Reed & Huffman. It subsequently passed into the hands of David Brown, who operated it until 1867, when it was purchased by Frederick C. Dentler, by whom it is now conducted. The amount of merchant work in 1876 was two thousand five hundred barrels; that of custom work, fifteen thousand bushels.

### PARK PRESBYTERIAN CHURCH.

The first services under the ministry of the Presbyterian church were held in the old school-house, which stood about two miles south of the village of Parkville, by Rev. Albert H. Gaston, in 1843.

We copy the subjoined list of articles paid Mr. Gaston for his pastoral labors during the year 1844, from Mr. John Lomison's memoranda, by whom they were paid:

| | | |
|---|---|---|
| To 4½ pounds of tallow, at 10 cents per pound | - - | $ 45 |
| To 2 bushels of oats, at 20 cents per bushel | - - | 40 |
| To 12 bushels of oats, at 20 cents per bushel | - - | 2 40 |
| To 2 bushels of wheat, at 50 cents per bushel | - - | 1 00 |
| To hauling one load of goods from Marshall | - - | 3 50 |
| To 7 pounds of butter at 12½ cents per pound | - - | 87½ |
| Total | - - - - - - | $8 62½ |

Services continued to be held in the place above designated until about 1850, when most of those who were accustomed to worship there united themselves with the church at Three Rivers. In 1854 steps were taken for the regular organization of a Presbyterian church at Parkville, as the annexed " minutes" will show:

"Previous notice having been given, a meeting of the trustees of the Presbyterian church of Three Rivers and the Reserve was held at Parkville, January 11, 1854, whereupon L. E. Schellhous was called to the chair, and E. S. Moore, clerk of the session, acted as secretary.

"Resolved, That the bequest of the late Samuel Fisher (of Park township) in his will appropriating a sum of money for 'the purpose of erecting a Presbyterian church edifice in Parkville, or within two miles distant,' shall be located at Parkville.

"Resolved, That the trustees of said church or society proceed immediately to draw the money so appropriated, and apply the same to the erection of said building, and that a committee be added to act with the trustees as a building committee, and that L. E. Schellhous, Charles Ackenbach, and J. F. Williams, M. D.,* be said committee.'

"Resolved, That the trustees, together with such committee, be authorized to solicit additional aid for the purpose of enlarging the amount already bequeathed for said building, and then the plan shall be so proportioned to the amount raised."

The first trustees of the church were John Lomison, John Troy, A. C. Prutzman, J. E. Kelsey, Burden Hix.

In 1858 several members were dismissed from the church at Three Rivers for the purpose of effecting the organization in accordance with the meeting above mentioned. The church was, therefore, regularly organized in 1858, and the building completed in 1860. The first members were John Lomison, John Troy, O. H. P. Blue, John Hutchison, Jacob Jones, L. H. Fort, with their wives and families; Mrs. Jane Campbell, Mrs. Charlotte Blue, Mrs. Sarah McCracken, Mrs. Ann Campbell—in all, twenty souls. The present membership is thirty-five.

The elders elected at the first meeting were John Lomison, O. H. P. Blue, John Troy. The first pastor was Rev. A. G. Martin, and the present (occasionally officiating) minister is Rev. William A. Masker, acting pastor of the First Presbyterian church of Three Rivers.

### PARKVILLE METHODIST EPISCOPAL CHURCH.

From the records of the Methodist Episcopal church of Parkville, now in the possession of Richard Dougherty, we learn that the society was organized in the year 1844. We subjoin the early minutes, as subscribed to by one Peter Sabin, with all its legal verbiage:

"I, Peter Sabin, preacher in charge of Centreville circuit, Kalamazoo district and Michigan conference, do hereby certify that I have, and by these presents do, in accordance with the rules and regulations of the Methodist Episcopal church, make, constitute, and appoint Simeon L. Frost, Amos Reed, Jesse Fisher, Michael L. Flower, Philip Felker, Isaac F. Ulrich, Percifer Hewer, Nelson Healy, Isaiah Reed, they and each of them being members of the Methodist Episcopal church, trustees of a certain church of the Methodist order, to be known, designated, and described as the 'First Methodist Episcopal of the township of Park,' which said church is to be situated in said township, in the county of St. Joseph and State of Michigan, and within the boundaries of the said Centreville circuit, of which said circuit I, Peter Sabin, am preacher in charge.

"In witness whereof, I, Peter Sabin, have hereunto set my signature and affixed my seal at Centreville, this the 23d day of January, A. D. 1844.

"PETER SABIN.

"Signed, sealed, and delivered in the presence of A. Bonham and Christiana Bonham, the day and date above mentioned."

On the 2d of February, 1844, at a meeting called for the purpose, the following officers were elected: Isaiah Reed, moderator; Isaac F. Ulrich, clerk; Michael L. Hower, treasurer. At the same meeting a building-committee was elected, being composed of the following: Amos Reed, Jonas Fisher and Simeon L. Frost. February 19, 1844, this committee met at the house of Isaac F. Ulrich, and proceeded to consider the best means by which a church-edifice could be built, Mr. Isaac Mowrey and Catharine his wife having donated an acre of land located one and a half miles south of Parkville for the purpose. It was finally agreed that contributions of materials and labor should be solicited, which was accordingly done. The frame of the sacred edifice was begun in 1844, and the entire building was completed in 1846, having cost in money only seven hundred and two dollars. Among the first members were Jonas Fisher and wife, Michael Hower, Sr., and family, Amos Reed and wife, S. L. Frost and wife, George Wilson and wife, and others. The first pastor was Rev. Richard C. Meek. In 1867 the present church-edifice at Parkville was completed, and the old building is now used only occasionally. This was under the pastorate of the Rev. D. D. Gillett. The present officers are Richard Dougherty, Andrew Perrin, Benjamin Perrin, E. Bodmer, L. B. Perrin, George Good, Jacob Carr, trustees; Richard Dougherty, Solomon Sterner, Grenthan Deats, Michael Hower and John Holliday, stewards; L. Bodmer, class-leader. The present membership is eighty; pastor, Rev. S. S. Wilson.

PARKVILLE GRANGE, NO. 22.

This grange was regularly organized in October, 1872, with thirty-three members. The first officers were: Richard Dougherty, master; David Handshaw, overseer; Solomon Sterner, treasurer; S. H. Angevine, secretary; Mrs. Susan Dougherty, Ceres; Mrs. Ann Campbell, Flora; Mrs. Sarah K. Leland, Pomona. The grange has been in successful operation since its organization, most of the prominent farmers of the township evincing a commendable interest in its meetings. The present officers are: George W. Osborn, master; Samuel H. Angevine, secretary; John B. Norton, treasurer; Wesley Shannon, overseer; Mrs. S. H. Angevine, lecturer; John Detwiler, steward; Orville Dougherty, assistant steward; W. P. Leland, gate-keeper; Mrs. G. W. Osborn, Ceres; Mrs. Ann Campbell, Flora; Mrs. W. P. Leland, Pomona; Mrs. S. H. Angevine, lady assistant.

MOORE PARK

is a station on the Michigan Southern and Lake Shore railroad, established in 1871, and so named from the picturesque homestead of Hon. Edward S. Moore, a short distance therefrom. The side-track was laid down in 1868. A very neat and tasteful station-house was built in 1871, which has a capacity of storage in the upper story of eight thousand bushels. The warehouse is thirty-five by forty feet, and the ticket-office twenty-five by forty feet. Thirty-seven thousand bushels of wheat and other grain and one thousand two hundred barrels of flour, four car-loads of wool and six car-loads of fruit were shipped from the station in 1876. Moore & Weinberg are the shippers of wheat, and the Parkville mills of flour. Three or four very neat cottages are clustered about the station.

PARK IN THE REBELLION

bore no inconspicuous part in defense of the national authority, but filled her quotas upon demand, uncomplainingly, and with promptness. Her citizens vied with their fellows of the county to place the record of the same high among those of the rest of the State.

We here append a list of those of her citizens who left the comforts and endearments of home to go in defense of the government which had secured to them "life, liberty, and the pursuit of happiness," that all men might taste the sweets thereof, black or white. Should any name be missing, which properly ought to be in the list, if the reader will refer to the several township histories and the general military history of the county, he may find them there.

SECOND MICHIGAN INFANTRY.

Private Stephen Baker, Company I; mustered-out.

FOURTH INFANTRY.

Second Lieutenant B. F. Gruner, Company C; first lieutenant; discharged at expiration of service.

SIXTH INFANTRY.

Private Samuel Bond, Company C; died at Camp Mars, November 11, 1862.

Private John Collar, Company C.
Private Franklin Felker, Company C; discharged for disability.
Private Isaac Hilliard, Company C; discharged at expiration of service.
Private Conrad A. Lamberson, Company C; discharged at expiration of service.
Private Christian Schraeder, Company C; mustered-out.
Private William H. Woodward, Company C; mustered-out.

ELEVENTH INFANTRY.

Private Charles Carter, Company B; mustered-out.
Private Henry M. Woodward, Company C; died of typhoid fever, April 16, 1862.
Corporal John M. Day, Company E; killed at Chattanooga.
Private David Clingeman, Company E; discharged at expiration of service.
Private Hiram I. Evart, Company E; died at Stone River, December 31, 1862.
Private Solomon Shirley, Company E; discharged at expiration of service.
Private Aaron Wilhelm, Company E; discharged by Colonel May, September, 1861.
Private Robert S. Day, Company E; mustered-out.
Private James Slote, Company E; mustered-out.
Private Manasseh Clingeman, Company E; mustered-out.
Private Joseph S. Brown, Company E; mustered-out.

TWELFTH INFANTRY.

Private William Greiner, Company E; died at Duvall's Bluff, Arkansas.

THIRTEENTH INFANTRY.

Private Horace Cotherman, Company E; mustered-out.
Private Samuel P. Holben, Company K; veteran reserve corps.
Private John Shick, Company K; re-enlisted, and mustered-out.

SEVENTEENTH INFANTRY.

Private Frank H. Osborn, Company C; died in action, October 4, 1862, at Middletown, Maryland.
Private George A. Osborn, Company C; mustered-out.
Private John A. Troy, Company C; killed at South Mountain, September 14, 1862.

NINETEENTH INFANTRY.

First Lieutenant John Whaley, Company K.
Sergeant Robert McElrath, Company K; mustered-out.

TWENTY-FIFTH INFANTRY.

Private Henry Barnes, Company D.
Private Andrew Gonever, Company D; mustered-out.
Private Wesley N. Hower, Company D; died at Bowling Green, Kentucky.
Private Southard Perrin, Company D; killed at Tebbs' Bend, July 4, 1863.
Private Elijah Reed, Company D.
Private Samuel Stecker, Company D; mustered-out.
Private Francis C. Koch, Company G; died at Bowling Green, Kentucky, April 7, 1863.
Private Welton Smith, Company G; mustered-out.

TWENTY-EIGHTH INFANTRY.

Private Daniel Sidler, Company I; mustered-out.

FOURTH CAVALRY.

Private John Ballow, Company G; mustered-out.

FIRST LIGHT ARTILLERY.

Private Adam Bloom, Battery Fourteen; mustered-out.
Private Simeon Bloom, Battery Fourteen; mustered-out.
Private Daniel Hartranft, Battery Fourteen; mustered-out.
Private William Hopper, Battery Fourteen; discharged for disability.

PROVOST-GUARD.

Henry Kimple; mustered-out.

UNITED STATES NAVY.

Christopher Schrader; re-enlisted in Sixth Infantry.
Theodore Luckwick; died, August, 1862, at Helena.
William Woodruff; died, September, 1862, at Helena.

We are under obligations (and tender our thanks for the same) to I. F. Ulrich, Esq., John Lomison, Esq., Andrew M. Leland, Esq., Richard Dougherty, and Mrs. James Hutchison, for information and assistance in compiling the history of Flowerfield.

JAMES HUTCHINSON.

RESIDENCE OF STEPHEN D. HUTCHINSON,
PARK TP, ST JOSEPH CO, MICH.

FLOWERFIELD STATION.

RESIDENCE OF ALEXANDER FRAZIER,
PARK TP, ST JOSEPH CO, MICH.

# BIOGRAPHICAL SKETCHES.

## RICHARD DOUGHERTY.

Richard Dougherty was born June 8, 1823, in the town of Hector, Schuyler county, State of New York. In the fall of 1840 he removed with his father John B. Dougherty, and his family, to Branch county, in the State of Michigan. In the year 1843 he came to St. Joseph county, where he has resided ever since.

In January, 1846, he married Susan Leland, daughter of George and Lydia Leland, and together they have raised a large family, grown and growing up. The oldest three children are girls. The oldest daughter died in her twenty-fourth year. There are eight sons and two daughters still living, and all at home except the oldest daughter, who is married and lives in Three Rivers.

Mr. Dougherty is a breeder of Durham cattle and merino sheep, and has some most excellent stock of both varieties.

## JOHN LOMISON.

Of the very few pioneers of Park township now remaining, none stand higher in the estimation of the public than does the subject of this sketch; hence, a representation on the pages of our history is but a fitting tribute to his general worth.

John Lomison was born in Turbet township, Northumberland county, Pennsylvania, November 14, 1807. He comes of a good old Scottish family, and bears the impress of the careful training he received at the hands of his parents, as his entire life has fully demonstrated. Until his nineteenth year he worked on his father's farm, and then apprenticed himself to one Jacob Hibler, under whom he learned the trade of tanner and currier. His industry and close application to his trade early won for him the good opinion of his master, and at the close of his apprenticeship he was made foreman of the establishment, and subsequently became a partner in it. He remained in this position about seven years and then worked at the business on his own account for four years.

In 1836 he abandoned this trade and turned his attention to farming. For the furtherance of this new vocation he returned to Michigan, and on the 1st of September, 1836, he arrived at his new home, entering eighty acres at first, and subsequently the same amount adjoining his first purchase. He has added to this until he now owns one hundred and eighty-four acres of highly-cultivated land, having thereon good substantial buildings.

On the 17th of March, 1833, he married Miss Sarah Fisher, by whom he has had an interesting family of eight children—four sons and four daughters. Of the sons, two, Franklin and Clarence, served in the rebellion; Franklin in the Sixth Michigan Infantry (afterwards heavy cavalry), under General Benjamin Butler, and was killed at Port Hudson, May 27, 1863; Clarence served in the Twenty-fourth Michigan Infantry, and received an honorable discharge.

Mr. Lomison has been several times elected to the offices of supervisor, town clerk and justice of the peace, and also once a representative in the State legislature. He served in these various capacities of trust with honor to himself and to the satisfaction of his constituents. His character for honesty and business ability is well known; and perhaps no man in St. Joseph county has been oftener selected by those leaving fortunes, to administer on their estates, than he. And we know that none have fulfilled the trusts committed to their care with greater integrity or more to the satisfaction of those interested. We mention one instance of an estate he administered on, not because we wish to make any particular merit of it, but simply as illustrating his character as a business man and as a faithful trustee: we

refer to the estate of John H. Bowman, of Three Rivers, which, when probated, was assessed at twenty-two thousand dollars. After paying the debts of the estate and some bequests amounting to over twenty thousand dollars, he handed over to the heirs property assessed at twenty-two thousand dollars, being equal to the entire estate when coming under his administration, after settling everything.

In politics Mr. Lomison is a Republican, and while never having sought political preference, yet he has always earnestly served the best interests of the party when chosen by it to fill any office. In religion he is a Presbyterian, having been a member of that church for thirty-five years, and an elder in it for more than thirty.

By thrift and economy he has accumulated a neat fortune, and now, at the age of three-score years, he enjoys the fruits of a well-spent life. Looking back over the past, he harbors no regrets, and looking to the future, he has no fears. Having always enjoyed good health, great energy and keen enterprise, and having been blessed with an admirable wife, who fearlessly shared his many trials, rejoicing ever at his success, and cheering him on in all his difficulties (and in the life of the pioneer they are many), they won a mutual triumph, and will finally reap a great reward.

## JAMES HUTCHISON.

Among the truly representative men of St. Joseph county, none were more prominently connected with its early improvement than was James Hutchison. He was one of the pioneers of Park township, and was in every respect adapted to the duties of the early settler. He had a robust constitution, excellent health, great intelligence, and a knowledge of men and things well calculated to inspire energy into those less able to cope with the trials incident to a new settlement.

His virtues were soon recognized by his fellow-pioneers, for we find him at an early day county surveyor, and also one of the county commissioners, which offices he was abundantly qualified to fill, being a man possessing considerable more than an average education for those days.

James Hutchison was born in Columbia county, Pennsylvania, November 14, 1799, and died February 2, 1866. At an early age he evinced a desire for study, and although his father's circumstances would not admit of his attending school for more than about six months, yet we find him often poring over such books as he could procure, having a particular preference for those treating on civil engineering and mathematics, in which sciences he became tolerably proficient. He was pre-eminently a self-made man, and although commencing life quite poor, he left at his death a very fair competency.

On the 11th of May, 1837, he married Rosanna S. Fortner, a native of Pennsylvania, who still survives. She proved to him a true and faithful wife; sharing his toils and cares, and doing all in her power to assist him in his struggles in the development of a new country. Three children were sent to gladden the hearts of the good couple, of whom but one survives, Oliver H. P. died when he was in his twenty-seventh year, and Epaphroditus in his infancy, leaving but Stephen W., who now resides on the old homestead, and is well-known throughout the county as a raiser of poultry and bees.

In politics Mr. Hutchison was a Democrat, having voted for Andrew Jackson in 1832, and always remained true to the old Jacksonian political principles.

In religion he was a Presbyterian, and though never making any ostentatious display of his religious views, yet was ever a devout Christian; a good citizen; a firm friend, and, in fine, a true specimen of nature's noblemen. (See portrait and illustration.)

# MENDON.

THE territory now included in the township of Mendon, and a portion of western and eastern Leonidas and Park, was included in, and formed the portion of the Nottawa-seepe reservation lying within St. Joseph county. Its surface is level generally, though somewhat rolling as it borders on the river St. Joseph. The township was originally covered with oak-openings, rather heavy than otherwise, except that portion of the southern sections which embrace the northern part of Nottawa prairie, some two thousand acres.

The soil is remarkably fertile and productive; the prairie being a black sandy loam, capable of producing large crops of corn and wheat, and the openings being a lighter yellowish soil. In the northern part of the township it is heavily timbered with oak, walnut, whitewood, black and white ash, sycamore, elm, maple, etc., and has and still does furnish large quantities of fine timber.

The area of the township includes twenty-two thousand three hundred and forty-two acres of land, and six hundred and forty acres of water-surface. It is drained by the St. Joseph, Big and Little Portage rivers and Bear creek. The former enters the township on the northeast quarter of section twenty-five, and runs westerly and southwesterly through sections twenty-five, twenty-six, twenty-seven and thirty-three, skirting the prairie on its southern bank, and passes into Nottawa township on the southeast quarter of section thirty-two. The Big Portage enters the township in the northwest, and passing through Portage lake makes its exit into Park on section nineteen. Bear creek also empties into Portage lake, a fine body of water in the northern part of the township, the creek coming in from the northeast. The Little Portage enters the township on the southeast quarter of section one and runs southwest through sections twelve and fourteen, thence westerly through sections twenty-three, twenty-two, twenty-one, twenty-nine, thirty and nineteen, into Park.

The water-power at Mendon village was created by damming the Little Portage on the southwest corner of the southeast quarter of the northeast quarter of section twenty-two, and cutting a race one-half mile south to a series of marshes, and thence by a short flume to the St. Joseph, securing a head of sixteen feet of water. There is little or no stone in the township. A series of marshes lie along the Little Portage, which are the only lands in the township that are not susceptible of cultivation.

## FIRST SETTLEMENTS.

The first white settler in the present territory of Mendon was Francois Moutau, a Frenchman, who, with his family, consisting of his wife and two or three children, one of them Frances, now the wife of Hon. Patrick Marantette, came to the reservation in charge of the trading-post established by Peter and J. J. Godfroi, in 1831, near Mr. Marantette's present residence, on the south bank of the St. Joseph. Mr. Moutau subsequently purchased lands of the government, when the same came into the market, and settled permanently, his descendants still living in the township. Mr. Moutau was born in Fort Wayne, Indiana, in 1770, and he died in 1853.

At the first court held in the district of Erie, set off by the governor of the territory of Michigan (Hull), April 7, 1805, which district comprised all the present southern tier of counties in the State and north to Huron river, Mr. Moutau was a grand juror. This court was held at Monroe, September 2, 1805, at the house of John Baptiste Jeraume, by Augustin B. Woodward, chief justice of the territory.

In the month of August, 1833, Mr. P. Marantette came and assumed charge of the post for the Godfrois. He was then an unmarried man, but in 1835 he married a daughter of Mr. Moutau. He subsequently bought a section of land on the reservation, which was reserved to him when the Indians sold their claims to the same in September following. Mr. Marantette possessed a great influence over the Nottawa Indians, and it was by his endeavors, largely, that they were finally gathered together in 1840 and removed to the west. His history in connection with them is given in the general history of the county. Mr. Marantette was born of French parents, about 1808, in or near Detroit, and his father before him was a man possessing the unbounded confidence of the Indians, with whom he was for years

in contact daily in Canada, where he is, or was but a short time previous to this writing, living.

Peter Neddeaux came to the Reservation in 1833, during the fall of the year, and located near the fort. He also was a Frenchman, as was the next comer, Leander Metha, who came in from Monroe in 1834, and settled on the north side of the river, on the present site of Mendon village.

A Mr. Miller also came in 1834, and located near Mr. Marantette's, on section thirty-five.

In 1835 Moses Taft, one of Mendon's worthiest citizens, came into the township with his family from Massachusetts, and located on the farm where he lived to the day of his death, which occurred in the year 1874. His son Seth now occupies the old homestead. William Harrington, Abram H. Voorhees, and A. Wesley Maring married daughters of Mr. Taft, all of whom are now living in the township. Mr. Taft was a native of Mendon, Worcester county, Massachusetts, where he was born July 8, 1792. He came to Leonidas in 1834. In an early day he made the journey down the Ohio and up the Mississippi as far as the falls of St. Anthony, the latter part of the trip being made in an Indian canoe. James S. Barnabee also married a daughter of Mr. Taft, who, alone of all her sisters, is now deceased. Mr. Taft was noted for his charitable and generous disposition, and is said never to have turned away distress unrelieved.

Stephen Barnabee was also an early settler, and Fordyce Johnson, the latter locating on section thirty-five in 1834. Samuel E. Johnson and his family of six boys, of whom Sherlock and Fordyce are now residents of Mendon, came from Livingston county, New York, to Nottawa prairie, November, 1833, and located on section one in Nottawa, south of the reservation-line. Mr. Johnson died in 1839.

Rowell came to the reservation in 1835, and Oliver H. Foote the same year, with his family of six children, and located where Elisha Foote now lives.

The Wakemans came to Nottawa prairie in 1833-6, Adams being the advance of the three brothers—Hiram the main body in 1834, and Mark the rear-guard in 1836. They settled in Mendon in 1837.

Benjamin Peter House came in from Mendon, New York, in 1837-8; N. Chapman in 1836; B. B. Bacon, 1837—the latter from New York; Ephraim K. Atkinson, from Pennsylvania, in 1837; James Van Buren, 1837-8; Abram H. Voorhees, 1841; Ira Pellett, 1837, and William Pellett, his brother, the same year, came in from Pennsylvania, and Joseph Woodward, also, who settled that year on Portage lake. A Mr. Curtis came in 1834; Abner Moore came in from Pennsylvania in 1834, and Harvey White in 1836 located in the same neighborhood,—southwest part of township, where he now lives. Ezra Brown came to the township in 1840; Pattee came in 1836-7, and Timothy Kimball and Van Buskirk before that time.

## THE FIRST FARM

was opened by Mr. Moutau in 1832-3, who raised a crop of corn. Mr. Marantette raised the first wheat, sowing two bushels of a spring variety, in 1835. In 1873 there were four thousand and forty-five acres of wheat sown, which produced forty-four thousand and forty-one bushels, and one thousand six hundred and eighty-six acres of corn planted, which yielded forty-eight thousand five hundred and seventy-five bushels. The crop of 1873 also produced ten thousand six hundred and fifty-six bushels of other grain, three thousand nine hundred and fifteen bushels potatoes, one thousand two hundred and seventy-three tons hay, fifteen thousand six hundred and sixty-seven pounds wool, one hundred and twenty-two thousand four hundred and fifty-two pounds pork, twenty-nine thousand and sixty pounds butter, five thousand five hundred and eighty pounds dried fruit, and three hundred and seventy-eight barrels of cider. Three hundred and forty-seven acres in orchards produced six thousand five hundred and sixty-one bushels of apples, valued at five thousand and forty-three dollars.

The first entries of public lands in the township were made in the year of 1835. The locations made previously were all by pre-emption, the land not coming into market until after the time had expired during which the Indians were promised quiet and undisturbed possession of their reservation

A. P. EMERY.

MRS. A. P. EMERY.

RESIDENCE OF A. P. EMERY, MENDON, ST. JOSEPH CO, MICHIGAN.

after the sale thereof to the government in 1833. Notwithstanding this guaranty the choice lands were all pre-empted before the expiration of the stipulated period of two years, or at least were located and occupied much to the discontent of the tawny possessors of the reservation, but the strife to secure the best possessions regarded not the conditions of treaties or rights of the natives of the soil, but in face of them all the choice lands of the Nottawas were appropriated by the Anglo-Saxon who has made the township what it is, one of the best in the county. There were but two entries in 1836, and both were made by Samuel T. Larkin on section twenty-six,—the northeast fractional quarter on September 22, and the southwest quarter September 29. In 1837 and '38 there was a rush for the land-office, and large tracts of the township were located. In 1876 there twenty-two thousand one hundred acres of land assessed for taxation, valued by A. P. Emery, supervisor of the township, at four hundred and thirty-six thousand and thirty dollars, which is about one-quarter its real value.

### THE LEADING FARMERS OF 1876

are Mr. Marantette, who is the heaviest land-owner in the township; E. L. Yaples and sons, A. H. Voorhees, Reuben Estes, Ira Pellett, G. C. Bennett, the McAllisters, Andrew M. Leland (who came in 1835), A. P. Emery, Eli Beebee's sons, Hiram Wakeman, Leonard Osgood, Maxwell Olney, Seth Taft, John Hamilton, A. Wesley Maring, James Barnabee and David Embly.

### THE FIRST HOUSES

built by a white man for a shelter were those erected by the Godfrois for a trading-post in 1831. They were two log houses, one for a store and another for a blacksmith-shop. Mr. Moutau built a log-cabin the same year, a rude, rough structure. Mr. Marantette built the first frame house erected in the township in 1835, which was named by Adams Wakeman, after the custom of the country, "The Queen of the Prairie." The first brick building in the township was built by Hosea Barnabee and William Pellett in the village, and which is now a part of the Commercial Hotel. The first hewed-log house was built by Leander Meths in 1834, near where the Wakeman House now stands.

### THE FIRST FRUIT-TREES

set out in Mendon were apples, which were in bearing when Mr. Moutan came to the Indian village in 1831, and were at least twenty years old; whether they were set out by the Indians or the missionaries, is not known. Mr. Moutan was the first settler among them to plant an orchard, from which the first fruit was raised, aside from those trees first named. Mr. Marantette planted the first peach-orchard and raised the first of that variety of fruit. He made charcoal-pits in 1833, and on the beds thereof, in 1834, he planted the stones or pits from which the trees grew, and ate the fruit thereof in 1838.

Whitefield Troy began a nursery in a small way after 1850, and now has a fine collection of ornamental fruit-trees, the only nursery in the township.

Mint-oil is now an important item of production in the township, three thousand five hundred pounds having been produced in 1876. The first distillery of peppermint oil was built in the township in 1856, by S. D. Angevine, who came to the township in 1840. A. P. Emery is the heaviest producer and dealer. His purchases, in 1876, aggregated seven thousand pounds.

Oliver H. Foote built a blacksmith-shop in his son's present location, in 1836.

### IMPROVED LIVE-STOCK ·

was first introduced into the township by the Wakeman brothers in 1851,— the same being thorough-bred "short-horn," or Durham cattle, from the Ohio Shakers. A. Wesley Maring, who came to the township in 1853, and located on sections twenty-five and thirty-six (a view of whose fine farm, dwelling and barns may be seen on another page), in 1861 began the improvement of sheep, and introduced pure blood (American merinos) into his flocks in 1875. He is also engaged in breeding polled (or muley) cattle. Mr. Marantette has been largely interested in the breeding of blooded horses, and has introduced some very fine stock.

The leading stock-raisers and breeders of the present, are: Hiram Wakeman, in blooded cattle; A. H. Voorhees and Mr. Marantette, in horses; A. Wesley Maring, McAllister and Maxwell Olney, in fine-wooled sheep. There is no association formed especially for the purpose of breeding, though Mr. Marantette has a private racing-track where his neighbors can, and do, speed their horses and colts ad libitum. In 1874 there were owned in the township five hundred and forty-seven horses, six mules, sixteen oxen, five hundred and eight cows, four hundred and forty-one other cattle, one thousand and nine hogs, and three thousand one hundred and ninety sheep.

### IMPROVED FARM-MACHINERY

was first introduced into the township in 1840, or thereabouts, in the shape of open-cylinder threshers. Separators were brought in by the Johnsons or Wakemans in 1842, and the first reaper was one manufactured by John M. Leland, and used in 1844 on the Wakeman farm.

### THE FIRST MERCHANT

in the township was Mr. Moutan, who was the agent of the Godfroi, at their trading-post in 1831. He was succeeded by Mr. Marantette in the agency in 1833. The business was principally confined to the Indian trade, though the settlers found many articles suitable to their needs in Marantette's stock. No whisky was allowed to be sold to the Indians under penalty of seven thousand dollars, which Mr. Marantette was under to Governor Porter.

### THE FIRST MANUFACTURES

established in the township, outside of the village, were blacksmithing, coopering and lime-burning. Oliver Delei was the first blacksmith, and worked in Godfroi's shop at the post in 1831. The first cooper was Abner Moore, who, in 1834-5, made half-bushel measures and churns. L. Salisbury had a cooper-shop (the first regular and full-fledged one in the township) before 1840, and in that shop the first meeting was held looking to the formation of the township.

Joseph Woodward burned the first lime made in the township, on the shore of Portage lake, using marl taken from the marsh on its borders, for the raw-material. The first wagon-maker was Stephen Barnabee, and Bowen was the first shoemaker, in 1838. Curtis Lewis, in the same years, made shoes also.

### THE FIRST WHITE CHILD

born in the township, was a child of Mr. and Mrs. Marantette, in 1836.

### THE FIRST MARRIAGE

of white persons in the township, was the one celebrated between Mr. P. Marantette and Miss Frances Moutan by J. W. Coffinberry, Esq., and afterwards ratified by the bishop of Detroit, at Bertrand's, on the St. Joseph. The legal marriage transpired November 23, 1835.

### THE FIRST DEATH

of a white person that occurred in the township was in 1838,—the person being the wife of Alexander C. Meths, and daughter of Colonel Lasell, of Monroe, she being accidentally shot by her husband. Peter Neddeaux died the same year.

### THE CEMETERY

is located about one and a half miles west of the village, and contains three acres,—being a part of the Estes farm. It was bought by the township in 1859. Before this plat was bought the burials were made either in Nottawa or at the west end of the town, and also in the northwest part of the township, where a burying-ground had been located long before the village was platted.

### THE FIRST SCHOOL-HOUSE

was built in the fall of 1837 in the township, near the Bacon homestead. Miss Weatby Hunt taught school in a log building near Meths's in the winter of 1836-7, and Mrs. Hosea Barnabee, now of Mendon, was a pupil of that school. A school was also taught about this time in one of the log buildings of the trading-post. The first frame school-house was built in 1841 in that village.

The statistics of 1876 show the following exhibit of educational privileges of the present: There are eight school-houses, five frames and three brick, valued at eighteen thousand three hundred and fifteen dollars, and containing seven hundred and thirty-eight sittings. There are six hundred and sixty-seven children between five and twenty years in the township, six hundred and two of whom attended the schools, which were in session an average of eight and three-quarter months. Six male teachers were paid one thousand nine hundred and ninety-one dollars and fifty cents, and three times as many females received two thousand dollars and seventy cents. The total income of the districts was seven thousand six hundred and forty-six dollars and forty-six cents, which was all expended except six hundred and seventy-two dollars and twenty-nine cents. District number three has an excellent brick school-house which cost about two thousand two hundred dollars.

### THE FIRST RELIGIOUS SERVICES

were held by the Roman Catholic missionaries at the trading-post in 1831-2, though the first mass was not celebrated until 1839, when Father Boss, of Detroit, on his way to Grand Rapids stopped at Marantette's. The first meeting among the settlers was a service held by Rev. John Ercanbrack in Mr. Pattee's house in 1838.

The first Methodist Episcopal church of West Mendon was organized in 1857 by the Rev. M. Gee, though as early as 1843 preaching was had in school-district number three, where the church edifice is situated, by Reverends Kellogg, Wilson, Duncan and Goodrich, in the school-house. The class organized by Mr. Gee was composed of the following members: Joseph Woodward, Maria Woodward, Mrs. Snow, Edward Snow, Mrs. Carey, William Embly and Mrs. Embly (now Barrett), Mrs. Maria Doan, Mrs. Jacob Peterman, Mrs. Van Buren, formerly Mrs. William Simpson, and about forty others, of whom many are now deceased. Mr. Joseph Woodward was the first leader of the class. In the spring of 1872 the society erected their present very neat and substantial brick chapel, thirty-two by forty-eight feet, which contains two hundred and fifty sittings and is a marvel of economical construction, costing about two thousand three hundred dollars. That it was built at all is largely owing to the liberality of A. P. Emery, Esq., on whose farm it stands. The first trustees of the society were Joseph Woodward, A. P. Emery, D. W. Embly, V. O. Doan and Ambrose McElrath. The church building was dedicated on the 25th day of January, 1873, and belongs to the Parkville charge. The preachers in charge have been Reverends William I. Cogshall, H. H. Parker, and the present incumbent, Rev. Mr. Wilson. The society is in a prosperous condition, having a membership of sixty. There is a flourishing Sunday-school connected with the church, which was organized in 1853 by Rev. Mr. Boyington in the old school-house, and has been kept in operation ever since. Mr. Boyington was the first superintendent, but Mr. Emery has had charge of the school since 1864. In 1848-9 Mrs. Shug, assisted by Mr. Calvin Snow, began a school, but it failed for want of pupils. It now numbers eighty scholars and teachers.

THE EVANGELICAL ASSOCIATION.

The Mendon class of this association was organized in 1868 by Rev. C. S. Brown, and comprised the following members: J. J. Miller and wife, Thomas Goodacre and wife, Reuben Andre and wife, and George Finister and wife. The first church, and in which this class now worships, was erected in 1871, and called "the Zion Evangelical church," and is situated on Joseph J. Miller's farm. It is a frame building thirty-four by forty-eight feet, with about two hundred and fifty sittings, and cost one thousand eight hundred dollars. The church was dedicated in November, 1871, by Rev. J. Stell. The building-committee consisted of Rev. M. J. Miller, Rev. F. N. Davis, J. J. Miller, H. S. Anderson, and Thomas Goodacre. The first trustees were Reuben Andre, George Finister and Thomas Goodacre. The present trustees are Thomas Goodacre, Reuben Andre and H. S. Anderson. The present membership of the church is twenty-seven. The Sunday-school was first organized in 1871, and has been in operation ever since, J. J. Miller being the superintendent from first to last. The following ministers of the St. Joseph circuit have had charge of this society: Rev. C. S. Brown, 1868; E. B. Miller, 1869, and his colleagues T. N. Davis, P. West, 1870; S. Copley and J. W. Loose, 1871-2. But Copley's health failing, Alonzo Russell and P.Swille came to the circuit in 1872; Reverends E. B. Miller and J. W. Loose, 1873; J. H. Keeler, 1874, and also the present pastor, Rev. B.F. Wade, 1875. The first Sunday-school held in the township was in 1850, in the school-house in the Angevine district.

CIVIL ORGANIZATION.

In the first organization of townships in St. Joseph county, the first four townships being numbered, five were included in and formed one township, called Flowerfield. This constitution remained unchanged until 1833, when Leonidas and Colon were constituted a separate township, and township five of range two, now known as Mendon, was attached to and became a part of Nottawa township. The township remained an integral part of the latter, until 1843, when it was set off into a separate and independent sovereignty, under the name of Wakeman, in honor of its largest land-holder. But this name was not satisfactory to the majority of the people of the township, and a meeting was called at the cooper-shop of L. Salisbury to select another name for the same, and memorialize the legislature to change it accordingly. Several names were suggested at the meeting; Peter House, who came from Mendon, New York, and Moses Taft, who came from Mendon, Massachusetts, suggested and moved the town be called Mendon; the motion was carried almost unanimously, and the name was accordingly changed from Wakeman to Mendon, in 1844, and the first town-meeting held at the school-house near T. Kimball's.

The first supervisor was Joseph Jewett. He was succeeded by Joseph Woodward, 1845; Patrick Marantette, 1846-47 and 1849-50; Moses Taft, 1848;

Norman Hill, 1851; Benjamin Osgood, 1852; Cyrus Dutton, 1853-54 and 1874; Ira Pellett, 1855; Abram H. Voorhees, 1856-58 and 1860-62-63; Stephen Barnabee, 1859-1861-1864-1867; H. H. Bourn, 1868-73, and A. P. Emery, 1875-77.

The town clerks have been as follows: E. Kellogg, 1844; Joseph Jewett, 1845-46; William Pellett, 1847-49 and 1852; B. P. Doan, 1850-51 and 1863; Edwin Stewart, 1853-58 and 1866; A. Crandall, 1859 and 1862; George B. Reed, 1860-1868 and 1870; H. S. Doan, 1864-65 and 1867; O. J. Fast, 1869; J. Wirt Hyatt, 1871; J. B. Anderson, 1872-73; A. H. Vose, 1874-76.

The principal justices of the peace have been Timothy Goodwin, Rensselaer Teffl, Hosea Barnabee, Fordyce Johnson, D. K. Van Ness, William Harrington, Lentulus Huntley and Rodney E. Fletcher.

AN ESTRAY WAIF

was picked up November 11, 1844, by James McElrath, and a description of the same left with the town clerk, which was a steer-calf, which the clerk said, was "read, with a line of white on the back, and some white spots scattered over it, said calf, he (McElrath), supposes to be an early calf, not one year old yet."

THE FIRST ROAD

laid out in the township was the territorial road, which passed along the southern line of the same, bounding the reservation on that side. It was laid out in 1832-33.

The first bridge built over the St. Joseph in the township was in the year 1839, at the village, near the present state-works. Another near the west end of the township, called the Wakeman bridge, was built in 1843, and the one in the village, the Marantette bridge, was built in 1873, and the old one first erected rebuilt in 1876.

POPULATION.

In 1850 Mendon contained a population of eight hundred and sixty-two. In 1870 the inhabitants numbered one thousand nine hundred and nine, of whom nine hundred and eighty-five were males and nine hundred and twenty-four females. In 1874 the State census-taker returned but one thousand seven hundred and forty-eight persons, nine hundred and twenty-three being males and eight hundred and twenty-five females. There were two hundred and ninety-two males between twenty-one and forty-five years, one hundred and fifty-six between twenty-five and seventy-five years, and twelve over seventy-five but under ninety years. Two hundred and ninety-four females were between eighteen and forty years, one hundred and seventy-nine between forty and seventy-five, and three over seventy-five years of age. There were four hundred and sixty-three boys under twenty-one and three hundred and forty-four girls under eighteen years. There were three hundred and fifty-five married men, eighty single ones who had never married, and of the same classes the females numbered three hundred and fifty-six and seventy-eight respectively. The widowed males were twenty-five to forty-two of the other sex.

THE POLITICAL BIAS

of the township sets strongly Republican, as will be seen by the presidential votes cast therein. In 1844 the Whigs cast sixty and the Democrats sixty-six votes. In 1848 the same parties cast seventy-four and seventy-two votes respectively, and the Free-Soilers polled eight. In 1852 the vote stood sixty-two Whig, ninety Democratic, and three Abolition. In 1856 the Republicans polled one hundred and fifty votes and the Democrats one hundred and seven. In 1860 the same parties polled two hundred and twenty and one hundred and forty-four respectively, and in 1864 one hundred and ninety-three and one hundred and eighteen, and in 1868 two hundred and sixty-seven and one hundred and eighty votes. In 1872 the Republicans cast two hundred and twenty-six votes, the Democrats one hundred and forty-five, and O'Conor had a trio of supporters. In 1876 the Republicans cast two hundred and thirty-eight votes, the Democrats two hundred and twenty-three, and Peter Cooper had twenty-eight ballots cast for him. This last vote would indicate a population of two thousand four hundred and more.

THE PEOPLE'S TAXES

have been laid on their property as follows: The first ones were levied in 1844 as a separate assessment on an assessment of thirty-six thousand two hundred and ninety-six dollars and seventy-one cents, the assessment as returned by Mr. Jewett being fifteen per cent higher. The State tax apportioned to Mendon amounted to ninety-three dollars and ninety-seven cents, and county two hundred and thirty-four dollars and ninety-four cents. In 1876 the total assessment was five hundred and fifteen thousand eight hundred and twenty dollars; other taxes for State and county purposes, two

MRS. A. H. VOORHEES.

ABRAM H. VOORHEES.

RESIDENCE of ABRAM H. VOORHEES,
MENDON ST. JOSEPH CO., MICHIGAN

thousand six hundred and thirty-five dollars and two cents—one-half to each. Other township taxes, including schools, amounted to six thousand eight hundred and eighty-eight dollars and seventy-three cents, making a grand total of nine thousand five hundred and twenty-three dollars and seventy-five cents.

### INCIDENTS.

In the fall of 1838 Mr. Woodworth, then living on what is now known as the Van Ness farm, on the west side of Portage lake, went out early one morning duck-shooting along the lake. Succeeding in shooting one, he took an old boat near by and paddled out to get his game, and as he reached over to get it he was seen to fall out of the boat into the water, and though an expert swimmer he went to the bottom, at a depth of one hundred and fifty feet, and was not seen again for several days, when his body was found floating down the current.

In the winter of 1854 Edgar, a son of Joseph Woodward, aged five years, broke through the ice near the site of Kenney's saw-mill, on what is now known as the Parkville mill-pond, and was drowned.

In 1845 William Simpson, while pitching grain, fell from a loft into a threshing machine at work on James Van Buren's farm, and was so severely mangled and crushed that he died in a short time afterwards.

As an instance of what pluck and determination will do, we recall an incident related by Mr. Marantette. He had been dragged down to Centreville with his witnesses to attend court on the suit brought against him by Hecox for breaking in the heads of his whisky-kegs and spilling the fiery stuff on the ground, by order of Governor Porter, Hecox being a trespasser on the reservation. While he was gone his men had taken the occasion to get more liquor than was good for them, and the result was they were quarrelsome when they returned home. They sat down to the table, four or five of them, and began to find fault with the food, when Mr. Marantette rebuked them for going to the groceries and getting drunk and quarrelsome. Two or three made some insulting reply and sprang to their feet and drew their knives, when Mr. Marantette seized his rifle and drew a bead on the ringleader and commanded them to sit down. They looked at the wiry little Frenchman, and then at the long shining rifle at full-cock, the hammer of which was drawn back at full-cock, and a steady finger laid against the trigger, and then they looked at the door, but "sit down I tell you!" came once more from the lips of Marantette, and they sat down and finished their supper, Mr. Marantette doing likewise, but keeping his gun within easy reach.

Comfort Tyler on the night of the 19th day of June, 1835, came up to the bank of the St. Joseph, at Mendon village, with his cattle, and shouted for assistance to cross the stream, but could bring no one to his relief and was compelled to stay out all night, and nearly perished with the cold. This was the date of the severe frost which cut down the crops, killing the wheat and corn.

Dr. Duncan came in from the south bringing his slaves with him, but they did not remain long under his care, preferring liberty to even the doctor's kindness. He subsequently went to preaching.

### THE VILLAGE OF MENDON

was first surveyed and platted in 1845, on the 23d day of November, by Leander Metha, the first settler on its territory. The original plat was laid on the east half of section twenty-seven, township five, range ten. Marantette has laid out additions since, as have others.

The first settler, as before stated, was Leander Metha, who built the first house on the present plat, in 1834, the same being a rough cabin of logs, and which was subsequently replaced by a hewed-log cabin of more comfortable dimensions, the old one being subsequently used for school-purposes.

The village began to gather to itself "a local habitation and a name" in 1844, when Brownson & Doan dammed the Little Portage and brought its waters through the marshes to the bank of the St. Joseph and built a saw-mill. This was the first of the

### MANUFACTURING INTERESTS

of Mendon. Into this saw-mill was also put an iron-mill for corn-grinding, and in 1845 the proprietors added a carding-machine to their manufacturing business, putting the same into the basement of the building they had put up and were occupying as a store. This carding-machine was run three years by Brownson & Doan, when, in 1848, they sold their buildings and water-power to Melvin and Eldredge Brown, of Centreville, who put in a turning-lathe and other machinery, and manufactured chairs and cabinet-work, and subsequently put in a planing-mill and sash, door and blind-

28

machinery, and operated the factory thus until 1855, when the cabinet-making was discontinued, and the firm changed to Brown, Fisk & Mason, who continued in the old building until 1870, when Brown & Bourn built the present factory opposite the Wakeman House.

In 1860 N. S. Harvey & Co. built a planing-mill and sash and door and blind factory on the bank of the river near the lower bridge. Subsequently S. M. Williams introduced stave-machinery, and the factory at present in the ownership of Wakeman & Lewis is turning out staves and heading in large quantities, from seven to eight hundred cords per year.

A foundry was built in 1860 by Gilbert E. Dart, and Richards put in machinery and ran it a short time only. Mr. Dart manufactured edged tools largely in 1845 and afterwards, his power being horse, and, later steam.

G. P. Doan began wagon-manufacturing in 1854, and continued therein until 1861. Rockwood was in the same business two years, and also Auten & Engle and White & Co. F. Glafke began the business in 1867, and still continues.

Andrew Kellicut in 1872 built a flouring-mill just opposite the Wakeman House, which is now owned by Adams Wakeman. It has three run of stones and is operated by Nelson Farquhar, lessee.

### THE FIRST CARPENTERS

who made their trade their principal business were two brothers L'istenbarger who had their shop in one of the buildings of the trading-post.

### THE FIRST BLACKSMITH-SHOP

in the village was Doan's, who was also the first shoemaker in the village. Mr. Sherman was the first harness-maker, and opened his shop in 1845.

### TRADE.

The first merchants after Mr. Marantette were Brownson & Doan, who built a store on the bank of the river, and which is still standing in the rear of the planing-mill of Bourn and others, in 1845, and put in a stock of goods. The leading merchants since then to the present have been Barnabee & Gillett, who succeeded H. H. Winsley in 1849, the latter being the successors of Doan & Kellogg, who succeeded Brownson & Doan. Hosea Barnabee succeeded Barnabee & Gillett, and remained in trade till his death in 1875, and was a successful trader.

Yaple & Wakeman built the Lewis & Van Ness store of the present in 1858, or thereabouts, and were succeeded by Wakeman & Lewis, Wakeman, Lewis & Co. (William Harrington), Lewis, Stowell & Co., and Lewis & Van Ness, the present firm. In several names, in which the senior partner of the present firm has been a member since 1860, the house has been the foremost merchants of the village for twenty years.

### THE EXCHANGE BANK

of Mendon was established in 1866 as a private bank, J. J. McAllister, president; A. N. McAllister, cashier. The bank drew thirty-five thousand dollars in exchange, in 1876, besides doing a handsome collection and discount business.

E. L. Yaple is a heavy lumber-dealer, his sales in 1876 amounting to twenty-eight thousand dollars, which is under the sales of 1875.

J. B. Anderson and Lewis & Van Ness are grain-buyers. In 1876 they bought one hundred and forty thousand three hundred and fifty bushels. The shipments of 1876 exceed those of 1875 by about fifty thousand bushels.

### THE FIRST HOTEL

was opened by Lewis B. Lyman in the eastern part of the village, near the bridge. The first building built expressly for hotel purposes was erected by Lyman near his first tavern, and called the Eastern. Taft kept a little house formerly on the same site. George Van Buren built one afterwards on the present site of the Wakeman House, and called it the Western. Both of these hotels were burned, and in 1873 the present commodious brick edifice was built by Adams Wakeman, he burning the brick for the same himself. Mr. Van Buren leased the new house and operated it until June, 1876, when his lease expired, and Mr. Wakeman entered upon the duties of host with W. M. Marantette as manager, and keeps a fine hostelry. Mr. Van Buren in the meantime opened the Commercial Hotel, which he is at present conducting successfully.

### THE POST-OFFICE

was not established in the village until 1839, the mail for the people thereof coming to Nottawa post-office, two miles to the south, and brought from thence by private hands. Joseph Bacon was the first mail-carrier from Mendon to White Pigeon. In 1858, December 17, William Pellett was commissioned as postmaster, and on May 23 following, the Nottawa post-office was discontinued. Mrs. Harriet E. Smith was appointed assistant post-mistress February 28, 1859, and managed the office for several years, having been previously employed in the same position at the Corners by Dr. Hyatt, the postmaster of the Nottawa office. The mail was to be supplied to the Mendon office, when it was first established, from Three Forks, meaning doubtless Three Rivers, but, in February, 1859, the supply was changed to Nottawa. Mr. Pellett was succeeded by William Harrington in 1860, and he by Hosea Barnabee in 1861, who held it until 1870, when A. Crandall, the present incumbent, was appointed. The business of the office in 1876 was as follows: Stamps sold, one thousand two hundred and three dollars and ten cents; registered letters sent, nine hundred and thirty-five; money-orders issued, twelve thousand and thirty-one dollars and eighty-one cents; money-orders paid, two thousand five hundred and fifty dollars and sixty-nine cents.

### THE RAILROAD

which passes through the village was secured by the liberality of the citizens of the same, and of the township. Adams Wakeman, Mr. Marantette, Estes, Harrington, and Mr. Taft were prominent in securing the requisite aid, giving largely of their own means to effect the passage of the road—the Grand Rapids and Indiana—through the village. In 1864 the townspeople voted twenty thousand dollars in aid of the road, and in June, 1866, increased the loan or donation twenty-five thousand dollars. In December of the same year the people also voted fifty thousand dollars in aid of the Grand Trunk railroad, on condition that it passed through the township near the village, but it did not accept the conditions, and the loan was never made.

The business transacted by the railroad at the Mendon station in 1876 will be seen by the following exhibit, kindly furnished by Mr. E. Baker, the station-agent in the village: Freight forwarded, eight millions four hundred and forty thousand eight hundred and sixty-one pounds, two-thirds of which was grain. The ticket-sales for the year amounted to five thousand one hundred and thirty-five dollars and eighty-five cents.

### THE UNITED STATES EXPRESS COMPANY

have an office in the village, and the agent, Mr. J. B. Anderson, has courteously furnished the following statement of the company's business for 1876: The value of the receipts, which are principally composed of money-packages, amounted to one hundred and eighteen thousand nine hundred dollars, and that of the forwarding to eighty-three thousand six hundred dollars,—making a total value of goods and money transferred of two hundred and two thousand five hundred dollars.

### THE PROFESSIONS.

The first physician who ministered to the "ills that flesh is heir to," was Dr. Rose, who prescribed for his patients after the method of the botanic school. Dr. Bennett, on the prairie, was also of that school. In 1844 Dr. Richardson administered his lotions and pills, and diagnosed his patients according to the allopathic or regular school of medicine. Dr. Israel Purchell, who followed him, was of the same practice, and died in Mendon after 1851.

Dr. Edwin Stewart came in 1852, and is there yet, being a most worthy citizen. In 1852 Dr. Harra was in the village for a few months. Dr. Loftus Hyatt, who had been in company with Dr. Mottram in Nottawa previously for some years, came to Mendon in 1859, and is still a resident there. Dr. H. C. Clapp located in the village in 1860, and is still in practice therein. Dr. Hamlin (eclectic) was also a dweller in the village in 1860, for a short time only. Dr. Corbin came in 1870, and Dr. Samuel H. Bennett (homeopathic), who is still a resident of the village, came before Corbin. Dr. Charles W. Shepherd, a partner of Dr. Stewart, came in 1874.

### THE FIRST LAWYER

who put out his "shingle" in Mendon was G. P. Doan, and he is still blooming in the village. Orla J. Fast came next, and is now the prosecuting attorney of the county, and is a very successful lawyer. A. J. Reeves was also a resident attorney of the village for a brief period.

Dr. J. E. Fuller was a dentist in the earlier history of the village, but Dr. A. J. Benedict is the only surgeon-dentist here at present, and he came in 1859.

### THE PRESS.

The Mendon *Eagle* spread his wings and screamed defiance to slow-going villages elsewhere, in 1857-8, under the management of N. D. Glidden and A. C. Miles. The bird subsided after a year's exhibit of his high-flying qualities, and Burlingame & Rockwell brought out the fowl again under the name of the Mendon *Independent*, which held the even tenor of its way

for about two years, when it ceased to illumine the horizon with its rays. Burlingame publishes a paper at present in Lenawee county.

The office was sold and finally passed into the hands of Mr. Marantette, and the material and presses were used by several different parties, spasmodically, as they found means sufficient to pay the rental therefor.

In 1871 Charles P. Sweet published the *Mendonian* for about three years. It professed independence in politics, and supported Mr. Greeley in 1872 for the presidency. Mr. Sweet went to Vicksburg, Kalamazoo county. In the fall of 1874 Mr. Alfred Rindge began the publication of

### THE MENDON WEEKLY TIMES,

the first number appearing October 2 of that year. The *Times* is a seven-column folio, gotten up in good style, and presents a neat appearance. Its record of local happenings is its best feature, though it by no means confines its columns to those alone. Its office is a well-stocked one, with new type and material, three good and new presses,—one the Centennial Nonpareil, the latest style out,—and does job-work with neatness and dispatch. The *Times* has a healthy patronage, and in politics is independent.

### THE UNION SCHOOL

of Mendon was first organized as such September 3, 1866. The first board of trustees were Dr. Edwin Stewart, Dr. H. C. Clapp, A. H. Voorhees, D. K. Van Ness, O. M. Beal, and Enoch Healey. .

The present site of the school-house, known as "The Park," was, after much negotiation and discussion, bought, and the present fine and airy structure erected in 1873. The plan of the White Pigeon union school-house was adopted after a full examination of several others. The building committee were H. H. Bourn, Benjamin Will and George Van Buren. Adams Wakeman supplied the brick from his own kilns.

The school-house and lots are valued at twelve thousand dollars, and the house furnishes three hundred and twenty sittings. The bonded indebtedness of the district is nine thousand seven hundred dollars. The first frame school-house erected in district number six was built in 1841, and the second about 1857.

The school was in session for the year ending September, 1876, ten months, two hundred and eighty-one pupils being in attendance. One male teacher was paid one thousand dollars, and three females one thousand three hundred and forty-four dollars. The total income of the district was four thousand eight hundred and fifty-two dollars and eighty-two cents, including one hundred and forty-four dollars and forty-five cents tuition fees from non-resident scholars. The present board of trustees is as follows: Dr. Edwin Stewart, Dr. H. C. Clapp, Dr. R. Beckley, R. E. Fletcher, G. W. Van Buren, and W. P. Custard.

The present corps of teachers comprises J. W. Bentley, principal; Annie H. Warner, assistant; Nettie Hazen, grammar department; Imogene Cross, intermediate; Hattie E. Blakely, primary. The principals of the school have been: David W. Herman, 1866-7; J. W. Bentley, 1868-73; Ira L. Forbes, 1874-5; C. B. Van Slyke, 1875-6.

### THE CHURCHES

in Mendon village are the Catholic, Episcopal, Methodist and Baptist denominations.

#### THE CATHOLIC CHURCH SOCIETY

was organized in 1837-38 by Father Charles Bose. The Moutan family, Mr. Marantette and family, Mr. Metta and family, the Neddeaux family and the French residents generally forming the nucleus of the society, afterwards known in 1858, as at present, as St. Martin's church. Mr. Marantette furnished a chapel until 1866 for several years, either at his house or in his store-building. The present church-building was erected in 1866, has about three hundred sittings and is valued at four thousand dollars. There are some forty-five or fifty families at present connected with the church. In 1840 Father Barnie visited the church here, and Father E. Soren, of Notre Dame, in 1842. The other priests who ministered to the charge, none of whom have remained more than one year, have been Fathers Quentin, Borreau, Schilling, Granger, Murriveaux, Labelle, Richards and Kurst.

#### THE METHODIST EPISCOPAL CHURCH SOCIETY

of Mendon was organized in 1856-58, the class being formed somewhere between those dates. The church-building was erected by a layman, Ezra Bourn, in 1860. The early members were: Ezra Bourn and wife, A. J. Troy and wife, George Maring and wife, L. Blyman and wife, Ziba White and wife, Mrs. Adaline Pellett, Gilbert Bennett and wife, Lentulus Huntley and wife,—Ezra Bourn being the class-leader and steward. The church contains

Res. of HIRAM WAKEMAN, Mendon, St. Joseph County, Michigan.

RESIDENCE of A. WESLEY MARING,
MENDON, ST JOSEPH CO., MICH.

WAKEMAN HOUSE,
MENDON, MICHIGAN.

about three hundred sittings, and is valued at five thousand dollars, and its parsonage at one thousand eight hundred dollars.

It is a brick building, and situated on the main street of that village. It was built on a broad catholic principle, for everybody to use who chose to occupy it. The Sunday-school connected with the church was organized in 1860, a union school being in operation earlier. Its superintendent is Mr. Anderson, and it has one thousand volumes in its library, the largest in the county, and which has been provided for by a most zealous and worthy sister of the church, Paulina (Harmon) McMillan, who endowed the library with eight hundred dollars, the interest of which is to be expended annually for books perpetually. Miss McMillan inherited a snug fortune from Mr. Harmon, who adopted her as his child and made her his heir, and she has been a most liberal donor to the Methodist Episcopal society, giving them a parsonage, valued at two thousand dollars, besides numerous other benefactions. A. J. Troy was the superintendent of the Sunday-school for six years, previous to J. C. Abbott, present incumbent.

The Mendon society was formerly the appointment of the Centreville charge, and afterwards in the circuit of Colon, Leonidas, and Park. Mr. J. C. Abbott, an old veteran in the cause, established preaching in Colon, in 1843, in a cooper-shop. At Watervliet, in Berrien county, Mr. Abbott preached a temperance sermon and pledged the ladies of the village to refuse to board the only liquor-seller in the village, a bachelor, and per consequence he was obliged to leave. Mr. Abbott immediately called a meeting in the quondam saloon, and turning the bar into a desk, he preached therefrom, dispensing truths where drink had been dispensed before. The ministers who have had charge of this society are Reverends Patterson, 1860-61 ; E. Kellogg, 1862 ; Beach, 1863-65 ; Joseph Jones, 1866-68 ; James L. Childs, 1868-69 ; William Mathias, 1869-70 ; William Rice, 1870-71 ; R. C. Welch, 1872 ; W. I. Cogshall, 1873 ; J. C. Abbott, 1874-75, and J. E. White, present incumbent. The church numbers eighty-four members.

### ST. PAUL'S (EPISCOPAL) CHURCH,

of Mendon, was organized September 8, 1866, with the following members: O. M. Beall, A. M. Townsend, William Harrington, Samuel C. Hodgman, Charles H. Lewis, James E. Fuller, George E. Sanford, Hazard L. Stowell, Peter R. Hall, Edwin Stewart and Levi Cole. Vestryman, William Harrington ; senior warden, Edwin Stewart ; junior warden, Charles H. Lewis ; S. C. Hodgman, secretary, and Levi Cole, treasurer. The present church was built in 1868. It contains two hundred and twenty-five sittings, and is furnished with a fine portable pipe-organ. It is valued at six thousand dollars.

The female members at the time of the organization were : Mrs. John Holden, Mrs. William Harrington (who subsequently donated to the church the organ, valued at six hundred dollars), Mrs. Edwin Stewart, Mrs. D. K. Van Ness, Mrs. Levi Cole, Mrs. I. J. McLellan, Mrs. Mary Stowell, Mrs. H. L. Stowell, Mrs. C. H. Lewis, Mrs. L. B. Lyman and Mrs. George Sanford.

A Sunday-school was organized when the parish was instituted, J. B. Anderson being the present superintendent. There are now forty scholars enrolled, and papers take the place of books.

At the bishop's first visit,—January 6, 1867,—he (McCroskry) confirmed a class of twenty-four, and the January following, six ; May 29, 1869, three ; in 1870, four, and in 1872, four. Dr. Gillespie, bishop of western Michigan, in May 23, 1875, confirmed a class of ten.

The ladies aid-society has been very efficient in aiding the building of the church, and is supporting a rector. Mrs. Van Ness is the president. The rectors of the society have been : Rev. William Charles, 1866-7 ; Rev. Augustus Bush, 1869-72 ; Abraham Reeves, 1873 ; L. D. Ferguson, 1875. The present rector, Rev. A. E. Bishop, began his labors over the church January 1, 1877.

The present vestry is as follows: D. K. Van Ness, S. W. ; J. B. Anderson, J. W. ; C. H. Lewis, secretary ; I. J. McLellan, treasurer ; Levi Cole, Edwin Stewart, Loftus Hyatt, John Holden, O. S. Morton and Homer Randall.

### THE BAPTIST CHURCH.

The early members of this organization include J. B. Taber and wife, Elisha Foote, Elisha Foote, Jr., Miss J. P. Tomlinson, P. Crandall, Mrs. L. Crandall, Osborn and others.

### SOCIETIES—MASONIC.

Mendon Lodge, No. 137, F. A. M., was instituted under dispensation in 1861-2, and chartered in 1863, with N. S. Johnson, W. M., who has been succeeded in the "East" by Horace C. Clapp in 1864-7 and 1870-5 ; by

Charles Palmer, 1868-9. The present officers are Charles A. Palmer, W. M.; A. H. Voorhees, S. W.; S. H. Bennett, J. W.; D. K. Van Ness, treasurer ; N. N. McAllister, secretary. The craft number eighty-five.

### I. O. O. F.

Morrison Lodge, No. 136, was organized January 7, 1870, its charter-members being William Harrington, N. G.; Rev. William Mathias, V. G.; G. Engle, treasurer ; T. H. Toby, secretary, and I. N. Caldwell. Its present membership is sixty-two. The hall where the lodge meets is the property of Morrison Lodge stock company, and was built in 1875, and is valued at one thousand dollars. The present officers are John Wolford, N. G.; Wallace Langdon, V. G.; Charles Wellesley, secretary ; S. P. Baird, treasurer.

Morrison Encampment of Patriarchs, No. 57, was instituted February 14, 1873, with J. Foreman, C. P.; Lewis H. Fort, H. P.; John Wolford, J. W.; William Osgood ; J. C. Blue, treasurer ; Julius B. Anderson, scribe, and C. B. Kenyon, S. W. It numbers at present thirty-five members, and its present officers are George Van Buren, C. P.; J. N. Caldwell, H. P.; Wallace Langdon, S. W.; S. Coon, J. W.; Charles Wellesley, scribe ; John Wolford, treasurer.

Both lodge and encampment were named in honor of R. H. Morrison, of Sturgis, an eminent member of the order.

### PATRONS OF HUSBANDRY.

Mendon Grange, No. 111, P. of H., was organized October 25, 1873, with A. H. Voorhees, master ; L. B. Osgood, overseer ; A. P. Emery, secretary, and twenty-seven charter-members, which were increased to fifty-three at the close of the first meeting. The membership at one time was as high as one hundred and five, but numbers at present only fifty-five,—the loss being the usual result by death, removal, and dismission. The grange is in good working order at present, and owns a warehouse on the railroad-grounds or near by, in which the members handle their own grain, plaster, etc. Three hundred tons of plaster passed through the building the first year. The present officers are J. W. Bentley, master ; Frank Butler, overseer ; A. H. Voorhees, secretary ; Mrs. Margaret Lohr, Ceres ; Mrs. Maria Manning, Pomona ; Mrs. Maria L. Fletcher, Flora ; Miss Ellen S. Voorhees, stewardess.

### GOOD TEMPLARS.

A lodge of Good Templars was organized August 14, 1867, and flourished finely, gaining a membership of one hundred and fifty and over, but it began to decline in 1869. The meeting was held May 3, 1870. It was re-organized a few months after, but led a sickly existence for a short time, finally sinking past recovery. Among its members were A. Crandall, Dr. H. C. Clapp, Prof. B. F. Fast, O. J. Fast, E. D. White, A. Gaines, J. E. Embly and wife, Mrs. Crandall, Mrs. B. F. Hills, and A. H. Vose.

### THE MUNICIPALITY.

Mendon village was first incorporated in 1858, the first president being William Miner ; G. P. Doan, clerk, and O. S. Norton, marshal. G. P. Doan was president in 1863 and in 1867. The corporation lapsed and the village was re-incorporated in 1870. The meeting of the city-board December 14, 1870, showed George B. Reed, S. Barnabee, George Van Buren, R. E. Fletcher, Levi Cole and Frederick Glefke to be the trustees, and B. S. Howe, the clerk. In 1871, O. J. Fast was the president, and again in 1875. Dr. H. C. Clapp filled the office in 1872, and J. W. Hyatt was the clerk. In 1875, A. N. McAllister was clerk. In 1875 the village re-incorporated by special act. The present board of village officers is as follows : Nathan S. Johnson, president ; Samuel Cross, recorder ; Homer Randall, treasurer ; Homer G. Fuller, Lentulus Huntley and O. M. Beall, trustees ; E. Whiting, marshal. The corporation own ladders and trucks to put fires out, and a calaboose to put rogues in.

### THE BUSINESS OF THE PRESENT

is conducted as follows :

#### Trade.

General Merchandise—Lewis Van Ness & Co., O. A. House, O. M. Lyman, Hasbrouck & Dukitte, Miner & Lester.

Groceries and Crockery—Levi Cole, C. L. Hasbrouck, Philip Ernst, Nelson Howard, T. S. Riley, O. M. Beall.

Drugs—C. L. Hasbrouck, O. M. Beall, Nelson Howard.

Hardware—J. A. Wallace & Co., Stephen Barnabee.

Books and Stationery—Alfred Crandall.

Clothing and Gents' Furnishing Goods—O. G. & J. Bond.

Millinery and Ladies' Furnishing Goods—Mrs. T. S. Riley and Miss Hattie Dean.

Not'ons and Fancy Goods—George H. Hart.
Bakery and Restaurant—I. J. McLelland.
Dress-making—Mrs. Mary Knox.
Markets—Whiting & Doan, and Cool & Tase.
Hotels—Adams Wakeman, George Van Buren.
Lumber—E. L. Yaple.
Grain and Produce—Lewis Van Ness & Co., J. B. Anderson, William Leidy.
Livery—J. M. Laird & Co., John Tompkins.
Seeds, Farming Implements and Plaster—Custer Brothers.

*Manufacturers.*

Flour-Mill—Nelson Farquhar.
Staves and Headings—Wakeman & Lewis.
Planing and Saw-Mill—Peck, Brown & Co., H. H. Brown, etc.
Furniture—G. Ernst & Kuhn.
Wagons—F. Glafke, William Dutton.
Blacksmithing—Ziba White, Howard & Gifford, W. W. Whiting, Joel Rose, Antell & Cleveland.
Cooperage—Schuyler Greene and Greene & Stimpson.
Harnesses—George S. Root, John C. Ziegler.
Shoes and Boots—George Ernst, Wolford & Slayton.
A fair estimate, made by competent business men in the village, places the capital invested in business in the village at one hundred and fifty thousand dollars.

MENDON IN THE REBELLION

has as proud a record as any of her sister towns in the county. She sent her sons to the front as promptly and as numerously, according to her population, as any, and they bore upon their shields as bravely, gallantly, and steadfastly as any of Michigan's soldiers the honor of the State. Mendon's citizen-soldiery in the war for the Union against treason and secession, as gathered from the official records, were as follows:

FOURTH MICHIGAN INFANTRY.

Private George Cook, Company C; discharged at expiration of service.
Private Addison J. Carpenter, Company C; discharged at expiration of service.
Private Eugene Garvin, Company C; discharged at expiration of service.
Private James K. Rockwell, Company C; discharged for disability.
Private William Stevens, Company C; discharged for disability.
Private John Sergeant, Company C; discharged at expiration of service.

SIXTH INFANTRY.

Private Vintroy Greene, Company B; discharged.
Private John E. Hall, Company B; discharged.
Private Eaton D. Slayton, Company B; mustered-out.
Private Silvanus S. Chapman, Company C; discharged for disability.

SEVENTH INFANTRY.

Private Winslow Brown, Company I; discharged for disability.
Private James H. Phillips, Company I; discharged June 2, 1862.
Private Holly Corwin, Company K; mustered-out.

TENTH INFANTRY.

Private Anson Sweet, Company K; mustered-out.

ELEVENTH INFANTRY.

Sergeant Cuthbert Dixon, Company A; discharged at expiration of service.
Corporal Aaron B. White, Company A; discharged at expiration/of service.
Corporal Edwin D. White, Company A; discharged at expiration of service.
Private Leonard F. Carknard, Company A; died at Stevenson, Alabama, October 15, 1863.
Private Nicholas C. Carknard, Company A; discharged.
Private Thelismar A. Church, Company A; discharged at expiration of service.
Private Ephraim Gibson, Company A; died at Elizabethtown, Kentucky.
Private John R. Hamlin, Company A; discharged at expiration of service.
Private William F. Patterson, Company A; discharged at expiration of service.
Private David Rockwell, Company A; discharged at expiration of service.
Private Daniel D. V. Rose, Company A; discharged at expiration of service.
Private Thomas A. White, Company A; discharged for disability.
Private James K. Woodward, Company A; mustered-out.
Private Henry A. Key, Company A; mustered-out.
Private Martin H. Glover, Company A; mustered-out.

Private Richard H. Welch, Company A; mustered-out.
Private Harrison Auten, Company C; died May 2, 1862.
Private Nelon Bacon, Company C; discharged at expiration of service.
Private William F. Y. Bournes, Company C; discharged at expiration of service.
Private Anthony Worthington, Company E; discharged at expiration of service.
Private Thomas Crow, Company G; discharged November 30, 1861.
Private Harvey Bates, Company G; mustered-out.
Private General V. Bland, Company I; mustered-out.
Private William H. Auten, Company C; veteran reserve corps.

TWELFTH INFANTRY.

Private Martin Nehrus, Company K; discharged for disability.

THIRTEENTH INFANTRY.

Private John S. Vandebogart, Company A; mustered-out.

FIFTEENTH INFANTRY.

Private John Jones, Company A; re-enlisted and mustered-out.
Private George H. Butler, Company D; mustered-out.

SIXTEENTH INFANTRY.

Private Benjamin Horton, Company I; mustered-out.

NINETEENTH INFANTRY.

Private James McIntyre, Company C; died at Smithville, North Carolina.
Private A. D. Mason, Company D; veteran reserve corps; mustered-out.
Corporal James E. Embly, Company D; mustered-out.
Private John Boyer, Company D; mustered-out.
Private John W. Barrett, Company D; died at Nicholasville, Kentucky.
Private John M. Culver, Company D; mustered-out.
Private George B. Crandall, Company D; mustered-out.
Private Theodore Neddo, Company D; mustered-out.
Private Robert Huff, Company C; died at Nashville.
Private Levi Hendrickson, Company C; killed at Thompson's Station, Tennessee, March 5, 1863.
Private Darius S. Cook, Company E; mustered-out.
Private Ira E. Dexter, Company D; mustered-out.
Corporal W. T. Huff, Company K; first lieutenant and mustered-out.
Private Sylvester E. Barretti, Company K; died of wounds at McMinnville.
Private Elijah Bowerman, Company K; mustered-out.
Private James Bradford, Company K; died at Murfreesboro, August 23, 1863.
Private George W. Doan, Company K; mustered-out.
Private Justin B. Doan, Company K; mustered-out.
Private James M. Dawley, Company K; killed at Chattanooga.
Private Elisha Dawley, Company K; mustered-out.
Private George Finnister, Company K; mustered-out.
Private Charles H. Greene, Company K; mustered-out.
Private James M. Huff, Company K; mustered-out.
Private Peter R. Hall, Company K; mustered-out.
Private Andrew Hughes, Company K; mustered-out.
Private Daniel W. Miner, Company K; mustered-out.
Private Charles M. Rose, Company K; mustered-out.
Private Hiram G. Stickney, Company K; died October 9, 1862.
Private Elisha E. Woodward, Company K; mustered-out.
Private George W. Wing, Company K; mustered-out.
Private Ira J. White, Company K; mustered-out.
Private John B. White, Company K; mustered-out.
Private Peter Vandebogart, Company K; mustered-out.
Private Martin Summiller, Company K; died.
Private Charles Z. Miller, Company K; died at Nicholasville, Kentucky, December 13, 1862.

TWENTY-FIFTH INFANTRY.

Private Frank Hendrickson, Company D; discharged.
Private Charles F. Johnson, Company G; discharged.

TWENTY-EIGHTH INFANTRY.

Private Cortlandt Chapman, Company C; mustered-out.
Private George Chapman, Company C; mustered-out.
Private John Libhart, Company C; mustered-out.
Private William I. Smalley, Company C; mustered-out.
Private I. Libhart, Company C; mustered-out.

THIRD CAVALRY.

Private Charles Huff, Company I; died at St. Louis.
Private Samuel Johnson, Company A; mustered-out.

# THE WAKEMAN BROTHERS.

Among the heaviest farmers of Nottawa Prairie, the Wakeman brothers, Mark H., Adams, and Hiram, stand in the foreground. The brothers owned at one time over twelve hundred acres in the townships of Nottawa and Mendon, and the farms now owned by Hiram and the estate of Mark number ten hundred and forty-nine acres. They were the first to introduce blooded cattle into the county, from which the improvement of that variety of stock began in St. Joseph. The first reaper introduced into the county was first operated on their farm in 1845.

## MARK HOAG WAKEMAN

was the oldest of the brothers, and the leader in all of their enterprises while he lived. He was born in August, 1799, in Bedford, Westchester county, New York. In 1818 he went to Savannah, Georgia, and engaged in the wholesale hat and shoe business, in which he continued successfully for several years. He sold out his business in Savannah, and went to New Orleans in 1834, and engaged in the ship chandlery business with a person named Palme, and in 1836 the establishment was burned, entailing a loss of forty thousand dollars. That year he came to St. Joseph County, Michigan, whither his brothers had preceded him, and entered into business with them in farming and stock raising extensively, in which connection he remained until his death, which occurred in June, 1866. Mr. Wakeman was married in 1856 to Annette Anderson, who died before her husband. By this marriage two children were born. —Mary, who now lives with Hiram, her uncle, and Alice, who died while a child.

## ADAMS WAKEMAN

was the first of the brothers to locate in St. Joseph County, whither he came in the fall of 1833. He located his first tract of land on Section 4, in Nottawa township, on the prairie, buying two hundred and forty acres the same fall. He was born in Bedford, Westchester county, New York, December 1, 1804. On July 1, 1830, he was united in marriage with Mrs. Eliza Hartley, of Philadelphia, but who removed from thence to Centreville, St. Joseph County, in October, 1832, being a member of the first family which settled in that village, that of T. W. Langley. Mrs. Wakeman died in the year 1845. Mr. Wakeman led a lonely life of twelve years, Mr. Wakeman took to himself another companion,—Mrs. Susan B. Reeves,—by whom two children were born,—Belle and Jessie,—both of whom have passed away from all suffering and care, leaving behind them naught but pleasing memories. In 1855 Adams sold his interest in the farming business to his brothers, and removed to the village of Mendon, and entered into a business co-partnership with E. L. Yaple in the dry goods and grocery line, the firm building the present store of Lewis, Van Ness & Co. The partnership continued three years, when Mr. Wakeman bought the interest of his partner, Yaple, and formed a new connection with Charles H. Lewis, the firm being Wakeman & Lewis, which continued three years, at the end of which time William Harrington came into the firm, that partnership continuing for four years, when Mr. Wakeman and Harrington closed their connection with the firm. Wakeman then gave his attention to manufacturing, owning and operating the saw-mill for some seven years. He also built the Western Hotel, which was burned in 1873. Mr. Wakeman at once proceeded to rebuild the hotel, the present fine building known as the Wakeman House, a view of which we present to our readers on another page of our work. He also assisted in the building of the flouring-mill in Mendon, and is now the proprietor of the same. He is also largely interested in the stave and heading factory, which is doing a thriving business in the village. In June, 1876, the lease of the hotel expiring, Mr. Wakeman took charge of it, and, under the management of W. M. Marantette, it is at this writing conducted in an admirable and satisfactory manner.

M. H. WAKEMAN.

## HIRAM WAKEMAN,

the sole representative of the farming interest of the brothers, was born in Carmel, Putnam county, New York, in October, 1808, and was married to Miss Sarah Jewett on the 9th day of December, 1840. He removed to Nottawa township with his family in the fall of 1834, keeping the house on the original location for a time. One child was born to Mr. and Mrs. Wakeman, which died in infancy.

The parents of these brothers were David and Elizabeth Wakeman, of Delaware county, New York. The brothers were members of the Whig party, and after that party was succeeded by the Republican organization they became zealous partisans in the latter, the surviving brothers still remaining members of the same. The brothers gave their attention wholly to their private business, and only played the honorable part of the private citizen in politics. In religious sentiment, the brothers were of the liberal school of doctrine.

HIRAM WAKEMAN.

ADAMS WAKEMAN.

Private Alfred Levere, Company K; mustered-out.
Private Charles Ney, Company K; mustered-out.
Private Oliver Neddo, Company K; mustered-out.
Private Franklin Neddo, Company K; mustered-out.

NINTH CAVALRY.

Private Francis M. Cleveland, Company E; mustered-out.
Private Thomas L. Miles, Company E; discharged for disability.
Private Charles H. Brown, Company G; mustered-out.
Private Abner Tuttle, Company K; died at Marietta, Georgia.
Private Jerome Brown, Company G; mustered-out.
Private Francis Moutan, Company K; mustered-out.
Private James Auten, Company K; mustered-out.
Private Samuel Methey, Company K; mustered-out.
Private Charles Scott, Company K; mustered-out.
Private Daniel Baker, Company K; died in Libby Prison, Richmond.
Private Alfred Butler, Company K.
Private Alanson L. Mason, Company E; Seventh veteran reserve corps.

FIRST LIGHT ARTILLERY.

Private William H. Stevens, Battery F; mustered-out.
Private George R. Stevens, Battery K; mustered-out.

Private William G. Cook, Battery L; mustered-out.
Private Samuel T. Watkins, Battery L; mustered-out.

FIRST MICHIGAN SHARP-SHOOTERS.

J. Baker, Company H; mustered-out.
Joel Rose, Company H; mustered-out.

ONE HUNDRED AND SECOND U. S. COLORED TROOPS.

Private Cornelius Brown, Company B; died at Beaufort, South Carolina.

PROVOST-GUARD.

Mahlon Huff; mustered-out.
Isaac Huff, Jr.; mustered-out.
John Reemer; mustered-out.
Private Frank M. Tuttle, Forty-fourth Illinois; mustered-out.

THIRTY-SEVENTH ILLINOIS.

Private Charles Dukitte, Company C; re-enlisted, and mustered-out.

We tender our acknowledgments for assistance received in the compilation of the history of Mendon, to Hon. P. Marantette, A. H. Voorhees, Esq., Lewis, Esq., Dr. Edwin Stewart, Lentulus Huntley, Esq., A. P. Emery Esq., A. M. Leland, Esq., and others.

# BIOGRAPHICAL SKETCHES.

MR. WILLIAM HARRINGTON.

MRS. WILLIAM HARRINGTON.

## WILLIAM HARRINGTON

was born in Utica, New York, April 15, 1812. He was a son of John and Amenah (Marvin) Harrington, with whom he removed, when fifteen years of age, to Akron, Ohio, where he resided until 1834, when he migrated to St. Joseph county, Michigan, and located on Nottawa prairie within the present limits of the township of Mendon. He attended the district-school in Utica until his removal to Ohio, from which time he was thrown upon his own resources for his support. He followed the business of farming in Mendon, Nottawa and Leonidas, and also the business of hotel-keeper in Centreville, and in Pawpaw, Van Buren county.

In 1855 he was elected sheriff of St. Joseph county, which position he held for four years ending December 31, 1858. From the fall of 1861 to the close of the year 1865, he was a member of the mercantile firm of Wakeman, Lewis & Co., of Mendon, who were the leading merchants of that village during that period. He was postmaster, also, of Mendon for a time, and justice of the peace for several years.

On the 19th day of January, 1840, Mr. Harrington married Lydia A., daughter of Moses Taft, one of Mendon's earliest, as well as worthiest citizens. Mrs. Harrington was born in Ellicott, Chautauqua county, New York, November 18, 1820, and removed with her father to Mendon in the year 1835. No children were born to Mr. and Mrs. Harrington.

In politics Mr. Harrington acted with the Whig, and afterwards with the Republican party from its organization till his death.

Mr. and Mrs. Harrington were members of the Protestant Episcopal church of Mendon, and were confirmed January 6, 1867, by Bishop McCrosky; and Mr. Harrington died in its communion on the 12th day of October, 1873. He was a member of Mount Hermon Lodge, A. F. and A. M., of Centreville, also a member of Centreville Chapter, R. A. M., and Columbia Commandery of Knights Templar of Sturgis, and the esteem in which he was held by his companions of the Masonic brotherhood will be seen by the following resolution adopted, with others, by Centreville Chapter, expressive of the sentiments of the members toward him on his decease. The committee of the chapter were: Judges J. Eastman Johnson, S. C. Coffinberry, and Samuel Frankish, who paid their deceased brother the following tribute:

"Companion Harrington was among the very best known men in this county. He possessed a very sanguine temperament; was endowed with a remarkable degree of energy of character; and in his emotional nature was full of the keenest and kindest sensibilities. He was one of nature's nobility, and ever ready to extend the hand of charity to the needy. * * *

"A man of his activities, of course, had faults,—it would be strange if he had not,—but whatever they were, they were far over-balanced by his amenities, his grand and noble sentiments, his firmness in adhering to what he thought was right, his active benevolence, and his Christian demeanor."

MR. JOHN HOLDEN.

MRS. JOHN HOLDEN.

## JOHN HOLDEN.

The old geographies used to declare that the chief products of Vermont were men and good horses. We present a sketch of one of those products in the person of John Holden, who was born in Sunderland, Bennington county, May 3, 1801, and removed in infancy to Arlington, in the same State, where he resided until 1838. He was the son of John and Abigail (Chipman) Holden. His father's business was that of a farmer and brickmason. John attended the district school in Arlington for a time, after which he worked by the month from an early age till twenty-three years old, when he followed the trade of a shoemaker, which he had previously learned.

June 25, 1838, he located in Pavilion township, Kalamazoo county, Michigan, two uncles on his mother's side having previously settled there, one of whom died, leaving his family to his nephew to care for in a great measure, and which care was most faithfully given. One of the sons has been in the United States treasury department since 1862.

Mr. Holden resided in Pavilion township twelve years, and then removed to Climax township, and from thence removed to Mendon, in 1867, where he has since resided. Besides his farming operations he followed his trade at shoemaking in the winter season for a time, walking to Kalamazoo and back every week, a distance of sixteen miles each way, and making twelve pairs of shoes per week. He has acquired, by steady industry and frugal habits, a comfortable competency, and is enjoying a respite from active labor now in his old days.

On the 9th day of September, 1824, he married Mrs. Laura (Hard) Canfield, in Arlington, Vermont, a daughter of Nobles Hard, of that place. She was born in October, 1794. By her he had born to him two children, Sarah, now Mrs. Nelson Eldred, a prominent citizen of Battle Creek, and John Nobles, who died in infancy soon after his removal to Michigan. Mrs. Holden died in Arlington, June 19, 1828.

Mr. Holden was again married on May 2, 1831, to Phebe, daughter of Raswell Webster, of Arlington, who was born February 22, 1811. The fruits of this marriage were: Frances Amelia, now the wife of Dr. Edw. Stewart, one of Mendon's most enterprising citizens; Clarissa A., now Mrs. Levi Wilson, of Galesburg, Michigan, and Phebe M., now Mrs. Hiram F. Husted, of Nebraska.

In politics Mr. Holden has been a member of the Whig and Republican parties, and is still connected with the latter organization.

Mr. Holden and his former and present wife were all members of the Protestant Episcopal church, and were confirmed when sixteen years old by Bishop Griswold, whose diocese, at the time, included all New England except Connecticut.

Mr. Holden was one of the justices of the peace in Kalamazoo county, for twelve years, but he gave his efforts more to *settle* difficulties between individuals, than to try lawsuits engendered by those difficulties, and rarely failed to effect a just settlement. A life of general usefulness has been his, and it is now crowned with years of honor, backward upon which he may look with pleasure and satisfaction.

## AARON P. EMERY.

The subject of this sketch is one of the leading agriculturists of Mendon, and the heaviest mint-producer in the township. Aaron P. Emery was born in Upper Mount Bethel, Northumberland county, Pennsylvania, November 3, 1832. He was the oldest child of Philip S. and Elizabeth (Miller) Emery, with whom he lived until the year 1853, where he came to St. Joseph county, Michigan, and remained till the spring of 1854, at which time he returned to finish his studies at Belvidere, New Jersey, where he was educated for surveying and the profession of a teacher, which professions he followed, more or less, until 1860. In 1855 he returned to St. Joseph county and bought a portion of the tract of land on which he now resides, on sections seventeen and eighteen. He now owns two hundred acres in his homestead, all under cultivation, with convenient dwelling and spacious barns thereon, a view of which we present on another page. He owns, besides his homestead, large tracts elsewhere. He began the cultivation of peppermint and its distillation in 1867, and has made that business a specialty ever since; being now, also, a heavy dealer in the oil.

On the 10th day of March, 1855, Mr. Emery was united in marriage to Elizabeth J., a daughter of John Hutchinson, of Park township, a pioneer of 1834. She was born June 8, 1838, being among the first white children born in that township. Her mother's maiden name was Caroline Krader, of Bucks county, Pennsylvania. The children of this marriage were Emma E., who died in 1875, aged eighteen years, Lewis, Alice, Georgia, Charlotte, and Ella, all of whom are living at home with their parents. Mr. Emery has held the office of supervisor of Mendon for two terms, the last one just closing; and notwithstanding that he is, and always has been, a Democrat in politics, and Mendon is a Republican town, yet he was elected by a handsome majority at his second election. He was also re-elected in 1877.

Mr. and Mrs. Emery are both members of the Methodist church of West Mendon, for the building up of which society and erection of the neat church Mr. Emery has been a most efficient aid.

Mr. Emery has been and is a very successful farmer, and anything he undertakes he generally completes, being sure first that he is all right in the beginning.

MR. ANDREW M. LELAND.

MRS ANDREW M. LELAND.

## ANDREW M. LELAND.

Among the many thrifty farmers in the township of Mendon, Andrew Moore Leland stands prominent. He was born April 3, 1816, in Liberty township, Columbia county, Pennsylvania, where he resided with his father and mother, George and Lydia Leland, until the summer of 1834, when he came to St. Joseph county, Michigan, arriving at Three Rivers June 10, where he remained with his brother, John M. Leland, until the fall of that year, when he returned to Pennsylvania, and, with his father's family, removed to Park township, in St. Joseph county, in the fall of 1835. The trip was overland in wagons, and occupied twenty-six days of steady travel. The first location Mr. Leland made in the county was on section thirty-six, township of Park. In 1863–4 he purchased land on section thirty in Mendon township, since which time he has resided thereon. He owned in Park and Mendon some four hundred acres, but has divided the tract among his boys, retaining about one hundred acres for himself, on which he resides.

Mr. Leland's father died in Park, May 3, 1860, and his mother a few months afterwards, August 5, the same year.

On the 9th day of September, 1841, Mr. Leland was united in marriage to Sarah K., a daughter of William Pellett. She was born July 13, 1824,

in Paupack township, Pike county, Pennsylvania, and removed to Michigan with her parents in 1837, who settled in Mendon in September of that year.

The children of this marriage are William P., George W., and Charles W., all of whom are married and live near the present homestead of the parents. Also, Albert, Hosea and an infant, all of whom are now deceased.

In politics Mr. Leland was originally a Whig, and cast his first presidential vote for "Tippecanoe and Tyler too" in 1840. He has been a Republican since the organization of that party.

Mr. Leland is not a member of any church, but Mrs. Leland is a member of the Methodist Episcopal church in Park.

Coming from a long-lived ancestry, his father dying at the age of ninety-one, and uncles nearly as old, Mr. Leland has inherited an abundant vital force, and possesses a fine physical endowment that bids fair to carry him up to the last decade of a century.

In 1859, at the age of forty-three years, he cradled nine acres of wheat and bound up one acre; his oldest son, then sixteen years old, and another boy of the same age, binding the balance in one day, from sun to sun.

## ABRAM H. VOORHEES.

Abram H. Voorhees was born in Lysander, Onondaga county, New York, March 23, 1824. He was a son of William and Alche (Van Doren) Voorhees, who were born in New Jersey. The father died when Abram was but four years old, and the mother, taking her son and a younger daughter, returned to her father's house in the village of Lysander, for a home, where they remained until Abram was twelve years old. He then went to live with a farmer named David Relyea, with whom he remained three years, when his mother marrying again (Jacob Springstedt) he returned to her and remained with her one year, coming west to Washtenaw county, Michigan, with the family, in 1840. The next year he came to Mendon, arriving there on the 4th day of March, working by the month the first season, but striking out for himself the next with a single yoke of oxen, and working land on shares for Moses Taft for two years, when he married Mr. Taft's daughter Sophia, on the 27th day of February, 1844. After his marriage he continued to farm Mr. Taft's land for three years, and then built a house on a location he had bought before his marriage on section twenty-six, in the winter of 1846–7, and removed into it the same winter. In the year 1851 ill-health compelled him to sell out his farm and stock and go to California, where he remained about a year. In the year 1854 he bought, and removed to, his present location near the village of Mendon, a view of which, and his

trotting stallion Hero, we present on another page. Mr. Voorhees in the year 186– conducted as marshal and captain a large company to the mines. Mr. Voorhees has been and is a very successful farmer. His fields show excellent culture, and his well-filled barns and sleek-coated cattle and blooded horses exhibit the legitimate results of his care and skill. He has paid considerable attention to stock-raising, but latterly is more interested in improving horses, and has a fleet stallion and several colts of the Messenger-Hambletonian stock now in his stables.

Mrs. Voorhees was born in Ellicott, Chautauqua county, New York, February 4, 1825, and removed to Mendon with her father, Mr. Taft, in 1835. Mr. and Mrs. Voorhees have had born to them four children—Charles G., now on his own farm in Mendon, and a part of Mr. Taft's original location; Maria L., now Mrs. E. A. Fletcher, of Mendon; Alche E., who died in infancy; and Ellen S., now at home, and an accomplished pianist.

Mr. Voorhees was a member of the old Whig organization, and joined the Republican party at its organization, remaining a member of it ever since. He has served his township as supervisor for six years, and justice of the peace for four years, besides serving in other minor offices at many different times. He was deputy sheriff of the county several years, and assistant United States marshal during the war of the rebellion. In religious sentiment Mr. and Mrs. Voorhees are liberal in their inclinations.

JACOB VAN NESS.

Nathan Osborn

GEORGE W. COODEN.

## HON. NATHAN OSBORN.

He, of whose life we write a brief sketch, was born in Windham, Green county, New York, on the 10th day of March, 1803. His father was the Rev. Enos Osborn, a minister of the Methodist Episcopal church, and who was born in Middlebury, Connecticut, in 1774, and removed to St. Joseph county, Michigan, with his son Nathan in 1838. He preached for several years to the people of St. Joseph county, among whom he lived nearly forty years, dying in their midst in February, 1876, at the advanced age of ninety-two years and six months. His wife was Naomi Wooster (a descendant of General Wooster, of Revolutionary memory). Nathan Osborn was the youngest of her four children, and was educated in the district-schools of Catskill, New York. He studied surveying, however, under Professor Gilbert and Surveyor-General Campbell, of Otsego county, New York.

Judge Osborn moved from Windham to Milford, Otsego county, and engaged in the manufacture of woolen goods for about two years, removed thence to Cooperstown for a short time, thence to Middlefield, in the same county, and began the study of law in the office of James Brackett, of Cherry Valley. In the spring of 1831 he removed to Harnellsville, New York, where he read law in the office of Judge Baldwin, and was admitted to the bar of Steuben county in the year 1836. On his first arrival in St. Joseph county he located in Florence, on section sixteen, and began the life of a farmer. In 1842 he removed to Park township, on the "Reserve," where he lived a few years, going from thence to South Bend for a time, and finally removed to Marcellus, Cass county, where he still resides. He was admitted to practice in the St. Joseph county courts in 1839, but did not give his attention to the legal profession as a business.

He was elected county surveyor of St. Joseph county in 1842, and also an associate-justice of the circuit court of the county subsequently; and, when the county court was reorganized, was elected its first second-judge, and then to the position of presiding or county judge of the same court.

Judge Osborn was united in marriage, February 15, 1821, to Miss Polly Claflin, in Catskill, who was born February 15, 1804. Their children were: JEANNETTE, now Mrs. Robert Crawford, of Kansas; AMANDA, afterwards Mrs. Lewis Kimball, but now dead; and JAMES D., now a leading lawyer of Goshen, Indiana (and former circuit judge of that State). Mrs. Osborn died February 8, 1852.

On the 1st day of November following, Judge Osborn took another companion, Mrs. Rebecca B. Foster, of Ottawa, Illinois, a daughter of Christian Adler, of Philadelphia. Two children were the fruits of this marriage, LIZZIE and BELL, the former now Mrs. George W. Jones and the latter Mrs. L. Poorman, both residing at Marcellus, Cass county.

On the 3d of February, 1862, Mrs. Rebecca Osborn died, and Judge Osborn, finding a lonely life insupportable, brought to his hearth another to make glad his desolate home,—Miss Emma J. Blowers, of Lake county, Illinois,—whom he married January 22, 1863, and by whom he has had one child born to him, IDA L., who resides at home.

Judge Osborn has always been a staunch Democrat in politics, and was an ardent supporter of General Jackson. He is liberal in his religious views, and looks for the elucidation of the mystery concerning man's past and future in a correct knowledge of the laws of nature rather than in theological dogmatising or deductions.

---

## GEORGE W. OSBORN.

The subject of the present sketch was born August 30, 1827, in Middlefield, Otsego county, New York. With his parents, Nathan and Polly Osborn, he came to St. Joseph county at the age of eleven years, settling with them in Florence, and four years later removing to Park, where he lived at the parental home till 1849, and after his marriage returned again and assisted his father on his farm until 1853. From that time until 1863 he pursued the avocation of a farmer in Mendon and Nottawa, and also engaged in machine-work in Goshen, Indiana. After a short sojourn in the latter place, he returned to Parkville, where he followed the trade of a shoemaker until April, 1876, when he again returned to Mendon, and leased the farm of Jacob Van Ness, on which he now resides.

Mr. Osborn was elected supervisor of the township of Park in 1866, and was retained in the office until he removed from the township, ten years afterwards. He held also the office of justice of the peace in that township eight years, besides other minor offices. He has invented lately an improvement on grain-drills, which bids fair to be of great advantage to the farmer.

Mr. Osborn was married January 24, 1849, to Ann Eliza, daughter of Jacob Van Ness, of Mendon.

Mrs. Osborn was born in Victor, Ontario county, New York, September 4, 1831. Mr. and Mrs. Osborn's children are: MORRIS, now married, and residing in Parkville; CATHARINE C., now Mrs. Albert Perrin; FITZ ROY and AL ZOA,—the two latter at home with their parents.

In politics, like his father before him, Mr. Osborn is Democratic, and he and his wife are both liberal in their religious views.

---

## JACOB VAN NESS.

Jacob Van Ness comes of the old Knickerbocker stock, who followed Hendrik Hudson up the noble river which he discovered and named, and settled on its banks eastward and westward, and wrested from hardy old nature farms and well-tilled fields. He was born in Hoosac, Rensselaer county, New York, February 5, 1805, where he lived under the old homestead-roof with his father and mother, John and Alida Van Ness, till he was twenty-two years old, when he removed to Rochester, New York, and from thence (in 1846) to St. Joseph county, Michigan, arriving at Centreville February 9. He settled in Mendon that year, on section seven, which location (one hundred and sixty-two acres) he still owns, his son-in-law, George W. Osborn, at present occupying it. He had very slender opportunities to get an education, and followed the occupation of a farmer throughout to the present time.

In 1827 he married Maria Morrison, of Pittstown, New York, who was born February 15, 1805, and to them have been born the following children: DANIEL K., now of the firm of Lewis Van Ness & Co., of Mendon; CORNELIA, afterwards Mrs. Lawrence, now deceased; ANN ELIZA, now Mrs. George W. Osborn; ANDREW, ALIDA, now Mrs. Beebe; SARAH CATHARINE, now deceased, and ABRAM, who was a soldier in the Sixth Michigan Infantry, and died in the service.

Mr. Van Ness was originally a member of the old Whig party, and on the organization of the Republican party, joined it, and has ever remained steadfast to its principles.

Mr. and Mrs. Van Ness are members of the Methodist Episcopal church of Vicksburg, Kalamazoo county, where they have resided since 1873.

---

## LEWIS B. LYMAN.

The subject of the present sketch (Lewis B. Lyman) was born in Fenner, New York, in the year 1821, where he lived with his parents, receiving a very meagre school education, and supporting himself by his own resources after he was fifteen years of age. At the age of twenty-five years he married Mary Wightman, of Bethany, New York, the interesting ceremony being performed by the Rev. Mr. Hart, at the residence of Mrs. McCleUr, a sister of the bride. In the year succeeding their marriage the young couple came to Mendon village, which, at the time (1846), contained but three log-dwellings,—into one of which they moved, and where their oldest child (now Mrs. R. C. Fletcher, of Mendon,) was born the same year, on the 31st day of March.

The next year Mr. Lyman built a frame-house, and opened the first hotel in the village, and also sold goods. Some three years after he moved to Coldwater and opened a hotel in that place, which shortly after burned,—by which disaster Mr. Lyman was swept of all his property. He came back to Mendon and rented a farm east of the village, and the second year the house and all it contained was destroyed by fire, and again his accumulations were swept away. Undaunted and undismayed, Mr. Lyman returned to the village, where he formed a mercantile connection,—in which business he continued for twenty years.

His courage and persistency were unbounded, and disaster served only to awake new energies and open new fields of conquest for his enterprise and ability. He was intimately connected with every leading movement in which the prosperity of Mendon was interested.

Besides the first child before mentioned, who married Roderick C. Fletcher, a son of the old pioneer, John W. Fletcher, two other children blessed the union consummated by Mr. and Mrs. Lyman,—Oliver Marcellus, born September 19, 1853, and Myrtle, September 10, 1860, the latter dying when four years old. Oliver M., familiarly known as "Sellie" Lyman, exhibits the dash and enterprise of his father, and is a leading merchant in the village at the present time. Being taken from his studies at the high-school in Grand Rapids, before his course was completed, by the death of his father in 1870, he settled up the estate, and entered business for himself when but twenty-one years old, and at the end of a year bought out his partner, and now manages his increasing and prosperous business alone. He was married on the 6th of February, 1877, to Miss Mary True, daughter of Samuel True, of Kalamazoo.

In politics Mr. L. B. Lyman was a Republican, staunch and ardent. His religious preferences were towards the Methodist belief, but he was a member of no church organization. His wife is a member of the Episcopal church at Mendon, in which village she at present resides.